CW01513201

THE PROTECTIONS FOR RELIGIOUS RIGHTS

Law and Practice

THE PROTECTIONS FOR RELIGIOUS RIGHTS

Law and Practice

SIR JAMES DINGEMANS
One of Her Majesty's Judges of the Queen's Bench Division

CAN YEGINSU
Barrister, 4 New Square

TOM CROSS
Barrister, 11KBW

HAFSAH MASOOD
Barrister, 3 Hare Court

OXFORD
UNIVERSITY PRESS

OXFORD
UNIVERSITY PRESS

Great Clarendon Street, Oxford, OX2 6DP,
United Kingdom

Oxford University Press is a department of the University of Oxford.
It furthers the University's objective of excellence in research, scholarship,
and education by publishing worldwide. Oxford is a registered trade mark of
Oxford University Press in the UK and in certain other countries

© James Dingemans, Tom Cross, Can Yeginsu and Hafsah Masood, 2013

The moral rights of the authors have been asserted

First edition published in 2013

Impression: 1

All rights reserved. No part of this publication may be reproduced, stored in
a retrieval system, or transmitted, in any form or by any means, without the
prior permission in writing of Oxford University Press, or as expressly permitted
by law, by licence, or under terms agreed with the appropriate reprographics
rights organization. Enquiries concerning reproduction outside the scope of the
above should be sent to the Rights Department, Oxford University Press, at the
address above

You must not circulate this work in any other form
and you must impose this same condition on any acquirer

Crown copyright material is reproduced under Class Licence
Number C01P0000148 with the permission of OPSI
and the Queen's Printer for Scotland

Published in the United States of America by Oxford University Press
198 Madison Avenue, New York, NY 10016, United States of America

British Library Cataloguing in Publication Data
Data available

Library of Congress Control Number: 2013940572

ISBN 978–0–19–966096–4

Printed in Great Britain by
CPI Group (UK) Ltd, Croydon, CR0 4YY

Links to third party websites are provided by Oxford in good faith and
for information only. Oxford disclaims any responsibility for the materials
contained in any third party website referenced in this work.

UNIVERSITY
OF YORK
LIBRARY

FOREWORD

This is an important work on what is, somewhat strange to say, essentially a new subject to English law. Sir James Dingemans and his co-authors have performed a service to all those who are interested in the field of law and religion. They have created, in one substantial volume, a restatement, in the form of a critical treatise, of the current law in twenty-first century Britain on the protections for religious rights. More than that, they have set their restatement in its necessary international context.

Thus, after an introductory chapter, in which some of the critical issues of the subject in the modern world are highlighted, and a whirlwind but fascinating sketch of the history of English law and religious rights is given, the authors turn in their next few chapters to discuss the modern international and European setting for the standards which operate in this field. Both in terms of the standards emerging from the United Nations, and in terms of the teaching of the European Convention on Human Rights, it is perhaps noticeable that this modern setting derives almost entirely from the catastrophe of the relatively recent period of the Holocaust. It is noticeable, however, that despite that circumstance, the dominant court in this field, namely the European Court of Human Rights sitting in Strasbourg, has—at any rate until very recently, I have in mind cases such as *Lautsi v Italy* (2012) and *Eweida v United Kingdom* (2013)—on the whole given only at most lukewarm support to the protection of religious rights to be found in the Convention's Article 9.

In the past, at least in Britain and in Europe, the relevant law was mainly concerned with the entrenchment of the dominant religion and the disabilities of other religions. Increasingly, however, in the modern, more secular and pluralist, world, the law has adopted a more neutral role. Perceptively, the authors point out that 'neutral' may be a better word than 'secular' to describe the attitude of the law and the courts which are called on to apply it. In that, however, the authors may be speaking as it should be, rather than as it is.

Before turning to domestic law, in a major chapter called 'Comparative Perspectives', the authors have co-opted a team of distinguished scholars to write about the law as found and practised in other parts of the world, mainly in other common law jurisdictions, but also in Turkey. In this respect, it may be observed that the United States (also included in this survey), because of its First Amendment's prohibition on the free exercise of religion and its tradition of separation of church and state, has one of the oldest, richest, and most refined jurisprudence on the subject to be found anywhere in the world. In a field in which it is necessary to have as broad a view of the subject as possible, this chapter sets a benchmark for a work of this kind in its provision of valuable insights into the relevant law across major parts of the globe.

It is against this background that the authors turn their attention to the domestic scene. There are chapters on the Human Rights Act 1998 and on the Equality Act 2010. In the latter case, as the authors observe, the most important protections for religious rights are to be found, almost perversely, in the exceptions to the discrimination provisions for protected characteristics. The difficulties created by the tension between equality and non-discrimination law, on the one hand, and legal protection for religious rights on the other, are well demonstrated in the unhappy decision in the *Jewish Free School* case, where even the majority in the Supreme Court are to be found wringing their hands at their conclusion.

Having set out the statutory background, the authors then adopt a functional approach to their remaining chapters, which helpfully cover such discrete areas as services and public functions, employment, education, religious expression, and the family. There are also appendices which contain within them much of the relevant statutory and constitutional texts not only from Britain but also from around the world.

This is a difficult and developing area of the law, and, for Britain, with its unwritten constitution and (prior to the Human Rights Act) quiescent common law, a relatively new one. It still remains to be seen how the traditional British virtues of democratic pluralism and tolerance will work out the tensions created by a new era in which religious fundamentalism poses grave risks to social cohesion and world peace. Sometimes the law is needed to protect and mediate between religious and other freedoms, or to assist real victims. Often, however, the law is used, not always successfully, due to the intractable nature of the problems, by litigants whose main interest is to espouse an extreme point of view. In such circumstances, much jurisprudence in the field has sought, in my respectful view wrongly, to find instant and artificial tests to eliminate proper enquiry. However, it is rather in the tools of justification, proportionality, and reasonable accommodation that a way forward can be provided. As it has been said, 'Come, let us reason together'[1](Isaiah 1:18).

This is an important modern work on an age-old problem which is becoming increasingly topical in its legal perspectives. I congratulate the authors on its production and wish it the success which it deserves.

Sir Bernard Rix
August 2013

---

[1] *The Holy Bible, King James Version*. New York: Oxford Edition: 1769; *King James Bible Online*, 2008. <http://www.kingjamesbibleonline.org/>.

PREFACE

In the twenty-first century, courts and tribunals around the world have to adjudicate on sensitive issues relating to the freedom of religion or conscience. The initiative for this book came because there was no single textbook which set out, in one place, the protections for religious rights available in international and domestic law.

It had become apparent from the submissions made in cases raising issues of religious freedoms that there were other jurisdictions which offered interesting perspectives and guidance in these cases. However, it had also become clear that it was necessary to have a better understanding of the constitutional and legal context in which those decisions had been made, so that the respective judgments might be accorded their proper weight. We were therefore keen to include comparative perspectives in this work. In this respect, we have been very lucky to secure contributions from expert commentators from Australia, Canada, India, New Zealand, Northern Ireland, the Republic of Ireland, South Africa, Turkey, and the United States.

There have been times during the research and writing of this book when we wondered whether it was a sensible thing to have started. But the hope that this book might help to avoid litigation for those blessed or burdened (we will not really know which it is until later) with a religious belief, and those in legal conflict with them, has kept us all going.

It is the aim of this book, which has been written and contributed to by persons with a wide range of beliefs, views, and perspectives, to set out what is the law in this area. Our principal hope is that you find this book both interesting and helpful. As there is such a diversity of writers and contributors we should state that the views expressed in the text are ours alone, although not necessarily shared by us all.

It is, of course, not possible to write a book of this nature without the help of others. We would like to thank Jessica Elliott and Jack Williams, who provided us with invaluable assistance on this project. We are also indebted to Christopher Knight, Hagen Kruger, Daniel Lewis, Michael Waibel, and Andrew Young for taking the time to review parts of our manuscripts and for providing us with valuable comments.

We would also like to thank all of those involved in this project at Oxford University Press—Zoe Organ, Vicky Pittman, Rachel Holt, and Matthew Humphrys—for their patience and support.

While Oxford University Press may have tolerated our failings, our families and friends have to live with them, and we thank them knowing that without them this book would not have been written.

The responsibility for errors and omissions is, of course, entirely ours. We have attempted to state the law as at 1 May 2013, but we have managed to include some later developments.

James Dingemans
Royal Courts of Justice, London, WC2A 2LL

Can Yeginsu
4 New Square, Lincoln's Inn, London, WC2A 3RJ

Tom Cross
11KBW, Temple, London, EC4Y 7EQ

Hafsah Masood
3 Hare Court, Temple, London, EC4Y 7BJ

30 June 2013

CONTENTS

II DOMESTIC PROTECTIONS

5. The Human Rights Act 1998

Contents

TABLE OF CASES

TABLE OF LEGISLATION

NORTHERN IRELAND *SEE*
UNITED KINGDOM

RUSSIAN FEDERATION

SOUTH AFRICA

TURKEY

INTERNATIONAL TREATIES AND CONVENTIONS

LIST OF ABBREVIATIONS

General

AHRC	Australian Human Rights Commission
CAT	Convention Against Torture and Other Cruel, Inhuman or Degrading Treatment or Punishment
CERD	International Convention on the Elimination of All Forms of Racial Discrimination
CJEU	Court of Justice of the European Union
CRC	Committee on the Rights of the Child (under the UNCRC)
CRTF	Country Report Task Force (established by the Human Rights Committee (of the United Nations))
DPP	Director of Public Prosecutions
EAT	Employment Appeal Tribunal
ECOSOC	Economic and Social Council (of the United Nations)
ECHR	European Convention on Human Rights (the Convention for the Protection of Human Rights and Fundamental Freedoms)
ECtHR	European Court of Human Rights
EHRC	Equality and Human Rights Commission
EIA 2006	Education and Inspections Act 2006
ESC	European Security Council
HRA 1998	Human Rights Act 1998
HRC	Human Rights Committee (of the ICCPR)
ICCPR	International Covenant on Civil and Political Rights
ICESCR	International Covenant on Economic, Social and Cultural Rights
LBC	London Borough Council
OSCE	Organization for Security and Co-operation in Europe
PWRA 1855	Places of Worship Registration Act 1855
SCC	Supreme Court of Canada
SSFA 1998	School Standards and Framework Act 1998
TCC	Turkish Constitutional Court
TEU	Treaty of the European Union
UNCRC	UN Convention on the Rights of the Child 1989
UNTS	United Nations Treaty Series

Journals

AJIL	American Journal of International Law
BYBIL	British Yearbook of International Law
Cardozo L Rev	Cardozo Law Review
CLJ	Cambridge Law Journal
Corn L Rev	Cornell Law Review
Ecc LJ	Ecclesiastical Law Journal
ECL Rev	European Constitutional Law Review

EHRLR	European Human Rights Law Review
Georgia JICL	Georgia Journal of International and Comparative Law
GYBIL	German Yearbook of International Law
Harv HRJ	Harvard Human Rights Journal
Harv JL&PP	Harvard Journal of Law and Public Policy
Harv L Rev	Harvard Law Review
HRLR	Human Rights Law Review
HRQ	Human Rights Quarterly
Israel YBHR	Israel Yearbook of Human Rights
McGill LJ	McGill University Law Journal
MLR	Modern Law Review
OJLR	Oxford Journal of Law and Religion
OJLS	Oxford Journal of Legal Studies
Texas ILJ	Texas International Law Journal
U Chi L Rev	University of Chicago Law Review
Va JIL	Virginia Journal of International Law
Va L Rev	Virginia Law Review
YBHRC	Yearbook of the Human Rights Committee

1

INTRODUCTION

A. Preamble

The law is more piecemeal than philosophy, and it is necessarily constrained by many **1.01** things others than philosophical truth: for example by the facts of any given case; by the evidence adduced; and by the doctrine of precedent. There have, however, been some interesting judicial statements about religious beliefs. In *United States v Kauten*, Judge Augustus N Hand said:

> Religious belief arises from a sense of the inadequacy of reason as a means of relating the individual to his fellow-men and to his universe—a sense common to men in the most primitive and in the most highly civilized societies. It accepts the aid of logic but refuses to be limited by it[1]

Mason ACJ and Brennan J expressed similar sentiments in *Church of the New Faith v* **1.02** *Commissioner of Pay-Roll Tax* when they said:

> In all societies and in all ages man has pondered upon the explanation of the existence of the phenomenological universe, the meaning of his existence and his destiny...For some, the natural order, known or knowable by use of man's senses and his natural reason, provides a sufficient and exhaustive solution to these great problems; for others, an adequate solution can be found only in the supernatural order, in which man may believe as a matter of faith, but which he cannot demonstrate to others who do not share his faith.[2]

Religious beliefs engage most aspects of everyday life. If the purpose of religion is to enable **1.03** mankind to seek ultimate truth this is not particularly surprising. Reported cases from all over the world show that religious beliefs will raise issues, from appearance (for example whether to shave, cover the head, or wear a cross), to eating (whether to eat meat only prepared in a certain way) and drinking (normally in relation to alcohol). Religious belief may affect aspects of general behaviour (from providing services to the sick and infirm or refusing

---

[1] *US v Kauten* (1943) 133 F (2d) 703, 708.
[2] *Church of the New Faith v Commissioner of Pay-Roll Tax* (1983) 154 CLR 120.

to carry arms) to sexual behaviour. It will affect beliefs about when life begins, and issues about dying. If persons of a particular religion believe that they have found real truth, experience shows that they will want to share that truth, and seek to live their lives in accordance with that truth.

1.04 In these circumstances there is little doubt that it would make states easier to govern if everyone either shared the same religious belief, or had no religious beliefs. However, at least since the Treaties of Westphalia signed between May and October 1648, Western Europe has recognized that rulers cannot compel everyone living in one state to believe the same thing or share a certain religious belief.

1.05 For many years it was not particularly necessary to study the protections available for those with a religious belief in England and Wales. As a matter of social history the laws were informed by an orthodox Judaeo-Christian approach, and this reduced potential areas of conflict with the actions of the majority of the population having those beliefs. But there have been some important developments.

1.06 First, new laws promoting individual self-determination have been enacted. According to some commentators, these laws themselves owe much to religious teaching about tolerance, and have been informed by a better understanding that law needs to protect minorities as well as majorities, but the laws have also raised issues relating to religious freedom. The reality of permissive legislation (as it has sometimes been called) is that it sometimes requires others (who believe the permitted act to involve sinful or religiously wrong behaviour) to become party to the relevant permitted behaviour. So, for example, the statutory right to abortion is capable of engaging the religious conscience of doctors who believe that life begins at conception (this issue was at least addressed in the legislation). If future laws are enacted permitting assisted dying, it is certain that they will engage the religious freedoms of persons who are involved in the nursing or treatment of the dying.

1.07 Secondly, new equality laws have been passed. These prevent discrimination on the basis of protected characteristics. As one of the protected characteristics is religion or belief (along with (currently) race, sex, age, disability, sexual orientation, gender reassignment, and marriage and civil partnership) it might be wondered why equality laws should cause difficulties for religious freedoms, and it is apparent that many of those debating religious freedoms in Parliament have made this working assumption. However, the reason that religious freedoms are still affected is because just as religious beliefs engage all areas of life, so do the other protected characteristics. For example, a religious belief about whether a woman should be a priest, rabbi, or imam will engage the protected characteristic of sex. A religious belief that sexual relations should be restricted to heterosexual marital relations will engage the protected characteristic of sexual orientation. This means, almost perversely, that the most important protections for religious rights in the Equality Act 2010 are set out in the schedules containing exceptions to the discrimination provisions for protected characteristics.

1.08 All of this means that there are now an increasing number of cases raising issues of religious freedom. This might be all well and good for the lawyers involved, but it is hardly satisfactory from the point of view of society generally, or those involved with the relevant disputes.

1.09 It is hoped that a clear explanation of the law might also assist those legislating in this area to understand why equality laws need careful drafting to avoid creating inequality.

This book starts with a historical review of some of the main provisions relating to religious **1.10** freedoms in England and Wales. It then looks at protections available through international treaties, working down to international regional protections, before considering some interesting comparative jurisdictions, before turning—finally—to the domestic law in England and Wales. The reason for looking at international and comparative experiences is because this is likely to assist in an understanding of comparative cases, which are frequently cited and considered in this area of law. For example, if a decision involving Turkey has been cited, either at the domestic level in Turkey or at the level of the European Court of Human Rights (ECtHR), it is necessary to understand the secular nature of the Turkish Constitution and state. It is then important to understand from recent ECtHR cases, such as *Lautsi v Italy*, that secularism is itself a world view which is entitled to the same respect from the law, but no more nor less, as that to be accorded to religious beliefs, and that a neutral approach is not necessarily always the same as a secular approach.[3] It might be thought that there has been confusion in terminology between neutrality and secularism. It is the duty of all courts to demonstrate neutrality towards all religions or beliefs whatever the starting point for that society (whether it is a religious starting point, such as in the Republic of Ireland, or a secular starting point, such as in France), but that does not mean that the courts are secularist.

Where suggestions are made for the future development of the law, the aim is to make these **1.11** clearly so that the suggestions can be distinguished from statements about the current state of the law. Any suggestions for the future development of the law are themselves informed by the proposition that understanding and tolerance for everyone, whether with or without a religious belief, is the best way for lasting truth to emerge, and for society to survive and flourish.

B. A Short History of English Law and Religious Rights

(1) Medieval England

Before the Reformation in the sixteenth century, Catholicism represented the religious **1.12** orthodoxy in England and had done so since the late seventh century. The Norman Conquest in 1066 resulted in the strengthening of ties between Rome and the Church of England. Tensions soon emerged between the authority of the monarchy and the Papacy, including over the appointment of bishops.[4] The centuries that followed saw various clashes between the monarchy and the Church over the extent of Papal intervention and, as the system of church courts became established, the scope of the ecclesiastical jurisdiction. A number of measures were introduced with a view to managing the relationship between the Church and state.[5]

If religious liberty was on the agenda at all in this period it was only to secure greater auton- **1.13** omy for the Church. There were calls by churchmen that 'the Church should be free', which for them included at least 'benefit of clergy' (immunity from being tried and punished in the ordinary courts) and freedom of canonical election.[6] The guarantee of freedom for the

---

[3] See Ch 3.
[4] The so-called 'investiture controversy' of the 12th and 13th centuries was a dispute about the rights of secular rulers to make appointments to church offices.
[5] eg the Constitutions of Clarendon passed by Henry II; and the Statutes of Praemunire passed in the 14th century.
[6] W McKechnie, *Magna Carta: A Commentary on the Great Charter of King John* (2nd edn, Maclehose, 1914) 18.

Church came to be enshrined in the first article of the Magna Carta (1215) which declared that 'the English church shall be free, and shall have her rights entire, and her liberties inviolate'.[7] This guarantee is one of the few that remains on the statute book today. The charter went on to set out the liberties granted to 'all freemen of our kingdom'; however, freedom of conscience and religion did not feature.

1.14 The Church was itself intolerant of those who held unorthodox Christian beliefs, particularly where they threatened the Church's authority and power. In 1401 the *de haeretico comburendo* was passed by Henry IV on the advice of the clergy. The statute was aimed at crushing Lollardy, a Christian reform movement which emerged in the fourteenth century and criticized corruption in the Catholic Church. The Lollards also believed in a lay priesthood, challenging the Church's authority to invest the divine authority to make a man a priest.

1.15 The *de haeretico comburendo* prohibited, among other things, the preaching, holding, teaching, or writing of any book contrary to the Catholic faith, or the making of conventicles. It sanctioned the burning of those who refused to abandon their heresy. The measures were expressed by the statute to be for 'the conservation of the Catholic faith' but also 'the safeguard of the estate, rights and liberties of the Church of England'. It was not just the integrity of the Church which was threatened. The statute acknowledged a concern that the Lollards would 'excite and stir' people to 'sedition and insurrection'. It has been said that in this way Lollardy 'cemented a connection between heresy and sedition which ensured the cooperation of the State in repressing dissent for another three centuries'.[8] Many Lollards were burned in the centuries that followed.

1.16 The Jews were the other significant religious minority in medieval England. They had settled in England following the Norman Conquest and were afforded a degree of religious freedom. However, their position was unique. The Jews were afforded privileges principally because of the useful economic function they performed. Being the only persons authorized to lend money at interest they provided money lending services to the general population and were a significant source of revenue for the Crown. The monarchy had a clear interest in securing their protection and ensuring that the community flourished. Successive monarchs, from Henry I onwards, issued charters of protection granting the Jews various rights and liberties, such as the freedom of movement throughout the country and free recourse to royal justice. They were also permitted to practise their faith relatively freely. Until the thirteenth century there was no prohibition on the building of synagogues and, while their conversion was encouraged, the employment of force for this purpose was prohibited.[9] The charter of Henry II even extended to Jews the privilege of internal jurisdiction in accordance with Talmudic law.[10]

1.17 This is not to say that the Jewish community faced no disadvantage or discrimination. They were financially exploited by the Crown and faced hostility from the Christian population and Church. Their religious freedom proved fragile and was increasingly restricted in the

---

[7] This was by no means an innovation. The Charters of Henry I, Stephen Blois, and Henry II guaranteed the freedom of the Church. However, what this freedom meant in practice differed from reign to reign: see McKechnie (n 6). The Magna Carta made clear that the freedom included freedom of elections 'which is reckoned most important and very essential to the English church'.

[8] J Rivers, *The Law of Organised Religions* (OUP, 2010) 9.

[9] C Roth, *A History of Jews in England* (3rd edn, Clarendon Press, 1964) 103.

[10] Roth (n 9) 10.

course of the thirteenth century.[11] In 1219 a royal decree was issued requiring all Jews to wear a distinguishing badge so that they could be differentiated from Christians. In 1222 a deacon who had converted to Judaism and married a Jewish woman was burnt for heresy.[12] Further restrictions were imposed on the Jewish community in 1253, including restrictions on where they could live and the building of new synagogues.[13] They were also prohibited from certain activities which risked offending Christian sensibilities, such as eating meat during Lent.

By 1275 Jews had been prohibited from lending money at interest. As their economic util-   **1.18**
ity diminished they were finally expelled from England in 1290, after anti-Jewish pogroms in London and York, and would not be formally readmitted for another four centuries.

(2) The English Reformation and establishment of the Church of England

The ties between Rome and the English Church were severed in the early sixteenth century   **1.19**
under Henry VIII. This was not for doctrinal reasons but because of the Pope's refusal to annul Henry's first marriage to Catherine of Aragon and assist him in obtaining a legitimate male heir through marriage to Anne Boleyn. The Ecclesiastical Appeals Act 1532 declared that England was 'an empire' governed by 'one supreme head and king'.[14] All matters were to be 'definitively adjudged and determined within the king's jurisdiction and authority' without resort to the Pope or any other foreign courts. A year later, in 1534, the Act of Supremacy declared that the King was the 'supreme head in earth of the Church of England, called *Anglicans Ecclesia*'.[15] It was this process that resulted in the 'establishment' of the Church of England and the special position it enjoys today.

As the head of the Church of England, the monarch now had greater freedom to control mat-   **1.20**
ters of religion. The Act of Supremacy 1534 expressly granted the king, his heirs, and successors 'full power and authority' to 'visit, suppress, redress, reform, order, correct, restrain and amend all such errors, heresies, abuses, offences, contempts and enormities' where necessary for 'the increase of virtue in Christ's religion, and for the conservation, peace, unity and tranquillity of this realm'.

Religious observance came to be tightly regulated by the state in the centuries that followed.   **1.21**
Significant reforms were instituted under Edward VI when Catholic doctrines and practices came to be rejected.[16] By the Act of Uniformity 1552 a uniform liturgy in the Protestant tradition was imposed.[17] This Act decreed that the Book of Common Prayer, annexed to the statue, was to be used within the Church of England. Attendance at church, or 'some usual place' where the prescribed common prayer was used, was made compulsory on Sundays and holidays. Attendance was compulsory for all regardless of their religious beliefs and preferences. The statute set down severe penalties for those present at any other manner and form of common prayer.

---

[11] These restrictions tended to emulate the regulations of the Fourth Lateran Council in Rome, which issued a series of anti-Jewish regulations.
[12] It has been suggested that this incident served as a common law precedent for the punishment of heretics by burning, for which the *de heretico comburendo* was unnecessary: Roth (n 9) 41.
[13] Roth (n 9) 58–9 and 76–8.
[14] Ecclesiastical Appeals Act 1952 (24 Hen VIII c 12).
[15] Act of Supremacy 1534 (26 Hen VIII c 1).
[16] After a period of uncertainty, Henry VIII had reasserted Catholicism as the orthodoxy by the Act of Six Articles 1539 (the long title of which was 'An Act abolishing diversity in Opinions').
[17] Act of Uniformity 1552 (5 & 6 Edw V1 c 1).

Those found guilty of their third offence faced life imprisonment.[18] These measures significantly curtailed the religious freedom of those whose beliefs did not coincide with those of the Church of England. While individual domestic worship was not affected by the Act of Uniformity, people were required publicly to engage in practices and rituals contrary to their consciences and were prevented from practising their religion in community with others.

1.22 The legislation was repealed during the brief reign of Mary I when Papal authority was restored. This was far from a triumph for religious freedom. The *de haertico comburendo* (which had been repealed by Edward VI) was restored and Protestants were executed for heresy. It was during this time that Archbishop Cranmer and Bishops Ridley and Latimer were burnt at the stake in Oxford.

1.23 The changes were reversed by Elizabeth I and new Acts of Supremacy and Uniformity were passed in 1558.[19] Attendance at church was once again made compulsory with more severe penalties set down for those failing to attend.[20] It has been suggested that, in practice, little attempt was made to deal with Catholic recusants during the first decade of Elizabeth's reign.[21]

1.24 More stringent measures were introduced following Elizabeth's excommunication by the Pope in 1570, as Catholic dissent became a more acute threat to the security of the state. Those who failed to attend church as required by law, or those found present at unlawful 'assemblies, conventicles or meetings' for the exercise of religion, faced imprisonment without any right of bail until they conformed.[22] 'Popish recusants' were also restricted to certain places of abode in an attempt to prevent them from corrupting others and stirring sedition and rebellion.[23]

1.25 Religious disputes continued during the reign of James I, although on the whole his approach was more moderate and tolerant. Following the Gunpowder Plot the Popish Recusants Act 1605 was passed imposing various penalties and restrictions on recusant Catholics. Among other things it provided rewards for those who reported Catholic priests or mass, it required all convicted Catholic recusants to depart from London and prohibited them from practising certain professions or entering into public office.[24] Controversially a new oath of allegiance was also introduced denying the Pope's authority.[25] Catholics who took the oath and displayed outward obedience to the law were tolerated. There were also clashes with the Presbyterians and Puritans. It was during James' reign that a group of Puritans, known as the Pilgrims, left England in the hope that they could practice their faith more freely in the New World.

1.26 Clashes with Puritans and their emigration continued during the reign of Charles I. Charles I was considered to be more authoritarian than his father, James I, and also alienated Parliament by trying to reign without it.

---

[18] The statute provided for six months' imprisonment for a first offence, imprisonment for a whole year for a second offence, and life imprisonment for a third offence.

[19] Act of Supremacy 1558 (1 Eliz I c 1) and Act of Uniformity (1 Eliz I c 2). Elizabeth I did make some concessions to Catholicism, including in the liturgy prescribed, eg abuse of the Pope was removed from the litany.

[20] Recusants (those who failed to attend church as required) faced a fine of 12 pence. Under the Act of Uniformity 1552, recusants had simply faced the 'censures of the Church'.

[21] Rivers (n 8) 12.

[22] Religion Act 1592 (35 Eliz I c 1). A conventicle is an unofficial meeting to discuss religious issues.

[23] Popish Recusants Act 1592 (35 Eliz I c 1).

[24] Popish Recusants Act 1605 (3 Jac I c 5).

[25] Popish Recusants Act 1605 (3 Jac I c 4). See further the Oath of Allegiance Act 1609.

The Civil War, which saw the breakdown of censorship and the collapse of the Church, created **1.27**
a climate in which religious dissent flourished[26] and calls for toleration could be more openly
canvassed.[27] The Commonwealth period saw greater toleration of Protestant dissenters; however, restrictions on religious freedom were reinforced following the restoration of the monarchy.
Although King Charles II appeared receptive to the idea of religious toleration,[28] the Cavalier
Parliament introduced a raft of draconian legislation which severely restricted the political and
religious rights of non-conformists. A new Act of Uniformity was passed.[29] The Conventicles
Acts of 1664 and 1670 reinforced the prohibition against unlawful assembly, making it a punishable offence to attend an assembly of five persons or more 'under colour or pretense of any
exercise of religion, in other manner than according to the liturgy and practice of the Church
of England'.[30]

The ability of non-conformists to participate in public life was also severely curtailed. Under the **1.28**
Corporation Act 1661 and the Test Acts of 1673 and 1678 no person could take up public office
unless he had received the Holy Communion 'according to the rites of the Church of England'.[31]
Public office holders were also required to take oaths of allegiance and supremacy and to make a
declaration against transubstantiation, which imposed a particular burden on Catholics. These
restrictions on public office were antithetical to religious freedom and toleration.[32] Moreover,
any person convicted of an offence under the Blasphemy Act 1698 faced severe disabilities.
The Act made made it an offence for any person educated in, or having made profession of,
the Christian religion, to deny the Holy Trinity, to assert that there was more than one god, or
to deny that the Christian religion was true or the Holy Scriptures to be of divine authority.[33]
A person convicted of their first offence was adjudged incapable and disabled in law to have or
to enjoy any office or employment, ecclesiastical, civil, or military. A person convicted of their
second offence was disabled to sue, prosecute, or plead any legal action or to be guardian of any
child, or executor or administrator of any person, among other things. It has been observed that
'the Legislature, in passing this Act, had not the punishment of blasphemy so much in view as
the protecting the Government of the country, by preventing infidels from getting into places
of trust.'[34]

It has been suggested that in practice this body of draconian legislation was not strictly **1.29**
enforced and in some places non-conformists were even able to establish their own places of

---

[26] There was 'an explosion' in the numbers and variety of Protestant groups: Rivers (n 8) 13.

[27] eg there were calls for religious toleration by the Levellers, a political movement that achieved some
prominence during the Civil War.

[28] In the Declaration of Breda, 1660, Charles II declared: 'liberty to tender consciences and that no man
shall be disquieted or called in question for differences of opinion in matter of religion, which do not disturb
the peace of the kingdom...'. In 1972 he issued his Declaration of Indulgence purporting to extend religious
freedom to Catholics and Protestant dissenters but was eventually forced to withdraw the Declaration by the
Cavalier Parliament.

[29] Act of Uniformity 1662 (14 Char II c 4).

[30] The Conventicle Act 1664 (16 Char II c 4) and the Conventicle Act 1670 (22 Char II c 1). The Conventicle
Act 1670 did not prohibit the assembly of five or more persons of the same household if the assembly was in a
house where there was a family inhabiting.

[31] The Corporation Act 1661 (13 Char II St 2 c 1) imposed the requirement on members of all corporations,
the Test Act 1673 (25 Char II c 2) extended it to all those holding any civil or military office, and the Test Act
1678 (30 Char II St 2 c 1) to all peers and members of the House of Commons.

[32] It is hoped that well-intentioned legislation does not create a modern day bar to public office for those
holding orthodox religious beliefs.

[33] Blasphemy Act 1698 (9 Gul III c 32).

[34] *R v Carlile* (1819) 3 B & Ald 161. In its working paper on Offences against Religion and Public Worship,
the Law Commission observed that there were few if any prosecutions under the Blasphemy Act 1968: Law

worship.[35] Moreover, the Jews remained unaffected by the Conventicles Acts, which were directed at Christian non-conformists. Following their expulsion in the thirteenth century, Jews had re-established themselves in England by 1656[36] and were able to practise their religion relatively freely.[37] Efforts to implicate or prosecute them for non-conformity generally failed. For example, in 1664 the Jewish community was threatened with prosecution under the Conventicle Act 1664 and petitioned the King. The Privy Council affirmed that no instructions had been given for disturbing them and that they could 'promise themselves the effects of the same favour as formerly they have had'. In 1685 there was an express recognition of their right to practise their religion freely. Legal proceedings had been commenced against forty-eight Jews for failure to attend church. The King, upon being petitioned by the wardens of the congregation, issued an Order in Council instructing the Attorney-General to suspend all proceedings: 'His Majesty's Intention being that they should not be troubled upon this account, but quietly enjoy the free exercise of their Religion, whilst they behave themselves dutifully and obediently to his Government.'[38]

1.30 There were other examples of attempts to accommodate the religious differences of Jews. In 1667 the Court of the King's Bench decided that Jews could be sworn on the Old Testament in accordance with their own practices, whilst in 1677 the venue of a case was altered so that a Jewish witness would not have to appear on a Saturday.[39]

1.31 Again, this is not to say that the Jewish community suffered no disadvantage or discrimination. Jews were subject to the same civil disabilities as Christian non-conformists. The Corporation and Test Acts applied to Jews, precluding them from taking public office. They were also unable to acquire the Freedom of the City of London, which inhibited their economic endeavours. However, on the whole, during this period Jews enjoyed more freedom in England than in any other country in Europe.[40]

(3) The dismantling of restrictions on religious freedom

1.32 In the course of the sixteenth and seventeenth centuries a significant body of legislation had built up impinging on the religious and other freedoms of those who held views different from those of the established Church. Although the legislation was not always rigorously enforced and Declarations of Indulgence were issued by Charles II and James II purporting to limit its effect, the legislation remained a potential tool for persecution subject to the whims of the established order.

1.33 The process of dismantling this body of legislation began in earnest upon the accession of William III and Mary II in 1689. The changes that followed were piecemeal, taking the form

---

Commission of England and Wales, Working Paper No 79, Offences against Religion and Public Worship (1981) para 2.24. The Act was only repealed in 1967.

[35] J Rivers (n 8) 14–15. Rivers suggests that 'generally speaking, rigorous application of the law was the exception, not the rule'.

[36] The Jews were never formally re-admitted by legislative instrument or otherwise. The most that can be said is that their presence was first recognized as legitimate in 1656: Roth (n 9) 166.

[37] Unlike before, no charter was issued setting out their rights and privileges; rather, they were given informal assurances of security.

[38] For other examples, see Roth (n 9) 180–4; TM Endelman, *The Jews of Britain 1656 to 2000* (University of California Press, 2002) 27–8.

[39] Roth (n 9) 180.

[40] Endelman (n 38) 257.

of exemptions carved out for individual groups rather than wholesale change or the creation of any positive rights to religious freedom.

The first significant piece of legislation was the Toleration Act 1689. The Act sought to provide 'some ease to scrupulous consciences in the exercise of religion';[41] however, it applied only to Trinitarian Protestants.[42] Those who took the oaths and subscribed to the declaration specified in the Act were exempted from the rigours of certain statutes including the Acts of Uniformity 1558 and 1662, the Religion Act 1592, and the Conventicle Act 1670. The Act made specific provision for Quakers by setting down an alternative declaration for those who scrupled 'the taking of any Oath'. Congregations or assemblies for religious worship were permitted under the Act but only if the place of worship was certified and registered and doors remained unlocked at the time of such meeting. Those present at a meeting where the doors were 'locked, barred or bolted' forfeited the concessions granted by the Act.

1.34

The Toleration Act 1689 went further than simply relaxing restrictions on religious observance. It also conferred a degree of positive protection by making it an offence to 'willingly and of purpose, maliciously or contemptuously come into any Cathedral or Parish Church, Chapel or other Congregation permitted by this Act, and disquiet or disturb the same, or misuse any Preacher or Teacher'. This represented for the first time recognition that the religious practice of non-conformists was deserving of positive legal protection.

1.35

While the Toleration Act went some way in establishing freedom of worship for Protestant dissenters, it provided no relief from the requirements imposed by the Corporation Act 1661 and the Test Acts 1673 and 1678, thereby maintaining the link between civic liberties and religious identity.[43] Indeed, in 1711 an attempt was made to discourage the practice of some dissenters who took Holy Communion simply to qualify for public office. The Occasional Conformity Act 1711 set down penalties for those in public office found present at any 'conventicle, assembly or meeting' for the exercise of religion other than according to the liturgy and practice of the Church of England.[44] Another restrictive step was the bar on Roman Catholics becoming monarch. This was introduced by the Bill of Rights which was passed around the same time as the Toleration Act.

1.36

As for freedom of worship, the concessions granted to Trinitarians by the Toleration Act were not extended to Catholics until 1791, over a century later.[45] The Conventicle Act 1670 was finally repealed in 1812 by the Places of Religious Worship Act.[46] The 1812 Act required congregations or assemblies for religious worship of Protestants (at which more than twenty

1.37

---

[41] Toleration Act 1689 (1 Will & Mar c 18), Preamble.

[42] The Act expressly provided that it did not extend and was not to be construed to extend 'to give any ease, benefit or advantage to any papist or popish recusant whatsoever, or any person that shall deny in his preaching or writing the doctrine of the blessed trinity...'.

[43] J Champion, 'Toleration and Citizenship in Enlightenment England: John Toland and the Naturalisation of the Jews' in OP Grell and R Porter, *Toleration in Enlightenment Europe* (CUP, 2000). According to Champion, this compromise 'was the result of the theological origins of the Toleration Act itself. The statutory legislation of 1689 was the result of complex and careful negotiation between Anglican and dissenting interests rather than a conclusion of conceptual considerations about the rights of conscience. Such statutory provisions were calculated to avoid much more dangerous alternatives being advanced: the overwhelming imperative was to preserve the authority and legitimacy of the "true" Anglican religion.'

[44] Occasional Conformity Act 1711 (10 Anne C 6).

[45] By the Roman Catholic Relief Act 1791 (31 Geo III c 32).

[46] The Act also repealed the Quakers Act 1662 (52 Geo III c 155).

people were present) to be certified and registered.[47] Again, doors had to remain unlocked or preachers faced considerable fines and the Act made it an offence to disturb religious assemblies authorized by the Act.[48] By 1813 toleration had also been extended to non-Trinitarian Protestants[49] and in 1846 the Religious Disabilities Act put Jews on the same footing as Protestant dissenters.[50]

1.38 The restrictions on participation in public life began to be dismantled by the late eighteenth century. The Corporation Act 1661 and Test Act 1673 were repealed in 1828 by the Sacramental Test Act but the relief offered was limited.[51] The necessity of receiving Holy Communion as a prerequisite to taking up public office was replaced with a declaration. This required office holders to declare that they would not exercise their power, authority or influence so as 'to injure or weaken the Protestant Church as it is by Law established in England'. Significantly, the declaration had to be made 'upon the Faith of a Christian', which meant that all but Christians remained excluded from public office.

1.39 The exclusion of Catholics from Parliament also remained in place. Catholics were not admitted to Parliament until 1829,[52] a privilege that was not extended to Jews until 1858.[53] However, an elected member still had to take an oath and was not permitted to affirm. Charles Bradlugh, MP for Northampton, was refused permission to take up his seat in the House of Commons on five occasions because of his refusal, as an atheist, to take the oath. After a lengthy campaign by Bradlugh, the law of oaths was completely neutralized in 1888.[54] Anyone who objected to being sworn was permitted to affirm whenever an oath was required.

1.40 Therefore by the end of the nineteenth century considerable progress had been made in extending religious and political freedom to all religious and non-religious groups. The Church of England no longer had a monopoly on public worship, and diversity of religious practice was tolerated. Religious liberty existed as a largely residual and negative freedom— people were free to do what they liked unless prohibited by the law.[55] It was not until the twentieth century that religious liberty came to be guaranteed and promoted as a positive legal right.

---

[47] ie 20 people besides the family and servants of the occupier.

[48] Quakers were expressly exempt from the requirements imposed by the Act.

[49] Unitarian Relief Act 1813 (53 Geo III c 160).

[50] Religious Disabilities Act 1846 (9 & 10 Vic c 159). The Places of Religious Worship Act 1812, the Roman Catholic Relief Act 1791, and the Religious Disabilities Act 1846 remained on the statute book until 1977 when they were repealed by the Statute (Law Repeals) Act 1977. However, in practice, prosecutions died out in the mid-19th century: Rivers (n 8) 149.

[51] Sacramental Test Act 1828 (9 Geo IV c 17).

[52] The Roman Catholic Relief Act 1829 (10 Geo IV c 7). This repealed the Test Act 1678.

[53] Jewish Relief Act 1858 (21 & 22 Vic c 49).

[54] The Oaths Act 1888 (51 & 52 Vic c 46).

[55] M Hill and R Sandberg, 'Is nothing sacred? Clashing symbols in a secular world?' (2007) Public Law 488. In the case of Jews, this was reflected in a ruling of Lord Brougham in 1833: 'His Majesty's subjects professing the Jewish religion are born to all the rights, immunities and privileges of His Majesty's other subjects, excepting so far as positive enactments of law deprive them of those rights, immunities, and privileges.' Roth (n 9) 248 and 292, note XI (c). As to the position generally, see the observations in *Attorney-General v Observer Ltd* [1990] 1 AC 109 (HL): 'the starting point of our domestic law is that every person has a right to do what he likes, unless restrained by the common law . . . or by statute'.

(4) Religious freedom in the twentieth and twenty-first centuries

The promotion and protection of religious liberty as a positive right finds its origins in **1.41** international law and the human rights movement that developed following the Second World War under the auspices of the United Nations. The UN Charter, signed in 1945, stated that the purposes of the United Nations included 'promoting and encouraging respect for human rights and for fundamental freedoms for all without distinction as to race, sex, language, or religion'. In 1948 the General Assembly of the United Nations adopted the Universal Declaration of Human Rights, Article 18 of which provided a right of 'freedom of thought, conscience and religion' and 'freedom, either alone or in community with others and in public or private, to manifest one's religion or belief in teaching, practice, worship and observance'. Article 2 provided a that everyone was entitled to all the rights and freedoms set forth in the Declaration 'without distinction of any kind, such as race, colour, sex, language, religion, political or other opinion, national or social origin, property, birth or other status'.[56]

However, the Universal Declaration of Human Rights was simply a declaration and unlike **1.42** a treaty was not binding on states in the formal sense.[57] While work on drafting a binding international treaty continued,[58] the newly formed Council of Europe resolved to draft a binding human rights treaty for Europe conferring enforceable rights upon individuals in Member States. Drafting was completed by 1950 and the European Convention on Human Rights came into force in 1953. The Convention established the European Commission of Human Rights and the European Court of Human Rights ('the ECtHR') so that individuals could enforce rights guaranteed by the Convention, including the right to freedom of religion enshrined in Article 9. The right was set out in the same terms as Article 18 of the Universal Declaration of Human Rights, except that it contained its own limitation clause.[59] The right to manifest one's religion and belief was expressly made subject 'to limitations as are prescribed by law and are necessary in a democratic society in the interests of public safety, for the protection of public order, health or morals, or the protection of rights and freedoms of others'.

The United Kingdom was closely involved with the drafting of the Convention as well as the **1.43** project's inception. However, the proposals were controversial in Britain, facing opposition from members of government and the judiciary. In particular there were concerns about the jurisdiction of the European Court of Human Rights ('the ECtHR') and the potential for interference by foreign judges. Although, in 1951, the United Kingdom became the first state to ratify the Convention, it did not accept the optional right of individual petition to the European Commission and the jurisdiction of the ECtHR until 1966. The Convention was not incorporated into domestic law until 1998.

Until its incorporation into domestic law, the Convention could not be invoked and enforced **1.44** directly in English courts. Courts could nevertheless have regard to Convention rights in interpreting legislation and applying common law principles. In *Ahmad v Inner London*

---

[56] See Ch 2, part B.

[57] For discussion of whether certain provisions of the Universal Declaration of Human Rights have binding status, see Ch 2, para 2.10.

[58] This would eventually culminate in two treaties—the International Covenant on Civil and Political Rights and the International Covenant on Economic, Social and Cultural Rights—which came into effect in 1976. The right to religious freedom was enshrined in the International Covenant on Civil and Political Rights, Art 18. See further Ch 2, part C.

[59] Although Art 18 of the Universal Declaration of Human Rights does not have its own limitation clause, it is subject to the general limitations in Art 29.

Education Authority the Court of Appeal had regard to Article 9 in a claim for constructive dismissal by a Muslim teacher whose employer had refused to accommodate his absence every Friday afternoon to attend mosque.[60] The majority took the view that Article 9 did not entitle Mr Ahmad to absent himself from work for the purposes of religious worship. Lord Denning advocated a cautious approach:

> Whilst upholding religious freedom to the full, I would suggest that it should be applied with caution, especially having regard to the setting in which it is sought. Applied to our educational system, I think that Mr. Ahmad's right to 'manifest his religion in practice and observance' must be subject to the rights of the education authorities under the contract and to the interests of the children whom he is paid to teach. I see nothing in the European Convention to give Mr. Ahmad any right to manifest his religion on Friday afternoons in derogation of his contract of employment: and certainly not on full pay.[61]

1.45 In some cases domestic law provided more generous protection than Article 9. For example, in 1976 Parliament enacted the Motorcycle Crash Helmets (Religious Exemption) Act which exempted Sikhs from the statutory requirement that motorcyclists wear crash helmets. Notwithstanding the importance of countervailing considerations, such as road safety, Parliament recognized the need to safeguard the religious freedom of adherents of the Sikh religion, a principle of which was that turbans had to be worn by men in public. The European Commission of Human Rights, on the other hand, ruled inadmissible a claim by a Sikh who had been convicted for not wearing a helmet before the exemption was introduced in 1976. The Commission held that the obligation to wear a helmet was a necessary safety measure and that any resulting interference with the applicant's freedom of religion was justified for the protection of health.[62]

1.46 There were, and remain, various other examples of legislative exemptions from the general law on grounds of religion and conscience reflecting specific policy choices by Parliament in favour of religious and conscientious freedom.[63]

1.47 When the Convention was incorporated into domestic law by the Human Rights Act 1998, the Act did not alter the substance of the rights but it did provide easier access to rights which already existed. The effect of the Act is that Convention rights, including Article 9, can now be directly enforced in domestic courts.[64]

1.48 Section 13 of the Human Rights Act provides that courts must pay particular regard to the importance of the right to freedom of religion:

> If a court's determination of any question arising under this Act might affect the exercise by a religious organisation (itself or its members collectively) of the Convention right to freedom of thought, conscience and religion, it must have particular regard to the importance of that right.

1.49 Section 13 was included in the Act to meet concerns of religious organizations about the impact of the Act on churches and other bodies of a religious character. There were concerns,

---

[60] *Ahmad v Inner London Education Authority* [1978] QB 36 (CA). See also *Blathwayt v Lord Crawley* [1976] AC 397 (HL).
[61] *Ahmad* (n 60) 41. Mr Ahmad's claim was also dismissed by the European Commission of Human Rights: *Ahmad v UK* (1981) 4 EHRR 126.
[62] *X v UK* (App 7992/77), Commission decision of 12 July 1978, 14 DR 234).
[63] See Ch 10, part D and Ch 6, part E.
[64] See further Ch 5, part C.

for example, that the Act would require ministers of religion to do things that were contrary to their doctrine or belief. During the passage of the Bill a number of amendments were adopted in an attempt to meet these anxieties, which included the exclusion of specified acts by religious bodies from the scope the Act. The measures were generally expressed to be for the benefit of 'Christian or other principal religious tradition represented in the United Kingdom', which raised issues about discrimination against minority religious traditions. The government eventually secured the removal of the amendments. It provided reassurance that much of what churches did was essentially private in nature and would not be affected by the Act.[65] The government expressed concern that amendments 'raised the prospect of some actions being protected by the provisions that certainly ought to be amenable to correction on human rights grounds'.[66] Section 13 was a compromise, intended to meet the concerns of the Churches 'without violating the Convention or compromising the integrity of the Bill'.[67] The intention was to make it clear that the 'Churches were to have protection consistent with the convention'.[68] Perhaps unsurprisingly, section 13 has added little value in practice.[69]

Article 9 has been invoked in various cases since the Human Rights Act 1998 came into force, including claims concerning religious dress and symbols in schools,[70] religious expression and association,[71] the use of corporal punishment in Christian schools,[72] conscientious objection in the military context,[73] and a claim by Hindus and Sikhs seeking to have cremations on open air funeral pyres.[74] However, before the judgment of the ECtHR in *Eweida v United Kingdom*[75] in January 2013, claims brought under Article 9 have seldom been successful.[76] **1.50**

Another significant development has been the recognition of 'religion and belief' as a protected characteristic in discrimination law. Historically, some religious groups enjoyed a degree of protection under the Race Relations Act 1976, which prohibited discrimination on racial grounds. The Act did not specifically prohibit religious discrimination; however, Jews and Sikhs were held to qualify as a racial group within the meaning of the Act.[77] The impetus to extend discrimination law to religion and belief initially came from the European **1.51**

---

[65] *Hansard* HC, col 1017 (20 May 1998).

[66] *Hansard* HC, col 1021 (20 May 1998).

[67] *Hansard* HC, col 1021 (20 May 1998).

[68] *Hansard* HC, col 1021 (20 May 1998).

[69] See further Ch 5, paras 5.30-5.31.

[70] eg *R (on the application of Begum) v Denbigh High School* [2007] 1 AC 100 (HL); *R (on the application of X) v Headteachers and Governors of Y School* [2008] 1 All ER 249 (QB) (Admin); *R (on the application of Playfoot) v Governing Body of Millais School* [2007] 3 FCR 754 (QB).

[71] eg *Hammond v DPP* (2004) 168 JP 601 (DC); *R (Singh) v Chief Constable of West Midlands Police* [2006] 1 WLR 3374 (CA); *Connolly v DPP* [2008] 1 WLR 276 (DC).

[72] *R (on the application of Williamson) v Secretary of State for Education and Employment* [2005] 2 AC 246 (HL).

[73] *Khan v Royal Air Force Summary Appeal Court* [2004] HRLR 40 (DC).

[74] *R (on the application of Ghai) v Newcastle City Council* [2011] QB 591 (CA).

[75] *Eweida and ors v UK* (2013) 57 EHRR 8. For further discussion see Chs 3 and 5.

[76] An example of a case in which Art 9 was successfully invoked is *R (on the application of Bashir) v Independent Adjudicator* [2011] HRLR 30 (QB) which concerned interference with a Muslim prisoner's religious fasting.

[77] *Seide v Gillette Industries* [1980] IRLR 427; *Mandala v Dowell Lee* [1983] 2 AC 548. Adherents of other faiths qualified for protection under the Race Relations Act 1976 if it could be shown that the adverse treatment suffered in a particular case was on the grounds of their race rather than their religion or religious beliefs. See eg *JH Walker Ltd v Hussain and ors* [1996] ICR 291 (EAT).

Union at least in the employment field.[78] The Employment Equality (Religion or Belief) Regulations 2003 prohibited discrimination, victimization, and harassment on grounds of 'religion or belief' in relation to employment and vocational training. The prohibition was later extended to the provision of goods and services by the Equality Act 1996.[79]

1.52 Discrimination law has become an important tool for those wishing to assert their religious rights; however, it is also a source of tension. Alongside religion or belief, the protected characteristics include age, disability, gender re-assignment, marriage and civil partnership, pregnancy and maternity, race, sex, and sexual orientation.[80] Parliament has sought to strike a balance between competing rights by carving out limited religious-based exceptions to the non-discrimination provisions.[81] Where employment is 'for the purposes of organised religion', for example, an employer can discriminate on grounds of sex or sexual orientation provided certain criteria are met.[82] However, these exceptions are narrow in scope, applying in carefully defined circumstances. In all other cases courts and tribunals are left to adjudicate between different interests. Recent years have seen a proliferation of cases involving a tension between the manifestation of religious beliefs and the protected characteristic of sexual orientation.[83] As these cases and cases concerning Article 9 show, religion and matters of conscience continue to raise difficult and sensitive questions.

(5) The position of the Church of England in the twenty-first century

1.53 In Wales the Church of England was disestablished at the beginning of the twentieth century following the growth of non-conformist churches.[84] In England the Church of England remains 'established', occupying a unique constitutional position which distinguishes it from other religious groups.[85] The Sovereign remains the supreme head of the Church of England[86] with responsibility for a range of functions within the Church, including the appointment of bishops and archbishops. Twenty-six bishops sit in the House of Lords as Lords Spiritual, able to participate in the legislative process. While representatives of other religious groups can be granted life peerages, only the Church of England enjoys guaranteed representation in the Lords.[87] Changes to the internal laws of

---

[78] EU Directive 2000/78/EC sought to 'put in place a general framework to ensure equal treatment of individuals in the European Union, regardless of their religion or belief, disability, age or sexual orientation, as regards access to employment or occupation and membership of certain organisations'. The Directive provided that discrimination 'based on religion or belief, disability, age or sexual orientation as regards the areas covered by this Directive should be prohibited throughout the Community'.

[79] The current law is to be found in the Equality Act 2010 which replaced previous discrimination legislation and put in its place a new harmonized scheme. See Ch 6.

[80] Equality Act 2010, s 4.

[81] See further Ch 6, part E.

[82] Equality Act 2010, Sch 9, para 2.

[83] See eg *Ladele v Islington LBC* [2010] 1 WLR 955 (CA); *McFarlane v Relate Avon Ltd* [2010] ICR 507 (EAT) and [2010] IRLR 872 (CA); *R (on the application of Johns) v Derby City Council* [2011] 1 FLR 2094 (QB); *Hall v Bull* [2012] 1 WLR 2514 (CA).

[84] The Welsh Church Act 1914.

[85] It has been said that 'a useful way of looking at establishment is as a special relationship, consisting of both benefits and burdens, between the Church of England and the English State'. P Cumper and P Edge, 'First Amongst Equals: The English State and the Anglican Church in the 21st Century' (2006) 83 University of Detroit Mercy Law Review 601.

[86] See para 1.20.

[87] Cumper and Edge (n 85) 601. Research conducted by a group of academics in 2007 revealed that the majority of bishops purported to act as a voice for all faith communities. However, at the same time they

the Church of England require Royal Assent and once passed form part of the law of the state.[88]

While the Church of England continues to occupy this unique constitutional position, the **1.54** religious rights of its members do not enjoy any greater protection in law than those of other faiths. One of the last vestiges of the privileged position historically enjoyed by members of the Church of England was removed in 2008 when the common law offences of blasphemy and blasphemous libel were abolished.[89] The offences, which had an ecclesiastical origin, were directed at attacks on the beliefs of the Church of England. Other religious groups were protected only to the extent that their beliefs were those which were held in common with the established Church.[90] In contrast, the new offences of incitement to religious hatred do not discriminate between religions.[91] In this and other respects the law has become both more neutral and equal in its treatment of different faiths.

---

recognized that there were factors limiting the extent to which this could be achieved: see A Harlow, F Cranmer, and N Dow 'Bishops in the House of Lords: a critical analysis' (2008) Public Law 490.

[88] Measures, which also require Parliamentary approval, have the full force and effect of primary legislation, whilst Canons are regarded as a form of secondary legislation.

[89] Criminal Justice and Immigration Act 2008, Part 5. See further Ch 10, part B.

[90] *William's case* (1797) 26 St Tr 654. See also *R v Chief Magistrate Stipendiary Magistrate, ex p Choudhury* [1991] 1 QB 429 (QB).

[91] See the Racial and Religious Hatred Act 2006.

PART I

INTERNATIONAL STANDARDS AND PROTECTIONS

2

THE UNITED NATIONS STANDARDS AND PROTECTIONS

A. Introduction

(1) The importance of international law in the protection of religious rights

2.01 International human rights treaties and the ideals they embody have exercised a marked influence over domestic law from the latter half of the twentieth century. In an era that has witnessed a rapid expansion of human rights law and brought about a far-reaching change to the ideological bases of international law[1] itself, domestic courts are being invited to pay increasing attention to sources of law and jurisprudence emanating from beyond their national borders. This is especially so for issues concerning religious rights which, by their very nature, transcend national considerations and boundaries.

2.02 The fundamental importance of religious rights is recognized in international instruments and has been restated time and again by the international and regional supervisory bodies in their jurisprudence. The right to freedom of religion has been described as 'far-reaching and profound',[2] 'one of the foundations of a "democratic society"...one of the most vital elements that go to make up the identity of believers and of their conception of life'.[3] Its 'fundamental character' is 'reflected in the fact that [it] cannot be derogated from, even in time of public emergency';[4] 'the pluralism indissociable from a democratic society, which has been dearly won over the centuries, depends on it'.[5]

2.03 Notwithstanding numerous statements to this effect, and notwithstanding the fact that all international and regional human rights treaties contain provisions for their protection, religious rights have often been constrained in their application and limited in their effect. The effective application of the rights is often impaired by the limitations in—or the complete absence of—meaningful mechanisms and procedures for their implementation and enforcement.

2.04 The protections for religious rights in international instruments necessarily set minimum standards and protections. They are important ones for legal practitioners: all of the protections and mechanisms—at the multilateral and/or UN level as discussed in this chapter, or on a regional level as discussed in Chapter 3—represent globally or regionally agreed standards which should influence decision-making at a national level while providing criteria against which domestic law may be evaluated. While certain provisions are declaratory of international norms rather than strictly enforceable, other provisions form the basis of legal obligations for states vis-à-vis their citizens and can be enforced through domestic courts or through international complaints procedures.

(2) The role of international law in domestic courts

2.05 Unlike their counterparts in domestic law, protections for religious rights in international law do not emanate from a single unified legislature or from a judiciary with jurisdiction to decide upon particular disputes. Rather, these protections have their origins primarily in international treaties,[6] which are also varyingly described as covenants, charters, pacts,

---

[1] All references to international law in this chapter are to be understood to be references to public international law. Private international law (also known as conflicts of laws) represents a distinct system wherein domestic courts operating within a national legal system are required to deal with cases with a foreign element. For a definition of private international law, see JJ Fawcett and JM Carruthers, *Cheshire, North & Fawcett's Private International Law* (OUP, 2008) 3–5.

[2] General Comment 22, UN Doc CCPR/C/21/Rev.1/Add.4 (1993) para 1.

[3] *Kokkinakis v Greece*, Series A No 260-A, (1994) 17 EHRR 397, para 31. Restated by the ECtHR and Grand Chambers on numerous occasions since.

[4] General Comment 22 (n 2) para 1. See also ICCPR, Art 4.2; see para 2.32.

[5] *Kokkinakis* (n 3) para 31.

[6] International treaties form only one of a number of sources of international law. The Statute of the International Court of Justice, Art 38(1) (adopted at San Francisco, 26 June 1945; entered into force 24 October 1945, 59 Stat 1055, 3 Bevans 1179) authoritatively sets out the sources of international law:

The Court, whose function is to decide in accordance with international law such disputes as are submitted to it, shall apply: (a) international conventions, whether general or particular, establishing

protocols, and conventions.[7] Religious rights are provided for in all major international and regional human rights treaties, both in explicit terms as well as indirectly, through associated provisions such as those protecting minorities or prohibiting discrimination. Those provisions bind states parties as treaty obligations, but they are also capable of binding non-states parties as part of customary international law.[8]

States take one of three approaches to the recognition of rights in international law.[9] A state **2.06** adopting a monist approach, such as the Netherlands, recognizes the terms of international treaties automatically as part of its domestic law; the act of ratification immediately incorporates the relevant treaty provisions into domestic law; and those provisions in turn become enforceable in the domestic courts.[10] A State adopting a dualist approach, such as the United Kingdom, recognizes the terms of international treaties once ratified as binding obligations in international law but not directly enforceable domestically. In addition to ratification, the relevant international instrument must be specifically incorporated into domestic law through legislative enactment before it can be applied by domestic courts.[11] Finally, there are some states, such as the United States, that chart a middle way between monist and dualist approaches.[12]

---

rules expressly recognized by the contesting states; (b) international custom, as evidence of a general practice accepted as law; (c) the general principles of law recognised by civilized nations; (d) subject to the provisions of Article 59, judicial decisions and the teachings of the most highly qualified publicists of the various nations, as subsidiary means for the determination of rules of law.

[7] A 'treaty' is defined in the Vienna Convention on the Law of Treaties, Art 2 (concluded at Vienna 23 May 1969, 1155 UNTS 331, 8 ILM 679, entered into force 27 January 1980) as: 'an international agreement concluded between States in written form and governed by international law, whether embodied in a single instrument or in two or more related instruments and whatever its particular designation'.

[8] Customary international law, as defined in the Statute of the International Court of Justice, Art 38(1) (b) ('international custom, as evidence of a general practice accepted as law') represents a key basis upon which today's human rights system is based. It has two constituent elements: (a) uniform and consistent conduct of states ('State practice'); and (b) the subjective acceptance that such conduct is required by law ('*opinio juris*'). I Brownlie, *Principles of Public International Law* (8th edn, OUP, 2012) 23; J Rehman, *International Human Rights Law* (Harlow: Longman/Pearson, 2010) 22; *Asylum Case (Colombia v Peru)*, Judgment 20 November 1950, (1950) ICJ Reports 266, 276–7. Treaty provisions may constitute customary international law: *North Sea Continental Shelf Cases (Federal Republic of Germany v Denmark; Federal Republic of Germany v Netherlands)* ICJ Reports 1969, 3, 41 ILR 29, para 71.

[9] See M Kirby, 'The growing rapprochement between international law and national law' in G Sturgess and A Anghie (eds), *Legal Visions of the 21st Century: Essays in Honour of Judge Christopher Weeramantry* (Kluwer International, 1998) 333–54; Brownlie (n 8), 48.

[10] Brownlie (n 8) 48–50; see G Williams and D Hovell, 'A Tale of Two Systems: The Use of International Law in Constitutional Interpretation in Australia and South Africa' (2005) 29 Melbourne University Law Review 95. See eg the Lithuanian 1992 Constitution, art 138(3) ('International agreements which are ratified by the Parliament of the Republic of Lithuania shall be the constituent part of the legal system of the Republic of Lithuania.'); the French 1958 Constitution, art 55 ('Les traités ou accords régulièrement ratifiés ou approuvés ont, dès leur publication, une autorité supérieure à celle des lois, sous réserve, pour chaque accord ou traité, de son application par l'autre partie.'); the German 1949 Constitution, art 25 ('Die allgemeinen Regeln des Völkerrechtes sind Bestandteil des Bundesrechtes. Sie gehen den Gesetzen vor und erzeugen Rechte und Pflichten unmittelbar für die Bewohner des Bundesgebietes.'); the Russian Federation 1993 Constitution, art 15(4) ('The generally recognised principles and norms of international law and international treaties of the Russian Federation are a constituent part of its legal system. If an international treaty of the Russian Federation stipulates rules other than those stipulated by the law, the rules of the international treaty apply.')

[11] See *JH Rayner (Mincing Lane) Ltd v Department of Trade and Industry* [1990] 2 AC 418 (HL), 476F–477A *per* Lord Templeman. See also R O'Keefe, 'The Doctrine of Incorporation Revisited' (2008) 79(1) BYBIL 7.

[12] US Constitution, Art VI, Section 2; see *Medellín v Texas* 552 US 491 (2008); BA Geslison, 'Treaties, Execution, and Originalism in *Medellín v. Texas* 128 S. Ct. 1346 (2008)' (2009) 32(2) Harv JL&PP 767; S Charnovitz, 'Revitalizing the U.S. Compliance Power' (2008) 102(3) AJIL 551.

(3) The UN framework of protection for religious rights

2.07 The impact of international legal protections for religious rights on particular jurisdictions is considered elsewhere in this book.[13] This chapter is concerned with the standards set by the United Nations in both its multilateral treaties and declarations. The starting point is the UN Charter,[14] drafted in 1945, which provides in Article 1, among the purposes and principles of the United Nations:

> (3) To achieve international co-operation in solving international problems of an economic, social, cultural, or humanitarian character, and in promoting and encouraging respect for human rights and for fundamental freedoms for all without distinction as to race, sex, language, or religion.

2.08 The United Nations has four instruments that include specific provisions focused on the protections for religious rights. First, there is Article 18 of the Universal Declaration of Human Rights 1948, which, although not binding, has become an important reference point for the protection of universal human rights and, according to some, may have become customary international law.[15] Secondly, there is the International Covenant on Civil and Political Rights 1966, which binds states parties and by its Article 18 offers a more detailed provision for the protection of religious freedom than in the Universal Declaration.[16] The Covenant is subject to the supervision of the United Nations Human Rights Committee, which has produced an important explanation of the scope of Article 18 rights in its General Comment 22. The Committee also has jurisdiction to receive interstate applications and to determine individual complaints in connection with alleged religious rights violations by states, where those states have ratified its first Optional Protocol establishing the individual complaints mechanism.[17] Thirdly, there is the Declaration on Elimination of All Forms of Intolerance and Discrimination Based on Religion or Belief 1981, a non-binding General Assembly resolution which deals specifically with religious freedom and with religious discrimination.[18] A UN Special Rapporteur was appointed to implement the 1981 Declaration and the mandate has grown in scope over time.[19] Finally, there is the Convention on the Rights of the Child 1989, which deals in its Article 14 with the religious freedom of parents and children and religious discrimination in relation to children.[20]

B. Universal Declaration of Human Rights 1948

(1) An important reference point for the protection of religious rights

2.09 While the regulation of religion, including some degree of religious toleration or liberty, has been included in international treaties for hundreds of years, the modern approach to the protections for religious rights has its roots in the Universal Declaration of Human Rights

---

[13] See Ch 4.

[14] The UN Charter is the founding document of the United Nations. Although its provisions relate primarily to the regulation of the United Nations and its constituent bodies, its significant also lies in setting out the fundamental values upon which the United Nations is premised.

[15] See para 2.10.

[16] See para 2.31.

[17] See para 2.103.

[18] See para 2.112.

[19] See para 2.126.

[20] See para 2.137.

('the Universal Declaration').[21] Although not a binding treaty, the impact of the Universal Declaration has been profound:

> No other document has so caught the historical moment, achieved the same moral and rhetorical force, or exerted as much influence on the [human-rights] movement as a whole. Parent to the two major covenants that followed it and grandparent to the many specialised treaties in the field, the Declaration expressed in lean, eloquent language the hopes and idealism of a world released from the grip of World War II. However self-evident it may appear today, the Declaration bore a more radical message than many of its framers perhaps recognised. It proceeded to work its subversive path through many rooted doctrines of international law, forever changing the discourse of international relations on issues vital to human decency and peace. It underscored the need for international human-rights institutions that could exercise novel jurisdictions over states. It animated peoples in many countries to rethink their plight and to demand of their leaders an unprecedented recognition of their human rights. This remarkable Declaration has become the constitution of the universal human-rights movement.[22]

The Universal Declaration was not intended to be legally binding but rather 'a common standard of achievement for all peoples of all nations'.[23] There are, however, strong arguments for the proposition that certain provisions of the Universal Declaration now enjoy binding status.[24] First, the Universal Declaration is arguably an authoritative interpretation of the meaning of human rights as prescribed within the UN Charter, which binds its member states.[25] This point is supported both by the *travaux préparatoires*[26] of the Universal Declaration and from its text.[27] Secondly, it has been argued that, in the light of state practice, a majority of the

2.10

---

[21] 10 December 1948, GA Resolution 217 A(III), UN Doc A/810, at 71 (1948). Adopted in Paris with 48 votes in favour, 0 against, and 8 abstentions (Byelorussia, Czechoslovakia, Poland, Ukraine, USSR, Yugoslavia, Saudi Arabia, and South Africa).

[22] HJ Steiner, 'Securing Human Rights: the First Half-Century of the Universal Declaration and Beyond', *Harvard Magazine*, September–October 1998, cited in Rehman (n 8) 83. see also B Simmons, *Mobilizing for Human Rights: International Law in Domestic Politics* (CUP, 2009).

[23] The Universal Declaration, para 8. This was certainly the intention of the drafters: '[the Universal Declaration] is not, and does not purport to be a statement of law or of legal obligation', Mrs Eleanor Roosevelt, Chairperson of the Human Rights Commission, quoted in MM Whiteman, *Digest of International Law*, Vol 1 (Washington, DC: US Government Printing Office, 1963) 55. For an analysis of the effect of the Universal Declaration at the time of its adoption, see H Lauterpacht, 'The Universal Declaration of Human Rights' (1948) 25 BYBIL 354. Not only did Professor Lauterpacht conclude that the Universal Declaration was devoid of legal effect, he expressed the view (at 369–70) that 'not being a legal instrument, the Declaration would appear to be outside international law and its provisions cannot properly be the subject matter of legal interpretation... There is a tendency—which ought to be resisted—to indulge in a legal interpretation of what is not a legal instrument.'

[24] Rehman (n 8) 79–82.

[25] UN Charter, Art 103.

[26] eg the Chinese Representative, Dr Peng-chun Chang, was of the view that while the Charter placed member states under an obligation to observe human rights, the Universal Declaration 'stated these rights explicitly': see J Humphrey, 'The UN Charter and the Universal Declaration of Human Rights' in E Laurd (ed), *The International Protection of Human Rights* (Thames & Hudson, 1967) 50. According to Professor René Cassin, the French member of the Human Rights Commission and the Drafting Committee, the Universal Declaration 'could be considered as an authoritative interpretation of the Charter': see Humphrey at 51. The Chilean Representative, Mr Hernan Santa Cruz, was of view that 'violations by any State of the rights enumerated in the Declaration would mean violation of the principles of the United Nations': UN Doc A/C.3/S.R 91, at 50. The Egyptian Representative, Abedel Hamid Badawi, remarked that the Universal Declaration was an 'authoritative interpretation of the Charter': UN Doc A/C.3/SR 92, at 61. It was the concern that the non-binding General Assembly resolution might come to have binding effect, through its recognition as an authoritative interpretation of the Charter, that lead South Africa to abstain from the vote: see Humphrey at 32–3.

[27] The Preamble to the UDHR makes reference to Arts 55 and 56 of the Charter, leading one commentator to take the view that 'each right is effectively incorporated into Charter articles 55 and 56': NS Rodley, *Treatment of Prisoners in International Law* (Clarendon Press, 1999) 63.

Universal Declaration's provisions represent customary international law.[28] That such state practice amounts to law (*opinio juris*) is confirmed by, for example, the Preambles to the European Convention on Human Rights, 1950[29] and the African Charter on Human and People's Rights 1981[30] and the constant invocation and reaffirmation of the Universal Declaration by the General Assembly.[31] There is also consistent reference to the Universal Declaration in bi-lateral agreements,[32] multilateral human rights treaties[33] and other international instruments. In the context of the latter, both International Covenants and three regional human rights treaties[34] make specific reference to the Universal Declaration. Further instances of *opinio juris* can be found either by replication of, or reference to, the Universal Declaration's provisions in national constitutions.[35] The Universal Declaration has also been treated as an authoritative document

---

[28] H-J Heitze, 'The UN Convention and the Network of International Human Rights Protection by the United Nations' in M Freeman and P Veerman (eds), *Ideologies of Children's Rights* (Martinus Nijhoff, 1992) 71–8. See Heitze (at 72): 'the Universal Declaration is the ius constituendum of the United Nations Charter to the term "human rights" and most of the international lawyers support the opinion that its principles are customary international law'.

[29] European Convention on Human Rights, ETS 5; 213 UNTS 221, Preamble: 'Considering the Universal Declaration of Human Rights proclaimed by the General Assembly of the United Nations on 10th December 1948'.

[30] African Charter on Human and People's Rights, June 27, 1981, 1520 UNTS 217, Preamble:

> Reaffirming the pledge they solemnly made in Article 2 of the said Charter to eradicate all forms of colonialism from Africa, to coordinate and intensify their cooperation and efforts to achieve a better life for the peoples of Africa and to promote international cooperation having due regard to the Charter of the United Nations, and the Universal Declaration of Human Rights.

See also ACHPR, Art 60:

> The Commission shall draw inspiration from international law on human and peoples' rights, particularly from the provisions of various African instruments on human and peoples' rights, the Charter of the United Nations, the Charter of the Organization of African Unity, the Universal Declaration of Human Rights, other instruments adopted by the United Nations and by African countries in the field of human and peoples' rights as well as from the provisions of various instruments adopted within the Specialized Agencies of the United Nations of which the parties to the present Charter are members.

[31] See eg The Declaration on the Rights of Persons Belonging to National or Ethnic, Religious and Linguistic Minorities 1992, Resolution adopted by the General Assembly on the Holocaust Remembrance, A/RES/60/7, 1 November 2005; see also Declaration on Granting Independence to Colonial Countries, which provides: 'All States shall observe faithfully and strictly the provisions of the Charter of the United Nations, the Universal Declaration of Human Rights and the present Declaration', GA Res 1514 (XV) 1960, para 7. The Universal Declaration was cited no fewer than 75 times by the General Assembly in its first 21 years: see SA Bleicher, 'The Legal Significance of Recitation of General Assembly Resolutions' (1969) 63 AJIL 444, 456.

[32] See eg the Franco-Tunisian Convention (1955) UNYBH (1955) 340, 342 as cited in Rehman (n 8) 81.

[33] Professor Brownlie points in addition to the Final Act of the Conference on Security and Co-operation in Europe, adopted by the Conference on Security and Co-operation in Europe at Helsinki, 1 August 1975 (reprinted in 14 ILM (175) 1292), and the Proclamation of Tehran, *The Final Act of the United Nations Conference on Human Rights*, Tehran, 22 April–13 May 1968, UN Doc A/CONF.32/41 (New York) E 68, XIV 2. To this, Professor Rehman adds the Vienna Declaration and Programme of Action, adopted by a consensus of representatives from 171 states by the World Conference on Human Rights, UN Doc A/CONF.157/23, 12 July 1993, which refers to the Universal Declaration a number of times and stresses in its preamble that:

> ... the Universal Declaration of Human Rights, which constitutes a common standard of achievement for all peoples and all nations, is the source of inspiration and has been the basis for the United Nations in making advances in standard setting as contained in the existing international human rights instruments, in particular the International Covenant on Civil and Political Rights and the International Covenant of Economic, Social and Cultural Rights.

[34] See n 32 above; see also AH Robertson and JG Merrills, *Human Rights in the World: An Introduction to the Study of International Protection of Human Rights* (Manchester University Press, 1996) 29, and J Humphrey, 'The International Bill of Rights: Scope and Implementation' (1975–76) 17 William and Mary Law Review 527.

[35] Constitution of Bosnia and Herzegovina (1995), Preamble; Constitution of the Second Republic of Guinea (1990), Preamble.

by national[36] and international tribunals[37] alike. Finally, some commentators have argued that provisions of the Universal Declaration are *jus cogens*; peremptory norms of law from which no state may derogate.[38] There is little doubt that certain provisions[39] of the Universal Declaration enjoy *jus cogens* status,[40] but equally, there are other provisions which it would be very difficult to argue constitute customary international law[41] or carry non-derogable status.

(2) Article 18[42]

(a) *The scope of the right*

Article 18 of the Universal Declaration sets out the right to freedom of thought, conscience **2.11** and religion. The provision has provided the basis for subsequent protections of religious rights at both international and domestic levels. It provides as follows:

> Everyone has the right to freedom of thought, conscience and religion; this right includes freedom to change his religion or belief, and freedom, either alone or in community with others and in public or private, to manifest his religion or belief in teaching, practice, worship and observance.

Article 18 marks two firsts in the development of religious rights. It is the first occasion on which religious rights were considered separately from the rights of minorities:[43] proposals for a minority protection provision in the Universal Declaration were rejected.[44]

---

[36] *Indian Express Newspapers (Bombay) Private Ltd and ors v Union of India and ors* 1986 AIR 515; 1989 SC 190 (14); *Filártiga v Pena-Irala* 630 F 2d 876 (1980); 19 ILM 966, US Circuit of Appeals, 2nd Circuit.

[37] *United States Diplomatic and Consular Staff in Tehran (US v Iran)*, Judgment 24 May 1980, (1980) ICJ Reports 3, para 91, where the ICJ notes 'wrongfully to deprive human beings of their freedom and to subject them to physical constraint in conditions of hardship is in itself manifestly incompatible with . . . the fundamental principles enunciated in the Universal Declaration of Human Rights'.

[38] For discussion of the classification and operation of peremptory norms, see Brownlie (n 8) 594–7.

[39] Right to Equality (Art 2); right to life, liberty and security (Art 3); freedom from slavery or servitude (Art 4); freedom from torture or cruel, inhuman or degrading treatment or punishment (Art 5); right to a fair trial (Art 10); the presumption of innocence and the prohibition of retroactive criminal law (Art 11).

[40] See MS McDougal, HD Lasswell, and L-C Chen, *Human Rights and World Public Order: The Basic Policies of an International Law of Human Dignity* (Yale University Press, 1980) 64.

[41] It must not be assumed without more that every right in the Universal Declaration is part of customary international law. There is debate about the legal content of a number of rights, particularly in respect of economic, social, and cultural rights; see P Thornberry, *International Law and the Rights of Minorities* (Clarendon Press, 1991) 322; J Edwards, 'Rights: Foundations, Contents, Hierarchy' (2006) 12 Res Publica 277. For argument in favour of customary nature, see JR Humphrey, 'The Universal Declaration of Human Rights: Its History, Impact and Judicial Character' in BG Ramcharan (ed), *Human Rights: Thirty Years after the Universal Declaration Commemorative Volume on the Occiasion of the Thirtieth Anniversary of the Universal Declaration of Human Rights* (Martinus Nijhoff, 1979) 21. Also H Hannum, 'The Status of the Universal Declaration of Human Rights in National and International Law' (1995–96) 25(1) Georgia JICL 287; the Universal Declaration was even quoted as containing rules of *jus cogens*: McDougal, Lasswell, and Chen (n 40) 272.

[42] M Scheinin, 'Article 18' in G Alfredsson and A Eide (eds), *The Universal Declaration of Human Rights: A Common Standard of Achievement* (Martinus Nijhoff, 1999) 379.

[43] For an examination of the background to this, see Thornberry (n 41) 133–7. See also GA Resolution 217C(III), adopted on the same day as the Universal Declaration, which provided:

> *Considering* that the United Nations cannot remain indifferent to the fate of Minorities,
> *Considering* that it is difficult to adopt a uniform solution of this complex and delicate question, which has special aspects in each State in which it arises,
> *Considering* the universal character of the Declaration of Human Rights,
> *Decides* not to deal in a specific provision with the question of minorities in the text of this Declaration.

[44] Mrs Roosevelt, Chairperson of the Committee of Human Rights, was strongly opposed to the idea of minority rights, believing that the 'best solution of the problem of minorities was to encourage respect for human rights': A/C.3/SR.161, at 726. Instead, the Commission on Human Rights established a Sub-Commission on

Furthermore, this was the first time that religious rights distinguished between the passive right to freedom of thought, conscience and religion, referred to sometimes as the *forum internum*, and the active right to manifest religion or belief in worship, teaching, practice, and observance, sometimes referred to as the *forum externum*. The unconditional nature of the *forum internum* was stressed in the drafting of the Universal Declaration.[45] Article 18 does not contain its own limitation clause. It is, however, subject to the general limitations in Article 29, which provides:

...

> (2) In the exercise of his rights and freedoms, everyone shall be subject only to such limitations as are determined by law solely for the purpose of securing due recognition and respect for the rights and freedoms of others and of meeting the just requirements of morality, public order and the general welfare in a democratic society.

> (3) These rights and freedoms may in no case be exercised contrary to the purposes and principles of the United Nations.

(b) Travaux préparatoires

2.12 Although Article 18 has been referred to as an 'easy case in the human rights catalogue',[46] a review of the drafting history indicates that there was no clear consensus as to what was embraced by the right in its final form, or how it should be interpreted.[47]

2.13 The 'Secretariat Outline', produced by John Humphrey, the Director of the UN Human Rights Division,[48] proposed the following wording in what was then Article 14: 'there shall be freedom of conscience and belief and of private and public religious worship'. The Universal Declaration Drafting Committee[49] decided to expand on that wording, presenting alternative drafts to the UN Commission on Human Rights.[50] The first, drafted in the main by the French representative, René Cassin, provided:

> Individual freedom of thought and conscience, to hold and change beliefs, is an absolute and sacred right. The practice of a private or public worship, religious observances, and manifestations of differing convictions, can be subject only to such limitations as are necessary to protect public order, morals and the rights and freedom of others.

Prevention of Discrimination and Protection of Minorities which assisted in developing ICCPR, Art 27 which grants the right to ethnic, religious, and linguistic minorities to enjoy their own culture, profess and practise their own religion, and use their own language. See J Humphrey, 'The United Nations Sub-Commission on the Prevention of Discrimination and the Protection of Minorities' (1968) 62 AJIL 869.

[45] Professor Cassin of France, member of the Sub-Committee that proposed the final text of Art 18, stressed the sacred and inviolable character of the right to freedom of thought, which he emphasized was the basis and origin of all other rights and had 'a metaphysical significance'. Professor Cassin was supported by Mr Pavlov, the Soviet Representative. Mr Malik of Lebanon expressed the view that the passive right was 'above the law' and Mr Fontana of Uruguay, also a member of the Sub-Committee, highlighted the fundamental nature of the freedom of thought. See UN Doc E/CN.4/SR.60.

[46] Scheinin (n 42) 379.

[47] For detail on the drafting of Art 18, see M Evans, 'The United Nations and the Freedom of Religion: the Work of the Human Rights Committee' in R Adhar (ed), *Law and Religion* (Ashgate, 2000) 183–93. See also Scheinin (n 42) 380–2.

[48] The Secretariat Outline E/CN.4/AC.1/3, reproduced as Annex A to the Report of the Drafting Committee (E/CN.4/21) and also reproduced in the 1947 UN Yearbook on Human Rights, 484.

[49] Chairman (Mrs Eleanor Roosevelt, US), Vice-Chairman (Mr Peng Chun Chang, China), and Rapporteur (Mr Charles Malik, Lebanon), and representatives from Australia (Mr William Hodgson), Chile (Mr Hernan Santa Cruz), France (Mr René Cassin), UK (Mr Charles Dukes), and the USSR (Mr Alexei Pavlov).

[50] Report of the Drafting Committee, E/CH.4/21, paras 13–17 and Annex F, Art 20. The UN Commission on Human Rights had been established in 1946 under the terms of the UN Charter.

The alternative, submitted by the United Kingdom, provided as follows:

1. Every person shall be free to hold any religious or other belief dictated by his conscience and to change his belief.

2. Every person shall be free to practise, either alone or in community with other persons of like mind, any form of religious worship and observance, subject only to such restrictions, penalties or liabilities as are strictly necessary to prevent the commission of acts which offend laws passed in the interests of humanity and morals, to preserve public order and to ensure the rights and freedoms of other persons.

3. Subject only to the same restrictions, every person of full age and sound mind shall be free to give and receive any form of religious teaching and to endeavour to persuade other persons of full age and sound mind of the truth of his beliefs, and in the case of a minor the parent or guardian shall be free to determine what religious teaching he shall receive.

2.14 The alternative drafts were considered by the Commission and amalgamated into what was then Article 16 of the Draft Universal Declaration which provided:

1. Individual freedom of thought and conscience, to hold and change beliefs, is an absolute and sacred right.

2. Every person has the right, either alone or in community with other persons of like mind and in public or private, to manifest his beliefs in worship, observance, teaching and practice.[51]

2.15 Although the Drafting Committee did not alter the text of Article 16 when it met in May 1948, the representative from the USSR took the opportunity to propose an alternative text:

Everyone must be guaranteed freedom of thought and freedom to perform religious services in accordance with the laws of the country concerned and the requirement of public morality.

This proposal was rejected when considered by the Commission in its third session in June 1948, by 10 votes to 5, with 1 abstention,[52] but it was pursued nevertheless by the USSR representative when the Draft Universal Declaration was considered by the Third Committee of the General Assembly during its third session on 9 November 1948.[53] The USSR placed great emphasis on the importance of the freedom of thought 'in order to promote the development of modern sciences and which took into account of the existence of free-thinkers whose reasoning had led them to discard old fashioned beliefs and religious fanaticism'. The USSR's proposed formulation plainly subjected the freedom to perform religious services to domestic law limitations which the USSR said would be required to allow the State to take action against 'certain religious practices . . . contrary to the requirements of morality and [which]could have deplorable effects on society', such as human sacrifice, flagellation, and savage mortification.[54] The USSR proposal was criticized by Mrs Roosevelt, who pointed out there was already a public morality restriction in draft Article 27 (subsequently Article 29); she also opposed the idea that the right should be subjected to provisions of national law. Her views were echoed by other delegates[55] and the USSR's proposal was rejected.[56]

---

[51] See Report of the Commission on Human Rights, 2nd Session, 1947, E/600, Annex A.

[52] Evans (n 47) 185.

[53] General Assembly Official Records, 3rd Session, 1949, Part I, Third Committee, 127th and 128th Meetings, A/C.3/SR.127–128, 390–408 (hereinafter 'GAOR, 3rd Session, 1949').

[54] GAOR, 3rd Session, 1949 (n 53) 391.

[55] GAOR, 3rd Session, 1949 (n 53) Mrs Corbet, UK, 393; Mr Contoumas, Greece, 394; Mr Aquino, Phillipines, 396; Mr Cassin, France, 396–7; Mr Beaufort, Netherlands, 397; Mrs Ikramullak, Pakistan, 399; Mr Azkoul, Lebanon, 399; Mr García Bauer, Guatemala, 402.

[56] GAOR, 3rd Session, 1949 (n 53) 405.

UNIVERSITY OF YORK LIBRARY

2.16 Considered alongside the Russian proposal were amendments submitted by Sweden, Saudi Arabia, Cuba, and Peru:

The Swedish Amendment. Sweden sought to place limits upon the freedom to manifest, suggesting that the words 'provided that this does not interfere unduly with the personal liberty of anybody else' be suffixed to draft Article 16(2). The reason for this amendment was 'to protect individuals who have religious beliefs different from the officially recognised religion, or who have no religious belief whatever, against manifestations of religious fanaticism'.[57] The Swedish proposal differed from the USSR's in scope, the latter permitting State interference with ritual practices considered to be an offence but which did not in themselves affect the rights of others. The Swedish amendment was mainly concerned with the need to protect against excessive manifestations of religious zeal and proselytism. It received some sympathy[58] but it was rejected for much the same reasons as the Soviet proposal.[59]

The Saudi Arabian Amendment. Saudi Arabia[60] omitted Article 16(2) in its entirety and suggested that Article 16(1) should be amended so as to read: 'Everyone has the right to freedom of thought, conscience or religion.'[61] This meant that no reference was to be made to the right to change one's religion, a point Saudi Arabia explained by observing that 'throughout history missionaries have often abused their rights by becoming the forerunners of a political intervention, and there were many instances where peoples had been drawn into murderous conflict by the missionaries' efforts to convert them'.[62] The Saudi proposal brought to the fore the irreconcilable conflict between some States which were not prepared to accept a right to change religion and others for whom that right was a *sine qua non* in the protection of religious rights and freedoms. When it came to a vote, almost half of the Committee failed to endorse the right to change one's religion: the proposal was rejected by 22 votes to 12, with 8 abstentions.[63]

The Cuban Amendment.[64] Cuba criticized the drafting of the opening phrase of Article 16(1)[65] and proposed to amend it to read: 'Every person has the right freely to profess a belief or conviction in any subject.' The proposal was rejected by 26 votes to 5, with 10 abstentions.[66]

The Peruvian Amendment.[67] 'Every person has the right freely to profess a religious faith, and to express it in thought and in practice, both in public as well as in private.' This

---

[57] UN Doc A/C.3/252.

[58] Mr Dehousse, Belgium: 'In professing or propagating a faith one could, to a certain extent, interfere with the freedom of others by seeking to impose an unfamiliar idea upon them. But proselytism was not limited to only one faith or religious group. If it was an evil, it was an evil from which all sides had to suffer'. GAOR, 3rd Session, 1949 (n 53) 395. See also Mr Contoumas, Greece, 393–4; Mr Aquino, Philippines, 396.

[59] See GAOR, 3rd Session, 1949 (n 53) Mrs Roosevelt, US, 393; Mrs Corbet, UK, 393; Mr Aquino, Phillipines, 396; Mr Cassin, France, 396; Mrs Ikramullak, Pakistan, 399; Mr Azkoul, Lebanon, 399; Mr García Bauer, Guatemala, 402.

[60] Represented by Mr Baroody, a Lebanese Christian.

[61] UN Doc A/C.3/247.

[62] cf GAOR, 3rd Session, 1949 (n 53) Mr Aquino, Philippines, 396 who argued that such incidents support the call for the provision's inclusion and not exclusion.

[63] GAOR, 3rd Session, 1949 (n 53) 405.

[64] UN Doc A/C.3/232.

[65] GAOR, 3rd Session, 1949 (n 53) Mr Pérez Cisneros, Cuba, 404, stating that the opening words of Art 16(1) 'mean nothing, as it stated a right which was evident, which existed a priori and which need not be defended'.

[66] GAOR, 3rd Session, 1949 (n 53) 405.

[67] UN Doc A/C.3/225.

was criticized by the Committee on the basis that it opened up the possibility of a prohibition on the teaching of religion[68] and excluded freedom of conscience in regard to philosophical and scientific concepts.[69] It was withdrawn by Peru.

All proposed amendments were rejected and a drafting Sub-Committee[70] was appointed **2.17** that unanimously recommended a one-paragraph article, practically identical to the final wording of Article 18. The text was approved by the Commission by 11 votes to 0, with 4 abstentions and the article was adopted as a whole by 38 votes to 3, with 3 abstentions.[71]

The word 'religion' was conspicuous by its absence from the wording of the draft Article 16. **2.18** The discussions surrounding its adoption provide little clarification with respect to the intended scope of the rights embodied. Almost all states agreed that freedom of thought, conscience, and religion should be assured to all[72] but, equally, considered that these rights could not be unconditional. However, there was little agreement as to the extent of any potential restrictions.

Views on the relationship between the inter-related notions of thought and conscience and **2.19** the freedom of religion differed vastly. For instance, Mr Pavlov of the USSR, expressed the view[73] that 'freedom of thought' encompassed scientific, philosophical, and religious thought whereas Mr Jimenéz de Aréchaga from Uruguay expressed the need to extend the 'freedom of thought' to embrace science and politics.[74] The Peruvian representative, Mr Encinas,[75] considered all three concepts as distinct.

Similarly, state representatives differed on the meaning to be ascribed to the term 'belief'. **2.20** For instance, the Chinese representative, Mr Chang, affirmed the original view of the Commission that freedom of belief (meaning *religious* belief) was encompassed by freedom of thought and conscience.[76] By contrast, Mr Cassin of France worked on the assumption that 'belief' was a broader concept, expressing the view that the freedom to manifest a 'belief' included the right to manifest one's thoughts through being able to change one's opinion, a right not otherwise included in the Article.[77] At the same time, other voices expressed concern that the draft Article did not go far enough to protect the manifestation of non-religious beliefs. For that reason Mr Pavlov, of the USSR,[78] Mr Saint-Loi of Haiti,[79] Mr Jimenez de Aréchaga[80] of Uruguay, and Mr Cassin of France[81] asked that the word used in the French text for 'belief' to be changed from *croyance* to *conviction*; the former term having 'an essentially religious flavour'.[82]

---

[68] GAOR, 3rd Session, 1949 (n 53) Mrs Roosevelt, US, 392.

[69] GAOR, 3rd Session, 1949 (n 53) Mr Dehousse, Belgium, 394; Mrs Corbet, UK, 393; Mr Aquino, Philippines, 395.

[70] Composed of representatives of France, Lebanon, the UK and Uruguay: UN Doc E/CN.4/SR.60.

[71] GAOR, 3rd Session, 1949 (n 53) 406; UN Doc E/CN.4/SR.62, see Scheinin (n 42) 381.

[72] Votes were taken on each part of the text and the first phrase was adopted with 44 votes for, Cuba abstaining on grounds that it was meaningless. GAOR, 3rd Session, 1949 (n 53) 405–6.

[73] GAOR, 3rd Session, 1949 (n 53) 402, supported by Mr Plaza, Venezuela, 400.

[74] GAOR, 3rd Session, 1949 (n 53) 401.

[75] GAOR, 3rd Session, 1949 (n 53) 398.

[76] GAOR, 3rd Session, 1949 (n 53) 398.

[77] GAOR, 3rd Session, 1949 (n 53) 397.

[78] GAOR, 3rd Session, 1949 (n 53) 391.

[79] GAOR, 3rd Session, 1949 (n 53) 399.

[80] GAOR, 3rd Session, 1949 (n 53) 401.

[81] GAOR, 3rd Session, 1949 (n 53) 397.

[82] GAOR, 3rd Session, 1949 (n 53) 397.

2.21   Despite some agreement that *non*-religious beliefs should also be protected, there was still little agreement on what was encapsulated by the notion of religious beliefs. Mr Baroody, the Saudi Arabian representative, expressed the view that 'religion was essentially a manifestation of an emotion',[83] whereas for Mr Aquino of the Philippines it was the 'expression of faith' and therefore it was 'inevitable that the definition of freedom of religion should give rise to differences of opinion'.[84] Mr Chang of China noted that 'a man's actions are more important than metaphysics'.[85]

2.22   Ultimately the draft Article was adopted without any uniformity of view as to its precise meaning or scope.[86] What became the final Article 18 was presented as a compromise text that should not be subject to further dissection. No fewer than 12 delegates[87] gave the consensual nature of the text as one of the reasons for supporting its adoption.

2.23   Against that background, there was little discussion when the draft Article was tendered to the General Assembly. The main exception was Egypt, which asserted that it was 'not entirely in agreement' with the right to change one's religion, suggesting that the right might encourage 'the machinations of certain missions, well known in the Orient, which relentlessly pursued their efforts to convert to their own beliefs the masses of the population'.[88] This point was supported by Sir Mohammad Zafrullah Khan of Pakistan, who argued that 'it was undeniable that their activity had sometimes assumed a political character which had given rise to justifiable objections'.[89] The General Assembly adopted draft Article 16 (which had, by that stage, been renumbered as draft Article 19) by 45 votes in favour and 4 abstentions, and went on to adopt the Universal Declaration as a whole (at which stage the article was renumbered again as Article 18), by 48 votes in favour, eight abstentions.[90] Article 18 was a consensus text.

(3) Indirect protections

2.24   The Universal Declaration contains other references to rights which reinforce religious freedoms. The opening sentence of the preamble to the Universal Declaration links the notion of inalienable rights to inherent human dignity, stating: 'Whereas recognition of the inherent dignity and of the equal and inalienable rights of all members of the human family is the foundation of freedom, justice and peace in the world.' Freedom of religion or belief can therefore be understood as a fundamental and inalienable human right to freedom and

---

[83]   GAOR, 3rd Session, 1949 (n 53) 392.

[84]   GAOR, 3rd Session, 1949 (n 53) 395.

[85]   GAOR, 3rd Session, 1949 (n 53) 398.

[86]   GAOR, 3rd Session, 1949 (n 53), some were satisfied, eg Mr De Athayde, Brazil, who (at 401) thought that 'Article 16 was the most important in the entire declaration' and that the 'basic text of the article was complete and that the detailed enumeration which followed the declaration of principle constitutes the essence itself of the philosophy which should be at the basis of that article'.

[87]   GAOR, 3rd Session, 1949 (n 53) Mrs Roosevelt, US, 393; Mrs Corbet, UK, 393, Mr Contoumas, Greece, 292; Mr Santa Cruz, Chile, 395; Mr Aquino, Phillipines, 395; Mr Cassin, France, 396; Mr Kural, Turkey, 397; Mr Encinas, Peru, 398; Mr Matienzo, Bolivia, 400; Miss Bernardino, Dominican Republic, 401; Mr Garciá Bauer, Guatemala, 401; and, with regard to its second part, Mr Pérez Cisneros, Cuba, 404.

[88]   GAOR, 3rd Session, 1949 (n 53) Mr Raafat, 913.

[89]   GAOR, 3rd Session, 1949 (n 53) 891. For the work and impact of the Muslim States on the drafting of the UDHR, see J Kelsey, 'Saudi Arabia, Pakistan and the Universal Declaration of Human Rights' in D Little, J Kelsey and AA Sachedina (eds), *Human Rights and the Conflict of Cultures: Western and Islamic Perspectives on Religious Liberty* (University of South Carolina Press, 1988) 33.

[90]   GA Res 217A (III) of 10 December 1949. See GAOR, 3rd Session, 1949 (n 53) 933.

equality, held by all human beings by virtue of their inherent dignity.[91] Freedom of belief and the word 'conscience' are also referred to in the second paragraph of the Preamble, which sets out the broad values and goals that underpin the Universal Declaration as a whole. Article 1 echoes the fundamental nature of these values: 'All human beings...are endowed with reason and conscience...'. Freedom of opinion and expression (Article 19) and freedom of assembly and association (Article 20) fortify the right to manifestation. Article 26(3) specifically provides for a parental right to choose the kind of education their children shall receive.

2.25 The prohibition against discrimination provides further protection for religious rights. Article 2 provides: 'Everyone is entitled to all the rights and freedoms set forth in this Declaration, without distinction of any kind, such as race, colour, sex, language, religion, political or other opinion, national or social origin, property, birth or other status.' This point is reinforced in turn by Article 7 which proclaims: 'All are equal before the law and are entitled without any discrimination to equal protection of the law. All are entitled to equal protection against any discrimination in violation of this Declaration and against any incitement to such discrimination.' Unlike Article 2, Article 7 is not confined to the rights and freedoms set out elsewhere in the Universal Declaration. It states on a more general basis that a person's personal attribute, such as his or her religion, must not be permitted to affect his or her entitlement to the equal protection of the law.

C. International Covenant on Civil and Political Rights 1966

(1) The framework of protection

2.26 The International Covenant on Civil and Political Rights 1966[92] (ICCPR) is one of two[93] treaties drafted following the adoption of the Universal Declaration to establish human rights protections that bind states parties.[94] The ICCPR consists of a preamble and eight parts comprising 53 articles. It provides for rights associated with freedom of thought, conscience, and religion in its Article 18. An infringement of one's right under Article 18 may also involve a simultaneous infringement of other rights under the ICCPR which may also overlap with religious rights, including the right to liberty of movement (Article 12); the right to privacy (Article 17); the rights to hold opinions and freedom of expression (Article 19); the right of peaceful assembly (Article 21); the right to freedom of association (Article 22); and the right to equal protection of the law without discrimination (Article 26). In addition to these indirect protections, Article 27 provides for a right for persons belonging to religious minorities to enjoy their own culture and to profess and practice their

---

[91] H Bielefeldt, 'Freedom of Religion or Belief: A Human Right under Pressure' (2012) 1(1) OJLR 15, 18–19.

[92] Adopted at New York, 16 December 1966, entered into force 23 March 1976. GA Res 2200A (XXI) UN Doc A/6316 (1966) 999 UNTS 171; 6 ILM (1967) 368.

[93] The other treaty, The International Covenant on Economic, Social and Cultural Rights (ICESCR) was adopted at New York on 16 December 1966 too, but entered into force earlier than the ICCPR, on 3 January 1976. GA Res 2200A (XXI) UN Doc A/6316 (1966) 993 UNTS 3; 6 ILM (1967) 360. There is a degree of overlap between the rights in the two treaties but there are also substantial differences in their content, the nature of the obligations, and the mechanisms for implementation. The ICESCR does not provide for religious rights but does stipulate that all of the rights provided therein must be exercised without discrimination on religious grounds: see Art 2(2).

[94] For an overview of the drafting process, see MJ Bossuyt, *Guide to the 'Travaux Préparatoires' of the International Covenant on Civil and Political Rights* (Martinus Nijhoff, 1987) 351–71; Evans (n 47) 194–201.

own religion. State parties are obliged to 'respect and ensure' these rights in favour of all individuals within their territory and subject to their jurisdiction irrespective of the religion of such individuals.[95]

2.27 As of 20 August 2012, 167 states had signed and ratified the ICCPR,[96] undertaking thereby to 'respect and ensure' the rights contained therein (Article 2(1)). The legal obligation under Article 2(1) is both negative and positive in nature:

> States Parties must refrain from violation of the rights recognised by the Covenant, and any restrictions on any of those rights must be permissible under the relevant provisions of the Covenant. Where such restrictions are made, States must demonstrate their necessity and only take such measures as are proportionate to the pursuance of legitimate aims in order to ensure continuous and effective protection of Covenant rights. In no case may the restrictions be applied or invoked in a manner that would impair the essence of a Covenant right.[97]

2.28 While ratification of the ICCPR commits a state party to honour its terms as a treaty-based obligation, there is no obligation on states parties to incorporate the provisions of the ICCPR directly into their domestic law. Some have, thereby rendering the treaty provisions enforceable in their domestic courts;[98] others have not.[99] It is arguable that non-states parties, and even those states parties who have ratified the ICCPR subject to reservations, may be bound by some of its provisions as a matter of customary international law.[100] However, the ICCPR also establishes international monitoring and complaints mechanisms that exist outside the realm of domestic courts.

2.29 The ICCPR is monitored and its implementation overseen by the Human Rights Committee (HRC), a body of experts consisting of 18 members elected from among the states parties. The HRC implements the treaty in three ways. First, it requires all states parties to present reports demonstrating their compliance with the terms of the treaty.[101] Secondly, it provides commentary in the form of General Comments, which seek to interpret and to explain treaty provisions.[102] Thirdly, it acts as the tribunal before which states parties[103] and

---

[95] ICCPR, Art 2(1).

[96] For a full list of those states that have signed and ratified, see <http://treaties.un.org/pages/ViewDetails.aspx?src=TREATY&mtdsg_no=IV-4&chapter=4&lang=en> (accessed 17 July 2013). Signed but not ratified: People's Republic of China; Comoros; Cuba; Nauru; Palau; Sao Tome and Principe; Saint Lucia. Neither signed nor ratified: Antigua and Barbuda; Bhutan; Myanmar; Fiji; Kiribati; Malaysia; Marshall Islands; Federated States of Micronesia; Oman; Qatar; Saint Kitts and Nevis; Saudi Arabia; Singapore; Solomon Islands; Tonga; Tuvalu; United Arab Emirates. Non-members of the UN: Taiwan; Kosovo; Vatican City.

[97] General Comment 31 [No 80] Nature of the General Legal Obligation Imposed on States Parties to the Covenant: 26 May 2004. CCPR/C/21/Rev.1/Add.13.

[98] Within Europe, the ICCPR has been ratified and is court-enforceable in Belgium, Bulgaria, Cyprus, the Czech Republic, Denmark, Estonia, Finland, Germany, Greece, Hungary, Latvia, Lithuania, the Netherlands, Poland, and Spain. Invoked in national courts: Romania: HC of Cassation, Decision 1088/2006 invoked ICCPR, Art 18; Netherlands: HR 19 January 1962, NJ 1962, 107, also invoking Art 18); Poland: CCt, K 26/00, invoking Art 22; as set out in N Doe, *Law and Religion in Europe: A Comparative Introduction* (OUP, 2011) 20, fn 75. For a comprehensive table of the status of the ICCPR in all state parties, see C Harland, 'The Status of the ICCPR in the Domestic Law of State Parties: An Initial Global Survey Through UN Human Rights Committee Documents' (2000) HRQ 201.

[99] But not court-enforceable in Austria, France, Ireland, Italy, Luxembourg, or Sweden; see also Harland (n 98).

[100] See para 2.73; see also S Joseph, J Schultz, and M Castan, *The International Covenant on Civil and Political Rights, Cases, Materials, and Commentary* (OUP, 2000) 13.

[101] Pursuant to ICCPR, Art 40(1).

[102] Pursuant to ICCPR, Art 40(4).

[103] Pursuant to ICCPR, Arts 41 and 42. See para 2.100.

individuals[104] can seek redress by lodging 'communications' concerning alleged violations of treaty rights. Although the communications procedure is quasi-judicial in nature, the HRC is not a court of law and its views are not binding upon relevant parties.

So far as religious rights are concerned, the HRC has considered a number of communica- **2.30**
tions in which issues have been raised in terms of Article 18 and/or Article 27. More important than those decisions, at least as sources of interpretation, are the General Comments it has issued: General Comment 22[105] on Article 18, adopted in July 1993 and General Comment 23[106] on Article 27, adopted in April 1994. It is therefore important that Article 18 is read in conjunction with General Comment 22 and, equally, that Article 27 is read together with General Comment 23.

(2) Substantive protections: Article 18[107] and General Comment 22

(a) *The scope of the right*

Article 18 ICCPR provides as follows: **2.31**

1. Everyone shall have the right to freedom of thought, conscience and religion. This right shall include freedom to have or to adopt a religion or belief of his choice, and freedom, either individually or in community with others and in public or private, to manifest his religion or belief in worship, observance, practice and teaching.

2. No one shall be subject to coercion which would impair his freedom to have or to adopt a religion or belief of his choice.

3. Freedom to manifest one's religion or beliefs may be subject only to such limitations as are prescribed by law and are necessary to protect public safety, order, health, or morals or the fundamental rights and freedoms of others.

4. The States Parties to the present Covenant undertake to have respect for the liberty of parents and, when applicable, legal guardians to ensure the religious and moral education of their children in conformity with their own convictions.

The rights set out in Article 18 are non-derogable,[108] and are subject to very few reserva- **2.32**
tions by states parties.[109] The right to freedom of thought, conscience, and religion under Article 18(1) is 'far reaching and profound'[110] and none of the rights provided for under Article 18 may be restricted, save for the right to manifest one's religion or belief, and then only on the grounds enumerated in Article 18(3).

---

[104] Pursuant to the First Optional Protocol to the ICCPR, Art 1. The HRC can consider claims from individuals in signatory states who claim to be 'victims' of a violation of any rights set out in the ICCPR. Individuals are referred to as 'authors' and can lodge communications for determination. See para 2.103.

[105] General Comment 22 (n 2), *The right to freedom of thought, conscience and religion (Art 18)*, para 2.

[106] General Comment 23, *The Rights of Minorities (Art 27)*, Fiftieth Session, 1994, 8 April 1994.

[107] P Radan, 'International Law and Religion: Article 18 of the International Covenant on Civil and Political Rights' in P Radan, D Meyerson, and RF Atherton (eds), *Law and Religion* (Routledge, 2005) 8–24; Evans (n 47) ch 8.

[108] Pursuant to ICCPR, Art 4(2). Para 1 of the General Comment says that its non-derogable nature reflects 'the fundamental character of these freedoms'.

[109] Mauritania and the Republic of Maldives are currently the only states with reservations in respect of Art 18. Both reservations have been subject to objections on the grounds of incompatibility by multiple states parties (for legal principles relating to the validity of reservations in respect of international treaties, see the Vienna Convention on the Law of Treaties, Art 19). Mexico is the only state party to have issued an interpretative statement on Art 18, and the Lao People's Democratic Republic is the only state party to have issued a declaration on Art 18. See <http://treaties.un.org/pages/ViewDetails.aspx?src=TREATY&mtdsg_no=IV-4&chapter=4&lang=en> (accessed 14 June 2013); see also Radan (n 107) 315, fn 3.

[110] General Comment 22 (n 2) para 1.

2.33   *Thought, conscience, religion, and belief.* Article 18 is not confined to the protection of religious rights. Although its drafters equated the words 'thought', 'conscience', and 'belief' with 'religion',[111] the HRC has made it plain that non-religious convictions fall within the article's scope. In *Yong-Joo Kang v Republic of Korea*,[112] the complainant (called the author of the communication) was imprisoned and forced to undertake a programme of ideological 'conversion' pursuant to South Korean national security legislation due to his alleged links with North Korea. The communication did not involve religious rights. The HRC found, nevertheless, that the 'ideology conversion system' constituted an impermissible restriction on the author's 'freedom of expression and of manifestation of belief on the discriminatory basis of political opinion', contrary to Article 19(1) and Article 18(1).[113]

2.34   In the earlier decision of *MA v Italy*,[114] the author argued that his right to freedom of expression under Article 19(1) had been violated by his conviction for attempting to re-establish the Fascist Party in Italy. The HRC found that the restriction on the author's right to freedom of expression was justified under Article 19(3), but noted in passing that the limitations set out in Article 18(3) would also have provided a permissible basis for restriction. Since Article 18(3) concerns only the manifestation of 'religion' and 'belief', the decision suggests that fascism qualified as a form of 'belief'. Moreover, General Comment 22 provides that Article 18 'encompasses freedom of thought on all matters, personal conviction and the commitment to religion or belief' and that 'freedom of thought and the freedom of conscience are protected equally with the freedom of religion and belief'.[115]

2.35   The term 'religion' remains undefined as a matter of international law.[116] Since Article 18 is not limited to freedom of religious belief, the HRC has only to be satisfied that a communication engages an issue of thought, conscience, belief, or religion. It is therefore unsurprising that the HRC's decisions have provided little guidance as to the meaning of 'religion'. However, paragraph 2 of General Comment 22 is more helpful:

> Article 18 protects non-theistic and atheistic beliefs, as well as the right not to profess any religion or belief. The terms belief and religion are to be broadly construed. Article 18 is not limited in its application to traditional religions or to religions and beliefs with institutional characteristics or practices analogous to those of traditional religions.

2.36   Despite this expansive interpretation, there are limits to what falls within the ambit of Article 18. In *M A B, W A T and J-A Y T v Canada*,[117] the HRC did not accept that the beliefs and practices of the Assembly of the Church of the Universe pertaining to the care, cultivation, possession, distribution, maintenance, integrity, and worship of marijuana as 'God's tree of life' constituted a religion or a belief for the purposes of Article 18. The communication was dismissed as inadmissible, with the HRC finding that 'a belief consisting primarily or exclusively in the worship and distribution of a narcotic drug cannot conceivably be brought

---

[111] The earliest drafts of UDHR, Art 18 suggest this and the draft produced by the Commission on Human Rights in December 1947 did not refer to religion. Evans (n 47) 56, fnn 36 and 37.

[112] *Yong-Joo Kang v Republic of Korea*, Comm No 878/1999, UN Doc CCPR/C/78/D/878/1999 (2003).

[113] *Yong-Joo Kang* (n 112) para 7.2.

[114] *MA v Italy*, Comm No 117/1981, Views of 10 April 1984, HRC Report, 1984, GAOR A/39/40, Annex XIV, Selected Decisions, Vol II, 31.

[115] General Comment 22 (n 2), para 1.

[116] J Gunn, 'The Complexity of Religion and the Definition of "Religion" in International Law' (2003) 16 Harv HRJ 189.

[117] *M A B, W A T and J-A Y T v Canada*, Comm No 570/1993, UN Doc CCPR/C/50/D/570/1993 (1994).

within the scope of Article 18'.[118] This decision has been described by commentators as unduly restrictive.[119]

Members of the HRC have expressed the view that Article 18 is restricted in scope to the **2.37** rights of individuals and '[does] not deal with the freedom of Churches or religious organisations with which religion could not be identified'.[120] Religious and other organizations would appear, therefore, to fall outside the scope of protection. In any event, a church or similar organization is not entitled to utilize the communications procedure under the First Optional Protocol since this is only open to individuals.[121] The practical way round this is for churches and religious organizations to try to persuade individual members to make the communication.

Manifestation. Article 18(1) provides that the right to freedom of religion includes an **2.38** individual's right to 'manifest his religion...either individually or in a community with others...in public or private', which may take the form of 'worship, observance, practice and teaching'. Further elaboration is provided in paragraph 4 of General Comment 22:

> ...The freedom to manifest religion or belief in worship, observance, practice and teaching encompasses a broad range of acts. The concept of worship extends to ritual and ceremonial acts giving direct expression to belief, as well as various practices integral to such acts, including the building of places of worship, the use of ritual formulae and objects, the display of symbols, and the observance of holidays and days of rest. The observance and practice of religion or belief may include not only ceremonial acts but also such customs as the observance of dietary regulations, the wearing of distinctive clothing or headcoverings, participation in rituals associated with certain stages of life, and the use of a particular language customarily spoken by a group. In addition, the practice and teaching of religion or belief includes acts integral to the conduct by religious groups of their basic affairs, such as, *inter alia*, the freedom to choose their religious leaders, priests and teachers, the freedom to establish seminaries or religious schools and the freedom to prepare and distribute religious texts or publications.

In *Clement Boodo v Trinidad and Tobago*,[122] the author, a Muslim prisoner, complained that **2.39** he was forbidden by the prison authorities from worshipping at Muslim prayer services, his prayer books were taken from him and on two occasions his beard was shaved off.[123] The HRC found that such actions constituted a violation of Article 18, observing that 'the freedom to manifest religion or belief in worship, observance, practice and teaching encompasses a broad range of acts and that the concept of worship extends to ritual and ceremonial acts giving expression to belief, as well as various practices integral to such acts'.

---

[118] *M A B, W A T and J-A Y T v Canada* (n 117) para 4.2.

[119] Joseph, Schultz, and Castan (n 100), 373–4; Evans (n 47) 43–4. The principal criticism is that the HRC could have accepted that the beliefs of the Assembly fell within the scope of religion or belief but could have justified the restrictions imposed by the Canadian authorities as justifiable limitations under Art 18(3).

[120] Mr Graefrath, comments with respect to the 2nd Periodic Report of the Ukrainian SSR (1985–86) I YBHRC 266. Hence it did not entail 'any freedom for the churches from domestic law, not to speak of any particular Church'. Mr Graefrath, comments with respect to the 2nd Periodic Report of Czechoslovakia (1985–86) I YBHRC 470. See also Mr Opsahl, who noted with respect to the 2nd Periodic Report of Hungary that Art 18 'provides for the rights of individuals and not religious groups' (1985–86) I YBHRC 493. This contrasts with the position under the ECHR; see M Evans, *Religious Liberty and International Law in Europe* (CUP, 1997) 286.)

[121] In *Hartikainen v Finland*, Comm No 40/1978 (Views adopted on 9 April 1981), SD I, 74, the General Secretary of the Union of Free Thinkers was not able to submit a communication alleging a violation of Art 18(4) in his official capacity but only as a representative of other individuals.

[122] *Clement Boodo v Trinidad and Tobago*, Comm No 721/1996, CCPR/C/74/D/721/1996.

[123] See *Clement Boodo v Trinidad and Tobago* (n 122) para 3.2.

2.40 *Adoption.* Article 18(1) provides for the freedom to 'have or adopt' a religion or belief of one's own choice. This freedom 'necessarily entails the freedom to choose a religion or belief, including the right to replace one's current religion or belief with another or to adopt atheistic views, as well as the right to retain one's religion or belief'.[124] The inclusion of an explicit right of this nature was prompted by a desire to protect apostates as well as those in danger of discrimination living in states with established religions.[125] The latter concern is dealt with in paragraph 9 of General Comment 22:

> The fact that a religion is recognized as a state religion or that it is established as official or traditional or that its followers comprise the majority of the population, shall not result in any impairment of the enjoyment of any of the rights under the Covenant, including articles 18 and 27, nor in any discrimination against adherents to other religions or non-believers.

2.41 *Coercion.* Article 18(2) prohibits the use of 'coercion which would impair [an individual's] freedom to have or to adopt a religion or belief of his choice'. This obligation is absolute and 'cannot be restricted'.[126] 'Coercion' includes 'the use of threat of physical force or penal sanctions to compel believers or non-believers to adhere to their religious beliefs and congregations, to recant their religion or belief or to convert'.[127] The prohibition also applies to 'policies or practices having the same intention or effect, such as for example those restricting access to education, medical care, employment or the rights guaranteed by article 25 and other provisions of the Covenant.... The same protection is enjoyed by holders of all beliefs of a non-religious nature'. Paragraph 3 of General Comment 22 goes even further, expressing the view that 'in accordance with articles 18(2) and 17, no one can be compelled to reveal his thoughts or adherence to a religion or belief'.

2.42 *Conscientious objection.* The absolute right to freedom of thought, conscience, and religion under Article 18(1) includes the 'inherent' right to conscientious objection to military service. The HRC's determination of complaints brought in relation to conscientious objection under Article 18 indicates that individuals are entitled to an exemption from compulsory military service but may be compelled to undertake a civilian alternative to military service. In *Atasoy and Sarkut v Turkey*,[128] the authors were Jehovah's Witnesses who complained that their Article 18(1) rights had been violated after they were prosecuted for their refusal to

---

[124] General Comment 22 (n 2) para 5.

[125] The *travaux préparatoires* of Art 18 showed that there was no consensus on the existence of a right to change one's religion. Egypt proposed that the reference to this right be deleted on the grounds that it was implicit within the concept of freedom of religion (see UN Doc E/CN.4/253); this proposal was defeated, by 7 votes to 2. At the Fifteenth Session (1960), Mr Baroody, representing Saudi Arabia, proposed that the reference to the right to change one's religion or belief be deleted (UN Doc A/C.3/L.876), but withdrew this in favour of a compromise proposal from the Philippines and Brazil that the text should read 'to have a religion or belief of his choice' (UN Doc A/C.3/L.877). Divergent opinion was resolved by the UK delegation, which sought to insert the expression 'or to adopt' into the amendment (UN Doc A/C.S/SR.1027, section 2); this was the solution ultimately employed. Muslim countries continue to express dissent in this regard, eg Sudanese justification for the retention of the death penalty for apostasy (1990–91) I YBHRC 291–2. The HRC has underlined the absolute right to change one's religion in numerous Concluding Observations: see eg Concluding Observations on the Islamic Republic of Iran (1993) UN Doc CCPR/C/79/Add.53, para 10; Concluding Observations on Libyan Arab Jamahiriya (1994) UN Doc CCPR/C79/Add.45, para 11; and Concluding Observations on Yemen, (2002) UN Doc CCPR/CO/75/YEM, para 20.

[126] General Comment 22 (n 2) para 8.

[127] General Comment 22 (n 2) para 5.

[128] *Atasoy and Sarkut v Turkey*, Comm Nos 1853/2008 and 1854/2008, UN Doc CCPR/C/104/D/1853-1854/2008 (2012).

comply with military service obligations in Turkey, where there were no alternatives to compulsory military service. The HRC held this to be a violation of the authors' rights to freedom of thought, conscience, and religion, finding:

> ...although the Covenant does not explicitly refer to a right to conscientious objection, the Committee reaffirms its view that such a right derives from Article 18, inasmuch as the obligation to be involved in the use of lethal force may seriously conflict with the freedom of conscience. The Committee reiterates that the right to conscientious objection to military service is inherent to the right to freedom of thought, conscience and religion. It entitles any individual to any exemption from compulsory military service if the latter cannot be reconciled with the individual's religion or beliefs...A State party may, if it wishes, compel the objector to undertake a civilian alternative to military service, outside of the military sphere and not under military command. The alternative service must not be of a punitive nature, but must rather be a real service to the community and compatible with respect for human rights.[129]

A further explanation of the HRC position is provided in the individual concurring opinion of HRC member Sir Nigel Rodley:[130]

> ...freedom of thought, conscience and religion embraces the right not to manifest, as well as the right to manifest, one's conscientiously held beliefs. Compulsory military service without possibility of alternative civilian service implies that a person may be put in a position in which he or she is deprived of the right to choose whether or not to manifest his or her conscientiously held beliefs by being under a legal obligation, either to break the law or to act against those beliefs within a context in which it may be necessary to deprive another human being of life...

> ...there is a certain lack of reality in basing the violation on an analysis of article 18, paragraph 3. The implication of relying on that provision is that circumstances could be envisaged in which the community interests contemplated by the provision could override the individual's conscientious objection to military service. This goes against all our experience of the phenomenon of conscientious objection. It is precisely in time of armed conflict, when the community interests in question are most likely to be under greatest threat, that the right of conscientious objection is most in need of protection, most likely to be invoked and most likely to fail to be respected in practice.[131]

The finding that the right of conscientious objection is subject to robust protections under **2.43** Article 18 marks a wholesale shift in the HRC's approach to the issue. In an early decision, the HRC explicitly stated that 'the Covenant does not provide for conscientious objection; neither article 18 nor article 19 of the Covenant, especially taking into account

---

[129] *Atasoy and Sarkut* (n 128) para 10.4.

[130] Jointly with members Mr Krister Thelin and Mr Cornelis Flinterman.

[131] Unlike the HRC majority, Sir Nigel draws a link between Art 18 and Art 6:

> In my view, the underlying issue concerns not only article 18 alone, but article 18 in the penumbra of article 6, the right to life, the right that from its earliest days the Committee described as the 'supreme right' (Human Rights Committee, general comment No. 6 (1982) on the right to life, para. 1. Official Records of the General Assembly, Thirty-seventh Session, Supplement No. 40 (A/37/40), annex V.). Of course, not every deprivation of human life in armed conflict (or otherwise) is to be considered a violation of article 6, and deprivation of life (killing) is not the same as deprivation of the right to life. But the value underlying that right—the sanctity of human life—puts it on another plane than that of other deep human goods protected by the Covenant. Paragraphs 1 and 2 of article 18 acknowledge that completely; paragraph 3 cannot but acknowledge it incompletely. This right to refuse to kill must be accepted completely. That is why article 18, paragraph 3, is the less appropriate basis for the Committee's decision.

paragraph 3(c)(ii) of article 8,[132] can be construed as implying that right'.[133] This position was maintained in a number of subsequent decisions,[134] although the HRC did go on, in *JP v Canada*,[135] to acknowledge that Article 18 did extend to protect 'the right to hold, express and disseminate opinions and convictions, including conscientious objection to military activities and expenditures'.[136] This did not go as far as to say that individuals had the right to manifest their conscientious objection to military service by abstaining from it.

2.44   The question of conscientious objection to military service was revisited in the drafting of paragraph 11 of General Comment 22, which observes:

> The Covenant does not explicitly refer to a right of conscientious objection, but the Committee believes that such a right can be derived from article 18, inasmuch as the obligation to use lethal force may seriously conflict with the freedom of conscience and the right to manifest one's religion or belief.[137]

Following its explicit recognition—in contrast to its earlier decisions—that a right to conscientious objection could be derived from Article 18, the HRC applied Article 18 in *Yoon and Choi v Republic of Korea*[138] to hold, for the first time, that punishing conscientious objectors for their refusal to perform military service amounted to a restriction on their ability to manifest their religion or belief:

> 8.2 …the present claim is to be assessed solely in the light of article 18 of the Covenant, the understanding of which evolves as that of any other guarantee of the Covenant over time in view of its text and purpose.
>
> 8.3 The Committee recalls its previous jurisprudence on the assessment of a claim of conscientious objection to military service as a protected form of manifestation of religious belief under

---

[132] Article 8(3) provides:

> 3. (a) No one shall be forced to perform forced or compulsory labour.
>
>   (b) …
>
>   (c) For the purpose of this paragraph, the term, forced or compulsory labour shall not include:
>   (i) …
>   (ii) any service of a military character and, in countries where conscientious objection is recognised, any national service required by law of conscientious objectors.

[133] *LTK v Finland*, Comm No 185/1984 (Decision of 9 July 1985), SD II, 61, para 5.2, the communication was held to be inadmissible.

[134] See *RTZ v Netherlands*, Comm No 245/1987 (Decision of 5 November 1987), SD II, 73, para 3.2; *MJG v Netherlands*, Comm No 267/1987 (Decision of 24 March 1988), SD II, 74, para 3.2; *Jarvinen v Finland*, Comm No 295/1988 (Decision of 25 July 1990), HRLJ 11 (1990) 324, para 6.1; *CBD v Netherlands*, Comm No 394/1990 (Decision of 22 July 1992), A/47/140, Annex (P), para 6.3; *JPK v Netherlands*, Comm No 401/1990 (Decision of 7 November 1991), A/47/40, Annex (t), para 6.5. See also *Brinkhof v Netherlands*, Comm No 402/1990 (Views adopted on 27 July 1993), IHRR 1(2) (1994) 92, para 6.2, in which the HRC recalled its refusal to declare admissible the claim that, because the author would be required to participate in plans which envisaged the use of nuclear weapons, he was being required to conspire in plans to commit crimes against humanity, illegal under international law, and hence his domestic conviction breached Arts 6 (the right to life) and 7 (prohibition on torture or cruel, inhuman or degrading treatment or punishment) of the ICCPR. This line of argument was again rejected in *ARU v Netherlands*, Comm No 509/1992 (Decision of 19 October 1993), IHRR 1(2) (1994) 55.

[135] *JP v Canada*, Comm No 446/1991 (Decision of 7 November 1992), A/47/40, Annex X.

[136] *JP v Canada* (n 135) para 4.2. This was endorsed by the HRC in *JvK and CMGvK-S v Netherlands*, Comm No 483/1991 (Decision of 23 July 1992), A/47/40, Annex X, section cc, para 4.2, and *KV and CV v Germany*, Comm No 568/1993 (Decision of 8 April 1994), IHRR 1(3) (1994) 54, para 4.3.

[137] The HRC also noted that 'a growing number of States have in their laws exempted from compulsory military service citizens who genuinely hold religious or other beliefs that forbid the performance of military service'.

[138] *Yoon and Choi v Republic of Korea*, Comm No 1321–1322/2004 (Views adopted on 3 November 2006).

article 18, paragraph 1. It observes that while the right to manifest one's religion or belief does not as such imply the right to refuse all obligations imposed by law, it provides certain protection, consistent with article 18, paragraph 3, against being forced to act against genuinely-held religious belief. The Committee also recalls its general view expressed in General Comment 22 that to compel a person to use lethal force, although such use would seriously conflict with the requirements of his conscience or religious beliefs, falls within the ambit of article 18. The Committee notes, in the instant case, that the authors' refusal to be drafted for compulsory service was a direct expression of their religious beliefs, which it is uncontested were genuinely held. The authors' conviction and sentence, accordingly, amounts to a restriction on their ability to manifest their religion or belief. Such restriction must be justified by the permissible limits described in paragraph 3 of article 18, that is, that any restriction must be prescribed by law and be necessary to protect public safety, order, health or morals or the fundamental rights and freedoms of others. However, such restriction must not impair the very essence of the right in question.

2.45 The HRC also explicitly addressed the relevance of Article 8, the prohibition on forced labour, concluding:

The Committee . . . notes that article 8, paragraph 3, of the Covenant excludes from the scope of 'forced or compulsory labour', which is proscribed, 'any service of a military character and, in countries where conscientious objection is recognized, any national service required by law of conscientious objectors'. It follows that article 8 of the Covenant itself neither recognizes nor excludes a right of conscientious objection. Thus, the present claim is to be assessed solely in the light of article 18 of the Covenant, the understanding of which evolves as that of any other guarantee of the Covenant over time in view of its text and purpose.

2.46 In March 2010, the HRC unanimously reiterated its position against Korea in a similar communication concerning objectors who included a Buddhist, a Catholic, and a number with conscientious objections not based in a specific religion. The HRC found:

. . . an infringement of their freedom of conscience and a restriction on their ability to manifest their religion or belief. The Committee finds that as the State party has not demonstrated that in the present cases the restrictions in question were necessary, within the meaning of article 18, paragraph 3, it has violated article 18, paragraph 1, of the Covenant.[139]

2.47 The HRC went further still in *Min-Kyu Jeong et al v The Republic of Korea*[140] by attributing the right of conscientious objectors to decline military service directly to the unconditional right to freedom of conscience.[141] This was the approach endorsed again in *Atasoy and*

---

[139] *Eu-min Jung, Tae-Yang Oh, Chang-Geun Yeom, Dong-hyuk Nah, Ho-Gun Yu, Chi-yun Lim, Choi Jin, Taehoon Lim, Sung-hwan Lim, Jae-sung Lim, and Dong-ju Goh v Republic of Korea*, Comm Nos 1593 to 1603/2007 (Views adopted on 23 March 2010), UN Doc CCPR/C/98/D/1593–1603/2007.

[140] *Min-Kyu Jeong et al v The Republic of Korea*, Comm No 1642–1741/2007 (Views adopted on 24 March 2011).

[141] The ground had been prepared for this shift in the dissent in *Yoon and Choi* from Committee member Mr Hipólito Solair-Yrigoyen:

8.2 . . . the fundamental human right to conscientious objection entitles any individual to an exemption from compulsory military service if this cannot be reconciled with that individual's religion or beliefs. The right must not be impaired by coercion. Given that the State party does not recognise this right, the present communication should be considered under paragraph 1 of article 18, not paragraph 3.

8.3 The right to conscientious objection to military service derives from the right to freedom of thought, conscience and religion. As stated in article 4, paragraph 2, of the Covenant, this right cannot be derogated from even in exceptional circumstances which threaten the life of the nation and justify the declaration of a public emergency. When a right to conscientious objection is recognised, a State may, if it wishes, compel the objector to undertake a civilian alternative to military service, outside the military sphere and not under military command. The alternative service must

Sarkut,[142] but it did not receive unanimous backing from HRC members: both decisions featured concurring Opinions from HRC members expressing a preference for the manifestation-based reasoning in *Yoon and Choi*.[143]

2.48 The HRC's Concluding Observations[144] have included specific recommendations to states to introduce legislation to provide for conscientious objection, as well as to address discriminatory practices where some recognition existed. For example, in the case of Chile:

> The State party should expedite the adoption of legislation recognising the right of conscientious objection to military service, ensuring that conscientious objectors are not subject to discrimination or punishment and recognising that conscientious objection can occur at any time, even when a person's military service has already begun.[145]

2.49 The Grand Chamber of the European Court of Human Rights (ECtHR) has followed the approach of the HRC to conscientious objection in the case of *Bayatyan v Armenia*.[146] In that case a Jehovah's Witness had been imprisoned because he had refused to perform military service.

2.50 Where a state provides an alternative to military service, differentiation in terms or length of service between military service and the alternative service must be reasonably and objectively justifiable. In *Foin v France*,[147] a length of 24 months for national alternative service rather than 12 months for military service was held to be discriminatory under Article 26:

> The Committee reiterates its position that article 26 does not prohibit all differences of treatment. Any differentiation, as the Committee has had the opportunity to state repeatedly, must however be based on reasonable and objective criteria. In this context, the Committee recognizes that the law and practice may establish differences between military and national alternative service and that such differences may, in a particular case, justify a longer period of service, provided that the differentiation is based on reasonable and objective criteria, such as the nature of the specific service concerned or the need for a special training in order to

---

not be of a punitive nature. It must be a real service to the community and compatible with respect for human rights. .

The mention of freedom to manifest one's religion or belief in article 18, paragraph 3, is a reference to the freedom to manifest that religion or belief in public, not to recognition of the right itself, which is protected by paragraph 1. Even if it were wrongly supposed that the present communication does not concern recognition of the objector's right, but merely its public manifestation, the statement that public manifestations may be subject only 'to such limitations as are prescribed by law' in no way implies that the existence of the right itself is a matter for the discretion of States parties.

[142] See *Atasoy and Sarkut* (n 128).

[143] eg Individual opinion of Committee member Mr Gerald L Neuman, jointly with members Mr Yuji Iwasawa, Mr Michael O'Flaherty, and Mr Walter Kaelin, in *Atasoy and Sarkut* (n 128) third para:

> Refusal to perform military service for reasons of conscience is among the 'broad range of acts' encompassed by the freedom to manifest religion or belief in worship, observance, practice and teaching. Such refusal involves not merely the right to hold a belief, but the right to manifest the belief by engaging in actions motivated by it. Article 18 of the Covenant does permit limitations on this freedom if the high standard of justification in paragraph 3 can be met. The majority's Views in the present case do not provide any convincing reason for treating conscientious objection to military service as if it were an instance of the absolutely protected right to hold a belief. Nor does the majority clarify how conscientious objection to military service can be distinguished in this respect from other claims to exemption on religious grounds from legal obligations.

[144] Originally, the Committee members expressed individual comments on states' reports; it was only in 1991 that the Committee as a whole started adopting Concluding Observations, which are agreed unanimously.

[145] Chile: 17 April 2007, UN Doc CCPR/C/CHL/CO/5, section 13.

[146] *Bayatyan v Armenia* (App 23459/03) (2011) para 105. See Ch 3, para 3.22.

[147] *Foin v France* (666/1995), ICCPR, A/55/40 Vol II (3 November 1999) 30, para 10.3

accomplish that service. In the present case, however, the reasons forwarded by the State party do not refer to such criteria or refer to criteria in general terms without specific reference to the author's case, and are rather based on the argument that doubling the length of service was the only way to test the sincerity of an individual's convictions. In the Committee's view, such argument does not satisfy the requirement that the difference in treatment involved in the present case was based on reasonable and objective criteria. In the circumstances, the Committee finds that a violation of article 26 occurred, since the author was discriminated against on the basis of his conviction of conscience.[148]

Religious and moral education of children. Article 18(4) obliges states parties to 'undertake to have respect for the liberty of parents and ... legal guardians to ensure the religious ... education of their children in conformity with their own convictions'. As with the prohibition on coercion set out in Article 18(2), this obligation is absolute and 'cannot be restricted'.[149] In practice, Article 18(4) permits the founding of religious schools in the private sector. It does not extend to requiring the state to fund such schools or to provide for religious education in the public sector. **2.51**

A state party's choice to fund private schools of one faith but not another can constitute discriminatory treatment. In *Arieh Hollis Waldman v Canada*,[150] the provincial government of Ontario offered funding to Roman Catholic private schools but not to Jewish private schools. A parent whose child attended a Jewish private school claimed that Ontario's policy constituted a violation of Article 26, the ICCPR's equality clause, as well as Article 18(4). The HRC upheld the author's claim on Article 26 grounds but did not address the Article 18(4) complaint. In a concurring opinion, one HRC member[151] did, however, stress the implied fundamental requirement of non-discrimination under Article 18(4): **2.52**

> There is a considerable degree of interdependence between [Article 18] and the non discrimination clause in article 26. In general, arrangements in the field of religious education that are in compliance with article 18 are likely to be in conformity with article 26 as well, because non-discrimination is a fundamental component in the test under Article 18(4). In the cases of *Blom v. Sweden* (Communication No. 191/1985) and *Lundgren et al. and Hjord et al. v. Sweden* (Communications 288 and 299/1988) the Committee elaborated its position in the question what constitutes discrimination in the field of education. While the Committee left open whether the Covenant entails, in certain situations, an obligation to provide some public funding for private schools, it concluded that ... the fact that private schools, freely chosen by the parents and their children, do not receive the same level of funding as public schools does not amount to discrimination.[152]

The position of states parties that choose to provide for religious education within their state school system is set out in paragraph 6 of General Comment 22: **2.53**

> The Committee is of the view that article 18.4 permits public school instruction in subjects such as the general history of religions and ethics if it is given in a neutral and objective way. The liberty of parents or legal guardians to ensure that their children receive a religious

---

[148] *Foin* (n 147) para 10.3. See also *Maille v France* (689/1996), ICCPR, A/55/40 Vol II (10 July 2000) 62, para 10.4; *Venier and Nicolas v France* (690/1996 and 691/1996), ICCPR, A/55/40 Vol II (10 July 2000) 75, para 10.4.

[149] General Comment 22 (n 2) para 8.

[150] *Waldman v Canada* (694/1996), ICCPR, A/55/40 Vol II (3 November 1999) 86 (CCPR/C/67/D/694/1996) paras 10.2, 10.4–10.6 and Individual Opinion by Martin Scheinin (concurring) 100, paras 3–5.

[151] *Waldman* (n 150) Individual Opinion by Martin Scheinin (concurring) 100, paras 3–5.

[152] *Waldman* (n 150) Individual Opinion by Martin Scheinin (concurring) 100, paras 3–5.

and moral education in conformity with their own convictions, set forth in article 18.4, is related to the guarantees of the freedom to teach a religion or belief stated in article 18.1. The Committee notes that public education that includes instruction in a particular religion or belief is inconsistent with article 18.4 unless provision is made for non-discriminatory exemptions or alternatives that would accommodate the wishes of parents and guardians.

2.54 This reflects the position of the HRC in the pre-General Comment 22 communication of *Erkki Hartikainen v Finland*.[153] The state school system in Finland provided religious education to students. Parents were, however, permitted to opt out in favour of instruction in the history of religion and ethics or opt out entirely. The HRC found that this scheme did not violate Article 18(4):

> 10.4 The Committee does not consider that the requirement of the relevant provisions of Finnish legislation that instruction in the study of the history of religions and ethics should be given instead of religious instruction to students in schools whose parents or legal guardians object to religious instruction is in itself incompatible with article 18 (4), if such alternative course of instruction is given in a neutral and objective way and respects the convictions of parents and guardians who do not believe in any religion. In any event, paragraph 6 of the School System Act expressly permits any parents or guardians who do not wish their children to be given either religious instruction or instruction in the study of the history of religions and ethics to obtain exemption therefrom by arranging for them to receive comparable instruction outside of school.

> 10.5 The State party admits that difficulties have arisen in regard to the existing teaching plan to give effect to these provisions, (which teaching plan does appear, in part at least, to be religious in character), but the Committee believes that appropriate action is being taken to resolve the difficulties and it sees no reason to conclude that this cannot be accomplished, compatibly with the requirements of article 18 (4) of the Covenant, within the framework of the existing laws.

(b) Justifiable limitations

2.55 None of the rights contained in Article 18 can be subject to limitations, save for the right to manifest one's belief or religion under Article 18(1). Manifestation can only be restricted pursuant to Article 20 and the limited grounds set out in Article 18(3).

2.56 Article 20 prohibits 'any propaganda for war' and the advocacy of, *inter alia*, 'religious hatred that constitutes incitement to discrimination, hostility or violence'. That this provision applies to the right to manifestation under Article 18(1) is made plain by paragraph 7 of General Comment 22.[154] The inclusion of Article 20 within the ICCPR was controversial[155] and the provision is subject to 16 reservations.[156]

2.57 Article 18(3) permits restrictions on the right to manifest one's religion where such restrictions 'are prescribed by law and are necessary to protect public safety, order, health or morals

---

[153] *Hartikainen v Finland* (R.9/40), ICCPR, A/36/40 (9 April 1981) 147, paras 10.4 and 10.5.

[154] General Comment 22 (n 2) para 7:

> In accordance with article 20, no manifestation of religion or belief may amount to propaganda for war or advocacy of national, racial or religious hatred that constitutes incitement to discrimination, hostility or violence. As stated by the Committee in its General Comment 11 [19], States parties are under the obligation to enact laws to prohibit such acts.

[155] See M Nowak, *UN Covenant on Civil and Political Rights: CCPR Commentary* (NP Engel, 2005) 479; Joseph, Schulz, and Castan (n 100), 544.

[156] Australia, Belgium, Denmark, Finland, France, Iceland, Ireland, Luxembourg, Malta, the Netherlands, New Zealand, Norway, Sweden, Switzerland, the UK, and the US.

or the fundamental rights and freedoms of others'. The article is 'to be strictly interpreted' so that 'restrictions are not allowed on grounds not specified [therein]'.[157] The grounds of restriction set out in Article 18(3) are narrower in scope than those found elsewhere in the ICCPR: for example see Articles 12 (freedom of movement and choice of residence), 19 (right of opinion and expression), 21 (right of peaceful assembly), and 22 (freedom of association), where restrictions are permitted 'in the interests of national security', and to protect the 'rights and freedoms of others'.

The General Comment expands upon Article 18(3) in paragraph 8: **2.58**

> Article 18.3 permits restrictions on the freedom to manifest religion or belief only if limitations are prescribed by law and are necessary to protect public safety, order, health or morals, or the fundamental rights and freedoms of others. The freedom from coercion to have or to adopt a religion or belief and the liberty of parents and guardians to ensure religious and moral education cannot be restricted. In interpreting the scope of permissible limitation clauses, States parties should proceed from the need to protect the rights guaranteed under the Covenant, including the right to equality and non-discrimination on all grounds specified in articles 2, 3 and 26. Limitations imposed must be established by law and must not be applied in a manner that would vitiate the rights guaranteed in article 18. The Committee observes that paragraph 3 of article 18 is to be strictly interpreted: restrictions are not allowed on grounds not specified there, even if they would be allowed as restrictions to other rights protected in the Covenant, such as national security. Limitations may be applied only for those purposes for which they were prescribed and must be directly related and proportionate to the specific need on which they are predicated. Restrictions may not be imposed for discriminatory purposes or applied in a discriminatory manner. The Committee observes that the concept of morals derives from many social, philosophical and religious traditions; consequently, limitations on the freedom to manifest a religion or belief for the purpose of protecting morals must be based on principles not deriving exclusively from a single tradition. Persons already subject to certain legitimate constraints, such as prisoners, continue to enjoy their rights to manifest their religion or belief to the fullest extent compatible with the specific nature of the constraint. States parties' reports should provide information on the full scope and effects of limitations under article 18.3, both as a matter of law and of their application in specific circumstances.

Discussions surrounding the adoption of paragraph 8 of General Comment 22 were long **2.59** and complex.[158] However, there are few concrete examples of the HRC having to consider the scope of permissible restrictions.

Prescribed by law and necessary. As a matter of form, restrictions must be set down in law. **2.60** In terms of their substance, the requirement of necessity means that 'limitations must be directly related and proportionate to the specific need on which they are predicated'.[159] Furthermore, the limitations 'must not be applied in a manner that would vitiate the rights guaranteed in Article 18'[160] and 'may not be imposed for discriminatory purposes or applied in a discriminatory manner'.

Public safety. The rights in Article 18 may be subject to limitation where the manifestation **2.61** of one's religion threatened the safety of others. In *Karnel Singh Bhinder v Canada*,[161] the

---

[157] General Comment 22 (n 2) para 8.
[158] BG Tahzib, *Freedom of Religion or Belief, Ensuring Effective International Legal Protection* (Kluwer Law International 1996) 334–43.
[159] General Comment 22 (n 2) para 8.
[160] General Comment 22 (n 2) para 8.
[161] *Karnel Singh Bhinder v Canada*, Comm No 208/1986, UN Doc CCPR/C/37/D/208/1986 (1989).

author—a Canadian Sikh maintenance electrician—claimed that Canadian occupational safety legislation which required him to wear a hard hat was an impermissible restriction of his right to manifest his religion by wearing a turban, as required by his religion. Canada argued that the restriction was for the purpose of protecting public safety and was proportionate in the circumstances. The HRA agreed, also examining the issue in relation to Article 26:

> Whether one approaches the issue from the perspective of article 18 or article 26, in the view of the Committee the same conclusion must be reached. If the requirement that a hard hat be worn is regarded as raising issues under article 18, then it is a limitation that is justified by reference to the grounds laid down in article 18, paragraph 3. If the requirement that a hard hat be worn is seen as a discrimination de facto against persons of the Sikh religion under article 26, then, applying criteria now well established in the jurisprudence of the Committee, the legislation requiring that workers in federal employment be protected from injury and electric shock by the wearing of hard hats is to be regarded as reasonable and directed towards objective purposes that are compatible with the Covenant.[162]

This decision, pre-General Comment 22, has been subject to criticism by commentators on the grounds that: (a) the HRC failed adequately to consider the proportionality of the restriction in relation to its purpose;[163] and (b) the public safety restriction should not apply to cases where the manifestation in question poses only a danger to the author/complainant and not to his colleagues or the wider public.[164]

2.62 A more exacting approach was adopted by the HRC in the case of *Ranjit Singh v France*.[165] The author was an Indian Sikh with refugee status in France, who sought to renew his permanent residence permit for which he was required to provide the French authorities with two photographs. The French authorities refused to accept the author's photographs as they failed to meet the requirements set in a French Decree governing the conditions applying to foreign nationals' admission to and residence in France, which stipulated that individuals must appear full face and bareheaded in the photographs destined for the residence permits. In the photographs he submitted, the author was wearing a Sikh turban. His request for an exemption from the provisions of the Decree was rejected. The author claimed that the requirement that he appear bareheaded in the identity photograph violated his right to freedom of religion under Article 18 and could not, as France sought to argue, be justified as: (i) necessary for the protection of public safety and order; and (ii) a proportionate measure for purposes of identification. The HRC upheld the author's complaint:[166]

> The Committee recognises the State party's need to ensure and verify, for the purposes of public safety and order, that the person appearing in the photograph on a residence permit is

---

[162] *Karnel Singh Bhinder* (n 161) para 6.2.
[163] Evans (n 47) 51.
[164] Tahzib (n 158) 296.
[165] *Ranjit Singh v France*, Comm No 1876/2000, UN Doc CCPR/C/102/D/1876/2009 (Views adopted on 22 July 2011).
[166] In his concurring opinion, HRC Member Mr Fábian Omar Salvioli found that France had acted in breach of Article 2(2) inasmuch as it had not taken the requisite action under its domestic law to give effect to the right covered by Article 18:

> The legislation is in itself incompatible with the Covenant and, as a result, in order to guarantee that such events would not recur, the Committee ought to have indicated that the State party must

in fact the rightful holder of that document. It observes, however, that the State party has not explained why the wearing of a Sikh turban covering the top of the head and a portion of the forehead but leaving the rest of the face clearly visible would make it more difficult to identify the author than if he were to appear bareheaded, since he wears his turban at all times. Nor has the State party explained how, specifically, identity photographs in which people appear bareheaded help to avert the risk of fraud or falsification of residence permits. Consequently, the Committee is of the view that the State party has not demonstrated that the limitation placed on the author is necessary within the meaning of article 18, paragraph 3, of the Covenant. It also observes that, even if the obligation to remove the turban for the identity photograph might be described as a one-time requirement, it would potentially interfere with the author's freedom of religion on a continuing basis because he would always appear without his religious head covering in the identity photograph and could therefore be compelled to remove his turban during identity checks. The Committee therefore concludes that the regulation requiring persons to appear bareheaded in the identity photographs used on their residence permits is a limitation that infringes the author's freedom of religion and in this case constitutes a violation of article 18 of the Covenant.

The scrutiny the HRC applied in *Ranjit Singh*—in particular in its assessment of the cogency of France's arguments justifying the restriction on grounds of public safety and order—can be contrasted to the inadmissibility decisions of the ECtHR in *Karaduman v Turkey*, *Phull v France*, *El Morsli v France*, and *Mann Singh v France*.[167]

Public order. A recent communication concerning public order and religious dress can also be **2.63**
contrasted with the approach of the ECtHR.[168] In *Bikramjit Singh v France*[169] the 17-year-old
Sikh author[170] complained that he had been prevented from manifesting his freedom of religion by Act No 2004-228 of March 2004, which introduced rules prohibiting 'the wearing of symbols or clothing by which pupils manifest their religious affiliation in a conspicuous manner'.[171] In particular, he stated that at the start of the school year in which the legislation was passed (September 2004), he had been prevented from entering the classroom in his *keski* and was sent to the canteen to study without assistance for three weeks. He was eventually expelled after he refused to remove his religious headgear. Multiple appeals finally resulted in a dismissal of his case by the Council of State in a ruling of December 2007. In his presentation of the facts, the author noted the following unchallenged points about the wearing of the turban and *keski*:

> The wearing of the turban is a categorical, explicit and mandatory religious precept in Sikhism ... Asking a Sikh to remove his turban is therefore tantamount to asking him to perform an impossible act. The *keski* (like the turban for adult men) is not meant as an external display of faith but is rather intended to protect the long uncut hair, which is considered as a sacred, inherent and intrinsic part of the religion. The turban is not worn with a view to proselytize—a concept which is foreign to the Sikh religion.[172]

---

amend [the relevant] Decree to remove the requirement that applicants must be photographed 'bareheaded'.

The majority View is silent on the Article 2(2) point.

[167] See Ch 3, para 3.99 (*Karduman v Turkey*), para 3.105 (*Phull v France*), and (n 352) para 3.105 (*El Morsli v France*).

[168] See Ch 3, paras 3.106–3.110.

[169] *Bikramjit Singh v France*, Comm No 1852/2008 (2012), UN Doc CCPR/C/106/D/1852/2008.

[170] Complainants are referred to as 'authors' in HRC communications.

[171] Education Code, art L.141–5-1.

[172] *Bikramjit Singh* (n 169) para 2.3.

2.64 As it was not in dispute that the legislation constituted an interference with the author's freedom of religion, it fell to the Committee to decide whether the limitation was necessary and proportionate to a legitimate end. First, it was accepted that the legislation served purposes relating to the rights and freedoms of others, public order, and public safety.[173] However, the HRC did not find for the state party beyond that point:

> The Committee is of the view that the State party has not furnished compelling evidence that by wearing his *keski* the author would have posed a threat to the rights and freedoms of other pupils or to order at the school. The Committee is also of the view that the penalty of the pupil's permanent expulsion from the public school was disproportionate and led to serious effects on the education to which the author, like any person of his age, was entitled in the State party. The Committee is not convinced that expulsion was necessary and that the dialogue between the school authorities and the author truly took into consideration his particular interests and circumstances.[174]

2.65 With regard to the effect of the legislation in general, the HRC made the following observations:

> ...the Committee notes the State party's assertion that the broad extension of the category of persons forbidden to comply with their religious duties simplifies the administration of the restrictive policy. However, in the Committee's view, the State party has not shown how the sacrifice of those persons' rights is either necessary or proportionate to the benefits achieved.[175]

2.66 In conclusion, the Committee advised that 'the State party is also under an obligation to prevent similar violations in the future and should review Act No. 200-228 in light of its obligations under the Covenant, in particular article 18'.[176]

2.67 The approach of the HRC in *Bikramjit Singh v France* appears to be inconsistent with the jurisprudence of the ECtHR.[177] Indeed, Strasbourg case law was referred to unsuccessfully by the state party in argument;[178] the author responded by stating that the French's government's attempts at justifying the interference were as insufficient in the ECtHR cases as they were in the present communication,[179] and the Committee itself did not comment on the issue. What impact, if any, this recent view will have on Strasbourg jurisprudence is difficult to determine. The Court has on a previous occasion taken heed of the HRC's comments and case law on Article 18;[180] however, for the ECtHR to adopt this approach would represent a departure from its previous approach to the issue of religious dress.

2.68 In *AR Coriel and MAR Aurik v the Netherlands*,[181] the authors were Dutch citizens who applied to change their surnames after their conversion to Hinduism in order to become priests. The change of name was a requirement imposed by Indian Hindu leaders upon those who wished to study to enter the priesthood. The applications to change their names were refused by the Dutch authorities pursuant to the 'Guidelines for the change of surname'

---

[173] *Bikramjit Singh* (n 169) para 8.6.
[174] *Bikramjit Singh* (n 169) para 8.7.
[175] *Bikramjit Singh* (n 169) para 8.7.
[176] *Bikramjit Singh* (n 169) para 10.
[177] See Ch 3, paras 3.99–3.100 (approach of ECtHR on religious dress).
[178] *Bikramjit Singh* (n 169) paras 4.2, 5.5.
[179] *Bikramjit Singh* (n 169).
[180] *Bayatyan v Armenia* (App 23459/03) (2011), para 105. See para 2.49.
[181] *AR Coriel and MAR Aurik v Netherlands*, Comm No 453/1991, UN Doc CCPR/C/52/D/1991 (1994).

(*Richtlijnen voor geslachtsnaamwijziging* 1976). The HRC found no breach of Article 18,[182] finding that 'the regulation of surnames and the change thereof was eminently a matter of public order and restrictions were therefore permissible under [18(3)]'. The HRC noted that the Netherlands 'could not be held accountable for restrictions placed upon the exercise of religious offices by religious leaders in other states'. The fact that the rules of admission into the Hindu faith were imposed from outside the Netherlands seemed central to the HRC's reasoning. This aspect of the HRC's decision has been strongly criticized for limiting the effectiveness of Article 18, given that religious requirements very often find their roots outside the geographical bounds of states parties. It is in situations where a person's religion *is* considered foreign in that person's country of residence that the protection of religious freedoms becomes important. As pointed out by Evans (at p 51 of his essay 'The United Nations and the Freedom of Religion: the Work of the Human Rights Committee' (see n 48)), the HRC also failed to carry out any meaningful proportionality analysis to determine whether the restriction was sufficiently tailored to the nature of the perceived public order interest.

AR Coriel and MAR Aurik can be contrasted again with the approach of the HRC in *Ranjit* **2.69** *Singh*, where public order was put forward as a justifiable limitation on the right but rejected by the HRC. In *Singh*, the HRC was willing to look behind the reasons advanced by the state for limiting the right and assess whether they indeed reflected a compelling basis for limitation.

Public morals. Paragraph 8 of General Comment 22 deals with permissible restrictions **2.70** on religious manifestation on the grounds of protecting public morals: 'The Committee observes that the concept of morals derives from many social, philosophical and religious traditions; consequently, limitations on the freedom to manifest a religion or belief for the purpose of protecting morals must be based on principles not deriving exclusively from a single tradition.' This provision attempts to ensure the neutrality of restrictions imposed on the manifestation of religious beliefs.

Fundamental rights and freedoms of others. Article 18 rights may also be restricted in order to **2.71** protect the rights and freedoms of others, provided they are 'fundamental'. In *Malcolm Ross v Canada*,[183] the author was a teacher in a private Jewish school. He was dismissed after publishing several books and pamphlets and making public statements on the subjects of abortion, conflicts between Judaism and Christianity, and the defence of the Christian religion.[184] None of these statements was made at the school where he was working, nor were they reflected in his work as

---

[182] The authors were successful under Art 17, see para 10.5:

> In the present case, the authors' request for recognition of the change of their first names to Hindu names in order to pursue their religious studies had been granted in 1986. The State party based its refusal of the request also to change their surnames on the grounds that the authors had not shown that the changes sought were essential to pursue their studies, that the names had religious connotations and that they were not 'Dutch sounding'. The Committee finds the grounds for so limiting the authors' rights under article 17 not to be reasonable. In the circumstances of the instant case the refusal of the authors' request was therefore arbitrary within the meaning of article 17, paragraph 1, of the Covenant.

For dissenting opinions in this context, see *Coeriel and Aurik v Netherlands* (453/1991), ICCPR, A/50/40 Vol II (31 October 1994) 21 (CCPR/C/52/D/453/1991) Individual Opinion by Mr Nisuke Ando, at 28 and Individual Opinion by Mr Kurt Herndl, also at 28.

[183] *Ross v Canada* (736/1997), ICCPR, A/56/40 Vol II (18 October 2000) 69, paras 2.1–2.3, 3.2–3.6, 4.1–4.8, 6.2, 6.8, 10.5, 10.6, and 11.1–11.7.

[184] *Ross* (n 183) para 2.1.

a teacher. His statements were not contrary to Canadian law and he was not prosecuted for the expression of his opinions. The author advanced his case before the HRC on the grounds that the act of dismissal constituted a violation of his rights under Article 18 and Article 19 (right to hold opinions and freedom of expression).[185] The HRA found that the author's dismissal was justified in order to protect the fundamental rights and freedoms of others. Given the widespread publicity given to the author's remarks, it was reasonable to assume that those remarks had caused 'the poisoned school environment' experienced by the Jewish students in the school district. His dismissal was 'necessary to protect the right and freedom of Jewish children to have a school system free from prejudice and intolerance'. The HRC noted that the rights under both Articles 18 and 19 carry with them 'special duties and responsibilities [that] are of particular relevance within the school system, especially with regard to the teaching of young students ... The influence exerted by school teachers may justify restraints in order to ensure that legitimacy is not given by the school system to the expression of views which are discriminatory'. The restrictions permitted in Article 19(3) in relation to freedom of expression must be 'provided by law' and 'necessary ... for respect of the rights or reputations of others'. In contrast, Under Article 18(3) restrictions must be 'prescribed by law' and 'necessary' to protect 'the *fundamental* rights and freedoms of others'. The HRC did not, however, examine the meaning of the word 'fundamental' in Article 18(3) as it qualifies the rights and freedoms of others, and concluded: 'The freedom to manifest religious beliefs may be subject to limitations which are prescribed by law and are necessary to protect the fundamental rights and freedoms of others, and in the present case the issues under paragraph 3 of article 18 are therefore substantially the same as under article 19. Consequently, the Committee holds that article 18 has not been violated.'[186]

2.72 *Limitations imposed by religious authorities.* In a case where a religious authority takes actions which may have the effect of denying or restricting an individual's freedom of manifestation, the state party is not in violation of its obligations under Article 18. In *W Delgardo Páez v Colombia*,[187] it was found that: 'Columbia may, without violating this provision of the Covenant, allow the Church authorities to decide who may teach religion and in what manner it should be taught ...'.[188]

(c) Treaty obligations and customary international law

2.73 As noted previously,[189] there is a widely held view that, despite its non-binding status as a declarative General Assembly resolution, many of the core protections outlined in the Universal Declaration should be considered binding on all states. This is irrespective of

---

[185] The right of freedom of expression in Art 19(2) is also subject to limitations. Art 19(3) provides: 'The exercise of the rights provided for in paragraph 2 of this article carries with it special duties and responsibilities. It may therefore be subject to certain restrictions, but these shall only be such as are provided by law and are necessary.'

[186] Ross (n 183) para 11.8. For dissenting opinion in this context, see *Ross* (n 183) 87, Individual Opinion by Hipólito Solari Yrigoyen (dissenting).

[187] *W Delgardo Páez v Colombia*, ICCPR, A/45/40 Vol II (12 July 1990) 43, paras 2.1, 2.2, 2.4, 5.7, and 5.8.

[188] *W Delgardo Páez* (n 187) para 5.7. Challenge on the Article 19 ground was also unsuccessful (at para 5.8):

> Article 19 protects, *inter alia*, the right of freedom of expression and of opinion. This will usually cover the freedom of teachers to teach their subjects in accordance with their own views, without interference. However, in the particular circumstances of the case, the special relationship between Church and State in Colombia, exemplified by the applicable Concordat, the Committee finds that the requirement, by the Church, that religion be taught in a certain way does not violate article 19.'

[189] *W Delgardo Páez* (n 187) para 2.10.

whether those states have ratified the ICCPR. With respect to the protections of Article 18 of the ICCPR, there is a strong argument that Article 18 had the effect of crystallizing a principle of customary international law.[190] This is supported by the fact that derogation from Article 18 is not permitted (see Article 4.2). Secondly, relatively few states parties have entered reservations. States that entered substantive reservations were subject to objections that such reservations were incompatible with the object and purpose of the Covenant itself.[191] Thirdly, a significant number of states have legislative provisions pertaining to the right to religious freedom, many of them in their seminal rights laws and constitutions. All regional human rights treaties contain provisions guaranteeing the right to freedom of religion. Finally, Article 18 finds its genesis in Article 18 of the Universal Declaration, an instrument in large part accepted as being reflective of principles of customary international law.

(d) Differences from Article 18 UDHR

Article 18 ICCPR clearly follows the text of its namesake in the Universal Declaration. However, it is distinguishable from Article 18 of the Universal Declaration in four central ways.[192] The first is the modification of the language in 18(1) where 'freedom to change his religion or belief' in the Universal Declaration has been replaced by 'freedom to have or adopt a religion or belief of his choice' in the ICCPR. This drafting reflected a compromise based on objections raised by Islamic states.[193] The second is the protection found in Article 18(2) ICCPR against coercion. This protection is aimed at situations where states seek to use force, the threat of physical force, penal sanctions, or policies and practices, in order to make citizens adhere to specific religious beliefs.[194] The third point of difference is that Article 18(3) provides a specific limitations clause in relation to the right to manifest. Finally, Article 18(4) requires states parties to have respect for the liberty of parents and legal guardians to ensure the religious and moral education of their children in conformity with their own convictions.

2.74

(e) Conclusions on Article 18 and the approach of the HRC

Early decisions of the HRC that deal with Article 18 issues are of only limited assistance to practitioners. They typically consist of a short recitation of the facts; an account of the efforts of the author to seek domestic remedies; a synopsis of submissions made to the HRC; followed by a decision which often lacks detailed reasoning or explanation. Given this approach, it is often difficult to distil principles for future application. This lack of clarity is compounded in cases where a number of different rights violations are alleged, when the decisions of the HRC have tended not to address those grounds of challenge separately. The situation has, however, improved with time and the advent of General Comment 22.[195] More recent communications have typically contained cogent reasoning not only by the majority but also in reasoned dissents. Notwithstanding the very helpful guidance found in General Comment 22, it was infrequently referred to in HRC decisions. That too has been

2.75

---

[190] Radan (n 107) 10.

[191] For instance, a number of states objected to the reservations initially entered by the Maldives and the Islamic Republic of Pakistan in relation to Art 18. Pakistan ultimately withdrew its reservation in June 2011.

[192] M Hill QC, R Sandberg, and N Doe, *Religion and Law in the United Kingdom* (Kluwer Law International, 2011) para 144.

[193] P Taylor, *Freedom of Religion: UN and European Human Rights Law and Practice* (CUP, 2005) 28, 30, 31.

[194] Taylor (n 193) 25.

[195] Radan (n 107) 13.

changing, as evidenced in the communications on conscientious objection, where it has in effect precipitated a shift in the HRC's reasoning as to the proper scope of the protections in Article 18.

(3) Substantive protections: Article 27 and indirect protections

(a) Article 27

2.76 Article 27 ICCPR provides:

> In those States in which ethnic, religious or linguistic minorities exist, persons belonging to such minorities shall not be denied the right, in community with the other members of their group, to enjoy their own culture, to profess and practise their own religion, or to use their own language.

2.77 Article 27 does not recognize or protect group rights. Article 27 was deliberately phrased to enunciate a right relating to the individual.[196] In any event, the individual communication procedure[197] of the ICCPR does not allow for group actions or actions brought by an individual as representative of a class or group.[198] The opening phrase 'in those States in which ethnic, religious or linguistic minorities exist' raises the possibility of states arguing that there are no such sufficiently identified minorities residing in their territories, so that the Article could not be invoked.

(b) Indirect protections

2.78 Article 20 ICCPR provides that:

1. Any propaganda for war shall be prohibited by law.
2. Any advocacy of national, racial or religious hatred that constitutes incitement to discrimination, hostility or violence shall be prohibited by law.

2.79 Rather than setting out a specific right for protection, Article 20 establishes limitations on other human rights (particularly freedom of expression and information). It not only

---

[196] The Sub-Commission on Prevention of Discrimination and Protection of Minorities discussed drafts of Art 27 (Report of Sub-Commission UN Doc E/CN.4/358, paras 39–48) submitted to it (pursuant to UNGA Res 217c(III), adopted 10 December 1948). The Sub-Commission in fact changed the wording from a collective wording: 'Ethnic, religious and linguistic minorities shall not be denied the right to enjoy their own culture, to profess and practice their own religion, or to use their own language' to the individual subject: 'persons belonging to minorities shall not be denied the right'.

[197] See para 2.103.

[198] See *Fatima Andersen v Denmark* (1868/2009), CCPR/C/99/D/1868/2009 (7 September 2010), para 6.4:

> The Committee observes that no person may, in theoretical terms and by *actio popularis*, object to a law or practice which he holds to be at variance with the Covenant. Any person claiming to be a victim of a violation of a right protected by the Covenant must demonstrate either that a State party has by an act or omission already impaired the exercise of his right or that such impairment is imminent, basing his argument for example on legislation in force or on a judicial or administrative decision or practice. In the Committee's decision regarding *Toonen v. Australia*, the Committee had considered that the author had made reasonable efforts to demonstrate that the threat of enforcement and the pervasive impact of the continued existence of the incriminated facts on administrative practices and public opinion had affected him and continued to affect him personally. In the present case, the Committee considers that the author has failed to establish that the statement made by Ms. Kjærsgaard had specific consequence for her or that the specific consequences of the statements were imminent and would personally affect the author. The Committee therefore considers that the author has failed to demonstrate that she was a victim for the purposes of the Covenant. This part of the communication is therefore inadmissible under article 1 of the Optional Protocol.

authorizes interference with those rights, but also imposes an obligation on states parties to enact prohibitory legislation.[199] The inevitable conflict with freedom of expression has prompted numerous reservations to Article 20,[200] causing the issue to be expressly addressed by the Committee in General Comment 11: 'in the opinion of the Committee, these required prohibitions are fully compatible with the right of freedom of expression as contained in article 19, the exercise of which carries with it special duties and responsibilities'. Very often, the Committee's assessment of whether Article 20(2) can operate as a defence to alleged restrictions of freedom of expression (Article 19) is subsumed within the analysis of the restriction criteria under Article 19(3).

Article 20(2) has particular relevance for freedom of religion. It seeks to ensure that no **2.80** speech, whether itself religiously motivated or not, operates to advocate religious hatred. Precisely what is included in the scope of 'advocacy' is unclear. In *Andersen v Denmark*,[201] the state party sought to argue that 'such advocacy must constitute incitement to discrimination, hostility or violence';[202] the Committee did not address the issue, and the reason for this alleged criterion is not set out in the Committee's summary.

Article 20(2) protects characteristics such as race and religion through the compromise of **2.81** free speech. Free speech can itself, of course, be religiously motivated, and authors of communications seeking protection of religious rights can therefore fall on both sides of the provision. They may either seek to allege that their right to freedom of (religiously-motivated) speech has been unlawfully violated by a state party, to which Article 20(2) may be raised as a defence; or, they may seek to allege that a state party is not giving proper effect to Article 20(2), and consequently they are the victims of advocacy of religious hatred.

An example of the former is *Ross v Canada*,[203] where it can be seen that in practice, the **2.82** HRC subsumes the question of a defence to restricting an alleged victim's freedom of speech under Article 20(2) within the question of justification of that restriction under Article 19(3).[204] The facts were set out earlier, at paragraph 2.71. In summary, Mr Ross was a school teacher in a private Jewish school who published a number of books and pamphlets reflecting anti-Semitic beliefs. As a result of the complaints of several parents to a Human Rights Inquiry Board (the Board), the school was ordered to place Mr Ross on leave of absence; to appoint him to a non-teaching position; and to dismiss him after 18 months if such a position could not be found. Mr Ross sought judicial review of the Board's decision, but the order was ultimately upheld by the Supreme Court of Canada. Mr Ross then submitted a communication to the HRC. He complained that he had been refused the right freely to express his religious opinions, and therefore his rights under Articles 18 and 19 ICCPR had been violated. In response, the state party submitted that his publications in fact fell within the scope of Article 20(2) because they constituted 'advocacy of national, racial or religious hatred',

---

[199] See General Comment 11, UN Doc A/38/40(SUPP): 'States parties are obliged to adopt the necessary legislative measures prohibiting the actions referred to therein. However, the reports have shown that in some States such actions are neither prohibited by law nor are appropriate efforts intended or made to prohibit them', para 1.

[200] Mostly by Western states parties, eg the US, Belgium, Denmark, Finland, and Iceland.

[201] *Andersen v Denmark*, Comm No 1868/2009, UN Doc CCPR/C/99/D/1868/2009 (2010).

[202] *Andersen* (n 201) para 4.3.

[203] *Ross* (n 183) 69.

[204] Art 19(3) provides: 'The exercise of the rights provided for in paragraph 2 of this article carries with it special duties and responsibilities. It may therefore be subject to certain restrictions, but these shall only be such as are provided by law and are necessary.'

and that therefore the communication was inadmissible.[205] The Committee responded that 'restrictions on expression which may fall within the scope of article 20 must also be permissible under article 19, paragraph 3, which lays down requirements for determining whether restrictions on expression are admissible', and therefore stated that consideration on the merits was required.[206] Ultimately the actions of the state party were considered to be justified under Article 19(3) (see paragraph 2.71).

2.83 The only communication in which the state party is alleged not to have complied with Article 20(2), and has thus failed to protect the author's religious rights, is *Andersen v Denmark*.[207] Mrs Andersen, a practising Muslim, contended that a leading figure of the Danish People's Party (DPP) was in breach of Article 20(2) when making statements comparing Muslim headscarves with Nazi swastikas. She claimed that 'her case [was] based on a clear pattern of Islamophobic statements amounting to hate propaganda against Muslims in Denmark carried out by leading members of the DPP'.[208] She asserted that Danish authorities had failed to acknowledge the need to protect Muslims against hate speech.[209] The Committee did not consider this question on the merits, and instead held that the communication was inadmissible because Mrs Andersen could not be considered a 'victim' for the purposes of the Covenant: 'the Committee considers that the author has failed to establish that the statement made by Ms. Kjærsgaard [a DPP leader] had specific consequence for her or that the specific consequences of the statements were imminent and would personally affect the author'.[210] This approach is difficult to reconcile with the content of the obligations in Article 20. 'Advocacy of religious hatred' does not of itself presume an immediate or specific consequence, and the focus of the Article is on measures taken to prohibit the act itself, rather than on preventing a particular outcome caused by that act. It is, therefore surprising that the Committee did not consider its earlier approach in holding authors susceptible to the 'pervasive impact of the continued existence of administrative practices and public opinion' to be victims for the purposes of the Covenant.[211]

(4) Practice and procedure

2.84 The implementation of the rights contained in the ICCPR is intended to be a domestic matter.[212] Nonetheless, there exists a secondary source of protection via the international enforcement mechanisms of the HRC. This body exercises a supervisory function which involves regular interaction with the states parties, and also has jurisdiction to receive complaints from individuals once they have exhausted domestic remedies. Whilst this bipartite system manifests a concession to State sovereignty, the Committee is able to influence and guide the states parties' domestic translation of the Covenant's guarantees through the issue of reports and General Comments.

---

[205] *Ross* (n 183) para 6.2.
[206] *Ross* (n 183) para 10.6.
[207] *Andersen* (n 201).
[208] *Andersen* (n 201) para 3.1.
[209] *Andersen* (n 201) para 3.2.
[210] *Andersen* (n 201) 6.4.
[211] *Toonen v Australia*, Comm No 488/1992, UN Doc CCPR/C/50/D/488/1992 (1994) para 5.1. This approach is also followed by the Committee on the Elimination of Racial Discrimination (see eg *The Jewish Community of Oslo et al v Norway*, Comm No 30/2003, UN Doc. CERD/C/67/D/30/2003 (2005)).
[212] See Nowak (n 155) 22-75.

(a) The Human Rights Committee[213]

The functions of the HRC are set out in the ICCPR, the First Optional Protocol and rules **2.85**
of procedure.[214]

Part IV, which consists of Articles 28 to 45, provides for the establishment of the HRC, the **2.86**
appointment of its members, its role and activities. The HRC is constituted of 18 members,[215] elected[216] from among nationals of states parties,[217] but serving in their personal
capacity[218] for four-year terms.[219] Members are anticipated to be 'persons of high moral
character and recognized competence in the field of human rights, consideration being given
to the usefulness of the participation of some persons having legal experience'.[220] In the elections, consideration is given to 'equitable geographic distribution of membership and to
the representation of the different forms of civilisation and of the principal legal systems'.[221]
Each state party may nominate no more than two nationals;[222] the HRC may not include
more than one national from the same state party.[223] The persons elected are those nominees
who receive the largest number of votes of the representatives of states parties present and
voting.[224] Each HRC member upon election is obliged to make a solemn declaration that he
or she will perform his or her duties impartially and conscientiously.[225] HRC members work
part time and receive emoluments from UN resources.[226]

The HRC meets three times a year: in spring in New York, and in Geneva in summer and **2.87**
autumn for three-week sessions.[227] The meetings of the HRC, and any subsidiary body, are
held in public unless the HRC decides otherwise, save that the adoption of Concluding
Comments under Article 40 take place *in camera*.[228] Twelve members constitute a quorum
for the conduct of HRC business.[229]

The HRC performs four essential functions in order to implement the Covenant. Under **2.88**
the reporting procedure set out in Article 40, it conducts dialogues and draws conclusions
from obligatory reports produced by states parties in order to show their compliance with

---

[213] T Opsahl, 'The Human Rights Committee' in P Alston (ed), *The United Nations and Human Rights: A Critical Appraisal* (Clarendon Press, 1992) 369–443; BG Ramcharan, 'Implementing the International Covenants on Human Rights' in BG Ramcharan (ed), *Human Rights: Thirty Years after the Universal Declaration Commemorative Volume on the Occasion of the Thirtieth Anniversary of the Universal Declaration of Human Rights* (Martinus Nijhoff, 1979) 159–95; HJ Steiner, P Alston, and R Goodman, *International Human Rights in Context: Law, Politics, Morals* (OUP, 2007) 844–924.
[214] Rules of Procedure of the Human Rights Committee (hereinafter 'Rules of Procedure'), UN Doc CCPR/C/3/Rev.10 (January 2012).
[215] ICCPR, Art 28(1).
[216] By secret ballot at meetings convened by the UN Secretary General at the Headquarters of the UN in New York: ICCPR, Art 30(4).
[217] ICCPR, Art 28(2).
[218] ICCPR, Art 28(3).
[219] ICCPR, Art 32(1), which also provides that they are eligible for re-election if re-nominated and that half of the members of the HRC are elected every two years.
[220] ICCPR, Art 28(2).
[221] ICCPR, Art 31(2).
[222] ICCPR, Art 29(2).
[223] ICCPR, Art 31(1).
[224] ICCPR, Art 30(4).
[225] Rules of Procedure (n 214) r 16.
[226] ICCPR, Art 35.
[227] Rules of Procedure (n 214) r 2(1).
[228] Rule of Procedure (n 214) r 33.
[229] Rules of Procedure (n 214) r 37.

the ICCPR. The same Article also authorizes the Committee to issue General Comments, which interpret and explain the meaning of the Covenant's provisions. Article 41 sets out the interstate complaints procedure, and the First Optional Protocol gives the HRC authority to hear complaints received by way of 'communications' from individuals. These mechanisms are largely replicated by other treaty bodies, although not all such bodies have jurisdiction to hear individual complaints.

(b) The reporting procedure

2.89 *Introduction.* Article 40 sets out the states parties' obligation to present reports which demonstrate their compliance with the ICCPR. The associated procedural rules[230] address questions of timing, public examination, and the Committee's response, and also consider in detail the procedure to be adopted when states parties default on their reporting obligations. These rules are regularly adapted in order to provide a realistic procedural framework for the HRC's response to non-performance, and to address the persistent lack of respect demonstrated by some states parties to the Committee and other treaty bodies.[231] The HRC has also issued 'Revised Reporting Guidelines' which provide the states with further information on how to prepare adequate submissions for the HRC's monitoring purposes.[232]

2.90 *Timing.* States must submit their initial report within a year of the entry into force of the Covenant,[233] and further periodic reports are to be submitted at the Committee's request thereafter.[234] These requests may be made 'in accordance with the periodicity of the Committee, or at any other time the Committee may deem appropriate';[235] generally, states parties are informed of the next date for submission when the HRC imparts its concluding observations on their current report.[236] Specific procedures exist to deal with the scenario where states parties have failed to comply with these requirements (see paragraph 2.96). Furthermore, Rule 66(2) of the Rules of Procedure provides for an emergency request procedure when the Committee is not in session. The practice of calling for emergency reports from states encountering acute human rights crises was initiated in 1992, and has been rarely used.[237]

2.91 *Content.* Paragraph 1 of Article 40 requires states to report on 'the measures they have adopted which give effect to the rights recognised herein and on the progress made in the enjoyment of those rights'. Reports should include an indication of any factors and difficulties

---

[230] Rules of Procedure (n 214) Part II, XV, rr 66–73.

[231] See Joseph, Schultz, and Castan (n 100) 48. See also the Working Methods of the Human Rights Committee, Pt V, available at <http://www2.ohchr.org/english/bodies/hrc/workingmethods.htm#a2> (accessed 1 February 2013) (hereinafter 'the Working Methods').

[232] UN Doc CCPR/C/2009/1, 22 November 2010 (hereinafter 'the Reporting Guidelines'). Further information relating to practice and procedure is available in the Working Methods, available at <http://www2.ohchr.org/english/bodies/hrc/workingmethods.htm> (last accessed 6 March 2013). While this section of the OHCHR website is a useful guide, it should be noted that the Rules of Procedure references were to an outdated revision as at the date of last access.

[233] ICCPR, Art 40(1)(a).

[234] ICCPR, Art 40(1)(b). The previous requirement was that the states parties submit periodic reports every five years, but this was altered to a case-by-case basis after HRC's 66th Session in 1999. See the 2000 Annual Report of the HRC (Report of the Human Rights Committee, UN Doc A/55/40, Vol I).

[235] Rules of Procedure (n 214) r 66(2).

[236] Rules of Procedure (n 214) r 71(3).

[237] Bosnia-Herzegovina, Croatia, and the former Republic of Yugoslavia (Serbia-Montenegro) are examples of states receiving emergency requests in 1992. See Joseph, Schultz, and Castan (n 100) 18.

affecting the implementation of the Covenant,[238] and the Committee may make known further specific requirements as to their form and content through the Secretary-General.[239] According to the Reporting Guidelines, reports should contain factual information on the overall framework of protection of human rights, non-discrimination, and equality and effective remedies, as well as specific information on the implementation of the Covenant and relevant general comments of the Committee.[240]

Reports on Article 18. The Reporting Guidelines set out 'possible topics for discussion' in **2.92** relation to states parties' reports on each Article of the Covenant. Under Article 18, it is suggested that the report provide information on the following:

- The existence of different religions within the State party's jurisdiction.
- The publication and circulation of religious material.
- The measures taken to prevent and to punish offences against the free exercise of one's religion.
- In cases where a State religion exists, how a person's freedom to practice another religion, to convert to another religion, or not to have a religion is guaranteed and on how the application of the principle of non-discrimination on religious grounds is ensured.
- Any procedures that must be followed for the legal recognition and authorization of various religious denominations in the country and their practical application, including information on any refusal of recognition that might have occurred during the reporting period.
- The main status differences between the dominant religion and other denominations, in particular with regard to the granting of subsidies and the protection of, and access to, places of worship, in particular for those belonging to religious minorities.
- The legal regulation and the practice of religious education, in particular where religion is taught in State schools, the possibility for children not to attend religious classes and how the right of parents to ensure the religious education of their children in conformity with their own convictions is guaranteed.
- The fiscal provisions applicable to religions.
- The status and legal position of conscientious objectors.
- The number of persons that applied for the status of, and those that were actually recognized as, conscientious objectors.
- The reasons considered to justify conscientious objection and the rights and duties of conscientious objectors as opposed to those of persons who serve in military service.[241]

Specific further procedures are in place for the event of a State party providing insufficient information (see paragraphs 2.93 and 2.96).

Focus-based reports. In order to address the problems of frequent delay and deficient detail in **2.93** states parties' reports,[242] a new procedure was adopted at the Committee's 97th Session in October 2009. To streamline the reporting process, the HRC will now generally send states parties a list of issues in advance, to which a reply is then given.[243] Where this procedure is adopted, the state party's response will constitute their periodic report for the purposes of Article 40(b).

---

[238] Rules of Procedure (n 214) r 66(1).
[239] Rules of Procedure (n 214) r 66(4).
[240] Reporting Guidelines (n 232) para 7 (see also, in more detail, paras 18–22).
[241] Reporting Guidelines (n 232) paras 83–84.
[242] See eg Rehman (n 8) 116–17.
[243] Reporting Guidelines (n 232) para 14.

2.94 *Procedure upon submission.* Reports are examined in a public dialogue between the HRC and the representatives of each state party.[244] Prior to the session, the HRC establishes a Country Report Task Force (CRTF), which is made up of four to six members of the HRC and at least one member of the state party concerned. This body will generally review the 'country profile' based on previous reports and concluding observations, and will prepare a list of questions arising out of the current report. The format of the session is as follows: the state party representative makes introductory comments, followed by replies to the first group of questions included in the list of issues. The Committee will then comment or issue further questions on the basis of the replies received, during which time the relevant members of the CRTF have priority in determining what questions should be put.[245]

2.95 *Concluding Observations.* The final phase of the Committee's examination of states parties' reports is the drafting and adoption of written concluding observations. The agreed structure is as follows: introduction; positive aspects; factors and difficulties impeding implementation of the Covenant; principle subjects of concern; and suggestions and recommendations.[246] The observations will include a paragraph requesting wide dissemination of the observations in the state party concerned, as well as a paragraph requesting an interim report on specific issues raised within a certain period (usually one year).[247]

2.96 *Delay, non-submission, and absence of representatives.* Non-compliance with the basic framework of requirements is an issue which plagues the reporting procedure.[248] In the event that a state party fails to submit a report or any further information requested, the Committee may issue a reminder. If the state fails to submit following this reminder, the HRC will make a statement to that effect in its annual report to the UN General Assembly.[249] After issuing reminders, the Committee may also notify the state party that it intends to conduct a public examination of the measures taken by that state to give effect to the rights enshrined in the Covenant.[250] The state party's next periodic report must then be within two years of this procedure.[251] If a state party has submitted a report but fails to send a representative to the interactive session, the Committee may notify the state party that it intends to proceed with the examination of the report at the pre-decided session or at a later session.[252]

2.97 *Provision of information by specialized agencies.* Specialized agencies may comment on states parties' reports if the Committee decides to transmit copies of such parts of the document as fall within their competence;[253] these comments will often be by way of oral representation at each plenary session.[254]

---

[244] Rules of Procedure (n 214) r 68.

[245] Working Methods (n 231) Section B.

[246] Working Methods (n 231) Section C.

[247] Rules of Procedure (n 214) r 71 addresses the consideration of reports and the requests for interim reports. While the rule suggests that the request for an interim report is discretionary, it appears from the Working Methods that provision of supplementary information is general practice.

[248] See Rules of Procedure (n 214).

[249] Rules of Procedure (n 214) r 69.

[250] Rules of Procedure (n 214) r 70.

[251] Rules of Procedure (n 214) r 70(3).

[252] Rules of Procedure (n 214) r 68(2).

[253] ICCPR, Art 40(3), supplemented by Rules of Procedure (n 214) r 67.

[254] Working Methods (n 231) Pt VIII.

(c) General comments

Introduction. Article 40(4) provides that the Committee 'shall transmit its reports, and any **2.98** such general comments as it may consider appropriate, to the State parties'. The HRC has interpreted this to mean that the Committee is authorized to issue 'General Comments' addressed to all state parties, and has presently issued 34 such comments.[255] Most expand on the meaning of specific Covenant rights,[256] while some address a particular theme encompassing a broader range of rights.[257]

Purpose, development, and use. Ghandi has provided a useful summary of the various pur- **2.99** poses served by the issue of General Comments.[258] His list reads as follows:

> To make the Committee's experience available for the benefit of all States Parties, so as to promote more effective implementation of the Covenant; to draw the attention of States parties to insufficiencies disclosed by a large number of reports; to suggest improvements in the reporting procedure; to clarify the requirements of the Covenant; and to stimulate the activities of States Parties and International Organisations in the promotion and protection of human rights. General Comments are intended also to be of interest to other States, especially those preparing to become parties to the Covenant. They are intended in addition to strengthen cooperation amongst States in the universal protection and promotion of human rights.

Earlier Comments were generally less detailed than the comprehensive Comments which followed in later years. The Committee is now replacing earlier versions with more relevant and elaborate Comments: General Comment 10 on the freedom of expression, for example, has been expanded upon in the most recent Comment 34 on the same subject.[259] The flexibility of this mandate of the Committee, in many respects unique in comparison with corresponding functions in other conventions,[260] has meant that General Comments have become a valuable jurisprudential resource. The HRC itself has made increasing reference to its Comments in the consideration of state reports, cementing their significance as a general interpretative resource for the implementation of the Covenant.

(d) Interstate applications

Introduction. The Covenant's interstate complaints procedure is provided for by Articles 41 **2.100** to 43, and has never been used.[261] This lack of participation has persisted despite exhortations in General Comment 31[262] for states to avail themselves of the procedure, and to consider the usage of the mechanism not as 'an unfriendly act', but as a 'reflection of legitimate community interest'.[263] The complaints process comprises several phases, each of which is

---

[255] There was an initial suggestion that Art 40(4) authorized the Committee to make a consensus evaluation on a particular state's report, but it was felt that this practice would be too invasive with regard to that state's internal affairs; see Joseph, Schultz, and Castan (n 100) 20.

[256] See eg the last general comment, General Comment 34, UN Doc CCPR/C/GC/34 (September 2011), which concerned Art 19 on the freedoms of opinion and expression. General Comment 22 on the freedom of religion (n 2) is a further example of this type of comment.

[257] See eg 'The position of Aliens under the Covenant' (General Comment 15, HRI/GEN/1/Rev.9 (Vol I) (1986) 189).

[258] PR Ghandi, *The Human Rights Committee and the Right of Individual Communication: Law and Practice* (Ashgate, 1998) 25.

[259] General Comment 34 (n 256).

[260] See Nowak (n 155) 747.

[261] See <http://www2.ohchr.org/english/bodies/petitions/index.htm#interstate> (accessed 1 February 2013).

[262] General Comment 31 (n 97).

[263] General Comment 31 (n 97) para 2.

consequential on the failure of the former. The ultimate destination of an interstate complaint is a non-binding recommendation by a five-member ad hoc Conciliation Commission, with the matter also being referred to the General Assembly by the HRC in its annual report.

2.101 *Initial procedure.* States parties cannot avail themselves of, or be subject to, the interstate complaints procedure without first making an additional declaration that the HRC is competent to hear such complaints.[264] Thereafter, any State (A) having made this declaration may bring another State's (B) perceived violations of the Covenant to the latter's attention. State B must then present a written explanation to State A within three months which clarifies the matter and sets out, *inter alia*, any remedies taken or pending.[265] If the issue is not resolved to the parties' satisfaction within six months, either then has the right to refer the matter to the Committee;[266] once the Committee has ascertained that all domestic remedies have been exhausted,[267] it will examine the communications in closed meetings.[268] It will subsequently make available its good offices with a view to friendly resolution of the issue[269]—during which time the states parties concerned have the right to be represented and to make oral or written submissions[270]—and is obliged to produce a written report within 12 months of receiving the notice of complaint.[271]

2.102 *No amicable resolution.* Under Article 42, if the matter has not been resolved to the satisfaction of all the parties, an ad hoc Commission of five members shall be formed ('the Commission').[272] Its object is to continue the pursuit of an amicable resolution,[273] and to issue a report on the matter for communication to the parties.[274] If no solution has been reached, the report must contain findings of fact and must express a view on the possibility of an amicable solution.[275] The state parties must notify the Commission within three months as to whether they accept the contents of the report,[276] and the matter will in each case be referred to the General Assembly by the HRC in its annual report.

(e) The Individual complaints procedure

2.103 *Introduction.* The first Optional Protocol to the ICCPR sets out the Individual Complaints Procedure, which is the third and arguably the most significant mechanism under the Covenant.[277] States may elect whether or not to sign up to the Protocol, and at the time of writing there are 114 states parties to it.[278] Under this procedure, individuals subject to the HRC's jurisdiction are able to send written communications to the Secretariat of the Office of the High Commissioner for Human Rights claiming that they are the victims of violation by a state party of any of the rights enshrined in the Covenant. The relevant state party must

---

[264] ICCPR, Art 41(1).

[265] ICCPR, Art 41(1)(a).

[266] ICCPR, Art 41(1)(b).

[267] ICCPR, Art 41(1)(c).

[268] ICCPR, Art 41(1)(d).

[269] ICCPR, Art 41(1)(e).

[270] ICCPR, Art 41(1)(f).

[271] ICCPR, Art 41(1)(g).

[272] ICCPR, Art 42(1). Details of the Commission's constitution are contained in Art 42(2)–(5).

[273] ICCPR, Art 42(1)(a).

[274] ICCPR, Art 42(7).

[275] ICCPR, Art 42(7)(c).

[276] ICCPR, Art 42(7)(d).

[277] See also Rules of Procedure, (n 214) XVII, rr 84–104.

[278] <http://treaties.un.org/Pages/ViewDetails.aspx?src=TREATY&mtdsg_no=IV-5&chapter=4&lang=en> (accessed 12 July 2013). The UK is not a state party to the First Optional Protocol.

be a party to the Protocol to be subject to the complaint. The procedure comprises the following broad stages: submission of the communication; seeking of information (and interim measures, where necessary) from the state party; response to the state party's information from the author of the complaint; consideration on admissibility by the Working Group on Communications; further consultation with the author and the state party; formulation of a view by the HRC; and finally, the forwarding of the HRC's view to the state party and the individual.

Submission of the communication. Communications must be in written form in any language, **2.104** and must be sent to the Secretariat of the Office of the High Commissioner for Human Rights. For a long time, it was the case that there were no time limits on the submission of a complaint after the exhaustion of domestic remedies;[279] however, the revised Rules of Procedure state that a communication may constitute an abuse of the right of submission when it is 'submitted after 5 years from the exhaustion of domestic remedies by the author of the communication, or, where applicable, after 3 years from the conclusion of another procedure of international investigation or settlement, unless there are reasons justifying the delay...'.[280] The communication must include clear information on the victim and the author, and must identify the state against which the complaint is being made. It must include a statement confirming that it has met the admissibility requirements (see paragraph 2.111).[281]

Response from state party. The procedure for communications is dealt with by a Working **2.105** Group on Communications established under Rule 95(1) of the Rules of Procedure. The Working Group consists of five members of the HRC and meets for one week before the session. As soon as possible after the receipt of a communication,[282] the Working Group will request the state party concerned to submit a written response to the communication.[283] This response must address both the merits and admissibility of the submission, unless otherwise requested, and must be sent to the Committee within six months.[284] The author of the communication is then given the opportunity to respond within a fixed time limit,[285] and there is a general power to allow each party to make further submissions upon receipt of information from the other side.[286]

Declaration of admissibility and consideration by the HRC. After the initial exchanges **2.106** between the parties, the communication is passed to the Working Party and can only be declared admissible by their unanimous decision.[287] Thereafter it is considered by the HRC in closed session, and the pleadings are treated as confidential.[288] The parties

---

[279] See eg *Víctor Villamón Ventura v Spain*, Comm No 1305/2004, UN Doc CCPR/C/88/D/1305/2004 (2006) para 6.4.

[280] Rules of Procedure, (n 214) r 96(c). This rule in its amended form came into effect as of 1 January 2012.

[281] See Rules of Procedure (n 214) r 96.

[282] In order to proceed at all, the communication must have been registered by the Special Rapporteur on New Communications. He may only register communications where he is satisfied that the preliminary admissibility requirements have been complied with (on admissibility, see paras 2.108–2.111).

[283] Rules of Procedure (n 214) r 97(1).

[284] Rules of Procedure (n 214) r 97(2).

[285] Rules of Procedure (n 214) r 99(3).

[286] Rules of Procedure (n 214) r 99(6).

[287] Rules of Procedure (n 214) r 99(2) and (3). The decision is transmitted to the Committee, who will generally endorse it without a plenary session, but discussion is obligatory once requested by any Committee member.

[288] The rules of confidentiality are set out in the Rules of Procedure (n 214) rr 102–103.

are both informed once the communication has been declared admissible, and further consultation is carried out prior to the HRC formulating its views.[289] In reaching a conclusion, the Committee will take all written information received into account.[290] There are no apparent mechanisms for oral or onsite investigations.[291] The HRC is not bound by the doctrine of precedent,[292] and presents its views though consensus; individual members may nonetheless write concurring or dissenting opinions.[293] The views, once formulated, are forwarded to the state party and to the individual,[294] and are not legally binding. However, the HRC has stated that their views 'exhibit some important characteristics of a judicial decision', pointing out that: 'They are arrived at in a judicial spirit, including the impartiality and independence of committee members, the considered interpretation of the language of the Covenant, and the determinative character of the decisions.'[295] The decisions often resemble legally-binding findings, not least in the range of remedies suggested.[296]

2.107 *Ensuring compliance.* Early procedure between 1982 and 1990 involved sending letters to states parties urging them to take action on the HRC's decisions. After this proved ineffective, an additional step was introduced whereby a Committee Member designated 'Special Rapporteur for the Follow-Up of Views' is given the task of monitoring the implementation process.[297] This Committee Member has a wide mandate,[298] and may make such further recommendations as he or she considers necessary as regards action by the Committee.[299] The Special Rapporteur must report to the HRC on the progress of any dialogue on a regular basis.

2.108 *Admissibility: who may submit?*[300] The HRC may only receive communications from individuals who are within the respondent state's jurisdiction. The complaint may come from a group of individuals who claim to be similarly affected,[301] and the Committee has been flexible in allowing others to petition on behalf of victims who are subject to, *inter alia*, arbitrary detention, censorship, or incapacitating illness.[302] As Articles 1 and 2 of the Protocol explicitly refer to 'individuals', NGOs and organizations in general are not permitted to act as authors of communications. The alleged victim must establish that a violation of the

---

[289] Rules of Procedure (n 214) r 99.

[290] Rules of Procedure (n 214) r 99(4).

[291] S Lewis-Anthony and M Scheinin, 'Treaty-Based Procedures for Making Human Rights Complaints within the UN System' in H Hannum (ed), *Guide to International Human Rights Practice* (Transnational Publishers, 2004) 48–50.

[292] See *Roger Judge v Canada*, Comm No 829/1998, UN Doc CCPR/C/78/D/839/1998 (2003) para 10.3: 'The Committee considers that the Covenant should be interpreted as a living instrument and the rights protected under it should be applied in context and in the light of present-day conditions.'

[293] Rules of Procedure (n 214) r 104.

[294] Rules of Procedure (n 214) r 100(3).

[295] General Comment 33, 'The Obligation of States Parties under the Optional Protocol to the International Covenant on Civil and Political Rights', UN Doc CCPR/C/GC/33 (5 November 2008) para 11.

[296] See Rehman (n 8) 124.

[297] Rules of Procedure (n 214) r 101.

[298] The Special Rapporteur may make such contacts and take such action as appropriate for the due performance of the follow-up mandate. The Special Rapporteur shall make such recommendations for further action by the Committee as may be necessary.

[299] Rules of Procedure (n 214), r 101(2).

[300] See Rehman (n 8) 125–37.

[301] *Lubicon Lake Band v Canada* (167/1984) para 32.1.

[302] See Ghandi (n 258) 85. See also Rules of Procedure (n 214) r 96(b).

Covenant has prevented the enjoyment of his rights,[303] and fulfilment of the requirement is not invalidated by virtue of the victim's own behaviour.[304] An alleged victim may only complain of violation of the rights enshrined within the Covenant,[305] and must establish a *prima facie* case.[306]

Admissibility: who can be subject to a communication? Actions under the Protocol must be **2.109** brought against a state party and not against an organization.[307] As a general principle, the state party in question must be the one which has violated the victim's rights,[308] and it is important to verify that the state is a party to the ICCPR and the Optional Protocol. It then remains to be determined that the organ in alleged violation is a public and not a private body.[309]

Admissibility: existence of other international procedures. A communication under the **2.110** Protocol cannot be considered if it is being examined by another international procedure.[310] Only procedures implemented by interstate or inter-governmental organizations are relevant for the purposes of this provision, and complaints are barred only when the matter is being concurrently considered by another international procedure.[311] Communications may be submitted subsequent to exhaustion of another procedure, or subsequent to withdrawal.[312]

Admissibility: non-exhaustion of domestic remedies. The provision under Article 5(2)(b) that **2.111** a victim must have exhausted all domestic remedies is a significant admissibility requirement.[313] The rationale is to ensure that state parties have had the opportunity to examine their own implementation of the provisions of the Covenant and to remedy any violations where necessary.[314] The applicant has the initial burden of proof, and is relieved of his obligation to exhaust domestic remedies where they are ineffective,[315] unreasonable in nature or excessively onerous,[316] unduly prolonged, or no longer open to the victim.[317] On a number of occasions, the Committee has required the state to show that the remedies are available and effective.

---

[303] *Morrison v Jamaica*, Comm No 663/1995, UN Doc CCPR/C/64/D/663/1995 (25 November 1998) para 6.4.

[304] *Michael and Brian Hill v Spain*, Comm No 526/1993, UN Doc CCPR/C/59/D/526/1993 (2 April 1997) para 9.1.

[305] *KL v Denmark*, Comm No 59/1979 (26 March 1980), UN Doc CCPR/C/OP/1 (1984) 24. Overlap with other Human Rights instruments does not render the application inadmissible.

[306] 'The case must not be entirely without merit or legal principle', Ghandi (n 258) 181.

[307] *H v Netherlands*, Comm No 217/1986 (24 March 1988) UN Doc CCPR/C/OP/1 (1984) 70.

[308] *Carmen Améndola and Graciela Baritussio v Uruguay*, Comm No 25/1978 (26 July 1982), UN Doc CCPR/C/OP/1 (1985) 136, para 7.2.

[309] See Rehman (n 8) ch 1.

[310] ICCPR, Art 5(2)(a).

[311] *LESK v Netherlands*, Comm No 381/1989, UN Doc CCPR/C/45/D/381/1989 (1992) para 5.2.

[312] See Rehman (n 8) 134.

[313] *NS v Canada*, Comm No 26/1978 (28 July 1978), Un Doc CCPR/C/OP/1 (1984) 19.

[314] See PR Ghandi, 'Some Aspects of the Exhaustion of Domestic Remedies Rule Under the Jurisprudence of the Human Rights Committee' (2001) 44 GYBIL 485.

[315] *Guillermo Ignacio Dermit Barbato and Hugo Haroldo Dermit Barbato v Uruguay*, Comm No 84/1981 (27 February 1981), UN Doc Supp No 40 (A/38/40) (1983) 124.

[316] *TK v France*, Comm No 220/1987 (8 December 1989) UN Doc CCPR/C/37/D/220/1987 (1989) para 8.2

[317] *Eduardo Bleier v Uruguay*, Comm No R.7/30 (23 May 1978), UN Doc Supp No 40 (A/37/40) (1982) 130.

D. UN Declaration on the Elimination of All Forms of Intolerance and of Discrimination Based on Religion or Belief 1981

2.112 It was originally intended that the protections for religious rights set out in the Universal Declaration and ICCPR would be followed by a detailed treaty on religious freedom and non-discrimination.[318] Such a treaty has not materialized.[319] Instead, the UN General Assembly has passed a non-binding declaration: the UN Declaration on the Elimination of All Forms of Intolerance and of Discrimination based on Religion and Belief 1981 ('the 1981 Declaration').[320] Notwithstanding its non-binding status, the 1981 Declaration, adopted by consensus, is significant. It provides the basis for the work of the UN Special Rapporteur[321] and it complements Article 18 of the Universal Declaration, Article 18 ICCPR, and General Comment 22 to form the basis for the promotion of religious freedom and religious tolerance within the UN framework.[322]

2.113 The 1981 Declaration consists of a ten-paragraph preamble and eight articles.[323] The Preamble invokes the principles of equality and dignity set out in the UN Charter, and through it the General Assembly stresses that 'religion or belief, for anyone who professes

---

[318] See GA Resolution 1781, 17 UN GAOR Supp (No 17) at 33, UN Doc A/5217 (1962), requesting that ECOSOC prepare a draft declaration and a draft convention on the elimination of religious intolerance. The Sub-Commission on Prevention of Discrimination and Protection of Minorities had earlier appointed a Special Rapporteur, Arcot Krishnaswami, to study religious rights. His report presented an analysis of norms and state practice, see A Krishnaswami, 'Study of Discrimination in the Matter of Religious Rights and Practices', UN Doc E/CN.4/Sub.2/200/Rev.1, UN Sales No 60.XIV.2 (1960), and draft principles prepared by the Sub-Commission on the basis of the Report, at Annex I.

[319] The international consensus or political will for any such treaty has to date been absent. GA Resolution 1781 was transmitted by ECOSOC to the Commission on Human Rights and the Sub-Commission. In 1964 the Sub-Commission transmitted a preliminary draft declaration to the Commission: see 37 UN ESCOR Supp (No 8), para 294, UN Doc E/3873 (1964). The working group formed in the Commission considered only six of the 14 articles in the Sub-Commission's draft. The Commission forwarded that draft, together with a modified text proposed by the working group to ECOSOC for referral to the General Assembly. The General Assembly did not consider the preliminary drafts but asked ECOSOC to invite the Commission to start work on a draft convention to be submitted to the Assembly together with the draft declaration. In 1965 the Sub-Commission presented a preliminary draft convention to the Commission, which the latter considered over the following two years. In 1967 ECOSOC transmitted the Commission's draft convention, consisting of a preamble and 12 articles on which the Commission had reached agreement, to the General Assembly: see Note by the Secretary General: Elimination of All Forms of Religious Intolerance, UN Doc A/8330, Annex III (1971). The General Assembly discussed the draft convention in 1967, but thereafter postponed consideration of the convention and decided in 1972 to accord priority to the completion of a draft declaration: GA Resolution 3027, 27 UN GAOR Supp (No 30), 72, UN Doc A/8730 (1972). Work on the draft declaration progressed with difficulty in the Commission from 1974 until a text was adopted in 1981; it was transmitted by ECOSOC to the General Assembly in the same year. See DJ Sullivan, 'Advancing the Freedom of Religion or Belief through the UN Declaration on the Elimination of Religious Intolerance and Discrimination' (1988) 82(3) AJIL 487–520, fnn 1–3. For the history of the Declaration and the draft convention, see S Liskofsky, 'The UN Declaration on the Elimination of Religious Intolerance and Discrimination: Historical and Legal Perspectives' in J Wood (ed), *Religion and the State: Essays in Honor of Leo Pfeffer* (Baylor University Press, 1985) 441, 460–3; N Lerner, 'Toward a Draft Declaration Against Religious Intolerance and Discrimination' (1981) 11 Israel YBHR 82; and N Lerner, 'The Final Text of the UN Declaration Against Intolerance and Discrimination Based on Religion or Belief' (1982) 12 Israel YBHR 185. For the drafting history of the Declaration, see *United Nations Action in the Field of Human Rights* (2nd edn, United Nations, 1988) 92–4.

[320] GA Resolution 36/55, 36 UN GAOR Supp (No 51) 171, UN Doc A/36/684 (1981).

[321] See below para 2.126.

[322] See generally Sullivan (n 319) 487–520.

[323] UN Declaration on the Elimination of All Forms of Intolerance and of Discrimination Based on Religion or Belief 1981, UN Doc A/RES/36/55, 25 November 1981. The full text of the 1981 Declaration can be found in Appendix I to this work.

either, is one of the fundamental elements in his conception of life'[324] and expresses concern at 'manifestations of intolerance and by the existence of discrimination in matters of religion or belief still in evidence in some areas of the world'.[325]

Article 1 of the 1981 Declaration echoes the terms of Article 18 ICCPR. Its first **2.114** paragraph reads:

> Everyone shall have the right to freedom of thought, conscience and religion. This right shall include freedom to have a religion or whatever belief of his choice, and freedom, either individually or in community with others and in public or private, to manifest his religion or belief in worship, observance, practice and teaching.

The second paragraph then contains the prohibition on coercion which forbids the use or threat of physical force to compel believers or non-believers to recant or to convert. The general wording of this provision does not elucidate what other conduct, conditions, or forms of communication would constitute coercion.[326] The right to change one's religion, as provided for in the Universal Declaration, or the right to adopt a religion or belief, as set out in the ICCPR, is not expressly referred to in the 1981 Declaration. One could assume that this right remains implicit in the broader right to have a religion or belief. The third and final paragraph sets out the familiar permissible limitations to the freedom to manifest one's religion or beliefs: public safety, order, health or morals, or the fundamental rights and freedoms of others.

Article 2 is a codification of the prohibition of discrimination on the grounds of religion or **2.115** belief. It additionally defines the phrase 'intolerance and discrimination based on religion or belief' in its paragraph 2 as 'any distinction, exclusion, restrictions or preference based on religion or belief and having as its purpose or as its effect nullification or impairment of the recognition, enjoyment or exercise of human rights and fundamental freedoms on an equal basis'. Article 2 is more comprehensive than Article 26 ICCPR relating to discrimination on grounds of religion, using language borrowed from the definition of racial discrimination in Article 1 of the International Convention on the Elimination of All Forms of Racial Discrimination.[327]

Article 2(2) does not address the intended reach of the prohibition of discrimination. **2.116** However, if Article 2(1) is read in conjunction with Article 3 and Article 4(1), the prohibition must be interpreted to apply to both public and private action. Article 2(1) forbids discrimination by 'any State, institution, group of persons, or person'. This formulation

---

[324] 1981 Declaration, Preamble, para 4.
[325] 1981 Declaration, Preamble, para 8.
[326] The draft principles prepared by the Sub-Commission included a more specific definition: 'No one shall be subjected to *material or moral coercion* likely to impair his freedom to maintain or to change his religion or belief' (emphasis added): See draft principles UN Doc E/CN.4/Sub.2/200/Rev.1, UN Sales No 60.XIV.2 (1960), Pt I(3). On the need for a more specific definition, see 34 UN ESCOR Supp (No 4) 57–8, UN Doc E/1978/34, discussing a proposal to include a fuller statement of the various kinds of coercion, such as legal, economic, and administrative coercion; see also 36 UN ESCOR Supp (No 6) 72, UN Doc E/1979/36, definition proposed by Cyprus.
[327] International Convention on the Elimination of All Forms of Racial Discrimination, 660 UNTS 195 (1965), reprinted in 5 ILM 352 (1966). ICCPR, Art 1(1) defines racial discrimination as:

> ...any distinction, exclusion, restriction or preference based on race, colour, descent, national or ethnic origin which has the purpose or effect of nullifying or impairing the recognition, enjoyment or exercise, on an equal footing, of human rights and fundamental freedoms in the political, economic, social, cultural or any other field of public life.

echoes Article 2(1) of the UN Declaration on the Elimination of All Forms of Racial Discrimination, which proscribes discrimination by any 'State, institution, group or individual'.[328] The conduct of private, non-governmental institutions and groups, as well as that of governmental authorities, thus falls within the scope of Article 2. As the word 'person' in the singular indicates, acts of discrimination committed by one individual against another are also encompassed by Article 2. The language of Article 3 confirms this interpretation, by condemning discrimination 'between human beings'. In a departure from the definition set out in the Racial Discrimination Convention, Article 2(2) omits the clause that extends the prohibition of discrimination to the 'political, economic, social, cultural or any other field of *public life*' (emphasis added).[329] Consequently, interpersonal and familial relationships are subject to the strictures of Article 2.

2.117　Neither Article 1 nor Article 2 defines 'religion' or 'belief', nor are these terms defined elsewhere in the 1981 Declaration. Although none of the definitions that were proposed at various stages of the drafting process won acceptance, the *travaux préparatoires* reveal a general agreement that 'theistic, non-theistic and atheistic beliefs' are all embraced by the phrase 'religion or belief'.[330]

2.118　Article 3 reiterates that discrimination between human beings on grounds of religion or belief 'constitutes an affront to human dignity and a disavowal of the principles of the Charter of the United Nations, and shall be condemned as a violation of the human rights and fundamental freedoms proclaimed' in the Universal Declaration and ICCPR and represents 'an obstacle to friendly and peaceful relations between nations'.

2.119　Article 4 lists the states parties' obligations in relation to the duty to eliminate religious discrimination. States parties are obliged not only to punish discrimination, but also to take preventive measures against it. The mandatory language and all-encompassing terms adopted by the General Assembly are notable:

> Article 4
> 1. All States *shall* take *effective* measures to prevent and eliminate discrimination on the grounds of religion or belief in the recognition, exercise and enjoyment of human rights and fundamental freedoms in *all* fields of civil, economic, political, social and cultural life.
> 2. All States *shall* make *all* efforts to enact or rescind legislation where necessary to prohibit any such discrimination, and to take *all* appropriate measures to combat intolerance on the grounds of religion or other beliefs in this matter (emphasis added).

---

[328] GA Resolution 1904, 18 UN GAOR Supp (No 15) 35–7, UN Doc A/5515 (1963).

[329] The phrase 'public life' was included in proposed versions of the definition of discrimination that reproduced the definition contained in the Racial Discrimination Convention, but was deleted from the final version of Art 2(2): see 1979 UN ESCOR Supp (No 6) 70, UN Doc E/1979/36.

[330] During drafting discussions, it was asserted that 'religion or belief' should be understood to include, *inter alia*, monotheism, polytheism, atheism, agnosticism, free thought, and animistic beliefs: see UN Doc E/3925 (1964) Annex, 1, 3–4; 1978 UN ESCOR Supp (No 4) 62, UN Doc E/1978/34. Conversely, some governments identified systems of thought that should be specifically excluded from the definition, such as racism, Nazism, and apartheid, UN Doc A/C.3/L.2033 (1973), and theories on subjects such as philosophy, history, politics, art, and science. See Analytical Presentation of the Observations received from Governments Concerning the Draft Declaration on the Elimination of All Forms of Religious Intolerance, Note by the Secretary General, UN Doc A/9135 (1973) 11. The view that the phrase 'religion or belief' was well understood to refer to both religious and non-religious beliefs prevailed, and the proposed definitions (which continued to be offered as late as 1981) were rejected: see UN Docs E/3925/Add.1 (1964) 10; A/9135 (1973) 10–11; E/CN.4/1146/Add.3 (1974) 1; 1981 UN ESCOR Supp (No 5) 149, UN Doc E/1981/25.

Article 5 contains provisions pertaining to the rights of the child in relation to the right **2.120** to freedom of religion or belief, including the right to organize the life within a family in accordance with the religious convictions of the parents or legal guardians; the right of the child to have access to religious instruction; protection from discrimination on the ground of religion or belief; and protection from practices of a religion or belief which are injurious to a child's physical or mental health or to his or her full development—the 'best interests of the child being the guiding principle'.[331] Article 5 further provides that children have a right of access to a religious education that is consistent with the wishes of their parents. Decisions concerning children's education in religion or belief are again guided by the 'best interests of the child'[332] (Article 5(2)). As stated previously, the only restriction upon the control that parents or other custodians may exercise over their children's upbringing in matters of religion or belief is an injunction against practices that are 'injurious to [their] physical or mental health or to [their] full development' (Article 5(5)). Because the 1981 Declaration fails to define 'child' or to specify the age at which children are entitled to decide matters of religion or belief for themselves, parental rights under the 1981 Declaration may conflict with their children's rights if the children's preferences in these matters differ from those of their parents or legal guardians.[333]

Article 6 provides a non-exhaustive list of which sorts of acts fall under the scope of the right **2.121** to freedom of religion or belief:

Article 6

In accordance with Article 1 of the present Declaration, and subject to the provisions of Article 1, paragraph 3, the right to freedom of thought, conscience, religion or belief shall include, inter alia, the following freedoms:

(a) To worship or assemble in connection with a religion or belief, and to establish and maintain places for these purposes;

(b) To establish and maintain appropriate charitable or humanitarian institutions;

(c) To make, acquire and use to an adequate extent the necessary articles and materials related to the rites or customs of a religion or belief;

(d) To write, issue and disseminate relevant publications in these areas;

(e) To teach a religion or belief in places suitable for these purposes;

(f) To solicit and receive voluntary financial and other contributions from individuals and institutions;

(g) To train, appoint, elect or designate by succession appropriate leaders called for by the requirements and standards of any religion or belief;

---

[331] UN Declaration on the Elimination of All Forms of Intolerance and of Discrimination Based on Religion or Belief, Art 5(2) and (4).

[332] cf Declaration of the Rights of the Child, Principle 7, GA Resolution 1386, 14 UN GAOR Supp (No 16) 19, UN Doc A/4354 (1959). Principle 7(2) provides that: 'The best interests of the child shall be the guiding principle of those responsible for his education and guidance; that responsibility lies in the first place with his parents.' In contrast, ICCPR, Art 18(4) makes no reference to considerations other than the convictions held by parents or guardians: 'The States Parties to the present Covenant undertake to have respect for the liberty of parents and, when applicable, legal guardians to ensure the religious and moral education of their children in conformity with their own convictions.'

[333] The failure to address the rights of children themselves was noted during drafting discussions: see UN Doc A/C.3/SR.2011 (1973) 15, comments by the representative of Japan. Regarding the need to define 'child' or to specify the age at which a child is entitled to make decisions concerning religion or belief, see UN Docs A/C.3/SR.2010 (1973) 9; A/C.3/SR.2013 (1973) 9–11; E/CN.4/1146/Add.3 (1974) 4.

(h) To observe days of rest and to celebrate holidays and ceremonies in accordance with the precepts of one's religion or belief;

(i) To establish and maintain communications with individuals and communities in matters of religion and belief at the national and international levels.

2.122   Article 7 mandates states parties to harmonize their domestic legislation so as to accord with the 1981 Declaration 'in such a manner that everyone shall be able to avail himself of such rights and freedoms in practice'. Article 8 is a savings clause intended to guarantee that the 1981 Declaration is not interpreted so as to lower the standards provided for religious rights in the other UN instruments, such as the Universal Declaration and ICCPR.

2.123   Much of the 1981 Declaration overlaps with and mirrors the provisions of Article 18 ICCPR. In places it develops those rights, for instance by including not only a right to non-discrimination on the basis of religion (Article 2), but also creating a positive obligation on states to 'take effective measures to prevent and eliminate discrimination on the grounds of religion or belief in the recognition, exercise and enjoyment of human rights and fundamental freedoms in all fields of civil, economic, political, social and cultural life' (Article 4(1)). The 1981 Declaration further elaborates on the right of parents/guardians to have their children educated according to their religious beliefs and includes the right to organize family life according to religious beliefs (Article 5(1)). However, it adds the limitation that 'practices of a religion or belief in which a child is brought up must not be injurious to his physical or mental health or to his full development' (Article 5(5)). The most significant development in the 1981 Declaration is that a more detailed list of manifestations of religion is set out in Article 6 in addition to the traditional formulation of 'worship, observance, practice, and teaching' set out in the Universal Declaration and ICCPR. The manifestations set out in Article 6 are inclusive, rather than exhaustive, and thus only represent a partial picture of the possible range of manifestations that are protected. The manifestations set out therein are particularly focused on the rights of religious groups and organizations; there is less detail on individual manifestations of religion or belief.

2.124   The positive features of the ICCPR are mirrored in the 1981 Declaration, Article 1 of which is almost identical to Article 18 ICCPR. But the 1981 Declaration extends the duties of states parties in a very important respect. When Articles 2(1), 4, and 7 are read together, it is plain that national laws are to protect all persons against religious discrimination practised by all other persons. This represents a bold attempt to require countries to outlaw private discrimination as well as discrimination at the hands of the state. This it is not a strategy mirrored in the UN Conventions on racial or gender discrimination. Also, the argument can be made that for those states which have approved the 1981 Declaration as well as the ICCPR, the Declaration essentially has a binding effect in international law. This appears to follow from Article 3 of the Declaration, which states that discrimination between human beings on the grounds of religion or belief constitutes a disavowal of the principles of the UN Charter. While a disavowal of principles is not of itself the same as a violation of rights, Article 3 goes on to say that religious discrimination 'shall be condemned as a violation of human rights and fundamental freedoms proclaimed in the Universal Declaration of Human Rights and enunciated in detail in the International Covenants on Human Rights', equating a violation of the Declaration with a violation of the ICCPR, which is binding on states parties. Further, comments of the HRC illustrate how the scope of Article 18 ICCPR has been expanded by the 1981 Declaration. Both in its reaction to the periodic reports submitted by state governments, and in its views on individual complaints lodged under the Optional Protocol to the

ICCPR, the HRC has adopted an interpretation of Article 18 which indicates that the 1981 Declaration is largely, if not entirely, declarative of existing law. The fact that no state has ever taken exception to the HRC's method of interpretation is perhaps some indication that this is regarded as uncontroversial.

The lack of specific guidance concerning measures to prevent discrimination in the 1981 **2.125** Declaration is matched by an absence of measures to provide redress for existing discrimination. The 1981 Declaration makes no mention of the right to equality before the law or any obligation to provide effective remedies for violations of its principles. Moreover, the 1981 Declaration does not state a right to effective administrative and judicial remedies for harm suffered as a result of discrimination on the basis of religion or belief and violations of the freedom of religion or belief.[334] As such, it lacks an enforcement machinery. To this extent, religious discrimination can still be seen as the poorer cousin when compared to racial and gender discrimination; both of these forms of discrimination have specially appointed Committees on the Elimination of Discrimination which, although unable to deal with individual complaints, can exercise considerable influence through the comments they issue on the country reports which have to be periodically submitted to them.[335]

E. UN Special Rapporteur on Freedom of Religion or Belief[336]

The UN Special Rapporteur on Freedom of Religion or Belief ('the Rapporteur') is an inde- **2.126** pendent expert appointed by the UN Human Rights Council.[337] The mandate holder is invited to identify existing and emerging obstacles to the enjoyment of the right to freedom of religion or belief and to present recommendations on ways and means to overcome such obstacles. Including the current incumbent, there have been four Rapporteurs to date:

---

[334] The 1964 Commission Draft Declaration, 37 UN ESCOR Supp (No 8) para 294, UN Doc E/3873 (1964). Art III(2), provided: 'Everyone has the right to effective remedial relief by the competent national tribunals against any acts violating the rights set forth in this Declaration or any acts of discrimination he may suffer on the grounds of religion or belief...'. The 1967 Draft Convention (n 319), Art X similarly addressed the availability of remedies, requiring states to:

... ensure to everyone within their jurisdiction effective protection and remedies, through the competent national tribunals and other State institutions against any acts, including acts of discrimination...which violate his human rights and fundamental freedoms contrary to this Convention, as well as the right to seek from such tribunals just and adequate reparation or satisfaction for any damage suffered as a result of such acts.

Examples of provisions asserting a right to effective remedies appear in several international human rights instruments, including the UDHR, Art 8; the ICCPR, Art 2(3); and the Racial Discrimination Declaration, Art 7(2).

[335] See B Dickson, 'The United Nation and Freedom of Religion' (1995) 44(2) ICLQ 338.

[336] See generally, M Wiener, 'The Mandate of the Special Rapporteur on Freedom of Religion or Belief—Institutional, Procedural and Substantive Legal Issues' (2007) 2 Religion and Human Rights 3; C Evans, 'Strengthening the Role of the Special Rapporteur on Freedom of Religion or Belief' (2006) 1 Religion and Human Rights 75.

[337] The United Nations Commission on Human Rights appointed further to Resolution 1986/20 (10 March 1986) a 'Special Rapporteur on religious intolerance'. In 2000, the Commission on Human Rights (the predecessor to the Human Rights Council) decided to change the mandate title to 'Special Rapporteur on freedom of religion or belief', which was subsequently endorsed by ECOSOC decision 2000/261 and welcomed by GA Resolution 55/97 (UN Doc A/RES/55/97). On 18 June 2010, the Human Rights Council adopted Resolution 14/11 (UN Doc A/HRC/RES/14/11) which, *inter alia*, extended the mandate of the Special Rapporteur for a further period of three years.

Mr Angelo d'Almeida Ribeiro,[338] Mr Abdelfattah Amor,[339] Ms Asma Jahangir,[340] and Mr Heiner Bielefeldt.[341]

(1) The mandate

2.127 The role of the Rapporteur was established by the UN Commission on Human Rights in its Resolution 1986/20,[342] to investigate governmental actions that were inconsistent with the rights set out in the 1981 Declaration and to recommend measures to remedy any such breaches.[343] The mandate has been gradually expanded since then and is now reflected in the Human Rights Council Resolutions 6/37 and 4/11. The aims of the Rapporteur are:

- to promote the adoption of measures at the national, regional and international levels to ensure the promotion and protection of the right to freedom of religion or belief;
- to identify existing and emerging obstacles to the enjoyment of the right to freedom of religion or belief and present recommendations on ways and means to overcome such obstacles;
- to continue his/her efforts to examine incidents and governmental actions that are incompatible with the provisions of the 1981 Declaration and to recommend remedial measures as appropriate;
- to continue to apply a gender perspective, *inter alia*, through the identification of gender-specific abuses, in the reporting process, including in information collection and in recommendations.

2.128 The international standards that inform the Rapporteur as the basis of his work have also evolved since the mandate's establishment. The 1986 resolution did not refer—unlike its first draft—to Article 18 of the Universal Declaration or to Article 18 ICCPR. The first Rapporteur therefore took the 1981 Declaration as his single point of reference in his work. Step by step, the second Rapporteur incorporated further international protections— especially Article 18 of the UDHR, Articles 4, 18 and 20 ICCPR and Article 13 of the International Covenant on Economic, Social and Cultural Rights—into the mandate. Subsequent Rapporteurs have extended the framework of reference further still, referring to General Comments of the HRC, as well a number of Declarations and Guidelines. The practice under the initial mandate of citing provisions of the 1981 Declaration has gradually declined.

(2) Working methods

2.129 In the discharge of the mandate, the Rapporteur:

- transmits urgent appeals and letters of allegation to states with regard to cases that represent infringements of or impediments to the exercise of the right to freedom of religion and belief;
- undertakes fact-finding country visits; and

---

[338] Portugal, March 1986 to March 1993.

[339] Tunisia, April 1993 to July 2004.

[340] Pakistan, August 2004 to July 2010.

[341] Since August 2010.

[342] 10 March 1986. Initially the mandate holder was the Special Rapporteur on Religious Intolerance. In 2001, at the request of the Rapporteur, his title was changed to the Special Rapporteur on Freedom of Religion or Belief: see Commission on Human Rights, UN Doc E/CN.4/RES/2001/42 (2001) para 11.

[343] For a discussion of the establishment of the role of Rapporteur and of the first nine reports, see Tahzib (n 158) 198–212.

- submits annual reports to the Human Rights Council, and General Assembly, on the activities, trends, and methods of work.

The various resolutions relating to the Special Rapporteur by the Economic and Social **2.130** Council (ECOSOC),[344] the General Assembly, the Commission on Human Rights, and (latterly) the Human Rights Council have not proscribed procedural guidelines for the mandate. The Rapporteur's activities and working methods have therefore been developed by the individual mandate holders themselves.

Urgent appeals/letters of allegation. The key fact-finding tool for the Rapporteur is the infor- **2.131** mation[345] submitted to his or her office by governmental organizations or NGOs, religious or belief communities, and also individuals, with regard to potential or actual violations of the right to freedom of religion or belief. Having evaluated the allegations, the Rapporteur may decide to send either a letter of allegation or an urgent appeal concerning pressing issues to the government concerned. The standard practice suggests the following applicable principles:[346]

- The non-exhaustion of domestic remedies does not prevent the Rapporteur from dealing with a case.
- The Rapporteur may send letters of allegation or urgent appeals even when the matter has already been submitted to another procedure for international investigation or settlement.
- Contrary to the enumeration of legitimate sources for the carrying out of the mandate in the initial resolution of the Commission of Human Rights, the Rapporteur has also considered information from individual persons who are not affiliated with an NGO.
- Complainants neither need to prove a personal, current injury, nor do they need to establish reasons for acting in the name of the alleged victim.
- Governments are given a period of two months to respond to letters of allegation and a period of two weeks to respond to urgent appeals.[347]
- Allegations are published in the annual reports, even when the government concerned has not reacted on the Rapporteur's letter.

Country visits. In addition to correspondence with governments, the Rapporteur undertakes **2.132** country visits, which represent one of his or her fundamental activities. Pursuant to paragraph 14 of Report E/CN.4/2005/61, the Special Rapporteur undertakes country visits to get an in-depth understanding of specific contexts and practices and to provide constructive feedback to the given country and report to the Council or the General Assembly. During country visits, the Special Rapporteur holds meetings with representatives of relevant state bodies, representatives of religious and belief communities present on the territory, associations of religious groups and other NGOs, as well as persons who may be interested or

---

[344] The body responsible for coordinating the economic, social, and related work of 14 UN agencies.
[345] The Rapporteur has developed a model questionnaire to facilitate the submission of information, see <http://www.ohchr.org/Documents/Issues/Religion/questionnaire-e.doc>.
[346] Wiener (n 336) 8–9.
[347] These time-periods were established in the 1994 annual report, UN Doc E/CN.4/1994/79. However, between 1998 and 2004, addressee states achieved only a 38.8% response rate within the specified periods, and a 61.6% response rate overall. Upon assuming the mandate in 2004, Special Rapporteur Jahangir sent the majority of her urgent appeals jointly with other special procedure holders, leading to a slightly improved response rate. The figures available in the latest joint communications reports (UN Doc A/HRC/18/51) show a current response rate of 50%.

affected by the mandate. The Special Rapporteur also undertakes field visits during these country missions in order to be completely acquainted with the surrounding circumstances.

2.133 The Special Rapporteur has also re-established the initial approach of sending follow-up letters after country visits in order to receive updated information about the implementation of recommendations at the national level (see paragraph 15 of A/HRC/13/40). In this regard, in November 2009 the Special Rapporteur transmitted follow-up tables to the governments of the eight countries which she had visited from 2005 to 2007. These tables contain the conclusions and recommendations from her mission report and follow-up information from relevant UN documents, including from the universal periodic review, special procedures, and treaty bodies. A third column includes information provided by the State on the consideration given to these recommendations, the steps taken to implement them, and any constraints which may prevent their implementation.

2.134 'Terms of reference for fact-finding missions by special Rapporteurs/representatives of the Commission on Human Rights' were adopted during the 1997 annual meeting of the Commission, which set out minimum standards for the mandate holders and the UN staff accompanying them. These terms of reference provide that governments guarantee minimum standards for in situ visits, which has led some governments not to make the required invitation. The most important of these conditions is that the Rapporteur can meet with critics or possible victims of the government and not only government officials. Such meetings should be in conditions that allow for frank and free communication without government interference or threat of retaliation against those who communicate their views to the Rapporteur.

2.135 *Annual reports.*[348] The approach adopted by the Rapporteur in his or her annual reports has changed over time. In his first report, the first Rapporteur was asked only to report on the general situation regarding religious discrimination and intolerance worldwide. He kept the scope of his report limited to generalities and did not raise particular allegations against states.[349] By his second report the Rapporteur had, however, moved to a discussion of the situation in particular states.[350] In his final report, the Rapporteur emphasized the 'dynamic nature' of his mandate and the increased importance of identifying 'more precisely particular situations where inconsistencies with the Declaration might have to be reported'.[351] Under subsequent Rapporteurs this approach of identifying and dealing with particular allegations has continued. Typically the Rapporteur's reports outline the allegation and also record the response, if any, from the state against which the allegation has been levelled. Increasingly, reports deal with the details of complex legal issues and their application to specific circumstances.[352]

---

[348] See <http://www.ohchr.org/EN/Issues/FreedomReligion/Pages/Annual.aspx> to download annual reports. For a general overview of the types of complaints investigated by the Rapporteur, see Evans (n 120) 245–50.

[349] A Vidal d'Almeida Ribeiro, 'Implementation of the Declaration on the Elimination of All Forms of Intolerance and of Discrimination Based on Religion or Belief', UN Doc E/CN.4/1987/35 (1986).

[350] A Vidal d'Almeida Ribeiro, 'Implementation of the Declaration on the Elimination of All Forms of Intolerance and of Discrimination Based on Religion or Belief', UN Doc E/CN.4/1988/45 (1988) para 9.

[351] A Vidal d'Almeida Ribeiro, 'Implementation of the Declaration on the Elimination of All Forms of Intolerance and of Discrimination Based on Religion or Belief', UN Doc E/CN.4/1993/62 (1993) para 10. At para 11, the Rapporteur sets out the way in which the Human Rights Commission extended his mandate to make this increased role possible.

[352] See eg the sophisticated analysis of the various types of rights at stake in conversion cases, A Jahangir, 'Elimination of All Forms of Religious Intolerance', UN Doc A/60/399 (2005) para 39.

The principal weakness with the reporting and complaints procedure is the extent to **2.136** which the Rapporteur relies on the cooperation of states. The capacity of the Rapporteur to undertake fact-finding is limited and his or her power to require cooperation by states is non-existent. States are able to respond in a perfunctory manner or simply refuse to respond at all, with no threat of sanction. In particular, the Rapporteurs have no power to require states to comply with his or her recommendations or to respond to his or her requests. The Rapporteur therefore has no real remedies other than condemnation of wrong-doing. Given these operating constraints, the Rapporteurs have attempted to work with governments to promote religious rights and tolerance.

F. UN Convention on the Rights of the Child 1989

The majority of international instruments that provide for a right to freedom of thought, **2.137** conscience, and religion explicitly recognize the right of parents and legal guardians to ensure the religious education of their children in conformity with their own convictions.[353] Article 14 of the UN Convention on the Rights of the Child 1989 (UNCRC),[354] while making reference to parental rights, provides for religious rights that apply to children as autonomous subjects of the law.[355] The United Kingdom has agreed to be bound by the UNCRC.[356]

The UNCRC is supervised and implemented by the Committee on the Rights of the Child **2.138** (CRC). The CRC was established through Article 43, and it has no mandate to accept and review individual complaints. There is a reporting system under Article 44(1) according to which states parties undertake to submit to the CRC reports on measures they have adopted which give effect to the rights recognized in the Convention and on the progress made on the enjoyment of those rights. The CRC holds three sessions a year; it has published ten General Comments.

Article 14 of the UNCRC provides: **2.139**

1. States Parties shall respect the right of the child to freedom of thought, conscience and religion.
2. States Parties shall respect the rights and duties of the parents and, when applicable, legal guardians, to provide direction to the child in the exercise of his or her right in a manner consistent with the evolving capacities of the child.

---

[353] See ICCPR, Art 18(4), paras 2.51–2.54; ICESCR (n 93), Art 13(3).

[354] New York, 20 November 1989 UNTS, Vol 1577, 3 (entry into force 2 September 1990, in accordance with Art 49). There is also an Optional Protocol on the sale of children, child prostitution, and child pornography (entry into force 18 January 2002) and an Optional Protocol on the involvement of children in armed conflict (entry into force 12 February 2002).

[355] Several states parties have exhibited reluctance to accept the autonomous right of the child in this field. Some have referred in general terms to national legislation and traditions (eg Indonesia, Malaysia, and Poland); some to the existence of a state religion (eg Algeria and the Maldives); some have pointed to the fact that a child's autonomous right with regard to religion runs counter to Islamic Sharia (eg Iraq and Jordan); and the Holy See has indicated a wish to safeguard the rights of parents in this sphere. For the full text of reservations made by states parties, see <http://treaties.un.org/untc/Pages/ViewDetails.aspx?src=TREATY&mtdsg_no=IV-11&chapter=4&lang=en> (accessed 12 July 2013).

[356] There are 193 states parties to the UNCRC. Within Europe, the Convention has been ratified and is court-enforceable in Belgium, Bulgaria, Cyprus, the Czech Republic, Denmark, Estonia, Finland, Germany, Greece, Hungary, Latvia, Lithuania, the Netherlands, Poland, and Spain. It is ratified but not enforceable in Austria, Ireland, and Sweden, see <http://treaties.un.org/untc/Pages/ViewDetails.aspx?src=TREATY&mtdsg_no=IV-11&chapter=4&lang=en> (accessed 12 July 2013).

> 3. Freedom to manifest one's religion or beliefs may be subject only to such limitations as are prescribed by law and are necessary to protect public safety, order, health, or morals or the fundamental rights and freedoms of others.

Article 14 is subject to widespread reservations from states parties.

(1) Article 14(1)

2.140 *Introduction.* Paragraph 1 of Article 2 states that: 'States Parties shall respect the right of the child to freedom of thought, conscience and religion.' The undertaking to 'respect' these rights appears to impose a negative obligation which does not require states to take active steps. However, although there is a growing distinction in international law generally between negative duties to respect rights as opposed to positive undertakings to protect and fulfil the same,[357] the jurisprudence of the ECtHR with respect to Article 9 supports the idea that active measures can be required under the former.[358] This is reflected in the approach of the CRC. The Guidelines for Periodic Reports (first revision) asked states to submit information on the 'measures adopted to ensure the child's freedom to manifest his or her religion or beliefs',[359] and the reports referred to in the following sections often request information about positive steps taken to ensure the protection of children's rights. The Committee thus reject an interpretation of the provision which simply requires states parties to refrain from interference with those rights under Article 14.

2.141 *Freedom of Thought and Conscience.* Freedom of thought concerns only the *forum internum*. This right is not subject to the restriction clause at Article 14(3); a child may therefore never be forced to reveal his or her thoughts.[360] The freedom is, however, subject to the rights and duties of the child's legal guardians under Article 14(2) to provide direction in accordance with the child's evolving capacities (see discussion at paragraph 2.149). Freedom of conscience is a narrower right, as it is restricted to ethical or philosophical convictions, and it does not require a supernatural element.[361] Like freedom of thought, it is not subject to the restrictions in paragraph 3 of Article 14, but is subject to the rights and duties of the child's legal guardians under paragraph 2 of the article.

2.142 *Scope of Freedom of Religion.* In comparison with other human rights instruments,[362] Article 14 of the Convention contains one of the most minimally defined rights to freedom of religion. The only indication that it includes a right to manifestation is given in Article 14(3), which sets the limits to the authorities' permissible interferences with that freedom. The difference between the wording in force and the earlier proposals made during the *travaux préparatoires*[363]

---

[357] See E Brems, 'Article 14: The Right to Freedom of Thought, Conscience and Religion', *A Commentary on the United Nations Convention on the Rights of the Child*, Vol 14 (Martinus Nijhoff, 2005) 10.

[358] See eg *X v UK*, ECmHR (App 8160/78) (1981), 22 DR, para 3, and now *Eweida v UK* (2013) 57 EHRR 213.

[359] UN Doc CRC/C/58 (1996). The latest revision of these guidelines (UN Doc CRC/C/58/Rev.2, November 2010) refers simply to the provision of 'information' on Article 14, at para 4(d).

[360] As is the case for adults; see General Comment 22 on Article 18 ICCPR (n 2) para 3.

[361] Brems (n 357) 12.

[362] See eg Art 18 ICCPR: 'This right shall include the freedom to have or to adopt a religion or belief of his choice, and freedom, either individually or in community with others, and in public or private, to manifest his religion or belief in worship, observance, practice and teaching.' See also UDHR, Art 18 and ECHR, Art 9.

[363] See eg the comprehensive US proposal (E/1982/12/Add.1, Pt C, para 118):

> 1. The States Parties to the present Convention shall ensure that the child has the right to freedom of thought, conscience and religion, including the freedom to have or to adopt a religion or belief of his choice, and freedom, either individually or in community with others and in public or

is a result of the states parties' inability to reach a consensus: precisely what practices are covered by Article 14(1) must be divined from the reports of the Committee.

Choice and adoption. The Committee has interpreted Article 14 as including the right of **2.143** children to choose their religion: 'The freedom of religion include[s] freedom to choose and change one's religion. No interpretation of such freedoms could restrict it to the possibility of holding one specific religion.'[364] Within the context of Article 14(1), this freedom of choice is as against public authorities, rather than as against their legal guardians under Article 14(2).[365] The Committee has shown a willingness not only to ensure that the freedom exists, but also to ensure that active steps are taken to promote the choice: it asked South Korea, for example, about measures taken to familiarize children with other cultures and about legislative provisions which allow children freely to choose their own religion.[366] The Committee has also made it clear that a child must be free not to have a religion,[367] and insofar as the choice or adoption of a religion is an internal freedom and not a manifestation per se, it constitutes a right which cannot be interfered with by the state as set out in Article 14(3). However, the adoption of a religion can rarely be divorced from its manifestation, and the Committee has exhibited a cautious attitude towards New Religious Movements (NRMs) where their practices are considered to have a pernicious influence upon children's behaviour.[368] Where the nature of the manifestation is not in issue, however, the Committee has been concerned not to limit the application of Article 14 to traditional religions to avoid discriminating against minority religions on account of their size or longevity.

Manifestation. Despite the difference in wording, the commentaries of the HRC on Article 18 **2.144** ICCPR[369] and of the Strasbourg Court on Article 9 ECHR[370] are of assistance. For the former provision, the HRC has included a broad range of practices:

> The concept of worship extends to ritual and ceremonial acts giving direct expression to belief, as well as various practices integral to such acts, including the building of places of worship, the use of ritual formulae and objects, the display of symbols, and the observance of holidays and days of rest. The observance and practice of religion or belief may include not only ceremonial acts but

---

private, to manifest his religion or belief in worship, observance, practice and teaching.... 4. The States Parties to the present Convention shall ensure that the child has: (a) the freedom to make, to acquire and to use to an adequate extent the necessary articles and material related to the rites or customs of a religion or belief; (c) the freedom to observe days of rest and to celebrate holidays and ceremonies in accordance with the precepts of his religion or belief; and (d) the freedom to establish and maintain communications with individuals and communities in matters of religion and belief at the national and international levels.

[364] UN CRC, Summary Record of the 317th meeting: Morocco, UN Doc CRC/C/SR.317 (1996) paras 51 and 60.

[365] One of the earlier objections to a wording which expressly included the right to 'have or adopt a religious belief of their choice' was from the Bangladeshi and Moroccan representatives, who commented that the article 'appears to infringe upon the sanctioned practice of a child being reared in the religion of his parents'. UN Doc E/CN.4/1986/39, Annex IV. This concern is met by the uneasy compromise in Art 14(2) as it now stands (see para 2.150).

[366] UN CRC, Summary Record for the 277th meeting: Republic of Korea, UN Doc CRC/C/SR.277 (1996) para 44.

[367] UN CRC, Summary Record of the 255th meeting: Holy See, UN Doc CRC/C/SR.255 (2005) para 17.

[368] The Committee was concerned by new religious sects targeting children in Ukraine, Bulgaria, and Lithuania (UN CRC, Summary Record of the 240th meeting: Ukraine, UN Doc CRC/C/SR.240 (1993) para 10; UN CRC, Summary Record of the 346th meeting: Bulgaria, UN Doc CRC/C/SR.1068 (1997) para 73; UN CRC, Summary Record of the 684th meeting: Lithuania, UN Doc CRC/C/SR.684 (2001) para 10).

[369] General Comment 22 (n 2).

[370] See Ch 3.

also such customs as the observance of dietary regulations, the wearing of distinctive clothing or head-coverings, participation in rituals associated with certain stages of life, and the use of a particular language customarily spoken by a group. In addition, the practice and teaching of religion or belief includes acts integral to the conduct by religious groups of their basic affairs, such as the freedom to choose their religious leaders, priests and teachers, the freedom to establish seminaries or religious schools and the freedom to prepare and distribute religious texts or publications.[371]

This detailed list can helpfully be divided into the broad headings of worship, observance, practice, and education, which are useful groupings under which to consider the approach of the Committee. The jurisprudence of the ECtHR has also traditionally made the distinction between acts that are 'intimately linked' to religion or belief, and those that are simply motivated or influenced by a religion or belief;[372] this distinction between linked and motivated action is borne out in the CRC's reports.

2.145 *Worship*. The CRC has taken the right to worship very seriously, emphasizing in particular the fact that the mere freedom to worship in private surroundings is not sufficient.[373] Questions were asked of Japan as to what legislative protection a pupil had to manifest his religion where he was marked absent from a class whilst attending mass on a Sunday,[374] while Indonesia, which had indicated that freedom of religion only applied to recognized religions, was asked to give details of the rights of children belonging to the unrecognized Bahai faith to worship or go to school.[375] Active steps were required of Turkmenistan to prevent and punish any attack on religious activities and places of worship.[376] Recommendations to abstain from worship have been strongly discouraged: school teachers in Kyrgyzstan had recommended children not to pray at home, and the Committee stated in response that it was essential that teachers imparted positive messages about all religions.[377]

2.146 *Observance*. As with ECHR jurisprudence, the CRC's focus on the child's right to observe his religion has centred on religious clothing. Questions were asked of Tunisia regarding how the authorities dealt with instances of exclusion of girls from school for not wearing veils,[378] while Germany was told that banning teachers from wearing headscarves in school injured the child's understanding of freedom of religion.[379] In the latter case, the CRC added that the ban hindered the development of an attitude of tolerance in a child, which forms one of the aims of education under Article 29. The CRC's response to the 2004 French law prohibiting the wearing of religious symbols in state schools was framed in cautious and diplomatic language, but nonetheless underlined clearly that 'the enjoyment of children's rights, as enshrined in the Convention, [should be used] as crucial criteria in the evaluation process [of the effects] of the legislation'.[380]

---

[371] HRC, General Comment 22 (n 2) para 4.

[372] See Ch 3, paras 3.33–3.43. See also S Stavros, 'Freedom of Religion and Claims for Exemption from Generally Applicable, Neutral Laws: Lessons from across the Pond?' (1997) 6 EHRLR, 607, 616–17.

[373] The Committee inquired about the fact that non-Mulsims are able to practise their religion 'in the privacy of their homes' in the Maldives, and whether this was in fact a restriction on public worship (UN CRC, Summary Record of the 466th meeting: Maldives, UN Doc CRC/C/SR.466 (1998) 75 and 81).

[374] UN CRC, Summary Record of the 465th meeting: Japan, UN Doc CRC/C/SR.465 (1998) 6.

[375] UN CRC, Summary Record of the 80th meeting: Korea, UN Doc CRC/C/SR.80 (1993) para 67.

[376] UN CRC, Concluding Observations: Turkmenistan, UN Doc CRC/C/TKM/CO/1 (2006) paras 33–34.

[377] UN CRC, Summary Record of the 988th meeting: Kyrgyzstan, UN Doc CRC/C/SR.988 (2005) para 23.

[378] UN CRC, Summary Record of the 789th meeting: Tunisia, UN Doc CRC/C/SR.789 (2002) para 13.

[379] UN CRC, Summary Record of the 927th meeting: Germany, UN Doc CRC/C/SR.927 (2004) para 36.

[380] UN CRC, Concluding Observations: France, UN Doc CRC/C/15/Add.240 (2006) para 25.

Practice. The right to practise a religion functions as a catch-all provision, and includes the **2.147** right not to practise a religion. Colombia was told in straightforward terms that to prevent a child from enjoying either the positive or negative freedom was contrary to Articles 12 and 14,[381] while a child's right not to be forced to practise a religion was underlined in the Committee's summary record on the Comoros.[382] In this instance, children had been forced to attend services in a mosque. Particular scrutiny has been exercised with regard to minority religions: China was asked whether it recognized the right of minority children to practise their religion; whether religious practices were authorized in the family; and whether children were arrested because of their own religious practice or that of their parents.[383] State religions too have been subject to close scrutiny: the CRC was concerned with how children practising different religious beliefs in Libya could be accommodated when Islam was the only religion in the state.[384]

Education. A child's educational environment will almost inevitably raise the issue of religious **2.148** freedom and preferences, and the CRC has considered multiple different issues under this heading. The first question is whether a child is able to receive instruction in his or her own religion.[385] The Committee has often used this as a basic test to measure the state of religious freedom for children in schools, as international law traditionally does not place a positive duty upon the state to provide tailored religious education.[386] With regard to the question of choice, the CRC's main concerns have been focused on compulsory religious education without exemption (which is contrary to Article 14).[387] The Committee will not be satisfied where religious education is virtually compulsory on the basis that any exemption requires a written objection,[388] and if alternatives are provided, they must be provided in an adequate way.[389] The conflict between the rights of children and parents with regard to choice in religious instruction is explored later, at paragraph 2.150. The CRC has also expressed concern as to the type, content, and aims of religious education given in schools: this has involved inquiries into training,[390] the curriculum,[391] and teachers' employment status.[392] Cyprus was asked for information on the aims of its religious education curricula, and in particular on whether religious equality was promoted,[393] while it was suggested to Finland that values

---

[381] UN CRC, Summary Record of the 114th meeting: Colombia, UN Doc CRC/C/SR.114 (1995) para 28.

[382] UN CRC, Summary Record of the 666th meeting: Islamic Federal Republic of the Comoros, UN Doc CRC/C/SR.666 (2001) para 10.

[383] UN CRC, Summary Record of the 1063rd meeting: China, UN Doc CRC/C/SR.1063 (2005) para 64.

[384] UN CRC, Summary Record of the 432nd meeting: Libya, UN Doc CRC/C/SR.432 (1998) para 45.

[385] See eg requests made of North Korea for information on the provision of religious instruction to children in religious minorities (UN CRC, Summary Record of the 277th meeting: Democratic People's Republic of Korea, UN Doc CRC/C/SR.277 (1996) para 26), and the concern expressed to Poland that Catholic children in state schools could receive religious instruction while children of other religions could not (UN CRC, Summary Record of the 827th meeting: Poland, UN Doc CRC/C/SR.827 (2002) para 50).

[386] See S Langlaude, *The Right of the Child to Religious Freedom in International Law* (Martinus Nijhoff, 2007) 141.

[387] See eg the Committee's concern over compulsory religious and ethics education in Turkey (UN CRC, Summary Record of the 701st meeting: Turkey, UN Doc CRC/C/SR.701 (2001) para 60).

[388] UN CRC, Initial Report of States Parties Due in 1992: Belize, UN Doc CRC/C/SR.513 (1999) para 19.

[389] UN CRC, Concluding Observations: Poland, UN Doc CRC/C/15/Add.194 (2002) para 32.

[390] UN CRC, Summary Record of the 323rd meeting: Nigeria, UN Doc CRC/C/SR.323 (1996) para 53.

[391] UN CRC, Summary Record of the 685th meeting: Lesotho, UN Doc CRC/C/SR.685 (2001) para 50.

[392] UN CRC, Summary Record of the 785th meeting: Niger, UN Doc CRC/C/SR.785 (2002) para 57.

[393] UN CRC, Summary Record of the 310th meeting: Cyprus, UN Doc CRC/C/SR.310 (1996) paras 9 and 47.

common to all religions should be presented in order to encourage the social integration of all believers.[394]

(2) Article 14(2)

2.149 *Introduction.* Paragraph 2 of Article 14 reads as follows: 'States Parties shall respect the rights and duties of the parents and, when applicable, legal guardians, to provide direction to the child in the exercise of his or her right in a manner consistent with the evolving capacities of the child.' The provision addresses the complex balance of rights between the child, his or her parents (hereinafter including legal guardians), and the state authorities with regard to the child's exercise of religious freedom, and is particularly remarkable for its imposition of obligations on third parties.[395] In essence, it seeks to resolve the tension between the parents' and children's rights by shifting the distribution of control in accordance with the child's 'evolving capacities'. Parents may direct the child's religious choices and instruction insofar as the child is not yet competent to do so, and the state is prohibited from interfering with the religious direction given by parents other than by reference to this benchmark. Such a broad term obviously does not provide a readily ascertainable dividing line for where the parents' rights end and the child's rights begin: the Committee has taken a case-by-case approach which does not demonstrate a consistent theme, and often defaults to age boundaries as indicators of where the child's freedom supersedes the parents' rights of guidance.

2.150 *Tensions between children and parents.* The *travaux préparatoires* show the history of the uneasy balancing exercise performed by Article 14(2).[396] The prevailing theme is that the rights of the child are to be *subject* to the rights of the parents,[397] which reflects the concerns raised by several states parties with regard to the parents' (invariably the father's) authority to determine the child's religion. Algeria's interpretative declaration, for example, states that Article 14(2) will be read in accordance with the Family Code, and in particular with the stipulation that 'a child's education is to take place in accordance with the religion of its father',[398] while Syria adopted a similar position with regard to the principles of the Islamic Sharia.[399] In both instances the CRC encouraged the states to withdraw their reservations and declarations by reaffirming that Article 14(2) protected parental rights.[400] However, this conciliatory attitude in responding to states' specific concerns is not consistently borne out in the Committee's records; in any event, an approach which favoured the parents' authority to the exclusion of the child's autonomy would undermine the protection of Article 3(1), which places the child's interests as paramount.[401]

---

[394] UN CRC, Summary Record of the 284th meeting: Finland, UN Doc CRC/C/SR.284 (1996) para 28.

[395] See generally, D Gomien, 'Whose Right (and Whose Duty) Is It? An Analysis of the Substance and Implementation of the Convention on the Rights of the Child' (1989–90) 7 New York Law School Journal of Human Rights 161–75.

[396] For a detailed exploration of the provision's drafting, see Langlaude (n 386) 103.

[397] See eg the introductory Canadian proposal in the 1984 report of the Working Group, UN Doc E/CN.4/1984/71, para 13.

[398] See <http://treaties.un.org/Pages/ViewDetails.aspx?src=TREATY&mtdsg_no=IV-11&chapter=4&lang=en#EndDec> (accessed 3 February 2013).

[399] See n 398.

[400] In responding to Algeria's declaration, the Committee stated that Art 14 granted parents the right to provide direction to the child in the exercise of their right to freedom of thought, conscience, and religion, and that this provision, therefore, was not at variance with the Algerian Family Code. UN CRC, Summary Record of the 387th meeting: Algeria, UN Doc CRC/C/SR.387 (2005) paras 14 and 27.

[401] See also UN CRC, Summary Record of the 456th meeting: Uganda, UN Doc CRC/C/SR.410 (1997) para 3.

Protection of parental rights. The CRC has on a number of occasions made direct suggestions **2.151** to states that parents have a Convention right to raise children according to their own religious beliefs.[402] The issue has arisen most frequently with regard to conflicts between parents' beliefs and religious instruction in schools, meaning that the question concerns the parents' rights of guidance as opposed to the state's rights. The Committee held that parents in Norway should not have to disclose their children's faith when applying for exemption from traditional religious education;[403] the right to withdraw children from compulsory religious education was referred to in the record of the meeting with Turkey;[404] and Japan was asked whether children were permitted, at their own or their parents' request, to withdraw from religious instruction.[405] However, the Committee has been careful not to accord parents full freedom in determining the religion of their child when addressing the rights of the latter against the former, emphasizing to South Korea that Article 14 gives parents an entitlement 'to provide *direction* to the child in the exercise of their right'.[406] The manner in which parents guide their children must also be consistent with the Convention as a whole: the bests interests of the child must be taken into account in accordance with Article 3, while Article 12 provides that the child's views must be given due weight in accordance with the age and maturity of the child.[407] Indeed, several reports expressly support the freedom of the child against the parents' rights, as explored in the following section.

The child's autonomy. The CRC has addressed the rights of the child as against the choices **2.152** of the parent on a number of occasions. Chile was asked whether a child's freedom of religion was accepted by family and society when children chose a religion different from that of their parents,[408] and the fact that parental authority prevailed even after the child had been removed from his or her parents in Burkina Faso was of 'particular concern'.[409] The Committee suggested to Djibouti that the child's freedom of religion, depending on their development, should not be tied to parental authority,[410] and Croatia was asked why its Constitution guaranteed parents the right to choose the religion of the child without even mentioning that the child's views should be taken into consideration.[411] The delegation of Malaysia was told simply that the provision in their Constitution for the complete freedom of the parent or legal guardian to decide the religion of the child was at variance with Articles 12 and 14.[412]

Boundaries by age-limit. The CRC has often commented on the inappropriateness of **2.153** age-limits adopted by states parties as thresholds for the assumption of free religious choice

---

[402] See eg UN CRC, Summary Record of the 333rd meeting: Mauritius, UN Doc CRC/C/SR.333 (1996) para 64.

[403] UN CRC, Summary Record of the 150th meeting: Norway, UN Doc CRC/C/SR.150 (1994) para 9.

[404] UN CRC, Summary Record of the 701st meeting: Turkey, UN Doc CRC/C/SR.701 (2001) para 60.

[405] UN CRC, Summary Record of the 465th meeting: Japan, UN Doc CRC/C/SR.465 (1998) para 6.

[406] UN CRC, Summary Record of the 277th meeting: Republic of Korea, UN Doc CRC/C/SR.277 (1996) para 31.

[407] See R Hodgkin and P Newell, *Implementation Handbook for the Convention on the Rights of the Child* (New York: UNICEF, 2002) 198.

[408] UN CRC, Summary Record of the 147th meeting: Chile, UN Doc CRC/C/SR.147 (1996) para 44.

[409] UN CRC, Summary Record of the 136th meeting: Burkina Faso, UN Doc CRC/C/SR.136 at 34 (1994) para 34.

[410] UN CRC, Summary Record of the 638th meeting: Djibouti, UN Doc CRC/C/SR.638 (2000) para 10.

[411] UN CRC, Summary Record of the 638th meeting: Djibouti (n 410) para 10.

[412] UN CRC, Summary Record of the 1216th meeting: Malaysia, UN Doc CRC/C/SR1216 (2007) para 33.

by children (vis-à-vis both parents and the state); it has not, however, provided a consistent framework of guidance.[413] Indeed, the 'evolving capacities' of the child suggest a proportionate increase and decrease of the child's and parents' rights respectively over time,[414] and a single dividing line would therefore be an inappropriate determiner. The Committee's comments are nevertheless instructive. For instance, it has found that the age-limit in Iceland for the child's ability to select or join a religious institution (it is unclear in the report whether the limit was 16 or 18) was too high;[415] while the prevention of minors under the age of 15 from joining in religious rituals without parental consent was found to be an infringement of their religious freedom in Belarus.[416] The Committee said that children should be able to choose their religion before the age of majority in Finland,[417] and it expressed concern that persons below the age of 18 in Denmark could not join a religious community against their parents' wishes.[418] Poland was asked why parental consent was required when students wished to attend ethics courses instead of religious courses, and the Committee referred in its report to the fact that parents were entitled to provide 'direction'.[419]

(3) Article 14(3)

2.154 *Introduction.* Article 14(3) provides that: 'Freedom to manifest one's religion or beliefs may be subject only to such limitations as are prescribed by law and are necessary to protect public safety, order, health, or morals or the fundamental rights and freedoms of others.' These delimited circumstances for the restriction of children's Article 14 rights apply only to freedom of religion and beliefs; not to freedom of thought or conscience, or to the parents' rights under Article 14(2). The paragraph has been interpreted strictly by the CRC.[420] The list of possible purposes to be served by limitations is more restrictive than under other articles,[421] and the terms themselves are more narrowly expressed (the rights and freedoms of others protected by the limitation must be 'fundamental', while 'public order' does not cover the abstract societal values included under '*ordre public*').[422] Any instances of limitation have been held up to close scrutiny, and broad-brush restrictions, such as the Indonesian authority's wide interpretation of limitations (possible 'for lawful purposes'), have given the Committee particular cause for concern.[423] Beyond the specific protected interests, the three-part checklist for limitation—prescription by law, serving of an enumerated interest, and necessity—is almost identical to the criteria under limitation clauses in other treaties.[424]

2.155 *Effect of narrow formulation.* Under UN and regional human rights conventions generally, where a violation of a limitation clause is found, it is often because the restriction in question is not

---

[413] See Langlaude (n 386) 113.

[414] See Brems (n 357) 29–30.

[415] UN CRC, Summary Record of the 856th meeting: Iceland, UN Doc CRC/C/SR/856 (2003) para 16.

[416] UN CRC, Summary Record of the 786th meeting: Belarus, UN Doc CRC/C/SR.786 (2002) para 70.

[417] UN CRC, Summary Record of the 1068th meeting: Finland, UN Doc CRC/C/SR.1068 (2005) para 17.

[418] UN CRC, Summary Record of the 1072nd meeting: Denmark, UN Doc CRC/C/SR.1072 (2005) para 54.

[419] UN CRC, Concluding Observations: Poland, UN Doc CCRC/C/15/Add.69 (1997) para 33.

[420] See eg UN CRC, Concluding Observations: Saudi Arabia, UN Doc CRC/C/15/add.148 (2001) para 31.

[421] Art 15(2), for example, provides that 'no restrictions may be placed on the exercise of these rights other than those imposed in conformity with the law and which are necessary in a democratic society in the interests of national security or public safety, public order (ordre public), the protection of public health or morals or the protection of the rights and freedoms of others'.

[422] See Brems (n 357) 33.

[423] UN CRC, Concluding Observations: Indonesia, UN Doc CRC/C/15/Add.25 (1994) para 13.

[424] See eg ICCPR, Art 18(3) and Article 9(2) ECHR, Art 9(2).

proportionate, rather than because one of the enumerated interests is not served.[425] It is therefore arguable that the narrow formulation of the clause under Article 14(3) has little extra protective effect. Indeed, where the CRC has linked the enjoyment of religious freedom with other freedoms, it has on at least one occasion extended the grounds of limitation to include those listed under other relevant articles. In its Concluding Observations to Kyrgyzstan, when commenting on the ability of persons under the age of 18 to associate for religious purposes, the Committee stated that the limitation clauses under Article 15(2) (freedom of association) needed to be complied with.[426] If links such as this are developed, it could lead to grounds of limitation such as national security being employed in addition to Article 14(3) grounds. This might undermine the apparent textual purpose of the differentiated limitation grounds under separate articles.

Specific instances. The CRC held that the arrest of Jehovah's Witnesses (including children) **2.156** in Eritrea was a limitation of religious freedom; assuming that the arrests were as a result of a religious manifestation, this would suggest that Article 14(3) conditions were not fulfilled.[427] The Committee also expressed concern that regulations prohibiting the wearing of a headscarf by schoolgirls in Tunisia,[428] and by teachers in Germany,[429] did not fulfil the criteria under Article 14(3). A more general reminder was issued to China that the criteria under Article 14(3) must be observed in each instance of limitation,[430] with similar reiterations being made to Saudi Arabia[431] and Iran.[432] However, the CRC issued no comment when informed that the national constitutions of Lebanon and Panama provided for limitations on freedom of religion on the grounds of public order/morals and Christian morals.[433]

(4) Related provisions

Article 2 prohibits discrimination, among others, on the basis of the religion of the child or **2.157** his or her parents or legal guardians. Article 8 protects the child's right to preserve his or her identity, which may include religious identity. Article 13 protects freedom of expression, which extends to expression in the religious sphere, similarly the freedoms of association and of peaceful assembly (Article 15) include applications in the context of religion. The child's right of access to information (Article 17) applies to information about religious matters.

The child's privacy right may also be related to his or her freedom of religion, for instance **2.158** when the mention of religious affiliation is mandated in an official document.[434]

---

[425] See Brems (n 357) 36.
[426] UN CRC, Concluding Observations: Kyrgyzstan, UN Doc CRC/C/15/Add.127 (2000) paras 31–32.
[427] UN CRC, Summary Record of the 865th meeting: Eritrea, UN Doc CRC/C/SR.865 (2003) para 86.
[428] UN CRC, Concluding Observations: Tunisia, UN Doc CRC/C/15/add.181 (2002) para 29.
[429] UN CRC, Concluding Observations: Germany, UN Doc CRC/C/15/add.226 (2004) para 30.
[430] UN CRC, Concluding Observations: China, UN Doc CRC/C/15/add.56 (1996) para 17.
[431] UN CRC, Concluding Observations: Saudi Arabia, UN Doc CRC/C/15/add.148 (1996) para 31.
[432] UN CRC, Concluding Observations: Islamic Republic of Iran, UN Doc CRC/C/15/add.123 (2000) para 35. Within a general admonition, the Committee highlighted restrictions on the enjoyment of religious freedom among the Bahais, citing discrimination in the areas of education, employment, travel, housing, and the enjoyment of cultural activities.
[433] UN CRC, Summary Record of the 289th meeting: Lebanon, UN Doc CRC/C/SR.289 (1996) para 42; Summary Record of the 354th meeting: Panama, UN Doc CRC/C/SR.354 (1997) para 84.
[434] The CRC objected in this respect to the requirement in Greece that a student's secondary school graduation certificate indicate, where applicable, that the student does not practise the Greek Orthodox religion.

3

THE EUROPEAN STANDARDS AND PROTECTIONS

A. The European Convention on Human Rights

(1) Introduction

3.01 Article 9 is the main protection available for religious freedom under the European Convention on Human Rights and Fundamental Freedoms (ECHR).[1] Article 9 is often considered in conjunction with Article 14 (protection against discrimination),[2] and Article 10 (freedom of expression) is also particularly important in many cases in respect of the right to express religious opinions.[3] This chapter concentrates on Article 9.

(2) Article 9 ECHR: an overview[4]

3.02 Article 9 ECHR provides:

1. Everyone has the right to freedom of thought, conscience and religion; this right includes freedom to change his religion or belief and freedom, either alone or in community with

---

[1] 4 November 1950, 213 UNTS 221. For a historical analysis of the Convention and its ratification, see AWB Simpson, *Human Rights and the End of Empire* (OUP, 2001).

[2] See paras 3.115 ff.

[3] See Ch 10, part C(4).

[4] For a general introduction to ECHR, Art 9, see A Mowbray, *Cases, Materials and Commentary on the ECHR* (OUP, 2012) ch 11; FG Jacobs, RCA White, and C Ovey, *The European Convention on Human Rights* (4th edn, OUP, 2010) ch 17; MW Janis, RS Kay, and AW Bradley, *European Human Rights Law: Text and Materials* (OUP, 2008), ch 7; R Clayton and H Tomlinson, *The Law of Human Rights* (OUP, 2008) paras 14.87 ff; S Knights, *Freedom of Religion, Minorities and the Law* (OUP, 2007) ch 2; C Evans, *Freedom of Religion under the European Convention on Human Rights* (OUP, 2001); B Emmerson and J Simor, *Human Rights Practice*

others and in public or private, and to manifest his religion or belief, in worship, teaching, practice and observance.

2. Freedom to manifest one's religion or beliefs shall be subject only to such limitations as are prescribed by law and are necessary in a democratic society in the interests of public safety, for the protection of public order, health or morals, or for the protection of the rights and freedoms of others.

The study of Article 9 ECHR is fascinating: it necessarily entails exploration of religious, political, cultural, sociological, philosophical, and historical diversity. As one author has put it: **3.03**

> The particular context of many of the cases provides an insight into the rich tapestry of European...diversity. Nevertheless, the [Strasbourg] Court has sought to impress upon the Continent a unifying set of values which will help Europe to prepare for and be at ease with the challenges posed by an increasingly secular but also increasingly multi-faith society. The clarion-call is to respect and to value pluralism and tolerance. The right to freedom of conscience cannot be taken for granted.[5]

The importance of Article 9 is obvious. The protection of a freedom to hold personal beliefs and thoughts and to manifest the values inherent in them, is a fundamental part of both individual human dignity and a liberal, democratic society.[6] The European Court of Human Rights (ECtHR) stated this in *Kokkinakis v Greece*,[7] the first case concerning freedom of religion to have come before the Court:[8] **3.04**

> As enshrined in Article 9, freedom of thought, conscience and religion is one of the foundations of a 'democratic society' within the meaning of the Convention. It is, in its religious dimension, one of the most vital elements that go to make up the identity of believers and their conception of life, but is also a precious asset for atheists, agnostics, sceptics and the unconcerned. The pluralism indissociable from a democratic society, which has been dearly won over the centuries, depends on it.[9]

There are two distinct justifications for Article 9, as set out in the *Kokkinakis* and developed in the subsequent case law of the ECtHR.[10] The first could be called the 'personal development argument'. This views the freedoms secured by Article 9 as providing scope for personal development and self-definition. For example, it could be said that to 'search for an understanding of the ultimate meaning of life in one's own way is among the most important aspects of a life that is truly human'.[11] The second could be called 'the social justification'. **3.05**

(Sweet & Maxwell, 2000) ch 9; and M Evans, *Religious Liberty and International Law in Europe* (CUP, 1997), chs 11 and 12.

[5] J Murdoch, *Protecting the right to freedom of thought, conscience and religion under the European Convention on Human Rights, Council of Europe Human Rights handbooks* (Council of Europe, 2012) 8.

[6] See also A Krishnaswami, 'Study of Discrimination in the Matter of Religious Rights and Practices', UN Doc E/CN.4/Sub.2/200/Rev.1 (1960):

> The right to freedom of thought, conscience and religion is probably the most precious of all human rights, and the imperative need today is to make it a reality for every single individual regardless of religion or belief that he professes, regardless of his status, and regardless of his condition in life. The desire to enjoy this right has already proved itself to be one of the most potent and contagious political forces that the world has ever known.

[7] *Kokkinakis v Greece* (1994) 17 EHRR 397.

[8] *Kokkinakis* (n 7) para 25 per Pettit J.

[9] *Kokkinakis* (n 7) para 31.

[10] See eg *Leyla Şahin v Turkey* (2007) 44 EHRR 5, para 104. For discussion, see PW Edge, 'Current Problems in Article 9 of the European Convention on Human Rights' [1996] Juridical Review 42, 47.

[11] MC Nussbaum, *Women and Human Development: The Capabilities Approach* (CUP, 2000) 179.

This views the freedoms secured by Article 9 as helping to provide the necessary platform for a functioning, pluralist, and democratic society where all can feel part of the community. This aspect of Article 9 was referred to by the ECtHR in *Moscow Branch of the Salvation Army v Russia*:[12]

> …For pluralism is also built on the genuine recognition of, and respect for, diversity and the dynamics of cultural traditions, ethnic and cultural identities, religious beliefs, artistic, literary and socio-economic ideas and concepts. The harmonious interaction of persons and groups with varied identities is essential for achieving social cohesion. It is only natural that, where a civil society functions in a healthy manner, the participation of citizens in the democratic process is to a large extent achieved through belonging to associations in which they may integrate with each other and pursue common objectives collectively.[13]

3.06 On its face,[14] Article 9 is potentially very broad in scope: it covers *thoughts, consciences, religions*, and *beliefs*, to which *everyone* has the absolute right, whether that be *alone or in community*, or in *public* or *private*. It also covers *manifestations* of those religions or beliefs which might comprise the broad acts of *worship, teaching, practice*, or *observance*, each of which can be limited in defined circumstances. These rights to manifestation have the potential to raise controversial issues, for example the competing definitions of religion and belief; the role of courts in determining issues in such fields;[15] the differing constitutional traditions pertaining to religion in society in Member States; the competing rights and values of different individuals and groups; and the use of available justifications for state interference in religious rights. It is therefore perhaps surprising that Article 9 case law is not as voluminous as that relating to other articles of the Convention, and that much of the ECtHR's jurisprudence is of relatively recent origin.[16] An increasing interest in, and discussion of,[17] Article 9 has, however, developed in recent years in response to fresh case law and a growing debate about how the policy concerns at issue are being satisfied by the current law.[18]

3.07 Another feature of Article 9 is that it is closely related, both textually and substantively, to other ECHR rights. These include: Article 6[19] (right of access to a court), Article 8 (respect

---

[12] *Moscow Branch of the Salvation Army v Russia* (2007) 44 EHRR 46.

[13] *Moscow Branch of the Salvation Army v Russia* (n 12) para 61.

[14] The *travaux préparatoires* relating to Art 9 are of very limited value as an aid to interpretation: see C Evans, 'Religious Freedom in European Human Rights Law: The Search for a Guiding Conception' in MW Janis and C Evans (eds), *Religion and International Law* (Martinus Nijhoff, 2004) 385, 388–9.

[15] See further A Scolnicov, 'Does Constitutionlisation Lead to Secularisation?' in I Katzenelson and G Stedman-Jones (eds), *Religion and the Political Imagination* (CUP, 2010) 295.

[16] There have been 40 judgments finding violations of Art 9 between 1959 and 2011 (one each in respect of Armenia, Austria, France, Georgia, Poland, San Marino, and Switzerland; three each in respect of Latvia, Moldova, and Ukraine; four in respect of Turkey; five each in respect of Bulgaria and Russia; and 10 in respect of Greece: European Court *Annual Report 2011* (2012) 160–1. The first judgment establishing a violation was delivered in 1993 (see nn 7 and 8). On why it may have taken so long for the Strasbourg Court to apply Art 9, see D Gomien, *Short Guide to the European Convention on Human Rights* (1991) 69 and MW Janis, 'Introduction' in Janis and Evans (n 14) xiii. The UK was found to have violated Art 9 in 2013.

[17] See further R Uitz, *Europeans and their Rights—Freedom of Religion* (Council of Europe, 2007), and J-F Renucci, *Article 9 of the European Convention on Human Rights: Freedom of Thought Conscience and Religion* (Council of Europe, 2005).

[18] C McCrudden, 'Religion, Human Rights, Equality and the Public Sphere' (2011) 13(1) Ecc LJ 38.

[19] See eg *Canea Catholic Church v Greece* (1997) 27 EHRR 521 regarding the right of access to a court for the determination of a religious community's rights.

for family life), Article 10[20] (freedom of expression), Article 11[21] (right of association), and Article 2 of Protocol No 1 (parents' philosophical and religious beliefs respected in provision of education to their children). The ECtHR has generally taken an exclusionary approach to Article 9 by resisting applicants' attempts to raise issues under Article 9 in circumstances where those issues may have been considered as falling to be determined under one of these other ECHR articles.[22]

Article 9 itself establishes two separate rights. The first is an absolute right to freedom of **3.08** thought, conscience, and religion and relates to what is often called the *forum internum*[23] of the individual. The second is a qualified right to manifest the religion or belief by worship, teaching, practice, and observance. This second right is qualified in that it is subject to the limitations set out in Article 9(2). These limitations provide that the right to manifestation may need to be balanced against other needs of society which are listed as: 'public safety', 'the protection of public order, health or morals', and 'the protection of the rights and freedoms of others'. These limitations must be 'prescribed by law' and 'necessary in a democratic society'.

Article 9 claims follow an analysis in which the ECtHR may, depending on the circum- **3.09** stances of any one case, ask up to three questions of the parties: (a) Is Article 9 engaged on the facts? (b) If so, has there been an interference with a right underArticle 9 on the facts? (c) If so, and a right to manifestation is engaged, is the interference with Article 9 justified?

(3) When is Article 9 engaged?

As a matter of historical practice the Commission and ECtHR have used various means to **3.10** delimit the scope of claims under Article 9.

a) What is meant by 'thought, conscience and religion' and 'belief'?[24]

In general, these terms have been used in a notably broad fashion; there has been an under- **3.11** standable reluctance to limit the concepts of religion and belief in particular. Traditionally,

---

[20] See eg *Feldek v Slovakia* (App 29032/95) (2001); *Van Den Dungen v Netherlands* (1995) 80 DR 147; *Vereiniging Rechtswinkel Utrecht v Netherlands* (1986) 46 DR 200; *Hazar v Turkey* (1990) 72 DR 200; *Otto-Preminger-Institut v Austria* (1994) 19 EHRR 34; and *Wingrove v UK* (1997) 24 EHRR 1. See further M Evans, 'The Freedom of Religion or Belief and the Freedom of Expression' (2009) 4(2–3) Religion and Human Rights 197.

[21] See eg *Religionsgemeinschaft der Zeugen Jehovas v Austria* (App 40825/98) (2008) paras 60–61; *Refah Partisi (the Welfare Party) and ors v Turkey* (2003) 37 EHRR 1; and *Hasan and Chaush v Bulgaria* (2002) 34 EHRR 55, 62 where the ECtHR emphasized that where the organization of a religious community is in issue, Art 9 must be interpreted in the light of Art 11.

[22] See *Hoffmann v Austria* (1993) 17 EHRR 293 (custody of children: Arts 8 and 14); *Zengin v Turkey* (2008) 46 EHRR 44 (exemptions from lessons in religious culture and ethics: Art 2 of Protocol No 1); *Glas Nadezha Eood and Elenkov v Bulgaria* (2007) 24 BHRC 239 (refusal of broadcasting licence: Art 10); *Young, James and Webster v UK* (1981) 4 EHRR 38 (joining trade unions: Art 11); *Darby v Sweden* (1990) 13 EHRR 774 (maintenance of an established church: Art 1 of Protocol No 1 and Art 14); and *Khan v UK* (1986) 48 DR 253 (right of marriage: Art 12). Also see A Lester and D Pannick, *Human Rights Law and Practice* (LexisNexis, 2009) para 4.9.2.

[23] See eg *Van Den Dungen* (n 20) para 1. See also P van Dijk, G van Hoof, A van Rijn, and L Zwaak (eds), *Theory and Practice of the European Convention on Human Rights* (4th edn, Intersentia, 2006) 752–3.

[24] Whilst the following analysis *formally* separates 'religion' and 'belief' for clarity and simplicity in exploration of the composite parts of the article, one author has cogently argued that in any *substantive* sense: 'It is preferable not to seek to distinguish between religion and beliefs, since nothing turns on the distinction . . . and an attempt to categorise certain beliefs as either being, or not amounting to, a religion is likely to provoke unnecessary disagreement.' (M Evans (n 4) 289).

the ECtHR has been careful not to make determinations of a precise definitional and delimiting nature.[25] However, there are naturally parameters and inherent limits involved in Article 9 as it is concerned with fundamental freedoms and rights: a wholly subjective test would be unjustifiably wide and unsuitable for adjudication.[26]

3.12 *Religion.* The ECtHR has never categorically defined 'religion'. Naturally, the well-established and mainstay religions have all been identified as falling within the ambit of Article 9, for example Buddhism,[27] Christianity (of many denominations),[28] Hinduism,[29] Islam,[30] Jehovah's Witnesses,[31] Judaism,[32] and Sikhism.[33]

3.13 Less well known and more recently established religions have also been held to fall within the ambit of Article 9. In *Kimlya and others v Russia*,[34] the question arose as to whether the Church of Scientology could be recognized as a religion. Holding that it could, the ECtHR noted[35] that where there is no European consensus on the religious nature of a body, the Court should be 'sensitive to the subsidiary nature of its role' and may simply rely upon the position taken by the domestic authorities. The ECtHR said: 'it is clearly not the Court's task to decide *in abstracto* whether or not a body of beliefs and related practices may be considered a religion'.[36] The following have also been held, or assumed to be,[37] religions for the purposes of Article 9: Druidism,[38] the Divine Light Zentrum,[39] the Moon Sect,[40] and the Osho movement.[41] Recent decisions of the ECtHR suggest a more generous acknowledgement of non-mainstream religions than those of the former Commission.[42]

3.14 Article 9 also provides protections for non-believers.[43] As the ECtHR stated in *Kokkinakis v Greece*, the protections in Article 9 are 'also a precious asset for atheists, agnostics, sceptics and the unconcerned'.[44]

---

[25] See J Hedigan, 'Religious Advertising and the European Convention on Human Rights', Congrès des Droits de l'Homme, Istanbul (2006), who states that: 'In matters pertaining to religion, it is perhaps better not to stray too far from home.' However, see McCrudden (n 18) 30, who suggests that courts' previous reticence has been replaced by a 'much more self-confident willingness to adjudicate contested issues touching on the religious sphere' in recent years.

[26] See R Allen and G Moon, 'Substantive rights and equal treatment in respect of religion and belief: towards a better understanding of the rights, and their implications' (2000) 6 EHRLR 580.

[27] *X v UK* (1974) 1 DR 41.

[28] *Knudsen v Norway* (1985) 42 DR 247.

[29] *ISKCON and ors v UK* (1994) 76-A DR 41.

[30] *Karaduman v Turkey* (1993) 74 DR 93.

[31] *Kokkinakis* (n 7).

[32] *D v France* (1983) 35 DR 199.

[33] *X v UK* (1982) 28 DR 5 38.

[34] *Kimlya and ors v Russia* (Apps 76836/01 and 32782/03) (2009).

[35] *Kimlya* (n 34) para 79.

[36] *Kimlya* (n 34) para 79.

[37] See *Chappell v UK* (1987) 53 DR 241 (druidism); *Omkarananda and Divine Light Zentrum v Switzerland* (1981) 25 DR 105 (Divine Light Zentrum); and *X and Church of Scientology v Sweden* (1979) 16 DR 68 (Scientology).

[38] *Chappell v UK* (App 10461/83) (1989).

[39] *Omkarananda and Divine Light Zentrum* (n 37).

[40] *X v Austria* (App 8652/79) (1981).

[41] *Leela Forderkreis EV and ors v Germany* (App 58911/00) (2008).

[42] See M Taylor, *Freedom of Religion: UN and European Human Rights Law and Practice* (CUP, 2005).

[43] See *Buscarini v San Marino* (1999) ECHR 7, para 34.

[44] *Kokkinakis* (n 7) para 31.

Attempts have been made by legal academics to define 'religion' for the purposes of the **3.15** ECHR.[45] Professor Nafziger suggests that the term 'religion' 'may be described as a practice of ultimate concern about our nature and obligations as human beings, inspired by experience and typically expressed by members of a group or community sharing myths and doctrines whose authority transcends both individual conscience and the state'.[46] However, he goes on to caveat this attempt (and indeed any definition of 'religion') as 'apt to be inadequate and culturally biased'.

There are at least a further four reasons why the definition of 'religion' in the Article 9 juris- **3.16** prudence is justifiably wide and not precisely limited. First, different communities based upon the same religion or belief tend to be highly differentiated.[47] Differences may be linked to the geographical origins of particular communities or religious traditions. Secondly, perspectives between adherents of the same religion or belief may vary according to generation, ethnicity, gender, and sexual orientation.[48] Thirdly, not all religious groups have identifiable leaders or representatives, especially those which are non-hierarchical. Even where they do, their positions may be contested by others with the same stated affiliation or may not represent the views of 'dissidents' or of relatively powerless or minor groups, such as women or those who are lesbian, gay, bisexual, or transgender.[49] Fourthly, it would be virtually impossible to arrive at a definition that is flexible enough to cover the wide range of faiths in the world but also precise enough to be capable of practical application.[50] This has led the ECtHR to limit attempts at a definition and refrain from a 'one size fits all' paradigm. The Court's reluctance to proffer a definition has also been the subject of criticism.[51]

There must still be proof that a religion is in question; whilst the freedom, and religious **3.17** beliefs themselves, are inherently subjective, if there were no evidential requirements, then the freedom would be made worthless. Therefore, if the matter is controversial, an applicant may be expected to establish that a particular 'religion' does actually exist.[52] The ECtHR will usually seek to avoid being drawn into definitional pursuits by simply accepting that a

---

[45] See further N Smart, *The Philosophy of Religion* (OUP, 1979) 4–34; K Greenawalt, 'Religion as a Constitutional Concept' (1984) 72 California Law Review 753; and PW Edge, *Legal Responses to Religious Difference* (Kluwer Law International, 2002) 5–17.

[46] JAR Nafziger, 'The Functions of Religion in the International Legal system' in Janis and Evans (n 14) 155, 158.

[47] See eg A Dinham, R Furbey, and V Lowndes, *Faith in the Public Realm: Controversies, Policies and Practices* (Policy Press, 2009); A Dinham, *Faith, Public Policy and Civil Society: Policies, Problems and Concepts in Faith-based Public Action* (Palgrave Macmillan, 2009); and J Beckford, R Gale, D Owen, C Peach, and P Weller, *Review of the Evidence Base on Faith Communities* (London: Office of the Deputy Prime Minister, 2006).

[48] Equality and Human Rights Commission Research Report 84, 'Religion or belief, equality and human rights in England and Wales', Human Rights and Social Justice Research Institute, London Metropolitan University (2012).

[49] F Panjwani, 'Because My Religion Says So: Democratic Theory and Internal Diversity in Religions' in H Ansari and D Cesarani (eds), 'Muslim-Jewish Dialogue in a 21st Century World', Egham: Centre for Minority Studies, History Department (2007) 38–51.

[50] See N Bratza, 'The "Precious Asset": Freedom of Religion Under the ECHR' (2012) 14 Ecc LJ 256. Also see TJ Gunn 'The Complexity of Religion and the Definition of Religion in International Law' (2003) 16 Harv HRJ 189.

[51] See eg Jacobs, White, and Ovey (n 4) 402: 'rather loose guidelines... [and] minimalist reasoning', and at 403: 'rather loose and ill-defined'.

[52] *X v the UK* (1977) 11 DR 55 (the applicant was unable to adduce evidence which established the essential elements of Wicca); and *X v Germany* (1970) 37 Coll 119 (the applicant, a light worshipper, did not provide sufficient evidence of his beliefs or how they were infringed). For discussion of this requirement, see C Evans (n 4) 58.

religion or belief is covered.[53] The applicant is also expected to show that he or she is genuinely an adherent of a particular religion.[54] This is a low burden of proof considering the Court's remarks in *Folgero v Norway*[55] that 'information about personal, religious and philosophical convictions concerns some of the most intimate aspects of private life'.

3.18 *'Belief'*.[56] For a 'belief' to fall within Article 9 it must satisfy three requirements.[57] First, the belief must 'attain a certain level of cogency, seriousness, cohesion and importance'.[58] Secondly, it must relate to a 'weighty and substantial aspect of human life and behaviour'.[59] Thirdly, it 'must also be worthy of respect in a democratic society and not be incompatible with human dignity'.[60] As the Court said in *Refah Partisi (The Welfare Party) v Turkey*,[61] the 'belief' must be:

> . . . in harmony with the rule of law and respect for human rights and democracy. An attitude which fails to respect that principle will not necessarily be accepted as being covered by the freedom to manifest one's religion and will not enjoy the protection of Article 9.

It follows that if a 'belief' does not respect the rule of law, human rights, or democracy then it will not fall within the protection of Article 9 for failing the third requirement.

3.19 Applying these requirements, the following beliefs have been held by the Strasbourg Court to fall within Article 9's ambit: pacifism,[62] atheism,[63] veganism,[64] political ideologies such as communism,[65] the Salvation Army,[66] pro-life,[67] secularism,[68] and conscientious objection.[69]

3.20 By contrast, the Court has held that the following 'beliefs' do not fall within the scope of Article 9: belief in assisted suicide,[70] belief in language preference,[71] belief in disposal

---

[53] See *Chappell v UK* (n 37) (druidism); *Omkarananda and Divine Light Zentrum* (n 37) (Divine Light Zentrum); and *X and Church of Scientology* (n 37) (Scientology).

[54] See *X v UK* (1981) 22 DR 27.

[55] *Folgero v Norway* (2008) 46 EHRR 47, 98.

[56] See further R Sandberg, 'Defining Religion: Towards An Interdisciplinary Approach' (2008) 17 Revista General de Derecho Canonico y Derecho Elesiastico del Estado 1; R Ahdar and I Leigh, *Religious Freedom in the Liberal State* (OUP, 2005) 124; and Taylor (n 42) 207.

[57] For an interesting thesis that individual 'sincerity' and 'consistency' have become the most significant determinants of whether or not a religious or philosophical belief is to be recognized as such for the purposes of accessing putative legal protections for individuals, see A Hambler, 'Establishing Sincerity in Religion and Belief Claims: A Question of Consistency' (2011) 13(2) Ecc LJ 146.

[58] *Campbell and Cosans v UK* (1982) 4 EHRR 293, para 36.

[59] *Campbell and Cosans* (n 58) para 36.

[60] *Campbell and Cosans* (n 58) para 36.

[61] *Refah Partisi (The Welfare Party) v Turkey* (2003) 37 EHRR 1, para 93, regarding secularism, which was held to satisfy this third requirement.

[62] *Arrowsmith v UK* (1978) 3 EHRR 218.

[63] *Angelini v Sweden* (1988) 10 EHHR 123.

[64] *H v UK* (1993) 16 EHRR CD 44 (a prisoner who refused to work in the prison print shop as he objected to working with animal products).

[65] *Hazar, Hazar and Acik v Turkey* (Apps 16311/90, 16312/90, and 16313/90) (1992).

[66] *Moscow Branch of the Salvation Army v Russia* (2007) 44 EHRR 912.

[67] *Plattform Ärzte für das Leben v Austria* (1991) 13 EHHR 204 (1986) 51 DR 41.

[68] *Lautsi v Italy* (2012) 54 EHRR 3 (App 30814/06) (2011) para 58.

[69] *Bayatyan v Armenia* (2012) 54 EHRR 15.

[70] *Pretty v UK* (2002) 35 EHRR 1, para 82. See, more generally, J Keown, 'Death in Strasbourg: Assisted Suicide' (2003) 1 International Journal of Constitutional Law 722; D Morris, 'Assisted Suicide under the European Convention on Human Rights: A Critique' (2003) 1 EHRLR 65; A Pedain, 'The Human Rights Dimensions of the Diane Pretty Case' (2003) 62 CLJ 181; and E Wicks, *The Right to Refuse Medical Treatment under the ECHR* (2001) 9 Medical Law Review 17.

[71] *Belgian Linguistic case* 1968 1 EHRR 252.

of human remains after death,[72] prisoners' preferences regarding their uniform,[73] and the idealistic aims of a not-for-profit organization which provided legal advice to prisoners and looked after their interests.[74]

It is evident that Article 9 does not grant the right to manifest a purely personal view-   **3.21**
point; the position was probably best summarized by the UK government's submission in *Arrowsmith v United Kingdom*:[75] 'the word "belief" connotes and requires the holding and expression of spiritual or philosophical convictions which, while not necessarily organised in the same sense of a religion, nevertheless have an identifiable formal content'.[76] The overall lack of clarity in the case law as to what precisely constitutes a 'belief',[77] and the instability that this creates, is commonly discussed in academic commentaries.[78] Identifying a belief as being within the bounds of an already accepted and well-established religious belief ensures that it will most certainly cross the threshold of 'seriousness'.[79] However, for those whose beliefs might fall within minority groups[80] or sects of which there is no mainstream knowledge or which do not have a long history,[81] the lack of clarity might create problems.

Conscientious objection. In the recent case of *Bayatyan v Armenia*,[82] the applicant was arrested   **3.22**
and charged with draft evasion for refusing to perform military service. He had, however, offered to perform civilian service instead. At paragraph 110 of its judgment, the Grand Chamber of the ECtHR stated:

> …Article 9 does not explicitly refer to a right to conscientious objection. However, it considers that opposition to military service, where it is motivated by a serious and insurmountable conflict between the obligation to serve in the army and a person's conscience or his deeply and genuinely held religious or other beliefs, constitutes a conviction or belief of sufficient cogency, seriousness, cohesion and importance to attract the guarantees of Article 9…Whether and to what extent objection to military service falls within the ambit of that provision must be assessed in light of the particular circumstances of the case.

The Grand Chamber, by a 16 to 1 majority, went on to hold that there had been a violation   **3.23**
of Article 9 as the state's actions were disproportionate and not necessary in a democratic society. Paragraph 110 is interesting for two reasons. First, it replaces earlier Commission

---

[72] *X v Germany* (1981) 24 DR 137 (but the matter can fall within the scope of Art 8)

[73] *McFeely et al v UK* (1980) 20 DR 44.

[74] *Vereniging Rechtswinkel Utrecht* (n 20).

[75] *Arrowsmith* (n 62).

[76] *Arrowsmith* (n 62) para 42.

[77] In *Chassagnou v France* 1999-III 19 EHRR 615, in a separate opinion, Fischbach J suggested that even 'environmentalism' or 'ecological' beliefs might come within the scope of Art 9 where they are informed by a 'truly societal stance'.

[78] See, *inter alia*, R Sandberg, *Law and Religion* (CUP, 2011) ch 3; L Vickers, *Religious Freedom, Religious Discrimination at the Workplace* (Hart Publishing, 2008) ch 2; Knights (n 4) 4–43; P Griffith, 'Protecting the Absence of Religious Belief? The New Definition of Religion or Belief in Equality Legislation' (2007) 2(3) Religion and Human Rights 149; and Ahdar and Leigh (n 56) 110–24.

[79] See M Evans (n 24) 290; K Rimanque, 'Freedom of Conscience and Minority Groups' in *Freedom of Conscience, Leiden Seminar Proceedings* (Council of Europe: Strasbourg, 1993) 144, 155; and TJ Gunn, 'Adjudicating Rights of Conscience Under the ECHR' in JD Van der Vyver and J Witte (eds), *Religious Human Rights in Global Perspective: Legal Perspectives* (Martinus Nijhoff, 1996) 329.

[80] For detailed discussion of the meaning of 'minority groups' see M Malik, 'Minority Legal Orders in the UK: Minorities, Pluralism and the Law', The British Academy, London (2012).

[81] See Z Machnyikova, 'Religious Rights' in M Weller (ed) *Universal Minority Rights* (OUP, 2007) 179, 183.

[82] *Bayatyan* (n 69). For discussion, see P Muzny, '*Bayatyan v Armenia*: The Grand Chamber Renders a Grand Judgment' (2012) 12(1) HRLR 135.

and ECtHR jurisprudence that conscientious objection was not protected under Article 9.[83] In that respect, the Grand Chamber's decision is another instance of the living instrument doctrine in which the Court has revised its jurisprudence to reflect contemporary standards.[84] The second point of interest is the final sentence of paragraph 110—'to what extent [a 'belief'] falls within the ambit of [Article 9] must be assessed in light of the particular circumstances'— which might be seen to be introducing a fourth requirement whereby, depending on the particular situation, the same substantive 'belief' may or may not fall within the ambit of Article 9. It is hoped that the Court will not enter into separate interference or justification questions at this preliminary stage: those sorts of questions fall to be determined at a later stage.

3.24 *Bayatyan v Armenia* has since been followed. In *Ercep v Turkey*[85] the Court found violations of Articles 6 and 9 in a case regarding the refusal of a Jehovah's Witness (who was a conscientious objector) to perform military service; the Court invited Turkey to enact legislation concerning conscientious objectors and to introduce an alternative form of service.[86] In *Savda v Turkey*,[87] the Court noted that since *Bayatyan*, opposition to military service (where motivated by a serious and insurmountable conflict between the obligation to serve in the army and a person's conscience or his deeply and genuinely held beliefs) constituted a conviction of sufficient cogency, seriousness, cohesion, and importance to attract the guarantees of Article 9. It went on to hold that there was a violation of the Convention as there was no procedure which would have enabled the applicant to establish whether he was entitled to conscientious-objector status in domestic law.

3.25 *'Thought' and 'conscience'.* There has been little case law on what is meant by 'thought' and 'conscience'. In *Johnston v Ireland*,[88] a restrictive meaning was adopted. It was held that the inability to obtain a divorce (which resulted in Johnston being unable to live with the second applicant except in an extra-marital relationship) was not a complaint about an interference with his 'conscience' as, in effect, the applicant was really complaining about the non-availability of divorce under Irish law—a matter which did not engage Article 9.[89] It has also been held that a mere 'consciousness' of belonging to a minority group (and in consequence, the aim of seeking to protect a group's cultural identity) does not in itself give rise to an Article 9 issue.[90]

3.26 In *Herrmann v Germany*,[91] the applicant attempted to raise Article 9 in the context of compulsory membership of a hunting association and the obligation for him to tolerate hunting on his property. The majority of the Grand Chamber did not consider in any detail the applicant's complaint that his Article 9 rights had been violated and instead decided the case under Article 1 of the First Protocol (property rights). However, in an interesting partially concurring and partially dissenting opinion, Judge Albuquerque disagreed with the majority's finding that it was unnecessary to examine the complaints under Article 9 separately. Citing numerous cases in which the Court had previously accepted arguments in various matters

---

[83] *Grandrath v Germany* (1966) 10 Yearbook 626, and *Autio v Finland* (1992) 72 DR 245.
[84] See eg *Tyrer v UK* (1970) 2 EHRR 1, para 31. See also, Mowbray (n 4) 609–10.
[85] *Ercep v Turkey* (App 2226/10) (2011).
[86] See further *Johansen v Norway* (1985) 44 DR 155 for the fact that the state is permitted to take measures to enforce *civilian* service without breaching Art 9. See also *Autio v Finland* (1991) 72 DR 245.
[87] *Savda v Turkey* (App 42730/05) (2012).
[88] *Johnston v Ireland* (1986) 9 EHRR 203, para 63.
[89] *Johnston* (n 88) para 63.
[90] *Sidiropoulos et al v Greece* (1999) 27 EHRR 633, para 41.
[91] *Herrmann v Germany* (App 9300/07) (2012).

concerning animal welfare,[92] he considered the right to object to hunting on conscientious grounds as falling within the Article 9's ambit. At page 43 of the judgment, he stated:

> Like Antigone, who buried her brother Polynices in compliance with the laws of the gods but against the laws of the city of Thebes forbidding the mourning of a traitor, the applicant faced a conflict of conscience between a legal rule and a higher ethical value. It is time to release him from this conflict by affirming that his claim is right and the impugned legal rule is wrong.

b) What is meant by 'manifestation'?[93]

Manifestation of religion or belief is the second aspect of the religious freedom protected **3.27** by Article 9. On its face, Article 9 only protects the manifestation of 'religion or belief', and not the manifestation of 'thought or conscience'.[94] In practice nothing has turned on this point. The rationale for protecting manifestation of religion or belief is twofold. First, actions and manifestations are intimately bound up with the existence of religious convictions or beliefs[95]—if the latter is protected, then it is logical to protect the former. Secondly, any right to hold and have beliefs or convictions would in practice be worthless if one could not express or fulfil those beliefs in any practical or real sense.

The right to manifestation is not absolute. Interferences with manifestations are subject **3.28** to the permissible justifications set out in Article 9(2). Moreover, the wide interpretations afforded by the Court to the terms 'religion' and 'belief' are in contrast to the narrow scope that has been given to the right to manifest that religion or belief.[96] As will be seen, there is a distinction drawn in the Strasbourg case law between, on the one hand, the holding and communication of a belief, and, on other hand, acts motivated by the belief but which are not central to its expression. It is this second aspect, the definitional issue, which concerns us in this section; the justifications for interference with the right under Article 9(2) will be discussed separately later in this chapter.[97]

One can manifest in 'private or in public' and 'in community with others'.[98] Article 9 there- **3.29** fore has a strong collective aspect.[99] As religious beliefs are very often manifested in communities,[100] Article 9 also includes the right to organize such religious communities.[101] It is

---

[92] *Herrmann* (n 91) the Judgment, at 39.

[93] See further P Cumper, 'The public manifestation of religion or belief: challenges for a multi-faith society in the twenty-first century' in A Lewis and R O'Dair (eds), *Law and Religion* (OUP, 2001) 311.

[94] But see Edge (n 10) 42, which might be seen to suggest otherwise.

[95] See eg *Kokkinakis* (n 7) para 31: 'Bearing witness in words and deeds is bound up with the existence of religious convictions.'

[96] See C Evans (n 4) 200.

[97] See para 3.72.

[98] See further J Rivers 'From Toleration to Pluralism: Religious Liberty and Religious Establishment under the UK's Human Rights Act' in R Ahdar (ed), *Law and Religion* (Ashgate, 2000) 138.

[99] For discussion of this collective dimension to religious freedom, see J Rivers, *The Law of Organised Religions: Between Establishment and Secularism* (OUP, 2010). On the relationship between individual rights and group rights, see A Scolnicov, *The Right To Religious Freedom in International Law: Between Group Rights and Individual Rights* (Routledge, 2011).

[100] For the communal nature of Art 9, see also *Hasan and Chaush* (n 21) para 62 and *Cyprus v Turkey* (2002) 35 EHRR 731, para 245 (Art 9 violated because Greek Cypriots living in Northern Cyprus did not have free access to places of worship outside their villages).

[101] *Church of Scientology Moscow v Russia* (2008) 46 EHRR 16, para 72:

> . . . Since religious communities traditionally exist in the form of organised structures, Article 9 must be interpreted in the light of Article 11 of the Convention . . . the right of believers to freedom of religion, which includes the right to manifest one's religion in community with others, encompasses the expectation that believers will be allowed to associate freely, without arbitrary State intervention.

necessary for the state not to ignore this communal nature of Article 9.[102] It has also been held that the rights set out in Article 9(1) are not mutually exclusive; this means that the right to manifest 'alone or in community with others' is a double right: the state cannot choose which one to grant.[103] The importance of the collective aspect to Article 9 was discussed by the ECtHR in *Supreme Holy Council of the Muslim Community v Bulgaria*[104] at paragraph 93:

> ... the autonomous existence of religious communities is indispensible in a democratic society ... What is at stake here is the preservation of pluralism and the proper function of democracy, one of the principal characteristics of which is the possibility it offers of resolving a country's problems through dialogue, even when they are irksome.

3.30 In theory, there are arguably three forms that manifestation can take.[105] The first is 'negative manifestation': this might take the form of a request for time off to fulfil religious obligations, or an abstention from certain duties for reasons of religious conviction. Secondly, there is 'passive manifestation': this might include wearing certain religious clothing or symbols. Thirdly, there is 'active manifestation': this would include distributing literature promoting a religion or belief and other proselytizing activities. These forms of manifestation appear across the ECtHR's case law. However, the text of Article 9 categorizes 'manifestation' differently, and more specifically, as entailing 'worship', 'teaching', 'practice', or 'observance'. The Strasbourg Court has tended to treat each category as exclusive.[106]

3.31 *'Worship'.* There have been cases from CIS states where the freedom to worship has been the subject of unjustifiable interference by licensing requirements.

3.32 *'Teaching'.* This covers the activities undertaken in religious establishments[107] and includes those conducted in schools with a religious foundation.[108] It also includes teaching of the unconverted (ie proselytizing) as well as the converted.[109] However, this will not be the case if the proselytizing is deemed 'improper',[110] for example where there is a hierarchical relationship between the converter and the potential convertee, such as in a military context.[111] Improper proselytism:

> ... represents a corruption or deformation of [freedom to choose religion]. It may ... take the form of activities offering material or social advantages with a view to gaining new members

---

Indeed, the autonomous existence of religious communities is indispensable for pluralism in a democratic society and is thus an issue at the very heart of the protection which Article 9 affords.

[102] See *Kokkinakis* (n 7) para 31, and *X v UK* (n 54).

[103] *X v UK* (n 54) 374, para 34.

[104] *Supreme Holy Council of the Muslim Community v Bulgaria* (2005) 41 EHRR 3.

[105] A Hambler, 'A Private Matter? Evolving Approaches to the Freedom to Manifest Religious Convictions in the Workplace' (2008) 3(2) Religion and Human Rights 111.

[106] C Evans (n 4) 106.

[107] See *Al-Nashif v Bulgaria* (2003) 36 EHRR 37.

[108] The ability for a registered religious society to found its own schools was one of the factors which engaged the state's duties under Art 9 when granting registered status in the case of *Religionsgemeinschaft der Zeugen Jehovas* (n 21) para 92. However, in *Savez Crkava 'Riječ Života' and ors v Croatia* (App 7798/08) (2010), the Court held that the right to manifest religion in teaching does not go so far as to entail an obligation on states to allow religious education in public schools or nurseries (para 57).

[109] *Kokkinakis* (n 7) (the applicant's criminal conviction by the Greek courts for proselytism, after engaging in a conversation about religion with a neighbour, was held not to have been justified in the circumstances of the case; no improper means had been established). For discussion, see Gunn (n 79) 329.

[110] For the distinction between 'proper' and 'improper' proselytism, also see Parliamentary Assembly Recommendation 1412 (1999).

[111] *Larissis v Greece* (1997) 4 BHRC 370 (there was violation of Art 9 where the three applicants were air force officers trying to convert a number of people to their faith, including three airmen who were their

for a Church or exerting improper pressure on people in distress or in need; it may even entail the use of violence or brainwashing; more generally it is not compatible with respect for the freedom of thought, conscience and religion of others.[112]

'Practice'. This is by far the largest category of 'manifestation' and the majority of the Court's **3.33** case law has been decided in this area. Strasbourg jurisprudence has drawn a distinction between a practice which was deemed to be an actual manifestation of a belief or religion (falling within the ambit of Article 9), and conduct which was merely motivated by a religion or belief (falling outside the ambit of Article 9). The leading case in expounding this difference is *Arrowsmith v United Kingdom*.[113] The pacifist applicant had been convicted for handing out leaflets. These leaflets did not focus on the promotion of non-violent means for dealing with political issues (as it was argued), but instead were critical of government policy. At paragraph 71, the Commission stated:

> . . . the term 'practice' as employed in Article 9(1) does not cover each act which is motivated or influenced by a religion or belief. It is true that public declarations proclaiming generally the idea of pacifism and urging the acceptance of a commitment to non-violence may be considered as a normal and recognised manifestation of pacifist belief. However, when the actions of individuals do not actually express the belief concerned they cannot be considered to be as such protected by Article 9(1) even when they are motivated or influenced by it.[114]

The leaflets in question did not reflect pacifist views per se, but were policy-based oppositions to British military involvement in Northern Ireland. The applicant's conviction did not therefore violate Article 9: distributing these leaflets was not a manifestation of a protected belief under Article 9, it was merely motivated by that belief.

The Commission's decision in *Arrowsmith* did not give extensive guidance as to what sepa- **3.34** rates those practices which are manifestations of a religion or belief from those which are merely motivated by it. The minimum threshold, positively formulated, is that the action should 'actually express the belief concerned', which points to the need for a direct link between the practice and the belief in question. This was interpreted by Mr Opsahl in his dissenting opinion as a requirement that the action '*necessarily* manifest a belief';[115] ie that it is a manifestation of the belief rather than of anything else. There is some support for this in the case law, particularly where the act in question might be better protected by other Convention rights. In *Khan v United Kingdom*,[116] for example, the applicant argued that his marriage to a girl aged 12, as permitted by Islam, was a manifestation of his religious beliefs. The Court held that 'while the applicant's religion may allow the marriage of girls at the age

---

subordinates; it was held to be necessary for the state to protect junior airmen from being put under undue pressure by seniors. However, the Court did not find a violation of Art 9 with regard to the measures taken against two of the applicants for the proselytizing of civilians as they were not subject to pressure and constraints like the airmen.) For discussion, see JW Montgomery, 'When is Evangelism Illegal?' (1998) New Law Journal 524. See also *Kalac v Turkey* (1997) 27 EHRR 552.

[112] *Kokkinakis* (n 7) para 48.
[113] *Arrowsmith* (n 62).
[114] The distinction between mere motivation and manifestation has been repeated and endorsed on numerous occasions: *Kalac v Turkey* (n 111); *Metropolitan Church of Bessarabia v Moldova* (2002) 35 EHRR 13, 114; *Şahin* (n 10), 105; *C v UK* (1983) 37 DR 142; *Vereniging Rechtswinkel Utrecht* (n 20); *Yanasik v Turkey* (1993) 47 DR 14; *Karaduman* (n 30); and *Van Den Dungen* (n 20).
[115] *Arrowsmith* (n 62), Separate Opinion, in part dissenting, of Mr Opsahl, para 2.
[116] *Khan v UK* (11579/85) (1986).

of 12, marriage cannot be considered simply as a form of expression of thought, conscience or religion, and is governed specifically by Article 12'.[117]

3.35 In a number of cases, the Commission has asked whether the act is 'required by' or 'necessary to' the belief in question. One example is *X v United Kingdom*,[118] where the applicant failed to establish that his publication of religious articles was a manifestation of his religion for the purposes of Article 9. The Commission held that 'he has failed to prove that it was a *necessary* part of this practice that he should publish articles in a religious magazine. Viewed in the light of Article 9 the complaint is manifestly ill-founded'.[119] Similarly, in *Logan v United Kingdom*,[120] visits to Buddhist priories were held by the Commission not to constitute an indispensable element of a Buddhist's religious worship.[121] Such a restrictive approach has not become a consistent theme of the case law;[122] indeed, the notion is expressly dismissed in the recent judgment of the ECtHR in *Eweida* (see paragraphs 3.39–3.42).

3.36 Further illustrations of the distinction between, on the one hand, a practice which is deemed an actual manifestation of a belief or religion, and, on the other hand, conduct which is merely motivated by a religion or belief, can be seen in the following cases. In *Kosteski v the former Yugoslav Republic of Macedonia*,[123] the refusal to work on a particular day was deemed not to be a manifestation of religious belief, even though it may have been motivated by such. In *Pastor X and the Church of Scientology v Sweden*,[124] it was held that words in an advertisement for the sale of Hubbard Electrometers by the Church of Scientology were 'more a manifestation of a desire to market goods for profit than the manifestation of a belief in practice'. In *Valsamis v Greece*,[125] pacifist students refused to take part in a parade to commemorate the Greek National day. However, the ECtHR concluded that taking part in the parade did not have a particular ideological connotation and therefore was not contrary to the pacifist beliefs of the students.[126]

3.37 There has been much criticism[127] of the restrictive manifestation requirements in general. They seem to discriminate against religions without an established cultural base or long history in Europe.[128] Deciding whether a practice is core or peripheral to a religion or belief also raises difficult questions as to how far judges can, or should, comprehend religions and beliefs as normative systems on their own terms and how far the law can accommodate and understand the degree of subjectivity and variety involved.[129] Furthermore, limiting the definition of

---

[117] *Khan* (n 116) 255.

[118] *X v UK* (App 8652/79) (1986).

[119] *X v UK* (n 118) 42.

[120] *Logan v UK* (1996) 22 EHRR CD 178, para 82.

[121] This reasoning follows the approach of the much earlier decision in *X v Austria* (App 1753/63) (1965), where the applicant failed to establish that th use of a prayer chain was an 'indispensible element in the proper exercise of the Buddhist religion' at 184.

[122] See Bratza (n 50).

[123] *Kosteski v the Former Yugoslav Republic of Macedonia* (2007) 45 EHRR 712, para 38.

[124] *Pastor X and the Church of Scientology v Sweden* (1979) 22 Yearbook 244, 250.

[125] *Valsamis v Greece* (App 21787/94) (1996).

[126] *Valsamis* (n 125), however, see the dissenting judges Thor Vilhjalmsson and Jambrek at para 32.

[127] See eg Knights (n 4) 45.

[128] Edge (n 10) 45–7.

[129] McCrudden (n 18) 26–38; C Stychin, 'Faith in the Future: Sexuality, Religion and the Public Sphere' (2009) 29(4) OJLS 755; and D Harris, M O'Boyle, and E Bates, *Law of the European Convention on Human Rights* (2nd edn, OUP, 2009) 433, suggest that this might be bringing the Court 'dangerously close to adjudication on whether a particular practice is formally required by a religion—a task which its judges, given the relevant theological issues, appear ill-equipped to handle'.

'manifestation' itself arguably confounds the issue with that of the permissible limitations and balancing exercise undertaken under Article 9(2).[130] The test is unclear in scope and has been inconsistently applied,[131] since the Court has not always asked the same questions of applicants.[132] For example, in *Knudsen v Norway*[133] it was asked whether the actions 'give expression' to the religion or belief in question, and in *Hasan and Chaush v Bulgaria*[134] the question was whether the acts were 'intimately linked' to personal conviction.[135] It is interesting to note that in *Şahin v Turkey*[136] no point was taken about whether wearing a hijab was required by the Muslim faith or not.[137] Finally the restrictive manifestation requirements make it almost impossible to show a breach of Article 9 arising from a general and neutral law.[138]

The ECtHR has signalled a substantial change in its approach to Article 9 in its recent decision in *Eweida*.[139] There were in fact four joined applications from Nadia Eweida, Shirley Chaplin, Lillian Ladele, and Gary McFarlane respectively. The applicants claimed that English law had failed adequately to protect their right to manifest their religion in the workplace, or that they had suffered unlawful discrimination, under Articles 9 and 14 read together. The Court upheld Ms Eweida's complaint (by a majority), dismissed Ms Ladele's complaint (by a majority), and dismissed the complaints of Chaplin and McFarlane (unanimously). **3.38**

In *Eweida*, a member of the check-in staff for British Airways plc was prohibited by the company's uniform policy from wearing a crucifix visibly around her neck. Her claim for indirect discrimination failed at the domestic level[140] on the grounds that that she had failed to show that that Christians as a group were put at a disadvantage by the uniform policy.[141] Article 9 was relied upon in argument, but the Court of Appeal held that the ECtHR's **3.39**

---

[130] J Martinez-Torron and R Navarro-Valls, 'Protection of Religious Freedom in the System of the Council of Europe' in T Lindhom, WC Durham, and BG Tahzib-Lie (eds), *Facilitating Freedom of Religion or Belief* (Martinus Nijhoff, 2004) 234; and Allen and Moon (n 26).

[131] C Evans (n 4) 202.

[132] See further R Sandberg, 'The Changing Position of Religious Minorities in English Law: The Legacy of Begum' in R Grillo et al., *Legal Practice and Cultural Diversity* (Ashgate, 2009); and M Evans (n 24) 307–14.

[133] *Knudsen v Norway* (n 28), regarding the distribution of anti-abortion materials outside a clinic which was held not to involve manifestation of religious or philosophical beliefs.

[134] *Hasan and Chaush* (n 21).

[135] See also *C v UK* (n 114) 147, regarding a Quaker's unwillingness to pay the portion of his taxes that would be used to pay for armament research:

> Article 9 primarily protects the sphere of personal beliefs and religious creeds, i.e. the area that is sometimes called the *forum internum*. In addition, it protects acts which are intimately linked to these attitudes, such as acts of worship or devotion which are aspects of the practice of a religion or belief in a generally recognised form.

[136] *Leyla Şahin v Turkey* (2005) 41 EHRR 8.

[137] Bratza (n 50) 256, with reference to the new Court, comments that 'it is perhaps possible to detect a shift in approach and a greater reluctance to enter into the question of whether a particular practice is an indispensible element of a religion or system of belief'.

[138] C Evans (n 4) 205.

[139] *Eweida and ors v UK* (Apps 48420/10, 59842/10, 51671/10, and 36516/10) (2013), (2013) 57 EHRR 213.

[140] *Eweida v British Airways plc* [2010] EWCA Civ 80. The domestic claim was not for discrimination under Article 14 in combination with Article 9, but was in fact brought under under the Employment Equality (Religion or Belief) Regulations 2003.

[141] Employment Equality (Religion or Belief) Regulations 2003, reg 3 (1)(b) provides:

> (1) For the purposes of these Regulations, a person ('A') discriminates against another person ('B') if—
>> (b) A applies to B a provision, criterion or practice which he applies or would apply equally to persons not of the same religion or belief as B, but—
>>> (i) which puts or would put persons of the same religion or belief as B at a particular disadvantage when compared with other persons,

jurisprudence on Article 9 did nothing to advance her case with regard to either manifestation or interference.[142]

3.40 Ms Eweida complained to the ECtHR, relying on Article 9 alone and in conjunction with Article 14. The Court reconsidered the approach previously taken to Article 9 claims arising in the employment context. First, it examined and clarified its approach to manifestation. The Court outlined familiar tests which it had used to determine what fell within and outside the scope of Article 9 at paragraph 82:

> ... acts or omissions which do not directly express the belief concerned or which are only remotely connected to a precept of faith fall outside the protection of Article 9 § 1... In order to count as a 'manifestation' within the meaning of Article 9, the act in question must be intimately linked to the religion or belief. An example would be an act of worship or devotion which forms part of the practice of a religion or belief in a generally recognised form.

3.41 After setting out these restrictions to what constitutes a manifestation, the Court then went on to express the boundaries of Article 9(1) in a far more expansive formulation:

> However, the manifestation of religion or belief is not limited to such acts; the existence of a sufficiently close and direct nexus between the act and the underlying belief must be determined on the facts of each case. In particular, there is no requirement on the applicant to establish that he or she acted in fulfilment of a duty mandated by the religion in question.[143]

3.42 An important part of the Court's reasoning was to set the limits of Article 9 not by reference to the criteria the applicant must satisfy, but by reference to the hurdles which do *not* need to be overcome. Applying these principles to the facts of Ms Eweida's case, the Court found that the wearing of a cross visibly was a manifestation of her religious belief.[144] Neither this finding nor its jurisprudential basis marks a drastic departure in ECtHR case law on manifestation, other than to dismiss the idea that the act must be *mandated* by the religion in question. Nonetheless, this expansive formulation of Article 9's scope may assist in focusing attention on subsequent filtering devices rather than on whether the act itself qualifies for protection.[145] The question of interference in Ms Eweida's case, and in the cases of her co-applicants, is considered at paragraphs 3.53–3.54.

(ii) which puts B at that disadvantage, and
(iii) which A cannot show to be a proportionate means of achieving a legitimate aim.

[142] *Eweida v British Airways* (n 140) para 22. With regard to manifestation, Sedley LJ quoted a passage from *Kalaç v Turkey* (1997) 27 EHRR 552, para 27: 'Article 9 does not protect every act motivated or inspired by a religion or belief. Moreover, in exercising his freedom to manifest his religion, an individual may need to take his specific situation into account'. With regard to interference, he quoted from *R (SB) v Governors of Denbigh High School* [2007] 1 AC 100, para 23 *per* Lord Bingham:

> The Strasbourg institutions have not been at all ready to find an interference with the right to manifest religious belief in practice or observance where a person has voluntarily accepted an employment or role which does not accommodate that practice or observance and there are other means open to the person to practise or observe his or her religion without undue hardship or inconvenience.

[143] *Eweida and ors v UK* (n 139) para 82.
[144] *Eweida and ors v UK* (n 139) para 89.
[145] This is particularly relevant for domestic case law; indeed, the UK government had argued that 'behaviour which was motivated or inspired by religion or belief, but which was not an act of practice of a religion in a generally recognised form, fell outside the protection of Article 9', and had relied on the fact that the wearing of a cross was not 'regarded as a mandatory requirement': *Eweida and ors v UK* (n 139) para 58. The impact of *Ewieda* on the the restrictive direction of domestic law is considered in Ch 5.

Of significance is the ECtHR's acknowledgement in *Eweida* that the right to manifest one's **3.43**
religious belief is a fundamental right not only because a healthy democratic society needs to
tolerate and sustain pluralism and diversity, but also because of 'the value to an individual who
has made religion a central tenet of his or her life to be able to communicate that belief to others'.[146] The ECtHR went on to emphasize that the importance for Ms Eweida and Ms Chaplin
of being permitted to manifest their religion by wearing a cross visibly must weigh heavily in the
balance.[147] This gives some recognition to the role and, more importantly, the value in Article 9
terms of religious dress and symbols as means of expression and bearing witness to one's faith.[148]

'*Observance*'. There has been a lack of case law or jurisprudence on this aspect of 'manifesta- **3.44**
tion'. In *Jewish Liturgical Association Cha'are Shalom Ve Tsedek v France*,[149] it was held that the
ritual slaughter of animals in accordance with religious requirements falls within Article 9.

(4) Has there been an interference with Article 9 rights?

Article 9 is broad in scope: the range of issues that may be brought to the Court under both **3.45**
the *forum internum* and *forum externum* is very wide. Interferences may involve impositions,[150]
restrictions,[151] burdens,[152] limitations,[153] pressurizations,[154] sanctions,[155] indoctrinations,[156]
expropriations,[157] or other forms of requirements.[158] Instead of analysing when an interference

---

[146] *Eweida and ors v UK* (n 140) para 94.

[147] *Eweida and ors v UK* (n 140) para 99.

[148] It will be recalled that in *Kokkinakis* (n 7), the ECtHR recognized this as an aspect of the freedom of religion and the right protected by Art 9: 'While religious freedom is primarily a matter of individual conscience, it
also implies, inter alia, freedom to "manifest [one's] religion". Bearing witness in words and deeds is bound up
with the existence of religious convictions.'

[149] *Jewish Liturgical Association Cha'are Shalom Ve Tsedek v France* (App 27417/95) (2000) para 73: '... It is
not contested that ritual slaughter, as indeed its name indicates, constitutes a rite ... whose purpose is to provide
Jews with meat from animals slaughtered in accordance with religious prescriptions, which is an essential aspect
of practice of the Jewish religion.'

[150] *Buscarini* (n 43) paras 34–41 (imposition of a requirement to take a religious oath); and *Chauhan v UK*
(1990) 65 DR 41, 44 (compulsory association, though cf *Revert and Legallais v France* (1988) 62 DR 309, 318).

[151] *Kokkinakis* (n 7) paras 31–33 (restrictions placed upon individual action or behaviour mandated by
belief, such as seeking to persuade others to follow a particular faith).

[152] *Manoussakis and ors v Greece* (1995) 23 EHRR 387, paras 36–53 (burdens placed upon the rights of members to exercise collective freedom of worship, such as restrictions on the establishment of places of worship).

[153] *Cyprus v Turkey* (App 25781/94) (2001) paras 242–246 (limitations on freedom of movement preventing members of a community from gathering to worship).

[154] *Ivanova v Bulgaria* (2008) 47 EHRR 54 (a teacher was dismissed solely on the grounds of religious beliefs
which had no impact on her performance, and was pressurized by officials to renounce her beliefs).

[155] *Hazar, Hazar and Acik v Turkey* (1992) 72 DR 200 (arrest on the basis of membership of a particular
party violated Art 9).

[156] See *Kjeldsen, Busk Madsen and Pedersen v Denmark (Danish Sex Education case)* (1976) 1 EHRR 711,
para 53. The right to change one's religion or belief is, in effect, a bulwark against 'indoctrination of religion by
the state' (*Angelini v Sweden* (1986) 51 DR 41, para 48); see also *CJ, JJ and EJ v Poland* (1996) 84A DR 46. The
use of physical threats or sanctions that force people to deny or adhere to a particular religion or belief is clearly
forbidden; for discussion, see BG Tahzib, *Freedom of Religion or Belief: Ensuring Effective International Protection*
(Martinus Nijhoff, 1996) 26.

[157] cf *Holy Monasteries v Greece* (1995) 20 EHRR 1, para 87, where general expropriation of agricultural and
pasture land belonging to monasteries was held not to constitute interference since the legislative provisions
did not concern objects intended for the celebration of divine worship and there had been no hindrance of the
exercising of the right to freedom of religion.

[158] *Sinan Işik v Turkey* (App 21924/05) (2010) paras 37–53 (a requirement to have religious faith disclosed
in identity documents such as identity cards). See also *Folgero v Norway* (2008) 46 EHRR 1147, finding that
a state cannot dictate or demand to know what an individual believes. However, see *X v Austria* (1972) 15
YB EHRR 498, where it was held that compulsory voting will not violate Art 9 as it only requires attendance at
the polls rather than actual registration of a vote.

will be found in the abstract, it is necessary to consider situations which have led to an interference being found by the Court. As previously noted, Article 9 establishes two separate rights: first, what can be called the 'internal aspect' (an absolute right to freedom of thought, conscience, and religion and relates to what is often called the *forum internum*[159] of the individual) and secondly, the 'external aspect' (a qualified right to manifest the religion or belief in worship, teaching, practice, and observance). This latter right is qualified in that it is subject to the limitations set out in Article 9(2), and has to be balanced against the other needs of society; therefore, if found, interferences with the right to manifest may be justified by the state under Article 9(2), leading to no violation of the Convention. The issue of justification will be separately analysed later.[160] The present section is subdivided into examples in which interferences have been found. The section will close with a discussion of the positive obligations placed on states.

3.46 It is possible to make two general preliminary points. First, the onus is on the applicant to demonstrate and prove that there has been an interference with his or her Article 9 rights. Secondly, the Court's approach to when interferences will be found is generally much narrower and more restrictive than might have been anticipated from the broad interpretation of the Article's scope. This was due to the application of a doctrine which, in the English Courts, has been called the doctrine of 'non-interference':[161] so long as there was a possibility that religious believers could act in the way that they desired somewhere, there was no material interference with their beliefs. The high water mark of the application of the doctrine was in *Jewish Liturgical Association v France*,[162] where the Grand Chamber considered that ultra-orthodox Jews would need to show that it was 'impossible' to eat meat slaughtered in accordance with their religious prescriptions before it could be shown that there was an interference with a freedom to manifest their beliefs.[163]

3.47 The doctrine was inconsistent with a principled approach to religious rights for three reasons. First, it seemed impossible to reconcile with the general points of principle made by the ECtHR about the importance of religious rights.[164] Secondly, there was no other ECHR right or freedom which was subject to this doctrine. Thirdly, it was contrary to the well-established principle that a broad and purposive approach needs to be taken to the interpretation of fundamental rights and freedoms guaranteed in the ECHR.

3.48 The Court's own use of the doctrine of 'non-interference' was not uniform,[165] and it now seems that, following the recent judgment of the ECtHR in *Eweida*, the doctrine can be considered a matter of jurisprudential history.

a) Circumstances in which interferences have been found

3.49 *Employment and voluntary assumption.* Traditionally, the 'specific situation' rule[166] applied where someone had voluntarily submitted themselves to a system where their manifestation

---

[159] See eg *Van Den Dungen* (n 20) para 1.
[160] See paras 3.72–3.73.
[161] See Ch 5, para 5.14.
[162] *Jewish Liturgical Association v France* (2000) 9 BHRC 27, para 81.
[163] *Jewish Liturgical Association* (n 162) para 80.
[164] See discussion at paras 3.04–3.05.
[165] See, and cf *Cyprus v Turkey* (2002) 35 EHRR 30, paras 243–246; *Metropolitan Church of Bessarabia* (n 114); *Moscow Branch of Salvation Army* (n 12); *Dahlab v Switzerland* (App 42393/98) (2001); and *Leela Forderkreis* (n 41) para 83.
[166] I Leigh, 'Balancing Religious Autonomy and Other Human Rights under the ECHR' (2012) OJLR 109, 116.

was restricted. In such circumstances, the ECtHR used to hold that there was no interference with Article 9 since there was no restriction on manifestation—the applicant had voluntarily accepted some sort of personal sacrifice. In this way, the specific situation rule recognized that a person's Article 9 rights may be influenced by the particular situation of the individual claiming that freedom. Therefore, where the applicant had entered into a contract of employment,[167] enrolled at a university,[168] submitted themselves to military service,[169] or been detained,[170] that person could not (legitimately) manifest their religion or belief.

However, it was questionable whether such situations were truly voluntary and whether **3.50** surrendering one's rights was consistent with the absolute right to change one's religion. When two basic rights are at stake for an individual (ie the right to freedom of religion and belief, and the right to work), that individual should be allowed to find a personal balance, rather than have an institution dictate the alternatives available with the potential consequences that individuals with strong beliefs may feel distanced from society.[171] Arguments have been made that a person can choose his or her religion, in contrast to race, gender, and disability which are immutable characteristics and therefore deserve greater protection. This approach has not been adopted by the Strasbourg Court, and the jurisprudence shows that interference with any of the protected characteristics requires weighty reasons, or serious justification. The argument that religious rights justified lesser protection mischaracterized the way in which religious beliefs were instilled in individuals in the way that they think and ultimately act, which are rooted in years of personal upbringing, community values, and (potentially) centuries of religious tradition; any change would involve a thorough transformation in ways of thought, values, and lifestyle. Further, the argument characterizes the meaning of choice by taking an entirely external viewpoint of the nature of the commitment involved in religious belief. The terminology of choice results in the user having to hold a rather thinly-veiled relativism between religions, and misunderstands what religious belief involves. The possession of a religious belief is a commitment to truth (from the perception of the believer), not an exchangeable value fit for selection.

More recent decisions of the ECtHR indicate that it no longer endorses the 'specific situa- **3.51** tion' approach.[172] As Sir Nicholas Bratza[173] has commented extra-judicially, 'the assumption that, in the modern employment market, such a choice is a real one has been questioned, and there are perhaps indications in the more recent case law that the freedom to resign from employment will no longer be seen as 'the ultimate guarantee of…freedom of religion'.[174] For example, interference has been found, despite the appellants' apparent acceptance of a restriction, in cases concerning the prohibition on wearing headscarves in universities in the

---

[167] *Stedman v UK* (1997) 5 EHRLR 544, and *Ahmad v UK* (1981) 4 EHRR 126.
[168] *Karaduman* (n 30).
[169] *Kalac v Turkey* (App 20704/02) (1997) paras 27–28.
[170] *X v UK* (n 27), 41–2; for criticism, see M Evans (n 24) 310.
[171] See S Leader, 'Freedom and Futures: Personal Priorities, Institutional Demands and Freedom of Religion' (2007) 70(5) MLR 713, 725.
[172] For discussion, see M Hill, R Sandberg, and C Doe, *Religion and Law in the United Kingdom* (Kluwer Law International, 2011) 53–6, and Knights (n 4) 44.
[173] Bratza (n 50) 256.
[174] See the older case law making this sort of claim: *Konttinen v Finland* (App 24949/94) (1996) 87-A DR, 68; *Karlsson v Sweden* (App 12356/86) (1988), unreported; *Knudsen v Norway* (App 11045/84) (1985) 42 DR 247. Compare with the newer approach in *Ivanova v Bulgaria* (2007) 47 EHRR 1173 (App 52435/99) (2007).

cases of *Şahin v Turkey*,[175] *Dahlab v Switzerland*,[176] and *Dogru v France*.[177] The specific situation rule was also not applied in *Lautsi v Italy*,[178] which concerned a non-religious applicant who had voluntarily submitted to a religious situation.

3.52   Furthermore, after reviewing and comparing two Article 8 cases, *Obst v Germany*[179] and *Schuh v Germany*,[180] and one Article 9 case, *Siebenhaar v Germany*[181] (involving the dismissal of the appellant by the Baden Protestant Church following her involvement with a different religious community, the Universal Church, which had incompatible teachings with those of her employers), Leigh suggests that there is a new 'balancing approach' now undertaken by the Strasbourg Court.[182] This approach recognizes that it is 'preferable to treat employment disputes with a religious element as involving clashing rights that need to be appropriately balanced rather than treating some of them as a zone in which human rights do not apply in the first place'.[183] Thus, for example, in *Siebenhaar v Germany*, instead of simply ruling that the rights in Article 9 do not apply, *in toto*, in a voluntary employment context, the Court balanced the rights in holding that the applicant's claim failed: she should have been aware that membership of the Universal Church was incompatible with her commitments under her contract of employment to the religious ethos of the Protestant Church.[184]

3.53   The Court's more recent rulings evidence a new development of balancing religious autonomy against other rights. This new approach can be seen in the *Eweida* case. After finding that wearing a cross at work was indeed a manifestation of Ms Eweida's religious belief, the Court went on to consider whether her right to do so had been interfered with. It held that where an individual complains of a restriction on his or her freedom of religion in the workplace, rather than holding that the possibility of changing job would negate any interference with the right, the better approach would be to weigh that possibility in the overall balance when considering whether or not the restriction was proportionate.[185] The Court found that the refusal by her employer to allow Ms Eweida to remain in her post while visibly wearing a cross amounted to an interference with her right to manifest her religion. This represents a significant departure from the Court's previous position. Similarly in Mr McFarlane's case, the Court accepted that Article 9 was engaged despite the fact that Mr McFarlane had voluntarily enrolled on Relate's post-graduate training programme knowing Relate's policy (that he would be required to provide counselling to same-sex couples).

---

[175]   *Şahin v Turkey* (n 136).
[176]   *Dahlab v Switzerland* (App 42393/98) (2001).
[177]   *Dogru v France* (App 27058/05) (2008).
[178]   *Lautsi* (n 68).
[179]   *Obst v Germany* (App 425/03) (2010), involving the dismissal of an employee of the Mormon church for adultery.
[180]   *Schuh v Germany* (App 1620/03) (2010), involving the dismissal for adultery of an organist employed by the Catholic church.
[181]   *Siebenhaar v Germany* (App 18136/02) (2011) para 46.
[182]   Leigh (n 166) 123–4.
[183]   Leigh (n 166) 123–4.
[184]   See *Siebenhaar* (n 181) paras 41–44.
[185]   *Eweida and ors v UK* (n 139). In so holding (at para 83), the Court distanced itself from the approach of the Commission (see eg *Konttinen v Finland* (1996) 87 DR 68), and had reference instead to its own approach in employment cases involving other fundamental rights.

The most definitive statement of the change in approach is found in the minority judgment **3.54**
of that case:

> A restriction on the manifestation of a religion or belief in the workplace may amount to
> an interference with Article 9 rights which requires to be justified even in a case where the
> employee voluntarily accepts an employment or role which does not accommodate the prac-
> tice in question or where there are other means open to the individual to practise or observe
> his or her religion as, for instance, by resigning from the employment or taking a new posi-
> tion...Insofar as earlier decisions of the Commission and the Court would suggest the con-
> trary, we do not believe that they should be followed.[186]

Recognition. Where issues regarding recognition of religions are raised, the Court often reads **3.55**
Articles 9 and 11 together.[187] The right to freedom of religion excludes any discretion on the
part of the state to determine whether religious beliefs or the means used to express beliefs
are themselves legitimate.[188] Furthermore, the state has no right to interfere with the internal affairs of the religious community by withholding or enforcing state recognition of the
organization or its religious leaders. For example, in *Hasan and Chaush v Bulgaria*,[189] the
national leader of the Bulgarian Muslim community was effectively replaced by the government with another candidate, which the Court held was tantamount to the state favouring
one faction to the complete exclusion of the hitherto acknowledged leadership.[190] This was
held to violate Article 9.

In *Metropolitan Church of Bessarabia and others v Moldova*,[191] the Metropolitan Church of **3.56**
Bessarabia was refused recognition by the authorities on the ground that it had split up
from the Metropolitan Church of Moldova. The Court noted that under relevant domestic
legislation the church's priests could not take divine service without official recognition, so
that its members could not meet to practise their religious beliefs;[192] furthermore, without
legal personality, the Church was not entitled to protection of its assets.[193] The Court also
emphasized that, whilst the imposition of a requirement of state registration is not in itself
incompatible with freedom of religion, the state must remain neutral and impartial by not
appearing to be assessing the comparative legitimacy of different beliefs.[194]

Oaths. Requiring prospective members of parliament to swear an oath on a certain religion's **3.57**
holy book or gospel in order to take their seats in Parliament,[195] and requiring a person to be
admitted to the legal profession to take an oath which would require them to reveal that they

---

[186] *Eweida and ors v UK* (n 139), partly dissenting opinion, para 2(b).

[187] See *Moscow Branch of the Salvation Army v Russia* (2007) 44 EHRR 912, paras 58 and 61. See also *Church of Scientology Moscow v Russia* (2008) 46 EHRR 304.

[188] *Manoussakis* (n 152), para 47. See also *Regionsgemeinschaft der Zeugen Jehovas and ors v Austria* (App 40/825/98) (2008) paras 87–99, which established a violation of Art 9 where, for some 20 years, the authorities had refused to grant legal personality to Jehovah's Witnesses.

[189] *Hasan and Chaush* (n 21).

[190] See *Hasan and Chaush* (n 21) para 78 Also see *Serif v Greece* (1999) 31 EHRR 561, regarding an applicant who had been elected as a mufti, a Muslim religious leader, without securing state authority to do: found
to be a violation; and *Agga v Greece (No 2)* (Apps 50776/99 and 52912/99) (2002), the applicant's election to
the post of mufti by worshippers at a mosque was annulled by state officials who thereafter appointed another
mufti: violation was also found.

[191] *Metropolitan Church of Bessarabia* (n 114).

[192] *Metropolitan Church of Bessarabia* (n 114) para 105.

[193] *Metropolitan Church of Bessarabia* (n 114) para 105.

[194] *Metropolitan Church of Bessarabia* (n 114) paras 116 and 117.

[195] *Buscarini* (n 43); note also that it was held that the obligation to take the oath was also not necessary in
a democratic society under Art 9(2), as making the exercise of a mandate intended to represent different views

are not Orthodox Christians,[196] are both interferences and violations of Article 9 rights. In *Dimitras v Greece*,[197] the Court held that there was also an inference and violation of Article 9 where the state required the applicants to reveal their religious convictions in order to be allowed to make a solemn declaration in Court in conformity with Article 218 of the Code of Criminal Procedure, which asked them to take the oath by placing their right hands on the Bible. The applicants informed the authorities that they were not Orthodox Christians and preferred to make a solemn declaration instead, which they were authorized to do. However, the applicants had been considered as Orthodox Christians as a matter of course, and had been obliged, sometimes in hearings, to point out that they did not subscribe to that faith and, in some cases, to specify that they were atheists or Jews in order to have the standard wording of the minutes amended. The effect of this judgment is not that religious oaths cannot be used in court; rather, it is that where religious oaths are used, witnesses have to be given the choice of making a solemn affirmation without giving any explanation of their reasons for doing so.

3.58   *Official documents.* It is an interference with Article 9 rights to make it mandatory to indicate one's religious affiliation on official documents. In *Sinan Işik v Turkey*,[198] the Court found a violation of Article 9 had arisen from the fact that the applicant's identity card contained an indication of religion, regardless of whether it was obligatory or optional (ie where the card could be left blank).[199] The Court stressed that the freedom to manifest one's religious beliefs has a negative aspect which includes the right not to be obliged to disclose one's religion.[200] In *Wasmuth v Germany*,[201] it was held that there was an interference with the applicant's Article 9 rights where the authorities issued a wage-tax card with reference to the fact the applicant did not belong to a religious society authorized to levy religious tax. In that case, however, the compulsory information on the tax card leading to an interference with the applicant's religious rights was held to be justifiable under Article 9(2)[202] so there was no violation of the Convention.[203]

3.59   *Conscientious objection.* This is discussed at paragraph 3.22. As has already been seen, the Court has held that there was an interference with Article 9 rights where: an applicant was convicted of a felony offence for having refused to enlist in the army during a time when the state in question did not offer alternative service for conscientious objectors;[204] an applicant, a Jehovah's Witness,

---

of society within Parliament subject to a prior declaration of commitment to a particular set of beliefs was contradictory.

[196]   *Alexandridis v Greece* (App 19516/06) (2008).

[197]   *Dimitras v Greece* (Apps 42837/06, 3237/07, 3269/07, 35793/07, and 6099/08) (2010). The Court also held that there had been a violation of Art 13. For comment see (2010) 5 EHRLR 542–5.

[198]   *Sinan Işik v Turkey* (App 21924/05) (2010).

[199]   See also *Grezlak v Poland* (App 7710/02) (2010), where the Court found that not giving the child of agnostic parents, who had withdrawn him from religion classes, a mark on his school report for 'religion/ethics' and simply leaving the relevant box blank violated Art 14 taken with Art 9.

[200]   See *Sinan Işik* (n 198) paras 38, 50–53.

[201]   *Wasmuth v Germany* (App 12884/03) (2011).

[202]   The Court held that the interference had served the legitimate aim of ensuring the right of churches and religious societies to levy religious tax. It was proportionate to that aim as the reference at issue was only of limited informative value concerning the religious or philosophic conviction, since it only indicated to the fiscal authorities that he did not belong to one of the churches or religious societies which were authorized to levy tax.

[203]   See the dissent of Judge Berro-Lefevre, joined by Judge Kalaydjieva, for the argument that the majority failed to take into account the potential difficulties that the disclosure to a person's employer of his/her religious affiliation, or lack of the same, may cause.

[204]   *Thlimmenos v Greece* (2001) 31 EHRR 411—in conjunction with Art 14. The applicant's exclusion from the profession of chartered accountants was disproportionate, under Art 9(2), to the aim of ensuring

was convicted of draft evasion and sentenced to prison for refusing to perform military service even though he was prepared to undertake alternative civil service;[205] and where an applicant, again a Jehovah's Witness, was convicted for refusing to perform military service for reasons of conscience.[206]

Taxation and state funding. Since the decision in *Darby v Sweden*,[207] the ECtHR has shown itself   **3.60** to be more willing to entertain challenges to fiscal discrimination in ecclesiastical taxation. In *Association Les Témoins de Jéhovah v France*,[208] the Court held that a supplementary tax demand for €57.5 million was a violation of Article 9. The association claimed that the procedure in question was flawed and, given its scale, had infringed its freedom of religion.[209] The Court noted that the supplementary tax assessment in question had concerned the entirety of the manual gifts received by the association, which represented the main source of its funding.[210] Furthermore, the relevant provisions of the tax code under which the gifts to the association were automatically taxed were not sufficiently foreseeable.[211] Its operating resources having thus been cut, the association had not been able to guarantee the free exercise of religion in practical terms to its followers. There had therefore been an interference with the applicant association's right to freedom of religion.[212]

Although domestic law must not impose an obligation to support a religious organization by   **3.61** means of taxation without recognizing the right of an individual to leave the organization and thus obtain an exemption from that requirement,[213] this principle does not extend to general legal obligations falling exclusively in the public sphere: so that taxpayers cannot demand that their payments are not allocated to particular purposes.[214]

In *Bruno v Sweden*,[215] the Court drew a distinction between taxation for the discharge of   **3.62** public functions (no interference), and functions purely associated with religious belief (interference).[216] In this case, legislation allowed exemption from the church tax for the majority, but nevertheless required the payment of a dissenter tax to meet the costs of tasks which had a non-religious nature and were performed in the interest of society (such as

---

appropriate punishment of persons who refuse to serve their country as he had already served his prison sentence.

[205] *Bayatyan v Armenia* (App 23459/03) (2011).

[206] *Ercep v Turkey* (App 43965/04) (2011). The Court invited Turkey to enact legislation concerning conscientious objectors and to introduce an alternative form of service. It also found a violation of Art 6.

[207] *Darby v Sweden* (n 22) , domestic law must not impose an obligation to support a religious organization by means of taxation without recognizing the right of an individual to leave the church and thus obtain an exemption from that requirement.

[208] *Association Les Témoins de Jéhovah v France* (App 8916/05) (2011).

[209] See *Témoins de Jéhovah* (n 208) paras 45–46.

[210] See *Témoins de Jéhovah* (n 208) para 49.

[211] See *Témoins de Jéhovah* (n 208) para 70.

[212] See *Témoins de Jéhovah* (n 208) para 53.

[213] *Darby v Sweden* (n 22); *Gottesmann v Switzerland* (1984) 40 DR 284; and *E and GR v Austria* (1984) 37 DR 42. Where administrative conditions must be fulfilled before an individual can leave the church, those conditions must not hinder the individual from exercising his right to leave (*Gottesmann v Switzerland* (1984) 40 DR 284, 289).

[214] *C v UK* (n 114); and *Ortega Moratilla v Spain* (1992) 72 DR 256, 262. The Commission has also emphasized the neutral nature of obligations to pay compulsory social security contributions (*Bouessel du Bourg v France* (1992) 16 EHRR CD 49), to pay child maintenance (*Karakuzey v Germany* (1997) 23 EHRR CD 92, 94), and to participate in a compulsory pension scheme (*V v Netherlands* (1983) 39 DR 267, 268).

[215] *Bruno v Sweden* (App 32196/96) (2001).

[216] See *Bruno* (n 215) 7.

burials, maintenance of historically valuable buildings, and the care of old population records). The Court confirmed that state authorities have a wide margin of appreciation in determining the arrangements for such responsibilities,[217] and that the proportion of the full amount of church tax payable by members of the church was proportionate to the costs of the Church's civil responsibilities.[218] Furthermore, public bodies were responsible for monitoring the expenditure and determining the taxation payable. The Court therefore held that the measures in question did not compel the applicant to contribute to religious activities of the Church.[219]

3.63   In *Asatruarfelagid v Iceland*,[220] the applicant (a religious association) complained that it was discriminated against compared with the National Church of Iceland, which received funding from the state in addition to parish charges. The Court declared this application inadmissible as there was no visible breach of the applicant association and its members' rights to practise their religion.[221] The Court upheld the Icelandic courts' view that the National Church's tasks could not be compared to those of the applicant association so the allocation of additional funding to the former could not constitute discrimination.[222]

3.64   *Religious holidays.* In *Sessa v Italy*,[223] the Court held that there had been no violation of Article 9 where the judicial authority had refused to adjourn a hearing on the date of a Jewish holiday. The Court was not persuaded that holding this amounted to an interference by restricting the applicant's right to manifest his faith.[224] This was for three reasons. First, it was not disputed that the applicant, a representative for one of the parties, had been able to carry out his religious duties.[225] Secondly, he should have known that his request would be refused on the basis of the statutory provisions in force and could have arranged to be replaced at the hearing in order to comply with his professional obligations.[226] Thirdly, the applicant had not shown that pressure had been exerted on him to change his religious beliefs or to prevent him from manifesting his religion or beliefs.[227] In *Kosteski v the Former Yugoslav Republic of Macedonia*,[228] it was held that Article 9 of itself does not give any entitlement to time off work for religious festivals. The applicant's complaint, after he had been fined for taking time off work to observe Muslim religious festivals, was that he had to substantiate his claims to his employer that he was a practising Muslim. This complaint was rejected as the requirement was not held to be disproportionate.[229]

---

[217]   See *Bruno* (n 215) 7.

[218]   See *Bruno* (n 215) 7.

[219]   See *Bruno* (n 215) 7.

[220]   *Asatruarfelagid v Iceland* (App 22897/08) (2012).

[221]   See *Asatruarfelagid* (n 220) paras 31–32.

[222]   See *Asatruarfelagid* (n 220) para 34.

[223]   *Sessa v Italy* (App 28790/08) (2012).

[224]   Notwithstanding this, the Court went on to analyse the situation on the *assumption* that there might have been an interference. Even then, the Court held that there was no violation of Art 9 because the interference was justified under Art 9(2): it was prescribed by law, based on the legitimate aim of protecting the rights and freedoms of others (in particular the public's right to the proper administration of justice) and was proportionate to that aim.

[225]   See *Sessa* (n 223) para 37.

[226]   See *Sessa* (n 223) para 37.

[227]   See *Sessa* (n 223) para 37.

[228]   *Kosteski* (n 123).

[229]   See *Kosteski* (n 123) para 39.

Immigration. Article 9 does not guarantee foreign nationals a right to obtain a residence **3.65** permit for work if the employer is a religious association.[230] Nor is Article 9 likely to be relevant in most immigration contexts. In *Z and T v United Kingdom*,[231] where a couple's applications for asylum in the United Kingdom were rejected after they left Pakistan due to attacks on Christian churches in Bahwalpur, the applicants claimed that having to return to Pakistan would violate their Article 9 rights. The ECtHR ruled that it was highly improbable that Article 9 could ever be used for this purpose as such matters would most likely fall to be considered under Articles 2 or 3 of the Convention. The Court stated:

> ... protection is offered to those who have a substantiated claim that they will either suffer per-secution for, inter alia, religious reasons or will be at a real risk of death or serious ill-treatment, and possibly flagrant denial of a fair trial or arbitrary detention because of their religious affilia-tion (as for any other reason). Where ... an individual claims that on return to his own country he would be impeded in his religious worship in a manner which falls short of those proscribed levels, the Court considers that very limited assistance, if any, can be derived from Article 9 by itself. Otherwise, it would be imposing an obligation on Contracting States effectively to act as indirect guarantors of freedom of worship for the rest of the world.

However, if the deportation itself was directly aimed at the religious activities of the deportee **3.66** or an organization of which he or she was a member, then Article 9 issues will arise and the Court will determine whether the deportation constitutes an interference with the right to manifestation of religion and belief.[232]

Religious dress codes and religious symbols. The Court has been reluctant to enter into debates **3.67** about whether particular practices are a required element of a particular religion. This may reflect the fact that persons sharing the same religious belief may have different interpreta-tions about what that religion requires as a matter of obligation. This is particularly so in cases involving the wearing of the Islamic headscarf. In recent cases, the Court has usu-ally accepted that there has been an interference with the manifestation of the applicant's religious belief in such cases, and then proceeded to examine whether the interference has been justified by reference to the limitations set out in Article 9(2). For example, in *Şahin v Turkey*,[233] the Grand Chamber refused to adjudicate on the contested question as to whether the applicant was fulfilling a religious duty, and thus manifesting her faith, by wearing the Islamic headscarf. The Court proceeded on the basis that regulations prohibiting the wearing of a headscarf interfered with the applicant's right to manifest her religion, and ultimately went on to hold that the prohibition in question was indeed justified.[234] This approach by the Court is both principled and pragmatic. The Court is concerned with the religious belief of the relevant individual. It is plain that members of the same religion may have differing interpretations of what that religion requires.

Positive obligations.[235] Under Article 1 ECHR, contracting states undertake to 'secure to **3.68** everyone within their jurisdiction' the rights and freedoms set out in the Convention. The

---

[230] *El Majjaoui and Stichting Touba Moskee v Netherlands* (App 25525/03) (2007). See also *Nolan and K v Russia* (App 2572/04) (2009) paras 61–79.
[231] *Z and T v UK* (App 27034/05) (2006). See *Chahal v UK* (1996) 23 EHRR 413.
[232] See *Omkarananda and Divine Light Zentrum* (n 37) 118.
[233] *Şahin* (n 136).
[234] See para 3.100.
[235] See generally A Mowbray, *The Development of Positive Obligations under the European Convention on Human Rights by the European Court of Human Rights* (Hart, 2004). See also *Thlimmenos* (n 204), where it was

Court has held that there are therefore situations in which states are obliged to take measures to safeguard the Article 9 rights of specific persons,[236] for example from hostile attacks by other private individuals. In *Otto-Preminger-Institut v Austria*,[237] the Court stated:

> ...the manner in which beliefs and doctrines are opposed or denied is a matter which may engage the responsibility of the State, notably its responsibility to ensure the peaceful enjoyment of the right guaranteed under Article 9 to the holders of those beliefs and doctrines. Indeed, in extreme cases the effect of particular methods of opposing or denying religious beliefs can be such as to inhibit those who hold such beliefs from exercising their freedom to hold and express them.[238]

3.69 This doctrine that the state must ensure that competing groups tolerate each other was affirmed in *97 Members of the Gldani Congregation and 4 others v Georgia*,[239] where the Court held that the Georgian authorities had violated Article 9 because of their failure to take the necessary measures to ensure that an Orthodox religious group tolerated the existence of the applicants' religious community.[240] The role of the authorities in such a situation is not to remove the cause of the tension completely, thereby eliminating pluralism, but instead to ensure tolerance.[241]

3.70 In *Savda v Turkey*,[242] a case about conscientious objection, the Court went on to hold that there was a violation of the Convention as there was no procedure which would have enabled the applicant to have established whether he was entitled to conscientious objector status in domestic law. In the light of its case law on Article 8, which had repeatedly emphasized the state's positive obligation to provide a regulatory framework of adjudicatory and enforcement machinery to protect the right to private life,[243] the Court considered that there was a positive obligation on the authorities to make available to the applicant an effective and accessible procedure which would have enabled him to establish whether he was entitled to conscientious objector status.[244] Another example is *Ercep v Turkey*,[245] in which, after finding violations of Articles 6 and 9 in a case regarding the refusal of a Jehovah's Witness to perform military service, the Court invited Turkey to enact legislation concerning conscientious objectors and to introduce an alternative form of service.[246]

3.71 In *Eweida* the ECtHR accepted that Article 9 imposes positive obligations on the state. However, as with all positive obligations, there are proper limits to those obligations. The positive obligations under Article 9 do not include a right for individuals to bring a specific form of domestic proceedings[247] or to have a particular form of proceedings brought on

---

acknowledged in the context of Art 14 and discrimination that different categories of persons may need to be treated differently.

[236] See *X v UK* (n 54).

[237] *Otto-Preminger-Institut* (n 20).

[238] *Otto-Preminger-Institut* (n 20) para 47.

[239] *97 Members of the Gldani Congregation and 4 others v Georgia* (App 71156/01) (2007).

[240] See *97 Members of the Gldani Congregation* (n 239) para 134.

[241] See *Serif* (n 190) para 31. See also *Metropolitan Church of Bessarabia* (n 114), and *Holy Synod of the Bulgarian Orthodox Church (Metropolitan Inokentiy) v Bulgaria* (22 January 2009) (Apps 412/03 and 35677/04) (2009).

[242] *Savda* (n 87).

[243] See eg *Strömblad v Sweden* (App 3684/07) (2012) para 74.

[244] See *Savda* (n 87) para 98.

[245] *Ercep v Turkey* (n 85).

[246] See *Ercep* (n 85) para 80.

[247] *Choudhury v UK* (1993) 12 HRLJ 172.

their behalf by the state.[248] Nor does Article 9 include the right to any protection from criticism.[249]

(5) Is the interference justified under Article 9(2)?

The freedom of thought, conscience, and religion (the 'internal aspect' of Article 9 or *forum internum*) is an absolute right which may not be subject to any limitation or restriction.[250] It is only the manifestation of religion or beliefs (the 'external aspect' or *forum externum*) which may be restricted, by reference to the limitations set out in Article 9(2). **3.72**

Article 9(2) provides: 'Freedom to manifest one's religion or beliefs shall be subject only to such limitations as are prescribed by law and are necessary in a democratic society in the interests of public safety, for the protection of public order, health or morals, or for the protection of the rights and freedoms of others.' There are therefore three cumulative tests to establish justification: is the measure: (1) prescribed by law; (2) in pursuit of a legitimate aim; and (3) necessary in a democratic society? The onus is on the state to satisfy these tests in order to prove justification and thereby to show that the interference with the applicant's right to manifestation is lawful. **3.73**

a) 'Prescribed by law'[251]

This requirement necessitates that there is some law on which the interference is based; without a legal basis, the interference will lead to an automatic violation of the Convention.[252] 'Law' has been defined broadly. It includes: statute, written enactments of lower rank than statute,[253] settled and published national case law which supplements statutory provisions,[254] and delegated regulatory measures taken by professional bodies.[255] In *Şahin v Turkey*,[256] the Court clarified the term of 'law' as follows: **3.74**

> ... the Court observes that it has always understood the term 'law' in its 'substantive' sense, not its 'formal' one; it has included both 'written law' ... and regulatory measures taken by professional regulatory bodies under independent rule-making powers delegated to them by parliament..., and unwritten law... In sum, the 'law' is the provision in force as the competent courts have interpreted it.[257]

---

[248] *Dubowska and Skup v Poland* (1997) 24 EHRR CD 75; and *Kubalska v Poland* (App 35579/97) (1997).

[249] *Church of Scientology v Sweden* (1978) 21 DR 109, 111.

[250] See *Darby v Sweden* (n 22) para 44.

[251] This requirement can also be found in Arts 10(2) and 11(2); the expression 'in accordance with law' in Art 8(2) is also understood as meaning the same.

[252] eg *Perry v Latvia* (App 30273/03) (2007) 62, finding that the prohibition of a pastor from exercising his ministry had not been based on any provision of law in force at the material time; *Kuznetsov and ors v Russia* (App 184/02) (2007), a legal basis for breaking up a religious event conducted on the premises lawfully rented was 'conspicuously lacking'; *Biserica Adevarat Ortodoxa din Moldova v Moldova* (2009) 48 EHRR 20, 36, involving the government's disobeying of a court order to register a church as an official religious denomination; and *Poltoratskiy v Ukraine* (2003) 39 EHRR 916, 170, where it was found that there was no legal basis for refusing a prisoner access to priest.

[253] *De Wilde, Ooms and Versyp v Belgium* (1979) 1 EHRR 373.

[254] *Kokkinakis* (n 7) paras 37–41, noting that it is inevitable that statutory wording may not always attain absolute precision.

[255] *Barthold v Germany* (1985) 7 EHRR 383.

[256] *Şahin* (n 136).

[257] *Şahin* (n 175) para 88.

3.75 To be 'prescribed by law', the interference in question must satisfy a number of requirements. First, it must be easily or adequately accessible,[258] and secondly, it must be formulated with sufficient precision to enable the citizen to regulate his conduct[259]—he must be able reasonably to foresee the consequences of his actions[260] (even if this might require some legal advice). In *Sunday Times v United Kingdom (No 1)*,[261] the Court stated:

> ...consequences need not be foreseeable with absolute certainty: experience shows this to be unattainable. Again, whilst certainty is highly desirable, it may bring in its train excessive rigidity and the law must be able to keep pace with changing circumstances. Accordingly, many laws are inevitably couched in terms which, to a greater or lesser extent, are vague and whose interpretation and application are questions of practice.[262]

3.76 Thirdly, the law must avoid excessive executive discretion and arbitrary interferences by public authorities with the rights safeguarded by the Convention. In *Hasan and Chaush v Bulgaria*,[263] this requirement was not satisfied where a governmental agency had favoured one faction over another in the appointment of a religious leader. There were no substantive criteria in the law and no procedural safeguards. The Court stated that:

> ...it would be contrary to the rule of law, one of the basic principles of a democratic society enshrined in the Convention, for a legal discretion granted to the executive to be expressed in terms of an unfettered power. Consequently, the law must indicate with sufficient clarity the scope of any such discretion conferred on the competent authorities and the manner of its exercise. The level of precision required of domestic legislation—which cannot in any case provide for every eventuality—depends to a considerable degree on the content of the instrument in question, the field it is designed to cover and the number and status of those to whom it is addressed.[264]

b) Does the interference pursue a legitimate aim?

3.77 Article 9(2) lists the legitimate aims which the state action may pursue when curtailing the right to manifestation: public safety, protection of public order, health or morals, and rights and freedoms of others. This list is narrower than the permissible limitations in Articles 8, 10, and 11 which include national security as a further potentially-legitimate aim. The case law shows that the Court tends to accept the aim claimed by the state rather easily. At times it has skipped over detailed analysis of this requirement rather swiftly.[265] It should also be noted that Article 15 permits states to derogate from their obligations, including Article 9, 'in times of war or other public emergency threatening the life of the nation'.

---

[258] *Sunday Times v UK (No 1)* (1979–80) 2 EHRR 245, para 49; *Silver and ors v UK* (1983) 5 EHRR 347, para 87, where unpublished instructions to prison governors did not satisfy this requirement.

[259] *Sunday Times (No 1)* (n 258), para 49. See also *Barthold* (n 255) para 47 and *Ezelin v France* (1991) 14 EHRR 362, para 45.

[260] eg *Svyato-Mykhaylivska Parafiya v Ukraine* (App 77703/01) (2007), where failure to register amendments to statutes of a religious organization had been based upon domestic law which had not been sufficiently foreseeable. Furthermore, the 'lack of safeguards against arbitrary decisions by the registering authority were not rectified by the judicial review conducted by the domestic courts, which were clearly prevented from reaching a different finding by the lack of coherence and foreseeability of the legislation' (at para 152).

[261] *Sunday Times (No 1)* (n 258).

[262] *Sunday Times (No 1)* (n 258) para 49.

[263] *Hasan and Chaush* (n 21). This was the first case in which the 'prescribed by law' requirement was held not to have been satisfied.

[264] *Hasan and Chaush* (n 21) para 84. A further illustration of this approach is *Kuznetsov v Russia* (n 252) para 74, where the Court stated that the breaking up of a meeting of a group of Jehovah's Witnesses by an official purporting to act in her official capacity had a 'conspicuously lacking' legal basis.

[265] See Taylor (n 42) 301–2.

'Public safety' and 'protection of public order'. These two aims are usually analysed together in **3.78** the case law. 'Public order' was defined in *Engel v The Netherlands*[266] as: 'the order that must prevail within the confines of a specific social group [where] disorder in that group can have repercussions on order in society as a whole'. The definition is rather broad.

These two legitimate aims have served to justify restrictions on access to a Druid festival at **3.79** Stonehenge;[267] a public protest against alcohol and pornography;[268] and a Buddhist prisoner growing a beard in order to enable the authorities to identify him.[269] The aims have also justified the removal from a prisoner of a religious book which contained a chapter on martial arts;[270] a government campaign which described the Osho movement associations as a 'youth sect' and 'psycho sect' and warned the public about their practices;[271] a conviction for the offence of usurping the functions of a minister of a known religion;[272] and holding in solitary confinement a serial murderer who had given evidence against a number of inmates and stopping him from attending chapel services.[273] The grounds of public safety and public order have also been used to justify holding that free expression of belief does not include incitement to desert the army, to murder officers, or to supply weapons to the IRA.[274]

The ECtHR has sometimes accepted that the interference is for a legitimate aim in circum- **3.80** stances where the aim has not seemed particularly convincing. In *Metropolitan Church of Bessarabia and others v Moldova*,[275] the Court stated:

> ... the refusal to allow the application for recognition lodged by the applicants was intended to protect public order and public safety. The Moldovan State ... had an ethnically and linguistically varied population. That being so, the young Republic of Moldova, which had been independent since 1991, had few strengths it could depend on to ensure its continued existence, but one factor conductive to stability was religion, the majority of the population being Orthodox Christians. Consequently, recognition of the Moldovan Orthodox Church, which was subordinate to the patriarchate of Moscow, had enabled the entire population to come together within that Church. If the applicant Church were to be recognised, that tie was likely to be lost and the Orthodox Christian population dispersed among a number of Churches. Moreover, under cover of the applicant Church, which was subordinate to the patriarchate of Bucharest, political forces were at work, acting hand-in-glove with Romanian interests favourable to reunification between Bessarabia and Romania. Recognition of the applicant Church would therefore revive old Russo-Romanian rivalries within the population, thus endangering social stability and even Moldova's territorial integrity.

The Court has taken care not to blur the distinction between, on the one hand, tensions **3.81** which may be seen in a truly pluralistic society, and on the other, the need to protect public order and safety:

> Although the Court recognises that it is possible that tension is created in situations where a religious or any other community becomes divided, it considers that this is one of the

---

[266] *Engel v Netherlands* (1976) 1 EHRR 647, para 98.
[267] *Chappell v UK* (n 37).
[268] *Hakansson v Sweden* (1983) 5 EHRR 297.
[269] *X v Austria* (n 121) 174 (inadmissibility decision).
[270] *X v UK* (1976) 5 DR 100.
[271] *Leela Forderkreis* (n 41).
[272] *Serif* (n 190).
[273] *Childs v UK* (1982) 5 EHRR 513.
[274] *X v UK* (1975) 3 DR 62.
[275] *Metropolitan Church of Bessarabia* (n 114) paras 111–113.

unavoidable consequences of pluralism. The role of authorities in such circumstances is not to remove the cause of tension by eliminating pluralism, but to ensure that the competing groups tolerate each other.[276]

In pluralist societies, the Court will need to continue to scrutinize these two aims to ensure that they are legitimate. In *Arslan v Turkey*,[277] the Court held that the applicants who had been convicted for contravening the legal dress code in public by wearing black headbands, harem trousers, and tunics did not pose any threat to the public because of their attire.

3.82 *Protection of 'health or morals'.* This aim has been used to justify a Sikh prisoner being required to clean the floor of his prison cell;[278] requiring all drivers, including Sikhs, to wear crash-helmets when riding motorcycles;[279] the conviction of a Dutch dairy farmer for refusing to participate in a compulsory health scheme to prevent tuberculosis in cattle;[280] and the state organizing the exercise of worship to ensure harmony and tolerance.[281]

3.83 *'Rights and freedoms of others'.* This restriction, mirroring restrictions under other ECHR articles, is of obvious importance and sometimes overused. It has been used to justify silencing those conveying their religious messages where the actions of that person were likely to provoke public indignation;[282] controls on planning;[283] restrictions on religious dress;[284] enforcing compulsory motor insurance;[285] the termination of a pregnancy where necessary for the protection of the rights of the mother;[286] and a statutory provision which precluded the applicants from being granted general dispensation from the obligation to ensure that their son, a minor, attended school on Saturdays on grounds of the right to education of the minor.[287]

c) Is the interference 'necessary in a democratic society'?

3.84 The third and final requirement is for the State to show that the interference in question is 'necessary in a democratic society'. The rationale for this is that the freedoms contained in Article 9 are some of 'the most vital elements that go to make up the identity of believers and their conception of life ... The pluralism indissociable from a democratic society, which has been dearly won over the centuries, depends on it'.[288] Therefore, in order for the state's interference to be 'necessary', it must satisfy a pressing social need. As stated in *Handyside v United Kingdom*:[289]

> ... whilst the adjective 'necessary', within the meaning of [this provision] is not synonymous with 'indispensible', neither has it the flexibility of such expressions as 'admissible', 'ordinary', 'useful', 'reasonable' or 'desirable'. Nevertheless, it is for the national authorities to make the

---

[276] *Serif* (n 190) para 53.
[277] *Arslan v Turkey* (App 22497/93) (1995).
[278] *X v UK* (n 33).
[279] *X v UK* (1978) DR 14 234.
[280] *X v Netherlands* (1963) 5 YB 278.
[281] *Cha'are Shalom Ve Tsedek v France* (n 149) para 84.
[282] *X v Sweden* (1984) 5 EHRR 297. See also *X Ltd and Y v UK (Gay News)* (App 8710/79) (1982).
[283] *Vergos v Greece* (2004) 41 EHRR 913; and *ISKON v UK* (1994) 90 DR 90.
[284] See eg *Karaduman* (n 30); *Dahlab v Switzerland* (n 165); and *Şahin* (n 10). The controversy of these decisions will be analysed in detail at paras 3.103–3.105.
[285] *X v Netherlands* (1967) 10 YB 472.
[286] *H v Norway* (1992) 73 DR 155, 170.
[287] *Martins Casimiro and Cerveira Ferreira v Luxembourg* (App 44888/98) (1999).
[288] *Şahin* (n 30) para 104.
[289] *Handyside v UK* (1979–80) 1 EHRR 737, para 48.

initial assessment of the reality of the pressing social need implied by the notion of 'necessity' in this context.

The measure in question must also be proportionate. As stated in *X and the Church of Scientology v Sweden*:[290] **3.85**

> ...the 'necessity' test cannot be applied in absolute terms, but requires...the assessment of various factors. Such factors include the nature of the right involved, the degree of interferences i.e. whether it was proportionate to the legitimate aim pursued, the nature of the public interest and the degree to which it requires protection in the circumstances of the case.

Proportionality, which is 'inherent in the whole of the Convention',[291] requires a 'balancing exercise' during which the Court asks 'whether the interference with the right is more extensive than is justified by the legitimate aim'.[292] Therefore, 'concrete evidence to substantiate the alleged damage'[293] must be adduced by the state, and the state's position 'must be convincingly established'.[294] An interference with a right may only stand upon proof being adduced that less restrictive means[295] are not available with which to satisfy the legitimate aim. **3.86**

A recent example of the balancing exercise can be seen in the case of *Eweida*.[296] After finding that Ms Eweida's right to manifest her religion had been interfered with by British Airways' decision to prohibit her from wearing her cross, the ECtHR went on to consider whether a fair balance had been struck between the aim of the prohibition and Ms Eweida's interests. The ECtHR went on to find that it had not. On one side of the scales was Ms Eweida's desire to manifest her religious belief, which was a fundamental right. On the other was her employer's wish to project a certain corporate image. While this aim was undoubtedly legitimate, in the Court's view the domestic courts had accorded it too much weight. Ms Eweida's cross was discreet and did not detract from her professional appearance. There was no evidence that the wearing of other previously authorized items of religious clothing, such as turbans and *hijabs*, had any negative impact on British Airways' brand or image. The Court also referred to the fact that British Airways was later able to amend its uniform code to allow for the visible wearing of religious symbolic jewellery which, in its view, demonstrated that the earlier prohibition was not of crucial importance.[297] **3.87**

In contrast, the ECtHR dismissed the application of Ms Chaplin, a nurse who had been prevented by her employer's uniform policy from wearing a cross on a chain around her neck. The purpose of the policy was to prevent the risk of injury when handling patients. The Court held the reason for asking Ms Chaplin to remove the cross, namely the protection of health and safety in a hospital ward, was 'inherently of a greater magnitude' than that which applied in respect of Ms Eweida.[298] It followed that the interference with Ms Chaplin's freedom to manifest her religion was necessary in a democratic society. **3.88**

---

[290] *X and the Church of Scientology* (n 37) para 73.
[291] *Sporrong and Lonroth v Sweden* (1983) 5 EHRR 35, para 69.
[292] D Feldman, *Civil Liberties and Human Rights in England and Wales* (OUP, 2002) 57.
[293] *Smith and Grady v UK* (2000) 29 EHRR 493, para 99.
[294] *Autronic v Switzerland* (1990) 12 EHRR 485, para 61.
[295] However, the court has not always utilized this requirement; see *James v UK* (1986) 8 EHRR 123, para 51: 'The availability of alternative solutions does not in itself render the...legislation unjustified...'; and *Chappell v UK* (1990) 12 EHRR 1, para 65.
[296] *Eweida and ors v UK* (2013) 57 EHRR 213.
[297] *Eweida and ors v UK* (n 296) para 94.
[298] *Eweida and ors v UK* (n 296) para 99.

3.89 A further example of proportionality in action can be seen in *Jakóbski v Poland*.[299] Here, the refusal by the authorities to provide a Buddhist prisoner with a vegetarian diet (to which he was required to adhere as part of his faith) was held to violate Article 9. A key factor in the ECtHR reaching this decision was the very limited (ie proportionate) burden involved in accommodating the applicant's religious practices. Unlike in earlier cases,[300] his meals did not have to be prepared, cooked, and served in a prescribed manner and did not require any special products. Furthermore, unlike in *X v United Kingdom*,[301] the applicant was not offered any alternative diet, and nor was the Buddhist Mission consulted on the issue. Therefore, the authority's actions in refusing the Buddhist prisoner a vegetarian diet were held to be disproportionate.[302]

3.90 The proportionality requirement also entails insisting that the state or its authorities fulfil fair procedural safeguards in order that their interferences are deemed justified. In *Manoussakis v Greece*,[303] whilst the requirement of prior authorization for use of a building for public worship pursued a legitimate aim, the conviction of the applicants for operating an unauthorised place of worship was held to be disproportionate to this aim because the applicants' attempts to get registration had been thwarted by Ministry delays (of over 18 months) and there was evidence that the state had used its law to impose rigid conditions on non-Orthodox movements.[304]

3.91 *Margin of Appreciation.*[305] A recent statement of this doctrine was issued by the Strasbourg Court in *Schilder v The Netherlands*:[306]

> Where questions concerning the relationship between State and religions are at stake, on which opinion in a democratic society may reasonably differ widely, the role of the national decision-making body must be given special importance. Rules in this sphere will consequently vary from one country to another according to national traditions and the requirements imposed by the need to protect the rights and freedoms of others and to maintain public order.

3.92 The margin of appreciation doctrine is the process by which the Court affords discretion to the state in order to decide what is 'necessary in a democratic society'.[307] It allows the Court to take into account the fact that the Convention rights may be interpreted differently

---

[299] *Jakóbski v Poland* (2012) 55 EHRR 8. This judgment is also relevant for noting that the European Prison Rules (Recommendation Rec 2006(2)) can be cited by the Court in its judgments (see para 53).

[300] See eg *D and ES v UK* (App 13669/88) (1990); and *X v UK* (App 5947/72) (1976).

[301] *X v UK* (n 301).

[302] See *X v UK* (n 300) paras 52–54.

[303] *Manoussakis* (n 152).

[304] See *Manoussakis* (n 152) paras 44–48. See also *Vergos* (n 283), finding no violation of Art 9 in refusing permission to build a prayer-house where the applicant was the only member of his religious community in his town; and *Johannische Kirche & Peters v Germany* (App 41754/98) (2001), where planning permission for a new cemetery was rejected.

[305] See generally RJ MacDonald, 'The Margin of Appreciation in the Jurisprudence of the European Convention on Human Rights' in *International Law at the Time of its Codification: Essays in Honour of Roberto Ago* (Guiffrè, 1987) 187; TH Jones, 'The devaluation of human rights under the European convention' (1995) Public Law 430; TA O'Donnell, 'The Margin of Appreciation Doctrine: Standards in the Jurisprudence of the European Court of Human Rights' (1982) 4 HRQ 474; F Matscher, 'Methods of Interpretation' in R St J MacDonald, F Matscher, and H Petzold (eds), *The European System for the Protection of Human Rights* (Martinus Nijhoff, 1993) 79; Y Arai-Takahashi, *The Margin of Appreciation Doctrine in the Jurisprudence of the ECHR* (Intersentia, 2002).

[306] *Schilder v The Netherlands* (App 2158/12) (2012) 22. See also *Şahin* (n 136) para 109 and *Dogru v France* (n 177) para 63.

[307] For criticism of the doctrine, see C Evans (n 4) 203.

in different Member States. This way judges sitting on a transnational court such as the ECtHR are obliged to take into account the cultural, historic, and philosophical differences between Member States and therefore respect and defer to a given state's greater understanding, knowledge, and expertise in certain areas. This rationale was explained by the Court in *Handyside v United Kingdom*:[308]

> By reason of their direct and continuous contact with the vital forces of their countries, state authorities are in principle in a better position than the international judge to give an opinion on the exact content of these requirements as well as on the 'necessity' of a 'restriction' or penalty' intended to meet them.[309]

The margin of appreciation doctrine allows for the differing degrees of importance accorded **3.93** to religions within varying societies and also the inherent difficulties of ruling in the sphere of religion as there are no set moral answers accepted across the 47 Council of Europe states. As stated in *Otto-Preminger-Institut v Austria*:[310]

> As in the case of 'morals' it is not possible to discern throughout Europe a uniform conception of the significance of religion in society; even within a single country such conceptions may vary. For that reason it is not possible to arrive at a comprehensive definition of what constitutes a permissible interference with the exercise of the right to freedom of expression where such expression is directed against the religious feeling of others. A certain margin of appreciation is therefore to be left to the national authorities in assessing the existence and extent of the necessity of such interference.

This was reiterated again in *Leyla Şahin v Turkey*:[311] **3.94**

> 'It is not possible to discern throughout Europe a uniform conception of the significance of religion in society... and the meaning or impact of the public expression of a religious belief will differ according to time and context... Rules in this sphere will consequently vary from one country to another according to national traditions and the requirements imposed by the need to protect the rights and freedoms of others and to maintain public order... Accordingly, the choice of the extent and form such regulations should take must inevitably be left up to a point to the State concerned, as it will depend on the specific domestic context...

Therefore, where there is no universal European approach regarding the interference in ques- **3.95** tion, there is likely to be a wide margin of appreciation afforded to the Member State in question.[312] The opposite is also true, so that there is likely to be a narrower margin of appreciation where there is a wide consensus among states on a particular issue. A good example of this is *Bayatyan v Armenia*,[313] where almost all Member States of the Council of Europe which had ever had, or still have, compulsory military service had introduced alternatives in order to reconcile the possible conflict between individual conscience and military obligations.

Recent examples of the application of the margin of appreciation doctrine can be seen in the **3.96** cases of *Ladele*[314] and *McFarlane*.[315] In both cases, conflicts had arisen between the religious beliefs of the applicants, and the respective desire of their employers to require all employees

---

[308] *Handyside* (n 289).
[309] *Handyside* (n 289) para 48.
[310] *Otto-Preminger-Institut* (n 20) para 50.
[311] *Şahin* (n 10) para 109.
[312] See also *Muller v Switzerland* (1988) 13 EHRR 212, para 35.
[313] *Bayatyan* (n 69).
[314] *Ladele v UK* (App 51671/10) (2013).
[315] *McFarlane v UK* (App 36516/10) (2013).

to register civil partnerships and to provide counselling to same-sex couples. In *Ladele* the Court accepted that Articles 9 and 14 were applicable, but by a majority considered that the decision of the local authority to require Ms Ladele to register civil partnerships, and the domestic courts to uphold that requirement, was within the wide margin of appreciation accorded to national authorities when striking a balance between competing rights. The decision of the ECtHR to rely on the margin of appreciation in the case of *Ladele* was not surprising in circumstances where a Dutch court, confronted with a very similar set of circumstances to that in *Ladele*, decided that the authority employing the registrar had a duty to come to a reasonable accommodation of the registrar's views.

3.97 The extent of the margin of appreciation in any given case depends on the context and the circumstances;[316] for example, the nature of the expression in question may be relevant. In *Wingrove v United Kingdom*,[317] the Court stated:

> Whereas there is little scope under Article 10(2) of the Convention for restrictions on political speech or on debate on questions of public interest, a wider margin of appreciation is generally available to the Contracting states when regulating freedom of expression in relation to matters liable to offend intimate personal convictions within the sphere of morals or, especially, religion. Moreover, as in the field of morals, and perhaps to an even greater degree, there is no uniform European conception of 'the requirements of the protection of the rights of others' in relation to attacks on their religious convictions. What is likely to cause substantial offence to persons of a particular religious persuasion will vary significantly from time to time and from place to place, especially in an era characterised by an ever-growing array of faiths and denominations. By reason of their direct and continuous contact with the vital forces of their countries, State authorities are in principle in a better position than the international judge to give an opinion on the exact content of these requirements with regard to the rights of others as well as on the 'necessity' of a 'restriction' intended to protect from such material those whose deepest feelings and convictions would be seriously offended.[318]

The ECtHR is likely to scrutinize cases more closely where criminal sanctions are imposed, as opposed to civil or administrative penalties.[319]

3.98 There are limits to the doctrine. Even where there is a wide margin of appreciation, it must be stressed that this does not mean a complete absence of European supervision.[320] In *Handyside v United Kingdom*[321] it was noted that the margin of appreciation:

> . . . does not give the Contracting States an unlimited power of appreciation. The Court . . . is responsible for ensuring the observance of those States' engagements, is empowered to give the final ruling on whether a 'restriction' or 'penalty' is reconcilable with [the Convention provisions]. The domestic margin of appreciation thus goes hand in hand with a European supervision. Such supervision concerns both the aim of the measure challenged and its 'necessity'; it covers not only the basic legislation but also the decision applying it, even one given by an independent court . . . It follows from this that it is in no way the Court's task to take the place of the competent national courts, but rather to review under [the Convention provisions] the decisions they delivered in the exercise of their power of appreciation.

---

[316] See also *Rasmussen v Denmark* (1985) 7 EHRR 371 para 40.
[317] *Wingrove* (n 20).
[318] *Wingrove* (n 20) para 58.
[319] See *Mehmet Agga v Greece (Nos 3 & 4)* (Apps 32186/02 and 33331/02) (2006).
[320] See *Lehideux and Isorni v France* (2000) 30 EHRR 665, para 51.
[321] *Handyside* (n 289) paras 49–50.

d) Case study: religious dress[322]

The first case in which the issue of prohibitions on the wearing of religious dress arose was **3.99**
Karaduman v Turkey,[323] where the Commission rejected the applicant's Article 9 complaint
after her university degree certificate had been withheld because she had refused to supply an
identity photograph showing herself bare-headed. In *Dahlab v Switzerland*,[324] the Courtheld
that there was no violation of Article 9, this time regarding the banning of a female teacher
from wearing the Islamic veil in a primary school. The state's action was held to be justified
as it pursued the legitimate aim of obtaining religious neutrality in classrooms. This was
because it was feared that the wearing of a headscarf whilst teaching might have a proselytising effect on the pupils[325] because it appeared to be imposed on women by a precept which,
the Swiss Federal Court noted, was hard to square with the principle of gender equality. The
ECtHR therefore felt it was difficult to reconcile the garment with the messages of tolerance,
respect for others, and equality and non-discrimination—messages which all teachers must
convey to their pupils.[326]

The Grand Chamber followed this approach in *Leyla Şahin v Turkey*[327] where, by 16 votes to **3.100**
1, it held that there was no violation of Article 9 where a university had prohibited students
from wearing Islamic headscarves in its grounds and had refused access to a written examination for a student not complying with this rule. The prohibition was found to have served
the legitimate aim of 'protecting the rights and freedoms of others and of protecting public
order'[328] and was compatible with Convention values since it was designed to uphold the
principle of secularism,[329] and was proportionate[330] as secularism was seen as a key element
in Turkey remaining a liberal democracy. It should be noted that Turkey was specifically
declared to be a secular state in each of its four constitutions since its founding as a Republic
in 1923. The Grand Chamber accepted the Turkish government's submission that the headscarf had taken on political significance in recent years through association with extreme
fundamentalist groups; referred to Turkey's commitment to gender equality; and pointed to
the impact of the headscarf on those women choosing not to wear it.[331] This represented a
difference in approach from that adopted by the Court in *Dahlab v Switzerland* (where the
focus had been on the impact on pupils) by introducing a new focus on the potential political consequences of allowing religious clothing to be worn in state institutions in a secular
society.[332] Furthermore, the ban was seen to be necessary in a democratic society considering

---

[322] See further I Gallala, 'The Islamic Headscarf: An Example of Surmountable Conflict between Shari'a and the Fundamental Principles of Europe' (2006) 12 ELJ 593; S Langlaude, 'Indoctrination, Secularism, Religious Liberty and the ECHR' (2006) 55 ICLQ 929; M Evans, *Manual on the Wearing of Religious Symbols in Public Areas* (Council of Europe, 2009); G Van der Schyff and A Overbeeke, 'Exercising Religious Freedom in the Public Space: A Comparative and European Convention Analysis of General Burqa Bans' (2011) 7(3) ECL Rev 424; and M Hunter-Henin, 'Why the French Don't Like the Burqa: Laïcité, National Identity and Religious Freedom' (2012) 61(3) ICLQ 613. For a jurisprudential analysis, see R Plant, 'Religion, Identity and Freedom of Expression' (2011) 17(1) Res Publica 7–20.
[323] *Karaduman* (n 30).
[324] *Dahlab v Switzerland* (n 165).
[325] See *Dahlab* (n 165) para 13.
[326] *Dahlab* (n 165) 13.
[327] *Şahin* (n 10).
[328] See *Şahin* (n 10) paras 99.
[329] See *Şahin* (n 10) para 116.
[330] See *Şahin* (n 10) paras 118–121.
[331] See *Şahin* (n 10) paras 111–116.
[332] See M Evans, '*Lautsi v Italy*: An Initial Appraisal' (2011) 6 Religion and Human Rights 237, 238.

the wide margin of appreciation states have in the area of dress codes in such a context.[333] *Şahin* has been followed in subsequent cases such as *Kurtulmus v Turkey*[334] and *Dogru v France*.[335]

3.101 The Grand Chamber decision in *Şahin* has been criticized[336] on a number of grounds including: the application of the margin of appreciation doctrine; the interpretation of the freedom of religion; its use of secularism; adverse implications on Muslim women's rights; and promotion of the image of Islam as a threat to democracy. The judgment of dissenting Judge Tulkens made these criticisms, and itself seems to have influenced the approach of the Court in later cases. For this reason this dissenting judgment is addressed in the following paragraphs.

3.102 First, there are a number of issues with the Court's use of gender arguments.[337] The Court cited a passage from *Dahlab v Switzerland* which referred to the Islamic headscarf as a 'powerful external symbol' that 'appeared to be imposed on women by a religious precept that was hard to reconcile with the principle of gender equality' and which 'could not easily be reconciled with the message of tolerance, respect for others and, above all, equality and non discrimination'.[338] As dissenting Judge Tulkens remarked, it questionable whether it is within the Court's role to 'make an appraisal of this type' on religious practices,[339] and whether paternalism is the right approach for the Court to take in these matters.[340] It is for evidence to establish whether the applicant freely adopted wearing the headscarf. Paternalism runs counter to the case law of the Court, which has developed a right of personal autonomy. The wearing of the veil has a much more complex meaning attributed to it, by both the wearer and society. Other critics have suggested that the result of the Grand Chamber's analysis may be counterproductive in that gender equality is unlikely to be enhanced by forcing Muslim

---

[333] See *Dahlab* (n 165) 12–13.

[334] *Kurtulmus v Turkey* (App 65500/01) (2006), concerning a university professor refused authorization to wear a headscarf.

[335] *Dogru v France* (n 177), concerning the (rejected) challenge of an 11-year-old girl excluded for refusing to remove her headscarf during sports lessons; finding that the national court's reasoning relating to health and safety reasons was not unreasonable, and that the applicant had been made aware of the school rules. See further *Aktas v France* (App 43563/08) (2009); *Bayrak v France* (App 14308/08) (2009); *Gamaleddyn v France* (App 18527/08) (2009); *Ghazal v France* (App 29134/08) (2009); and *Singh v France* (Apps 25463/08 and 27561/08) (2009), which concerned expulsions from school for wearing religious symbols and which were all declared inadmissible.

[336] See, *inter alia*, T Lewis, 'What not to wear: Religious rights, the European Court, and the margin of appreciation' (2007) 56 ICLQ 395; A Vakulenko, ' "Islamic Headscarves" and the European Convention on Human Rights: An Intersectional Perspective' (2007) 16(2) Social and Legal Studies 190; N Gibson, 'Faith in the Courts: Religious Dress and Human Rights' (2007) 66(3) CLJ 657; J Martinez-Torron, 'The (Un)protection of Individual Religious Identity in the Strasbourg Case Law' (2012) 1(2) OJLR 363; and T Hoopes, 'The *Leyla Şahin v Turkey* Case Before the European Court of Human Rights' (2006) 5(3) Chinese Journal of International Law 719.

[337] See further: A Blair and W Aps, 'What Not to Wear and Other Stories: Addressing Religious Diversity in Schools' (2005) 17(1) Education and the Law 1; J Marshall, 'Freedom of Religious Expression and Gender Equality: *Şahin v Turkey*' (2006) 69(3) MLR 452; S Mullallay, 'Civil Integration, Migrant Women and the Veil: at the Limits of Rights' (2011) 74(1) MLR 27; M Malik, 'Feminism and its "Other": Female Autonomy in an Age of Difference' (2008–09) 30 Cardozo L Rev 2613; M Borovali, 'Islamic Headscarves and Slippery Slopes' (2008–09) 30 Cardozo L Rev 2601; D Lyon and D Spini, 'Unveiling the Headscarf Debate' (2004) 12 Feminist Legal Studies 33; and L Abu-Odeh, 'Post-colonial Feminism and the Veil' (1993) 43 Feminist Review 26.

[338] *Şahin* (n 136) para 111.

[339] *Şahin* (n 136) para 12.

[340] *Şahin* (n 136) para 12.

women themselves to choose between restrictions imposed by a religious belief and restrictions imposed on them by the state. Restrictions may result in women not leaving their homes, instead of leaving their veils at home.[341]

Secondly, the Court's use of the principle of secularism[342] has been criticized. The Court did **3.103** not analyse why the wearing of headscarves at university could objectively be regarded as a threat to Turkish secularism; instead it seemed to defer to the state's interpretation of the principles of neutrality and secularism. Dissenting Judge Tulkens was of the view that the applicant had never had any intention of calling into question the principle of secularism and that there was no evidence to indicate that she had contravened that principle, nor that her wearing the headscarf had led to any disruption.[343]

Thirdly, the quality of the evidence for the decision and the proportionality of it have been **3.104** questioned.[344] It appears that the Court has reduced the intensity of its own supervisory review to a very low level. The Court accepted a hypothetical argument based on consideration of 'the impact which wearing such a symbol, which is presented as a compulsory religious duty, may have on those who chose not to wear it'.[345] However, it is not clear what the evidence for this is. The 'religious peace' of the school or university in question did not seem to have been threatened in any way. In endorsing statements from *Dahlab v Switzerland* that Islamic headscarves are 'powerful symbols' associated with extreme religious fundamentalist movements,[346] the Court might be considered to have moved into the political realm by passing judgment on a religious practice. As dissenting Judge Tulkens stated, under the Convention, 'only indisputable facts and reasons whose legitimacy is beyond doubt—not mere worries or fears—are capable of . . . justifying interference with a right guaranteed by the Convention . . . Such examples do not appear to have been forthcoming in the present case'.[347]

Some of the criticisms of the *Şahin* decision seem to have been recognized by the ECtHR in **3.105** *Arslan v Turkey*.[348] In this case a group of men were found to be in contravention of national laws prohibiting religious headgear and dress being worn in public places. In following their interpretation of their faith, the applicants wore black headbands, harem trousers, and tunics and used walking sticks. The court distinguished these cases on the grounds that the applicants in *Arslan v Turkey* were ordinary citizens with no public functions, posed no threat to

---

[341] See I Radacic, 'Religious Symbols in Educational Institutions: Jurisprudence of the European Court of Human Rights' (2012) 7 Religion and Human Rights 133, 141–3; BD Bleiberg, 'Unveiling the Real Issue: Evaluating the European Court of Human Rights' Decision to Enforce the Turkish Headscarf Ban in *Leyla Şahin v Turkey*' (2005) 91 Corn L Rev 129, 162; and E Chamblee, 'Rhetoric or Rights? When Culture and Religion Bar Girls' Rights to Education' (2004) 44 Va JIL 1073, 1110.

[342] On the problematic nature of secularism in general, see further D McGoldrick, *Human Rights and Religion: The Islamic Headscarf Debate in Europe* (Hart Publishing, 2006) 22–8; M Freeman, 'The Problem of Secularism in Human Rights Theory' (2004) 26(2) HRQ 375; and M Rosenfield, 'Can Constitutionalism, Secularism and Religion be Reconciled in an Era of Globalisation and Religious Revival?' (2008–09) Cardozo L Rev 2333.

[343] See *Şahin* (n 136) para 13.

[344] See T Gunn, 'Fearful Symbols: The Islamic Headscarf and the European Court of Human Rights in *Şahin v Turkey*' (2008) Droit et Religion 339, and Gibson (n 336) 670 ff.

[345] *Şahin* (n 136) para 115.

[346] *Şahin* (n 136) para 111.

[347] *Şahin* (n 136) para 5.

[348] *Arslan v Turkey* (App 41135/98) (2010).

the public order, their presence alone could not put any pressure on passers-by nor amount to improper proselytism, and they were in a fully public space.[349] This approach is principled and readily comprehensible: where the activity has little relevant connection with the state, the margin of appreciation afforded to the state is necessarily reduced.[350] By contrast in *Phull v France*,[351] where security checks at airports were in issue, the interest of the state was necessarily more engaged. In that case it was held that there was no relevant restriction of freedom of movement, and requiring someone during a check to remove a turban worn for religious purposes fell within the state's margin of appreciation.[352]

3.106 *Inconsistencies with Human Rights Committee jurisprudence.* A recent decision from the United Nations-based Human Rights Committee (HRC)[353] is at odds with the jurisprudence of the ECtHR on issues of religious dress. In *Bikramjit Singh v France*,[354] the 17-year-old Sikh author[355] complained that he had been prevented from manifesting his freedom of religion by Act No 2004-228 of March 2004, which introduced rules prohibiting 'the wearing of symbols or clothing by which pupils manifest their religious affiliation in a conspicious manner'.[356] In particular, he stated that at the start of the school year in which the legislation was passed (September 2004), he had been prevented from entering the classroom in his *keski* and was sent to the canteen to study without assistance for three weeks. He was eventually expelled after he refused to remove his religious headgear. Multiple appeals finally resulted in a dismissal of his case by the Council of State in a ruling of December 2007. In his presentation of the facts, the author noted the following unchallenged points about the wearing of the turban and *keski*:

> The wearing of the turban is a categorical, explicit and mandatory religious precept in Sikhism . . . Asking a Sikh to remove his turban is therefore tantamount to asking him to perform an impossible act. The *keski* (like the turban for adult men) is not meant as an external display of faith but is rather intended to protect the long uncut hair, which is considered as a sacred, inherent and intrinsic part of the religion. The turban is not worn with a view to proselytize—a concept which is foreign to the Sikh religion.[357]

3.107 As it was not in dispute that the legislation constituted an interference with the author's freedom of religion, it fell to the Committee to decide whether the limitation was necessary and proportionate to a legitimate end. First, it was accepted that the legislation served purposes relating to the rights and freedoms of others, public order, and public safety.[358] However, the HRC did not find for the state party beyond that point:

> The Committee is of the view that the State party has not furnished compelling evidence that by wearing his *keski* the author would have posed a threat to the rights and freedoms of other pupils or to order at the school. The Committee is also of the view that the penalty of the pupil's permanent expulsion from the public school was disproportionate and led to serious

---

[349] *Arslan* (n 348) para 49.
[350] *Arslan* (n 348) para 49.
[351] *Phull v France* (App 35753/03) (2005).
[352] See also *El Morsli v France* (App 15585/06) (2008), where an applicant's claim regarding being required to remove her headscarf for an identity check was held to be inadmissible.
[353] See Ch 2, para 2.29.
[354] *Bikramjit Singh v France*, Comm No 1852/2008 (2012), UN Doc CCPR/C/106/D/1852/2008.
[355] Complainants are referred to as 'authors' in HRC communications.
[356] Education Code, Art L.141-5-1.
[357] *Bikramjit Singh* (n 354) para 2.3.
[358] *Bikramjit Singh* (n 354) para 8.6.

effects on the education to which the author, like any person of his age, was entitled in the State party. The Committee is not convinced that expulsion was necessary and that the dialogue between the school authorities and the author truly took into consideration his particular interests and circumstances.[359]

With regard to the effect of the legislation in general, the HRC made the following observations: **3.108**

> ... the Committee notes the State party's assertion that the broad extension of the category of persons forbidden to comply with their religious duties simplifies the administration of the restrictive policy. However, in the Committee's view, the State party has not shown how the sacrifice of those persons' rights is either necessary or proportionate to the benefits achieved.[360]

In conclusion, the Committee advised that 'the State party is also under an obligation to prevent similar violations in the future and should review Act No. 200-228 in light of its obligations under the Covenant, in particular article 18'.[361] **3.109**

The approach of the HRC in *Bikramjit Singh v France* appears to be inconsistent with the jurisprudence of the ECtHR. Indeed, Strasbourg case law was referred to unsuccessfully by the state party in argument;[362] the author responded by stating that the French's government's attempts at justifying the interference were as insufficient in the ECtHR cases as they were in the present communication,[363] and the Committee itself did not comment on the issue. What impact, if any, this recent view will have on Strasbourg jurisprudence is difficult to determine. As noted in Chapter 2, the Court has on a previous occasion taken heed of the HRC's comments and case law on Article 18;[364] however, for the ECtHR to adopt this approach would represent a departure from its previous approach to the issue of religious dress. **3.110**

e) Case study: religious symbols

In *Lautsi v Italy*[365] the Grand Chamber, by 15 votes to 2, held that the presence of a crucifix in an Italian state school classroom did not breach the right of a parent to have her children (aged between 11 and 13) to be educated in accordance with her religious or philosophical convictions (a right provided for in Article 2 of Protocol and taken in conjunction with Article 9). This reversed the earlier Chamber's decision. The Grand Chamber stated that there is no European consensus on the issue of the display of religious symbols[366] and that the display of the crucifix therefore falls within the state's margin of appreciation.[367] Furthermore, the visibility of the symbol in classrooms was held not to reach the level of a process of indoctrination of young pupils.[368] **3.111**

The Chamber's mistake, according to the Grand Chamber,[369] was the *non sequitur* of considering that the mere presence of a crucifix was incompatible with the state's duty to respect **3.112**

---

[359] *Bikramjit Singh* (n 354) para 8.7.
[360] *Bikramjit Singh* (n 354) para 8.7.
[361] *Bikramjit Singh* (n 354) para 10.
[362] *Bikramjit Singh* (n 354) paras 4.2, 5.5.
[363] *Bikramjit Singh v France* (n 354).
[364] *Bayatyan v Armenia* (n 205) para 105. See Ch 2, para 2.49.
[365] *Lautsi v Italy* (2010) 50 EHRR 42. The Italian government's referral of the case to the Grand Chamber attracted interventions by ten states, 33 Parliamentarians, and six NGOs.
[366] *Lautsi* (n 365) paras 26–28.
[367] *Lautsi* (n 365) paras 68–70.
[368] *Lautsi* (n 365) para 71.
[369] See *Lautsi* (n 365) para 73.

neutrality.[370] The Court had previously held that whilst parents have the right to ensure that regard is paid to their religious or philosophical convictions, this did not mean that they had the right to ensure that the educational curriculum only included material which accorded with their pattern of belief.[371] Thus, whilst accepting that the context of education in a state school clearly engages the responsibility of the state,[372] the Grand Chamber held that, like the curriculum, this was a matter in which the state enjoys a wide margin of appreciation to decide whether or not to perpetuate a tradition,[373] particularly as a result of large diversity in practice across Europe[374] and as there was no evidence of indoctrination.[375] This approach to state neutrality represents a move to place substance over appearance by the Strasbourg Court: whilst 'states have a responsibility for ensuring, neutrally and impartially, the exercise of various religions, faiths and beliefs',[376] this does not necessarily mean that the public realm need be a completely religiously neutral space for that obligation to be fulfilled—what matters is the effect and impact of the symbol in question. The decision in *Lautsi* is also interesting for its recognition of the fact that secularism as a principle is entitled to no greater or lesser respect than religious beliefs. The true principle is toleration, and not elimination, of the inevitable differences between persons.

3.113 The decision has been criticized[377] because of the distinctions drawn between the symbol of the crucifix in *Lautsi v Italy* (allowed in classrooms), and the symbol of the Islamic headscarf in *Dahlab v Switzerland* (banned from classrooms). In the latter case, the religious clothing was seen as powerful, as it was 'a sign that is immediately visible to others and provides a clear indication that the person concerned belongs to a particular religion'.[378] It is not altogether clear what makes the Islamic headscarf an 'active' symbol, and in *Dahlab v Switzerland* there was no evidence of the impact of the headscarf on children: the applicant had not received any complaints from either the children or parents.

3.114 The use of the margin of appreciation doctrine in *Lautsi v Italy* has also been criticized.[379] The principle is mentioned 27 times in the whole judgment and features eight times in the final paragraphs alone. Judge Malinverni,[380] in his dissenting opinion, stated that in the vast majority of the Council of Europe Member States, the presence of religious symbols is not specifically regulated at all.[381] It is only in Italy, Australia, certain German states,

---

[370] For discussion of neutrality and secularism in relation to the case, see I Leigh and R Ahdar, 'Post-secularism and the European Court of Human Rights: or how God never really went away' (2012) 75(6) MLR 1064.

[371] See *Kjeldsen, Busk Madsen and Pedersen v Denmark* (App 2095/71) (1976) paras 50–53; *Folgero v Norway* (App 15472/02) (2007) paras 78 and 84; and *Zengin v Turkey* (App 1448/04) (2007) paras 51–52.

[372] See *Lautsi* (n 365) para 64.

[373] Though the Court also accepted that the reference to the historical tradition within a state could not by itself relieve the state of its obligations to respect the rights and freedoms under the ECHR.

[374] See *Lautsi* (n 365) para 68.

[375] See *Lautsi* (n 365) para 69.

[376] *Lautsi* (n 365) para 60.

[377] See P Ronchi, 'Crucifixes, Margin of Appreciation and Consensus: The Grand Chamber Ruling in *Lautsi v Italy*' (2011) 13 Ecc LJ 287–97; Radacic (n 341); and F Cortese, 'The *Lautsi* Case: A Comment from Italy' (2011) 6 Religion and Human Rights 221.

[378] *Dahlab v Switzerland* (n 165) 2.

[379] See Ronchi (n 377); and Radacic (n 341). However, for a different view, see D McGoldrick, 'Religion in the European Public Square and in European Public Life—Crucifixes in the Classroom?' (2011) HRLR 11, 451, 502.

[380] Joined by Judge Kalaydjieva.

[381] *Lautsi* (n 365) para 1.

and Poland that the display of crucifixes is explicitly regulated. In some other countries (such as Ireland, Greece, and Malta) religious symbols are tolerated, and in others supreme courts have enforced their removal (Spain, Switzerland, and Germany). In only three countries are religious symbols strictly forbidden (France, Macedonia, and Georgia). Thus, as Judge Malinverni stated, it is difficult 'to draw definite conclusions regarding a European consensus'.[382] It is also interesting to note the difference in approach between this case and the case of *A, B and C v Ireland*,[383] decided by the Grand Chamber just a few months prior to it. There, despite broad consensus on the issue in question, the Court disregarded the notion of consensus and instead relied predominantly on Irish moral views.[384]

(6) Article 14 ECHR

a) Operation of Article 14

Article 14 provides: The enjoyment of the rights and freedoms set forth in this Convention shall be secured without discrimination on any ground such as sex, race, colour, language, religion, political or other opinion, national or social origin, association with a national minority, property, birth or other status. **3.115**

Article 14 is not a free-standing right. It protects against discrimination in respect of the other rights in the Convention. It is not necessary for such a right to be breached in order for there to be a breach of Article 14.[385] Article 14 has been described as being 'complementary' to the other Convention articles.[386] Even if a measure conforms with the free-standing Convention rights, it may yet violate Article 14 when read together with one or more of those rights if it operates in a discriminatory way.[387] **3.116**

It is necessary to consider whether there has been a breach of Article 14 in a number of different stages. **3.117**

The first question is whether the facts in issue fall within the 'ambit' of the free-standing right of the Convention which is relied on in conjunction with Article 14. The expression 'ambit' has generally been interpreted generously. The ECtHR has said that the facts will fall within the ambit of a Convention right where the disadvantage caused by the measure is 'linked to the exercise of the right guaranteed',[388] although it is not the case that any link, however tenuous, will suffice.[389] Article 14 may also apply where the state has provided for rights additional to those guaranteed by the Convention, where they are 'within the general scope of any Convention article'.[390] **3.118**

In the present context the most likely question will be whether the facts in issue fall within the 'ambit' of Article 9, although it may also be relevant to consider other articles.[391] The **3.119**

---

[382] *Lautsi* (n 365) para 1.
[383] *A, B and C v Ireland* (2011) 53 EHRR 13.
[384] See *A, B and C* (n 383) paras 226–228.
[385] See *Belgian Linguistics* (n 71) ('The Law', Part 1(B), para 9); *Van der Mussele v Belgium* (1983) 6 EHRR 163, para 43.
[386] See eg *National Union of Belgian Police v Belgium* (1975) 1 EHRR 578.
[387] *Marckx v Belgium* (1979) 2 EHRR 330.
[388] *Schmidt and Dalhlstrom v Sweden* (1976) 1 EHRR 632, para 39.
[389] eg *Botta v Italy* (1998) 26 EHRR 241.
[390] *Clift v UK* (App 7205/07) (2010); *EB v France* (2008) 47 EHRR 41, para 48.
[391] See eg *Paroisse Greco-Catholique Sambata Bihor v Romania* (App 48107/99) (2010), in which there was found a breach of Art 14 taken together with Art 6 as a result of national courts' inconsistent decisions on whether to judge disputes brought by Greek Catholic parishes (see especially paras 79–82).

ambit of Article 9 has been interpreted generously by the ECtHR. In *Thlimmenos v Greece*,[392] the applicant was prevented from being a chartered accountant because of a criminal conviction resulting from the fact that, as a Jehovah's Witness, he had refused to wear military uniform. The Court held that the facts fell within the ambit of Article 9 because his conviction was the result of the exercise of his Article 9 right.[393]

3.120 The second question is whether there is a difference of treatment between the claimant and other persons in relevantly similar or analogous situations. Not every difference in treatment is capable of amounting to a breach of Article 14. The ECtHR does not always engage in a separate analysis as to whether persons are in relevantly similar or analogous situations, sometimes focusing on whether the discriminatory effect of a measure is justifiable (the fourth question, see paragraph 3.123). Nevertheless, the Court has often dismissed complaints on the basis that the applicant has not identified a suitable comparator.[394]

3.121 A measure can give rise to a difference in treatment whether or not it is specifically aimed at a particular group. Article 14 prohibits unjustifiable discrimination. The ECtHR has not generally adopted an analysis depending on whether the discrimination is direct or indirect.[395]

3.122 The third question is whether the difference of treatment is on a ground protected by Article 14. Protection against discrimination on grounds of 'religion' is expressly forbidden by Article 14.

3.123 The fourth question is whether the difference in treatment is justifiable, in the sense of having 'no reasonable and objective justification'.[396] The existence of such justification is assessed in relation to the 'aims and effects' of the measure under consideration, with regard being had to the principles which normally prevail in democratic societies.[397] Justification requires that the measure in question have a legitimate aim and be proportionate to that aim.[398] The Court will rarely look behind the state's given explanation for the aim behind a measure. Where a case turns on justification, it will generally turn on whether a measure is a proportionate means of meeting the aim advanced.

3.124 The intensity of review of the proportionality of a measure will vary from case to case. However, in cases concerning differential treatment on grounds of religion, 'very weighty reasons' are required to justify the difference.[399] The margin of appreciation accorded to states in such cases will ordinarily be narrow. However, states are not required to show that there was no alternative non-discriminatory means of achieving the same aim.[400]

---

[392] *Thlimmenos v Greece* (2001) 31 EHRR 15, paras 41–42.

[393] See also *Kosteski v Former Yugoslav Republic of Macedonia* (2007) 45 EHRR 31, in which the ECtHR accepted that Art 9 did not provide for a right to take time off work to celebrate religious holidays, but held that Art 14 applied to national proceedings which related to the applicant's decision to take time off for those purposes and in which findings were made concerning the apparent genuineness of the applicant's beliefs.

[394] eg people in different types of occupation (eg *Van der Mussele* (n 385)), or having different residence (*Carson v UK* (2010) 51 EHRR 13), or with different property rights (*Palumbo v Italy* (App 15919/89) (2000)). See also the cases on the situations of married and unmarried couples, eg *PM v UK* (2006) 42 EHRR 45.

[395] It may be noted that the text of Article 14 draws no express contrast between direct and indirect discrimination.

[396] *Belgian Linguistics* (n 71) 284, para 34.

[397] *Belgian Linguistics* (n 71) para 34.

[398] *Belgian Linguistics* (n 71) para 34.

[399] See eg *Hoffmann v Austria* (n 22) para 36.

[400] *Rasmussen v Denmark* (1984) 7 EHRR 371, para 41.

b) The ECtHR's Approach

Breaches of Article 14 have been found where Jehovah's Witnesses had to perform civilian service but members of other religions did not;[401] where a Jehovah's Witness had been detained for refusing to undertake military service;[402] where particular churches were denied privileges concerning education and marriage that were available to other equivalent religious bodies;[403] and where particular churches did not have legal personality to take proceedings to protect their land and buildings although the Orthodox Church and Jewish Synagogue did.[404]

3.125

97 Members of the Gldani Congregation of Jehovah's Witnesses v Georgia[405] concerned an attack on the applicants which resulted in severe physical injuries and the confiscation and burning of their Bibles and other religious materials by a group of Orthodox believers. Although they had been alerted to the attack, the police had not intervened. Instead they took one of the victims into custody where he was again attacked by one of the Orthodox assailants. Little or no action was taken against the assailants, even though it was possible to have identified them, but one of the victims of the attack was prosecuted. The Court found breaches of Article 14 with Article 9 and Article 3 in its procedural aspects.[406]

3.126

In *Hoffmann v Austria*,[407] Articles 9 and 14 were found to have been breached by the refusal of custody to a mother on the basis that she was a Jehovah's witness. Her husband and children were Catholics. The Court held that although the protection of the children's rights was a legitimate aim, a distinction based essentially on a difference in religion alone was not acceptable.[408] In other cases, no breach has been found where a Jehovah's Witness mother has not been given custody because of objective facts about the mother's lifestyle rather than her religion as such.[409]

3.127

In *Thlimmenos v Greece*,[410] the Court upheld a complaint that the state had breached Articles 9 and 14 by *not* treating the applicant differently from others who were convicted of criminal offences. The applicant had been denied access to his accountancy profession because his conscientious objection had earned him a criminal record. The Court considered that this had no proper bearing on his fitness to be an accountant.

3.128

However the Court had not always found that differential treatment on grounds of religion breaches Article 14.

3.129

---

[401] *Gutl v Austria* (App 49686/99) (2009); *Loffelmann v Austria* (2010) 51 EHRR 37 (App 42967/98) (2008); *Lang v Austria* (2010) 51 EHRR 29 (App 28648/03) (2009).

[402] *Tsirlis and Koulompas v Greece* (1997) 25 EHRR 198 (see the Commission's Report, paras 117–120). The Court, having considered that there was a breach of Art 5, did not consider that a separate issue arose under Art 14.

[403] *Savez Crkva 'Riječ Života* (n 108) paras 85–93.

[404] *Canea Catholic Church* (n 19) breach of Art 14 read together with Art 6.

[405] *97 Members of the Gldani Congregation of Jehovah's Witnesses v Georgia* (2008) 46 EHRR 30.

[406] See also *Milanovic v Serbia* (App 44614/07) (2010), in which it was found that the authorities had failed to carry out their obligation to investigate whether attacks on the Hare Krishna community were religiously motivated, in breach of Article 14.

[407] *Hoffmann v Austria* (n 22).

[408] See also *Palau-Martinez v France* (2005) 41 EHRR 9.

[409] *Deschomets v France* (App 31956/02) (2006); *Islmailova v Russia* (App 37614/02) (29 November 2007) paras 58–63; *M and C v Romania* (App 29032/04) (2011) paras 140–149.

[410] *Thlimmenos* (n 204).

3.130   A nature of the historical relationship between the state and a particular established religion may justify favoured treatment for that religion. Thus, in *Moratilla v Spain*,[411] the exemption of the Catholic Church from tax was compatible with Articles 9 and 14, because the Catholic Church had entered into a concordat with the government that gave it obligations as well as advantages.[412] It may also be consistent with Article 14 for certain religions to be afforded special status, provided there is a fair mechanism for applying for that status. Thus in *Religionsgemeinschaft der Zeugen Jehovas v Austria*,[413] it was held to be contrary to Article 14 that Jehovah's Witnesses, as a registered religious community, were subject to more severe state control than religious societies.[414]

3.131   National circumstances may justify measures primarily directed at particular religious groups. In *Şahin v Turkey*,[415] students wearing the Islamic headscarf, or other symbols of religious faith, were prohibited from being admitted to educational activities at Istanbul University. The Grand Chamber of the ECtHR considered that the rule was not contrary to Article 14 for the same reasons that it was not contrary to Article 9 or Article 2 of the First Protocol to the Convention read on their own, namely the importance of the secular principle under the Turkish constitution, the need to ensure gender equality, and the need to protect people who chose not to wear headscarfs. The rule was intended to protect order and the secular nature of educational institutions.[416] In a series of admissibility decisions concerning France, it has been held that it is compatible with Article 14 to expel pupils from school for wearing religious symbols, because the national laws were designed to preserve the secular nature of the education system and applied equally to all conspicuous symbols.[417]

3.132   In *Cha'are Shalom Ve Tsedek v France*,[418] it was held to be not contrary to Article 14 read together with Article 9 for the authorities to refuse to allow a Jewish association to access slaughterhouses to perform ritual slaughter, but to grant approval to another Jewish association. The different treatment was justified by the need to protect public health and public order.

3.133   In *Eweida*,[419] it was unnecessary for the Chamber of the ECtHR to consider whether there was a breach of Article 14 read together with Article 9, given its finding that Article 9 had been breached.[420] In the cases of *Chaplin*[421] and *McFarlane*,[422] it similarly engaged in no

---

[411] *Moratilla v Spain* (App 17522/90) (1992) 72 DR 256.
[412] See further *Holy Monasteries* (n 157), finding it to be compatible with Art 14 for only property belonging to the monasteries of the Greek Orthodox church to be appropriated by the state, because of the close links between the church and the state; *Alujer Fernandez and Caballero Garcia v Spain* (App 53072/99) (2001), finding that it was justified for tax rules to favour donations to the Catholic church but not to other churches, in circumstances where there was a reciprocal arrangement between Spain and the Holy See and donations were voluntary.
[413] *Religionsgemeinschaft der Zeugen Jehovas v Austria* (n 21) paras 97–99.
[414] See also *Koppi v Austria* (2011) 52 EHRR 10.
[415] *Şahin* (n 10). See paras 3.100–3.104.
[416] See paras 3.112–3.149, 3.183–3.188, 3.191.
[417] *Aktas v France* (n 335); *Bayrak v France* (n 335); *Gamaleddyn v France* (App 18527/08) (2009); *Ghazal v France* (n 335); *Jasvir Singh v France* (n 335); *Ranjit Singh v France* (App 27561/08) (2009).
[418] *Cha'are Shalom Ve Tsedek v France* (n 149).
[419] *Eweida and ors v UK* (2013) 57 EHRR 213.
[420] *Eweida* (n 419) para 95.
[421] *Eweida and ors v UK* (App 59842/10) (2013).
[422] *McFarlane* (n 315).

separate analysis of Article 14 from that of Article 9.[423] Notably, Ms Ladele's case[424] was argued solely on the basis that the termination of her employment because she refused to be designated as a registrar of civil partnerships was in breach of Article 14 taken together with Article 9.[425] The Court accepted that Article 14 was applicable on the basis that that the applicant's objection to participating in the creation of same-sex civil partnerships was directly motivated by her religious beliefs.[426] It considered that the relevant comparator was a registrar with no religious objection to same-sex unions, and agreed that the local authority's rule requiring her designation had a particularly detrimental impact on her because of her religious beliefs.[427] However, it found that the aim pursued by the authority, which included the provision of a service which complied with the policy of being committed to the promotion of equal opportunities and non-discrimination against others (including on the basis of sexual orientation), was legitimate,[428] and the termination of Ms Ladele's employment proportionate to that aim. In particular, the local authority's policy aimed to secure the rights of others which are also protected under the Convention.[429]

(7) Bringing an ECHR claim: procedure and remedies[430]

The Strasbourg court faces an unprecedented level of demand and has serious caseload issues **3.134** with a substantial backlog of cases having built up.[431] It is unsurprising that there are a number of admissibility and procedural hurdles for applicants to satisfy.

a) Who is entitled to bring a claim?

Article 9 states that 'everyone' has the benefit of the freedoms which it protects.[432] However, **3.135** elsewhere in the Convention more exacting requirements are set out which applicants must satisfy before they can bring a claim to the Court. Specifically, Article 34 sets out the standing requirements for who is entitled to bring a claim under the Convention:

> The Court may receive applications from any person, non-governmental organisation or group of individuals claiming to be the victim of a violation by one of the High Contracting Parties of the rights set forth in the Convention or the Protocols thereto. The High Contracting Parties undertake not to hinder in any way the effective exercise of this right.

---

[423] *McFarlane* (n 315) paras 101 and 109 respectively.

[424] *Ladele* (n 314).

[425] *Ladele* (n 314) para 103.

[426] *Ladele* (n 314) para 103.

[427] *Ladele* (n 314) para 104.

[428] *Ladele* (n 314) para 105.

[429] *Ladele* (n 314) para 106.

[430] For a full analysis see: L Zwaak, 'The Procedure before the European Court of Human Rights' in van Dijk, van Hoof, van Rijn, and Zwaak (eds) (n 23) 95–290; K Reid (ed), *A Practitioner's Guide to the European Convention on Human Rights*, (4th edn, Sweet & Maxwell, 2011) 7–56; and P Leach, *Taking a Case to the European Court of Human Rights* (OUP, 2011) 16–77.

[431] See, *inter alia*, <http://assembly.coe.int/Communication/pressajdoc29_2012rev.pdf>; Keller et al, 'Debating the future of the European Court of Human Rights after the Interlaken conference: two innovative proposals' (2010) 21(4) EJIL 1025; A Lester, 'The European Court of Human Rights after 50 years' (2009) 4 EHRLR 461; L Caflisch, 'The reform of the European Court of Human Rights: Protocol No. 14 and beyond' (2006) 6(2) HRLR 403; and L Wildhaber, 'The European Convention on Human Rights and international law' (2007) 56(2) ICLQ 217.

[432] See *Kustannus AB v Finland* (1996) 85 A DR 29, 43.

This Article therefore has two components: first, an applicant must be a person, an NGO, or group of individuals; and secondly, the applicant must be a 'victim'. Each will be dealt with in turn.

3.136 Initially, the Commission refused standing to churches.[433] However, this position was reversed in *X and the Church of Scientology v Sweden*,[434] so that it is now established that a Church body,[435] or an association with religious and philosophical objects,[436] is capable of possessing and exercising the rights to manifest beliefs contained in Article 9.[437] Church or religious bodies also have the right to exercise the rights guaranteed by Article 9 on behalf of their adherents.[438] At paragraph 70 of *X and the Church of Scientology v Sweden* the Commission remarked:

> The [Commission] is now of the opinion that the... distinction between the Church and its [individual] members under Article 9(1) is essentially artificial. When a church body lodges an application under the Convention, it does so in reality, on behalf of its members. It should therefore be accepted that a church body is capable of possessing and exercising the rights contained in Article 9(1) in its own capacity as representative of its members.

3.137 This approach is welcome.[439] It ends refusals to deal with cases of potentially widespread government action against particular religious groups on technical grounds. Churches or religious bodies may be in a stronger position to bring a case than private individuals. It strengthens the positions of vulnerable groups.

3.138 However, representative religious status has not been extended to commercial bodies. In *Kustannus Oy Vapaa Ajattelija Ab v Finland*,[440] the applicant company (set up with the primary aim of publishing and selling books promoting the aims of the free-thinkers' philosophical movement) had been required to pay a church tax, a requirement upheld by the domestic courts as the company was a commercial enterprise rather than a religious community. In holding that there was no Article 9 violation, the Commission stated:

> ... The Company form may have been a deliberate choice on the part of the applicant association and its branches for the pursuance of part of the freethinkers' activities. Nevertheless, for the purposes of domestic law this applicant was registered as a corporate body with limited liability. As such it is in principle required by domestic law to pay tax as any other corporate body, regardless of the underlying purpose of its activities on account of its links with the applicant association and its branches and irrespective of the final receiver of the tax revenues collected from it.

---

[433] *Church of X v UK* (1968) 13 YB 306.

[434] *X and the Church of Scientology* (n 37).

[435] This includes church parishes: *Hautaniemi v Sweden* (1996) 85 A DR 94, 96. For the fact that legal status or personality can be given to a religious organization, see *Metropolitan Church of Bessarabia* (n 114).

[436] *Omkarananda and Divine Light Zentrum* (n 37).

[437] See also *Chappell v UK* (n 37); *Moscow Branch of the Salvation Army* (n 12); *Church of Scientology Moscow* (n 101); *Religionsgemeinschaft der Zugen Jehovas* (n 21); and *Leela Forderkreis EV and ors v Germany* (2009) 49 EHRR 117, para 79.

[438] *Supreme Holy Council of the Muslim Community v Bulgaria* (2005) 41 EHRR 3, para 74; *Cha'are Shalom Ve Tsedek* (n 149) para 72; and *Canea Catholic Church* (n 19) para 31.

[439] See C Evans (n 4) 15. Cf P Van Dijk and JGH Van Hoof, *Theory and Practice of the ECHR* (2nd edn, Kluwer, 1990) 405.

[440] *Kustannus Oy Vapaa Ajattelija Ab v Finland* (1996) 2 ECHR CD 69.

Thus, the limited liability company, although just an umbrella organization for the Finnish freethinkers movement, was held to be liable for the church tax as a corporate body regardless of its links with the philosophical association.

Furthermore, only individuals can have thoughts or consciences so these freedoms can-**3.139** not be relied on by corporations[441] or associations.[442] In *Kontakt-Infromation-Thereapie and Hagen v Austria*,[443] the applicant association was a private, non-profit making organization operating drug abuse rehabilitation centres, which had imposed upon it a duty to disclose information relating to their clients. The Commission rejected this part of the application *ratione personae*:

> …the association does not claim to be a victim of a violation of its own Convention rights. Moreover, the rights primarily invoked, i.e. the right to freedom of conscience…are by their very nature not susceptible of being exercised by a legal person such as a private association. Insofar as Article 9 is concerned, the Commission considers that a distinction must be made in this respect between the freedom of conscience and the freedom of religion, which can also be exercised as a church as such…[444]

The religious group must be a non-governmental body, albeit the fact that there may be a close **3.140** connection between the religious group and the state does not necessarily preclude the group from seeking redress.[445]

Turning to the second requirement in Article 34 that the applicant[446] must be a 'victim',[447] the **3.141** Court has taken a rather restrictive reading of this condition.[448] This can be seen from *Swiss Muslim League v Switzerland*,[449] which concerned a challenge under Articles 9 and 14 about a constitutional amendment to ban the construction of minarets which was passed after a referendum. The action was brought by three associations and a foundation whose aims included promoting the understanding of culture in Switzerland and the integration of Muslims in Swiss society. Under Convention law, one can be a 'victim' in three senses: directly,[450] indirectly,[451] or potentially. It was held that the association fell into none of these categories. None of the

---

[441] *Company X v Switzerland* (1981) 16 DR 85.

[442] *Kontakt-Infromation-Therapie and Hagen v Austria* (1988) 57 DR 81.

[443] *Kontakt-Infromation-Therapie and Hagen* (n 442). For the fact that associations are not capable of exercising the right of freedom of conscience, see also *Vereniging Rechtswinkels Utrecht* (n 20) (prisoners' rights association).

[444] *Kontakt-Infromation-Thereapie and Hagen* (n 442) 6.

[445] *Holy Monasteries* (n 157) 20 EHRR 1; and *Finska Forsamlingen I Stockholm and Hautaniemi v Sweden* (App 24019/94) (1996).

[446] Applications can be brought only by living persons or on their behalf; a deceased person cannot lodge an application even through a representative—see *Kaya and Polat v Turkey* (App 22729/93) (1998). However, the victim's death does not automatically mean that a case is struck out of the Court's list.

[447] The notion of 'victim' is interpreted autonomously and irrespective of domestic rules—see *Gorraiz Lizarraga and ors v Spain* (App 62543/00) (2004) para 35. The applicant must retain the status as 'victim' throughout the proceedings—see *Burdov v Russia* (App 59498/00) (2002) para 30.

[448] However, the Court has stated that the interpretation of the term 'victim' is liable to evolve over time in the light of conditions in contemporary society—see *Monnat v Switzerland* (App 73604/01) (2006) paras 30–33, and *Stukus and ors v Poland* (App 12534/03) (2008) para 35.

[449] *Swiss Muslim League v Switzerland* (App 66274/09) (2011), unreported 28 June 2011 ECtHR. See also *Ouardiri v Switzerland* (App 65840/09) (2011), regarding a Muslim resident who challenged the same constitutional ban on the building of minarets under Arts 9 and 14, whose application was rejected for similar reasons.

[450] See eg *Ammur v France* (App 19776/92) (1996) para 36, and *Karner v Austria* (App 40016/98) (2003) para 25.

[451] See eg *Yasa v Turkey* (App 1709/05) (1999) para 66.

associations had the aim of constructing mosques with minarets so they were therefore not direct victims. Since they were legal entities they could not be indirect victims. As for being potential victims, the case law has recognized a number of situations as falling under this category: those who are unable to show whether they have been a victim of a breach of the Convention because of the secrecy of the measure in question; those who have been forced to modify their behaviour under pain of criminal sanctions; and those who fall within a category of people who may become directly affected by the legislation under scrutiny. None of the associations could show that the constitutional amendment had any real effect on them: there had been no reduction in their memberships nor a loss of prestige. They were therefore not potential victims either, since Article 34 does not allow abstract complaints alleging a violation simply because domestic law appears to contravene the Convention.[452]

b) Admissibility criteria[453]

3.142 *Non-exhaustion of domestic remedies.* Article 35(1), states that the Court 'may only deal with the matter after all domestic remedies have been exhausted'. This rule affords the national authorities the opportunity to prevent or to put right the alleged violations of the Convention before a case is brought to the ECtHR. The requirement to exhaust domestic remedies may be waived by the state in question.[454] Both the Commission and the Court have applied the rule flexibly in circumstances where its application would have been excessively formalistic.[455] Thus, the Court has held that it would be unduly formalistic to require the applicants to avail themselves of a remedy which even the highest court of the country had not obliged them to use.[456] The rule is also inapplicable where seeking the domestic remedy is futile or ineffective due to a repetition of acts incompatible with the Convention or official tolerance by the State authorities has been shown to exist,[457] and where requiring the applicant to use a particular domestic remedy would be unreasonable in practice or provide a disproportionate obstacle.[458]

3.143 *Time limit.* According to Article 35(1) the Court can only deal with the matter 'within a period of six months from the date on which the final [domestic] decision was taken'. This ensures that cases are examined within a reasonable time and protects the authorities from being in a position of uncertainty for a long period of time. The sixth-month period starts running from the date on which the applicant or his representative has sufficient knowledge of the final domestic decision.[459]

3.144 *Redundancy.* As stated in Article 35(2)(b), the Court 'shall not deal with any application...that...is substantially the same as a matter that has already been examined by the Court or has already been submitted to another procedure of international investigation or settlement and contains no relevant new information'. An application is considered 'substantially the same' where the parties, the complaints, and the facts are identical.[460]

---

[452] See *Monnat v Switzerland* (n 448) paras 21–32.
[453] Under ECHR, Art 32, it is the Court itself that is judge of its own jurisdiction.
[454] See *De Wilde, Ooms and Versyp v Belgium* (Apps 2832/66, 2835/66, and 2899/66) (1972) para 55.
[455] See *Ringeisen v Austria* (App 2614/65) (1972) para 89; and *Kozacioglu v Turkey* (App 2334/03) (2009).
[456] *DH and ors v the Czech Republic* (2006) 43 EHRR 41, paras 116–118.
[457] See *Aksoy v Turkey* (App 21987/93) (1996) para 52.
[458] See *Veriter v France* (App 31508/07) (2010) para 27, and *Gaglione and ors v Italy* (App 45867/07 and 69 more) (2010) para 22.
[459] See *Koc and Tosun v Turkey* (App 23852/04) (2008).
[460] See *Verein gegen Tierfabriken Schweiz (VgT) v Switzerland (No 2)* (App 32772/02) (2009) para 63.

Abuse of application. According to Article 35(3)(a), the Court will 'declare inadmissible any **3.145** individual application ... if it considers that ... the application is incompatible with the provisions of the Convention or the Protocols thereto, manifestly ill-founded or an abuse of the right of individual application'. Any applicant's conduct that is contrary to the purpose of the right of individual application or impedes the proper function of the Court or its proceedings will constitute an abuse.[461] This can happen in four situations: (a) misleading the Court;[462] (b) using vexatious, insulting, threatening, or provocative language;[463] (c) breaching confidentiality;[464] and (d) advancing an application which is manifestly vexatious or devoid of any real purpose.[465] 'Manifestly ill-founded' complaints are those which treat the Court as one of first instance,[466] complaints where there has clearly been no violation, unsubstantiated complaints,[467] and confused or far-fetched complaints.

No significant disadvantage. With the entry into force of Protocol No 14[468] on 1 June 2010, **3.146** a new admissibility criteria was added to Article 35(3)(b). This now provides:

> The Court shall declare inadmissible any individual application ... if it considers that ... the applicant has not suffered a significant disadvantage, unless respect for human rights as defined in the Convention and the Protocols thereto requires an examination of the application on the merits and provided that no case may be rejected on this ground which has not been duly considered by a domestic tribunal.

This criterion of 'significant disadvantage' hinges on the idea that a violation of a right, however real from a strict legal perspective, should attain a minimum level of severity to warrant consideration by an international court.

Strike Out. At any stage of the proceedings, the Court can decide to strike an application out **3.147** of its case list,[469] for example where the applicant does not intend to pursue his application, or the matter has been resolved.

c) Future admissibility criteria developments

Brighton Declaration.[470] At the High Level Conference of the Council of Europe at the insti-**3.148** gation of the UK Presidency, 19–20 April 2012, the Brighton Declaration was made and subsequently adopted by all 47 Council of Europe Member States. The relevant paragraphs, in summary, highlight the following themes: that states parties should bear the primary burden of implementing the Convention, and should thereby reduce the number of cases which proceed to the ECtHR (paragraph 7); that states parties enjoy a margin of appreciation in their implementation of Convention rights (paragraph 11); and that the Convention system is subsidiary to the safeguarding of human rights at national level and that national

---

[461] See *Mirolubovs and ors v Latvia* (App 798/05) (2009), para 62, which also states that the rejection of an application on the grounds of abuse is an exceptional measure.

[462] See eg *Varbanov v Bulgaria* (App 31365/96) (2000) para 36.

[463] See eg *Duringer and Grunge v France* (Apps 61164/00 and 18589/02) (2003); and *Stamoulakatos v UK* (App 27567/95) (1997).

[464] See eg *Popov v Moldova* (App 74153/01) (2005) para 48.

[465] See eg *Philis v Greece* (App 18989/91) (1994).

[466] See eg *Kemmache v France (No 3)* (App 17621/91) (1994) para 44. The Court may not, therefore, question the findings and conclusions of the domestic court regarding: facts of the case, interpretation of domestic law, admissibility of evidence at trial, or the guilt or innocence of the accused in criminal proceedings.

[467] See Rules of Court, r 47, and r 44C(1).

[468] See <http://www.coe.int/t/dghl/standardsetting/cddh/GT_GDR_A/R2ADDII_e.pdf>.

[469] See ECHR, Art 37.

[470] See further M Elliott, 'After Brighton: between a rock and a hard place' (2012) Public Law 619.

authorities are in principle better placed than an international court to evaluate local needs and conditions (paragraph 11). In the light of these principles, the following key recommendations are made: (1), that a power to issue advisory opinions be granted to the Court (paragraph 12(d)); (2) that the time limit under Article 35(1) of the Convention be shortened (paragraph 15(a)); (3) that the proviso in Article 35(3)(b) of the Convention that no application be declared inadmissible on 'serious disadvantage' grounds where there has been no due consideration by a domestic court be deleted (paragraph 15(d)); (4) that the Court be empowered to make a separate decision on admissibility at the request of the respondent government when there is a particular interest in having the Court rule on the effectiveness of a domestic remedy which is at issue in the case (paragraph 15(f)); and (5) that the Court should not consider domestic remedies to be exhausted unless the applicant has argued the Convention point in front of national courts (paragraph 15(g)).

3.149   *Draft Protocols 15.* This is the first of two new proposed Protocols which will amend the admissibility criteria. Article 1 makes reference to the principle of subsidiarity and the margin of appreciation doctrine, emphasizing that it is the contracting states that have 'the primary responsibility to secure the rights and freedoms defined in this Convention and the Protocols thereto'.

3.150   The remainder of the Protocol has two effects. First, it will amend Article 35(1) by reducing the period following the date of the final domestic decision within which an application must be made to the Court from six months to four (Article 4 of the Protocol). This is predicated on the grounds that the development of swifter communications technology, along with the time limits of similar length in force in the Member States, allow for the reduction of the time limit. Secondly, it will amend Article 35(3)(b) containing the admissibility criterion concerning 'significant disadvantage' by deleting the proviso that the case has to have been duly considered by a domestic tribunal (Article 5 of the Protocol). This amendment is intended to give greater effect to the maxim *de minimis non curat praetor*.

3.151   *Draft Protocol 16.* This is the second of two new proposed Protocols which will amend the admissibility criteria. This draft Protocol introduces the 'advisory opinion' (at Article 1(1)). By stating that relevant courts or tribunals 'may' request that the Court give an advisory opinion (Article 1(2)), this amendment makes clear that it is optional for them to do so and is not in any way obligatory, in accordance with the principle of subsidiarity. The Court also has a discretion to accept a request or not, although in principle a request should be accepted if it satisfies the relevant criteria by relating to an appropriate question (as defined in Article 1(1)) and the requesting court or tribunal fulfilling the procedural requirements (Article 1(2) and (3)). The panel must give reasons for any refusal to accept a national court or tribunal's request for an advisory opinion. This is intended to reinforce dialogue between the Court and national judicial systems.

d) Remedies

3.152   *Just satisfaction.* Article 41 ECHR reads as follows: 'If the Court finds that there has been a violation of the Convention or the Protocols thereto, and if the internal law of the High Contracting Party concerned allows only partial reparation to be made, the Court shall, if necessary, afford just satisfaction to the injured party.'

3.153   The award of just satisfaction is not an automatic consequence of a finding that there has been a violation of a Convention right—it will only be provided if domestic law does not allow complete reparation to be made and, even then, only 'if necessary' and if the award is considered 'just'. For this latter requirement the Court will take into account the context of the case, including whether a mere finding of a violation is a satisfactory result, the applicant's own conduct, and the local economic circumstances. Formal requirements for submitting claims for just satisfaction are laid down in rule 60 of the Rules of Court. Of more immediate assistance is the Practice Direction, issued by the President of the Court in accordance with rule 32 of the Rules of Court on 28 March 2007, on just satisfaction claims. This identifies the formal requirements, and then addresses the substantive requirements for submitting claims. The jurisprudence of the Court on issues of just satisfaction is remarkably undeveloped.

Just satisfaction can be afforded in respect of pecuniary damage, non-pecuniary damage (such as mental or physical suffering), and costs and expenses. A clear causal link must be established between the damage claimed and the violation of the Convention. The purpose of just satisfaction is not to punish the responsible state, but instead to compensate the applicant for the actual consequences of the Convention violation. No claims for 'punitive', 'aggravated', or 'exemplary' damages will be entertained.   **3.154**

If the Court finds there has been a violation, it may award the applicant 'just satisfaction',   **3.155** usually a sum of money in compensation for certain forms of damage. The Court may also require the state concerned to refund the applicant's expenses incurred in presenting his or her case. If the Court finds that there has been no violation, the applicant will not have to pay any additional costs, such as those incurred by the respondent state. Although just satisfaction is normally in the form of a sum of money to be paid by the respondent Member State to the victim, in rare cases the Court can consider a consequential order aiming to put an end to a violation or to remedy it.

The judgment of the Court is binding. As stated in Article 46(1): 'The High Contracting   **3.156** Parties undertake to abide by the final judgment of the Court in any case to which they are parties.'

The Court is not empowered to annul national laws. Furthermore, the Court is not responsi-   **3.157** ble for the execution of its judgments; as soon as it has given judgment, responsibility passes to the Committee of Ministers of the Council of Europe, which has the task of supervising execution and ensuring that any compensation is paid.[471]

e) Level of damages in Article 9 cases

Recent findings of violations in respect of Article 9 alone have tended to result in awards not   **3.158** exceeding €5,000–6,000 for non-pecuniary damage. In *Eweida*, Ms Ewieda was awarded €2,000 for the anxiety, frustration, and stress caused by the violation of Article 9 she had suffered,[472] while in *Jakóbski v Poland*,[473] the applicant was awarded €3,000 after alleging he was forced to survive on food parcels from his family when prison authorities refused to meet his dietary requirements. The award in *Lautsi v Italy* (subsequently overturned by the Grand Chamber),[474], amounted to €5,000 for breach of Ms Lautsi's right to educate her children in line with her own religious convictions; and in *Tsatsuryan v Armenia*,[475] the applicant was

---

[471] See ECHR, Art 46(2), (3), (4), and (5).
[472] *Eweida and ors v UK* (n 419) para 114.
[473] *Jakóbski v Poland* (App 18429/06) (2010).
[474] *Lautsi* (n 365).
[475] *Tsatsuryan v Armenia* (App 37821/03) (2012).

awarded €6,000 for a punishment for conscientious objection forced on him which was found to be 'wholly disproportionate in a modern democratic state'.[476]

3.159 A combination of different violations will be considered an aggravating factor, and will often result in a higher reward. Two applicants in *O'Donoghue and others v United Kingdom*[477] received €8,500 jointly in respect of non-pecuniary damage for violations of Article 12 and Article 9 caused by an Approval Scheme for marriages to foreign nationals. A noticeably higher award was made in the case of *Metropolitan Church of Bessarabia v Moldova*,[478] where the applicant church was awarded €20,000 as a result of being prohibited from conducting divine service, meeting to worship, and having judicial protection of their assets (the court found a violation of Articles 9 and 13).

3.160 Findings of violations of Article 14 in conjunction with Article 9 result in a similar level of award. In *Religionsgemeinschaft der Zeugen Jehovas and others v Austria*,[479] the applicants were awarded €10,000 non-pecuniary damages as a result of inability to register under the Religious Communities Act 1998. With regard to the first two applicants in *Kimlya and others v Russia*,[480] the Court awarded €5,000 in respect non-pecuniary damage for refusal to be registered as a local religious organization, but held that a finding of violation was sufficient just satisfaction for the third applicant (a religious group without any legal status).

3.161 Recent conscientious objection cases have resulted in non-pecuniary damage awards between €6,000 (for a violation of Article 9 alone)[481] and €15,000 (for a violation of Article 3, Article 9, and Article 6(1)).[482] For a violation of Articles 9 and 6, the Court made an award of €10,000.[483]

B. Religious Rights in the Context of the European Union

(1) Introduction

3.162 The role in EU law of religious rights, and of human rights as a whole, has changed dramatically since the Communities were first founded. While the EEC and Euratom Treaties were almost exclusively economic in focus, the central position of fundamental rights is now expressly recognized both in EU primary law and in the jurisprudence of the Court of Justice of the European Union (CJEU). The Court's case law in this regard was initially developed by reference to 'general principles of EU law' and to the ECHR; as of 2009, the European Charter of Fundamental Rights (the 'Charter') has represented a binding codification of these developments which is part of the body of EU primary law.

3.163 Religious rights form part of the body of fundamental rights protected by EU law. As well as having been considered in express terms for over 30 years by the CJEU[484] and having

---

476 *Tsatsuryan v Armenia* (n 475) para 40.
477 *O'Donoghue and ors v UK* (App 34848/07) (2010).
478 *Metropolitan Church of Bessarabia v Moldova* (App 45701/99) (2001).
479 *Religionsgemeinschaft der Zeugen Jehovas* (n 21).
480 *Kimlya & ors v Russia* (App 76836/01) (2009).
481 *Bukharatyan v Armenia* (App 37819/03) (2012).
482 *Feti Demirtaş v Turkey* (App 5260/07) (2012).
483 *Ercep v Turkey* (n 206).
484 See para 3.179.

always had a place in the European Union's anti-discrimination principles, rights relating to freedom of religion and belief now enjoy express protection by virtue of Article 10 of the Charter. This section will consider the interaction of the elements which have contributed to developing the framework for the protection of fundamental rights as a whole in European law, and will then explore the substantive and practical principles which govern the approach to religion in that context.

(2) Overview: fundamental rights within the EU framework

a) Introductory comments

Section (b) (paragraphs 3.165–3.168) provides an overview of the development of fundamental rights in the context of the European Union, and sets out some background to the relationship between the EU and ECHR systems.[485] Section (c) (paragraphs 3.169–3.171) will consider their current role in the light of the fact that the European Charter of Fundamental Rights (hereinafter, 'the Charter') has become primary law, and the fact that the European Union[486] is now required to become a party to the ECHR.[487]

3.164

b) The development of fundamental rights in the European Union

Originally, the two supranational European legal systems established in the aftermath of the Second World War had entirely distinct competences. The European Economic Community focused on the harmonization and protection of transnational trade and industry, while the purpose of the ECHR was to encourage cooperation in the field of human rights. Given these separate spheres of protection, there was almost no concern for fundamental rights in the Treaty of Rome and the Euratom Treaty.[488] However, as the European Communities grew more integrated and the scope of their competences increased, interference with the interests of individuals became increasingly common when implementing Community Law. After initial resistance to attempts by litigants to invoke fundamental rights, the CJEU signalled a marked change in attitude when referring to 'the fundamental human rights enshrined in the general principles of Community law' in *Stauder v City of Ulm*;[489] from this point onwards, the Community took an increasingly active approach in terms of both the jurisprudence of the European Court, and the substantive protection afforded by the Treaties themselves. The ECHR and the case law of the Strasbourg Court formed a natural point of reference throughout this development, although the CJEU was conscious of the difficulties inherent in purporting to bind Member States to ECHR provisions by virtue of its interpretation of EU law (but see paragraph 3.171 for the current negotiation process for the European Union's accession to the ECHR).

3.165

---

[485] An exhaustive survey of this complex area is beyond the scope of this section; for an in-depth analysis, see P Craig and G De Búrca (eds), 'Human Rights in the EU' in *EU Law: Text, Cases and Materials* (5th edn, OUP, 2011) ch 11.

[486] The EU has gained its own legal personality by virtue of TFEU, Art 47.

[487] By virtue of TEU, Art 6(2).

[488] There was concern from the start to protect rights that affected workers; see, notably, TEEC, Art 119 (now TFEU, Art 157) guaranteeing equality between men and women in respect of pay. See also AG Toth, 'The Individual and European Law' (1975) 24 ICLQ 659, 667: 'the essentially economic character of the Communities...[made] the possibility of their encroaching upon fundamental human values, such as life, personal liberty, freedom of opinion, conscience etc very unlikely'.

[489] Case 29/69 *Erich Stauder v City of Ulm* [1969] ECR 419, para 7. In this decision, an EU measure concerning a subsidized butter scheme for welfare recipients was construed in a manner consistent with protection for human dignity.

3.166 After *Stauder*,[490] references to the importance of fundamental human rights in CJEU judgments became more assertive. In *Internationale Handelsgesellschaft*,[491] the Court stated that human rights formed an 'integral part of the general principles of European law', and that their protection 'must be ensured within the framework of the structure and objectives of the Community'.[492] However, the judgments stopped short of detailing principles beyond the scope of Community competence;[493] and the Court was careful to set the boundaries of fundamental rights under EU law in line with the common protection afforded by Member States' national legal systems.[494] Where claimants sought to rely on protection with regard to activities which fell outside the scope of EU law, general principles had no effect.[495]

3.167 As fundamental human rights assumed an increasingly important role in the Community (and later, the Union), it was natural that they should be developed by reference to the coexisting system of human rights protection in Europe. The ECHR had always been of particular significance in the CJEU's jurisprudence,[496] and the Court stated in *Johnston v Ulster Constabulary* that 'as the European Parliament, Council and Commission recognised in their joint declaration of 5 April 1977 . . . and as the Court has recognised in its decisions, the principles on which [the ECHR] is based must be taken into consideration in Community Law'.[497] This falls short of suggesting that ECHR principles are binding, but the CJEU often ruled that particular aspects of EU legislation constituted the Union's manifestation of general principles enshrined in the ECHR.[498] The Court asserted in a judgment underlining its commitment to fundamental rights, that 'international treaties for the protection for human rights on which the Member States have collaborated or of which they are signatories, can supply guidelines which should be followed within the framework of Community law',[499] and it is clear that the CJEU was willing to look closely at ECtHR case law for guidance. However, the Court was careful not to rule that the ECHR was formally incorporated into the EU legal order, as this would have equated to judicial incorporation of an international

---

[490] See *Erich Stauder* (n 489).

[491] Case 11/70 *Internationale Handelsgesellschaft GmbH v Einfuhr- und Vorratsstelle für Getreide und Futtermittel* [1970] ECR 1125.

[492] *Internationale Handelsgesellschaft mbH* (n 491) para 4.

[493] A paradigmatic example of this tension can be found in the reaction of the German court upon the return of *Internationale Handelsgesellschaft*, known as the *Solange I* judgment: 'in the hypothetical case of a conflict between Community law and . . . the guarantees of fundamental rights in the Constitution . . . the guarantee of fundamental rights in the Constitution prevails as long as the competent organs of the Community have not removed the conflict of norms in accordance with the Treaty mechanism' [1974] CMLR 540, 550.

[494] See eg Cases 46/87 and 227/88 *Hoechst AG v Commission* [1989] ECR 2859, where the Court surveyed the protection offered in different Member States concerning the inviolability of the home and ruled that EU protection of that right must be recognized only insofar as it is recognized by all Member States in common (at para 17); a similar principle with regard to the scope of protection for the confidentiality of written communications between lawyers and their clients was upheld in Case 155/79 *AM & S Europe Ltd v Commission* [1982] ECR 1575.

[495] See eg Case 159/90 *Society for the Protection of the Unborn Child v Grogan* [1999] ECR I-04685, paras 30–31.

[496] And in the Treaties themselves; see para 3.168.

[497] Case 222/84 *Marguerite Johnston v Chief Constable of the Royal Ulster Constabulary* [1986] ECR 1651, para 18.

[498] See judgments concerning EU legislation on, for example, powers to limit free movement and residence (Case 36/75 *Rutili v Minister for the Interior* [1974] ECR 1219), rights concerning access to judicial protection (Case C-424/99 *Commission v Austria* [2001] ECR I-9285, paras 45–47), rights against sex discrimination (Case C-185/97 *Coote v Granada Hospitality* [1988] ECR I-5199, paras 21–23), and privacy and data protection (Cases C-465/00, 138, and 139/01 *Rechnungshof v Österreichischer Rundfunk* [2003] ECR I-2629, para 14).

[499] Case 4/73 *J Nold, Kohlen- und Baustoffgroßhandlung v Commission* [1974] ECR 491, para 13.

agreement into EU law without the consent of Member States.[500] Now the status of ECHR provisions with regard to the interpretation of EU legislation has become more certain, at least insofar as they correspond with provisions in the Charter (see paragraph 3.170).

The increasing significance of fundamental rights in the Community (and later, Union) legal order has not been purely as a result of the efforts of the CJEU: their progressive importance is reflected in amendments to the Treaties.[501] Equality in pay between men and women was a feature of the Treaty of Rome,[502] and the institutions had competence to combat discrimination in general (including on religious grounds).[503] By the time of the Maastricht Treaty, human rights were sufficiently on the Community agenda that a duty to protect them was inserted into the preamble of the founding treaty; this did not confer a legal obligation, but was a significant step towards recognition of the importance of fundamental rights in the exercise of the Union's competences. The Treaty of Amsterdam eventually recognized human rights and fundamental freedoms as guaranteed by the ECHR, as well as the constitutional traditions of the Member States, as being one of the foundations of the Union under Article 6(2) TEU. It removed the employment-focused parameters from the protection against all forms of discrimination in primary European law by virtue of Article 13.[504] By this time it was evident that human rights were high on list of the Union's priorities, and all Member States had by this point become parties to the ECHR, the European Social Charter (ESC), and the Organization for Security and Co-operation in Europe (OSCE). Nonetheless, it was not until recently that the European Union adopted its own comprehensive code of human rights within its body of primary law.

c) Current status of fundamental rights: the Treaties, the Charter and Accession to the ECHR

The year 2000 saw the proclamation of the Charter of Fundamental Rights of the European Union at the Nice European Council Summit.[505] It represented a codification of the existing CJEU and ECtHR case law, the ECHR, the EU Treaties, the Social Charters, and the common traditions of the Member States.[506] It did not become a part of EU primary law at that time, nor was it in any way legally binding; nonetheless, the European Court immediately started to refer to it in its judgments.[507] The ratification of the Treaty of Lisbon saw the Charter become primary EU law.[508]

3.168

3.169

---

[500] See eg AG Trabucchi's discussion in Case 118/75 *Watson and Belmann* [1976] ECR 1185, 1207.

[501] See in general P Twomey, 'The European Union: Three Pillars without a Human Rights Foundation' in D O'Keefe and P Twomey (eds), *Legal Issues of the Maastricht Treaty* (Chancery, 1994) 121–31.

[502] See n 488.

[503] TEEC, Art 13.

[504] TEEC, Art 13 (now TFEU, Art 19):

> Without prejudice to the other provisions of this Treaty and within the limits of the powers conferred by it upon the Community, the Council, acting unanimously on a proposal from the Commission and after consulting the European Parliament, may take appropriate action to combat discrimination based on sex, racial or ethnic origin, religion or belief, disability, age or sexual orientation.

[505] See generally (2001) 8(1) Maastricht Journal of European and Comparative Law (this issue is dedicated entirely to the EU Charter); E Eriksen, J Fossum, and A Menéndez (eds), 'The Chartering of Europe', Arena Report No 8/2001; K Feus (ed), *An EU Charter of Fundamental Rights: Text and Commentaries* (Federal Trust, 2000).

[506] Preamble to the Charter of Fundamental Rights, para 5.

[507] See eg Case 173/99 *Broadcasting, Entertainment, Cinematographic and Theatre Union (BECTU) v Secretary of State for Trade and Industry* [2001] ECR I-04881, para 28 *per* AG Tizzano, where he argued that while the charter was not binding, the statement of existing rights which it constitutes cannot be ignored when they concern the scope and nature of an existing fundamental right.

[508] See TEU, Art 6(1).

3.170 As a result, the provisions of the ECHR are now more closely tied to the EU system.[509] Article 52(3) of the Charter provides that: 'Insofar as this Charter contains rights which correspond to rights guaranteed by the Convention for the Protection of Human Rights and Fundamental Freedoms, the meaning and scope of those rights shall be the same as those laid down by the said Convention.' It adds that: 'This provision shall not prevent Union law providing more extensive protection.' Article 52(3) of the Charter is important in several respects. First, when there are 'corresponding' rights in the ECHR, the Convention sets the minimum standard for human rights protection. Secondly, where this is the case, it is possible to rely directly on ECHR provisions when interpreting the EU Charter. Although the Charter does not state that the Strasbourg Court's interpretation of those provisions is binding upon the CJEU, it seems likely that the Luxembourg Court is intended to pay very close attention to the jurisprudence of the ECtHR in this regard.[510] This should lead to an increased degree of predictability when considering the nature and scope of corresponding rights (as is the case with Article 10 of the Charter on religious freedom; see paragraph 3.174).

3.171 In addition, Article 6(2) declares that the European Union is now required to become a party to the ECHR. The terms of the European Union's accession to the ECHR are still being negotiated,[511] and it is not yet clear how far the accession might lead to a different standard of human rights protection in terms of the Union's actions. This is particularly so given the fact that the ECHR and the jurisprudence of the ECtHR already play a prominent role as regards EU fundamental rights.[512] At the very least, the European Union's accession will send an important political signal as regards the Union's commitment to human rights by subjecting its acts, including the acts of the Court, to review by the ECtHR. It may lead to a new hierarchy of the Courts.

(3) Religion in European law: provisions and substantive principles

a) The importance of religion in EU law

3.172 The prominent references to religion in primary EU law reflect the important position it holds in the European Union's legal order. The preamble to the Lisbon Treaty names the European 'cultural, religious and humanist inheritance' as a source of inspiration, 'from which have developed the universal values of the inviolable and inalienable rights of the human person, freedom, democracy, equality and the rule of law'.[513] The principle of non-discrimination, which takes a prominent position in EU law and is closely intertwined with the protection of religious rights, is also part of this heritage. Article 10 TFEU states that: 'In defining and implementing its policies and activities, the Union shall aim to combat discrimination based on sex, racial or ethnic origin, religion or belief, disability, age or sexual orientation.'

---

[509] See generally W Weiss, 'Human Rights in the EU: Rethinking the Role of the European Convention on Human Rights after Lisbon' (2011) 7(1) European Constitutional Review 64.

[510] This has indeed been the approach of the Court thus far: see eg Case C-400/10 PPU *J McB v LE* [2010] CMR I-08965, para 53; Case C-279/09 *DEB v Bundesrepublik Deutschland* [2010] ECR I-13849, paras 35–52.

[511] On 13 June 2012, the Committee of Ministers instructed the Steering Committee for Human Rights (CDDH) to pursue negotiations with the EU, in an ad hoc group, with a view to finalizing the accession instruments. That ad hoc group has so far held five meetings in Strasbourg (21 June 2012, 17–19 September 2012, 7–9 November 2012, 21–23 January 2013), and 2–5 April 2013).

[512] See para 3.167.

[513] Preamble to the European Union Reform Treaty (Lisbon) (2007) para 1.

b) Religion in the Treaties and in the Charter

Although Article 19 TFEU provides the European Union with competence to 'take appro- **3.173**
priate action to combat' the discrimination contemplated in Article 10,[514] the provisions
themselves confer no substantive rights upon individuals. Stand-alone protection is now
incorporated into primary law by virtue of the Charter:[515] Article 21 complements the general non-discrimination principle and provides explicit protection against discrimination on
religious grounds. This provision reinforces a human rights approach which had arguably
been overtaken by the focus on the economic rationale behind non-discrimination.[516] The
Charter goes beyond providing protection against discrimination, by expressly guaranteeing
the right to freedom of religion in Article 10(1):

> Everyone has the right to freedom of thought, conscience and religion. This right includes
> freedom to change religion or belief and freedom, either alone or in community with others
> and in public or in private, to manifest religion or belief, in worship, teaching, practice and
> observance.

As discussed previously, at paragraph 3.170, Article 52(3) of the Charter provides that the **3.174**
meaning and scope of any rights contained in its provisions shall be the same as that of any
corresponding right guaranteed by the ECHR. In a judgment of September 2012, the CJEU
confirmed that 'The right to religious freedom enshrined in Article 10(1) of the Charter corresponds to the right guaranteed by Article 9 of the ECHR',[517] and the *Explanations Relating
to the Charter of Fundamental Rights* (the '*Explanations*') state that 'The right guaranteed in
paragraph 1 corresponds to the right guaranteed in Article 9 of the ECHR and, in accordance
with Article 52(3) of the Charter, has the same meaning and scope.'[518] The consequences of
these findings also extend to potential justifications for interferences with freedom of religion. As the *Explanations* state, limitations to the freedom of religion 'must therefore respect
Article 9(2) of the Convention [ECHR]'.[519] The scope and meaning of religious freedom as

---

[514] TFEU, Art 19 reads:

1. Without prejudice to the other provisions of the Treaties and within the limits of the powers
conferred by them upon the Union, the Council, acting unanimously in accordance with a special legislative procedure and after obtaining the consent of the European Parliament, may take
appropriate action to combat discrimination based on sex, racial or ethnic origin, religion or belief,
disability, age or sexual orientation.

2. By way of derogation from paragraph 1, the European Parliament and the Council, acting in
accordance with the ordinary legislative procedure, may adopt the basic principles of Union incen-
tive measures, excluding any harmonisation of the laws and regulations of the Member States, to
support action taken by the Member States in order to contribute to the achievement of the objectives referred to in paragraph 1.

[515] While TFEU, Art 19 grants competence to the EU institutions, the Charter of Fundamental Rights is
addressed both to those institutions and to Member States 'when they are implementing Union law' (Art 51).

[516] See eg Recital 11 of Council Directive (EC) 2000/78 of 27 November 2000 establishing a general framework for equal treatment in employment and occupation:

Discrimination based on religion or belief, disability, age or sexual orientation may undermine
the achievement of the objectives of the EC Treaty, *in particular* the attainment of a high level of
employment and social protection, raising the standard of living and the quality of life, economic
and social cohesion and solidarity, and the free movement of persons (emphasis added).

[517] Judgment of the Court (Grand Chamber), 5 September 2012, Joined Cases C-71/11 and C-99/11 *Y and
Z v Bundesrepublik Deutschland*, para 56.

[518] Explanations Relating to the Charter of Fundamental Rights, 2007/C 303/02, 14 December 2007,
Explanation on Article 10.

[519] Explanations (n 518) Explanation on Article 10.

set out in the ECHR and as interpreted by the ECtHR will therefore play a fundamental role in the protection of religious freedoms within the EU system in the future.

3.175 Finally, Article 22 of the Charter calls upon the European Union to respect cultural, religious, and linguistic diversity,[520] while Article 14(3) demands the same for the rights of parents to ensure that their children are educated in conformity with their religious, philosophical, and pedagogical convictions. In answer to the concern that the provisions of the Charter would greatly expand the scope of operation of EU law, Article 6(1) TEU provides that: 'The provisions of the Charter shall not extend in any way the competences of the Union as defined in the Treaties.' Respect for the principle of subsidiarity is highlighted in the Charter itself,[521] and the provisions are to apply to Member States 'only when implementing European law'.[522]

c) Definition of religion

3.176 As with the ECHR system and the other regional human rights systems discussed in the following, primary EU law does not define the term 'religion'. The absence of a definition demonstrates neutrality towards different religions; no particular religious or spiritual heritage is specified in the Preamble to the Lisbon Treaty, and there is no differentiation between different beliefs in the protective framework.[523] Indeed, religious diversity must be respected under Article 22 of the Charter. This neutrality can also be seen in legislation protecting the status of religious associations: Article 17(1) TFEU states that: 'The Union respects and does not prejudice the status under national law of churches and religious associations or communities in the Member States',[524] while philosophical and non-confessional organizations are to be treated the same way by virtue of Article 17(2) TFEU.

3.177 For the most part, decisions, directives, and regulations contemplate the concept of religion in as broad a manner as the Treaties themselves.[525] An exception is the attempt in Directive (EU) 2011/95 to give the term more defined content for the purposes of refugee law:

> The concept of religion shall in particular include the holding of theistic, non-theistic and atheistic beliefs, the participation in, or abstention from, formal worship in private or in public, either alone or in community with others, other religious acts of expressions of view, or forms of personal or communal conduct based on or mandated by any religious belief.[526]

---

[520] Explanations (n 518) Explanation on Article 22.

[521] See Charter of Fundamental Rights, Art 51(2).

[522] See Charter of Fundamental Rights, Art 51(1).

[523] Council decisions expressly recognize 'religious diversity' (Decision (EC) 2006/320 [2006] OJ L/118/9, 13) and the need to work with 'religious pluralism' (Decision (EC) 1982/2006 [2006] OJ L412/1).

[524] There are also special provisions within the EU non-discrimination framework explicitly allowing certain differences of treatment on the grounds of religion and belief when it comes to churches and other religion- or belief-based organizations. See Directive (EC) 2000/78 of November 2000 establishing a general framework for equal treatment in employment and occupation, Art 4(2). Moreover, the special needs of both churches and religious communities in terms of working time are recognized, see Directive (EC) 2003/88 of 4 November 2003 concerning certain aspects of the organisation of working time, Art 17(1)(c).

[525] See eg the decisions pertaining to circumstances under which legislation protecting animal welfare rights (eg TFEU, Art 13) can be derogated from (eg Council Regulation (EC) 1099/2009 of 24 September on the protection of animals at the time of killing; Council Directive (EC) 2007/43 of 28 June 2007 laying down minimum rules for the protection of chickens kept for meat production; and Council Directive (EC) 93/119 of 22 December 1993 on the protection of animals at the time of slaughter or killing). All refer simply to 'religion' or to 'religious rituals' without further definition, despite the frequent conflict between the two systems of protection.

[526] Art 10(b), Directive (EU) 2011/95 of 13 December 2011 on standards for the qualification of third-country nationals or stateless persons as beneficiaries of international protection, for a uniform status for

Although the majority of these elements presuppose that the existence of a religion has **3.178** already been established, the list provides a helpful summary of the external actions which will be brought under the scope of the Directive's protection. The CJEU recently had cause to issue a preliminary ruling which expanded further upon the detail in Directive (EU) 2011/95.[527] It found, *inter alia*, that the Directive's scope of protection 'extends both to forms of personal or communal conduct which the person concerned considers to be necessary to him—namely those "based on ... any religious belief"—and to those prescribed by religious doctrine—namely those "mandated by any religious belief" '.[528] While this provides a clearer picture as to what the concept of religion involves, it is questionable to what extent this interpretation will carry weight with the definition of religion more generally under EU law, given that it deals only with a specific provision of secondary legislation.

d) Religious freedom

As a result of Article 10 of the Charter, the protection of religious freedom is now part of **3.179** primary European law. However, the CJEU first ruled upon the concept more than 30 years ago in the case of *Vivian Prais*.[529] Ms Prais had applied to the Council for a position as a translator, and was invited to participate in an entry examination. As the date of the examination coincided with a Jewish religious festival during which she would not be allowed to travel or write, she asked for an alternative test date. When her request was declined, she challenged the Council's actions before the Court. She claimed, *inter alia*, that: 'The Community institutions are ... bound to respect freedom of religion and such respect must imply a readiness to make the necessary administrative arrangements to enable candidates to take examinations in accordance with their religious convictions.'[530]

The Court's judgment did not deal directly with the existence or scope of religious freedom **3.180** under EU law, but held simply that where the testing authority has knowledge of a candidate's religious commitments, 'it should take this into account in fixing the date'.[531] Ms Prais' claim was ultimately rejected because she had only informed the Council about the religious festival after the date had been set and the other candidates had been invited.[532] The opinion of Advocate General Warner did consider the scope of the freedom as set out under Article 9 ECHR, thus suggesting that he found its application to EU law appropriate; however, he held in this case that the provision could not bear the interpretation for which Ms Prais was contending.[533]

The principle is also embedded in numerous regulatory instruments,[534] and is evident in **3.181** decisions on the administration of justice. For example, a Member State has no duty to

---

refugees eligible for subsidiary protection, and for the content of the protection granted. The Directive replaces Council Directive (EC) 2004/83 of 29 April 2004, which contained the same definition of religion.

[527] Judgment of the Court (Grand Chamber), 5 September 2012, Joined Cases C-71/11 and C-99/11, *Y and Z v Bundesrepublik Deutschland*.

[528] *Y and Z* (n 527) para 71.

[529] *Vivian Prais v Council* [1976] ECR 1589.

[530] *Vivian Prais* (n 529) 1594.

[531] *Vivian Prais* (n 529) para 16.

[532] *Vivian Prais* (n 529) para 19.

[533] *Vivian Prais* (n 529) Opinion of AG Warner.

[534] Respect for religious freedom appears in the directive on freedom of movement of EU citizens (Corrigendum to Directive (EC) 2004/58, Preamble (32)), while the directive on the equal treatment of men and women in the supply of goods and services makes explicit reference to respect for the freedom of religion (Directive (EC) 2004/113, Preamble (3)).

extradite where it has 'substantial grounds' to believe that the request has been made to 'prosecute or punish a person on religious grounds' or would 'cause prejudice to the position of that person for this reason'.[535] The European Union commonly makes religious freedom or equality a condition in its policies on external relations with non-Member States.[536]

e) Equality and non-discrimination

3.182 There is a broad range of secondary legislation dealing with religious discrimination over various areas of EU competence. Different regimes exist for various classes of individual in certain spheres: union personnel are protected as regards their recruitment process;[537] third country nationals are protected for the purposes of admission for study, exchanges, and voluntary service;[538] and families of EU citizens are protected as regards their freedom of movement.[539] Non-discrimination regulations are in place with regard to healthcare and the application of funds. Regulation (EC) 1905/2006 promotes healthcare services for lower income population groups and marginalized groups, including 'persons belonging to groups suffering religious discrimination',[540] while a number of different instruments are in place to deal with implementing funds (such as the European Agricultural Fund for Rural development,[541] or the European Globalisation Adjustment Fund to support workers affected by major structural changes in world trade).[542]

3.183 There are also various regulatory instruments in place as part of a wider programme to eliminate discrimination. Each measure seeks to combat discrimination generally, with explicit reference to grounds of religion or belief. The list includes the Culture Programme;[543] the decision establishing the Youth Action Programme;[544] and the 'year of equal opportunities' programme.[545]

f) Special privileges and exemptions

3.184 One means of protecting religion in EU law is the use of privileges and exemptions. While the main domain of these measures is the functional instruments of EU law, there does now exist a special protection for conscientious objectors in Article 10(2) of the Charter: 'The right of conscientious objection is recognised, in accordance with the national laws governing the exercise of this right.' Similarly, Article 14(3) protects the rights of parents to ensure the education and teaching of their children in conformity with their religious, philosophical, and pedagogical beliefs. The underlying idea is to reinforce the protection of religious belief in the face of rules of general applicability which would otherwise put religious individuals at a disadvantage.

---

[535] Decision (EC) 2004/579. Further examples include Council Framework Decision (EC) 2005/214, Preamble (5), refusal to execute a decision or financial penalty if the Member State believes (objectively) that the aim is to punish a person on the grounds of religion; and Council Framework Decision (EC) 2006/783, 13, a Member State may refuse to confiscate property if confiscation is to punish or prosecute a person on account of their religious belief.

[536] See eg Common Position on Nigeria, 2002/401; see generally, Doe (n 172) 246.

[537] Decision (EC) 2002/621 (Personnel Selection Office).

[538] Directive (EC) 2004/114.

[539] Corrigendum to Directive (EC) 2004/58, Preamble (32).

[540] Council Regulation (EC) 1905/2006, Art 5(2)(b)(i).

[541] Council Regulation (EC) 1698/2005, Art 8.

[542] Regulation (EC) 1929/2006, Art 2(1)(b)(iii).

[543] Decision (EC) 1855/2006, Art 12(d).

[544] Decision (EC) 1719/2006.

[545] Decision (EC) 771/2006, Art 2 (on the basis of Directive (EC) 2000/78).

As with rules protecting against discrimination in general, different instruments exist to pro- **3.185**
tect different classes. For religious associations, two directives ensure that religious symbols
cannot be used in trademarks[546] and prohibit the use of advertisements in any broadcast of
a religious service.[547] Individuals are granted exemptions and privileges in a wide variety of
ways, for example in the fight against racial hatred and discrimination in electronic commerce regulations;[548] while religious property is granted special protection under regulations
dealing with the export of cultural goods[549] and with the rehabilitation of damaged and
destroyed properties.[550]

Special privileges are also a feature of EU religious protection. Examples are the exemption **3.186**
of 'mobile churches' from vehicle harmonization,[551] and tax exemption in relation to 'sup-
plies of staff by religious or philosophical institutions for medical, welfare, child protection
and educational purposes with a view to spiritual welfare'.[552] Privileges with regard to the
working time requirements for those officiating at religious ceremonies[553] and exceptions
to copyright harmonization law for the purposes of articles on 'religious topics'[554] are at the
discretion of Member States.

(4) Religion in European law: practical principles

a) Subsidiarity

EU law concerning religious protection engages the question of subsidiarity[555]—it is an area **3.187**
where established practices of great importance to individual nations can vary considerably
across Member States. The general principle of subsidiarity first appeared in the Maastricht
Treaty,[556] and means, in essence, that the Union will not take action in areas which do not
fall within its exclusive competence unless the proposed objectives cannot be adequately
achieved by the Member States.

The regulation of religion is not expressly listed among the competences of the European **3.188**
Union, although subjects associated with religion are, such as culture and education.[557]
On the whole, the European Union prefers to leave specific regulation up to Member
States, and the examples of latitude granted to national law are numerous: the morality of
prostitution,[558] Sunday trading laws,[559] and religious and ethical issues about abortion[560]
have all been held in CJEU jurisprudence to fall within the discretion of Member States.[561]

---

[546] Directive (EEC) 89/104, Art 3(2)(b).
[547] Directive (EEC) 89/552 (amended by (EC) 97/36), Art 11(5).
[548] Directive (EC) 2000/31, Article 3(4)(a).
[549] Regulation (EEC) 3911/92, Annex, Art 1(2).
[550] Decision (EC) 2006/56, conditions for EU partnership with Serbia and Montenegro.
[551] Directive (EC) 2001/85, Annex 1, para 1.3.2.
[552] Council Decision (EC) 2006/35.
[553] Directive (EC) 2003/88, Art 17(1)(c).
[554] Directive (EC) 2001/29, Art 5(3)(c) and (g).
[555] See eg TFEU, Art 17(1): 'The Union respects and does not prejudice the status under national law of
churches and religious associations or communities in the Member States.'
[556] Maastricht Treaty, Art 3A.
[557] TFEU, Art 6.
[558] See Case C-268/99 *Jany and ors v Staatssecretaris van Justitie* [2001] ECR I-8615, para 56: 'it is not for
the Court to substitute its own assessment for that of the legislatures of Member States'.
[559] See Case C-145/88 *Torfaen BC v B&Q plc* [1989] ECR I-3851.
[560] See Case 159/90 *Society for the Protection of the Unborn Child v Grogan* [1999] ECR I-04685, paras 19
and 20.
[561] For further examples, see Doe (n 172) 241–3.

b) Cooperation

3.189 Article 17(3) TFEU calls upon the Union to 'maintain an open, transparent and regular dialogue with these churches and organisations', and to do so 'recognising their identity and their specific contribution'.[562] To facilitate this process, the Catholic Church, Protestant Churches, and Jewish, Muslim, Orthodox, and other religious groups all have full-time representation in Brussels. This obligation goes beyond the requirements of the ECHR, and is not generally found in national law; commentators have argued that the process is a useful way to mitigate the difficulty religions face in accepting the marginal role they have been assigned as a result of the adoption of the constitution.[563]

c) Autonomy of religious associations

3.190 The autonomy of religious associations is not a feature of the Treaties,[564] but it is assumed in numerous regulatory instruments. For example, the Turkey Accession Partnership Decision requires Turkey to establish conditions for the functioning of religious communities, including legal and judicial protection.[565] Certain instruments on foodstuffs dealing with religious rights assign exclusive competence to religious authorities for the task of carrying out public EU functions; for example Directive (EC) 93/119 states that 'the religious authority on whose behalf slaughter is carried out shall be competent for the application and monitoring of the special provisions which apply to slaughter according to religious rights'. Rules on the description and presentation of wines furthermore permit recommendations to the consumer on the question of a given wine's suitability for religious purposes.[566]

3.191 The best known expression of the religious autonomy principle concerns the freedom of religious organizations to discriminate on grounds of religion in the employment sphere. Discrimination in this area is generally prohibited, but may be permitted in 'the case of occupational activities within churches and other public or private organisations the ethos of which is based on religion or belief'.[567] This is because the religion or belief can constitute 'a genuine, legitimate and justified occupational requirement, having regard to the organisation's ethos'.[568]

---

[562] This idea is also enshrined in the legal framework surrounding the European Union Agency for Fundamental Rights: Art 10, sentence 2 of Council Regulation (EC) 168/2007 of 15 February 2007 establishing a European Union Agency for Fundamental Rights states that: '…the Agency shall establish a cooperation Network (Fundamental Rights Platform), composed of…churches, religious, philosophical and non-confessional organisations…'.

[563] See in particular, Doe (n 172) 253.

[564] It is possible that it is implicit in the Lisbon Reform Treaty, Art 17 on the status of religious associations.

[565] Council Decision (EC) 2006/35 [2006] OJ L22/34, 38.

[566] Regulation (EEC) 3201/90, Art 10(1).

[567] Directive (EC) 2000/78, Art 4(1).

[568] Directive (EC) 2000/78, Art 4(2).

4

COMPARATIVE PERSPECTIVES

A. AUSTRALIA

Paul Babie[1]

(1) Introduction

4.01 Modern Australia is a plural, multicultural, multi-faith society comprising approximately 22.7 million people.[2] While early religious traditions include the 40,000 years of Australia's Indigenous culture and brief contacts with Islam via Indonesia in the last 300 years, today, through English-European settlement,[3] more than half of Australians identify as Christian. At the 2011 Census,[4] 61.1 per cent of Australians identified themselves as Christian (which reflects a long-term decrease from 96 per cent in the first national Census in 1911),[5] 2.5 per cent as Buddhist, 2.2 per cent as Muslim, 1.3 per cent as Hindu (the fastest growing religion in Australia since the 2001 Census, increasing from 148,130 to 275,534),[6] and 0.5 per cent as Jewish. A small percentage (0.8 per cent) of the population indicated that they adhere to another religion; 8.6 per cent did not specify;[7] and 22.3 per cent indicated that they practice no religion, up from approximately 15 per cent at the 2001 Census.[8] Table 4.1 summarizes these trends.

4.02 While the 2011 Census data indicate a large percentage of the population adhering to some form of religious tenets, Australia protects human rights generally, and religious freedom specifically, through a minimal patchwork of constitutional, legislative, and common law provisions differing not only in their applications to the Commonwealth,[9] state, and territory governments in the Australian federation, but also in the scope and strength of protection afforded. Given the complexity of this piecemeal approach, this chapter has two objectives.

---

[1] Adelaide Law School, The University of Adelaide, Australia. For earlier versions of some of the material presented in this chapter, see also P Babie and J Krumrey-Quinn, 'Religious Symbols and Autonomy in Australia' in C McCrudden and L Lazarus (eds), *Adjudicating Human Rights Diversely* (Hart Publishing, forthcoming 2013); P Babie and B Mylius, 'Religious Education in Australian Schools' in D Davis and E Miroshnikova (eds), *The Routledge International Handbook of Religious Education* (Routledge, 2013) 23–31; P Babie and B Mylius, 'The Future of Religious Freedom in Australian Schools' (2012) 21 International Journal of Educational Reform 173; P Babie and N Rochow, 'Religious Freedom and Bills of Rights: Australia as Microcosm' in P Babie and N Rochow (eds), *Freedom of Religion Under Bills of Rights* (The University of Adelaide Press, 2012) 1; P Babie and N Rochow, 'Feels Like Déjà vu: Religious Freedom under a Proposed Australian Bill of Rights' (2010) BYU Law Review 821. Richard Sletvold (LLB, 2013) provided outstanding comments and research assistance in the preparation of this chapter, for which I am extremely grateful.

[2] For a real-time population projection, see Australian Bureau of Statistics, 'Population Clock', 3 October 2010, available at <http://www.abs.gov.au/AUSSTATS/abs@.nsf/Web+Pages/Population+Clock>.

[3] Department of Foreign Affairs and Trade, 'About Australia: Religious Freedom', Factsheet, February 2008, available at <http://web.archive.org/web/20110806061716/.dfat.gov.au/facts/religion.html>.

[4] Australian Bureau of Statistics, 'Reflecting a Nation: Stories from the 2011 Census, 2012–2013: Cultural Diversity in Australia', Statistics Catalogue No 2071.0, 21 June 2012, available at <http://www.abs.gov.au/ausstats/abs@.nsf/Latestproducts/2071.0Main%20Features902012%E2%80%932013>.

[5] This figure is divided among denominations as follows: Catholic 25.3%, Anglican 17.1%, Uniting Church 5.0%, Presbyterian and Reformed 2.8%, Eastern Orthodox 2.6%, Lutheran 1.2%, Pentecostal 1.1%, and other Christian 4.5% (Australian Bureau of Statistics, 'Reflecting a Nation' (n 4)).

[6] Australian Bureau of Statistics, '2011 Census Reveals Hinduism as the Fastest Growing Religion in Australia', Media Release, CO/61, 21 June 2012, available at <http://www.abs.gov.au/websitedbs/censushome.nsf/home/CO-61>.

[7] Australian Bureau of Statistics, '2011 Census' (n 6).

[8] Australian Bureau of Statistics, 'Reflecting a Nation' (n 4).

[9] In this chapter, 'Commonwealth' refers to the federal form of government established for Australia in 1901 by the Commonwealth of Australia Constitution Act 1901 ('Australian Constitution').

First, in section (2), to provide an overview of the protections of religious freedom in Australia, outlining the protections found in the Australian Constitution, Commonwealth, state and territory legislative anti-discrimination regimes, emerging protections under state legislative human rights charters, and possible protection found in common law rules of statutory interpretation. Secondly, having outlined the limited Australian protection of religious freedom, section (3) explores the three principal areas of religious freedom that have recently gained most attention in Australia: education, employment, and religious dress. Section (4) offers some brief conclusions.[10]

Table 4.1 *Religious Affiliations Indicated in the 2011 Census*[11]

Religion	Percentage of population
Christian	61.1
Catholic	25.3
Anglican	17.1
Uniting Church	5.0
Presbyterian and Reformed	2.8
Eastern Orthodox	2.6
Baptist	1.6
Lutheran	1.2
Pentecostal	1.1
Other Christian	4.5
Non-Christian	7.2
Buddhism	2.5
Islam	2.2
Hinduism	1.3
Judaism	0.5
Other non-Christian	0.8
No Religion	22.3
Not Specified	8.6

(2) Protecting religious freedom

This Part contains four sections, each considering a different dimension of Australian protection of religious freedom: (a) the Australian Constitution;[12] (b) Commonwealth, state and territory legislative anti-discrimination regimes; (c) state legislative human rights charters; and (d) common law rules of statutory interpretation.   **4.03**

---

[10] For a more extensive recent overview of religious freedom in Australia, see eg CM Evans, *Legal Protection of Religious Freedom in Australia* (Federation Press, 2012); see also AHRC, 'Freedom of Religion and Belief in the 21st Century', Research Report (2012), and the papers commissioned for the report which are collected on the website AHRC, *Freedom of Religion and Belief in the 21st Century* <http://www.hreoc.gov.au/frb/>.

[11] Table 4.1 is adapted from a table appearing in Australian Bureau of Statistics, 'Reflecting a Nation' (n 4). The 'missing' percentage reflects individuals who inadequately identified their religious affiliation, ie they attempted to provide one, but their response could not be classified.

[12] The Australian Constitution is enacted by the Commonwealth of Australia Constitution Act 1900 (Imp) 63 & 64 Vict, c 12, s 9.

a) The Australian Constitution

4.04 While the Australian Constitution empowered the Federal Australian Parliament to make laws 'with respect to...external affairs',[13] enabling it to implement by way of legislation international treaties and covenants, including those that contain human rights norms,[14] the framers of the Constitution ultimately included no bill of rights in Australia's Constitution,[15] providing only the barest of protection of rights, with religion finding protection only in section 116.

4.05 Section 116, which expressly deals with religious freedom,[16] reads as follows:

> The Commonwealth shall not make any law for establishing any religion, or for imposing any religious observance, or for prohibiting the free exercise of any religion, and no religious test shall be required as a qualification for any office or public trust under the Commonwealth.

4.06 This provision found its way into the Constitution as a result of petitions circulated by Christian organizations during the Constitutional Conventions of the 1890s. The petitions 'asked for the recognition of God as the supreme ruler of the universe; for the declaration of national prayers and national days of thanksgiving and "humiliation"'.[17] The essence of the petitions was to demand that the Constitution include reference to the Christian identity of the new nation. Difficult though drafting such reference was, the framers settled on including these words in the Preamble: 'Whereas the people of New South Wales, Victoria, South Australia, Queensland, and Tasmania, humbly relying on the blessing of Almighty God'.[18]

4.07 The mention of 'Almighty God' reopened a debate about prohibiting religious tests and religious establishment, on the one hand, and a concern to limit restrictions on the free exercise of religion, on the other.[19] Ultimately, this settled itself in the compromise of section 116, which struck a balance between the two sets of interests and the opposing fears they represented.[20]

4.08 Yet, because it operates as a constraint only upon the federal legislature,[21] section 116 prohibits the Commonwealth, but not the States, from legislating to establish a religion or from limit the free exercise of religion.[22] And while the Australian provision goes further than the First Amendment to the Constitution of the United States, prohibiting not only federal laws 'establishing any religion', but also the use of law to impose religious observance or to

---

[13] Australian Constitution, s 51(xxix).

[14] See *Commonwealth v Tasmania* (1983) 158 CLR 1; *Koowarta v Bjelke-Petersen* (1982) 153 CLR 168.

[15] A Byrnes, H Charlesworth, and G McKinnon, *Bills of Rights in Australia: History, Politics and Law* (UNSW Press, 2009) 24–5.

[16] On the history of this provision, see JA La Nauze, *The Making of the Australian Constitution* (Melbourne University Press, 1972) 228–9; H Irving, *To Constitute a Nation: A Cultural History of Australia's Constitution* (CUP, 1999) 165–8; J Quick and RR Garran, *The Annotated Constitution of the Australian Commonwealth* (Australian Book Company, 1901) 951–3.

[17] Irving (n 16) 166.

[18] Irving (n 16) 166; Commonwealth of Australia Constitution Act 1900 (Imp) 63 & 64 Vict, c 12.

[19] Irving (n 16) 167.

[20] Irving (n 16) 167–8; see also R Ely, *Unto God and Caesar: Religious Issues in the Emerging Commonwealth, 1891–1906* (Melbourne University Press, 1976).

[21] See *Kruger v Commonwealth* (1997) 190 CLR 1; see also *Grace Bible Church v Reedman* (1984) 36 SASR 376.

[22] See La Nauze (n 16) 228–9; Irving (n 16) 165–8.

administer a religious test as a qualification for public office, the potential contained in the text, unlike its counterpart American provision, remains largely unrealized.[23]

Responsibility for the limited use of section 116 lies squarely with the Australian courts. **4.09** While the American judiciary invokes the First Amendment to the US Constitution to protect the right to freedom of religion, Australian judges historically treat its counterpart, notwithstanding its remarkably similar wording, as part of a nineteenth century British statute, rendering it a virtual dead letter as a means of conferring any substantive rights, and rendering it of little practical import as a tool for the protection of religious freedom in Australia. Paradoxically, this narrow interpretation flows from the judicial assertion that section 116 is dislocated from a bill of rights, properly understood. In the celebrated *DOGS Case*,[24] for example, the High Court noted that:

> [Section 116] does not form part of a Bill of Rights. The plaintiff's claim that it represents a personal guarantee of religious freedom loses much of its emotive and persuasive force . . . [when it is recognised that] s 116 is a denial of legislative power to the Commonwealth, and no more.[25]

Despite its being the most direct adoption of an American constitutional provision, the **4.10** narrow construction of section 116 confines its operation when compared to its American counterpart,[26] despite an apparent expectation on the part of some framers that American jurisprudence might influence its interpretation.[27] This has led the High Court to reject claims that legislation infringes upon the freedom of religion when it has been argued that:

(1) compulsory peacetime military training offends the religious convictions of persons who believe that military service is opposed to the will of God;[28]

---

[23] *A-G (Vic) ex rel Black v Commonwealth* (1981) 146 CLR 559, 579 (Barwick CJ) ('*DOGS Case*'); see also *Lemon v Kurtzman*, 403 US 602 (1971); *Everson v Board of Education*, 333 US 1 (1947); F Gedicks, *The Rhetoric of Church and State: A Critical Analysis of Religion Clause Jurisprudence* (Duke University Press, 1995) 44–61.

[24] *DOGS Case* (1981) 146 CLR 559, 579.

[25] *DOGS Case* (n 24) 652 (Wilson J).

[26] See CL Pannam, 'Travelling Section 116 with a US Road Map' (1963) 4 Melbourne University Law Review 41; Gedicks (n 23) chs 1, 5, 6.

[27] In their discussion of the anticipations expressed in the constitutional debates on s 116, Quick and Garran (n 16) refer to the debates which considered its inclusion (at 952):

> The strongest argument, however, for the adoption of the earlier part of sec 116, was found in the special form of the preamble of the Constitution Act, which recites that the people of the colonies, 'humbly relying on the blessing of Almighty God, have agreed to unite in one indissoluble Commonwealth'. Referring to this recital, it was stated by Mr Higgins that, although the preamble to the Constitution of the United States contained no such words as these, it had been decided by the courts in the year 1892 that the people of the United States were a Christian people; and although the Constitution gave no power to Congress to make laws relating to Sunday observance, that decision was shortly afterwards followed by a Federal enactment declaring that the Chicago exhibition should be closed on Sundays.

Quick and Garran go on to discuss how it is a matter of conjecture as to why s 116 was limited to the Commonwealth and did not extend its prohibition to the States. The debate cited in this connection again makes reference to American First Amendment jurisprudence (at 953); see *Bradfield v Roberts*, 175 US 291 (1899); *Davis v Beason*, 133 US 333 (1890); *Reynolds v US*, 98 US 145 (1879); *Ex p Garland*, 71 US (4 Wall) 333 (1866); *Permoli v Municipality No 1 of New Orleans*, 44 US (3 How) 589 (1845). It seems, though, that not all framers took the view that s 116 would protect all manner of religious practice. Tasmania's Premier, Sir Edward Braddon, for instance, argued during the Convention Debates for an amendment that 'shall prevent the performance of any such religious rites as are of a cruel or demoralising character or contrary to the law of the Commonwealth': Irving (n 16) 168, citing *Official Record of the Debates of the Australasian Federal Convention, Adelaide, Sydney, Melbourne, 1897–1898* (Legal Books, 1986) 657.

[28] *Krygger v Williams* (1912) 15 CLR 366.

(2) the use of legislation for compulsory removal of Aboriginal children from their families prohibited them from access to and free exercise of their tribal religion;[29] and

(3) government funding of religiously-based schools amounted to an establishment of religion.[30]

4.11 In its origin, its text, and its judicial interpretation, then, section 116 fails to provide a robust protection of religious freedom.

b) Commonwealth, state, and territory legislation

4.12 In the absence of comprehensive Constitutional protection, in Australia, one finds protection for religious freedom largely in a patchwork of Commonwealth, state, and territory legislation and institutional arrangements.[31] This section contains two parts, corresponding to the two levels of protection.

4.13 **(i) Commonwealth** At the international level, Australia accepts the procedures which allow UN human rights bodies to provide redress to individuals who claim violations of their rights under the International Convention on the Elimination of All Forms of Racial Discrimination (CERD),[32] the International Covenant on Civil and Political Rights (ICCPR),[33] the Optional Protocol to the ICCPR,[34] and the Convention Against Torture and Other Cruel, Inhuman or Degrading Treatment or Punishment (CAT).[35] At the Commonwealth level, the Racial Discrimination Act 1975 (Cth) and the Sex Discrimination Act 1984 (Cth) are the primary legislative protections for human rights.

4.14 Institutionally, the Human Rights and Equal Opportunity Commission Act 1986 (Cth) established the Human Rights and Equal Opportunity Commission—since renamed the Australian Human Rights Commission (AHRC)[36]—and conferred upon it a number

---

[29] *Kruger v Commonwealth* (n 21).

[30] *A-G (Vic) ex rel Black v Commonwealth* (n 23).

[31] See ACT Bill of Rights Consultative Committee, 'Towards an ACT Human Rights Act' (Information Planning and Services, 2003). For some of the history, see R Piotrowicz and S Kaye, *Human Rights in International and Australian Law* (Butterworths, 2000).

[32] Opened for signature 7 March 1966, 660 UNTS 195 (entered into force 4 January 1969). See especially, at Art 5(d)(vii) (protecting the right to freedom of thought, conscience and religion); at Preamble para 1 (noting that one of the UNs' purposes is 'to promote and encourage universal respect for and observance of human rights and fundamental freedoms for all, without distinction as to . . . religion').

[33] Opened for signature 19 December 1966, 999 UNTS 171 (entered into force 23 March 1976). See especially at Arts 2(1) (preventing discrimination on the ground of religion in respect of ICCPR rights); 4(1) (preventing discrimination solely on the ground of religion in states of emergency where a state derogates from ICCPR obligations); 18 (providing that every person has the 'right to freedom of thought, conscience and religion'); 24 (preventing discrimination on the basis of religion in respect of the rights of a child 'to such measures of protection as are required by his status as a minor'); 26 (requiring that the law of the State party 'shall prohibit any discrimination and guarantee to all persons equal and effective protection against discrimination on any ground such as . . . religion'); 27 (guaranteeing the right of ethnic, religious or linguistic minorities to 'profess and practise their own religion').

[34] Optional Protocol to the International Covenant on Civil and Political Rights, opened for signature 16 December 1966, 999 UNTS 302 (entered into force 23 March 1976) ('Optional Protocol to the ICCPR'). In particular, the Optional Protocol allows communications to be brought before the Human Rights Committee in respect of alleged violations of the ICCPR by Australia. In the religious context, this allows individuals to bring complaints especially in respect of the articles listed in n 33.

[35] Opened for signature 10 December 1984, 1465 UNTS 85 (entered into force 26 June 1987); see also Byrnes, Charlesworth, and McKinnon (n 15) 37. In the religious context, this offers protection against torture used as a means of punishing and persecuting religious minorities, for example. In this way, it strengthens the existing protections against such persecution that appear more expressly in other human rights instruments.

[36] The Disability Discrimination and Other Human Rights Legislation Amendment Act 2009 (Cth) Sch 3, s 1 amended the Human Rights and Equal Opportunity Commission Act 1986 (Cth) by renaming it the Human Rights Commission Act 1986 (Cth), and renaming the Commission the Australian Human Rights Commission.

of functions concerning human rights. These functions include research and education, examining existing and proposed legislation for consistency with such rights, reporting to Parliament on the need for laws or other actions to implement international obligations, and examining Acts or practices of Commonwealth authorities for consistency with protected rights.[37]

In 2011, the Commonwealth Parliament enacted the Human Rights (Parliamentary Scrutiny) Act 2011 (Cth), which requires that all new Bills (and disallowable legislative instruments) introduced must be accompanied by a Statement of Compatibility with the seven core human rights treaties to which Australia is a party.[38] The Act also established a new Parliamentary Joint Committee on Human Rights.[39] This forms part of Australia's Human Rights Framework, which is the response of the federal government to the recommendations of the National Human Rights Consultation Committee's Final Report.[40] In particular, this means that all new Bills (and disallowable legislative instruments) are scrutinized with regard to the religious freedom protections that appear in the treaties discussed previously. This includes the important protection conferred, for example, by Article 18(1) of the ICCPR—the right to 'freedom of thought, conscience and religion'. The rationale behind the Act is, of course, to bring the issue of legislative incompatibility with such fundamental rights to the forefront of political debate in the process of introducing new Bills to the Commonwealth Parliament. **4.15**

(ii) State and territory   The states and territories provide somewhat wider legislative protection against discrimination than that found in Commonwealth legislation. More importantly, the advent of human rights legislation in the Australian Capital Territory (ACT) and Victoria—the Human Rights Act 2004 (ACT) ('ACT HRA 2004') and the Charter of Human Rights and Responsibilities Act 2006 (Vic) ('Victorian Charter')—expands the power of administrative bodies in those jurisdictions to monitor human rights violations.[41] This section considers both forms of legislative protection. **4.16**

Anti-discrimination legislation   Most Australian jurisdictions prohibit discrimination on the basis of religion,[42] including a lack of religious belief.[43] Discrimination may be either direct or indirect, with the former focusing upon the purpose of the conduct and the latter on its effect.[44] Where no such prohibition exists, as in the Commonwealth and New South Wales jurisdictions, some religious groups have been held to fall within the definition of race and therefore anti-race discrimination legislation may apply in some cases.[45] **4.17**

---

[37]   Human Rights Commission Act 1986 (Cth), s 11(e).

[38]   Attorney-General's Department, 'Australia's Human Rights Framework', available at <http://www.ag.gov.au/RightsAndProtections/HumanRights/HumanRightsFramework/Pages/default.aspx>.

[39]   See Attorney-General's Department, 'Australia's Human Rights Framework' (n 38).

[40]   National Human Rights Consultation Committee, 'National Human Rights Consultation: Report' (Attorney-General's Department, 2009).

[41]   Byrnes, Charlesworth, and McKinnon (n 15) 14, 40–3.

[42]   See eg Equal Opportunity Act 2010 (Vic), s 6(1)(n); Fairwork Act 2009 (Cth), ss 153, 195, 351, 772. Religious discrimination is not prohibited under the New South Wales or Commonwealth anti-discrimination regimes.

[43]   See eg Equal Opportunity Act 2010 (Vic), s 4(1). See also *Dixon v Anti-Discrimination Commissioner (Qld)* [2005] 1 Qd R 33, para 21.

[44]   See eg Equal Opportunity Act 2010 (Vic), s 8.

[45]   See eg *Jones v Scully* (2002) 120 FCR 243, 272; *Haider v Combined District Radio Cabs Pty Ltd* [2008] NSWADT 123 (24 April 2008). Further, in New South Wales the obligation extends to ethno-religious discrimination, although this has not been held to extend to discrimination on religious grounds: *A on behalf of V and A v Department of School Education* [1999] NSWADT 120 (12 November 1999), affd *A obo V and A v*

4.18 Still, the prohibition of discrimination on the basis of religion is typically far from the primary purpose of such legislation. Rather, such regimes normally afforded protection in the form of specific exemptions for religion found in general anti-discrimination[46] and employment legislation.[47] The significant overlap between Commonwealth, state, and territory anti-discrimination regimes,[48] as well as between anti-discrimination and employment regimes,[49] means that actions are generally capable of being brought under more than one regime, save for those where the alleged discrimination involves a Commonwealth officer or department.[50]

4.19 In order to engage in lawful discriminatory conduct, the party seeking to rely upon it[51] must establish that the discriminatory conduct conforms to the doctrines of that religion;[52] is necessary to avoid injury to the religious susceptibilities of the adherents of that religion;[53] or is based on the inherent requirements of a particular position of employment.[54] The

---

NSW Department of School Education [2000] NSWADTAP 14 (1 September 2000), where the point was made (at para 20) that:

> It is not a legitimate construction of the [Anti-Discrimination Act] to import, by the back door, a prohibition on religious discrimination by including the practice of the religion generally associated with or observed by a particular ethno-religious group within the concept of 'a characteristic that appertains generally to persons of that race.

[46] See eg Anti-Discrimination Act 1977 (NSW); Equal Opportunity Act 2010 (Vic); Age Discrimination Act 2004 (Cth); Equal Opportunity for Women in the Workplace Act 1999 (Cth); Disability Discrimination Act 1992 (Cth); Sex Discrimination Act 1984 (Cth); Racial Discrimination Act 1975 (Cth). The federal government announced in 2010 its intention to streamline the commonwealth anti-discrimination laws as part of Australia's Human Rights Framework: R McClelland (A-G) and L Tanner (Minister for Finance and Deregulation), 'Reform of Anti-Discrimination Legislation', Media Release, 29/2010, 21 April 2010; see also Attorney-General's Department, 'Consolidation of Commonwealth Anti-Discrimination Laws', Discussion Paper (September 2011), as well as the submissions made as a result of the Discussion Paper, which are collected at Attorney-General's Department, 'Consolidation of Commonwealth Anti-Discrimination Laws', 18 November 2011, at <http://www.ag.gov.au/Humanrightsandantidiscrimination>. A draft bill consolidating the commonwealth's anti-discrimination laws was released in 2012 for further public consultation: Exposure Draft Human Rights and Anti-Discrimination Bill 2012 (Cth).

[47] Fairwork Act 2009 (Cth). This legislation applies to the states, as all (bar Western Australia) have for this purpose conferred the commonwealth with industrial relations powers pursuant to the Commonwealth Constitution, s 51 (xxxvii): T Blackshield and G Williams, *Australian Constitutional Law and Theory: Commentary and Materials* (5th edn, Federation Press, 2009) 995. Additionally, the word 'exemption' has been criticized as not appropriately recognizing the importance of religious groups' ability to discriminate in accordance with their religious commitments: N Foster, 'Freedom of Religion in Practice: Exemptions under Anti-Discrimination Laws on the Basis of Religion', Paper presented at Law and Religion: Legal Regulation of Religious Groups, Organisations and Communities, The University of Melbourne, 15–16 July 2011, at 28. The AHRC prefers the use of the term 'accommodations': AHRC, 'Freedom of Religion Research Report' (n 10) 9, 33.

[48] B Gaze and R Hunter, *Enforcing Human Rights: An Evaluation of the New Regime* (Themis Press, 2010) 52–4, 138–9.

[49] See eg Fairwork Act 2009 (Cth), s 351(2)(a) which permits an exception for discriminatory conduct that is lawful under anti-discrimination law of the commonwealth or states or territories. See also C Sappideen et al, *Macken's Law of Employment* (7th edn, Lawbook, 2012) 606–7, who questions whether this limits the scope of the subsequent exceptions within the same provision.

[50] Gaze and Hunter (n 48) 52–4, 138–9.

[51] Equal Opportunity Act 2010 (Vic), s 13(2); Anti-Discrimination Act 1977 (NSW), s 104; Sex Discrimination Act 1984 (Cth), s 7C.

[52] The conformity test has been noted as 'singularly undemanding' for its requirement that an act or practice be merely in conformity with rather than a breach of the doctrine: *OW v Members of the Board of the Wesley Mission Council* [2010] NSWADT 293 (10 December 2010) para 35. See also *OV v Members of the Board of Wesley Mission Council* (2010) 270 ALR 542, 560, para 72 (Basten JA and Handley AJA). Cf *Cobaw Community Health Services Ltd v Christian Youth Camps Ltd* [2010] VCAT 1613 (8 October 2010) para 317.

[53] 'Injury' requires something more than mere offence: *Hozack v Church of Jesus Christ of Latter-Day Saints* (1997) 79 FCR 441, 444.

[54] Fairwork Act 2009 (Cth), ss 153(2)(a) and 195(2)(a) (discriminatory terms), s 351(2)(b) (discriminatory actions against a staff member), s 772(2)(b) (discriminatory termination).

exemptions operate to the benefit of religious orders, bodies, or institutions more generally,[55] as well as religious and non-religious educational institutions more specifically.[56] The granting of an exemption to a religious educational institution specifically permits discrimination in relation to student enrolments, students' access to benefits or detriments, and student expulsion,[57] as well as student dress and appearance,[58] and the employment of staff.[59]

In short, rather than offering a carte blanche to discriminate, exemptions are generally limited **4.20** to particular grounds, differing as between jurisdictions. Whereas most permit discrimination on the basis of sex, religious belief, marital status, sexual orientation, pregnancy, and gender identity, Commonwealth employment legislation also permits discrimination as to race, colour, age, physical or mental disability, political opinion, national extraction, and social origin.[60]

Human rights legislation   The ACT HRA 2004—Australia's first bill of rights of any kind— **4.21** protects a range of human rights and freedoms. In relation to religious freedom, for example, section 14 enshrines the right to freedom of thought, conscience, religion, and belief, while section 27 protects the rights of minorities to enjoy their own culture, religion, and language. In addition to these specific religious rights, the ACT HRA 2004 also covers the right to equality before the law,[61] the right to life,[62] the right to privacy,[63] freedom of peaceful assembly and association,[64] freedom of expression, the right to take part in public life,[65] and the right to liberty and security of the person.[66]

While the legislation preserves parliamentary sovereignty by leaving ultimate decisions con- **4.22** cerning the violation of human rights to the ACT Legislative Assembly, there nonetheless exists a range of enforcement mechanisms:[67]

(1) an obligation on decision-makers to interpret ACT laws (excluding the common law) to be consistent so far as possible with human rights;[68]

---

[55] Anti-Discrimination Legislation 1977 (NSW), s 56(a)–(d); Equal Opportunity Act 2010 (Vic), s 82; Fairwork Act 2009 (Cth), ss 153(2)(c), 195(2)(c), 351 (2)(c), 772(2)(c); Sex Discrimination Act 1984 (Cth), s 37(a), (b), (d).

[56] Anti-Discrimination Legislation 1977 (NSW), ss 31A, 31K, 46A, 49ZO; Equal Opportunity Act 2010 (Vic), ss 39, 83; Sex Discrimination Act 1984 (Cth), s 38.

[57] Anti-Discrimination Legislation 1977 (NSW), ss 31A, 31K, 46A, 49ZO; Sex Discrimination Act 1984 (Cth), s 38, 7(a), (b), (d).

[58] Equal Opportunity Act 2010 (Vic), s 42.

[59] Fairwork Act 2009 (Cth), ss 153(2)(a) and 195(2)(a) (discriminatory terms), s 351(2)(b) (discriminatory actions against a staff member), s 772(2)(b) (discriminatory termination); Sex Discrimination Act 1984 (Cth), s 38.

[60] The extent to which discrimination on bases other than religious grounds is permitted in schools (especially in employment) has been questioned: see C Evans and L Ujvari, 'Non-Discrimination Laws and Religious Schools in Australia' (2009) 30 Adelaide Law Review 31, 55–6; M Thornton, 'Excepting Equality in the Victorian Equal Opportunity Act' (2010) 23 Australian Journal of Labour Law 240, 245–6.

[61] ACT HRA 2004, s 8.

[62] ACT HRA 2004, s 9.

[63] ACT HRA 2004, s 12.

[64] ACT HRA 2004, s 15.

[65] ACT HRA 2004, s 16.

[66] ACT HRA 2004, s 18.

[67] See Byrnes, Charlesworth, and McKinnon (n 15) 14, 74–9, for the history and legislative background to the ACT HRA 2004. The ACT government itself commissioned a study into the options for human rights legislation prior to the enactment of the ACT HRA 2004: see ACT Bill of Rights Consultative Committee (n 31).

[68] ACT HRA 2004, s 30; for a detailed discussion of the operation of this provision, see Byrnes, Charlesworth, and McKinnon (n 15) 14, 83–5.

(2) jurisdiction vested in the ACT Supreme Court to issue declarations of incompatibility in cases where legislation cannot be interpreted so as to be consistent (not, however, affecting the validity of the legislation);[69]

(3) a duty on the Attorney-General to present written statements on the compatibility of each government Bill presented to the Legislative Assembly;[70] and

(4) the office of Human Rights Commissioner, which has the power to review laws for compatibility with the ACT HRA 2004.[71]

4.23 The ACT HRA 2004 does, however, contain two significant limitations. First, section 6 provides that 'Only individuals have human rights'.[72] Secondly, and more significantly, none of the enumerated rights is absolute—section 28(1) imposes a general qualification on each of the rights found in the Act: 'Human rights may be subject to reasonable limits set by Territory laws that can be demonstrably justified in a free and democratic society'.[73] As such, any limitations placed upon enumerated rights must be proportionate to the objective sought to be achieved by the legislation; a list of factors contained in section 28(2) assists in determining proportionality:[74]

> In deciding whether a limit is reasonable, all relevant factors must be considered, including the following:
> (a) the nature of the right affected;
> (b) the importance of the purpose of the limitation;
> (c) the nature and extent of the limitation;
> (d) the relationship between the limitation and its purpose;
> (e) any less restrictive means reasonably available to achieve the purpose the limitation seeks to achieve.[75]

4.24 Critics predicted an increase in litigation following the enactment of the ACT HRA 2004; however, this prediction proved to be unfounded. Indeed, some supporters might have hoped for a more vigorous invocation of the Act by the courts rather than the cautious, often superficial consideration given to enumerated rights, usually to bolster decisions reached on other grounds. While several decisions considered the interpretive provision of section 30,[76] and other important issues relating to the application of the ACT HRA 2004,[77] there has been only one judicial decision that has issued a declaration of incompatibility,[78] and only two cases have referred briefly to section 14 of the ACT HRA 2004.[79]

4.25 Following broad community consultation, with the ACT HRA 2004 serving as an impetus, in 2006 the Victorian Parliament enacted the Victorian Charter, which shares many of its

---

[69] ACT HRA 2004, ss 32, 39, and 33.

[70] ACT HRA 2004, s 37.

[71] ACT HRA 2004, s 41; see also ACT HRA 2004, ss 38, 43, 44 and Sch 2.

[72] ACT HRA 2004, s 6.

[73] This is similar in its terms to the limitation found in s 1 of the Canadian Charter of Rights and Freedoms: Canada Act 1982 (UK) c 11, Sch B, Pt I ('Canadian Charter of Rights and Freedoms').

[74] Byrnes, Charlesworth, and McKinnon (n 15) 82.

[75] ACT HRA 2004, s 28(2).

[76] Byrnes, Charlesworth, and McKinnon (n 15) 99–104; see *Commissioner for Housing (ACT) v Y* [2007] ACTSC 84 (12 October 2007); *SI bhnf CC v KS bhnf IS* (2005) 195 FLR 151.

[77] See *R v YL* (2004) 187 FLR 84; *Hausmann v Shute* (2007) 227 FLR 368; *Stevens v McCallum* [2006] ACTCA 13 (30 June 2006); *R v Griffin* [2007] ACTCA 6 (5 April 2007); *Capital Property Projects (ACT) Pty Ltd v ACT Planning and Land Authority* [2008] ACTCA 9 (21 May 2008).

[78] *Re Islam* (2010) 244 FLR 158.

[79] *Buzzacott v The Queen* [2005] ACTCA 7 (1 March 2005); *R v AM* (2010) 245 FLR 410.

characteristics with its ACT counterpart. The parliamentary scrutiny and compatibility processes found in the Victorian Charter came into effect on 1 January 2007, while provisions relating to public authorities and the courts—the interpretation of law, declarations of inconsistent interpretation, and new obligations on public authorities[80]—commenced on 1 January 2008.[81]

The Victorian Charter applies to Parliament, courts, tribunals, and to public authorities in **4.26** order to protect human persons.[82] Most of the same human rights found in the ACT HRA 2004 are also protected by the Victorian Charter. These include: the right to recognition and equality before the law;[83] the right to life;[84] freedom of thought, conscience, religion, and belief;[85] freedom of expression;[86] freedom of assembly and association;[87] and cultural rights (affirming the rights of members of all cultural, religious, racial, or linguistic communities to exercise various rights related to membership in those communities).[88]

As with the ACT HRA 2004, section 7 of the Victorian Charter provides that its enumer- **4.27** ated rights are subject to such reasonable limits as can be demonstrably justified in a free and democratic society based upon human dignity, equality, and freedom. Additionally, the same non-exhaustive set of factors used to determine whether a limitation is reasonable found in the ACT HRA 2004 is found in the Victorian Charter.

The enforcement provisions of the Victorian Charter are also similar to those found in the **4.28** ACT HRA 2004, for instance compatibility statements must be prepared when legislation is introduced into Parliament;[89] legislation may be overridden for a period of five years;[90] and all statutory provisions must be interpreted by the courts and any other decision-maker in a way compatible with human rights, so far as it is possible to do that consistently with their purpose and, if that is not possible, the court or decision-maker may make a declaration of inconsistent interpretation.[91] Remedies for breaches of obligations of public authorities are limited to those causes of action and grounds for review that exist outside the Charter.[92]

To date, as with the ACT HRA 2004, the most significant impact of the Victorian Charter **4.29** has been in the executive and legislative spheres.[93] Use of the Charter in the courts has been limited primarily to criminal matters.[94]

---

[80] Victorian Charter, Pt 3, div, 3–4.
[81] For the background to the enactment of the Victorian Charter, see Byrnes, Charlesworth, and McKinnon (n 15) 109–14; A Pound and K Evans, *An Annotated Guide to the Victorian Charter of Human Rights and Responsibilities* (Lawbook, 2008); C Evans and S Evans, *Australian Bills of Rights: The Law of the Victorian Charter and ACT Human Rights Act* (LexisNexis, 2008); G Taylor, *The Constitution of Victoria* (Federation Press, 2006) 51–2.
[82] Victorian Charter, ss 6–7.
[83] Victorian Charter, s 8.
[84] Victorian Charter, s 9. By virtue of s 48, the Victorian Charter does not affect any law applicable to abortion or child destruction passed before or after the Charter.
[85] Victorian Charter, s 14.
[86] Victorian Charter, s 15.
[87] Victorian Charter, s 16.
[88] Victorian Charter, s 19.
[89] Victorian Charter, ss 28, 30.
[90] Victorian Charter, s 31. On these grounds, see Byrnes, Charlesworth, and McKinnon (n 15) 123–33.
[91] Victorian Charter, ss 32, 36–7.
[92] Victorian Charter, s 39.
[93] Byrnes, Charlesworth, and McKinnon (n 15) 123–33.
[94] See eg *R v Benbrika (Ruling No 20)* (2008) VSC 80; *R v Williams* (2007) VSC 2; *R v White* (2007) VSC 142.

c) Common law

4.30 Although recognized as being of fundamental importance to a free society,[95] there is no 'inalienable right of religious freedom and expression' under the common law of Australia.[96] Nevertheless, such a freedom does form the basis of a principle of construction that legislation can only take away long established rights and freedoms where clear words are used,[97] sometimes referred to as the 'common law bill of rights',[98] and recently judicially outlined,[99] in which the court rendered invalid a provision of delegated legislation restricting annoying conduct, which could have included the actions of a religious group protesting during the Pope's visit to Australia. The court considered that the legislation was to be interpreted having regard not only to the freedom of expression but also to the 'freedom of people to adhere to the religion of their choice and the beliefs of their choice and to manifest their religion or beliefs in worship, observance, practice and teaching',[100] finding that the latter freedom had been 'generally accepted in Australian society'.[101] Thus, as the delegated legislation violated those freedoms in a manner that went beyond the scope of delegated legislative power, the legislation was held invalid.[102] Still, the common law is easily modified by a contrary statutory intention and so fails to provide a robust bulwark against any intended legislative incursions into the freedom of religion.[103]

(3) The principal Australian contexts in which religious rights arise

a) Education

4.31 **(i) Background** Education at the primary[104] and secondary[105] levels in Australia may be very broadly categorized as either 'Government'[106] or 'Non-government'.[107] The majority of non-government schools in Australia are Catholic,[108] although schools representing many other faiths, denominations, and philosophies—including Lutheran, Anglican, Uniting, 'Christian', Islamic, Jewish, Greek Orthodox, Non-denominational, and secular (Montessori, Waldorf/Steiner, and other) are also in operation nationally.[109] In 2011,

---

[95] *Church of the New Faith v Commissioner of Pay-roll Tax (Vic)* (1983) 154 CLR 120, 130 (Mason ACJ and Brennan J); *Aboriginal Legal Rights Movement Inc v South Australia (No 1)* (1995) 64 SASR 551, 552 (Doyle CJ, Bollen J agreeing), 554 (Debelle J); *Canterbury Municipal Council v Moslem Alawy Society Ltd* (1985) 1 NSWLR 525, 544 (McHugh J).

[96] *Grace Bible Church v Reedman* (1984) 36 SASR 376, 389 (Millhouse J), 385 (Zelling J).

[97] *Evans v New South Wales* (2008) 168 FCR 576, 580, para 8 ('*Evans*'); *Aboriginal Legal Rights Movement Inc v South Australia (No 1)* (1995) 64 SASR 551, 552 (Doyle CJ, Bollen J agreeing).

[98] J Spiegelman, 'The Common Law Bill of Rights' (Speech delivered at McPherson Lectures on Statutory Interpretation and Human Rights, University of Queensland, 10 March 2008).

[99] *Evans* (2008) 168 FCR 576.

[100] *Evans* (n 97) 580, para 8.

[101] *Evans* (n 97) 596, para 79.

[102] *Evans* (n 97) 596, para 83.

[103] *Aboriginal Legal Rights Movement Inc v South Australia (No 1)* (1995) 64 SASR 551, 552 (Doyle CJ, with whom Bollen J agreed), 554 (Debelle J).

[104] 'Primary' schools correspond approximately to US elementary schools, typically catering for students from Reception (ages 5–6) to Grade 6 or 7 (ages 11–13).

[105] Secondary schools typically cater for students from Grade 7 or 8 (ages 12–14) to Grade 12 or 13 (ages 17–19).

[106] Sometimes referred to as 'state' or (in contrast to the UK) 'public'.

[107] Non-government schools are variously referred to as 'independent', 'religious', 'church', or 'private' schools, depending on the particular school.

[108] See Australian Bureau of Statistics, '4221.0—Schools, Australia, 2011: Schools', Statistics Release No 4221.0, 21 March 2012, available at <http://www.abs.gov.au/AUSSTATS/abs@.nsf/Previousproducts/4221.0Main%20Features12011>.

[109] By way of example, a directory of non-Catholic non-government schools in South Australia is available at The Association of Independent Schools of South Australia, 'Member School Directory' (Directory,

there were 9,435 schools operational across the country: 6,705 Government schools, and 2,730 non-government schools (comprising 1,710 Catholic schools and 1,020 independent schools),[110] catering to around 3,541,809 students (including 22,277 part-time students).[111]

(ii) Government schools Funding for government schools comes primarily from state **4.32** governments, with the commonwealth government providing supplementary assistance.[112] Non-government educational institutions are predominantly privately funded, though they receive some public funding, primarily from the commonwealth government.[113] Australian students generally begin school with a kindergarten or preparatory school year, and then undertake 12 years of primary and secondary schooling; ten years of schooling is generally the minimum, although there is some variation in this and in school starting and leaving ages from state to state.[114]

Australian state government approaches to religious education in government schools are **4.33** broadly similar; in South Australia,[115] for instance, provision for religious education is made by section 102 of the Education Act 1972 (SA):

102—Religious education

(1) Regular provision shall be made for religious education at a Government school, under such conditions as may be prescribed, at times during which the school is open for instruction.

(2) The regulations shall include provision for permission to be granted for exemption from religious education on conscientious grounds.

Beyond this enabling provision, the content and conduct of religious education in gov- **4.34** ernment schools is provided for by the Education Regulations 2012 (SA) which are made under the Act.[116] Among other things, the regulations provide for the establishment of

---

January 2012) <http://www.ais.sa.edu.au/__files/f/93172/AISSA%20Member%20School%20Directory%20 January%202012>.

[110] Or, expressed differently: 6,312 primary schools, 1,396 secondary schools, 1,305 combined primary-secondary schools, and 422 special schools: Australian Bureau of Statistics, 'Schools' (n 108).

[111] Australian Bureau of Statistics, '4221.0—Schools, Australia, 2011: Students', Statistics Release No 4221.0, 21 March 2012, available at <http://www.abs.gov.au/ausstats/abs@.nsf/Latestproducts/4221.0Main %20Features302011>.

[112] Department of Education, Employment and Workplace Relations, 'Funding for Schools' (2011), available at <http://deewr.gov.au/funding-schools>; Review of Funding for Schooling Expert Panel, 'Review of Funding for Schooling—Final Report' (2011) ch 2, especially at 38–42, paras 2.1.2–2.1.3 ('*Gonski Review*'). The *Gonski Review,* the final report of the commissioned review into funding of schooling in Australia, which was undertaken by an expert panel chaired by David Gonski AC, is the best resource currently available on school funding in Australia.

[113] See *Gonski Review* (n 112) ch 2.

[114] Department of Education, Employment and Workplace Relations, 'Overview' (n 112).

[115] It is noted that, while the relevant legislative provisions of other states' Acts are broadly similar, they differ in detail, and the following discussion should be read with this in mind. Relevant similar legislation in other Australian states and territories includes the Education Act 2004 (ACT), s 29; the Education Act 1990 (NSW), ss 32–33A; the Education Act (NT), s 73; the Education (General Provisions) Act 2006 (Qld), s 76; the Education Act 1994 (Tas), s 34; the Education and Training Reform Act 2006 (Vic), s 2.2.11; and the School Education Act 1999 (WA), ss 69, 71. For an older, though still informative, detailed overview of the area, see G Rossiter, *Religious Education in Australian Schools* (Curriculum Development Centre, 1981). For further discussion, see M Crawford and G Rossiter, 'The Nature of Religious Education in Public Schools: The Quest for an Educational Identity' (1994) 5 Panorama: International Journal of Comparative Religious Education and Values 77.

[116] These are further reflected in Department of Education and Children's Services policies on the topic: Department of Education and Children's Services (SA), 'Religious Activities in Government Schools',

standing committees[117] and school-specific religious education committees,[118] and for the development of course modules for distribution to schools.[119] Most significantly, they also provide for the conduct of both 'religious education' and 'religious seminars' in schools.[120]

4.35 However, this broad similarity in the approach to religious education in government schools is beginning to diverge. In 2010 New South Wales passed the Education Amendment (Ethics) Act 2010 (NSW), which inserted a new section 33A into the Education Act 1990 (NSW). This section creates a secular alternative to special religious education, an ethics course, for students whose parents object to special religious education. This amendment has garnered some controversy in NSW, but the NSW government remains committed to it.[121] Conversely, the Victorian government rejected an attempt by the Humanist Society of Victoria to have its course on 'humanist applied ethics' approved for delivery in government schools during special religious instruction time in 2010.[122]

4.36 In 2012, two developments in different Australian jurisdictions emerged to threaten the status of religious education in Australian government schools. The first was a High Court Challenge to the constitutionality of federal government funding of the National Schools Chaplaincy Program (NSCP)[123] in government schools. The second was a challenge in the Victorian Civil and Administrative Tribunal (VCAT) to the alleged discriminatory nature of a state government-funded chaplaincy programme in Victorian government schools. Both carried implications for religious education programmes (specifically chaplaincy programmes) in Australian government schools.

Administrative Instructions and Guidelines (May 2007), available at <http://www.decs.sa.gov.au/volunteers/files/links/Religious_activities_in_Go.pdf>.

[117] Education Regulations 2012 (SA), reg 87. The Standing Committee on Religious Education in Government Schools is composed of departmental, ecumenical, parent organization, and tertiary education course representatives, and is charged with advising the Minister on various matters concerning religious education in schools.

[118] Education Regulations 2012 (SA), reg 88. The school-specific religious education committees are composed of not more than two teachers, not more than two parents from the school council, and not more than four local clergy. These committees are established by the head teacher or principal of the school, in consultation with the school council, and are charged with advising and assisting the head teacher or principal 'in such matters concerning religious education in the school as the head teacher and the committee shall determine'.

[119] Education Regulations 2012 (SA), reg 89. Pursuant to reg 90, only persons registered as teachers may teach the classes.

[120] Education Regulations 2012 (SA), regs 91(1), (2).

[121] See eg A Shanahan, 'Godless Ethics Classes Pointless', *The Australian*, 1 May 2010, available at <http://www.theaustralian.com.au/opinion/columnists/godless-ethics-classes-are-pointless/story-fn562txd-1225860481656>; Education Amendment (Ethics Classes Repeal) Bill 2011 (NSW), which seeks to repeal the amendment; S Nicholls, 'Premier Says Ethics Pledge Still Intact Despite Nile "Process"', *The Sydney Morning Herald*, 3 August 2011, available at <http://www.smh.com.au/nsw/premier-says-ethics-pledge-intact-despite-nile-process-20110802-1i9tx.html#ixzz1U96JAxYg>; S Nicholls, 'Class of His Own: Nile Pushes for Ethics Review', *The Sydney Morning Herald*, 4 August 2011, available at <http://www.smh.com.au/nsw/class-of-his-own-nile-pushes-for-ethics-review-20110803-1ibpk.html>.

[122] M Bachelard, 'Thou Shall Not Teach Humanism: ALP', *The Age*, 7 November 2010, available at <http://www.theage.com.au/victoria/thou-shall-not-teach-humanism-alp-20101106-17i8t.html>.

[123] Department of Education, Employment and Workplace Relations, 'National School Chaplaincy and Student Welfare Program Overview' (June 2012), available at <http://www.deewr.gov.au/Schooling/NSCSWP/Pages/NSCSWP_Overview.aspx> (from 1 January 2012 this became the National School Chaplaincy and Student Welfare Program, and under this retitled programme schools could choose between engaging a school chaplain or a secular student welfare worker).

Williams *Williams v Commonwealth*[124] involved a recent constitutional challenge to the   **4.37**
Commonwealth government's NSCP. The plaintiff, Mr Williams, was a father of four children who attended Darling Heights State School in Queensland. The school participated in
the NSCP. One of the defendants, the Scripture Union of Queensland ('Scripture Union'),
had entered into a funding agreement with the commonwealth government to provide chaplaincy services to the school under the NSCP guidelines. The guidelines required that school
chaplains would, among other things: '[provide] general religious and personal advice to
those seeking it'; and would '[work] in a wider spiritual context to support students and
staff of all religious affiliations and not [seek] to impose any religious beliefs or persuade an
individual toward a particular set of religious beliefs'.[125] The funding pursuant to which the
Scripture Union was contracted to provide the chaplaincy services had no statutory basis.
Rather, the NSCP was administered by the commonwealth government purely by way of a
series of funding agreements.

Mr Williams argued: **4.38**

(1) that the Commonwealth had no executive power to enter into the NSCP funding agree-
    ment with the Scripture Union; and
(2) that the Commonwealth had no authority to draw money from the Consolidated
    Revenue Fund, and to pay such funds over to the Scripture Union.

These arguments were based on section 61 of the Australian Constitution—which vests   **4.39**
executive power in the commonwealth government that 'extends to the execution and maintenance of [the] Constitution, and of the laws of the Commonwealth'—which Mr Williams
argued did not empower the commonwealth to enter into such funding agreements in the
absence of a statutory basis. He also relied upon section 116 of the Constitution, which
relevantly provides that 'no religious test shall be required as a qualification for any office or
public trust under the Commonwealth'.[126] He argued that the definition of 'school chaplain'
in the NSCP guidelines—which required that the person be recognized 'through formal
ordination, commissioning, recognised qualifications or endorsement by a recognised or
accepted religion institution or a state/territory approved chaplaincy service'[127]—imposed a
religious test for that particular Commonwealth office, contrary to the Constitution.[128] The
Attorneys-General of each state intervened, and the Churches' Commission on Education
Incorporated appeared as *amicus curiae*, with some 16 counsel in total appearing before
the Court.

The High Court found for Mr Williams, holding that the executive power in section 61 of   **4.40**
the Constitution did not permit the commonwealth to enter into the NSCP funding agreements, or to authorize the payments from the Consolidated Revenue Fund. The executive
power found in section 61 did not extend to authorizing the commonwealth government
to do what the Commonwealth Parliament could authorize it to do by means of passing

---

[124] *Williams v Commonwealth* (2012) 288 ALR 410. See also the case notes: BB Saunders, 'The
Commonwealth and the Chaplains: Executive Power after *Williams v Commonwealth*' (2012) 23 Public Law
Review 153; A Sapienza, 'Using Representative Government to Bypass Representative Government' (2012) 23
Public Law Review 161.
[125] *Williams* (n 124) 494, para 305 (Heydon J), quoting the NSCP guidelines.
[126] This section is analogous to US Constitution, art VI, cl 3.
[127] See eg *Williams* (n 124) 446, para 107 (Gummow and Bell JJ), quoting the NSCP guidelines.
[128] *Williams* (n 124) 446, para 107.

legislation.[129] However, Mr Williams failed at the threshold on the section 116 ground. The High Court found that the 'chaplains engaged by [Scripture Union held] no office under the Commonwealth'.[130] The commonwealth's funding provided to the Scripture Union by way of the NSCP was 'insufficient to render a chaplain engaged by [the Scripture Union] the holder of an office under the Commonwealth'.[131] There needed to be a 'closer connection to the Commonwealth' in order for the religious test under section 116 of the Constitution to be enlivened.[132] Justice Heydon, whilst not expressly agreeing with the reasoning of Gummow and Bell JJ (as had the other members of the Court), nevertheless reached a similar conclusion. His Honour held that the Commonwealth had 'no legal relationship with the "chaplains"', and that they had no control over them, since they were overseen and controlled by the school engaging their services;[133] this meant that the office was not 'in direct relationship with the Commonwealth'.[134] Whilst his Honour indicated that it was unnecessary to decide the point, he appeared to doubt whether the NSCP even imposed a 'religious test', because the work provided by the school chaplains could have been done not only by persons who met a religious test, but also by persons who did not.[135]

4.41 The result of the case was that a vast number of commonwealth funding programmes (including the NSCP) were constitutionally invalid, for want of statutory authorization for their expenditures. The commonwealth government responded by rushing through emergency legislation in the form of the inconspicuously titled Financial Framework Legislation Amendment Act (No 3) 2012 (Cth), which purports to validate all such expenditures by the commonwealth government,[136] and has allowed the NSCP to continue in its slightly altered form as the National School Chaplaincy and Student Welfare Program (NSCSWP).[137] The Act has caused considerable controversy,[138] and Mr Williams has already indicated that he will again seek to challenge the constitutionality of the NSCSWP in the High Court.[139] It remains to be seen what will become of the NSCSWP.

4.42 *Aitken* The *Aitken v Department of Education and Early Childhood Development* ('*Aitken*') VCAT challenge to the discriminatory nature of the state government-funded chaplaincy programme in Victorian government schools involved Victorian legislation which, like the

---

[129] *Williams* (n 124) 446, para 107. The reasons of French CJ, Gummow, and Bell JJ, Hayne, Crennan, and Kiefel JJ all illustrate this reasoning; see eg at 433, para 60, 441, para 83 (French CJ). Heydon J dissented on this point.

[130] *Williams* (n 124) 446, para 109 (Gummow and Bell JJ; French CJ, Hayne, Crennan, and Kiefel JJ agreeing).

[131] *Williams* (n 124) 447, para 110.

[132] *Williams* (n 124) 447, para 110.

[133] *Williams* (n 124) 532, para 445 (Heydon J).

[134] *Williams* (n 124) 532, para 444 (Heydon J).

[135] *Williams* (n 124) 495, paras 306–307 (Heydon J).

[136] See generally Sapienza (n 124).

[137] See 'National School Chaplaincy and Student Welfare Program Overview' (n 123).

[138] See 'National School Chaplaincy and Student Welfare Program Overview' (n 123); S Breheny, 'Democracy Sidelined in Panic Over Chaplains', *The Sydney Morning Herald*, 5 July 2012, available at <http://www.smh.com.au/opinion/politics/democracy-sidelined-in-panic-over-chaplains-20120704-21his.html>;LMezrani,'Academic Says Chaplaincy Rescue Bill Flawed', *Lawyers Weekly*, 28 June 2012, available at <http://www.lawyersweekly.com.au/news/academic-says-chaplaincy-rescue-bill-is-flawed>; A Twomey, 'Bringing Down the House? Keeping School Chaplains Means a Surrender to the Executive', *The Conversation*, 27 June 2012, available at <http://theconversation.edu.au/bringing-down-the-house-keeping-school-chaplains-means-a-surrender-to-the-executive-7926>.

[139] J Lee, 'Father to Take on Canberra Again Over Chaplains', *The Age*, 7 July 2012, available at <http://www.theage.com.au/opinion/political-news/father-to-take-canberra-on-again-over-chaplains-20120706-21mop.html>.

South Australian legislation considered earlier, allows for the provision of Special Religious Instruction (SRI) in Victorian government schools.[140] Significant controversy has arisen over the past year with regard to the provision of this special religious education by the multi-denominational coalition ACCESS Ministries,[141] which teaches the majority of SRI courses in Victorian government schools. Specifically, a cross-section of parents—most clearly represented by the organization Fairness in Religions in School (FIRIS)—object to instances of alleged discriminatory treatment of students who opt out of SRI,[142] as well as the alleged evangelical conduct of ACCESS Ministries' representatives delivering SRI.[143]

Victorian lawyer Andrea Tsalamandris, working with FIRIS,[144] requested a hearing before **4.43** VCAT following a determination by the Victorian Equal Opportunity and Human Rights Commission that a case exists to be answered,[145] as well as the apparent unwillingness of the Victorian Department of Education to conciliate in the matter.[146] FIRIS, while remaining 'supportive of education *about* religion reflective of Australia's multicultural traditions', seeks to bring about the cessation of SRI 'designed to instruct children in a particular faith'.[147]

The *Aitken* matter was heard by VCAT from 1 to 9 March 2012, and the Tribunal handed **4.44** down its decision on 18 October.[148] VCAT found against FIRIS, holding that children who opt out of special religious instruction classes in state primary schools are not being discriminated against under the Equal Opportunity Act.

(iii) **Non-government schools**[149]   As might be expected, the scope for religious education **4.45** in non-government schools is greater than the scope for the same in government schools. In

---

[140] Education and Training Reform Act 2006 (Vic), s 2.2.11. Section 2.2.10 of the same Act provides that 'education in Government schools must be secular and not promote any particular religious practice, denomination or sect'; but note that general religious instruction/education—civics—is expressly allowed by this section.

[141] ACCESS Ministries, 'Special Religious Instruction—The Facts', ACCESS Ministries Fact Sheet (August 2011) 6, available at <http://www.accessministries.org.au/sitebuilder/media/knowledge/asset/files/1/aug2011factsheetsri.pdf>:

> ACCESS ministries is the trading name of the Council for Christian Education in Schools, which is made up of the Anglican Church, Australian Christian Churches, Baptist Union, Christian Brethren Fellowships of Victoria, Christian Reformed Churches, Churches of Christ in Australia, CRC International, Lutheran Church, Presbyterian Church, Salvation Army, Uniting Church, [and the] Wesleyan Methodist Church.

[142] Parental anecdotes include stories of children who have been opted out of SRI being asked to sit in corridors or even in the same classroom as the SRI teaching; of SRI sessions that were not attended by regular teachers, in breach of SRI guidelines; and of opted-out students being forbidden to work on school work during the SRI sessions: see S Warhaft, 'Interview with Sophie Aitken' (Radio Interview, 20 May 2011, available at <http://religionsinschool.com/2011/06/03/sophie-aitken-interview-abc-melbourne>; see also FIRIS, 'Parents' Stories' (2011), available at <http://religionsinschool.com/parents-stories>.

[143] Warhaft (n 142). The relevant legislation on discrimination in Victoria is the Equal Opportunity Act 1995 (Vic) and Equal Opportunity Act 2010 (Vic) (the latter being intended, according to its purposes (s 1), to 're-enact and extend the law relating to equal opportunity and . . . discrimination'). Cf generally AHRC, 'A Guide to Australia's Anti-discrimination Laws, Information for Employers: Good Practice, Good Business', 24 January 2007, available at <http://www.hreoc.gov.au/info_for_employers/law/index.html#VIC>.

[144] Cf FIRIS, 'Fairness in Religion in School' (2011), available at <http://religionsinschool.com>.

[145] Cf Warhaft (n 142). According to this interview, a VCAT directions hearing was scheduled for 6 June 2011.

[146] Cf L Hobday, 'Investigation Ordered into Religious Educator', 13 May 2011, ABC PM, available at <http://www.abc.net.au/pm/content/2011/s3216526.htm>.

[147] Cf FIRIS, 'Parents' Stories' (n 142).

[148] *Aitken v Victoria* [2012] VCAT 1547 (18 October 2012).

[149] As with the discussion of government schools, examples in this discussion of non-government schools will also be drawn from South Australia.

South Australia, for example, all curricula in non-government schools must conform to the South Australian Curriculum Standards and Accountability Framework;[150] but beyond this, the intensity and purpose of religious education may be determined by the individual school, and will vary depending on the faith or denomination (if any) of the particular school.

4.46 As noted previously, the commonwealth provides the majority of any public funding to non-government schools.[151] Currently, the provision of such funding is made pursuant to the Schools Assistance Act 2008 (Cth).[152] This Act provides for both recurrent funding (calculated by reference to enrolments and a complex set of other criteria)[153] and capital funding,[154] funding for non-government schools with significant proportions of Indigenous students,[155] and funding for targeted programmes including the 'Literacy, Numeracy and Special Learning Needs' programme, the 'Country Areas' programme and the 'English as a Second Language' programme.[156]

4.47 As a prerequisite to funding, non-government schools or non-government school bodies (where they exist) must sign funding agreements that accord with the School Assistance Regulations 2009 (Cth).[157] These agreements place a number of conditions on funding, including requirements for school performance and transparency, grant acquittal and reporting, and monitoring and evaluation.[158] The agreements also stipulate the uses to which funds may be put: recurrent grant funds, which are most material to the present discussion, may be used for 'teaching and ancillary staff salaries . . . professional development of teachers . . . curriculum development . . . [and] maintenance and general operation'.[159]

b) Employment

4.48 Given the level of financial support provided by state and commonwealth governments, religious schools have received criticism for their discriminatory employment practices so as to maintain their religious ethos on the basis that this subverts multi-faith and multi-cultural Australian ideals and undermines the promotion of equality through anti-discrimination laws.[160] While religious institutions tend to accept non-religious students,[161] maintenance of

---

[150] For a discussion of the sometimes complex relationship between religious non-government schools and anti-discrimination laws, see Evans and Ujvari (n 60).

[151] See n 113 and accompanying text.

[152] A useful discussion and breakdown of the Act is contained in Department of Education, Employment and Workplace Relations (Cth), 'Schools Assistance Act 2008 Administrative Guidelines: Commonwealth Programs for Non-Government Schools, 2009 to 2012: 2010 Update', Administrative Guideline (2010), available at <http://www.deewr.gov.au/Schooling/Programs/Documents/SchoolAdminGuidelines2010.pdf>. Useful further discussion, with a focus on emerging issues and community concerns, may be found in 'Review of Funding for Schooling' (n 112).

[153] 'Review of Funding for Schooling' (n 112) 12–13.

[154] Schools Assistance Act 2008 (Cth) Pts 4, 5.

[155] Schools Assistance Act 2008 (Cth) Pt 4, div 9.

[156] Schools Assistance Act 2008 (Cth) Pt 6.

[157] Administrative Guidelines (n 152) 4.

[158] Administrative Guidelines (n 152) 4.

[159] Administrative Guidelines (n 152) 14.

[160] AHRC, 'Freedom of Religion Research Report' (n 10) 62–3. See, also, D Cahill et al, *Religion, Cultural Diversity and Safeguarding Australia: A Partnership under the Australia Government's Living in Harmony Initiative* (Department of Immigration and Multicultural and Indigenous Affairs and Australian Multicultural Foundation, 2004) 118.

[161] See eg the submission of the Anglican Education Commission to the AHRC: Bryan Cowling, Submission No 1536 to AHRC, 'Freedom of Religion and Belief Project', (2008–09), available at <http://www.hreoc.gov.au/frb/frb_submissions.html>.

the religious ethos through setting faith-based criteria for the employment of teachers and other staff remains of importance to religious institutions.[162]

Due to the limited application of commonwealth constitutional protections, the primary **4.49** source for the ability of religious schools to discriminate in hiring practices comes through the application of the exemptions to anti-discrimination and employment legislation. Exemptions in Australia take a 'group-oriented approach', focusing on the effect of the failure to permit discrimination on the group and its members.

A recent interpretation by the New South Wales Court of Appeal of the 'religious bod- **4.50** ies' exemption in section 56 of the Anti-Discrimination Act 1977 (NSW) in 2010 may prove significant for the provision of religious education in Australian non-government schools. *OV v Members of the Board of Wesley Mission Council*[163] arose after Wesley Mission, a publicly-funded body, refused to authorize OV and OW as foster carers on the grounds that their relationship was a homosexual one. When the couple challenged the decision, alleging that it constituted discrimination on the basis of homosexuality and marital status,[164] Wesley Mission sought to rely on the 'religious bodies' exception contained within section 56 of the Anti-Discrimination Act 1977 (NSW), which provides that the Act does not apply to 'a. any other act or practice of a body established to propagate religion that conforms to the doctrines of that religion or is necessary to avoid injury to the religious susceptibilities of the adherents of that religion'.

The case began in the Equal Opportunity Division of the NSW Administrative Decisions **4.51** Tribunal (NSWADT), where the couple's complaint was upheld with respect to homosexuality.[165] Wesley Mission appealed to the Appeal Panel of the Tribunal (NSWADTAP), with the NSW Attorney-General intervening in support of their contentions. The Appeal Panel set aside the NSWADT's decision[166] and OW and OV appealed to the NSW Court of Appeal.[167]

The New South Wales Court of Appeal held that the exemption contained in section 56 **4.52** protected Wesley Mission's decision to refuse the authorization of OV and OW to become foster carers due to their same-sex relationship. In deciding the case, Basten JA and Handley JA (with Allsop P concurring) concluded that the correct construction of section 56 requires decision-makers to consider whether any allegedly discriminatory act conforms, at the time it is made, with the particular religious doctrines that the relevant organization was established to propagate.[168]

---

[162] See generally AHRC, 'Freedom of Religion Research Report' (n 10) 63–5.
[163] *OV v Members of the Board of Wesley Mission Council* (2010) 79 NSWLR 606 ('*OV*').
[164] Discrimination on such grounds is prohibited by the Anti-Discrimination Act 1977 (NSW), Pts 3 and 4.
[165] *OV v QZ (No 2)* [2008] NSWADT 115 (1 April 2008).
[166] *Members of the Board of the Wesley Mission Council v OV* [2009] NSWADTAP 57 (27 January 2009).
[167] *OV* (n 163). It should be noted that the NSWCA ultimately remitted the case to the NSWADT, which reconsidered the matter and held that the actions of Wesley Mission fell *within* the exemption properly construed: *OW v Members of the Board of the Wesley Mission Council* [2010] NSWADT 293 (10 December 2010). For a perspective on the potentially divisive nature of the case within the Uniting church, cf 'Gay Foster Care Ban Divides Uniting Church', *The Sydney Morning Herald*, 27 December 2010, available at <http://news.smh .com.au/breaking-news-national/gay-foster-care-ban-divides-uniting-church-20101227-1988l.html>.
[168] Specifically, 'the question the Tribunal needed to address was whether a refusal in 2003 to consider an application to authorise a same-sex couple to foster a child conformed at that time with the doctrines of the religion which the Wesley Mission was as at 2003, established to propagate': *OV* (n 163) 621, para 54.

4.53 In response to this decision, the body Christian Schools Australia ('CSA') (which describes itself as a peak body serving independent Christian schools)[169] suggests that the decision may have implications for allegedly discriminatory acts occurring in non-government schools across Australia.[170] It asserts that schools seeking to rely on the section 56 exemption or an analogous provision would be required to demonstrate, first, that they seek to ('were established to') propagate a religion, and secondly, that the relevant religion contains particular doctrines relevant to the act in question.[171] CSA further suggests that standard 'Statement of Faith' documents in school constitutions may be inadequate, and forecasts the adoption of 'more expansive and codified "doctrinal statements"'.[172]

4.54 The NSW Court of Appeal's interpretation of section 56 may therefore operate as a double-edged sword: while it provides an extra avenue of argument for religious non-government schools being accused of discrimination, there may also be the potential for insincere uses of the exception in cases where discrimination has occurred and where legal recourse therefore ought rightly be granted.

c) Religious dress

4.55 An emerging issue in law and religion discourse in Australia is the regulation of religious dress in specific situations.[173] Given international developments and the current international political climate, it is perhaps unsurprising that the Australian jurisprudence has concerned itself largely with the Muslim *burqa* and *niqab*.[174] An example will serve to illustrate the emergence of this issue.

4.56 In 2011, a Muslim woman, Carnita Matthews, was travelling along a road by car when she was stopped for a breathalyser check by a police officer.[175] Ms Matthews was wearing her *niqab* at the time, which covered her whole face but for her eyes. The next day a person claiming to be Ms Matthews made a statutory declaration, which asserted that the police officer from the day before had tried to remove her *niqab* against her will. The police investigated the matter, and found CCTV footage from the police car in question was not consistent with the statutory declaration that had been made. As a result, Ms Matthews was charged with having made a false statement to the police.

---

[169] CSA, 'About CSA' (2011), available at <http://csa.edu.au/csa/about>.

[170] M Spencer, 'Court of Appeal Decision Impacts All Christian Schools' on CSA, Blogs: Comment, Opinion and Features, 17 August 2010, available at <http://archive.csa.edu.au/blogs/staff/378-court-of-appeal-decision-impacts-all-christian-schools>. Cf also E Turnour, 'Religious Body Exemptions Under Anti-Discrimination Legislation' in Moores Legal, 'Not for Profit Briefing' Newsletter (August 2010), available at <http://www.mooreslegal.com.au/uploadedFiles/Newsletters/NotForProfit/nl/NFP_Briefing_August_2010.pdf>.

[171] Spencer (n 170).

[172] Spencer (n 170).

[173] See eg R Barker, 'The Full Face Covering Debate: An Australian Perspective' (2012) 36(1) University of Western Australia Law Review 143; R Barker, 'Full Face Covering Legislation' (2012) 37(1) Alternative Law Journal 62; A Gray, 'Section 116 of the Australian Constitution and Dress Restrictions' (2011) 16(2) Deakin Law Review 293; A Hewitt and C Koch, 'Can and Should Burqas Be Banned? The Legality and Desirability of Bans of the Full Veil in Europe and Australia' (2011) 36(1) Alternative Law Journal 16; C Koch, A Hewitt, and M Lum, 'Do *Burqas* Bite? National and International Perspectives on Bans of Religious Dress', Paper presented at The South Australian Chapter of the Australian Association of Constitutional Law and The Research Unit for the Study of Society, Law and Religion at The University of Adelaide: Joint Seminar, Adelaide Law School, 20 July 2010; S Remond, 'The Niqab in the Courtroom' (2010) 48(9) Law Society Journal 36.

[174] See the papers listed at n 173.

[175] This example is drawn from Barker, 'Full Face Covering Legislation' (n 173).

Having been found guilty, Ms Matthews appealed on the basis that the Justice of the Peace **4.57** who had witnessed the declaration had failed to identify the person making the declaration—who was wearing a *niqab*, thus obscuring their face—as Ms Matthews when the declaration was made. The appeal was granted and the conviction quashed. In consequence, the New South Wales Parliament passed an Act[176] to enable police and other designated public officers to request an individual to remove a face covering in order for them to be identified. The removal is limited to the period of identification, after which the individual may replace their face covering. The legislation, whilst based on this particular incident, is drafted in general terms, so as to cover circumstances such as individuals wearing 'dark sunglasses'.[177] The new powers are currently under review by the New South Wales Ombudsman, which is expected to release its report by mid-2013.[178]

This example shows one of the emerging real-world aspects of the debate in Australia. **4.58** Meanwhile, scholarly commentary has focused largely on the extent to which it would be within the powers of the various state parliaments, and the federal Parliament, to enact an outright complete ban on full-face coverings.[179] The views expressed have been mixed: some commentators have reasoned that 'there is no legal limitation on the Commonwealth's power to implement legislation banning the wearing of the *burqa* and *niqab* and it is unlikely that there is any real limitation on the enactment of an effective state or territory ban';[180] whilst others have argued that 'the High Court should read the principle of religious freedom in section 116 broadly', so as to invalidate such a law.[181] Ultimately, these conflicting views will only be resolved as and when specific religious dress matters come before the courts.

As this, and other, religious legal issues emerge, it will be interesting to observe whether **4.59** the Australian jurisprudence continues to develop in a piecemeal fashion—adding patches as necessary to protect religious freedoms—or moves towards a more cohesive, holistic approach. These issues are likely to test, in particular, the outer limits of the narrow constitutional protection found in section 116.

(4) Conclusion

The available constitutional guarantees, combined with a piecemeal legislative anti- **4.60** discrimination regime, make it difficult to find comprehensive protection for religious rights in Australia. This firmly places the protection of religious freedom in the hands of the State and Territory legislatures for the moment. Yet, current developments may drive comprehensive national responses in the future.

---

[176] Identification Legislation Amendment Act 2011 (NSW), which amends the Amendment of Law Enforcement (Powers and Responsibilities) Act 2002 (NSW); Children (Detention Centre) Act 1987 (NSW); Court Security Act 2005 (NSW); Crimes (Administration of Sentences) Act 1999 (NSW); Oaths Act 1990 (NSW); Children (Detention Centres) Regulation 2010 (NSW); and Crimes (Administration of Sentences) Regulation 2008 (NSW).

[177] Barker, 'Full Face Covering Legislation' (n 173) 62.

[178] D Carter, 'Review of Police Powers Requiring Removal of Face Coverings' (2012) 27(3) Alternative Law Journal 206.

[179] See the papers listed at n 173.

[180] Hewitt and Koch (n 173) 20.

[181] Gray (n 173) 324.

B. CANADA

Howard Kislowicz[182]

(1) Main provisions and brief historical perspective

4.61 There are two main legislative protections for the exercise of religious rights in Canada. First, the Canadian Charter of Rights and Freedoms protects the 'freedom of conscience and religion'.[183] This constitutionally entrenched provision applies to legislation and government action,[184] and effectively requires governments to justify infringements of religious liberties. Secondly, religious rights are protected by federal and provincial human rights statutes. These instruments are generally aimed at eliminating discriminatory treatment and apply in both private and public contexts.

4.62 Some religious rights have been protected in Canada since before the country's 1867 confederation, though these applied only to Catholic and Protestant Christians. The Treaty of Paris 1763, for example, guaranteed religious freedom to Catholics; this right was preserved by the Québec Act of 1774, the Constitutional Act of 1791, and the Act of Union of 1840.[185] While the Constitution Act, 1867, did not guarantee religious freedom per se, it preserved the denominational schooling rights that existed at the time of confederation.[186] In 1960, the Canadian Bill of Rights specifically protected freedom of religion;[187] though not constitutionally entrenched, this act applied to all subsequent federal legislation.[188]

4.63 An early example of the judicial protection of religious freedom in Canada is the 1953 decision of *Saumur v City of Québec*.[189] There, in the absence of an explicit constitutional right of religious freedom, the Supreme Court of Canada (SCC) exempted a group of Jehovah's Witnesses from a municipal by-law that limited the distribution of written materials on city streets.[190]

(2) Key constitutional and statutory materials

4.64 The Canadian Charter of Rights and Freedoms, which forms part of the Constitution Act, 1982, protects 'freedom of conscience and religion'.[191] As already noted, this provision binds

---

[182] Assistant Professor, Faculty of Law, University of New Brunswick. Thanks to the editors of this work for including me in the project, and to Professor Ran Hirschl for considering me up to the task. Thanks also to Jonathan Rabinovitch for assistance with the section on employment. Mistakes are mine.

[183] The Canadian Charter of Rights and Freedoms, Pt I of the Constitution Act, 1982, being Sch B to the Canada Act 1982 (UK), 1982, c 11, s 2(a).

[184] Constitution Act, 1982, s 32.

[185] Québec Act of 1774, 14 Geo III, c 83; Constitutional Act of 1791, 31 Geo III, c 31; British North America Act, 1840, 3 & 4 Victoria, c 35; see *Saumur v City of Québec* [1953] 2 SCR 299, 358.

[186] The Constitution Act, 1867, 30 & 31 Vict, c 3, s 93.

[187] SC 1960, c 44, s 1(c).

[188] SC 1960, c 44, s 2. Subsequent legislation could avoid the application of the Bill of Rights if it contained a specific derogation.

[189] See n 185.

[190] Rand, Estey, and Kellock JJ ruled on federalism grounds (the province was incompetent to legislate in relation to religion and free speech); Locke J suggested that the right to religious freedom was implicit in the Constitution Act, 1867; and Kerwin J held that the right was protected by the Freedom of Worship Act, RSQ 1941, c 307.

[191] See n 183.

all government actors, federal and provincial. Though the right is framed expansively, governments may limit the freedom of conscience and religion if the limitation is 'within the reasonable limits prescribed by law as can be demonstrably justified in a free and democratic society'.[192] This complex phrase is addressed in paragraphs 4.70–4.74.

As also noted previously, federal and provincial human rights legislation prohibits religious **4.65** discrimination. The prohibitions take various forms across the country. Some human rights codes prohibit discrimination in various situations (for example discriminatory publications, discrimination in accommodations, in the purchase of property, etc), and in each situation lists religion as one of the prohibited grounds of discrimination.[193] Others take a substantially similar approach, including 'religion' in the general definition of 'prohibited grounds' of discrimination.[194]

Québec's Charter of Human Rights and Freedoms has a broad prohibition against discrimi- **4.66** nation on the basis of religion, but differs from most other provincial human rights documents in that it also guarantees religious and conscientious freedom.[195]

(3) Leading cases

a) When is a religious right held to be exercised?

R v Big M Drug Mart,[196] the SCC's first decision regarding the Charter's protection of reli- **4.67** gious freedom, provides the foundational definition of religious freedom in Canadian law. There, Justice Dickson held:

> The essence of the concept of freedom of religion is the right to entertain such religious beliefs as a person chooses, the right to declare religious beliefs openly and without fear of hindrance or reprisal, and the right to manifest religious belief by worship and practice or by teaching and dissemination.[197]

From this broad definition, it is clear that a religious right can be exercised in at least four **4.68** ways: (1) by holding beliefs, (2) by declaring those beliefs openly, (3) by observing religious practices, and (4) by proselytizing.

In *Syndicat Northcrest v Amselem*,[198] the majority of the SCC elaborated on the foundations **4.69** laid in *Big M*. The majority adopted 'a personal or subjective conception of freedom of religion . . . [which is] a function of personal autonomy and choice'.[199] This led the majority to hold that 'claimants seeking to invoke freedom of religion should not need to prove the objective validity of their beliefs in that their beliefs are objectively recognized as valid by

---

[192] Constitution Act, 1982, s 1.

[193] Human Rights Code, RSBC 1996, c 210; Alberta Human Rights Act, RSA 2000, c A-25; Human Rights Act, RSNB 2011, c 171. Ontario's Human Rights Code, RSO 1990, c H.19 uses the same model, except that it employs the term 'creed' instead of religion.

[194] Human Rights Code SS 1979, c S-24.1, s 2(m.1); Human Rights Code, CCSM c H175, s 9(2)(d); Canadian Human Rights Act, RSC 1985, c H-6; Human Rights Act, RSNS 1989, c 214; Human Rights Act, 2010, SNL 2010, c H-13.1; Human Rights Act, RSPEI 1988, c H-12; Human Rights Act, SNu 2003, c 12; Human Rights Act, SNWT 2002, c 18.

[195] Charter of human rights and freedoms, RSQ, c C-12, ss 3, 10. Yukon's Human Rights Act, RSY 2002, c 116 works similarly, see ss 3, 7. Interestingly, the latter accords the right of religious freedom to both individuals and groups.

[196] *R v Big M Drug Mart* [1985] 1 SCR 295.

[197] *Big M* (n 196) 336.

[198] *Syndicat Northcrest v Amselem*, 2004 SCC 47.

[199] *Amselem* (n 198) para 42.

other members of the same religion, nor is such an inquiry appropriate for courts to make'.[200] Relatedly, religious freedom protection extends to both mandatory and voluntary religious practices, as determining the obligatory nature of a practice requires an objective determination as to what a religion requires. Accordingly, the central evidentiary requirement in a religious freedom case is proof that a claimant has a sincere belief that a practice has religious significance.[201] As a balance to this highly subjective test, a claimant must demonstrate that the alleged interference with religious freedom is 'non-trivial.'[202]

b) Justifying infringements

4.70 Given the broad scope of religious freedom set by the SCC, it is perhaps unsurprising that most of the determinative legal analysis centres on whether the infringement of religious freedom is justified. In the constitutional context, section 1 of the Charter of Rights and Freedoms structures this analysis. The central question of this analysis is whether the rights infringement is within the 'reasonable limits ... [of] a free and democratic society'.[203] Notably, while it is the claimant's obligation to prove that his or her rights have been infringed, the burden of proof shifts to the government actor once the analysis moves to the justificatory phase.

4.71 The limitation set out in section 1 applies to all rights enshrined in the Charter, and the framework that structures the analysis has its origins in *R v Oakes*,[204] a drug prosecution. The test contains two main parts. First, the government must show that an infringing law has a pressing and substantial objective. Secondly, the government must show that the law is proportionate to its objectives. This part of the analysis is further broken down into three questions:

- Is there a rational connection between the impugned law and a valid purpose?
- Is the *Charter* right infringed in the least drastic way that allows the government to achieve its objective? and
- Do the salutary effects of the law outweigh its detrimental effects?

4.72 In general, it is unlikely that laws or government actions will fail the first branch of the *Oakes* test, as courts usually defer to legislatures on whether an objective is sufficiently important. However, the SCC has held that a law with a specifically religious purpose is invalid. This was the case with the federal Lord's Day Act,[205] which mandated Sunday closure for retail establishments in an effort to enforce observation of the Christian Sabbath.[206]

4.73 Most religious freedom claims under the Charter are fought on the proportionality branch of the test, and, more specifically, on the question of whether the impugned action abridges the constitutional right as little as possible. For example, in *Multani v Commission scolaire*

---

[200] *Amselem* (n 198) para 43.

[201] *Amselem* (n 198) para 47.

[202] *Amselem* (n 198) para 58. See also *R v Jones* [1986] 2 SCR 284, para 65.

[203] By the terms of Charter of Rights and Freedoms, s 1, limitations on rights must be 'prescribed by law'. As leading Canadian constitutional scholar Peter Hogg notes, in order to have the benefit of s 1, laws must be 'adequately accessible to the public, and ... formulated with sufficient precision to enable people to regulate their conduct by it': P Hogg, *Constitutional Law of Canada*, 2010 Student edn (Thomson Reuters Canada Ltd, 2010) para 38.7(a). Government policies (rather than enactments) can fall within this definition, see *Greater Vancouver Transportation Authority v Canadian Federation of Students*, 2009 SCC 31.

[204] *R v Oakes* [1986] 1 SCR 103.

[205] Lord's Day Act, RSC 1970, c. L-13.

[206] *R v Big M Drug Mart* [1985] 1 SCR 295. See also *R v Edwards Books and Art Ltd* [1986] 2 SCR 713, where the Court upheld Sunday closing legislation found to have a secular purpose.

Marguerite-Bourgeoys,[207] the SCC held that a total ban on the wearing of a *kirpan* (Sikh ceremonial dagger) in a public high school failed on the minimal impairment analysis. Less drastic measures that would have ensured safety were available, such as the student's commitment to wear the *kirpan* secured in a particular way underneath his clothes.[208] This said, the SCC recently reaffirmed the relevance of the weighing of salutary and deleterious effects of government actions or legislation. The majority of the SCC held that this was 'decisive' in its validation of Alberta's elimination of a religious exemption from the photo requirement on driver's licences (see paragraphs 4.116–4.117 for further discussion of this case).[209]

A separate form of justification applies in the application of human rights legislation (usually in the employment context); this is discussed later, at paragraphs 4.83–4.85. **4.74**

c) Premises and associations

(i) **Shared ownership** The *Amselem* case,[210] referred to earlier in respect of its influential **4.75** holdings on the scope of religious rights, stemmed from a dispute in a condominium-style complex.[211] The by-laws at the heart of the controversy prohibited 'decorations, alterations and constructions' on co-owners' balconies and terraces. A conflict arose when Orthodox Jewish co-owners of three units erected *succoth* (singular: *succah*) on their balconies or terraces. *Succoth* are huts constructed by some Jews during the annual nine-day holiday of *Succoth*. The condominium syndicate (Québec's equivalent to the board of directors) sought an injunction requiring these co-owners to dismantle their *succoth*.[212]

The lower courts favoured the position of the syndicate of co-owners. In their view, the **4.76** restrictions on the ordinary rights of ownership were justified by aesthetic and safety-related concerns. Ultimately, however, a 5 to 4 majority of the SCC held that the religious freedom interests of the Orthodox Jewish co-owners outweighed the concerns of the other co-owners, especially given the short span of the holiday and the dearth of evidence that other co-owners were materially affected by the installation of *succoth*. Notably, the effect of this ruling on condominium-type properties outside Québec is unclear. As noted previously, Québec's Charter of Human Rights and Freedoms binds both public and private actors, and guarantees the right of religious freedom. Human rights legislation in the other provinces centres on the prevention of discrimination, rather than on religious freedom per se. It remains to be seen whether a court or tribunal would apply *Amselem*'s logic directly to a religious discrimination claim.

---

[207] *Multani v Commission scolaire Marguerite-Bourgeoys*, 2006 SCC 6.

[208] Following *Multani*, there was some controversy as to whether the notion of 'reasonable accommodation' borrowed from the employment context was applicable under s 1 of the Charter. In *Multani*, the SCC drew on that notion. In *Alberta v Hutterian Brethren of Wilson Colony*, 2009 SCC 37, the Court held that the reasonable accommodation analysis was applicable only to government action, rather than legislation.

[209] *Wilson Colony* (n 208) paras 78, 79–99. See B Berger, 'Section 1, Constitutional Reasoning and Cultural Difference: Assessing the Impacts of *Alberta v Hutterian Brethren of Wilson Colony*' (2010) 51 Supreme Court Law Review (2d) 25.

[210] *Amselem* (n 198).

[211] Québec law uses the term 'divided co-ownership' rather than the more familiar term, 'condominium'. For ease of reading, I employ the term condominium. Property rights in such cases are regulated by the Civil Code of Québec, arts 1038–1109.

[212] For an analysis of *Amselem* through the lens of the common law of nuisance and the Québec civil law concept of 'voisinage,' see S Van Praagh, 'View from the *Succah*: Religion and Neighbourly Relations' in R Moon (ed), *Law and Religious Pluralism in Canada* (UBC Press, 2008) 21.

4.77 **(ii) Zoning disputes** *Congrégation des témoins de Jéhovah de St-Jérôme-Lafontaine v Lafontaine (Village)*[213] was a dispute between a congregation of Jehovah's Witnesses and the village of Lafontaine, Québec. The congregation set out to purchase land for a new Kingdom Hall,[214] and searched for property in the area properly zoned for a place of worship. Having concluded that there was no available property in the zone, the congregation entered into a purchase agreement of a property in a residential zone, conditional on the congregation obtaining re-zoning approval from the municipality.[215]

4.78 The municipality referred the matter to its Consultative Committee for Urban Planning,[216] which commissioned a study 'on the financial impact upon city taxpayers of granting the Congregation's request'.[217] Because places of worship are generally exempt from property taxes, the study concluded that granting the congregation's re-zoning request would 'result in increased property taxes for neighbouring residents'.[218] On this basis, the municipality denied the congregation's re-zoning request at a public meeting, and gave detailed reasons in support of its action.

4.79 The congregation twice renewed its search for land in the proper zone, and was unsuccessful both times. The congregation presented two additional zoning variance requests to the municipality for a property in a commercial area located 400 metres from another place of worship. The municipality summarily rejected the congregation's requests. The congregation then instituted litigation, arguing that the municipality's actions infringed its freedom of religion.

4.80 A narrow majority of the SCC disposed of the case on the basis of administrative law principles of procedural fairness. Chief Justice McLachlin, for the majority, reasoned that, in failing to provide reasons for its denials of the congregation's second and third requests for zoning variances, the municipality did not meet its duty to 'exercise the powers conferred upon it fairly, in good faith and with a view to the public interest'.[219] Accordingly, the Court remitted the matter back to the municipality for reconsideration.[220] Within the context of its analysis of the duty of fairness, the majority took into account that the congregation was seeking to exercise its religious beliefs. This aided only in supporting the majority's conclusion that the congregation's interests were important.

4.81 The four dissenting judges treated the matter as a question of religious freedom. In essence, this view held that municipalities must adapt their zoning by-laws to 'evolving community needs'.[221] A case where a congregation cannot find a suitably zoned piece of land for its place of worship is an 'exceptional situation' that mandates some positive action on the municipality's part.[222] In this case, because there was land available for purchase in the properly zoned area (a factual determination by the trial judge), there was no infringement of religious freedom.

---

[213] *Congrégation des témoins de Jéhovah de St-Jérôme-Lafontaine v Lafontaine (Village)* [2004] 2 SCR 650.

[214] Kingdom Hall is the term adopted by Jehovah's Witnesses for their communal places of worship: see Jehovah's Witnesses, Authorized Site of Office of Public Information of Jehovah's Witnesses, 'Worship and Conventions', available at <http://www.jw-media.org/people/worship.htm>.

[215] *Témoins de Jéhovah* (n 213) para 18.

[216] Original French: *Comité consultatif d'urbanisme.*

[217] *Témoins de Jéhovah* (n 213) para 19.

[218] *Témoins de Jéhovah* (n 213) para 19.

[219] *Témoins de Jéhovah* (n 213) para 2.

[220] *Témoins de Jéhovah* (n 213) para 31.

[221] *Témoins de Jéhovah* (n 213) paras 73–75.

[222] *Témoins de Jéhovah* (n 213) para 79.

Though the dissenting view is not formally binding on lower courts, the Québec Court of **4.82** Appeal applied its reasoning in *Congregation of the Followers of the Rabbis of Belz to Strengthen Torah v Val-Morin (Municipalité de).*[223] There, a Hasidic Jewish congregation engaged in a dispute with a municipality over the zoning of two buildings. The buildings were located in a residential zone, but the congregation had used the buildings as a synagogue and a religious school for some 20 years. Though the congregation owned other land in an area of the municipality that was properly zoned for these purposes, the congregation argued that the enforcement of the zoning regulation infringed its freedom of religion. It claimed that the costs of building a new place of worship and school in the proper zone were prohibitive, and that the municipality was obligated, in the circumstances, to accommodate the congregation. A unanimous Court of Appeal held that the municipality was under no obligation to accommodate the congregation.

d) Employment

In the employment context, religious rights are usually based in human rights legislation as **4.83** opposed to constitutional provisions. A leading case in this field is *Ontario Human Rights Commission v Simpsons-Sears.*[224] There, an employee who joined the Seventh Day Adventist Church during the course of her employment sought a change in work schedule on the basis of her religious beliefs, which prohibited work on Saturdays. The SCC held that, where the employee establishes a *prima facie* case of discrimination, the employer is under a duty to take reasonable steps to offer the employee an accommodation. The employer's duty ends where the accommodation gives rise to 'undue interference in the operation of the employer's business . . . [or] undue expense to the employer'.[225] The onus is on the employer to prove undue hardships. However, more recent case law has emphasized that all parties must contribute to the search for accommodation; employees, employers, and unions (where relevant) all have a duty to facilitate this search.[226] In *Simpsons-Sears*, the employer had not submitted evidence of undue hardship, and the employee was successful in obtaining monetary relief.[227]

In recent case law surrounding employers' duty of accommodation, the SCC has streamlined **4.84** what was once a more complex legal analysis. Whereas, in older cases, the Court distinguished between 'direct' and 'adverse effects' discrimination, and the relationship between bona fide occupational requirements and employers' duty to accommodate was complicated,[228] the current approach is unified.[229] The analysis of the employer's duty to accommodate is guided by three questions:

(1) Did the employer adopt the standard for a purpose rationally connected to the performance of the job?
(2) Did the employer adopt the particular standard in an honest and good faith belief that it was necessary to the fulfilment of that legitimate work-related purpose; and

---

[223] *Congregation of the Followers of the Rabbis of Belz to Strengthen Torah v Val-Morin (Municipalité de)*, 2008 QCCA 577, leave to appeal to the SCC denied, 2008 CanLII 48619.

[224] *Ontario Human Rights Commission v Simpsons-Sears* [1985] 2 SCR 536.

[225] *Simpsons-Sears* (n 224) para 23.

[226] *Central Okanagan School District No 23 v Renaud* [1992] 2 SCR 970, 994.

[227] See also *Commission scolaire régionale de Chambly v Bergevin* [1994] 2 SCR 525, where the SCC found that a school calendar, though neutral on its face, discriminated against Jewish teachers by not providing a day off for Yom Kippur; the teachers successfully recovered a day's wages on the basis of their collective agreement.

[228] *Bhinder v CN* [1985] 2 SCR 561; *Central Alberta Dairy Pool v Alberta (Human rights commission)* [1990] 2 SCR 489; see also G England, *Individual Employment Law* (2nd edn, Irwin Law, 2008) 172–5.

[229] *British Columbia (Public Service Employee Relations Commission) v BCGSEU* [1999] 3 SCR 3.

(3) Is the standard reasonably necessary to the accomplishment of that legitimate work-related purpose? To show that the standard is reasonably necessary, it must be demonstrated that it is impossible to accommodate individual employees sharing the characteristics of the claimant without imposing undue hardship upon the employer.[230]

4.85 In addition to these considerations, about one-third of Canadian employees belong to union and work under a collective agreement.[231] Collective agreements generally provide employees with rights beyond those provided in human rights legislation.

e) Education

4.86 Religious rights litigation in the Canadian education context can be divided into five types of cases: (1) religious exercises in public schools; (2) religious instruction in public schools; (3) students' religious apparel; (4) teachers' religious rights; and (5) the rights of faith-based schools to government funding. This section deals with each of these in turn.

4.87 **(i) Religious exercises** Challenges to religious exercises in Canadian public schools have generally been aimed at schools that commenced their morning assembly with a biblical reading and/or a recitation of the Lord's Prayer. The SCC has never decided the issue definitively. However, *Zylberberg v Sudbury Board of Education*,[232] a decision of the Ontario Court of Appeal, has been followed by courts in other jurisdictions,[233] and can be considered the prevailing statement of Canadian law on the question. In that case, a group of parents challenged a school jurisdiction's practice of commencing each day with the singing of 'O Canada' and the recitation of the Lord's Prayer. In some schools, this was supplemented by the reading of biblical passages. At the request of a parent, students could be exempted from attending or participating in the exercises.[234] The litigant parents had not sought to have their children excused from the exercises, 'because they did not want [the children] singled out from their peers because of their religious beliefs'.[235]

4.88 The *Zylberberg* Court held that religious freedom implies that the practices of a dominant religion 'cannot be imposed on religious minorities'.[236] It follows, on this view, that the rights of non-believers to refuse to participate in religious activities must be protected. The Court further held that whether pressure or compulsion existed had to be assessed from the standpoint of members of religious minorities, and 'in particular, from the standpoint of pupils in the sensitive setting of a public school'.[237] In the Court's view, that the parents did not seek the exemption for their children showed that the children and their parents felt compelled to conform to the religious practices of the majority.[238] Moreover, the exemption procedure required students to 'make a religious statement' and publicly declare their faith. The Court found that this procedure infringed the students' freedom of religion in this 'broader

---

[230] *British Columbia* (n 229) para 54.
[231] Human Resources and Skills Development Canada, 'Work—Unionization Rates', available at <http://www4.hrsdc.gc.ca/.3ndic.1t.4r@-eng.jsp?iid=17>.
[232] *Zylberberg v Sudbury Board of Education* (1988), 65 OR (2d) 641 (CA).
[233] See *Russow v BC (Attorney General)* (1989), 62 DLR (4th) 98; *Manitoba Assn for Rights and Liberties Inc v Manitoba (Minister of Education)* (1992), 94 DLR (4th) 678.
[234] *Zylberberg* (n 232) 645.
[235] *Zylberberg* (n 232) 647.
[236] *Zylberberg* (n 232) 647.
[237] *Zylberberg* (n 232) 647.
[238] *Zylberberg* (n 232) 655.

sense'.[239] Though the school board argued that the parents had failed to prove any actual harm to their children, the Court determined that no such proof was required.

The Court concluded by holding that the religious exercises could not be justified as being a 'reasonable limit' of religious freedom. The purpose of the regulation authorizing the exercises was clearly religious, and, as noted in paragraph 4.72, legislation with a religious purpose cannot be justified under section 1 of the Charter. Further, even if section 1 were applicable, the Court held that the legislation failed to impair the rights of students of religious minorities as little as possible, and thus could not be saved.[240]   **4.89**

(ii) Religious instruction and curriculum design   In *Canadian Civil Liberties Association v Ontario (Minister of Education)* (the *Elgin County* case),[241] the issue was whether the curriculum of religious studies prescribed by the Elgin County Board of Education infringed the freedom of religion and equality rights of students. At the time, Ontario's Education Act provided that students were allowed to receive the religious instruction that their parents desired, but that no student could be required to 'read or study in or from a religious book, or to join in an exercise of devotion or religion'.[242] School boards were allowed to select a 'clergyman' or lay person to give religious instruction in lieu of the teacher, and there was some flexibility in the regulation to allow for multiple clergy members or lay people of 'different denominations' to provide religious education.   **4.90**

In rendering its decision, the Ontario Court of Appeal made a critical distinction between indoctrination and education. Religious instruction that amounts to indoctrination falls foul of the constitutional protection of freedom of religion, while education may not. In the Court's view, 'teaching students Christian doctrine as if it were the exclusive means through which to develop moral thinking and behaviour amounts to religious coercion in the class-room'.[243]   **4.91**

Interestingly, the Court held that the availability of an exemption from religious instruction provided in the legislation 'strongly suggests something other than pure education'.[244] Thus, whereas with respect to religious exercises, exemption provisions were seen as well-intentioned but ineffective because of the pressures to conform in elementary and high schools, with respect to religious education, they were seen as indicia of the indoctrinating intent of the curriculum. With respect to the actual Elgin County curriculum, the Court found that it crossed into indoctrination at several points. Bible stories were included in the curriculum 'for their own sake, rather than as general illustrations to enhance the teaching about values'.[245] Some exercises treated biblical texts as authoritative sources of guidance for the children's lives. Other exercises were even more clearly aimed at indoctrination: 'At the intermediate level, there are included student worksheets which require the pupil to read passages in the Bible and then fill blanks in sentences such as 'Jesus Christ is the... way to God.' The word to be inserted is 'only'.[246]   **4.92**

---

[239] *Zylberberg* (n 232) 655.
[240] *Zylberberg* (n 232) 659–62.
[241] *Canadian Civil Liberties Association v Ontario (Minister of Education)* (1990), 71 OR (2d) 341 (CA) (*Elgin County*).
[242] Education Act, RSO 1980, c 129, s 50.
[243] *Elgin County* (n 241) 363.
[244] *Elgin County* (n 241) 362.
[245] *Elgin County* (n 241) 376.
[246] *Elgin County* (n 241) 376.

4.93 Finally, the Court held that section 1 of the Charter was not applicable because the purpose of the legislation and curricula infringed freedom of religion. It further held that curricula aimed at indoctrination in a particular religion could never be saved by section 1, because they cannot be rationally connected to a valid legislative purpose, nor can they be said to meet a 'minimal impairment' test.[247]

4.94 More recently, in *SL v Commission scolaire des Chênes*,[248] the controversy centred on a course titled 'Ethics and Religious Culture' that had been made compulsory in Québec high schools. The claimants sought to have their children exempted from the course, arguing that participation in the course would expose their children 'to a form of relativism, which would interfere with [the parents'] ability to pass their faith on to their children'.[249] The SCC found that the course was designed as 'a comprehensive presentation of various religions without forcing the children to join them'.[250] The course, therefore, did not cross the line from education into indoctrination, and it fell to the claimants to prove how the course infringed their religious freedom, which they failed to do. In rejecting the claim, the Court went on to hold that:

> … the suggestion that exposing children to a variety of religious facts in itself infringes their religious freedom or that of their parents amounts to a rejection of the multicultural reality of Canadian society and ignores the Québec government's obligations with regard to public education. Although such exposure can be a source of friction, it does not in itself constitute an infringement of [freedom of religion and conscience].[251]

4.95 One other decision bears mentioning on the issue of curriculum design. In *Chamberlain v Surrey School District No 36*,[252] the SCC reviewed a British Columbia school board's decision to exclude books about same-sex families from a kindergarten curriculum. The Court's quashing of this decision was based on the legislation applicable to British Columbia schools, rather than on the notion of freedom of religion. However, in applying British Columbia's School Act, the Court relied heavily on a provision requiring that: 'All schools and Provincial schools must be conducted on strictly secular and non-sectarian principles.'[253] The Court's interpretation of the term 'secular' is notable. Chief Justice McLachlin held for the majority of the Court:

> The Act's insistence on strict secularism does not mean that religious concerns have no place in the deliberations and decisions of the Board … Religion is an integral aspect of people's lives, and cannot be left at the boardroom door. What secularism does rule out, however, is any attempt to use the religious views of one part of the community to exclude from consideration the values of other members of the community. A requirement of secularism implies that, although the Board is indeed free to address the religious concerns of parents, it must be sure to do so in a manner that gives equal recognition and respect to other members of the community.[254]

---

[247] *Elgin County* (n 241) 380.

[248] *SL v Commission scolaire des Chênes* 2012 SCC 7.

[249] *SL* (n 248) para 29.

[250] *SL* (n 248) para 37.

[251] *SL* (n 248) para 40. In *Loyola High School v Courchesne*, 2012 QCCA 2139, a Catholic high school in Québec was unsuccessful in obtaining an exemption from teaching the same curriculum; at the time of writing, the SCC had granted leave to appeal and scheduled the hearing for April 2014.

[252] *Chamberlain v Surrey School District No 36* [2002] 4 SCR 710. For a more in-depth discussion of this case, see IT Benson, 'Considering Secularism' in Douglas Farrow (ed), *Recognizing Religion in a Secular Society: Essays in Pluralism, Religion, and Public Policy* (McGill-Queen's University Press, 2004).

[253] School Act, RSBC 1996, c 412, s 76.

[254] *Chamberlain* (n 252) para 19. Notably, the books depicting same-sex parents were eventually excluded from the curriculum on the basis of problems with punctuation, spelling, and grammar. The board also found

(iii) Students' religious apparel In the 1990s, following a similar controversy in France,[255] there was public debate in Québec about whether students in public schools should be allowed to wear a *hijab*.[256] However, according to two noted academics tasked with examining the notion of reasonable accommodation in Québec, 'fairly broad agreement was reached then to allow students wearing headscarves to attend public schools rather than excluding them and thus steering them to private denominational schools'.[257] Further, the Québec Human Rights Commission has issued an opinion to the effect that private denominational schools were 'bound to accommodate students of other religious faiths, for example by allowing the wearing of a headscarf, unless they could show that the confessional status of these establishments demands certain exclusions or preferences'.[258]   **4.96**

None of the debate surrounding the *hijab* resulted in a decision from a Canadian court. In contrast, as mentioned at paragraph 4.73, the SCC has addressed whether a Sikh student could carry a *kirpan*[259] in a public school setting, in apparent contravention of a no-weapons policy. In *Multani v Commission scolaire Marguerite-Bourgeoys*,[260] the Court held that an absolute prohibition against wearing *kirpans* was an unjustifiable violation of a Sikh student's freedom of religion. The issue arose when a student, Gurbaj Singh Multani, accidentally dropped his *kirpan* while in the schoolyard. The Multani family initially reached a compromise arrangement with the local school board; Gurbaj Singh could wear his *kirpan* to school provided that it was sealed inside his clothing.[261] However, the school's governing board refused to ratify this agreement on the basis that it conflicted with the school's prohibition on weapons and dangerous objects.[262] In a set of concurring opinions, the SCC found in favour of the Multanis. The Court held that Gurbaj Singh had established the sincerity of his religious beliefs, and that the interference with his religious freedom was not trivial; it had effectively deprived him of the right to attend a public school.   **4.97**

The Court then turned to balancing this right against the objective in banning *kirpans* from schools. The Court held that though the creation of a safe school environment is a laudable goal, the actual prevailing practice was to create a reasonably safe environment, rather than an absolutely safe one. For example, there were no metal detectors nor was there a prohibition on all potentially dangerous objects such as scissors and compasses.[263] The majority   **4.98**

---

fault with the way the books depicted men, addressed the issue of sexual orientation for the age of the audience, and raised the subject of dieting, see 'School board rejects books with gay parents for bad grammar', *CBC News*, 13 June 2003, available at <http://www.cbc.ca/canada/story/2003/06/13/samesex_books030613.html>.

[255] See ET Beller, 'The Headscarf Affair: The Conseil d'Etat on the Role of Religion and Culture in French Society' (2004) 39 Texas ILJ 581 for a discussion of what has come to be known as the '*Affaire du foulard*' or '*Affaire des voiles.*'

[256] A *hijab* (sometimes spelled *hidjab*) is a headscarf worn by some Muslim women.

[257] Québec, Commission de consultation sur les pratiques d'accommodement reliées aux différences culturelles, *Building the Future: A Time for Reconciliation* (Québec: Gouvernement du Québec, 2008) 141 (Co-Chairs: G Bouchard and C Taylor) (*Bouchard-Taylor Report*). Bouchard and Taylor note, however, that Muslim girls in Québec have been confronted with prohibitions on wearing their *hijabs* in soccer matches and *tae kwon do* tournaments, at 57, 71, 73; see also L Barnett, *Freedom of Religion and Religious Symbols in the Public Sphere* (Canada: Parliamentary Information and Research Service, Law and Government Division, 2006) available at <http://www.parl.gc.ca/Content/LOP/ResearchPublications/2011-60-e.htm>.

[258] *Bouchard-Taylor Report* (n 257) 51.

[259] A *kirpan* is a ceremonial dagger traditionally carried by Orthodox Sikhs who have been baptized.

[260] *Multani v Commission scolaire Marguerite-Bourgeoys* [2006] 1 SCR 256.

[261] *Multani* (n 260) para 3.

[262] *Multani* (n 260) para 4.

[263] *Multani* (n 260) paras 46–48.

of the Court noted that there was no evidence supporting the view that the *kirpan* would present a risk to the goal of ensuring a reasonable level of safety. There was no proof that this particular student constituted a danger, nor was there any evidence of a violent incident involving a *kirpan* in any Canadian school.[264] In the majority's view, an absolute prohibition on *kirpans* was contraindicated by the special duty of schools to foster respect for the constitutional rights of others and teach 'civic virtue and responsible citizenship'.[265]

4.99   **(iv) Teachers' religious beliefs**   In *Ross v New Brunswick School District No 15*,[266] a public school teacher had publicly expressed the view that 'Christian civilization was being undermined and destroyed by an international Jewish conspiracy'.[267] Though these activities occurred outside the classroom, a Jewish family complained to the New Brunswick Human Rights Commission. The family argued that, in failing to take disciplinary action against the teacher, the school board had condoned his views and thereby discriminated against Jewish and other minority students. The SCC held that the most appropriate solution in such a case was to remove the teacher from the classroom, and provide him with the opportunity to hold a non-teaching position in the School Board.

4.100   More recently, in *Trinity Western University v British Columbia College of Teachers*,[268] the question was whether the College of Teachers had acted appropriately in refusing to approve a teacher-training programme provided by a private religious university. The approval would have qualified graduates from the programme to teach in British Columbia's public school system. The College of Teachers was concerned with the university's policy of requiring students to sign a 'community standards' document that condemned, among other things, 'homosexual behaviour'. The College of Teachers argued that it was against the public interest to approve a programme at a university that adopted discriminatory practices. Instead, the College of Teachers preferred a programme wherein aspiring teachers spent the last year of the programme at a public university. The SCC held that the College of Teachers had acted inappropriately, and that the Trinity Western training programme should be approved.

4.101   The SCC's responses to these two cases illuminate the legal boundaries of teachers' freedom of religion. In both cases, the court held that public schools are meant to transmit civic values. This requires, in the Court's view, 'an environment free of bias, prejudice and intolerance'[269] and that the school 'be premised upon principles of tolerance and impartiality so that all persons within the school environment feel equally free to participate'.[270]

4.102   Accordingly, in *Ross*, where there was evidence that the teacher's off-duty activities contributed to a poisoned environment in the school, the teacher's freedom of religion could not suffice to keep him in a teaching position; students' right to learn in an environment free from discrimination prevailed.[271] In contrast, in *Trinity Western*, where there was no evidence that teachers' professed religious beliefs would create a discriminatory environment in schools, the teachers' rights to hold their religious beliefs prevailed.[272]

---

[264] *Multani* (n 260) paras 57–60, 67.
[265] *Multani* (n 260) para 78.
[266] *Ross v New Brunswick School District No 15* [1996] 1 SCR 825. For subsequent treatment of this case by the UN-based Human Rights Committee (HRC, see Ch 2, paras 2.71 and 2.82).
[267] *Ross* (n 266) para 3.
[268] *Trinity Western University v British Columbia College of Teachers* [2001] 1 SCR 772.
[269] *Trinity Western* (n 268) para 13.
[270] *Ross* (n 266) para 42.
[271] *Ross* (n 266) paras 40, 45, 47.
[272] *Trinity Western* (n 268) para 36.

(v) Faith-based schools   The availability of public funding for faith-based schools var-   **4.103**
ies by province. Nova Scotia, New Brunswick, Prince Edward Island, and Newfoundland
provide no funding; Québec, British Columbia, and Manitoba provide partial funding;
Alberta and Saskatchewan provide a mix of full and partial funding, depending on the
school; Ontario provides full funding to Catholic schools, but does not fund any other
faith schools.[273] As noted at paragraph 4.62, Canada's constitution initially protected the
funding of Catholic and Protestant schools as it existed at the time of confederation or at
the time that a province joined the federation. Some jurisdictions, such as Québec and
Newfoundland, have altered this by constitutional amendment and done away with confessional school boards.

Ontario's practice of funding only Catholic schools was the subject of litigation in *Adler v*   **4.104**
Ontario.[274] Non-Catholic litigants challenged this policy on the basis of the equality guarantee in the Charter of Rights and Freedoms. The SCC held that one constitutional provision
could not be used to invalidate another. This effectively forecloses the possibility of making
a constitutional argument that these differential rights should be abolished; such change can
only come through constitutional amendment.[275]

f) Expression

Chief Justice McLachlin of the SCC has held that the ambit of expressive freedom is broader   **4.105**
'than freedom of conscience and religion, in that even harmful expression may be protected'.[276] That said, cases related to both constitutional rights tend to be determined with
reference to the Charter's 'reasonable limits' clause.

The relationship between the two constitutional freedoms is illustrated well by an example   **4.106**
discussed at paragraph 4.99. In *Ross*, a teacher who was disciplined for religiously-based
anti-Semitic views sought redress on the basis of both freedom of expression and freedom
of religion.[277] The teacher was moved to a non-teaching position. Though the SCC found
that the order removing the teacher from the classroom violated both freedoms, it upheld
the teacher's removal from the classroom through section 1 of the Charter (the 'reasonable
limits' clause), ultimately treating the rights of religious and expressive freedom together. In
this analysis, the Court held that the teacher's expression 'undermine[d] democratic values
in its condemnation of Jews and the Jewish faith [and impeded] meaningful participation
in social and political decision-making by Jews'.[278] Similarly, the Court also held that 'any
religious belief that denigrates and defames the religious beliefs of others erodes the very basis
of the guarantee' of religious freedom.[279]

---

[273] See J Wilson, 'Faith-based schools', 17 September 2007, available at <http://www.cbc.ca/
ontariovotes2007/features/features-faith.html>.
[274] *Adler v Ontario* [1996] 3 SCR 609. See also *Waldman v Canada*, Communication 694/1996, UN
Doc CCPR/C/67/D/694/1996 (5 November 1999), available at <http://www.unhchr.ch/tbs/doc.nsf/0/
b3bfc541589cc30f802568690052e5d6>, where the UN Human Rights Committee held that the funding
of Catholic schools in Ontario violated the International Covenant on Civil and Political Rights. Ontario
continues to provide funding to Catholic schools, but no other faith-based schools.
[275] This kind of constitutional amendment requires majority votes of the provincial legislature and the two
federal houses of Parliament, see Constitution Act, 1982, Sch B to the Canada Act 1982 (UK), 1982, c 11, s 43.
[276] *Young v Young* [1993] 4 SCR 3, para 219.
[277] *Ross* (n 266).
[278] *Ross* (n 266) para 93.
[279] *Ross* (n 266) para 94.

4.107   More recently, in *Saskatchewan (Human Rights Commission) v Whatcott*,[280] the SCC considered the interaction of religious and expressive freedom with a hate speech prohibition. Whatcott had distributed flyers on behalf of a group called Christian Truth Activists. Two of the flyers contained arguments aimed at keeping LGBT issues out of public schools, and were titled 'Keep Homosexuality out of Saskatoon's Public Schools!' and 'Sodomites in our Public Schools' respectively.[281] Other flyers reprinted a page of classified ads from a magazine with handwritten comments advocating the prohibition of ads for 'men seeking boys'. Four complainants alleged that the flyers violated the Saskatchewan Human Rights Code's prohibition on the publication or display of material 'that exposes or tends to expose to hatred, ridicules, belittles or otherwise affronts the dignity of any person or class of persons on the basis of a prohibited ground [of discrimination]'.[282] The Saskatchewan Human Rights Tribunal found that the flyers contravened the hate speech prohibition, and that the prohibition was a reasonable limit on Whatcott's expressive and religious rights. The Tribunal issued an order prohibiting Whatcott and the Christian Truth Activists from distributing the flyers or similar material, and ordered Whatcott to pay compensation to the complainants in the amount of $17,500.

4.108   On appeal, the SCC held that the objectives of the legislation, 'reducing the harmful effects and social costs of discrimination by tackling certain causes of discriminatory activity,'[283] were sufficient to justify an infringement of Whatcott's *Charter* rights to freedom of expression and religion. However, consistent with previous jurisprudence,[284] the Court held that, in order to pass constitutional muster, hate speech laws must be interpreted to set a high bar on the meaning of 'hatred'. An impugned publication must (a) be assessed from the perspective of a reasonable observer, (b) rise to the level of inciting the extreme emotions of detestation or vilification, and (c) be likely to 'expose the targeted group or person to hatred by others'.[285] On this basis, the Court found that the provision at issue was only partly valid. It struck the phrase 'ridicules, belittles, or otherwise affronts the dignity of' from the Human Rights Code as setting the bar too low on hate speech, and not being rationally connected to the goal of addressing systemic discrimination. Based on the newly worded legislation, the Court found that the flyers 'Keep Homosexuality out of Saskatoon's Public Schools!' and 'Sodomites in our Public Schools' violated the prohibition, while the magazine reprints with handwritten comments did not. The SCC allowed only the publication prohibition and compensation linked to the first two flyers to stand.

g) Family

4.109   **(i) Marriage**   Since 2005, same-sex marriages have had legal validity in Canada.[286] This has raised two main questions for religious rights in the appellate courts. First, can religious

---

[280] *Saskatchewan (Human Rights Commission) v Whatcott* 2013 SCC 11.
[281] *Whatcott* (n 280) para 8.
[282] Saskatchewan Human Rights Code, SS 1979, c S-24.1, s 14(1)(*b*).
[283] *Whatcott* (n 280) para 71.
[284] See *Canada (Human Rights Commission) v Taylor* [1990] 3 SCR 892; *R v Keegstra* [1990] 3 SCR 697.
[285] *Whatcott* (n 280) para 58.
[286] *Reference re Same-Sex Marriage*, 2004 SCC 79; Civil Marriage Act, SC 2005, c 33. This followed a number of provincial appellate and trial court decisions that restricting marriage to opposite-sex couples violated the Charter right to equality, see *Halpern v Canada (Attorney General)* (2003), 65 OR (3d) 161; *Barbeau v British Columbia*, 2003 BCCA 406; *Hendricks v Québec (Procureure générale)* [2001] JQ no 3350 (QL); *Dunbar v Yukon*, 2004 YKSC 54; *Vogel v Canada (Attorney General)* [2004] MJ No 418 (QL) (QB); *Boutilier v Nova Scotia (Attorney General)* [2004] NSJ No 357 (QL) (SC); and *NW v Canada (Attorney General)*, 2004 SKQB 434.

officials who conduct marriage ceremonies be required, contrary to their religious beliefs, to conduct same-sex marriages? The SCC held that the religious freedom guarantee in the Charter would prevent a government from implementing such a requirement,[287] though no government has suggested that it would attempt to do so.

The second question regards civil marriage commissioners who may object, on religious grounds, to performing same-sex marriages. On this issue, the Saskatchewan Court of Appeal held that such officials can validly be compelled to perform same-sex marriages, or, in the alternative, cease acting as a marriage commissioner.[288] Essentially, the Court held that same-sex couples' equality rights would be infringed if marriage commissioners could opt out of performing same-sex marriages, and that this infringement outweighed marriage commissioners' rights of religious freedom. The case was not appealed, and the SCC has not yet ruled on this issue.

4.110

(ii) Divorce There has been significant debate in Ontario as to whether divorcing couples can have their disputes decided by religious arbitrators applying religious law.[289] The issue attracted attention when Syed Mumtaz Ali, a retired Ontario lawyer committed to a conservative form of Islam, announced the creation of the Islamic Institute of Civil Justice, a Sharia-based arbitral tribunal. Though this raised much public concern, it was not a truly novel issue for Ontario law. Marion Boyd, commissioned by Ontario's Attorney General to report on the matter, noted that 'family matters have been arbitrated based on religious teachings for many years in Jewish, Muslim and Christian settings'.[290] Boyd recommended that the practice of faith-based arbitration should continue, though with added judicial safeguards to protect against unconscionable awards. However, the government chose a different course, announcing that there would be no more religious arbitration of family disputes in the province, and amended the province's arbitration legislation accordingly.[291] Some have questioned, however, the scope of this change, as religious families may still be able to put their religious norms into a pre-nuptial or separation agreement, which could then be

4.111

---

[287] *Reference re Same-Sex Marriage* (n 286) para 58.

[288] *Marriage Commissioners Appointed Under The Marriage Act (Re)*, 2011 SKCA 3.

[289] There has been much nuanced commentary on this debate, see eg M Boyd, *Dispute Resolution in Family Law: Protecting Choice, Promoting Inclusion* (Toronto: Ministry of the Attorney General, 2004) 89–92, available at <http://www.attorneygeneral.jus.gov.on.ca/english/about/pubs/boyd/fullreport.pdf> (*Boyd Report*); J-F Gaudreault-Desbiens, 'Constitutional Values, Faith-Based Arbitration, and the Limits of Private Justice in a Multicultural Society' (2005) 19 National Journal of Constitutional Law 155; A Shachar, 'Religion, State, and the Problem of Gender: New Modes of Citizenship and Governance in Diverse Societies' (2005) 50 McGill LJ 49; LE Weinrib, 'Ontario's Sharia Law Debate: Law and Politics under the Charter' in R Moon (ed), *Law and Religious Pluralism in Canada* (UBC Press, 2008) 239; V Bader, 'Legal Pluralism and Differentiated Morality: Shari'a in Ontario' in R Grillo et al (eds), *Legal Practice and Cultural Diversity* (Ashgate, 2009) 49–72; S Razack, 'Between a Rock and Hard Place: Canadian Muslim Women's Responses to Faith-Based Arbitration' in R Mehdi et al (eds), *Law and Religion in Multicultural Societies* (DJØF Publishing, 2008) 83–94; A Emon, 'Islamic Law and the Canadian Mosaic: Politics, Jurisprudence, and Multicultural Accommodation' (2009) 87 Canadian Bar Review 391; B Ryder, 'The Canadian Conception of Equal Religious Citizenship' in R Moon (ed), *Law and Religious Pluralism in Canada* (UBC Press 2008) 87–109; F Ahmed and S Luk, 'Religious Arbitration: A Study of Legal Safeguards' (2011) 77 Arbitration 290.

[290] *Boyd Report* (n 289) 4.

[291] 'McGuinty rules out use of sharia law in Ontario', 12 September 2005, available at <http://www.ctv.ca/CTVNews/TopStories/20050912/mcguinty_shariah_050911>. The amended legislation requires that family arbitrations be conducted 'exclusively in accordance with the law of Ontario or of another Canadian jurisdiction,' Arbitration Act, 1991, SO 1991, c 17, s 1. For practical consideration of this change in family law, see PM Epstein and SR Gibb, 'Family Law Arbitrations: Choice and Finality under the Amended Arbitration Act, 1991 and Family Law Act' in *The Law Society of Upper Canada Special Lectures 2006: Family Law* (Thomson Carswell, 2007).

enforced by an arbitrator or court.[292] Moreover, the legislation allows couples to mediate their disputes upon marriage breakdown, and clerics can act as mediators.[293]

4.112   In addition, Canada's law of divorce has an interesting overlap with religious laws of divorce. In legislation similar to that prevailing in New York State, the federal Divorce Act provides incentives for divorcing spouses to remove barriers to religious remarriage.[294] Where a spouse fails to remove such barriers, courts may dismiss that spouse's application or strike out his or her pleadings. Parliament adopted these provisions at the behest of members of the Jewish community.[295] In Orthodox Judaism, a husband must provide a religious divorce (a *get*) and a wife must accept it in order to end the religious marriage. Without a *get*, an Orthodox Jew (usually the woman) cannot remarry within his or her community and any children born of another partner will be considered illegitimate. This kind of legislation can encourage recalcitrant spouses to provide a *get*, lest they incur the civil consequences just outlined.

4.113   A related situation was at issue in *Bruker v Marcovitz*.[296] There, a husband and wife agreed in the context of their civil separation agreement that the husband would provide a *get*. However, the civil divorce was granted before the husband provided the *get*, which he then withheld for some 15 years. The wife sought damages for the husband's failure to perform his contractual obligation; the husband invoked his religious freedom as a bar to a court's enforcements of the contractual provision. The majority of the SCC held that, though the contract required the husband to perform a religious act, the husband had converted this into an enforceable civil obligation by signing the separation agreement. The Court ordered damages in the amount of $47,500.[297]

4.114   **(iii) Children**   Questions of religious significance may also arise with respect to child custody and access disputes, as was the case in *Young v Young*.[298] There, some two years before the couple's separation, the father had become involved in the Jehovah's Witnesses. In deciding the conditions of the father's access rights, the trial judge prohibited the father from discussing his religious beliefs with his three daughters, reasoning that the discussions caused stress for the children. However, as the father had undertaken not to bring his children to religious services or on proselytizing activities, the majority of the SCC held that the restrictions on the father's access should be removed. Only one judge made this decision on the basis of the Charter right to religious freedom. The other majority judges reasoned that the restrictions were not in the children's best interests, as there was no evidence of harm flowing from discussions about the father's religion.

4.115   Another issue that has been litigated several times in Canada relates to the medical treatment of children. In *B (R) v Children's Aid Society*,[299] parents of a 1-month-old child refused blood transfusions on the basis of their religious beliefs as Jehovah's Witnesses. When physicians concluded that the child's life was in danger and might require blood transfusions, the

---

[292] Ahmed and Luk (n 289) 292; Ryder (n 289) 105.
[293] Emon (n 289) 394.
[294] Divorce Act, RSC 1985, c 3 (2nd Supp), s 21.1.
[295] *Bruker v Marcovitz*, 2007 SCC 54, paras 3–9.
[296] *Bruker* (n 295) paras 3–9.
[297] *Bruker* (n 295) paras 33, 97. Whether a court might order specific performance of this type of contract remains an open question.
[298] *Young* (n 276).
[299] *B (R) v Children's Aid Society* [1995] 1 SCR 315. See also *AC v Manitoba (Director of Child and Family Services)*, 2009 SCC 30.

Ontario Provincial Court made the child a ward of the province's Children's Aid Society for 72 hours, during which the Society consented to blood transfusions on the child's behalf. The majority of the SCC held that this action was a serious infringement of religious freedom. However, the Court upheld the state actions and the legislative scheme on which they were based through section 1 of the Charter. The majority reasoned that the state has an interest in protecting children, and that the legislation had sufficient procedural safeguards to protect parents' interests.

(h) Miscellaneous

(i) **Driver's licence photographs**   In *Alberta v Hutterian Brethren of Wilson Colony*,[300] a dis-   **4.116**
pute arose between a small group of Hutterian Brethren and the Alberta government about the photographs that appear on driver's licences.[301] Some Hutterites believe that the Bible's Second Commandment, which forbids graven images, prohibits them from having their photographs taken.[302] Though the Alberta government had allowed Hutterites an exemption from the driver's licence photograph requirement since 1974, in 2003 the province amended its regulations to eliminate this exemption. The province conceded that the newly universal photograph requirement infringed religious freedom, but argued that photographs of all drivers were necessary to create a secure digital databank that would be used to combat identity fraud.

The majority of the SCC upheld the new regulation under section 1 of the Charter. In the   **4.117**
majority's view, there were important salutary effects of the photo requirement, namely: '(1) enhancing the security of the driver's licensing scheme; (2) assisting in roadside safety and identification; and (3) eventually harmonizing Alberta's licensing scheme with those in other jurisdictions.'[303] The majority held that these outweighed the Hutterian Brethren of Wilson Colony's inability to drive on the highway.[304]

(ii) **Police officers' apparel**   In *Grant v Canada (Attorney General)*,[305] a group of citizens   **4.118**
who had connections with the Royal Canadian Mounted Police (RCMP) challenged a policy allowing Sikh officers to wear turbans instead of the felt hat ordinarily required. These citizens argued that allowing RCMP officers to wear turbans was a violation of the state's religious neutrality and the religious freedom rights of those who interact with the RCMP officers. The Federal Court held that, to the extent that there was a requirement of religious neutrality in police uniforms, this was a convention and thus not legally enforceable. The Court further held that interactions with police officers wearing turbans did not involve any religious coercion; members of the public were only required to 'observe the officer's religious

---

[300] *Alberta v Hutterian Brethren of Wilson Colony*, 2009 SCC 37.

[301] The Hutterite faith, like the Amish and Mennonite faiths, stems from the Anabaptist tradition. For a more thorough account of the Hutterite faith in relation to litigation, see AJ Esau, *The Courts and the Colonies: The Litigation of Hutterite Church Disputes* (UBC Press, 2004).

[302] The text of the biblical commandment that the Wilson Colony members submitted to the Court provides: 'You shall not make for yourself an idol, or any likeness of what is in heaven above or on the earth beneath or in the water under the earth' (Exodus 20:4); see *Wilson Colony* (n 300) para 29.

[303] *Wilson Colony* (n 300) para 79. For discussion of this proportionality analysis, see PW Hogg, *Constitutional Law of Canada*, Vol 2, looseleaf (ThomsonCarswell, 2007) 38–44; H Kislowicz, R Haigh, and A Ng, 'Calculations of Conscience: The Costs and Benefits of Religious and Conscientious Freedom' (2011) 48 Alberta Law Review 679. See also RE Charney, 'How Can There Be Any Sin in Sincere? State Inquiries into Sincerity of Religious Belief' (2010) 51 Supreme Court Law Review (2d) 47, 65.

[304] *Wilson Colony* (n 300) para 96.

[305] *Grant v Canada (Attorney General)* [1995] 1 FC 158.

affiliation',[306] and not share in his beliefs. As such, the Court found no infringement of the right to religious freedom. The Federal Court of Appeal upheld this ruling, and the SCC denied leave to appeal.[307]

4.119 **(iii) Prayers in legislative bodies** In *Freitag v Penetanguishene (Town)*,[308] the claimant challenged the town council's practice of commencing meetings with a reading of the Lord's Prayer. The town argued that the practice was not intended to indoctrinate people into the Christian faith, but rather to 'have the Council take a moment's pause to recognize the importance of our deliberations, the moral values that should be brought onto our deliberations and the fact that we are serving the public when we deliberate'.[309] It also provided evidence that another non-Christian resident of the town was a long-standing member of the town council who did 'not feel compelled to stand when called upon by the Mayor, but [chose] to stand and take a moment for silent reflection'.[310]

4.120 Ontario's Court of Appeal held that the purpose of the prayer was to 'to impose a Christian moral tone on the deliberations of council',[311] noting that the town had refused to adopt a practice that would set a moral tone without reciting a Christian prayer. The Court held that this religious purpose was enough to invalidate the practice. The Court went on to find fault with the effects of the recitation of the Lord's Prayer on the claimant. While the recitation of the Lord's Prayer did not cause the applicant to avoid public council meetings altogether, he was 'singled out as being not part of the majority recognized officially in the proceedings' and dissuaded from running for public office.[312] These are clear violations of religious freedom.

4.121 *Ontario (Speaker of the Legislative Assembly) v Ontario (Human Rights Commission)*[313] began with a complaint to Ontario's Human Rights Commission. At the time, Ontario's legislature began every day with both a 'non-denominational' prayer and the Lord's Prayer. The claimant's[314] concern was with the latter. On this occasion, however, the Ontario Court of Appeal held that the Human Rights Commission did not have jurisdiction to intervene. The requirement that the Ontario legislature begin every day with the recitation of prayers is embodied in the Standing Orders of Legislative Assembly. These are immune from judicial scrutiny on the basis of parliamentary privilege, which protects matters essential to the internal functioning of legislative assemblies from judicial review. The Court distinguished the case from its previous holding in *Freitag* on the basis that a provincial legislative assembly enjoys constitutional status, while a town council does not.

---

[306] *Grant* (n 305) para 84.

[307] *Grant v Canada (Attorney General)* (1995), 125 DLR (4th) 556; [1995] SCCA No 394 (QL).

[308] *Freitag v Penetanguishene (Town)* (1999), 47 OR (3d) 301 (CA).

[309] *Freitag* (n 308) para 6.

[310] *Freitag* (n 308) para 8.

[311] *Freitag* (n 308) para 18.

[312] *Freitag* (n 308) para 36. For another case regarding a prayer in a town council, see *Allen v Renfrew (Corporation of the County)* (2004), 69 OR (3d) 742 (SC); the Québec Court of Appeal has also recently granted leave to a similar case in *Saguenay (Ville de) v Mouvement laïque québécois*, 2011 QCCA 583.

[313] *Ontario (Speaker of the Legislative Assembly) v Ontario (Human Rights Commission)* (2001), 54 OR (3d) 595 (CA).

[314] The same claimant brought the suit as in *Freitag* (n 308). More recently, the same litigant convinced the Ontario Human Rights Tribunal that his town's newly adopted prayer, identical in wording to the prayer recited to open sittings in the House of Commons, was discriminatory on the basis of creed because it 'derived at least in part from Judeo-Christian values and beliefs', negatively affected the applicant who did not share those beliefs: *Freitag v Penetanguishene (Town)* 2013 HRTO 893, paras 46–53.

Ontario's legislature still begins its days with a recitation of the Lord's Prayer, as do several other provincial legislatures.[315]

C. INDIA

Mara Malagodi[316]

(1) Introduction

This part of Chapter 4 analyses the protection of religious rights under the Indian legal sys-   **4.122**
tem; it focuses on the articulation of India's peculiar notion of secularism and its impact on the negotiation of the individual and collective dimensions of religious rights and their legal protection. It is divided into five sections. Section (2) provides a historical background to the Indian legal system and the development of the framework protecting religious rights. Section (3) analyses the manner in which religious rights are given effect by investigating their constitutional regulation, the competence of the various legislative bodies within the Indian federal system, the powers of the Supreme Court together with the array of remedies at its disposal when fundamental rights are violated, and the position of international law within India's legal system. Section (4) illustrates the various constitutional and statutory materials protecting religious rights, the nature of their limitations, and the leading cases interpreting these provisions. Eight issues are explored in detail within this section: secularism; freedom of religion; right to equality; discrimination on the basis of religion in employment; the issue of 'untouchability'; the personal laws system and the demand for a Uniform Civil Code; criminal law provisions related to religion; and the special treatment of the cow. The final section offers brief concluding observations.

(2) Background

The legal treatment of religion in contemporary India reflects the peculiar notion of secular-   **4.123**
ism developed post-independence and the legacy of pre-colonial and colonial legal institutions. The Preamble to the Indian Constitution expressly provides that India is a secular state; however, it has been argued that India is not truly secular for a number of reasons. First, the Indian legal system does not feature the 'wall of separation' between state and religion prescribed by the modern Western model(s).[317] Secondly, recurring bouts of communal violence have taken place in India since independence and religious minorities often suffer discriminatory treatment.[318] Thirdly, the Hindu Right (*Hindutva*) rose to power at the centre in the mid-1990s and has in the process appropriated the meaning of and demand for secularism.[319]

In response to such points, it is fair to note that India has devised its own version of secular-   **4.124**
ism, which has been pivotal in preserving democracy and national unity since independence

---

[315] R Benzie, 'Lord's Prayer review ordered' *The Toronto Star*, 13 February 2008, available at <http://www.thestar.com/News/Ontario/article/303245>.

[316] Dr Mara Malagodi is British Academy Postdoctoral Fellow in the Law Department of the London School of Economics and Political Science (LSE), University of London.

[317] TN Madan, 'Secularism in Its Place' (1987) 46(4) Journal of Asian Studies 747.

[318] S Tambiah, 'The Crisis of Secularism in India' in R Bhargava (ed), *Secularism and Its Critics* (OUP, 1998) 418.

[319] B Cossman and R Kapur, *Secularism's Last Sigh? Hindutva and the (Mis)Rule of Law* (OUP, 1999).

and has over the years guaranteed the protection of religious rights. Such protection has been articulated through an institutional framework in which the state both recognizes and protects the country's religious plurality, while at the same time frequently intervening in the religious domain. Religious law is part of the official Indian legal framework, directly recognized by—and often legislated for—by state actors. In fact, alongside uniform legislation, there exists a personal law system under which private legal matters in the areas of family, succession, and inheritance law are regulated by separate bodies of law which do not apply to individuals on the basis of their citizenship, but apply to four groups defined in terms of their religious affiliation (Hindu, Muslim, Christian, and Parsi). Indian citizens can choose the 'secular option'—which applies directly in case of inter-religious marriage or marriage to a foreigner—but the striking majority of the Indian population chooses to be regulated by their respective personal laws. This phenomenon has resulted in a renegotiation of the private/public divide in religious matters dealt with by the law and has engendered a peculiar system in which the Indian state directly engages with issues pertaining to religion.

4.125 India gained independence from Britain in August 1947 after a protracted anti-colonial struggle led by the All-India National Congress. The Indian Republic emerged from the bloodshed of the Partition of the Indian subcontinent, which created the sovereign states of India and Pakistan. Partition led to approximately a million casualties and the migration of over ten million people between the two newly created states, which soon went to war against each other in 1948 over the disputed territory of Kashmir. This outcome followed from the decision to accept the demand for Pakistan—a separate country deputed to be the homeland of the Muslim population of the subcontinent. Partition also shaped Indian nationalism, the peculiarly Indian notion of secularism, and the institutional treatment of the country's vast religious diversity.[320] The development of post-1947 Indian state-framed nationalism[321] and the design of independent India's legal structures to accommodate the polity's extraordinary socio-cultural and religious diversity are inextricably intertwined as both stemmed from the fear of enduring communal violence, stark opposition to the ethno-cultural nationalist discourse of Islamic Pakistan, and resistance to the demands for Hindu majoritarianism advocated by the Hindu Right. India's commitment to the institutionalization of secularism was already tangible during the life of the Constituent Assembly (1946–49); Indian constitution-makers with radically different political affiliations—from liberals to Gandhians, from Marxists to the Hindu Right—rallied around secularism as a tool of nation-building to the point that the term 'secularism' became then antithetical to the term 'communalism'.[322]

4.126 India's founding fathers were acutely aware of the importance of religion in Indian society and its pervasive nature in people's lives. Therefore, their efforts in institutional design were aimed at devising a constitutional edifice not hostile to religion, but one which could best manage the post-independence challenges faced by a deeply religious, utterly unequal, and internally plural society. The protection of minorities and the idea of religious tolerance

---

[320] The data on India's religious composition from the 2001 Census indicate that 80.5% of the total population (approximately 1.03bn people) was Hindu, 13.4% Muslim, 2.3% Christian, 1.9% Sikh, 0.8% Buddhist, 0.4% Jain, and 0.6% of other denominations or persuasions. See <http://www.censusindia.gov.in/Census_Data_2001/India_at_glance/religion.aspx> (accessed 30 September 2012).

[321] R Brubaker, 'The Manichean Myth: Rethinking the Distinction between "Civic" and "Ethnic" Nationalism' in H Kriese et al (eds), *Nation and National Identity* (Verlag Ruegger, 1999) 55.

[322] R Bajpai, *Debating Difference: Groups Rights and Liberal Democracy in India* (OUP, 2011) 94–6.

played a pivotal role in designing institutions capable of guaranteeing the inclusion of all religious groups in a polity with an absolute Hindu majority of over 80 per cent of the total population. As Bose suggests, it is because of this official representation of India as secular and inclusive that the retention of Indian-controlled Kashmir as the only Muslim-majority Indian state is so important in the construction of Indian nationhood.[323] Thus, the bases for the institutional treatment of religious diversity in India are to be found in the idea of 'ameliorative secularism' propounded by Jacobsohn, who defines it as:

> A model of the secular constitution as a conceptual projection of the multifaceted character of the Indian nationhood... the Constitution seeks an amelioration of the social conditions of people long burdened by the iniquities of religiously based hierarchies, but also embodies a vision of intergroup comity whose fulfilment necessitates cautious deliberation in the pursuit of abstract justice.[324]

This approach has been translated in institutional terms into what Bhargava has termed **4.127** as a 'strategy of principled distance', which features a combination of strict intervention, non-interference, and equidistance, as the case may be.[325]

In this regard, it is of pivotal importance to highlight that at the time of independence, India **4.128** retained the British colonial legal system and judicial structure almost intact. Partial reform initially took place within Hindu law, and from the mid-1980s in Islamic law. The Indian state also attempted several bouts of legislative activity to curb discrimination of the basis of caste and 'untouchability' in the light of the modernist imperatives that accompanied decolonization. It is such mix of continuity and change, preservation of historical legacies and innovation, that best characterizes Indian post-colonial legal developments in the matter of the institutional treatment of religion.

(3) The constitutional framework

The Constitution of India came into force on 26 January 1950 and remains to this day the **4.129** fundamental law of the land—notwithstanding the fact that it has been amended almost a hundred times since its inception. It comprises 395 articles and 12 Schedules. It is an entrenched, written document expressly committed to constitutional democracy.

Part III of the Constitution of India guarantees extensive and justiciable fundamental rights **4.130** (articles 12–35). A number of rights deal specifically with matters pertaining to religion and they will be discussed in detail in section (4). The application of fundamental rights in India is not always confined to actions of the state as defined under article 12 (vertical application), but in more limited circumstances a breach of fundamental rights by non-state actors also gives rise to a cause of action against non-state actors (horizontal application), mostly under article 21 (Right to Life) and when the constitutional text makes certain fundamental rights expressly applicable to non-state actions or the article is not expressly confined to state actions.[326]

Part IV of the Constitution contains extensive directive principles of state policy (articles **4.131** 36–51), which are not enforceable in a court of law, but are of fundamental importance in

---

[323] S Bose, *Kashmir: Roots of Conflict, Paths to Peace* (Harvard University Press, 2005) 8.
[324] GJ Jacobsohn, *The Wheel of Law: Indian Secularism in Comparative Constitutional Context* (OUP, 2003) 93–5.
[325] R Bhargava, 'What Is Secularism for?' in Bhargava (ed) (n 318) 520.
[326] M Singh, *V.N. Shukla's Constitution of India* (Eastern Book Company, 2010) 24.

giving direction to the governance of the country (article 37). For instance, article 44 prescribes that the state shall endeavour to secure a Uniform Civil Code applicable throughout India, thus there is an implied commitment on the part of the state to repeal the various personal laws operating in post-independence India, which are based on the affiliation to a particular religious community (Hindu, Muslim, Parsi, and Christian) and devise a uniform secular law regulating family, inheritance, and succession matters. The Supreme Court also established that the Constitution prescribes a harmony between fundamental rights and direct principles,[327] and that the directive principles should be used to aid the interpretation of fundamental rights.[328]

4.132 Article 13 specifies that laws in derogation to fundamental rights shall be void. Article 32 confers the right to move to the Supreme Court 'by appropriate proceedings' to enforce the fundamental rights enshrined in Part III. The Supreme Court[329] is empowered to issue directions or orders or writs, including writs in the nature of *habeas corpus* (to order the release of a person detained unlawfully), *mandamus* (to order a public authority to perform its duty), prohibition (to prohibit a lower court from proceeding on a case), *quo warranto* (to order a person to vacate a wrongfully assumed office), and *certiorari* (to order the removal of a proceeding from a lower court and bring it before itself), for the enforcement of Fundamental Rights.[330] Article 226 grants Indian High Courts the same powers as the Supreme Court under article 32, making the Higher Judiciary the guardian of the Constitution and the protector of fundamental rights. To safeguard the independence of the judiciary from undue executive influence, the appointment procedure for Supreme Court judges under article 124(2), and for High Court judges under article 217, has been interpreted by the Supreme Court in the following manner: the judges of the Higher Courts are appointed by a warrant of the President of India who must act on the recommendation of a collegium comprising the Chief Justice and the four seniormost judges of the Supreme Court. The Court itself overruled its earlier decision in which the President of India was given primacy in the appointment process.[331] The Supreme Court's interpretation of the constitutional provision pertaining to judicial appointments to the Higher Courts in the first *Judges Case* (1981) was confirmed in two later decisions in 1993 and 1998.[332]

4.133 Since the late 1960s, Indian Courts have adopted a more activist stance and a shift from parliamentary to judicial supremacy progressively took place. The judicial review of legislation in India evolved through tensions between Parliament and the Supreme Court over property rights and the Indian Congress government's programme of land redistribution.[333] Judicial review in India resulted in a *de facto* limitation of the doctrine of parliamentary sovereignty,

---

[327] *Minerva Mills Ltd v Union of India* AIR 1980 SC 1789.

[328] *Bandhua Mukti Morcha v Union of India* AIR 1984 SC 802.

[329] The Supreme Court also features jurisdiction as provided for by statute. Importantly, art 141 of the Indian Constitution makes the law declared by the Supreme Court binding on all courts, but not on the Supreme Court itself, which may overrule its previous decisions, while art 142 makes any order passed by the Supreme Court enforceable throughout the territory of India.

[330] These provisions are limited by art 359 of the Indian Constitution, which allows during emergency rule for the suspension of any of the Fundamental Rights guaranteed in Part III—except art 20 (Lawful Punishment for Criminal Offences, Rule against Double Jeopardy, and Protection against Self-Incrimination) and art 21 (Right to Life and Personal Liberty)—including the Right to Constitutional Remedies.

[331] *SP Gupta v Union of India* AIR 1981 SC 149.

[332] *Supreme Court Advocates-On-Record Association (SCAORA) v Union of India* AIR 1994 SC 268; *Special Reference No 1 of 1998* AIR 1999 SC 1.

[333] *Golakh Nath v State of Punjab* AIR 1967 SC 1643.

especially with the establishment of the basic structure doctrine in the 1973 *Kesavananda Bharati* case.[334] This doctrine limits the power of Parliament to amend the Constitution and empowers the Supreme Court to strike down legislation—even a constitutional amend-ment—if it violates the basic structure of the Constitution. The basic structure is understood as formed by the following principles enunciated by Chief Justice Sikri in his opinion in the *Kesavananda Bharati* judgment: supremacy of the Constitution; republican and democratic form of Government; secular character of the Constitution; separation of powers; and fed-eral character of the Constitution.[335] Following the development of the judicial review of legislation since the late 1960s with the *Golakh Nath* and *Kesavananda Bharati* decisions, the Indian Supreme Court has progressively acquired power and legitimacy as the protector of fundamental rights. In the two years of emergency rule (1975–1977) under Indira Gandhi, the position and credibility of the Court was, however, considerably weakened, especially following the *Shukla* judgment.[336] In the late 1970s, India's apex court was determined to redeem itself from the dark days of the Emergency and a new generation of judges substi-tuted on the bench the old guard, whose majority had been trained during colonial times.

It was at this point that India's most well-known judicial contribution to world jurispru-dence was created: public interest litigation (PIL). The Supreme Court revolutionized its approach to fundamental rights by relaxing the rules concerning *locus standi*. The Court ruled that in the judicial interpretation of the expression 'by appropriate proceedings' con-tained in article 32(1):   **4.134**

> ...our approach must be guided not by any verbal or formalistic canons of construction, but by the paramount object and purpose for which this Article has been enacted as a Fundamental Right in the Constitution...It is clear on the plain language of clause (1) of Article 32 that whenever there is a violation of a Fundamental Right, any one can move to the Supreme Court for enforce-ment of such Fundamental Right.[337]

Progressively PIL became a new kind of constitutional litigation *tout court* which abandoned the adversarial system as the Court could then initiate proceedings *suo motu* or entertain the petition of any individual acting out of public concern. This form of judicial activism produced a vast array of case law, ranging from issues of bonded labour to environmental protection.[338] A great number of PIL cases pertaining to religious rights have been filed in the Supreme Court; for instance in 1997 the Ahmedabad Women's Action Group (AWAG) brought a constitutional challenge under PIL against a number of personal law provisions deemed discriminatory against women. The Supreme Court did not, however, get embroiled in the political controversy and

---

[334] *Kesavananda Bharati v State of Kerala* AIR 1973 SC 1461.
[335] *Kesavananda Bharati v State of Kerala* AIR 1973 SC 1535.
[336] *ADM Jabalpur v Shivkanta Shukla* AIR 1976 SC 1207.
[337] *Bandhua Mukti Morcha v Union of India* AIR 1984 SC 806.
[338] For instance, see *Dr Upendra Baxi v State of UP* (1984) 4 SCC 104 on the inhuman conditions of deten-tion in the Agra Protective Home for Women; *People's Union for Democratic Rights v Union of India* AIR 1982 SC 1473 on child labour; *Bhandua Mukti Morcha v Union of India* AIR 1984 SC 802 on bonded labour; *Olga Tellis v Bombay Municipal Corporation* AIR 1986 SC 180 on the rights of Bombay slum dwellers; *MC Mehta v Union of India* AIR 1987 SC 1086 on the disastrous Shriram pesticide plant gas leak in Bhopal, Madhya Pradesh; *MC Mehta v Union of India* AIR 1988 SC 1115 on the pollution of the Ganga river; *People United for a Better Living in Calcutta v State of WB* AIR 1993 Cal 215 on the preservation of Calcutta's wetlands; *Vellore Citizens Welfare Forum v Union of India* AIR 1996 SC 2715 on the pollution caused by tanneries' discharge in Tamil Nadu; *MC Mehta v Union of India* AIR 1997 SC 734 on protecting the Taj Mahal from pollution; *Vishaka v State of Rajasthan* AIR 1997 SC 3011 on sexual harassment in the workplace; *MC Mehta v Union of India* AIR 2002 SC 1696 on public transport in Delhi to run solely on natural gas.

declined to exercise its jurisdiction on the matter, stating that is was for the legislature to lay down the policy the state should pursue.[339]

4.135 In addition to the extensive guarantees contained in the fundamental rights section of the Constitution, India is a signatory to a number of international conventions devoted to the protection of human rights. India adopts a dualist approach in the implementation of international law at the domestic level; thus, international treaties do not automatically become part of Indian national law, but legislation passed by Parliament under article 253 is needed to enforce the international obligations contracted by the executive. Thus, in the absence of domestic legislation incorporating international obligations into the national legal system, international legal instruments are in principle unenforceable by Indian courts. However, article 51 of the Constitution prescribes respect for the international obligations to which India is party. Article 51 is part of the Directive Principles of State Policy—and hence non-justiciable—but through the case law the principle that Indian domestic statutory provisions ought to be interpreted consistently with international obligations progressively became the norm. This results from a *prima facie* presumption that Parliament would not act in breach of international law. As a result, Indian courts may construe the Constitution itself or statutory provisions pre-dating any contraction of international obligations so as to render them consistent with such international law instruments to which India is party.[340] Thus, the Indian judiciary has played a critical role in the domestic implementation of international law instruments, especially in the areas of human rights and environmental law, fostering harmonization between domestic and international legal norms.[341] It is in the light of these extensive constitutional guarantees, legal procedures, and institutional mechanisms that the protection of religious rights in India ought to be considered, without losing sight of the severe limitations imposed by security laws in conflict areas throughout independent Indian history.

(4) Key constitutional provisions, statutes, and case law

4.136 The protection of religious rights in India is enshrined both in the Constitution and in a number of statutory provisions, interpreted by the country's Higher Judiciary.

a) Secularism

4.137 Secularism is a fundamental principle of India's legal system and is set out in the Preamble to the Constitution, which states that India is a 'Sovereign Socialist Secular Democratic

---

[339] *Ahmedabad Women's Action Group (AWAG) v Union of India* AIR 1997 SC 3614.

[340] Main International Legal Instruments to which India is party: Universal Declaration of Human Rights; International Covenant on Economic, Social and Cultural Rights (1979); International Covenant on Civil and Political Rights (1979); International Convention on the Elimination of All Forms of Racial Discrimination (1968); Convention on Rights of the Child (1992); Convention on Elimination of all Forms of Discrimination Against Women (1981); Convention against Torture and other Cruel, Inhuman or Degrading Treatment or Punishment (1997); International Covenant on Suppression and Punishment of the Crime of Apartheid (1977); Convention on the Prevention and Punishment of the Crime on Genocide (1959); Convention on the Non-Applicability of Statutory Limitations to War Crimes and Crimes against Humanity (1971); Slavery Convention (1927); Protocol amending the Slavery Convention (1926); Supplementary Convention on the Evolution of Slavery, Slave Trade and Institutions and Practice similar to Slavery (1960); Convention for the Suppression of the Traffic in Persons and of the Exploitation of the Prostitution of Others (1953); Convention on the Nationality of Married Women (1957); Convention on the Political Rights of Women (1961), available at <http://mha.nic.in/uniquepage.asp?Id_Pk=235> (accessed 5 October 2012).

[341] SK Agarwal, 'Implementation of International Law in India: Role of Judiciary', available at <http://oppenheimer.mcgill.ca/IMG/pdf/SK_Agarwal.pdf> (accessed 5 October 2012).

Republic'.[342] As Bajpai explains, the principle of secularism was interpreted, first, as 'disestablishment', ie the Constitution makes no reference to God and institutes no official religion.[343] Secondly, it was understood as 'non-sectarianism' in the sense that the State did not afford preferential treatment to any religion. Thirdly, it was taken to mean 'exclusion of religion from politics', for instance, by barring separate electorates on the basis of religious affiliation, as had occurred during colonial times, especially along the Hindu-Muslim divide. In fact, India's founding fathers, in the early years of independence, strived to institutionalize a framework in which religion was not to be the basis for identity politics. Notwithstanding the fact that the Constitution did not expressly define the state as secular, secularism was of fundamental constitutional importance as recognized by Chief Justice Sikri when he singled it out as one of the five pillars of the 'basic structure' of the Indian Constitution as early as 1973 in his opinion in the *Kesavananda Bharati* case.[344] The reasons behind Indira Gandhi's decision to include 'secularism' in the Preamble during the Emergency remain, however, unclear.

With regard to the judicial interpretation of secularism, the Supreme Court found itself **4.138** entangled in difficult political controversies with the rise of *Hindutva* and various bouts of communal violence. The meaning of secularism and its constitutional significance were elucidated in the 1994 *Bommai* case, in which the Supreme Court upheld the validity of the declaration of presidential rule in four states and the suspension of their respective Hindu Right state governments under article 356, following the destruction of the Babri mosque in Ayodhya in 1992 and the ensuing communal riots.[345] The Supreme Court confirmed that secularism forms part of the basic structure of the Constitution; it also held that:

> ... in matters of State, religion has no place. No political party can simultaneously be a religious party. Politics and religion cannot be mixed. Any State Government which pursues unsecular policies or unsecular course of action acts contrary to the constitutional mandate and renders itself amenable to action under Article 356.

It is striking to compare the outcome of the *Bommai* case with the *Ayodhya* decision, in which **4.139** the Supreme Court upheld the constitutional validity of the Acquisition of Certain Area at Ayodhya Act 1993, enacted to manage the land upon which the Babri mosque stood before being demolished by a Hindu mob on the basis that the site was the birthplace of Hindu God Ram. The Supreme Court held that the Act did not violate the constitutional principle of secularism.[346]

The ambivalence of the Supreme Court in dealing with questions of communalism is evident **4.140** in the batch of *Hindutva* cases, in which the 1987 election of 12 Hindu Right politicians to the state legislature of Maharashtra was challenged as violating section 123 (3) of the Representation of the People Act 1951, which prohibits the use of religion in electoral propaganda.[347] The Supreme Court upheld the election of some politicians, while it invalidated

---

[342] Significantly, the adjectives 'socialist' and 'secular' were absent in the promulgated original text of the Constitution and were inserted in 1976 by the 42nd Amendment Act during Indira Gandhi's Emergency. However, as illustrated previously, the secular nature of the Indian State was made clear already during the debates of the Constituent Assembly.

[343] R Bajpai, *Debating Difference: Group Rights and Liberal Democracy in India* (OUP, 2011) 100–2.

[344] *Kesavananda Bharati* (n 335).

[345] *SR Bommai v Union of India* AIR 1994 SC 1918.

[346] *Ismail Faruqui v Union of India* (1994) 6 SCC 361.

[347] *Manohar Joshi v Nitin Bhaurao Patel* AIR 1996 SC 796.

the election of others; however, these cases are significant in that the Court interpreted the notion of *Hindutva* as secular and not associated with Hinduism, but with 'the way of life of the Indian people'.[348]

b) Freedom of religion

4.141   Part III of the Constitution on Fundamental Rights contains extensive guarantees protecting religious rights. Articles 25 to 28 of the Constitution form the basis for the protection of religious rights. The analysis of the aforementioned constitutional provisions and of the leading cases pertaining to the protection of religious rights reveals a complex and nuanced approach to the institutional management of India's religious diversity, of the politicization of identity on a religious basis, and of the competing claims that emerge in such a plural society.

4.142   **(i) Freedom of religion and the individual**   Article 25 guarantees to all persons the 'freedom of conscience and free profession, practice and propagation of religion' and the right is not confined to Indian citizens:

> *Article 25. Freedom of conscience and free profession, practice and propagation of religion.*—(1) Subject to public order, morality and health and to the other provisions of this Part, all persons are equally entitled to freedom of conscience and the right freely to profess, practise and propagate religion.
>
> (2) Nothing in this article shall affect the operation of any existing law or prevent the State from making any law—
>
> > (*a*) regulating or restricting any economic, financial, political or other secular activity which may be associated with religious practice;
> >
> > (*b*) providing for social welfare and reform or the throwing open of Hindu religious institutions of a public character to all classes and sections of Hindus.
>
> *Explanation I*—The wearing and carrying of *kirpans* shall be deemed to be included in the profession of the Sikh religion.
>
> *Explanation II*—In sub-clause (*b*) of clause (2), the reference to Hindus shall be construed as including a reference to persons professing the Sikh, Jaina or Buddhist religion, and the reference to Hindu religious institutions shall be construed accordingly.

4.143   India's Supreme Court has defined the right to 'profess a religion' as the right to declare one's religious beliefs in a free and open manner.[349] The right to 'practise' one's religion, instead, has seen a long string of Supreme Court decisions. As highlighted by Singh, the Supreme Court interpreted the Constitution as offering protection only to the 'rituals and observances, ceremonies and modes of worship considered by a religion to be its integral and essential part'; the Supreme Court subsequently interpreted 'integral and essential' on an ad hoc basis in respect of a particular religion.[350] For instance in the notorious *Ayodhya* decision, the Supreme Court held that 'a mosque is not an essential part of the practice of the religion of Islam and *namaz* (prayer) by Muslims can be offered anywhere, even in the open'.[351] Similarly, the Supreme Court ruled that public performance of the *Tandava* dance does not constitute an essential practice of the Ananda Marga,[352] and that gifts for a charitable

---

[348] *Manohar Joshi* (n 347) 1129–30.

[349] *Punjabrao v DP Meshram* AIR 1965 SC 1179.

[350] Singh (n 326) 240.

[351] *Faruqui* (n 346).

[352] *Acharya Jagdishwarand Avandhuta v Commander of Police* AIR 1984 SC 51; *Commander of Police v Acharya Jagdishwarand Avandhuta* AIR 2004 SC 2984.

purpose do not form an essential part of the Christian religion.[353] The Supreme Court also went as far as distinguishing religion from philosophy in adjudicating that the teachings of Sri Aurobindo did fall within the latter categorization and hence did not enjoy the protection offered by articles 25 and 26 of the Constitution.[354]

With regard to the question of religious conversion in India, the Supreme Court interpreted **4.144** the right to 'propagate' one's religion in article 25 as the right to 'propagate' one's religion only by divulging its tenets, not as the right to convert another person's to one's own religion, because actively seeking to convert another person would impinge on the 'freedom of conscience' of that person, which is guaranteed by the same article.[355] The explicit limitations to religious freedom contained in article 25(1) 'subject to public order, morality and health' provide the state with a constitutional basis on which to restrict freedom of religion. Paragraph (2), instead, has been interpreted by Jacobsohn (at 93) as instrumental to accommodating the state's provision for 'social welfare and reform'. The link to article 17 (Abolition of 'Untouchability') and the desire to reform caste-based discrimination can be evinced from article 25(2)(b), which provides for the reform of Hindu religious institutions of a public character. Significantly, Explanation II defines 'Hindus' as including 'persons professing the Sikh, Jain or Buddhist religion'.

(ii) Rights of religious groups   Article 26 establishes the constitutional rights of religious **4.145** denominations:

> 26. *Freedom to manage religious affairs.*—Subject to public order, morality and health, every religious denomination or any section thereof shall have the right—
> (*a*) to establish and maintain institutions for religious and charitable purposes;
> (*b*) to manage its own affairs in matters of religion;
> (*c*) to own and acquire movable and immovable property; and
> (*d*) to administer such property in accordance with law.

While article 25 provides guarantees for individuals, article 26 establishes the constitutional **4.146** rights of religious groups. In this way, a distinction is drawn between individual and collective freedom of religion.[356] The Supreme Court held that three conditions ought to be satisfied for a religious denomination to be recognized as such in constitutional terms: common faith, common organization and designation by a distinctive name.[357] It is important to note that the guarantees under article 26 are extended also to a section of any given denomination.[358] Indian courts have interpreted the expression 'religious matters' in the light of the judicial doctrine that distinguishes essential from non-essential practices of any given religion.[359]

Potential clashes between articles 25 and 26 ought to be highlighted. Article 26(b) grants **4.147** the right to any religious denomination to 'manage its own affairs in matters of religion'; this clause is engaged in cases concerning temple entry and the exclusion of members of the public from worshipping on the basis of caste and/or 'untouchability'. As Singh explains, article 26(b) must yield to the overriding non-discriminatory provision enshrined in article

---

[353] *John Vallamotton v Union of India* AIR 2003 SC 2902.
[354] *SP Mittal v Union of India* AIR 1983 SC 1.
[355] *Rev Stanislaus v State of MP* AIR 1977 SC 908.
[356] Jacobsohn (n 324) 92.
[357] *SP Mittal v Union of India* AIR 1983 SC 1
[358] *Commander HRE v Sri Lakshmindra Thirtha Swamiar of Sri Shirur Mutt* AIR 1954 SC 282.
[359] *Syedna Taher Saifuddin Saheb v State of Bombay* AIR 1962 SC 853.

25(2)(b), but also observe the right that 'during certain ceremonies and on special occasions it is only members of a certain community that have the right to take part therein and that on those occasions all other persons would be excluded'.[360]

4.148 A similar conflict may arise in the interpretation of Article 17 (Abolition of 'Untouchability') in relation to Article 26(b). Singh explains that:

> ... there is a fundamental distinction between excluding persons from temples open for the purpose of worship to the Hindu public in general on the ground that they belong to the excluded communities and excluding persons from denominational temples on the ground that they are not objects within the benefit of the foundation.[361] The former will be covered by Article 17 and the latter protected by Article 26.[362]

Thus, the issue of temple entry has been skilfully negotiated by Indian courts by interpreting in conjunction different constitutional provisions under articles 17, 25, and 26 in order to devise a legal framework capable of distinguishing various factual situations in which both the religious rights of the individual and of denominations are respected. Additionally, both Articles 25 and 26 are subject to limitations pertaining to 'public order, morality and health', which have been interpreted purposively to cover issues ranging from inciting hatred among people professing different religions[363] to noise pollution.[364]

4.149 **(iii) Religion and taxation** Article 27 prohibits the state from levying taxes deputed to financially support any particular religion or religious denomination.

> 27. *Freedom as to payment of taxes for promotion of any particular religion.*—No person shall be compelled to pay any taxes, the proceeds of which are specifically appropriated in payment of expenses for the promotion or maintenance of any particular religion or religious denomination.

4.150 Article 27 was inserted ultimately to protect secularism and shield the state from allegations of supporting any particular religion. The case law draws a distinction between 'taxes' and 'fees' in the application of article 27: 'fees' do not fall within the prohibition of article 27. For such a payment to be classified as a fee, it must, first, be paid in consideration for some special services/work for the benefit of the payee; and, secondly, 'fees' are only levied for that specific consideration and ought not to merge with general state revenues.[365]

4.151 **(iv) Religion and education** Article 28 regulates religious instruction only in educational institutions entirely supported by state funds.

> 28. *Freedom as to attendance at religious instruction or religious worship in certain educational institutions.*—(1) No religious instruction shall be provided in any educational institution wholly maintained out of State funds.
> (2) Nothing in clause (1) shall apply to an educational institution which is administered by the State but has been established under any endowment or trust which requires that religious instruction shall be imparted in such institution.

---

[360] Singh (n 326) 248.
[361] Singh (n 326) 114.
[362] *Venkataramana Devaru v State of Mysore* AIR 1958 SC 255.
[363] *Subhash Desai v Sharad J Rao* AIR 1994 SC 2277.
[364] *Church of God (Full Gospel) in India v Majestic Colony Welfare Association* (2000) 7 SCC 282; *Noise Pollution (V) In re* (2005) 5 SCC 733.
[365] *Jagannath Ramanuj Das v State of Orissa* AIR 1954 SC 400.

(3) No person attending any educational institution recognised by the State or receiving aid out of State funds shall be required to take part in any religious instruction that may be imparted in such institution or to attend any religious worship that may be conducted in such institution or in any premises attached thereto unless such person or, if such person is a minor, his guardian has given his consent thereto.

Article 28 prohibits religious instruction in any educational institutions wholly maintained **4.152** out of state funds, but not in educational institutions recognized or managed by the state but set up by a trust or endowment requiring religious instruction to be imparted. In the latter kinds of institutions, participation in religious instruction is strictly voluntary.

Article 29 provides a constitutional guarantee against discrimination solely based on religion **4.153** in the admission to educational institutions supported by state funds.

> 29. *Protection of interests of minorities.*—(1) Any section of the citizens residing in the territory of India or any part thereof having a distinct language, script or culture of its own shall have the right to conserve the same.
> (2) No citizen shall be denied admission into any educational institution maintained by the State or receiving aid out of State funds on grounds only of religion, race, caste, language or any of them.

Article 29(2), Cultural and Educational Rights, forbids the exclusion from admission to **4.154** any wholly or partly state-funded educational institution 'on grounds only of religion, race, caste, language or any of them'.[366] Importantly, article 29(2) gives horizontal application to the right it enshrines and bestows such right upon individuals on the basis of their citizenship rather than their communal affiliation.[367]

From the analysis of the fundamental rights pertaining to religion it is clear that the strategy **4.155** adopted by Indian state-actors to manage religious diversity institutionally, alternates a strict exclusion of religion from politics and firm 'colour-blind' anti-discrimination policies, with more or less direct interference in religious matters and positive discrimination measures under the right to equality discussed later. Such approach combines a pragmatic attitude towards India's social realities and the importance of religion within the polity, with an aspirational reformism aimed at eradicating certain social evils associated with religion and communalism. The ultimate goal of this approach is to cement the basis of the Indian nation by creating a common 'legal' benchmark for all the different communities, without alienating them through excessive state interference in purely private matters. In fact, the provisions pertaining to the protection of religious rights contained in the Directive Principles of State Policy are in line with the approach illustrated previously. Article 38 provides that 'the State shall strive to promote the welfare of the people by securing and protecting as effectively as it may a social order in which justice—social, economic and political—shall inform all the institutions of the national life'. Equality is pivotal to the conception of justice espoused by the Indian Constitution; it is equality among individuals and also among groups.

c) Right to equality

The Indian Constitution contains extensive guarantees pertaining to equality of treatment **4.156** and non-discrimination. Religion is both an identity marker in respect of which individuals ought not to be discriminated against and a basis for collective entitlements:

---

[366] Singh (n 326) 259.
[367] *State of Madrasa v Srt Champakam* AIR 1951 SC 226.

14. *Equality before law.*—The State shall not deny to any person equality before the law or the equal protection of the laws within the territory of India.

15. *Prohibition of discrimination on grounds of religion, race, caste, sex or place of birth.*—(1) The State shall not discriminate against any citizen on grounds only of religion, race, caste, sex, place of birth or any of them.

(2) No citizen shall, on grounds only of religion, race, caste, sex, place of birth or any of them, be subject to any disability, liability, restriction or condition with regard to—

    (*a*) access to shops, public restaurants, hotels and places of public entertainment; or

    (*b*) the use of wells, tanks, bathing *ghats*, roads, and places of public resort maintained wholly or partly out of State funds or dedicated to the use of the general public.

(3) Nothing in this article shall prevent the State from making any special provision for women and children.

(4) Nothing in this article or in clause (2) of Article 29 shall prevent the State from making any special provision for the advancement of any socially and educationally backward classes of citizens or for the Scheduled Castes and the Scheduled Tribes.

(5) Nothing in this article or in sub-clause (g) of clause (1) of Article 19 shall prevent the State from making any special provision, by law, for the advancement of any socially and educationally backward classes of citizens or for the Scheduled Castes or the Scheduled Tribes in so far as such special provisions relate to their admission to educational institutions including private educational institutions, whether aided or unaided by the State, other than the minority educational institutions referred to in clause (1) of Article 30.

4.157 Article 15 prohibits discrimination against Indian citizens by the state on grounds only of religion, race, caste, sex or place of birth; it acts as an important corollary to article 14, which establishes equality before the law of all persons, not just citizens. Discrimination in this context implies a sense of prejudice.[368] The removal of prejudice is pivotal to independent India's process of nation-building; the creation of a modern polity required the undermining of the politicization of inter-religious communal identities and the removal of forms of intra-religious discrimination—such as 'untouchability'. As a result, article 15(1) applies directly to state actors and it is on its basis that, for instance, the Supreme Court invalidated an Act of the Legislature of Uttar Pradesh creating separate electorates for different religious communities.[369] Article 15(2) prohibits entry refusal into shops, public restaurants, hotels, and public entertainment and denial of usage of wells, tanks, bathing ghats, etc maintained wholly/partly by state funds or for the usage of the general public. Significantly, article 15(2) does not specify that its guarantees against discrimination are restricted to state actions and its horizontal application clearly aims at removing disabilities based on the Hindu caste system.

4.158 The formulation of the right to equality includes positive discrimination measures for *Dalits* (former 'untouchables') only after the 1st Amendment of the Constitution in 1951, when the Congress government sought to overturn the Supreme Court decision in the *State of Madrasa v Srt Champakam* on reservations in student admission to state-run medical colleges.[370] As a result, the Nehru government reasserted parliamentary sovereignty and inserted paragraph (4) in article 15 spelling out that 'nothing...shall prevent the State from making any special provisions for the advancement of any socially and educationally backward classes of citizens or for the Scheduled Castes or Scheduled Tribes'. The expression 'Scheduled Castes'

---

[368] Singh (n 326) 82.
[369] *Nain Sukh Das v State of UP* AIR 1953 SC 384.
[370] *State of Madrasa v Srt Champakam* AIR 1951 SC 226.

exclusively indicates *Dalits*. With regard to the third category of people identified by paragraph (4)—Other Backward Classes (OBC)—a more precise definition was only arrived at
in the early 1990s, following the government's decision to implement the findings of the
Mandal Commission on OBC. In a lengthy case on OBC quotas, the Supreme Court held
that caste is not a criterion to identify OBC and that the OBC category can include religious
minorities such as Muslims and Christians.[371] As a result, religious affiliation may form the
basis for the identification of social groups entitled to positive discrimination measures in
education and public service employment. The notion of equality in the Indian Constitution
under articles 14 to 18 contains both a negative and positive connotation. Negative equality
requires the enforcement on the part of the state of a strictly non-discriminatory approach by
which individuals are entitled to be protected from exclusion from public educational institutions and public employment only on the basis of religion.[372] Conversely, positive equality
mandates positive discrimination and state action in order to secure the inclusion into the
public sphere of individuals and groups belonging to different religions through reservations
for Scheduled Castes and OBC.[373]

d) Discrimination in employment

Article 16 secures to Indian citizens equality of opportunity in matters of public employ-   **4.159**
ment and forbids discrimination on a number of grounds, including religion; significantly
this constitutional guarantee extends only to employment or office under the state. Singh
clarifies that 'there is no constitutional prohibition against private persons or bodies employing people on grounds prohibited by Article 16(2)'.[374]

> *Article 16. Equality of opportunity in matters of public employment*—(1) There shall be equality
> of opportunity for all citizens in matters relating to employment or appointment to any office
> under the State.
>
> (2) No citizen shall, on grounds only of religion, race, caste, sex, descent, place of birth,
>   residence or any of them, be ineligible for, or discriminated against in respect of, any
>   employment or office under the State.
>
> (3) Nothing in this article shall prevent Parliament from making any law prescribing,
>   in regard to a class or classes of employment or appointment to an office under the
>   Government of, or any local or other authority within, a State or Union territory, any
>   requirement as to residence within that State or Union territory prior to such employ-
>   ment or appointment.
>
> (4) Nothing in this article shall prevent the State from making any provision for the reserva-
>   tion of appointments or posts in favour of any backward class of citizens which, in the
>   opinion of the State, is not adequately represented in the services under the State.
>
> (4A) Nothing in this article shall prevent the State from making any provision for reservation
>   in matters of promotion, with consequential seniority, to any class or classes of posts in
>   the services under the State in favour of the Scheduled Castes and the Scheduled Tribes
>   which, in the opinion of the State, are not adequately represented in the services under
>   the State.

Article 16(2), prohibiting discrimination, ought to be read in conjunction with paragraphs   **4.160**
(4) and (4A) of article 16, which grant to the state the right to pass legislation for positive
discrimination measures for the benefit of specified classes of Indian citizens. The Supreme

---

[371] *Indra Sawhney v Union of India* AIR 1993 SC 477.
[372] *B Venkataramana v State of Madras* AIR 1951 SC 229.
[373] *State of Madrasa v Srt Champakam* AIR 1951 SC 226; *Indra Sawhney v Union of India* AIR 1993 SC 477.
[374] Singh (n 326) 107.

Court interpreted these provisions as early as 1951 in the *Venkataramana v State of Madras* case, where the State of Madras had allocated public sector jobs on the basis of fixed quotas to various communities, some of which did not fall under the constitutional definition of 'Backward' in article 16(4). The Court held that the allocation of posts to Hindus, Muslims, and Christians violated article 16(2) and was therefore unconstitutional.[375] In a similar case a number of teachers employed in state schools in Jammu and Kashmir were promoted on the basis that 50 per cent of the promotions were reserved to Muslims, as they represent a 'Backward Class' in the state within the meaning of article 16(4). The Supreme Court allowed the petition, did not recognize all the Muslims of Jammu and Kashmir as a 'Backward Class', and held that the discrimination measure based solely on religion violated article 16(2).[376]

4.161 With regard to employment discrimination in the private sector, India has neither a constitutional ban nor a comprehensive statutory framework dealing with such issue. The Constitution concentrates on state actions and reservations in public employment and education, while the statutory framework contains different Acts dealing with separate issues, such as discrimination on the basis of gender and disability. Significantly, there are no specific provisions that deal with discrimination on the basis of religion (other than 'untouchability') in the private sector.

e) 'Untouchability'

4.162 Article 17 of the Constitution abolishes 'untouchability' and forbids its practice in any form. It provides the constitutional basis for the criminalization of discrimination on the ground on 'untouchability'.

> *Article 17. Abolition of Untouchability*—'Untouchability' is abolished and its practice in any form is forbidden. The enforcement of any disability rising out of 'Untouchability' shall be an offence punishable in accordance with law.

4.163 Article 17 is the only constitutional provision pertaining to equality that binds both the public and private sectors. This highlights the reformist commitment of the Indian constitution-makers to the eradication of the social evil of discrimination on the basis of 'untouchability'. Article 17 forms the constitutional basis of a cause of action for discrimination against *Dalit*, of judicial review of discriminatory legislation, and the criminalization of the practice of 'untouchability'. It is useful to read articles 15 and 16 in conjunction with article 17 with specific reference to positive discrimination measures for Scheduled Castes, as discussed previously.

4.164 The interventionist and reformist approach of the Indian state towards religion is well attested in the criminal law field by the Untouchability (Offences) Act 1955—renamed in 1976 as the Protection of Civil Rights Act 1955—and the later Prevention of Atrocities Act 1989. The rationale of these Acts is to discourage, penalize, and ultimately eradicate discriminatory behaviour towards *Dalit*. Mendelsohn and Vicziany argue that the main effect of this legislation was to contribute to the de-legitimation of the practice of 'untouchability', but only in the areas where state control is more substantial.[377] *Dalit* political efforts have also concentrated on certain issues, such as the treatment of *Dalit* women and the way in

---

[375] *Venkataramana v State of Madras* AIR 1951 SC 229.
[376] *Triloki Nath v State of Jammu & Kashmir* AIR 1967 SC 1283.
[377] O Mendelsohn and M Vicziany, 'The Untouchables' in O Mendelsohn and U Baxi (eds), *The Rights of Subordinated People.* (OUP, 1994) 107.

which *Dalit* have been addressed, rather than sharing common spaces such as temples and wells with upper castes. For instance, the issue of access to water has been largely sidestepped by creating separate water facilities for *Dalit*: 'provided one has convenient access to water, it seems not so vital to insist on using a well where again one will feel unwelcome'.[378]

f) Personal laws and the Uniform Civil Code

The most significant area of law in India dealing specifically with religion is the personal law system. India's personal law system regulates the domains of family, inheritance, and succession law separately for four communities defined on the basis of religion: Hindus (including also Sikhs, Buddhists, and Jains); Muslims; Parsi; and Christians. Indian citizens are also afforded the opportunity to opt for a secular legal framework under the Special Marriage Act 1954. At Independence, India's constitution-makers envisioned the supersession of the various personal laws in favour of a secular Uniform Civil Code.   **4.165**

> *Article 44. Uniform Civil Code for the citizens.*—The State shall endeavour to secure for the citizens a uniform civil code throughout the territory of India.

Article 44 is part of the Constitution's Directive Principles of State Policy and as such it is not justiciable. This provision is indicative of the desire of India's founding fathers to attain legal equality and national unity by means of legal uniformity. The programmatic nature of the Directive Principles of State Policy provision is confirmed by article 372, which guarantees the continuance in force of existing laws, including the personal law system.   **4.166**

The history of personal laws in India goes back to Mughal times and the early colonial period. At the time of the Constituent Assembly, Indian reformists, including Nehru, wished to establish a modern uniform legal system, but they were unable to pass a Uniform Civil Code overriding the country's various personal laws. Hence, they resigned themselves to enshrining the ideal of legal uniformity in the Directive Principles of State Policy. As a result, the strategy of the Indian state was to reform the law of the majority of the population, Hindu law, while opting for a policy of non-interference in Islamic law and leaving the Muslim community, the second biggest religious group in independent India, regulated under largely uncodified Sharia law. As a result, in the early 1950s the Nehru government passed the Hindu Code Bills: the Hindu Marriage Act 1955; the Hindu Succession Act 1956; the Hindu Minority and Guardianship Act 1956; and the Hindu Adoptions and Maintenance Act 1956.[379]   **4.167**

Two areas of family law in India are of particular importance in understanding the interplay of religious law and state reformist intervention. First, the issue of the legal validity of marriage: so far, the validity in the eyes of the law of a matrimonial union is not to be found in the formal process of registration with state authorities (unless contracted under the secular Special Marriage Act 1954), but in the correct ritual solemnization of the marriage under section7 of the Hindu Marriage Act 1955 and uncodified Sharia provisions. Indian reformists have endeavoured to alter this balance between religion and state and, as a result, the Compulsory Registration of Marriages Bill 2006—a piece of uniform legislation—was introduced in Parliament, but at the time of writing is still pending. If passed, the Bill would make the legal validity of a marriage contracted under personal laws entirely dependent on   **4.168**

---

[378] Mendelsohn and M Vicziany (n 377) 107.
[379] RV Williams, *Postcolonial Politics and Personal Laws. Colonial Legal Legacies and the Indian State* (OUP, 2006) 106.

the procedural criteria of registration with state authorities; hence, non-compliance would render the marriage void *ab initio*.

4.169 Secondly, the issue of post-divorce maintenance has been progressively streamlined across the various personal laws. In traditional Islamic law, women are generally entitled to post-divorce maintenance only in the *iddat* period of three menstrual cycles. The most important case on this issue was the 1985 *Shah Bano* decision in which a divorced, elderly Muslim woman won her legal battle to obtain the entitlement to maintenance extending beyond the *iddat* period from her former husband. The husband's appeal was dismissed by the Supreme Court in a path-breaking judgment, which denied any conflict between Muslim personal law and the provisions of Indian general law contained in sections 125 and 127 of the Criminal Procedure Code 1973, entitling to post-divorce maintenance a 'divorced wife' who cannot support herself.[380] Moreover, the Supreme Court made it very clear that section 125—being part of Indian general law—would in any case override Muslim personal law, were there any conflict between the two. The Supreme Court also reiterated the necessity of bypassing the various personal laws and framing a Uniform Civil Code for the entire territory of India in conformity with article 44. The fact that the Supreme Court bench that decided the *Shah Bano* case was composed by five Hindu judges, together with growing Hindu nationalism, fuelled a series of protests on the part of the Indian Muslim community, demanding that the regulation of such matters should remain under the purview of their personal law. The issue of streamlining personal laws and creating a sort of uniformity of norms across the laws applying to the various religious communities has been a recurrent theme in Indian adjudication, as the relationship between state-made law and religious norms has always been a most intractable matter.

4.170 Following the *Shah Bano* decision,[381] the Gandhi government passed the Muslim Women (Protection of Rights on Divorce) Act 1986, which has been interpreted progressively by the courts, to extend the post-divorce maintenance provisions for Muslim women beyond the *iddat* period, hence creating the same legal obligation on the divorced parties across the various personal laws.[382] The 1986 Act was constitutionally challenged a number of times; however, the petitions were kept pending by the Supreme Court for several years. In the meantime, the majority of the decisions at High Court-level promoted the concept that a divorced Muslim husband is liable for his former wife's financial support.[383] In 2001, the Supreme Court heard the *Danial Latifi* case and interpreted, for the first time, the controversial section 3(1)(a) of the 1986 Act. The apex court confirmed the interpretation offered by the Kerala High Court in *Ali v Sufaira* establishing the right of divorced Muslim women to maintenance post-*iddat* period.[384] It is now generally accepted in India that a divorced husband is liable for maintaining his children and former wife, irrespective of which personal law applies to him, as clearly stated in the *Geeta Gladstone* decision on a Christian divorce: 'every Indian citizen is bound to maintain his wife and children. This is a tradition of the society'.[385]

---

[380] *Mohammed Ahmed Khan v Shah Bano Begum* AIR 1985 SC 945.
[381] *Mohammed Ahmed Khan* (n 380).
[382] W Menski, *Modern Indian Family Law* (Curzon, 2001) 239–94.
[383] *Ali v Sufaira* 1988 (2) KLT 94; *Ahammed v Aysha* 1990 (1) KLT 172.
[384] *Danial Latifi v Union of India* AIR 2001 SC 3958.
[385] *Gladstone v Geeta Gladstone* 2002 (2) KLT SN 126 (Case No 155).

g) Criminal law

Criminal Law in India has been regulated through uniform legislation since colonial times, **4.171**
when the most important statute was introduced: the Indian Penal Code (IPC) 1860. The
IPC contains an extensive section (Chapter XV) on Offences Relating to Religion, which
identifies five offences: injuring or defiling place of worship with intent to insult the religion
of any class (section 295); deliberate and malicious acts intended to outrage religious feelings
of any class by insulting its religion or religious beliefs (section 295A); Disturbing religious
assembly (section 296); Trespassing on burial places (section 297); and uttering, words, etc,
with deliberate intent to wound the religious feelings of any person (section 298). During
colonial times, the scope of Chapter XV was to cordon, control, and sanction all behaviour
potentially inciting communal violence. Very little changed after independence, when the
IPC was kept in force and Chapter XV barely amended. It is striking to compare the trajec-
tory of the same Chapter of the Penal Code in the neighbouring jurisdiction of Pakistan,
where a series of amendments in the 1980s transformed a useful criminal law instrument,
devised to protect various religions, into the notorious 'blasphemy laws' used to entrench the
primacy of Islam and to criminalize the country's religious minorities.

In India, the constitutional validity of section 295A of the IPC 1860 was constitutionally **4.172**
challenged as a violation of the fundamental right to freedom of speech and expression
conferred by article 19(1)(a) of the Constitution. The Supreme Court upheld the constitutional validity of section 295A because it was absurd to suggest that insult to religion as an
offence could have no bearing on public order since the provisions of articles 25 and 26 of
the Constitution, while guaranteeing freedom of religion, expressly made it subject to public
order.[386]

h) Cow protection

The cow is Hinduism's sacred animal and thus it has been accorded special status and protec- **4.173**
tion within India's constitutional framework and legal system:

> *Article 48. Organisation of agriculture and animal husbandry*—The State shall endeavour to
> organise agriculture and animal husbandry on modern and scientific lines and shall, in par-
> ticular, take steps for preserving and improving the breeds, and prohibiting the slaughter, of
> cows and calves and other milch and draught cattle.

Article 48 is part of the Constitution's Directive Principles of State Policy and as such it is not **4.174**
justiciable. It provides for special protection of cows and other bovine specimens. Article 48
exemplifies the tension between the protection of religious norms and their reform in modernist terms, especially in the part concerning animal husbandry, with its special reference to
the preservation of cows, calves, and milch and draught cattle. The protection of Hinduism's
sacred animal is couched in the modernist language of science and effectively implies a ban
on cow slaughter. The extension of such ban is defined by the Supreme Court as state-level
legislation prohibiting cow slaughter, and has been interpreted by the Supreme Court in the
light of article 48 in a number of cases.[387] The Court ruled in 1958 that the protection of cows
under article 48 does not extend to cattle that are no longer milch or draught cattle, but the
Court also held that cow slaughtering was an 'optional' Muslim practice and not an essential
one.[388] Over 40 years later, the Supreme Court overruled itself and upheld the validity of an

---

[386] *Ramji Lal Modi v State of UP* AIR 1957 SC 620.
[387] Singh (n 326) 358–9.
[388] *Mohammad Hanif Quareshi v State of Bihar* AIR 1958 SC 731.

Act that imposes a complete ban on cow slaughter in Gujarat.[389] The Supreme Court later clarified in a different judgment that article 48 did not impose a total ban on bovine cattle slaughter and that bovine cattle may be slaughtered after they cease to breed or yield milk on grounds of public policy, rather than on grounds of protecting religious rights.[390]

(5) Conclusions

4.175 This overview has sought to illustrate India's 'strategy of principled distance' towards the various religions present in the country; such a strategy adopted by Indian state actors—including the courts—combines a degree of strict intervention, non-interference, and equidistance, with the aim of securing justice for Indian citizens. To conclude, the protection of religious rights in India since independence in 1947 has been articulated through a sophisticated institutional framework informed by a *sui generis* notion of secularism inextricably intertwined with the imperative of preserving national unity. As a result, different strategies have been deployed, ranging from strict non-intervention to a selective intervention, hence leading at times to ambiguous and contradictory outcomes. It seems that the comment made by Cossman and Kapur about the Supreme Court's *Hindutva* decisions appropriately illustrates such tensions also in other areas of law investing the question of religious rights and their protection: 'the decision was thus a contradictory one, in which the Hindu Right was both condemned and condoned. It is, moreover, the contradictory nature of the inroads made by the Hindu Right that continues to make law and legal discourse an important site of contestation in the struggle for Indian secularism'.[391]

D. New Zealand

Saeeda Verrall[392]

(1) Introduction

4.176 Domestic jurisprudence relating to the protection of religious freedoms in New Zealand is somewhat conspicuous in its absence. More than 20 years into the lifespan of New Zealand's seminal rights document, the New Zealand Bill of Rights Act 1990 (NZBORA), there is a relative paucity of case law exploring the parameters of the rights to hold and manifest one's religious beliefs. Notwithstanding, a number of judicial decisions have emerged across a range of social and legal contexts, highlighting what could be described as a pragmatic approach adopted by the New Zealand courts; giving recognition and effect to the relevant rights where applicable, balancing these against competing rights or public policy interests transparently, and not shying away from concluding that in certain instances, the asserted right cannot sensibly be understood to be engaged at all. While the New Zealand courts have adjudicated matters of religious freedom when they have intersected with the public sphere, there have also been decisions reflecting the reluctance of the judiciary to intervene in ecclesiastical concerns or matters of religious doctrine.

---

[389] *State of Gujarat v Mirzapur Moti Kureishi Kassab Jamat* (2005) 8 SCC 534.
[390] *Akhil Bharat Goseva Sangh (3) v State of AP* (2006) 4 SCC 162.
[391] Cossman and Kapur (n 319) 138.
[392] Saeeda Verrall is a New Zealand qualified lawyer currently practising as an appellate lawyer in the Office of the Prosecutor at the United Nations International Criminal Tribunal for the Former Yugoslavia. The views

Despite the modest number of cases engaging the religious protection clauses in NZBORA, **4.177** New Zealand nonetheless provides an interesting illustration of the interplay between law and religion in a contemporary western society, with the unique, additional consideration of the religious and spiritual beliefs and practices of New Zealand's indigenous people, the Maori.

With immigration now bringing a greater diversity of faiths into New Zealand, a growing **4.178** rights culture and a maturing body of rights jurisprudence may provide ground for increased litigation in this field.

(2) New Zealand's religious landscape at a glance

As one of the leading NZBORA texts succinctly states: 'Religious conflict looms large in **4.179** world history but, happily, not so much in New Zealand.'[393] British settlement throughout the nineteenth century imported what has variously been referred to as a *de facto*[394] or generalized[395] Christianity into New Zealand.[396] The role of Christianity in public life has historically been reflected in practices such as the public observance of Christian holidays, which continues today. However, as noted by the New Zealand Court of Appeal: 'Unlike England and Scotland, New Zealand does not have a national established church.'[397] As such, while New Zealand's Christian history played a role in shaping social and cultural mores, religion typically played little role in the institutions of government.[398]

Throughout the twentieth century, the number of New Zealanders who identified with an **4.180** organized religion gradually declined.[399] While Christian denominations still account for the majority of religious faiths, the growth of other religions, together with a gradual move towards secularization in the public sphere, led to the emergence of what some have termed a post-Christian society, where 'generic Christianity' no longer assumes a position of *de facto* ascendancy.[400] In an oft-cited example, in 2002 the then Prime Minister, Helen Clark, decided not to include the saying of grace at the Commonwealth Heads of Government banquet, explaining 'we're not only a society of many faiths, but we're also increasingly secular. In order to be inclusive, it seems to me to be better not to have one faith put first'.[401]

---

expressed herein are those of the author alone and do not necessarily reflect the views of the International Criminal Tribunal for the Former Yugoslavia or the United Nations in General.

[393] P Rishworth, G Huscroft, S Optican, and R Mahoney, *The New Zealand Bill of Rights* (OUP, 2003) 280. However, there have historically been some notable exceptions, such as the Tohanga Suppression Act of 1907, prohibiting the practice of Maori indigenous religion through superstition-based or purportedly supernatural medical practices or fortune telling.

[394] See R Ahdar, 'Religious Liberty in a Temperate Zone: A Report from New Zealand', (2007) 21 Emory International Law Review 205, 211.

[395] Rishworth et al (n 393) 280.

[396] See Sir Ivor Richardson's survey, 'Religion and the Law' 61 (1962), noting that 'there is a certain amount of truth in the statement that Christianity is part of our law. In the first place, the Christian religion has played an important part in shaping our culture, our tradition, and our law'.

[397] *Mabon v Conference of the Methodist Church of New Zealand* [1998] 3 NZLR 513.

[398] There are, however, exceptions. New Zealand's national anthem is 'God Defend New Zealand'. The Parliamentary prayer is also Christian. Members of Parliament were questioned in 2007 as to whether they wanted to amend the prayer but the majority wished to retain it in its current form: See New Zealand Human Rights Commission, *Human Rights in New Zealand 2010*, ch 10, 'Freedom of Religion and Belief'. See further, Rishworth et al (n 393) 280, giving the examples of legal prohibitions on Sunday trading, or trading at Easter and Christmas, as well as the criminalization of blasphemous libel.

[399] The 1996 Census recorded 18.42% of the population as identifying as Anglican, 13.79% as Catholic, 13.36% as Presbyterians; 33.54% professed to have 'no religion' or otherwise objected to answering the question.

[400] See Ahdar (n 394) 213.

[401] See R Ahdar, 'Reflections on the Path of Religion-State Relations in New Zealand' (2006) 3 Brigham Young University Law Review 619, 642.

4.181   While general religious adherence declined throughout the twentieth century, what is often referred to as the Maori Renaissance simultaneously saw a revival of Maori language and cultural institutions from the 1980s onwards. This was echoed by a range of legislative measures giving effect to Maori rights and interests, including the establishment of institutions and legal procedures to redress Maori for historical grievances perpetrated by the Crown and the integration of Maori considerations into New Zealand's legislative framework. Maori spiritual and religious practices such as *karakia* (prayers) before meetings and the blessing of public buildings were increasingly incorporated into public life. Perhaps in contrast to the experience of other post-colonial countries, the beliefs and practices of New Zealand's indigenous population were often viewed as a matter of uniqueness and pride for many New Zealanders, and came to form part of New Zealand's collective cultural identity. This simultaneous move towards state secularism while increasingly embracing Maori spiritual values in the public sphere led one leading commentator to note that the: 'New Zealand Government's recognition has, to be fair, never been entirely neutral or consistent'.[402]

4.182   One view of Maori ceremonial protocol or religious expression is that it has come to be seen as culture rather than religion per se, or alternatively, that it has come to represent a form of civic religion 'in which a spiritual element is acknowledged through references to God in a "non-sectarian manner" that is potentially inclusive of many religious traditions'.[403] However, notwithstanding the potential mainstreaming of Maori spiritual observances and their intermingling with Christian traditions, in recent years, the special status given to Maori spiritual practices in public life has come under increased scrutiny and criticism.[404]

4.183   Moving forward, the twenty-first century has witnessed an increasingly diverse religious landscape in New Zealand, commensurate with increased immigration from Asia and the Middle East. While the number of New Zealanders who identify with a religion has continued to decline overall, the last population census results saw an increase in the numbers of Sikhs, Hindus, and Muslims.[405]

---

[402] R Ahdar, 'Indigenous Spiritual Concerns and the Secular State: Some New Zealand Developments' (2003) 23 OJLS 611, 626.

[403] Rishworth et al (n 393) 306.

[404] eg controversy arose in 2001 over the publicly-funded exercise of sending Maori elders to New Zealand embassies and consular offices to carry out 'cleansings'. The Complaints Review Tribunal also adjudicated over a complaint from an applicant who objected to a Regional Council permitting a *karakia* (prayer) to be recited before a public meeting, alleging violations of the Human Rights Act 1993. The Tribunal found that his 'level of discomfort' during the *karakia* practice did not constitute a form of discrimination on the basis of religion under the Human Rights Act: *Church v Hawkes Bay District Council, Complaints Review Tribunal*, CRT 04/01, 26 March 2001. It has been noted that in other jurisdictions, such as the US, this would constitute an obvious infringement of the anti-establishment clause: P Rishworth, 'Notes for Public Address at New Zealand Diversity Forum on Religion and Schools', 14 September 2007. Cf *Mair v Wanganui District Court* [1996] 1 NZLR 556, where the High Court upheld a conviction for contempt of court after the defendant attempted to perform a *karakia* against the express order of the District Court Judge. In language that can be seen as more consistent with anti-establishment jurisprudence, the Judge noted that courts are secular institutions and that 'involving any person in a karakia against their personal wishes is insensitive and unacceptable'.

[405] Statistics New Zealand, 'Quickstats about Culture and Identity, Summary of 2006 Census of Populations and Dwellings' (the 5-yearly census was not carried out in 2011 due to the Canterbury earthquakes). From 2011 the number of New Zealanders born overseas increased by 3.4%, the number of people that identified as Sikhs, Muslims, and Hindus increased by 83%, 52.6%, and 61.8% respectively. The percentage of people identifying with one of the Christian denominations was 55.6%, down from 60.6% in 2001, although there was simultaneously an increase within minority Christian denominations (Orthodox, Born Again, Pentecostal, and 'fundamentalist' Christian faiths). The number of people stating that they had no religion continued to increase, up to 34.7% of the population. See also New Zealand Human Rights Commission, *Human Rights in New Zealand 2010*, ch 10, 'Freedom of Religion and Belief'.

(3) Legislation relating to religious rights and freedoms

a) *The New Zealand Bill of Rights Act 1990*

(i) Provisions relevant to religious freedoms   NZBORA is New Zealand's primary rights **4.184**
document. Adopted in part to give domestic effect to New Zealand's obligations under the
ICCPR,[406] it applies to all acts performed by the legislative, executive, and judicial branches
of government and by any person or body in the performance of a statutory function.[407]

Sections 13 and 15 are the core provisions relating to religious rights and fall under the **4.185**
penumbra of Democratic and Civil Rights contained in Part 2 of the Act:

> 13 Freedom of thought, conscience, and religion
>
> Everyone has the right to freedom of thought, conscience, religion, and belief, including the
> right to adopt and to hold opinions without interference.
>
> …
>
> 15 Manifestation of religion and belief
>
> Every person has the right to manifest that person's religion or belief in worship, observance,
> practice, or teaching, either individually or in community with others, and either in public
> or in private.

With respect to minorities, including religious minorities, section 20 provides: **4.186**

> 20 Rights of minorities
>
> A person who belongs to an ethnic, religious, or linguistic minority in New Zealand shall not
> be denied the right, in community with other members of that minority, to enjoy the culture,
> to profess and practise the religion, or to use the language, of that minority.[408]

The division between sections 13 and 15 reflects the distinction between the right to hold **4.187**
beliefs without interference and the right to the manifestation of those beliefs. The intervening section 14 is consistent with this gradient from internal belief to outward manifestation,
dealing with freedom of expression.[409]

The language of sections 13 and 15 comes from Articles 18(1) and 19(1) and (2) of the **4.188**
ICCPR. To the extent that the text deviates from that of the ICCPR, NZBORA provisions
do not replicate Article 18(2), the right to be free from coercion that would impair the
freedom to adopt religion or beliefs, nor Article 18(4) relating to the liberty of parents and
guardians to ensure the religious and moral education of their children.[410] In keeping with
the ICCPR, the rights enumerated in NZBORA reflect the freedom of religion, rather than
a freedom from religion. Consistent with this, there is no anti-establishment clause such as
that found in the First Amendment of the US Constitution.[411]

---

[406] See *White Paper, A Bill of Rights for New Zealand*, para 10.1. The NZBORA's long title is: 'to affirm New
Zealand's commitment to the International Covenant on Civil and Political Rights'. Treaties and other international instruments do not have automatic effect; to be enforceable, the rights and obligations in them must
be implemented into domestic law.

[407] NZBORA, s 3: Application.

[408] cf ICCPR, Art 27.

[409] See Rishworth et al (n 393) 278, rejecting the idea that s 14 should be seen as freedom of expression for
'secular ideas' while s 15 encompasses religious expression. Whenever expression is involved, it is anticipated
that s 14 would be the primary section invoked.

[410] Nor does the NZBORA replicate Art 18(3) of the ICCPR, which speaks to limitations on the right. As
discussed later, limitations are dealt with in NZBORA, s 5.

[411] The White Paper introducing the proposed Bill of Rights legislation before Parliament noted that the
issue of an official state religion 'does not appear to be a real question to address in New Zealand': *White Paper,*

4.189 (ii) **Status and operation of NZBORA**   When initially proposed, it was envisaged that NZBORA would constitute a supreme law for New Zealand; a constitutional document that would empower courts to strike down inconsistent legislation. However, despite general support for the affirmation of most of the rights contained in the proposed bill, there was strong resistance to the proposal for an entrenched Bill of Rights with supreme status. In a legal system premised upon Parliamentary supremacy, fears of judicial activism and a wariness of undermining the legislature's hold on the balance of power ultimately led to a severe watering down of the bill's potency. Interestingly, religious groups were among those critical of the potential reach of NZBORA, with some arguing that vesting such power in the judiciary could result in courts determining matters of social policy.[412]

4.190 What emerged as the final NZBORA was a non-entrenched statute that not only lacked supremacy over inconsistent legislation, but was expressly subject to it. Section 4 of NZBORA provides:

> 4. Other enactments not affected
>
> No court shall, in relation to any enactment (whether passed or made before or after the commencement of this Bill of Rights),—
>
> (a) hold any provision of the enactment to be impliedly repealed or revoked, or to be in any way invalid or ineffective; or
>
> (b) decline to apply any provision of the enactment—
>
> by reason only that the provision is inconsistent with any provision of this Bill of Rights.

4.191 Thus in the case of inconsistency between NZBORA and other legislation, a Court cannot decline to apply the latter, or hold any provision of it to be impliedly revoked or ineffective.

4.192 Section 5 of NZBORA is the limitations provision and states that 'subject to section 4 the rights and freedoms contained in this Bill of Rights may be subject only to such reasonable limits prescribed by law as can be demonstrably justified in a free and democratic society'. While this aims to place a boundary on the permissible limitations that can be placed on NZBORA rights, section 5 is expressly subject to section 4. Meaning that again, if legislation directly sought to directly limit, exclude, or contradict NZBORA rights, that legislation would have to prevail.

4.193 Section 6 of the Act does, however, give NZBORA some teeth, albeit as an 'interpretive document'. Section 6 provides:

> 6. Interpretation consistent with Bill of Rights to be preferred
>
> Wherever an enactment can be given a meaning that is consistent with the rights and freedoms contained in this Bill of Rights, that meaning shall be preferred to any other meaning.

para 10.60. However, see A Butler and P Butler, *The New Zealand Bill of Rights Act 1990: A Commentary* (LexisNexis Butterworths, 2006) para 14.6.15, noting that the right to hold religious beliefs or opinions without interference under NZBORA, s 13 would also preclude state endorsement of a particular religion or favour one religion over another 'and so indirectly exert pressure to believe'. See also P Rishworth, 'The Religion Clauses of the New Zealand Bill of Rights' [2007] New Zealand Law Review 631, 642, arguing that the reasoning of the White Paper was superficial: an anti-establishment clause goes much further than prohibiting the unlikely event of a state-established religion, 'it speaks to laws and practices that suggest state support, endorsement or non-neutrality in matters of religion'.

[412] Simultaneously, other religious groups were concerned that the Bill did not recognize God as the ultimate source of rights, unlike the Canadian Charter upon which much of NZBORA is based. For further discussion see R Ahdar, 'Ruminations from the Shaky Isles on Religious Freedom in the Bill of Rights Era' in P Babie and N Rochow (eds), *Freedom of Religion under Bills of Rights* (University of Adelaide Press, 2012) 374–5.

Although section 6 provides that legislation should be given a meaning consistent with **4.194**
NZBORA, in keeping with the premise of section 4 that contrary legislation must prevail
when inconsistent with NZBORA rights, a section 6 approach to interpretation is only available where legislation *can* be given a meaning consistent with NZBORA. While ambiguous
legislation would therefore be subject to a rights-interpretive approach, legislation explicitly
abridging rights would take precedence.[413]

Aside from an inability to strike down inconsistent legislation, NZBORA also lacks a rem- **4.195**
edies provision. In the first few years of NZBORA's tenure the New Zealand Court of Appeal
found an *implied* power to grant financial remedies,[414] which has subsequently been upheld
and applied in a number of cases.[415] However, despite initial predictions, the availability of
compensatory damages for breaches of NZBORA has not resulted in a vast increase in the
number of claims, nor a proliferation in financial awards. The absence of a clear mechanism
for financial remedies both in NZBORA and in practice may further explain the relative lack
of litigation arising out of the Act.

In addition, before legislation can come into effect, section 7 of NZBORA requires the **4.196**
Attorney-General to submit a report to Parliament in any instance where any part of a leg-
islative bill 'appears to be inconsistent with any of the rights and freedoms contained in this
Bill of Rights'.

In contrast to Article 18(3) of the ICCPR, sections 13 and 15 of NZBORA do not contain **4.197**
their own limitations clauses. Rather, section 5 acts as a general limitations provision for all
rights contained in NZBORA. It has been noted that, as section 13 applies to the *forum internum* (the realm of personal thought), there would be little space for justified infringements
into this realm.[416] As noted by District Court Judge Lindsay Moore 'the rights of thought,
conscience, religious and other belief affirmed by s 13 can be regarded as absolute'.[417]

---

[413] Although, see para 4.196, the Attorney-General considers legislation for consistency with NZBORA
before it enters into force.

[414] See eg *Simpson v Attorney-General* [1994] 3 NZLR 667 ('Baigent's case'). In *Baigent* the Court of Appeal
held that compensation was available as a discretionary remedy for breaches of NZBORA where there was no
existing cause of action or remedy, or where the existing remedy or cause of action was inadequate.

[415] The majority of such claims under NZBORA have dealt with the deprivation of liberty or invasion of
privacy in the criminal justice context, although it has been noted that the Act offers the potential for compensation in areas such as the non-observance of natural justice or preventing freedom of movement. On the whole,
the potential for financial remedies under the Act has not expanded significantly over time. The quantum of
damages awarded is discretionary and has generally been quite modest. For instance, in *Attorney-General v
Udompun* [2005] 3 NZLR 204 (CA), the plaintiff, a Thai national, was ultimately awarded NZ$4,000 for
'procedural failings' leading to her being denied entry into New Zealand twice and for the manner in which
she was treated during her detention. In a major case involving financial damages under NZBORA, *Taunoa v
Attorney-General* [2008] 1 NZLR 429 (SC), the plaintiffs were awarded damages for their time spent in incar-
ceration on a 'behaviour modification regime', which included solitary confinement, deprivation of privileges,
and various indignities for badly-behaved inmates. The Supreme Court upheld the award of damages to the five
plaintiffs but reduced the quantum for the totality of damages from NZ$140,000 awarded in the High Court,
to NZ$86,000 on appeal, with the plaintiffs receiving different amounts depending on their time spent on the
regime and the resultant harm. For further discussion, see G McLay, 'Damages for Breach of the New Zealand
Bill of Rights—Why Aren't They Sufficient Remedy?' [2008] NZLR 333.

[416] Butler and Butler (n 411) para 14.8.1.

[417] *Police v Razamjoo* [2005] DCR 408, discussed at para 4.228. There is no separate constitutional court
system in New Zealand for determining NZBORA cases. The principles of NZBORA must be applied by all
levels of the judicial branch of government. Cases with an NZBORA element to them will be determined by the
Court in which they would regularly be heard. For instance, criminal cases such as *Razamjoo* may be heard at
first instance in either the District Court or High, and NZBORA issues could be raised at first instance, before

4.198 In a situation where rights in NZBORA may clash with each other, the Act does not provide a hierarchy of rights or a method for their reconciliation. Courts have generally sought to reconcile competing rights on a case-specific basis.[418]

b) Human Rights Act 1993

4.199 Alongside the rights and protections set out in NZBORA, the Human Rights Act 1993 aims to 'provide better protection of human rights in New Zealand in general accordance with United Nations Covenants or Conventions on Human Rights'.[419] The thrust of the Act is to prohibit various forms of discrimination. It also regulates the operation of the Human Rights Commission[420] and sets up a framework for investigating and resolving complaints, including through the Human Rights Review Tribunal.[421] Unlike NZBORA, which is limited in its application to the branches of government or those exercising a statutory power, the Human Rights Act extends its coverage to other situations, such as employment relationships.

4.200 The prohibited grounds of discrimination include 'religious belief' and 'ethical belief', the latter defined as 'the lack of a religious belief, whether in respect of a particular religion or religions or all religions'.[422] However, the Act also sets out a number of exceptions where discrimination, or differential treatment, is effectively permissible. With respect to religious affiliation, exceptions include employment in the field of national security;[423] employment in work performed outside New Zealand, where the customs of the country in which the work is performed are ordinarily carried out by persons of a particular religious group;[424] employment in a private household;[425] and employment in an organized religion, as teacher in a private school, or as a social worker in a religious organization.[426] The usual prohibition on discrimination in the provision of land, housing, and accommodation also carries an exception for religious institutions,[427] and the prohibition against discrimination in access to education carries an exception for restricted admission on the basis of religious belief in the case of religious educational institutions.[428]

c) The education regime

4.201 The interplay between religion and public education has been one of the few areas of ongoing tension in New Zealand. From the Education Act of 1877, the New Zealand primary

---

being appealed to the Court of Appeal and potentially the Supreme Court. As seen at paras 4.244–4.245, other judicial bodies, such as the Environment Court, are also competent to determine cases with an NZBORA element.

[418] See eg *Re J (an infant)* [1996] 2 NZLR 134, discussed at paras 4.208–4.211, where the Court of Appeal adopted a 'definitional balancing' approach which defined the scope of the substantive rights so that they did not clash with each other, as opposed to determining the permissible restrictions on any given right with reference to NZBORA, s 5, the limitations clause.

[419] Human Rights Act (HRA 1993).

[420] HRA 1993, ss 4, 5.

[421] HRA 1993, Pt 3: Resolution of disputes about compliance with Part 1A and Part 2. Cases from the Human Rights Review Tribunal can be appealed to the High Court and, with leave, to the Court of Appeal on a question of law. There is a further possibility of appeal to the Supreme Court if the requisite criteria are met.

[422] HRA 1993, s 21(1), (c), (d).

[423] HRA 1993, s 25(a)(i).

[424] HRA 1993, s 26.

[425] HRA 1993, s 27(2).

[426] HRA 1993, s 28. An exemption also exists regarding membership in a qualifying body which facilitates engagement in or calling for the purposes of organized religion: Section 39.

[427] HRA 1993, s 55.

[428] HRA 1993, s 58.

education system was required to provide a minimum of four hours of educational instruction per day, being 'entirely of a secular character'.[429] However, the school day routinely ran longer than four hours and the practice was established of providing religious instruction during school hours (beyond the four-hour minimum) and deeming the school to be notionally closed for the period of such instruction.[430]

The Education Act of 1964 essentially formalized this arrangement.[431] The Act provided, **4.202** however, that religious instruction was not to be compulsory and that a student's parents or guardians could seek to exempt them,[432] thus establishing an opt-out procedure.[433] The Education Act of 1989 supplemented this with further opt-out procedures for students holding religious beliefs, allowing them to be excused from tuition in a particular subject, including on the basis of 'sincerely held religious or cultural views'.[434]

Alongside the public school system, the Private Schools Conditional Integration Act 1975 **4.203** permits state funding of schools that reflect 'special character' education, including religious schools. However, even where religious instruction forms part of a school's special character education, the school must be 'responsive to the sensitivities of pupils and parents of different religious or philosophical affiliations, and shall not require any such pupil to participate...'.[435]

d) Other legislation

Blasphemous libel. A miscellany of other legislation also touches upon religious beliefs or **4.204** rights. For instance, blasphemous libel remains an offence under the Crimes Act 1961, punishable by up to one year's imprisonment.[436] Leave of the Attorney-General is required to pursue a prosecution and none have been brought in recent times. The continued presence of this offence in the criminal law has been described by one commentator as 'probably something of an embarrassment'.[437]

Exemption from statutory/legal obligations. A number of other laws create exceptions where **4.205** individuals can exempt themselves from certain statutory obligations on the basis of their religious beliefs. The Law Practitioners Act 1982 permitted a person to object to being a

---

[429] Education Act 1877, s 84(2).

[430] Religious 'instruction' in schools is exactly that; 'instruction in as opposed to about a religion. It is not, in other words, comparative religion': Rishworth (n 404).

[431] Education Act 1964, ss 77, 78.

[432] Education Act 1964, s 79.

[433] One of the earliest (pre-NZBORA) cases touching on this issue was *Rich v Christchurch Girls' High School Board of Governors (No 1)* [1974] 1 NZLR 1, holding that religious readings and prayers at state schools were permissible so long as an 'opt-out' existed. Although the majority of the 1964 Act has been repealed, the provisions for religious instruction remain operative. Commentators expressed the view that this is likely to remain the case under NZBORA. Moreover, as it is regulated by statute, the provision would trump the rights in NZBORA by virtue of NZBORA, s 4. It is likely that this would be the same for secondary schools if a suitable opt-out procedure existed: Rishworth et al (n 393) 301.

[434] Education Act 1989, s 25A. Section 25AA also allows students to be exempt from parts of the health curriculum relating to sexual education. The system of 'opting out' of religious instruction in schools remains in place, notwithstanding some challenges. In 2006 the Ministry of Education sought to revise this practice, circulating draft guidelines suggesting that schools should instead adopt 'opt-in' procedures, so as to avoid the possibility of peer-pressure or coercion, which the Ministry noted could be in violation of NZBORA. Ultimately, the level of public opposition to these guidelines led the Ministry to quickly withdraw them. For more, see Ahdar (n 394) 219.

[435] Private Schools Conditional Integration Act 1975, s 32(2).

[436] Crimes Act 1961, s 123.

[437] R Ahdar, 'The Right to Protection of Religious Feelings' (2008) 11(4) Otago Law Review 629, 641.

member of a District Law Society on the basis of a genuine 'conscientious belief', 'whether or not the grounds of the belief are of a religious character, and whether or not the belief is held as part of the doctrine of a religion, religious denomination, or sect'.[438] The Employment Relations Act 2000 permits workplaces to deny union access where the employer is a 'practising member of a religious society or order whose doctrines or beliefs preclude membership of any organisation or body other than the religious society or order of which the employer is a member'.[439] The Statistics Act 1975 makes it an offence to refuse to provide information lawfully requested by a person or body authorized under the Act, but creates an exemption for those who object to stating their religious denomination.[440] The Contraception, Sterilisation and Abortion Act 1977 permits medical practitioners to object to performing abortion or sterilization procedures on the grounds of conscience,[441] implicitly exempting those whose faiths do not condone such procedures.

4.206 *Maori spiritual interests.* A range of legislation also requires consideration to be given to Maori interests, which may include customs, practices, or beliefs that explicitly or implicitly involve a spiritual or religious element. One such example is the Resource Management Act 1991, New Zealand's seminal environmental planning statute, which requires certain matters of national importance to be taken into consideration when exercising any functions under the Act. Those matters include 'the relationship of Maori and their culture and traditions with their ancestral lands, water, sites, waahi tapu, and other taonga'.[442] A further example is the obligation of persons exercising functions under the Hazardous Substances and New Organisms Act 1996 (which regulates genetically modified organisms) to take into account 'the relationship of Maori and their culture and traditions with their ancestral lands...and other taonga'.[443]

(4) Jurisprudence considering religious rights

4.207 The jurisprudence concerning the protection of religious freedoms in New Zealand, while in its infancy, touches upon a wide range of legal and social issues. The scarcity of case law somewhat frustrates the ability to draw finite conclusions about when such rights are understood to be engaged, or the methodology used adjudicate them. However, a study of the cases nonetheless provides some insight into the scope of the rights and provides a tentative platform for predicting how related issues might be determined in the future.

a) Defining the scope of the rights

4.208 *Religious rights and refusal of medical treatment for children.* Not long into NZBORA's tenure, the boundaries of the right to the manifest one's religious beliefs—and its intersection

---

[438] Law Practitioners Act 1982, s 24(1). The Law Practitioners Act was repealed by virtue of the Lawyers and Conveyancers Act 2006. Under s 386 of the Lawyers and Conveyancers Act, persons who were members of a District Law Society under the old scheme continue by default as members of a branch of the New Zealand Law Society, but membership is voluntary.

[439] Employment Relations Act 2000, s 23, 24.

[440] Statistics Act 1975, s 43(3). The five-yearly national census permits people to decline to answer questions relating to their religious affiliation.

[441] Contraception, Sterilisation and Abortion Act 1977, s 46.

[442] Resource Management Act 1991, s 6(e).

[443] Resource Management Act 1991, s 6. Early in the Act's tenure, an application regarding genetically modified cows was unsuccessfully contested by Maori, arguing that genetic engineering was contrary to their customs and spiritual principles: see *Bleakley v Environmental Risk Management Authority* [2001] 3 NZLR 213, 227.

with other rights and public policy considerations—were tested in the case of *Re J*.[444] J, the 3-year-old son of Jehovah's Witnesses, required a life-saving blood transfusion. In the face of the parents' refusal of consent, the hospital obtained a Court order permitting the blood transfusion and placing J under the guardianship of the Court.

The parents appealed to the Court of Appeal, arguing that the order breached their rights **4.209** under sections 13 and 15 of NZBORA and could not be considered to be a justified limitation on those rights pursuant to section 5. In dismissing the appeal, the Court of Appeal noted that the rights in question were not absolute, as reflected in the limitations provision in Article 18(3) of the ICCPR, on which the rights were modelled. Ordinarily, the rights included a parent's ability to bring up children and educate them within their religion, and to make decisions as to children's health and medical treatment. However, in a case where those medical decisions had the potential to impact upon the child's own right not to be deprived of life (enshrined in section 8 of NZBORA),[445] the Court declined to invoke section 5 of NZBORA to assess whether intervening to protect the child was a justifiable limitation on the rights of religious freedom.

Rather, the Court adopted a 'definitional balancing' approach; construing the scope of the right **4.210** under section 15 so as to exclude matters implicating another's life or health and thus defining the right of religious manifestation compatibly with the coexisting right not to be deprived of life. The Court considered that this definitional balancing approach was preferable to 'ad hoc balancing' under the section 5 limitations provision. On the Court's approach, the right to manifest one's religious beliefs did not, by definition, extend to imperilling the health of a child, and thus no reasonable limitations on the right were required.

In adopting this methodology, the Court of Appeal declined to follow the approach taken by the **4.211** Canadian Supreme Court in *B(R) v Children's Aid Society of Metropolitan Toronto*.[446] In a similar factual scenario, the majority in *B(R)* adopted a balancing approach, considering whether a limitation on the right to manifest one's religious beliefs was reasonable ('demonstrably justified in a free and democratic society') under section 1 of the Charter, rather than limiting the scope of the right from the outset. In *Re J*, Gault J considered that either approach ultimately led to the same conclusion:

> It is to be expected whether approached by reference to the principles of fundamental justice, to limits on absolute rights that can be justified in a free and democratic society, or to the scope appropriate for competing fundamental rights, the result should be the same.[447]

Following *Re J*, the potential for development or even further discussion of the definitional ver- **4.212** sus ad hoc modes of balancing might have been expected. However, this has not been borne out in the case law. The result in *Re J* has been echoed in similar cases,[448] but the rationale for adopting this approach to reconciling competing rights has not been subject to detailed exploration.[449]

---

[444] *Re J (an infant)* [1996] 2 NZLR 134.

[445] The reference to NZBORA, s 8 in this context has been criticized, given that NZBORA only protects against state intrusion into the right to life, not that of the parents.

[446] *B(R) v Children's Aid Society of Metropolitan Toronto* [1995] 1 SCR 315.

[447] *Re J (an infant)* [1996] 2 NZLR 134, 145.

[448] eg in *Auckland Healthcare Services Ltd v Liu* [1998] NZFLR 998, the High Court defined the scope of the parents' right under NZBORA, s 15 so as to exclude any acts or omissions that would place the health, welfare, or life of their child at risk.

[449] The Court of Appeal has applied ad hoc balancing in other instances, eg when reconciling freedom of expression under NZBORA, s 14 and restrictions on objectionable publications: see eg *Living Word Distributors Ltd v Human Rights Action Group* [2000] 3 NZLR 570.

Scholars have expressed some scepticism at the Court's methodology, arguing in favour of an ad hoc balancing approach that would 'ensure the state carries the onus of establishing that a fundamental civil right really warrants restriction rather than, with definitional balancing, the state not being put to the task of discharging the onus by virtue of a court's initial defining away of the disputed scope of the right'.[450]

4.213 *A duty to protect religion?* The scope of the NZBORA rights of religious freedom—and specifically, whether they include a positive obligation on the state to protect religion—was considered in *Mendelssohn v Attorney-General*.[451] Mendelssohn was a member of Centrepoint, a religious commune established in the late 1970s under Herbert 'Bert' Potter. The religion became embroiled in controversy in 1990 when Potter was convicted for drug offences and then for widespread sexual abuse within the commune.

4.214 Centrepoint had been formally structured as a charitable trust. The trust's operation ran into difficulties as the commune became caught up in scandal. Mendelssohn petitioned the Attorney-General to restore the operation of the trust to its proper purposes. The Attorney-General declined to do so, ordering an inquiry into the trust's affairs, which ultimately resulted in the appointment of a Public Trustee. Mendelssohn brought an action against the Attorney-General, arguing, *inter alia*, an obligation under NZBORA to protect his freedom of religion[452] by taking 'position steps to protect that freedom and abstaining from conduct that would damage that freedom'.[453]

4.215 The Court of Appeal gave short shrift to Mendelssohn's proposition that the state was under a duty to take positive steps to protect his freedom of religion, noting 'those provisions do not impose positive duties on the State, at least in any sense relevant to this case. Rather, they affirm freedoms of the individual which the State is not to breach. The very nature of these rights and freedoms means that they are freedoms from state interference'. The Court distinguished this from other rights in NZBORA that explicitly contained a positive aspect, such as the criminal justice provisions imposing procedural obligations on the state. Supporting this conclusion, the Court referred to Article 18 of the ICCPR and foreign constitutional provisions, which also primarily placed restraints on the state rather than obligations (noting that the United States, in particular, 'strongly heads in the opposite direction', given the anti-establishment clause in the First Amendment).

4.216 While the Court did not rule out circumstances in which the state could take positive steps to, for instance, repress the imparting of ideas incompatible with respect for the freedom of religion of others, this was more appropriately viewed as a power of the state; not a duty.

4.217 *Shop trading hours.* One of the instances where New Zealand's Christian roots have been granted legislative recognition is the regulation of shop trading hours. The Easter trading ban has been an ongoing source of contention in New Zealand, but careful judicial analysis has been lacking and the courts have yet to consider in this context whether New Zealand's freedom of religion provisions implicitly include a right to be free from coerced observance of religious practices through state recognition or endorsement of them.

---

[450] Ahdar (n 412) 386. See also A Butler, 'Limiting Rights' (2002) 33 Victoria University of Wellington Law Review 537, 547–8.

[451] *Mendelssohn v Attorney-General* [1999] 2 NZLR 268.

[452] Mendelssohn relied on NZBORA, ss 13, 14, 15, 17 (freedom of association), and 20 (minority rights).

[453] *Mendelssohn* (n 451) para 6.

In *Department of Labour v Books and Toys Wanaka Ltd*,[454] a local business sought relief **4.218** from incurring a penalty for staying open on Easter Sunday by seeking the Court to grant a Declaration of Inconsistency with section 15 of NZBORA. The District Court found it lacked jurisdiction to grant such a remedy.[455] However, it went on to note that, in any case, it would have declined to grant relief since the defendant opened their business for economic reasons and not religious reasons.[456] Unfortunately, this limited reasoning failed to consider the more pertinent issue of whether the religious freedoms under NZBORA encompassed a right to be free from religion, and whether state laws endorsing a particular religious practice amounted to a form of coercion. Thus, the issues considered by the Canadian Supreme Court in *R v Big M Drug Mart Ltd*,[457] in a similar context, did not fall for consideration.[458]

Exorcisms and consent to bodily harm. One of the few cases where the right protecting mani- **4.219** festation of religion appears to have been construed broadly is the case of *R v Lee*.[459]

Lee held a probationary ministerial credential from the Assembly of God in New Zealand **4.220** and founded the 'Lord of All's' church, of which one Joanna Lee was also a member. Lee was convicted of the manslaughter of Joanna, who died at Lee's hand during an exorcism ('deliverance'). Lee was charged with manslaughter through an unlawful act—assault. Joanna's deliverance had taken place over several hours and involved Lee applying weight to parts of her body, bouncing on her stomach and chest area and applying sustained pressure to her neck.

In appealing his conviction, Lee argued that the trial judge erred in failing to put consent **4.221** to the jury as a defence for the underlying act of assault.[460] In considering this question, the Court of Appeal was called to consider the intersection of common law jurisprudence removing consent as a defence to assault in certain circumstances with the NZBORA section 15 right to manifestation of religious beliefs.

Counsel for Lee argued that the section 15 right extended to the practices of 'fringe religions' **4.222** and that the public interest was properly protected by permitting consent to exorcisms in circumstances short of consent to death or the application of force likely to cause grievous bodily harm (those being factual issues to be left to the jury). The Crown conceded that section 15 would protect certain forms of religious ritual involving physical contact and that the provision informed the common law as to the limitations of consent. However, it argued

---

[454] *Department of Labour v Books and Toys Wanaka Ltd* (2005) 7 HRNZ 931 (DC).

[455] Recall that legislation inconsistent on its face with NZBORA 'trumps' NZBORA by virtue of section 4. Declarations of Inconsistency are not foreshadowed in the provisions of NZBORA. Despite discussions earlier in the NZBORA's tenure regarding the ability of Courts to issue such Declarations, the procedure has never gained traction in New Zealand: see C Geiringer, 'On a Road to Nowhere: Implied Declarations of Inconsistency and the New Zealand Bill of Rights Act' (2009) 40 Victoria University of Wellington Law Review 613.

[456] *Books and Toys Wanaka Ltd* (n 454) para 25. Nonetheless, the judge proceeded to discharge the defendant without penalty.

[457] *R v Big M Drug Mart Ltd* [1985] 1 SCR 295, finding that there was no true secular basis for Sunday trading restrictions and that they coerced non-Christians to observe the Christian Sabbath.

[458] Rishworth (n 411) 642, noting that the NZBORA *White Paper* failed to consider the value of an anti-establishment clause in determining whether state actions were coercive through their implicit endorsement of a particular religion.

[459] *R v Yong Bum Lee*, CA 437/04, 7 April 2006.

[460] The Crown had argued that Joanna did not consent, at least from the point where her death was imminent. Alternatively, the procedure went beyond the bounds of any legitimate religious practice, and public policy grounds excluded consent as an available defence.

that the deliverance carried out by Lee either fell outside the bounds of legitimate religious conduct protected by section 15,[461] or if it was protected, limitation of the right was justified in terms of section 5 of NZBORA.

4.223 As a starting point, the Court recognized the clear right to manifestation of religious beliefs under section 15, which included religious practices such as ritual circumcision or religious flagellation. While the availability of consent as a defence to harm arising from religious rituals would be a fact-specific inquiry, the Court declined to endorse a blanket exclusion of exorcisms on the basis of their inherent potential for harm, or to limit permissible exorcisms to those of 'mainstream' religions. Reviewing the evidence from the trial, the Court of Appeal concluded there was an evidential basis for consent and that it should have been put to the jury as a defence. The Court quashed Lee's conviction and remitted the case for a re-trial.

b) Religious rights in the criminal justice context

4.224 The Courts have rejected religious beliefs as a defence per se in the criminal justice context.

4.225 *A religious basis for the use cannabis?* The contention that a individual's Rastafarian beliefs provided a defence to cannabis charges under the Misuse of Drugs Act 1975 was sharply dismissed before the Court of Appeal in *R v Anderson*.[462] On appeal, the defendant asserted that the trial judge's failure to direct the jury on the relevance of his religious beliefs constituted a breach of section 15 of NZBORA (and section 21(1)(c) of the Human Rights Act 1993). Putting it simply, the Court of Appeal noted: 'There is nothing in the Bill of Rights Act . . . that enables the appellant to set up his beliefs as a defence to particular crimes. He is entitled to hold these beliefs but he is obliged to abide by the law.'[463]

4.226 *Religious exemptions from tax procedures?* Likewise, an individual's religious beliefs were not considered to be a defence to charges under the Tax Administration Act 1994 in *Tahaafe v Commissioner of Inland Revenue*,[464] relating to improper claims for tax rebates, many of which were deposited into the pastor's personal bank account. Tahaafe argued that the Court at first instance failed to appreciate his actions in the context of the culture and practices of the Tongan Anglican Mission Church, which differed greatly from mainstream Christian cultures and from the secular population, and that viewed in context, it was entirely reasonable for the appellant to believe Church members had intended the money to be a personal donation to him. Again, the High Court judge dealt with the NZBORA argument swiftly, concluding: 'While ss13, 14, or 15 of the Bill of Rights Act conferred freedoms on the appellant in terms of religion, they did not provide him with a defence to the charges that he faced.'[465]

4.227 *Religious exemption from sentencing conditions?* Criminal justice procedures also trumped the rights of religious observance in *Feau v Department of Social Welfare*.[466] The appellant was sentenced to periodic detention, which involved an induction programme on a Saturday. The appellant appealed his sentence on the basis that—as a Seventh Day Adventist—it

---

[461] The Crown led evidence of other religious practitioners regarding the manner in which exorcisms are ordinarily carried out, arguing the procedure was customarily limited to the moderate application of force to the body.

[462] *R v Anderson* CA 27/04, 23 June 2004.

[463] *Anderson* (n 462) para 9.

[464] *Kinelotti Tahaafe v Commissioner of Inland Revenue* (HC Auckland, CRI-2009-404-102, 10 July 2009).

[465] *Kinelotti Tahaafe* (n 464) para 69.

[466] *Feau v Department of Social Welfare* (1995) 2 HRNZ 528, 529–30.

interfered with his right under section 15 of NZBORA by compelling him to work on the Sabbath. Accepting at face value the sincerity of the appellant's claim, the Court found that the infringement on the right was minimal (he only had to attend once on a Saturday and the induction meeting did not involve 'work'), and was justified under section 5 as a limitation on his right and as an inevitable consequence of his penalty. However, the High Court judge did note that rights should be accommodated to the extent possible and expressed some concern at the periodic detention centre for its inflexible approach.

Allowances for witnesses in court wearing burqas. In contrast to the aforementioned cases, **4.228** *Police v Razamjoo*[467] provides an illustration of how the manifestation of religious beliefs has been accommodated in a pragmatic manner, in a different aspect of the criminal justice process.

In a criminal trial at the District Court, the issue arose of whether prosecution witnesses, **4.229** both Afghan Muslims, could be permitted to give evidence wearing *burqas*, so that their faces would be entirely covered. The defendant argued that this would hinder the court's ability to assess their credibility through their demeanuours and expressions.[468] Defence counsel took an inflammatory stance, submitting voluminous material regarding the evils of Islamic fundamentalism and arguing that to permit the *burqa* to be worn in court 'must be seen in the context of the political expression of the Muslim religion or Islamism which aims to relegate the Western world back to the dark ages through bombings of innocent people, televised executions and general dehumanization of women'.[469] These submissions were strongly criticized by the District Court judge, calling them 'political rather than legal in nature'[470] and dependent upon factual assertions 'for which there was no evidential foundation'.[471] The judge concluded that the defence submissions were 'extravagant and often needlessly offensive in both scope and expression. There were numerous appeals to ignorance and prejudice'.[472]

The District Court judge reviewed a number of foreign decisions, emphasizing the signifi- **4.230** cance of the right to manifest one's religious beliefs and challenging the basis for the assumed connection between perceptible demeanour and credibility, and was 'reluctantly forced to the conclusion that there could be a fair trial' even if the witness wore a *burqa*. However, fair trial rights were not the only consideration to be weighed; the public right to the open and transparent administration of justice meant that the public should also be able to see and hear participants. Concerned with striking an appropriate balance between these competing rights and interests, the judge noted:

> Whilst the Court needs to take into account the special characteristics (whether expressed as rights or otherwise) of a witness which may make their giving evidence in the ordinary way an unreasonable burden so that either or both of their rights and interests of a fair trial require that burden to be reduced, care has to be taken to try and avoid the adoption of procedures which are so obviously out of keeping with the expectation of the community generally so as to seriously call into question confidence in the judicial system.

---

[467] *Police v Razamjoo* [2005] DCR 408.
[468] NZBORA, s 25(f) also provides for the right of persons charged to examine witnesses for the prosecution. The defendant did not raise the right to confrontation as such.
[469] *Razamjoo* (n 467) para 53.
[470] *Razamjoo* (n 467) para 53.
[471] *Razamjoo* (n 467) para 55.
[472] *Razamjoo* (n 467) para 73.

4.231   Striking a practical balance, the judge ordered that the witnesses would be required to give evidence without their faces covered, but behind a screen where they were only visible to the judge, counsel, and female court staff. This solution—adopted as an ad hoc procedural measure—was praised by commentators as an 'excellent example of how potentially "conflicting" rights can be balanced with each other and a practical solution found which maximises the rights of the parties involved'.[473]

c) Family law

4.232   *Best interests of the child.* In the context of child custody, a parent's religious beliefs may be relevant to the court's assessment of what constitutes the 'best interests of the child'. In the early case of *N v N*,[474] the Family Court noted the difficulty in adjudicating a dispute when parents advance conflicting religious beliefs as part of their custody applications or seek to impugn the religious beliefs of the other. The Family Court judge went on to state that 'it is not the concern of the Family Court to say which of two different methods of practising Christianity is better, for the Court cannot take sides on matters of religion'. However, while courts are understandably reluctant to endorse a particular faith over another when determining what is in the best interests of the child, Courts have nonetheless recognized that the religious practices of parents and their impact on children may nonetheless be *relevant* to this assessment.[475]

d) Distinguishing between the public and private affairs of a religious organization

4.233   Despite a willingness to adjudicate on the protection of religious freedoms when they concern an individual's rights in the public sphere, New Zealand courts have been reluctant to intervene in ecclesiastical issues or legal matters turning upon matters of faith.

4.234   *Employment relationships within religious organizations.* In *Mabon v The Conference of the Methodist Church of NZ*,[476] the Court of Appeal considered that a Methodist minister who had been dismissed from his parish position was not considered an 'employee', who would otherwise have recourse to bring a complaint under the relevant employment legislation. The Court found that the parties had not entered into an employment relationship with the intent to be legally or contractually bound. Rather, the Court conceptualised the minister's employment as a 'calling of God'. The Court's reluctance to intervene in the internal operations of the Church was readily apparent, as it stated: 'clearly and reflecting the separation of church and state, Courts must be reluctant to determine what are at heart ecclesiastical disputes where matters of faith or doctrine are at issue'.[477]

4.235   *Application of privacy laws to religious organizations.* In *The Director of Human Rights Proceedings v The Catholic Church for New Zealand*,[478] the plaintiff alleged that the Catholic Church was in breach of its obligations under the Privacy Act 1993 for refusing to disclose documents which contained personal information regarding her application for an

---

[473] Butler and Butler (n 411) para 14.11.4.

[474] *N v N* (1987) 2 FRNZ 534, 536.

[475] See eg *Hill v Hill* (DC Taupo, FP-069-111-92, 24 January 1996) Whitehead DCJ, where the Court declined to strike out parts of a mother's affidavit relating to her concerns about the children's father seeking to raise them as Jehovah's Witnesses, with the Court noting that evidence relating to religious upbringing was not irrelevant to the issue at hand.

[476] *Mabon v Conference of the Methodist Church of NZ* [1998] 3 NZLR 513.

[477] *Mabon* (n 476) 523.

[478] *Director of Human Rights Proceedings v Catholic Church for New Zealand*, High Court Auckland, CIV-2006-404-006162, 19 February 2008.

annulment of marriage. Under the Privacy Act 1993, 'agencies' are required to provide an individual with access to personal information relating to them that is held by the agency. The Catholic Church resisted the plaintiff's application on the basis that the Church—and in particular the Catholic Tribunal responsible for the dissolution of marriages—should be excluded from the definition of agency and exempt from the disclosure and access procedures under the Act as a matter of public policy.

Relying on section 15 of NZBORA, the Church argued that an obligation to provide access **4.236** to personal information could have a detrimental impact on the operation of the Church Tribunal and the manner in which its proceedings were conducted, and 'perhaps also inhibit their freedom to conduct those proceedings in a manner which was consistent with the teaching of the Church'.[479] The Church averred that section 6 of NZBORA dictated that the Privacy Act 1993 should be read in a manner consistent with the right, so as to exclude the Tribunal from the obligations under the Act.

The High Court judge recalled *Mabon* and the common law principles under which courts **4.237** had traditionally declined to become involved in matters that touched upon the private or domestic procedures of religious organizations.[480] The judge also referenced the earlier case of *Marshall v National Spiritual Assembly of the Baha's of New Zealand Inc*,[481] where the High Court heard an application by a plaintiff who had been dismissed from the Baha'i Church, following an allegation that he failed to carry out the religion according to its tenets. While *Marshall* was resolved by reference to the constitution of the Church, the presiding judge subsequently noted that generally 'a determination of matters of faith is at the very margins of justiciability'.[482]

Returning to the case at hand, the High Court resolved the issue primarily through canons **4.238** of statutory interpretation, determining that the Church's Tribunal fell within the plain wording of the Privacy Act 1993 and was thus caught by its access and disclosure procedures. The judge was not persuaded that there were any 'real policy justifications for [the Church Tribunal's] exclusion from the definition of "agency" '.[483] The Court accepted at face value the Church's argument that the sacrament of marriage—and the steps required to dissolve it—were central to the Church's doctrine, but failed to see how the plaintiff's request for personal information could raise any implications which could affect religious belief, or its manifestation, or any other issue of Church doctrine. As such, the judge considered that section 15 of NZBORA was not in fact engaged, precluding the need to resort to section 6 of the Act as an interpretative exercise.

e) Maori spiritual beliefs

A unique element within the New Zealand legal landscape is the recognition and treatment **4.239** of tikanga Maori,[484] which is often intertwined with practices or beliefs that have a spiritual or religious element. The intersection between Maori spiritual beliefs and public life in New Zealand has led to some interesting—and to an outsider, perhaps curious—cases.

---

[479] *Catholic Church for New Zealand* (n 478) para 33.

[480] *Catholic Church for New Zealand* (n 478) para 65, citing *Mabon*, which is discussed at para 4.234.

[481] *Marshall v National Spiritual Assembly of the Baha's of New Zealand Inc* [2003] NZLR 205, para 31.

[482] AP Randerson, 'Law and Religion in the South Pacific', Background Material Prepared for a Symposium to be held at Brigham Young University, Utah, 2–5 October 2011.

[483] *Catholic Church for New Zealand* (n 478) para 65.

[484] A term that has been understood to embrace customs, values, protocols, and beliefs.

4.240 The relevance of Maori beliefs regarding the natural environment with respect to New Zealand's environmental planning regime was highlighted in the *New Zealand Underwater Association*[485] case. Ports of Auckland sought a permit to discharge water and dredged sediment into the Hauraki Gulf as part of ongoing maintenance of the commercial port area. Before the Planning Tribunal, substantial opposition was advanced by the Hauraki Maori Trust Board, the Ngai Tai Tribe, and the Ngati Paoa Tribe.

4.241 Having considered the potential biological, geological, and ecological impacts of the proposed venture, the Planning Tribunal turned to consider the 'Effect of Discharge on Maori Cultural Values'. The Tribunal noted that the waters of the proposed discharge site—the Hauraki Gulf—had for generations been a source of 'physical and spiritual sustenance to the tangata whenua'.[486] Witnesses testified that the discharge of dredgings would be 'offensive to the spiritual values of the Tikapa Moana; a direct attack on its mauri, its wairua, and its Tapu; and an affront to the Maori customary practice with respect to the sea; and would cause much grief'.[487] The Maori groups also relied upon the Treaty of Waitangi as justifying why weight should be afforded to these considerations, and upon the rights enshrined in NZBORA.[488]

4.242 Although the Tribunal accepted that the waters of the Hauraki Gulf were considered *taonga*[489] and that Maori spiritual and cultural considerations were to be taken into account in the Tribunal's deliberations, it ultimately found that 'the evidence does not support the claims that exercise of the right sought [to discharge water into the Gulf] would necessarily deny their enjoyment of that culture or the practice of their religion'.[490] Moreover, the specific statutory regime for water usage did not give primacy to considerations of 'national importance' found in other environmental legislation, which included conservation of the cultural environment and the 'relationship of the Maori people and their culture and traditions with their ancestral land'.[491]

4.243 Subsequently, a major overhaul of New Zealand's environmental planning legislation resulted in the Resource Management Act 1991, which specifically incorporates Maori concerns—including their culture, traditions, and relationship to *taonga*—as a 'Matter of National Importance'[492] that must be taken into account in the exercise of any statutory functions under the Act. As noted by commentator Paul Rishworth, this has had the effect that 'Maori concerns, including spiritual concerns, were mainstreamed into the ordinary operation of the law, and not made a Bill of Rights matter'.[493]

4.244 Maori spiritual and cultural concerns have remained pertinent in the new environmental planning context. For instance, the Environment Court considered, but ultimately rejected,

---

[485] *New Zealand Underwater Association*, Planning Tribunal, A131/91, 16 December 1991.

[486] *New Zealand Underwater Association* (n 485) 30. *Tangata whenua* is generally understood to mean 'people of the land'.

[487] *New Zealand Underwater Association* (n 485) 30.

[488] Although the intervening Maori groups relied on notions of belief, spirituality, and customary practice, their NZBORA claim relied on s 20, relating to the protection of minority rights.

[489] This term is often translated into English to mean 'treasure'; something particularly sacred to Maori.

[490] *New Zealand Underwater Association* (n 485) 49.

[491] This language was found in the Town and Country Planning Act 1977, s 3(1) under 'matters of national importance'.

[492] Resource Management Act 1991, s 6.

[493] P Rishworth, 'Indigenous Peoples and Bills of Rights' in P Babie and N Rochow (eds), *Freedom of Religion under Bills of Rights* (University of Adelaide Press, 2012) 408.

a claim by local Maori opposed to the expansion of a dairy factor on the basis that the discharge of wastewater into the Waikato River would constitute an abuse of their ancestors and constitute a desecration of the 'spiritual power, sacredness and standing of the river'.[494]

In 1999, the Northland Regional Council declined to grant resource consent for the con-   **4.245**
struction of a prison building, based on the harmful effects it would have on the cultural and spiritual interests of local Maori. One of the objections of local Maori was that the prison site would interfere with a *taniwha*[495] named Takauere, which was the spiritiual guardian of the area. On appeal, the Environment Court[496] gave close consideration to witness evidence regarding the role of the *taniwha* and recognized the importance of sections 13 and 15 of NZBORA with respect to Maori spiritual beliefs. However, the Court ultimately overturned the Council's decision, noting the difficulty in evaluating questions about 'mythical, spiritual, symbolic or metaphysical beings',[497] referring to the conflicting evidence regarding the precise nature and role of the *taniwha*. Ultimately, the Court concluded that on the evidence: 'None of us has been persuaded . . . that, to whatever extent Takauere may exist as a mythical, spiritual, symbolic or metaphysical being, it would be affected in pathways to the surface or in any way at all by the proposed prison.'[498]

Despite the difficulties posed to the courts in adjudicating over such matters, similar chal-   **4.246**
lenges continue to arise. For instance, in 2002 the media seized on similar Maori opposition to the construction of a motorway, which was initially planned to run through the lair of a one-eyed *taniwha*.[499]

(5) Conclusions

While the aforementioned cases provide some elucidation on the scope and application   **4.247**
of the rights, many questions remain. Notwithstanding the lack of an anti-establishment clause, the disestablishment potential[500] of NZBORA rights with respect to freedom *from* religion and potentially coercive state endorsement of religion is yet to be fully explored. While courts have found rights to be engaged in certain instances, not properly engaged in others, and elsewhere engaged but subject to limitations or counterveiling public policy considerations, the methodology is inconsistent. Leading commentator Paul Rishworth has described the varied outcome of these cases as 'ad hoc and unreasoned, but generally satisfactory settlements . . . with no necessary determination of how such issues should be resolved for the future'.[501]

However, despite the general absence of litigation to date, issues touching upon reli-   **4.248**
gious freedoms have continued to affect New Zealand society,[502] perhaps foreshadowing

---

[494] *Mahuta v Waikato Regional Council* (Environment Court, A 91/98, 29 July 1998), paras 165–168.
[495] *Taniwha* are generally understood to be spiritual creatures or monsters, which sometimes perform a guardianship role.
[496] *Beadle v Minister of Corrections* [2002] NZRMA 401.
[497] *Beadle* (n 496) para 440.
[498] *Beadle* (n 496) para 443.
[499] See, 'Second Home Puts Taniwha Out of the Way', *New Zealand Herald*, 9 November 2002.
[500] Ahdar (n 412) 390; Ahdar (n 402) 624.
[501] P Rishworth, 'Human Rights and the Reconstruction of the Moral High Ground' in R Bigwood (ed), *Public Interest Litigation: New Zealand Experience in International Perspective* (LexisNexis NZ, 2006) 115, 124–5.
[502] See eg Ahdar (n 412) 390–1.

increased litigation in the future. Many such controversies have centred on the role of religion and spirituality in public life, including continued questioning over whether Parliament should commence with a Christian prayer; whether the Lord's Prayer could be recited in public school assemblies; the legitimacy of a lunchtime Christian Club for students;[503] the appropriateness of Muslim prayer rooms in state schools; displays of religious adornments in schools; and sending Maori elders to perform spiritual cleansings at foreign embassies.[504]

4.249 Similarly, the frequent collision between freedom of expression and insult to religious sentiments has sparked debate in New Zealand as it has elsewhere. Public outcry erupted following the decision of the national museum, Te Papa, to host a visiting exhibition in 1998 that included the controversial 'Virgin in a Condom' statue.[505] A resulting application by a National Party Member of Parliament and a Catholic Priest for blasphemous libel under the Crimes Act 1961 was rejected by the Solicitor-General, who noted that NZBORA protected such freedom of expression. Two of New Zealand's major newspapers reprinted the Danish cartoons depicting the Prophet Mohammed as a terrorist, prompting further controversy. The screening of the 'Bloody Mary' episode of South Park depicting the Virgin Mary spraying menstrual blood on the Pope also polarized New Zealanders. New Zealand's then Prime-Minister, Helen Clark (a self-described agnostic), commented that she found it personally 'quite revolting', although it survived a number of complaints to the Broadcasting Standards Authority and an appeal to the High Court.[506]

4.250 Despite the ongoing public discourse, a number of reasons have been advanced for why few challenges have been brought before the courts. Arguably, New Zealand does not have the litigious culture that characterizes other Western legal systems and lacks the type of well-organized and funded pressure groups to drive litigation.[507] As noted, NZBORA contains no remedies provisions and cannot be used to invalidate primary legislation. Moreover, section 7 already requires draft statutes to be 'NZBORA vetted' before they are passed into law, arguably defusing potential conflicts before they arise.

4.251 The legal and socio-cultural landscape in New Zealand continues to evolve. New Zealand's relative religious homogeneity and the default acceptance of Christian traditions is coming under increasing challenge. As noted by New Zealand's Justice Randerson:

> The relative lack of flashpoint freedom of religion issues in New Zealand might be considered cause for the celebration of the tolerance of New Zealanders. On the other hand, as Stanley Fish puts it, tolerance is exercised in inverse proportion to there being anything at stake. In

---

[503] A Wellington state primary school Board of Trustees banned the school's long-running 'KidsKlub', a Christian club run in the school lunchtime. The Board pointed to the Education Act 1964 and the requirement to provide a secular education. A group of parents sough a legal opinion from the architect of NZBORA, Sir Geoffrey Palmer, who opined that the ban breached NZBORA's right to manifest one's religious beliefs. As long as an 'opt-out' procedure existed, there was no compusion or coercion on children to attend: see Ahdar (n 394) 211.

[504] See further, Rishworth (n 411) 631, 635.

[505] Ahdar (n 437) 642.

[506] Broadcasting Standards Authority, Decision 2006-022, 26 June 2006; *Browne v CanWest TV Works Ltd* (HC Wellington, CIV-2006-485-1661, 31 July 2007). The Broadcasting Standards Authority also dismissed complaints regarding the satirical documentary Super Size Me, where the presenter ate only Middle Eastern food over the period of a month and became a terrorist by the end: Broadcasting Standards Authority, Decision 2004-152, 4 November 2004.

[507] Rishworth (n 411) 631, 636.

other words, it is easy to be tolerant where there are not real (or perceived) threats to the majority position.[508]

The majority position is coming under increased challenge: 'the last vestiges of public Christian ritual and symbolism are just that. There is a steady pattern of dismantling these historic Christian remnants from the public square'.[509] Increased overall secularization (coupled with simultaneous growth of non-Christian faiths); the increasing reach of the law into the private sphere;[510] a heigtened rights consciousness among New Zealanders; and an expanding body of rights jurisprudence, are cited as potential catalysts for increased litigation. The question remains as to whether that is the inevitable—or indeed the best—path for New Zealand. Commentators have noted the possibility for principled solutions that do not always call for litigation, positing that delineating the scope of religious freedoms does not necessarily need to fall within the realm of the judiciary.[511] However, the conclusion that religious rights and freedoms will continue to be tested in the current social climate is inescapable. **4.252**

E. Northern Ireland

Claire Archbold[512]

(1) Constitutional law

As part of the United Kingdom, Northern Ireland does not have a single written constitution, but as a separate jurisdiction within the United Kingdom, the common law has evolved with some distinctive differences, and the Northern Ireland statute book has developed similarly but not identically to that for England and Wales.[513] In relation to religious rights, the Human Rights Act 1998 applies the European Convention on Human Rights to Northern Ireland in the same way as in the other jurisdictions of the United Kingdom. Other international treaties bind the UK government in relation to Northern Ireland. Given the particular history of Northern Ireland, where religious affiliation has been seen as an identifier of community background, the Northern Ireland Act 1998 provides additional protections from discrimination on the ground of religious belief in relation to the operation of the Assembly and other public bodies created as part of the devolution settlement of 1998. **4.253**

An Act of the Northern Ireland Assembly is outside its legislative competence and therefore void if, *inter alia*, it is incompatible with a Convention Right,[514] or if it discriminates **4.254**

---

[508] Randerson (n 482). Justice Randerson currently sits as a Judge on the Court of Appeal.

[509] Ahdar (n 394) 236.

[510] Rishworth (n 411) 631, 633. See also Ahdar (n 412) 388–9.

[511] Rishworth (n 411) 631, 633, 640, 649.

[512] Barrister-at-law, Inn of Court of Northern Ireland. Thanks are due to Eileen McBride of the Equality Commission for Northern Ireland for her comments on the section on employment and anti-discrimination law, to Professor Laura Lundy of Queen's University, Belfast for her comments on the section on education law, and to Alistair Butler, Assistant Registrar General for Northern Ireland for the useful information he provided on marriage law and practice.

[513] Differences have existed between the statute books applicable in the two jurisdictions throughout our constitutional history. Most recently, the Northern Ireland Act 1998 has devolved legislative power in relation to 'transferred matters', and in certain circumstances 'other matters' to the Northern Ireland Assembly. Under s 4 a transferred matter is defined as any matter not listed as 'excepted' or 'reserved' to the UK Parliament by Schs 2 and 3 of the Act. See further B Dickson, in Lester, Pannick, and Herberg, *Human Rights Law and Practice* (3rd edn, LexisNexis, 2009) ch 6.

[514] Northern Ireland Act 1998, s 6(2)(c).

against any person or class of person on the ground of religious belief or political opinion.[515] Ministers or departments of the devolved Executive are similarly described as having no power to make subordinate legislation or do any act which discriminates on these grounds.[516] A complex system of checks and balances provides for human rights certification and monitoring of Assembly legislation by a range of persons and bodies including the sponsoring Minister,[517] the Presiding Officer,[518] the Attorney General,[519] the Secretary of State,[520] and the Northern Ireland Human Rights Commission.[521]

4.255 Section 76 of the Northern Ireland Act 1998 also creates a statutory tort where 'any public authority[522] carrying out functions relating to Northern Ireland' discriminates, or aids or incites another person to discriminate on the ground of religion or political belief. Such action is described as 'unlawful', and damages or an injunction are available.

4.256 In both cases, discrimination is defined as treating a person or class of people less favourably in any circumstances than one treats or would treat other persons in those circumstances.[523] The Northern Ireland Act 1998 draws a careful boundary[524] between the acts covered by these provisions, which are effectively public law functions, and those functions such as provision of employment, goods, facilities, and services to which the Fair Employment and Treatment (NI) Order 1998 applies.[525]

4.257 At the time of its passage, one of the most novel provisions of the Northern Ireland Act 1998 was section 75, which set out two positive duties on public authorities, namely that:

(1) A public authority shall in carrying out its functions relating to Northern Ireland have due regard to the need to promote equality of opportunity—

    (a) between persons of different religious belief, political opinion, racial group, age, marital status or sexual orientation;

    (b) between men and women generally;

    (c) between persons with a disability and persons without; and

    (d) between persons with dependants and persons without.

---

[515] Northern Ireland Act 1998, s 6(2)(e).

[516] Northern Ireland Act 1998, s 24(1)(a) and (c). See also the prohibition on incitement or aid of others to discriminate in s 24(1)(d).

[517] Northern Ireland Act 1998, s 24(1)(a), (c), (d), and (e). The Minister must make a statement of compliance similar to that in the Human Rights Act 1998, s 19(2).

[518] The Presiding Officer must make a determination as to legislative competence before the bill is introduced into the Assembly (Northern Ireland Act 1998, s 10(1)).

[519] The Attorney General can refer legislation to the Supreme Court if he considers it to be outside the Assembly's legislative competence (Northern Ireland Act 1998, s 11(1)). The Attorney General must also be notified if an issue as to legislative competence (a 'devolution issue') arises in any proceedings (Northern Ireland Act 1998, Sch 10).

[520] The Secretary of State can refuse to submit a Bill for Royal Assent if he believes it to be incompatible with any international treaty obligations. This is a general reference to international treaties, which Dickson (n 513) argues include international human rights norms other than the Convention Rights.

[521] The Presiding Officer has a duty to send a copy of each Bill to the NI Human Rights Commission to advise whether it is compatible with the Convention rights (Northern Ireland Act 1998, s 13(5)). The Commission must advise him of its view as soon as is reasonably practicable (Northern Ireland Act 1998, s 69(4)(1)). The Commission's full range of powers is set out in the Northern Ireland Act 1998, s 69 and there is a useful commentary in Dickson (n 513) paras 6.19–6.30. The Commission's website is at <http://www.nihrc.org>.

[522] A public authority is defined by list, see Northern Ireland Act 1998, s 75(3).

[523] Northern Ireland Act 1998, s 98(5).

[524] But see the Fair Employment and Treatment (NI) Order 1998, SI 1998/3162 (NI 21), art 37 which states that judicial review is available even for actions which fall within the Order's scope.

[525] Northern Ireland Act 1998, ss 24(2) and 76(4).

(2) Without prejudice to its obligations under subsection (1), a public authority shall in carrying out its functions relating to Northern Ireland have regard to the desirability of promoting good relations between persons of different religious belief, political opinion or racial group.

The duties are in part fulfilled by drawing up an Equality Scheme and carrying out Equality Impact Assessments of new policies, in line with the Commission's guidance.[526] The guidance is in part binding[527] but courts have indicated that the main remedy for breach of these duties should be via the Equality Commission's enforcement procedures,[528] and they have been infrequently litigated in court. The Equality Commission's remit extends across the protected dimensions of equality and anti-discrimination law (religious belief, political opinion, racial group, age, marital status, sexual orientation, sex, disability, and having or not having dependents) and it replaces the bodies which previously had responsibility for issues affecting those dimensions.[529] The Commission takes on the oversight, reporting, and investigative functions of those bodies, and has further duties to keep under review the effectiveness of the duties imposed by section 75 of the Northern Ireland Act 1998, to advise public authorities on it and to investigate and adjudicate on complaints relating to it.[530]   **4.258**

a) Religious bodies and the law

There is no established church in Northern Ireland. The (Anglican) Church of Ireland was disestablished in 1871.[531]   **4.259**

(2) Human rights

The Human Rights Act 1998 applies in Northern Ireland as elsewhere in the United Kingdom. Northern Ireland legislation made either by Act of the Assembly or by Order-in-Council, although it has the subject matter of primary legislation, is in the form of delegated legislation and so may be struck down by the courts.[532] The status of the Convention Rights under the Northern Ireland Act 1998, as outlined previously, give added strength to the remedies available for breach of a Convention Right by a public body. There is as yet no decided case law on the significance, if any, of the distinction between the description of acts of the Assembly, Ministers and Departments in contravention of the Convention Rights as 'unlawful' under section 6 of the Human Rights Act 1998, and as 'not law' in the case of legislation,[533] or outside the Minister or Department's power in the case of other acts.[534] It is arguable that the unequivocal classification as void and of no effect in these provisions limits the powers of the courts by comparison with the wide discretion in section 8(1) of the Human Rights Act 1998:   **4.260**

(1) In relation to any act (or proposed act) of a public authority which the court finds is (or would be) unlawful, it may grant such relief or remedy, or make such order, within its powers as it considers just and appropriate.

---

[526] The Guide for Public Authorities can be found at <http://www.equalityni.org/archive/pdf/S75GuideforPublicAuthoritiesApril2010.pdf>

[527] Guide for Public Authorities, Chs 5, 6, and 7 provide guidelines on the form and content of an Equality Scheme as required by Northern Ireland Act 1998, Sch 9, para 4(3)(a).

[528] See comments of Girvan J in *Re Peter Neill's Application* [2005] NIQB 66, reiterated by the Court of Appeal at [2006] NICA 5.

[529] Northern Ireland Act 1998, ss 73, 74.

[530] Northern Ireland Act 1998, Sch 9 sets out the Commission's powers and obligations in relation to the 'section 75 duties'.

[531] Irish Church Act 1869.

[532] As was done in *Re G* [2008] UKHL 38.

[533] Northern Ireland Act 1998, s 6(1).

[534] Northern Ireland Act 1998, s 24(1).

a) Significant case law on human rights and religion in Northern Ireland

4.261   There have been a small number of human rights cases brought within the rubric of Article 9 ECHR in Northern Ireland. One of the most significant is perhaps *Re Christian Institute's Application*,[535] in which a consortium of religious interest groups sought to challenge the legality of the Equality Act (Sexual Orientation) Regulations 2006. These prohibited discrimination on the grounds of sexual orientation in the provision of goods, facilities, and services in Northern Ireland. Regulation 16 of the Regulations provided for an exemption for religious bodies, but this did not extend to the provision of goods, facilities, and services on a commercial basis or under contract with a public authority, or to certain matters in the field of education. Weatherup J refused to carry out an analysis of whether the regulations were a proportionate interference with rights under Article 9 ECHR *in abstracto*, holding that such argument was better located within specific proceedings when any example of interference with Article 9 rights manifested itself. He struck down provisions on harassment for inadequacy of consultation.

4.262   *Re Parsons' Application*[536] was a human rights challenge to the positive discrimination measures[537] which permitted '50/50' recruitment of Protestant and Catholic police officers for a period following the replacement of the Royal Ulster Constabulary with the Police Service of Northern Ireland in 2001. The Court of Appeal held that the decision complained of did not reach the level of interference with the applicant's right to hold, manifest, and express his religious beliefs to result in a breach of Article 9 ECHR.

4.263   The question of what constitutes a religious belief was raised in *Re Dowdell's Application*,[538] in which the prisoner's belief that he was not guilty of the offences of which he had been convicted was held not to come within the rubric of Article 9 ECHR.

4.264   The withdrawal of discretionary funding by Belfast City Council from the publisher of an iconoclastic arts magazine, *The Vacuum*, after it published two simultaneous, satirical editions of the magazine, entitled 'God' and 'Satan', which linked religious and sexual imagery and satirised religion, in ways which were offensive to members of the Council, was held by Deeny J in *Re West's Application*[539] to breach neither the publisher's rights under Article 9 nor Article 10 ECHR. The magazine continued to be published without the funding. Deeny J found the decision to be within a range of legitimate decisions (including a decision to continue funding) which the Council could have made. He observed that the awarding of discretionary funding was already sufficiently difficult without the courts interfering too readily. There was no right to the discretionary funding, and in any event, the level of interference had not reached the threshold identified in *Parsons*.

4.265   In *Re Sandown Free Presbyterian Church's Application*,[540] the applicant placed an advertisement in a local publication asking people to join a demonstration against the Belfast Gay Pride festival, responding to a banner displayed about Jesus in the previous year's march. The advertisement described homosexuality as 'an abomination', language which it said it took from the Bible, but,

---

[535] *Re Christian Institute's Application* [2008] NI 86.
[536] *Re Parsons' Application* [2004] NI 38.
[537] Police (NI) Act 2000, s 46, permitted pursuant to a specific exemption in Council Directive (EC) 2000/78 of 27 November 2000 establishing a general framework for equal treatment in employment and occupation.
[538] *Re Dowdell's Application* [2003] NIJB 177.
[539] *Re West's Application* [2006] NIQB 39.
[540] *Re Sandown Free Presbyterian Church's Application* [2011] NI 242.

as the judge said, the advertisement 'contained no exhortation to violence or other improper or illegal activity. Indeed it referred to the sometimes violent antagonism displayed towards homosexuals which it describes as an "unacceptable and totally unjustifiable response"'.

Complaints were made to the Advertising Standards Agency, which found against the appli- **4.266** cant. Treacy J granted the application in part, not on Article 9 grounds, but on the basis that the Advertising Standards Agency had failed to show the necessity of the limits placed on the future freedom of expression of the applicant under Article 10 ECHR. However, the context of religious belief was important to this assessment. He said:

> I have taken into account the very particular context in which the advertisement was placed, the fact that the advertisement did not condone and was not likely to provoke violence, contained no exhortation to other improper or illegal activity, constituted a genuine attempt to stand up for their religious beliefs and to encourage others to similarly bear witness and did so by citing well known portions of scripture which underpinned their religious faith and their call to bear witness. Whilst such views and scriptural references may be strongly disdained and considered seriously offensive by some, this does not justify the full scope of the restrictions contained in the impugned determination.[541]

The conditions imposed by the Parades Commission on a parade by members of the Orange **4.267** Order were argued by the Order to constitute an illegitimate interference with the rights of marchers under Articles 9, 10, and 11 ECHR,[542] but were found to be legitimate and proportionate by Weatherup J in *Re Tweed's Application for judicial review*.[543]

Some cases in Northern Ireland, like *Parsons*, arise from situations in which religious affiliation **4.268** as a marker of community identity is relevant, but in these other cases, Article 9 rights have not formed part of the argument. One noteworthy case was *E v Chief Constable*,[544] in which the House of Lords found that the police had not done enough to protect Catholic children walking to and from a church school from abuse and missiles hurled by loyalist 'protesters'.

Other cases which were not argued on Article 9 grounds, but which have related to issues **4.269** of particular interest to religious groups in Northern Ireland, include *Northern Ireland Commissioner for Children and Young People's Application*,[545] *Dudgeon v UK*,[546] *Family Planning Association of NI v Minister for Health Social Services and Public Safety*,[547] *Re G (Adoption, unmarried couple)*,[548] and *Belfast City Council v Miss Behavin' Ltd*.[549]

---

[541] *Re Sandown Free Presbyterian Church's Application* [2011] NI 242, 266.

[542] And in particular, the compatibility of the enabling legislation, the Public Processions (Northern Ireland) Act 1998, s 8(6)(c), with the Convention.

[543] *Re Tweed's Application for judicial review* [2007] NIQB 69.

[544] *E v Chief Constable* [2008] UKHL 66.

[545] *Northern Ireland Commissioner for Children and Young People's Application* [2009] NICA 10 (physical punishment of children).

[546] *Dudgeon v UK* (App 7525176) (1981) 4 EHRR 149 (criminalization of homosexual behaviour).

[547] *Family Planning Association of NI v Minister for Health Social Services and Public Safety* (2005) NI 188 (failure to produce guidelines on abortion). See also *Society for the Protection of Unborn Children's application* [2009] NIQB 92. It might be noted that another application has been brought by the Family Planning Association which is before the courts, but on hold pending the outcome of the DHSSPS consultation on the draft guidelines: Department of Health and Social Services and Public Safety, The Limited Circumstances for a Lawful Termination of Pregnancy in Northern Ireland (April 2013).

[548] *Re G (Adoption, unmarried couple)* [2008] UKHL 38 (adoption law failing to permit unmarried couples to adopt), followed in the context of same-sex couples by the Northern Ireland Court of Appeal in *Re NI Human Rights Commission's Application* (27 June 2013), judgment of Girvan LJ.

[549] *Belfast City Council v Miss Behavin' Ltd* [2007] UKHL 19 (failure to grant a licence to a sex shop).

(3) Discrimination law

4.270 Anti-discrimination law in relation to religion in Northern Ireland is largely on the same EU-derived equal treatment model with judicial enforcement as applies elsewhere in the United Kingdom. Because of the historical context of Northern Ireland, the Fair Employment and Treatment (NI) Order 1998 and its predecessor, the Fair Employment Act 1976, prohibit discrimination on the grounds of religious belief or political opinion, the first jurisdictions in the United Kingdom to do so. The two grounds are freestanding, although they may be interrelated in some fact situations. One might say that the main target of the legislation is not discrimination on the ground of religion, but on the ground of perceived community background.[550]

4.271 It is perhaps for this reason that there has been remarkably little case law on what amounts to a religious belief under the legislation. However, in three cases on political opinion, the Northern Ireland Court of Appeal found that the concepts are not limited to the context of Northern Ireland and explored the scope of 'political opinion' under the legislation. Thus, membership of a particularly left-wing trade union[551] or the holding of 'independent and radical' views about policing policy[552] could both be relevant political opinions for the purposes of the legislation. What was required was an opinion 'relating to the conduct of the government of the state or matters of public policy'.[553]

4.272 The Fair Employment and Treatment (NI) Order 1998 (FETO), goes beyond the standard EU model of anti-discrimination legislation and imposes a number of significant duties on employers. All private sector employers with more than ten full-time employees must register with the Equality Commission and submit an annual monitoring return giving details of the community background, sex, and occupational classification of their workforce, as well as applicants and appointees to jobs. Community background means those staff who are treated as belonging to either the Protestant or Roman Catholic community in Northern Ireland.

4.273 At least every three years, a registered employer must carry out a review to determine if there is fair participation in employment by both Protestants and Roman Catholics. If it appears that this is not the case, he is under a duty to determine what affirmative action would be reasonable and appropriate. FETO permits only limited affirmative action, by encouraging job applications from members of under-represented groups, by targeted training, and by targeted redundancy (in consultation with the Equality Commission) to help ensure fair participation.

4.274 In addition to this self-reporting, the Equality Commission can investigate the employment practices of any Northern Ireland employer at any time, and can seek an undertaking or issue a legally enforceable direction to take affirmative action to ensure fair participation. In addition to a potential fine of up to £5,000, an employer in default of the registration or

---

[550] A good example of the dynamic is provided by *Smyth v Croft Inns* (1996) IRLR 84, in which a claim was made in relation to the failure by an employer to take any action to assist a Roman Catholic barman who was facing threats and sectarian abuse by a largely Protestant and loyalist clientele. The Northern Ireland Court of Appeal held that the appropriate comparator in the case was not a Protestant barman in the same bar, but a Protestant barman in a bar with a Roman Catholic and Irish Republican clientele.

[551] *McKay v Northern Ireland Public Service Alliance* [1994] NI 103.

[552] *Ryder v Policing Board of Northern Ireland* [2007] NICA 43.

[553] *Gill v Northern Ireland Council on Ethnic Minorities* [2002] IRLR 74 *per* Carswell LCJ.

monitoring provisions may be excluded from public contracts or government grant-awarding programmes.

a) Effectiveness of the fair employment legislation

The registration and monitoring provisions of FETO have been subject to some criticism **4.275** as being unduly draconian, and as reinforcing stereotypes by the monitoring of community background. However, a major study led by Professor Bob Osborne of Queen's University, Belfast in 2004,[554] found that while some areas of under-representation remained for Catholics, and some were developing for Protestants, there had been a substantial improvement in the employment profile of Catholics, who were now well represented in managerial, professional, and senior administrative posts. He concluded that strong legislation had played a role in the achievement of a situation where educational attainment rather than community background was the key determinant of workplace success in Northern Ireland.

b) Equality of outcome—50/50 recruitment to the Police Service of Northern Ireland

Perhaps the strongest piece of affirmative action legislation in Europe, for which special **4.276** dispensation from the European Union was required, is that in relation to the police service in Northern Ireland. Unlike almost all other law in the European Union, it focuses not on equality of opportunity, but on equality of outcome, which is largely impermissible under EU law.[555] This was particularly connected to circumstances in Northern Ireland. Following the recommendations of the review of policing in Northern Ireland led by Chris Patten (the Patten Commission), section 46(1) of the Police (NI) Act 2000 provided that in making appointments of trainee police officers, the chief constable of the Police Service of Northern Ireland was under a duty to appoint from a pool of qualified candidates an even number of persons of whom one-half were to be persons treated as Catholic and one-half were to be persons not so treated.[556]

(4) Education

The main statutes governing education law in Northern Ireland are the Education and **4.277** Libraries (NI) Order 1986, the Education (NI) Orders 1993, 1996, 1997, and 1998, and the Education Reform (NI) Order 1989. One of the most distinctive features of the education system is that selection of pupils by academic ability at age 11 is still permitted, although the examinations are now run by consortia of state-funded grammar schools rather than by the state. Another is that education in Northern Ireland is *de facto* religiously segregated, due in large part to the churches' response to education reform in the 1920s and 1930s. At that time, schools which had previously had a charitable status were offered the opportunity to transfer their assets to the state in order to secure full funding. Most Protestant or non-denominational schools did this, while most Catholic schools did not. The former today have *controlled* status, while the latter retain their *voluntary* status, receiving a lower level of state funding.[557] More recently, religiously integrated schools and Irish language

---

[554] Osborne et al, *Fair Employment in Northern Ireland: a generation on* (Blackstaff Press/Equality Commission for Northern Ireland, 2004).

[555] For the EU case law on positive discrimination in gender cases, see A McColgan, *Discrimination Law, Text, Cases and Materials* (2nd edn, Hart Publishing, 2005) 162–4.

[556] See *Parsons' Application for judicial review* [2003] NICA 20.

[557] See L Lundy; *Education Law, Policy and Practice in Northern Ireland* (SLS Legal Publications, 2000) paras 1.09–1.10

schools have been created in response to parental demand. Funding for integrated schools is provided either through the controlled mechanism or by a new grant-maintained status.[558]

4.278 While admission to controlled or voluntary schools may be determined in large part by parental choice based on religious background, the only sector in Northern Ireland which uses religious denomination as a selection criterion is the integrated sector, which is required by articles 66 and 88 of the Education Reform (NI) Order 1989 to use its best endeavours to ensure that 'the management, control and ethos of the school are such as are likely to attract to the school reasonable numbers of both Protestant and Roman Catholic pupils'. The Northern Ireland Council on Integrated Education's policy is that the balance should not fall below 60/40 either way. Admissions criteria which restricted the school to certain percentages of pupils from Catholic and Protestant community backgrounds have been found to be legally problematic,[559] but so far no reported case has challenged the legal validity of criteria which positively favour one religion over another.[560]

4.279 All schools in receipt of public funds in Northern Ireland must provide a daily period of collective worship in an assembly or assemblies.[561] While context suggests that the drafters intended the worship to be Christian in nature in controlled schools, it is stated that it must not be distinctive of any particular religious denomination.[562] The curriculum of all grant-aided schools must also include provision for the religious education of all registered pupils[563] and must follow the core syllabus provided by the main church bodies in Ireland,[564] which is of a Christian but broadly non-denominational character.[565] Schools may go beyond this syllabus, and while in controlled schools the content must remain non-denominational, denominational religious instruction may be given in integrated and voluntary schools.[566]

4.280 All grant-aided schools are required to have a curriculum which meets the following criteria:

> 4(2) The curriculum for a grant-aided school satisfies the requirements of this Article if it is a balanced and broadly based curriculum which—
> (a) promotes the spiritual, moral, cultural, intellectual and physical development of pupils at the school and thereby of society; and

---

[558] See Education Reform (NI) Order 1989, SI 1989/2406 (NI 20), and for more detail on integrated education, see Lundy (n 557) ch 9.

[559] *Re Patten's Application for judicial review*, NI Queen's Bench Division (30 September 1994).

[560] See Lundy (n 557) paras 9.37–9.38.

[561] Education and Libraries (NI) Order 1986, SI 1986/594 (NI 3), art 21(1).

[562] SI 1986/594 (NI 3) (n 561) art 21(2). Note that this differs from Education Reform Act 1988, s 7(1) which requires the collective worship to be 'wholly or mainly of a broadly Christian character' in England and Wales.

[563] SI 1989/2406 (NI 20) (n 558) art 5(1).

[564] The Church of Ireland, Methodist, Presbyterian, and Roman Catholic churches ('the four main churches') are organized on an all-island basis. Historically, these four denominations have been treated as the 'main' churches in Northern Ireland. The figures for the 2001 and 2011 censuses indicate the percentages of religious affiliation in the jurisdiction to be Catholic 41% in 2001 and 42% in 2011 (a slight increase); while over the same period, the other three main churches suffered a slightly larger decrease, with Church of Ireland falling from 15% to 14%, Methodist from 3.5% to 3%, and Presbyterian from 21% to 19%. Other Christian and Christian-related religious denominations also decreased slightly over the period (from 6.1% to 5.8%), while the percentage of the population adhering to non-Christian religions rose slightly, but given the numbers, significantly (from 0.3% to 0.8%), this is believed largely to be due to inward migration. The most marked increase was in those professing no religious belief (from 14% to 17%). See <http://www.nisra.gov.uk/Census/detailedcharacteristics_stats_bulletin_2011.pdf>.

[565] SI 1989/2406 (NI 20) (n 558) art 13.

[566] SI 1986/594 (NI 3) (n 561) art 21(2) and (7).

(b) prepares such pupils for the opportunities, responsibilities and experiences of adult life.[567]"

In addition, article 8 of the Education Reform (NI) Order 1989 requires all grant-aided **4.281** schools to meet the following requirements:

8.—(1) The curriculum for a grant-aided school shall not, in so far as it relates to pupils of compulsory school age, be taken to satisfy the requirements of Article 4(2) unless it promotes, wholly or mainly through the teaching of the contributory subjects and religious education, the attainment of the objectives of the following educational themes, namely—
(a) Information Technology;
(b) Education for Mutual Understanding;
(c) Cultural Heritage;
(d) Health Education;
(e) Economic Awareness;
(f) Careers Education.

Parents have the right to withdraw children from religious education classes,[568] and children who **4.282** are withdrawn have the right not to be excluded from any other advantage the school offers.[569] Teachers in controlled schools have a right to be excused from conducting or attending collective worship or providing non-denominational religious education[570] on the grounds of conscience, but this right does not extend to teachers in voluntary schools. Article 21 of the 1986 Order requires non-denominational religious education in controlled schools. In *Brudell v Governors of Ballykelly Primary School*,[571] a controlled school which had pupils of mixed religions, offered separate religious education for Catholic and Protestant pupils to be taught by teachers of the same religion. While numbers had been evenly balanced, the school roll was declining, particularly in relation to Protestant pupils. The school was required to make four teachers redundant and chose four Protestant teachers, although all were senior to three Catholic teachers in years of service. This was done to preserve the school's policy of maintaining staffing in line with the religious make-up of the pupils. The applicant was qualified to teach RE in all schools. The claim of direct and indirect discrimination was found proved. Indirect discrimination is unlawful unless the criterion applied is objectively justifiable by factors unrelated to religion, and must be proportionate to the reasonable needs of the employer. There is no statutory requirement in a controlled school to give separate RE teaching to Catholic pupils and the applicant was qualified to teach RE to all children. Other means of providing specific religious instruction to Catholic pupils, for example using local clergy, were not considered by the governors. Their motivation of acting in the best interests of the school provided no defence.

(5) Family law

a) Marriage

Historically, the law of Northern Ireland, as of the jurisdication of Ireland before **4.283** 1922, recognized as legal marriages contracted according to the rites of the Church of

---

[567] SI 1989/2406 (NI 20) (n 558) art 4(2). See Kerr J's analysis of art 4(2) in *Re Ferris's Application* [2001] NIQB 22.

[568] SI 1989/2406 (NI 20) (n 558) art 21(5).

[569] SI 1986/594 (NI 3) (n 561) art 21(4), and see *Re Cecil's Application for judicial review*, NIQB (27 January 1989). Lundy (n 557) para 5.52, observes that the possible conflict between the parents' right to have the child educated in accordance with parental religious views and the child's right to freedom of thought, conscience, and religion has not yet come before the Northern Ireland courts.

[570] SI 1989/2406 (NI 20) (n 558) art 22(2).

[571] *Brudell v Governors of Ballykelly Primary School* [2010] NIFET [2010] 6 BNIL 33.

Ireland,[572] Methodist, Presbyterian, or Roman Catholic churches. Jewish and Quaker marriages were also legally recognized,[573] and those who could officiate at 'mixed' marriages involving one Catholic or one Episcopalian partner were also regulated.[574] While civil ceremonies were also permitted, the Marriages (NI) Order 2003 ('the 2003 Order')[575] removed this discrimination against other faiths and Christian denominations. All religious marriages in Northern Ireland are now of full legal effect if the officiant is registered as a person empowered to solemnize marriages (the 2003 Order, article 10). A secular civil marriage may also be contracted by a registrar of marriages for the local area (article 31) and may be in a registry office or an approved place, such as a hotel (article 18(2)). The widening of places where a civil marriage may take place has been extremely popular among couples planning weddings. As in other parts of the United Kingdom, same-sex couples may contract a civil partnership but not a marriage in Northern Ireland.[576]

4.284 The 2011 Census indicates that 47.03 per cent of the population of NI aged 16 and over were married or in a civil partnership and living together, while 6.4 per cent reported themselves to be cohabiting. There is likely to be significant under-reporting of cohabitation.[577] The Registrar General's Annual Report indicates the method of celebration of marriages in Northern Ireland. In 2011 there were 8,366 marriages, 2,732 (32.7 per cent) of which were civil ceremonies. This compares to 1986 (25 years previously) when 1,421 (13.9 per cent) of the 10,225 marriages were civil ceremonies and 1961 (50 years previously), when only 520 (5.3 per cent) of the 9,861 marriages were civil ceremonies. It is interesting to note the growth in popularity of approved venues for civil ceremonies. In 2004 there were 323 such marriages and in 2011 there were 1,291. As in other jurisdictions, the average age at which a person marries has also increased from 27 to 33 for men and from 25 to 31 for women since 1961.[578]

b) Adoption

4.285 Adoption in Northern Ireland is governed by the Adoption (NI) Order 1987. Adoption services are provided directly by the Health and Social Services Trusts and by voluntary

---

[572] Matrimonial Causes and Marriage Law (Amendment) Act (Ireland) 1870, s 33 (see also the Marriages (Ireland) Act, 1844, and the Marriage Law (Ireland) Amendment Act, 1863).

[573] The Matrimonial Causes and Marriage Law (Amendment) Act (Ireland) 1870, s 37 permits special licences to be issued by the following:

> The moderator of the General Assembly of the Presbyterian Church in Ireland: The moderator of the Remonstrant Synod of Ulster: The moderator of the Presbytery of Antrim: The moderator of the Northern Presbytery of Antrim: The moderator of the Synod of Munster: The moderator of the Eastern Reformed Presbyterian Synod: The moderator of the United Presbyterian Presbytery of Ireland: The moderator of the Secession Church in Ireland: The moderator of the Reformed Presbyterian Synod of Ireland: The chairman of the Congregational Union of Ireland: The secretary of the Conference of the Methodist or Wesleyan Church in Ireland: The president or head of the Methodist New Connexion Church: The president or head of the Association of the Baptist Churches in Ireland: The clerk to the yearly meeting of the Society of Friends in Ireland.

[574] Matrimonial Causes and Marriage Law (Amendment) Act (Ireland) 1870, s 38. 'Mixed marriages' involving a Quaker are dealt with in the Marriage (Society of Friends) Acts 1860 and 1872.

[575] Marriage (NI) Order 2003, SI 2003/413 (NI 3), and see the Marriage Regulations (NI) 2003, SR 2003/468.

[576] Civil Partnership Act 2004, s 2. Due to the earlier commencement date of the legislation in Northern Ireland, the first civil partnerships in the UK were celebrated in Belfast on 19 December 2005 <http://news.bbc.co.uk/2/hi/uk_news/northern_ireland/4540226.stm>.

[577] See the NI Census Key Report at <http://www.nisra.gov.uk/Census/key_report_2011.pdf>. Note that while 47.52% of the population over 16 had a married status, only 0.09% had a civil partnership status in 2011.

[578] The Registrar General's Annual Reports are available at <http://www.nisra.gov.uk>.

adoption agencies, some of which are faith based.[579] The legislation requires the court, in deciding on any course of action in relation to the adoption of a child, to regard the child's welfare as the 'most important' consideration, having regard to the need to be satisfied that adoption, or adoption by a particular person, is in the best interests of the child, the need to safeguard the welfare of the child throughout his or her childhood, and the importance of providing the child with a stable and harmonious home. Due consideration must be given to the wishes and feelings of the child, having regard to his or her age and understanding.[580] An adoption order may contain such terms and conditions as the court may think fit[581] and a birth parent's consent to freeing for adoption may be given conditionally on the religious persuasion in which the child is to be brought up.[582]

c) Placement of children

Religious background may be a cause of conflict between different members of the child's family when resolving private law contact and residence issues, as was the case in *Re H and P (Residence Application)*.[583]   **4.286**

In making any decision about looked-after children, Health and Social Services Trusts are enjoined by the Children (NI) Order 1995 to give due consideration: **4.287**

(a) having regard to his age and understanding, to such wishes and feelings of the child as the authority has been able to ascertain;
(b) to such wishes and feelings of any person mentioned in paragraph (2)(b) to (d) as the authority has been able to ascertain; and
(c) to the child's religious persuasion, racial origin and cultural and linguistic background.[584]

When children are placed with family members or foster parents under the Children (NI) Order 1995, guidance enjoins social workers to assess and ensure that carers fully understand the child's cultural, religious, and linguistic needs and emphasizes that: **4.288**

> The importance of religion as an element of culture should never be overlooked. To some children and families it may be the dominant factor so that the religion of foster parents, for example, may in some cases be more important than their ethnic origin. Where it has not proved possible to make a placement which entirely reflects the child's religion or racial background, an independent visitor could provide a link with the religious or racial background (if the criteria for appointing an independent visitor apply).[585]

The guidance indicates that in most cases, continuity in life and care: 'suggests a need for placement with a family of the same religion, race and culture in a neighbourhood within reach of family, school or day nursery, church, friends and leisure activities'.[586]   **4.289**

Regulation 2(2)(c) of the Children (Private Arrangements for Fostering) Regulations 1996 makes specific reference to the needs of the child arising from religion, culture, language,   **4.290**

---

[579] A list of adoption agencies with contact details can be found at <http://www.dhsspsni.gov.uk/adoption _contacts.htm>.
[580] Adoption (NI) Order 1987, SI 1987/2203 (NI 22), art 9.
[581] SI 1987/2203 (NI 22) (n 580) art 12(6).
[582] SI 1987/2203 (NI 22) (n 580) art 17(1). The test of whether a mother is unreasonably withholding her consent has been held to be whether the advantages of adoption are sufficiently strong to override the views and interests of the objecting parent—*Down and Lisburn Health and Social Services Trust v H* [2007] 1 FLR 121, *Re JL (Unreasonable Witholding of Consent)* [2008] NIFam 11.
[583] *Re H and P (Residence Application)* [2011] NIFam 16.
[584] Children (NI) Order 1995, SI 1995/755 (NI 2), art 26(3).
[585] Children (NI) Order 1995 Guidance and Regulations, Vol 3, para 2.39.
[586] Guidance and Regulations (n 585) para 5.4.

and race and a Trust's duty to satisfy itself that these needs are being met by the particular arrangements made for fostering the child.

4.291 Volume 4 of the Department of Health and Social Services Guidance on the Children (NI) Order 1995, which deals with looked-after children, also emphasizes that regard must be had to the child's cultural, religious and linguistic needs in assessment and planning for a child who will be in the direct care of a Trust.

(6) Wills, trusts, and property law

4.292 Religion may be relevant to the avoidance of dispositions of property in wills or trusts in two main ways in Northern Ireland. Although the law is not dissimilar to that in England, the particular circumstances in Northern Ireland provide a number of striking examples.

4.293 The first issue relates to ministers of religion and other religious advisers, who are a group of people in relation to whom undue influence may be proven in the disposition of an estate[587] or an *inter vivos* transfer. The law is the same as that in England and Wales.

4.294 The second issue relates to dispositions of property dependent on religious conditions, either precedent or subsequent. While the law in Northern Ireland does not differ materially from that in England and Wales, social conditions in this jurisdiction mean that in the past the case law often focused on requiring legatees to adhere to, or prohibiting them from converting to, the Roman Catholic faith or the faith of a particular Protestant denomination. Although such clauses may or may not be void for uncertainty, the case law pre-dates the introduction of the Human Rights Act 1998[588] and there may be a question as to whether they will be void for public policy or unenforceable by a court as a result of the court's duties with regard to the Convention Rights.

4.295 After the disestablishment of the Church of Ireland, the church's Representative Church Body was incorporated by Royal Charter, and given powers to deal with church lands in the Glebe Lands, Representative Church Body, Ireland Act 1875. The value and sale of tithe rent charges, and the conversion of renewable leases by tenants of lands owned by ecclesiastical bodies is dealt with in the Irish Church Act 1869 (Amendment) Act 1872.

4.296 Long leases of land (not exceeding 5 acres) for the construction of a 'place of worship for a congregation', a dwelling for a clergyman, minister or pastor, a school, a burial ground, and any other relevant buildings, are governed by the Leasing Powers Act for Religious Worship in Ireland, 1855. Interestingly, the provisions are not limited to Christian denominations.

4.297 The question of what exact denomination of non-conformist congregation is meant in legal deeds and documents relating to the places where they meet, where the deeds or documents do not specify the doctrinal basis of the body or organization owning or using the premises 'shall not be called in question on account of the doctrines or opinions or mode of worship so taught or observed in such meeting house' and can be proved by 25 years' usage by a group following particular doctrines, etc.[589]

---

[587] As was attempted in the case of *Thompson and anor v Thompson* [2003] NIFam 3.

[588] For discussion of this issue, see H Conway and S Grattan, 'Testamentary Conditions in Restraint of Religion in the Twenty-First Century: An Anglo-Canadian Perspective' (2005) 50 McGill LJ 511.

[589] The Nonconformist Chapels Act 1844, which makes this provision, still applies in Northern Ireland.

(7) Charities

The law of charities in Northern Ireland is governed by the Charities Act (NI) 2008, as **4.298** amended by the Charities Act (Northern Ireland) 2013 which is partially in force.[590] It defines charitable purposes as including both the advancement of religion[591] and the advancement of 'human rights, conflict resolution or reconciliation or the promotion of religious or racial harmony or equality and diversity'.[592] Religion is defined as including both monotheism and polytheism as well as 'any analogous philosophical belief (whether or not involving belief in a god)'.[593] This is materially similar to provision elsewhere in the United Kingdom. The previous common law definition of charitable purposes in Northern Ireland was also similar to that elsewhere in the United Kingdom.[594]

(8) Planning

Churches still in ecclesiastical use cannot be scheduled as historic monuments[595] and Article **4.299** 44(8) of the Planning (NI) Order 1991 provides an exemption to the requirement for consent before demolition, alteration, or extension of an ecclesiastical building which is in current use as a church.

(9) Criminal law

Where an offence was motivated by hostility based on, *inter alia*, the victim's membership or **4.300** presumed membership of a religious group (defined by reference either to religious belief or lack of religious belief), the sentencing judge should treat this as an aggravating factor and state in open court that he or she has done so.[596]

Stirring up fear or hatred of a group by reason of characteristics including their religion is **4.301** an offence,[597] as is publishing or broadcasting a document or recording to stir up fear or hatred,[598] or possessing documents to stir up fear or hatred.[599]

The common law offence of blasphemy still applies in Northern Ireland. **4.302**

The Sunday Observance Act 1833 provides that election of officers of corporations and **4.303** other public companies which are required to take place on a Sunday shall take place on the

---

[590] More information can be obtained from the Charities Commission for Northern Ireland at <http://www.charitycommissionni.org.uk>

[591] Charities Act (NI) 2008, art 2(2)(c).

[592] Charities Act (NI) 2008, art 2(2)(h).

[593] Charities Act (NI) 2008, art 2(3).

[594] Halsbury states that the Charitable Uses Act 1601 (43 Eliz 1 c 4 (1601)) did not extend to that country, an Irish statute of Charles I (10 Car 1 (1634)) contained a closely similar list of purposes which were regarded as charitable in Ireland: see *Incorporated Society in Dublin v Richards* (1841) 1 Dr & War 258, 324 *per* St Leonards LJ; *Income Tax Special Purposes Comrs v Pemsel* [1891] AC 531, 544–6, HL *per* Halsbury LJ.

[595] Department for the Environment for NI, Planning Policy Statement 6, 'Planning, Archaeology and the Built Heritage', Appendix B, para B2.

[596] Criminal Justice (No 2) Order 2004, SI 2004/1991 (NI 15), art 2(2) and see the definition in art 2(5).

[597] Public Order (NI) Order 1987, SI 1987/463 (NI 7), art 9. Note that legislation equivalent to Criminal Justice and Immigration Act 2008, s 74 and Sch 16, which amends the Public Order Act 1986 and introduces a new offence of incitement to hatred on the grounds of sexual orientation, does not yet appear to have been introduced in Northern Ireland. An exception relating to the teaching of orthodox religious doctrine is included in the Public Order Act 1986, s 29JA.

[598] SI 1987/463 (NI 7) (n 597) arts 10–12.

[599] SI 1987/463 (NI 7) (n 597) art 13.

Saturday before or the Monday after the date in question, and any meetings transacting such business on a Sunday shall be void.

4.304 The prohibition on executing legal processes on a Sunday in section 7 of the Sunday Observance Act 1695 was put to ingenious use in *Re Farrell*,[600] in which the applicant arranged to call to the police station to collect a summons for drink driving on a Sunday. In the magistrates' court, his counsel argued that the summons had not been validly served, as a result of section 7 of the 1695 Act.

4.305 Girvan J held that Parliament has never amended or repealed it and indeed made some limited amendments to it in 1967, and has made specific exemptions to it in other statutes. Section 7 is drawn in very wide and prohibitive terms to prevent the service of all court-related documents on a Sunday. A summons is process for the purposes of section 7. If it is not properly served the court has no jurisdiction to proceed to a hearing in his absence. Giving of the document to the applicant at the police station constituted service although he knew of the document's existence in advance. This service occurred on a Sunday in breach of the 1695 Act.

F. Republic of Ireland

James Anderson and Claire Archbold[601]

(1) Constitutional law[602]

4.306 The Republic of Ireland has a written Constitution—the Constitution of Ireland (*Bunreacht na hÉireann*)—which provides for the institutions of the state and guarantees certain fundamental rights. It may only be amended by national referendum initiated by the Parliament (*Oireachtas*). The Constitution consists of a Preamble and 50 articles arranged under 16 headings.

4.307 A distinctive feature of the Irish Constitution, drafted in 1937, is its approach to religion. The Preamble is explicitly Christian, and article 6 states that 'all powers of government, legislative and judicial, derive under God, from the People'. The statements of principles in the Preamble are used as a dynamic tool for judicial activism and 'no interpretation of the Constitution is intended to be final for all time'.[603] The religious dimension of the Preamble has been used in this way as an interpretive tool, and the Constitution has been interpreted by courts in the past as 'reflecting a firm conviction that we are a Christian people',[604] as demonstrating an intention, *inter alia*, to express natural human rights 'as being in the category of natural law derived from God's law',[605] and as 'proclaiming a deep religious conviction

---

[600] *Re Farrell* [2005] NIJB 357 (Girvan J).

[601] Barristers-at-law of the Inn of Court of Northern Ireland. Thanks are due to Dr Conor O'Mahoney of University College Cork and Catherine-Ellen O'Keeffe, Solicitor for their comments on the text, and in particular to Richard McNamara, Solicitor for his comments and wisdom. Any remaining errors or omissions are the authors' own.

[602] A useful introduction to this material may be found in GW Hogan and GF Whyte, *JM Kelly: The Irish Constitution* (4th edn, Lexis Nexis Butterworths, 2003) or O Doyle, *Constitutional Law: Text, Cases and Materials* (Clarus Press, 2009). For a more detailed consideration of the subject of religion and law in Ireland, see E Daly, *Religion, Law and the Irish State* (Clarus Press, 2012).

[603] Hogan and Whyte (n 602) para 2.1.11.

[604] *Quinn's Supermarket Ltd v Attorney General* [1972] IR 1 *per* Walsh J.

[605] *McGee v Attorney General* [1974] IR 284 *per* Walsh J.

and faith and an intention to adopt a Constitution consistent with that conviction and faith and with Christian beliefs'.[606]

There is a doctrine of harmonious interpretation of the Constitution, and competing rights should be interpreted so as to support this where possible. Where it is not possible a hierarchy of rights was recognized in *The People v Shaw*,[607] in which Kenny J states: **4.308**

> There is a hierarchy of constitutional rights and, when a conflict arises between them, that which ranks higher must prevail... The decision on priority of constitutional rights is to be made by the High Court and, on appeal by this Court. When a conflict of constitutional rights arises, it must be resolved by having regard to (a) the terms of the Constitution, (b) the ethical values which all Christians living in the State acknowledge and accept and (c) the main tenets of our system of constitutional parliamentary democracy.

Fundamental rights are dealt with in articles 40 to 44 of the Constitution. The right to life of the unborn, with an equal right to life of the mother, is specifically protected by article 40.3.3, introduced after a referendum in 1983 when the Irish electorate approved an Eighth Amendment to the Constitution. In 1992, a 13-year-old girl became pregnant following rape and, after confessing suicidal thoughts to her parents, went to England for an abortion. The Attorney General obtained an injunction from the High Court prohibiting the procedure, which was overturned by the Supreme Court.[608] Subsequently, by referendum, the electorate voted for the Thirteenth and Fourteenth Amendments which inserted a protection on the freedom to travel. Article 40.3.3 presently reads: **4.309**

> The State acknowledges the right to life of the unborn and, with due regard to the equal right to life of the mother, guarantees in its laws to respect, and, as far as practicable, by its laws to defend and vindicate that right.
>
> This subsection shall not limit freedom to travel between the State and another state.
>
> This subsection shall not limit freedom to obtain or make available, in the State, subject to such conditions as may be laid down by law, information relating to services lawfully available in another state.

Article 40.3.3 has again come to public attention following the decision of the European Court of Human Rights (ECtHR) in *A, B and C v Ireland*,[609] and the death in 2012 of Savita Halappanavar in University Hospital Galway.[610] The independent report into Mrs Halappanavar's death, under the chairmanship of Professor Sir Sabaratnam Arulkumaran, and the Protection of Life During Pregnancy Bill 2013 were published on the same day, 13 June 2013. The Bill was intended to provide clarity as to the law for patients and doctors, as required by the ECtHR in *A, B and C* and recommended by the report, and was passed into law on 30 July 2013.   **4.310**

Article 40.6.1 guarantees freedom of expression, subject to public order and morality and to some specific limitations: **4.311**

> The right of the citizens to express freely their convictions and opinions.

---

[606] *Norris v Attorney General* [1984] IR 36 *per* O'Higgins CJ. See further Hogan and Whyte (n 602) paras 2.1.19–2.1.22.

[607] *The People v Shaw* [1982] IR 1.

[608] *Attorney General v X* [1992] 1 IR 1.

[609] *A, B and C v Ireland* [2010] ECHR 2032.

[610] The death of Mrs Halappanavar in hospital, having sought medical attention related to her pregnancy, is the subject of the independent report, published on 13 June 2013 by the Health and Safety Executive, available at <http://www.hse.ie/eng/services/news/nimtreport50278.pdf>.

The education of public opinion being, however, a matter of such grave import to the common good, the State shall endeavour to ensure that organs of public opinion, such as the radio, the press, the cinema, while preserving their rightful liberty of expression, including criticism of Government policy, shall not be used to undermine public order or morality or the authority of the State.

The publication or utterance of blasphemous, seditious, or indecent matter is an offence which shall be punishable in accordance with law.

4.312   The law relating to blasphemy is dealt with at paragraphs 4.328–4.329, in the section on criminal law.

4.313   Articles 41 and 42 relating to the family (described as the 'natural, primary and fundamental unit group of society' by Article 41.1 and limited by judicial interpretation to the married family), the role of women in the home, and education (including the right and duty of parents to undertake the religious education of the child) have been described both as reflecting Catholic morality and as designed to protect the interests of the Protestant minority in the state.[611] Hardiman J has stated that he does not regard articles 41 and 42 as 'reflecting uniquely any confessional view'.[612]

4.314   Until recently, article 42.5 of the Constitution, provided that:

> In exceptional cases, where the parents for physical or moral reasons fail in their duty towards their children, the State as guardian of the common good, by appropriate means shall endeavour to supply the place of the parents, but always with due regard for the natural and imprescriptible rights of the child.

4.315   Following deep public concern about the abuse and mistreatment of children in orphanages and other institutions run by religious bodies on behalf of the state in the past, the electorate voted in a referendum on 10 November 2012, that article 42.5 should be removed and replaced by a new article 42A entitled 'Children'. This affirms the 'natural and imprescriptible' rights of the child and lays the foundation for modern adoption and public law children proceedings, based on the best interests of the child and stating the child's right to have a voice where appropriate.[613] The issues of same-sex marriage and the provisions in Article 42 about women in the home, as well as provisions about increasing participation in public life by women are among those under discussion by the Convention on the Constitution set up by the *Oireachtas* in 2012. The Convention is described as an exercise in participative democracy, being a forum comprising 66 randomly selected citizens and 33 Parliamentarians, including four representatives of the political parties from Northern Ireland, under the independent chairmanship of Tom Arnold, which seeks widespread participation from the public, interest groups, and the Irish Diaspora.[614]

4.316   Religion is dealt with expressly by Article 44, which provides that:

> 1. The State acknowledges that the homage of public worship is due to Almighty God. It shall hold His Name in reverence, and shall respect and honour religion.

---

[611] B Moriarty and E Massa (eds), *Human Rights Law* (OUP/Law Society of Ireland, 2011) 167, para 3.5.7.
[612] *North West Health Board v HW* [2001] 3 IR 622.
[613] Article 42A of the Constitution has come into effect following the approval of the Thirty-First Amendment to the Constitution (Children) Bill 2012 by the People in a referendum held on 10 November 2012. The Supreme Court delivered its opinion in this case on 11 December 2012, see *McCrystal v Minister for Children* [2012] IESC 53. The text of article 42A can be accessed at the Referendum Commission's specially designed website for the referendum, see <http://www.refcom.ie>.
[614] See the Convention's website at <https://www.constitution.ie>.

2. 1° Freedom of conscience and the free profession and practice of religion are, subject to public order and morality, guaranteed to every citizen.

2° The State guarantees not to endow any religion.

3° The State shall not impose any disabilities or make any discrimination on the ground of religious profession, belief or status.

4° Legislation providing State aid for schools shall not discriminate between schools under the management of different religious denominations, nor be such as to affect prejudicially the right of any child to attend a school receiving public money without attending religious instruction at that school.

5° Every religious denomination shall have the right to manage its own affairs, own, acquire and administer property, movable and immovable, and maintain institutions for religious or charitable purposes.

6° The property of any religious denomination or any educational institution shall not be diverted save for necessary works of public utility and on payment of compensation.

There has not been much litigation about article 44.1, but in the leading case of *Quinn's* **4.317**
Supermarket v Attorney General,[615] Walsh J said that:

> Our Constitution reflects a firm conviction that we are religious people. The preamble to the Constitution acknowledges that we are a Christian people and Article 44, s. 1, sub-s. 1, acknowledges that the homage of public worship is due to Almighty God but it does so in terms which do not confine the benefit of that acknowledgment to members of the Christian faith. In Article 44, s. 1, of the Constitution the State recognises the existence of the several religious denominations there named, including the Jewish Congregations, as well as all other unnamed ones existing at the date of the coming into operation of the Constitution. This declaration is an express recognition of the separate co-existence of the religious denominations, named and unnamed. It does not prefer one to the other and it does not confer any privilege or impose any disability or diminution of status upon any religious denomination, and it does not permit the State to do so.

Quoting this dictum, the Supreme Court in *Corway v Independent Newspapers (Ireland)* **4.318**
Limited[616] found that it could not determine what religions were to be protected by the constitutional prohibition on blasphemy, and stated that this was a matter for the legislature.

Articles 44.1.2 and 44.1.3 previously explicitly recognized 'the special position' of the **4.319**
Catholic Church, and the Church of Ireland, Presbyterian and Methodist churches as well as the Religious Society of Friends,[617] the Jewish congregations, and all other religious denominations existing in Ireland at the date of coming into operation of the Constitution. These articles were deleted in 1972, following a referendum.[618]

There is consequently now no constitutional definition of religion. On the one hand, in **4.320**
Quinn's Supermarket v Attorney General, Walsh J did not confine article 44 to members of the Christian faith,[619] but on the other, in *Johnston v Church of Scientology Mission of Dublin Ltd*,[620] Geoghegan J did not recognize Scientology as a religion. The question of the definition of a religion has yet to be definitively ruled on by the courts in Ireland.

---

[615] *Quinn's Supermarket v Attorney General* [1972] IR 1.
[616] *Corway v Independent Newspapers (Ireland) Ltd* [1999] 4 IR 485.
[617] Usually known as Quakers in everyday speech.
[618] The case law considering the effect (if any) of these provisions is considered by Hogan and Whyte (n 602) paras 7.8.16–7.8.17.
[619] *Quinn's Supermarket v Attorney General* [1972] IR 1.
[620] *Johnston v Church of Scientology Mission of Dublin Ltd* [2001] IESC 25.

4.321 The constitutional guarantees in article 44.2 can be largely divided into two categories: freedoms of religion[621] and freedoms from religion.[622] In a significant number of cases the Irish courts have held that the overriding purpose of article 44 is to protect religious freedom and that religious discrimination may be permitted for this purpose. In the leading case of *Quinn's Supermarket v Attorney General*,[623] the constitutionality of article 2 of the Victuallers' Shops (Hours of Trading on Weekdays) (Dublin and Dun Laoghaire and Bray) Order 1948 was challenged. This Order exempted kosher butcher shops from a ban on evening opening which generally applied to other businesses in the area. The Supreme Court held that article 44.2.3 *prima facie* prohibited discrimination. Notwithstanding that article 2 of the Order aimed to assist a religious minority, it potentially infringed article 44.2.3. Walsh J reasoned, however, that the guarantee of freedom of religious practice could, in such circumstances, justify discrimination.

4.322 In *Re Article 26 and the Employment Equality Bill 1996*,[624] the Supreme Court considered the constitutionality of, among other matters, an exemption to the general prohibition on discrimination in the Bill which allowed certain vocational training bodies and religious bodies operating religious, educational, or medical institutions to discriminate on the grounds of religion in order to maintain the religious ethos of the institution. The Court stated:

> It is constitutionally permissible to make distinctions or discriminations on grounds of religious profession, belief or status insofar—but only insofar—as this may be necessary to give life and reality to the guarantee of the free profession and practice of religion in the Constitution.[625]

(2) Human rights[626]

4.323 The European Convention on Human Rights Act 2003 is an Act of the *Oireachtas* which incorporated the European Convention on Human Rights (ECHR) into Irish law. The Act is an example of an interpretive incorporation of the Convention similar to the Human Rights Act 1998 in the United Kingdom. Unlike the United Kingdom, which does not have a written constitution, the interpretation of the Act by the Irish Superior Courts, ie the High Court and the Supreme Court, is subject to the provisions of the Constitution, which would take precedence in the event of conflict.[627] The duty on the Court is an interpretative one only.[628] As the Constitution takes precedence over the Convention (as stated in the long title to the Act), section 1 of the European Convention on Human Rights Act 2003 does not include courts in the definition of those 'organs of the State' which are obliged to exercise functions in a manner compatible with the Convention. The courts must interpret domestic law in accordance with the Convention insofar as and subject to the Constitution.

---

[621] Articulated as as freedom of conscience, free practice of religion, the right of every religious denomination to manage its own affairs, the protection of the property of every religious denomination.

[622] Articulated as guarantees against state endowment of religion, against state imposition of disabilities or discriminations on the ground of religion, the right of a child to attend a school receiving public money without attending religious instruction at that school.

[623] *Quinn's Supermarket* (n 619).

[624] *Re Article 26 and the Employment Equality Bill 1996* [1997] 2 IR 321.

[625] *Re Article 26* (n 624) 358.

[626] For a useful introduction to this subject, see H Becker et al, *Human Rights Law* (3rd edn, Oxford University Press/Law Society of Ireland, 2011); and U Kilkelly (ed), *ECHR and Irish Law* (2nd edn, Jordan Publishing, 2009).

[627] See Hogan and Whyte (n 602) para 7.1.158.

[628] European Convention on Human Rights Act 2003, s 2.

This is the limit of the courts' power in relation to the Convention. There must be a domestic law which can be interpreted in accordance with it (or otherwise). They have no jurisdiction to consider a freestanding argument based on the Convention Rights. The principal remedy, as in the United Kingdom, is a declaration of incompatibility. The interpretive duty and the availability of remedies are discussed in *Foy v An t-Ard Chláraitheoir & ors*.[629] Further to section 4 of the European Convention on Human Rights Act 2003 the courts are required to take 'due account' of the jurisprudence of the ECtHR and decisions, opinions, etc of the European Commission on Human Rights and the Council of Ministers of the Council of Europe.

The question of the inter-relationship of the Constitutional rights and the ECHR rights where differences exist, was dealt with by the Supreme Court in *Carmody v Minister for Justice*.[630] It was held that Constitutional questions should be determined first as 'it hardly needs to be said that the provisions of the Act of 2003 cannot compromise in any way the interpretation or application of the Constitution'. The implications of this are seen in *McD v L*,[631] in which the Supreme Court refused to recognize a woman and her same-sex partner as a family enjoying rights under Article 8 ECHR. There was no provision of domestic law to which the interpretive obligation could apply. The constitutional protection extended only to the married family, and this took precedence. **4.324**

A number of cases in the ECtHR, although not directly concerned with religion, demonstrate the religious framework for debate on many socially sensitive subjects in the jurisdiction. In *Johnston v Ireland*,[632] it was ruled that Articles 8 and 12 ECHR do not give rise to a right to divorce. In the case of *Murphy v Ireland*,[633] it was alleged that the prohibition of the broadcast of a religious advertisement pursuant to section 10(3) of the Radio and Television Act 1988 constituted a violation under Articles 9 and 10 ECHR. The Court held that Article 10 (freedom of expression) was not breached by the prohibition on religious advertising. Member States had a wide margin of appreciation on this sensitive subject. In *Keegan v Ireland*,[634] the applicant successfully argued that the failure of the Adoption Acts to make provision for consulting the natural father of a child placed for adoption infringed his right to respect for family life under Article 8 ECHR. In the case of *Open Door Counselling Ltd and Dublin Well Woman Ltd v Ireland*,[635] a majority of the Court ruled that the restriction on the freedom of the applicants to impart information about access to termination of pregnancy services abroad was in breach of Article 10 ECHR. The measure was disproportionate to the government's stated aim of protecting the life of the unborn and upholding the Constitution, in particular as the information was freely available elsewhere and the service was legal in other parts of Europe. In *Norris v Ireland*,[636] the ECtHR held that the criminalization of homosexuality is a breach of Article 8 ECHR. In *Airey v Ireland*,[637] the ECtHR stated, in an application relating to non-availability of legal aid for judicial separation, that the right of effective access to a court may, in some civil proceedings, require the **4.325**

---

[629] *Foy v An t-Ard Chláraitheoir & ors* [2007] IEHC 470.
[630] *Carmody v Minister for Justice* [2009] IESC 71.
[631] *McD v L* [2007] IESC 81.
[632] *Johnston v Ireland* [1986] 9 EHRR 203.
[633] *Murphy v Ireland* (App 44179/98) (10 July 2003).
[634] *Keegan v Ireland* [1994] 18 EHRR 342.
[635] *Open Door Counselling Ltd and Dublin Well Woman Ltd v Ireland* [1993] 15 EHRR 244.
[636] *Norris v Ireland* [1991] 13 EHRR 186.
[637] *Airey v Ireland* [1979] 2 EHRR 305.

state to provide publicly-funded legal aid. In *A, B and C v Ireland*,[638] the ECtHR held there is no right for women to have an abortion, and that the first two applicants' rights were not violated by being forced to travel for an abortion. The protection of a moral belief in the right to life of the unborn held by the majority of the Irish population was a legitimate aim of the state, and the action taken was within the margin of appreciation. It found, however, that Ireland had violated Article 8 ECHR by failing to provide an accessible and effective procedure by which a woman could establish whether she qualified for a legal abortion under current Irish law.[639]

4.326   International human rights standards also impact on Irish law by another route, through the European Union. The Charter of Fundamental Rights of the European Union[640] has been part of EU law since the entry into force of the Treaty of Lisbon on 1 December 2009, and the Charter has the same legal status as the Treaties.[641] The Irish Constitution required a referendum to ratify the Lisbon Treaty and after the initial 'no' vote on 12 June 2008, the European Council gave a number of guarantees to Ireland, including the guarantee that nothing in the Lisbon Treaty or the Charter of Fundamental Rights affects in any way the scope and applicability of the provisions of the Irish Constitution relating to the protection of the right to life or family.[642] Article 6(1) provides that 'the provisions of the Charter shall not extend in any way the competences of the Union as defined in the Treaties'.

4.327   Article 6(2) provides a legal basis for EU accession to the ECHR which, once ratified, will form part of EU law. The EU institutions and Member States are both subject to EU human rights acquis when dealing with matters within the competence of the European Union and it will be interesting to see how domestic and international courts deal with any potential fault-lines between the Irish Constitution and the EU's human rights acquis.

(3) Criminal Law[643]

4.328   Blasphemy is a criminal offence in Ireland. Article 40.6.1.i of the Constitution provides that 'the publication or utterance of blasphemous, seditious, or indecent matter is an offence which shall be punishable in accordance with law'. In *Corway v Independent Newspapers Ltd*,[644] it was alleged that a cartoon was a blasphemous libel. The Supreme Court ruled that it was impossible to say of what this offence consisted, and whether it applied only to Christianity or to other world religions. The task of defining this crime was one for the government and not the courts.

4.329   Following *Corway* and a Law Reform Commission report,[645] the constitutional guarantee was given statutory embodiment as a criminal offence of blasphemy punishable by a fine[646]

---

[638] *A, B and C v Ireland* [2010] ECHR 2032.

[639] The government established an Expert Group to report on how to implement the ruling, under the chairmanship of Ryan J. The Group reported in November 2012 and their report can be accessed at <http:www .dohc.ie>. It is understood that the Department of Health is currently preparing draft legislation following the Report's recommendations.

[640] Charter of Fundamental Rights of the European Union of 18 December 2000, [2000] OJ C364/01.

[641] TEU, Art 6(1).

[642] Moriarty and Massa (n 611).

[643] On Irish Criminal Law, see C Hanly, *An Introduction to Irish Criminal Law* (2nd edn, Gill and McMillan, 2006)

[644] *Corway v Independent Newspapers Ltd* [2000] 1 ILRM 426.

[645] Law Reform Commission, 'Report on the Crime of Libel' (LRC 41-1991).

[646] Currently of €25,000.

in section 36 of the Defamation Act 2009. Blasphemy is not limited to material likely to outrage members of the Christian religion. The removal of blasphemy from the Constitution is one of the questions being considered by the Constitutional Convention set up by the *Oireachtas* in 2012.[647]

Hate crime is dealt with in the Prohibition of Incitement to Hatred Act 1989 which pro- **4.330** scribes in section 2 words or behaviours that are: 'Threatening, abusive or insulting and are intended or, having regard to all the circumstances, are likely to stir up hatred.'

Hatred is defined in section 1 of the Act as being hatred directed: '...against a group of per- **4.331** sons in the State or elsewhere on account of their race, colour, nationality, religion, ethnic or national origins, membership of the travelling community or sexual orientation.'

Prior to the Protection of Life during Pregnancy Act 2013, abortion was regulated within **4.332** the criminal law in Ireland. Now, the Act (s 22) states the intentional destruction of unborn human life to be an offence, but sections 7–9 permit and set out the decision-making process for abortion where the life of the woman is at risk from physical illness or suicide.[648] Provision of information about abortion services abroad is underpinned by a series of statutory prohibitions on providing information 'advocating or promoting the termination of pregnancy', breach of which is an offence.[649]

As an interesting side note, in the case of *People (DPP) v Draper*,[650] a man was prosecuted for **4.333** criminal damage of religious statues. The defence raised was that the defendant believed that he had been 'sent by God'. The court rejected this on the basis that while his freedom of conscience and freedom to practice religion was protected by Article 44.2 of the Constitution, such rights were expressly subjugated to public order.

(4) Family law[651]

Although religion is not directly relevant to Irish family law, the religious and social context **4.334** of Ireland at the time of drafting is strongly reflected in articles 41 and 42 of the Constitution, which govern the area. In particular, the statement in article 41.1 that the family is 'a moral institution possessing inalienable and imprescriptible rights antecedent and superior to all positive law' has resulted in some distinctive features of Irish family law. Law in the area has also been marked by the social change in Ireland during the past quarter century. A brief summary of developments in relation to family relationships between adults and the law relating to children is illustrative.

---

[647] The new coalition government elected in 2011 has agreed in its Programme for Government to remove blasphemy from the Constitution. Such an amendment is likely to occur within a range of constitutional reforms currently being considered by the Constitutional Convention which has been set up by the new government (see the Convention's website at <https://www.constitution.ie>).

[648] This is a codification of the position set out in *Attorney General v X* [1992] IESC 1.

[649] Regulation of Information (Services Outside the State for the Termination of Pregnancies) Act 1995, s 10.

[650] Reported in *The Irish Times*, 24 March 1988.

[651] Two useful texts on this subject are J Nestor, *Introduction to Irish Family Law* (Gill and McMillan, 2007; 4th edn, Gill and Macmillan, 2011) and G Shannon, *Family Law* (4th edn, OUP/Law Society of Ireland, 2011). Also see Hogan and Whyte (n 602) ch 7. See also G Shannon, *Child Law* (2nd edn, Round Hall, 2010) and AJ Shatter, *Family Law* (4th edn, Tottel Publishing, 1997).

a) Relationships between adults

4.335 The unit of the family is stated to have 'natural and imprescriptible rights' in article 41.1 of the Constitution,[652] and in article 41.3 the state pledges itself to 'guard with special care the institution of Marriage, on which the Family is founded, and to protect it against attack'. Marriage was defined by Costello J in *Murray v Ireland*[653] as derived from the Christian idea of 'a partnership based on an irrevocable personal consent given by both spouses which establishes a unique and very special life-long relationship'. The unenumerated rights protected by article 40.3.1 of the Constitution, when construed in the light of article 41, have been interpreted by the Supreme Court as conferring upon spouses a broad right to privacy in marital affairs.[654] In 2006, in *Zappone and Gilligan v Revenue Commissioners*,[655] Dunne J considered constitutional and human rights law and refused to recognize a Canadian same-sex marriage as giving rise to legal consequences in Irish law, but civil partnerships have been available in Ireland since 1 January 2011[656] and same-sex marriage is a subject under discussion by the Constitutional Convention established by the *Oireachtas* in 2012.[657]

4.336 Divorce was introduced in Ireland by the Family Law (Divorce) Act 1996, following the amendment of article 41.3.2 after a referendum in 1995. Article 41.3.2 previously prohibited the issue of decrees of dissolution of marriage, but now permits divorce on the ground of four years' separation in the previous five years where there is no reasonable prospect of reconciliation between the parties and proper provision has been made for the spouses and their children.

b) The law relating to children

4.337 The position of the child in Irish law has been located firmly within the (married) family by articles 41 and 42 of the Constitution. Welfare of the child is paramount in custody cases.[658] The historic position of the child of unmarried parents was described by O'Higgins CJ in *G v An Bord Uchtála*:

> At common law an illegitimate child was termed 'filius nullius' and regarded as being no more than the 'unfortunate offspring of the common failing of a man and woman', a burden on the locality and a person to be shunned. In this unchristian treatment of a human being natural rights were, of course, forgotten and a lonely life was ordained merely because of the accident of birth. Not only is this not so now under the Constitution, but the State has the added obligation to defend and vindicate in its laws all natural rights of all citizens. In relation to illegitimate children and certain others the State has by the Adoption Acts endeavoured to discharge this obligation. The purpose of these Acts is to give to these children the opportunity of becoming members of a family and to have the status and protection which such membership entails.[659]

4.338 The Adoption Act 1952 permitted the adoption only of children of unmarried parents. When adoption of the children of married parents was proposed in the Adoption Bill 1987,

---

[652] The doctrine of unenumerated rights is discussed and developed by the Supreme Court in the context of water fluoridation in the important case of *Ryan v Attorney General* [1965] IESC 1, [1965] IR 294.

[653] *Murray v Ireland* [1985] IR 532.

[654] *McGee v Attorney General* [1974] IR 284.

[655] *Zappone and Gilligan v Revenue Commissioners* [2006] IEHC 404.

[656] Civil Partnership and Certain Rights and Obligations of Cohabitants Act 2010, Pt 3.

[657] See the Convention's website at <https://www.constitution.ie>.

[658] The Guardianship of Infants Act 1969, s 3, as amended by the Children Act 1997, s 12.

[659] *G v An Bord Uchtála* [1980] IR 32, 56.

a court challenge claimed this amounted to an attack on the unenumerated rights of the original family. In *Re Article 26 and the Adoption (No 2) Bill*, the Supreme Court stated:

> The court rejects the submission that the nature of the family as a unit group possessing inalienable and imprescriptible rights makes it constitutionally impermissible for a statute to restore to any member of an individual family constitutional rights of which he has been deprived by a method which disturbs or alters the constitution of that family if that method is necessary to achieve that purpose. The guarantees afforded to the institution of the family by the Constitution, with their consequent benefit to the children of a family should not be construed so that upon the failure of that benefit it cannot be replaced where the circumstances demand it by incorporation of the child into an alternative family.[660]

The state's duty, in exceptional cases where 'the [married] parents for physical or moral rea- **4.339** sons fail in their duty towards their children' to 'endeavour to supply the place of the parents, but always with due regard for the natural and imprescriptible rights of the child' as expressed in article 42.5 has been deleted by the Thirty First Amendment to the Constitution in 2012, passed following the deep public concern in recent years about the past treatment of looked-after children in institutions run by religious orders. The balance between parental rights and the rights of children is encapsulated in the new article 42A(2)(1) which replaces Article 42.5. It provides that:

> In exceptional cases, where the parents, regardless of their marital status, fail in their duty towards their children to such extent that the safety or welfare of any of their children is likely to be prejudicially affected, the State as guardian of the common good shall, by proportionate means as provided by law, endeavour to supply the place of the parents, but always with due regard for the natural and imprescriptible rights of the child.

The recalibration of the Constitutional approach to children in a modern, child-centred way **4.340** in article 42A, also includes the restatement of the paramountcy of the welfare principle, the right of the child to be consulted in decisions affecting him or her, and a revised framework for adoption and public law proceedings.

The constitutional rights in articles 41 and 42 have not led to any different application **4.341** of the general rule of the comity of courts in Ireland in relation to parental child abduction.[661] Finlay P (as he then was) delivered the *ex tempore* judgment of the Supreme Court in *Saunders v Mid-Western Health Board*:[662]

> Where... parents having no connection with Ireland bring their children unlawfully from the country in which they are, into the jurisdiction of this court, in breach of an order made by the court in the jurisdiction in which they were domiciled and in which the children were being reared, I do not accept that they can by that act alone confer on themselves and their children constitutional rights under Articles 41 and 42 of the Constitution.

---

[660] *Re Article 26 and the Adoption (No 2) Bill* [1989] IR 656, 663.

[661] See: *Kent County Council v CS* [1984] ILRM 292. The extent of constitutional rights in their application to non-Irish citizens who abduct their children from the place of the child's habitual residence into Ireland was the subject of an interesting analysis by O'Donnell J in the recent case of *Nottinghamshire County Council v B* [2011] IESC 48. In this case, the Hague Convention was interpreted and enforced in accordance with its intention such that the place of the child's habitual residence is the most appropriate jurisdiction to determine the welfare and best interests of the child.

[662] *Saunders v Mid-Western Health Board*, Supreme Court judgment of 23 June 1987. For subsequent case law, see the Law Reform Commission, 'Aspects of Inter Country Adoption Law', Consultation Paper CP47-2007, at 59 ff; and the Law Reform Commission, 'Aspects of Inter-Country Adoption', Report 89-2008, at 52 ff.

4.342   The law in relation to residency rights of aliens who are married to an Irish citizen or whose children are born in Ireland, however, is distinctive, and the role of the rights in articles 41 and 42 are considered by the Supreme Court in a number of significant immigration cases.[663]

(5) Education law[664]

4.343   Commentators see the constitutional provisions on education as particularly demonstrative of the Irish Constitution's distinctive features. Gerry Whyte has argued that:

> The Constitution addresses the issue of education in two different Articles—Article 42 dealing with education generally and Article 44 dealing with religion. This arrangement is not without significance for the former Article is largely informed by Roman Catholic social teaching while the ideological ancestry of Article 44 lies in nineteenth century liberalism. Thus constitutional policy on education straddles an ideological fault line in the Irish Constitution.[665]

4.344   Article 42.1 of the Constitution provides an acknowledgement from the state that:

> … the primary and natural educator of the child is the Family and guarantees to respect the inalienable right and duty of parents to provide, according to their means, for the religious and moral, intellectual, physical and social education of their children.

4.345   The family therefore enjoys a protected status as the primary educator of the child, and such education includes religious education. Parents possess the constitutional right to decide the religion of their children and the state cannot interfere. The principle was explained by Murnaghan J in the Supreme Court decision in *Re Tilson, infants*.[666]

4.346   The Guardianship of Infants Act 1964, as amended, allows the court to make a custody order which secures the religious upbringing of the children. The High Court decided in *H v H*,[667] among other grounds, to grant custody of a two-year-old boy, baptised a Catholic, to the father and not the mother, who had formed an attachment with a Jewish man whom she proposed to marry, and intended to alter the child's religion accordingly. While the state cannot dictate the religion in which parents are to instruct their children, neither can anyone else.[668]

4.347   Article 42.3 provides that:

> 1° The State shall not oblige parents in violation of their conscience and lawful preference to send their children to schools established by the State, or to any particular type of school designated by the State.
>
> 2° The State shall, however, as guardian of the common good, require in view of actual conditions that the children receive a certain minimum education, moral, intellectual and social.[669]

---

[663] A useful starting point may be found in the following cases: *Fajujonu v Minister for Justice* [1990] 2 IR 151; *Osayande v Minister for Justice, Equality and Law Reform* [2003] 1 IR 1; *Oguekwe v Minister for Justice Equality and Law Reform* [2008] 3 IR 795, [2008] IESC 25; and *Okunade v Minister for Justice Equality and Law Reform & the Attorney General* [2012] IESC 49.

[664] On education law generally, see C O'Mahoney, *Educational Rights in Irish Law* (Thompson Round Hall, 2006); D Glendinning, *Religion, Education and the Law* (Tottell, 2008); and A Lodge and K Lynch, *Diversity at School* (Equality Authority, 2004).

[665] Paper to the TCD/IHRC Conference on Religion and Education: A Human Rights Perspective, held on 27 November 2010.

[666] *Re Tilson, infants* [1951] IR 1.

[667] *H v H* [1978] IR 138.

[668] See *Re Blake* [1955] IR 89.

[669] Art 42.3 of the Constitution.

The state is also required, by article 42.4 to provide free primary education, and it was **4.348**
held constitutional to provide this through a denominational education system in *Crowley*
v Ireland.[670] Constitutionally controlled secondary education was deemed constitutional
by Barrington and Keane JJ in *Campaign to Separate Church and State Ltd v Minister for*
Education.[671]

The Education Act 1998 provides for religious education and religious instruction. The **4.349**
board or management of schools should uphold 'the characteristic spirit of the school as
determined by the cultural, educational, moral, religious, social, linguistic and spiritual values and traditions which inform and are characteristic of the objectives and conduct of the
school'.[672]

The balancing act required of the board is indicated in that the board has a duty to have **4.350**
regard to 'the principles and requirements of a democratic society and have respect and
promote respect for the diversity of values, beliefs, traditions, languages and ways of life in
society'[673] and its admissions and participation policies, while reflecting its characteristic
spirit, must also respect constitutional rights, the policy principle of equality, and the right
of parents to send a child to a school of their choice, as well as any relevant Ministerial directions.[674] The school's admissions policy must provide maximum accessibility.[675]

Section 30 of the Education Act 1998 provides that the Minister may prescribe the subjects **4.351**
to be offered, the syllabus of each secular subject, and the amount of instruction time for each
subject, including the time to be spent on religious instruction, but not the content of religious
instruction. Although this section of the Act provides for a period of religious instruction in
recognized denominational schools, the content and supervision of such instruction falls to
the various religious authorities. The instruction is given by the teachers, who are employees
of the school boards who are in turn remunerated by the state. Section 30(4) confers considerable discretion on schools, provided they discharge their obligations to teach the full state
curriculum. The Minister is required to have regard to the characteristic spirit of a school.

In order to give effect to Article 44.2.4 of the Constitution, section 30(2)(e) of the 1998 Act **4.352**
provides that the Minister shall 'not require any student to attend instruction in any subject
which is contrary to the conscience of the parent of the student or, in the case of a student
who has reached the age of 18 years, the student'.

In *Campaign to Separate Church and State Ltd v Minister for Education*,[676] the Supreme Court **4.353**
considered article 44.2.4 and found in support of the proposition that the public funding
of denominational schools (by paying the wages of school chaplains) did not constitute an
endowment of religion contrary to article 44.2.2 of the Constitution.[677] Keane J said:

> [Article 44.2.4] makes it clear beyond argument, not merely that the State is entitled to pro-
> vide aid to schools under the management of different religious denominations, but that such

---

[670] *Crowley v Ireland* [1980] IR 102.
[671] *Campaign to Separate Church and State Ltd v Minister for Education* [1998] 2 ILRM 81.
[672] Education Act 1998, s 15(2)(b).
[673] Education Act 1998, s 15(2)(e).
[674] Education Act 1998, s 15(2)(d).
[675] Education Act 1998, s 9(m).
[676] *Campaign to Separate Church and State Ltd v Minister for Education* [1998] 3 IR 321, [1998] 2 ILRM 81.
[677] On the prohibition of religious endowment, see also *McGrath v Trustees of Maynooth College* [1979]
1 LRM 166.

schools may also include religious instruction as a subject in their curricula. It is subject to two qualifications; first, the legislation must not discriminate between schools under the management of different religious denominations and, secondly, it must respect the right of a child not to attend religious instruction in a school in receipt of public funds.[678]

4.354 Barrington J observed that while there exists a constitutional right for a child not to attend religious instruction at school, the 'Constitution cannot protect him from being influenced, to some degree, by the religious "ethos" of the school'.[679] Some commentators see this as having the practical effect of making it 'virtually impossible for some parents and children to fully exercise their rights with respect to religious freedom in education'.[680]

4.355 Every recognized school is required to publish its 'Admissions and Participation Policies' in accordance with section 15(2)(d) of the Education Act 1998. To date there has been no judicial interpretation of this provision although there have been referrals to the Equality Authority under the Equal Status Acts 2000 to 2011, which prohibit discrimination on eight substantive grounds, including that of religion. Section 7 of the Equal Status Act 2000 (as amended) provides that no school, whether or not supported by public funds, shall discriminate in relation to admission to, access to, or expulsion from such school, but may give preference to pupils of one religion over another in cases of over-subscription or, more generally, may refuse admission where to do so is necessary to uphold the ethos of the school.

4.356 The provisions of article 44.2.3, which prohibits discrimination by the state on the grounds of religious belief, have been held to be secondary to the right to freedom of religion,[681] and this principle may be seen in the field of education. Section 37 of the Employment Equality Act 1998 permits religious ethos schools (and section 12 permits vocational colleges) to discriminate on the ground of religion in the selection of staff. The Supreme Court upheld these provisions on a constitutional challenge in *Re Article 26 and the Employment Equality Bill 1996*,[682] stating that such provisions were permissible if they were necessary to give 'life and reality' to the constitutional guarantee of freedom of religion. In *Greally v Minister of Education*,[683] Geoghegan J upheld a recruitment scheme for teachers to state-funded Catholic secondary schools which gave preference to teachers who had taught for two years in that school or for three years in another Catholic school, saying that:

> It is true that by its express terms the Constitution only requires funding of primary education…But if the State in fact decides to fund secondary education by paying the salaries of teachers it cannot impose conditions to that funding which would effectively destroy the denominational nature of schools requiring such funding.[684]

4.357 There is no express right for teachers not to teach religious education on grounds of conscience. Speaking extra-judicially, Walsh J has said 'it is doubtful if any teacher can be

---

[678] *Campaign to Separate Church and State* (n 676) [1998] 3 IR 321, 360 and [1998] 2 ILRM 81, 84.

[679] *Campaign to Separate Church and State* (n 676) [1998] 3 IR 321, 358.

[680] C O'Mahony, 'Religious Education in Ireland' in D Davies and E Miroshnikova (eds), *Routledge International Handbook of Religious Education* (Routledge, 2012).

[681] *Quinn's Supermarket v Attorney General* [1972] IR 1.

[682] *Re Article 26* (n 624).

[683] *Greally v Minister of Education* [1999] 1 IR 1.

[684] *Greally* (n 683) 10–11.

permitted to refuse to teach [religion] simply because he or she does not believe it, as distinct from having a conscientious objection to teaching it'.[685]

In *Mulloy v Minister for Education*,[686] a scheme which gave salary credits to lay teachers who **4.358** served abroad and which denied the plaintiff, a teacher who was a Catholic priest and who had served abroad, was declared unconstitutional. Walsh J held that:

> The reference to religious status, in both the Irish text and the English text of the Constitution, relates clearly to the position or rank of a person in terms of religion in relation to others either of the same religion or of another religion or to those of no religion at all. Thus it ensures that, no matter what is one's religious profession or belief or status, the State shall not impose any disabilities upon or make any discrimination between persons because one happens to be a clergyman or a nun or a brother or a person holding rank or position in some religion which distinguishes him from other persons, whether or not they hold corresponding ranks in other religions or whether or not they profess any religion or have any religious belief, save where it is necessary to do so to implement the guarantee of freedom of religion and conscience already mentioned.[687]

(6) Employment and discrimination law[688]

Article 40 of the Constitution provides that 'All citizens shall, as human persons, be held **4.359** equal before the law' and article 42.2.3 provides that 'The State shall not impose any disabilities or make any discrimination on the ground of religious profession, belief or status'.[689] This provision was discussed earlier in the context of education.

The constitutional protections have in more recent years been augmented by the provisions **4.360** of the Employment Equality Acts 1998 to 2004 and the Equal Status Acts 2000 to 2004.

The Employment Equality Act 1998 prohibits discrimination in employment and voca- **4.361** tional training on the full grounds of anti-discrimination law common to other European jurisdictions, with some additions for the domestic situation (notably the express addition of Irish Travellers). Section 6(2) of the 1998 Act sets out the grounds, which are gender, marital status, family status, sexual orientation, religious belief, age, disability, race, or being a member of the Irish Traveller community. Religious belief is defined as including religious background or outlook.[690]

The Equal Status Act 2000, which deals with discrimination in the provision of goods and **4.362** services, defines the protected grounds in the same way. Religious belief is again defined to include religious background or outlook.[691]

Ireland, like other EU Member States, is bound to implement EU Directives, and the **4.363** Employment Equality Act 1998 and the Equal Status Act 2000 were amended by the Equality Act 2004 to ensure that they were fully compliant with the Framework Employment Equality Directive (Directive (EC) 2000/78).

---

[685] B Walsh, 'The Constitution and Constitutional Rights' in F Litton (ed), *The Constitution of Ireland 1937–1987* (Institute of Public Administration, 1988) 100.

[686] *Mulloy v Minister for Education* [1975] IR 88.

[687] *Mulloy* (n 686) 96–7.

[688] For an introduction to this subject, see B Daly and M Doherty, *Principles of Irish Employment Law* (Clarus Press, 2010).

[689] Article 44.3 of the Constitution.

[690] Employment Equality Act 1998, Pt II.

[691] Equal Status Act 2000, s 2.

4.364 Both Acts contain a range of exemptions in relation to religion which may be argued to be wider than the religious exemption in Article 4(2) of the Framework Directive.[692] Section 12(4) of the Employment Equality Act 1998 permits discrimination in vocational education:

> (4) For the purposes of ensuring the availability of nurses to hospitals and teachers to primary schools which are under the direction or control of a body established for religious purposes or whose objectives include the provision of services in an environment which promotes certain religious values, and in order to maintain the religious ethos of the hospitals or primary schools, the prohibition of discrimination in *subsection (1)*, in so far as it relates to discrimination on the religion ground, shall not apply in respect of—
>
> (*a*) the nomination of persons for admission to the School of Nursing… or
> (*b*) places in a vocational training course specified in an order made under *subsection (5)*.

4.365 Section 37 of the Employment Equality Act 1998 provides for a number of exemptions for genuine occupational qualification, and also that:

> (1) A religious, educational or medical institution which is under the direction or control of a body established for religious purposes or whose objectives include the provision of services in an environment which promotes certain religious values shall not be taken to discriminate against a person for the purposes of this Part or *Part II* if—
>
> (*a*) it gives more favourable treatment, on the religion ground, to an employee or a prospective employee over that person where it is reasonable to do so in order to maintain the religious ethos of the institution, or
> (*b*) it takes action which is reasonably necessary to prevent an employee or a prospective employee from undermining the religious ethos of the institution.

4.366 The constitutionality of this provision was unsuccessfully challenged in *Re Article 26 and the Employment Equality Bill 1996*.[693]

4.367 The Equal Status Act 2000 contains a number of exemptions on the ground of religion for goods and services provided 'for religious purpose',[694] the provision of accommodation or the disposal of premises which are reserved to a religious purpose,[695] and the provision of both vocational religious education and religious-ethos education in schools.[696] Section 8 provides an exception for clubs whose 'principal purpose' is to cater for persons of one particular, *inter alia*, religious belief.[697]

---

[692] The argument is made by Gerry Whyte in the Paper to the TCD/IHRC Conference on Religion and Education: A Human Rights Perspective, held on 27 November 2010. Art 4(2) provides that:

Member States may maintain national legislation in force at the date of adoption of this Directive or provide for future legislation incorporating national practices existing at the date of adoption of this Directive pursuant to which, in the case of occupational activities within churches and other public or private organisations the ethos of which is based on religion or belief, a difference of treatment based on a person's religion or belief shall not constitute discrimination where, by reason of the nature of these activities or of the context in which they are carried out, a person's religion or belief constitute a genuine, legitimate and justified occupational requirement, having regard to the organisation's ethos. This difference of treatment shall be implemented taking account of Member States' constitutional provisions and principles, as well as the general principles of Community law, and should not justify discrimination on another ground.

[693] *Re Article 26* (n 624).
[694] Equal Status Act 2000, s 5(2)(e).
[695] Equal Status Act 2000, s 6(5).
[696] Equal Status Act 2000, s 7(3)(b) and (3)(c).
[697] The provision relating to clubs was considered in detail by the Supreme Court in the context of gender-segregated golf clubs in *Equality Authority v Portmarnock Golf Club and ors* [2009] IESC 73.

The case of *McKeever v Board of Management of Knocktemple National School*[698] was one of the **4.368** first successful claims of religious discrimination under the Employment Equality Acts, but the matter has subsequently been considered by the courts in a number of notable cases.[699]

(7) Charity law

The Charities Act 2009 reformed the law relating to charities by ensuring greater account- **4.369** ability, transparency, and protection against the abuse of charitable status and fraud. The Act, together with the Charities Acts 1961 and 1973, provides for a composite regulatory framework for charities in Ireland.[700] The advancement of religion is one of the four stated charitable purposes in section 3 of the Act.

G. South Africa

Waheeda Amien[701]

(1) Introduction

Under colonialism and apartheid, Christianity was the favoured religion in South Africa. For **4.370** instance, education encompassed Christian principles; blasphemy included vilification of the Christian God; restraints on trade covered Christian days; and unions not conforming to Christian requisites for marriage were treated as uncivilized and invalid.[702] Essentially, norms not conforming to Christian ideals were marginalized.[703] So in addition to racially-based dis- crimination, apartheid also entrenched religious discrimination.[704] Since the introduction of democracy in 1994 and under the guidance of the post-apartheid Constitutions,[705] there is greater appreciation of South Africa's religious diversity. In particular, the judiciary is forging a more accommodative path in relation to religious rights.[706]

---

[698] *McKeever v Board of Management of Knocktemple National School* [2011] ELR 86.

[699] See *The Irish Prison Service v Fr Donal Morris*, Determination No EDA074, Labour Court 2007 (on the interpretation of what constitutes 'religious belief'); *Department of Defence v Barrett* EET081 (on the issue of humanism and whether it may constitute a religious belief for the purposes of the Acts); and *Hassan v Western Union Financial Services (Ireland) Ltd* DEC-S2006-004 (on direct discrimination).

[700] Legislative reform of charity law followed extensive legal research and consultation by the Law Reform Commission of Ireland, which produced a Consultation Paper and Report on charity law prior to the enact- ment of the Act of 2009: 'Report on Charitable Trusts and Legal Structures for Charities', LRC 80-2006. The Report is available at <http://www.lawreform.ie>.

[701] BA LLB (Cape Town), LLM (Western Cape), PhD (Ghent). Senior Lecturer in Law, University of Cape Town.

[702] *S v Lawrence, Negal, Solberg* 1997 (4) SA 1176 (CC), paras 123, 149–151; *Bronn v Frits Bronn's Executors and ors* 1860 3 Searle 313, 318, 320, 321, 333; *Seedat's Executors v The Master (Natal)* 1917 AD 302, 307–8; *Ismail v Ismail* 1983 (1) SA 1006 (AD) 1024D–F. For harms caused by non-recognition of Muslim marriages, see W Amien, 'A South African case study for the recognition and regulation of Muslim family law in a minority Muslim secular context' (2010) 24(3) International Journal of Law, Policy and the Family 361, 363.

[703] *Lawrence* (n 702) para 123.

[704] W Amien, 'Overcoming the conflict between the right to religious freedom and women's rights to equal- ity—a South African case study of Muslim marriages' (2006) 28 HRQ 729, 730.

[705] The 1993 Constitution was the interim Constitution. The 1996 Constitution is the final Constitution. The latter Constitution is currently applicable.

[706] South Africa has multitudes of religious communities of which the majority is Christian-based, compris- ing about 80% of the total population. Several minority religions make up the balance, consisting of Muslims

4.371 This contribution provides a synopsis of South Africa's jurisprudence on religious rights. Section 2 explains the relevant constitutional provisions. This is followed by section 3, which presents the Constitutional Court cases dealing with religious freedom. Section 4 offers a discussion of the main themes emerging from the case law. Finally, section 5 presents the conclusions. While there are lower court decisions dealing with religious freedom,[707] this contribution focuses on Constitutional Court decisions, since the jurisprudence on religious freedom has been developed mainly in that forum.

(2) Constitutional provisions

4.372 Religious freedom is defined as the right to have or not have beliefs, to pronounce those beliefs publicly without fear of retaliation, and to exhibit those beliefs through practice, worship, education, and propagation.[708] Religious beliefs and practices are afforded constitutional protection because they comprise core components of one's identity and are therefore important for the protection of human dignity, which is a key constitutional value.[709] Sections 15 and 31 are the main constitutional provisions that entrench the right to religious freedom.

4.373 Section 15 reads:

    (1) Everyone has the right to freedom of conscience, religion, thought, belief and opinion.

    (2) Religious observances may be conducted at state or state-aided institutions, provided that—

        (a) those observances follow rules made by the appropriate public authorities;

        (b) they are conducted on an equitable basis; and

        (c) attendance at them is free and voluntary.

    (3) (a) This section does not prevent legislation recognising—

            (i) marriages concluded under any tradition, or a system of religious, personal or family law; or

            (ii) systems of personal and family law under any tradition, or adhered to by persons professing a particular religion.

        (b) Recognition in terms of paragraph (a) must be consistent with this section and the other provisions of the Constitution.

4.374 Section 31 reads:

    (1) Persons belonging to a cultural, religious or linguistic community may not be denied the right, with other members of that community—

        (a) to enjoy their culture, practice their religion and use their language; and

---

(1.5%), African traditional beliefs (0.3%), Judaism (0.2%), Hinduism (1.2%), and other unidentified faiths (0.6%). See <http://www.statssa.gov.za/census01/html/RSAPrimary.pdf> (accessed 11 January 2011).

[707] *Worcester Muslim Jamaa v Valley and ors* [2002] JOL 9538 (C); *Antonie v Governing Body, the Settlers High School and ors* [2002] JOL 9663 (C); *Taylor v Kurtstag NO and ors* 2005 (1) SA 362 (W); *Department of Correctional Services and anor v POPCRU and ors* ('*Popcru*') [2012] 2 BLLR 110 (LAC)(S Afr).

[708] *S v Lawrence, Negal, Solberg* 1997 (4) SA 1176 (CC), paras 92, 94. The Court adopted this definition from the Canadian Supreme Court in *R v Big M Drug Mart Ltd* (1985) 18 DLR (4th) 321 (SCC) ('*Big M*'). The latter defines freedom of religion as 'the right to entertain such religious beliefs as a person chooses, the right to declare religious beliefs openly and without fear of hindrance or reprisal, and the right to manifest religious belief by worship and practice or by teaching and dissemination' (*Big M*, para 94).

[709] *Christian Education South Africa v Minister of Education* 2000 (4) SA 757 (CC), para 36; *Prince v President, Cape Law Society, and ors* 2002 (2) SA 794 (CC), para 49; *MEC for Education, KwaZulu-Natal, and ors v Pillay* 2008 (1) SA 474 (CC), para 62. N Smith, 'Freedom of Religion Under The Final Constitution' (1997) 114 South African Law Journal 217, 224–5.

(b) to form, join and maintain cultural, religious and linguistic associations and other organs of civil society.

(2) The rights in subsection (1) may not be exercised in a manner inconsistent with any provisions of the Bill of Rights.

Section 15(1) protects the individual right to religious freedom, which relates to personal **4.375** belief. Section 31(1) recognizes the collective nature of religious freedom by protecting the right of individuals to practice their religion collectively with other members of their religious community.[710] The section 31(1) right to practice religion and establish, join, and maintain religious associations is internally limited so that it cannot conflict with any other right in the Bill of Rights.[711] This internal limitation is a necessary addition because it can potentially prevent the privatization of harmful group practices.[712] Notably, the judiciary interprets the limitation as not permitting reliance on section 31(1) 'to shield practices which offend the Bill of Rights'.[713]

Section 18 entrenches a further collective right, namely, freedom of association. The latter **4.376** includes the right of individuals to practice their religion in association with others and the right of religious organizations to function independently within civil society.[714] Freedom of association also means that religious bodies can require those who join their organizations to comply with their rules and to choose which individuals may associate with them just as individuals can choose to associate with a religious organization.[715]

The judiciary recognizes the interrelatedness of the individual and collective components of **4.377** religious freedom and the complexity of that relationship:

> ... it is not easy to separate the individual religious conscience from the collective setting in which it is frequently expressed. Religious practice often involves interaction with fellow believers. It usually has both an individual and a collective dimension and is often articulated through activities that are traditional and structured, and frequently ritualistic and ceremonial.[716]

Since the particular interest protected by the individual's right to practice her religion **4.378** in community with others is based on respect for diversity,[717] the individual and collective aspects of religious freedom are important in achieving the constitutional aspiration of 'an open and democratic society based on human dignity, equality and freedom'.[718] Given South Africa's historical legacy of religious discrimination, protection of diversity

---

[710] *Christian Education* (n 709) para 20; *Prince* (n 709) paras 110, 143, 146; *Taylor* (n 707) para 38. C Heyns and D Brand, 'The Constitutional Protection of Religious Human Rights in Southern Africa' (2000) 14 Emory International Law Review 699, 748.

[711] Section 31(2) of the Constitution.

[712] *Christian Education* (n 709) para 26.

[713] *Christian Education* (n 709) para 26.

[714] *S v Lawrence, Negal, Solberg* 1997 (4) SA 1176 (CC), para 142; *Taylor v Kurtstag NO and ors* 2005 (1) SA 362 (W), paras 36–37. LWH Ackermann, 'Some reflections on the Constitutional Court's Freedom of Religion Jurisprudence' (2002) 43 (1–2) Dutch Reformed Theological Journal 177, 179.

[715] *Wittmann v Deutscher H Schulverein, Pretoria, and ors* 1998 (4) SA 423 (T), 451D; *Taylor* (n 714) para 37.

[716] *Christian Education South Africa v Minister of Education* 2000 (4) SA 757 (CC), para 19.

[717] *Christian Education* (n 716) paras 19–20, 23, 25. D Meyerson, 'Multiculturalism, Religion and Equality' (2001) Acta Juridica 104, 117.

[718] *Prince v President, Cape Law Society, and ors* 2002 (2) SA 794 (CC), para 114. Section 39(1)(a) of the Constitution reads: 'When interpreting the Bill of Rights, a court, tribunal or forum must promote the values that underlie an open and democratic society based on human dignity, equality and freedom.'

is key to an open and democratic society.[719] In fact, the judiciary adopts the view that mere tolerance of diversity is insufficient; diversity must be respected, celebrated, and promoted.[720]

4.379 Constitutional appreciation of diversity is also expressed through section 15(3)(a). The latter facilitates development of a legally pluralistic society by permitting the enactment of legislation to recognize, among others, religious marriages or systems of religious personal and family law. As with section 31(1), recognition of religious marriages or religious personal and family law systems is required, through section 15(3)(b), to be consistent with the provisions of the Bill of Rights and other provisions of the Constitution.

4.380 Additional constitutional provisions relating to religious freedom include: section 9(3), which identifies religion as a ground for unfair discrimination;[721] section 9(1), which guarantees equal treatment of different religions;[722] section 16(2)(c), which through freedom of expression prohibits the promotion of hatred on religious grounds; section 35(2) (f)(iii), which affords detained and imprisoned persons the right to interact with their religious counsellors; and section 235, which does not preclude religious communities from claiming a right of self-determination.[723] Provision is further made for the establishment of a Commission for the Promotion and Protection of the Rights of Cultural, Religious and Linguistic Communities to strengthen constitutional democracy, and a Pan South African Language Board to promote respect for languages used for, among others, religious purposes.[724] In the case of official oath-taking, the Constitution gives the oath-taker the option of taking the oath in the name of God.[725] Reference to 'God' also appears in the Preamble.[726]

4.381 The protection of religious freedom encompassed in the array of provisions to which reference has just been made, indicates a constitutional acknowledgement that religion plays a valuable role in peoples' lives.[727] When interpreting those rights, the judiciary must promote the values that underlie an open and democratic society based on human dignity, equality, and freedom.[728] In the cases discussed in the next section, the judiciary has endeavoured to frame its developing jurisprudence on religious freedom by keeping the values of human dignity, equality, and freedom foremost in mind.

---

[719] *Christian Education* (n 716) para 23; *Prince* (n 718) para 49.

[720] *MEC for Education, KwaZulu-Natal, and ors v Pillay* 2008 (1) SA 474 (CC), para 65.

[721] Section 9(3) of the Constitution reads: 'The state may not unfairly discriminate directly or indirectly against anyone on one or more grounds, including...religion.'

[722] Section 9(1) of the Constitution reads: 'Everyone is equal before the law and has the right to equal protection and benefit of the law.' L Du Plessis, 'Religious freedom and equality as celebration of difference: A significant development in recent South African constitutional case-law' (2009) (12)4 Potchefstroom Electronic Law Journal 10, 12.

[723] J Van der Vyver, 'Constitutional Perspective of Church-State Relations in South Africa' (1999) Brigham Young University Law Review (1999) 635, 647.

[724] Sections 6(5)(b)(ii) and 181(1)(c) of the Constitution. *S v Lawrence, Negal, Solberg* 1997 (4) SA 1176 (CC), para 144; *Christian Education South Africa v Minister of Education* 2000 (4) SA 757 (CC), para 23. C Rautenbach, N Goolam, and N Moosa, 'Constitutional Analysis' in (eds) JC Bekker, C Rautenbach and NMI Goolam (eds), *Introduction to Legal Pluralism in South Africa* (Lexis Nexis/Butterworths, 2006) 149, 152.

[725] Sch 2 of the Constitution.

[726] The Preamble concludes with the words 'May God protect our people' and 'God bless South Africa'.

[727] *S v Lawrence, Negal, Solberg* 1997 (4) SA 1176 (CC), para 116.

[728] Section 39(1)(a) of the Constitution.

(3) Jurisprudence

Four cases have been adjudicated in the Constitutional Court that deal with religious free- **4.382**
dom, namely, *S v Lawrence, Negal, Solberg* ('*Lawrence*');[729] *Christian Education South Africa*
v Minister of Education ('*Christian Education*');[730] *Prince v President, Cape Law Society and*
ors ('*Prince*');[731] and *MEC for Education, KwaZulu-Natal, and ors v Pillay* ('*Pillay*').[732] The
following paragraphs present the facts, decisions, and reasoning of these cases, followed in
section 4 by a discussion of the main themes emerging from the case law.

a) S v Lawrence, Negal, Solberg

Lawrence is the first case where the Constitutional Court dealt with, *inter alia*, the right to **4.383**
religious freedom. Solberg (appellant) was an employee of a Seven Eleven franchise. She was
convicted of contravening section 2 of the Liquor Act 27 of 1989 under which it is an offence
for grocers to sell liquor on closed days, which include Sundays, Good Friday, and Christmas
Day.[733] Although Solberg did not indicate that she adhered to any particular religion, she
contended that the prohibition infringed her right to religious freedom because its purpose
is to coerce observance of the Christian Sabbath and Christian holidays.[734]

Since Solberg's conviction related to trading in liquor on Sundays, the majority of the Court **4.384**
(*per* Chaskalson P) confined its assessment to Sunday as a closed day.[735] The Court decided
that there was no infringement of religious freedom because the effects of the Liquor Act do
not coerce people to act or prevent people from acting in a manner contrary to their religious
beliefs.[736] The Court also viewed Sundays as having acquired secular and religious underpin-
nings, where many South Africans treat Sundays as convenient days of rest, not just out of a
desire to observe the Christian Sabbath.[737]

Sachs J (with Mokgoro J concurring), in his minority judgment, disagreed with the idea **4.385**
that there is no infringement. He thought it important to consider the impact of all the
closed days on religious freedom, which he viewed as state endorsement of Christianity.[738]
However, he held that the infringement is justifiable, thereby concurring with the majority
that the legislation is constitutional.[739] In coming to this conclusion, Sachs viewed all three
closed days as having become secularized as days of common rest.[740] He also regarded the
link between alcohol consumption and violence, deaths resulting from drunken driving,
and economic disempowerment as strong factors for justifying the choice of closed days.
Moreover, he was perturbed by the fact that the appellant's claim was not based in any religious belief.[741]

---

[729] *Lawrence* (n 727).
[730] *Christian Education South Africa v Minister of Education* 2000 (4) SA 757 (CC).
[731] *Prince v President, Cape Law Society, and ors* 2002 (2) SA 794 (CC).
[732] *MEC for Education, KwaZulu-Natal, and ors v Pillay* 2008 (1) SA 474 (CC).
[733] *S v Lawrence, Negal, Solberg* 1997 (4) SA 1176 (CC) paras 1, 2.
[734] *Lawrence* (n 733) para 85.
[735] *Lawrence* (n 733) para 91.
[736] *Lawrence* (n 733) paras 90, 94, 97, 105. Sachs J departed from the majority by not expecting coercion to
be proven before religious freedom is infringed (para 179).
[737] *Lawrence* (n 733) para 95.
[738] *Lawrence* (n 733) paras 160, 163, 178.
[739] *Lawrence* (n 733) paras 172–178.
[740] *Lawrence* (n 733) paras 172–175.
[741] *Lawrence* (n 733) paras 140, 175.

4.386   While the reasons identified by Sachs to limit sales of alcohol on specific days are valid, his overall reasoning that the infringement of religious freedom is justifiable is problematic. Sachs admitted that at weekends, drinking usually starts on Friday night and continues until Sunday. The same reasoning applies to Christmas Day. Goodwill Day and New Year's Day follow Christmas Day, so any drinking that happens on Christmas Day does not end on Goodwill Day and New Year's Day. Similarly, any drinking that happens over the Easter weekend does not stop when Good Friday ends. It continues until Family Day, which is the Monday that follows Easter Sunday.[742] So why not make all those public holidays closed days too? The only reason for their exclusion from the list of closed days must be because Christian norms are favoured above other norms. This is precisely the conclusion that O'Regan J reached in her dissenting judgment when she held that the infringement is unjustifiable.[743] In fact, she found that the preference for Christian norms in the identification of closed days is the primary purpose of the legislation.[744] In her view, inequitable state endorsement of religion results in direct or indirect coercion of religious beliefs or practices, which is constitutionally proscribed.[745]

4.387   The *Lawrence* judgment laid an important foundation for the development of the Court's jurisprudence on religious freedom, which was followed three years later by the *Christian Education* case.

b)   Christian Education

4.388   In *Christian Education*, the appellant was a voluntary association that represented 196 independent Christian schools in South Africa, which strove to maintain an active Christian ethos in the schools. This included the use of corporal punishment, which they claimed is an integral part of the Christian belief system and which they had delegated to the school's teachers to impose on their children.[746] The appellant challenged section 10 of the Schools Act 84 of 1996, which prohibits corporal punishment against learners in schools on the basis that it infringes their individual and communal rights to freely practice their religion.[747]

4.389   A unanimous Court (*per* Sachs J) denied their appeal and found that the section justifiably infringes sections 15 and 31 of the Constitution.[748] In reaching his decision, Sachs considered the historical context of South Africa in which the use of force against youths protesting against apartheid was particularly pernicious and South Africa's current context where child abuse is rampant.[749] Sachs viewed the state ban on corporal punishment in schools as a measure to break from South Africa's totalitarian past, to promote the principle that problems should be solved through processes of reason rather than force, to introduce an alternative paradigm to dealing with challenges of discipline, and to garner respect for the dignity of children.[750]

---

[742] *Lawrence* (n 733) paras 175–177.

[743] *Lawrence* (n 733) paras 125, 132.

[744] *Lawrence* (n 733) para 132.

[745] *Lawrence* (n 733) para 123.

[746] *Christian Education South Africa v Minister of Education* 2000 (4) SA 757 (CC), paras 2, 5.

[747] Section 10 of the Constitution reads: '(1) No person may administer corporal punishment at a school to a learner. (2) Any person who contravenes ss (1) is guilty of an offence and liable on conviction to a sentence which could be imposed for assault.' (*Christian Education* (n 746) paras 2, 7).

[748] *Christian Education* (n 746) para 52.

[749] *Christian Education* (n 746) para 49.

[750] *Christian Education* (n 746) paras 41, 50.

Sachs also spent a great deal of time discussing the limitability of religious freedom. He high- **4.390** lighted section 36 as a general limitation on religious freedom.[751] An application of section 36 entails a balancing exercise to determine whether or not the limitation is reasonable and justifiable in an open and democratic society based on human dignity, freedom, and equality.[752] The balancing exercise is context-driven, nuanced, and is employed on a case-by-case basis.[753] It involves a consideration of the nature and importance of the right; the extent to which the right is limited; the purpose, importance, and effect of the legislation; and the availability of less restrictive means to achieve the legislative purpose.[754] Through his analysis of section 36 in the context of religious beliefs and practices, Sachs introduced the principle of reasonable accommodation, which is implicit in the balancing exercise.[755] In the form of reasonable accommodation, the balance lies in the expectation that citizens are bound by certain basic norms so that religious adherents 'cannot claim an automatic right to be exempted by their beliefs from the laws of the land', while the state simultaneously should not, wherever reasonably possible, put 'believers to extremely painful and intensely burdensome choices of either being true to their faith or else respectful of the law'.[756]

Two years later, the Court again had occasion to consider a challenge to religious freedom **4.391** in the *Prince* matter. This time, pragmatism rather than a principled approach informed the Court's decision.

c) Prince

The appellant, Gareth Prince, was a law graduate who applied to the Cape Law Society **4.392** to have his articles of clerkship registered, without which he could not be admitted as an attorney. The Law Society refused his application claiming that he was not a fit and proper person because he had two convictions for the possession and use of cannabis and he had indicated that he would continue to break the law by continuing to use it. The possession and use of cannabis is prohibited by section 4(b) of the Drugs and Drug Trafficking Act 140 of 1992 and section 22A(10) of the Medicines and Related Substances Control Act 101 of 1965. The legislation permits an exception for cannabis to be used for medicinal, analytical, or research purposes.[757] The appellant did not dispute that the legislation serves a legitimate

---

[751] Section 36 of the Constitution reads:

    (1) The rights in the Bill of Rights may be limited only in terms of law of general application to the extent that the limitation is reasonable and justifiable in an open and democratic society based on human dignity, equality and freedom, taking into account all relevant factors, including
        (a) the nature of the right;
        (b) the importance of the purpose of the limitation;
        (c) the nature and extent of the limitation;
        (d) the relation between the limitation and its purpose; and
        (e) less restrictive means to achieve the purpose.
    (2) Except as provided in subsection (1) or in any other provision of the Constitution, no law may limit any right entrenched in the Bill of Rights.

[752] *Christian Education South Africa v Minister of Education* 2000 (4) SA 757 (CC), para 32.
[753] *Christian Education* (n 752) para 30. See also *Prince v President, Cape Law Society, and ors* 2002 (2) SA 794 (CC), para 155.
[754] *Christian Education* (n 752) para 31.
[755] In *Prince* (n 753) para 76, the Court stated that the balancing exercise 'requires a degree of reasonable accommodation from all concerned'.
[756] *Prince* (n 753) para 35. In the context of culture, this approach is formulated as 'either your culture or your rights'. A Shachar, *Multicultural Jurisdictions. Cultural Differences and Women's Rights* (CUP, 2001) 3, 25–32.
[757] *Prince* (n 753) paras 1, 22, 51.

governmental purpose in the war against drugs, which seeks to clamp down on trafficking in dependence-producing drugs and prevent harm caused by the abuse of those drugs.[758] However, as a Rastafarian, he claimed that the laws were overbroad and challenged them on the basis that a failure to provide an exemption for the use of cannabis for religious purposes infringed religious freedom.[759] Nine judges, making up the majority of the Court, agreed that the legislation infringed religious freedom.[760] With an almost equal split among them as to whether or not the infringement was justifiably limited, Chaskalson CJ, Ackermann J and Kriegler J (on behalf of five judges) held that the infringement was justified, while Ngcobo J (on behalf of four judges) decided that it was not.[761]

4.393   Chaskalson et al viewed the appellant's contention that the legislation was overbroad as an argument that the government should employ less restrictive means to achieve the legislative aims.[762] However, they felt that if an exemption were permitted, it would be almost impossible for the state to police by distinguishing between recreational and religious use of cannabis.[763] In contrast, Ngcobo reasoned that since there was already infrastructure in place to regulate the exemption against dependence-producing drugs on the basis of medical and other reasons, it would not be a substantial burden to require the government to apply its mind to an exemption for the use of cannabis by Rastafarians.[764] In fact, Sachs J, in a separate judgment, offered a useful balancing approach, namely, a '*continuum*' that ranges from 'easily controllable and manifestly religious use' of cannabis to 'difficult-to-police utilisation that is barely distinguishable from recreational use'. Based on Sach's continuum, cannabis that is used on public religious occasions would be exempted while the use of cannabis in the privacy of a home would not.[765]

4.394   The Court observed that Rastafarians use cannabis in various ways, such as smoking it, burning it as incense, bathing in it, eating it, and drinking it.[766] Ngcobo's position was that not all forms of consuming cannabis present a risk of harm, such as burning it as incense or bathing in it. There was also evidence summarized by the Court suggesting that if limited amounts of cannabis were smoked, it was not harmful.[767] Ngcobo therefore found that a blanket prohibition against the use of cannabis would not achieve the legislative objectives.[768] Instead, by not distinguishing between Rastafarians who use cannabis for religious purposes and drug abusers, the prohibition against cannabis effectively stigmatizes all Rastafarians as criminals, thereby increasing their marginalization as a minority religious community.[769] The degradation they consequently suffer 'strikes at the very core of their human dignity . . . [and] says that their religion is not worthy of protection'.[770] In the context of this case, the appellant suffered the additional burden of being prevented from practising his chosen career.[771]

---

[758] *Prince* (n 753) paras 52, 113–114.
[759] *Prince* (n 753) paras 35, 91–94.
[760] *Prince* (n 753) paras 44, 111.
[761] *Prince* (n 753) paras 81, 111.
[762] *Prince* (n 753) para 114.
[763] *Prince* (n 753) para 142.
[764] *Prince* (n 753) paras 69–70.
[765] *Prince* (n 753) para 148.
[766] *Prince* (n 753) paras 28, 55.
[767] *Prince* (n 753) para 74.
[768] *Prince* (n 753) paras 58–62.
[769] *Prince* (n 753) para 51. The Court noted that there are only about 12,000 Rastafaris in South Africa (para 15).
[770] *Prince* (n 753) para 51.
[771] *Prince* (n 753) para 51.

The pragmatic approach adopted by the majority of the Court left all uses of cannabis **4.395** prohibited.

d) *Pillay*

Unlike previous cases where the issue of religion arose in the context of religious freedom, **4.396** in *Pillay*, it was framed within an equality claim. Sunali Pillay was a learner at Durban Girls High School, which is a partially state-funded school.[772] In 2004, she began wearing a nose stud as an expression of her South Indian Tamil Hindu culture.[773] This contravened the school's code of conduct, which permitted learners to wear only ear studs or sleepers and a wristwatch.[774]

Sunali's mother, Navaneethum Pillay (respondent), launched an equality challenge on **4.397** Sunali's behalf. She claimed that the school's code of conduct contravened section 6 of the Promotion of Equality and Prevention of Unfair Discrimination Act 4 of 2000 ('Equality Act') by unfairly discriminating against her daughter on the basis of religion and culture.[775] The respondent explained that according to South Indian Tamil Hindu culture, when females reach puberty, they should wear a nose stud at all times to indicate that they are responsible young adults of marriageable age.[776]

A Hindu expert testified that the practice is an expression of Hindu culture, and that it is **4.398** neither religious nor obligatory.[777] However, he admitted that it is difficult to distinguish between Hindu culture and Hindu religion.[778] Although Sunali did not testify, the majority of the Court (*per* Langa CJ), comprising 10 out of 11 judges, accepted the respondent's evidence that Sunali approached the practice as an expression of both her religious and cultural convictions.[779] Langa noted that while religion and culture are viewed as distinct concepts, they are sometimes interlinked, as he found them to be in this case:

> …religion is ordinarily concerned with personal faith and belief, while culture generally relates to traditions and beliefs developed by a community. However, there will often be a great deal of overlap between the two; religious practices are frequently informed not only by faith but also by custom, while cultural beliefs do not develop in a vacuum and may be based on the community's underlying religious or spiritual beliefs. Therefore, while it is possible for a belief or practice to be purely religious or purely cultural, it is equally possible for it to be both religious and cultural.[780]

The Court viewed the school's refusal to permit Sunali to wear her nose stud as a message **4.399** that her religion and culture were unwelcome, thereby marginalizing her.[781] In contrast, if

---

[772] *MEC for Education, KwaZulu-Natal, and ors v Pillay* 2008 (1) SA 474 (CC), para 4.

[773] *Pillay* (n 772) paras 5, 60.

[774] *Pillay* (n 772) para 5.

[775] *Pillay* (n 772) paras 9, 135–136. Discrimination must be unfair before it contravenes the Equality Act. Section 6 provides: 'Neither the State nor any person may unfairly discriminate against any person.' Section 1(1)(viii) defines discrimination as meaning 'any act or omission, including a policy, law, rule, practice, condition or situation which directly or indirectly— (a) imposes burdens, obligations or disadvantage on; or (b) withholds benefits, opportunities or advantages from, any person on one or more of the prohibited grounds'. Religion and culture are included as grounds for unfair discrimination (s 1(1)(xxii)(a)). Section 14 provides guidance for determining unfairness.

[776] *Pillay* (n 772) paras 7, 11, 60, 85.

[777] *Pillay* (n 772) para 13.

[778] *Pillay* (n 772) para 13.

[779] *Pillay* (n 772) para 58.

[780] *Pillay* (n 772) para 47.

[781] *Pillay* (n 772) paras 85, 90, 112.

an exemption were granted on religious or cultural grounds, Langa suggested that it would provide a learning environment that would function as a microcosm of South Africa where different religions and cultures coexist.[782] This would ensure that learners' education in practice encompasses values of diversity, freedom, dignity, and equality.[783] Despite the school's fear that an exemption for wearing a nose stud might result in other contraventions of the code, such as wearing of dreadlocks, etc, Langa considered such an outcome as positive. He thought it would encourage learners to publicly express their cultures and religions, which is a step in the right direction to achieving a society that promotes respect and appreciation for diversity.[784]

4.400 Langa found that failure to reasonably accommodate Sunali's sincerely held religious and cultural beliefs, which were compromised by the school's code, resulted in her being treated differently from learners whose sincerely held religious and cultural beliefs were not compromised by the code.[785] Langa accordingly decided that Sunali had been unfairly discriminated against on the basis of religion and culture.[786]

(4) Main principles emerging from the case law

4.401 This section draws attention to several themes arising from the case law on religious freedom, some of which have been alluded to previously and some that have not been explicitly mentioned. The themes that have been introduced in the preceding sections include the core components of religious freedom and the relationship between religious freedom, equality, diversity, and human dignity. The remaining themes that are not as obvious from the earlier sections, relate to the link between religious freedom, judicial engagement with religious doctrine, and secularism.

a) Core components of religious freedom

4.402 The elements identifiable from the case law as crucial for successful reliance on the right to religious freedom are eloquently summarized by Sachs J:

> [The freedom of religion clause] was intended at least to uphold the following principles and values: South Africa is an open and democratic society with a non-sectarian state that guarantees freedom of worship; is respectful of and accommodatory towards, rather than hostile to or walled-off from religion; acknowledges the multi-faith and multi-belief nature of the country; does not favour one religious creed or doctrinal truth above another; accepts the intensely personal nature of individual conscience and affirms the intrinsically voluntary and non-coerced character of belief; respects the rights of non-believers; and does not impose orthodoxies of thought or require conformity of conduct in terms of any particular world view. The Constitution, then, is very much about the acknowledgement by the state of different belief systems and their accommodation within a non-hierarchical framework of equality and non-discrimination. It follows that the state does not take sides on questions of religion. It does not impose belief, grant privileges to or impose disadvantages on adherents of any particular belief, requires conformity in matters simply of belief, involve itself in purely religious controversies, or marginalize people who have different beliefs.[787]

---

[782] *Pillay* (n 772) para 102.
[783] *Pillay* (n 772) para 104.
[784] *Pillay* (n 772) para 109.
[785] *Pillay* (n 772) paras 44, 79, 115.
[786] *Pillay* (n 772) para 68. Although O'Regan J in her minority judgment agreed that Sunali had been unfairly discriminated against, she thought the practice was only cultural and therefore identified culture as the ground of unfair discrimination (paras 162, 166).
[787] *S v Lawrence, Negal, Solberg* 1997 (4) SA 1176 (CC), para 148.

The first core component of religious freedom is thus that the belief or practice must be **4.403** based in a religion.[788] The Constitutional Court does not, however, provide guidelines to determine what would constitute a religion that is constitutionally protected. Secondly, the protection of religious freedom is of particular significance to marginalized religious minorities, which are not part of the mainstream religious communities.[789] Thirdly, only sincerely held religious beliefs or practices are constitutionally protected regardless of whether they are irrational or shared by anyone else.[790] This involves a subjective inquiry into the sincerity of the claimant's beliefs or practices. Fourthly, if it is unclear whether or not a belief or practice forms part of a religion, the judiciary must not pronounce on the issue unless the dispute relates to how central the belief or practice is to the religion.[791] To do otherwise requires a court to substitute its own understanding of a religious belief or practice for that of the claimant.[792] A subjective inquiry must also be undertaken to determine whether or not a religious belief or practice forms a central tenet of the religion. The inquiry involves a consideration of how important the belief or practice is to the claimant's religious identity.[793] An objective inquiry can also be applied provided it supplements the subjective inquiry.[794] Van der Schyff argues that reliance on a subjective inquiry to determine the centrality of a belief or practice indicates that religious autonomy is a fundamental feature of religious freedom.[795] But whose religious autonomy would that be: the individual's understanding of her religion; the understanding of religious leaders; or the general belief and practice systems of the religious community? The Constitutional Court favours the subjective position of the individual, which is problematic because it ignores the reality that religious beliefs and practices are grounded in communal contexts.[796] A more appropriate approach would be to apply an objective inquiry to ascertain if the belief or practice is a central tenet of the religion followed by a subjective inquiry to establish if the claimant sincerely adheres to that belief or practice. The objective inquiry should verify that the belief or practice is reasonably justifiable within the religion and the subjective inquiry should ensure that the claimant accepts the belief or practice as a religious tenet. Where varying interpretations exist, the court should recognize the interpretation that is religiously justifiable and sincerely held by the claimant within the context of the case. If varying interpretations are religiously justifiable, the court should accept the one that most accords with the provisions of the Constitution, including gender equality.

The fifth core component is that religious freedom protects both obligatory and volun- **4.404** tary religious beliefs or practices.[797] Sixthly, the principle of non-coercion informs religious freedom. This means that the state may not compel people into acting or constrain people

---

[788] HMThD ten Napel and FHK Theissen, 'The Judicial Protection of Religious Symbols in Europe's Public Educational Institutions: Thank God for Canada and South Africa' (2011) 8(1) Muslim World Journal of Human Rights 1, 19.

[789] *Prince v President, Cape Law Society, and ors* 2002 (2) SA 794 (CC), paras 112, 160.

[790] *MEC for Education, KwaZulu-Natal, and ors v Pillay* 2008 (1) SA 474 (CC), para 146.

[791] *Prince* (note 789) paras 42, 75. G Van der Schyff, 'Freedom of Religious Autonomy as an Element of the Right to Freedom of Religion' (2003) 3 TSAR 512, 524.

[792] *Pillay* (n 790) para 87.

[793] *Pillay* (n 790) para 88.

[794] *Pillay* (n 790) para 88.

[795] Van der Schyff (n 791) 538. Napel and Theissen also think this approach reflects the Court's respect for religious diversity. Napel and Theissen (n 788) 21.

[796] IT Benson, 'The case for religious inclusivism and the judicial recognition of religious associational rights: A response to Lenta' (2008) 1 Constitutional Court Review 297, 308–10.

[797] *MEC for Education, KwaZulu-Natal, and ors v Pillay* 2008 (1) SA 474 (CC), paras 61, 65–66.

from acting in a manner that is contrary to their religious beliefs.[798] Thus, the 'free exercise of religion' forms part of the right to religious freedom, whereby religious adherents are allowed to practice their beliefs free from state coercion.[799] In contrast, the right to religious freedom does not contain an 'establishment clause', which prevents state establishment of religion and prohibits the state from promoting, funding, or inhibiting religion.[800] In South Africa, religious freedom does not preclude the state from subsidizing independent religious educational institutions and permitting religious observances from being conducted at state institutions.[801] Yet, the right to religious freedom would be infringed if the state were to promote and support religion in a coercive manner.[802]

4.405   Where the state promotes and supports religion, the seventh core component of religious freedom requires that it must do so equitably. Thus, state endorsement of one religion over another is prohibited.[803] In the light of South Africa's tyrannical history, which did not respect the multiplicity of religions in the country and marginalized those who adhered to anything other than Christianity, it is not surprising that the Constitution, as a transformative document, requires that all religions be treated equally.[804] As Sachs wrote, the effect of state endorsement of a particular religion 'divides the nation into insiders who belong, and outsiders who are tolerated [which] is impermissible in the multi-faith, heterodox society contemplated by our Constitution'.[805] The requirement for equal treatment of religions therefore necessarily involves acceptance of religious diversity. This is critical for the achievement of an open and democratic society based on human dignity, equality, and freedom.[806] In particular, religious freedom is integrally linked to an appreciation of the importance of diversity where the 'right to be different' is 'the most treasured aspect of [South Africa's]...constitutional order'.[807] The preferred approach is to afford maximum protection to religious freedom; but since it is not an absolute right,[808] where substantial competing interests exist, religious freedom can be limited. In that case, the employment of a balancing exercise must involve 'maximum harmonisation of all the competing considerations...without losing sight of the

---

[798] *S v Lawrence, Negal, Solberg* 1997 (4) SA 1176 (CC), paras 92, 104; *Christian Education South Africa v Minister of Education* 2000 (4) SA 757 (CC), para 19. P Fourie, 'The SA Constitution and Religious Freedom: Perverter or Preserver of Religion's Contribution to the Public Debate on Morality?' (2003) 82 Scriptura: International Journal of Bible, Religion and Theology in Southern Africa 94, 101.

[799] *Lawrence* (n 798) para 100. The Court referred to the 'free exercise' and 'establishment' clauses in the First Amendment of the US Constitution, which reads: 'Congress shall make no law respecting an establishment of religion, or prohibiting the free exercise thereof.' Meyerson (n 717) 109.

[800] *Lawrence* (n 798) paras 99–101, 116, 118. Van der Vyver (n 723) 653, 655–6.

[801] Section 29(3)–(4) of the Constitution reads: '(3) Everyone has the right to establish and maintain, at their own expense, independent educational institutions...(4) Subsection (3) does not preclude state subsidies for independent educational institutions.' Section 15(2) of the Constitution reads: 'Religious observances may be conducted at state or state-aided institutions, provided that—those observances follow rules made by the appropriate public authorities; they are conducted on an equitable basis; and attendance at them is free and voluntary.' *Lawrence* (n 798) para 143. Heyns and Brand (n 710) 748, 762–3.

[802] *Lawrence* (n 798) paras 89, 120.

[803] *Lawrence* (n 798) paras 121–123, 128. Van der Vyver (n 723) 656.

[804] *Lawrence* (n 798) para 123; *Pillay* (n 797) para 147.

[805] *Lawrence* (n 798) para 179.

[806] *Lawrence* (n 798) paras 145–146, 148. Section 36(1) of the Constitution. See also *Christian Education South Africa v Minister of Education* 2000 (4) SA 757 (CC), para 23.

[807] *Christian Education* (n 806) para 24; *Prince v President, Cape Law Society, and ors* 2002 (2) SA 794 (CC), para 170; *Pillay* (n 797) para 92.

[808] *Christian Education* (n 806) para 41.

ultimate values highlighted by our Constitution'.[809] So where possible, religious freedom must be reasonably accommodated.[810]

Reasonable accommodation is the eighth core component of religious freedom. In the context of unfair discrimination on the ground of religion, it is applicable in two instances: when a neutral rule or practice marginalizes certain sections of society; and in localized contexts, such as schools, where a reasonable balance between conflicting interests may more easily be achieved.[811] In these instances, schools can be expected to incur hardships to accommodate diversity so that everyone can enjoy all their rights equally.[812] This would ensure that marginalized sections of society that cannot conform to certain social norms would still be able to function with their dignity intact.[813]

4.406

Where the right to religious freedom is at issue, reasonable accommodation involves balancing religious freedom with a compelling interest served by the law and the means used to achieve a legitimate purpose of the law.[814] So the judiciary will always check to see if less restrictive means could be employed to achieve a legislative aim. The main difficulty in trying to balance religious rights with most other rights is that they usually represent differing interests, which emanate from different paradigms.[815] For instance, the Constitutional Court suggests that religious adherence derives from faith, while public or private concerns are usually assessed on reasonableness.[816] Yet, religion is an integral part of people's existence and therefore it weaves its way into the public aspect of their lives. This is where the balancing act becomes tricky because, in the Court's view, trying to weigh faith against reason or separate the religious from the secular is not always possible.[817] The Court further recognizes that there is a fine and somewhat artificial line between public and private domains, so the normative question is how far a democracy should permit its religious communities to decide which laws they are prepared to obey and which not.[818] As mentioned previously, the balance lies in the expectation that individuals should not be put to the onerous test of having to choose between their religion and the law. At the same time, harmful religious practices cannot be protected under the auspices of religious freedom.[819] Since an application of this approach depends on the facts of each situation, the outcome of cases involving a conflict between religious freedom and laws will depend on the circumstances of those cases.

4.407

b) Religious freedom, equality, diversity, and human dignity

Although the relationship between religious freedom, equality, diversity, and human dignity has been alluded to throughout this contribution, this section attempts to describe the connection more succinctly. In South Africa, the inseparable link between protecting religious freedom, promoting equality among different religions, celebrating religious diversity, and

4.408

---

[809] *Prince* (n 807) para 155.
[810] *Prince* (n 807) para 76.
[811] *Prince* (n 807) para 78.
[812] *Prince* (n 807) paras 73, 75.
[813] *Prince* (n 807) paras 73, 75.
[814] *Department of Correctional Services and anor v POPCRU and ors* ('*Popcru*') [2012] 2 BLLR 110 (LAC) (S Afr), para 43.
[815] *Christian Education South Africa v Minister of Education* 2000 (4) SA 757 (CC), para 33.
[816] *Christian Education* (n 815) para 33.
[817] *Christian Education* (n 815) paras 34, 36.
[818] *Christian Education* (n 815) para 35.
[819] *Christian Education* (n 815) para 35.

maintaining human dignity does not imply an attempt to eradicate religious differences.[820] Instead, revelling in our religious diversity is symbolic of the South African struggle to defeat apartheid. Although it has been just under 20 years since apartheid was formally dismantled, this is not nearly a long enough time for its discriminatory effects to have been appropriately remedied. Religious freedom cannot therefore be addressed without considering the country's historical context, which was riddled with numerous forms of discrimination, including the religious type. This is why one of the determining factors for an infringement of the right to religious freedom is whether or not the claimant is located within a historically marginalized religious community. As Sachs observes:

> Religious marginalisation in the past coincided strongly in our country with racial discrimination, social exclusion and political disempowerment... Thus, any endorsement by the State today of Christianity as a privileged religion not only disturbs the general principle of impartiality in relation to matters of belief and opinion, but also serves to activate memories of painful past discrimination and disadvantage based on religious affiliation... [The] [p]ainful history in our country... reminds us that the values underlying [our freedom of religion clause] can never be taken for granted, and must always be jealously guarded.[821]

4.409 To deal with the effects of religious marginalization and to ensure that it is not repeated, it is important to value religious diversity and encourage an appreciation of it because it is one guarantee for a free society.[822] Promoting respect for religious diversity is achievable by aiming to prevent religious discrimination and ensuring that all religions are afforded equal treatment.[823] In fact, in its equality analysis, the Constitutional Court adopts a substantive approach to equality where it is not required to treat likes alike.[824] Instead, the focus is on achieving substantive justice, which requires a context- and impact-driven approach that sometimes requires people to be treated differently in order to achieve a fair and just result.[825] In its conception of equality, the Court therefore endorses appreciation of difference.

4.410 The protection of human dignity is also central to the Constitutional Court's equality jurisprudence.[826] One of the significant factors by which to determine unfair discrimination is whether or not the challenged rule or conduct impairs human dignity.[827] As mentioned earlier, religious freedom is integrally linked to the protection of human dignity. Therefore, a celebration of religious diversity through the principles of religious freedom and equality affirms human dignity.[828]

---

[820] *National Coalition for Gay and Lesbian Equality and ors v Minister of Home Affairs and ors* 1999 (3) SA 173 (C), paras 22, 112, 132.

[821] *S v Lawrence, Negal, Solberg* 1997 (4) SA 1176 (CC), paras 152–153.

[822] *Prince v President, Cape Law Society, and ors* 2002 (2) SA 794 (CC), para 49.

[823] *National Coalition for Gay and Lesbian Equality and ors v Minister of Home Affairs and ors* 1999 (3) SA 173 (C), paras 22, 112, 132.

[824] *President of the Republic of South Africa v Hugo* 1997 (4) SA 1 (CC), para 41.

[825] *MEC for Education, KwaZulu-Natal, and ors v Pillay* 2008 (1) SA 474 (CC), para 103; *Harksen v Lane* 1997 (11) BCLR 1489 (CC), para 53; *Daniels v Campbell NO and ors* 2004 (5) SA 331 (CC), para 22; *Prinsloo v Van Der Linde* 1997 (3) SA 1012 (CC), para 20. C Albertyn and J Kentridge, 'Introducing the Right to Equality in the Interim Constitution' (1994) 10 South African Journal of Human Rights 149, 161.

[826] LWH Ackermann, 'Equality and Non-Discrimination: Some Analytical Thoughts' (2006) 22 South African Journal of Human Rights 597, 598–9, 602, 609. CRM Dlamini, 'Equality Or Justice? Section 9 of the Constitution Revisited—Part I' (2002) 27(1) Journal for Juridical Science 14, 17.

[827] Section 14(3)(a) of the Promotion of Equality and Prevention of Unfair Discrimination Act of 2000. See also *Harksen* (n 825) para 51; *President of the Republic of South Africa v Hugo* 1997 (4) SA 1 (CC), para 43. T Deane and R Brijmohanlall, 'The Constitutional Court's Approach to Equality' (2003) 44(2) Codicillus 92, 94.

[828] *Prince v President, Cape Law Society, and ors* 2002 (2) SA 794 (CC), para 49; *Pillay* (n 825) para 62.

c) Religious freedom, doctrine of religious entanglement, and secularism

South Africa deals with its religious diversity by adopting a form of secularism that is inclusive **4.411**
of religions in the public sphere.[829] This could be referred to as *inclusive secularism*, as opposed
to *exclusive secularism*. Exclusive secularism embodies the French understanding of *laïcité* that
promotes an absolute separation between state and religion.[830] The range of constitutional provisions dealing with religious rights, including the absence of an establishment clause and the
Constitutional Court's approach to religion, suggests that South Africa does not require a strict
separation between religion and state.[831] For instance, as indicated previously, the state is permitted to promote religion in the public sphere by supporting religious observances at state or state
aided institutions, provided it is done in an equitable and non-coercive manner. The state may
also legislate on religious marriages and/or religious personal and family law systems. If such
assistance were to be provided or such legislation were to be enacted, it would entail some degree
of intervention by the state.[832]

In fact, the enactment of legislation regulating religious marriages or personal and family law **4.412**
systems would effectively bring religion within the judiciary's purview where courts would
be competent to examine and pronounce on religious doctrine.[833] Prior to the promulgation
of the Constitution, the apartheid era judiciary was not prepared to engage with religious
doctrine.[834] However, in *Ryland v Edros*,[835] a case that dealt with the recognition of terms and
customs of Muslim marriages, the Western Cape High Court observed that the constitutional provision relating to religious freedom might now have opened the possibility for the
judiciary to become engaged in religious doctrinal issues.[836] Yet, the judiciary remains reluctant to actually do so, as is evidenced by Ngcobo's obiter remark in *Prince*: 'It is undesirable
for the Courts to be concerned with questions as to what, as a matter of religious doctrine,
would be an effective practice of a particular religion.'[837]

---

[829] Benson (n 796) 303. SE Dangor, 'The Establishment and Consolidation of Islam in South Africa: From
the Dutch Colonisation of the Cape to the Present' (2003) 48(1) Historia 203, 215.

[830] The manifestation of secularism as a collaboration between state and religion is described in various
terms: 'Cooperation model', which recognizes cooperation between religious communities and the secular
state; 'non-discriminatory neutrality', which involves equitable state accommodation of religious symbols or
practices in the public sphere; 'benevolent neutrality', which requires the state to respect religious diversity and
actively accommodate religious practices and beliefs of minority religious communities; 'assimilation' where
one religion dominates in the public sphere even though policy-making is determined by secular principles, eg
where exclusively Christian religious holidays are celebrated as public holidays. Van der Schyff (n 791) 515–7,
520. Meyerson (n 717) 104, 115. P Coertzen, 'Christian Freedom and Freedom of Religion with Reference
to the South African Constitution (1996)' (2005) 46(3–4) Dutch Reformed Theological Journal 351, 358.
W Kymlicka, *Multicultural Citizenship* (OUP, 1995) 3.

[831] *S v Lawrence, Negal, Solberg* 1997 (4) SA 1176 (CC), para 119.

[832] *Lawrence* (n 831) para 143. Van der Schyff (n 791) 519–20.

[833] The Indian Supreme Court and Indian authors such as Danial Latifi express similar opinions in the
context of India, where religious marriages and personal law systems have been regulated for several decades.
Pannal Bansilal Pitti and ors v State of AP and anor (1996) 2 SCC 498, 511, para 14. Danial Latifi, 'Muslim
Jurisprudence and Shah Bano Case' (March 1986) Radical Humanist 11, 13.

[834] *Ryland v Edros* 1997 (2) SA 690 (C) 86F.

[835] *Ryland* (n 834).

[836] *Ryland* (n 834) 86F. See also C Rautenbach, 'Some Comments on the Current (and Future) Status
of Muslim Personal Law in South Africa' (2004) 2 Potchefstroom Electronic Law Journal 1, 8. J Church,
'The Dichotomy of Marriage Revisited: A Note on *Ryland v Edros*' (1997) 60 Tydskrif vir Hedendaagse
Romeins-Hollandse Reg 292, 293.

[837] *Prince v President, Cape Law Society, and ors* 2002 (2) SA 794 (CC), para 75. See also *Ryland* (n 834) 86G;
Taylor v Kurtstag NO and ors 2005 (1) SA 362 (W), para 61.

4.413 The judiciary's cautious approach to religion is illustrated by its preference to adopt a subjective approach to determine the centrality of beliefs or practices to a religion. It will therefore be interesting to see how it grapples with religious doctrinal engagement if legislation is enacted to regulate religious marriages and/or personal and family law systems.

(5) Conclusion

4.414 The inclusion of religious rights in the Constitution symbolizes a break from South Africa's oppressive past. In particular, religious freedom is essential to transform South Africa into the constitutional aspiration for an open and democratic society based on human dignity, equality, and freedom.[838] The manner in which provisions protecting religious freedom are interpreted is responsive to the historical marginalization of minority religions and denotes commitment to embrace religious diversity as one of the key features of South African society. Yet, limitations imposed on religious freedom signal awareness that not all religious practices and beliefs will be permitted; certainly not those that negate one's dignity.

4.415 Part of South Africa's promise to celebrate religious diversity is reflected in the possibility for introducing official plural legal systems that are inclusive of religion. This type of manifestation of religious freedom as *inclusive secularism* distinguishes South Africa from countries that attempt to keep religion out of the public sphere. Despite constitutional enablement for religion to operate in the public domain and while the judiciary has laid important and extensive groundwork for developing its jurisprudence on religious freedom, it is cautious about how it approaches religion. South Africa's judiciary has attempted to convey the message that religious diversity is something to be proud of, not shunned; and that where necessary, it will not protect harmful religious beliefs and practices.

H. Turkey

Mine Yildirim[839]

4.416 Successor to the Ottoman Empire,[840] the Turkish Republic is a relatively young constitutional parliamentary democracy. Its establishment in 1923 was coupled with sweeping measures taken to eliminate the influence of religion from state affairs, including in the law, state administration, and education.[841] Laicism is one of the six official pillars of the Republic, protected by the Constitution and by laws the constitutionality of which cannot be challenged. The collective dimension of freedom of religion or belief, in particular, has been subject to state control with a view to diminishing the political influence of religious communities (the *cemaat*). In contrast to the measures taken to break away from the

---

[838] *Prince* (n 837) para 49. F Cachalia, 'Citizenship, Muslim Family Law and a Future South African Constitution: A Preliminary Enquiry' (1993) 56 Tydskrif vir Hedendaagse Romeins-Hollandse Reg 392, 395.

[839] Abo Akademi, Institute for Human Rights.

[840] On law and justice in the Ottoman Empire, see H İnalcık, *Osmanlı'da Devlet, Hukuk, Adalet* [Law and Justice in the Ottoman State] (Eren, 2000). B Eryılmaz, *Osmanlı Devletinde Gayrimüslim Tebaanın Yönetimi* [The Administration of the non-Muslim community in the Ottoman State] (Risale, 1990) 31. G Bozkurt, *Gayrimüslim Osmanlı Vatandaşlarının Hukuki Durumu* [The Legal Status of non-Muslim Ottoman Citizens] (Türk Tarih Kurumu, 1989).

[841] Ç Özek, *Türkiye'de Laiklik Gelişim ve Koruyucu Ceza Hükümleri* [Laiklik in Turkey] (İstanbul Üniversitesi Hukuk Fakültesi Yayınları, İstanbul, 1962).

theocratic Ottoman state tradition in the pursuit of the elimination of religious influence in state affairs, the Ottoman arrangement for providing centrally organized religious (strictly Sunni-Hanafi school) public services has been maintained through the establishment of the institution of the Presidency of Religious Affairs.[842]

While ostensibly committed to strict separation of state and religious affairs, practice has included arrangements that raise questions about the compatibility of Turkish secularism (*laiklik*),[843] with international standards relating to the right to freedom of religion or belief and to neutrality and impartiality on the part of the state. Generally speaking there seems to be an agreement in Turkey that *laiklik* has, at least, two requirements, namely freedom of religion or belief and the separation of state and religious affairs.[844] **4.417**

(1) General framework

a) *Turkish secularism: laiklik*

The term *laiklik* (French term *laïcité*) formally entered the Turkish legal system through its inclusion in the Constitution in 1937.[845] The paramount place and particular meaning given to the principle in the Turkish Constitution and its interpretation by the higher courts—in particular the Turkish Constitutional Court,[846] and the Council of State[847]—form the general legal framework for cases that raise issues of religious freedom or belief in Turkey. **4.418**

Under the 1982 Turkish Constitution[848]—in force at the time of writing—*laiklik* is directly or indirectly protected through a number of provisions. The principle is one of the attributes of the Republic (article 2) that cannot be amended (article 4), and no activity that is contrary to republican principles and reforms based on *laiklik* can attract constitutional protection (Preamble, paragraph 5). The state's fundamental social, economic, political, and legal order cannot be based on religious tenets.[849] Reform laws,[850] most of which are directly or **4.419**

---

[842] İ Gözaydın, *Diyanet Türkiye Cumhuriyeti'nde Dinin Tanzimi* [The Presidency of Religious Affairs—The Arrangement of Religion in the Turkish Republic] (İletişim Publications, 2009).

[843] I will use the word '*laiklik*' throughout the text in order to emphasize the autonomous meaning the term has in the Turkish context.

[844] See among others, E Özbudun, *Türk Anayasa Hukuku* (Yetkin Yaylınları, 2013) s 54–58. K Gözler, *Türk Anayasa Hukuku* [Turkish Constitutional Law] (Ekin, 2000).

[845] The principle of *laïcité* had been part of public discussion during various attempts to modernize the Ottoman Empire in the mid-nineteenth century. Many measures had been taken to eliminate the influence of religion from state affairs before *laïcité* was expressly acknowledged in the Constitution. For a relatively recent discussion, see K Ersin, 'Democracy, Islam and secularism in Turkey' in NJ Brown and E Shahin (eds), *The Struggle Over Democracy in the Middle East: Regional Politics and External Policies* (Routledge, 2009) 153–86.

[846] According to art 148 of the Turkish Constitution, the Constitutional Court examines the constitutionality, in respect of both form and substance, of laws, decrees having the force of law, and the Rules of Procedure of the Turkish Grand National Assembly. Constitutional amendments are examined and verified only with regard to their form. The judgments of the Constitutional Court are final.

[847] Administrative courts deal with cases which are brought against the administrative organs because of the implementation of administrative legislation. The administrative decisions and judgments of courts can be appealed to the Council of State. The Council of State is the last instance for reviewing decisions and judgments given by administrative courts and cases which are not referred by law to other administrative courts.

[848] 1982 Turkish Constitution, art 24(5).

[849] 1982 Turkish Constitution, available at <http://www.constitution.org/cons/turkey/turk_cons.htm>. (last accessed 17 June 2013).

[850] Reform Laws include revolutionary laws adopted in the early years of the Turkish Republic. These are Tevhid-i Tedrisat Kanunu [Law on the Unification of the Educational System] Act No 430 of 3 March 1340 (1924); Şapka Kanunu [Law on Wearing Hats] Act No 671 of 25 November 1341 (1925); Tekke ve Zaviyelerin Kapatılmasına İlişkin Kanun [Closure of Dervish Monasteries and Tombs, the Abolition of the Office of Keeper of Tombs and the Abolition and Prohibition of Certain Titles] Act No 677 of 30 November 1341

indirectly linked to *laiklik*, are under Constitutional protection and cannot be understood as contradictory to the Constitution (article 174). Political parties must also abide by the principle of *laiklik* or risk closure (article 68). Fundamental rights cannot be relied on in order to establish a state order, or any part of this order, based on religion (article 14/1).

4.420 The principle of non-interference in the affairs of religious communities that follows from the notion of separation of state and religious affairs is not set out in the Constitution.[851] This has significant implications for the freedom of religion or belief, particularly in its collective dimension for religious/belief groups—in their associative rights. This is particularly evident in the restrictions on the autonomy of religious communities as well as the state monopoly on certain religious services/activities, such as those provided by the Presidency of Religious Affairs (Diyanet) and religious education provided by the Ministry of Education. In effect, religious education may only be administered under the supervision and control of the state.

4.421 The Turkish Constitutional Court (TCC) was set up in 1962. It has interpreted the principle of *laiklik* to mean first, that religion cannot in any way interfere in state affairs and secondly, taking into account historical realities, that the state will be permitted to adopt an interventionist, restrictive, controlling approach towards the manifestation of religion or belief.[852] This position is often justified by the TCC by reference to Turkey's unique background.[853] The TCC has also highlighted important differences between belief systems. For instance, the lack of a hierarchical class of clergy in Islam has been said to make it impossible to grant independence in internal affairs for those involved in places of worship and religious affairs.[854] Since Islam regulates not only individual religious belief but also social relations, state affairs, and the law, the TCC has held that an unlimited freedom of religion and independent religious associative freedom would be dangerous for Turkey.[855]

4.422 The TCC has expressed the view that the principle of *laiklik* holds a privileged position in the Constitution.[856] The TCC mandates itself with what Dinçkol refers to as an 'active' approach towards the protection of the principle of secularism and views it as the 'heart' of the constitutional system in Turkey.[857]

b) The Presidency of Religous Affairs: the Diyanet

4.423 Article 136 of the Turkish Constitution places the Presidency of Religious Affairs (*Diyanet*) in the general state administration under the Prime Minister's Office. The *Diyanet* is to work

---

(1925); art 110 of Medeni Kanun [Civil Code] No 743 of 17 February 1926, Yeni Türk Harflerinin Kabulü ve Tatbiki Hakkında Kanun [Law on the Adoption and Application of the Turkish Alphabet] Act No 1353 of 1 November 1928, Efendi, Bey, Paşa gibi Lakap ve Ünvanların Kaldırılmasına Dair Kanun [Law on the Abolition of Titles and Appellations such as Efendi, Bey or Pasa] Act No 2590 of 26 November 1934; Bazı Kisvelerin Giyilemeyeceğine Dair Kanun [Law on the Prohibition of the Wearing of Certain Garments] Act No 2596 of 3 December 1934.

[851] B Tanör and N Yüzbaşıoğlu, *1982 Anayasasına Göre Türk Anayasa Hukuku* [Turkish Constitutional Law According to the 1982 Constitution] (YKY Publications, 2005) 89.

[852] B Dinçkol, *1982 Anayasası Çerçevesinde ve Anayasa Mahkemesi Kararlarında Laiklik* [Secularism Within the Framework of the 1982 Constitution and the Judgments of the Constitutional Court] (Kazancı Kitap, 1992) 182.

[853] 21 October 1971, E/1970/53 and K/1971/76, Anayasa Mahkemesi Kararları Dergisi [Journal of Judgments of the Constitutional Court] (AMKD) No 10 (1971).

[854] AMKD No 10, 61–2.

[855] AMKD No 10, 66.

[856] Date 07.03.1989, E/1989/1 and K/1989/12, AMKD No 12 (1991), 133–65.

[857] Dinçkol (n 852) 178 and 212.

in line with the principle of *laiklik* removed from all political views and ideas, and to seek to ensure national solidarity and unity.[858] The purpose of the *Diyanet* is stipulated in its own law: 'carrying out activities related to the beliefs, worship and ethics of the Islamic religion, enlightening the society about religion and administering worship places'.[859]

The fact that the state provides certain religious services as a 'public service' through the **4.424** *Diyanet* raises particular issues. Ensuring the neutrality required of 'public service' would seem to be difficult, considering that the *Diyanet* has been criticized for serving only the needs of the Sunni-Muslims.[860] On the one hand, the *Diyanet* is the only religious institution that receives financial state support for all of its activities and personnel, yet on the other, it is under the control of the state—enjoying limited autonomy.[861] Through this arrangement the Turkish state is closely involved in the religious affairs of a particular Islamic tradition. No other belief or religion receives support for its services from the state. This arrangement may been seen to undermine the constitutional principle of impartiality.

Yet, in a decision that has caused controversy, the TCC found that the *Diyanet* and in **4.425** particular the civil servant status of its personnel is compatible with the principle of *laiklik*.[862] The decision was based on the consideration of first, the country's experience that an understanding of 'uncontrolled religious freedom and independent religious association' is loaded with serious dangers and, secondly, the nature of Islam, which regulates social relations, state affairs, and the law. The TCC held that there is no doubt that the regulation of the *Diyanet* in the Constitution and the 'civil servant' status of its personnel is a requirement for historical reasons and in the light of the facts and circumstances of the country.[863] This decision has been criticized for itself being inconsistent with the principle of *laiklik*.[864]

c) *Religious minorities*[865]

Turkey's national and international obligations relating to the protections for religious minori- **4.426** ties are not reflected in state practice. The Lausanne Peace Treaty is the founding document of modern Turkey,[866] as well as a treaty establishing a minority protection regime for Turkey's non-Muslims. Articles 37 to 45 of the Lausanne Treaty provide for the protection of non-Muslim minorities. The principle place given to the protection scheme within the Turkish legal system is explicitly mandated through Article 37 by obliging Turkey to recognize Articles 38 to 44 as basic law. Article 37 stipulates that there shall not be any laws or regulations or official acts that run contrary to—or take priority over—the said provisions. This explicit prohibition has not prevented state restrictions that have served to prevent non-Muslim minorities in Turkey from fully enjoying their rights. In contrast to the contemporary minority protection schemes that protect

---

[858] Turkish Constitution, art 136.

[859] Law No 633, art 1 *Official Gazette* No 12038, 2 July 1965.

[860] R Çakır and İ Bozan, *Sivil, Şeffaf ve Demokratik bir Diyanet İşleri Başkanlığı Mümkün mü?* [Is a Civil, Transparent and Democratic Presidency of Religious Affairs Possible?] (TESEV, 2005) 38.

[861] For discussion on various proposals for the transformation of the *Diyanet* into an autonomous institution within the state administration, see Gözaydın (n 842) 279–83.

[862] Constitutional Court Judgment, 21 October 1971, E.1970/53, K.1971/76, AYMD, No 10, 67–8.

[863] AYMD, No 10, 60–70.

[864] Gözler (n 844).

[865] It is not possible to do justice to the topic of the protection of minorities, and religious minorities in particular, in Turkey within the confines of this contribution.

[866] The Lausanne Peace Treaty is ratified in domestic law by Law No 340 and is thus part of domestic law.

racial, linguistic, and religious minorities, the Lausanne Treaty identifies solely non-Muslim minorities as minority right holders, and there are certain rights that are protected only for these communities.[867] In practice, the Turkish government extended the protections to the Armenian Orthodox, Greek Orthodox, and Jewish communities, in spite of the fact that these communities are not mentioned by name in the Lausanne Treaty. Other non-Muslim groups, such as the Syrian Orthodox and Syrian Chaldean, Latin Catholic, and those of the Bahai faith, were not granted the same rights protected under the Lausanne Peace Treaty. For example, Syrian and Chaldean Christians are not able to establish their own schools in accordance with Article 40 of the Lausanne Treaty.[868]

d) The principle of equality

4.427 The principle of equality is protected under article 10 of the 1982 Constitution, which provides for equality before law without distinction based on, *inter alia*, religion. Gözler has observed that the Turkish Constitutional Court has adopted a relative understanding of the equality principle, one that allows for differentiated treatment in cases where there are 'rightful reasons'. In cases where a 'rightful reason' does not exist and the legislator has discriminated arbitrarily, the TCC may then annul a legal provision.

4.428 In Turkey, at the intersection of the protection of equality, *laiklik*, and the right to freedom of religion there is the issue that the state provides services based on one religion and in particular to one denomination of this religion.[869] However, as has already been noted, in a case concerning the civil servant status of the *Diyanet* personnel, this is not viewed as a violation of the principle of equality by the Turkish judiciary.

4.429 The TCC has relied on article 10 to find a provision providing broader legal protection for members of theistic religions, as opposed to non-theistic religions, to be in contradiction with the principle of equality.[870] The TCC held that: 'In a *laic* society differences based on religion or denomination cannot be the reason of any distinction.'[871] Dinçkol argues that through this decision not only traditional theistic religions but all religion or beliefs are equally protected.[872] Nonetheless, the legal practice in Turkey is such that—as will be seen—while there may be formal equality, substantive equality is arguably yet to be achieved.

(2) The constitutional protection of freedom of religion or belief: article 24

4.430 The right to freedom of religion or belief is enshrined in article 24 of the Constitution:

> Everyone has the right to freedom of conscience, religious belief and conviction.
>
> Acts of worship, religious services, and ceremonies shall be conducted freely, provided that they do not violate the provisions of Article 14.

---

[867] Baskın Oran attributes this 'victory' on the part of Turkish authorities, to the fact that they represented Turkey as the victor of the National Indepence War. B Oran, *Türkiye'de Azınlıklar: Kavramlar, Teori, Lozan, İç Mevzuat, İçtihat, Uygulama* [Minorities in Turkey: Concepts, Theory, Lausanne National Legislation, Case Law, Practice] (İletişim, 2004) 64.

[868] The explanation given by the state for this anomaly is that Syrians had given up these rights after the establishment of the Turkish Republic.

[869] A Sezer, 'Türkiye'de Din-Vicdan Özgürlüğü ve Din Devlet İlişkisi' [Freedom of Religion—Conscience and Religion State Relations in Turkey] in *Prof. Dr Bülent TANÖR Armağanı*, (Legal Publications, Istanbul, 2004) 561–609.

[870] 4 Kasım 1986 tarih ve K.1986/26 (AMKD).

[871] 4 Kasım 1986 tarih ve K.1986/26 (AMKD).

[872] Dinçkol (n 852).

No one shall be compelled to worship, or to participate in religious ceremonies and rites, to reveal religious beliefs and convictions, or be blamed or accused because of his religious beliefs and convictions.

Education and instruction in religion and ethics shall be conducted under state supervision and control. Instruction in religious culture and moral education shall be compulsory in the curricula of primary and secondary schools. Other religious education and instruction shall be subject to the individual's own desire, and in the case of minors, to the request of their legal representatives.

No one shall be allowed to exploit or abuse religion or religious feelings, or things held sacred by religion, in any manner whatsoever, for the purpose of personal or political influence, or for even partially basing the fundamental, social, economic, political, and legal order of the state on religious tenets.

The first paragraph of article 24 provides for the inviolable right to freedom of conscience, **4.431** religion, belief and convictions. This right includes the right not to believe, and also the right to change one's religion or belief. While the notion of conscience has not been invoked as a separate component, it is usually referred to together with religion as 'freedom of religion and conscience', which seems to point to the individual's inner sphere made up of deep convictions that may not necessarily be religious. It is, however, not so broad as to include the protection against being compelled to act against one's conscience.[873]

The second paragraph of article 24 suggests that the scope of the protection accorded to **4.432** manifestations—even though this term is absent from the provision—which is limited to 'worship, religious services and ceremonies', in contrast to the protection afforded to the non-exhaustive list of manifestations of religion or belief in 'worship, observance, practice and teaching' stipulated in Article 9 ECHR. The narrow scope of protection here, generally restricting manifestations to places of worship, is in line with the restrictions on manifestations of religion in the public sphere, in the context of religious symbols, and with regard to the teaching of religion. Sezer observes that it is necessary to differentiate between 'worship' and 'practice': it is only the right to worship that the Constitution guarantees, a 'practice' that is not worship is not protected.[874] This is difficult to reconcile with the non-exclusive list of manifestations enshrined in the international protections to which Turkey is a signatory, such as Article 9 ECHR and Article 18 ICCPR.[875]

Teaching as a form of manifestation of religion is not provided for as a right. Instead it is **4.433** referred to in the context of the institution of strict state control in paragraph 3 of article 24 through the regulation concerning compulsory religious education classes and other religious instruction which can only be carried out under state control. Through this provision the state takes upon itself the role of teaching religion.[876] In addition, all 'other' religious teaching or instruction that may be carried out by private individuals or religious groups must take place under state supervision.

---

[873] eg the right to conscientious objection to compulsory military service is not recognized. M Yildirim, 'Conscientious Objection to Military Service: International Human Rights Law and the Case of Turkey' (2010) 5 Religion and Human Rights 65–91.

[874] Sezer (n 869).

[875] ECHR, Art 9; ICCPR, Art 18. See Ch 2, paras 2.11–2.23 and Ch 3, paras 3.02–3.114.

[876] The content of RCMK classes are not specified in the Constitution. This was later defined by jurisprudence, see the decision of the Council of State, 8th Chamber, E2006/4107, K.2007/481, 28 December 2007, E.2007/679 K.2008/1461, 29 February 2008.

4.434　Until relatively recently, in reaching its decisions, the TCC seldom considered Strasbourg case law and other international instruments providing for fundamental rights. Article 90 of the Turkish Constitution deals with international treaties. Article 90(5) provides:

> International agreements duly put into effect carry the force of law. No appeal to the [TCC] can be made with regard to these agreements, on the ground that they are unconstitutional. In conflicts arising between different provisions of a domestic law and an international agreement related to fundamental rights and freedoms, the provisions of the international agreement will be taken as the basis.

Turkey's international human rights commitments are therefore relevant to the domestic protections for religious freedom.

4.435　Article 24 of the Constitution is subject to a number of limitations. The limitation enshrined in article 24 itself provides that: 'no one shall be allowed to exploit or abuse religion or religious feelings or things held sacred by religion'. The purpose of this provision is to restrict the use of religion to gain personal or political influence as well as to prohibit the 'abuse' of religion in order to base the order of the state on religious tenets.

4.436　The general restrictions clause that is applicable to all fundamental rights is set out at article 13 of the Constitution. It stipulates that fundamental rights may be restricted, 'only by law', without 'infringing upon their essence' and restrictions may not be 'in conflict with the letter and spirit of the Constitution and the requirements of the democratic order of society and the secular Republic and the principle of proportionality'.[877] The 'essence' of rights is a somewhat vague notion which has not been defined by the TCC for the purposes of the right to freedom of thought, conscience, and religion.

4.437　An additional restriction clause is found in article 14, which provides: 'None of the rights and freedoms embodied in the Constitution shall be exercised with the aim of violating the indivisible integrity of the state with its territory and nation, and endangering the existence of the democratic and secular order of the Turkish Republic based upon human rights.'[878] The requirement of a democratic order of society has been used to restrict the state, whereas the requirement of a secular Republic has been used to restrict fundamental freedom.[879] The same provision goes on to create a restriction preventing the state and individuals from destroying fundamental rights and freedoms embodied in the Constitution. This creates an obligation both for the state and the individual.

4.438　So far as the suspension of fundamental rights is concerned, even in times of war, mobilization, martial law, or in times of emergency, 'no one may be compelled to reveal his/her religion, conscience, thought and convictions or be accused because of them'.[880]

4.439　The unalterable nature of the Reform Laws that are protected under article 174 of the Constitution may also be construed as an additional limitation clause. The Reform Laws protected under this provision relate to a number of different areas,[881] including the direct

---

[877] As amended on 17 October 2001.
[878] As amended on 17 October 2001.
[879] O Can, 'Anayasa Değişiklikleri ve Düşünceyi Açıklama Özgürlüğü' (Constitutional Amendments and the Freedom to Express One's Thoughts) (2002) 19 Anayasa Yargısı 503.
[880] Turkish Constitution, art 15.
[881] Act No 430 of 3 March 1340 (1924) on the Unification of the Educational System; 2. Act No 671 of 25 November 1341 (1925) on the Wearing of Hats; Act No 677 of 30 November 1341 (1925) on the Closure

and indirect protection of the principle of *laiklik*. As a result of this clause, for example, the prohibition against wearing religious garments for clergy of any religion or the prohibition of the use of certain religious leadership titles and the closure of certain places of worship, such as dervish lodges, may not be challenged on grounds of their constitutionality. These laws therefore enjoy absolute protection in domestic law.

(3) The approach of the higher courts to religious rights

a) Compulsory religious culture and ethics classes

In spite of the domestic and international court decisions that have found current practice in Turkey to be incompatible with Turkey's human rights commitments under the ECHR, the issue of compulsory religion classes continues to be an unresolved domestic issue. The National Security Council (NSC),[882] acknowledging that religion is a unifying factor in society, advised the drafters of the 1982 Constitution that compulsory religious education under state control was acceptable, but that it should be taught as a cultural subject.[883] Not surprisingly, the compulsory nature of the education has been viewed by many as a practice that is irreconcilable with the *laic* nature of the state.[884] The constitutional provision on religious education stipulates: **4.440**

> Education and instruction in religion and ethics shall be conducted under state supervision and control. Instruction in religious culture and moral education shall be compulsory in the curricula of primary and secondary schools. Other religious education and instruction shall be subject to the individual's own desire, and in the case of minors, to the request of their legal representatives.

The Constitution therefore provides for two different kinds of religious instruction and education and creates different legal regimes for each. First, there is a reference to 'Religious Culture and Moral Education' (RCME) classes that are deemed compulsory in primary and secondary schools. Secondly, the third sentence refers to 'other religious education and instruction' and makes them subject to the individual's own desire and, in the case of children, the wishes of their legal representatives. However, both kinds of religious instruction and education have one common element: both are subject to state supervision and control. **4.441**

The higher courts have had to give meaning to RCME. It has been observed that the key word here is 'culture', which seems to indicate that 'religious culture' lessons must provide content that is relevant for all and not only for members of a particular religion.[885] Thus it would follow from the text, and such an interpretation would exclude, first, that the 'religious culture' **4.442**

---

of Dervish Monasteries and Tombs, the Abolition of the Office of Keeper of Tombs and the Abolition and Prohibition of Certain Titles; The principle of civil marriage according to which the marriage act shall be concluded in the presence of the competent official, adopted with the Turkish Civil Code No 743 of 17 February 1926, and art 110 of the Code; Act No 1288 of 20 May 1928 on the Adoption of International Numerals; Act No 1353 of 1 November 1928 on the Adoption and Application of the Turkish Alphabet; Act No 2590 of 26 November 1934 on the Abolition of Titles and Appellations such as Efendi, Bey or Pasa; Act No 2596 of 3 December 1934 on the Prohibition of the Wearing of Certain Garments.

[882] See art 187 of the Constitution. The NSC develops national security policy.

[883] *Cumhuriyet* Daily, 27 June 1987.

[884] Dinçkol (n 852) 64. See the case of *Hasan and Eylem Zengin v Turkey* on the compulsory nature and content of Religious Culture and Ethics classes and the inadequate provision for exemption in Turkey. *Hasan and Eylem Zengin v Turkey*, ECtHR, 9 January 2008 (App 1448/04), paras 58–76.

[885] K Gözler, '1982 Anayasası'na Göre Din Eğitim ve Öğretimi', Prof Dr Tunçer Karamustafaoğlu'na Armağan, Adalet Yayınevi, 2010, 317–34, available at <http://www.anayasa.gen.tr/din-egitimi.htm> (accessed 19 October 2011).

lessons would be compulsory for all—without any exemption—and that they would be compulsory in all primary and secondary schools. In practice, there is a general impression that the RCME lessons are not about the culture of religion but are about Sunni Islam. This is evidenced by the Ministry of Education's curricula,[886] the objections of atheist and Alevi parents,[887] as well as the possibility of exemption for Christian and Jewish students.[888] On the other hand, surveys have shown that the majority of the people in Turkey consider the RCME as a course in religion and wish them to continue in their compulsory form.[889]

4.443 The ECtHR has ruled that the compulsory RCME lessons in Turkey amounted to religious instruction in the case of *Hasan and Eylem Zengin v Turkey*.[890] The case concerned the request of an Alevi parent for the exemption of his daughter from the compulsory RCME lessons. The ECtHR held that the 'religious culture and ethics' classes could not be considered to meet the criteria of objectivity and pluralism, and held that there had been a violation of the right to education protected under Article 2 of Protocol No 1 ECHR.[891]

4.444 In Turkey, the Council of State (CS) has also ruled that the books taught in RCME classes are based on the teachings of a particular religion. Practices such as doing the Muslim prayer and memorizing Arabic prayers are part of these lessons.[892] Thus in the light of its content, the CS held that they could not be accepted as teaching on religious culture and moral education but were in fact 'religious instruction'.[893] The CS held that according to article 24 of the Constitution, this kind of religious instruction may only be given subject to the desire of the individual, and that rules that make it compulsory without a request from parents for such instruction were in violation of the Constitution as well as the ECHR.[894] Sezer asks the crucial question, 'what can be the reason for a secular state to desire to give all of its citizens religious information in a compulsory manner?' and proposes that 'compulsory religion' lies behind this practice.[895]

4.445 The second kind of religious education is allowed by the Constitution, however, subject to individual desire and under state supervision and control. A separate regulation concerning 'other religious education' also reinforces the interpretation that the 'Religious Culture' classes ought not to be 'instruction in a certain religion'. There is no constitutional restriction concerning either the content of 'other religious education' or state supervision and control. If such education is provided by public institutions one may assume that state supervision

---

[886] <http://www.dkab.org>.

[887] 'Aile Çocuğun Dışlanmaması için Dava Açmak İstemiyor' (Parents Do not Want to Sue because they Do not want their Children to be Excluded), 22 June 2011, Bianet, available at <http://bianet.org/bianet/insan-haklari/130932-aile-cocugun-dislanmamasi-icin-dava-acmak-istemiyor> (accessed 13 December 2011).

[888] On 9 July 1990, the Education and Teaching High Council took a decision regarding religious culture and moral education classes and the right of Christian and Jewish students to be exempted from these classes.

[889] According to a survey 82.1% of the people in Turkey think that there should be compulsory religious education in public schools; 85.5% think that worship practices, such as ritual ablution and *namaz*, should be taught as part of general teaching about Islam. A Çarkoğlu and B Toprak, *Religion, Society and Politics in a Changing Turkey* (TESEV Publications, 2007) 60.

[890] *Hasan and Eylem Zengin v Turkey*, ECtHR Judgment, 9 October 2007 (App 1448/04).

[891] *Hasan and Eylem Zengin* (n 890).

[892] The Council of State, 8th Chamber, E2006/4107, K.2007/481, 28 December 2007; E.2007/679 K.2008/1461, 29 February 2008.

[893] The Council of State, 8th Chamber, E2006/4107, K.2007/481[14] 28 December 2007; E.2007/679 K.2008/1461, 29 February 2008.

[894] See n 893.

[895] Sezer (n 869).

and control is present; however, there is no constitutional rule concerning how the state supervision and control can be exercised if such education is provided in the family, under informal arrangements, or in religious establishments. Legal regulation exists concerning 'Quran courses'.[896] On the other hand, it is not possible for children to receive religious education in an institutional framework, apart from the summer Quran courses that are organized by the *Diyanet*. For non-Muslims an option similar to the summer Quran courses does not exist.

b) Coercion to disclose religion or belief

The prohibition of a requirement to declare one's religion or belief is a fundamental compo- **4.446**
nent of the right to have a thought, religion, or belief.[897] The TCC had the opportunity to address this issue for the first time in an appeal case that concerned the request of three individuals to change the religion that was indicated on their national identity cards.[898] The case was taken to the TCC with the claim that the relevant provisions of the Public Registration Law violated the Constitution, in particular the provisions protecting the right to freedom of religion or belief, the right to freedom of expression, the principle of secularism, and the principle of equality. The fundamental question was whether the requirement to register one's religion on a national identity card constitutes coercion to disclose one's convictions and opinions. The TCC did not think so. The decisive factor for the TCC was that the provisions in question did not require the disclosure of religious convictions and opinions, but instead 'just the religion'. The distinction between 'religious convictions and opinions' on the one hand, and, 'just religion' on the other, was not clarified by the TCC. In contrast, the dissenting judges drew attention to the fine that is due for the non-disclosure of religion or belief, holding that 'there is no doubt that there is coercion'.[899] They also found the requirement to register one's religion or belief incompatible with the principle of secularism, saying, 'for whatever reason and regardless of at what level, the coercion of citizens to disclose religious convictions and opinions means nothing short of an infringement of secularism'.[900]

In a more recent case dating to 1995 the Constitutional Court maintained its previously held **4.447**
position on the constitutionality of the requirement in the Public Registration Law to register religion in a public register.[901] This time the TCC elaborated on the difference between 'religion' and 'religious conviction and opinion', noting that religious conviction and opinion is a broader term including one's religious views on a variety of issues, whereas religion amounts only to demographic or personal information. Hence the Court maintained that what was prohibited in article 24 of the Constitution, protecting the right to freedom of religion or belief, was not the 'noting of one's religion', but rather 'the disclosure of one's religious convictions and opinions in a coercive manner'. Bearing in mind the possibilities of

---

[896] Diyanet İşleri Başkanlığı Kur'an Kursları ile Öğrenci Yurt ve Pansiyonlarına ilişkin Yönetmelik [Regulation on the Presidency of Religious Affairs Quran Courses and Dormitories and Hostels], RG No 23982, 3 March 2000. Upon completion of Grade 5, children can take part in these courses. Turkish Constitution, art 4(k).

[897] General Comment 22 of the Human Rights Committee on Article 18, UN Doc HRI/GEN/1/Rev.1 at 35 (1994) para 5.

[898] Constitutional Court Judgment, E1979/9, K1979/44, 27 November 1979.

[899] Judgment E1979/9, K1979/44 (n 898).

[900] Judgment E1979/9, K1979/44 (n 898).

[901] Constitutional Court, E1995/17, K1995/16, 21 June 1995. The case involved the referral of a case by the Council of State arguing that the requirement to register 'religion' in the population register is contrary to the Constitution. The case considered by the Council of State involved a Bahai citizen requesting a change in the religions section of his ID case from Islam to 'Bahai'.

changing the religion or erasing it through administrative action, the Court found that the coercive element was non-existent.[902]

4.448 The Turkish practice concerning the registration of religious affiliation in public registers and on ID cards was considered and found to be in violation of Article 9 ECHR by the ECtHR in *Sinan Işık v Turkey*.[903]

4.449 The Law on Legal Procedures (LLP) requires individuals to take an oath on 'God and honour' in court.[904] This provision makes it compulsory for everyone, including non-believers, to take an oath by reference to one's God. This provision has not been the subject of consideration by the TCC.

c) Manifestation of religion—religious symbols—in the public sphere

4.450 *Public work place—Civil servants and dress code.*[905] The Turkish Constitution recognizes the right of all Turkish citizens to enter public service and stipulates that no criterion other than the qualifications for the office concerned may be taken into consideration for recruitment into public service.[906] The general provisions of the Law on Public Servants, however, have implications for the restriction of manifestations of religion or belief.[907] So far as public servants working in schools connected to the Ministry of Education are concerned, they are subject to a regulation requiring the head to be uncovered.[908]

4.451 The dress code of public servants is regulated by the Framework Regulation of October 1982 (the Regulation of October 1982).[909] The purpose of the Regulation of October 1982 is to ensure that public servants have uniformity in terms of clothing and wear modest and contemporary clothes that are in line with the reforms and principles of Atatürk.[910]

4.452 The higher courts have interpreted *laiklik* functionally so as to exclude not only the headscarf, but also 'persons with certain religious affiliations' (*dinci*), in general, from the public workplace.[911] This was done by attributing manifestations of religion a meaning and

---

[902] The dissenting judges held that there was a clear coercive element in the requirement to register one's religion.

[903] *Sinan Işık v Turkey* (App 21925/05) (2010).

[904] Article 339 of Law No 1086. Hukuk Usulü Muhakemeleri Kanunu [Law on Legal Procedures], 18 June 1927, RG No 622, 623, 624, 2, 3, and 4 July 1927.

[905] This section is based on an article which is yet to be published; M Yildirim, 'Religion in the Public and Private Turkish Workplace: the Approach of the Turkish Judiciary' in K Alidadi, MC Foblets, and J Vrielink (eds.) *A Test of Faith? Religious Diversity and Accommodation in the European Workplace* (Ashgate, forthcoming).

[906] Turkish Constitution, art 70.

[907] Devlet Memurları Kanunu [Law on Public Servants] No 657, 14 July 1965, Resmi Gazete [Official Gazette] RG No 12056, 23 July 1965, art 6.

[908] Milli Eğitim Bakanlığına ve Diğer Bakanlıklara Bağlı Okullardaki Memurların ve Öğrencilerin Kılık Kıyafetine İlişkin Yönetmelik [Regulation on Attire and Clothing for Officials and Students in Schools Under the Ministry of Education and Other Ministries], No 8/3349, December 1981, RG No 17537, 7 December 1981.

[909] Kamu Kurum ve Kuruluşlarında Çalışan Personelin Kılık ve Kıyafetine Dair Yönetmelik [Regulation Pertaining to the Attire of Personnel Employed at Public Institutions] (October 1982 Regulation), RG No 17849, 25 October 1982.

[910] October 1982 Regulation, art 16. Art 5 of the Regulation regulates many aspects of appearance, *inter alia*, the length and form of hair, moustache, beard, shirts, ties, how much a shirt or blouse can reveal, how loose or tight trousers can be, heels of shoes, nails, make-up, etc.

[911] It has been observed that the Turkish judiciary has a strong tendency to protect the state and sanction severely what it perceives as a threat to the state. M Sancar and EÜ Atılgan, *Adalet Biraz Es Geçiliyor* [Justice is Somewhat Overlooked] (TESEV Publications, 2009) 124–50.

significance that is ideologically incompatible with *laiklik* and by the imposition of serious sanctions upon persons who wear or use these symbols. For instance, the courts equated the act of wearing the headscarf in a public workplace with disrupting the order of an institution for ideological or political purposes, thus warranting dismissal from work.[912]

Factors that may be taken into account in the assessment of the compatibility of a civil serv-   **4.453**
ant's actions with the dress code regulations and the principle of *laiklik*, include: dress outside the public workplace;[913] 'sincerity' in abiding by the relevant regulations;[914] manifestations of religion or belief outside the workplace; and affiliations with certain groups and religious world views. The assumed connection between these factors seems to be based on general perceptions and presuppositions rather than the concrete acts of individuals that pose an immediate and material threat to the secular nature of the public service they are delivering.

Interestingly, the relationship of religious symbols and neutrality find limited reflection in   **4.454**
the jurisprudence of the Turkish higher courts. Demir argues that the ban on religious symbols for public servants is a requirement of the principle of *laiklik* since the neutrality of the public servant will be undermined if he or she wears religious symbols or clothes.[915] Religious symbols and/or practices are not assessed as legally protected manifestations of religion or belief, but as indicators of certain religious affiliations that are viewed as inconsistent with preserving the principle of *laiklik*.

d) Manifestations of religion or belief in the Turkish schools—the headscarf

Dress codes for teachers, whether in public or private educational institutions, prohibit the   **4.455**
wearing of the headscarf.[916] Students in primary or secondary education may not enter school wearing a headscarf,[917] and it is only recently that university students have been allowed to enter university wearing the headscarf.[918] The only exception here are schools where religious vocational training takes place.[919] School administrations may not display any religious symbols in either public or private schools. The state's obligation to respect parents' religious or

---

[912] The case of Züheyla Zeybel set the precedent for this interpretation, E2000/1244, K2001/474, 25 January 2001, Council of State, General Council of Chambers of Administrative Cases. A report by AK-DER claims that during the period 1998–2002 approximately 5,000 public servants were dismissed and another 10,000 were forced to resign. A Report by AK-DER, 'İstatistiki Verilere Göre Türkiye'de Kadınların Genel Konumu ve Başörtüsü Yasağının Cinsiyet Endekslerine Etkileri' [A Statistical Analysis of the Situation of Women in Turkey and the Effect of the Headscarf Ban on Gender Index] (AK-DER, 2008) 7.

[913] The judgment of the Council of State demonstrates that the headscarf, even though it was worn outside the workplace, is viewed by the judiciary as a religious manifestation that undermines certain qualities that are expected from teachers, *inter alia*, 'being a good example', and the secular character of public education. It was specifically mentioned that she did not wear the headscarf at her workplace. The Case of Aytaç Altındağ, Council of State Judgment, 8th Chamber, E2004/4051, K2005/3366, 26 October 2005.

[914] The wearing of a wig over the headscarf by a teacher was considered as a sign that the applicant was not really sincere in abiding by the applicable dress code. The Case of Kevser Sönmez, Sakarya Second Administrative Court, E2001/14, K2001/2854, 26 December 2001.

[915] HS Demir, *Avrupa İnsan Hakları Mahkemesi Kararları Işığında Türkiye'de Din ve Vicdan Özgürlüğü, Adalet*, s. 127.

[916] See Yildririm (n 905).

[917] See Yildririm (n 905).

[918] The Head of the Higher Education Council (YÖK) Professor YZ Özcan, announced that instructors in universities may no longer take action against students wearing the headscarf. BBC News, 31 December 2001, 'Quiet End to Turkey's Headscarf Ban', avaialble at <http://www.bbc.co.uk/news/world-europe-11880622> (accessed 15 December 2011).

[919] Art 12 stipulates that during courses on the Koran female students may cover their hair with an Islamic veil.

philosophical beliefs in education generally becomes an issue in the context of parents whose daughters wear the headscarf and are not allowed entry into school.

4.456 The common element in all such cases relates to the privileged protection and particular under-standing of *laiklik*. The wearing of the headscarf has been held to be inconsistent with *the principle*. The jurisprudence of the CS in a case concerning disciplinary measures against a university student who wore the headscarf at university is instructive.[920] The CS considered the wearing of the headscarf to be a symbol that shows a strong objection to the *laik* nature of the Turkish Republic and proof that the students in question embrace a state order that is based on religion.[921] The connection drawn between the act of wearing the headscarf and thus being a threat to the *laik* or secular state is not fully explained but appears to be drawn with certain assumptions or perceptions.

4.457 Proposed constitutional amendments relaxing the restrictions on university students wearing the headscarf were also made ineffective by the TCC. The adoption of Law No 3511 in 1989,[922] and after its annulment,[923] the adoption of the Law No 5735 in 2008,[924] failed to lead to a solution. The TCC held that the proposed constitutional amendments had the main aim of de-restricting the display of religious symbols in higher education institutions without eliminat-ing public fears, foreseeing safeguards against abuses, and putting in place measures necessary for the protection of third party rights.[925] According to the TCC, the use of the religious symbols would create pressure on non-believers and on Muslim females and would also damage state neutrality by opening a pathway for religion to be used for political purposes.[926]

e) The collective dimension

4.458 The collective dimension of the right to freedom of religion or belief is based on protection of the manifestation of religion or belief 'in community' with others, recognizing the nature of believers who generally engage in activities that they do together.[927] Such actions include, but are not limited to, assembly for the purposes of worship, establishing and maintaining places of worship, establishing charitable institutions, and maintaining educational facilities.[928]

4.459 *Legitimacy of religion.* In international law it is well established that the state cannot evalu-ate the legitimacy of a religion. In *Metropolitan Church of Besserabia v Moldova*, the ECtHR observed that neutrality and impartiality as defined in its case law is incompatible with the state having a role in assessing the legitimacy of religious beliefs.[929] In the Turkish system,

---

[920] Council of State, 8th Chamber, E1983/207, K1984/330, 23 December 1984.

[921] Council of State, 8th Chamber, E1983/207, K1984/330, 23 December 1984, paras 1–10.

[922] This Law added a new art 16 to Law No 2547 on Higher Education. Art 16 stipulated that: 'Within higher education establishments, classrooms, laboratories, clinics, and policlinics and in corridors it is obliga-tory to be in modern clothing and looks. The closing of the neck and hair with a cloth or with a turban due to religious reasons is unrestricted.'

[923] The TCC annulled the Law on grounds that it was contrary to the Preamble and arts 2, 10, 24, and 174 of the Constitution. Turkish Constitutional Court Judgment, E1989/1, K1989/12, 7 March 1989.

[924] No one can be denied, for any reason at all, the right to higher education in cases not openly stipulated by law.

[925] Turkish Constitutional Court Judgment, E1989/1 K1989/12, 7 March 1989. Turkish Constitutional Court Judgment, E1990/36, K1991/8, 9 April 1991.

[926] *Svyato-Mikhaylivska Parafiya v Ukraine* (App 77703/01) (2007).

[927] *Svyato-Mikhaylivska Parafiya* (n 926) para 117.

[928] 1981 Declaration on the Elimination of All Forms of Intolerance and of Discrimination Based on Religion or Belief, 25 November 1981, A/RES/36/55, art 6.

[929] *Metropolitan Church of Besserabia v Moldova* (App 45701/99) (2001) para 123.

while there is no specific recognition procedure for religions, there are certain circumstances where such recognition has a legal significance. In this context the situation of the Bahai and the Jehovah's Witnesses in Turkey stand out. In the case of a Bahai who wanted to have the Bahai religion stated in the religion section of his national identity card, the CS held that the Bahai faith was not a 'religion' as such.[930] This decision was based on the opinion requested from the Presidency of Religious Affairs, which stated that the Bahai faith was a 'sect'—*tari-kat*[931]—not an independent religion.[932] In two decisions concerning similar cases, this time initiated by Jehovah's Witnesses, the CS recognized this religion on the basis of the opinion of the Turkish Rabbinate and Greek Orthodox Patriarchate.[933] These decisions demonstrate that for the CS the claim of members of a religion as to whether their belief system is a religion or not is not determinative; instead the CS chooses to rely on the opinion of the already established religious authorities or theological faculties. Bearing in mind that new or minority religious groups may be considered heterodox in relation to established religions, the practice adopted by the CS places the members of unrecognized religions at the mercy of recognized ones. A similar dispute concerned the *Gök Tanrı* (the faith of Göktürks) and the Jehovah's Witnesses; the administrative courts held that they were not religions.[934] In the former the administrative court decided on its own, in the latter it based its decision on the opinions of the Rabbinate and the Greek Orthodox Patriarchate.

Legal personality. The right of belief groups to acquire legal personality has been recognized in international court decisions[935] and political instruments.[936] The lack of legislation pertaining to the legal personality of belief communities in Turkey rules out the possibility of acquiring legal personality as such.[937] A related issue concerns the legal status of the leadership of certain belief communities. Even though no religious leadership enjoys a public or private legal status, case law and administrative practice demonstrate that there is no consistent legal solution or approach to the question of whether the Patriarchate,[938] or Chief Rabbinate have legal status or not.[939] **4.460**

---

[930] Council of State, 10th Chamber, E1992/3226, K1995/4872, 25 October 1995.

[931] *Tarikat* literally means 'path', a path within a belief; however, in Turkish it may sometimes have a negative conotation implying that the belief in question is a radical closed community or that it is heterodox.

[932] Council of State, 8th Chamber, E1983/207, K1984/330, 23 December 1984.

[933] Council of State, 10th Chamber, E2003/2029, K2006/6340, 13 November 2006 and Council of State, 10th Chamber, E2003/2040, K2006/6339, 13 November 2006.

[934] Council of State, 10th Chamber, E1994/8030, K1996/719, 15 February 1996; Council of State, 10th Chamber, E2003/2029, K2006/6340, 13 November 2006; and Council of State, 10th Chamber, E2003/2040, K2006/6339, 13 November 2006.

[935] *Metropolitan Church of Bessarabia* (n 929) para 105. Other examples include *Fener Rum Erkek Lisesi Vakfı v Turkey Fener Boys High School Foundation v Turkey*, Judgment (App 34478/97) (2007); *Apostolidi and ors v Turkey* (App 45628/99) (2007); *Fener Rum Patrikligi (Ecumenical Patriarchate) v Turkey* (App 14340/05) (2008); and the cases of *Yedikule Surp Pirgiç Ermeni Hastanesi Vakfı v Turkey* (App 36165/02) (2008); *Samatya Surp Kevork Ermeni Kilisesi, Mektebi Ve Mezarligi Vakfı Yönetim Kurulu v Turkey* (App 1480/03) (2008); and *Bozcaada Kimisis Teodoku Rum Ortodoks Kilisesi Vakfı v Turkey (No 2)* (Apps 37639/03, 37655/03, 26736/04, and 42670/04) (2009).

[936] OSCE/ODIHR Guidelines for legislative reviews of laws affecting religion or belief (CDL-AD (2004)028).

[937] See European Commission for Democracy Through Law (the Venice Commission), Opinion on the Legal Status of Religious Communities in Turkey, CDL-AD(2010)005, Opinion 535/2009, 15 March 2010.

[938] On the legal status of the Greek Orthodox Patriarchate and relevant discussion, see E Macar, *Cumhuriyet Döneminde İstanbul Rum Patrikhanesi* [Istanbul Greek Orthodox Patriarchate in the Republic Period] (İletişim, 2004) 267–9.

[939] Council of State, 10th Chamber, E2003/2029, K2006/6340, 13 November 2006 and Council of State, 10th Chamber, E2003/2040, K2006/6339, 13 November 2006.

4.461   The existing forms of legal status constitute an inadequate legal framework in the context of the exercise of associative rights of belief communities. Members of belief communities may establish associations or foundations and gain a limited legal personality and an indirect means of, *inter alia*, owning property or establishing places of worship or charity institutions.

4.462   Article 101(4) of the Civil Code prohibits the establishment of a foundation 'contrary to the characteristics of the Republic as defined by the Constitution, Constitutional rules, laws, morals, national integrity and national interest, or with the aim of supporting a distinctive race or community'. This provision has not been evoked to try to close the community foundations established before the Republic, since they enjoy a special protection based on Turkey's obligations under the Lausanne Treaty. However, it might, depending on interpretation and application, be an obstacle to the setting up of *new* foundations to support the activities of a given religious community, especially if the purpose of the foundation goes beyond support for a specific building or institution set aside for religious purposes. This provision has been applied inconsistently by the High Court of Appeals in cases dealing with the establishment of foundations having the purpose of meeting the religious needs of new religious groups.[940]

4.463   The Law on Foundations, dated 20 February 2008, includes provisions that provide solutions to a number of issues concerning community foundations.[941] Some of these provisions facilitate the return of properties of foundations that were confiscated as a result of the judicial practice based on the 1974 jurisprudence of the Court of Appeals.[942] Despite certain positive changes, measures necessary to fully correct the unjust treatment of community foundations over decades are not complete.[943]

4.464   The establishment of an association is another private law legal entity option available for members of belief communities. It is, however, not an option that is designed particularly as a legal entity for religious groups, nor is it necessarily suitable to the nature and needs of religious communities in the exercise of the right to manifest their religion or belief together. An association is a private law legal person that is formed by real or legal persons with the objective of realizing a certain purpose, which is not contrary to law, by bringing together their knowledge and efforts.[944] The possibility for members of belief communities to establish ordinary associations with religious purposes is a relatively recent development. The Law on Associations, which was adopted in 2004 in accordance with the Harmonization Process for Turkey's accession to the European Union, omits the explicit prohibition on establishing associations based on a certain religion or denomination that was found in the previous law. In addition, there is no explicit prohibition in the Turkish Civil Code analogous to that

---

[940]   See the inconsistent decisions of the High Courts of Appeals in the cases of Istanbul Protestant Foundation and the 7th Adventists Foundations.

[941]   Law on Foundations No 5737, adopted on 20 February 2008, RG No 26800, 27 February 2008.

[942]   The High Court of Appeals unanimously decided that: 'The legal entities formed by those who are not Turks are prohibited from acquiring property'; High Court of Appeals, 2nd Chamber, E/4449, K/4399, 6 July 1971. Hence an innovative yet explicitly discriminatory legal categorization was created by case law. Those who formed non-Muslim community foundations were considered non-Turks, and thus subject to laws that were applicable to foreigners in the sphere of property rights.

[943]   M Yildirim and O Oering, 'What does Turkey's Restitution Decree mean?', Forum 18 News, 6 October 2011, available at <http://forum18.org/Analyses.php?region=68> (accessed 15 December 2011).

[944]   Dernekler Kanunu (Law on Associations), No 5253, 4 November 2004, RG No 25649, 23 November 2004, art 2. Turkish Civil Code, art 56.

which applies to foundations in article 101(4) of the Turkish Civil Code. The Turkish Civil Code stipulates that associations 'contrary to law and morals' may not be established.

Even though it is not explicitly protected, the right of religious congregations to assemble **4.465** for traditional gatherings is an exception to meetings that generally require permission.[945] However, they must abide by laws in general. Prevention of religious services or worship through the use of violence or threat or any other action contrary to law is subject to punishment.[946] On the other hand, it has been reported that belief groups that gather for worship, for example, in an association building, have been prosecuted for conducting illegal worship activity in a place that is not assigned as a place of worship.[947]

In 2003 it became legally possible to establish places of worship other than mosques.[948] The **4.466** right to establish places of worship is partly regulated by the Zoning Law which stipulates that: 'In the development of zoning plans, the required places of worship shall be designated taking into account the conditions of the planned districts and regions and their future needs.'[949] In addition, the permission of the highest civilian administrator is required.

Mosques are subject to a different regulation based on the requirements of the Presidency **4.467** of Religious Affairs or *Diyanet*. It is not possible to establish a mosque and appoint religious personnel outside the *Diyanet* structure. The regulation singles out the *Diyanet* as the sole subject of the exercise of the right to establish places of worship and appoint religious leaders in the context of Sunni-Muslim practice.

f) Freedom of expression and freedom of religion or belief

The Turkish Constitution protects everyone's right to express and disseminate his thoughts **4.468** and opinions by speech, in writing, in pictures, or through other media, individually or collectively.[950] The Former Turkish Criminal Code treated blasphemy under crimes against freedom of religion or belief; however, the new Turkish Criminal Code treats blasphemy under provisions relating to crimes against honour as an aggravated form of insult.[951] Article 125(b) and (e) of the Code impose a sentence of up to a year of imprisonment for the crime of insult when the crime is committed against a person because of the expression of his/her ideas or religious, social, political, and philosophical beliefs or the change of these; latter, or his/her behaviour that derive from the requirements of a religion; or when the crime is committed with reference to the values considered sacred by the religion to which the victim belongs. Critics of religion—particularly of Islam—are frequently prosecuted; even if such cases may not lead to convictions, it would not be unreasonable to surmise that such prosecutions might cause self-censorship.[952]

---

[945] Toplantı ve Gösteri Yürüyüşleri Kanunu (Law on Meetings and Demonstrations), Law No 2911, 6 October 1983, RG No 18185, 8 October 1983, art 4(b).

[946] Turkish Criminal Code (Türk Ceza Kanunu), Law No 5237, 26 September 2004, RG No 25611, 12 October 2004, art 115(2).

[947] Interview with Umut Şahin from the Association of Protestant Churches, November 2011.

[948] İmar Kanunu (Public Works Law), Law No 3194, 3 May 1985, RG No 18749, 9 May 1985, Additional Provision 2 (amending art 9), 15 July 2003.

[949] See n 951.

[950] Turkish Constitution, art 26.

[951] Türk Ceza Kanunu [Turkish Criminal Code] Law No 5237, 26 September 2004, entered into force on 1 June 2005. RG No 25611, 12 October 2004.

[952] The Turkish media reports such cases frequently, see among others, 'Bu Dava "İllallah" dedirtir', 12 December 2011, Bianet, available at <http://www.bianet.org/bianet/ifade-ozgurlugu/134708-bu-dava-illallah-dedirtir> (accessed 15 December 2011); 'Savcılık Dine Hakaret Eden Sav Hakında 1 Yıl Hapis

I. United States

Nicholas Hatzis[953]

(1) The First Amendment

a) Introduction

4.469 The religion clauses of the First Amendment provide: 'Congress shall make no law respecting an establishment of religion, or prohibiting the free exercise thereof.' The former is the Establishment Clause, and the latter the Free Exercise Clause. Broadly speaking, the Establishment Clause regulates church-state relations while the Free Exercise Clause guarantees a right to religious freedom. This does not mean that the relevant cases and the principles underlying them should be seen as unconnected. By contrast, they are closely linked and operate together in pursuance of the constitutional objective of protecting freedom of religion.[954] In the context of the American tradition of separation of church and state, privileging one (or more) religious group is seen as a restriction of the religious freedom of others. Thus, the Establishment Clause has been relied upon by the Supreme Court to invalidate provisions which subjected religious groups to unjustified differential treatment.[955]

4.470 Sometimes, though, there is dissonance between the two clauses. The most characteristic example concerns the issue of religious exemptions from general laws. Where such a law makes the practice of religion more difficult, is it legitimate for the government to exempt believers from the obligation to comply with it while expecting everyone else to respect it? If the Free Exercise Clause requires the government to take into account religious needs and accommodate them, how far can this accommodation go before becoming an establishment of religion prohibited by the Establishment Clause?

4.471 The aim of this contribution is to provide a discussion of the main rules governing the protection of religious freedom under the Free Exercise Clause; it refers to Establishment Clause points where they are relevant for religious claims but does not examine issues concerning the separation of church and state. Given the limited space available, it is impossible to discuss all relevant cases or even all the issues to which the cases which are discussed give rise. The focus, therefore, is on Supreme Court free exercise case law and the constitutional principles it developed.

b) The scope of the Free Exercise Clause: belief and practice

4.472 The first major Supreme Court case on the Free Exercise Clause was *Reynolds v United States*[956] decided in 1878. It concerned a challenge to a federal law making bigamy a criminal offence. The claimant, a Mormon, argued that practising polygamy was his religious duty. The Court rejected the claim, holding that 'Congress was deprived of all legislative power over mere opinion but was left free to reach actions which were in violation of social duties or

---

İstedi', 26 November 2011, Zaman Daily, available at <http://www.zaman.com.tr/haber.do?haberno=1206533&title=savcilik-dine-hakaret-eden-sav-hakkinda-1-yil-hapis-istedi> (accessed 15 December 2011).

[953] City University London; University of Oxford.

[954] K Greenawalt, *Religion and the Constitution: Free Exercise and Fairness* (Princeton University Press, 2006) 3.

[955] *Larson v Valente* 456 US 228 (1982), discussed at para 4.479.

[956] *Reynolds v US* 98 US 145 (1878). See also *Davis v Beason* 133 US 333 (1890).

subversive of good order'.[957] Given the pernicious effects of polygamy on society, the Court continued, the legislature was justified in prohibiting it: 'laws are made for the government of actions, and while they cannot interfere with mere religious belief and opinions, they may with practices'.[958]

The effect of *Reynolds* was to introduce into religious freedom jurisprudence the dichotomy **4.473** between religious belief and action and the principle that while the state cannot interfere with the former, the latter can be legitimately restricted in pursuance of valid public interests.[959] This is now the rule in most constitutional systems and in the European Convention on Human Rights. The Strasbourg organs have developed the rule that Article 9 ECHR protects, on the one hand, 'the sphere of personal beliefs and religious creeds, this being the area which is sometimes called the *forum internum*', and, on the other, 'acts which are intimately linked to these attitudes, such as acts of worship or devotion which are aspects of the practice of a religion or belief in a generally recognised form', without 'always guarantee[ing] the right to behave in the public sphere in a way which is dictated by such a belief'.[960]

The Supreme Court affirmed the distinction between belief and action in *Cantwell v* **4.474** *Connecticut*.[961] The petitioners were Jehovah's Witnesses who had been convicted of engaging in door-to-door canvassing without having the required permit which the local council had discretion to grant or not. In reversing the convictions as incompatible with the First Amendment, the Supreme Court noted: ... the Amendment embraces two concepts,—freedom to believe and freedom to act. The first is absolute but, in the nature of things, the second cannot be. Conduct remains subject to regulation for the protection of society ... In every case the power to regulate must be so exercised as not, in attaining a permissible end, unduly to infringe the protected freedom.[962]

Thus, *Cantwell* relaxed the strictness of the *Reynolds* rule:[963] the constitutional guarantee of religious freedom could be relied upon even where the state was restricting religiously-motivated conduct (as opposed to religious belief) in pursuance of a legitimate public aim.

(2) Direct interference with freedom of religion

The state may restrict religious freedom in a direct or indirect manner. Direct interferences **4.475** involve a law or measure which seeks to regulate in some way the exercise of religion. A classic example would be a law making membership in a religious community compulsory or banning a religious group. By contrast, indirect interferences flow from general and neutral laws which pursue non-religious objectives but restrict religious freedom because they require the performance of an act which is religiously prohibited or forbid the performance of an act which is religiously required. For example, a statute making school attendance compulsory until a certain age constitutes an indirect restriction of the freedom of a religious group with the fundamental belief that salvation requires living in a community away from worldly influences.[964]

---

957 *Reynolds* (n 956) 164.
958 *Reynolds* (n 956).
959 Greenawalt (n 954) 28.
960 For a recent authority see *Schilder v Netherlands* (App 2158/12), decision of 16 October 2012, para 18.
961 *Cantwell v Connecticut* 320 US 296 (1940).
962 *Cantwell* (n 961) 303–4.
963 Greenawalt (n 954) 29.
964 The case is *Wisconsin v Yoder* 406 US 205 (1972), discussed at paras 4.498–4.501.

4.476   This section discusses the case law on direct interferences with religious practice. There are only a few such cases; they attract strict scrutiny, which is the most intensive form of constitutional judicial review. *Torcaso v Watkins*[965] provides a typical example. According to the state constitution of Maryland, public officials had to declare their belief in God. The appellant was refused a commission as notary public because he would not make the required declaration. The Supreme Court held that this compulsory profession of a religious belief was unconstitutional: 'neither a State nor the Federal Government can constitutionally force a person to profess a belief or disbelief in any religion. Neither can constitutionally pass laws or impose requirements which aid all religions as against non-believers, and neither can aid those religions based on a belief in the existence of God as against those religions founded on different beliefs'.[966] Thus, the First Amendment prevents the state from disfavouring not only those with certain religious beliefs, but also those who hold no such beliefs at all.[967] Further, the Court rejected the argument that the requirement to profess belief in God was constitutional because no citizen was compelled to hold public office against his will, noting that: 'The fact . . . that a person is not compelled to hold public office cannot possibly be an excuse for barring him from office by state-imposed criteria forbidden by the Constitution.'[968] Justice Black's opinion concluded that the Maryland rule 'unconstitutionally invade[d] the appellant's freedom of belief and religion'.[969] As this formulation implies, requirements to make a profession of belief violate not only the Free Exercise Clause but also the Establishment Clause of the First Amendment, as state power is used to support a particular religious viewpoint.[970]

4.477   In *McDaniel v Paty*,[971] the appellant, an ordained Baptist minister, challenged a Tennessee law which prohibited 'priests of any denomination' from serving as delegates to the state's constitutional convention. The provision applied to all religious groups so there was no discrimination among religions; rather, it disfavoured religion itself.[972] The Court's decision to strike down the law as incompatible with the Free Exercise Clause was unanimous, but there were two views as to the character of the religious classification the law made. Justice Burger's plurality opinion held that, unlike *Torcaso v Watkins*, *McDaniel* did not involve an interference with religious *belief*; if that were the case the Tennessee law would have been declared unconstitutional without any further inquiry because: 'The Free Exercise Clause categorically prohibits government from regulating, prohibiting, or rewarding religious beliefs as such.'[973] The law, he continued, defined 'ministerial status . . . in terms of conduct and activity rather than in terms of belief'[974] and was 'directed primarily at status, acts and conduct'.[975] Then he proceeded to balance the appellant's religious freedom against the state

---

[965]   *Torcaso v Watkins* 367 US 488 (1960).

[966]   *Torcaso* (n 965) 495 (citations and internal quotation marks omitted).

[967]   See N Tebbe, 'Nonbelievers' (2011) 97 Virginia Law Review 1111, 1149.

[968]   *Torcaso* (n 965) 405–96.

[969]   *Torcaso* (n 965) 496.

[970]   Greenawalt (n 954) 36.

[971]   *McDaniel v Paty* 435 US 618 (1978).

[972]   In his concurring opinion, Brennan J doubted whether the law really avoided discrimination among religions given that 'ministers of faiths with established, clearly recognizable ministries' would be at a disadvantage compared to 'members of nonorthodox humanistic faiths having no "counterpart" to ministers' and given that the latter, by not being ministers in a traditionally understood sense, would be able to escape the disqualification: *Paty* (n 971) 633, fn 4 (Brennan J, concurring).

[973]   *Paty* (n 971) 626 (citation omitted).

[974]   *Paty* (n 971) 627.

[975]   *Paty* (n 971) 627.

interest pursued by the impugned law. Tennessee had argued that disqualifying the clergy was necessary in order to prevent the legislative process from becoming a means of promoting sectarian interests in violation of the Establishment Clause.[976] But the Court found that, while the aim was indeed legitimate, there was no evidence that such a prohibition was necessary in modern America: 'the American experience provides no persuasive support for the fear that clergymen in public office will be less careful of anti-establishment interests or less faithful to their oaths of civil office than their unordained counterparts'.[977]

In a concurring opinion, Justice Brennan disagreed with the plurality's characterization of the law, explaining that the only reason for the appellant's disqualification was not that he had engaged in a particular activity but that he was a priest: 'The purpose of the Tennessee provision [was] not to regulate activities associated with a ministry . . . but to bar from political office persons regarded as deeply committed to religious participation because of that participation.'[978] Therefore, he found that *Torcaso* was the controlling precedent as the law's effect was to burden people whose deeply-held religious faith had led them to priesthood. **4.478**

While *McDaniel v Paty* concerned a burden imposed on all religions, the provisions at stake in *Larson v Valente*[979] introduced a preference of some religions over others. A Minnesota statute imposed onerous registration and disclosure requirements on charities. At first, all religious charities were exempted but later the exemption was limited to those which received more than half of their contributions from members and affiliated organizations; religious groups unable to satisfy this fifty per cent rule became subject to the statute, which was challenged by the Unification Church of the Reverend Moon. Justice Brennan's majority opinion framed the issue as one concerning discrimination against some religions in violation of the Establishment Clause and therefore calling for strict scrutiny review. The legislative history of the law showed that the legislators intended to regulate the activities of non-traditional religions while making certain that mainstream religious organizations, such as the Roman Catholic Archdiocese, were exempted. The rule, Justice Brennan concluded, created an 'official denominational preference'[980] in violation of the Establishment Clause.[981] **4.479**

The more pernicious practice of targeting a religious group by prohibiting its worship rituals came before the Supreme Court in *Lukumi*.[982] The city of Hialeah in Florida passed a series of ordinances prohibiting the ritual slaughter of animals. This practice was followed by the Santeria religion, a traditional African religion with elements of Roman Catholicism, which originates in Cuba. Justice Kennedy noted that a law which restricts the religious practice will attract strict scrutiny unless it is neutral and applies in a general manner. However, **4.480**

---

[976] On the history and justifications for clergy disqualification and the relationship between clergy political activity and democratic politics, see K Greenawalt, 'Religion and American Political Judgments' (2001) 36 Wake Forest Law Review 401; M Cordes, 'Politics, Religion and the First Amendment' (2000–01) DePaul Law Review 111; P Weithman, 'May Clergy Seek Elective Office?' (1999) 74 Notre Dame Law Review 1737.

[977] *Paty* (n 971) 629 (citation omitted).

[978] *Paty* (n 971) 634 (Brennan J, concurring).

[979] *Larson v Valente* 456 US 228 (1982).

[980] *Larson* (n 979) 255.

[981] While the focus of the opinion is on the Establishment Clause, Brennan J also noted that the 'constitutional prohibition of denominational preferences is inextricably connected with . . . the Free Exercise Clause': *Larson* (n 979) 245. The idea underlying this statement is that a law which treats a specific group less favourably restricts its right to religious practice.

[982] *Church of Lukumi Babalu Aye v City of Hialeah* 508 US 520 (1993).

no law can be neutral if it 'restricts practices because of their religious motivation'.[983] The defendants argued that the law passed the neutrality threshold because it made no direct reference to religious beliefs and practices. The Court rejected this restriction of the neutrality requirement to the face of the statute:

> Facial neutrality is not determinative. The Free Exercise Clause, like the Establishment Clause, extends beyond facial discrimination. The Clause forbids subtle departures from neutrality and covert suppression of particular religious beliefs. Official action that targets religious conduct for distinctive treatment cannot be shielded by mere compliance with the requirement of facial neutrality. The Free Exercise Clause protects against governmental hostility which is masked, as well as overt.[984]

4.481 What is necessary is to look beyond the face of the law, to its actual operation. Here, the prohibition was drafted in a way which excluded, in practice, all other instances of animal killing from its scope, catching only the Santeria ritual sacrifices.

4.482 Further, Justice Kennedy looked at the legislative history of the ordinances. The minutes of the meetings of the local council contained numerous hostile references to the Santeria religion and its adherents which clearly demonstrated that the motive of city officials in passing the ordinances was to prohibit its rituals and target a group that was very unpopular among local residents.[985] The Hialeah restrictions, Justice Kennedy held, constituted a 'religious gerrymander, an impermissible attempt to target petitioners and their religious practices'.[986]

4.483 The judgment in *Lukumi* demonstrates how equality considerations operate in modern Free Exercise law.[987] Genuine respect for religious freedom requires *equal* freedom for all. This is a particularly valuable guarantee for small and non-traditional religious groups which are often the victims of hostile treatment by state institutions and religious majorities. Hostile treatment of this type operates as an exclusion mechanism from the political community: certain groups are marginalized and their members' status as equal citizens is undermined.[988] In such cases, religious freedom reaches beyond the individual believer who is prevented from practicing his religion to encompass a broader concern about the fate of non-mainstream groups.

(3) Indirect interference with freedom of religion

4.484 The great majority of contemporary cases involving free exercise claims arise in relation to laws which neither target, covertly or overtly, a particular religion nor do they seek to regulate behaviour by referring to religious criteria. Rather, they are general and neutral laws: they pursue a non-religious objective, apply to everybody, and do not involve any religious distinctions or classifications. They become relevant for religious practice because some of the obligations they impose conflict with religious requirements. Most religions expect their believers not only to believe, but also to behave in a certain way. General and neutral laws can

---

[983] *Lukumi* (n 982) 533.

[984] *Lukumi* (n 982) 534 (internal citations and quotation marks omitted).

[985] Scalia J did not join that part of Kennedy's J's opinion which examined the legislators' intentions, taking the view that the only criterion which mattered for the assessment of the Hialeah ordinances was their effect; this was enough for the Court to strike them down as incompatible with the Free Exercise Clause: *Lukumi* (n 982) 558–9 (Scalia J, concurring in part and concurring in the judgment).

[986] *Lukumi* (n 982) 534 (internal citations and quotation marks omitted).

[987] For a theory of religious freedom based on equality see C Eisgruber and L Sager, *Religious Freedom and the Constitution* (Harvard University Press, 2007).

[988] See K Karst, 'Religious Freedom and Equal Citizenship: Reflections on *Lukumi*' (1994) 69 Tulane Law Review 335, 350 ff.

restrict their freedom to do so where they require all citizens to perform an act which is prohibited by some religions or prevent all citizens from performing an act which is mandated by some religions; thus, the adherents of those religions are prevented from conforming to the requirements of their faith. In this sense, general and neutral laws impose an indirect or incidental burden on religious freedom: they do not single out religious conduct but make it more difficult to engage in such conduct.[989]

The constitutional question, then, becomes whether the Free Exercise Clause *requires* the state to exempt religious individuals from the scope of general laws which impinge on the freedom to practice their religion. This is different from (but related to) the issue of legislative religious exemptions; the latter are not mandated by the Constitution, so the legislature has *discretion* to grant them or not to believers.[990] This section discusses *constitutionally mandated* exemptions. **4.485**

a) Early developments

We have already seen that the first major case on the Free Exercise Clause, *Reynolds v United States*[991] (1878), was an exemption case about a Mormon claimant who was prevented from engaging in religiously-required polygamy by a law which criminalized bigamy, and that his challenge was rejected by the Supreme Court on the basis that the legislature could interfere with religious conduct (as opposed to belief) in pursuance of a legitimate aim. But in *Cantwell v Connecticut*[992] (1940) the Court accepted that conduct also enjoyed the protection of the First Amendment. **4.486**

The case law that followed was not consistent. A number of cases were brought in the 1940s by Jehovah's Witnesses who found some of their practices being restricted by general laws. In *Minersville School District v Gobitis*,[993] the claimants were Jehovah's Witnesses who wished their children to be exempted from the obligation to salute the flag at school. In an opinion by Justice Frankfurter the Supreme Court rejected the claim, reasoning that judges should not interfere with the educational authorities' assessment about the appropriate methods to promote patriotism and national unity among pupils, provided that 'the remedial channels of the democratic process remain open and unobstructed'.[994] Granting the exemption, he continued, 'might introduce elements of difficulty into the school discipline, might cast doubts in the minds of the other children which would themselves weaken the effect of the exercise'.[995] Justice Stone, the sole dissenter, replied to the argument that Jehovah's Witnesses could use the democratic process to obtain a legislative exemption. He explained that the issue was whether the government could compel the expression of a belief contrary to the individual's religious convictions, which the First Amendment protects. Jehovah's Witnesses were a 'politically helpless minorit[y]',[996] so leaving the protection of their religious freedom to politics was 'no more than the surrender of the constitutional protection of the liberty of small minorities to the popular will'.[997] **4.487**

---

[989] See M Dorf, 'Incidental Burdens on Fundamental Rights' (1996) 109 Harvard Law Review 1182.
[990] How far the legislature can go in accommodating religious claims by granting exemptions from general laws is a particularly vexed issue in Establishment Clause jurisprudence.
[991] *Reynolds v US* 98 US 145 (1878).
[992] *Cantwell v Connecticut* 310 US 296 (1940).
[993] *Minersville School District v Gobitis* 310 US 586 (1940).
[994] *Gobitis* (n 993) 599.
[995] *Gobitis* (n 993) 600.
[996] *Gobitis* (n 993) 604.
[997] *Gobitis* (n 993) 606.

4.488 *Gobitis* was overruled in *West Virginia Board of Education v Barnette*,[998] decided in 1943. Justice Jackson, who wrote the majority opinion, took the view that the issue of the compulsory flag salute was not merely whether a religious exemption was mandated but whether the state had the power to coerce people into affirming a belief against their conscience and opinion. While the authorities could fashion educational policy as they saw fit, they had to do so within the constraints of the Constitution. In response to Justice Frankfurter's argument that Jehovah's Witnesses should lobby the government for an exemption, he said that:

> The very purpose of a Bill of Rights was to withdraw certain subjects from the vicissitudes of political controversy, to place them beyond the reach of majorities and officials...One's right to life, liberty, and property, to free speech, a free press, freedom of worship and assembly, and other fundamental rights may not be submitted to vote.[999]

Finally, he rejected the view, adopted in *Gobitis*, that the pursuit of national unity justified compulsory expressions of belief. In doing so, he provided one of the classic, and most eloquent, expositions of First Amendment doctrine:

> ...freedom to differ is not limited to things that do not matter much. That would be a mere shadow of freedom. The test of its substance is the right to differ as to things that touch the heart of the existing order. If there is any fixed star in our constitutional constellation, it is that no official, high or petty, can prescribe what shall be orthodox in politics, nationalism, religion, or other matters of opinion or force citizens to confess by word or act their faith therein.[1000]

4.489 A year later Jehovah's Witnesses challenged, this time unsuccessfully, a child labour law which made it a criminal offence for parents to allow their children to sell any merchandise, newspapers, or magazines in the streets or other public places. In *Prince v Massachusetts*,[1001] the Supreme Court held that while minors too benefited from the right to freedom of religion, the 'state's authority over children's activities is broader than over like actions of adults'.[1002] Preaching and religious canvassing in the street could create difficult situations where children might suffer psychological or physical harm. The fact that some parents might be wiling to take that risk was not decisive: 'Parents may be free to become martyrs themselves. But it does not follow they are free, in identical circumstances, to make martyrs of their children before they have reached the age of full and legal discretion when they can make that choice for themselves.'[1003]

4.490 A challenge to a Sunday closing law came before the Supreme Court in *Braunfeld v Brown*.[1004] The appellants were Orthodox Jews who wished to be allowed to open their stores on Sundays, given that they were religiously required to close them on Saturdays. Their claim was that the law violated their free exercise rights because it obliged them either to give up their Sabbath observance or suffer a serious economic disadvantage which might make it impossible for them to continue in their business. In a plurality opinion by Chief Justice Warren the Court upheld the law. It noted that 'the statute...does not make criminal the holding of any religious belief or opinion, nor does it force anyone to embrace any religious belief or to say or

---

[998] *West Virginia Board of Education v Barnette* 319 US 624 (1943).
[999] *Barnette* (n 998) 638.
[1000] *Barnette* (n 998) 642.
[1001] *Prince v Massachusetts* 321 US 158 (1944).
[1002] *Prince* (n 1001) 168.
[1003] *Prince* (n 1001) 171.
[1004] *Braunfeld v Brown* 366 US 599 (1961).

believe anything in conflict with his religious tenets'.[1005] Reiterating the distinction between belief and practice announced in *Reynolds* and affirmed in *Cantwell*, it stated that 'legislative power over mere opinion is forbidden but it may reach people's actions'.[1006] The law at stake did not prohibit a religious practice; it only made it more expensive for some believers. Having a common day of rest which 'eliminates the atmosphere of commercial noise and activity'[1007] was a legitimate secular goal. While it was true that the statute imposed an indirect economic burden on the appellants:

> ...in cosmopolitan nation[s] made up of people of almost every conceivable religious preference...it cannot be expected, much less required, that legislators enact no law regulating conduct that may in some way result in an economic disadvantage to some religious sects and not to others because of the special practices of the various religions.[1008]

In dissent, Justice Brennan stated that the main issue concerned the appropriate standard of **4.491** constitutional review. Citing *West Virginia Board of Education v Barnette* he held that where a law restricts religious freedom, strict scrutiny is called for. In the present case there was no 'compelling state interest'[1009] which could justify denying an exemption; rather, it was 'the mere convenience of having everyone rest on the same day'.[1010] The majority, Justice Brennan concluded, had 'exalted administrative convenience to a constitutional level high enough to justify making one religion economically disadvantageous'.[1011]

b) The 'compelling interest' test: Sherbert v Verner

Adell Sherbert was a Seventh-day Adventist who lost her job after refusing to work on **4.492** Saturday, her religion's Sabbath. Being unable to find other work because of her unavailability on Saturdays, she applied for unemployment benefits. South Carolina authorities rejected her application because the relevant law stated that those who had refused to accept suitable work that had been offered to them were not eligible. In *Sherbert v Verner*[1012] the Supreme Court found for Ms Sherbert. The opinion, by Justice Brennan, is a particularly important Free Exercise Clause judgment.

Justice Brennan's starting point was that although the law did not compel her to work on **4.493** Saturdays it constituted a burden on the free exercise of religion. The burden was 'indirect'[1013] but this did not change the fact that her 'ineligibility for benefits derive[d] solely from the practice of her religion'.[1014] She had the choice of either remaining true to her religious convictions and forgoing the benefits, or accepting Saturday work and violating a religious obligation. 'Governmental imposition of such a choice', Justice Brennan concluded, 'puts the same kind of burden upon the free exercise of religion as would a fine imposed against appellant for her Saturday worship'.[1015]

[1005] *Braunfeld* (n 1004) 603.
[1006] *Braunfeld* (n 1004) 603.
[1007] *Braunfeld* (n 1004) 608.
[1008] *Braunfeld* (n 1004) 606 (citation omitted).
[1009] *Braunfeld* (n 1004) 613 (Brennan J, concurring in part and dissenting in part).
[1010] *Braunfeld* (n 1004) 614 (Brennan J, concurring in part and dissenting in part).
[1011] *Braunfeld* (n 1004) 615–16 (Brennan J, concurring in part and dissenting in part).
[1012] *Sherbert v Verner* 374 US 398 (1963).
[1013] *Sherbert* (n 1012) 404.
[1014] *Sherbert* (n 1012) 404.
[1015] *Sherbert* (n 1012) 404.

4.494   Next, he subjected the South Carolina law to strict scrutiny. This form of judicial review requires the state to show that it pursues a compelling state interest using the least intrusive means. Justice Brennan found that the defendants had failed the test. They had argued that, if an exemption had been granted, there would be a danger of fraudulent claims being submitted by people who had no real religious objections to Saturday work. However, there was nothing in the record to suggest that such fears were justified, and, even if that had been the case, the burden was on the government to demonstrate that 'no alternative forms of regulation would combat such abuses without infringing First Amendment rights'.[1016]

4.495   *Sherbert*'s innovation lies in the express adoption of the compelling interest test for religious exemption claims. This test is particularly exacting and in most cases the government will fail to satisfy it.[1017] Thus, where a general law restricts freedom of religious practice, the judgment requires the government to carve out an exemption for believers. The accommodation of religious claims, then, becomes not a matter of legislative discretion but an obligation imposed by the Constitution.

c)   The application of the compelling interest test

4.496   Following *Sherbert*, a series of claims for religious exemptions came before the courts. Not surprisingly, the judgment was held to be controlling precedent in cases concerning unemployment benefits. Thus, in *Thomas v Review Board of the Indiana Employment Security Division*,[1018] the Supreme Court dealt with a claim by a Jehovah's Witness who had left his job in a steel factory when he was transferred to a department producing turrets for military tanks because his religious pacifist beliefs prevented him from manufacturing war materials. Under the relevant Indiana law his application for unemployment compensation had to be rejected because he had left his job. The defendants argued that this was only an indirect burden on religion made necessary by the state interest in managing effectively the unemployment fund. Chief Justice Burger pointed out that this was the type of argument that *Sherbert* had rejected. Making the claimant chose between his religious convictions and unemployment compensation constituted a burden on religion: 'While the compulsion may be indirect, the infringement upon free exercise is nonetheless substantial.'[1019] As the defendants were unable to demonstrate that granting the benefit would lead large numbers of employees to leave their jobs and make similar requests, their refusal was not based on a compelling interest and, therefore, breached the claimant's religious freedom.[1020]

4.497   Another employment case, *Frazee v Illinois Department of Employment Security*,[1021] presented the Supreme Court with slightly different facts from *Sherbert*. The claimant was a Christian who had refused to accept employment requiring him to work on Sundays. The state authorities in Illinois rejected his application for unemployment compensation because he based

---

[1016] *Sherbert* (n 1012) 407 (citation omitted). Brennan J tried to distinguish *Sherbert* from *Braunfeld v Brown*, saying that the latter involved a 'less direct burden' on religious practice and a more overwhelming state interest (the need for a common day of rest) which could not have been achieved by a different form of regulation. However, as Harlan J noted in his dissent, *Braunfeld* was essentially overruled: see *Sherbert* 421 (Harlan J, dissenting).

[1017] Greenawalt (n 954) 30.

[1018] *Thomas v Review Board of the Indiana Employment Security Division* 450 US 707 (1981).

[1019] *Thomas* (1018) 718.

[1020] The second reason put forward by the defendants as a justification for the law was that granting the benefit to believers would lead to excessive probing by employers into job applicants' religious beliefs. Again, Burger CJ found that there was no evidence to support this argument.

[1021] *Frazee v Illinois Department of Employment Security* 489 US 829 (1989).

his objection on the fact that as a Christian 'he could not work on the Lord's day'[1022] without claiming that he was a member of a particular Christian denomination which prohibited work on Sunday. The Supreme Court held that what mattered in such cases was the existence of a sincere religious belief, without a further requirement to demonstrate that the religious objection was grounded on the official dogma of a specific religion. 'We reject the notion', Justice White wrote, 'that to claim the protection of the Free Exercise Clause, one must be responding to the commands of a particular religious organization.'[1023]

One of the most controversial judgments finding in favour of religious claimants was the one **4.498** in the case of *Wisconsin v Yoder*.[1024] The State of Wisconsin provided for compulsory school attendance until the age of 16. The defendants, members of the Old Order Amish, had been convicted of violating the relevant law as they had refused to allow their children to attend school beyond the eighth grade. They claimed that it was a fundamental tenet of their religion that salvation requires a return to 'the simple life of the early Christian era'.[1025] In turn, this meant that children had to be protected from influences which were incompatible with the Amish way of life. Chief Justice Burger, the author of the majority opinion, described the Amish objection to high-school education as follows:

> They object to the high school, and higher education generally, because the values they teach are in marked variance with Amish values and the Amish way of life; they view secondary school education as an impermissible exposure of their children to a 'worldly' influence in conflict with their beliefs. The high school tends to emphasize intellectual and scientific accomplishments, self-distinction, competitiveness, worldly success, and social life with other students. Amish society emphasizes informal learning-through-doing; a life of 'goodness,' rather than a life of intellect; wisdom, rather than technical knowledge, community welfare, rather than competition; and separation from, rather than integration with, contemporary worldly society.[1026]

The Court noted at the outset that the Amish way of life was 'not merely a matter of personal **4.499** preference, but one of deep religious conviction'.[1027] Where a general law restricted free exercise rights the compelling interest test of *Sherbert* was the appropriate standard of review.[1028] It was legitimate for the state to ensure that citizens had a degree of education which would permit them to participate in social and political life, and schooling beyond the eighth grade might be important for people who will live in modern society. But 'if the goal of education be viewed as the preparation of the child for life in the separated agrarian community that is the keystone of the Amish faith',[1029] the additional one or two years of high school, the Court continued, were not indispensable for the achievement of the state's educational aims.

The second state interest relied on by Wisconsin was the need to protect children from the **4.500** 'ignorance'[1030] that the Amish way of life promoted. The Court acknowledged that this was

---

[1022] *Frazee* (n 1021) 830 (internal quotation marks omitted).
[1023] *Frazee* (n 1021) 834.
[1024] *Wisconsin v Yoder* 406 US 205.
[1025] *Yoder* (n 1024) 210.
[1026] *Yoder* (n 1024) 210–11.
[1027] *Yoder* (n 1024) 216.
[1028] Wisconsin also argued that since the law did not affect belief but only conduct, it should pass constitutional muster. The Court reiterated its earlier rule that conduct too enjoyed protection under the Free Exercise Clause and stated that in the Amish case 'belief and action cannot be neatly confined in logic-tight compartments': *Yoder* (n 1024) 220.
[1029] *Yoder* (n 1024) 222.
[1030] *Yoder* (n 1024) 222.

a real interest but found that, on the facts, there was no such danger because the Amish were a 'highly successful social unit' and 'productive and very law-abiding members of society'.[1031] The Court then rejected the argument that the additional schooling was necessary for those children who might wish to leave the community, taking the view that the vocational training that the Amish provided to older children was enough to allow them to live in mainstream society: 'There is nothing in this record to suggest that the Amish qualities of reliability, self-reliance, and dedication to work would fail to find ready markets in today's society.'[1032] Finally, the Court distinguished *Yoder* from *Prince v Massachusetts*, the case concerning Jehovah's Witnesses' children who were engaging in religious canvassing in the streets together with their parents, taking the view the latter presented much more severe dangers for children, and therefore justified more extensive state intervention, than refusing to send children to school so that they could live in a closed community.

4.501   The majority's failure to take seriously into account the interests of the Amish children (as opposed to those of their parents who wished to preserve their traditional way of life) and protect their right to exit the community was criticized in Justice Douglas's dissent. He pointed out that it was a mistake to think that those interests were always identical, and that where the child is mature enough to have an opinion about his education his wishes should prevail over parental choice: 'the education of the child is a matter on which the child will often have decided views. He may want to be a pianist or an astronaut or an oceanographer. To do so he will have to break from the Amish tradition'.[1033] But breaking from that tradition is made more difficult by the lack of adequate education, the result being an early foreclosure of choices:

> If a parent keeps his child out of school beyond the grade school, then the child will be forever barred from entry into the new and amazing world of diversity that we have today . . . If he is harnessed to the Amish way of life by those in authority over him and if his education is truncated, his entire life may be stunted and deformed.[1034]

4.502   The strictness of the compelling interest test had the potential to lead to the invalidation of a wide range of neutral laws which burdened religious freedom. In practice, though, the Supreme Curt used a variety of methods to limit the test's effect. One such method was to find that the interest the government invoked to justify the law was indeed compelling and, thus, trumped the free exercise claim; in cases concerning special environments, such as the military and prisons, it deferred extensively to the government's judgment as to why the religious claim could not be accommodated; and in other cases it construed the concept of 'burden' to religion narrowly.[1035]

4.503   In *United States v Lee*,[1036] the Court dealt with a challenge to the compulsory participation in the social security system. A member of the Old Order Amish had refused to pay social security contributions for his employees, who were also Amish, because it was a fundamental tenet of their religion that the community should care for the elderly and, therefore, both the acceptance of state benefits and the payment of contributions were religiously prohibited. The Court accepted that the religious objection was sincere but rejected the challenge

---

[1031]   *Yoder* (n 1024) 222.
[1032]   *Yoder* (n 1024) 224.
[1033]   *Yoder* (n 1024) 244–5 (Douglas J, dissenting in part) (citation omitted).
[1034]   *Yoder* (n 1024) 245–6 (Douglas J, dissenting in part) (citation omitted).
[1035]   See K Sullivan and G Gunther, *Constitutional Law* (17th edn, Foundation Press, 2010) 1304 ff.
[1036]   *US v Lee* 455 US 252 (1982).

because when balanced against the state interest in maintaining a social security scheme the scales came down in favour of the latter; as Chief Justice Burger wrote: 'mandatory participation is indispensable to the fiscal vitality of the social security system'.[1037] It would be difficult for the government, he continued, to cope with 'myriad exceptions flowing from a wide variety of religious beliefs'.[1038] Thus, the mandatory scheme was a necessary means for the achievement of the overriding state interest in providing social security.

Exemptions in the context of the armed forces came up in *Goldman v Weinberger*.[1039] The claimant, an Orthodox rabbi and Air Force clinical psychologist, had been reprimanded for wearing a yarmulke in violation of a regulation which prohibited the wearing of headgear indoors. In an opinion by Justice Renquist, the Supreme Court rejected his free exercise claim. While not doubting that the regulation burdened his right to religious freedom, it did not interfere with the military authorities' judgment that it was necessary, stating that 'the desirability of dress regulations in the military is decided by the appropriate military officials, and they are under no constitutional mandate to abandon their considered professional judgment'.[1040] Similar reasoning was applied by the Court where prison regulations were concerned. In *O'Lone v Estate of Shabazz*,[1041] a Muslim prisoner had been prevented from attending *Jumu'ah*, a weekly service mandated by the Koran, because his classification did not allow him entry into the building where the service was held. The opinion was given again by Chief Justice Renquist, who held that prison authorities enjoyed wide discretion and that the appropriate level of review was 'a reasonableness test less restrictive than that ordinarily applied to alleged infringements of fundamental constitutional rights'.[1042]

4.504

The critical consideration in both cases was the standard of review. While the compelling interest test announced in *Sherbert* would have required the government to show that there existed no less restrictive means for the achievement of the relevant objective, the military and prison regulations at issue easily passed constitutional muster because the Court applied instead the feeble rational basis test which is characterized by extensive deference to the judgment of the administration.[1043] Actually, Justice Brennan, in his dissent in *Goldman*, forcefully criticized the majority for adopting what he described as a 'subrational-basis standard'[1044] which failed to require the government to provide even a '*credible* explanation of how the contested practice is likely to interfere with the proffered military interest'.[1045]

4.505

The concept of 'burden to religion' was discussed by the Supreme Court in *Lyng v Northwest Indian Cemetery Protective Association*.[1046] The Forest Service gave permission for timber

4.506

[1037] *Lee* (n 1036) 258.

[1038] *Lee* (n 1036) 260.

[1039] *Goldman v Weinberger* 475 US 503 (1986).

[1040] *Goldman* (n 1039) 509. Following the Supreme Court judgment, Congress passed legislation allowing military personnel to wear religious items of clothing provided that they did not interfere with the performance of their duties.

[1041] *O'Lone v Estate of Shabazz* 482 US 342 (1987).

[1042] *O'Lone* (n 1041) 349 (internal quotation marks omitted).

[1043] For an argument that in cases concerning the military the appropriate standard of review is an intermediate test which requires the government to establish that it has a substantial reason not to grant the exemption but does not necessitate the existence of a compelling interest, see Greenawalt (n 954) 164.

[1044] *Goldman* (n 1039) 515 (emphasis in the original) (footnote omitted).

[1045] *Goldman* (n 1039) 516 (emphasis in the original). Justice Brennan J also dissented in *O'Lone* (n 1041) 354.

[1046] *Lyng v Northwest Indian Cemetery Protective Association* 485 US 439 (1988). For an analysis of judicial determinations of burden, see Greenawalt (n 954) 202.

harvesting and road construction in a national forest that three Indian tribes had traditionally been using for religious purposes. In an opinion by Justice O'Connor the Court acknowledged that the project 'could have devastating effects on traditional Indian religious practices'[1047] but rejected the free exercise challenge because no coercion was involved. The Court referred to the principle that both direct and indirect coercion was caught by the First Amendment but took the view that:

> ...this does not and cannot imply that incidental effects of government programs, which may make it more difficult to practice certain religions but which have no tendency to coerce individuals into acting contrary to their religious beliefs, require government to bring forward a compelling justification for its otherwise lawful actions. The crucial word in the constitutional text is 'prohibit'.[1048]

Thus, burden was defined by reference to coercion, and coercion was defined narrowly to exclude measures which do not compel some form of action. It was this narrow construction which Justice Brennan criticized in his dissent. His view was that the 'distinction between governmental actions that compel affirmative conduct inconsistent with religious belief, and those governmental actions that prevent conduct consistent with religious belief' was 'without constitutional significance'.[1049] He agreed with the majority that the crucial word in the First Amendment was 'prohibit' but interpreted it much more broadly to include 'governmental action that makes the practice of one's chosen faith impossible'.[1050] The First Amendment, Justice Brennan thought, 'is directed against any form of governmental action that frustrates or inhibits religious practice'.[1051]

4.507   The *Lyng* Court refused to apply the compelling interest test and equated burden with compulsion to act. Justice O'Connor's view that 'government simply could not operate if it were required to satisfy every citizen's religious needs and desires'[1052] showed the Supreme Court's growing uneasiness about the *Sherbert* precedent and its effects on governmental action. Two years after *Lyng*, the test itself was overruled.[1053]

d) The Vietnam-era cases: defining 'religion'

4.508   Conscription legislation during the Vietnam War provided for an exemption for religious conscientious objectors. The statute, originating in the 1940s, exempted those 'who by reason of their religious training and belief are conscientiously opposed to participation in war in any form'; it defined the term 'religious training and belief' as 'an individual's belief in a relation to a Supreme Being involving duties superior to those arising from any human relation, but (not including) essentially political, sociological, or philosophical views or a merely personal moral code'. In several cases brought by conscientious objectors courts were asked to decide which forms of opposition to war fell within the scope of the exemption. Unlike *Sherbert* and its aftermath, the issue in these cases was not whether the First Amendment mandated an exemption, given that Congress had already provided for it in a statute; the question for the courts was how to interpret the requirement for 'religious training and belief'. Although they were not about constitutional exemptions, the cases are discussed here

---

[1047] *Lyng* (n 1046) 451.
[1048] *Lyng* (n 1046) 450–1.
[1049] *Lyng* (n 1046) 468 (Brennan J, dissenting).
[1050] *Lyng* (n 1046) 468 (Brennan J, dissenting).
[1051] *Lyng* (n 1046) 459 (Brennan J, dissenting).
[1052] *Lyng* (n 1046) 452.
[1053] With two exceptions, see para 4.552.

because they demonstrate the difficulties of defining religion in the context of conscientious objection claims.

In *United States v Seeger*,[1054] the Supreme Court joined three cases of objectors whose exemp-   **4.509**
tion claims had been rejected. The first claimant had stated that his opposition stemmed
from 'a belief in and devotion to goodness and virtue for their own sakes, and a religious faith
in a purely ethical creed . . . without belief in God, except in the remotest sense' and that he
preferred to 'leave the question as to his belief in a Supreme Being open'.[1055] The second had
affirmed that he believed in a 'Supreme Being who was the Creator of Man in the sense of
being ultimately responsible for the existence of man and who was the Supreme Reality'.[1056]
Finally, the third claimant had said that he adopted a definition of religion as 'the consciousness of some power manifest in nature which helps man in the ordering of his life in harmony
with its demands'.[1057]

In finding for the three claimants, the Supreme Court held that the test objectors had to   **4.510**
satisfy was whether they had 'a sincere and meaningful belief which occupies in the life of
its possessor a place parallel to that filled by the God of those admittedly qualifying for the
exemption'.[1058] Justice Clark, the author of the judgment, noted that sincere religious devotion takes many forms and believers use a wide variety of ways to express convictions which
are of paramount importance for their lives. The history of the statute demonstrated that
Congress's intention was to facilitate the accommodation of all religiously-inspired opposition to war, excluding only that based on sociological or philosophical beliefs or a personal
moral code. Accordingly, the question to ask in conscientious objection cases was: 'does the
claimed belief occupy the same place in the life of the objector as an orthodox belief in God
holds in the life of one clearly qualified for exemption?'[1059]

While *Seeger* was about individuals who subscribed to some form of religiosity, albeit with   **4.511**
non-traditional views about God, the claimant in *Welsh v United States*[1060] had struck the
word 'religious' from his draft exemption form and stated that his beliefs had been formed
'by reading in the fields of history and sociology'.[1061] In a plurality opinion by Justice Black,
the Supreme Court ruled that he could benefit from the exemption. The meaning of *Seeger*,
Justice Black wrote, was that an objection is 'religious' for the purposes of the statute if it
'stem[s] from the registrant's moral, ethical, or religious beliefs about what is right and wrong
and that these beliefs be held with the strength of traditional religious convictions'.[1062] The
critical consideration was whether the objector's beliefs imposed on him ethical duties similar to those imposed by mainstream religious convictions:

> If an individual deeply and sincerely holds beliefs that are purely ethical or moral in source and
> content but that nevertheless impose upon him a duty of conscience to refrain from participat-
> ing in any war at any time, those beliefs certainly occupy in the life of that individual 'a place
> parallel to that filled by . . . God' in traditionally religious persons. Because his beliefs function

---

[1054] *US v Seeger* 380 US 163 (1965). The text of the law at issue is cited at 165.
[1055] *Seeger* (n 1054) 166.
[1056] *Seeger* (n 1054) 167.
[1057] *Seeger* (n 1054) 169.
[1058] *Seeger* (n 1054) 176.
[1059] *Seeger* (n 1054) 184.
[1060] *Welsh v US* 398 US 333 (1970).
[1061] *Welsh* (n 1060) 341.
[1062] *Welsh* (n 1060) 340.

as a religion in his life, such an individual is as much entitled to a 'religious' conscientious objector exemption [under the statute] as is someone who derives his conscientious opposition to war from traditional religious convictions.

4.512 Justice Harlan concurred in the judgment but for different reasons. His view was that the law clearly privileged theistic beliefs and it was impossible to construe it in a manner which included non-religious objections to war. The question, therefore, was whether this distinction was constitutional. He concluded that it was not, because it violated the Establishment Clause of the First Amendment. Congress could not exempt only individuals with theistic beliefs and disadvantage those whose religious convictions did not include belief in a Supreme Being or secular objectors. The Constitution required equal treatment for all objectors irrespective of the source of their objection: 'The common denominator must be the intensity of moral conviction with which a belief is held'.[1063]

4.513 Both the plurality and the concurring opinions are motivated by a concern that it is impermissible to draw a distinction between religious and secular objectors. In effect, they made the 'religious training and belief' requirement in the statute irrelevant.[1064] More generally, *Welsh* and *Seeger* show that even if the legislature is free to grant or not to grant an exemption, the manner in which it structures the exemption (where it opts for one) is subject to significant constitutional constraints arising from a combination of religious freedom and non-discrimination principles.[1065]

e) The end of the compelling interest test: the Smith *case*

4.514 *Employment Division Department of Human Resources v Smith*,[1066] which has been described as 'one of the most important Free Exercise Clause cases of the twentieth century',[1067] was another unemployment compensation case. It concerned a member of the Native American Church whose rituals included the use of peyote, a drug prohibited in Oregon; he was fired because he ingested peyote during a religious ceremony. The authorities denied his claim for unemployment benefits because his dismissal was for work-related misconduct. Relying on cases such as *Sherbert* and *Thomas*, he argued that this was an unconstitutional restriction of his free exercise rights.

4.515 Writing for the majority, Justice Scalia rejected the claim. His starting point was the *Reynolds* distinction between belief and action and the rule that religious convictions were not valid reasons requiring an exception from general criminal prohibitions. Then he proceeded to discuss the cases where the Court had declined to uphold claims for exemptions, including *Prince v Massachusetts* and *Braunfeld v Brown*, and noted that even after *Sherbert* the Court had found that the compelling interest test was satisfied (as in *United States v Lee*) or had avoided it altogether (as in *Lyng*). What those judgments mean, he said, is that if the interference with religious practice is 'merely the incidental effect of a generally applicable and otherwise valid provision, the First Amendment has not been offended'.[1068]

[1063] *Welsh* (n 1060) 358, Harlan J concurring.

[1064] Greenawalt (n 954) 62–63.

[1065] In another judgment, *Gillette v US* 401 US 437 (1971), the Supreme Court upheld a refusal to exempt an objector who opposed some, but not all, wars. For discussion, see K Greenawalt, 'All or Nothing at All: The Defeat of Selective Conscientious Objection' (1971) Supreme Court Review 31.

[1066] *Employment Division Department of Human Resources v Smith* 494 US 872 (1990).

[1067] Eisgruber and Sager (n 987) 78.

[1068] *Smith* (n 1066) 878.

Sherbert itself, however, was not overruled, but distinguished. Justice Scalia said that the law at **4.516** stake in it (and also in *Thomas*) withheld unemployment benefits where the claimant had left his job or refused employment 'without good cause'. This required an individualized evaluation by the Employment Board of the reasons each claimant had for quitting or refusing employment, creating in essence a system of 'individual exemptions'.[1069] The effect of *Sherbert* was to extend the system to include religious reasons. By contrast, *Smith* involved 'an across-the-board criminal prohibition on a particular form of conduct';[1070] in such cases the *Sherbert* test did not apply.

The majority opinion also distinguished *Wisconsin v Yoder*, the compulsory education case, **4.517** because it did not rest exclusively on freedom of religion but rather combined a Free Exercise Clause ground with another constitutionally protected interest, namely the right of parents to make decisions about the education of their children.[1071] *Smith* was not such a 'hybrid situation'[1072] but a stand-alone religious freedom claim.

One of the opinion's main themes, reflecting Justice Scalia's more general hostility towards **4.518** judicial discretion, was that judges should not engage in the process of evaluating the importance of religious claims and weighing them against governmental interests. He said that 'it is horrible to contemplate that federal judges will regularly balance against the importance of general laws the significance of religious practice'.[1073] Given the strictness of the compelling interest test and the religious diversity prevalent in America it would be a 'luxury'[1074] to adhere to a standard of review which could be used to invalidate 'every regulation of conduct that does not protect an interest of the highest order'.[1075]

Justice Scalia's view of the judges' proper role explains why he was not hostile to *all* religious **4.519** exemptions but only to those which were *judicially* created by reference to the Constitution. If the legislature wished to accommodate religious practices by exempting believers from the scope of general, neutral laws it was free to do so. This is the difference between constitutionally mandated exemptions (which *Smith* rejects) and legislative exemptions (which *Smith* permits): 'to say that a nondiscriminatory religious-practice exemption is permitted, or even that it is desirable, is not to say that it is constitutionally required, and that the appropriate occasions for its creation can be discerned by the courts'.[1076] Therefore, individuals whose religious practice is burdened by general laws should have recourse to the legislature through the political process, not the courts. Justice Scalia admitted that this 'will place at a relative disadvantage those religious practices that are not widely engaged in'[1077] but found it to be an 'unavoidable consequence of democratic government'.[1078]

Both Justice O'Connor, who concurred in the result, and Justice Blackmun, who dissented, **4.520** were very critical of the majority's interpretation of past Free Exercise cases. Justice O'Connor pointed out that they contained no categorical rule that general laws were immune to First

---

[1069] *Smith* (n 1066) 884.
[1070] *Smith* (n 1066) 884.
[1071] Recognized by the Supreme Court in *Pierce v Society of Sisters* 268 US 510 (1925).
[1072] *Smith* (n 1066) 882. The majority opinion also described *Cantwell v Connecticut* as a hybrid case because it combined religious freedom and free speech.
[1073] *Smith* (n 1066) 889, fn 5.
[1074] *Smith* (n 1066) 888.
[1075] *Smith* (n 1066) 888.
[1076] *Smith* (n 1066) 890.
[1077] *Smith* (n 1066) 890.
[1078] *Smith* (n 1066) 890.

Amendment scrutiny but rather involved a careful 'weighing of the competing interests'.[1079] Deciding 'each case on its individual merits'[1080] was the judges' proper role. The Free Exercise Clause did not distinguish between general laws and laws that targeted religion, as its objective was to make religious practice a 'preferred constitutional activity',[1081] protected from governmental intrusion. Therefore, it was appropriate to subject laws that criminalized a religious activity to strict scrutiny. In the present case, she found that the *Sherbert* test had been met because Oregon had a compelling interest in controlling the use of drugs and the general ban was necessary for effective enforcement.

4.521 Justice Blackmun agreed that the majority opinion had mischaracterized precedents so as to effect a 'wholesale overturning of settled case law'[1082] but, unlike Justice O'Connor, held that Oregon had failed to satisfy the compelling interest test. He explained that what was at stake was not the 'State's broad interest in fighting the critical "war on drugs"'[1083] but 'the State's narrow interest in refusing to make an exception for the religious, ceremonial use of peyote'.[1084] Oregon had not tried to enforce its drug laws against religious users of peyote and had not prosecuted Smith. Further, 23 states had legislative or judicial exemptions for peyote use, which showed that it was possible to maintain and enforce a general policy against the use of drugs and accommodate religious needs at the same time. Oregon's interest amounted 'only to the symbolic preservation of an unenforced prohibition'[1085] but such symbolic reasons were not compelling enough to defeat a religious freedom claim.

4.522 *Smith* did away with constitutionally mandated religious exemptions from general laws. If such laws satisfied a very basic reasonableness requirement, the fact that they impinged on the free exercise of religion was not a violation of the First Amendment. Two exceptions to this rule were maintained: first, hybrid cases where the religious freedom claim is combined with another constitutionally protected interest; and secondly, cases concerning eligibility for unemployment benefits. The judgment did not affect the power of Congress and state legislatures to grant legislative exemptions. Also, state courts remained free to create judicial exemptions from state laws under the religious freedom provisions of state constitutions.

e) Post-Smith

4.523 The dramatic change to Free Exercise law introduced by *Smith* was met with negative reactions from both constitutional scholars[1086] and legislators. Congress and the state of Oregon passed legislation exempting the religious use of peyote from general criminal laws. Also, a number of state supreme courts interpreted their state constitutions as requiring strict

---

1079 *Smith* (n 1066) 896 (O'Connor J, concurring in the judgment).
1080 *Smith* (n 1066) 899 (O'Connor J, concurring in the judgment).
1081 *Smith* (n 1066) 902 (O'Connor J, concurring in the judgment).
1082 *Smith* (n 1066) 908 (Blackmun J, dissenting).
1083 *Smith* (n 1066) 909–10 (Blackmun J, dissenting).
1084 *Smith* (n 1066) 910 (Blackmun J, dissenting).
1085 *Smith* (n 1066) 911 (Blackmun J, dissenting).
1086 See eg M McConnell, 'Free Exercise Revisionism and the Smith Decision' (1990) 57 University of Chicago Law Review 1109; D Laycock, 'The Remnants of Free Exercise' (1990) Supreme Court Review 1. More recently, Eisgruber and Sager (n 987) 95 ff, although agreeing with the Court that religious reasons cannot justify the exemption of believers from general laws, criticized *Smith* for failing to ensure equal religious liberty for Native Americans because Oregon had a legislative exemption for the sacramental use of wine in localities where alcohol use was banned but not one for the sacramental use of peyote. For a more favourable view of *Smith*, see DP Marshall, 'In Defense of Smith and Free Exercise Revisionism' (1991) 58 University of Chicago Law Review 308. and MA Hamilton, *'Employment Division v Smith* at the Supreme Court: The Justices, the Litigants and the Doctrinal Discourse' (2011) 32 Cardozo Law Review 1771.

scrutiny review of rules which restricted religious practice.[1087] More importantly, Congress enacted the Religious Freedom Restoration Act (RIFRA) which reinstated the *Sherbert* compelling interest test for all cases where there was a substantial burden on religion.[1088] The Act was intended to apply to both federal and state authorities. However, the Supreme Court held in *City of Boerne v Flores*[1089] that the Act was unconstitutional in relation to its application to the states, because Congress lacked power under the Fourteenth Amendment to restrict state law beyond the limits imposed on it by the Constitution as interpreted by the Supreme Court itself. The issue of RIFRA's application to the federal government was raised in *Gonzales v O Centro Esperita Beneficente Uniao Do Vegetal*,[1090] which closely resembled the *Smith* case. It concerned a small Christian group whose members made sacramental use of a hallucinogenic tea. When the federal authorities confiscated a shipment of the tea, threatening to prosecute the members of the group under federal drug laws, the group claimed an exemption under RIFRA. In a unanimous decision the Supreme Court agreed, holding that the Act was a valid restriction of the power of the federal government and that the latter had failed to satisfy the compelling interest test.

Following the invalidation of the state component of RIFRA, Congress enacted the Religious **4.524** Land Use and Institutionalised Persons Act (RLUIPA). This was an attempt to reintroduce some restrictions on state laws impinging on religious practice but with a considerably narrower scope: the Act applied only to claims by institutionalized individuals and decisions concerning land development. As RIFRA had done a few years earlier, RLUIPA reinstated the *Sherbert* compelling interest test for cases falling under it. In order to avoid the problem of federal power over the states, which had proved fatal for RIFRA in *Boerne*, RUILPA was based not only on the Fourteenth Amendment but also on the Spending Clause and the Commerce Clause of the federal Constitution, which provide Congress with wide legislative power. This time the Supreme Court upheld the validity of the Act.[1091]

Three years after *Smith* the Supreme Court decided *Lukumi*,[1092] the Florida case on ritual **4.525** animal sacrifice discussed earlier. As we have seen, the Court held that the impugned city ordinances were not really neutral provisions of general applicability but constituted covert targeting of a specific religious practice, and struck them down, relying on the Free Exercise Clause.

The most recent free exercise case is *Hosanna-Tabor Evangelical Lutheran Church and School* **4.526** *v Equal Employment Opportunity Commission*.[1093] Here the Supreme Court held, for the first

---

[1087] See the discussion in A Carmella, 'State Constitutional Protection of Religious Exercise: An Emerging Post-Smith Jurisprudence' (1993) Brigham Young University Law Review 275.

[1088] On RFRA's provisions, see T Berg, 'What Hath Congress Wrought? An Interpretative Guide to the Religious Freedom Restoration Act' (1994) 39 Villanova Law Review 1.

[1089] *City of Boerne v Flores* 521 US 507 (1997). The case concerned a claim by a Catholic church in Texas for a religious exemption from planning law.

[1090] *Gonzales v O Centro Esperita Beneficente Uniao Do Vegetal* 546 US 418 (2006).

[1091] In *Cutter v Wilkinson* 125 S Ct 2113 (2005), which concerned religious claims by prisoners. On the place of RLUIPA in the broader scheme of religious exemptions, see IC Lupu and RW Tuttle, 'The Forms and Limits of Religious Accommodation: The Case of RLUIPA' (2010–11) 32 Cardozo Law Review 1907.

[1092] *Church of Lukumi Babalu Aye v City of Hialeah* 508 US 520 (1993).

[1093] *Hosanna-Tabor Evangelical Lutheran Church and School v Equal Employment Opportunity Commission* 132 S Ct 694 (2012). For discussion, see MW McConnell, 'Reflections on *Hosanna-Tabor*' (2012) 35 Harvard Journal of Law and Public Policy 821; D Laycock, '*Hosanna-Tabor* and the Ministerial Exception' (2012) 35 Harvard Journal of Law and Public Policy 839; CM Corbin, 'The Irony of *Hosanna-Tabor Evangelical Lutheran Church and School v EEOC*' (2012) 106 Northwestern University Law Review 951. For a comparison between

time, that the Free Exercise Clause and the Establishment Clause place the employment relationship between a religious group and its clergy beyond the reach of anti-discrimination law. This is usually referred to as the 'ministerial exemption'; it means that when making decisions about the appointment and dismissal of their ministers, religious groups do not need to comply with employment equality norms. The respondents had argued that *Smith* precluded a constitutionally mandated exemption since the anti-discrimination statute at issue, the Americans with Disabilities Act, was a neutral law of general applicability serving the legitimate governmental aim of eradicating discriminatory practices against disabled people. The Court rejected this argument with little discussion, distinguishing the two cases as follows: '*Smith* involved government regulation of only outward physical acts. The present case, in contrast, concerns government interference with an internal church decision that affects the faith and mission of the church itself.'[1094]

Hosanna-Tabor and the position of the House of Lords on the application of anti-discrimination law to the clergy, see N Hatzis, 'The Church-Clergy Relationship and Anti-Discrimination Law' (2013) 15 Ecclesiastical Law Journal 144.

[1094] *Hosanna-Tabor* (n 1093) 707.

PART II

DOMESTIC PROTECTIONS

5

THE HUMAN RIGHTS ACT 1998

A. Introduction

For centuries, religious rights in the United Kingdom existed as a broad-ranging but prin- **5.01** cipally negative set of freedoms at common law. Individuals were permitted to do as they pleased in matters of faith, unless the law stated otherwise.[1] Religious liberty, thus conceived, was more passive toleration of religion than any active promotion of religious freedom as a fundamental right. All that changed on 2 October 2000 when the Human Rights Act 1998 (HRA 1998)—the United Kingdom's *de facto* Bill of Rights—came into full force.

HRA 1998 indirectly incorporates Convention rights into domestic UK law,[2] requiring the **5.02** UK courts to apply and to enforce these rights by statutory interpretation where possible.

---

[1] See *Malone v Metropolitan Police Commissioner (No 2)* [1979] Ch 344, 357. See generally *AG v Guardian Newspapers Ltd (No 2)* [1990] 1 AC 109 (CA).

[2] Convention rights had already been given indirect force in Scotland (Scotland Act 1998, ss 29, 57, and 126(1)); Wales (Government of Wales Act 1998, Sch 8); and Northern Ireland (Northern Ireland Act 1998, ss 9–11, 13, 14, and 71).

HRA 1998 also renders unlawful any conduct of public authorities, including courts, which violates Convention rights, for which conduct they become liable.

5.03 Article 9 ECHR provides:

> 1. Everyone has a right to freedom of thought, conscience and religion; this right includes freedom to change his religion or belief, and freedom, either alone or in community with others and in public or private, to manifest his religion or belief, in worship, teaching, practice and observance.

> 2. Freedom to manifest one's religion or beliefs shall be subject only to such limitations as are prescribed by law and are necessary in a democratic society in the interests of public safety, for the protection of public order, health or morals, or for the protection of the rights and freedoms of others.

5.04 Religious liberty in the United Kingdom is now a positive right with two dimensions. Article 9(1) ECHR treats the right to hold a particular belief (the *forum internum*) as absolute, whilst the right to act on or manifest that belief (the *forum externum*) is subject to the limitations set out in Article 9(2). The latter provision is the principal battleground for religious freedoms, given the comparative rarity of interference with belief itself.[3]

5.05 The shift in UK law from a negative common law toleration of religious liberty to a positive legal right to religious freedom was initially hailed as 'a new dawn for freedom of religion... intended to symbolise the freedom of [the] individual'.[4] Article 9's rights and liberties were meant to offer more protection to individuals and change the relationship between the citizen and the state.[5] However, claims for breaches of Article 9 ECHR have tended to fail in practice.[6] Domestic courts have been influenced by the approach of the ECtHR, and have taken a very restrictive approach to Article 9. This approach has been disapproved in part by the ECtHR in *Eweida v United Kingdom*,[7] and it seems inevitable that the courts in England and Wales, which had questioned the restrictive approach (in particular in *Copsey* and *Williamson*) of the ECtHR, will now take a more liberal approach to religious rights. At present, claims for infringement of religious rights which have relied on a combination of ECHR rights (such as Articles 9, 10, and 14) have proved most successful: see, for instance, *Re Christian Institute and Others (Application for Judicial Review)*;[8] and *Sandown Free Church v ASA*.[9]

---

[3] The absolute right to hold a belief is incapable of being interfered with in a democratic society. See *Van Den Dungen v Netherlands* (App 22838/93) (1995), Comm Rep 80 DR 147, 150, which discusses the *internum/externum* distinction and summarizes Art 9 protection of each dimension. The complexities of trying to untangle belief and practice are explored well in G Moens, 'The Action-Belief Dichotomy and Freedom of Religion' (1989) 12 Sydney L Rev 195.

[4] M Hill, 'A New Dawn for Freedom of Religion: Grounding the Debate', in M Hill (ed), Religious Liberty And Human Rights Vol 1 (University of Wales Press, 2002).

[5] See Lord Lester, Address at the University of Cambridge Centre for Public Law, 'The Human Rights Act and the Criminal Justice and Regulatory Process', 9 January 1999.

[6] In the UK, see eg *R (Williamson) v Secretary of State for Education and Employment* [2005] 2 AC 246 (HL); *R (Shabina Begum) v Governors of Denbigh High School* [2007] 1 AC 100 (HL); *R (X) v Governors of Y School* [2007] EWHC (Admin) 298; *R (Playfoot) v Governing Body of Millais School* [2007] EWHC (Admin) 1698.

[7] *Eweida and ors v UK* (2013) 57 EHRR 213. See discussion at paras 5.13, 5.18 and Ch 3, paras 3.38–3.43.

[8] *Christian Institute and ors (Application for Judicial Review)* [2007] NIQB 66.

[9] *Kirk Session of Sandown Free Presbyterian Church (Application for Judicial Review)* [2011] NIQB 26.

B. Article 9

There are 4 conditions for a successful Article 9 claim. The Claimant must show that:[10]   **5.06**

(1) he or she has a religious belief;
(2) the act in question was a manifestation of his or her religion or belief;
(3) the respondent interfered with this manifestation; and
(4) this interference was unjustified.

(1) Religion or belief

The claimant will need to show that the relevant beliefs qualify for protection under Article 9   **5.07**
ECHR. The general approach to the issue of determining the religious nature of the beliefs
adopted by Arden LJ in the Court of Appeal in *Williamson*[11] was approved by Lord Nicholls
in the House of Lords.[12] Arden LJ stated (at paragraphs 251 and 252):

> In my judgment, it is a mixed question of fact and law whether a person has a religious belief
> for the purpose of article 9. Thus the first step is for the Judge to make findings on the evi-
> dence as to what are the actual beliefs of the complainant, so far as relevant... the second step
> is for the judge to decide whether those beliefs constitute religious beliefs for the purposes of
> the Convention. The latter is principally a question of law... Religious texts often form the
> basis from which adherents develop specific beliefs. It is not the Court's function to judge
> whether those beliefs are fairly based on the passages said to support them. Its function at the
> fact-finding stage is to decide what the beliefs are and whether they are genuinely held by the
> complainant. The fact that the beliefs are based on religious texts may help the Court reach its
> decision on this factual issue.

The integrity of the belief is tested: 'a belief must satisfy some modest, objective minimum   **5.08**
requirements... implicit in Article 9' before it qualifies for protection.[13] Lord Nicholls
imposes three such requirements: the belief must be 'consistent with basic standards of
human dignity or integrity' (dignity);[14] it 'must relate to matters more than merely trivial' by
possessing 'an adequate degree of seriousness and importance' (seriousness);[15] and finally, it
must be 'coherent in the sense of being intelligible and capable of being understood' (coherence).[16] The precise 'nature and scope of the belief'[17] must be articulated in the evidence
before it can be scrutinized according to these three requirements of dignity, seriousness, and
coherence. Lord Nicholl's approach has been followed in subsequent cases.

Relevant evidence of the religious belief needs to be adduced. In *McClintock v Department*   **5.09**
of Constitutional Affairs,[18] the Employment Appeal Tribunal rejected an agnostic discomfort
with same-sex adoption as a basis for a manifested belief, insisting upon the need for an actual
and positively asserted belief. The appellant in this case did not, as a matter of principle,

---

[10] *Williamson* (n 6) para 57 *per* Lord Walker.
[11] *R (Williamson) v Secretary of State for Education and Employment* [2002] EWCA Civ 1926.
[12] *Williamson* (n 6) paras 23–24.
[13] *Williamson* (n 6) para 23.
[14] As a hypothetical example, Lord Nicholls cites a belief in torture as ineligible for protection. *Williamson*
(n 6) para 23.
[15] *Williamson* (n 6) para 23.
[16] *Williamson* (n 6) para 23.
[17] *Williamson* (n 6) para 32.
[18] *McClintock v Department of Constitutional Affairs* [2008] IRLR 29, para 45.

reject the possibility that same sex parents could ever be in a child's best interests, but he felt that the evidence to support that view was unconvincing. The claim was brought under the Employment Equality (Religion or Belief) Regulations 2003, SI 2003/1660, but the Employment Appeal Tribunal drew on Article 9 case law for deciding the question of belief.[19]

5.10   As a general proposition, too many cases involving religious rights have suffered from an absence of evidence, and attempts by advocates to give evidence of the relevant religious belief. This has sometimes encouraged domestic courts to enter into their own assessment of the religious belief in question. Neither the giving of evidence by an advocate nor a subjective assessment of the religious belief by the court itself is permissible. The advocate is there to represent a party, and is not a witness. The court is a court of law, and it is not qualified to sit in judgment on the religious belief. That task is for the various structures of the relevant religious organization.

(2)   Manifestation of belief

5.11   For Article 9 ECHR to be engaged, the claimant must show that what he or she is being prevented from doing constitutes a manifestation of his or her religion or belief. This is not an onerous requirement. It is settled law, for example, that the wearing of various forms of Islamic and other traditional religious dress is a manifestation of religion for the purposes of Article 9, even where other, even most other, members of that faith regard such dress as unnecessary.[20]

5.12   Previous cases which had tended towards a more restrictive approach to finding a manifestation are now unlikely to survive the decision in *Eweida*.[21] In *R (Playfoot) v Governing Body of Millais School*,[22] for example, the claimant's wearing of a silver 'purity ring' as a symbol of her commitment to pre-marital sexual abstinence was held not to constitute a manifestation. The administrative court held that an activity did not automatically qualify for Article 9 protection simply because it was religiously motivated: the test was one of 'perceived obligation'.[23] This approach was far more restrictive than that adopted previously by the House of Lords in *Williamson*,[24] where the claimants' belief that corporal punishment should be administered at their children's school was held to be a manifestation of belief under Article 9. The House of Lords concluded in that case that the act must be shown to be 'intimately linked' to the relevant belief.[25] If the belief took the form of a perceived obligation to act in a specific way, then this test was passed.[26] A perceived obligation to act was held to be sufficient, but not necessary, for establishing an intimate link.[27] It was also sufficient, but not necessary, that the act reflected the practice of that belief in a 'generally recognised form'.[28] The House of Lords

---

[19]   *McClintock* (n 18) para 41.

[20]   *R (Shabina Begum) v Governors of Denbigh High School* [2007] 1 AC 100 (HL), para 50 *per* Lord Hoffmann.

[21]   *Eweida* (n 7) para 82. See also M Hill, 'Religious symbolism and conscientious objection in the workplace: an evaluation of Strasbourg's judgment in *Eweida and others v United Kingdom*' (2013) 15(2) Ecc LJ 191.

[22]   *R (Playfoot) v Governing Body of Millais School* [2007] EWHC (Admin) 1698.

[23]   *Playfoot* (n 22) para 21.

[24]   *Williamson* (n 6).

[25]   *Williamson* (n 6) para 32 *per* Lord Nicholls. For ECtHR authority relied on, see generally *X v UK* (1984) 6 EHRR 558; *Arrowsmith v UK* (App 7050/75) (1978), Comm Rep 19 DR 5.

[26]   *Williamson* (n 6) para 32 *per* Lord Nicholls.

[27]   *Williamson* (n 6) para 33.

[28]   *Kalaç v Turkey* (1997) 27 EHRR 552, 558.

found that the act in question was indeed a 'perceived obligation',[29] and did not explore further what the minimum threshold was in cases where that test was not passed.

In argument before the ECtHR in *Eweida*, the UK government sought to rely on the more **5.13** restrictive approach to manifestation. The government asserted the need for the act to be a 'mandatory requirement', and for it to be one 'of practice of a religion in a generally recognized form'.[30] However, the Strasbourg Court has made it clear that neither requirement was necessary,[31] stating in terms that 'there is no requirement on the applicant to establish that he or she acted in fulfilment of a duty mandated by the religion in question'.[32] The ECtHR was nonetheless careful to reiterate that there are boundaries to Article 9(1) within which an applicant must fall: the correct test was simply to establish 'a sufficiently close and direct nexus between the act and the underlying belief'.[33] In other words, the restrictive approach to manifestation adopted in cases such as *Playfoot* has been rejected by the ECtHR; but it remains the case that manifestation of belief is a matter that must be closely examined by the court.[34]

(3) Interference

Failing to find an interference has, until relatively recently, been the basis on which the **5.14** ECtHR has chosen to resolve most Article 9 claims. No interference was found, for example, where an employer refused to accommodate mosque attendance,[35] nor where a recent convert to Seventh Day Adventism was compelled to work after dusk.[36] The domestic courts had followed this approach, albeit with reluctance on occasion. In *Copsey v Devon Clays Ltd*,[37] the employer's denial of a Sabbath rest day to a Christian employee would have been deemed interference by the English court had it not been for the authority of Strasbourg's clear and strict stance on interference,[38] which the Court of Appeal termed the 'doctrine of non-interference'.

The House of Lords in *Williamson*[39] did not dismiss the claim on the basis of the doctrine **5.15** of non-interference, and found that there was an interference with the manifestation of the claimant's beliefs (which, in the event, was justifiable). The ECtHR also changed its approach. In *Şahin*,[40] the Grand Chamber considered a ban by a university on Islamic headscarves. The ban was found to be an interference under Article 9 (although, again, justifiable in the particular circumstances of the case).

Domestic law, however, in *Begum*, decided shortly after the Grand Chamber's judgment **5.16** in *Şahin* saw a 3 to 2 majority of the House of Lords effectively return to the doctrine of non-interference. In *Begum*, the majority held that there was no interference where

---

[29] *Williamson* (n 6) para 32.
[30] *Eweida* (n 13) para 58.
[31] *Eweida* (n 7) para 82.
[32] *Eweida* (n 7) para 82.
[33] *Eweida* (n 7) para 82.
[34] *Core Issues Trust v Transport for London* [2013] EWHC 651, para 165 *per* Lang J.
[35] *Ahmad v UK* (1981) 4 EHRR 126.
[36] *Konttinen v Finland* (App 24949/94) (1996), Comm Rep 87 DR 68 (1996).
[37] *Copsey v Devon Clays Ltd* [2005] EWCA (Civ) 932.
[38] *Copsey* (n 37) para 36 *per* Lord Mummery: 'In the absence of the Commission rulings, I would have regarded this as a case of material interference with Mr Copsey's Article 9 rights.'
[39] *Williamson* (n 6) paras 39, 48–52.
[40] *Leyla Şahin v Turkey* (2005) 44 EHRR 99.

claimants voluntarily accepted arrangements that they knew did not accommodate the activity by which they sought to manifest their beliefs.[41] Lord Bingham based this rule on a line of Strasbourg cases that deal with voluntary acceptance in the contexts of education, such as attending universities with secular dress codes[42] or schools with compulsory sex education;[43] employment, such as jobs which do not allow time off for prayers[44] and military careers with associated behavioural restrictions.[45] The House of Lords also held that there will be no interference if there are other means by which the claimant could manifest his or her belief without undue hardship or inconvenience. The speeches of Lords Hoffmann[46] and Scott[47] placed particular reliance on this latter principle in dismissing the *Begum* appeal on its facts. Whilst claimants no longer need to show that it is *impossible* to manifest their belief elsewhere,[48] a claim will continue to fall at the interference hurdle if the claimant could find alternative employment[49] or educational provisions[50] without substantial hardship or inconvenience.

5.17 The tests in *Begum* have been followed in subsequent cases. No interference was found in *Playfoot*.[51] In *R (X) v Governors of Y School*,[52] the defendant school's prohibition of the Islamic *niqab* veil did not constitute interference because the claimant could have manifested her belief at a comparable school without significant inconvenience.[53] Mr Justice Silber's judgment expressly followed both *Begum*[54] and the body of pre-*Şahin* ECtHR cases on non-interference.[55]

5.18 However, as discussed in Chapter 3,[56] the ECtHR has now repudiated the doctrine of non-interference in the recent case of *Eweida v United Kingdom*,[57] Ms Eweida worked for British Airways, which had a uniform policy. The Strasbourg Court accepted that the uniform policy interfered with Ms Eweida's desire to manifest her religious belief by wearing a cross, even in circumstances where it was common ground that Ms Eweida did not believe that there was a mandatory requirement to wear the cross. It seems very likely that the approach of the ECtHR in *Eweida* and the approach of the House of Lords in *Williamson* will now be followed by the courts in England and Wales.

---

[41] *R (Shabina Begum) v Governors of Denbigh High School* [2007] 1 AC 100 (HL), para 23.
[42] *Karaduman v Turkey* (App 16278/90) (1993), Comm Rep 74 DR 93.
[43] *Kjeldsen v Denmark* (1976) 1 EHRR 711.
[44] *Ahmad* (n 35).
[45] *Kalaç* (n 28).
[46] *Begum* (n 41) paras 50–52.
[47] *Begum* (n 41) paras 87–89.
[48] This ECtHR standard derives from *Cha'are Shalom Ve Tsedek v France* (App 7417/95) (2000) 9 ECtHR 27, para 80, in which the Grand Chamber held that 'there would be interference…only if the illegality of performing ritual slaughter made it impossible for ultra-orthodox Jews to eat meat from animals slaughtered in accordance with the religious prescriptions they considered applicable'. This 'impossibility' standard describes a limit so extreme as to deprive the right to manifest belief of any meaning. In *Begum*, Lord Hoffmann explicitly eschews the impossibility standard. *Begum* (n 41) 52.
[49] *Stedman v UK* (1997) 23 EHRR 168.
[50] *Valsamis v Greece* (1997) 24 EHRR 294.
[51] *R (Playfoot) v Governing Body of Millais School* [2007] EWHC (Admin) 1698, para 32.
[52] *R (X) v Governors of Y School* [2007] EWHC (Admin) 298.
[53] *X v Y School* (n 52) para 39.
[54] *X v Y School* (n 52) paras 31–32.
[55] *X v Y School* (n 52) paras 33–38.
[56] See paras 3.53–3.54.
[57] *Eweida* (n 7).

(4) Justification

If a claimant succeeds in showing that there is an interference with the manifestation of a **5.19** religious belief, the burden shifts to the defendant to show that the interference was justified according to the Convention. There are three requirements. First, Article 9(2) ECHR requires that the limitation be 'prescribed by law'. In other words, the measure must have a basis in domestic law and be sufficiently accessible, clear, and foreseeable to allow individuals to regulate their conduct accordingly.[58] This test is common to many articles and applies to ECtHR jurisprudence in general, without significant nuances peculiar to Article 9.

Secondly, the measure must be pursuant to a 'legitimate aim' or 'permissible purpose', ie in the **5.20** words of Article 9(2) 'necessary in a democratic society in the interests of public safety, for the protection of public order, health or morals, or the protection of the rights and freedoms of others'. In general, meeting the 'legitimate aim' test causes little controversy: it is settled law, for example, that school uniforms meet this condition.[59]

Thirdly, the limiting measure must be proportionate to its legitimate aim. Proportionality is a **5.21** generic and familiar ECtHR tool for the balancing of competing interests. In the ECtHR the application of the test can be qualified by the 'margin of appreciation', a judge-made doctrine of judicial deference whereby Member States are afforded a degree of latitude in how they protect their citizens' rights.[60] Domestic jurisprudence shows that heightened judicial vigilance is required when Convention rights are at stake. The principle that ECHR cases demand a greater 'intensity of review' than domestic judicial review[61] is established law in the United Kingdom.[62]

In *Surayanda v Welsh Ministers*,[63] proportionality was pivotal to the Court of Appeal's finding **5.22** that the defendant authority was justified, given the threat of bovine tuberculosis, in ordering the slaughter of a bullock held sacred by a religious community. All three judges in that case noted the doctrine of deference, but reached their proportionality conclusion without resort to that. Thomas LJ conducted a critical scrutiny,[64] whilst Lloyd LJ confined the doctrine of deference to 'appropriate cases'.[65]

In the recent case of *Hall v Bull*,[66] the Court of Appeal held that a hotel owner's refusal to **5.23** provide a double bed (as opposed to single beds) to civil partners was discriminatory pursuant to the provisions of the Equality Act (Sexual Orientation) Regulations 2007. The hotel owners had refused to provide the double bed because they believed that providing the double bed would involve them in the promotion of what they considered to be the sin of extra marital sexual relations (for this reason the hotel owners also refused to provide a double bed to unmarried heterosexual couples). Challenges to the Regulations on the basis that they infringed the hotel owners' Article 9 rights failed, but Rafferty LJ, giving a judgment with

---

[58] *Gorzelik and ors v Poland* (2005) 40 EHRR 4, 64; cited approvingly in *Şahin* (n 40) 84.

[59] Not materially an issue in *R (Shabina Begum) v Governors of Denbigh High School* [2007] 1 AC 100 (HL), para 26; *Şahin* (n 40) 99; or *X v Y School* (n 52) para 70.

[60] See generally Y Arai-Takahashi, *The Margin of Appreciation and the Principle of Proportionality in the Jurisprudence of the ECHR* (Intersentia, 2002); JA Sweeney, 'Margins of Appreciation: Cultural Relativity and the ECHR' (2005) 54 ICLQ 459.

[61] *R (Daly) v Secretary of State for the Home Department* [2001] UKHL 26, 27 *per* Steyn LJ.

[62] *Begum* (n 59) para 30 *per* Bingham.

[63] *Surayanda v Welsh Ministers* [2007] EWCA (Civ) 893.

[64] *Surayanda* (n 63) para 79.

[65] *Surayanda* (n 63) para 103.

[66] *Hall v Bull* [2012] EWCA Civ 83.

which both Hooper LJ and Sir Andrew Morritt Chancellor agreed, said that 'any interference with religious rights, specifically identified in article 9 and listed in article 14 of the Convention, must satisfy the test of "anxious scrutiny"'.[67] An appeal to the UK Supreme Court is due to be heard in October 2013.

(5) Article 9 in combination with Article 14

5.24 As explained more fully in Chapter 3,[68] Article 14 will apply where the facts in issue fall within the 'ambit' of a Convention right. In *Gallagher (Valuation Officer) v The Church of Jesus Christ of Latter-Day Saints*,[69] the House of Lords held that the different treatment of a Mormon Temple, which did not benefit from an exemption from council tax as a 'place of public religious worship' because it was not open to the public, fell outside the ambit of Article 9, on the basis that the difference in treatment arose not because of the Mormons' religion, but because their religion prevented them from providing the public benefit necessary to secure the tax advantage.[70] It might be thought that that aspect of the decision is not easy to reconcile with the general approach taken by the ECtHR as to the ambit of Article 9, namely that rules of general application having particular consequences for persons because of their religion may fall within its ambit.[71]

5.25 In *R (Playfoot) v Millais School Governing Body*,[72] a school uniform policy prevented a student from wearing a 'purity' ring at school, symbolizing her commitment to chastity before marriage. She argued that this was contrary to Article 14 read together with Article 9 on the basis that Muslim girls wore Islamic headscarves and Sikh girls could wear the *Kara* bangle. The Court held there was no breach of Article 14. The school had reached carefully considered decisions on each occasion it had been called upon to permit exceptions to the uniform policy, and had allowed the headscarves and the *Kara* because it considered these were required as part of the students' faiths.[73]

5.26 In *Gallagher*, the House of Lords took the view that it complied with Article 14 for an exemption from council tax only to be extended to places of 'public religious worship', even though that excluded Mormon Temples because they did not allow entry to the public.[74] At paragraph 51 Lord Scott of Foscote held justification to be established for a number of reasons:

> . . . First, states may justifiably take the view that the practice of religion is beneficial both to the individuals who practise it as well as to the community of whom the individuals form part, and that, therefore, relief from rating for premises where religious worship takes place is in the public interest. But, second, states may also recognise that, although religion may be beneficial both to individuals and to the community, it is capable also of being divisive and, sometimes, of becoming dangerously so. No one who lives in a country such as ours, with a community of diverse ethnic and racial origins and of diverse cultures and religions, can be unaware of this. Religion can bind communities together; but it can also emphasise their differences. In these circumstances secrecy in religious practices provides the soil in which suspicions and

[67] *Hall v Bull* (n 66) para 56.
[68] See Ch 3, paras 3.118–3.119.
[69] *Gallagher (Valuation Officer) v The Church of Jesus Christ of Latter-Day Saints* [2008] UKHL 56.
[70] See *Gallagher* (n 69) paras 13–14 *per* Hoffmann LJ and para 31 *per* Hope LJ. Cf para 49 *per* Scott LJ. The case is pending before the Strasbourg Court at the time of writing.
[71] cf the cases cited in Ch 3 at para 3.119.
[72] *R (Playfoot) v Millais School Governing Body* [2007] EWHC 1698 (Admin).
[73] *Playfoot* (n 72) para 41.
[74] *Playfoot* (n 72) paras 15, 31, and 51.

unfounded prejudices can take root and grow; openness in religious practices, on the other hand, can dispel suspicions and contradict prejudices. I can see every reason why a state should adopt a general policy under which fiscal relief for premises used for religious worship is available where the premises are open to the general public and is withheld where they are not.

Most of the domestic cases concerning religious rights have considered arguments involving **5.27** the combination of Articles 9 and 14. However, other substantive Articles may also have relevance. In *R (Baiai and ors) v Secretary of State for the Home Department*,[75] it was held to be contrary to Article 14 taken with Article 12 (right to marry) that the immigration regime designed to deal with sham marriages did not apply to Anglican weddings because there was no evidence to show why non-Anglican religious marriages should be treated any differently.[76] However, it was not contrary to Article 14 for the immigration regime to treat Anglican religious ceremonies differently from ceremonies in registry offices, because there was good evidence of sham marriages taking place in non-religious ceremonies.[77]

(6) Section 13 HRA 1998

During the passage of the HRA 1998, the fear that other Convention rights would threaten **5.28** religious beliefs and practices provoked extensive parliamentary debate.[78] Among the concerns raised was the possibility that priests might be forced to marry divorced or same-sex couples, or that churches might be forced to employ staff with different religious beliefs.[79] The government rejected an amendment designed to give absolute priority to Article 9,[80] and the House of Commons instead inserted section 13(1) in the following terms:

> If a court's determination of any question arising under this Act might affect the exercise by a religious organization (itself or its members collectively) of the Convention right to freedom of thought, conscience and religion, it must have particular regard to the importance of that right.

Section 13 is limited,[81] and the fact that the text refers only to 'a religious organisation' makes **5.29** it more restrictive than the rights under Article 9. It is not clear whether the section extends to bodies which are conducted in accordance with a set of religious beliefs.[82]

The practical purpose served by section 13 has perplexed the courts.[83] The essence of the pro- **5.30** vision seems to be that the courts should have particular regard to the undoubted importance of religious rights, rather than that the latter should enjoy any sort of priority. It is questionable whether freedom of religion could in fact be prioritized as against other Convention rights: Article 17 of the Convention contains a prohibition against limiting ECHR rights to

---

[75] *R (Baiai and ors) v Secretary of State for the Home Department* [2006] EWHC 823 (Admin).

[76] *Baiai* (n 75) paras 122–131, 138–150. The point was not contested on appeal: [2007] EWCA Civ 478, paras 38–40 [2008] UKHL 53, paras 26 and 29 or in the Strasbourg Court (*O'Donoghue v UK* (App 34848/07) (2010) paras 102–103 and 110).

[77] *Baiai* (n 75) para 59.

[78] For a detailed analysis, see P Cumper, 'The Protection of Religious Rights under the Human Rights Act' [2000] Public Law 254, 255.

[79] See *Hansard* HC, vol 306 (16 February 1998), especially the speeches of Sir Brian Mawhinney (cols 786–793), Ann Widdecombe (col 799), and Theresa May (col 850).

[80] Home Secretary (Jack Straw MP), *Hansard* HC, col 1340 (21 October 1998).

[81] cf HRA 1998, s 12.

[82] *R (Williamson) v Secretary of State for Education and Employment* [2003] QB 1300 (CA), para 48 *per* Buxton LJ: 'I am far from certain that Parliament intended the concept of "religious organisations" to extend as far as schools, or for that matter bodies such as sports clubs or benevolent associations, that are conducted according to religious principles.'

[83] See the discussion of the three Court of Appeal judges in *Williamson* (n 82) paras 48–9, 181, and 313.

a greater extent than the Convention provides. It is arguable[84] that to accord special protection to religious rights when they are held by an organization as opposed to an individual would be in contravention of Article 14 of the Convention.

5.31   Section 13 has not affected the outcome of any decided case involving freedom of religion, and is often given short shrift when raised in argument.[85] However, in *Wallbank v Aston Cantlow*,[86] section 13 contributed to the court's rationale in finding that a church could not be a core public authority (and therefore not a 'victim' for the purposes of bringing a claim under HRA 1998).[87] In *Williamson*, although deciding that the claimants were not a religious organization for the purposes of section 13, both Buxton and Rix LLJ made it clear that they did not accept that section 13 is devoid of substance.[88]

C. Remedies

(1) Available remedies and jurisdiction

5.32   When an act (or proposed act) of a public body is found to be in breach of Convention rights, the available remedies under the HRA 1998 include damages, injunctive and declaratory relief, prerogative remedies, and remedies in criminal proceedings. Furthermore, section 3 of the 1998 Act imposes an obligation on the courts to interpret legislation compatibly with Convention rights, while section 4 empowers the court to make a declaration of incompatibility where it is impossible to interpret the legislation in this manner. These provisions, although not strictly remedies in themselves, clearly have an important remedial purpose and are therefore also considered in this section. In *Hall v Bull* the Court of Appeal accepted that the County Court had jurisdiction to strike down secondary legislation pursuant to the primary legislation of the Act.[89]

5.33   The primary remedial mechanism of the HRA 1998 is contained in section 8. Section 8(1) provides that, where a court or tribunal finds that any act (or proposed act) of a public authority is (or would be) unlawful, it may grant such relief or remedy, or make such order, within its powers, as it considers just and appropriate. However, the Act does not confer a power to award such a remedy in every instance where HRA arguments are raised. Damages may only be awarded by a court or tribunal which has power to award damages, or to order the payment of compensation, in civil proceedings.[90] A declaration of incompatibility can only be granted by the higher courts,[91] and it continues to be the case that quashing regulations,

---

[84]   See J Beatson, S Grosz, T Hickman, and R Singh, *Human Rights: Judicial Protection in the United Kingdom* (Sweet & Maxwell, 2008) 415.

[85]   Most recently in *Hall v Bull* [2012] EWCA Civ 83, para 53, where Rafferty LJ made the following brief remark: 'it does not in my view on the facts of this case add to the requirements already set out in the Convention'.

[86]   *Wallbank v Aston Cantlow and Wilmcote with Billesley Parochial Church Council* [2003] UKHL 37.

[87]   *Wallbank* (n 86) para 15 *per* Nicholls LJ: 'The Human Rights Act goes out of its way, in section 13, to single out for express mention the exercise by religious organisations of the Convention right of freedom of thought, conscience and religion. One would expect that these and other Convention rights would be enjoyed by the Church of England as much as other religious bodies.'

[88]   *Williamson* (n 82) paras 49, 189.

[89]   *Hall v Bull* (n 85) para 28.

[90]   HRA 1998, s 8(2). This means that a criminal court will not be able to award damages for breach of Convention rights.

[91]   HRA 1998, s 4(5).

mandatory orders, and prohibiting orders are only available under proceedings for judicial review.

(2) Sections 3 and 4 HRA 1998

Taken together, sections 3 and 4 provide the courts with a mechanism for reviewing legislation which is potentially contrary to one or more Convention rights. The scheme attempts to strike a balance between allowing the courts to deal effectively with infringing legislation and maintaining the boundaries of their constitutional role. **5.34**

Section 3 of HRA 1998 provides that courts are required to construe any legislation in conformity with the Convention 'so far as it is possible to do so'. This confers a strong interpretative obligation, although the Courts are not permitted to legislate or to amend legislation.[92] If the measure of interpretation required is such that it is effectively a legislative act, the only option for the court is to issue a declaration of incompatibility under section 4. Such a declaration is intended as a measure of last resort.[93] Therefore the determination of the boundary of the interpretative obligation under section 3 is crucial. **5.35**

(a) Section 3

The obligation to interpret legislation in a Convention-compliant manner 'as far as it is possible to do so' was described in strong terms in the White Paper:[94] 'The courts will be required to interpret legislation so as to uphold Convention rights unless the legislation itself is so clearly incompatible with the Convention that it is impossible to do so.' The provision enjoyed mixed judicial reaction immediately following its coming into force. Lord Steyn was in favour of a broad interpretation of what was 'possible': he commented extra-judicially that the obligation amounted to a 'rebuttable presumption in favour of an interpretation consistent with convention rights',[95] and remarked in *R v A (No 2)*[96] that it was necessary 'sometimes to adopt a construction which is linguistically strained not only by reading down but by implication of provisions'. However, in the same case Lord Hope was clear that section 3 remained only an interpretive tool, and did not give the courts the right to legislate.[97] In *Re S*, Lord Nicholls stated that the courts should be mindful of the outer limit and the aim of HRA 1998 of preserving Parliamentary sovereignty.[98] In that case, the House of Lords held that the Court of Appeal had effectively legislated in relation to the Children Act 1989 by allowing applications to be made to the Court when a child was in the care of a local authority, and reversed the decision. **5.36**

The House of Lords settled its approach in *Ghaidan*, where more coherent principles for the boundary of what was 'possible' under section 3 were outlined in the majority judgments. Lord Nicholls said the answer was that Parliament could not be taken to 'have intended that in the discharge of this extended interpretative function the courts should **5.37**

---

[92] See eg *Re S (Minors) (Care Order: Implementation of Care Plan)* [2002] UKHL 10, 38–41.
[93] See eg *Ghaidan v Godin-Mendoza* [2004] 2 AC 557, para 39; this was also the view of the Secretary of State for the Home Department (Mr Jack Straw) in Parliamentary debates on the Human Rights Bill, *Hansard* HC, cols 421–422 (3 June 1998).
[94] Rights Brought Home: The Human Rights Bill (1997) Cm 3782, para 2.7.
[95] Lord Steyn, 'Incorporation and Devolution—a few reflections on the Challenging Scene' [1998] EHRLR 153.
[96] *R v A (No 2)* [2002] 1 AC 45, 45.
[97] *R v A (No 2)* (n 96) 88.
[98] *Re S* (n 92) 39.

adopt a meaning inconsistent with a fundamental feature of legislation',[99] while Lord Rodger said that the court must not ascribe a meaning which conflicts with 'essential principles' of the legislation concerned.[100] The conclusion given by Lord Nicholls was that the section 3 obligation:

> ...may require the court to depart from the unambiguous meaning that legislation would otherwise bear. In the ordinary course the interpretation of legislation involves seeking the intention reasonably to be attributed to Parliament in using the language in question. Section 3 may require the court to depart from this legislative intention, that is, depart from the intention of the Parliament which enacted the legislation.[101]

5.38 The House of Lords ultimately held in *Ghaidan* that the 'essential principles' of paragraph 2 of Schedule 1 to the Rent Act 1977 were not to be determined by reference to the gender-specific language employed, but instead by reference to the overall protective intention of the provision. The focus thereby shifted from the wording to the substance of the provision, allowing the courts more freedom in determining what was 'possible' for the purposes of their obligation under section 3.

5.39 The approach set out in *Ghaidan* is broad, but not without limits. The courts will refrain from adopting an interpretation that conflicts with a fundamental feature of the legislation concerned: *R (Anderson) v Secretary of State for the Home Department*[102] is a good illustration of this limitation. In *Anderson*, the role of the Home Secretary in the then-applicable regime governing the release of prisoners serving mandatory life sentences would have to have been written out of the legislation in order to render the provision compliant with Article 6 ECHR. Lord Bingham commented that this 'would not be judicial interpretation but judicial vandalism...and would go well beyond any interpretative process sanctioned by section 3'.[103] The courts will avoid any interpretation which represents a major change in the law: in *Bellinger v Bellinger*,[104] the House of Lords considered it could not construe the statutory word 'female' to include the meaning 'transsexual'. Lord Nicholls held:[105]

> [The interpretation] would have far-reaching implications. It raises issues whose solution calls for extensive inquiry and the widest public consultation and discussion.... The issues are altogether ill-suited for determination by courts and court procedures. They are pre-eminently a matter for Parliament.

It is clear that while courts are permitted to go to considerable lengths in carrying out their obligation under section 3,[106] they must stop short of interpreting contrary to fundamental principles of the legislation in question, and of ascribing any meaning to a provision which has far-reaching consequences for public policy.

---

[99] *Ghaidan* (n 93) 33.
[100] *Ghaidan* (n 93) 121.
[101] *Ghaidan* (n 93) 30.
[102] *R (Anderson) v Secretary of State for the Home Department* [2002] UKHL 46.
[103] *Anderson* (n 102) 30.
[104] *Bellinger v Bellinger* [2003] 2 WLR 1174.
[105] *Bellinger v Bellinger* (n 104) 36.
[106] The court 'can read in and read down; it can supply missing words, so long as they are consistent with the fundamental features of the legislative scheme; it can do considerable violence to the language and stretch it almost (but not quite) to breaking point'. *Ghaidan* (n 93) para 67 *per* Rodger LJ.

(b) Section 4

Where a court finds that a piece of legislation is incompatible with the Convention but has **5.40** no power to strike it down,[107] it may make a declaration that the legislation is incompatible with a Convention right.[108] County courts, magistrates' courts, and crown courts are not empowered to make such a declaration:[109] they are not, however, prevented from expressing a view that the legislation is incompatible.[110] The likely necessity of a declaration of incompatibility is something to which the High Court and the county court must have regard when considering making a transfer order to the High Court.[111]

Where a court makes a declaration of incompatibility, this does not affect the validity or **5.41** continuing operation or enforcement of the provision in respect of which it was given.[112] However, it does trigger the right of the government to use a 'fast-track' procedure to change the legislation under section 10 of HRA 1998.[113] Save in urgent cases, the draft of the remedial order is laid before Parliament for 60 days, after which it is approved by resolutions of both Houses.[114] A remedial order may have retrospective effect,[115] and it was intended that any changes would be limited to those which are necessary to correct the incompatibility.[116]

(3) Damages

(a) The award of damages

Section 8(1) of HRA 1998 itself does not specifically identify damages as a remedy, but it is **5.42** clear from a construction of section 8 as a whole, and established authority, that damages are intended to be available for the unlawful act of a public authority for the purposes of section 6(1). The 1998 Act does not create an ordinary tortious action for breach of statutory duty which gives rise to damages by right. Rather, it 'gives the court a special statutory discretion, modelled in relation to damages on the approach of the European Court of Human Rights'.[117] Section 8(3) provides that no award of damages is to be made unless, taking account of all the circumstances of the case, including any other relief or remedy granted, or order made, in relation to the act in question (by that or any other court or tribunal), and also taking into account the consequences of any decision in respect of that act, the court or tribunal is satisfied that the award is necessary to afford just satisfaction to the person in whose favour it is made. The court will consider whether other remedies suffice before coming to the question of monetary compensation.[118]

---

[107] As is the case for all primary legislation. Legislation emanating from Scotland, Northern Ireland, and Wales is regarded as secondary legislation (under HRA 1998, s 21 for Scotland and Ireland, and under the Government of Wales Act 1998, s107(1) for Wales).

[108] HRA 1998, s 4(2).

[109] HRA 1998, s 4(5).

[110] Indeed, such a view may be of assistance to the higher court; see *Wilson v First County Trust Ltd (No 2)* [2003] UKHL 40, para 14.

[111] CPR, r 30.3(2).

[112] HRA 1998, s 4(6)(a).

[113] Details of how remedial orders may be made are contained in HRA 1998, Sch 2.

[114] HRA 1998, Sch 2, paras 2, 3.

[115] HRA 1998, Sch 2, para 1(1)(b) and (4).

[116] *Hansard* HL, col 402 (29 January 1998).

[117] *Somerville v Scottish Ministers* [2007] UKHL 44, para 176 *per* Mance LJ.

[118] In *Anufrijeva v Southwark LBC* [2003] EWCA Civ 1406, para 53, Woolf LJ stated that 'where an infringement of an individual's human rights has occurred, the concern will usually be to bring the infringement to an end and any question of compensation will be of secondary, if any, importance'. This approach was appealed in *R (Greenfield) v Secretary of State for the Home Department* [2005] UKHL 14, para 9 *per* Bingham LJ.

5.43　In exercising the discretion to award damages, the court must have regard to the principles applied by the ECtHR in relation to the award of compensation under Article 41 ECHR.[119] This is made difficult by the fact that the ECtHR's explanation for the basis of its awards is often limited. The main principle is that compensation does not arise by right, and should be awarded only if 'necessary' to 'afford just satisfaction' to the injured party.[120] The decision is an equitable assessment as to whether compensation is appropriate in all the circumstances.[121]

5.44　Section 9 of HRA 1998 places express limitation on the jurisdiction to award damages for judicial acts. Where the act is done in good faith, damages may not be awarded otherwise than to compensate a person to the extent required by Article 5(5) ECHR.[122] The 1998 Act therefore reflects the general common law principle of judicial immunity against actions for damages. It is interesting to compare this approach with the approach to the award of damages for constitutional infringements by judicial authorities under written constitutions, as in *Maharaj v Attorney General of Trinidad and Tobago (No 2)*.[123]

(b) The assessment of damages

5.45　As with the award of damages, the court must take principles developed by Strasbourg case law into account when assessing the quantum of any award.[124] Section 8 damages should therefore not be assessed according to domestic tortious principles, but on the basis most likely to achieve 'just satisfaction' or 'fairness in the individual case'.[125]

5.46　In *Anufrijeva v Southwark*,[126] Lord Woolf identified four main principles underpinning the Strasbourg jurisprudence in this area.[127] The first and most important was that the ECtHR is to seek, so far as possible, to put the applicant in the position he would have enjoyed had there been compliance with the requirements of the Convention.[128] The second is that Strasbourg case law on damages for anxiety and distress is not consistent or coherent, although the ECtHR has been persuaded to award 'a just and equitable amount of compensation' for distress, disruption, lost opportunities of being released from detention, and other types of damage.[129] Thirdly, the ECtHR is disinclined to pay compensation for procedural

---

[119] *Greenfield* (n 118) para 6. This does not amount to an obligation to apply the principles, but see the speech by the Lord Chancellor, Lord Irvine, on the second reading of the Bill in the House of Lords on 3 November 1997: 'Our aim is that people should receive damages equivalent to what they would have obtained had they taken their case to Strasbourg', 582 HL Official Report (5th series) col 1232. For an assessment of the principles applied by the ECtHR under Art 41, see Ch 3, paras 3.152-3.157.

[120] See eg *Gazzardi v Italy* (1981) 3 EHRR 333.

[121] See eg *McCann v UK* (1995) 21 EHRR 97, para 219, after finding a breach of ECHR, Art 2, the court stated: 'having regard to the fact that the three terror suspects who were killed had been intending to plant a bomb in Gibraltar, the court does not consider it appropriate to make an award'.

[122] HRA 1998, s 9(3). ECHR, Art 5(5) reads: 'Everyone who has been the victim of arrest or detention in contravention of the provisions of this article shall have an enforceable right to compensation.'

[123] *Maharaj v Attorney General of Trinidad and Tobago (No 2)* [1979] AC 385.

[124] HRA 1998, s 8(4)(b).

[125] *R (Greenfield) v Secretary of State for the Home Department* [2005] 1 WLR 673, para 19 *per* Bingham LJ. For an analysis of Strasbourg pricniples, see Ch 3, paras 3.153–3.159.

[126] *Anufrijeva v Southwark LBC* [2003] EWCA Civ 1406.

[127] *Anufrijeva* (n 126) paras 52–56.

[128] *Kinglsey v UK* (2002) EHRR 177, para 40.

[129] Note, however, that in domestic application, Stanley Burton J stated in *R v Mental Health Review Tribunal* [2004] QB 976, para 71, that 'distress and disappointment are part of everyday life, and do not necessarily lead to claims for damages'. He furthermore concluded that it would be contrary to Strasbourg principles to award damages for loss of a chance of a favourable tribunal decision or for loss of opportunity as such.

errors, and finally, the Court's approach in assessing damages is an equitable one involving consideration of a range of factors, including the seriousness and manner of the violation.

A recent case concerning unnecessarily prolonged imprisonment provides a helpful exam- **5.47** ple of the domestic courts' approach. In *R (Faulkner) v Secretary of State for Justice*,[130] it was held that Mr Faulkner's rights under Article 5(4) ECHR had been violated.[131] The Supreme Court held, in reliance on an earlier case,[132] that such a violation could result in an award of damages under section 8 of HRA 1998. When assessing the measure of that award, Lord Reed held that the amount should be a matter of judgment, reflecting the facts of the case (which should be ascertained in the ordinary manner) and having regard to guidance from Strasbourg and the national courts in comparable cases.[133] The Supreme Court then proceeded to consider the approach of the ECtHR in a long line of authorities where a violation of Article 5(4) had been found: first, to determine in what circumstances different heads of loss could be compensated; and secondly, to determine the quantum of any compensation. The latter process involved distilling an appropriate bracket from the figures available,[134] but even extensive analysis precluded the derivation of precise guidance.[135] The Supreme Court took care to highlight that any conclusion reached would be 'what is just and appropriate in the individual case'.[136]

Exemplary damages have not been awarded, but awards for interest have been made where **5.48** this is necessary to avoid unfair diminution in the value of compensation.[137] Again, it is interesting to compare the approach of common law jurisdictions with written constitutions on the issue of 'vindication'.

(4) Prerogative orders

In judicial review proceedings, mandatory, prohibiting, and quashing orders are available in **5.49** HRA-based applications. As claims under section 7(1)(a) of HRA 1998 are in practice often brought by application for judicial review, these are likely to be the usual orders made following a challenge to the act of a public authority. A quashing order has the effect of quashing a decision of a public authority, a prohibiting order prevents a public body from acting beyond its jurisdiction, and a mandatory order compels a public body to do its duty.

A quashing order will often be a sufficient remedy in a claim brought under section 7(1)(a). **5.50** Although the court may not substitute its own decision for that of the public authority, once the decision has been set aside, the course which the public body should lawfully take is likely to be obvious from the reasoning of the judgment. It will usually, therefore, be unnecessary for the court to grant any further remedy by way of damages.[138]

---

[130] *R (Faulkner) v Secretary of State for Justice* [2013] UKSC 23.
[131] ECHR, Art 5(4) provides: 'Everyone who is deprived of his liberty by arrest or detention shall be entitled to take proceedings by which the lawfulness of his detention shall be decided speedily by a court and his release ordered if the detention is not lawful.'
[132] *R (James) v Secretary of State for Justice* [2010] 1 AC 553.
[133] *Faulkner* (n 130) para 39.
[134] The poles of the bracket in this case were themselves broad and imprecise: a violation under Art 5(4) 'could reasonably be expected to be significantly above awards for frustration and anxiety alone, but well below the level of awards for a loss of unrestricted liberty', *Faulkner* (n 130) para 75.
[135] *Faulkner* (n 130) para 75.
[136] *Faulkner* (n 130) para 75.
[137] See eg *Stran Greek Refineries v Greece* (1994) 19 EHRR 293, paras 82–83.
[138] See n 118.

5.51 A prohibiting order is often complementary to a quashing order, and prevents public bodies from acting unlawfully in the future. It has been said that there is little difference in principle between a quashing and a prohibiting order 'except that the latter may be invoked at an earlier stage'.[139]

5.52 A mandatory order can be granted in the claimant's favour if there is only one possible decision in the circumstances.[140] This is rarely the case, as a public body will often have a discretion in exercising its duties. In granting mandatory orders, the courts must be careful to avoid any appearance that they are 'assuming the function assigned by Parliament to the public body and exercising the discretion on their behalf'.[141]

(5) Declarations and injunctions

5.53 A court with the necessary jurisdiction[142] may grant the remedies of declarations and injunctions, whereby legal rights are declared or orders made to prevent or compel specified acts.

5.54 Although declaratory and injunctive relief are, in origin, private law remedies, a claimant may seek them in judicial review proceedings.[143] As with all public law remedies, the court has a broad discretion as to whether or not to grant declarations or injunctions in Part 54 applications. In practice, however, relief for breaches of HRA 1998 has nearly always been granted by the courts where an illegality challenge succeeds.[144] This compulsion stems from the fact that courts and tribunals are expressly categorized as public bodies for the purposes of section 6(1) of the Act, and would therefore be in breach of that obligation if the claimant remained a victim of a breach of a Convention right.

(6) Remedies in criminal proceedings

5.55 Potential remedies in criminal proceedings where a defendant's Convention rights have been violated include:

- an order withdrawing issue of a summons;
- a motion to quash in indictment;
- a stay of criminal proceedings;
- the dismissal of the prosecution;
- an order excluding the admission of evidence;
- an order requiring the inclusion of evidence;
- an order of the Court of Appeal quashing a conviction; and
- an order of the Divisional Court in judicial review quashing a conviction.

5.56 HRA 1998 does not grant criminal courts any new power to make compensatory awards. Where a defendant wishes to claim damages as a result of, for example, a judicial decision which has

---

[139] *R (London Electricity Joint Committee Company (1920) Ltd) v Electricity Commissioners* [1924] 1 KB 171, 206 *per* Atkin LJ.

[140] See eg *R (Stewart) v City of London Licensing Justices* [1954] 1 WLR 1325.

[141] *R (Nilish Shah) v Barnet LBC, ex p Nilish Shah* [1983] 2 AC 309, 350.

[142] The High Court has jurisdiction to grant declarations pursuant to the Supreme Court Act 1981, s 31 and injunctions pursuant to ss 30 and 31 of the same Act. County courts have the same powers as the High Courts in this regard: County Courts Act 1984, s 38.

[143] CPR, r 54(3)(1).

[144] A rare example of refusal to grant a declaration can be seen in *R (Rusbridger) v A-G* [2003] AC 357.

breached his Convention rights, he will need to commence proceedings in the civil courts. As these are proceedings under section 7(1)(a) in respect of a judicial act, such a claim may only be brought by application for judicial review (section 9(1)(b)).

D. Procedure

(1) Introduction

(a) General scheme

There is no prescribed procedure which must be followed in all HRA cases. The White Paper, *Rights Brought Home*, envisaged that Convention arguments would as far as possible be integrated into existing causes of action, but that if none were available, it would be possible for a complainant to bring proceedings on Convention grounds alone.[145] This approach is provided for by section 7 of HRA 1998, which first sets out the procedural mechanism for bringing a free-standing claim against a public authority for breach of their duty to act compatibly with Convention rights,[146] and secondly allows for HRA arguments to be relied upon in 'any legal proceedings', including as a defence and in the course of an appeal.[147] Free-standing claims can be brought either by way of the new statutory cause of action under section 7, or by way of judicial review. **5.57**

HRA 1998 therefore provides for Convention arguments to be relied on in every forum where legal rights are determined. By virtue of their status as public authorities,[148] courts are bound to act in a way which is compatible with ECHR rights wherever they undertake to interpret legislation, to exercise discretion, or to develop the principles of the common law.[149] In turn, the Courts themselves have made it clear that in many cases Convention arguments do not add anything to the rights and remedies available under the common law.[150] **5.58**

---

[145] *Rights Brought Home* (Cm 3782, 1997) para 2.3.

[146] HRA 1998, s 7(1)(a).

[147] HRA 1998, s 7(1)(b), as defined at s 7(6). Further procedural rules are contemplated under s 2 (governing citation of Convention authority); s 5 (regulating joinder in cases where a court is considering whether to make a declaration of incompatibility); s 7 (concerning the question of taking proceedings in the appropriate court); and s 9 (in relation to damages claims against judicial authorities under s 5).

[148] HRA 1998, s 6(3)(a).

[149] This has proved controversial with regard to disputes between private parties which are regulated by the common law. However, see *A v Secretary of State for the Home Department (No 2)* [2005] UKHL 71, para 7 *per* Bingham LJ: 'If, and to the extent that, development of the common law is called for, such development should ordinarily be in harmony with the United Kingdom's international obligations and not antithetical to them.'

[150] See eg *R (Bright) v Central Criminal Court* [2001] 1 WLR 662, 679 *per* Judge LJ:

> Our attention was drawn to a number of decisions of the European Court of Human Rights. I have considered them with care. That said, by now, we surely fully appreciate that the principles to be found in Articles 6 and 10 of the European Convention are bred in the bone of the common law and indeed, in some instances at any rate, the folk understanding of the community as a whole. I do not intend to imply any criticism of the submissions made by any of the counsel in this appeal, each of whom advanced submissions of great clarity and appropriate economy, when I say that generally, the vast and increasingly lengthy number of citations in numerous skeleton and oral arguments of the decisions of the European Court, simply repeating in different language long standing and well understood principles of the common law, suggests that perhaps we do not.

This was repeated recently in *J v Commissioner of Police of the Metropolis* [2013] EWHC 32 (QB), para 59.

5.59   The options open to individuals to enforce their Convention rights may be summarized as follows:

(1) as a head of illegality in an application for judicial review;

(2) as a free-standing claim in the ordinary courts against a public authority for breach of section 6(1) of the Act;

(3) as a claim against a public authority which indirectly relies on a Convention right by virtue of statutory interpretation, exercise of judicial discretion, or interpretation of common law principles;

(4) as a claim against a private party on the same basis;[151] and

(5) as a defence where a public authority has brought proceedings against an individual in breach of their Convention rights.

(b)   The role of judicial review

5.60   Part 54 proceedings will be appropriate where primary legislation is alleged to be incompatible with a Convention right (apart from in a dispute between two private parties),[152] or where the lawfulness (in terms of *vires*) of a particular decision is concerned.[153] Quashing, mandatory, or prohibiting orders continue to be exclusively available in judicial review proceedings, rendering Part 54 applications necessary where these remedies are sought.

5.61   Judicial review proceedings are less likely to be appropriate where there is a dispute of facts to be resolved. It has been observed that disputes involving a human rights element 'often require cross-examination which is more conveniently provided for outside the Administrative Court list';[154] in these cases, HRA cases can properly be commenced by ordinary action and then transferred to a High Court judge with administrative experience if necessary.[155] However, where this is impossible as a result of the remedies being sought, there is the increasing possibility that a cross-examination order will be made in judicial review proceedings.[156] The Administrative Court does not have jurisdiction to hear an action for damages alone, so any claim seeking an exclusively compensatory remedy must be brought as a private action.[157]

(2)   HRA-based judicial review

5.62   HRA 1998 has created a new illegality ground for judicial review applications. An individual can argue that a decision should be quashed because a public authority has acted incompatibly with one or more Convention rights, and has thereby contravened section 6(1) of HRA 1998. For the purposes of the 1998 Act, these are free-standing claims of the type envisaged by section 7(1)(a), and the specific standing requirements set out by that section therefore apply. General procedural points are covered by CPR Part 54, but there are some specific issues to note where the applications are HRA-based.

---

[151] See n 149.

[152] *R (Pearson) v Secretary of State for the Home Department* [2001] EWHC Admin 239, para 6.

[153] CPR, r 54.1.

[154] *D v Home Office* [2006] 1 WLR 1003, para 105.

[155] *D v Home Office* (n 154) para 129.

[156] See especially *R (Al-Sweady) v Secretary of State for Defence* [2009] EWHC 2387, 17–21; see also para 5.74.

[157] CPR, r 54.3(2). See also *D v Home Office* (n 154) para 58.

(a) Standing requirements

In order to bring HRA-based judicial review proceedings against a public body, a claimant **5.63** must satisfy the standing requirements listed under section 7.[158] These may be summarized as follows: a person who claims that a public authority has acted (or proposes to act) in a way which is made unlawful under the Act may bring proceedings in an appropriate court or tribunal[159] within the limitation period,[160] provided he is or would be a victim of the unlawful act[161] for the purposes of Article 34 ECHR.[162]

(i) Victim In HRA-based judicial review proceedings, the 'victim' requirement replaces **5.64** the 'sufficient interest' test for standing. In accordance with Article 34 ECHR, any private, natural, or legal person can bring a claim under HRA 1998, including NGOs and companies.[163] Unlike with other judicial review applications, NGOs may only invoke HRA 1998 where it is their own rights as an organization (or those of their members collectively) which are at stake (but see paragraph 5.69).[164] This more stringent approach for HRA-based claims has provoked judicial comment.[165] Core public authorities cannot be victims for the purposes of Article 34, and Strasbourg jurisprudence has been consistent in holding that local authorities are not 'non-governmental organisations or groups of individuals' for the purposes of the Article. This principle has been upheld in domestic law.[166]

The meaning of 'victim' under domestic law is autonomous with ECtHR jurisprudence:[167] **5.65** the basic test for any applicant is whether they are directly affected by the measure in question.[168] The requirement is thereby narrower than the traditional 'sufficient interest' requirement for judicial review. The test does, however, include the more general provision that an individual can be a 'victim' of the state of the law, even where that has not caused him specific detriment;[169] the direct effect on the applicant in this scenario stems from the very existence of the law in question.[170]

Where there is a real threat of a future violation of an applicant's Convention right, he or she **5.66** qualifies as someone who 'would be' a victim for the purposes of section 7(1) of HRA 1998.

---

[158] See, recently, the comments of Mrs Justice Lang in *Core Issues Trust v Transport for London* [2013] EWHC 651, para 9: 'Although the test for standing in judicial review claims under CPR Pt 54 is more liberal than under the ECHR, the human rights claim was at the core of this judicial review, and so the Claimant had to establish standing under the HRA 1998.'

[159] HRA 1998, s 7(1)(a).

[160] HRA 1998, s 7(5).

[161] HRA 1998, s 7(3).

[162] HRA 1998, s 7(7).

[163] Companies cannot rely on all Convention rights. For instance, they cannot rely on the right to freedom of conscience, but they do have a right to freedom of religion: see *X and Church of Scientology v Sweden* (1979) 16 DR 68, 70.

[164] See eg *Christians against Racism and Fascism v UK* (App 8840/78) (1980) 21 DR 138.

[165] *The Children's Rights Alliance for England v Secretary of State for Justice* [2012] EWHC 8 (Admin), para 223 *per* Foskett J: 'Shutting such an organisation out of raising issues of the kind that have been raised in this application is a very unfortunate consequence of section 7 of the Human Rights Act, but Parliament took the view it did at the time it passed the Act and the Act must be respected.'

[166] See eg *R (Medway Council) v Secretary of State for Transport* [2002] EWHC 2516 (Admin), para 20.

[167] See eg *Al Hassan-Daniel v Revenue and Customs Commissioners* [2010] EWCA Civ 1443, para 23.

[168] See eg *Sisojeva v Latvia* (2007) 45 EHRR 33, 92.

[169] *Eckle v Germany* (1982) 5 EHRR 1, 66.

[170] See eg *Norris v Ireland* (1988) 13 EHRR 186, para 31, where the applicant was considered a victim of a law criminalizing homosexual activity without ever having been prosecuted by it, and where the risk of prosecution was minimal.

This principle first emerges in ECtHR case law in *Campbell and Cosans v United Kingdom*,[171] where the Court observed obiter that 'a mere threat of conduct prohibited by Article 3 may itself conflict with that provision', provided the threat was sufficiently real and immediate. In *Soering v United Kingdom*,[172] the Court established, in an extradition decision, that the applicant could be a victim of a breach of Article 3 where there were 'substantial grounds for believing' that he faced a 'real risk' of being subjected to torture or inhuman or degrading treatment or punishment upon fulfilment of the extradition request. This element of ECtHR jurisprudence has been followed in the domestic case law.[173]

5.67   Although it was feared that the victim requirement in HRA-based judicial review proceedings would severely limit the participation of public interest groups, it was intended that these bodies would retain an important role through assisting and providing representation for individual victims and filing *amicus curiae* briefs.[174] Furthermore, the Equality and Human Rights Commission has special standing not only to intervene in existing proceedings, but also to take 'own name' proceedings, including judicial review, to prevent breaches of HRA 1998.[175]

5.68   (ii) **Limitation: judicial review**   Section 7(5)(a) and (b) of HRA 1998 state that proceedings under section 7(1)(a) must be brought within one year of the act complained of, or such longer period as the court or tribunal considers equitable having regard to all the circumstances.[176] These provisions are subject to any rule imposing a stricter time limit in relation to the procedure in question,[177] meaning that the time limit will remain no later than three months (after the grounds for which judicial review arose) when proceedings are brought by way of judicial review.

(b) Public authority

5.69   Section 6(1) makes it unlawful for public authorities to act (or fail to act) in a way which is incompatible with a Convention right.[178] 'Public authorities' for the purposes of the Act fall into three categories. 'Core' public authorities include all bodies which are obviously public in nature, and the Act regulates all their functions whether public or private. 'Hybrid' or 'functional' public bodies are also included by virtue of section 6(3)(b), which contemplates any person certain of whose functions are public in nature. It is only with regard to these public functions that hybrid authorities are subject to a duty under the Act.[179] Finally, section 6(3)(a) expressly provides for the fact that courts and tribunals are public bodies for the purposes of the HRA. There is no self-contained definition of 'public authority' within the section, and a body of case-law has been developed to determine the scope of the term in HRA proceedings.

---

[171] *Campbell and Cosans v UK* (1982) 4 EHRR 293, para 26.
[172] *Soering v UK* (1989) 11 EHRR 439.
[173] See *R (Countryside Alliance) v A-G* [2006] EWCA Civ 817, para 65.
[174] *Hansard* HL, col 810 (5 February 1998).
[175] Equality Act 2006, s 30.
[176] For a full discussion of limitation under HRA 1998, see para 5.79.
[177] HRA 1998, s 7(5).
[178] HRA 1998, s 6(2) provides that such an act is not unlawful in circumstances where the public authority could not have acted otherwise as a result of primary legislation; s 6(5) provides that an 'act' does not include a failure to legislate.
[179] HRA 1998, s 6(5).

(i) Core public authorities The House of Lords favoured a relatively narrow test with **5.70** regard to the definition of core public authorities under the HRA, as inclusion within this category prevents the body itself from bringing a claim for breach of its Convention rights.[180] Obviously governmental bodies such as government departments and ministers, local authorities and the police have been included, as well as NHS Trusts, coroners and bodies such as the General Medical Council and the Legal Services Commission. In *Aston Cantlow*, Lord Nicholls formulated the test as follows: 'the phrase "a public authority" in section 6(1) is essentially a reference to a body whose nature is governmental in a broad sense of that expression', and went on to include factors such as 'the possession of special powers, democratic accountability, public funding in whole or in part, an obligation to act only in the public interest, and a statutory constitution.'[181] The duty extends to all acts of the authority, including employment and contractual relationships which would not previously have been amenable to judicial review.[182]

(ii) Hybrid authorities With hybrid or functional public authorities, the question is **5.71** whether the act complained of is 'public' for the purposes of liability under section 6. In principle, this ensures that the scope of protection is not hindered by technical distinctions about the nature of the body exercising the function, and prevents the state from escaping liability by delegating essentially public functions to private bodies.[183] However, the definition has proved controversial in practice. Although the House of Lords in *Aston Cantlow* appeared to lay down a relatively broad test,[184] there has been disproportionate focus in the case law on institutional proximity to state bodies rather than on the substance and nature of the act.[185] The current state of the law is reflected in the decision of *YL v Birmingham City Council*,[186] where the House of Lords held that the provision of care for a vulnerable and elderly individual which was both arranged and paid for by the local authority was not a 'function of a public nature' when carried out by a privately-owned care home. While the dissenting speeches of the minority[187] focused on the importance of the public interest in the provision of such care, the public funding provided and the coercive powers of the state,[188] as well as on the general need to bring delegated public functions under the protection of the Act,[189] the majority[190] focused on the fact that the care was provided under a commercial contract rather than as a result of statutory duty.[191] With the case law as it currently stands, factors including

---

[180] *Aston Cantlow and Wilmcote with Billesley Parochial Church Council v Wallbank and anor* [2003] UKHL 37, para 8 *per* Nicholls LJ.

[181] *Aston Cantlow* (n 180) para 7.

[182] See eg *R (Lavelle) v BBC* [1983] ICR 99, 107H.

[183] See *eg Costello-Roberts v UK* (1995) 19 EHRR 112, where the UK was held liable under ECHR, Art 3 for corporal punishment inflicted in a private school.

[184] *Aston Cantlow* (n 180) para 12 *per* Nicholls LJ: 'Factors to be taken into account include the extent to which in carrying out the relevant function the body is publicly funded, or is exercising statutory powers, or is taking the place of central government or local authorities, or is providing a public service.'

[185] See eg 'The Meaning of public Authority under the Human Rights Act', 7th Report (2003–2004), HL 39, HC 382, February 2004, where the Joint Committee on Human Rights expresses concern about the deficit of protection where individuals received public services on a 'contracted-out' basis.

[186] *YL v Birmingham City Council* [2007] UKHL 27.

[187] *YL v Birmingham City Council* (n 186) dissenting speeches were given by Lord Bingham of Cornhill (paras 1–20) and Baroness Hale of Richmond (paras 36–75)

[188] *YL v Birmingham City Council* (n 186) paras 67–69 *per* Baroness Hale.

[189] *YL v Birmingham City Council* (n 186) para 20 *per* Bingham LJ.

[190] *YL v Birmingham City Council* (n 186) majority speeches were given by Lord Scott of Foscote (paras 21–35), Lord Mance (paras 76–123), and Lord Neuberger of Abbotsbury (paras 124–171).

[191] *YL v Birmingham City Council* (n 186) para 26 *per* Scott LJ.

delegation from the State (or supervision by a State regulatory body), public funding and the public interest in the activity will not in themselves be sufficient to establish liability for the act in question.

(c) Human Rights Act-specific issues

5.72 Applications made in relation to Article 9 ECHR rights will need, as with all qualified rights, to show arguable interference and an arguable absence of justification for the interference at the permission stage.

5.73 Rules on disclosure in judicial review proceedings are traditionally more restrictive than in ordinary actions.[192] However, the House of Lords has made it clear that those principles need to be adjusted to take account of HRA-based applications.[193] Judges may now decide on the need for disclosure on the facts of the particular case.

5.74 Finally, the HRA 1998 has had an impact on the use of cross-examination in judicial review hearings. There is a power to order cross-examination under CPR 56.16(1), although it has been used sparingly as a result of the fact that judicial review applications are generally made to determine points of law. It has nonetheless been recognized in HRA applications that a full merits review of the facts may well be required,[194] resulting in the more frequent exercise of this order.[195] Indeed, it has been expressly recognized that those HRA-based claims which are commenced by way of judicial review could also be brought as an action in tort under section 7(1)(a) of HRA 1998 (see paragraph 5.75);[196] such a claim would proceed as a usual Part 7 claim and is likely to involve the calling of oral evidence.

(3) Free-standing claims

5.75 As an alternative to bringing judicial review proceedings under section 7(1)(a) of HRA 1998, individuals have the option of bringing an ordinary action against a public authority for breach of the statutory duty imposed by section 6. For discussion as to where this is the appropriate course of action, see paragraph 5.61.

(a) Public authority and victim requirement

5.76 Individuals who seek to bring ordinary actions under section 7(1)(a) of HRA 1998 are subject to the victim requirement as set out at paragraph 5.64, and rely on the same body of case law for the purposes of defining a public authority, set out at paragraph 5.69.

---

[192] *The White Book* (Sweet & Maxwell, 2013) Vol I, para 54.16.2.

[193] *Tweed v Parades Commission for Northern Ireland* [2007] 1 AC 650, paras 29–32, given in the context of a decision concerning Convention rights and HRA 1998.

[194] See eg *R (Wilkinson) v Broadmoor Hospital Authority* [2002] 1 WLR 419, para 16 *per* Brown LJ: 'As to why it is now [subsequent to the passage of HRA 1998] essential for the proper determination of the claimant's judicial review challenge that the three doctors be cross-examined, Mr Bowen [for the Claimants] submits that article 6 requires the court to reach its own conclusions on the disputed issues of fact...'. Para 17 *per* Brown LJ: 'The respondents seek to resist this appeal... [on the basis that] this is a judicial review challenge in which, as ever, the critical question is whether those whose decisions are impugned have acted fairly, reasonably and lawfully, and where no issue of precedent fact arises for the court's determination.' Para 36 *per* Brown LJ: 'I have concluded that what would be required on a substantive challenge here would be a full merits review of the propriety of the treatment proposed and, for that purpose, cross-examination of the specialists.'

[195] Note, however, the admonitory comment in *R(N) v Dr M* [2003] 1 WLR 562, para 39: '[*Wilkinson* was not] a charter for routine applications to the court for oral evidence in human rights cases generally.'

[196] *Wilkinson* (n 194) para 24.

(b) Appropriate court or tribunal

A free-standing claim for breach of statutory duty under HRA 1998 must be brought in the **5.77** 'appropriate court or tribunal'.[197] Section 7(2) of HRA 1998 provides that the ' "appropriate court or tribunal" means such court or tribunal as may be determined in accordance with the rules' as defined at section 7(9), which states that 'rules' means 'in relation to proceedings before a court or tribunal outside Scotland, rules made by the Lord Chancellor, or the Secretary of State for the purpose of this section or rules of court…'. These include both rules which apply for the purposes of commencing free-standing HRA claims, and those which apply whenever HRA arguments are raised in legal proceedings.[198]

The relevant rule for free-standing proceedings under section 7(1)(a) is CPR Rule 7.11.[199] **5.78** This rule provides that where the act complained of is a judicial act, the claim must be brought in the High Court; any other claim under section 7(1)(a) may be brought in any court.[200] The overarching principle is that claims go to the court or tribunal most accustomed to dealing with claims analogous to the subject matter in question.[201] Proceedings are issued in the usual manner by way of a Part 7 claim form, and further procedural rules specific to human rights claims will then apply according to the court in question. Aside from the requirement to bring proceedings complaining of a judicial act in the High Court, there are just two specific provisions concerning the appropriate forum: where the claim is brought by way of judicial review, proceedings must be commenced in the Administrative Court by filing a claim form in accordance with CPR rule 54.6, while proceedings against the intelligence services must be brought in the Investigatory Powers Tribunal.[202]

(c) Limitation period

Section 7(5)(a) and (b) of HRA 1998 state that proceedings under section 7(1)(a) must be **5.79** brought within one year of the act complained of, or such longer period as the court or tribunal considers equitable having regard to all the circumstances.

When considering the exercise of discretion under section 7(5)(b), the burden of establish- **5.80** ing that it is equitable to extend time is on the claimant. Thomas LJ accepted, in *Dunn v Parole Board*,[203] that the court may have regard to factors listed in section 33(3) of the Limitation Act 1980 when the case involves personal injury or death, although a claimant has yet to be successful in extending the limitation period on those grounds. Otherwise, he stated, 'Parliament gave the court a wide discretion; I do not think that it would be helpful to list the factors taken into account or to state what should be given greater or lesser weight'.[204] Factors which have been considered by the courts include the time taken to obtain legal aid, the proportionality of the claim, and the length of the delay and the reasons for it.[205]

---

[197] HRA 1998, s 7(1)(a).

[198] For more general procedural rules, including rules concerning statements of case, see para 5.82.

[199] Inserted by Civil Procedure (Amendment No 4) Rules 2000, SI 2000/2092.

[200] HRA 1998, s7(1)(a) refers to the 'appropriate court or tribunal'; the Regulation of Investigatory Powers Act 2000, s 65(2) and (3) state that the jurisdiction of the Investigatory Powers Tribunal (IPT) shall be 'the only appropriate tribunal' for the purposes of s 7 in relation to any proceedings under s 7(1)(a) if such proceedings are proceedings against any of the intelligence services.

[201] See 'The Appropriate Forum for an Argument under the Human Rights Act' in J Wadham, H Mountfield, E Prochaska, C Brown (eds), *The Human Rights Act 1998* (6th edn, OUP, 2011) 67–9.

[202] Regulation of Investigatory Powers Act 2000, s 65(2) and (3).

[203] *Dunn v Parole Board* [2008] EWCA Civ 374.

[204] *Dunn* (n 203) paras 30–31.

[205] See generally *A v Essex County Council* [2007] EWHC 1652 (QB), paras 122–124.

5.81 On-going acts cause particular difficulty with regard to limitation. Section 7(5)(a) of HRA 1998 states that the limitation period starts to run on 'the date on which the act complained of took place'. For continuing acts, such as unlawful segregation or detention, this could mean either the date the act ceased or the date on which it began. The very serious problem with the latter is that if an individual fails to bring proceedings within one year of the unlawful act commencing, he remains without any means of redress not only after the conclusion of the act, but all the while that act continues after the first year. This important issue has yet to be conclusively decided, but in *A v Essex County Council*[206] Baroness Hale expressed the view (obiter) that time begins to run from the date the breach ended.[207] Similarly in *Somerville v Scottish Ministers*,[208] Lord Hope made the obiter statement that he would hold 'the phrase "the date on which the act complained of took place" in sec 7(5)(a) [to mean], in the case of what may properly be regarded as a continuing act of alleged incompatibility, that time runs from the date when the continuing act ceased, not when it began.'[209]

(d) Statements of case

5.82 The main rules beyond identification of the appropriate court or tribunal concern procedural requirements for statements of case. These are provided for by paragraph 15.1 of Practice Direction 16, and apply whenever any right arising under HRA 1998 is made in argument, or whenever any remedy available under the Act is sought.[210] The party seeking to do either of these things must:

(a) state that fact in his statement of case;
(b) give precise details of the Convention right which it is alleged has been infringed and details of the alleged infringement;
(c) specify the relief sought;
(d) state whether the relief sought includes a declaration of incompatibility pursuant to section 4 and, if so, give details of the legislative provision which is alleged to be incompatible and details of the incompatibility;
(e) state whether the relief sought includes damages in respect of a judicial act to which section 9(3) applies and, if so, give details of the judicial act complained of and the court or tribunal alleged to have made it; and
(f) give details of any finding of unlawfulness upon which the claim is based.

(4) Other legal proceedings

5.83 Section 7(1)(b) of HRA 1998 provides for the ability of parties to rely on Convention rights in 'any legal proceedings' where they are victims of the act or proposed act of a public authority. An example might be a claim in negligence against a public authority, where the claimant argues that the common law duty of care should be formulated in a manner compatible with his Convention rights. Furthermore, as stated previously, the courts are at all times under a duty to act compatibly with Convention rights by virtue of section 6(1), meaning in principle that arguments under the Act may be relied upon in proceedings of any nature.

---

[206] *A v Essex County Council* [2010] UKSC 33.
[207] *A v Essex County Council* (n 206) para 113.
[208] *Somerville v Scottish Ministers (No 2)* [2007] UKHL 44.
[209] *Somerville* (n 208) para 51.
[210] *The White Book* (n 192) PD 16, para 15.1.

Section 7(6) of the Act states that legal proceedings for the purposes of section 7(1)(b) **5.84** include proceedings brought by or at the instigation of a public authority, as well as appeals against the decision of a court or tribunal. The first limb is to ensure that Convention rights can be relied on by way of defence to a criminal charge, while the second ensures that arguments under HRA 1998 can be raised for the first time on appeal against a decision of a court or tribunal.

(a) Standing and limitation periods

A person wishing to rely on Convention rights under section 7(1)(b) of HRA 1998 must be **5.85** a victim of the act complained of.[211] There are no further procedural requirements beyond those for the statement of case, as set out at paragraph 5.82.

There is no limitation period for an individual wishing to rely on a Convention right during **5.86** other legal proceedings. The one-year time limit in section 7(5)(a) applies only to claims that directly allege a breach of the ECHR by a public body.

(b) Procedural rules

The fact that a Convention right is raised in argument to bolster an ordinary cause of action **5.87** has no impact on the court in which the proceedings are brought. Procedural rules relevant to statements of case are nonetheless engaged, as explored at paragraph 5.82.

Where issues arise under HRA 1998 in criminal proceedings, no specific rules apply. Thus, **5.88** when a Convention right is relied upon in a defence to a criminal charge, the issue will be raised in the Magistrates' Court or Crown Court where the case is being prosecuted without the triggering of further procedural steps.

(c) Declarations of incompatibility and the Crown

Section 3 of HRA 1998 makes specific provisions for the court's obligation to interpret leg- **5.89** islation in a manner that is compatible with Convention rights. Where this exercise leads a court to consider making a declaration of incompatibility under section 4(2), the Crown is entitled to receive notice. Section 5 provides that a Minister of the Crown or person entitled to be joined as a party to proceedings, thereby has the right to appeal against any declaration of incompatibility made.

---

[211] See para 5.64.

6

THE EQUALITY ACT 2010

A. Introduction

6.01 'Religion or belief' is a protected characteristic in discrimination law. The Equality Act 2010 repealed previous discrimination legislation, including the Employment Equality (Religion or Belief) Regulations 2003 and Part 2 of the Equality Act 2006, and put in its place a new harmonized scheme. Under the Equality Act 2010, 'religion or belief' forms part of the general framework of equality rights and is protected alongside several other characteristics, including age, disability, gender reassignment, marriage and civil partnership, pregnancy and maternity, race, sex, and sexual orientation.[1]

6.02 The scheme of the Equality Act 2010 is as follows:

(1) Chapter 1 of Part 2 lists and defines the 'protected characteristics', including 'religion or belief'.

(2) Chapter 2 of Part 2 sets out 'prohibited conduct', which includes direct discrimination, indirect discrimination, harassment, and victimization. Ancillary provisions are set out in Part 8, including, for example, the liability of employers for unlawful acts by their employees in the course of employment[2] and provisions concerning secondary liability.

(3) Parts 3 to 7 deal with specific areas where such conduct is prohibited: services and public functions (Part 3); premises (Part 4); work (Part 5); education (Part 6); and associations (Part 7).

---

[1] Equality Act 2010, s 4.
[2] Equality Act 2010, s 109.

(4) Part 9 deals with enforcement, including relevant procedure and remedies.

(5) Part 10 contains provisions relating to contracts, etc, including the enforceability of terms which constitute, promote, or provide for treatment prohibited under the Equality Act 2010, and those which seek to contract out of protection afforded by the 2010 Act.

(6) Chapter 1 of Part 11 sets out the public sector equality duty which has been extended to 'religion or belief' by the 2010 Act. Chapter 2 of Part 11 defines the circumstances in which positive action is permissible.

(7) Exceptions to the discrimination provisions (including religious-based exceptions) are set out in the Schedules to the 2010 Act, principally Schedules 9 and 23.

This chapter considers relevant provisions of the Equality Act 2010 and some of its key concepts. A detailed consideration of the protection afforded to religious rights in specific areas covered by the Equality Act can be found in Chapters 7, 8, and 9. **6.03**

This chapter begins in part B by charting the legislative development of the law relating to religious or belief discrimination and, briefly, the background to the Equality Act 2010. **6.04**

B. Background

The prohibition of discrimination on grounds of 'religion or belief' is a relatively recent development in domestic law.[3] Whilst legislation prohibiting discrimination on the grounds of sex, race, and disability has existed for some time,[4] discrimination law has historically protected religious interests only indirectly. For example, certain religious groups—principally Jews and Sikhs—were afforded a degree of protection under the Race Relations Act 1976 on the basis that they were mono-ethnic and qualified as a racial group within the meaning of the Act.[5] Even so, members of these groups would fall outside the protection of the Act if it could be shown that the discrimination suffered in a particular case was on the grounds of their religious beliefs and not race. Conversely, adherents of other faiths qualified for protection under the Race Relations Act 1976 if it could be shown that the adverse treatment suffered in a particular case was on the grounds of their race rather than their religion or religious beliefs.[6] In this way, religious interests were protected only to the extent they fell within the scope of racial discrimination laws. Religion or belief was not a protected characteristic in its own right. **6.05**

The impetus to extend discrimination law to cover religion or belief came from the European Community, itself acting under newly acquired powers in this field. The Treaty of Amsterdam **6.06**

---

[3] At least in England and Wales. Legislation prohibiting discrimination on the grounds of religious belief has existed in Northern Ireland since 1976. See Ch 4, para 4.270.

[4] Sex Discrimination Act 1975, Race Relations Act 1976, and Disability Discrimination Act 1995.

[5] *Seide v Gillette Industries* [1980] IRLR 427 (EAT); *Mandla v Dowell Lee* [1983] 2 AC 548 (HL).

[6] A rare example was *JH Walker Ltd v Hussain and ors* [1996] ICR 291 (EAT). Muslim employees requested time off for Eid (a religious festival) after their employer issued a notice stating that no holidays could be taken over the summer peak period of June, July, and August. Their request was refused. The claim for direct race discrimination failed on the grounds that the discrimination alleged was not on the grounds of colour, race, nationality, or ethnic or national origins, as 'the true nature of Islam is not within the Race Relations Act 1976'. The Race Relations Act 1976 did not mention religion and it was not possible to treat Muslims both as a religious grouping and as an ethnic grouping. However, the tribunal accepted that there had been indirect race discrimination. The work force was divided into roughly two halves: those of European origin and those from the Indian sub-continent. Almost half of the workers for whom the holiday embargo was intended consisted of non-Europeans, of whom almost all were Muslim. The number of people from the Asian group who could comply with the direction to work on Eid was considerably smaller than the proportion of Europeans who could comply with the direction to work on Eid.

entered into force on 1 May 1999, giving the Council of Ministers new powers to combat discrimination, including a power to 'take appropriate action to combat discrimination based on sex, racial or ethnic origin, religion or belief, disability, age or sexual orientation'.[7]

6.07 Acting pursuant to this power, the Council adopted two directives in 2000. The first laid down a framework for combating discrimination on grounds of 'racial or ethnic origin' in a range of fields, including employment and occupation, education, and the provision of goods and services ('the Race Directive').[8] The second laid down a general framework for combating discrimination on other grounds, specifically, 'religion or belief, disability, age or sexual orientation', but was limited to the fields of employment and occupation ('the Employment Directive').[9] The directives laid down minimum requirements expressly giving Member States the option of introducing or maintaining more favourable provisions.[10]

6.08 The provisions of the Employment Directive relating to 'religion or belief' were implemented by the Employment Equality (Religion or Belief) Regulations 2003, which came into force on 2 December 2003. These regulations prohibited direct and indirect discrimination, harassment, and victimization on grounds of religion or belief. Like the Employment Directive the reach of the Regulations was limited to the employment field. At the same time the law was extended to cover discrimination on grounds of sexual orientation by the Employment Equality (Sexual Orientation) Regulations 2003 which also sought to implement the provisions of the Employment Directive. The regulations included a limited exception to the non-discrimination provisions where employment was 'for purposes of an organised religion' in order to accommodate religious beliefs concerning same-sex sexual activity.[11]

6.09 Protection of 'religion or belief' was extended beyond the employment field by Part 2 of the Equality Act 2006, which came into force on 30 April 2007. The Equality Act 2006 made it unlawful to discriminate on the grounds of 'religion or belief' in the provision of goods, facilities, services, the disposal and management of premises, and in the exercise of the functions of public authorities. The 2006 Act prohibited direct and indirect discrimination and victimization only. Harassment was not covered because of concerns that the provisions could be used by religious groups to stop other religions staging events that they considered unlawful. There were also amendments to the definitions of 'religion or belief' and direct discrimination, the significance of which are considered in parts C and D of this chapter.

6.10 At the same time, the Equality Act (Sexual Orientation) Regulations 2007, which also came into force on 30 April 2007, prohibited discrimination on grounds of sexual orientation

---

[7] Treaty of Amsterdam, Art 13, now TFEU, Art 19. The Treaty of Amsterdam also affirmed in unequivocal terms that 'the Union is founded on the principles of liberty, democracy, respect for human rights and fundamental freedoms, and the rule of law, principles which are common to the Member States' (TEU, Art 6).

[8] Council Directive (EC) 2000/43 of 29 June 2000.

[9] Council Directive (EC) 2000/78 of 27 November 2000. Recital 9 of the Employment Directive states: 'Employment and occupation are key elements in guaranteeing equal opportunities for all and contribute strongly to the full participation of citizens in economic, cultural and social life and to realising their potential.' Recital 11 of the Employment Directive provides that 'discrimination based on religion or belief, disability, age or sexual orientation may undermine the achievement of the objectives of the EC Treaty, in particular the attainment of a high level of employment and social protection, raising the standard of living and the quality of life, economic and social cohesion and solidarity and the free movement of persons'.

[10] Council Directive (EC) 2000/78 of 27 November 2000, Art 8.

[11] Employment Equality (Sexual Orientation) Regulations 2003, SI 2003/1661, reg 7(3). The validity of this exception was challenged unsuccessfully in *R (Amicus) v Secretary of State for Trade and Industry* [2007] ICR 1176 (QB).

in the provision of goods, facilities, services, education, the disposal and management of premises, and in the exercise of the functions of public authorities. Again the regulations prohibited discrimination and victimization only. The regulations included an exception for the benefit of religious organisations.[12]

In the meantime, the discrimination law framework as a whole was under review. **6.11** Anti-discrimination laws covering sex, race, disability, religion or belief, and sexual orientation had developed in a piecemeal fashion and spanned several pieces of legislation. The government set up the Discrimination Law Review in 2005 to consider the opportunities for creating a clearer and more streamlined legislative framework, and eventually mooted the idea of a single equality act.[13]

These efforts culminated in the Equality Act 2010, the majority of which came into force **6.12** on 1 October 2010. The Equality Act 2010 repealed previous discrimination legislation, including the Employment Equality (Religion or Belief) Regulations 2003[14] and Part 2 of the Equality Act 2006,[15] and put in its place a new, harmonized scheme under which 'religion or belief' is protected alongside other characteristics.[16]

The Equality Act 2010 does more than simply replicate the protection afforded to 'religion **6.13** or belief' under the previous legislation. It also enhances protection in a number of respects. For example:

(1) The 2010 Act extends the public sector equality duty to 'religion or belief' (Part 11, Chapter 1). Previously, the law only imposed such a duty in relation to race, disability, and gender.

(2) The 2010 Act extends what is permissible by way of positive action to address inequalities (Part 11, Chapter 2).

(3) The 2010 Act seeks to prohibit combined discrimination (section 14), which occurs when a person is directly discriminated against because of a combination of two relevant protected characteristics.[17] For example, if a man is refused a service on the grounds that he may be a 'terrorist' simply because he is Muslim and male, the new provisions would permit him to bring a combined discrimination claim if the reason for his treatment was a combination of 'sex' and 'religion or belief' which resulted in his being stereotyped as a terrorist; it would not be necessary for him to bring separate claims for religion or belief and sex discrimination.[18] However, section 14 is not yet in force.[19]

---

[12] Equality Act (Sexual Orientation) Regulations 2007, SI 2007/1263, reg 14.

[13] The government published a Green Paper in June 2007, a White Paper in June 2008, and a response to the Discrimination Law Review in July 2009. For a detailed account of the background to the Equality Act 2010, see B Doyle et al, *Equality and Discrimination: the New Law* (Jordans, 2010) ch 1.

[14] Employment Equality (Religion or Belief) Regulations 2003, SI 2003/1660, Sch 27, Pt 2.

[15] Equality Act 2006, Sch 27, Pt 1.

[16] Equality Act 2010, s 4.

[17] The relevant protected characteristics are age, disability, gender reassignment, race, religion or belief, sex, and sexual orientation: Equality Act 2010, s 14(2).

[18] Equality Act 2010, Explanatory Notes, para 68. The combined discrimination provisions sought to address concerns about the difficulties of separating out the grounds to prove discrimination. For an exploration of the difficulties, see Citizens Advice, 'Potential Intersectional Discrimination Cases: Citizens Advice research for the GEO' (May 2009). For example, one adviser observed that 'in trying to separate out the grounds to prove the treatment you tend to lose the emphasis and essence of the discrimination. You dilute both the issues and the treatment, with the consequence that you may end up presenting two weak cases and losing both'.

[19] In March 2012, the government announced that it would delay commencement of the combined discrimination provisions as part of its package to reduce regulatory burdens on business. A written ministerial

(4) The 2010 Act gives employment tribunals the power to make a recommendation to a respondent, found liable under the Act, to take certain steps to remedy matters, not just for the benefit of the individual complainant, but the wider workforce (section 124(3)).[20] Previously recommendations could only be made for the benefit of the individual complainant.

(5) Other changes which may potentially impinge on religious interests include an amendment to the Civil Partnership Act 2004 which removes the prohibition on civil partnerships being registered on religious premises (section 202). However, the provision makes clear that this does not place an obligation on religious organizations to host civil partnerships if they do not wish to do so.[21]

C. Protected Characteristics

6.14 The following characteristics are protected characteristics: age, disability, gender reassignment, marriage and civil partnership, pregnancy and maternity, race, religion or belief, sex and sexual orientation.[22] The majority of religion- and conscience-based claims are brought on the grounds of 'religion or belief'; however, religious groups that qualify as a racial group can, and do, continue to rely on 'race' as the basis of their claims.[23]

(1) Religion or belief

6.15 'Religion or belief' is listed as a protected characteristic in section 4 of the Equality Act 2010 and is defined by section 10 as follows:

> (1) Religion means any religion and a reference to religion includes a reference to a lack of religion.
>
> (2) Belief means any religious or philosophical belief and a reference to belief includes a reference to a lack of belief.

(a) Definition of 'religion or belief'—legislative development

6.16 The term 'religion or belief' was lifted by the Employment Equality (Religion or Belief) Regulations 2003 from the Employment Directive[24] and has been adopted in all subsequent legislation.[25] While the Employment Directive leaves the term completely undefined, domestic legislation has sought to lay down a broad definition delineating the parameters

---

statement was laid in the House of Commons on 15 May 2012 by Theresa May, and in the House of Lords by Baroness Verma. The measure forms part of the 'Red Tape Challenge' equalities package.

[20] Following a consultation in May 2012, the government announced its intention to abolish the power of employment tribunals to make wider recommendations: Government Equalities Office, 'Equality Act 2010: employment tribunals' power to make wider recommendations in discrimination cases and obtaining information procedure: Government response to the consultation' (October 2012). The relevant amendment to the Equality Act 2010 has been included in the Draft Deregulation Bill published on 1 July 2013.

[21] Civil Partnership Act 2004, s 6A(3A). See also Marriages and Civil Partnerships (Approved Premises) Regulations 2005, SI 2005/3168, as amended, s 2B.

[22] Equality Act 2010, s 4.

[23] eg, *R (Watkins-Singh) v Governing Body of Aberdare Girls' High School* [2008] EWHC 1865 (Admin).

[24] The term 'religion or belief' also appears in the Universal Declaration of Human Rights, Art 18; the International Covenant on Civil and Political Rights, Art 18; the European Convention on Human Rights, Art 9; and the Treaty of Amsterdam.

[25] 'Religion or belief' is listed as a protected characteristic in the Equality Act 2010, s 4.

of the term while leaving the precise scope to be defined by the courts.[26] The Employment Directive does not, for example, limit the term 'belief' to 'religious or philosophical' beliefs. This is a domestic qualification.

The Equality Act 2010 adopts the same definition of 'religion or belief' as the Equality Act **6.17** 2006.[27] The original definition in the Employment Equality (Religion or Belief) Regulations 2003 was, however, different. Regulation 2(1) of the 2003 Regulations provided that 'religion or belief' meant 'any religion, religious belief, or similar philosophical belief'.[28] This made it plain that in order to qualify for protection under the 2003 Regulations, a philosophical belief had to be 'similar' to a religious belief.[29] The Explanatory Notes to the 2003 Regulations stated:

> That does not mean that a belief must include faith in a God/Gods or worship of a God/Gods to be 'similar' to a religious belief. It means that the belief in question should be a profound belief affecting a person's way of life, or perception of the world. Effectively, a belief should occupy a place in the person's life parallel to that filled by the God/Gods of those holding a particular religious belief. As with a religious belief, a similar philosophical belief must attain a certain level of cogency, seriousness, cohesion and importance, be worthy of respect in a democratic society, and not incompatible with human dignity (see judgment of the European Court of Human Rights in *Campbell and Cosans v UK* (1982) 4 EHRR 293 at 304). Examples of beliefs which generally meet this description are atheism and humanism; examples of beliefs which generally do not are support for a political party, support for a football team.[30]

Part 2 of the Equality Act 2006 amended the definition by removing the word 'similar' and by **6.18** providing expressly that a reference to 'religion' or 'belief' included a lack of religion or belief. This amended definition was substituted for the definition in the 2003 Regulations.[31] During the passage of the Equality Bill, the Government explained that the removal of the word 'similar' was of cosmetic significance only: it did not mean that a 'philosophical belief' no longer had to be of a similar nature to a religious belief; rather, this was clear from the context in which the term 'philosophical belief' appeared, ie as part of the legislation relating to discrimination on the grounds of religion or belief.[32] The need for a philosophical belief to have 'similar status or

---

[26] Originally, the purpose of setting down a definition in the legislation was to make clear that the term 'belief' did not extend to political belief which, in the government's view, was not covered by the Employment Directive: see Department for Trade and Industry, 'Towards Equality and Diversity: Implementing the Employment and Race Directives' (December 2003) paras 13.4–13.6. Generally, see also the comments of Lord Sainsbury during the passage of the Employment Equality (Religion or Belief) Regulations 2003: *Hansard* HL, vol 649, col 786 (17 June 2003).

[27] Equality Act 2006, s 44.

[28] Employment Equality (Religion or Belief) Regulations 2003, SI 2003/1660, reg 2(1).

[29] This caused unease among some atheists, agnostics, and humanists who were not happy with their beliefs being classified as 'similar' to religious beliefs. See eg the comments of Lord Wedderburn in the debate on the 2003 Regulations: *Hansard* HL, vol 649, col 788 (17 June 2003) and the comments of Lord Lester in the debate on the Equality Bill 2006: *Hansard* HL, vol 673, col 1109 (13 July 2005).

[30] See also the comments of Lord Brennan during the passage of the 2003 Regulations: *Hansard* HL, vol 649, col 788 (17 June 2003): 'the word "similar" in these regulations is used in relation to the quality of the belief, not its nature. The phrase "similar philosophical belief" addresses the state of mind in which someone holds that belief to the same thinking quality as a religious belief.'

[31] Equality Act 2006, s 77.

[32] See the comments of Baroness Scotland during the passage of the Equality Bill: *Hansard* HL, vol 649, cols 1109–1110 (12 July 2005):

> The intention behind the wording in Part 2 is identical to that in the employment regulations. However, in drafting Part 2, it was felt that the word 'similar' added nothing and was, therefore, redundant. This is because the term 'philosophical belief' will take its meaning from the context in

cogency' to a religious belief was confirmed by the EAT in *Grainger v Nicholson*.[33] However, as discussed later, the requirement has become somewhat diluted in practice.

6.19 The definition of 'religion or belief' has generated a number of decisions. While the terms 'religion' and 'religious belief' have attracted relatively little attention, the scope of the term 'philosophical belief' has been considered in a number of cases. Most of these cases were decided under the discrimination provisions in the Employment Equality (Religion or Belief) Regulations 2003 (as amended) and are first instance decisions of the employment tribunal. The issue has not yet been considered by the higher courts.

(b) Religion and religious belief

6.20 Section 10(1) of the Equality Act 2010 simply states that 'religion means any religion and a reference to religion includes a lack of religion', leaving the precise scope of the term to be determined by the courts.

6.21 The courts and tribunals have so far avoided the need to grapple with the question of what qualifies as a 'religion' for the purposes of the legislation, since any borderline cases are likely to be classified as a 'philosophical belief'.[34] The Explanatory Notes to the Equality Act 2010, however, offer examples of religions which qualify for the purposes of the Act: the Baha'i faith, Buddhism, Christianity, Hinduism, Islam, Jainism, Judaism, Rastafarianism,[35] Sikhism, and Zoroastrianism. Atheists, humanists, and secularists will fall within the statutory definition because of their lack of religion.[36]

6.22 As to whether or not a particular belief or a practice manifesting a particular belief forms part of a person's religion, in *Hussain v Bhuller* it was held that 'if a person genuinely believes that his faith requires a certain course of action then that is sufficient to make it part of his religion'.[37] It is not necessary for a belief to be shared by others for it to be a religious belief,

---

which it appears; that is, as part of the legislation relating to discrimination on the grounds of religion or belief. Given that context, philosophical belief must therefore always be of a similar nature to religious beliefs. It will be for the courts to decide what constitutes a belief for the purposes of Part 2 of the Bill, but case law suggests that any philosophical belief must attain a certain level of cogency, seriousness, cohesion and importance, must be worthy of respect in a democratic society and must not be incompatible with human dignity.

[33] *Grainger v Nicholson* [2010] IRLR 4 (EAT), para 26.

[34] See eg *Greater Manchester Police Authority v Power* [2009] UKEAT/0434/09 in which the claimant was an adherent of the Spiritualist Church which, according to census data from 2001, was the eighth largest faith group in Great Britain. The EAT upheld the employment tribunal's findings that the claimant's beliefs, which included a belief that the dead could be contacted through mediums or psychics, were capable of being religious beliefs, or alternatively they fell into the category of a philosophical belief for the purposes of the 2003 Regulations. It should be noted that whilst on one view the claimant's beliefs were unconventional, he did, in common with other spiritualists, believe in the existence of a God. For the definition of 'religion' in Art 9 ECHR see Ch 3 paras 3.12-3.17, and in international instruments see Ch 2 paras 2.33-2.37 and 2.117.

[35] In *Harris v NKL Automotive Ltd* [2007] UKEAT/0134/07/DM, the parties accepted that Rastafarianism was a 'philosophical belief' within the meaning of the 2003 Regulations.

[36] See eg *R (National Secular Society) v Bideford Town Council* [2012] 2 All ER 1175 (QB) in which the claimants argued that the holding of public prayers at full meetings of the Council placed a town councillor, and others who shared his lack of religious belief, at a particular disadvantage. Atheists, humanists, and secularists may also argue that their beliefs fall into the category of a 'philosophical belief'.

[37] *Hussain v Bhuller* ET 1806638/2004 (5 July 2005). The question in that case was whether attendance at home for bereavement purposes was part of the Muslim faith. The claimant had not been permitted to take time off work to take part in the mourning period following the death of his grandmother. He argued before the tribunal that the observance was part of Muslim culture and integral to the bereavement process. The tribunal stated:

It would be wrong to suggest that religion consists only of attending the mosque or other place of worship. In our view religion must extend outwards to its interaction with the everyday life of the

nor does it need to be a mandatory requirement of an established religion for it to qualify as a religious belief.[38]

The decision in *Devine v Home Office* suggests there are limits to the approach in *Hussain* **6.23**
v Bhuller. Mr Devine was rejected for a job at the Home Office on the basis that there was a potential conflict of interest arising as a result of his previous work advising asylum seekers in a Citizens' Advice Bureau. He brought a claim under the Employment Equality (Religion or Belief) Regulations 2003 on the grounds that his sympathy for underprivileged asylum seekers was a demonstration of the Christian virtue of charity and he had therefore been discriminated against on the grounds of his religion. The tribunal found that this was too vague or ill-defined to give rise to a claim for religious or belief discrimination.[39]

In *R (Williamson) v Secretary of State for Education and Employment*, Lord Nicholls empha- **6.24**
sized (in the context of Article 9 ECHR) that a belief must be coherent in the sense of being intelligible and capable of being understood, but that too much should not be demanded in this regard:

> Typically, religion involves belief in the supernatural. It is not always susceptible to lucid exposition or, still less, rational justification. The language used is often the language of allegory, symbol and metaphor. Depending on the subject matter, individuals cannot always be expected to express themselves with cogency or precision. Nor are an individual's beliefs fixed and static. The beliefs of every individual are prone to change over his lifetime.[40]

Courts will want to ensure that any assertion of religious belief is made in good faith and that **6.25**
the asserted belief is genuinely held. Where the genuineness of an asserted belief is in issue, a court or tribunal will inquire into and decide this as an issue of fact. In *Williamson* it was emphasized that this was properly a 'limited inquiry':

> The court is concerned to ensure an assertion of religious belief is made in good faith ... But, emphatically, it is not for the court to embark on an inquiry into the asserted belief and judge its 'validity' by some objective standard such as the source material upon which the claimant founds his belief or the orthodox teaching of the religion in question or the extent to which the claimant's belief conforms to or differs from the views of others professing the same religion. Freedom of religion protects the subjective belief of an individual ... religious belief is intensely personal and can easily vary from one individual to another ... The relevance of objective factors such as source material is, at most, that they may throw light on whether the professed belief is genuinely held.[41]

---

individual. We would conclude that attendance at home for bereavement purposes formed part of the Claimant's religion or religious belief.

[38] *Eweida v British Airways* [2009] ICR 303 (EAT), para 29. Where, however, a particular belief or practice is not recognized by the majority of adherents of a particular faith as a requirement of that faith, a claimant may struggle to demonstrate group disadvantage for the purposes of an indirect discrimination claim: *Eweida v British Airways* [2010] ICR 890 (CA).

[39] *Devine v Home Office* ET 2302061/2004 (9 August 2004).

[40] *R (Williamson) v Secretary of State for Education and Employment* [2005] 2 AC 246 (HL), para 23.

[41] *Williamson* (n 40) para 22 *per* Lord Nicholls. See also the comments of Baroness Hale at para 75. The courts have been mindful of the need to avoid getting embroiled in determining matters of religious doctrine and practice: see eg the recent decision in *Khaira v Shergill* [2012] PTSR 1697 (CA). A case which came close to treading this ground is *Watkins-Singh* (n 23), where the Court considered expert evidence relating to the significance of the Kara to Sikhs and found that, although the claimant was not obliged by her religion to wear the Kara, it was clearly an extremely important indication of her faith and this was a view shared for good reason by very many other Sikhs.

6.26   Finally, in *McClintock v Department of Constitutional Affairs* it was held that to constitute a belief there must be a viewpoint in which one actually believes; it is not enough to have an opinion based on some real or perceived logic or based on information or lack of information available.[42] The claimant was a Justice of the Peace who resigned from membership of the Family Panel because he could not in conscience agree to place children with same sex couples. He was a practising Christian, but the evidence he adduced made no suggestion that his views were based on religious grounds or a philosophical viewpoint. Rather, his asserted view was that the question of allowing same sex couples to adopt children had not been sufficiently researched and tested. The EAT affirmed that such views did not fall within the scope of the 2003 Regulations.

6.27   It should be noted that that the criteria for determining whether a belief amounts to a 'philosophical belief' include the following:[43]

(1) The belief must attain a certain level of cogency, seriousness, cohesion and importance; and
(2) It must be worthy of respect in a democratic society, not be incompatible with human dignity and not conflict with the fundamental rights of others.

6.28   Whether religious beliefs must also satisfy these requirements in order to qualify as beliefs for the purposes of the discrimination legislation has not yet been considered or authoritatively determined. The EAT in *Grainger* distilled these criteria from the decisions in *Campbell & Cosans v United Kingdom*[44] and *Williamson*,[45] which concerned Article 2 of the First Protocol, and in the latter case, also Article 9 ECHR. Whilst the majority in *Williamson* made no distinction between religious and other beliefs, Lord Walker questioned whether the requirements should apply to religious beliefs. The court was not, in his view, well equipped to weigh the cogency, seriousness, and coherence of theological doctrines. As for the requirement that the belief be worthy of respect in a democratic society, this begged too many questions, with Lord Walker expressing agreement with the proposition that, in matters of human rights, 'the court should not show liberal tolerance only to tolerant liberals'.[46]

6.29   The decision of the High Court of Northern Ireland in the *Application for Judicial Review by the Christian Institute* should be noted.[47] In this case, there was no dispute that the requirements applied in determining whether the applicant's religious beliefs qualified for protection under Article 9 ECHR. The religious belief in question was the orthodox Christian belief that the practice of homosexuality is sinful. The High Court rejected an argument that the belief was inconsistent with the basic standards of human dignity and integrity, stating that it was a long established part of the belief system of the world's major religions and was not unworthy of recognition. Article 9 was therefore engaged.[48]

(c) Philosophical belief

6.30   The scope of the term 'philosophical belief' was considered by the EAT in *Grainger v Nicholson*, in which an employee alleged that he had been discriminated against contrary to the Employment Equality (Religion or Belief) Regulations 2003 (as amended) because of

---

[42] *McClintock v Department of Constitutional Affairs* [2008] IRLR 29 (EAT).
[43] *Grainger v Nicholson* [2010] ICR 360 (EAT).
[44] *Campbell and Cosans v UK* (1982) 4 EHRR 293.
[45] *R Williamson* (n 40).
[46] *Williamson* (n 40), in particular paras 57–60.
[47] *An Application for Judicial Review by the Christian Institute* [2008] NI 86 (QB).
[48] *Christian Institute* (n 47) para 50.

his philosophical belief about climate change and the environment, namely, that 'we must urgently cut carbon emissions to avoid catastrophic climate change'.[49] He claimed this was not merely an opinion but a philosophical belief which affected how he lived his life, including his choice of home, the way he travelled, and what he consumed. The EAT accepted that the employee's asserted belief was capable of being a 'philosophical belief' within the meaning of regulation 2(1)(b).

In determining the proper scope of the term, the EAT found helpful and relied on the **6.31** authorities relating to Article 2 of the First Protocol and Article 9 ECHR.[50] Drawing on these and other authorities, the EAT distilled the following criteria for determining whether a belief amounts to a 'philosophical belief':

(1) The belief must be genuinely held;[51]
(2) It must be a belief and not an opinion or viewpoint based on the present state of information available;[52]
(3) It must be a belief as to a weighty and substantial aspect of human life and behaviour;[53]
(4) It must attain a certain level of cogency, seriousness, cohesion and importance;[54]
(5) It must be worthy of respect in a democratic society, not be incompatible with human dignity, and not conflict with the fundamental rights of others.[55]

The EAT went on to clarify that: **6.32**

(1) The belief must have a similar status or cogency to a religious belief. This is notwithstanding the amendment to the 2003 Regulations removing the word 'similar';[56]
(2) The belief does not need to be one which is shared by others;
(3) Moreover, the philosophical belief does not need to constitute or allude to a fully fledged system of thought provided that the five criteria set out above are satisfied;[57]
(4) The existence of a positive philosophical belief does not depend upon the existence of a negative philosophical belief to the contrary.

Although *Grainger v Nicholson* was decided under the 2003 Regulations (as amended), the **6.33** test set out in *Grainger* is likely to be applied beyond the employment context.[58]

---

[49] *Grainger* (n 43) para 3.

[50] Art 2 of the First Protocol protects the right to education and provides as follows: 'In the exercise of any functions which it assumes in relation to education and to teaching, the State shall respect the right of parents to ensure such education and teaching in conformity with their own religious and philosophical convictions.' The EAT relied in particular on *Campbell and Cosans* (n 44) and *Williamson* (n 40). Both cases concerned beliefs relating to the use of corporal punishment. It should be noted that breach of Art 9 was not alleged in *Campbell and Cosans*.

[51] In *Williamson* (n 40) para 22 Nicholls LJ emphasized that any inquiry into the genuineness of a professed religious belief should be a limited one. In *Grainger* (n 43) para 6, the EAT took the view that where the assertion is of a philosophical belief, 'it is plain that the limiting words of Lord Nicholls do not, or at any rate, may not, apply'.

[52] See *McClintock* (n 42).

[53] See *Campbell and Cosans* (n 44) para 36.

[54] *Campbell and Cosans* (n 44) para 36.

[55] *Campbell and Cosans* (n 44) para 36. See also *Williamson* (n 40) para 23.

[56] See para 6.18.

[57] The EAT was here seemingly responding to an argument raised on behalf of the employer that a philosophical belief must form part of a system of beliefs—that it must be based on a 'philosophy of life'. See *Grainger* (n 43) paras 25–27.

[58] The Explanatory Notes to the Equality Act 2010 state that the criteria for determining what is a 'philosophical belief' for the purposes of the Act are those set out in *Grainger*; See the Explanatory Notes, para 52.

6.34 Although in *Grainger*, the EAT made a point of emphasizing the need for a philosophical belief to have similar status or cogency to a religious belief, this requirement has been somewhat diluted in practice.[59] Protection has since been held to extend to beliefs which some may be surprised to find qualify as beliefs similar to religious beliefs. In *Hashman v Milton Park* the employment tribunal, having considered the criteria set out in *Grainger*, held that a belief in the sanctity of life which comprised beliefs in veganism, environmentalism, and animal rights activism, including anti-hunt activism, was capable of amounting to a 'philosophical belief'. The tribunal emphasized that the judgment was based on the particular facts of the case and should not be taken to mean that everyone opposed to fox hunting necessarily held a philosophical belief within the meaning of the 2003 Regulations.[60] In *Maistry v The BBC*, a former employee of the BBC claimed that his dismissal amounted to discrimination on the grounds of his philosophical belief in what was described, in short, as 'the higher purpose of public service broadcasting'. The tribunal held that the asserted belief satisfied all five criteria set out in *Grainger* and was therefore capable of amounting to a 'philosophical belief'.[61]

6.35 Beliefs that have been held not to qualify as a 'philosophical belief' include a belief underpinning the choice to wear a poppy,[62] beliefs in conspiracy theories concerning the attack on the World Trade Center on 9/11,[63] and Marxist/Trotskyite beliefs and membership of the Socialist Party.[64] In *Kelly v Unison*, the tribunal took the view that political beliefs were not protected by the Regulations, or alternatively, applying the *Grainger* criteria, the claimants' beliefs in a Marxist/Trotskyite system conflicted with the fundamental rights of others and were not worthy of respect in a democratic society. The tribunal referred in particular to the claimants' views concerning revolution the fundamental essence of which, in the tribunal's view, was undemocratic, and matters such as the deprivation of home and property from the individual which were not compatible with human dignity.

6.36 Whether a political opinion or belief in a political philosophy qualifies for protection remains unclear.[65] In *Grainger v Nicholson* it was held that the claimant's asserted belief in anthropogenic climate change was likely to be characterized as a political belief, but this was not a ground for excluding it if it otherwise qualified as a genuinely held philosophical belief. The EAT considered *Hansard* relating to the then Equality Bill and held as follows:

> As appears from the passage in Hansard, the Attorney General suggested that 'support of a political party' might not meet the description of a philosophical belief. That must surely be so, but that does not mean that a belief in a political philosophy or doctrine would not qualify...belief in the political philosophies of Socialism, Marxism, Communism or free market Capitalism might qualify. There is nothing in my mind in the make up of a philosophical belief—particularly against the background of Article 14 of the Convention... —which would disqualify a belief based on a political philosophy.

---

[59] The Explanatory Notes to the 2003 Regulations provided that, in order to qualify, 'a belief in question should be a profound belief affecting a person's way of life, or perception of the world. Effectively, a belief should occupy a place in the person's life parallel to that filled by the God/Gods of those holding a particular religious belief'. Earlier cases certainly appear to have required more by way of similarity: eg *Finnon v Asda Stores* ET 2402142/05 (4 January 2006).

[60] *Hashman v Milton Park* ET 3105555/2009 (31 January 2011).

[61] *Maistry v The BBC* ET 1313142/2010 (29 March 2011).

[62] *Lisk v Shield Guardian Co Ltd* [2011] ET 3300873/2011 (14 September 2011).

[63] *Farrell v South Yorkshire Police Authority* [2011] ET 2803805/2010 (24 May 2011).

[64] *Kelly v Unison* ET 2203854/08 (22 December 2009).

[65] Political opinion is protected in Northern Ireland.

In *Kelly v Unison*, the tribunal distinguished between political beliefs 'which involve the **6.37** objective of the creation of a legally binding structure by power of government regulating others' and beliefs 'such as those of Mr Nicholson where his beliefs are expressed by his own practices but where he has no ambition to impose his scheme on others'.[66] The tribunal held that the latter qualified for protection under the Regulations but the former did not.

The tribunal in *Kelly v Unison* was clearly concerned to ensure that protection was not **6.38** extended to those with extreme political views, for example those denying to a group of people the right to exist.[67] However, the distinction drawn between beliefs concerning the imposition of a system of government and those that do not have these aspirations, is a tenuous one and would not necessarily exclude those with extreme views.[68]

It is suggested that the approach in *Grainger v Nicholson*—that a belief should not be excluded **6.39** simply on the grounds that it can be characterized as 'political' or is rooted in political philosophy—is to be preferred. While the legislative intention may originally have been to exclude political beliefs,[69] this became less clear later.[70] Indeed the Explanatory Notes to the Employment Equality (Religion or Belief) Regulations 2003 suggested that the term 'similar philosophical belief' included a political belief, provided the belief was similar to a religious belief.[71] Early cases involving claims by members of the British National Party (BNP) were rejected on the basis that the asserted belief, whether in the BNP or British Nationalism, was not similar to a religious belief.[72] In *Grainger v Nicholson* it was suggested that the way to deal with an objectionable political belief would be to conclude that it offended the requirement that the belief must be worthy of respect in a democratic society and not be incompatible with human dignity.[73]

---

[66] *Kelly v Unison* (n 64).

[67] *Kelly v Unison* (n 64) see paras 106 and 133 in particular.

[68] In *Maistry v The BBC*, the tribunal held that the decision in *Kelly v Unison* could not be safely relied on. The tribunal observed that it was a first instance decision only and the question had not yet been definitively determined by appellate courts.

[69] Department for Trade and Industry, 'Towards Equality and Diversity: Implementing the Employment and Race Directives' (December 2003) paras 13.4–13.6.

[70] It is not possible to discern any clear legislative intention from *Hansard* that political beliefs were intended to be excluded altogether.

[71] The Explanatory Notes, which were published by the DTI, stated:

The reference to 'similar philosophical belief' does not include any philosophical or political belief unless it is similar to a religious belief . . . it means that the belief should be a profound belief affecting a person's way of life, or perception of the world. Effectively, a belief should occupy a place in the person's life parallel to that filled by the God/Gods of those holding a particular religious belief.

[72] See eg *Baggs v Fudge* ET 1400114/05 (24 March 2005) and *Finnon v Asda Stores* ET 2402142/05 (4 January 2006). It should be borne in mind, however, that early cases appeared to require a lot more by way of similarity with religious beliefs.

[73] It has been said that whilst this is an understandable way to avoid protecting 'unacceptable' political beliefs, it may limit the protection inappropriately: 'after all, the protection for freedom of speech under Article 10 ECHR is very clear that the protection of the Convention applies to speech that offends, shocks or disturbs, and not just to inoffensive matters . . . ': L Vickers, 'Religious discrimination in the workplace: an emerging hierarchy?' (2010) Ecc LJ 280. See also *Williamson* (n 40), in which Lord Nicholls emphasized that, pursuant to Art 9 ECHR, everyone is entitled to hold whatever beliefs they wish, and it is only when questions of manifestation arise that a belief must satisfy some modest objective minimum requirements.

6.40 Following the decision of the ECtHR in *Redfearn v United Kingdom*,[74] there is now the possibility that in appropriate cases the term 'belief' will have to be interpreted broadly to cover political beliefs and, more particularly, support of or affiliation to a political party, including those with policies and aims similar to those of the BNP.

6.41 Mr Redfearn was employed by a private company as a driver responsible for transporting children and adults with physical and mental disabilities. He was summarily dismissed after being elected as a local councillor for the BNP. Although there were no complaints about his work or his conduct at work, the majority of his passengers were of Asian origin and there was a concern that his continued employment would give rise to anxiety among service users, and would jeopardize the reputation of his employer. Mr Redfearn did not have the requisite one year's continuous service to bring a claim for unfair dismissal, and his claim of race discrimination failed, it being found that he had not suffered discrimination 'on racial grounds'.[75]

6.42 The ECtHR held there had been a violation of Mr Redfearn's rights under Article 11 ECHR. The Court stated that there was a positive obligation on authorities to provide protection against dismissal by private employers where dismissal was motivated solely by the fact that an employee belonged to a particular political party—or, at least to provide means by which the proportionality of such a dismissal could be evaluated.

6.43 The ECtHR considered that a claim for unfair dismissal would have been an appropriate domestic remedy. However, Mr Redfearn was unable to benefit as a result of the one-year qualifying period. The Court observed that the one-year qualifying period did not apply to all dismissed employees; a number of exceptions were created to offer additional protection to employees dismissed on certain prohibited grounds such as race, sex, and religion.[76] However, no additional protection was afforded to those dismissed because of their political opinion or affiliation. The Court emphasized that political parties were a form of association essential to the proper functioning of a democracy and that Article 11 was applicable not only to persons and associations whose views were favourably received or regarded as inoffensive, but also to those whose views offend, shock, or disturb.

6.44 The Court considered that it was incumbent upon the state to take reasonable and appropriate measures to protect employees, including those with less than one year of service, from dismissal on grounds of political opinion or affiliation, either through the creation of an exception to the one-year qualifying period or through a free-standing claim for unlawful discrimination on grounds of political opinion or affiliation.

6.45 The government has implemented the decision in *Redfearn v United Kingdom* by creating an exception to the need for a qualifying period of employment in claims of unfair dismissal (now two years[77]) where 'the reason (or, if more than one, the principal reason) for the dismissal is, or relates to, the employee's political opinions or affiliation'.[78] A claim

---

[74] *Readfearn v UK* (2013) 57 EHRR 2.

[75] *Redfearn v Serco* [2006] ICR 1367 (CA). The racial grounds relied on were those of the passengers and colleagues who were of Asian origin, and the fact that the BNP limited its membership to white people.

[76] This was a reference to the fact that there is no qualifying period for bringing a discrimination claim.

[77] Unfair Dismissal and Statement of Reasons for Dismissal (Variation of Qualifying Period) Order 2012, SI 2012/989, art 4; Employment Rights Act 1996, s 108(1).

[78] Enterprise and Regulatory Reform Act 2013, s 13; Employment Rights Act 1996, s 108(4). This provision came into force on 25 June 2013. The transitional provisions provide that the provision 'does not apply

of discrimination on grounds of 'religion or belief' is another option for those dismissed as a result of their affiliation to a political party. Where, as in *Redfearn*, Article 11 rights are engaged, a tribunal may be under an interpretative obligation pursuant to section 3 of the Human Rights Act 1998, to interpret the term 'belief' as covering support of or affiliation to a political party. Article 10 issues may also be engaged.[79]

(2) Race

The race discrimination provisions also afford a degree of protection to religious rights.

6.46

'Race' is defined by section 9(1) of the Equality Act 2010 as including 'colour', 'nationality', and 'ethnic or national origins'. Section 9(3) provides that a 'racial group' is 'a group of persons defined by reference to race; and a reference to a person's racial group is a reference to a racial group into which the person falls'.

6.47

For religious rights, there are two points of significance. First, religious groups that qualify as a 'racial group' can and continue to rely on 'race' as the basis of their claims even where religious rights are in issue. It has been held that Sikhs and Jews are a 'racial group' defined by reference to ethnic origins.[80]

6.48

In *Mandla v Dowell Lee*, a Sikh pupil who wore a turban in accordance with the tenets of his faith, was refused admission to a private school unless he removed the turban and cut his hair. It was found that there had been unlawful race discrimination contrary to the Race Relations Act 1976. Lord Fraser stated:

6.49

> For a group to constitute an ethnic group in the sense of the Act of 1976, it must, in my opinion, regard itself, and be regarded by others, as a distinct community by virtue of certain characteristics. Some of these characteristics are essential; others are not essential but one or more of them will commonly be found and will help to distinguish the group from the surrounding community. The conditions which appear to me to be essential are these: (1) a long shared history, of which the group is conscious as distinguishing it from other groups, and the memory of which it keeps alive; (2) a cultural tradition of its own, including family and social customs and manners, often but not necessarily associated with religious observance. In addition to those two essential characteristics the following characteristics are, in my opinion, relevant; (3) either a common geographical origin, or descent from a small number of common ancestors; (4) a common language, not necessarily peculiar to the group; (5) a common literature peculiar to the group; (6) a common religion different from that of neighbouring groups or from the general community surrounding it; (7) being a minority or being an oppressed or a dominant group within a larger community, for example a conquered people

---

where the effective date of termination of the contract of employment in question is earlier than the date on which that section comes into force': Enterprise and Regulatory Reform Act 2013, s 24(3). 'Effective date of termination' here has the meaning given by the Employment Rights Act 1996, s 97(1).

[79] While Mr Redfearn complained of a violation of rights under both Arts 10 and 11 ECHR, the Court considered it appropriate to examine his complaints under Art 11 and stated that it would do so in the light of Art 10. Mr Redfearn's complaint that his dismissal gave rise to a breach of Art 9 was dismissed as manifestly unfounded.

[80] In respect of Sikhs, see *Mandla* (n 5). In *Dhinsa v Serco* ET 1315002/2009 (18 May 2011) the tribunal considered whether Amritdhari Sikhs comprised a distinct ethnic group which was separate from Sikhs generally. In respect of Jews, see *Seide v Gillette Industries* [1980] IRLR 427 (EAT); *R (on the application of E) v Governing Body of JFS* [2010] 2 AC 728 (SC). Adherents of other faiths qualify for protection if it can be shown that the adverse treatment suffered was on grounds of their race, rather than their religion: eg *JH Walker Ltd v Hussain and ors* [1996] ICR 291 (EAT).

(say, the inhabitants of England shortly after the Norman conquest) and their conquerors might both be ethnic groups.[81]

6.50 In *R (Watkins-Singh) v Governing Body of Aberdare Girls' High School* the court found that the refusal to grant a Sikh pupil a waiver to permit her to wear the *Kara* (found to be an important indication of her faith) constituted indirect discrimination on grounds of race under the Race Relations Act 1976 and on grounds of religion under the Equality Act 1996. [82]

6.51 Claims of race and religious discrimination will not necessarily be coextensive, as the decision in *Dhinsa v Serco* demonstrates.[83] A trainee custody officer and a devout Amritdhari Sikh brought a claim for indirect discrimination on the grounds of race and religion or belief after he was dismissed for wearing a *kirpan* whilst on duty. In respect of the race discrimination claim the tribunal found that Amritdhari Sikhs were not a distinct and different racial group separate from Sikhs generally. The claimant did not therefore have the protection of the Race Relations Act 1976 in his capacity as an Amritdhari Sikh, only as a Sikh. This had implications for his claim, as the tribunal went on to find that there was no evidence that Sikhs generally were subjected to particular disadvantage in the application of the relevant provision, criterion, or practice (PCP). There was expert evidence that Amritdhari Sikhs only formed 10 per cent of the Sikh population and that non-Amritdhari Sikhs were not prevented from being employed as custody officers by the PCP. The claim for religious discrimination was rejected on different grounds. The tribunal accepted that Amritdhari Sikhs were placed at a particular disadvantage as a result of the application of the PCP, but went on to find that the indirect discrimination was justified.

6.52 Secondly, following the enactment of the Enterprise and Regulatory Reform Act 2013, 'caste' is to be added to the definition of 'race' in section 9(1) of the Equality Act 2010.[84] 'Caste' is in some cases (but not all) either rooted in religion or a religious concept.[85] Moreover there are some religions which are said to comprise solely members of low castes, and so discrimination against adherents may constitute both caste and religious discrimination.[86] The government has indicated that legislation will be implemented in one to two years,[87] during which time further consideration will be given to the definition of 'caste.'

---

[81] *Mandla* (n 5) 562. As to the position of Sikhs, Lord Fraser observed that:

> . . . they were originally a religious community founded about the end of the 15th century in the Punjab by Guru Nanak, who was born in 1469. But the community is no longer purely religious in character. Their present position is summarised sufficiently for present purposes in the opinion of the learned judge in the county court in the following passage: 'The evidence in my judgment shows that Sikhs are a distinctive and self-conscious community. They have a history going back to the 15th century. They have a written language which a small proportion of Sikhs can read but which can be read by a much higher proportion of Sikhs than of Hindus. They were at one time politically supreme in the Punjab.'

[82] *Watkins-Singh* (n 23).

[83] *Dhinsa v Serco* ET 1315002/2009 (18 May 2011).

[84] Enterprise and Regulatory Reform Act 2013, s 97. The Equality Act 2010, s 9(5) previously contained an enabling power which provided that a minister could by order amend the section so as to provide 'caste' to be an aspect of race. The Enterprise and Regulatory Reform Act 2013, s 97 amends the Equality Act 2010, s 9(5) and places a *duty* on a minister to make an order amending s 9 so as to prove 'caste' to be an aspect of race.

[85] As in the case of *Varna*, which is a Hindu religious concept. The four varnas of the Hindu tradition are the Brahmins, Kshatriyas, Vaishuas, and Shudras. See further the report by the National Institute for Economic and Social Research (NIESR): H Metcalf and H Rolfe, 'Caste discrimination and harassment in Great Britain' (December 2010).

[86] eg Ravidassia, Valmiki, and Ambedkarite Buddhists: see the NISER report, 'Caste discrimination and harassment in Great Britain' (n 85) para 9.4.

[87] *Hansard* HC, vol 561, col 795 (23 April 2013).

D. Prohibited Conduct

'Prohibited conduct' under the Equality Act 2010 includes direct discrimination (sec- **6.53**
tion 13), indirect discrimination (section 19), harassment (section 26), and victimization
(section 27).

The 2010 Act also prohibits combined discrimination (section 14), which is a form of direct **6.54**
discrimination. However, the provisions relating to combined discrimination have not yet
been brought into force.[88]

(1) Direct discrimination

Direct discrimination occurs when a person is treated less favourably because of a pro- **6.55**
tected characteristic. For example, if a hotelier refuses to provide someone with a room
because they are Hindu, he directly discriminates against that person because of religion
or belief.

The rule aims to achieve formal equality of treatment - there must be no less favourable treat- **6.56**
ment between otherwise similarly situated people on grounds of religion or belief. Indirect
discrimination, on the other hand, looks beyond formal equality towards a more substantive
equality of results. Criteria which appear neutral on their face may have a disproportionately
adverse impact upon people of a particular religion or belief.[89]

Unlike indirect discrimination, direct discrimination because of 'religion or belief' or 'race' **6.57**
cannot be justified. The intention or motive for discriminating is also irrelevant.[90] In other
words, whether there has been discrimination because of a protected characteristic depends
on whether the protected characteristic was the criterion applied as a basis for the discrimination; the motive for discriminating according to that criterion is not relevant.[91] Less favourable treatment because of religion or belief is not therefore saved from constituting unlawful
discrimination by the fact that the discriminator acted from a benign motive.[92]

Claims of direct discrimination on grounds of religion or belief have rarely succeeded in **6.58**
practice.[93]

---

[88] In March 2012, the government announced that commencement of the combined discrimination provisions in the Equality Act 2010 would be delayed as part of the package to minimize regulatory burdens on
business.

[89] In the context of race discrimination, see the comments in *R (Elias) v Secretary of State for Defence* [2006]
1 WLR 3213 (CA), para 119; and *R (E) v Governing Body of JFS* [2010] 2 AC 728 (SC), para 56.

[90] *R v Birmingham City Council, ex p Equal Opportunities Commission (No 1)* [1989] AC 1155 (HL); *James
v Eastleigh Borough Council* [1990] 2 AC 751 (HL); *Nagarajan v London Regional Transport* [2000] 1 AC 501;
R (E) v Governing Body of JFS [2010] 2 AC 728 (SC). It has been emphasized that there are two types of 'why'
question—one relevant and the other irrelevant. The relevant question is what caused the discriminator to act
as he did, and the irrelevant one is the discriminator's motive, intention, reason, or purpose: see *Nagarajan v
London Regional Transport* [2000] 1 AC 501 (HL); and *R (E) v Governing Body of JFS* [2010] 2 AC 728 (SC).

[91] *Application of E* (n 90) para 20 *per* Lord Phillips.

[92] *James v Eastleigh Borough Council* [1990] 2 AC 751 (HL).

[93] R Sandberg, *Law and Religion* (CUP, 2011) refers to the first instance decision of *Bodi v Teletext* [2005]
ET 3300497/2005 as a rare example of a direct discrimination claim. The claimant complained he had not
been shortlisted for a job on grounds of his race (Asian) and religion (Muslim). He compared his treatment with
that of shortlisted candidates with equivalent or lesser experience and successfully established that he had been
treated less favourably on grounds of his race and/or religion.

(a) Statutory definition

6.59 Direct discrimination is defined in section 13(1) of the Equality Act 2010: 'A person (A) discriminates against another (B) if, because of a protected characteristic, A treats B less favourably than A treats or would treat others.'

6.60 This definition is less comprehensive than the definition in section 45 of the Equality Act 2006.[94] The likely explanation is that section 13 is a generic definition intended to apply to all protected characteristics, whereas section 45 dealt specifically with direct discrimination on grounds of religion or belief.[95]

6.61 The following cases are covered by section 13:

(1) A treats B less favourably because of B's religion or belief. For example, A refuses to offer B a job because B is Jewish.

(2) A treats B less favourably because of B's association with someone who has a protected characteristic. For example, A refuses to offer B a job because B's wife is Jewish.[96]

(3) A treats B less favourably because of the protected characteristic of another person or persons. For example, A dismisses B because B refuses to follow A's unlawful discriminatory instruction not to serve Jewish people.[97]

(4) A treats B less favourably because of a religion or belief to which B is *thought to* belong or subscribe. For example, A refuses to offer B a job because he thinks B is Jewish even if in fact he is not.[98]

6.62 It should be noted that the word 'because' has replaced the words 'on grounds of' which were used in the Employment Equality (Religion or Belief) Regulations 2003 and the Equality Act 2006. According to the Explanatory Notes to the Equality Act 2010, this change in

---

[94] Equality Act 2006, s 45 provided:

(1) A person ('A') discriminates against another ('B') for the purposes of this Part if on grounds of the religion or belief of B or of any other person except A (whether or not it is also A's religion or belief) A treats B less favourably than he treats or would treat others (in cases where there is no material difference in the relevant circumstances);

(2) In subsection (1) a reference to a person's religion or belief includes a reference to a religion or belief to which he is thought to belong or subscribe.

[95] The Explanatory Notes provide that s 13 'replaces the definitions of direct discrimination in previous legislation and is designed to provide a more uniform approach . . .': see Equality Act 2010, Explanatory Notes, para 63.

[96] Unlike the 2006 Act, the 2010 Act does not state expressly that such cases are included. However, the Explanatory Notes to the Equality Act 2010 make clear that the definition in s 13 is broad enough to cover such cases: the Equality Act 2010, Explanatory Notes, para 59.

[97] See eg, in the context of race discrimination, *Showboat Entertainment Centre Ltd v Owens* [1984] IRLR 7 (EAT). In *Redfearn v Serco* [2006] ICR 1367 (CA), the claimant, an active member of the BNP, worked as a driver for a company providing transport services to public authorities. The majority of his passengers were of Asian origin. The Court of Appeal held that although racial considerations were relevant in the decision to dismiss the claimant, namely the fact that the employer's customers were mainly Asian as was a significant percentage of its workforce, the dismissal was not 'on racial grounds' for the purposes of the Race Relations Act 1976. While an employer was liable 'on racial grounds' within the meaning of the Race Relations Act 1976, s 1(1)(a) for the less favourable treatment of an employee who refused to implement the employer's racially discriminatory policy, or was affected by that policy, that principle could not be applied so as to make an employer who was not pursuing a policy of race discrimination, or who was pursuing a policy of anti-race discrimination, liable for race discrimination.

[98] The Equality Act 2006 expressly stated that a reference to a person's religion or belief included a reference to a religion or belief to which he is thought to belong or subscribe: Equality Act 2006, s 45(2). The Explanatory Notes to the Equality Act 2010 state that the definition in s 13 is broad enough to cover such cases: Equality Act 2010, Explanatory Notes, para 59.

wording does not change the legal meaning of the definition, but rather 'is designed to make it more accessible to the ordinary user of the Act'.[99]

Section 24 of the 2010 Act makes clear that, for the purpose of establishing direct discrimi- **6.63** nation, it does not matter whether A shares the protected characteristic. So in the examples above, it would make no difference if A was also Jewish. Whilst previous legislation also made clear that less favourable treatment could not be on grounds of A's own religion or belief,[100] the 2010 Act does expressly exclude such discrimination. The wording of section 13 is broad enough to cover discrimination on grounds of A's own religion or belief, although it is unlikely that it was intended to extend this far.

(b) Burden of proof

In direct discrimination claims the claimant must prove on the balance of probabilities, **6.64** facts from which the court or tribunal could conclude, in the absence of any other explanation, that the respondent has committed an act of unlawful discrimination. If the claimant establishes a *prima facie* case, the burden shifts to the respondent to prove that the treatment afforded to the claimant was not on a proscribed ground, for example religion or belief.[101]

(c) Comparator

Direct discrimination claims involve a comparison between A's treatment of B, and how **6.65** A treats or would treat others. The comparator may be actual ('treats') or hypothetical ('would treat'), but 'there must be no material difference between the circumstances relating to each case'.[102]

In claims concerning religious practices/manifestation of religious beliefs, the appropriate **6.66** comparator has been identified as a person engaging in the particular practice for reasons other than religious belief.[103] For example, in *Azmi v Kirklees Metropolitan Council*,[104] a bilingual support teacher was suspended when she refused to follow an instruction to remain unveiled at all times in the classroom. The EAT held that the correct comparator was a women who wears a face covering for a reason other than religious belief. Since on the evidence such a person would have been issued an instruction, and if she had refused to comply with it would have been suspended, it could not be said that the claimant had been treated less favourably on grounds of her religious belief.

In *Ladele v Islington London Borough Council*, a registrar complained of the treatment to **6.67** which she was subjected by the local authority and its officers when she refused to carry out the registration of civil partnerships on grounds of her religious beliefs. The local authority

---

[99] Equality Act 2010, Explanatory Notes, para 61.

[100] See the Employment Equality (Religion or Belief) Regulations 2003, SI 2003/1660, s 3(2) and the Equality Act 2006, s 45(1). Note that the Equality Act 2006, s 77, substituted s 45(1) for reg 3(1)(a) and deleted reg 3(2).

[101] Equality Act 2010, s 136 and *Igen v Wong* [2005] 3 All ER 812 (CA). It has been accepted that there are cases in which the court or tribunal may omit express consideration of the first stage of the test, moving straight to the second and concluding that the respondent has discharged the burden on him by proving that the treatment was not on the proscribed ground: *Brown v London Borough of Croydon* [2007] ICR 909 (CA).

[102] Equality Act 2010, s 23(1). The 2006 Act and the 2003 Regulations contained a similar requirement.

[103] In *McFarlane v Relate Avon Ltd* [2010] ICR 507 (EAT), the EAT rejected the argument that special considerations applied to the use of a comparator in cases of alleged discrimination on grounds of 'religion or belief'.

[104] *Azmi v Kirklees Metropolitan Borough Council* [2007] ICR 1154 (EAT).

maintained that its actions were not motivated by her religious beliefs but by her refusal to perform civil partnership duties. It was held that the proper comparator was another registrar who refused to conduct civil partnership work because of antipathy to the concept of same-sex relationships, such antipathy not being connected to or based on his or her religious belief.[105] If such a person would equally have been required to carry out civil partnership ceremonies and would have been subject to similar action if he or she had refused, this necessarily prevented a finding that there had been direct discrimination on grounds of religion or religious belief.[106]

(d) Reason for treatment

6.68 The purpose of a comparison between A's treatment of B and his treatment of others is to illuminate the answer to the question whether there has been less favourable treatment on grounds of religion or belief.[107] The use of a comparator is simply part of the process of identifying the reason for the claimant's treatment. Was it because of religion or belief or some other reason? This is the crucial question in a case of direct discrimination.[108] Direct discrimination is established if the treatment was because of religion or belief. It has been held that courts and tribunals may sometimes be able to avoid arid and confusing disputes about the identification of the appropriate comparator by concentrating primarily on why the claimant was treated as he or she was.[109]

6.69 In cases where the treatment complained of arises from an employee's insistence on manifesting his belief in the workplace, employers have generally succeeded in establishing that the action they took against the employee was not taken on grounds of religion or belief, but rather against the manifestation of that belief, for example the employee's unwillingness to counsel same sex couples[110] or to officiate at civil partnerships.[111] In *McFarlane*, the EAT rejected an argument that this approach involved an illegitimate distinction between the immediate conduct which led to the act complained of, and the belief of which that conduct was an outward and visible sign:

> It is of course correct that persons with a religious belief are likely to manifest that belief in conduct. We further accept that in some cases where an employer objects to such a manifestation it may be impossible to see any basis for the objection other than an objection to the belief which it manifests; and in such a case a claim by the employer to be acting on the grounds of the former but not the latter may be a regarded as a distinction without a difference. But in other cases there will be a clear and evidently genuine basis for differentiation between the two, and in such a case the fact that the employee's motivation for the conduct

---

[105] *Ladele v Islington LBC* [2009] ICR 387 (EAT) and *Islington LBC v Ladele* [2010] 1 WLR 955 (CA).

[106] See also the decision of the EAT in *McFarlane* (n 103), and the decision of the Court of Appeal dismissing a renewed application for permission to appeal in *McFarlane v Relate Avon Ltd* [2010] IRLR 872 (CA).

[107] *Azmi v Kirklees Metropolitan Borough Council* (n 104) para 54.

[108] *Nagarajan v London Regional Transport* [2000] 1 AC 501 (HL).

[109] *Shamoon v Chief Constable of the Royal Ulster Constabulary* [2003] ICR 337 (HL), para 11 and see also paras 7–10. It has been said that there are two 'why' questions: the irrelevant one is the discriminator's motive, intention, reason, or purpose and the relevant one is what caused him to act as he did: *Nagarajan* (n 108) and *R (E) v Governing Body of JFS* [2010] 2 AC 728 (SC), paras 62–64.

[110] *McFarlane* (n 103) and *McFarlane* (n 106).

[111] *Ladele v Islington LBC* [2009] ICR 387 (EAT) and *Islington LBC v Ladele* [2010] 1 WLR 955 (CA).

in question may be found in his wish to manifest his religious belief does not mean that belief is the ground of the employer's action.[112]

Cases concerning a failure to accommodate a religious difference—for example *Azmi*, *Ladele*, **6.70**
McFarlane, and *Eweida*—are generally considered on the basis of indirect discrimination.[113]

(2) Indirect discrimination

Indirect discrimination looks beyond formal equality towards a more substantive equality of **6.71**
results. It is concerned with 'the discriminatory impact of facially neutral requirements'.[114]
A provision, criteria, or practice which is ostensibly neutral may put persons of a particular religion or belief at a particular disadvantage when compared with others. This will constitute unlawful discrimination unless it can be shown that, despite its discriminatory impact, the provision, criteria, or practice constituted a proportionate means of achieving a legitimate aim.

The concept of indirect discrimination, which has its origins in US Supreme Court jurisprudence,[115] first appeared in the Sex Discrimination Act 1975 and later in the Race Relations Act 1976. The definition of indirect discrimination in this legislation was cast in different terms from current legislation ie in terms of an unjustified requirement or condition which a considerably smaller proportion of the protected group than the non-protected group could comply with, and which caused detriment to the claimant because he or she could not comply with it.[116] The definition in the Equality Act 2010 (as well as the Employment Equality (Religion or Belief) Regulations 2003 and Equality Act 2006) is cast in wider terms.[117]

---

[112] *McFarlane* (n 103), para 18. The EAT considered the example of an employee who wishes to wear an item of jewellery or clothing with a religious significance. The EAT observed that:

> ... in the absence of any other context, it may be permissible to infer that an employer who dismisses an employee for wearing the item in question does so because of an objection to the belief so manifested: the protestation 'I don't mind you being a Christian/Muslim, but I object to you wearing a cross/veil' might, without more, be rejected as spurious. If, however, it appeared from the context that there was some other ground for the objection—such as a general policy about the wearing of jewellery or practical reasons why the wearing of a veil was regarded as inappropriate—the position would be entirely different. In such a case any claim would have to be on the basis of indirect discrimination.

[113] Note the comments of Wilkie J in *Azmi v Kirklees Metropolitan Borough Council* (n 104) paras 75–76, that the question whether the claimant's conduct was properly a manifestation of a religious belief or religious belief is not determinative of whether the case is one of indirect or direct discrimination; there is no good reason for an *a priori* position that a manifestation of a religious belief always has to be dealt with as indirect discrimination.

[114] *Eweida v British Airways* [2010] ICR 890 (CA), para 13.

[115] In particular, the case of *Griggs v Duke Power Co Ltd* (1971) 401 US 424, in which the Supreme Court construed the Civil Rights Act of 1964 as covering not only 'overt' discrimination, but also 'practices that are fair in form but discriminatory in operation'. The case concerned a challenge by African American employees to a requirement imposed by their company of a high school diploma or passing of a general intelligence test as a condition of employment or promotion. The requirement was applied fairly to all but a disproportionate number of African Americans were rendered ineligible. For a more detailed account of the influence of US Supreme Court jurisprudence on discrimination law in Europe, see B Hepple, 'The European Legacy of Brown v Board of Education' (2006) 3 University of Illinois Law Review 605.

[116] See the observations in *Eweida v British Airways* [2009] ICR 303 (EAT), para 10 and *Eweida v British Airways* [2010] ICR 890 (CA), para 14.

[117] *Eweida v British Airways* [2009] ICR 303 (EAT), para 10.

(a) Statutory definition

6.73 Indirect discrimination is defined in section 19 of the Equality Act 2010 as follows:

(1) A person (A) discriminates against another (B) if A applies to B a provision, criterion or practice which is discriminatory in relation to a relevant protected characteristic of B's.
(2) For the purposes of subsection (1), a provision, criterion or practice is discriminatory in relation to a relevant protected characteristic of B's if—
   (a) A applies, or would apply, it to persons with whom B does not share the characteristic,
   (b) it puts, or would put, persons with whom B shares the characteristic at a particular disadvantage when compared with persons with whom B does not share it,
   (c) it puts, or would put, B at that disadvantage, and
   (d) A cannot show it to be a proportionate means of achieving a legitimate aim.[118]

6.74 Section 19 covers cases where (a) the provision, criterion, or practice is applied and puts a person at a disadvantage, and (b) where it would put a person at a disadvantage if it were applied. Where a Jewish applicant is deterred from applying for a job because a company invariably undertakes the selection exercises for the job on Saturdays, the company will have indirectly discriminated against the applicant unless the practice can be justified.[119]

6.75 It must be shown that the relevant provision, criterion, or practice is applied, or would be applied, to persons who do not share the claimant's religion or belief—in other words, it must be facially neutral.[120] A policy which is developed directly in response to a particular employee's conduct or request that his beliefs be accommodated will satisfy this requirement if can be shown that the policy is of general application and was not developed with the intention of targeting the employee's conduct.[121]

(b) Group disadvantage

6.76 In order to establish indirect discrimination, a claimant must show that the provision, criteria, or practice of which he complains:

(a) Puts persons, or would put persons, with whom he shares the characteristic at a particular disadvantage when compared with persons with whom he does not share it (section 19(2)(b)); and
(b) Puts him at a particular disadvantage (section 19(2)(c)).

6.77 As to section 19(2)(b), in *Eweida v British Airways* the Court of Appeal held that the natural meaning of the equivalent provision in the Employment Equality (Religion or Belief) Regulations 2003 (regulation 3(1)(b)(i)) was that 'some identifiable section of a workforce, quite possibly a small one, must be shown to suffer a particular disadvantage which the claimant shares'.[122] Indirect discrimination is not established where the claimant alone is disadvantaged by the provision, criterion, or practice. The wording of section 19(2)(b) of the Equality Act 2010 is materially the same as regulation 3(1)(b) and is likely to be interpreted in the same way.

---

[118] 'Religion or belief' is listed as a 'relevant protected characteristic' in Equality Act 2010, s 19(3).

[119] Equality Act 2010, Explanatory Notes, paras 79 and 81.

[120] The 2010 Act does not define 'provision, criterion or practice', nor was the phrase defined by the 2003 Regulations or the 2006 Act. However, see *British Airways v Starmer* [2005] IRLR 863 (EAT). The EAT confirmed, among other things, that a one-off discretionary decision can be a PCP.

[121] *Azmi v Kirklees Metropolitan Borough Council* (n 104) paras 60–62. In this case, the tribunal considered whether the policy had been adopted with the intention of 'targeting the veil'.

[122] *Eweida v British Airways* [2010] ICR 890 (CA), para 15.

There remains uncertainty about how this rule should be applied in practice.[123] The Court **6.78**
of Appeal in *Eweida* gave some consideration to the question but did not need to reach a
concluded view on the facts. Ms Eweida was a Christian who had been suspended when she
insisted on wearing a small visible cross with her uniform contrary to the staff dress code.
She alleged that the dress code, which forbade the wearing of visible neck adornment, placed
Christians as well as herself at a particular disadvantage. She accepted, however, that the visible display of the cross was a personal choice and not a requirement of the Christian faith.
Having found that the 2003 Regulations required evidence of group disadvantage, Sedley LJ
considered what this might require in practice:

> On the narrowest view, its practical application in a case like this would require evidence that
> other uniformed BA staff would, like Ms Eweida, have wished to wear a cross in a visible place but
> were deterred by the code from doing so: the fact that, unlike Ms Eweida, they had not chosen
> to provoke a confrontation would not count against them. On the widest view it would operate
> wherever evidence showed that there were in society others who shared the material religion or
> belief and so would suffer a disadvantage were they to be BA employees. On an intermediate view,
> it would operate by assuming, even if it is not the case, that the workforce includes such others and
> asking whether they too, or some of them, would be adversely affected by the relevant require-
> ment. All three have difficulties. The narrow view excludes the solitary individual from the protec-
> tion of the law against indirect discrimination—a result which the Disability Discrimination Act
> 1995 explicitly avoids but which the 2003 Regulations do not. The wide view places an impossible
> burden on employers to anticipate and provide for what may be parochial or even factitious beliefs
> in society at large. The intermediate view, despite its attractions, in practice risks becoming merged
> with the wide view by inviting proof that in the world outside the workforce are co-religionists or
> fellow believers, however few, who are to be assumed to have entered the same employment as the
> claimant and have become subject to the requirement to which the claimant objects... We do not
> have to resolve this issue because Ms Eweida's evidence failed all three tests.[124]

Even the wide view places those with unique or highly personal beliefs outside the protection **6.79**
of the 2010 Act, and places a heavy burden evidentially on those with minority views.

Ms Eweida successfully complained to the ECtHR. She argued that domestic law, as **6.80**
interpreted and applied by the domestic courts, had failed to give adequate protection to
her rights under Article 9.[125] The ECtHR, though ultimately upholding her complaint,

---

[123] See eg the comments of the EAT in *Chatwal v Wandsworth Borough Council* [2011] Eq LR 942 (EAT),
paras 25–27. The claimant's appeal was allowed on the grounds that the tribunal had failed to properly explain
why the claimant had failed to prove group disadvantage. The EAT observed that tribunal's task was not helped
by the fact that there was 'no consensus in law as to how large (or small) this cohort of others or "group" must
be in order to suffice'. The EAT found that the Court of Appeal's decision in *Eweida v British Airways* did not
assist in this regard. It held that in the absence of any specific guidance, the tribunal:

> ...could only take a 'steer' from the Court of Appeal's endorsement of what this Employment
> Appeal Tribunal had said in *Eweida*, namely that (at [60]): 'In our judgment, in order for indirect
> discrimination to be established, it must be possible to make some general statements which would
> be true about a religious group such that an employer ought reasonably to be able to appreciate that
> any particular provision may have a disparate adverse impact on the group.'

See also the decision in *Chaplin v Royal Devon and Exeter Hospital NHS Foundation Trust* ET 1702886/2009
(21 April 2010), in which the tribunal noted that the Court of Appeal in *Eweida* had given some obiter consideration to what might constitute a 'group' for the purposes of this exercise. The tribunal observed that the 2003
Regulations made no mention of 'group', but simply referred to persons in the plural rather than the singular.

[124] *Eweida v British Airways* [2010] ICR 890 (CA), paras 8 and 9.

[125] Ms Eweida invoked ECHR, Art 9 alone and in conjunction with Art 14. Since Ms Eweida's employer was
a private company, the question was whether her right to manifest her religion was sufficiently secured within
the domestic legal order.

was careful not to level criticism at the manner in which the 2003 Regulations had been applied.[126] The Court held that while the examination of Ms Eweida's case by the domestic tribunals and court focused primarily on the complaint of discriminatory treatment, it was clear that that the legitimacy of the of the uniform code and proportionality of the measures taken by British Airways were examined in detail. This glosses over the fact that consideration of proportionality was obiter, the claim having failed at the prior hurdle on grounds that Ms Eweida had not established group disadvantage. The Court went onto find that in the assessment of proportionality a fair balance had not been struck between Ms Eweida's rights and those of others. While her employer's desire to project a certain corporate image was no doubt a legitimate aim, the domestic courts had accorded it too much weight.

6.81 In view of the need to show group disadvantage it remains unclear how the rights of an employee in a situation like Ms Eweida's would be secured domestically.[127] The Equality Act 2010 must, so far as possible, be read in conformity with Convention rights.[128] This raises issues about whether section 19 will need to be read down in appropriate cases.

6.82 In a joint dissenting opinion, two of the judges acknowledged there was some force in the argument that to require evidence of group disadvantage discriminates against adherents of religions that are less prescriptive as regards the manner of dress or outward manifestations of faith, but did not find it necessary to resolve this question:[129]

> While it is true that the purpose of the indirect discrimination is to deal principally with the problem of group discrimination, it is also true that to require evidence of group disadvantage will often impose on an applicant an excessive burden of demonstrating that persons of the same religion or belief are put at a particular disadvantage. This may be especially difficult, as the applicant argues, in the case of a religion such as Christianity…[130]

(c) Establishing 'particular disadvantage'

6.83 The provision, criterion, or practice must put both the claimant and persons with whom he shares his religion or belief, at a 'particular disadvantage'.[131] This may be established even though the claimant has, or is able to, comply with the provision, criterion, or practice in issue.[132]

---

[126] *Eweida and ors v UK* (2013) 57 EHRR 8.

[127] The employment tribunal does not have jurisdiction to entertain a free-standing claim under the ECHR: see Ch 8, paras 8.55–8.58.

[128] See generally *Ladele v Islington LBC* [2010] 1 WLR 955 (CA), para 22, where Lord Neuberger MR acknowledged that Art 2(5) of the Employment Directive, particularly in the light of the recitals, suggested that the Employment Directive and any domestic legislation made thereunder should be read in conformity with Art 9 ECHR. He acknowledged that any such legislation would, if possible, have to be read in any event in conformity with Art 9 by virtue of the Human Rights Act 1998, s 3.

[129] The judges disagreed with the majority's view that a fair balance had not been struck in Ms Eweida's case. Even if the measure could, in principle, give rise to indirect discrimination, there was in their view, in the particular circumstances of the case, an objective and reasonable justification for the measure.

[130] *Eweida and ors v UK* [2013] IRLR 231, para 9, joint partly dissenting opinion of Judges Bratza and David Thor Bjorgvinsson.

[131] While the term 'particular disadvantage' was used in the 2003 Regulations, reg 3(1)(b), the Equality Act 2006, s 45(3) used the term 'disadvantage' rather than 'particular disadvantage'. The courts nevertheless appeared to read the word 'particular' into s 45(3) of the 2006 Act without expressly considering the issue: see eg *Watkins-Singh* (n 23); and *R (National Secular Society) v Bideford Town Council* [2012] 2 All ER 1175 (QB).

[132] *Eweida v British Airways* [2009] ICR 303 (EAT), para 44. The position was different under the old concept of indirect discrimination (see para 6.72) where, in order for detriment to be established, it was necessary that it should result from an inability to comply with a particular condition or requirement. In *Eweida*, the EAT observed that the new concept identifies particular disadvantage resulting from the application of a provision, criterion, or practice, but does not link it specifically to non-compliance with the provision or criterion in issue.

The inability to engage in a practice, such as wearing an item of jewellery, may amount to a   **6.84**
'particular disadvantage' even if it is not a requirement of the claimant's religion or belief.[133]
In *Watkins-Singh v The Governing Body of Aberdare Girls' High School* it was held that there
was a need to show that the item was a matter of 'exceptional importance' for the claimant's
religious belief, even if not an actual requirement of his or her religion. The importance of
the item was to be judged subjectively and objectively: 'there would be a "particular disadvantage"...if a pupil is forbidden from wearing an item when (a) that person genuinely
believed for reasonable grounds that wearing this item was a matter of exceptional importance to...his or her religious belief' and (b) if the wearing of the item could be shown
'objectively to be of exceptional importance to...his or her religion, even if it was not an
actual requirement of that person's religion'.[134]

The Court in *Watkins-Singh* emphasized that the decision was fact specific and should not be   **6.85**
taken to suggest that there would only ever be 'particular disadvantage' if the above elements
were proved.[135]

Later cases have doubted the requirement to show 'exceptional importance.' In *G v St*   **6.86**
Gregory's Catholic Science Governors, the Court held that the need to show 'particular disadvantage' for the purposes of indirect discrimination under the Race Relations Act 1976
conveyed the need for a 'high standard.' However, although more than choice was required,
the need to show 'exceptional importance' put the threshold too high.[136]

In *R (National Secular Society) v Bideford Town Council*, a case brought under Part 2 of the   **6.87**
Equality Act 2006, the Court accepted that there had to be a certain threshold, 'albeit not
a high one', before a set of circumstances can be described as a 'disadvantage' or 'particular
disadvantage'. These were 'ordinary words' which were to be applied 'without undue analysis
or with undue sensitivity'. While the analysis in *Watkins-Singh* was correct, there was a risk
it could be misinterpreted so as to lead to an inappropriately high standard. In the Court's
view, there was no requirement for exceptional disadvantage; the word 'particular' emphasized 'not exceptional, but specific or identifiable and more than objectively insignificant'.
It was observed that the decision in *Eweida v British Airways* showed 'that disadvantages can
exist from small distinctions, such as the prohibition on wearing a religious symbol outside
a civil uniform'.[137]

The Court found no disadvantage on the facts. The claimant was a former councillor who   **6.88**
challenged the Council's practice of holding of prayers as part of the formal business of
council meetings. He alleged that the practice placed him and other councillors who shared
his lack of religious belief at a particular disadvantage. In rejecting this argument, the Court

---

[133] *Watkins-Singh* (n 23) para 51. The court rejected the contention that there will only be 'particular disadvantage' where a member of the group is prevented from wearing something which he or she is required by his
or her religion to wear, as this would set the threshold too high.

[134] *Watkins-Singh* (n 23) para 56. It should be noted that the claimant brought the claim under the Race
Relations Act 1976 (alleging race discrimination) as well as the Equality Act 2006, Pt 2 (alleging religious or
belief discrimination).

[135] *Watkins-Singh* (n 23) para 57.

[136] *G v St Gregory's Catholic Science Governors* [2011] Eq LR 859 (QB). The claimant, who was
African-Caribbean, was turned away from school on his first day because of his cornrows. He alleged that the
school's failure to permit him to wear cornrows when they were of cultural and ethnic significance constituted
indirect discrimination.

[137] *R (National Secular Society) v Bideford Town Council* [2012] 2 All ER 1175 (QB), para 52.

observed that the claimant and other councillors who lacked religious belief were not compelled to participate in the meetings. The fact that they had to arrive after prayers or stay in silence, ignoring what was going on around them and seeming inadvertently disrespectful, or had to leave, disturbing their papers and concentration just before the substantial business began, with a degree of public embarrassment, was of 'no real significance' and did not amount to disadvantage.[138] On other grounds the Court accepted that there was no statutory power for the Council to hold prayers, a matter which was then altered by the earlier enactment of new statutory provisions in the Localism Act.

(d) Justification

6.89 Unlike direct discrimination, indirect discrimination can be justified. A provision, criterion, or practice which is discriminatory will not be unlawful if it can be shown that it is 'a proportionate means of achieving a legitimate aim'.[139] The onus of justifying the discrimination is on the alleged discriminator.[140]

6.90 The first task is to identify the aim which is sought to be achieved and to assess whether the aim is legitimate.[141] The provision, criterion, or practice must be rationally connected to the aim, and it must be no more than necessary to achieve the aim—in other words, it must be proportionate.[142] Applying EC jurisprudence, it has been held that 'the objective of the measure in question must correspond to a real need and the means used must be appropriate with a view to achieving the objective and be necessary to that end'.[143]

6.91 Whether the relevant provision, criterion, or practice is proportionate requires an objective balance between its discriminatory effect and the reasonable needs of the party applying it.[144] The discriminatory effect of a particular provision, criterion, or practice may entail an assessment of the number of people in a particular protected group that are, or are potentially, affected by the provision, criterion, or practice,[145] in addition to the quality and the seriousness of the

---

[138] *National Secular Society* (n 137) para 54 and see generally paras 53–57. The Court, at para 67, accepted that hostility towards non-participants or non-co-religionists would be 'strong evidence of real disadvantage'. However, the evidence suggested that, although that had occurred elsewhere, it had not occurred in Bideford.

[139] Again, the wording used in the Equality Act 2006 was different; s 45(3) referred to a provision, criterion, or practice which A could not 'reasonably justify by reference to matters other than B's religion or belief'.

[140] This is clear from the statutory wording itself: see the Equality Act 2010, s 19(2)(d) which provides that a provision, criterion, or practice is discriminatory where '*A cannot show* it to be a proportionate means of achieving a legitimate aim' (emphasis added).

[141] In *Ladele*, the characterization of Islington LBC's aim was one of the matters in dispute. The Court of Appeal upheld the EAT's finding that the tribunal had mischaracterized Islington's aim by treating it as a purely practical one of delivering an efficient system; Islington's aim was also to support their overarching policy of being an employer and public authority wholly committed to the promotion of equal opportunities and requiring all its employees to act in a way which did not discriminate against others. Lord Neuberger MR held that he found it very difficult to see how this aim could be challenged either as being Islington's actual aim in the light of the evidence, or a legitimate aim in the light of its 'Dignity for All' policy, current legislation, and mainstream thinking: *Islington LBC v Ladele* [2010] 1 WLR 955 (CA), paras 45–46.

[142] In *R (Elias) v Secretary of State for Defence* [2006] 1 WLR 3213 (CA), para 165, Mummery LJ set out a three-stage test: 'First, is the objective sufficiently important to justify limiting a fundamental right? Secondly, is the measure rationally connected to the objective? Thirdly, are the means chosen no more than is necessary to accomplish the objective?' The first question concerns the legitimacy of the aim.

[143] *Elias* (n 142) para 151. See also *R (E) v Governing Body of JFS* [2010] 2 AC 728 (SC).

[144] *Hampson v Department of Education and Science* [1989] ICR 179 (CA).

[145] See eg the first instance decision in *Dhinsa v Serco* ET 1315002/2009 (18 May 2011), para 80. The claimant, an Amritdhari Sikh, was employed as prison custody officer. He was prohibited from wearing a *kirpan* by the Prison Service's policy and was dismissed when he chose to do so. The tribunal found that Amritdhari Sikhs

disadvantage suffered.[146] In *MBA v the Mayor and Burgesses of the London Borough of Merton*, the EAT affirmed that what has to be considered is not the discriminatory impact of a provision, criterion, or practice on the particular employee but on the group as a whole and, that in assessing the discriminatory impact, a tribunal was entitled to consider the extent to which the employee's belief is shared by other adherents of the faith.[147]

In the employment context it has been held that it is for the employment tribunal to weigh **6.92** the needs of the business against the discriminatory effect of a provision, criterion, or practice. Although the principle of proportionality requires the tribunal to take into account the reasonable needs of the business, it has to make its own judgment, upon a fair and detailed analysis of the working practices and business considerations involved, as to whether the proposal is reasonably necessary.[148]

It has been suggested that the approach under the Employment Equality (Religion or Belief) **6.93** Regulations 2003, deriving as it did from the Employment Directive, was more stringent than is currently applied in considering Article 9 ECHR.[149]

(3) Harassment

The Equality Act 2010 prohibits harassment related to religion or belief, but only in the work- **6.94** place.[150] Harassment related to religion or belief is not prohibited in relation to the provision of services and public functions (Part 3),[151] premises (Part 4),[152] education (Part 6),[153] and associations (Part 7).[154] In this respect the position remains as before.[155]

Harassment is defined by section 26(1) of the Equality Act 2010 as follows:[156] **6.95**

A person (A) harasses another (B) if—
(a) A engages in unwanted conduct related to a relevant protected characteristic, and
(b) the conduct has the purpose or effect of—
   (i) violating B's dignity, or
   (ii) creating an intimidating, hostile, degrading, humiliating or offensive environment for B.

Section 26(4) provides that, in deciding whether conduct has this effect, each of the following **6.96** must be taken into account: (a) the perception of B; (b) the other circumstances of the case; and

---

formed a very small percentage of Sikhs generally and had heard evidence of only two examples of Amritdhari Sikhs being disadvantaged by the policy. The tribunal weighed this 'very small disparate impact' against the requirements of the national policy. See also *MBA v the Mayor and Burgesses of the London Borough of Merton* [2012] Eq LR 526 (EAT).

[146] See eg *R (National Secular Society) v Bideford Town Council* [2012] 2 All ER 1175 (QB), para 64.
[147] See *MBA* (n 145).
[148] *Hardys & Hansons v Lax* [2005] ICR 1565 (CA).
[149] *MBA* (n 145).
[150] The same is true of sexual orientation. Harassment related to all other protected characteristics (other than gender reassignment in the education context) is prohibited beyond the workplace.
[151] Equality Act 2010, s 29(8)(a).
[152] Equality Act 2010, s 33(6)(a).
[153] Equality Act 2010, s 85(10)(b).
[154] Equality Act 2010, s 103(2)(a).
[155] Harassment was prohibited by the Employment Equality (Religion or Belief) Regulations 2003; however, the Equality Act 2006 did not prohibit harassment. It should be noted that the Protection from Harassment Act 1997 covers all forms of harassment, including harassment taking place outside the workplace.
[156] There are three different types of harassment under the Equality Act 2010, but only the first, in s 26(1), applies to 'religion or belief'. The other two are types of sexual harassment.

(c) whether it is reasonable for the conduct to have that effect.[157] The effect of the conduct must therefore be subjectively and objectively assessed.[158]

6.97 In *Heafield v Times Newspaper Ltd*, a sub-editor, who was Roman Catholic, was upset and offended when an editor chasing a delayed article about the Pope shouted 'can anyone tell me what's happening to the fucking Pope?' The EAT upheld the tribunal's finding that this did not constitute harassment within the meaning of the Employment Equality (Religion or Belief) Regulations 2003.[159] To the extent that the sub-editor felt his dignity to be violated, or felt that that an adverse environment had been created, that was not a reasonable reaction. What was said was not only not ill-intentioned or anti-Catholic, or directed at the Pope or Catholics, it was *evidently* not any of those things. The EAT acknowledged that, in a perfect world, the editor would not have used an expletive, but it recognized that people are not perfect and sometimes use bad language thoughtlessly; a reasonable person would have understood that and made allowance for it. The EAT affirmed that the context in which words were used was relevant to their effect.

6.98 Like section 13 (direct discrimination), the wording of section 26(1) is broad enough to cover unwanted conducted relating not only to B's religion or belief, but also the religion or belief of another.[160] It is also broad enough to cover harassment related to A's religion or belief, which is not expressly excluded.

6.99 Any unwanted conduct must be 'related to' religion or belief. This is different from the wording used in the 2003 Regulations, which prohibited unwanted conduct 'on grounds of' religion or belief.[161] The term 'related to' is broader in scope in that it requires only a connection or association between the unwanted conduct and the protected characteristic rather than a causal link.[162] It therefore potentially captures a broader range of conduct.

6.100 Finally, it should be noted that the Equality Act 2010 also prohibits third party harassment. Where a third party harasses an employee in the course of the employee's employment, his employer will be liable for harassment where it has failed to take such steps as would have been reasonably practicable to prevent the third party from doing so.[163] A third party is a person other than the employer or another employee.[164] However, the provisions relating to third party harassment will be repealed.[165]

---

[157] The equivalent provision in the 2003 Regulations was formulated differently. Reg 5(2) provided that conduct should be regarded as having this effect 'only if, having regard to all the circumstances, including in particular the perception of B, it should reasonably be considered as having that effect'.

[158] In *Equal Opportunities Commission v Secretary of State for Trade and Industry* [2007] 2 CMLR 49 (QB), the objective test was unsuccessfully challenged in the context of sex discrimination as a gloss on the relevant framework directive.

[159] *Heafield v Times Newspaper Ltd* [2013] Eq LR 345 (EAT).

[160] *Saini v All Saints Haque Centre* [2009] IRLR 74 (EAT). The respondent wished to dismiss the claimant's colleague on the ground that he was a Hindu and subjected the claimant to harassment to this end. It was found that the claimant had been harassed on grounds of religion. The EAT held that reg 5(1)(b) of the 2003 Regulations was breached 'not only where an employee is harassed on the grounds that he holds certain religious or other relevant beliefs but also where he is harassed because someone else holds certain religious or other beliefs'.

[161] Employment Equality (Religion or Belief) Regulation 2003, reg 5(1). The term 'related to' is also used in the Employment Directive: see Council Directive (EC) 2000/78 of 27 November 2000, Art 2(3).

[162] See *Equal Opportunities Commission v Secretary of State for Trade and Industry* [2007] 2 CMLR 49 (QB). See also L Vickers, *Religious Freedom, Religious Discrimination and the Workplace* (Hart Publishing, 2008) 147.

[163] Equality Act 2010, s 40(2).

[164] Equality Act 2010, s 40(4). An employer is of course liable, in the normal way, for anything done by an employee in the course of employment: Equality Act 2010, s 109(1).

[165] Enterprise and Regulatory Reform Act 2013, s 65.

(4) Victimization

Victimization occurs when a person is mistreated because he or she seeks to rely on or enforce **6.101** rights under discrimination legislation. For example, if a person is denied a promotion because he makes a complaint of religious discrimination, the denial of promotion amounts to victimization.

A significant change under the Equality Act 2010 is that victimization is no longer treated as **6.102** a form of discrimination. Previous legislation required a claimant to show that they had been treated less favourably than others by reason of the fact that they had made a complaint of religious discrimination, for example.[166] Under the 2010 Act a claimant need only show that they have been subjected to 'detriment'. It is no longer necessary to compare the treatment of the claimant with other persons in order to establish a claim for victimization.

The definition of victimization can be found in section 27 of the Equality Act 2010 which **6.103** provides:

(1) A person (A) victimises another person (B) if A subjects B to a detriment because—
  (a) B does a protected act, or
  (b) A believes that B has done, or may do, a protected act.
(2) Each of the following is a protected act—
  (a) bringing proceedings under this Act;
  (b) giving evidence or information in connection with proceedings under this Act;
  (c) doing any other thing for the purposes of or in connection with this Act;
  (d) making an allegation (whether or not express) that A or another person has contravened this Act.[167]

The reference to contravening this Act in section 26(2)(d) includes a reference to committing a **6.104** breach of an equality clause or rule.[168]

Like previous legislation, the 2010 Act makes clear that giving false evidence or information, **6.105** or making a false allegation, is not a protected act if the evidence or information is given, or the allegation is made, in bad faith.[169]

E. Exceptions

Importantly, the Equality Act 2010 contains a number of religious-based exceptions to the **6.106** non-discrimination provisions.

(1) Employment

The relevant exceptions to Part 5 (work) are set out in Part 1 of Schedule 9 to the Equality **6.107** Act 2010:

(1) Where employment is 'for the purposes of an organised religion', an employer can discriminate on grounds of sex, gender reassignment, marriage, and sexual orientation so as to

---

[166] Employment Equality (Religion or Belief) Regulations 2003, SI 2003/1660, reg 4; Equality Act 2006, s 45(4).

[167] The transitional provisions contained in the Equality Act 2010 (Commencement No 4, Savings, Consequential, Transitional, Transitory and Incidental Provisions and Revocation) Order 2010/2317, art 8, provide that, for the purposes of s 27, a protected act includes acts done under previous enactments. For example, s 27 applies where A subjects B to detriment because B brought proceedings under the 2003 Regulations.

[168] Equality Act 2010, s 26(5).

[169] Equality Act 2010, s 26(3).

comply with doctrines of the religion, or so as to avoid conflicting with the strongly held religious convictions of a significant number of the religion's followers (Schedule 9, paragraph 2).[170] It has been held that, on its proper construction, this exception is very narrow.[171] It is intended to cover a narrow range of employment, such as ministers of religion and a small number of lay posts.[172]

(2) An employer with 'an ethos based on religion or belief' can lawfully apply, in relation to work, a requirement to be of a particular religion or belief if it can show that, having regard to that ethos and to the nature and context of the work, it is an occupational requirement, the application of the requirement is a proportionate means of achieving a legitimate aim, and the person to whom the requirement is applied does not meet it (or the employer has reasonable grounds for not being satisfied that the person meets it) (Schedule 9, paragraph 3).[173]

(3) Finally, there is a generally applicable exception. An employer can lawfully apply, in relation to work, a requirement to have a particular protected characteristic if it can show that, having regard to the nature and context of the work, it is an occupational requirement, the application of the requirement is a proportionate means of achieving a legitimate aim, and the person to whom the requirement is applied does not meet it (or the employer has reasonable grounds for not being satisfied that the person meets it) (Schedule 9, paragraph 1).[174] Under previous legislation, the requirement to have a particular characteristic had to be a *determining* occupational requirement.[175] This imposed a more stringent test than the exception now contained in paragraph 2 of Schedule 9 for the benefit of persons with an ethos based on religion or belief. This is no longer the case.

6.108 These exceptions are considered in more detail in part H of Chapter 8.

(2) Services and public functions, premises and associations

6.109 Paragraph 2 of Schedule 23 to the Equality Act 2010 contains a religious-based exception to the obligations in Part 3 (services and public functions), Part 4 (premises), and Part 7 (associations) so far as they relate to religion or belief or sexual orientation. It permits religious organizations to discriminate on grounds of religion or belief and sexual orientation in certain carefully defined circumstances.[176]

6.110 The exception applies to an organization the purpose of which is (a) to practise a religion or belief; (b) to advance a religion or belief; (c) to teach the practice or principles of a religion or belief; (d) to enable persons of a religion or belief to receive any benefit, or to engage in any

---

[170] Previously equivalent exceptions were to be found in the Sex Discrimination Act 1975, s 19, and the Employment Equality (Sexual Orientation) Regulations 2003, reg 7(3). The exception was intended to form part of the implementation of art 4(1) of Council Directive (EC) 2000/78 of 27 November 2000.

[171] *R (Amicus) v Secretary of State for Trade and Industry* [2007] ICR 1176 (QB), paras 89–91.

[172] Equality Act 2010, Explanatory Notes, para 790. For an example of a case where a lay post was held to fall within the scope of the exception, see *Reaney v Hereford Diocesan Board of Finance* ET 1602844/2006 (17 July 2007).

[173] The exception could previously be found in the Employment Equality (Religion or Belief) Regulations 2003, reg 7(3). It is intended to implement Art 4(2) of Council Directive (EC) 2000/78 of 27 November 2000.

[174] This exception could previously be found in the Employment Equality (Religion or Belief) Regulations 2003, reg 7(2) and the Employment Equality (Sexual Orientation) Regulations 2003, reg 7(2). It too forms part of the implementation of Art 4(1) of Council Directive (EC) 2000/78 of 27 November 2000.

[175] The term 'determining' occupational requirement appears in Council Directive (EC) 2000/78 of 27 November 2000, Art 4(1).

[176] As to its application to public authorities, see Equality Act 2010, Sch 23, para 2(10).

activity, within the framework of that religion or belief; or (e) to foster or maintain good relations between persons of different religions or beliefs.[177]

Any such organization can place restrictions relating to religion or belief or sexual orientation **6.111** on membership of the organization, participation in activities, the provision of goods and services in the course of its activities, or the use or disposal of premises owned or controlled by the organization.[178] Similarly, a minister can place restrictions relating to religion or belief or sexual orientation, on participation in activities or the provision of goods, facilities, or services carried on in the performance of the minister's functions in connection with or in respect of the organization.[179]

However, a restriction relating to religion or belief is permissible only if it is imposed (a) because **6.112** of the purpose of the organization, or (b) to avoid causing offence, on grounds of the religion or belief to which the organization relates, to persons of that religion or belief.[180] Restrictions relating to sexual orientation are permissible only if imposed (a) because it is necessary to comply with the doctrine of the organisation, or (b) to avoid conflict with strongly held convictions.[181]

This exception is considered in more detail in Chapter 7. **6.113**

(3) Services and public functions—specific exemptions from section 29

Section 29 of the Equality Act 2010 prohibits discrimination and victimization in the provision **6.114** of services to the public, as well as prohibiting discrimination, victimization, and harassment in the exercise of public functions that do not involve the provision of services to the public.[182]

There are a number of exceptions to this provision which are set out in Schedule 3 to the **6.115** 2010 Act:

(1) Section 29 does not apply, so far as it relates to religious or belief discrimination, to local authorities in the exercise of their functions relating to the provision of primary and secondary schools for children in a given catchment area (Schedule 3, paragraph 6). The purpose is to prevent a local authority from being bound to provide schools for pupils of different faiths, or of no faith, in every catchment area.[183]

(2) Section 29 does not apply, so far as it relates to religious or belief discrimination, to anything done in connection with the curriculum of a school, admission to a school with a religious ethos, acts of worship or other religious observance organized by or on behalf of a school, the responsible body of a school with a religious ethos, transport to and from school, and the establishment, alteration, or closure of schools (Schedule 3, paragraph 11). According to the Explanatory Notes, this provision means that, for example, a local authority can select a person of a particular religion or belief to be a governor of a school with a religious ethos.[184]

---

[177] Equality Act 2010, Sch 23, para 2(1). It does not apply to an organization whose sole or main purpose is commercial: Sch 23, para 2(2).
[178] Equality Act 2010, Sch 23, para 2(3).
[179] Equality Act 2010, Sch 23, para 2(5). 'Minister' is defined in Sch 23, para 2(8).
[180] Equality Act 2010, Sch 23, para 2(6).
[181] Equality Act 2010, Sch 23, para 2(7). Para 2(9) defines what 'strongly held convictions' means for these purposes.
[182] See Ch 7.
[183] Equality Act 2010, Explanatory Notes, para 685.
[184] Equality Act 2010, Explanatory Notes, para 695.

(3) Those providing foster care, or other similar forms of care, are exempted from the prohibition in section 29 (Schedule 3, paragraph 15).[185] This means, for example, that a Muslim family may lawfully agree to foster only Muslim children. However, there is no similar exemption in favour of public authorities, who are prohibited from discriminating in the provision of fostering services.[186]

(4) In certain circumstances, 'services' may be provided as part of a religious activity, for example a reception following a religious service. A minister does not breach section 29, so far as it relates to sex discrimination, by providing a service only to persons of one sex, or separate services for persons of each sex if: (a) the service is provided for the purposes of an organized religion; (b) it is provided at a place which is (permanently or for the time being) occupied or used for those purposes; and (c) the limited provision of the service is necessary in order to comply with the doctrines of the religion or for the purpose of avoiding conflict with the strongly held religious convictions of a significant number of the religion's followers (Schedule 3, paragraph 29). The provision makes clear that an organization is not a relevant organization in relation to a religion if its sole or main purpose is commercial.[187]

6.116 These exceptions are also considered in Chapters 7 and 9.

F. Advancement of Equality

6.117 The provisions discussed in part D provide protection by affording a remedy to individuals whose religious rights are compromised. While they are an important tool for the protection of religious rights, the scope for addressing structural and institutional inequalities through these provisions is limited.[188] These provisions are supplemented with provisions relating to advancement of equality which seek to encourage a more proactive approach to the achievement of equality:

(1) The public sector equality duty requires public authorities and other persons exercising public functions to have due regard to specified equality goals in the exercise of their functions. Previously, the law imposed such a duty in relation to race, disability, and gender only. The Equality Act 2010 extends the public sector equality duty to 'religion or belief'. It means that public authorities and others on whom the duty is imposed now have to consider how their policies, programmes, and service delivery will affect people of different religions or beliefs.

(2) The 2010 Act permits an employer, service provider, or other organization to take positive action to alleviate disadvantage suffered by persons of a particular religion

---

[185] As to adoption, it should be noted that when the Equality Act (Sexual Orientation) Regulations 2007 were passed Catholic adoption agencies sought an exemption which would permit them to opt out from having to place children with homosexual couples. The government refused to grant an exemption, although they were provided with a 20-month breathing space to allow them to comply with the Regulations. This ended on 31 December 2008.

[186] *R (Johns) v Derby City Council* [2011] HRLR 20 (QB).

[187] Equality Act 2010, Sch 3, para 29(4). Otherwise, the provision defines a relevant organization in relation to religion in para 29(3).

[188] There is some scope for addressing structural inequalities. For example, employment tribunals can make recommendations not only for the benefit of an individual complainant but also the wider workforce: see Equality Act 2010, s 124(3). However, the government has announced its intention to abolish the power of employment tribunals to make wider recommendations: Government Equalities Office, 'Equality Act 2010: employment tribunals' power to make wider recommendations in discrimination cases and obtaining information procedure: Government response to the consultation' (October 2012).

or belief, reduce their under-representation in a particular activity, or otherwise meet their needs.

(1) Public sector equality duty

The public sector equality duty comprises a general equality duty set out in section 149 of the Equality Act 2010, supported by specific duties imposed on certain public authorities by the Equality Act 2010 (Specific Duties) Regulations 2011 for the purpose of enabling them to better perform the general equality duty. **6.118**

(a) General duty

The public sector equality duty is set out in section 149 of the Equality Act 2010, which came into force on 5 April 2011. **6.119**

The duty, which is subject to limited exceptions set out in Schedule 18 to the Act,[189] is imposed on public authorities[190] and persons who are not public authorities but who exercise public functions.[191] Section 149 provides that such persons must, in the exercise of their functions,[192] 'have due regard' to the need to: **6.120**

(a) eliminate discrimination, harassment, victimization and any other conduct that is prohibited by or under the 2010 Act;
(b) advance equality of opportunity between persons who share a relevant protected characteristic and persons who do not share it;
(c) foster good relations between persons who share a relevant protected characteristic and persons who do not share it.

It makes clear that having due regard to the need to advance equality of opportunity involves having due regard, in particular, to the need to:[193] **6.121**

(a) remove or minimize disadvantages suffered by persons who share a relevant protected characteristic that are connected to that characteristic;
(b) take steps to meet the needs of persons who share a relevant protected characteristic that are different from the needs of persons who do not share it;
(c) encourage persons who share a relevant protected characteristic to participate in public life or in any other activity in which participation by such persons is disproportionately low.

Having due regard to the need to foster good relations involves having due regard, in particular, to the need to tackle prejudice and promote understanding.[194] **6.122**

---

[189] Equality Act 2010, s 149(9). For example, the duty does not apply in relation to the exercise of immigration and nationality functions (at least as far as the protected characteristics of race, religion or belief, or age are concerned), nor does it apply to the exercise of judicial functions or in connection with proceedings in the House of Commons or the House of Lords.

[190] Equality Act 2010, s 149(1). The public authorities subject to the duty are those listed in Sch 19 of the schedule; see Equality Act 2010, s 150(1).

[191] Equality Act 2010, s 149(2). 'Public function' is defined by s 150(5) which provides that 'a public function is a function of a public nature for the purposes of the Human Rights Act 1998'.

[192] Public authorities are subject to the duty in relation to all their functions unless they are specified in Sch 19 in respect of certain specified functions only, in which case they are subject to the duty only in respect of the exercise of those functions: see the Equality Act 2010, s 150(3) and (4). Persons who are not public authorities but who exercise public functions are only subject to the duty in the exercise of those functions: see the Equality Act 2010, s 149(2).

[193] Equality Act 2010, s 149(3).

[194] Equality Act 2010, s 149(5).

6.123 Guidance for public sector organizations published by the Government Equalities Office states that 'having due regard' means consciously thinking about the equality goals as part of the process of decision-making; this means that 'consideration of equality issues must influence the decisions reached by public bodies—such as how they act as employers; how they develop, evaluate and review policy; how they design, deliver and evaluate services, and how they commission and procure from others'.[195] The following example is given:

> When reviewing the services it provides, a public transport service provider finds that Sunday services are often used by people going to religious services. Reducing the Sunday service would therefore affect the ability of people belonging to certain religious groups to attend those services. The transport service provider considers this evidence along with any other relevant factors, such as the cost of providing the service, when arriving at its conclusions following the review.[196]

6.124 Case law concerning the equality duties imposed by previous legislation remains relevant in determining what is required by the duty. The following principles can be distilled from the case law:

(1) The duty is to 'have due regard' to the specified equality goals, rather than to take steps towards these goals or to achieve results.[197] For example, there is no duty to promote equality of opportunity; the duty is to *have due regard to the need* to promote equality of opportunity. This requires an authority to take that need into account, and in deciding how much weight to accord to the need, to have *due* regard to it.[198]

(2) *Due* regard is the regard that is appropriate in all the circumstances.[199] It does not exclude paying regard to countervailing factors. What the relevant countervailing factors are will depend upon the function being exercised and all the circumstances that impinge on it.[200]

(3) The duty must be performed with vigour and an open mind. It is not a matter of mere form or box-ticking. The question in every case is whether the decision-maker has in substance had due regard to the relevant statutory need.[201]

(4) The duty requires consideration to be given to equality goals in advance of a policy decision being made;[202] compliance should not be treated as a 'rearguard action following a concluded decision' but as an essential preliminary to such decision.[203] Moreover, the duty is a continuing one.[204] Authorities must have regard to the equality duty not only when a policy is developed but also when the policy is being implemented.[205]

---

[195] Government Equalities Office, 'Equality Act 2010: Public Sector Equality Duty, What Do I Need to Know? A Quick Start Guide for Public Sector Organisations' (June 2011) 4 and 5. The Equality and Human Rights Commission has also published guidance: Equality and Human Rights Commission, 'The essential guide to the public sector equality duty' (revised 2nd edn, January 2012).

[196] Government Equalities Office, 'Equality Act 2010: Public Sector Equality Duty, What do I need to Know? A Quick Start Guide for Public Sector Organisations' (last updated 30 June 2011) 7.

[197] *R (Baker and ors) v Secretary of State for Communities and Local Government* [2009] PTSR 809 (CA), para 31 (in respect of the equality duty under the Race Relations Act 1976); and *R (Brown) v Secretary of State for Work and Pensions* [2009] PTSR 1506 (QB), para 84 (in respect of the equality duty under the Disability Discrimination Act 1995).

[198] *Baker and ors* (n 197) para 31.

[199] *Baker and ors* (n 197) para 31.

[200] *Brown* (n 197) para 82.

[201] *R (Domb) v London Borough of Hammersmith* [2009] BLGR 843 (CA), para 52; and *R (Equality and Human Rights Commission) v Secretary of State for Justice* [2010] Eq LR 59 (QB), para 45.

[202] *Secretary of State for Defence v Elias* [2006] 1 WLR 3213 (CA).

[203] See *R (BAPIO Action Ltd) v Secretary of State for the Home Department* [2008] ACD 7, paras 2 and 3.

[204] *R (Kaur) v London Borough of Ealing* [2008] EWHC 2062 (Admin), para 19.

[205] See Equality and Human Rights Commission, 'The essential guide to the public sector equality duty' (revised 2nd edn, January 2012) 8.

An illustration of the continuing nature of the duty is the case of *Watkins-Singh*, which **6.125** concerned the equality duty under section 71 of the Race Relations Act 1976.[206] The claimant was a Sikh pupil who was prevented by the school uniform policy from wearing the Kara—an item of jewellery of exceptional significance to her for racial and religious reasons. Her request for a dispensation from the uniform policy was refused by the school. The court found that the defendant had failed to take into account the need to reconsider the uniform policy in the light of the obligations in section 71 or its race equality policy at any time before the claimant tried to wear the Kara. Furthermore, the school and the defendant had also failed to give any consideration to section 71 or the race equality policy when dealing with, and ultimately refusing, the claimant's application for dispensation, including the exceptional significance for racial or religious reasons to the claimant as a devout Sikh of wearing the Kara. The court observed that the attitude of the school and defendant was to regard race issues as completely distinct from uniform policy; it concluded that the school had 'clearly failed to comply with its section 71 obligations and race equality issues as unfortunately those issues played no part (although they should have done) in its decision making in relation to the claimant's wish to wear a Kara'.

A failure in respect of performance of a public sector duty does not confer a cause of action **6.126** in private law.[207] However, the duty can be enforced by means of an application for judicial review.

(b) Specific duties

The Equality Act 2010 (Specific Duties) Regulations 2011, which came into force on 10 **6.127** September 2011, impose specific duties on public authorities specified in the schedules of the Regulations for the purpose of enabling them to better perform the equality duty imposed on them by section 149 of the 2010 Act.[208] Specifically:

(1) Each public authority listed is required to publish information to demonstrate compliance with section 149 of the 2010 Act which must include information relating to persons who share a protected characteristic who are its employees (unless it has fewer than 150 employees) and other persons affected by their policies and practices.[209] The information must be published annually.[210]

(2) Each public authority listed must prepare and publish one or more objectives it thinks it should achieve to do any of the things listed in section 149(1)(a) to (c) of the 2010 Act.[211] Any objective published must be 'specific and measurable'.[212] The objective must be published every four years.[213]

---

[206] *Watkins-Singh* (n 23). The Race Relations Act 1976, s 71 required bodies on whom the duty was imposed to have due regard, in carrying out their functions, to the need to eliminate unlawful racial discrimination and to promote equality of opportunity and good relations between persons of different racial groups. The Race Relations Act 1976 (Statutory Duties) Order 2001, art 3 required specified bodies to prepare a race equality policy.

[207] Equality Act 2010, s 156.

[208] The Regulations were made pursuant to powers conferred by the Equality Act 2010, s 153 which gives Ministers the power to impose specific duties on certain public authorities for the purpose of enabling the better performance by them of the duty imposed by the Equality Act 2010, s 149(1). It should be noted that there are separate regulations for Wales: the Equality Act 2010 (Statutory Duties) Wales Regulations 2011, SI 2011/1064.

[209] The Equality Act 2010 (Specific Duties) Regulations 2011, SI 2011/2260, reg 2.

[210] SI 2011/2260, reg 2(2) and (3).

[211] SI 2011/2260, reg 3(1).

[212] SI 2011/2260, reg 3(3).

[213] SI 2011/2260, reg 3(2).

6.128   The objective of the specific duties is, in part, to increase transparency and public accountability. The Regulations therefore require public authorities to publish the information in such a manner that the information is accessible to the public.[214]

6.129   It should be noted that, in May 2012, the government announced a review of the public equality sector duty (including the specific duties imposed by the 2011 Regulations) with a view to establishing whether the equality duty is operating as intended.[215]

(2) Positive action

6.130   The Equality Act 2010 permits positive action to alleviate disadvantage experienced by persons of a particular religion or belief, to reduce their under-representation in any particular activity, or to meet their specific needs.

6.131   Section 158 provides that positive action may be taken where a person 'reasonably thinks' that:

(a) persons who share a protected characteristic suffer a disadvantage connected to the characteristic;

(b) persons who share a protected characteristic have needs that are different from the needs of persons who do not share it; or

(c) participation in an activity by persons who share a protected characteristic is disproportionately low.

6.132   In such circumstances, a person is not prohibited from taking any positive action which is a 'proportionate means' of achieving any of the following aims:

(a) enabling or encouraging persons who share the protected characteristic to overcome or minimize that disadvantage;

(b) meeting those needs; or

(c) enabling or encouraging persons who share the protected characteristic to participate in that activity.

6.133   Section 159 makes separate provision for recruitment and promotion.[216] It applies where an employer reasonably thinks that:

(a) persons who share a protected characteristic suffer a disadvantage connected to the characteristic, or

(b) participation in an activity by persons who share a protected characteristic is disproportionately low.

6.134   In such cases Part 5 (work) does not prohibit the employer from treating A more favourably in connection with recruitment or promotion than B because A has the protected characteristic but B does not, with the aim of enabling or encouraging persons who share a protected characteristic to overcome or minimize that disadvantage or participate in that activity.[217] However, such positive action is permitted only if:[218]

---

[214] SI 2011/2260, reg 4.

[215] Written Ministerial Statement by Theresa May, 15 May 2012. The review forms part of the 'Red Tape Challenge' equalities package which seeks to identify measures in the 2010 Act which are placing unnecessary or disproportionate burdens on business.

[216] 'Recruitment' for these purposes is defined by Equality Act 2010, s 159(5).

[217] Equality Act 2010, s 159(2) and (3).

[218] Equality Act 2010, s 159(4).

(a) A is as qualified as B to be recruited or promoted;

(b) the employer does not have a policy of treating persons who share a protected character-istic more favourably in connection with recruitment or promotion than persons who do not share it; and

(c) taking the action in question is a proportionate means of achieving the aim of enabling or encouraging persons who share a protected characteristic to overcome or minimize that disadvantage or to participate in that activity.

The Equality Act 2010 affords greater scope for positive action than previous legislation. **6.135** The Employment Equality (Religion or Belief) Regulations 2003, for example, permitted positive action only in connection with affording persons of a particular religion or belief access to facilities for training, or encouraging persons of a particular religion or belief to take advantage of opportunities for doing particular work.[219] The 2010 Act, on the other hand, allows positive action specifically in recruitment and promotion. The following example is given in guidance from the Government Equalities Office:

> A counselling service for teenagers has no employees who are Muslim, despite being located in an area of high Muslim population. When a vacancy arises, two candidates of equal merit are in a tie-breaker situation with the employer having to find some way to choose between them. One candidate is Muslim and the other candidate is not. The service manager could choose to offer the job to the Muslim candidate. This would be allowed under the positive action provi-sions, so the non-Muslim candidate could not claim unlawful religious discrimination.[220]

However, positive action is only permitted in carefully defined circumstances. Employers **6.136** must not adopt policies and practices designed routinely to give preference to candidates with a particular protected characteristic; candidates must be considered on their individual merits.[221] Positive action is lawful only where candidates of equal merit are in a 'tie-breaker' situation. Moreover, any positive action must be proportionate. The Explanatory Notes state:

> The extent to which it is proportionate to take positive action measures which may result in people not having the relevant characteristic being treated less favourably will depend, among other things, on the seriousness of the relevant disadvantage, the extremity of need or under-representation and the availability of other means of countering them. This provision will need to be interpreted in accordance with European law which limits the extent to which the kind of action it permits will be allowed.[222]

---

[219] Employment Equality (Religion or Belief) Regulations 2003, SI 2003/1660, reg 25.

[220] Government Equalities Office, 'Equality Act 2010: What Do I Need To Know? A Quick Start Guide to Using Positive Action in Recruitment and Promotion' (January 2011) 5.

[221] This point is emphasized in EU jurisprudence concerning the extent of positive action permitted by Council Directive (EC) 76/204 of 9 February 1976 which allowed policies 'designed to eliminate existing ine-qualities affecting women in the workplace and to promote a better balance between the sexes in employment'. The ECJ has held that laws which automatically and unconditionally give priority to women go beyond the lim-its of the exception from the principle of non-discrimination in Art 2(4): see eg Case C-450/93 *Kalanke v Freie Hansestadt Bremen* [1995] ECR I-3051; Case C-409/95 *Marschall v Land Nordrhein-Westfalen* ECR [1997] ECR I-6363; Case C-158/97 *Badeck v Landesan bein Staatsgerichtshof des Landes Hessen* [2000] ECR I-1875; and Case C-407/98 *Abrahamsson v Fogelqvist* [2000] ECR I-5539. Guidance prepared by the Government Equalities Office emphasizes that this does not prevent an employer having a routine policy of being prepared to use positive action where it is appropriate to do so: Government Equalities Office, 'Equality Act 2010: What Do I Need To Know? A Quick Start Guide to Using Positive Action in Recruitment and Promotion' (January 2011) 9.

[222] Equality Act 2010, Explanatory Notes, para 512. As to relevant European law, see n 221 and Case C-476/99 *Lommers v Minister Van Landbouw, Natuurbeheer en Visserij* [2002] ECR I-2891.

G. Procedure and Remedies

6.137 Part 9 of the Equality Act 2010 concerns enforcement of the provisions of the Act in the county court and employment tribunal.

6.138 Any proceedings relating to a contravention of the 2010 Act must be brought in accordance with Part 9.[223] This does not prevent a claim for judicial review, proceedings under the Immigration Acts, or proceedings under the Special Immigration Appeals Commission Act 1997.[224]

(1) Proceedings in the county court

6.139 Subject to limited exceptions,[225] a county court has jurisdiction to determine a claim in relation to contravention of Part 3 (services and public function), Part 4 (premises), Part 6 (education), and Part 7 (associations).

(a) Time limits

6.140 Proceedings must generally be brought within six months, starting with the date of the Act to which the claim relates, or such other period as the county court thinks just and equitable.[226]

6.141 For these purposes:

(1) Conduct extending over a period is to be treated as done at the end of the period.[227]
(2) A failure to do something is to be treated as occurring when the person in question decided on it.[228] In the absence of evidence to the contrary, a person is to be taken to decide on a failure to do something when that person does an act inconsistent with doing it, or, in the absence of an inconsistent act, on the expiry of the period in which he might reasonably have been expected to do it.[229]

(b) Remedies

6.142 If a county court finds that there has been a contravention, it has power to grant a remedy which could be granted by the High Court in proceedings in tort and/or a claim for judicial review.[230]

6.143 Any award of damages may include compensation for injured feelings whether or not it includes compensation on any other basis.[231]

6.144 Where the county court finds that there was indirect discrimination within the meaning of section 19 of the Equality Act 2010, but is satisfied that the provision, criterion, or practice was not applied with the intention of discriminating against the claimant, the

---

[223] Equality Act 2010, s 113(1).
[224] Equality Act 2010, s 113(3).
[225] Equality Act 2010, s 114(2)–(4).
[226] Equality Act 2010, s 118(1). There is a time limit of 9 months where a claim has been referred to a student complaints scheme within 6 months, or where a claim has been referred to the Equality and Human Rights Commission for conciliation: see Equality Act 2010, s 118(3) and (4).
[227] Equality Act 2010, s 118(6)(a).
[228] Equality Act 2010, s 118(6)(b).
[229] Equality Act 2010, s 118(7).
[230] Equality Act 2010, s 119(2).
[231] Equality Act 2010, s 119(4).

court must not make an award of damages unless it first considers what other remedies are available.[232]

(2) Proceedings in the employment tribunal

An employment tribunal has jurisdiction to determine a complaint relating to Part 5 (work). **6.145**

(a) *Time limits*

Proceedings in the employment tribunal must be brought within three months from the date **6.146** of the Act to which the complaint relates, or such other period as the employment tribunal thinks just and equitable.[233]

Where conduct extends over a period, or the complaint relates to the failure to do something, **6.147** the same rules set out at paragraph 6.141 apply.[234]

(b) *Remedies*

If an employment tribunal finds there has been a contravention of the Act, it may make a **6.148** declaration as to the rights of the complainant and respondent, award compensation, or make an appropriate recommendation.[235]

An appropriate recommendation is a recommendation that, within a specified period, the **6.149** respondent takes specified steps for the purpose of obviating or reducing the adverse effect of any matter to which the proceedings relate on the complainant and/or on any other person.[236] Previously, recommendations could only be made by the tribunal for the benefit of the individual complainant. Employment tribunals now have the power to make recommendations for the benefit of the wider workforce. At the end of 2012, following a consultation, the government announced its intention to abolish the power of employment tribunals to make wider recommendations.[237]

If the respondent fails without reasonable excuse to comply with an appropriate recom- **6.150** mendation so far as it relates to the complainant, the tribunal may increase the amount of any compensation already awarded or, if no compensation had previously been awarded, to award compensation.

Where a tribunal finds that there was indirect discrimination within the meaning of section **6.151** 19 of the Equality Act 2010, but is satisfied that the provision, criterion, or practice was not applied with the intention of discriminating against the complainant, the tribunal must not award compensation unless it first considers whether to make a declaration or an appropriate recommendation.[238]

---

[232] Equality Act 2010, s 119(5) and (6).
[233] Equality Act 2010, s 123(1).
[234] Equality Act 2010, s 123(3) and (4).
[235] Equality Act 2010, s 124(2).
[236] Equality Act 2010, s 124(3).
[237] Government Equalities Office, 'Equality Act 2010: employment tribunals' power to make wider recommendations in discrimination cases and obtaining information procedure: Government response to the consultation' (October 2012). The relevant amendment to the Equality Act 2010 was included in the Draft Deregulation Bill published on 1 July 2013.
[238] Equality Act 2010, s 124(4).

(3) Transitional provisions

6.152 The majority of the provisions in the Equality Act 2010 came into force on 1 October 2010.[239]

6.153 The transitional provisions are set out in the Equality Act 2010 (Commencement No 4, Savings, Consequential, Transitional, Transitory and Incidental Provisions and Revocation) Order 2010.

6.154 The transitional provisions provide that the 2010 Act does not apply where the act complained of occurs wholly before 1 October 2010.[240] Previous legislation, procedures, and remedies are applicable as if the 2010 Act had not been commenced.

6.155 There are specific transitional provisions relating to victimization. The Order makes clear that for the purposes of section 27 of the Equality Act 2010 (which defines what amounts to victimization)[241] a protected act includes acts done under previous enactments.[242] This means that section 27 applies where, for example, an employer subjects an employee to detriment because the employee brought proceedings under the Employment Equality (Religion or Belief) Regulations 2003.

6.156 Finally, the enforcement provisions in Part 9 of the 2010 Act apply where an act carried out before 1 October 2010 is unlawful under a previous enactment, and that act continues on or after 1 October 2010 and is unlawful under the 2010 Act.[243]

---

[239] The Equality Act 2010 (Commencement No 4, Savings, Consequential, Transitional, Transitory and Incidental Provisions and Revocation) Order 2010, SI 2010/2317, art 2.
[240] SI 2010/2317, art 15.
[241] See paras 6.101–6.105.
[242] SI 2010/2317, art 8.
[243] SI 2010/2317, art 7.

7

SERVICES AND PUBLIC FUNCTIONS, PREMISES, ASSOCIATIONS

A. Introduction

Two types of protection of religious rights in the areas of services (including in the exercise of a public function), premises, and associations may be seen to exist. First, various statutory provisions in Parts 3, 4, and 7 of the Equality Act 2010 provide protection against persons being discriminated against because of their particular religion or belief, or lack of religion or belief. Secondly, by virtue of exemptions from the provisions in those Parts of the Act, 'religious organisations', ministers, and certain others are given freedom to carry out certain religious activities which might otherwise be said to constitute religious or sexual orientation discrimination against others. In effect, therefore, the Equality Act 2010 protects religious rights both by preventing certain forms of discrimination on religious grounds, and permitting certain forms of discrimination undertaken in the name of religion. This Chapter describes and discusses the forms of discrimination in each case.   **7.01**

Part B of this Chapter contains a brief description of the legislation preceding the Equality Act 2010 under which much of the relevant case law has been decided. Part C describes the protection for religious rights in the relevant areas which exists in both of the ways identified earlier, including by reference to case law. Part D addresses relevant aspects of procedure and remedies.   **7.02**

B. Legislative History

It has for some time been unlawful to discriminate in relation to services and premises on the ground of sex, race, or disability. In summary: **7.03**

(1) sections 29 to 31of the Sex Discrimination Act 1975 prohibited discrimination on the grounds of sex in the provision of goods, facilities, or services (section 29), in the disposal or management of premises (section 30), and in relation to consent for assignment or sub-letting (section 31);

(2) sections 20 to 25 of the Race Relations Act 1976 prevented discrimination on the grounds of race in the provision of goods, services, and facilities (section 20), the disposal and management of premises (section 21), in relation to consent for assignment or sub-letting (section 24), and on the part of associations as defined (section 25);

(3) sections 19 to 24 of the Disability Discrimination Act 1995 prohibited discrimination on the grounds of disability in relation to goods, facilities and services (section 19), discrimination by employment services and public authorities (section 21), and discrimination by a person with power to dispose of any premises (section 22).

7.04 Prior to the Equality Act 2006, however, it was not unlawful to discriminate because of religion or belief in the fields with which this chapter is concerned, although such discrimination was prohibited in the employment field.[1] Under the 2006 Equality Act, it became unlawful for the first time to discriminate on the grounds of religion or belief in respect of the provision of goods, facilities, or services (section 46); in respect of premises (section 47); and in the exercise of the functions of public authorities (section 52).

7.05 The substance of most of these provisions in the 2006 Equality Act was carried forward into the Equality Act 2010. To that extent the present law remains largely unchanged from that which existed before the Equality Act 2010 came into force on 1 October 2010. Most of the cases decided under the religious discrimination provisions in the 2006 Act, or indeed the previous legislation insofar as it bears upon religious discrimination, remain relevant. This is reflected in the following discussion.

C. Who and What is Protected?

7.06 This section discusses the protection of religious rights contained in the Equality Act 2010 which prohibits discrimination and victimization. The concepts of 'discrimination' (direct and indirect), 'victimisation', 'protected characteristic', 'detriment', and other relevant concepts are discussed in Chapter 6.

(1) Provision of services and public functions

(a) Service provision

7.07 In relation to the protected characteristic of religion or belief,[2] a person (known as a 'service provider') concerned with the provision of a service[3] to the public or a section of the public (for payment or not) must not:

(1) discriminate[4] against a person requiring the service[5] by not providing the person with the service;[6]

---

[1] In particular the Employment Equality (Religion or Belief) Regulations 2003, now themselves overtaken by the Equality Act 2010 (in following notes 'EA 2010'). See Ch 8.

[2] 'Religion or belief', defined in EA 2010, s 10 and case law, is discussed fully at Ch 6, paras 6.15–6.45.

[3] 'Provision of a service' includes the provision of goods or facilities (EA 2010, s 31(2)) and the provision of a service in the exercise of a public function (s 31(3)), eg the provision of medical treatment on the NHS.

[4] The meaning of 'discrimination' (direct and indirect) is dealt with at Ch 6, 6.55–6.70 (direct) and 6.71–6.93 (indirect).

[5] 'A person requiring a service' includes a person who is seeking to obtain or use the service (EA 2010, s 31(6)).

[6] EA 2010, s 29(1). A service provider 'not providing a person with a service' includes (a) the service-provider not providing the person with a service of the quality that the service-provider usually provides to the public (or the section of it which includes the person), or (b) the service-provider not providing the person with the service

(2) in providing the service, discriminate against a person (a) as to the terms on which they provide the service to that person;[7] (b) by terminating the provision of the service to that person;[8] or (c) by subjecting that person to any other detriment;

(3) victimize[9] a person requiring the service by not providing the person with the service;[10]

(4) in providing the service, victimize a person (a) as to the terms on which they provide the service to that person;[11] (b) by terminating the provision of that service to that person;[12] or (c) by subjecting that person to any other detriment.[13]

Cases of indirect discrimination by service-providers because of religion or belief may be more common, and more difficult to spot, than cases of direct discrimination. For example, a requirement on the part of a company which organizes outdoor activities that participants wear protective headgear may be indirectly discriminatory against Sikhs unless it can be justified, for instance on health and safety grounds. An example of victimization would be a refusal to provide the outdoor activity service to a Sikh because he had made a complaint that the requirement to wear headgear was in breach of the Equality Act 2010.   **7.08**

There is no provision which makes harassment unlawful in relation to service provision as it would apply to religion or belief (although such harassment is unlawful in relation to all other protected characteristics save sexual orientation).[14] The legislation expressly makes clear, however, that this does not prevent conduct relating to religion or belief from amounting to less favourable treatment for the purposes of, for example, direct discrimination.[15]   **7.09**

There has been a large amount of case law decided under previous legislation on what constitutes provision of a 'service' for the purposes of non-discrimination obligations.   **7.10**

In the context of section 20 of the Race Relations Act 1976, now repealed, it was held that the police duties of assisting and protecting members of the public were 'services of any profession or trade, or any local or other public authority' so that officers were subject to the obligation.[16] The protection, assistance, and support afforded to victims and eye-witnesses by police officers in the investigation of crime was also held to constitute the provision of facilities and/or services.[17] The provision of access to a shopping centre fell within the scope of section 20(2) as access to and use of any place which members of the public are permitted to enter.[18] A local authority provided 'goods, facilities and services' for children 'looked after' by it, whether children in care (for whom the authority stood in *loco parentis*) or children   **7.11**

---

in the manner in which, or on the terms on which, the service-provider usually provides the service to the public (or the section of it which includes the person).

[7] EA 2010, s 29(2)(a).

[8] EA 2010, s 29(2)(b).

[9] The concept of 'victimisation' is discussed fully in Ch 6, paras 6.101–6.105.

[10] EA 2010, s 29(4).

[11] EA 2010, s 29(5)(a).

[12] EA 2010, s 29(5)(b).

[13] EA 2010, s 29(5)(c).

[14] EA 2010, s 29(8).

[15] See EA 2010, s 212(5).

[16] *Farah v Commissioner of Police for the Metropolis* [1998] QB 65. The performance of a public duty did not preclude the provision of a 'service'.

[17] *Brooks v Commissioner of Police for the Metropolis* [2002] Po LR 88.

[18] *CIN Properties Ltd v Rawlins* [1995] 2 EGLR 130.

accommodated by it.[19] Determining a marriage licence also fell within the scope of section 20.[20] A defendant's distribution of leaflets to residents calling upon them to voice to the planning authority objections to applications by Asians for planning approvals was held to amount to provision of a service to the public on the basis that it amounted to an indirect attempt to induce the authority to discriminate on racial grounds where the authority were providing a service to the public, namely town and country planning.[21]

7.12 In the context of sex discrimination, a local authority's charging arrangements relating to access to a leisure centre fell within the scope of the old section 29 of the Sex Discrimination Act 1975 which prohibited discrimination in the provision of goods, facilities, and services.[22] However, the Secretary of State's powers relating to immigration control were not concerned with the provision of facilities under section 29(1) of the 1975 Act,[23] and the grant of 'special vouchers' as part of immigration control did not fall within section 29(1), as the section applied to the direct provision of facilities and services, not to the mere grant of permission to use facilities, and was to be construed as applying only to acts that were at least similar to those of private persons.[24] It was similarly decided that immigration control did not amount to the provision of goods, services, or facilities for the purposes of section 20(1)(e) of the 1976 Race Relations Act, so that an investigation by the Commission into the Home Office's administration of immigration laws was not justified on the basis of investigating such discrimination (although it was justified on a different basis).[25]

7.13 It was also held that services provided to a person held in an immigration removal centre were 'services' within the meaning of section 19 of the Disability Discrimination Act 1995.[26]

7.14 *Re All Saints', Sanderstead* concerned the definitions of 'service' and 'service-provider' as they applied to a Church of England parish church. A vicar and churchwardens sought a faculty for the removal of communion rails and their incorporated kneelers from a church building. A disabled member of the congregation, who had difficulty taking communion standing and could not kneel to take it if there were no rails, objected that the petition was in breach of the disability discrimination provisions in the Equality Act 2010. Although expressing the view that, in permitting access to and use of a Church, an incumbent was a 'service-provider' for the purposes of section 29 of the Equality Act 2010, Petchey Ch held that neither a priest celebrating Holy Communion nor a church organization facilitating the celebration of Holy Communion could properly be said to be a 'service-provider', and the provision or otherwise of a communion rail was not a 'service' within the meaning of the Act.[27] It followed that there could be no direct discrimination, or failure to make reasonable adjustments, in respect of the petition to remove the rails.

---

[19] *Conwell v Newham LBC* [2000] 1 WLR 1.
[20] *Tejani v Superintendent Registrar for the District of Peterborough* [1986] IRLR 502.
[21] *Commission for Racial Equality v Riley* [1982] CLY 2558.
[22] *James v Eastleigh BC* [1989] 3 WLR 123.
[23] *R v Immigration Appeal Tribunal, ex p Kassam* [1980] 1 WLR 1037.
[24] *R v Entry Clearance Officer, ex p Amin* [1983] 3 WLR 258.
[25] *Home Office v Commission for Racial Equality* [1982] QB 385.
[26] *Gichura v Home Office* [2008] ICR 1287.
[27] *Re All Saints', Sanderstead* [2012] Fam 51, para 63.

Schedule 3 to the Equality Act 2010 provides for a number of relevant exceptions to the **7.15** prohibitions in Part 3 of the Act relating to service provision and public functions for those engaged in religious activities. Where the equality legislation has not provided for exceptions, difficult cases can arise.

Paragraph 15 of Schedule 3 exempts providers of foster and other forms of home care from **7.16** the prohibition in section 29 of the Equality Act 2010. This means, for example, that a Muslim family could agree to foster only Muslim children. However, as noted in *R (Johns and ors) v Derby City Council*,[28] there is no similar exemption in favour of a public authority which remains forbidden from discriminating in the provision of fostering services. In the view of the Court in that case, therefore, this gave rise to:

> ... what might be seen as a difficulty. For if the carer is allowed to agree only to foster on a ground that would otherwise be discriminatory, but the public authority is not allowed to discriminate in the provision of its services, it is difficult to see how the former can be permissible without the latter, unless [the exemption] is only to bite where no public authority is involved and the fostering agency is a private body.[29]

It was unnecessary to resolve that difficulty in this case.

Regulations 3 and 4 of the Equality Act (Sexual Orientation) Regulations 2007, made **7.17** under the Equality Act 2006, prohibited discrimination on grounds of sexual orientation in refusing to provide a person with goods, facilities, or services in a hotel. In *Hall v Bull*, an elderly couple, who ran a private hotel, operated a policy to restrict occupancy of their double-bedded rooms to married couples because of a sincerely held religious belief that it was sinful for persons, whether heterosexual or homosexual, to have sexual relations outside marriage. They refused to honour a booking for a double-bedded room made by a homosexual couple in a civil partnership. It was not possible for homosexuals to marry. In defence to a claim that their refusal constituted direct discrimination contrary to the 2007 Regulations, they argued that it was based on an objection to sexual practice outside marriage, rather than an objection to homosexuality.

The county court and court of appeal nevertheless held that the refusal constituted **7.18** direct discrimination under the 2007 Regulations, on the basis that the criterion at the heart of the policy—the need for marriage—was necessarily linked to the characteristic of homosexuality because a homosexual couple could not marry.[30] Further, the 2007 Regulations were compatible with the hotel operators' rights to manifest their religious belief under Article 9(2) ECHR, because they amounted to a proportionate limitation

---

[28] *R (Johns and ors) v Derby City Council* [2011] EWHC 375 (Admin). In this case, the claimants' application to a local authority to be short-term foster carers was proposed to be refused on the basis of concerns as to how they would foster a homosexual child. The claimants alleged that a refusal on that basis would constitute direct discrimination in service provision because of their religion or belief as Christians.

[29] *Johns and ors* (n 29) para 95.

[30] *Hall v Bull* [2012] 1 WLR 2514. In so holding, the Court of Appeal (at para 40) drew heavily on *James v Eastleigh Borough Council* [1990] 2 AC 751. There the plaintiff and his wife, both aged 61, used swimming baths run by the council. The council's policy was that persons would be admitted free when of state pension age. Facing an allegation of direct sex discrimination, the council argued that its policy was not based on sex so could not be directly discriminatory; it was simply based on whether or not a person had reached state pension age. The House of Lords held, however, that the policy constituted direct sex discrimination against men, because a man only reached state pension age at 65, whereas a woman did at 60. The fact that the council's policy had a benign motive was irrelevant.

to protect the Article 8 rights of homosexuals.[31] Rafferty LJ concluded her leading judgment by saying:

> Whilst the defendants' beliefs about sexual practice may not find the acceptance that once they did, nevertheless a democratic society must ensure that their espousal and expression remains open to those who hold them. It would be unfortunate to replace legal oppression of one community (homosexual couples) with legal oppression of another (those sharing the defendants' beliefs); rather there should be achieved respect for the broad protection granted to religious freedom... However, in a pluralist society, it is inevitable that from time to time, as here, views, beliefs and rights of some are not compatible with those of others... I do not consider that the defendants face any difficulty in manifesting their religious beliefs, they are merely prohibited from doing so in the commercial context they have chosen.[32]

7.19 The Supreme Court has given permission to appeal in *Hall v Bull*. It is yet to be heard at the time of writing.

7.20 A similar issue arose in *Black v Wilkinson*.[33] There an owner of a bed and breakfast restricted the sharing of her double rooms to heterosexual and preferably married couples. She denied that this constituted direct discrimination because of sexual orientation, merely sexual behaviour. In the County Court, Recorder Moulder held that there was, however, direct discrimination, either on the basis identified in *Hall v Bull*, or on the basis that the owner had treated the homosexual couple less favourably than she would have treated unmarried heterosexual couples in the same circumstances. Again it was held that the application of the 2007 Regulations did not involve a breach of the owner's rights under Article 9 ECHR. The judge granted permission to appeal to the Court of Appeal, which is yet to be heard at the time of writing.

7.21 It is important to recognize that acts of worship are not themselves 'services' within the meaning of the Equality Act 2010.[34] To that extent religious bodies may not be accused of discriminating through practices forming part of such acts.

7.22 In certain circumstances, however, services may be provided as part of religious activity. An example would be a reception following a religious service. As to this, paragraph 29(1) of Schedule 3 to the Equality Act 2010 provides that a minister[35] does not breach section 29, so far as it relates to sex discrimination, by providing a service only to persons of one sex, or separate services for persons of each sex, if (a) the service is provided for the purposes of an organized religion; (b) it is provided at a place which is (permanently or for the time being) occupied or used for those purposes; and (c) the limited provision of the service is necessary in order to comply with the doctrines of the religion or is for the purpose of avoiding

---

[31] See *Hall v Bull* (n 30) paras 45–51.

[32] *Hall v Bull* (n 30) para 56.

[33] *Black v Wilkinson* [2012] Eq LR 1090.

[34] EA 2010, Explanatory Notes, para 742.

[35] 'Minister' means minister of religion, or other person, who (a) performs functions in connection with the religion, and (b) holds an office or appointment in, or is accredited, approved or recognized for purposes of, a relevant organization in relation to the religion. An organization is a 'relevant organisation' in relation to a religion if its purpose is: (a) to practise the religion, (b) to advance the religion, (c) to teach the practice or principles of the religion, (d) to enable persons of the religion to receive benefits, or to engage in activities, within the framework of that religion, or (e) to foster or maintain good relations between persons of different religions, but an organization is not a relevant organization in relation to a religion if its sole or main purpose is commercial: EA 2010, Sch3, para 29(3) and (4).

conflict with the strongly held religious convictions of a significant number of the religion's followers.[36]

(b) Public functions

By section 29(6) of the Equality Act 2010, even if not providing a service to the public or a **7.23** section of the public, a person must not do anything constituting discrimination or victimization relating to the protected characteristic of religion or belief when acting in the exercise of a public function.[37] A public function is a function that is a function of a public nature for the purposes of the Human Rights Act 1998.[38] Examples of public functions not involving the provision of a service would be licensing functions, government and local authority public consultation exercises, the provision of public highways, planning permission decisions, and core functions of the prison service or probation service.[39]

In *Re All Saints', Sanderstead*, discussed earlier in the context of service provision,[40] also **7.24** considered whether a priest celebrating Holy Communion was exercising a 'public function' within the meaning of section 29 of the Equality Act 2010. The Consistory Court noted that in *Aston Cantlow and Wilmcote with Billesley Parochial Church Council v Wallbank* the House of Lords had emphasized that in order for the EHCR to apply a function needs to be of a *governmental* nature.[41] Petchey Ch held that, since the celebration of Communion was on that basis not a public function under section 29 of the Equality Act 2010, no duty not to discriminate because of disability or to make reasonable adjustments arose in respect of a petition to remove communion rails inside a church.

It should be noted that certain immigration decisions are exempt from the scope of religious **7.25** or belief-related discrimination under section 29 of the Equality Act 2010 (see paragraph 18 of Schedule 3). Specifically, the protection in section 29 does not apply to:

(1) a decision taken in accordance with immigration rules to refuse entry clearance or leave to enter the United Kingdom, or to cancel leave to enter or remain[42] in the United Kingdom, on the grounds that the exclusion of the person from the United Kingdom is conducive to the public good;[43]

(2) a decision taken in accordance with immigration rules to vary leave to enter or remain in the United Kingdom, or to refuse an application to vary leave to enter or remain in the

---

[36] EA 2010, Sch 3, para 29(1).

[37] It is not unlawful to harass in the exercise of a public function in relation to religion or belief: see EA 2010, s 28(8).

[38] EA 2010, s 31(4). Under the Human Rights Act 1998, s 6(3)(b) it is unlawful for any person certain of whose functions are 'functions of a public nature' to act in a way which is incompatible with a right in the ECHR. See generally *YL v Birmingham City Council* [2008] 1 AC 95; and cf *R (Weaver) v London & Quadrant Housing Trust* [2009] 1 All ER 17.

[39] See the Explanatory Notes to the Equality Act 2010, para 122.

[40] *Re All Saints'* (n 27). See previous discussion of the case at para 7.14.

[41] *Aston Cantlow and Wilmcote with Billesley Parochial Church Council v Wallbank* [2004] 1 AC 546. See especially the speech of Lord Rodger of Earlsferry at para 170 of *Aston Cantlow* (cited at *Re All Saints'* (n 27) para 66), and that of Lord Hobhouse of Woodborough at para 86 (cited at *Re All Saints'* (n 27) para 67).

[42] 'Immigration rules', 'entry clearance', 'leave to enter', and 'leave to remain' are to be construed in accordance with the Immigration Act 1971 (see EA 2010, Sch 3, para 19).

[43] EA 2010, Sch 3, para 18(3)(a). This means that decisions to refuse entry on conducive grounds to, for example, preachers holding extreme religious views who use the pulpit to incite violence, do not constitute unlawful discrimination because of religion or belief.

United Kingdom, on the grounds that it is undesirable to permit the person to remain in the United Kingdom;[44]

(3) a decision (whether or not taken in accordance with immigration rules) in connection with an application for entry clearance or for leave to enter or remain in the United Kingdom on the grounds that (a) a person holds an office or post in connection with a religion or belief or provides the service in connection with a religion or belief; (b) a religion or belief is not to be treated the same way as certain other religions or beliefs; or (c) the exclusion from the United Kingdom of a person to whom (a) applies is conducive to the public good;[45]

(4) anything done for the purposes of or in pursuance of the decisions mentioned in points (1) to (3);[46]

(5) a decision taken, or guidance given, by the Secretary of State in connection with a decision mentioned in points (1) to (3);[47]

(6) a decision taken in accordance with guidance given by the Secretary of State in connection with a decision mentioned in points (1) to (3).[48]

7.26 In *R (National Secular Society) v Bideford Town Council*, it was argued on behalf of a person without religious belief[49] that the practice of Bideford Town Council to hold prayers as part of the formal business of council meetings was indirectly discriminatory[50] in the exercise of its public function, contrary to its duty under section 52 of the Equality Act 2006 (the predecessor of the Equality Act 2010 section 29(6)).

7.27 Ouseley J held that the council's business was 'unquestionably' in the exercise of a public function,[51] but that the 'practice' properly defined was not applied to the claimant because he was free to leave or not to participate in the meeting during the part of it in which prayers were conducted.[52] Further, the fact that it might seem inadvertently disrespectful or be publicly embarrassing for those sharing the claimant's lack of religious belief, or the claimant himself, not to participate in that part of the meeting, did not constitute a disadvantage for

---

[44] EA 2010, Sch 3, para 18(3)(b).

[45] EA 2010, Sch 3, para 18(5) and (6). Explanatory Notes to the Equality Act 2010, para 711 explains that 'the immigration services may differentiate between certain religious groups in order to allow a person such as a minister of religion to enter the UK to provide essential pastoral services, without being challenged by groups which could operate against the public interest, but which might also claim to represent a religion'.

[46] EA 2010, Sch 3, para 18(2) and (4).

[47] EA 2010, Sch 3, para 18(7)(a).

[48] EA 2010, Sch 3, para 18(7)(b).

[49] *R (National Secular Society) v Bideford Town Council* [2012] EWHC 175 (Admin). It will be recalled that a lack of religious belief is a form of religious belief: see EA 2010, s 10(2).

[50] It was submitted that the requirements of indirect discrimination under either EA 2006, s 45 or EA 2010, s 19 were satisfied, notwithstanding the differences in wording between the two: see generally *National Secular Society* (n 49) paras 43–44.

[51] *National Secular Society* (n 49) para 37.

[52] *National Secular Society* (n 49) paras 47–49. Although not discriminatory, the Court nevertheless found the council's holding of prayers as part of its formal business to be *ultra vires*, on the basis that there is no specific statutory power to say prayers during council business and the prayers were not calculated to facilitate, or conducive or incidental to the discharge of, any of the council's functions under the Local Government Act 1972, s 111: see *National Secular Society* (n 49) paras 24–33. Permission to appeal on this point was granted, but was overtaken by further statutory provisions enacted so that there could be no doubt that there was a statutory power to say prayers. The discrimination argument was predicated on the basis that that was not so, ie that the practice was *intra vires* (see para 41), and the aspect of the judgment addressing discrimination must be read accordingly.

statutory purposes,[53] and, even were that not so, the practice was shown by the council to be a proportionate means of meeting a legitimate aim.[54]

In *R (Ghai) v Newcastle City Council*,[55] Cranston J disposed of an argument that a local **7.28** authority's refusal to provide a Hindu with land for an open air funeral pyre was unlawful under section 52(1) of the Equality Act 2006 as indirect discrimination on the ground of religion and belief in the exercise of a public function. Even if discrimination were established (which the Court did not decide), the local authority's refusal attracted the exemption in the Act for acts done with statutory authority, apparently because it had been based on the fact that the proposed use of the land would constitute a criminal offence under the Cremation Act 1902 and the Cremation (England and Wales) Regulations 2008.[56]

(2) Premises

The prohibitions on religious discrimination in Part 4 of the Equality Act 2010 fall upon **7.29** three main categories of person: persons who have the right to dispose of premises (section 33); persons whose permission is required for the disposal of premises (section 34); and persons who manage premises (section 35).

(a) Persons having the right to dispose of premises

A person who has the right to dispose[57] of premises[58] must not discriminate against or vic- **7.30** timize another (a) as to the terms on which they offer to dispose of the premises to that person;[59] (b) by not disposing of the premises to that person;[60] or (c) in their treatment of that person with respect to things done in relation to persons seeking premises.[61] There is, however, no provision rendering unlawful harassment in relation to premises disposal as it would apply to religion or belief (although such harassment is again unlawful in relation to all other protected characteristics save sexual orientation).[62]

---

[53] *National Secular Society* (n 49) paras 53–59.

[54] *National Secular Society* (n 49) paras 60–64. For the purpose of the discrimination argument, the legitimate aim was taken as that the saying of prayers was calculated to facilitate the conduct of the council's business, or was conducive or incidental to it (para 60). On the assumption (not upheld on the *vires* issue) that prayers could be a lawful part of the meeting, it was 'difficult to see how alternatives, which either involve no prayers or none in the formal meeting, can meet that aim at all' (para 63).

[55] *R (Ghai) v Newcastle City Council* [2009] EWHC 978; subsequently appealed to the Court of Appeal but on different grounds: see [2011] QB 591.

[56] *Ghai* (n 55) para 157.

[57] In the case of premises subject to a tenancy, disposing of premises includes (a) assigning the premises; (b) sub-letting them; or (c) parting with possession of them (s 38(3)), and also includes granting a right to occupy them (s 38(4)). 'Tenancy' means a tenancy created (whether before or after the passing of the EA 2010) (a) by a lease or sub-lease; (b) by an agreement for a lease or sub-lease; (c) by a tenancy agreement; or (d) in pursuance of an enactment (s 38(6)).

[58] 'Premises' means whole or part of the premises: EA 2010, s 38(2).

[59] EA 2010, s 33(1)(a) and (4)(a) ('discrimination' and 'victimisation', respectively).

[60] EA 2010, s 33(1)(b) (discrimination); EA 2010, s 33(4)(b) (victimisation). Where an interest in a commonhold unit cannot be disposed of unless a particular person is a party to the disposal, that person must not discriminate against or victimize a person by not being a party to the disposal (s 33(2) (discrimination); s 33(4) (victimisation)). Disposing of an interest in a commonhold unit includes creating an interest in a commonhold unit (s 38(5)). 'Commonhold unit' is to be construed in accordance with the Commonhold and Leasehold Reform Act 2002.

[61] EA 2010, s 33(1)(c).

[62] EA 2010, s 33(6).

7.31 It may be discrimination, therefore, for a landlord to refuse to let a property to a Muslim because he is a Muslim. However, the private[63] disposal of premises by an owner-occupier[64] is subject to a narrower range of obligations. Specifically:

(1) it is *not* unlawful for a person having the right to dispose of premises to discriminate against another in relation to religion or belief (a) as to the terms on which they offer to dispose of the premises to the other person, (b) by not disposing of the premises to the other person, or (c) in their treatment of the other person with respect to things done in relation to persons seeking premises;[65]

(2) it is *not* unlawful for a person whose permission is required for the disposal of premises to discriminate against another in relation to religion or belief by not giving permission for the disposal of the premises to the other.[66]

For example, if the situation arose, it would be lawful for a homeowner who has made known that he wants to sell his house privately to opt to sell it to a fellow Christian.

(b) Persons whose permission is required for disposal

7.32 A person whose permission is required for the disposal of premises must not discriminate against or victimize another by not giving permission for the disposal of the premises to the other.[67] For example, a landlord's refusing permission to a Jewish tenant to sublet a property would be victimization if the refusal was because the tenant had given evidence against the landlord in proceedings brought under the Equality Act 2010.[68]

7.33 Those prohibitions do not, however, apply to anything done in the exercise of a judicial function, so a judge refusing permission to dispose of premises in court proceedings could not be liable.[69] There is again no provision rendering unlawful harassment in relation to such a person as it would apply to religion or belief.[70]

(c) Persons managing premises

7.34 A person who manages premises must not discriminate against or victimize a person who occupies the premises (a) in the way in which they allow that person, or by not allowing that person, to make use of a benefit or facility;[71] (b) by evicting that person (or taking steps for the purpose of securing that person's eviction);[72] or (c) by subjecting that person to any other detriment.[73] Again there is no provision rendering unlawful harassment in relation to premises management as it would apply to religion or belief.[74]

---

[63] A disposal is a private disposal only if the owner-occupier does not (a) use the services of an estate agent for the purpose of disposing of the premises, or (b) publish (or cause to be published) an advertisement in connection with their disposal (EA 2010, Sch 5, para 1(2)).

[64] 'Owner-occupier' for those purposes means a person who (a) owns an estate or an interest in premises, and (b) occupies the whole of them (EA 2010, Sch 5, para 1(5)).

[65] EA 2010, Sch 5, para 1(3).

[66] EA 2010, Sch 5 para 1(4).

[67] EA 2010, s 34(1) (discrimination); s 34(3) (victimisation).

[68] This would be a 'protected act' under EA 2010, s 27(2)(b).

[69] EA 2010, s 34(5).

[70] EA 2010, s 4(4).

[71] EA 2010, s 35(1)(a) (discrimination); s 35(3)(a) (victimisation).

[72] EA 2010, s 35(1)(b) (discrimination); s 35(3)(b) (victimisation).

[73] EA 2010, s 35(1)(c) (discrimination); s 35(3)(c) (victimisation).

[74] EA 2010, s 35(4).

It may be possible, for example, that a manager's restriction on the use of communal facilities **7.35** such as a garden or kitchen by a particular occupier at a particular time might be indirectly discriminatory unless justifiable, or even constitute direct discrimination.

(d) The 'small premises' exception

The obligations not to discriminate against others under sections 33(1),[75] 34(1),[76] and **7.36** 35(1)[77] of the Equality Act 2010 do *not* apply to anything done by a person in relation to the disposal, occupation, or management of part of 'small premises', if (a) the person or a relative[78] of that person resides, and intends to continue to reside, in another part of the premises ('the resident'); and (b) the premises include parts (other than storage and means of access) shared with residents of the premises who are not members of the same household as the resident.[79]

Premises are 'small' for that purpose if (a) the only other persons occupying the accommo- **7.37** dation occupied by the resident are members of the same household; (b) the premises also include accommodation for at least one other household; (c) the accommodation for each of those other households is let, or is available for letting, on a separate tenancy or similar agreement; and (d) the premises are not normally sufficient to accommodate more than two other households.[80] Premises are also small if they are not normally sufficient to provide residential accommodation for more than six persons (in addition to the resident and members of the same household).[81]

This means, for instance, that a Jewish family who own a large house but live in only part **7.38** of it may lawfully let out an unoccupied floor only to a practising Jew or Jews. This avoids the problem of a non-Jewish resident of the house having to share kitchen facilities with the Jewish family, which wishes to keep its food kosher.

Examples from decided cases of discrimination in relation to affording access to premises are **7.39** where a Sikh man was refused entry to licensed premises because he was wearing a turban, which was discrimination because of race,[82] contrary to the now repealed section 21(2) (a) of the Race Relations Act 1976,[83] and where a local authority sought to impose more stringent contract terms on the hiring of council premises for a wedding on the ground that those attending would be gypsies, which was held to be contrary to section 21 of the 1976 Act (as well as section 20).[84] It was also held that section 21 of the Race Relations Act 1976

---

[75] See para 7.30.
[76] See para 7.32.
[77] See para 7.34.
[78] 'Relative' means (a) spouse of civil partner, (b) unmarried partner, (c) parent or grandparent, (d) child or grandchild (whether or not legitimate), (e) the spouse, civil partner, or unmarried partner of a child or grandchild, (f) brother or sister (whether of full blood or half-blood), or (g) a relative within (c), (d), (e), or (f) whose relationship arises as a result of marriage or civil partnership (see EA 2010, Sch 5, para 3(5)). 'Unmarried partner' for those purposes means the other member of a couple consisting of (a) a man and a woman who are not married to each other but are living together as husband and wife, or (b) two people of the same sex who are not civil partners of each other but are living together as if they were (EA 2010, Sch 5, para 3(6)).
[79] EA 2010, Sch 5, para 3(1) and (2).
[80] EA 2010, Sch 5, para 3(3).
[81] EA 2010, Sch 5, para 3(4).
[82] Sikhs had by then been established as a racial group for the purposes of race discrimination: *Mandla v Dowell Lee* [1983] 2 AC 548.
[83] *Gurmit Singh Kambo and ors v Nigel Vaulkhard*, The Times, 7 December 1984.
[84] *Hallam v Cheltenham BC*, appealed to the House of Lords on a different point: [2001] 1 WLR 655.

(as well as section 20) applied to prisoners applying for jobs allocated by the Prison Labour Board, because prisoners were a 'section of the public' and the prisoners were 'occupants' of a prison.[85]

(3) Associations

7.40 Historically, discrimination in the process of obtaining membership of a private club was held to lie outside the scope of section 20 of the Race Relations Act 1976 or section 29 of the Sex Discrimination Act 1975.[86] However, subject to the important exception for 'single characteristic associations' discussed later,[87] 'associations' are now subject to a range of obligations not to discriminate against others because of religion or belief. An 'association' for that purpose is an association of persons (a) which has at least 25 members,[88] and (b) admission to membership[89] of which is regulated by the association's rules and involves a process of selection.[90] It does not matter for definitional purposes whether an association is incorporated or whether its activities are carried out for profit.[91]

7.41 Obligations apply in relation to persons seeking membership, members, associates, and guests. There is no provision rendering unlawful harassment on the part of associations relating to religion or belief (although there is prohibition of harassment in relation to all other protected characteristics save sexual orientation).[92]

(a) Persons seeking membership

7.42 An association must not discriminate against or victimize a person (a) in the arrangements it makes for deciding who to admit for membership;[93] (b) as to the terms on which it is prepared to admit a person to membership;[94] or (c) by not accepting a person's application for membership.[95] So, for example, a gentlemen's club refusing to accept a man's application for membership, or charging him a higher subscription rate, because he is a Rastafarian will commit direct discrimination. Or a cricket club might commit indirect discrimination by only holding trials on Saturdays, precluding the attendance of Jewish candidates, unless the practice was justified, for instance because no other day of the week was found to be satisfactory for a trial day.

(b) Members

7.43 An association must not discriminate against or victimize a member (a) in the way it affords the member access, or by not affording the member access, to a benefit, facility or service;[96] (b) by depriving the member of membership;[97] (c) by varying the member's terms of

---

[85] *Alexander v Secretary of State for the Home Department* [1985] CLY 1669, appealed at [1988] 1 WLR 968 but only in relation to quantum.

[86] *Charter v Race Relations Board* [1973] AC 868.

[87] See paras 7.49 and 7.50.

[88] Note that a Minister of the Crown may by order amend this number (see EA 2010, s 107(3)).

[89] 'Membership' means membership of any description (EA 2010, s 107(5)).

[90] EA 2010, s 107(2). It is no longer a characteristic of an 'association' that 'admission to membership is so conducted that the members do not constitute a section of the public': see the old Race Relations Act 1976, s 25(1)(b) and *Ashan v Watt* [2007] UKHL 51, [2008] 1 AC 696.

[91] EA 2010, s 107(4).

[92] EA 2010, s 103(2).

[93] EA 2010, s 101(1)(a) and (5)(a) ('discrimination' and 'victimisation', respectively).

[94] EA 2010, s 101(1)(b) and (5)(b).

[95] EA 2010, s 101(1)(c) and (5)(c).

[96] EA 2010, s 101(2)(a) and (6)(a).

[97] EA 2010, s 101(2)(b) and (6)(b).

membership;[98] or (d) by subjecting the member to any other detriment.[99] A private members club expelling a member because she has brought religious discrimination proceedings against it under the Equality Act 2010 will commit victimization, for example.

Terms of admission to membership of the British National Party, said to be unlawful by   **7.44** the Commission for Equality and Human Rights, was addressed by the Divisional Court in failed committal proceedings in *Commission for Equality and Human Rights v Nicholas Griffin and ors.*[100]

(c) Associates

A person is an 'associate' in relation to an association, if, the person (a) is not a member of the   **7.45** association, but (b) in accordance with the association's rules, has some or all of the rights as a member as a result of being a member of another association. An example is a member of private members club X, who benefits from 'reciprocal arrangements' at club Y, allowing her to take hospitality at the latter. The member of club X is an associate of club Y.

An association must not discriminate against or victimize an associate (a) in the way it affords   **7.46** the associate access, or by not affording the associate access, to a benefit, facility or service;[101] (b) by depriving the associate of their rights as an associate;[102] (c) by varying the associate's rights as an associate;[103] (d) by subjecting the associate to any other detriment.[104] Thus, following from the example in paragraph 7.45, it is no more open to club Y to prohibit the member of club X from enjoying her hospitality rights at club Y because she had made a religious discrimination complaint against club Y, than it would be open to club X to do the same were her complaint to have been made against club X.

(d) Guests

An association must not discriminate against or victimize a person (a) in the arrangements   **7.47** it makes for deciding who to invite, or who to permit to be invited, as a guest;[105] (b) as to the terms on which it is prepared to invite that person, or to permit that person to be invited, as a guest;[106] or (c) by not inviting that person, or not permitting that person to be invited, as a guest.[107] For example, a requirement that guests comply with the members' dress code may constitute indirect discrimination unless that dress code allows for the wearing of religious dress.

Further, an association must not discriminate against or victimize a guest invited by the   **7.48** association or with the association's permission (whether express or implied) (a) in the way it affords the guest access, or by not affording the guest access, to a benefit, facility or service;[108] or (b) by subjecting the guest to any other detriment.[109]

---

[98] EA 2010, s 101(2)(c) and (6)(c).
[99] EA 2010, s 101(2)(d) and (6)(d).
[100] *Commission for Equality and Human Rights v Nicholas Griffin and ors* [2010] EWHC 3343 (Admin).
[101] EA 2010, s 101(3)(a) and (7)(a) ('victimisation' and 'discrimination', respectively).
[102] EA 2010, s 101(3)(b) and (7)(b).
[103] EA 2010, s 101(3)(c) and (7)(c).
[104] EA 2010, s 101(3)(d) and (7)(d).
[105] EA 2010, s 102(1)(a) and (4)(a).
[106] EA 2010, s 102(1)(b) and (4)(b).
[107] EA 2010, s 102(1)(c) and (4)(c).
[108] EA 2010, s 102(2)(a) and (5)(a).
[109] EA 2010, s 102(2)(b) and (5)(b).

(e) Single characteristic associations

7.49 A religious association may naturally wish to restrict its membership and benefits only to those of a particular religion or belief. This is catered for by paragraph 1 of Schedule 16 to the Equality Act 2010, which makes an exception from the obligations in Part 7 of the Act relating to associations for 'single characteristic associations'. Without breaching the Act, an association (unless it is a registered political party)[110] may:

(1) restrict its membership to persons who share the same religion or belief;[111] and

(2) if it restricts membership in that way: (a) restrict access by associates to a benefit, facility of service to such persons;[112] and (b) invite as guests, or permit to be invited as guests, only such persons.[113]

7.50 It is important to appreciate that the restrictions permitted by Schedule 16 can only be made by reference to a *single* protected characteristic. So, for example, an association's restricting its membership to Christians is lawful, as would be an association's restricting its membership to men only; but it is not lawful for an association to restrict its membership only to Christian men. Associations whose membership is limited only to persons of a particular religion or belief, and which may or may not also restrict associate access and the invitation of guests on the same basis, may not otherwise discriminate in respect of its membership or associate or guest arrangements.

(f) 'Selection arrangements' in political parties

7.51 It is possible that a political party may wish to make arrangements for selecting candidates to run for election which favour those of a particular religion or belief. Whether this is lawful is likely to turn on the type of election in question.

7.52 Section 104 of the Equality Act 2010 makes special provision for associations which are 'registered political parties'. Section 104 of the Equality Act 2010 exempts 'registered political parties' (ie a party registered in the Great Britain register under Part 2 of the Political Parties, Elections and Referendums Act 2000[114]) from the prohibitions in Part 7, where they are acting in accordance with 'selection arrangements'. Selection arrangements, for that purpose, are arrangements (a) which the party makes for regulating the selection of its candidates in a relevant election;[115] (b) the purpose of which is to reduce inequality in the party's representation in the body concerned;[116] and (c) which are a proportionate means of achieving that purpose (although this last requirement does not apply to short-listing[117]).[118]

---

[110] See EA 2010, Sch 16, para 1(5).

[111] EA 2010, Sch 16, para 1(1).

[112] EA 2010, Sch 16, para 1(2).

[113] EA 2010, Sch 16, para 1(3).

[114] EA 2010, s 107(7).

[115] 'Relevant elections' are (a) Parliamentary elections; (b) elections to the European Parliament; (c) elections to the Scottish Parliament; (d) elections to the National Assembly for Wales; (e) local government elections within the meaning of of the Representation of the People Act 1983, s 191, 203, or 204 (excluding elections for the Mayor of London): s 104(8).

[116] 'Inequality in a party's representation in a body' means inequality between (a) the number of the party's candidates elected to be members of the body who share a protected characteristic, and (b) the number of the party's candidates so elected who do not share that characteristic (EA 2010, s 104(4)).

[117] EA 2010, s 104(7).

[118] EA 2010, s 104(3).

Selection arrangements cannot include short-listing only such persons as are of a particular **7.53** religion or belief.[119] However, a qualifying party could choose to reserve a specific number of seats for candidates of a particular under-represented religion or belief in a by-election shortlist. This is because a by-election is not a 'relevant election' under section 104(8) of the Equality Act 2010.[120]

(g) *Charities*

It should also be noted that associations, such as religious associations, are often charities.[121] **7.54** Exemptions from the Equality Act 2010 obligations are conferred upon certain charities in certain circumstances by sections 193 to 194 of the Act. The effect of section 193(1) and (2) is that a person does not breach the Act only by restricting the provision of benefits to persons who share a particular religion or belief if (a) the person acts in pursuance of a charitable instrument;[122] and (b) the provision of the benefits is (i) a proportionate means of achieving a legitimate aim, or (ii) for the purpose of preventing or compensating for a disadvantage linked to the religion or belief.

Further, it is not a contravention of the Equality Act 2010 for a charity to require mem- **7.55** bers, or persons wishing to become members, to make a statement which asserts or implies membership or acceptance of a religion or belief. Restricting access by members to a benefit, facility, or service to those who make such a statement is treated as imposing such a requirement.[123] However, such a requirement is only lawful if (a) the charity, or an organization of which it is part, first imposed such a requirement before 18 May 2005; and (b) the charity or organization has not ceased since that date to impose such a requirement.[124]

In *Catholic Care (Diocese of Leeds) v Charity Commission for England and Wales*,[125] the Upper **7.56** Tribunal held that a Roman Catholic charity had failed to show the 'weighty and convincing reasons' necessary to justify a change to its memorandum of association to enable it to restrict its adoption services to heterosexual couples under the exemption in section 193 of the Equality Act 2010. Sales J accepted that the change had the legitimate aim of seeking to place more children with adoptive families overall (because, if allowed, the charity would be able to attract private funding and provide free services additional to those of the local authority), but considered that this was not a material probability. The possibility of free services was not in any event sufficient to discharge the heavy onus on the charity to show that its proposed discrimination would be objectively justified.

(4) The 'religious organisations' exception

The exceptions which have so far been addressed in this chapter have related to specific provi- **7.57** sions preventing discrimination on religious grounds. More widely, however, paragraph 2 of

---

[119] EA 2010, s 104(6).

[120] See n 116.

[121] A 'Charity' for this purpose has the meaning given in s 1 of the Charities Act 2011 (EA 2010, s 194(3) (a)). Charitable status is addressed at Ch 12, paras 12.47 ff.

[122] 'Charitable instrument' means an instrument establishing or governing a charity (EA 2010, s 194(4)). 'Charity', in relation to England and Wales, has the meaning given by s 1(1) of the Charities Act 2011, and, in relation to Scotland, means a body entered in the Scottish Charity Register (EA 2010, s 194(3)).

[123] EA 2010, s 193(5).

[124] EA 2010, s 193(6).

[125] *Catholic Care (Diocese of Leeds) v Charity Commission for England and Wales* [2012] Eq LR 1119.

Schedule 23 to the Equality Act 2010 provides for exceptions from obligations in Parts 3, 4, and 7 of the Act for a religious 'organisation', so far as they prevent discrimination because of religion or belief or sexual orientation. This is an organization, the sole or main purpose of which must not be commercial,[126] and the purpose of which is any one or more of the following:

(1) to practise a religion or belief;[127]
(2) to advance a religion or belief;[128]
(3) to teach the practice or principles of a religion or belief;[129]
(4) to enable persons of a religion or belief to receive any benefit, or to engage in any activity, within the framework of that religion or belief;[130]
(5) to foster or maintain good relations between persons of different religions or beliefs.[131]

7.58 An organization falling within the definition set out at paragraph 7.57, is to be contrasted with an 'association' as defined in Part 7 of the 2010 Act, which may not exist for any of the aforementioned purposes (and would therefore not fall within the definition) but may still be connected to religion or belief in some way (for example a purely social club whose members are all of a single religion). Subject to the 'single characteristic' exception discussed earlier,[132] such an association will still be subject to the obligations under Parts 3, 4, and 7 of the Act from which the previously mentioned organizations are exempted.

7.59 In contrast, an organization falling within the aforementioned definition, or a person acting on behalf of or under the auspices of the organization,[133] does not breach Part 3, 4, or 7, as far as these relate to religion or belief or sexual orientation, only by restricting:

(1) membership of the organization;[134]
(2) participation in activities undertaken by the organization or on its behalf or under its auspices;[135]
(3) the provision of goods, facilities, or services in the course of activities undertaken by the organization or on its behalf or under its auspices;[136]
(4) the use or disposal[137] of premises owned or controlled by the organisation.[138]

---

[126] EA 2010, Sch 23, para 2(2).
[127] EA 2010, Sch 23, para 2(1)(a).
[128] EA 2010, Sch 23, para 2(1)(b).
[129] EA 2010, Sch 23, para 2(1)(c).
[130] EA 2010, Sch 23, para 2(1)(d).
[131] EA 2010, Sch 23, para 2(1)(e). Organizations qualifying by sole dint of having such a purpose do not benefit from the exceptions set out in para 2 to the Schedule insofar as it applies in relation to sexual orientation: see Sch 23, para 2(11).
[132] See paras 7.49 and 7.50.
[133] EA 2010, Sch 23, para 2(4).
[134] EA 2010, Sch 23, para 2(3)(a). Cf the lawful requirement that members of an 'association' within the meaning of EA 2010, Pt 7 shall be only of a certain religion or belief.
[135] EA 2010, Sch 23, para 2(3)(b).
[136] EA 2010, Sch 23, para 2(3)(c).
[137] 'Disposal' is to be construed in accordance with EA 2010, s 38: see further n 58. However, in its application in relation to sexual orientation, 'disposal' does not here include disposal of an interest in premises by way of sale if the interest being disposed of is (a) the entirety of the organization's interest in the premises, or (b) the entirety of the interest in respect of which the organization has power of disposal (EA 2010, Sch 23, para 2(12)).
[138] EA 2010, Sch 23, para 2(3)(d).

Further, a minister[139] does not contravene Part 3, 4, or 7, so far as these relate to religion or **7.60** belief or sexual orientation, only by restricting:

(1) participation in activities carried on in the performance of the minister's functions in connection with or in respect of the organization;[140]

(2) the provision of goods, facilities, or services in the course of activities carried on in the performance of the minister's functions in connection with or in respect of the organization.[141]

However, a restriction described previously relating to organizations (and persons acting on **7.61** their behalf) and ministers is lawful only:

(1) relating to *religion or belief*, if it is imposed (a) because of the purpose of the organization, or (b) to avoid causing offence, on grounds of the religion or belief to which the organization relates, to persons of that religion or belief;[142]

(2) relating to *sexual orientation*, if it is imposed (a) because it is necessary to comply with the doctrine of the organization, or (b) to avoid conflict with 'strongly held convictions'.[143] In the case of a religion, 'strongly held convictions' mean the strongly held religious convictions of a significant number of the religion's followers; and in the case of a belief, refer to the strongly held convictions relating to the belief of a significant number of the belief's followers.[144]

So, for example, it would not be unlawful sexual orientation discrimination for a church to refuse to let out its hall for a Gay Pride celebration if this would conflict with the strongly held convictions of a significant number of its followers.

The legislation nevertheless recognizes that a public authority should not be able to avoid **7.62** its obligation not to discriminate in the exercise of public functions by hiding behind the exemptions given to religious organisations. Paragraph 2 of Schedule 23 to the Equality Act 2010 does not permit anything prohibited by section 29 of the Act,[145] so far as this relates to sexual orientation, if it is done (a) on behalf of a public authority, and (b) under the terms of a contract between the organization and the public authority.[146]

D. Procedure and Remedies

Subject to certain limited exceptions,[147] a county court or, in Scotland, the sheriff, has juris- **7.63** diction to determine a claim relating to a contravention of Parts 3, 4, and/or 7.[148] However,

---

[139] This means a minister of religion, or other person, who (a) performs functions in connection with a religion or belief to which the organization relates, and (b) holds an office or appointment in, or is accredited, approved or recognized for the purposes of the organization (see EA 2010, Sch 23, para 2(8)).

[140] EA 2010, Sch 23, para 2(5)(a).

[141] EA 2010, Sch 23, para 2(5)(b).

[142] EA 2010, Sch 23, para 2(6).

[143] EA 2010, Sch 23, para 2(7).

[144] EA 2010, Sch 23, para 2(9).

[145] See paras 7.07 ff.

[146] EA 2010, Sch 23, para 2(10).

[147] EA 2010, s 114(2) and (3).

[148] EA 2010, s 114(1)(a), (b), and (d).

that jurisdiction does not, for example, prevent a claim for judicial review,[149] or, in Scotland, an application to the supervisory jurisdiction of the Court of Session,[150] in appropriate cases.

7.64 Such a claim may generally not be brought after the end of (a) the period of six months starting with the date of the act to which the claim relates, or (b) such other period as the county court or sheriff thinks just and equitable.[151]

7.65 There is a presumption that a judge or sheriff will appoint an assessor to assist the court when hearing discrimination cases.[152] However, an assessor need not be appointed where there are good reasons not to (for example after an assessment of the judge's own level of experience, the nature of the case, and the wishes of the claimant).

7.66 If a county court finds that there has been a contravention of Part 3, 4, and/or 7, it has power to grant any remedy which could be granted by the High Court in proceedings in tort, and/or on a claim for judicial review.[153] Similarly, a sheriff in Scotland has power to make any order which could be made by the Court of Session in proceedings for reparation or on a petition for judicial review.[154]

7.67 An award of damages may include compensation for injured feelings (whether or not it includes compensation on any other basis).[155] If the county court or sheriff finds that there was indirect discrimination within the meaning of section 19 of the Equality Act 2010,[156] but is satisfied that the provision, criterion, or practice was not applied with the *intention* of discriminating against the claimant or pursuer, the court or sheriff must not make an award of damages unless it first considers whether to make any other disposal.[157]

---

[149] EA 2010, s 113(3)(a).
[150] EA 2010, s 113(3)(d).
[151] EA 2010, s 118.
[152] EA 2010, s 114(7) and (8).
[153] EA 2010, s 119(2).
[154] EA 2010, s 119(3).
[155] EA 2010, s 119(4).
[156] See further Ch 6, paras 6.71–6.93.
[157] EA 2010, s 119(5) and (6).

8

RELIGION AND EMPLOYMENT

A. Introduction

This chapter explores the protections for religious rights in the employment context. **8.01**

Parts B and C begin by providing an overview of the legal framework for the protection of **8.02** religious rights in this area, which principally comprises discrimination law and the law of unfair dismissal against the background of rights guaranteed by the European Convention on Human Rights and Fundamental Freedoms as scheduled to the Human Rights Act 1998.

Parts D to G consider specific issues that have arisen in the work context. Religious rights **8.03** may be engaged in the workplace in a number of ways. An employee may seek to manifest his religion or religious beliefs, for example, by wearing religious dress at work or by taking time off work for religious observance. This may conflict with his contractual duties or the policies and practices of the employer, or may otherwise impinge on the employer's commercial or economic interests. It may also affect the rights and interests of other employees and the wider community. The question in these cases is usually the extent to which an employer should accommodate the right of an employee to manifest his or her beliefs. In some cases the law provides a clear answer. For example, shop workers may opt out of Sunday working and dismissal by an employer on these grounds is automatically unfair; another example is the exception Sikhs enjoy from legal requirements relating to the wearing of safety helmets.

In most cases, however, courts and tribunals are left to adjudicate among the different interests involved.

8.04 The religious rights of employers may also be engaged. The law affords protection to a person refused a job because of his sex; however, a mosque may want to employ an imam who is male in accordance with Islamic teaching. Discrimination law seeks to protect the religious rights of employers by carving out limited religious-based exceptions to the non-discrimination provisions. These and other protections are considered in part H.

8.05 Finally, part I provides an overview of the procedure in the employment tribunal and the remedies available.

B. Discrimination Law

(1) Introduction

8.06 Discrimination law protects religious rights in the work context in broadly three ways:

8.07 First, the law prohibits discrimination, victimization, and harassment on grounds of 'religion or belief' and affords remedies to the victims of such conduct.[1] The concepts of 'discrimination' (direct and indirect), 'victimisation', and 'harassment' are considered in Chapter 6, as is the definition of 'religion or belief'. Provisions relating to discrimination, victimization, and harassment in the work context can be found in Part 5 of the Equality Act 2010.

8.08 Secondly, the law permits positive action by employers in connection with recruitment or promotion in order to alleviate disadvantage suffered by persons connected with their religion or belief and/or to enable or encourage persons with a particular religion or belief to participate in an activity in which they are under-represented.[2]

8.09 Thirdly, there are religious-based exceptions to the non-discrimination provisions. For example, discrimination on grounds of sex and sexual orientation is not unlawful where employment is for the purposes of an organized religion. This and other relevant exceptions are set out in Schedule 9 to the Equality Act 2010 and are considered in more detail in part H below.

8.10 This part begins by setting out the legislation preceding the Equality Act 2010 under which much of the relevant case law has been decided.

(2) Legislative history

8.11 The Equality Act 2010 repealed and replaced previous discrimination legislation with a new harmonized scheme. The law relating to religious discrimination in the employment field was previously to be found in the Employment Equality (Religion or Belief) Regulations 2003 as amended by the Equality Act 2006, with the religious-based exceptions spread across various pieces of legislation, including the Employment Equality (Sexual Orientation Regulations) 2003.

---

[1] Some religious groups—principally Sikhs and Jews—also qualify as a 'racial group' within the meaning of the Equality Act 2010, s 9 (previously, the Race Relations Act 1976). See Ch 6, para 6.05 and paras 6.46–6.52. Religious groups that qualify as a racial group can, and do, rely on the race discrimination provisions for the protection of their religious rights: see eg *Dhinsa v Serco* ET 1315002/2009 (18 May 2011).

[2] Equality Act 2010, s 159. See Ch 6, paras 6.133–6.136.

Before the Employment Equality (Religion or Belief) Regulations 2003 came into force on 2 **8.12**
December 2003, 'religion or belief' was not a protected characteristic in discrimination law.[3]
Discrimination, victimization, and harassment were prohibited only on grounds of sex, race,
and disability.[4] Religious interests were protected only to the extent they fell within the scope
of race discrimination laws.[5] The impetus to extend discrimination law to cover 'religion or
belief' came from the European Union.

(a) Council Directive (EC) 2000/78

The Treaty of Amsterdam entered into force on 1 May 1999 giving the Council of Ministers **8.13**
new powers to combat discrimination, including a power to 'take appropriate action to
combat discrimination based on sex, racial or ethnic origin, religion or belief, disability, age
or sexual orientation'.[6]

Acting pursuant to this power, the Council adopted Directive (EC) 2000/78 (hereinafter **8.14**
'the Employment Directive') the purpose of which, by Article 1, was 'to lay down a general
framework for combating discrimination on the grounds of religion or belief, disability, age
or sexual orientation as regards employment and occupation, with a view to putting into
effect in the Member States the principle of equal treatment'.[7]

The Employment Directive is not simply a matter of historical interest, since domestic legis- **8.15**
lation must, so far as possible, be construed to give effect to the Directive.[8]

The following provisions are of particular note: **8.16**

(1) Article 2(1) provides that the principle of equal treatment means that 'there shall be
    no direct or indirect discrimination whatsoever on any of the grounds referred to in
    Article 1'. Article 2(2) and (3) goes on to define direct and indirect discrimination and
    harassment. Article 2(5) provides that the Employment Directive 'shall be without prej-
    udice to measures laid down by national law which, in a democratic society, are necessary
    for public security, for the maintenance of public order and the prevention of criminal

---

[3] In the education context, Education Act 1944, s 30 was considered to be essentially a non-discrimination
provision, protecting teachers from being penalized for their religious beliefs: see *Ahmad v Inner London
Education Authority* [1977] 3 WLR 396 (CA). The equivalent provision is now to be found in the School
Standards and Framework Act 1998, s 59. This and other relevant provisions are considered in more detail in
part C of this chapter.

[4] Sex Discrimination Act 1975; Race Relations Act 1976, Pt 2; and the Disability Discrimination Act
1995, Pt 2.

[5] Some religious groups—principally Jews and Sikhs—were afforded a degree of protection under the Race
Relations Act 1976 on the basis that they were mono-ethnic and qualified as a racial group within the meaning
of the Act: see *Seide v Gillette Industries* [1980] IRLR 427 (EAT); *Mandla v Dowell Lee* [1983] 2 AC 548 (HL).

[6] Treaty of Amsterdam, Art 13. Now TFEU, Art 19. The Treaty of Amsterdam also affirmed in unequivocal
terms that '[t]he Union is founded on the principles of liberty, democracy, respect for human rights and fundamental freedoms, and the rule of law, principles which are common to the Member States' (TEU, Art 6). For a
detailed exposition of the development of fundamental rights in the EU, see Ch 3, part B.

[7] Council Directive (EC) 2000/78 of 27 November 2000. The Directive is wider in scope than the
Employment Equality (Religion or Belief) Regulations 2003, which concern only discrimination on grounds
of 'religion or belief'. The UK had already introduced legislation dealing with discrimination on grounds of
disability (Disability Discrimination Act 1995). The Employment Equality (Sexual Orientation) Regulations
2003, SI 2003/1661 made discrimination on the grounds of sexual orientation unlawful, and discrimination on the grounds of age was later covered by the Employment Equality (Age) Regulations 2006, SI
2006/1031: *Hashwani v Jivraj* [2011] 1 WLR 1872 (SC), para 10.

[8] See eg Case C-106/89 *Marleasing SA v La Comercial Internacional de Alimentacion SA* [1990] ECR I-4135,
ECJ; *Hashwani* (n 7) para 8.

offences, for the protection of health and for the protection of the rights and freedom of others'.[9]

(2) Article 3(1) states that the Employment Directive applies to all persons, in both the public and private sectors, including public bodies, in relation to:

(a) conditions for access to employment, to self-employment or to occupation, including selection criteria and recruitment conditions, whatever the branch of activity and at all levels of the professional hierarchy, including promotion;

(b) access to all types and to all levels of vocational guidance, vocational training, advanced vocational training and retraining, including practical work experience;

(c) employment and working conditions, including dismissals and pay;

(d) membership of, and involvement in, an organisation of workers or employers, or any organisation whose members carry on a particular profession, including the benefits provided for by such organisations.

(3) Article 4 makes provision for exceptions to the non-discrimination provisions based on occupational requirements. Article 4 is set out and considered in detail in part H of this chapter.

(4) Article 7 provides that the principle of equal treatment shall not prevent Member States from maintaining or adopting measures to prevent or compensate for disadvantages linked to any of the specified grounds.

(5) Article 11 makes provision for victimization.

8.17 The provisions of the Employment Directive (and the domestic legislation made thereunder) are to be interpreted in the light of the recitals and given their natural meaning consistent with the EC Treaty and the case law of the European Court of Justice.[10]

(b) Domestic legislation

8.18 The Employment Equality (Religion or Belief) Regulations 2003 were introduced to transpose the provisions of Council Directive (EC) 2000/78 ('the Employment Directive'), prohibiting for the first time discrimination, victimization, and harassment on grounds of 'religion or belief'.

8.19 The 2003 Regulations made it unlawful for employers to discriminate against applicants and employees on grounds of religion or belief.[11] This was subject to two exceptions which broadly emulated Article 4 of the Employment Directive. First, it was not unlawful to discriminate on grounds of religion or belief where being of a particular religion or belief was a genuine and determining occupational requirement. Secondly, there would be no discrimination where the employer had an ethos based on religion or belief and being of a particular religion or belief was a genuine occupational requirement.

---

[9] In *Azmi v Kirklees Metropolitan Borough Council* [2007] ICR 1154 (EAT), para 42 the EAT noted that 'article 2(5) replicates, in virtually identical terms, article 9(2) of the European Convention on Human Rights, article 9(1) of which protects the right to freedom of thought, conscience and religion'. The EAT went onto observe at para 47 that there was no equivalent in the 2003 Regulations of Art 2(5) replicating ECHR, Art 9(2). In *Islington LBC v Ladele* [2010] 1 WLR 955 (CA), para 22 the Court of Appeal held that Art 2(5), particularly in the light of Recitals (1) and (4) of the Preamble, suggests that the Employment Directive and any domestic legislation made thereunder should be read in conformity with the ECHR. It was acknowledged that any such legislation would have, if possible, to be read in any event in conformity with Art 9 by virtue of HRA 1998, s 3.

[10] *Hashwani* (n 7).

[11] The Employment Equality (Religion or Belief) Regulations 2003, SI 2003/1660, reg 6. The 2003 Regulations in fact covered a range of work relationships beyond the conventional employer–employee relationship, including contract workers, office holders, and barristers, among others.

At the same time the law was extended to cover discrimination on grounds of sexual ori- **8.20**
entation by the Employment Equality (Sexual Orientation) Regulations 2003, which also
implemented the provisions of the Employment Directive. This had implications for some
religious groups who believed that homosexual practice was contrary to their religious teachings with the regulations potentially imposing duties which were inconsistent with the practice of those beliefs.

A limited exemption from the non-discrimination provisions was introduced to accomodate **8.21**
religious beliefs concerning sexual orientation. It applied where employment was for the
purposes of an organized religion, emulating a similar provision in the Sex Discrimination
Act 1975.[12] The other exception was more generally drawn and applied where being of a
particular sexual orientation was a genuine and determining occupational requirement. The
validity of these provisions was challenged unsuccessfully in *R (Amicus) v Secretary of State
for Trade and Industry*, where it was held that the exceptions were not incompatible with
the Employment Directive.[13] It was, however, emphasized that the exceptions were to be
construed strictly.

The exceptions in both the Employment Equality (Religion or Belief) Regulations 2003 and **8.22**
the Employment Equality (Sexual Orientation) Regulations 2003 were carried forward into
the Equality Act 2010, and are considered in more detail in part H.

(3) Who and what is protected?

Part 5 of the Equality Act 2010 prohibits discrimination, victimization, and harassment on **8.23**
grounds of 'religion or belief' in the work context. It protects employees and job applicants,
imposing obligations on employers in respect of recruitment, the terms of employment
offered, access to promotion and other opportunities, and dismissal. It also covers a range
of work relationships beyond employment, extending protection to contract workers, barristers, and office-holders among others.

(a) Employees and applicants

The persons protected under the Equality Act 2010 include: (a) employees; (b) job appli- **8.24**
cants, including prospective applicants;[14] and (c) former employees where the discrimination or harassment arises out of and is closely connected to the former employment.[15]

Definition of employment. 'Employment' is defined in section 83(2) of the Equality Act **8.25**
2010 and includes 'employment under a contract of employment, a contract of apprenticeship or a contract personally to do work'.[16]

---

[12] Sex Discrimination Act 1975, s 19.

[13] *R (Amicus) v Secretary of State for Trade and Industry* [2007] ICR 1176.

[14] Employers are under an obligation not to discriminate against or victimize a person in the arrangements
they make for deciding whom to offer employment: Equality Act 2010, s 39(1) and (3). See further para 8.34.

[15] Equality Act 2010, s 108. It is clear that former employees are protected against post-termination discrimination and harassment: see Equality Act 2010, s 108(1) and (2). However, there is some uncertainty about
whether the protection extends to post-termination victimization: see the Equality Act 2010, s 108(7) and the
two conflicting decisions of the EAT in *Rowstock Ltd v Jessemey* [2013] IRLR 439 (EAT) and *Onu v Akwiwu*
[2013] IRLR 523 (EAT), both of which are being appealed.

[16] Equality Act 2010, s 83(2)(a). References to employer, employee, or to employing or being employed in
Pt 5 are to be read accordingly: Equality Act 2010, s 83(4). The definition of 'employment' in the Employment
Equality (Religion or Belief) Regulations 2003, s 2(3), was almost identical: ' "employment" means employ-
ment under a contract of service or of apprenticeship or a contract personally to do any work'.

8.26 The definition encompasses a wider range of persons than the unfair dismissal provisions, which are limited to persons engaged under a contract of employment, meaning a contract of service or apprenticeship.[17] Discrimination law extends protection to those engaged under 'a contract personally to do work'. In *Hashwani* the Supreme Court made clear that this did not encompass all those engaged under a contract for the provision of services.[18] The definition referred to 'employment under' a contract personally to do work. Drawing on the jurisprudence of the European Court of Justice,[19] the Supreme Court stated that the essential question in each case was whether a person performed services for and under the direction of another in return for which he or she receives remuneration, or whether he or she was an independent provider of services not in a relationship of sub-ordination with the person who receives the services. The latter would not be engaged in employment under a contract personally to do work for the purposes of the Employment Equality (Religion or Belief) Regulations 2003. It was held that this would remain the correct approach to the definition of employment in the Equality Act 2010.[20]

8.27 In this way discrimination legislation protects an intermediate class of person between those engaged under a contract of service and those who work for themselves/carry on business on their own account. It has been said in other contexts that such persons may be vulnerable to exploitation because of their subordinate position and may be in need of protection against inequality and discrimination.[21]

8.28 In *Hashwani* it was argued that an arbitration clause requiring the arbitrator appointed to be a member of the Ismaili community was discriminatory. The Supreme Court held that the 2003 Regulations did not apply since an arbitrator's role was that of an independent provider of services not in a relationship of subordination with the parties who received his services. It followed that an arbitrator was not engaged in employment under a contract personally to do work within the meaning of the 2003 Regulations.

8.29 Ministers of religion have been held to be employees employed both under a contract of service[22] and a contract personally to do work.[23] Historically, ministers of religion were generally held not to be employees on the basis that the relationship between a church and minister of religion was not contractual.[24] There were broadly two strands of reasoning. First, it was thought that, having been appointed to an ecclesiastical office, Ministers were office holders rather than employees whose functions were defined by contract.[25] Secondly, the special features of the arrangement between the church and minister, including the spiritual nature of the duties of a minister of religion, were thought to be

---

[17] Employment Rights Act 1996, s 230(1) and (2).

[18] *Hashwani* (n 7).

[19] In particular Case C-256/01 *Allonby v Accrington and Rossendale College* [2004] ECR I-873, an equal pay claim, in which the Court of Justice considered the concept of 'worker' within the meaning of the EC Treaty, Art 141(1).

[20] *Hashwani* (n 7) para 27.

[21] See eg Court of Appeal in Northern Ireland in *Perceval-Price v Department of Economic Development* [2000] IRLR 380 (an equal pay claim) and the Employment Appeal Tribunal in *Byrne Bros (Formworks) Ltd v Baird* [2002] IRLR 96 (a case under the Working Time Regulations 1998).

[22] See eg *New Testament Church of God v Stewart* [2008] ICR 282 (CA).

[23] *Percy v Board of National Mission of the Church of Scotland* [2006] 2 AC 28 (HL).

[24] For previous authorities, see *President of the Methodist Conference v Parfitt* [1984] QB 368 (CA); *Davies v Presbyterian Church of Wales* [1986] 1 WLR 323 (HL); *Diocese of Southwark v Coker* [1998] ICR 140 (CA).

[25] *Re National Insurance Act 1911* [1912] 2 Ch 563; *Scottish Insurance Comrs v Church of Scotland* 1914 SC 16.

inconsistent with the existence of a contractual relationship.[26] There was thought to be a presumption, albeit rebuttable, against an intention to create legal relations between ministers and a church.[27]

The decision of the House of Lords in *Percy v Board of National Mission of the Church of Scotland* marked an important shift in approach. A minister of the Church of Scotland brought a claim for sex discrimination after action was taken against her for having an extra-marital affair, when similar action had not been taken against male ministers. By a majority the House of Lords held that she was employed under a contract personally to execute work within the meaning of 'employment' under the Sex Discrimination Act 1975.[28] The majority held that holding an office and being an employee were not inconsistent.[29] Importantly, the case has also been taken as signalling the abandonment of the presumption against an intention to create legal relations.[30] Lord Nicholls stated that, given the context in which the issues normally arise today (statutory protection for employees), it was time to recognize that employment arrangements between a church and its ministers should not lightly be taken as intended to have no legal effect.[31] Lord Hope took the view that a presumption was tantamount to contracting out of the protection afforded by the discrimination legislation, which was not permitted.[32] In holding that there was no general presumption against an intention to create legal relations, Baroness Hale stated that she found it 'difficult to discern any difference in principle between the duties of the clergy appointed to minister to our spiritual needs, of the doctors appointed to minister to our bodily needs, and of the judges appointed to administer the law, in this respect'.[33]

8.30

This does not mean that the spiritual nature of the work of a minister is irrelevant. In *New Testament Church of God v Stewart*, Pill LJ emphasized that, although a spiritual motivation in working for a church does not necessarily preclude an intention to create legal relations, the spiritual nature of the work and the spiritual discipline under which it is performed remain relevant considerations when it is to be decided whether there is a contractual relationship.[34] This includes the religious beliefs held in a church, which may throw light on the nature of the relationship between it and its ministers.[35] In *Preston v President of the Methodist*

8.31

---

[26] *Davies* (n 24). See also *President of the Methodist Conference v Parfitt* [1984] QB 368 (CA).

[27] *Diocese of Southwark v Coker* [1998] ICR 140 (CA).

[28] *Percy* (n 23). The contract was with the Church of Scotland Board of National Mission and not 'the Church of Scotland'. Although the Church itself had a distinctive identity, it did not have the capacity to own any property or to enter into contracts in its own name. Ms Percy accepted that she did not enter into a contract of service.

[29] *Percy* (n 23) para 20 *per* Lord Nicholls; para 87 *per* Lord Hope; paras 142–143 *per* Baroness Hale.

[30] See *New Testament Church of God* (n 22), para 35; and *Preston v President of the Methodist Conference* [2013] 2 WLR 1350 (SC), paras 10, 26, and 30.

[31] *Percy* (n 23) para 20.

[32] *Percy* (n 23) paras 106–108.

[33] *Percy* (n 23) para 151. See also para 148.

[34] *New Testament Church of God* (n 22) paras 35 and 36. At para 64, Arden LJ emphasized that the weight to be given to such considerations depended on the overall assessment of the evidence.

[35] *New Testament Church of God* (n 22) paras 48, 61, and 66. The Court considered the Art 9 implications of imposing an employment relationship in circumstances where this was inconsistent with the religious beliefs held. Arden LJ held that Art 9 would be engaged, one aspect of freedom of religion being the right of a religious organization to be allowed to function peacefully and free from arbitrary state intervention. However, Lawrence Collins LJ doubted that imposing an employment relationship in this way could be regarded as a limitation on, or interference with, the right under Art 9. In *Preston v President of the Methodist Conference* [2012] QB 735 (CA). Maurice LJ agreed with Lawrence Collins LJ, taking the view that the potential role of Art 9 in such cases was modest.

Conference, Lord Sumption, with whom Lord Wilson and Lord Carnwarth agreed, held that the primary considerations in deciding whether a minister of religion served under a contract of employment are the manner in which the minister was engaged and the character of the rules or terms governing his or her service. He emphasized that, as with all exercises in contractual construction, these documents fall to be construed against their factual background, and part of that background is the fundamentally spiritual purpose of the functions of a minister of religion.[36]

8.32   As for the position of unremunerated volunteers, in *X v Mid Sussex Citizens' Advice Bureau* it was held that a volunteer working at the Citizens' Advice Bureau did not fall within the ambit of the Disability Discrimination Act 1995 when read together with Directive (EC) 2000/78.[37] The Supreme Court rejected an argument that the reference to 'occupation' in Article 3(1)(a) of the Directive covered voluntary work.[38]

8.33   The definition of 'employment' in section 83(2) of the Equality Act 2010 explicitly includes Crown employment and employment as a relevant member of the House of Commons and House of Lords staff.[39] The Act makes clear that Part 5 applies to service in the armed forces as it applies to employment by a private person[40] and makes specific provision for police cadets and police constables.[41]

8.34   Finally, it should be noted that, like its predecessors, section 39 of the Equality Act 2010 prohibits an employer from discriminating against or victimizing 'a person ... in the arrangements ... [it] makes for deciding whom to offer employment'. This has the potential to capture and extend protection to prospective job applicants. If an employer creates a position or positions (such as a volunteer post or internship) with the sole or dominant purpose of deciding to whom it should offer employment, the position may constitute a relevant arrangement within the meaning of section 39.[42] It would follow that the person holding that position would enjoy protection under the Act.

---

[36]   *Preston* (n 30) para 10. See also paras 26 and 33–35.

[37]   *X v Mid Sussex Citizens' Advice Bureau* [2013] 1 All ER 1038 (SC). It was common ground that had the claimant been protected, she and other similarly placed volunteer workers would also be protected from discrimination on the other grounds identified in the Directive, including religion or belief: *X v Mid Sussex Citizens' Advice Bureau* [2011] ICR 460 (CA) para 2.

[38]   The concept of 'occupation' is not found in domestic discrimination legislation. It was accepted by the appellant that if the post fell within the scope of the Directive, it could only be given effect either by interpreting domestic legislation in accordance with the Directive, or by giving direct effect to the Directive.

[39]   Equality Act 2010, s 83(2)(b)–(d).

[40]   Equality Act 2010, s 83(3).

[41]   Equality Act 2010, s 42. This identifies the employer, for the purposes of Pt 5, as the chief officer and/or responsible authority (both defined by s 43).

[42]   See *X v Mid Sussex Citizens' Advice Bureau* [2011] ICR 460 (CA), in which the Court of Appeal rejected an argument that a volunteer post at the Citizens' Advice Bureau was such an arrangement. It held that the purpose of the arrangement was to secure advisers to provide advice to clients of the Citizens' Advice Bureau, and not to create a potential pool from which full-time staff could be drawn. It observed that most voluntary advisers had no wish to obtain a permanent staff post. Moreover, all paid positions were externally advertised and were open to everyone, not just voluntary advisers. Nor was the purpose of the arrangement to improve the employment prospects of the relatively small proportion of volunteers who might at some future date seek a full-time position. That may be one of the effects or by-products of the arrangement, but it was not its purpose. It should be noted that the word 'purpose' (which appeared in the Disability Discrimination Act 1995 and other predecessor legislation) has been omitted from the Equality Act 2010, s 39(1) and (3). It is, however, unlikely that the omission is of significance.

Discrimination and victimization in recruitment and employment.   The Equality Act 2010   **8.35**
imposes obligations on employers in respect of recruitment and treatment of employees.

In respect of recruitment, an employer (A) must not discriminate against or victimize a   **8.36**
person (B):[43]

   (a)   in the arrangements A makes for deciding whom to offer employment;
   (b)   as to the terms on which A offers employment to B;
   (c)   by not offering B employment.

Arrangements include the policies, criteria, and practices used in the recruitment process as   **8.37**
well as advertisements for jobs, the application process, and the interview stage.[44]

Moreover, an employer (A) must not discriminate against or victimize an employee of   **8.38**
A's (B):[45]

   (a)   as to B's terms of employment,
   (b)   in the way A affords B access, or by not affording B access, to opportunities for promotion,
      transfer or training or for any other benefit, facility or service;[46]
   (c)   by dismissing B;[47]
   (d)   by subjecting B to any other detriment.

For the purposes of establishing 'detriment', it is not necessary to demonstrate some physical   **8.39**
or economic consequence. The question whether an employee has been subjected to detriment is not an entirely subjective one; the question is whether the treatment is of such a kind
that a reasonable worker would or might take the view that in all the circumstances it was to
his detriment.[48]

Harassment of employees and applicants.   It is unlawful for an employer to harass his employ-   **8.40**
ees and those who have applied for employment.[49]

An employer is also liable for harassment of its employees and applicants by third parties.[50]   **8.41**
A third party is any person other than the employer himself or another employee, for example customers or clients.[51] An employer's liability arises where:

(1)   the employee/applicant is harassed by the third party in the course of their
    employment;[52]

---

[43]   Equality Act 2010, s 39(1) (discrimination) and (3) (victimisation).
[44]   Equality and Human Rights Commission, Employment Statutory Code of Practice (2011) para 10.8.
[45]   Equality Act 2010, s 39(2) (discrimination) and (4) (victimisation).
[46]   Note the exception in Equality Act 2010, Sch 9, Pt 3, para 19 where the employer offers a benefit, facility,
or service of the same description to the public.
[47]   The reference to dismissing B includes termination of employment through the expiry of a fixed-term
contract (unless immediately after termination the employment is renewed on the same terms) and constructive
dismissal: see Equality Act 2010, s 39(7) and (8).
[48]   *Shamoon v Chief Constable of the Royal Ulster Constabulary* [2003] ICR 337 (HLNI).
[49]   Equality Act 2010, s 40(1). For the definition of 'harassment' see Equality Act 2010, s 26 and see
further Ch 6.
[50]   Equality Act 2010, s 41(2). Previously, such liability existed only under the Sex Discrimination Act 1975.
An employer was not liable for third party harassment under the Employment Equality (Religion or Belief)
Regulations 2003.
[51]   Equality Act 2010, s 40(4). Of course, an employer's liability for harassment by another employee is
covered by s 109(1), which provides that anything done by a person in the course of their employment must be
treated as also done by the employer.
[52]   Equality Act 2010, s 41(2)(a).

(2) the employer has failed to take such steps as would have been reasonably practicable to prevent the harassment;[53]

(3) the employer knows that the employee/applicant has been harassed in the course of their employment on at least two other occasions by the third party. It does not matter whether the third party is the same or different people on each occasion.[54]

8.42 The provisions in the Equality Act 2010 relating to third party harassment of employees have been repealed by the Enterprise and Regulatory Reform Act 2013.[55]

(b) Other work relationships

8.43 The Equality Act 2010 protects a range of relationships in the work context other than employment.

8.44 For example, it is unlawful for a principal to discriminate, victimize, or harass a contract worker.[56] A 'principal' is a person who makes work available for an individual who is employed by another person and supplied by that other person in furtherance of a contract to which the principal is a party.[57] A 'contract worker' is a person supplied to a principal in furtherance of such a contract.[58] This protects persons such as agency workers.

8.45 In addition, Part 5 extends protection to the following persons:

(1) partners in a firm, including those seeking to become partners;[59]
(2) members of limited liability partnerships, including those seeking to become members;[60]
(3) barristers, including pupils and tenants and applicants for pupillage and tenancy;[61]
(4) office-holders, including those seeking appointment to an office;[62]
(5) members of trade organizations, including applicants for membership;[63]
(6) local authority members in relation to the carrying out of official business.[64]

The 2010 Act imposes obligations on qualification bodies in relation to the conferment of qualifications,[65] and employment service providers in relation to the provision of employment services.[66]

---

[53] Equality Act 2010, s 40(2)(b).
[54] Equality Act 2010, s 40(3).
[55] The Enterprise and Regulatory Reform Act 2013, s 65. This is expected to come into force on 1 October 2013. For the government's consultation on the repeal of the third party harassment provisions in the 2010 Act, see Government Equalities Office, 'Equality Act 2010—employer liability for harassment of employees by third parties' (2012).
[56] Equality Act 2010, s 41(1) and (3).
[57] Equality Act 2010, s 41(5).
[58] Equality Act 2010, s 41(7). Of course, contract workers also enjoy separate protection from discrimination, victimization, and harassment by their employer.
[59] Equality Act 2010, s 44.
[60] Equality Act 2010, s 45.
[61] Equality Act 2010, s 47. Advocates are also protected: Equality Act 2010, s 48.
[62] Equality Act 2010, ss 49–52.
[63] Equality Act 2010, s 57.
[64] Equality Act 2010, s 58.
[65] Equality Act 2010, s 53.
[66] Equality Act 2010, s 55. The provision of employment services includes, among other things, the provision of vocational training and vocational guidance (including making arrangements for the provision of both), provision of a service for finding employment for persons, and supplying employers with persons to do work: see Equality Act 2010, s 56.

C. Unfair Dismissal and Other Protections

(1) Unfair dismissal

Employees enjoy statutory rights under the Employment Rights Act 1996, including the **8.46** right not to be unfairly dismissed.[67] Before the emergence of 'religion or belief' as a protected characteristic in discrimination law, the law of unfair dismissal was the principal means for the protection of religious rights in the employment context including the assertion of rights guaranteed by the ECHR. It remains an important tool in some cases.[68]

To qualify for protection under the unfair dismissal provisions, an employee must establish **8.47** the following:

(1) That he was engaged under a contract of employment, meaning a contract of service or apprenticeship.[69]
(2) That he was employed for the necessary qualifying period.[70] The qualifying period was reduced from two years to one year from 1 June 1999, but has been increased again to two years.[71] A qualifying period of two years applies to employees whose period of continuous employment begins on or after 6 April 2012.[72] In some cases there is no qualifying period.[73] This includes cases where the reason or principal reason for dismissal was a reason related with the refusal of Sunday work by a retail or betting shop worker or the employee's political opinions or affiliation.[74]
(3) That the employee was dismissed. An employee is treated as having been dismissed not only where his contract of employment is terminated by his employer, but also where an employee terminates his contract by reason of the employer's conduct (known as constructive dismissal).[75]

Once an employee has shown that the qualifying conditions are met, the burden shifts to the **8.48** employer to show the reason or principal reason for the dismissal, and that the reason was a fair reason. Potentially fair reasons include reasons related to the capability or qualifications of the employee, the conduct of the employee,[76] or some other substantial reason of a kind such as to justify the dismissal of an employee holding the position which that employee held.[77]

The Employment Rights Act 1996 sets out a number of circumstances in which a dismissal **8.49** will be deemed to be automatically unfair. This includes the dismissal of an employee who

---

[67] Employment Rights Act 1996, s 94(1).
[68] See paras 8.51–8.53.
[69] Employment Rights Act 1996, s 230(1) and (2).
[70] Employment Rights Act 1996, s 108(1).
[71] Unfair Dismissal and Statement of Reasons for Dismissal (Variation of Qualifying Period) Order 2012, SI 2012/989, art 3.
[72] SI 2012/989, art 4.
[73] Employment Rights Act 1996, s 108(3).
[74] Employment Rights Act 1996, s 108(3)(d) and s 103(4) respectively. Section 103(4) of the 1996 Act (exception to the need for a qualifying period where the dismissal is for political opinions) is an amendment introduced by the Enterprise and Regulatory Reform Act 2013, s 13 following the decision of the ECtHR in *Redfearn v UK* (2013) 57 EHRR 2. See further Ch 6, paras 6.40–6.45.
[75] Employment Rights Act 1996, s 95(1).
[76] Employment Rights Act 1996, s 98(2).
[77] Employment Rights Act 1996, s 98(1).

is a shop worker if the employee has opted out of Sunday working in accordance with the Sunday Working Act 1994 and the reason for dismissal is his refusal to work on Sunday.

8.50 If the employer establishes that the reason for dismissal was a potentially fair reason—for example the conduct of the employee—the employment tribunal will go on to consider whether the dismissal was fair having regard to that reason. The fairness of a dismissal 'depends on whether in the circumstances (including the size and administrative resources of the employer's undertaking) the employer acted reasonably or unreasonably in treating it as a sufficient reason for dismissing the employee', and is to be determined 'in accordance with equity and the substantial merits of the case'.[78] It is well established that the correct approach for a tribunal when applying this statutory test is to consider whether the employer's actions, including its decision to dismiss, fell within the band of reasonable responses which a reasonable employer could adopt.[79] It is not for the tribunal to substitute its decision for the employers—in other words, the fact that the tribunal would have assessed the case before it differently from the employer does not mean that the employer has acted unfairly.

8.51 These provisions can offer protection to employees who have been dismissed for reasons related to their religion or religious practices. For example, in *Chondol* a social worker was dismissed for gross misconduct when, among other things, he gave a bible to a service user and attempted to promote his religious beliefs to a different service user. The tribunal held that, having accepted the employee's explanation of these incidents, the employer was not reasonably entitled to conclude that he had committed misconduct.[80] In another case a shop assistant who was dismissed after wearing a headscarf to work succeeded in her claim for unfair dismissal, while her claim for direct discrimination failed.[81]

8.52 It has been suggested that an employer may be acting unfairly where he makes no attempt to accommodate an employee's religious needs. In *Copsey*, Rix LJ held that an employer who seeks to change an employee's working hours so as to prevent that employee from practising his sincere adherence to the requirements of his religion in the way of Sabbath observance, may be acting unfairly if he makes no attempt to accommodate his employee's needs, this being no more than what would be expected of a decent employer:

> To say in such a situation that the employee's religious needs simply lie outside the scope of what the law requires of a fair employer ought not to be acceptable. I do not think this places any burden on a decent employer that he does not already observe in practice... Such a requirement would, I venture to think, be easily fitted into the general law of unfair dismissal. An employer who had sought to find a reasonable accommodation for his employee would have nothing to fear. Provided his solution was one which a reasonable employer could require, in that it lay within the range of reasonable responses to the problem, it would not be for an employment tribunal to second-guess the employer.[82]

---

[78] Employment Rights Act 1996, s 98(4).

[79] *Iceland Frozen Foods Ltd v Jones* [1983] ICR 17 (EAT).

[80] *Chondol v Liverpool City Council* [2009] EAT 0298/08. Mr Chondol's dismissal was, however, found to be fair having regard to other incidents. For a more detailed discussion of this case, see paras 8.146–8.147.

[81] *Farrah v The Global Luggage Co Ltd* [2012] ET 2200147/2012. For a more detailed consideration of this case, see para 8.109. The tribunal indicated that a claim for indirect discrimination would have succeeded had it been pursued.

[82] *Copsey v WBB Devon Clays Ltd* [2005] ICR 1789 (CA), para 71. See also the comments of Neuberger LJ at paras 82–91.

The 'band of reasonable responses test' has, however, been criticized for being favourable **8.53** to the employer and not permitting sufficient scrutiny of decisions.[83] By comparison the approach when assessing proportionality in claims of indirect discrimination is more rigorous, requiring the tribunal to make its own judgment, on a fair and detailed analysis of the working practices and business considerations involved, as to whether the proposal is reasonably necessary.[84]

(2) Human rights law

For employees seeking protection of their religious rights the most important provision of **8.54** the ECHR is Article 9 (freedom of thought, conscience and religion), whether taken alone or in conjunction with Article 14 (prohibition of discrimination). These and other relevant provisions are dealt with extensively elsewhere in this work.[85] This section simply highlights some of the issues that have arisen in the employment context.

(a) Assertion of Convention rights in proceedings before the employment tribunal

Where an employer is a public authority within the meaning of section 6 of the Human **8.55** Rights Act 1998 it is unlawful for them to act in a way which is incompatible with Convention rights. However, the employment tribunal has no jurisdiction to entertain proceedings against a public authority under section 7 of the Human Rights Act 1998 for acting incompatibly with Convention rights. This is not to say that Convention rights are irrelevant in proceedings before the employment tribunal. Pursuant to section 3 of the 1998 Act, the employment tribunal must read and give effect to relevant legislative provisions in a way which is compatible with Convention rights.[86]

In claims of unfair dismissal it has been held that the tribunal should inject consideration of **8.56** Convention rights into section 98(4) of the Employment Rights Act 1996 (determination of whether dismissal is fair or unfair)[87] by interpreting the words 'reasonably or unreasonably' in that section as including 'having regard to the applicant's Convention rights'.[88] Moreover 'all the circumstances' envisaged by section 98(4) should be interpreted to include all those matters weighed in the balance in assessing whether there has been an interference with Convention rights under, for example, Article 9(1), and then those matters advanced as a justification pursuant to Article 9(2).[89]

Convention rights are relevant in proceedings before the employment tribunal even where **8.57** the claim for unfair dismissal is brought against a private sector employer, at least where the state has a positive obligation to secure enjoyment of the relevant Convention right between

---

[83] For discussion, see L Vickers, *Religious Freedom, Religious Discrimination and the Workplace* (Hart Publishing, 2008) 174–6. See also *Turner v East Midlands Trains Ltd* [2013] ICR 525 (CA) in which the Court of Appeal observed that the ECtHR has recognized that some leeway should be given to the employer in the discharge of his powers of dismissal. The ECtHR itself adopts a light touch when reviewing human rights in the context of the employment relationship.

[84] *Hardys & Hampson plc v Lax* [2005] ICR 1565 (CA). See also Ch 6, paras 6.89–6.92.

[85] See Chs 3 and 5.

[86] The employment tribunal does not have jurisdiction to make declarations of incompatibility.

[87] The Employment Rights Act 1996, s 98(4) provides that the determination of the question whether the dismissal is fair or unfair (having regard to the reason shown by the employer) (a) depends on whether in the circumstances the employer acted reasonably or unreasonably in treating it as a sufficient reason for dismissing the employee, and (b) shall be determined in accordance with equity and the substantial merits of the case.

[88] *Pay v Lancashire Probation Service* [2004] ICR 187 (EAT).

[89] *Pay* (n 88).

private persons.[90] Again, where applicable, Convention rights will be considered as part of the employment tribunal's determination of whether the dismissal was fair or unfair pursuant to section 98(4) of the Employment Rights Act 1996.[91] It has been held that there will not always be a need for an employee to expressly invoke Convention rights since the concept of unfairness in the law of unfair dismissal may by itself be apt to cover the particular situation.[92]

8.58   As for discrimination law, the recitals to Council Directive (EC) 2000/78 refer expressly to the European Convention for the Protection of Human Rights and emphasize the importance of respecting fundamental rights and freedoms.[93] Moreover, Article 2(5) of the Directive replicates in virtually identical terms Article 9(2) ECHR. In *Ladele*, Lord Neuberger MR stated that Article 2(5), particularly in the light of the recitals, suggested that the Directive and any domestic legislation made thereunder should be read in conformity with Article 9 ECHR. He acknowledged that any such legislation would, if possible, have to be read in any event in conformity with Article 9 by virtue of section 3 of the Human Rights Act 1998.[94]

(b) The scope of protection

8.59   In *Ladele*, Elias P giving the judgment of the Employment Appeals Tribunal, observed that the ECtHR has 'adopted a very narrow protection indeed for employees who seek to rely on their Article 9 rights'.[95] Where an employee's ability to observe a religious practice conflicts with the demands of his employment, the approach taken by Strasbourg has traditionally been that there is no interference with the employee's Article 9(1) rights since he is free to relinquish his post and take up other employment.[96] The Commission held that freedom to resign was the ultimate guarantee of his right to freedom of religion.[97] This approach became firmly entrenched in domestic law following the decision in *R (Begum) v Headteacher and Governors of Denbigh High School*, in which Lord Bingham observed as follows:

> The Strasbourg institutions have not been at all ready to find an interference with the right to manifest religious belief in practice or observance where a person has voluntarily accepted an employment or role which does not accommodate that practice or observance and there are other means open to the person to practise or observe his or her religion without undue hardship or inconvenience.[98]

---

[90] *X v Y (Employment: Sex Offender)* [2004] ICR 1634 (CA), para 64. This was a case concerning Arts 8 and 14, both of which, the Court of Appeal found, were not confined in their effect to relations between individuals and the state. It has been recognized that Art 9 also imposes positive obligations on the state: see *Eweida and ors v UK* (2013) 57 EHRR 8, para 84.

[91] In *X v Y* (n 90) para 59, Mummery LJ held that considerations of fairness, the reasonable response of a reasonable employer, equity, and substantial merits ought, when taken together, to be sufficiently flexible, without even minimal interpretative modification under HRA 1998, s 3 to enable the employment tribunal to give effect to applicable Convention rights.

[92] *Copsey* (n 82) paras 71–73 *per* Rix LJ. Neuberger LJ, at paras 91 and 93, also doubted whether Art 9 took matters much further. See also the observations of Mummery LJ in *X v Y* (n 90) para 59.

[93] See in particular recitals (1), (4), and (5).

[94] *Islington LBC v Ladele* (n 9) para 22.

[95] In *London Borough of Islington v Ladele* [2009] ICR 387 (EAT), para 119.

[96] See eg *Konttinen v Finland* (1996) 87 DR 68 and *Stedman v UK* (1997) 23 EHRR CD 168.

[97] *Konttinen* (n 96) para 75.

[98] *R (Begum) v Headteacher and Governors of Denbigh High School* [2007] 1 AC 100 (HL), para 23. See also para 50.

Domestic courts had felt unable to disregard what has been described variously as a 'clear line **8.60** of decisions' from Strasbourg and 'a coherent and remarkably consistent body of authority'.[99] Despite express reservations by judges,[100] domestic courts and tribunals adopted the same approach when determining the Article 9 rights of employees.[101]

However, in January 2013 the ECtHR expressly distanced itself from this approach. In **8.61** *Eweida and ors v the United Kingdom*, the Court acknowledged that it had not applied a similar approach in respect of employment sanctions imposed on individuals as a result of the exercise by them of other rights protected by the Convention, for example the right to respect for private life under Article 8, the right to freedom of expression under Article 10, and the freedom not to join a trade union under Article 11. It went on to state that:

> Given the importance in a democratic society of freedom of religion, the Court considers that, where an individual complains of a restriction on freedom of religion in the workplace, rather than holding that the possibility of changing job would negate any interference with the right, the better approach would be to weigh that possibility in the overall balance when considering whether or not the restriction was proportionate.[102]

Domestic courts and tribunals are bound to consider this new approach by the ECtHR[103] **8.62** and it would be surprising if they did not follow suit, particularly in the light of earlier concerns about the previous approach. If they do, it will mean that most cases will fall to be decided at the justification stage, permitting courts and tribunals to undertake a balancing of competing interests.[104] In *Eweida* it was suggested that the possibility of changing job will fall to be weighed in the balance, or at least will weigh more heavily in the balance, where an employee has made a decision to enter into a contract of employment and to undertake responsibilities which he knows will have an impact on his freedom to manifest his religious belief. This is to be contrasted with cases where the responsibility or duty to which the employee objects is introduced by his employer at a later date.[105]

Following the decision of the ECtHR in *Eweida*, the Equality and Human Rights Commission **8.63** published guidance for employers on 'Religion or Belief in the Workplace'.[106] Among other things, it provides guidance on how employers should deal with religion or belief requests by employees. It advises employers that they should take 'all requests seriously and should not make assumptions about the significance of a religion or belief, or disregard a request because it is made by one employee'. Moreover, employers are encouraged 'to take as their starting-point consideration as to how to accommodate the request unless there are cogent

---

[99] *Copsey* (n 82) para 31; and *Begum* (n 98) para 24 respectively. For a different analysis see *Copsey* at paras 60–65.

[100] *Copsey* (n 82) para 35 and *Begum* (n 98) para 24.

[101] See eg *Copsey* (n 82); *Eweida v British Airways plc* [2010] ICR 890 (CA), paras 22–23; and *Doogan v Greater Glasgow and Clyde Health Board* [2012] SLT 1041 (CSOH).

[102] *Eweida v UK* (n 90) para 83.

[103] Pursuant to HRA 1998, s 2(1).

[104] This is provided, of course, that other hurdles are met, eg that the wearing of a particular religious symbol or objection to a work task was a 'manifestation' of their religion or belief.

[105] See the observations in *Eweida v UK* (n 90) paras 106 and 109. See also the discussion in *Copsey* (n 82) paras 61–65, where Rix LJ advocated precisely this distinction.

[106] EHRC, 'Religion or Belief in the Workplace: A guide for employers following recent European Court of Human Rights judgments' (February 2013).

or compelling reasons not to do so, assessing the impact of the change on other employees, the operation of the business and other factors', which are outlined.

(3) Protections under the School Standards and Framework Act 1998

8.64　There is specific provision in the education context for the protection of religious rights. The School Standards and Framework Act 1998 ('SSFA 1998') includes provisions protecting teachers and other staff against discrimination on grounds of their religious opinions and attendance of religious worship.[107] At the same time, schools which have a religious character (ie faith schools)[108] are permitted, in defined circumstances, to give preference—in connection with the appointment, remuneration, or promotion of teachers—to persons whose religions opinions are in accordance with the religion or religious denomination of the school, or who attend religious worship, etc.[109] In dismissing a teacher, they can also have regard to any conduct on the teacher's part which is incompatible with the precepts or with the upholding of the tenets of the religion or religious denomination of the school.[110] Importantly, the law expressly provides that a person does not contravene the Equality Act 2010 by doing anything which is permitted by SSFA 1998.[111]

8.65　The scope of protection afforded by SSFA 1998 ultimately depends on the type of school.[112]

8.66　Section 59 of SSFA 1998 protects staff at maintained schools which are non-religious.[113] Section 59(2) concerns appointment and dismissal (including, potentially, promotion and demotion) and extends to all staff. It provides that: 'No person shall be disqualified by reason of his religious opinions, or of his attending or omitting to attend religious worship (a) from being a teacher at the school, or (b) from being employed or engaged for the purposes of the school otherwise than as a teacher.'

8.67　Section 59(4), which only extends to teachers, provides that: 'No teacher at the school shall receive any less remuneration or be deprived of, or disqualified for, any promotion or other advantage (a) by reason of the fact that he does not give religious education, or (b) by reason of his religious opinions or of his attending or omitting to attend religious worship.'

8.68　Section 59 of SSFA 1998 also applies to staff, other than 'reserved teachers', at foundation and voluntary controlled schools with a religious character.[114] Such schools must select a portion of teachers for their fitness and competence to give religious education, and specifically appoint them to do so.[115] Known as 'reserved teachers', they must not exceed one-fifth of the total number of teachers at the school.[116] Equivalent provision is made for staff at Academies

---

[107] SSFA 1998, s 59(2) and (4) (maintained schools) and s 124AA (Academies). These protections are not new. They were previously contained in the Education Act 1944, s 30 and later the Education Act 1996.

[108] Certain schools can be designated by Order of the Secretary of State as having a 'religious character': SSFA 1998, s 69.

[109] SSFA 1998, s 60 (maintained schools), s 124A (independent schools), and s 124AA (Academies).

[110] SSFA 1998 s 60(6) (maintained schools), s 124A(3) (independent schools), and s 124AA(7) (Academies).

[111] Equality Act 2010, Sch 22, para 4. Specifically, it is not a contravention of the Equality Act 2010 to do anything permitted for the purposes of SSFA 1998, s 60(4) and (5), s 124A and s 124AA(5)–(7).

[112] For an overview of educational provision in the UK, see Ch 9, part B.

[113] The section applies to community schools, community or foundation special schools, and foundation or voluntary schools which do not have a religious character. For an overview of educational provision in the UK, see Ch 9, part B.

[114] SSFA 1998, s 60(2) and (3).

[115] SSFA 1998, s 58(2).

[116] SSFA 1998, s 58(3).

by section 124AA of SSFA 1998.[117] The 1998 Act does not extend the same protection to staff at independent schools which are not Academies.[118]

As to the scope of sections 59 and 124AA, the equivalent, almost identically worded provision in the Education Act 1944 was narrowly construed by the Court of Appeal in *Ahmad v Inner London Education Authority*.[119] Mr Ahmad, employed as a teacher under a full-time contract, wished to take off every Friday afternoon for prayers. The local authority was willing to accommodate his request but only if he agreed to vary his contract to part-time with reduced pay. Mr Ahmad resigned in protest. In his claim for unfair dismissal he relied on section 30 of the Education Act 1944. **8.69**

Lord Denning MR accepted that if the words (which now appear in section 59(4) of SSFA 1998) were read literally without qualification, they would entitle Mr Ahmad to take time off every Friday afternoon without loss of pay. However, he did not think this could have been intended. He held that section 30 should be read subject to the qualification 'if the school timetable so permits'. So read, it meant that Mr Ahmad was entitled to attend for religious worship during the working week if it could be arranged consistently with performing his teaching duties under his contract of employment. **8.70**

Orr LJ agreed that section 30 could not be construed as authorizing a breach of contract by a teacher in absenting himself during school hours for the purposes of attending religious worship. He observed that if this was the intention he would have expected much clearer and more specific language to be used. He also expressed doubts as to whether the prohibition against receiving any less remuneration was directed at a case like this. In his view, it was more likely to have been inserted because there was a danger that a teacher might be offered a lower rate of remuneration either because he did or did not give religious instruction. **8.71**

The majority did not explicitly address an argument raised by the local authority that 'attending or omitting to attend religious worship' was a reference to the act of worship in school for which the Education Act 1944 made provision. By their reasoning, the majority appeared to accept, implicitly, that religious worship could include a reference to religious worship outside school.[120] **8.72**

Narrowly construed,[121] it is difficult to see what in practice section 59 adds to the protections in the Equality Act 2010. Of greater significance are the provisions in SSFA 1998 permitting schools with a religious character to impose requirements on teachers relating to religion and religious beliefs. These provisions are considered in part H. **8.73**

D. Time Off for Religious Observance

An employer's requirements in relation to working hours may be incompatible with an employee's wish to participate in religious observance at particular times or on particular **8.74**

---

[117] See in particular SSFA 1998, s 124AA(8) and (10).
[118] They are, in the normal way, governed by the provisions of the Equality Act 2010.
[119] *Ahmad* (n 3).
[120] Note that some provisions in the legislation refer expressly to 'religious worship in the school': see eg SSFA 1998, s 71(1)(b).
[121] It is unlikely that developments since 1977 would justify a broader construction. See generally the dissenting judgment of Lord Scarman in *Ahmad* (n 3).

days. For example, Christians may wish to avoid working on Sundays, while Muslims may request time off for Friday prayers. While the law makes specific provision in respect of Sunday working for retail and betting shop workers, others must rely on the general law for protection.

(1) Sunday working for shop workers

8.75 Until 1994 all shops were required by the Shops Act 1950 to close on a Sunday, subject to limited exceptions.[122] This protected those holding a belief that Sunday is a day of rest and religious observance even if only incidentally.

8.76 The rules relating to Sunday trading were relaxed by the Sunday Trading Act 1994, which permitted shops to open on a Sunday subject to some restrictions on the opening hours of large shops.[123] This had clear implications for religious rights. Importantly, the legislation contained a number of provisions which afford some protection to the religious interests of workers who wish to avoid Sunday working.

8.77 First, those employed as shop workers when the 1994 Act came into force have the option of opting into Sunday working but cannot be required by their employer to work Sundays.[124] Such workers are known as 'protected' workers.[125]

8.78 Secondly, employees who can lawfully be required to work on Sundays (for example those employed after the 1994 Act came into force) have the option of opting out of Sunday working by serving on their employer a written notice to the effect that they object to Sunday working.[126] They are not obliged to cite a reason for their objection, which may be religious or entirely secular. However, the effect is not immediate, with the notice only taking effect three months from the date on which it is given.[127]

8.79 This protection is supplemented by provisions in the Employment Rights Act 1996 which provide that that protected or opted-out workers have the right not to be subjected to any detriment or to be dismissed on the ground that they have refused to do Sunday work.[128] Dismissal on such grounds is deemed to be automatically unfair.[129]

8.80 It should be noted that the same protections apply for the benefit of betting shop workers.[130]

---

[122] Shops Act 1950, s 47.

[123] With some exceptions, large shops can open on a Sunday for a maximum period of six hours between the hours of 10am and 6pm: Sunday Trading Act 1994, Sch 1, para 2. Large shops are those shops with 'a relevant floor area exceeding 280 square metres': Sunday Trading Act 1994, s 1. There are no restrictions on the opening hours of shops with a relevant floor area of less than 280 square metres.

[124] Employment Rights Act 1996, ss 36–37. These provisions were originally contained in the Sunday Trading Act 1994, Sch 4. They do not apply to those employed to work on Sundays only.

[125] Employment Rights Act 1996, s 36(1).

[126] Employment Rights Act 1996, s 40. Again this does not apply if the employee is employed to do Sunday work only.

[127] Employment Rights Act 1996, s 41.

[128] Employment Rights Act 1996, ss 45 and 101.

[129] Employment Rights Act 1996, s 101(1). There is no qualifying period in such cases: s 108(3)(d). See para 8.47.

[130] The rules relating to betting on Sundays were relaxed by the Deregulation and Contracting Out Act 1994 which permitted betting on Sundays. Again, the relevant provisions were originally contained in the Deregulation and Contracting Out Act 1994, Sch 5A, but are now also set out in the Employment Rights Act 1996.

Finally, the Sunday Trading Act 1994 contains a specific exception for persons of the Jewish **8.81**
religion. The general rule prohibiting large shops from opening on Sunday for the serving of
retail customers (except for a maximum of six hours on Sunday between the hours of 10am
and 6pm)[131] does not apply where the shop is occupied by a person of the Jewish religion[132]
and that person gives to the local authority for the area a notice that he intends to keep the
shop closed for the serving of customers on the Jewish Sabbath.[133]

The protection afforded by these provisions is, in the end, limited. The provisions apply only **8.82**
to retail and betting shop workers, and even then they only protect the interests of those for
whom the day of religious observance is Sunday and, to a limited extent, those observing
the Jewish Sabbath. Non-retail employees and those observing a different day of religious
observance must rely on the general law for protection.

(2) Other requests for time off work

(a) The ECHR

For employees who wish to be excused from work for reasons connected to their religion or **8.83**
religious beliefs, the assistance afforded by Article 9 ECHR has historically been limited.
The approach traditionally taken by Strasbourg is that where an employee's working hours
are incompatible with his religious obligations, there is no interference with his rights under
Article 9(1) since he is free to relinquish his post.[134]

The same approach has been adopted by domestic courts. In *Copsey*, an employee was dis- **8.84**
missed when he refused on religious grounds to agree a contractual variation in his working hours which would have required him to work a seven-day shift, including Sunday if
needed. Mr Copsey was a Christian with a sincerely held belief that Sunday is a day of rest.
He claimed his dismissal was unfair on grounds that there had been an interference with his
right to manifest his religion contrary to Article 9.

Mummery LJ held that Article 9 ECHR was not engaged having regard to the 'clear line of **8.85**
decisions' of the Commission to the effect that Article 9 is not engaged where an employee
asserts Article 9 rights against his employer in relation to his hours of working.[135] He indicated, however, that in the absence of the Commission rulings he would have regarded this as
a case of material interference with Mr Copsey's Article 9 rights, where it would be necessary
to consider the justification arguments available to the employer under Article 9(2).[136] Rix
LJ disagreed with Mummery LJ's analysis, taking the view that the Commission decisions on
Article 9 in the employment context did not represent a body of consistent decisions which
required a conclusion that Article 9 was not engaged in a case such as Mr Copsey's where

---

[131] Sunday Working Act 1994, Sch 1, para 2(1).
[132] A shop occupied by a partnership or company shall be taken to be occupied by a person of a Jewish religion if the majority of the partners or the directors are persons of that religion: Sunday Working Act 1994, Sch
2, para 8(2). It should be noted that protection extends to members of any religious body regularly observing
the Jewish Sabbath as it applies to persons of the Jewish religion: Sch 2, para 9.
[133] Sunday Working Act 1994, Sch 1, para 2(2)(b) and Sch 2, para 8. The Shops Act 1950 also contained
an exception for the benefit of persons of the Jewish religion. While generally all shops were required to close
on Sundays, shops occupied by persons of the Jewish religion which were closed on Saturday were permitted to
open on Sundays until 2 pm: Shops Act 1950, s 53(1).
[134] *Konttinen* (n 96); *Stedman* (n 96); and *Ahmad v UK* (1981) 4 EHRR 126.
[135] This 'clear line of decisions' comprised *Ahmad* (n 134), *Konttinen* (n 96), and *Stedman* (n 96).
[136] *Copsey* (n 82) paras 30–39.

it was the employer and not the employee who was insisting on a contractual variation of agreed hours. Rix LJ held that, if the Commission's rationale was that an employee cannot complain of an interference in his rights of religious freedom if he binds himself by his own contract in a way which is inconsistent with those rights, then for the purposes of such a rationale there was a critical distinction between those cases where the employee was seeking to be excused from contractually agreed hours, and cases where it was the employer who was seeking a contractual variation of hours originally agreed.[137]

8.86 As noted earlier,[138] the ECtHR has recently distanced itself from its previous approach. In *Eweida and ors v United Kingdom*, the ECtHR accepted that where an individual complains of a restriction on freedom of religion in the workplace, rather than holding that the possibility of changing job would negate any interference with the right, the better approach is to weigh that possibility in the overall balance when considering whether or not a restriction was proportionate.[139] This paves the way for claims concerning working hours to be considered at the justification stage.

8.87 It should be noted that in *Copsey*, Mummery LJ indicated that even if the issue of justification arose for consideration, he would have regarded the dismissal as probably justified under Article 9(2). The employer had compelling economic reasons which made it necessary to change the working practices of the workforce to a seven-day shift. The alternatives to dismissal were fully explored with Mr Copsey, and the employer had done everything that it could to accommodate Mr Copsey's wish not to work on Sundays. For example, Mr Copsey had been offered but refused employment in another of the employer's operations which operated on a five-day operating shift pattern with some Saturday and Sunday overtime working.[140]

(b) Discrimination law

8.88 Due in part to the restrictiveness of human rights jurisprudence, most claims concerning working hours are generally brought as indirect discrimination claims and normally turn on whether the relevant provision, criterion, or practice—usually the requirement to work hours from which the employee is seeking to be excused—can be justified as being a proportionate means of achieving a legitimate aim. Relevant considerations include the discriminatory impact of the provision, criterion, or practice; the operational and business needs of the business; and what steps, if any, the employer has taken to accommodate an employee's request.

8.89 As to the discriminatory impact of a particular measure, in *MBA v the Mayor and Burgesses of the London Borough of Merton*, the EAT affirmed that what has to be considered is the discriminatory impact of a provision, criterion, or practice on the group as a whole and not the particular employee; further, that in assessing the discriminatory impact, a tribunal was

---

[137] *Copsey* (n 82) paras 43–65. Rix LJ took this to be the rationale of *Konttinen* (n 134), in which the applicant, a Seventh-day Adventist, refused to work after sunset on Friday evenings when his contract required him to so. In his view, the Commission's decision in *Stedman v UK* (n 134)—in which a Christian employee was dismissed when she refused to agree to sign a contract which required Sunday working—represented an unreasoned extension of the rationale in *Konttinen*.

[138] See paras 8.61–8.62.

[139] *Eweida v UK* (n 90).

[140] *Copsey* (n 82) para 41.

entitled to consider the extent to which the employee's belief is shared by other adherents of the faith.[141]

The case concerned a Christian employee who believed that Sunday was a day of rest and wor- **8.90** ship and wished to be excused from Sunday working. In considering whether the requirement to work on Sunday was justified, the tribunal had attached weight to the fact that her belief, whilst deeply held, was not 'a core component of the Christian faith'.[142] The EAT held that, although the tribunal's language was less than elegant, in using the word 'core' it had simply intended to reflect the evidence put before it from an Anglican bishop that only some Christians felt obliged to abstain from work on the Sabbath. Although a tribunal had no right to determine matters of faith qualitatively (by evaluating how important a belief was), a tribunal was properly entitled to consider how many adherents of a faith shared the particular belief and would be affected by the provision, criterion, or practice when assessing the discriminatory impact of a provision, criterion, or practice on a group.

The EAT also rejected an argument that an employer must make 'all possible' efforts to accom- **8.91** modate an employee's religious needs. While accepting the importance of eliminating discrimination on the ground of religion and belief, the EAT stated that this put the threshold too high.[143]

However, a failure by an employer to give any consideration to alternative solutions which would **8.92** have enabled an employee to meet his religious obligations may well justify a conclusion that the requirement to work on a particular day was not proportionate.[144]

While cases will turn on their individual facts, the following are examples of cases where employ- **8.93** ers have succeeded in showing that a requirement relating to working hours was justified.

In *Cherfi* the claimant was employed as a security guard and was refused permission to leave **8.94** the site on Friday afternoons to attend prayers at a mosque. As part of its contract with the employer, the client required a specified number of staff on site for the full duration of operating hours, which meant that security staff were required to remain on site throughout their shifts. Apart from financial penalties, the continuation of the contract was in danger if breaches occurred. In an attempt to support the claimant's wish to attend mosque on Friday, his employer offered to amend his contract to a Monday to Thursday pattern with the option of working one day at the weekend, which the claimant said he was not willing to do. It was found that the requirement for the claimant to remain on site was a proportionate means of achieving the employer's legitimate aim of meeting the operational needs which it had in complying with its contract.[145]

---

[141] *MBA v the Mayor and Burgess of the London Borough of Merton* [2012] Eq LR 526 (EAT).

[142] The tribunal placed reliance on the judgment of Lord Neuberger MR in *Islington LBC v Ladele* (n 9), where one of features he considered when assessing proportionality was the fact that Ms Ladele's objection to conducting civil partnerships was based on her view of marriage which was not a core part of her religion.

[143] *MBA* (n 141) para 52.

[144] See eg *Edge v Visual Security Services Ltd* [2006] ET 1301365/06, where an employer's failure to find alternative solutions because they were too much trouble meant that it could not show that the requirement for Sunday working was proportionate; and *Estorninho v Zoran's Delicatessen* [2006] ET 23014871/06 where a chef who was required by his employer to cover an additional shift on Sundays succeeded in his claim for indirect religious discrimination as his employer had failed to discuss the matter with the other chef or look for other ways to cover Sundays.

[145] *Cherfi v G4S Security Services Ltd* [2011] UKEAT 0379/10.

8.95 It has been held that requiring a Jehovah's Witness to work on a Sunday when he wished to worship and attend Kingdom Hall meetings on that day was justified where an employer had a contractual obligation to provide services to its customers on Sundays, which was a legitimate aim. The pool of employees was limited after a business decision had been made to stop using agency staff and, assuming the obligation to work on Sunday was distributed equitably, it was a proportionate means of achieving the legitimate aim.[146] Similarly, an employer was able to justify a requirement for Saturday morning working which disadvantaged a Seventh Day Adventist, whose faith required her to abstain from work from sunset on Friday to sunset on Saturday. The tribunal found that the requirement was based on a compelling business need.[147]

E. Religious Symbols and Dress

8.96 Religious symbols and dress constitute an important aspect of religious observance for adherents of many religions. However, an employee's desire to wear a particular item may come into conflict with an employer's insistence that staff observe a dress code at work for the purposes of presenting a particular image, or for practical reasons related to the role such as health and safety. Indeed, in some situations employers are under a legal obligation to ensure a certain dress code is adhered to. For example, employers must ensure that employees wear suitable head protection on construction sites where there is a foreseeable risk of head injury other than by falling.[148] Sikhs who wear turbans are exempted from any legal requirements to wear a safety helmet while on a construction site;[149] however, there are no exemptions for other religious groups.

(1) The ECHR

8.97 Historically, Article 9 ECHR has not been of significant assistance in cases involving religious symbols or dress.

8.98 First, an employee is required to show that the wearing of a particular item is a 'manifestation' of their religion or belief. Not every act which is motivated by religion or belief constitutes a manifestation of it.[150] The act in question must be intimately linked to the religion or belief.[151] The wearing of a purity ring was held not to be a manifestation of a belief in celibacy before marriage, since the claimant was under no obligation by reason of her belief to wear the ring, nor did she suggest that she was obliged to do so.[152] On the other hand, it has been accepted that the wearing of a *jilbab* by a Muslim girl was a manifestation of her religion, and the fact that most other Muslims might not have thought it necessary was irrelevant.[153] In *Eweida*, the wearing of a cross

---

[146] *Patrick v IH Sterile Services* [2011] ET 3300983/2011.

[147] *James v MSC Cruises Ltd* [2006] ET 22031/05.

[148] Construction (Head Protection) Regulations 1989, SI 1989/2209.

[149] Employment Act 1989, s 11.

[150] *Arrowsmith v UK* (1981) 3 EHRR 218; *R (Williamson) v Secretary of State for Education and Employment* [2005] 2 AC 246 (HL).

[151] *X v UK* (1983) 6 EHRR 558; *Williamson* (n 150).

[152] *R (Playfoot) v Governing Body of Millais School* [2007] EWHC 1698 (Admin). The court's approach to manifestation in Playfoot was more restrictive than that adopted previously by the House of Lords in *Williamson* (n 150): see Ch 5, para 5.12.

[153] *Begum* (n 98) para 50 *per* Lord Hoffman.

visibly by a Christian employee, and the wearing of a cross and chain by another, was held by the ECtHR to be a manifestation of their religious beliefs.[154] The Court confirmed that 'there is no requirement on the applicant to establish that he or she acted in fulfilment of a duty mandated by the religion in question'.[155]

Secondly, and more problematically, taking the historical lead from Strasbourg, courts and tribunals have applied the principle that interference with the right to manifest religious belief in practice or observance is not readily established where a person has voluntarily accepted employment or a role which does not accommodate that practice or observance, and there are other means open to the person to practise or observe his or her religion without undue hardship or inconvenience.[156]   **8.99**

For example, in *Eweida*, a member of the check-in staff for British Airways plc was prohibited by the company's uniform policy from wearing a crucifix visibly around her neck. Her claim for indirect discrimination failed at the domestic level on the grounds that that she had failed to show that that Christians as a group were put at a disadvantage by the uniform policy. Citing this principle, the Court of Appeal held that the jurisprudence on Article 9 did nothing to advance her case.   **8.100**

Ms Eweida complained to the ECtHR, invoking Article 9 alone and in conjunction with Article 14. The Court reconsidered the approach previously taken to Article 9 claims arising in the employment context. It held that where an individual complains of a restriction on freedom of religion in the workplace, rather than holding that the possibility of changing job would negate any interference with the right, the better approach would be to weigh that possibility in the overall balance when considering whether or not the restriction was proportionate. It found that the refusal by her employer to allow Ms Eweida to remain in her post while visibly wearing a cross amounted to an interference with her right to manifest her religion. This represents a significant departure from its previous position.   **8.101**

The Court went on to conclude that, on the facts, a fair balance had not been struck between Ms Eweida's interests and those of others. On one side of the scales was Ms Eweida's desire to manifest her religious belief, which was a fundamental right; on the other was the employer's wish to project a certain corporate image. While the employer's aim was undoubtedly legitimate, in the Court's view the domestic courts had accorded it too much weight. Ms Eweida's cross was discreet and cannot have distracted from her professional appearance. There was no evidence that the wearing of other previously authorized items of religious clothing, such as turbans and hijabs, had any negative impact on British Airways' brand or image. The Court also referred to the fact that British Airways was able to later amend its uniform code to allow for the visible wearing of religious symbolic jewellery which, in its view, demonstrated that the earlier prohibition was not of crucial importance.   **8.102**

The ECtHR, however, dismissed the application of Ms Chaplin, a nurse who had been prevented by her employer's uniform policy from wearing a cross on a chain around her neck. The purpose of the policy was to prevent the risk of injury when handling patients. The Court held the reason for asking Ms Chaplin to remove the cross, namely the protection of   **8.103**

---

[154] *Eweida v UK* (n 90) para 89.
[155] *Eweida v UK* (n 90) para 82. See Ch 5, para 5.13.
[156] *Begum* (n 98) para 23 *per* Lord Bingham.

health and safety in a hospital ward, was 'inherently of a greater magnitude' that than which applied in respect of Ms Eweida.[157] It followed that the interference with Ms Chaplin's freedom to manifest her religion was necessary in a democratic society.

8.104 Of some significance is the ECtHR's acknowledgement in *Eweida* that the right to manifest one's religious belief is a fundamental right not only because a healthy democratic society needs to tolerate and sustain pluralism and diversity, but because of 'the value to an individual who has made religion a central tenet of his or her life to be able to communicate that belief to others'.[158] The ECtHR went on to emphasize that the importance for Ms Eweida and Ms Chaplin of being permitted to manifest their religion by wearing a cross visibly must weigh heavily in the balance.[159] This gives some recognition to the role and, more importantly, to the value in Article 9 terms of religious dress and symbols as means of expression and bearing witness to one's faith.[160]

8.105 Perhaps precisely because of their power in this regard, the ECtHR has recognized that religious dress and symbols may impinge on the freedom of conscience and religion of others, particularly in a school environment. In *Dahlab v Switzerland*, the ECtHR considered the Article 9 complaint of a Muslim primary state school teacher who had been barred from wearing a headscarf whilst teaching in order to maintain the denominational neutrality required by the state.[161] The Court accepted that it was very difficult to assess the impact of 'a powerful external symbol such as the wearing of a headscarf' on the freedom of conscience and religion of very young children, however, it could not be denied outright that the wearing of the headscarf might have a form of proselytising effect on the children given that it appeared to be imposed on women by a precept which is laid down in the Koran and which the Swiss Federal Court had found was hard to square with the principle of gender equality. It appeared difficult to reconcile this with the message of tolerance, respect for others, and equality and non-discrimination that all teachers in a democratic society must convey to their pupils.[162]

8.106 This can be contrasted with the decision in *Lautsi v Italy* in which the Grand Chamber held that that there was no evidence that the display of a religious symbol on a classroom wall (in this case a crucifix) might have an influence on pupils.[163] The Grand Chamber observed that the crucifix on a wall was essentially a passive symbol and could not be deemed to have an influence on pupils comparable to that of didactic speech or participation in religious activities.[164]

8.107 Domestic courts have made some reference to the impact of wearing a religious symbol in a school environment on those who choose not to wear it. For example, in *R (X) v Head Teacher*

[157] *Eweida v UK* (n 90) para 99.
[158] *Eweida v UK* (n 90) para 94. Cf Ch 3, paras 3.04–3.05.
[159] *Eweida v UK* (n 90) para 99.
[160] It will be recalled that in *Kokkinakis v Greece* (1993) 17 EHRR 397 the ECtHR recognized this as an aspect of the freedom of religion and the right protected by Art 9: 'While religious freedom is primarily a matter of individual conscience, it also implies, inter alia, freedom to "manifest [one's] religion." Bearing witness in words and deeds is bound up with the existence of religious convictions.'
[161] *Dahlab v Switzerland* (App 42393/98) (2001).
[162] See generally Ch 3, paras 3.99–3.105 for Strasbourg jurisprudence relating to religious dress.
[163] *Lautsi v Italy* (2012) 54 EHRR 3, para 66.
[164] *Lautsi* (n 163) paras 72–73. The Grand Chamber distinguished *Dahlab v Switzerland* (n 161) on the grounds that the facts of that case were entirely different. However, it is difficult to see how the case is properly distinguishable on this point. The wearing of a headscarf is also, on one view, a passive symbol which, on its own, could not be deemed to have an influence on pupils comparable to that of didactic speech or participation in religious activities. Cf Ch 3, paras 3.103–3.105 and 3.113.

and Governors of Y School—a case concerning a school's refusal to allow a pupil to wear a *niqab* veil at school—the Court, when assessing justification under Article 9(2), had regard to the school's concern about the pressure that would be applied to other Muslim girls to wear a *niqab* if the claimant were allowed to do so.[165]

(2) Discrimination law

Claims concerning religious symbols and dress are commonly brought as claims of discrimination. In claims of direct discrimination, when determining the reason for an employer's treatment of an employee a distinction is drawn between an employer's objection to the symbol or form of dress on the one hand, and the religion or belief of which that symbol is a manifestation on the other.[166] In *Azmi* the claimant was suspended when she refused to comply with an instruction not to wear a veil (covering her head and face) when she was teaching children.[167] Her claim for direct discrimination failed. The EAT held that the correct comparator in such a case was a woman who, whether Muslim or not, for a reason other than religious belief wears a face covering. The tribunal, having identified the correct comparator, was entitled to conclude that on the evidence before it, such a person would have been issued with an instruction and, if she refused to comply with it, would have been suspended. **8.108**

In *Farrah* the claimant was employed as a shop assistant and was moved to another store when she wore a headscarf to work.[168] She was subsequently forced to resign after taking an unauthorized extended lunch break. The tribunal found the unauthorized absence was used as a pretext to dismiss her, the real reason being her employer's dislike for her wearing a headscarf, which was felt was to be contrary to the 'trendy' image they tried to maintain. She succeeded in her claim for unfair dismissal but her claim for direct discrimination failed. The tribunal held that although her employer did not like her headscarf there was no evidence that it did not like her religious faith as a Muslim woman.[169] **8.109**

A uniform or dress code imposed by an employer may be indirectly discriminatory where it puts persons of a particular religion, or those holding a particular belief, at a disadvantage when compared with those who do not—usually by preventing them from wearing an item which they wish to wear as a matter of religious observance.[170] There may be 'particular disadvantage' even when a person is prevented from wearing something which he or she is not required by his or her religion to wear.[171] In *Watkins-Singh* the court held that there was nevertheless a need to show that the item was a matter of 'exceptional importance' for the claimant's religious belief.[172] Later cases have suggested that while more than choice is required, the need to show 'exceptional importance' puts the threshold too high.[173] **8.110**

---

[165] See eg *R (X) v Head Teacher and Governors of Y School* [2008] 1 All ER 249, paras 91–95. See also *Begum* (n 98).

[166] See, however, the comments in *McFarlane v Relate Avon Ltd* [2010] ICR 507 (EAT), para 18 and, generally, Ch 6, para 6.69.

[167] *Azmi* (n 9).

[168] *Farrah v The Global Luggage Co Ltd* [2012] ET 2200147/2012.

[169] The tribunal indicated that a claim for indirect discrimination, had it been brought, would in all likelihood have succeeded.

[170] See generally Ch 6 for a discussion of direct discrimination.

[171] *R (Watkins-Singh) v Governing Body of Aberdare Girls' High School* [2008] EWHC 1865 (Admin).

[172] *Watkins-Singh* (n 171) paras 51–57.

[173] *G v St Gregory's Catholic Science Governors* [2011] Eq LR 859. See also *R (National Secular Society) v Bideford Town Council* [2012] 2 All ER 1175.

8.111 A claimant must show that the provision, criteria, or practice of which he complains not only puts him at a disadvantage but also puts, or would put, persons sharing his religion or belief at a particular disadvantage. This places those with unique or highly personal beliefs in some difficulty. In *Eweida*, it was held that a Christian employee had not suffered indirect discrimination by a uniform policy which prevented her from wearing a cross visibly over her uniform.[174] Ms Eweida accepted that it was not a requirement of her faith to wear a cross in this manner but she saw it as a personal expression of her faith. Her claim of indirect discrimination failed on the grounds that she had failed to show that Christians as a group were put at a disadvantage by the uniform policy.

8.112 The tribunal indicated that had a *prima facie* case of unlawful discrimination been made out, it would have found that the uniform policy restricting the visible display of religious symbols was not a proportionate means of achieving a legitimate aim, namely brand uniformity. The policy did not distinguish between an item which represented the core of an individual's being, such as a religious symbol, from an item worn as a piece of cosmetic jewellery. The blanket ban of everything classified as 'jewellery' did not strike the correct balance between corporate consistency, individual need, and the accommodation of diversity. On appeal, Sedley LJ expressed some reservations about the tribunal's finding on proportionality. He referred to the fact that the policy had been in force for some years and had apparently not caused Ms Eweida or anyone else at British Airways any problem, and when the issue was raised by her it had been conscientiously addressed. Moreover, he held that the reference to 'the core of an individual's being' had no place in a case in which it was not suggested that the visible wearing of the cross was no more than a personal preference on Ms Eweida's part.

8.113 Similarly, in *Chaplin* the tribunal found that a nurse who wished to wear a crucifix on a chain around her neck had failed to show that other persons were put at a disadvantage by her employer's uniform policy which prohibited her from doing so on health and safety grounds.[175] There was evidence of one other person to whom the policy was applied whose religious views were not so strong so as to lead her to decline to comply with the policy; this person had not therefore been placed at a 'particular' disadvantage. The tribunal indicated that if it had been necessary to decide the point it would have found, by a majority, that the policy was a proportionate means of achieving a legitimate aim.

8.114 Both Ms Eweida and Ms Chaplin complained to the ECtHR, invoking Article 9 alone and in conjunction with Article 14. For reasons detailed previously, Ms Eweida's application succeeded, while Ms Chaplin's application failed. The Court held that the reason for asking Ms Chaplin to remove her cross, namely the protection of health and safety, was inherently of a greater magnitude than that which applied in respect of Ms Eweida, namely her employer's wish to project a certain corporate image.

8.115 The Court was careful not to level criticism at the manner in which the Employment Equality (Religion or Belief) Regulations 2003 had been applied by the domestic tribunals and courts. Since Ms Eweida's employer was a private company, the question in her case was whether her right to manifest her religion was sufficiently secured within the domestic legal order. The Court stated that while the examination of Ms Eweida's case by the domestic tribunals and

---

[174] *Eweida v British Airways* (n 101). The uniform policy only permitted items to be worn visibly if wearing them was a mandatory requirement and the item could not be concealed under the uniform.

[175] *Chaplin v Royal Devon and Exeter Hospital NHS Foundation Trust* [2010] ET 1702886/2009.

court focused primarily on the complaint of discriminatory treatment, it was clear that that the legitimacy of the uniform code and the proportionality of the measures taken by British Airways were examined in detail. While true, this glosses over the fact that consideration of proportionality was obiter and in no way determinative of Ms Eweida's case. In a dissenting opinion,[176] two of the judges acknowledged that there was some force in the argument that to require evidence of group disadvantage would be to discriminate against adherents of religions that, like Christianity, are less prescriptive as regards the manner of dress or outward manifestations of faith. They did not, however, find it necessary to resolve the point.

A number of cases in the domestic context have turned on the question of justification. **8.116**

In *Azmi*, it was held that the requirement not to wear clothing which covered the face or **8.117** mouth and/or which interfered unduly with a teacher's ability to communicate with pupils was a proportionate means of achieving a legitimate aim, namely the need to raise the educational achievements of the children in school. The requirement (which prevented the claimant from wearing a veil) had not been imposed immediately, and there had been observations of the claimant assisting the children and teaching before the instruction had been issued. Moreover, the instruction that she must remove her veil was confined to those occasions when she was teaching children and the claimant had the freedom to wear the veil at other times. Finally, the council had considered alternative ways of accommodating the claimant's wish to wear her veil when in a classroom with a male teacher.[177]

In *Dhinsa* it was held that a policy operated by the Prison Service which restricted staff and **8.118** visitors, other than Sikh Chaplains, from wearing a *kirpan* inside a prison was justified.[178]

The claimant, a trainee custody officer and a devout Amritdhari Sikh, was dismissed when **8.119** he chose to wear a *kirpan* whilst on duty. The tribunal noted that 'it is the solemn duty of an Amritdhari Sikh to wear the *kirpan* at all times' and 'because of its religious significance it is not to be considered as a weapon, and it is offensive to Sikhs to refer to the *kirpan* merely as a knife or a dagger. Nonetheless it is effectively a bladed instrument made of steel or iron'. The tribunal found that the need to ensure the safety and security of all staff, visitors, and prisoners was a legitimate aim and that the policy restricting the wearing of a *kirpan* inside a prison was a proportionate means of achieving that aim. The discriminatory impact of the policy would be small, since Amritdhari Sikhs formed a small percentage of Sikhs and of all potential prison custody officers, applicants, or potential applicants for the position and there were only two other examples of Amritdhari Sikhs being disadvantaged by the policy.

---

[176] The judges disagreed with the majority's view that a fair balance had not been struck in Ms Eweida's case.

[177] *Azmi* (n 7).

[178] *Dhinsa v Serco and anor* [2011] ET 1315002/2009. The tribunal noted that the *kirpan*:

> ... is indicative of a ceremonial sword. There is a requirement that it is made of steel or iron. It does not have to be sharp, but it does have to consist of a handle and a blade... It is normally about six inches in length (including the handle). It would be a breach of the articles of faith to wear a miniature or replica kirpan, or one which was not made of steel or iron, or one which was welded closed.

It should be noted that, generally, it is not an offence for a Sikh to carry a kirpan in a public place. The Criminal Justice Act 1988, s 139(5)(b) provides that it is a defence for a person charged with an offence of having an article with a blade or point in a public place to prove that he had the article with him for 'religious reasons'. The same defence is available where a person is charged with an offence of having such an article on school premises: Criminal Justice Act 1988, s 139A(4)(c).

8.120 Moreover, the tribunal had regard to the compelling security reason that an item equivalent to a steel knife should not be introduced into the prison estate generally. It rejected an argument that the blanket ban was not appropriate and necessary considering the different treatment afforded to Sikh chaplains and the fact that prison officers carried ligature knives and prisoners had access to other items that could readily be used as weapons. The tribunal noted that chaplains had less contact with prisoners and their role was not one of potential conflict with prisoners, unlike the relationship between prisoners and prison custody officers. Moreover, ligature knives did not pose the same immediate and obvious threat as a stolen *kirpan*, and access to other potentially dangerous items was strictly controlled. The tribunal also had regard to the public interest in ensuring that the public had confidence in the prison system. It concluded that the policy restricting the wearing of *kirpans* was appropriate and necessary and a proportionate means of achieving the legitimate aim pursued.

8.121 In another case, a midwife wished to wear scrub dresses while working in an operating theatre rather than scrub trousers, on the grounds that the Old Testament forbids a woman to wear men's clothes. The tribunal found that the trust's dress code was a proportionate means of achieving the legitimate aim of preventing infection in operating theatres.[179]

8.122 Where a provision, criterion, or practice relating to the wearing of a safety helmet while on a construction site is applied to a Sikh, and there are no reasonable grounds for believing that the Sikh would not wear a turban at all times when on such a site, the provision, criterion, or practice is to be taken as one which cannot be shown to be a proportionate means of achieving a legitimate aim within the meaning of section 19(2)(d) of the Equality Act 2010.[180]

F. Refusal of Work Tasks

8.123 Employees holding particular beliefs may ask to be excused from certain types of work on the grounds that the work is incompatible with those beliefs.

(1) Conscientious objection clauses

8.124 In limited circumstances, individuals are given a specific right to refuse work tasks to which they have a conscientious objection whether on religious or other grounds.

8.125 Specific statutory provision is made for conscientious objection in the case of abortion. Section 4(1) of the Abortion Act 1967 provides that 'no person shall be under any duty, whether by contract or by any statutory or other legal requirement, to participate in any treatment authorised by this Act to which he has a conscientious objection'. Importantly, this right is not absolute. It does not affect any duty 'to participate in treatment which is necessary to save the life or to prevent grave permanent injury to the physical or mental health of a pregnant woman'.[181]

---

[179] *Adewole v Barking, Havering and Redbridge University Hospitals NHS Trust* [2011] ET (unreported).

[180] Employment Act 1989, s 12. Before amendment by the Equality Act 2010, this provision applied only to claims of indirect discrimination brought under the Race Relations Act 1976. In its amended form, while the heading of section 12 remains 'Protection of Sikhs from racial discrimination in connection with requirements as to wearing of safety helmets', there is nothing in the substance of the provision which limits its operation to claims of indirect race discrimination.

[181] Abortion Act 1967, s 4(2).

The Human Fertilisation and Embryology Act 1990—which regulates the creation, keep- **8.126**
ing, and use of embryos outside the human body, and the storage and use of gametes to create
embryos—contains a similar conscientious objection clause which provides that 'no person
who has a conscientious objection to participating in any activity governed by this Act shall
be under any duty, however arising, to do so'.[182]

The right of conscientious objection in section 4(1) of the Abortion Act 1967 applies where **8.127**
the person concerned is being asked 'to participate in any treatment authorised by this Act'.
ie treatment authorized by section 1 of the Abortion Act 1967. It has been held that the
word 'participate', in its ordinary and natural meaning, refers to 'actually taking part in treatment administered in a hospital or other approved place . . . for the purpose of terminating
a pregnancy'.[183]

It was found that a medical secretary required by her employer to type a letter referring a **8.128**
patient to a consultant with a view to termination of the patient's pregnancy was not participating in any treatment authorized by the Act within the meaning of section 4(1) and,
consequently, was not entitled to claim conscientious objection as a justification for her
refusal to do so.[184]

In *Doogan*, the Inner House of the Court of Session rejected an argument that the right of **8.129**
conscientious objection is limited to a right to refuse to participate only in those activities
which directly bring about the termination of the pregnancy.[185] The reclaimers in *Doogan*
were two Roman Catholic midwives who objected to participating in abortions on religious
grounds. They petitioned for judicial review of a decision by a local health board that section
4(1) did not confer on them any right to refuse to delegate to, supervise, or support staff
in the provision of nursing care to patients undergoing medical termination of pregnancy.
It had been accepted by the Outer House that the right of conscientious objection did not
apply since their roles, which were supervisory and administrative in nature, did not require
direct involvement in the termination process.

The Inner House disagreed, holding that 'the right of conscientious objection extends not **8.130**
only to the actual medical or surgical termination but to the whole process of treatment given
for that purpose'.[186]

The Court observed that the right of conscientious objection is given in section 4: **8.131**

> . . . because it is recognised that the process of abortion is felt by many people to be morally
> repugnant . . . it is a matter on which many people have strong moral and religious convictions,
> and the right of conscientious objection is given out of respect for those convictions and not
> for any other reason. It is in keeping with the reason for the exemption that the wide interpre-
> tation which we favour should be given to it. It is consistent with the reasoning which allowed

---

[182] Human Fertilisation and Embryology Act 1990, s 38(1).
[183] *Janaway v Salford Area Health Authority* [1988] 3 WLR 1350 (HL) para 570 *per* Lord Keith.
[184] *Janaway* (n 183).
[185] *Doogan v Greater Glasgow and Clyde Health Board* [2013] SLT 515 (CSIH).
[186] *Doogan* (n 185) para 37. At para 36, referring to the case of *Janaway* (n 183), it was observed that the
duties of the reclaimers were far removed from those of a secretary typing a letter of referral, and it had not been
argued that their duties involved anything other than treatment in the proper sense; the reclaimers were, in the
words of Keith LJ in *Janaway*, 'actually taking part in treatment administered in a hospital or other approved
place . . . for the purpose of terminating a pregnancy'.

such an objection in the first place that it should extend to any involvement in the process of treatment, the object of which is to terminate a pregnancy.[187]

(2) Work tasks and beliefs concerning same-sex couples

8.132 In a number of cases employees have sought to be excused from carrying out work tasks which conflict with a sincerely held belief that the practice of homosexuality is sinful. Although raising issues of controversy on both sides of the debate, the actual area of conflict has proved to be limited to activities which in some way involve taking an active part in promoting or facilitating the practice of homosexuality, for example officiating at civil partnerships and facilitating the formation of a same-sex union.[188]

8.133 Cases such as these have generally been approached not from the point of view of the practicability of accommodating the employee's views but whether, as a matter of principle, the employer could legitimately refuse to accommodate views which were incompatible with its declared principles relating to equality and diversity.[189] The answer has generally been an emphatic yes. This approach has meant that there has been no meaningful balancing exercise between competing interests.

8.134 In *Ladele* the claimant, a registrar of births, marriages, and deaths, was disciplined when she refused to officiate at civil partnerships on the grounds that she could not reconcile her faith with taking active part in enabling same-sex unions to be formed. In anticipation of the Civil Partnership Act 2004 coming into force, Ms Ladele had made her position clear to management and Islington Council which, as the registration authority, was required to ensure that there was a sufficient number of civil partnership registrars for its area to carry out the functions of civil partnership registrars.[190] Some registration authorities had decided not to designate registrars who shared Ms Ladele's beliefs as civil partnership registrars, which meant that such registrars were not put to a decision about whether they should conduct such registrations. Islington, however, made the decision to designate all their registrars as civil partnership registrars. Ms Ladele's continued refusal to perform civil partnership duties (which did not form part of her job description) prompted complaints from two gay registrars and was considered a breach of Islington's 'Dignity for All' equality and diversity policy. While Islington was prepared to excuse Ms Ladele from officiating at civil partnership ceremonies, it was their position that she would still be required to officiate at civil partnerships which involved no ceremonies. Ms Ladele rejected this offer on the grounds that she would still be facilitating the formation of a same-sex union. Upon being disciplined and threatened with dismissal, she brought a claim alleging direct and indirect discrimination on grounds of religion or belief.

8.135 Ms Ladele's claim for direct discrimination succeeded at first instance but the local authority's appeal was allowed by the EAT. The Court of Appeal endorsed the EAT's observation that Ms Ladele's complaint was about a failure to accommodate her difference, rather than discrimination because of that difference. In any case Ms Ladele was treated in the way she was not because of her religious belief with regard to same-sex unions, but her conduct, namely her refusal to carry out civil partnership duties.

---

[187] *Doogan* (n 185) para 38.
[188] *Islington LBC v Ladele* (n 9).
[189] See eg the observations of the EAT in *McFarlane v Relate Avon Ltd* [2010] ICR 507 (EAT), para 29.
[190] The Civil Partnership Act 2004, s 29(2).

Ms Ladele's claim of indirect discrimination turned on justification. The Court of Appeal **8.136** held that the aim Islington was seeking to pursue was to provide a service which was not only effective in terms of practicality and efficiency but also one which complied with their overarching policy of being an employer and public authority committed to the promotion of equal opportunities and fighting discrimination both externally and internally. This was a legitimate aim 'in light of Islington's "Dignity for All" policy, current legislation and mainstream thinking'.[191] Lord Neuberger MR endorsed the EAT's finding that that the only way Islington could achieve that aim was by requiring all registrars to conduct civil partnerships. He had little sympathy with the argument that this approach overlooked the requirement to show proportionality of means, stating that aim of the 'Dignity for All' policy was of general, overarching significance to Islington and also had fundamental human rights equality and diversity implications, whereas the effect of implementing the policy did not impinge on Ms Ladele's religious beliefs since she remained free to hold them and worship as she wished. Even assuming that argument could be run, the fact that Ms Ladele's refusal to perform civil partnerships was based on her religious view of marriage could not justify the conclusion that Islington should not be allowed to implement its aim to the full. Lord Neuberger highlighted the following features of the case:

> Ms Ladele was employed in a public job and was working for a public authority; she was being required to perform a purely secular task, which was being treated as part of her job; Ms Ladele's refusal to perform that task involved discriminating against gay people in the course of that job;[192] she was being asked to perform the task because of Islington's 'Dignity for All' policy, whose laudable aim was to avoid, or at least minimise, discrimination both among Islington's employees, and as between Islington (and its employees) and those in the community they served; Ms Ladele's objection was based on her view of marriage, which was not a core part of her religion; and Islington's requirement in no way prevented her from worshipping as she wished.[193]

There had, during the case, been no submissions about whether Ms Ladele's religious belief **8.137** had been 'a core part' of her religion. A finding that Ms Ladele's view of marriage was 'not a core part of her religion' might be considered an impermissible qualitative assessment of Ms Ladele's asserted belief of a kind discouraged by the House of Lords in *Williamson*.[194] Notably, no express consideration was given to how the 'Dignity for All' policy engaged or protected Ms Ladele's interests and religious rights.[195]

As for Article 9, the Court of Appeal held that this did not assist Ms Ladele since 'Article 9 **8.138** does not require that one should be allowed to manifest one's religion at any time and place of one's choosing'.[196] Ms Ladele's proper and genuine desire to have her religious views relating

---

[191] *Islington LBC v Ladele* (n 9) paras 45 and 46.

[192] It should be noted that later in his judgment, Lord Neuberger MR accepted that had Islington not designated Ms Ladele as a civil partnership registrar, there would have been a powerful case for saying that she would then have had no cause to refuse to officiate at civil partnerships and accordingly no problem of discrimination under the Equality Act (Sexual Orientation) Regulations 2007 could arise: see *Ladele* (n 188) paras 68–74.

[193] *Ladele* (n 188) para 52.

[194] See *R (Williamson) v Secretary of State for Education and Employment* [2005] 2 AC 246 (HL), para 22 *per* Lord Nicholls. For a discussion of this aspect of Lord Neuberger MR's judgment, see *MBA v the Mayor and Burgesses of the London Borough of Merton* [2012] Eq LR 526 (EAT).

[195] The Court's reasoning has been criticized for being one-sided: see eg R Sandberg, *Law and Religion* (CUP, 2011) 111.

[196] Here Lord Neuberger MR was quoting from the speech of Lord Hoffman in *Begum* (n 98) para 50.

to marriage respected should not be permitted to override Islington's concern to ensure that all its registrars manifest equal respect for the homosexual community as for the heterosexual community.

8.139   Finally, the Court of Appeal considered the effect of the Equality Act (Sexual Orientation) Regulations 2007 which prohibited discrimination on grounds of sexual orientation. Lord Neuberger MR accepted that, once Ms Ladele had been designated a civil partnership registrar, her refusal to perform civil partnerships when she was prepared to perform marriages amounted to unlawful discrimination contrary to the 2007 Regulations and that Islington was not merely entitled but obliged to require her to perform civil partnerships. He acknowledged that this argument effectively involved saying that the prohibition of discrimination by the 2007 Regulations takes precedence over any right which a person would otherwise have by virtue of his or her religious belief or faith to practice discrimination on the ground of sexual orientation. Importantly, Lord Neuberger MR added that had Islington not designated Ms Ladele as a civil partnership registrar, there would have been a powerful case for saying that no problem of discrimination under the 2007 Regulations could arise.

8.140   A similar approach was adopted in *McFarlane*, a case concerning a relationship counsellor who sought an exemption from providing psycho-sexual therapy to same-sex couples.[197] Mr McFarlane's employer made clear that this would conflict with its equal opportunities policy and refused his request. His employer subsequently doubted his willingness to offer psycho-sexual therapy to same-sex couples and dismissed him. At the EAT Mr McFarlane's claim of direct discrimination failed on the grounds that he was treated as he was not because of his Christian faith but because of his perceived unwillingness to provide psycho-sexual therapy to same-sex couples.[198]

8.141   His claim for indirect discrimination also failed. The legitimate aim on which the employer relied was the provision of a full range of counselling services to all sections of the community regardless, among other things, of their sexual orientation. Against this background, both the EAT and the Court of Appeal were expressly unwilling to countenance any balancing exercise. Drawing on its reasoning in *Ladele*,[199] the EAT observed that in a situation of this kind, detailed evaluations about the practicability of accommodating Mr McFarlane's views were out of place, the question being whether the employer was entitled to treat the issue as one of principle in which compromise was inappropriate.[200] Mr McFarlane's application for permission to appeal was dismissed by the Court of Appeal on the grounds that the case could not sensibly be distinguished from *Ladele*. According to Laws LJ, 'there is no more room here than there was there for any balancing exercise in the name of proportionality. To give effect to the applicant's position would necessarily undermine Relate's proper and legitimate policy'.[201]

8.142   Both Ms Ladele and Mr McFarlane complained to Strasbourg. While Mr McFarlane invoked Article 9 alone and in conjunction with Article 14, Ms Ladele complained only under Article 14 taken in conjunction with Article 9. Her complaint was that she had suffered

---

[197]   Mr McFarlane was willing to provide counselling where no sexual issues were involved.
[198]   *McFarlane v Relate Avon Ltd* [2010] ICR 507 (EAT).
[199]   The EAT's decision in *McFarlane* preceded the Court of Appeal's decision in *Ladele*.
[200]   *McFarlane* (n 198) para 29.
[201]   *McFarlane v Relate Avon Ltd* [2010] IRLR 872 (CA).

discrimination in being treated in the same way as employees who had no equivalent religious belief, and whose circumstances were therefore materially different from her own. The ECtHR affirmed that a failure to treat differently persons whose situations are significantly different is discriminatory if it has no objective and reasonable justification; in other words, if it does not pursue a legitimate aim or there is no reasonable relationship of proportionality between the means employed and the aim sought to be realized.[202] The Court held that the local authority's decision not to make an exception for Ms Ladele pursued a legitimate aim. As for proportionality, the Court attached weight to the serious consequences for Ms Ladele and the fact that there had been no requirement to officiate at civil partnerships when she entered into her contract of employment. On the other hand, the local authority's policy aimed to secure the rights of others, which were also protected under the Convention. National authorities had a wide margin of appreciation when it came to striking a balance between competing Convention rights. In the Court's view, the local authority had not exceeded that margin.

Mr McFarlane's application also failed. While the loss of a job was a severe sanction with grave consequences, the Court observed that Mr McFarlane had voluntarily enrolled on the training programme in psycho-sexual counselling knowing that his employer operated an equal opportunities policy and that the filtering of clients on grounds of sexual orientation would not be possible. However, the most important factor for the Court was that the employer's action was intended to secure the implementation of its policy of providing a service without discrimination. In all the circumstances, the state authorities had not exceeded the wide margin of appreciation available to them in deciding where to strike the balance between Mr McFarlane's right and the employer's interest in securing the rights of others. **8.143**

In Ms Ladele's case there was a joint dissenting opinion from Judges Vučinić and De Gaetano. They saw Ms Ladele's case as not so much one of freedom of religious belief but as one of freedom of conscience—ie that no one should be forced to act against his or her conscience or be penalized for refusing to act against his or her conscience. In their view, there was a fundamental difference between the two. They observed that the word 'conscience' was conspicuously absent from Article 9(2), but did not finally resolve the question of whether the limitations of Article 9(2) apply to prescriptions of conscience. They stated that once a genuine and serious case of conscientious objection was established, the state was obliged to respect the individual's freedom of conscience both positively and negatively. Ms Ladele's objection to officiating at civil partnerships was a genuine and serious one. They also referred to the following features of the case: the fact that her job did not include officiating at civil partnerships when she first joined the public service and therefore, unlike Mr McFarlane, it could not be said that she had waived her right to invoke conscientious objection; her case was not one of discrimination vis-à-vis a service user and therefore no balancing exercise could be carried out between Ms Ladele's concrete right to conscientious objection and a legitimate policy which protected rights in the abstract; and finally, treating Ms Ladele differently from those registrars who had no conscientious objection was something which could have been achieved without detriment to overall services, as evidenced by the experience of other local authorities. **8.144**

---

[202] *Eweida v UK* (n 90).

G. Expression of Religious Views in the Workplace

8.145 Employers may insist that employees refrain from promoting any religious views in the workplace. However, the courts and tribunals have been careful to distinguish between the promotion of religious views in the work context, and the simple expression of religious views.

8.146 In *Chondol*, a social worker was dismissed for gross misconduct for, among other things, giving a service user a bible and attempting to promote his religious beliefs to a different service user in breach of a management instruction prohibiting the overt promotion of religious beliefs by social workers. In the course of the disciplinary proceedings, Mr Chondol's employer accepted his explanation that, as regards the first incident, the service user had specifically asked him whether he had a bible, and as regards the second, all he had done was to ask the service user whether he had any belief in God or went to church. The tribunal found that, having accepted this version of events, his employer was not reasonably entitled to conclude that Mr Chondol had committed misconduct.[203]

8.147 Mr Chondol's claim for direct religious discrimination, however, failed. The tribunal found that the actual reason for the treatment he received was the employer's belief that he had been inappropriately promoting Christianity to service users (even if that belief was not a reasonable one), and not his religion. The EAT held that the distinction between, on the one hand, Mr Chondol's religious belief as such and, on the other, the inappropriate promotion of that belief was entirely valid in principle, although it acknowledged that in any case in which such a distinction is relied on it will be necessary to be clear that it reflects the employer's true reason.

8.148 *Smith* was a case concerning the expression of religious views by an employee on Facebook.[204] Mr Smith, a practising Christian, was employed in a managerial position at a private housing trust. He was made the subject of disciplinary proceedings after posting a comment on his Facebook wall page that 'gay marriage' was 'an equality too far' and, in response to a colleague's enquiry on Facebook, stating that the bible specified that marriage was for men and women and the state should not impose its rules on places of faith and conscience.

8.149 Mr Smith was found guilty of gross misconduct and demoted to a non-managerial position. The trust sought to maintain political and denominational neutrality. Its position was that by posting these comments on Facebook, which identified Mr Smith as a manager of the trust and in circumstances where a sizeable number of his Facebook friends were trust employees, he had acted contrary to the trust's equal opportunities policy and committed breaches of its code of conduct which prohibited employees from attempting to promote their political or religious views, or engaging in any activities which might bring the trust into disrepute either at work or outside work.

8.150 Mr Smith successfully brought a claim for damages for breach of his employment contract. The Court found that Mr Smith's postings about gay marriage were not such as to bring the trust into disrepute. Mr Smith used Facebook for personal and social purposes rather than work-related purposes, and no reasonable reader of his Facebook wall page could rationally

---

[203] *Chondol v Liverpool City Council* [2009] EAT 0298/08. The dismissal was found to be fair having regard to other incidents.
[204] *Smith v Trafford Housing Trust* [2013] IRLR 86.

conclude that the postings were in any relevant sense made on behalf of the trust. Quite apart from this, it was difficult to envisage how any loss of reputation would arise in the mind of any reasonable reader of Mr Smith's postings. The trust prided itself on encouraging diversity, which formed part of its reputation, but this inevitably involved employing persons with widely different religious and political beliefs and views, some of which, however moderately expressed, might cause distress among the holders of deeply felt opposite views.

As for the prohibition on the promotion of political and religious views, the Court held that this was plainly not designed to prohibit any discussion of politics and religion even in the workplace; rather, it was concerned with proselytizing, canvassing, and more generally with the advancement of religious or political views with a view to persuading recipients to accept them. Mr Smith's comments could not sensibly be regarded as promotion in this sense. **8.151**

The Court went on to consider the extent to which the prohibition on the promotion of political and religious views, properly interpreted, extended to an employee's personal social life. It observed that: **8.152**

> The right of individuals to freedom of expression and freedom of belief, taken together, means that they are in general entitled to promote their religious or political beliefs, providing they do so lawfully. Of course, an employer may legitimately restrict or prohibit such activities at work, or in a work related context, but it would be prima facie surprising to find that an employer had, by the incorporation of a code of conduct into the employee's contract, extended that prohibition to his personal or social life.[205]

It concluded that the prohibition on promoting religious views did not extend to Mr Smith's Facebook wall, which did not have the necessary work-related context. The Court reached the same conclusion in relation to the part of the code and equal opportunities policy which provided that employees should treat their colleagues with dignity and respect, being non-judgmental in their approach and not engaging in any conduct which may make another person feel uncomfortable, embarrassed, or upset. The Court observed that the lawful expression of religious or political views may frequently cause a degree of upset, and even offence, to those with deeply held contrary views, even where none was intended by the speaker. This was the price to be paid for freedom of speech, and to construe the provisions as having application to every situation outside the workplace where an employee came into contact with one or more work colleagues would be to impose a fetter on this freedom.[206] However, the Court went on to observe that the issue was of course a matter of fact and degree and it was not difficult to imagine the use of Facebook, for example, to pass judgment on the morality of a named work colleague, which would contravene this part of the code and equal opportunities policy.[207] Moreover, the Court emphasized that a degree of objectivity had to be applied to Mr Smith's posting. Statements about politics and religion were more prone to misinterpretation than others, and it would not be a reasonable interpretation of the code and policy that they should be taken to have been infringed if language which **8.153**

---

[205] *Smith* (n 204) para 66.

[206] *Smith* (n 204) para 82.

[207] See *Sanchez v Spain* (2012) 54 EHRR 24, in which the ECtHR held that an attack by a trade union publication on the respectability of employees by using grossly insulting or offensive expressions, overstepped the limits the right to freedom of expression. Such an attack in a professional environment, on account of its disruptive effects, amounted to a particularly serious form of misconduct justifying severe sanctions, including dismissal.

was non-judgmental, not disrespectful, nor inherently upsetting nonetheless caused upset merely because it had been misinterpreted.[208]

H. Religious Rights of Employers

(1) Exceptions under the Equality Act 2010

8.154 The Equality Act 2010 contains a number of exceptions to the non-discrimination provisions which afford limited protection to the religious rights of employers and, more broadly, the organization of religious communities.[209]

8.155 Two of the exceptions are specifically religion-based. The first applies where employment is 'for the purposes of an organised religion' (Equality Act 2010, Schedule 9, paragraph 2). Here an employer may discriminate on specified grounds so as to comply with the doctrines of the religion or so as to avoid conflicting with the strongly held convictions of a significant number of the religion's followers. The second exception permits an employer with 'an ethos based on religion or belief' to discriminate on grounds of religion or belief where being of a particular religion or belief is an occupational requirement and it can be justified (Equality Act 2010, Schedule 9, paragraph 3).

8.156 There is, in addition, a generally applicable exception which permits employers to impose a requirement that an employee have a particular protected characteristic where it can be shown that it is an occupational requirement (Equality Act 2010, Schedule 9, paragraph 1). Unlike previous legislation, the Equality Act 2010 does not require it to be a 'determining' occupational requirement.

8.157 The exceptions are intended to implement Article 4 of Council Directive (EC) 2000/78 and they must, so far as possible, be construed to give effect to the objective of the Directive.[210]

(a) Article 4 of Council Directive (EC) 2000/78

8.158 Article 4 has two sections. Whereas Article 4(1) is generally applicable, Article 4(2) makes provision for a more flexible occupational requirement exception for the benefit of churches and other organizations with an ethos based on religion or belief, but it only permits a difference of treatment on grounds of religion or belief.

8.159 Article 4(1) states that:

> ... Member States may provide that a difference of treatment based on a characteristic related to any of the grounds referred to in Article 1 shall not constitute discrimination where, by reason of the nature of the particular occupational activities concerned or of the context in which they are carried out, such a characteristic constitutes a genuine and determining occupational requirement, provided that the objective is legitimate and the requirement is proportionate.

8.160 Article 4(1) permits a more limited derogation than Article 4(2) in that it requires the characteristic on which the difference of treatment is based to be a 'determining' occupational requirement. Recital 23 to the Directive makes clear that the circumstances in which a difference of treatment is justified are 'very limited'.

---

[208] *Smith* (n 204) para 83.
[209] See discussion in *Amicus* (n 13) paras 42–44.
[210] See eg Case C-106/89 *Marleasing SA* (n 8); *Hashwani* (n 7) para 8.

Article 4(2), which is for the benefit of churches and organizations with an ethos based on **8.161** religion or belief, provides as follows:[211]

> Member States may maintain national legislation in force at the date of the adoption of this Directive or provide for future legislation incorporating national practices existing at the date of adoption of this Directive pursuant to which, in the case of occupational activities within churches and other public or private organisations the ethos of which is based on religion or belief, a difference of treatment based on a person's religion or belief shall not constitute discrimination where, by reason of the nature of these activities or of the context in which they are carried out, a person's religion or belief constitute a genuine, legitimate and justified occupational requirement, having regard to the organisation's ethos.

Article 4(2) goes onto clarify three points: first, that 'this difference in treatment shall be **8.162** implemented taking account of Member States' constitutional provisions and principles, as well as the general principles of Community law; secondly, that this difference in treatment 'should not justify discrimination on another ground'—ie any ground other than 'religion or belief'; and thirdly, it provides that:

> *Provided its provisions are otherwise complied with*, this Directive shall *thus* not *prejudice* the right of churches and other public or private organisations, the ethos of which is based on religion or belief, acting in conformity with national constitutions and laws, to require individuals working for them to act in good faith and with loyalty to the organisation's ethos. (emphasis added)

The wording (particularly the wording emphasized) suggests that this final section of **8.163** Article 4(2) is not an additional derogation. It simply clarifies that churches and organizations with an ethos based on religion or belief can require their employees to act consistently with the organization's ethos *provided* this does not breach the provisions of the Directive. It does not therefore permit the application of a requirement that is discriminatory.[212]

(b) Employment for the purposes of an organized religion

Provided specified criteria are met, the Equality Act 2010 permits discrimination against **8.164** employees, applicants, and office holders on grounds of sex, gender reassignment, marriage, and sexual orientation, where employment is 'for the purposes of an organised religion'.[213] This means that, for example, a mosque may require its imam to be male and heterosexual in accordance with Islamic teaching, without contravening provisions prohibiting discrimination on grounds of sex and sexual orientation.

This exception is intended to form part of the implementation of Article 4(1) of Council **8.165** Directive (EC) 2000/78.[214] Although the Equality Act 2010 (like the legislation it replaced) contains a general exception for occupational requirements intended to form part of the

---

[211] For a summary of the background to Art 4(2) see Y Stox, 'Religious-Ethos Employers and Other Expressive Employers under European and Belgian Employment Law' in K Alidadi et al (eds), *A Test of Faith? Religious Diversity and Accommodation in the European Workplace* (Ashgate, 2012).

[212] See generally *O'Neill v Governors of St Thomas More RCVA Upper School* [1996] IRLR 372 (EAT) and *Percy v Church of Scotland Board of Mission* [2006] 2 AC 28 (HL). In *O'Neill*, a teacher of religious education at a Roman Catholic school was constructively dismissed after she became pregnant by a Roman Catholic priest. The EAT found that dismissal was discriminatory on the grounds of sex; the circumstances relied on by the governors were all causally related to the claimant's pregnancy.

[213] Equality Act 2010, Sch 9, para 2. Equivalent exemptions could previously be found in the Sex Discrimination Act 1975, s 19 and the Employment Equality (Sexual Orientation) Regulations 2003, reg 7(3).

[214] *Amicus* (n 13) para 89.

implementation of Article 4(1),[215] the specific and separate exception for the benefit of organized religions was introduced—at least in respect of discrimination on grounds of sexual orientation—as a result of representations from the Churches, and the government's view that the delicate balance between the competing claims of those asserting rights in respect of sexual orientation and those asserting religious rights was properly one for the legislature.[216]

8.166 The exception is narrow in its scope. In *R (Amicus) v Secretary of State for Trade and Industry*, a challenge to the equivalent exemption in the Employment Equality (Sexual Orientation) Regulations 2003 failed. The Court held that exception had to be construed strictly, since it was a derogation from the principle of equal treatment, and purposively, so as to ensure compatibility with the Directive as far as possible. The exception was on its proper construction very narrow[217] and, so construed, it was a lawful implementation of Article 4(1) of Directive 2000/78. Any requirement that met the conditions in the exception pursued a legitimate aim for the purposes of Article 4(1) and, in the Court's view, the balance struck in this sensitive and difficult area was appropriate and proportionate. Moreover, there was said to be no incompatibility with Article 8 or 14 ECHR.[218]

8.167 The effect of the exception is that, provided specified criteria are satisfied, a person may lawfully apply, in relation to employment, a requirement to be of a particular sex, a requirement not to be a transsexual person, various specified requirements relating to marriage and civil partnership, and a requirement related to sexual orientation.[219] The choice of the wording 'related to sexual orientation' (rather than 'being of a particular sexual orientation') was deliberate so as to accommodate the concerns of some churches about certain forms of sexual *behaviour* rather than sexuality per se.[220]

8.168 The exception applies only where the following criteria are satisfied.

8.169 First, the employment must be 'for the purposes of an organised religion'.[221] This is a narrower expression than 'for the purposes of a religious organisation', or the expression 'where an employer has an ethos based on religion or belief' used in paragraph 3 of Schedule 9 to the Equality Act 2010.[222] The Explanatory Notes to the Equality Act 2010 explain that it is intended to cover a very narrow range of employment, such as ministers of religion and a small number of lay posts, including those that exist to promote and represent religion.[223] In *Reaney* it was held that employment as a Diocesan Youth Officer for the Diocese of Hereford was for the purposes of an organized religion, namely the religion of the Church of England. The role was not that of an ordained minister. However, having considered the substance of the work involved, the tribunal found that the role would be closely associated with the

---

[215] See Equality Act 2010, Sch 9, para 1.

[216] *Amicus* (n 13) paras 89–91. At para 123 Richards J noted that the 'exception involves a legislative striking of the balance between competing rights. It was done deliberately this way so as to reduce the issues that would have to be determined by courts or tribunals in such a sensitive field'.

[217] *Amicus* (n 13) para 115.

[218] *Amicus* (n 13) paras 176–199.

[219] See the Equality Act 2010, Sch 9, para 2(4).

[220] *Amicus* (n 13) paras 119 and 108.

[221] Equality Act 2010, Sch 9, para 2(1)(a).

[222] *Amicus* (n 13) para 116.

[223] Equality Act 2010, Explanatory Notes, para 790. See also *Hansard* HL, vol 649, cols 778–780 (17 June 2003).

promotion of the Church and fell within the small number of posts outside the clergy which were within the scope of the exception.[224]

The precise scope of the term has not yet received authoritative consideration, but it is likely **8.170** to be narrowly construed.[225]

Secondly, the employer must show that the application of the requirement engages 'the com- **8.171** pliance or non-conflict principle'.[226] The compliance principle is engaged if the requirement is applied so as to comply with the doctrines of the religion.[227] The non-conflict principle is engaged if, 'because of the nature or context of the employment, the requirement is applied so as to avoid conflicting with the strongly held religious convictions of a significant number of the religion's followers'.[228]

In *R (Amicus) v Secretary of State for Trade and Industry*, the Court held that the compliance **8.172** principle is to be read not as a subjective test concerning the motivation of the employer, but as an objective test 'whereby it must be shown that employment of a person not meeting the requirement would be incompatible with the doctrines of the religion'.[229] Similarly, the non-conflict principle was also an objective test. The Court observed that while the non-conflict principle was wider than the compliance principle, it was still hemmed about by restrictive language and was going to be a far from easy test to satisfy in practice.[230]

On a separate note, the Court held that reference to a 'significant number' of the religion's **8.173** followers rather than to all, or the majority of, a religion's followers ensured that proper account was taken of the existence of differing bodies of opinion even within an organized religion. It was legitimate to allow for the possibility of applying a relevant requirement even if the convictions in question are held only by a significant minority of followers.[231]

Finally, the employer must show that the person to whom the requirement is applied does not **8.174** meet it, or that he has reasonable grounds for not being satisfied that the person meets it.[232] The latter permits an employer to rely on the exemption based on their perception of the person's sexual orientation or marriage status for example, provided there is some reasonable basis for it. It does not apply where the employer applies a requirement to be of a particular sex.[233]

In *Reaney*, the employment tribunal held that on the facts of that case the employer could **8.175** not rely on the exception in the Employment Equality (Sexual Orientation) Regulations 2003 since the claimant, who had applied for the position of Diocesan Youth Officer, met the requirement for the post relating to sexual orientation. His relationship had ended some months before and he was committed to undertaking the work in the Church of England

---

[224] *Reaney v Hereford Diocesan Board of Finance* [2007] ET 1602844/2006.

[225] In *Amicus* (n 13) para 16, Richards J observed that the fact the exception in the Employment Equality (Sexual Orientation) Regulations 2003 applied only to employment for the purposes of an organized religion was an 'important initial limitation'. The implication was that, unless narrowly construed, there was a risk the exemption would be incompatible with the obligations imposed on the UK by Directive (EC) 2000/78.

[226] Equality Act 2010, Sch 9, para 2(1)(b). These terms are new to the Equality Act 2010, although the principles themselves are not.

[227] Equality Act 2010, Sch 9, para 2(5).

[228] Equality Act 2010, Sch 9, para 2(6).

[229] *Amicus* (n 13) para 117.

[230] *Amicus* (n 13) para 117.

[231] *Amicus* (n 13) para 118.

[232] Equality Act 2010, Sch 9, para 2(1)(c).

[233] Equality Act 2010, Sch 9, para 2(8).

in full compliance with the requirement not to enter into a sexual relationship with another person. He had indicated that he was happy to remain celibate for the duration of the post. Further, applying the second limb, the tribunal found that it was not reasonable for the Bishop to be unsatisfied in all the circumstances that the claimant met the requirement. He had no evidence to suggest that the claimant was not telling the truth when he said he did not have any present relationship.[234]

(c) Persons with an ethos based on religion or belief

8.176 The Equality Act 2010 contains a specific exemption for the benefit of persons with 'an ethos based on religion or belief'. A person with a religious ethos can lawfully apply, in relation to work, a requirement that a person be of a particular religion or belief.[235] For example, a religious organization may want to restrict applicants for the post of head of the organization to those people that adhere to a particular faith. The exception is intended to implement Article 4(2) of Directive (EC) 2000/78.

8.177 A rigorous approach must be adopted to the question of whether the particular exception applies.[236] The exception applies only where the following criteria are met:

8.178 First, in order to take advantage of the exception, a person must have 'an ethos based on religion or belief'. The Explanatory Notes provide that it is for an employer to show that it has an ethos based on religion or belief by reference to such evidence as the organization's founding constitution.[237]

8.179 Certain employers—such as local authorities—cannot, by their nature, have an ethos based on religion or belief. In *Glasgow v McNab* an atheist teacher working in a Roman Catholic school brought a claim for religious discrimination against the education authority which maintained the school, when he unsuccessfully applied for a post at the school which was reserved for Roman Catholic teachers. In considering whether the equivalent exemption under the Employment Equality (Religion or Belief) Regulations 2003 applied, the EAT upheld the decision of the tribunal that the education authority could not show that it was an employer which had an 'ethos based on religion or belief'. It took the view that an education authority does not have a religious ethos. The fact that it operated a statutory system under which it enabled denominations to advance their ethos through schools maintained by it, did not mean that it espoused the same ethos. Indeed, as a local authority it had no business seeking to follow or further any particular religious ethos at all.[238] The EAT also indicated that an organization would not qualify for the protection afforded by the exemption if only part of it had a religious ethos.[239]

8.180 A local education authority employer can, however, take advantage of the provisions in the School Standards and Framework Act 1998 which permit preference to be given, in

---

[234] *Reaney* (n 224).

[235] Equality Act 2010, Sch 9, para 3. The exemption could previously be found in the Employment Equality (Religion or Belief) Regulations 2003, reg 7(3). It should be noted that the wording of exemption in the Equality Act 2010 is not identical to the exemption in reg 7(3) of the 2003 Regulations. It is not clear whether the difference in wording is of any significance. In *Hashwani* (n 7), para 54, Clarke LJ observed that it had not been suggested that there was 'any significant difference' between the Equality Act 2010, Sch 9, para 3 and reg 7(3).

[236] *Hashwani* (n 7) para 53.

[237] Equality Act 2010, Explanatory Notes, para 795.

[238] *Glasgow City Council v McNab* [2007] IRLR 476 (EAT), para 61.

[239] *Glasgow v McNab* (n 238) para 61.

connection with appointment, remuneration, or promotion of teachers, to persons whose religious opinions are in accordance with the tenets of the religion or religious denomination specified in relation to the school.[240] Giving such preference would not contravene the provisions of the Equality Act 2010.[241]

Secondly, a person who wishes to take advantage of the exception in paragraph 3 of Schedule 9 to the Equality Act 2010 must show that, having regard to its religious ethos and to the nature or context of the work, the requirement to be of a particular religion or belief is 'an occupational requirement'.[242]   **8.181**

Under the Employment Equality (Religion or Belief) Regulations 2003 it was necessary to show that being of a particular religion or belief was a 'genuine' occupational requirement. The omission of the word 'genuine' in paragraph 3 of Schedule 9 to the Equality Act 2010 is unlikely to be of any real significance and is on any view implicit. Whether a particular religion or belief is an occupational requirement is to be assessed having regard to the employer's religious ethos and to the nature or context of the work. It is difficult to see how a requirement which has no connection with either an organization's religious ethos, or the nature or context of its work, can properly be said to be a *genuine* occupational requirement.   **8.182**

Thirdly, the employer must show that, having regard to its ethos and to the nature or context of the work, the application of the requirement to be of a particular religion or belief is a proportionate means of achieving a legitimate aim.[243]   **8.183**

Finally, it must be shown that the person to whom the employer applies the requirement does not meet it, or the employer has reasonable grounds for not being satisfied that the person meets it.[244]   **8.184**

It should be noted that a religious organization wishing to apply a requirement that its employees be of a particular religion or belief may find that it is more readily able to take advantage of the generally applicable exception in paragraph 1 of Schedule 9 to the Equality Act 2010. Historically, the generally applicable exception was narrower. The requirement to have a particular characteristic had to be a 'determining' occupational requirement. Under the Equality Act 2010 this is no longer required. This means that the criteria for the exceptions in paragraphs 1 and 3 are the same, save that paragraph 3 applies only where the employer has 'an ethos based on religion or belief'. In this respect, paragraph 3 imposes an additional requirement and is narrower in scope. The more flexible exception in paragraph 1 leaves paragraph 3 redundant in practice.[245]   **8.185**

(d) Occupational requirements—general

The Equality Act 2010 contains a generally applicable exception which allows a person to apply, in relation to work, a requirement to have a particular protected characteristic if it   **8.186**

---

[240] SSFA 1998, s 60(5). See paras 8.189–8.194.
[241] Equality Act 2010, Sch 22, para 4.
[242] Equality Act 2010, Sch 9, para 3(a).
[243] Equality Act 2010, Sch 9, para 3(b).
[244] Equality Act 2010, Sch 9, para 3(c).
[245] There may conceivably be cases where it is easier to show that the requirement to be of a particular religious belief is an occupational requirement having regard to the employer's ethos. But it is likely that the employer's ethos would, in any case, fall to be considered as part of the 'context' of the work.

can be shown that, having regard to the nature or context of the work, it is an occupational requirement, that the application of the requirement is a proportionate means of achieving a legitimate aim, and that the person to whom the employer applies the requirement does not meet it, or the employer has reasonable grounds for not being satisfied that the person meets it.[246] This exception also forms part of the implementation of article 4(1) of Directive (EC) 2000/78.

8.187 The exception in the Equality Act 2010 is broader than the equivalent exception under previous legislation, which applied only where having a particular characteristic was a 'genuine and *determining*' occupational requirement of the job. In other words, it had to be an essential requirement for the job.[247] This imposed a more stringent test than the exception for persons with an ethos based on religion or belief, where the requirement to be of a particular religion or belief needed to be no more than a genuine occupational requirement.

8.188 The words 'genuine' and 'determining' have both been dropped from paragraph 1 of Schedule 9 to the Equality Act 2010. An employer now only has to show that the requirement to have a particular protected characteristic is 'an occupational requirement'. This broadens the scope of the exception beyond that contemplated by Article 4(1) of the Directive.[248] It is likely that this provision will become the one most employed or relied on by religious organizations.[249]

(2) The School Standards and Framework Act 1998

(a) The relevant provisions

8.189 There is specific provision in the education context for the protection of religious rights. The School Standards and Framework Act 1998 (SSFA 1998) protects teachers and other staff employed at maintained schools and Academies against discrimination by reason of their religious opinions and attendance or non-attendance at religious worship. The relevant provisions—in section 59 of SSFA 1998 (maintained schools) and section 124AA of SSFA 1998 (Academies)—are considered in part C.

8.190 However, SSFA 1998 expressly permits schools with a religious character (ie faith schools)[250] to impose requirements relating to religion and religious belief on teachers, including applicants for teaching positions. The degree of freedom afforded depends on the type of school.[251]

8.191 If the school is a voluntary aided school[252] section 60(5)(a) of SSFA 1998 provides that:

> Preference may be given, in connection with the appointment, remuneration or promotion of teachers at the school, to persons—
> (i) whose religious opinions are in accordance with the tenets of the religion or religious denomination specified in relation to the school . . . or,

---

[246] Equality Act 2010, Sch 9, para 1. This exemption could previously be found in the Employment Equality (Religion or Belief) Regulations 2003, reg 7(2) and the Employment Equality (Sexual Orientation) Regulations 2003, reg 7(2).

[247] *Hashwani* (n 7) para 59.

[248] Council Directive (EC) 2000/78, Art 4(1) refers to 'genuine and determining occupational requirement'.

[249] See para 8.185.

[250] Certain schools can be designated by Order of the Secretary of State as having a 'religious character': SSFA 1998, s 69.

[251] For an overview of educational provision in the UK, including different types of school, see Ch 9.

[252] A voluntary aided school is maintained by the local authority, but the land and building are owned by a charitable foundation, usually a religious organization, and staff are employed by the school's governing body.

>   (ii) who attend religious worship in accordance with those tenets, or
>   (iii) who give, or are willing to give, religious education at the school in accordance with those
>   tenets.

Further, section 60(5)(b) provides that at voluntary aided schools: **8.192**

>   ... regard may be had, in connection with the termination of the employment or engage-
>   ment of any teacher at the school, to any conduct on his part which is incompatible with the
>   precepts, or with the upholding of the tenets, of the religion or religious denomination so
>   specified.

It should be noted that these provisions apply only to teachers. Section 60(6) of SSFA 1998   **8.193**
makes clear that a person shall not be disqualified by reason of his religious opinions, or of
attending or omitting to attend religious worship from being employed or engaged for the
purposes of the school otherwise than as a teacher.[253]

Foundation and voluntary controlled schools are not given the same freedom to impose   **8.194**
religious requirements in respect of their teachers.[254] Put simply, religious requirements can
only be imposed on a specified portion of the total number of teachers. Section 58(2) of
SSFA 1998 provides that the teachers at foundation and voluntary controlled schools must
include persons who are selected for their fitness and competence to give such religious education as is required under the Act and who are specifically appointed to do so.[255] Teachers
employed in pursuance of this section are known as 'reserved teachers'. Reserved teachers
in such schools cannot exceed one-fifth of the total number of teachers, including the head
teacher.[256] Section 60(5) applies only in relation to reserved teachers at the school.[257]

As for independent schools, section 124A of the SSFA 1998 replicates section 60(5) of   **8.195**
the SSFA 1998 in respect of employment of teachers at independent schools having a religious character. The position of Academies with a religious character is virtually the same
vis-à-vis appointment of staff as foundation or voluntary schools, in other words, religious
requirements can only be imposed on reserved teachers.[258] The main difference relates to
the appointment of a person to be the principal of the Academy. Where the principal of the
school is not to be a reserved teacher, regard may be had to an applicant's ability and fitness
to preserve and develop the religious character of the Academy.[259]

(b) Relationship with the Equality Act 2010

The Equality Act 2010 (Schedule 22, paragraph 4) provides that a person does not contra-   **8.196**
vene the Equality Act 2010 by doing anything which is permitted by SSFA 1998.[260]

Indeed, the provisions in SSFA 1998 permitting discrimination on grounds of religion or   **8.197**
religious belief are more generous to employers than the occupational requirement exceptions

---

[253] This replicates s 59(2) of SSFA 1998, s 59(2). See paras 8.64–8.73.
[254] Foundation and voluntary controlled schools are wholly maintained by the local authority. In voluntary
controlled schools, the local authority will also employ staff at the school. In foundations schools, staff are
employed by the school's governing body.
[255] This only applies where the number of teachers at a school exceeds two.
[256] SSFA 1998, s 58(3).
[257] SSFA 1998, s 60(3) and (8). Section 59(2) and (4) applies to all other teachers and staff: SSFA 1998,
s 60(2) and (3).
[258] SSFA 1998, s 124AA replicates the relevant provisions in SSFA 1998, ss 58 and 60(5).
[259] SSFA 1998, s 124AA(5).
[260] Specifically, it is not a contravention of the Equality Act 2010 to do anything permitted for the purposes
of SSFA 1998, ss 60(4) and (5), 124A, and 124AA(5)–(7).

in paragraphs 1 and 3 of Schedule 9 to the Equality Act 2010, particularly in respect of voluntary aided schools. For example, under SSFA 1998 an employer who sets a preference for its teachers to have religious opinions in accordance with the tenets of the religion/religious denomination of the school, is not required to show that this is an occupational requirement, or that it is a proportionate means of achieving a legitimate aim.[261]

8.198 Even more generous are the provisions permitting employers, when making a decision to dismiss, to take account of conduct on the part of a teacher which is incompatible with religious standards.[262] This may result in dismissals which are discriminatory but not unlawful. For example, the dismissal of a teacher at a faith school on the grounds that he has had a homosexual relationship contrary to the tenets of the religion specified in relation to the school, may be discriminatory on grounds of sexual orientation but it would not constitute unlawful discrimination by virtue of Schedule 22 to the Equality Act 2010. This raises questions about the compatibility of the provisions in SSFA 1998 with Council Directive (EC) 2000/78. Article 4(2) affirms that the Directive does not prejudice the right of an organization, the ethos of which is based on religion or belief, to require individuals working for it to act with loyalty to the organization's ethos 'provided that its provisions are otherwise complied with'.[263]

(3) Protections under the ECHR

8.199 Article 9 ECHR protects not only the individual but also religious communities. The ECtHR has stated that Article 9, interpreted in the light of Article 11, safeguards the autonomy of religious communities—including their internal organization—against unjustified state interference.[264] It is recognized that a religious employer that imposes a duty of loyalty on employees (requiring them to lead lives that are consistent with the teaching of the particular faith) enjoys rights under Article 9.[265] The imposition of a duty of loyalty may, however,

---

[261] Granted, it is unlikely this would be too difficult to show where the teacher is a teacher of religious education. During the passage of the Education Bill (which became the Education Act 2011), an amendment to SSFA 1998 s 60 was introduced in the Lords (on 22 June 2011), purporting to bring the provision in line with the Equality Act 2010 and Council Directive (EC) 2000/78.

[262] SSFA 1998, ss 60(5)(b) and 124AA(7).

[263] Council Directive (EC) 2000/78, Art 4(2). See paras 8.162–8.163.

[264] *Hasan v Bulgaria* (2002) 34 EHRR 1339. The ECtHR stated at para 62:

> Where the organisation of the religious community is in issue, Article 9 must be interpreted in the light of Article 11, which safeguards associative life against unjustified State interference. Seen in this perspective, the believer's right of freedom of religion encompasses the expectation that the community will be allowed to function peacefully, free from arbitrary State intervention. Indeed, the autonomous existence of religious communities is indispensable for pluralism in a democratic society and is thus an issue at the very heart of the protection which Article 9 affords. It directly concerns not only the organisation of the community as such but also the effective enjoyment of the right to freedom of religion by all its active members. Were the organisational life of the community not protected by Article 9 of the Convention, all other aspects of the individual's freedom of religion would become vulnerable.

Followed in *Obst v Germany* (App 425/03) (2010) and *Schüth v Germany* (App 1620/03) (2010). In the domestic context, see *New Testament Church of God* (n 22) para 60, where Arden LJ acknowledged:

> One aspect of freedom of religion is the freedom of a religious organisation to be allowed to function peacefully and free from arbitrary state intervention. This aspect of the freedom has been said to derive from Art.9, interpreted in the light of Art.11, but it is properly described as derived from Art.9: Hasan and Chaush v Bulgaria (2002) 34 EHRR 55 at [62] and [64].

[265] *Obst* (n 264) and *Schüth* (n 264).

impinge on the employee's right to freedom of religion under Article 9 or their right to respect for private or family life under Article 8. The ECtHR has considered a number of cases where these competing interests have been at stake and has affirmed that this is an area where the state enjoys a wide margin of appreciation.[266] In examining the balance struck by domestic courts between the competing interests of a religious employer and employee, it has held that the fact that the courts have attached more weight to the interests of the employer does not itself raise an issue under the Convention.[267]

In *Obst v Germany* there was found to be no violation of the Article 8 rights of a director **8.200** of public relations for the Mormon Church who was dismissed for having an extra-marital affair. The ECtHR held that the labour courts had taken account of all the relevant factors and carried out a detailed and meticulous balancing exercise between the applicant's rights to respect for private life under Article 8 and the rights enjoyed by the Church employer under Article 9. Relevant considerations included the nature of the applicant's post and the fact that as a director of public relations he had increased duties of loyalty. It was also relevant that he had grown up in the Mormon Church and should have been aware of the importance of marital fidelity to his employer when signing his employment contract, and the incompatibility of his conduct with his increased duties of loyalty.

On the other hand, in *Schüth v Germany* the ECtHR found that the labour courts had failed **8.201** to balance the interests of the Church and the employee in a manner compatible with the ECHR. The applicant had been an organist and a choirmaster in a Catholic parish and was dismissed when his employer discovered that he had a child with a woman who was not his wife. The Court held that the interests of the Church had not been weighed against the applicant's right to respect for his private and family life, nor had the labour courts examined the Church's view that the applicant's functions were so closely bound up with the Church's proclamatory mission that the parish could not continue employing him without losing all credibility. The ECtHR emphasized that a more detailed examination was required when weighing the competing rights and interests at stake, particularly where the individual right of an applicant had to be balanced against a collective right. Further, it observed that the courts had given only marginal consideration to the lack of media coverage in the case, the fact that after 14 years' service the applicant had not challenged the Church but simply failed to observe it in practice, and the fact that the impugned conduct was at the very heart of his private life. The fact that the applicant had limited opportunities of finding another job was also important. The ECtHR concluded that there had been a violation of the applicant's Article 8 rights.

In *Siebenhaar v Germany* the applicant complained of a violation of her rights under **8.202** Article 9. She had been employed as a childcare assistant in a day nursery run by a Protestant parish and later in a management position at a kindergarten run by another Protestant parish. Her employment contract required loyalty to the Protestant Church and she was not permitted to be a member of, or work for, organisations whose views or activities were in contradiction to the Church's mandate. The applicant was dismissed when her employer found out that she was an active member of the Universal Church. The ECtHR held that the labour courts had carried out a careful and thorough balancing exercise between the applicant's

---

[266] *Obst* (n 264) and *Schüth* (n 264).
[267] *Schüth* (n 264) *Siebenhaar v Germany* (App 18136/02) (2011).

right to freedom of religion under Article 9 and the rights of the Protestant Church under Article 9. The Federal Labour Court had found that, given her active commitment to the Universal Church, the applicant could no longer be trusted to respect her employer's ideals and her dismissal had been necessary to preserve the Church's credibility. The relatively short duration of her employment had also been taken into account. The ECtHR concluded that there had been no violation of Article 9.

8.203 It is clear from these decisions that the employee's role within the organization and the impact of the impugned conduct on the employer will be important considerations.

I. Procedure and Remedies

(1) Discrimination claims

8.204 An employment tribunal has jurisdiction to determine a complaint relating to Part 5 of the Equality Act 2010.[268]

(a) Time limit

8.205 Proceedings in the employment tribunal must be brought within three months from the date of the act to which the complaint relates, or such other period as the employment tribunal thinks just and equitable.[269] In other words, a complaint must be presented within three months. The tribunal has power to extend the time limit where it is just and equitable to do so.

8.206 For these purposes:

(1) Conduct extending over a period is to be treated as done at the end of the period.[270] Where there is a complaint of a number of instances of discrimination or harassment extending over a period of time, the tribunal will have to determine whether they constitute 'conduct extending over a period' or a series of discrete acts.

(2) A failure to do something is to be treated as occurring when the person in question decided on it.[271] In the absence of evidence to the contrary, a person is to be taken to decide on a failure to do something when that person does an act inconsistent with doing it, or, in the absence of an inconsistent act, on the expiry of the period in which he might reasonably have been expected to do it.[272]

(b) Remedies

8.207 If an employment tribunal finds there has been a contravention of the Equality Act 2010, it may:

(1) make a declaration as to the rights of the complainant and respondent;[273]

---

[268] Equality Act 2010, s 120(1). This includes complaints relating to a contravention of s 108 (relationships that have ended), s 111 (instructing, causing or inducing contraventions), and s 112 (aiding contraventions) relating to Pt 5. It does not include complaints against qualification bodies in so far as the act complained of may be subject to an appeal or proceedings in the nature of an appeal by virtue of an enactment: Equality Act 2010, s 120(7).

[269] Equality Act 2010, s 123(1).

[270] Equality Act 2010, s 123(3)(a).

[271] Equality Act 2010, s 123(3)(b).

[272] Equality Act 2010, s 123(4).

[273] Equality Act 2010, s 124(2)(a).

(2) award compensation to the complainant;[274] or

(3) make an appropriate recommendation.[275]

Where a tribunal finds that there was indirect discrimination within the meaning of section **8.208** 19 of the Equality Act 2010, but is satisfied that the provision, criterion, or practice was not applied with the intention of discriminating against the complainant, the tribunal must not award compensation unless it first considers whether to make a declaration or an appropriate recommendation.[276]

Appropriate recommendation. An appropriate recommendation is a recommendation that, **8.209** within a specified period, the respondent takes specified steps for the purpose of obviating or reducing the adverse effect of any matter to which the proceedings relate on the complainant and/or on any other person.[277] Previously, recommendations could only be made by the tribunal for the benefit of the individual complainant. The Equality Act 2010 gives tribunals the power to make recommendations for the benefit of the wider workforce. However, at the end of 2012 the government announced its intention to abolish the power of employment tribunals to make wider recommendations.[278]

If the respondent fails, without reasonable excuse, to comply with an appropriate recom- **8.210** mendation so far as it relates to the complainant, the tribunal may increase the amount of any compensation already awarded or, if no compensation had previously been awarded, may award compensation.[279]

Compensation. Unlike claims for unfair dismissal, there is no statutory cap on the amount **8.211** of compensation that can be awarded. The correct approach to assessing compensation in discrimination claims is to follow the ordinary principles of tort.[280] This means that the claimant should, so far as possible, be put back into the position he would have been in had no discrimination occurred.

As well as compensation for pecuniary loss, a claimant can recover compensation for injury **8.212** to feelings.[281] The assessment of compensation for injury to feelings is an exercise where precision is impossible. The following bands have been identified as a guide: an award of £500 to £6,000 for less serious cases where the act of discrimination was an isolated or one-off event; £6,000 to £18,000 for serious cases which do not merit an award in the highest band; and £18,000 to £30,000 for the most serious cases such as where there has been a lengthy campaign of discriminatory harassment against the claimant.[282]

---

[274] Equality Act 2010, s 124(2)(b).

[275] Equality Act 2010, s 124(2)(c).

[276] Equality Act 2010, s 124(4).

[277] Equality Act 2010, s 124(3).

[278] Government Equalities Office, 'Equality Act 2010: employment tribunals' power to make wider recommendations in discrimination cases and obtaining information procedure: Government response to the consultation' (October 2012). The relevant amendment to the Equality Act 2010 was included in the Draft Deregulation Bill published on 1 July 2013.

[279] Equality Act 2010, s 124(7).

[280] *Ministry of Defence v Cannock* [1995] All ER 449 (EAT).

[281] Compensation for injury to feelings cannot be awarded in claims of unfair dismissal: *Dunnachie v Kingston upon Hull City Council* [2005] 1 AC 226 (HL).

[282] *Vento v Chief Constable of West Yorkshire Police (No 2)* [2003] ICR 318 (EAT) as updated by the EAT in *Da'Bell v NSPCC* [2010] IRLR 19 to take account of inflation.

8.213   An employment tribunal can award compensation for personal injury where the act complained of results in psychiatric or physical injury.[283]

8.214   Aggravated and exemplary damages are also recoverable in appropriate cases. The purpose of an award of aggravated damages is compensatory.[284] It is to compensate the claimant for aggravation of the injury to feelings caused by the wrongful act as a result of some additional element.[285] In *Shaw*, Underhill P held that the circumstances attracting an award of aggravated damages fall into three categories:[286]

(1) *The manner in which the wrong was committed.* An award can be made in the case of any exceptional or contumelious conduct which has the effect of seriously increasing the claimant's distress.

(2) *Motive.* Underhill P observed that:

> ...discriminatory conduct which is evidently based on prejudice or animosity or which is spiteful or vindictive or intended to wound is, as a matter of common sense and common experience, likely to cause more distress than the same acts would cause if evidently done without such a motive—say, as a result of ignorance or insensitivity.

(3) *Subsequent conduct.* For example, where the employer plainly shows that he does not take the claimant's complaint seriously, or a failure to apologise.[287]

8.215   Exemplary damages can be awarded where there is oppressive, arbitrary, or unconstitutional action by servants of the government, or where the conduct of the alleged discriminator was calculated to make a profit for himself that may exceed any compensation payable to the claimant.[288]

(2) Claims for unfair dismissal

8.216   The employment tribunal has exclusive jurisdiction to hear complaints of unfair dismissal. For the tribunal's rules of procedure, reference should be made to the Employment Tribunals (Constitution and Rules of Procedure) Regulations 2004, or with effect from 29 July 2013, the Employment Tribunals (Constitution and Rules of Procedure) Regulations 2013.

(a) Time limit

8.217   A complaint of unfair dismissal must be presented to the tribunal before the end of the period of three months beginning with the effective date of termination.[289] The tribunal has no jurisdiction to hear a complaint presented out of time, unless it grants an extension of time. The tribunal may extend time where it is satisfied that it was 'not reasonably practicable' for the complaint to be presented before the end of the period of three months.[290]

---

[283] *Sheriff v Klyne Tugs (Lowestoft) Ltd* [1999] ICR 1170 (CA).

[284] See *Commissioner of Police for the Metropolis v Shaw* [2012] ICR 464 (EAT).

[285] *Shaw* (n 284).

[286] *Shaw* (n 284).

[287] For an example arising in the religious discrimination context, see *Bungay v Saini* [2011] Eq LR 1130 (EAT). The respondents in that case had been held liable for encouraging the operation of a discriminatory anti-Hindu policy which had resulted in the dismissal of two employees. In assessing aggravated damages, the tribunal took into account post-dismissal conduct.

[288] *Rookes v Barnard* [1964] AC 1129 (HL). For a discussion of the availability of such damages in the employment context, see *City of Bradford Metropolitan Council v Arora* [1991] 2 WLR 1377 (CA); *Virgo Fidelis Senior School v Boyle* [2004] IRLR 268 (EAT); and *Ministry of Defence v Fletcher* [2010] IRLR 25 (EAT).

[289] Employment Rights Act 1996, s 111(2)(a). For the meaning of 'effective date of termination' see Employment Rights Act 1997, s 97.

[290] Employment Rights Act 1996, s 111(2)(b).

(b) Remedies

Where the employment tribunal finds that the complaint of unfair dismissal is well founded, **8.218**
it may make an order for reinstatement or re-engagement, or an order for compensation.

Order for reinstatement or re-engagement.   An order for reinstatement is an order 'that the **8.219**
employer shall treat the complainant in all respects as if he had not been dismissed'.[291] In
deciding whether to make such an order, the tribunal must take into account whether the
claimant wishes to be reinstated, whether it is practicable for an employer to comply with
the order, and, in a case where the claimant caused or contributed to the dismissal, whether
it would be just to order reinstatement.[292]

If the tribunal decides not to make an order for reinstatement, it must go on to consider whether **8.220**
to make an order for re-engagement and on what terms.[293] An order for re-engagement is
'an order, on such terms as the tribunal may decide, that the complainant be engaged by the
employer, or by a successor of the employer or by an associated employer, in employment
comparable to that from which he was dismissed or other suitable employment'.[294] In deciding whether to make such an order, the tribunal must take into account the same factors as
those considered when deciding whether to make an order for reinstatement.[295]

Where an order for reinstatement or re-engagement is made and the employer either fails to **8.221**
reinstate or re-engage the employee, the tribunal can make an additional award of compensation over and above the ordinary award of compensation.[296] The tribunal can also award
compensation where the employee is reinstated or re-engaged but the employer fails to comply fully with the terms of the order.[297] The amount of the compensation (which is subject to
the statutory cap) may be such 'as the tribunal thinks fit having regard to the loss sustained by
the complainant in consequence of the failure to comply fully with the terms of the order'.[298]

Compensation.   Where the tribunal awards compensation, the award will consist of two **8.222**
components: the basic award[299] and the compensatory award.[300] The amount of the compensatory award will be 'such amount as the tribunal considers just and equitable in all the
circumstances having regard to the loss sustained by the complainant in consequence of
the dismissal in so far as that loss is attributable to action taken by the employer'.[301] The
loss recoverable includes (but is not limited to) any expenses reasonably incurred by the
employee in consequence of the dismissal, and loss of any benefit which he might reasonably be expected to have had but for the dismissal.[302] Only pecuniary losses are recoverable.
In *Dunnachie* the House of Lords confirmed that compensation for unfair dismissal cannot

---

[291] Employment Rights Act 1996, s 114(1).
[292] Employment Rights Act 1996, s 116(1).
[293] Employment Rights Act 1996, s 116(2).
[294] Employment Rights Act 1996, s 115(1).
[295] Employment Rights Act 1996, s 116(3).
[296] Employment Rights Act 1996, s 117(3) and (4). The additional award of compensation must be an
amount 'not less than twenty-six nor more than fifty-two weeks' pay'.
[297] Employment Rights Act 1996, s 117(1).
[298] Employment Rights Act 1996, s 117(2).
[299] Employment Rights Act 1996, s 118(1)(a). The basic award is to be calculated in accordance with ss
119–122 and s 126.
[300] Employment Rights Act 1996, s 118(1)(b).
[301] Employment Rights Act 1996, s 123(1).
[302] Employment Rights Act 1996, s 123(2).

include non-pecuniary losses, such as injury to feelings.[303] The position is different in discrimination claims where such losses are often awarded.[304]

8.223 An employee is under a duty to mitigate his losses, for example he must take reasonable steps to find alternative employment.[305] This will be taken into account when assessing compensation. Furthermore, where the tribunal finds that the dismissal was to any extent caused or contributed to by any action of the complainant, it can reduce the amount of the compensatory award 'by such proportion as it considers just and equitable having regard to that finding'.[306] The tribunal has a general discretion to adjust the award where it is 'just and equitable' to do so.[307]

8.224 Importantly, the compensatory award is subject to a statutory cap.[308] For dismissals on or after 1 February 2013 the maximum amount that can be awarded is £74,200. Pursuant to a new power conferred on the Secretary of State by the Enterprise and Regulatory Reform Act 2013,[309] an additional, alternative cap is being introduced, so that the maximum amount that can be awarded will be the prevailing statutory maximum (£74,200 for dismissals on or after 1 February 2013) or 52 multiplied by a week's pay of the employee concerned, whichever is lower.[310]

---

[303] *Dunnachie* (n 281).

[304] See para 8.212.

[305] Employment Rights Act 1996, s 123(4).

[306] Employment Rights Act 1996, s 123(6). The basic award can also be reduced where the tribunal considers that the conduct of the employee before the dismissal was such that it would be just and equitable to do so: Employment Rights Act 1996, s 122(2).

[307] Employment Rights Act, s 123(1).

[308] Employment Rights Act 1996, s 124(1).

[309] Enterprise and Regulatory Reform Act 2013, s 15. This gives the Secretary to State a power to amend, by order, 'section 124 of the Employment Rights Act 1996 (limit of compensatory award etc) so as to vary the limit imposed for the time being by subsection (1) of that section'.

[310] Draft Unfair Dismissal (Variation of the Limit of Compensatory Award) Order 2013.

9

RELIGION AND EDUCATION

A. Introduction

(1) Overview of this chapter

9.01 The purpose of this chapter is to describe the protections for religious rights in the context of education. The main focus is upon education in schools (including at sixth form level), although reference will also be made to issues which arise in higher education settings such as universities.

9.02 The chapter is divided into six parts. The remainder of this part A introduces the main domestic legislation, and provisions of the European Convention on Human Rights (ECHR), to which reference will be made throughout the chapter. Part B provides an overview of, and the religious rights implications for, the education system in the United Kingdom, including the role played by faith schools. Part C analyses religious rights as they are impacted in certain specific aspects of teaching and content in schools. Part D describes the protections and freedoms in schools afforded to the religious by the anti-discrimination legislation, and part E focusses on admissions. Finally, part F tackles the difficult issues of religious dress and symbols in schools.

(2) Key legal sources

9.03 Much of the domestic legislation relevant to the matters covered in this chapter is contained in the School Standards and Framework Act 1998 (SSFA 1998), the Education Act

1996, the Education and Inspections Act 2006 (EIA 2006), and the Equality Act 2010. In particular, SSFA 1998 and the Education Act 1996 contain provision concerning religious teaching in schools; EIA 2006 concerns the process for establishing new schools, including faith schools; and the Equality Act 2010 both prohibits discrimination against the religious in schools and allows faith schools freedom to discriminate within limits, including in relation to admissions.

9.04   Most of the issues discussed also require consideration of provisions of the ECHR. The most important provisions of the ECHR in this field are Article 9 (whether considered in isolation or read together with Article 14) and Article 2 of the First Protocol ('A2P1').

9.05   The fundamental principles underlying Articles 9 and 14 are dealt with extensively elsewhere in this work.[1]

9.06   A2P1 comprises two sentences. In full it provides that:

> No person shall be denied the right to education. In the exercise of any functions which it assumes in relation to education and teaching, the state shall respect the right of parents to ensure such education and teaching in conformity with their own religious and philosophical convictions.[2]

9.07   In respect of the principle affirmed in the second sentence of A2P1, the United Kingdom has entered a reservation. The principle is accepted by the United Kingdom only so far as is compatible with the provision of efficient instruction and training and the avoidance of unreasonable public expenditure.[3] To that extent the principle is a qualified one. The result is to achieve consistency with the qualified principle in section 9 of the Education Act 1996 that 'pupils are to be educated in accordance with the wishes of their parents, so far as that is compatible with the provision of efficient instruction and training and the avoidance of unreasonable public expenditure'.[4]

9.08   The leading case on the interpretation of A2P1 is *Belgian Linguistic Case (No 2)*.[5] There the European Court of Human Rights (ECtHR) held that the general right to education comprises four separate rights, none of which is absolute, namely: (1) A right of access to such educational establishments as exist; (2) A right to an effective (but not the most effective possible) education; (3) A right to official recognition of academic qualifications; and (4) a right, when read with the freedom from discrimination guaranteed by Article 14 of the Convention, not to be disadvantaged in the provision of education on any ground such as sex, race, colour, language, religion, political or other opinion, national or social origin, association with a national minority, property, birth or other status, without reasonable and objective justification.

9.09   What A2P1 does not do is guarantee a right for a pupil to be educated at or by a particular institution, or to receive education of a particular kind or quality, other than that prevailing

---

[1] See generally Chapter 3.

[2] For meaning of 'philosophical convictions' see *Campbell and Cosans v UK* (1982) 4 EHRR 293, para 36; *Valsamis v Greece* (1996) EHRR 294, para 25. See further *R (Williamson) v Secretary of State for Education and Employment* [2005] UKHL 15, para 60 *per* Lord Walker and para 23 *per* Lord Nicholls.

[3] See HRA 1998, s 15(5) and Sch 2, Pt II which expressly preserves the derogation.

[4] See generally *Watt v Kesteven County Council* [1955] 1 QB 408, 424 *per* Denning LJ and 429 *per* Parker LJ; *Cumings v Birkenhead Corporation* [1972] Ch 12, 36.

[5] *Belgian Linguistic Case (No 2)* (1968) 1 EHRR 252.

in the state. The purpose of the second sentence was described in *Kjeldsen, Busk Madsen and Pedersen v Denmark* as safeguarding the possibility of pluralism in education, which is essential to the preservation of a democratic society.[6]

In *A v Headteacher and Governors of Lord Grey School*,[7] Lord Bingham explained that: **9.10**

> ... the underlying premise of the Article was that all existing member states of the Council of Europe had, and all future member states would have, an established system of state education. It was intended to guarantee fair and non-discriminatory access to that system by those within the jurisdiction of the respective states. The fundamental importance of education in a modern democratic state was recognised to require no less. But the guarantee is, in comparison with most other Convention guarantees, a weak one, and deliberately so. There is no right to education of a particular kind or quality, other than prevailing in the state. There is no Convention guarantee of compliance with domestic law. There is no Convention guarantee of education at or by a particular institution ... The test, as always under the Convention, is a highly pragmatic one, to be applied to the specific facts of the case: have the authorities of the state acted so as to deny to a pupil effective access to such educational facilities as the state provides for such pupils?[8]

As will be seen later, A2P1 has been used to test the lawfulness of a state's arrangements in **9.11** respect of the funding of faith schools and admissions decisions. It also has relevance in relation to issues concerning religious education and worship in schools, school discipline, and school uniform.

B. Educational Provision in the United Kingdom

(1) The basic types of school

The United Kingdom has state-maintained and independent school sectors. In general, state-maintained schools are funded by the state, and independent schools are not. **9.12** Academies, of which there are ever-increasing numbers under the present government, are independent, state-funded schools, and will be addressed separately. In principle, all these types of school may be 'religious'.

The main types of state-maintained schools are: community schools (including special community schools), foundation schools (including special foundation schools), and voluntary **9.13** schools.[9]

In general, community and foundation schools are wholly maintained by a local authority. **9.14** Differences between them include that whereas community school staff are employed by the local authority,[10] foundation school staff are employed by the school's governing body (except where the school's delegated budget has been suspended);[11] and that, in contrast to

---

[6] *Kjeldsen, Busk Madsen and Pedersen v Denmark* (1976) 1 EHRR 711.
[7] *A v Headteacher and Governors of Lord Grey School* [2006] 2 AC 363. See further the subsequent judgment of the ECtHR in *Ali v UK* (App 40385/06) (2011) 53 EHRR 12, [2011] ELR 85 in which the Court confirmed that A2P1 did not guarantee a right of access to a particular institution.
[8] Lord Bingham's analysis was followed by the Supreme Court in *A v Essex County Council* [2010] UKSC 33, [2010] 3 WLR 509, [2010] ELR 531; and *Re JR17's Application for Judicial Review (2010)* [2010] UKSC 27 in the context of cases involving school exclusions.
[9] SSFA 1998, s 20.
[10] Education Act 2002, s 35.
[11] Education Act 2002, s 36 and Sch 2.

community schools, foundation schools have a body (not the local authority or the governing body) holding land on trust for the purposes of the school.

9.15 There are two kinds of voluntary schools: voluntary controlled schools and voluntary aided schools. In general, voluntary controlled schools do not enjoy as much freedom as voluntary aided schools. In particular, voluntary controlled schools are wholly maintained by their local authorities, whereas voluntary aided schools are mainly, but not wholly, so maintained. The governing bodies of voluntary aided schools employ the staff at those schools (except where the school's delegated budget has been suspended),[12] and are responsible for the schools' admissions policies.

9.16 Independent schools are defined by section 463 of the Education Act 1996.[13] The definition embraces Academies, although special considerations apply to Academies, and they will be addressed separately.[14] Independent schools may be managed by companies established under the Companies Acts, by registered charities, and by natural persons.

9.17 Whereas the rights and obligations of schools maintained by the state are fundamentally governed by statute, those of independent schools are not, in general,[15] so governed. Thus, for instance, independent schools are not subject to the detailed obligations in respect of religious education, worship, and sex education discussed later.[16] Further, whereas head teachers and governing bodies of maintained schools are public authorities for the purposes of section 6 of the Human Rights Act 1998 (HRA 1998) and will generally be amenable to judicial review in the exercise of their functions,[17] independent schools are almost certainly not public authorities for the purposes of section 6 of the 1998 Act and will not generally be amenable to judicial review.[18]

9.18 However, independent schools will be bound by such contractual obligations as they may be subject to between them and parents,[19] and will also have duties of care in the law of tort. Further, although independent schools may generally only be sued in private law, the court or tribunal hearing a complaint of a breach of human rights in an independent school setting

---

[12] Education Act 2002, s 36 and Sch 2.

[13] 'Independent school' means any school at which full-time education is provided for (a) five or more pupils of compulsory school age, or (b) at least one pupil of that age for whom a statement is maintained under s 324, or who is looked after by a local authority (within the meaning of the Children Act 1989, s 22), and which is not a school maintained by a local authority or a special school not so maintained.

[14] See paras 9.30 ff.

[15] Independent schools are nevertheless subject to a wide range of statutory obligations, for instance in relation to inspections (see eg the Education Act 2002, ss 157–174), and certain duties under the Children Act 1989.

[16] See paras 9.37 ff.

[17] *Ali v Headteacher and Governors of Lord Grey School* [2006] UKHL 14; *R (Begum) v Headteacher and Governors of Denbigh High School* [2006] UKHL 26.

[18] *R v Muntham House School, ex p R* [2000] ELR 287 (approved in *Poplar Housing and Regeneration Community Association Ltd v Donoghue* [2001] EWCA Civ 595, [2002] QB 48, 67); *R v Fernhill Manor School, ex p A* [1993] 1 FLR 620, [1994] ELR 67. Cf *R v Cobden Hall School, ex p S* [1998] ELR 488, where it was held that a pupil attending an independent school but on an assisted places scheme could judicially review a scheme to exclude him. For a discussion of the relationship between the factors relevant to whether a body is a public authority under HRA 1998, s 6 and those relevant to whether it is amenable to judicial review on a more general basis, see *R (Weaver) v London and Quadrant Housing Trust* [2009] EWCA Civ 587, [2010] 1 WLR 363.

[19] In *Gray v Marlborough College* [2006] EWCA Civ 1262, [2006] ELR 516 it was held, in the context of an exclusion, that there was a basic symmetry in essentials between a contractually implied obligation of fairness and that derived from statute or general public law. See further *R v Dunraven School Governors, ex p B (A Child)* [2000] BLGR 494.

will still be obliged, as a public authority itself under section 6(3)(a) of HRA 1998, to act compatibly with the ECHR and thus ensure the protection of ECHR rights through their determinations.[20] The effect is that in practice independent schools are subject to the same human rights obligations as maintained schools.[21]

(2) Faith schools

Faith schools existed long before the state decided to make elementary education compul-   **9.19**
sory. In that sense, they are the root from which the modern system of education grew. They increased significantly in number from the early part of the nineteenth century when the National Society for the Education of the Poor in the Principles of the Established Church undertook a significant programme for the provision of Church of England Schools. By 1870, nearly 900,000 children were being educated in Church of England schools, representing 70 per cent of the school population.[22] Other faiths were also represented at that time: from 1808 the British and Foreign School Society provided schools for Protestant dissenters, and the Catholic Poor School Committee was formed in 1847. The Methodist Church also provided schools.[23] The state provided grant funding for such schools.[24]

When the state made elementary education compulsory in 1880, it provided a large num-   **9.20**
ber of additional schools for that purpose. But these were not intended as secular schools. At that time, few were in favour of secular education. The non-church-sponsored schools were required to give a Christian education, although it was to be related to a Christianity not distinctive of any particular denomination.[25] Further, instead of 'nationalizing' the pre-existing schools being provided by the Church of England and other churches, the state continued to subsidize them. Although protestant dissenters were, from 1870, strongly opposed to the state funding schools of the established church, the principle of state funding for religious teaching was, at that time, essentially uncontroversial.[26] This is now no longer so.[27]

Today both state maintained and independent schools may be designated by Order of the   **9.21**
Secretary of State as having a 'religious character'.[28] In the state-maintained sector, although foundation schools, voluntary controlled schools, and voluntary aided schools may be designated as having religious character,[29] the majority of the United Kingdom's state-maintained religious schools are voluntary schools. Designation takes place in accordance with the Religious Character of Schools (Designation Procedure) Regulations 1998. Independent

---

[20] See *Williamson* (n 2).
[21] *Kjeldsen* (n 6) paras 50 and 51; *Begum* (n 17); and *Williamson* (n 2).
[22] The figures are taken from M Cruickshank, *Church and State in English Education* (Macmillan, 1964) 190.
[23] See Cruickshank (n 22) 2 and 8.
[24] Cruickshank (n 22) 3 and 10, notes that the first state grant for education (of £200,000) was made in 1833 to the two school societies then in existence, and that by 1857, the state was spending some £500,000 per annum on educational grants.
[25] Elementary Education Act 1870 (33 & 34 Vict, c 75), s 14(2).
[26] The history is summarized more fully in P Petchey, 'Legal Issues for faith schools in England and Wales' [2008] Ecc LJ 174–6.
[27] See eg J De Long and G Snik, 'Why should states fund denominational schools?' (2002) 36(4) Journal of Philosophy and Education 32; R Jackson, 'Should the state fund faith-based schools? A review of the arguments' (2003) 25(2) British Journal of Religious Education 89.
[28] Under SSFA 1998, s 69(3) and (5).
[29] SSFA 1998, s 69(2)(b) and (c) and s 69(3).

schools are designated under the Religious Character of Schools (Designation Procedure) (Independent Schools) (England) Regulations 2003.[30]

9.22   There are now about 7,000 faith schools designated by the Secretary of State, representing about a third of all schools and educating around a quarter of all pupils.[31] Current government policy is that there should be more of them.[32] Designation as such a school has significant implications for matters such as admissions, RE, and religious worship.

9.23   The proportion of schools representing particular faiths is, perhaps inevitably, a matter of some controversy. At the time of writing, Church of England and Roman Catholic schools continue to dominate the picture, as they have done historically. Of the 7,000 or so state-maintained faith schools nationwide, there are only about 50 that are Jewish, Muslim, Sikh or Hindu, and the majority of those are Jewish. Available statistics[33] suggest that the ratio of the number of Christian children to places available in Christian schools[34] bears no relation to the ratio of Muslim or Sikh children to places available in Muslim or Sikh schools[35] (although, out of all the religions, the ratio is most favourable to Jewish children[36]).

9.24   There is no legal reason why that should be so. Under section 13 of the Education Act 1996, local authorities are made responsible for contributing to the spiritual, moral, mental, and physical development of the community by securing that efficient primary, secondary, and (in England) further education is available to meet the needs of the population of their area. More specifically, under section 14(3A) of the Education Act 1996,[37] the general duty on a local authority to secure that sufficient schools for providing primary and secondary education are available for their area must be exercised 'with a view to (a) securing diversity in the provision of schools, and (b) increasing opportunities for parental choice'. In the exercise of a local authority's school planning functions, therefore, the extent to which existing schools represent diversity of faiths and/or allow for parental choice in respect of faith schools will be relevant considerations.

9.25   Nevertheless, the duties in sections 13 and 14 of the Education Act 1996 are 'target duties', leaving wide discretion to a local authority as to how they should be pursued and fulfilled.[38] Thus, the duty in section 14(3A), for instance, does not impose an obligation on a local authority to ensure that schools are provided in its area to meet every wish of parents for

---

[30]   Religious Character of Schools (Designation Procedure) Regulations 1998, SI 1998/2535; Religious Character of Schools (Designation Procedure) (Independent Schools) (England) Regulations 2003, SI 2003/2314. SSFA 1998, s 124B.

[31]   Standard Note (for Members of Parliament): SN/SG/4405: 'Faith schools: admissions and performance' (March 2009) 3. A useful and concise history of faith schools is contained in Petchey (n 26) 174–6.

[32]   The Coalition Agreement between the Conservatives and Liberal Democrats promises: 'we will work with faith groups to enable more faith schools and facilitate inclusive admissions policies in as many of these schools as possible', HM Treasury, 'The Coalition: Our Programme for Government' (May 2010) 29.

[33]   On schools, see Department for Education and Skills, 'Annual Schools Census' (January 2004); on numbers of children, see Office for National Statistics, 'Census' (April 2001), collated by the ONS.

[34]   In 2004, Christian schools had places for 1.7m children and, in 2001, 5.1m children aged 5 to 16 in England were described as Christian.

[35]   There were 371,000 school-aged (5 to 16-year-old) Muslim children in England in 2001 and four Muslim state-maintained schools in 2004, catering for around 1,100 children. There were 64,000 school-aged Sikh children and two Sikh state-maintained schools, catering for around 600 children.

[36]   There were 33,000 Jewish school-aged children in England in 2004 compared with 13,000 places in state-maintained Jewish schools.

[37]   Added by the Education and Inspections Act 2006.

[38]   *R v Inner London Education Authority, ex p Ali* (1992) 2 Admin LR 822, 827–8.

schools of particular kinds to provide school places for their children. Rather, it imposes a general objective at a high level of generality, leaving a wide discretion to local authorities as to what steps they adopt to pursue that objective.[39] Further, local authorities are exempt from claims of discrimination (for example against particular religious groups) in the exercise of their functions under sections 13 and 14, with the effect that they cannot be bound to provide schools for all pupils of different faiths or beliefs who may wish for there to be one.[40]

The right to education in A2P1 does not require contracting states to the ECHR to establish **9.26** at their own expense, or to subsidize, education of any particular type or at any particular level.[41] There is thus no obligation under the ECHR to fund faith schools per se. But the funding of faith schools is legally permissible, provided that it does not amount to unjustified discrimination.

In *Verein Gemeinsam Lernen v Austria*,[42] an attempt was made to challenge Austria's subsidiz- **9.27** ing of church schools on the basis that it was more favourable than for non-religious private schools, contrary to A2P1 read together with Article 14. The ECtHR held that the differential treatment was nevertheless justified, on the basis that church schools were a widespread phenomenon in the Austrian education system which had catered for large numbers of pupils for a considerable time, and that if the educational services provided by non-church schools fell to be met by the state, there would be a considerable burden on the state as it would have to make up the shortfall in schools.

In *X v United Kingdom*,[43] parents in Northern Ireland wanted to set up a non-denominational **9.28** school. They would have been required to provide part of the funding to do so. They argued that the state's failure to provide all the funding for their non-denominational school discriminated against them contrary to A2P1, read together with Article 14, given that the state wholly funded essentially Protestant schools. The Commission held that it was legitimate for the state to exercise substantial control in the ownership and management of schools for which it provided a full 100 per cent subsidy, and that it was reasonable for the state, in relation to bodies that seek ownership and decisive control over management policy in voluntary schools, to require some degree of financial contribution. The Commission did not consider that the requirement of a 15 per cent contribution towards the capital costs of the schools was an unreasonable or disproportionate requirement, taking into consideration that ownership of the school would be vested in trustees representative of the body concerned and the

---

[39] *R (BHA) v Richmond LBC* [2012] EWHC 3622 (Admin), [2013] 2 All ER 146, para 20.

[40] Equality Act 2010, Sch 3, para 6 disapplies the obligation on public authorities (such as local authorities) not to discriminate in the exercise of their public functions from (a) the exercise of the authority's functions under the Education Act 1996, s 14 and (b) the exercise of its function under s 13 of that Act insofar as this relates to a function under s 14 of that Act. Cf *R v Birmingham City Council, ex p Equal Opportunities Commission* [1989] AC 1155, where the House of Lords held that a local education authority breached the Sex Discrimination Act 1975, s 23 if it knowingly maintained a system of education in its area under which girls had considerably fewer opportunities for selective education than boys. For examples of unsuccessful challenges to decisions to cease to maintain single sex schools, see *R v Northamptonshire County Council, ex p K*, The Times, 27 July 1993; and *R v Secretary of State for Education, ex p Parveen Malik* [1994] ELR 121. In *R (McDougal) v Liverpool City Council* [2009] EWHC 1821 (Admin), [2009] ELR 510 the High Court held that a decision to close a non-faith comprehensive school did not interfere with the right of parents and pupils who were not Catholics not to be discriminated against under A2P1 of the ECHR read together with Art 14, given that the local authority would provide free travel to another non-faith school.

[41] *Belgian Linguistic Case (No 2)* (n 5) para 4.

[42] *Verein Gemeinsam Lernen v Austria* (1995) 20 EHRR CD 78.

[43] *X v UK* (App 7782/77) (1978) 14 DR 179.

exercise of two-thirds control in the governing body.[44] It has been suggested that *X v United Kingdom* provides a legal answer to the secularist who objects in principle to the state funding of faith schools: the state is not unfairly subsidizing faith schools, but granting a degree of autonomy to faith schools in return for funding from the faiths.[45]

9.29 Home schooling is lawful in the United Kingdom.[46] However, the ECtHR has held that in signatory states where education in school is compulsory, the Convention does not give parents a right to educate their children at home so as to school them in their religious beliefs if no faith school is available.[47]

(3) Academies

9.30 The promotion of academies has been the single most significant item on the education agenda of the coalition government which took power in the United Kingdom in 2010. Prior to the Academies Act 2010, academies existed[48] but were fewer in number. Under the 2010 Act, a significant number of maintained schools have converted to academy status,[49] and many academies have been created as new schools,[50] known colloquially as 'free schools'. The number is only likely to keep growing. Under section 6A of EIA 2006, if a local authority thinks it needs a new school in its area, it must first seek proposals for an academy school. This effectively constitutes a presumption in favour of academies in the exercise of a local authority's school planning functions under section 13 and 14 of the Education Act 1996.[51]

9.31 In law, academies (whether created prior to or under the Academies Act 2010) are independent schools. Unlike 'classic' independent schools, however, they are funded by the state by means of funding agreements between the academy proprietor (usually an academy trust) and the Secretary of State.[52] Strictly speaking, academies are not bound *by statute* by the raft of obligations applying to maintained schools discussed in this chapter (for example relating to admissions or the curriculum). Instead, the funding agreement will contain obligations which bind the academy as a matter of *contract* between it and the Secretary of

---

[44] See further *X and Y v UK* (App 9461/81) (1982) 31 DR 210; *W and DM and M and HI v UK* (1984) 37 DR 96 EComHR; *W and KL v Sweden* (App 10478/93) (1985) 45 DR 143.

[45] Petchey (n 26) 190.

[46] The authority for home schooling is the Education Act 1996, s 7 which provides that: 'The parent of every child of compulsory school age shall cause him to receive efficient full-time education suitable—(a) To his age, ability and aptitude, and (b) To any special educational needs he may have, *either* by regular attendance at school *or otherwise*' (emphasis added).

[47] *Konrad v Germany* (2007) 44 SE8. The Court held that the second sentence of A2P1 could not be read in isolation from the first sentence. Respect was only due to convictions on the part of the parents which did not conflict with the child's right to education. On the facts of the case, the parent's right to education in conformity with their religious convictions had not been restricted in a disproportionate manner, given in particular the general interest of society to avoid the emergence of parallel societies based on separate philosophical convictions, the importance of integrating minorities into society, and the fact that the applicant parents were free to educate their children after school and at weekends.

[48] See the Education Act 1996, s 482.

[49] In brief, the conversion process involves the Secretary of State making an 'Academy Order' in respect of the maintained school under the Academies Act 2010, s 4. There must be consultation on the question of whether the conversion should take place, whether before or after the making of the order (s 5). The school is converted when 'Academy arrangements' (usually, the funding agreement) are entered into under s 1 of the 2010 Act.

[50] See Academies Act 2010, ss 9 and 10.

[51] See *R (BHA) v Richmond LBC* [2012] EWHC 3622 (Admin), [2013] 2 All ER 146.

[52] In *R (Elphinstone) v City of Westminster* [2009] BLGR 158, Rix LJ described academies as a 'species' of independent school.

State. Although the Academies Act 2010 guarantees that an academy will teach a prescribed curriculum,[53] the detail of a number of important matters, such as the school's admission arrangements and obligations, are determined by the terms of the contract alone, which the academy proprietor and the Secretary of State are in principle free to negotiate. In practice, however, it is the expectation of the Secretary of State that the contract should impose obligations on academies broadly equivalent to those imposed upon maintained schools.

It is presently unclear how a parent, who will not be a party to the academy's contract with   **9.32**
the Secretary of State, may enforce a breach of its terms, for example in relation to admissions. As explained previously, academies are independent schools, and the acts of such schools have not generally been held to be amenable to judicial review. The position of academies is, however, different from that of 'classic' independent schools in that they are state funded. In *R v Governor of Haberdashers' Aske's Hatcham College, ex p T*,[54] Dyson LJ held that a city technology college was amenable to judicial review, having regard in particular to the facts that the city technology college was created through the exercise of public power (the entering into of the funding agreement between the Secretary of State and the school) and was publicly funded.[55] It is submitted that the same or similar principles apply to academies converted or created under the Academies Act 2010, and that they are both amenable to judicial review on conventional public law grounds and required to comply with human rights obligations as public authorities under section 6 of HRA 1998.[56] This is consistent with the government's position.

There is no reason why a faith school cannot be established as an academy. The nature of the   **9.33**
school would fundamentally be governed, as previously explained, by the terms of the funding agreement between the faith academy's proprietor and the Secretary of State. However, at the time of writing, it is the Secretary of State's expectation that funding agreements for faith academies contain provision to the effect that the academy will adopt admission criteria that provide that, if oversubscribed, at least 50 per cent of their places available each year will be allocated without reference to any faith-based admission criteria. Although there is nothing to stop negotiation for a different percentage, the Secretary of State's current policy may nevertheless lead proponents of faith schools to prefer to make a proposal for a voluntary aided school. Such proposals may be made by proposers to local authorities under section 11(1A) of the EIA 2006.

In *R (BHA) v Richmond LBC*,[57] the British Humanist Association sought to challenge a local   **9.34**
authority's decision to approve proposals made to it by the Diocese of Westminster for voluntary aided primary and secondary schools. The British Humanist Association argued that, on the facts, the Council had formed the view that there was a 'need' for a new school and

---

[53] The Academies Act 2010, s 1A(1)(b) requires an academy to have a curriculum satisfying the requirement of the Education Act 2002, s 78 to have a broad and balanced curriculum.

[54] *R v Governor of Haberdashers' Aske's Hatcham College, ex p T* [1995] ELR 350.

[55] See further *R v Governors of Bacon's City Technology College, ex p W* [1998] ELR 488.

[56] Note, however, that the soundness of Hatcham College has not been considered by the higher courts. Indeed, in *R v Bacon's City Technology College, ex p W* [1998] ELR 488, its correctness was not conceded by the CTC, which reserved its position in case the matter went to the Court of Appeal (which it did not). However in *R (Omotosho) v Harris Academy Crystal Palace* [2011] EWHC 3350 (Admin), in which a pupil challenged the decision by an admissions Independent Appeal Panel (IAP) refusing his appeal against the decision of an academy not to offer him a place, the academy conceded (at least in the High Court) that an academy and its IAP were amenable to judicial review.

[57] *R (BHA) v Richmond LBC* [2012] EWHC 3622 (Admin), [2013] 2 All ER 146.

should therefore have sought proposals for an academy under the presumption in section 6A of EIA 2006 before approving the diocese's proposals. The Court rejected that argument on the basis that Richmond had merely thought the diocese's proposals were beneficial or desirable but not necessary, so the academy presumption was not engaged. More significantly for present purposes, the Court also held that where a proposal for a voluntary aided school is made to a local authority by a proposer under section 11(1A) of EIA 2006, the authority must proceed to determine that proposal on its merits even if it does come to think, after the proposal is presented to it, that there is a 'need' for a new school. To that extent the academy presumption does not override the statutory process for determining proposals for voluntary aided schools made by proposers.[58] The decision in the *Richmond* case has, unsurprisingly, been widely welcomed by those who champion state-funded faith schools.

C. Teaching and Content

9.35 Four main issues concerning teaching and the content of education have arisen in the sphere of religious rights, namely religious education and collective worship, sex education, corporal punishment, and absence from school for religious holidays, festivals, and pilgrimages. This section addresses each of these in turn.

9.36 As explained in part B of this chapter, independent schools and academies are not generally subject to the various legislative provisions discussed in the following, but will be bound to act in conformity with the ECHR and may be subject to specific contractual obligations relevant to the matters which the legislation covers.

(1) Religious education and collective worship

9.37 The SSFA 1998 makes provision for the teaching of religious education (RE) and collective worship in state-maintained schools.

9.38 In state-maintained schools, the nature and amount of RE or worship to be provided depends, *inter alia*, on whether the school has been designated by the Secretary of State as having a 'religious character'.[59] Whether or not a school is so designated, the nature and amount of religious education and collective worship to be provided will depend on the type of school.

9.39 In the case of any community, foundation, or voluntary school not of designated religious character, RE lessons must be provided in accordance with an agreed syllabus adopted for the school or for those pupils.[60] The syllabus lies outside the National Curriculum; it is drawn up by Agreed Syllabus Conferences (ASCs) appointed by the local authority for that purpose, the committees of which include representatives of Christians and other religious denominations (whose selection must appropriately reflect the principal religious traditions in the area), representatives of the Church of England, teaching representatives, and representatives of the local authority itself.[61] Every agreed syllabus must reflect the fact that the religious traditions in Great Britain are in the main Christian, while taking account of the teaching and practices of the other principal religions represented in Great Britain.[62] The

---

[58] *Richmond* (n 57) paras 74–76.
[59] See para 9.21.
[60] SSFA 1998, Sch 19, para 2(1) and (2).
[61] Education Act 1996, s 375 and Sch 31.
[62] Education Act 1996, s 375(3).

agreed provision must not, however, be given by means of any catechism or formulary which is distinctive of a particular religious denomination (although this does not prohibit provision in the syllabus for the general study of such catechisms or formularies).[63] The agreed syllabus is subject to review by the local standing advisory committee, which comprises a committee whose membership is similar to that of the ASC.[64] The government has published non-statutory guidance in relation to RE.[65]

Provision must equally be made for collective worship in those schools. Subject to the exceptions set out in the following paragraphs, each pupil in attendance at a community, foundation, or voluntary school must on each school day take part in an act of collective worship.[66] In general terms, this must reflect the broad traditions of Christian belief without being distinctive of any particular denomination,[67] although not every act of worship need do so.[68] It does not matter that non-Christian children would be participating.[69] In the case of a voluntary school, the required collective worship must be in accordance with any provisions of the trust deed relating to the school, or where provision for that purpose is not made by such deed, in accordance with the tenets and practices of the religion or religious denomination specified in relation to the school.[70] To that extent, the law promotes RE and collective worship as something to which all pupils of such schools are entitled, even if religion plays no other part in their upbringing.   **9.40**

Importantly, however, if the parent of a pupil at a community, foundation, or voluntary school requests that he be wholly or partly excused from receiving RE,[71] or attending at religious worship,[72] the pupil must be excused unless or until the request is withdrawn. The result may be either that the pupil receives no RE (or participates in no worship) at all, or that, if certain criteria are fulfilled,[73] he receives specifically tailored religious education elsewhere.[74]   **9.41**

Moreover, a head teacher of any community school maintained by a local authority or any foundation school not designated as being of religious character may, after consultation with the governing body, which may consult parents, apply to the standing advisory committee to lift or modify the Christian requirement of collective worship for any class or description of pupil.[75] This happens in schools where there are children of different and often   **9.42**

---

[63] SSFA 1998, Sch 19, para 2(5).
[64] Education Act 1996, s 390(4).
[65] 'Religious education in English schools: Non-statutory guidance 2010', available at <http://media.education.gov.uk/assets/files/religious%20education%20guidance%20in%20schools.pdf>.
[66] SSFA 1998, s 70(1).
[67] SSFA 1998, Sch 20, para 3(2)–(3).
[68] SSFA 1998, Sch 20, para 3(4)–(6).
[69] *R v Secretary of State for Education, ex p R and D* [1994] ELR 495, QBD.
[70] SSFA 1998, Sch 20, para 5.
[71] SSFA 1998, s 71(1).
[72] SSFA 1998, s 71(1A). Note that under s 71(1B), sixth form pupils themselves (as opposed to their parents acting on their behalf) may opt out of religious worship.
[73] Namely that the local authority are satisfied—(a) that the parent of the pupil desires him to receive religious education of a kind which is not provided in the school during the periods of time during which he is so excused, (b) that the pupil cannot with reasonable convenience be sent to another community, foundation, or voluntary school where religious education of the kind desired by the parent is provided, and (c) that arrangements have been made for him to receive religious education of that kind during school hours elsewhere (SSFA 1998, s 71(3)).
[74] SSFA 1998, s 71(3).
[75] Education Act 1996, s 394; SSFA 1998, Sch 20, para 4.

non-Christian faiths. The decision must be reviewed on any application of the head teacher and in any event every five years.[76] The Secretary of State can intervene if she or he considers that a standing advisory committee is acting unreasonably in this regard.[77]

9.43 The opt-out is not without its critics,[78] but it serves to safeguard against a conflict between the education imparted to a child and his or her religious beliefs or practices in the vast majority of cases.

9.44 Different rules as to religious education and worship apply to schools designated as having a 'religious character'. Within that group, there is a distinction between foundation and voluntary controlled schools, and voluntary aided schools.

9.45 In the case of foundation and voluntary controlled schools with a designated religious character, RE is normally given in accordance with the provisions of any trust deed relating to the school or, where provision for that purpose is not made by such a deed, in accordance with the tenets of the religion or religious denomination specified in relation to the school. It may also be in accordance with an agreed syllabus adopted for the school or its pupils.[79]

9.46 In the case of voluntary aided schools with a religious character, the required RE is either in accordance with any provisions of the trust deed relating to the school, or, where provision for that purpose is not made by such a deed, in accordance with the tenets of the religion or religious denomination specified in relation to the school, or, where the parents of any pupils at the school wish them to receive religious education in accordance with any agreed syllabus adopted by the local authority, and cannot with reasonable convenience cause those pupils to attend a school at which that syllabus is in use, to be provided in accordance with that syllabus.[80]

9.47 In the case of a foundation school with a designated religious character, the required collective worship must be in accordance with any provisions of the trust deed relating to the school, or where provision for that purpose is not made by such deed, in accordance with the tenets and practices of the religion or religious denomination specified in relation to the school.[81]

9.48 The ECHR does not prevent states from requiring schools to teach RE. In *Kjeldsen* the ECtHR made clear that:

> . . . the setting and planning of the curriculum fall in principle within the competence of the Contracting States. This mainly involves questions of expediency on which it is not for the Court to rule and whose solution may legitimately vary according to the country and the era. In particular, the second sentence of Article 2 of the Protocol does not prevent States from imparting through teaching or education information or knowledge of a directly or indirectly religious or philosophical kind. It does not even permit parents to object to the integration of

---

[76] Education Act 1996, s 395.
[77] Education Act 1996, s 396.
[78] A Mawhinney, 'The Opt-Out Clause: Imperfect Protection for the Right to Freedom of Religion in Schools' (2006) 2(2) Educational Law Journal 102; A Bradney, *Religions, Rights and Laws* (Leicester University Press, 1993) 63, argues that withdrawal rights are divisive because, even where parents or teachers are aware of their rights, they are loath to use them.
[79] SSFA 1998, Sch 19, para 3(3).
[80] SSFA 1998, Sch 19, para 4(3).
[81] SSFA 1998, Sch 20, para 5.

such teaching or education in the school curriculum, for otherwise all institutionalised teaching would run the risk of proving impracticable.[82]

The ECtHR has upheld a requirement to provide religious teaching even in circumstances **9.49** where parents did not have the right to opt out of it.[83]

The Convention nevertheless compels that religious teaching not be imparted in an overly **9.50** dogmatic manner. As also explained in *Kjeldsen*:

> The second sentence of Article 2 implies on the other hand that the State, in fulfilling the functions assumed by it in regard to education and teaching, must take care that information or knowledge included in the curriculum is conveyed in an objective, critical and pluralistic manner. The State is forbidden to pursue an aim of indoctrination that might be considered as not respecting parents' religious and philosophical convictions. That is the limit that must not be exceeded.[84]

It is more difficult for a state to justify subjecting pupils to religious worship without the **9.51** possibility of opt-out, or where the right to opt out is qualified. *Folgero v Norway*,[85] arose as a result of Norway's primary school system being changed to include a subject called 'KRL', which covered Christianity, religion, and philosophy. Teaching about Christianity formed a greater part of the subject than teaching about any other religion and an 'object clause' explained that the subject's purpose was to give pupils 'a Christian and moral upbringing'. The subject also included participation in acts of worship. The European Court accepted that the Christian bias did not itself violate the Convention in the light of the place occupied by Christianity in Norway's national history and tradition,[86] but that it was necessary to examine the adequacy of Norway's partial exemption arrangements, particularly bearing in mind the effect that the acts of worship might have on the pupils' minds. The court found that the partial exemption (which among other things obliged parents to give reasons for an exemption request) was insufficient in practice to neutralize the religious impact of the subject to an acceptable degree. In all the circumstances, the refusal to grant the parents full exemption from KRL gave rise to a breach of A2P1.

There may also be circumstances where compulsorily subjecting a child to certain activities **9.52** without the possibility of opt-out gives rise to a breach of his Article 9 right or his parents' right under A2P1. In *Valsamis v Greece*,[87] the applicants, who were Jehovah's Witnesses, complained of the penalty of one day's suspension imposed on their daughter for refusing to take part in a school parade. They relied on A2P1 and Article 9 ECHR. They claimed that

---

[82] *Kjeldsen* (n 6), para 53.

[83] In *Angelini v Sweden* (1988) 10 EHRR 123 an atheist mother and daughter claimed a breach of Arts 9, 14 and A2P1 ECHR because the daughter was not given an exemption from religious instruction classes. The application under A2P1 was dismissed as the Swedish government had entered a reservation stating that exemptions from teachings in Christianity could only be granted to 'children of another faith than the Swedish Church in respect of whom a satisfactory religious instruction has been arranged'. In rejecting the Art 9 claim the Commission noted that Art 9 essentially afforded protection against indoctrination by the state. See also *CJ, JJ and EJ v Poland* (App 23380/94) (1996) 84-A DR 46, no discrimination or breach of Art 9 was found in a case where children were exempt from religious instruction but effectively required to reveal that fact in their class certificates. See also *Bernard v Luxembourg* (App 17187/90) (1993) 75 DR 57, an admissibility decision.

[84] *Kjeldsen* (n 6) para 53.

[85] *Folgero v Norway* (2008) 46 EHRR 47.

[86] See also *Zengin v Turkey* (2008) 46 EHRR 44, 63, giving greater priority to Islam than to other religions and philosophies could not itself be viewed as a departure from the principles of pluralism and objectivity, having regard to the fact that notwithstanding Turkey's secular nature, Islam was the major religion there practised.

[87] *Valsamis* (n 2).

participation by their daughter in a National Day parade violated their deeply held commitment to pacifism, which forbade any conduct or practice associated with war or violence. As to A2P1, the majority of the ECtHR expressed surprise that the state curriculum required a pupil to parade on a national holiday but stated that it could not discern anything, either in the purpose of the parade or in the arrangements made for it, that could offend the applicants' pacifist convictions. As regards Article 9, the ECtHR noted at the outset that the applicant was exempted from religious education and the Orthodox mass on the grounds of her own religious beliefs. Having already held that the obligation to take part in the parade was not such as to offend her parents' religious conviction, it rejected the claim under Article 9 ECHR.

(2) Sex education

9.53   In the United Kingdom, all pupils receiving secondary education must receive sex education as part of the basic curriculum.[88] Governing bodies of all maintained schools must make, and keep up to date, a written policy on sex education and its provision.[89] The statement must be made available for inspection (at all reasonable times) by parents of registered pupils at the school and a copy of the statement must be provided free of charge to any such parent who asks for one.[90]

9.54   Where sex education is given to any registered pupils at a maintained school, the head teacher and governing body must take such steps as are reasonably practicable to secure that it is given in such a manner as to encourage those pupils to have due regard to moral considerations and the value of family life.[91] There is a duty on the Secretary of State to issue guidance designed to secure that when sex education is given to registered pupils at maintained schools, they learn the nature of marriage and its importance for family life and the bringing up of children, and they are protected from teaching and materials which are inappropriate having regard to the age and the religious and cultural background of the pupils concerned.[92] The current guidance remains 'Sex and Relationship Education Guidance'.[93]

9.55   Sex education nevertheless remains a matter of obvious concern to religious parents and groups. However, as in relation to RE and religious worship, parents have the power to withdraw their child unconditionally from sex education lessons, so far as compatible with the requirements of the National Curriculum.[94] Thus, the withdrawal could not have the effect of excusing a pupil from biology lessons; its effect means that children may avoid teaching on the non-biological aspects of sex education, for example teaching about AIDS, HIV, and contraception.[95]

9.56   The ECtHR adopts a similar approach to sex education as it does to religious education. Thus, in *Kjeldsen*, it suggested that compulsory sex education in the state sector would be unlikely to

---

[88]   Education Act 2002, s 80(1)(c).
[89]   Education Act 1996, s 404(1)(a).
[90]   Education Act 1996, s 404(1)(b).
[91]   Education Act 1996, s 403(1).
[92]   Education Act 1996, s 403(1A).
[93]   Department for Education and Skills, 'Sex and Relationship Education Guidance', DfES 0116 2000 (July 2000).
[94]   Education Act 1996, s 405.
[95]   Education Act 1996, s 579 extends the definition of 'sex education' to include education about AIDS and HIV, and any other sexually transmitted disease.

violate A2P1 unless it was aimed at advocating a specific kind of sexual behaviour, and so constituted indoctrination.[96] States have to take care that information or knowledge included in the curriculum is conveyed in an objective, critical, and pluralistic manner. The fact that pupils may avoid sex education through a right to opt out, or through education otherwise than in a setting where sex education is compulsory, will also tell against any breach of religious rights.[97]

In *Dojan v Germany*,[98] parents who had been fined for keeping their children away from school on days when they were to study sex education, alleged a breach of their A2P1 rights. The parents were members of the Christian Evangelical Baptist Church, and asserted that the book that the teachers would be using was 'partly pornographic and contrary to Christian sexual ethics requiring that sex should be limited to matrimony... [I]t set forth a liberal, emancipatory image of sexuality which was not consistent with their religious and other moral beliefs and would lead to premature "sexualisation" of the children'. **9.57**

The Court rejected the complaints. It considered that the sex education in question amounted to the neutral transmission of knowledge regarding procreation, contraception, pregnancy, and childbirth and that the ensuing guidelines and curriculum were based on current scientific and educational standards.[99] There was no indication that the education had put into question the parents' sexual education of their children based on their religious convictions or that the children had been influenced to approve of or reject specific sexual behaviour contrary to their parents' religious and philosophical convictions.[100] Further, the parents were free to educate their children after school and at weekends, so that the parents' right to educate their children in conformity with their religious convictions was not restricted in a disproportionate manner.[101] *Dojan* is a further example of the considerable deference which the ECtHR is likely to show to states in complaints asserting a breach of religious rights in the area of school curricula. **9.58**

(3) Corporal punishment

The law in the United Kingdom on corporal punishment in schools is now essentially settled. **9.59**

It has been illegal for teachers to administer corporal punishment to pupils in state-maintained schools, or pupils in independent schools receiving public funding under the assisted places scheme, since the enactment of the Education (No 2) Act 1986, which came in response to the decision of the ECtHR in *Campbell and Cosans v United Kingdom*.[102] In 1993, in response to the decision of the ECtHR in *Costello-Roberts v United Kingdom*,[103] and in compliance **9.60**

---

[96] *Kjeldsen* (n 6) para 53.

[97] cf *Kjeldsen* (n 6) para 54, where the Court noted that the Danish state 'preserved an important expedient for parents who, in the name of their creed or opinions, wished to dissociate their children from integrated sex education by allowing them either to entrust their children to private schools, or to educate them at home'. See also *Alonso and Merino v Spain* (App 51188/99) (2000) unreported.

[98] *Dojan v Germany* [2011] ELR 511 (App 319/08).

[99] *Dojan* (n 98) para 64.

[100] *Dojan* (n 98) para 68.

[101] *Dojan* (n 98) para 69.

[102] *Campbell and Cosans* (n 2).

[103] *Costello-Roberts v UK* (1993) 19 EHRR 112. The ECtHR held that the corporal punishment comprising three 'whacks' of the slipper on his clothed buttocks for a series of minor breaches of school rules, which a 7-year-old boy had received from the headmaster of the independent school he was attending, was not a breach of his Art 3 (inhuman and degrading treatment) or Art 8 (respect for private and family life) ECHR rights. The Court held that for corporal punishment to be 'degrading', the humiliation or debasement involved must, taking all the circumstances of the case into account, attain a level of severity higher than that inherent in any

with Article 3 ECHR, which imposes upon states a positive obligation to ensure that individuals are not subjected to 'inhuman or degrading' punishment, Parliament intervened again with regard to those children at private schools who were not covered by the earlier legislation. Section 193 of the Education Act 1993 provided that the corporal punishment of children could not be justified if 'inhuman or degrading'. In 1998, the ban pursuant to the 1986 Act was extended to include privately-funded children attending independent schools.

9.61 Section 548(1)(a) of the Education Act 1996 now provides that corporal punishment given by, or on the authority of, a member of staff to a child for whom education is provided at any school cannot be justified in any proceedings on the ground that it was given in pursuance of a right exercisable by the member of staff by virtue of his position as such. The Act defines corporal punishment as 'doing anything for the purpose of punishing [a] child (whether or not there are other reasons for doing it) which, apart from any justification, would constitute battery'.[104]

9.62 In *R (Williamson) v Secretary of State for Education and Employment*, the ban in section 548(1)(a) of the Education Act 1996 was held by the House of Lords not to be incompatible with the Article 9 and A2P1 rights of head teachers, teachers, and parents at four independent Christian schools. The claimants believed that, correctly used, discipline of this type was an effective deterrent against behaviour that was unacceptable in the community. They claimed that some 40 schools were conducted in accordance with such beliefs, which were grounded in scripture.

9.63 The House of Lords held that the measure constituted an interference with the parents' beliefs for the purposes of Article 9 ECHR,[105] but that it was justified under Article 9(2). The ban was prescribed by law, was for the legitimate aim of protecting children, and the means chosen to achieve it were not disproportionate.[106] Further the ban engaged,[107] but did not infringe, the parents' rights under A2P1.

(4) Absence from school for religious holidays, festivals, and pilgrimages

9.64 A parent or pupil may wish the pupil to be absent from school in order to observe a religious holiday or to participate in a religious festival or pilgrimage. In practice this should create no difficulty in cases of sporadic and short absences, but may give rise to an issue if the absence is regular or lengthy.

9.65 If a child who is a registered pupil at a school fails to attend regularly at school, his parent is guilty of a strict-liability offence.[108] However, section 444(3)(c) of the Education Act 1996 provides a defence for the parent where the child is absent 'on any day exclusively set apart

---

punishment. The nature and context of the punishment, the manner and method of execution, its duration, its physical and mental effects, and, in some instances, the sex, age, and state of health of the victim must be taken into account (*Costello-Roberts*, paras 29–33).

[104] Education Act 1996, s 548(4).

[105] *Williamson* (n 2), paras 40–41 *per* Lord Nicholls. Their Lordships rejected the argument that there was no interference with the manifestation of the parents' religious beliefs because the parents could have attended school themselves to administer the punishment or could have administered the punishment after school at home, or indeed could have educated the child at home.

[106] *Williamson* (n 2) paras 49–50 *per* Lord Nicholls, and paras 81–86 *per* Baroness Hale.

[107] *Williamson* (n 2) para 27 *per* Lord Nicholls.

[108] Education Act, s 444. A parent is also under a general statutory duty to ensure that his child receives efficient full-time education (Education Act 1996, s 7). Where a parent fails to comply with that duty, the local authority may commence a process leading to a school attendance order under s 437 of the 1996 Act, and it is a criminal offence to fail to comply with such an order (s 443).

for religious observance by a religious body to which his parent belongs'.[109] The availability of this defence makes prosecution unlikely in circumstances where the absence is for bona fide religious observance, although it does not strictly excuse absence on days taken on which a pupil travels for the purpose of the observance, for instance on a visit to a holy site. It is therefore possible to envisage circumstances in which the legislation might have to be read down to achieve compatibility with (for instance) a parent's rights under Article 9 ECHR.

There is also a more serious offence, carrying a potential term of imprisonment, which is **9.66** committed where the parent *knows* that the child is failing to attend regularly and fails to cause him to do so.[110] In circumstances where a parent arranges for a child to participate in a regular or lengthy absence, the requirement of knowledge will almost certainly be satisfied. But the offence is subject to a general defence of reasonable justification.[111] It is submitted that absence for bona fide religious observance, including for travel for that purpose, is capable of amounting to such justification.

In *Casimiro and Ferreira v Luxembourg*,[112] parents and a pupil who were Seventh Day **9.67** Adventists complained to the ECtHR that requiring the pupil to attend school on a Saturday was an unjustified interference with his requirement of strict Sabbath observance. The relevant domestic legislation allowed pupils to be exempt from school for a period of between eight and 30 days for the celebration of religious rituals applicable to their particular beliefs. The ECtHR contrasted this with the taking off of one day every week, which had repercussions on the normal school timetable and amounted to a substantial proportion of school time. It declared the complaint inadmissible on the grounds that although there was an interference with freedom of religion it was justified with regard to the principle of respecting the right to education.

D. Discrimination in Education

The Equality Act 2010 protects religious freedom in the field of education both by prohib- **9.68** iting discrimination against people because of religion or belief and, through important exceptions to those provisions, allowing for discrimination so as to underpin faith-based education. The purpose of this part is to outline the key provisions in each case. The topic of admissions is dealt with separately in part E.

(1) Discrimination by schools

In England and Wales, responsible bodies of state-maintained[113] and independent schools[114] **9.69** (including academies)[115] must not discriminate against or victimize a pupil in the way they provide education for him;[116] in the way they afford the pupil access to a benefit, facility, or

---

[109] See *Marshall v Graham* [1907] 2 KB 112.
[110] Education Act 1996, s 444(1A).
[111] Education Act 1996, s 444(1B).
[112] *Casimiro and Ferreira v Luxembourg* (App 44888/98) (1999).
[113] Equality Act 2010, s 85(7)(a). The responsible body will be either the local authority or the governing body, depending on the type of state-maintained school in question (see s 85(9)(a)).
[114] Equality Act 2010, s 85(7)(b). The responsible body will be the proprietor of the school (see s 85(9)(b)).
[115] Equality Act 2010, s 89(6), read together with Education and Skills Act 2008, ss 92(1) and 168(2) and Education Act 1996, s 463.
[116] Equality Act 2010, s 89(2)(a) and (5)(a) (discrimination and victimization, respectively).

service;[117] by not providing education for the pupil;[118] by not affording the pupil access to a benefit, facility, or service;[119] by excluding the pupil from the school;[120] or by subjecting the pupil to any other detriment.[121] The prohibition against harassing a pupil, or a person who has applied for admission as a pupil,[122] does not extend to the protected characteristic of religion or belief.[123]

9.70 However, save in respect of excluding a pupil or subjecting him to 'any other detriment' because of religion or belief, which remains unlawful in all schools, it is not unlawful for faith schools (whether state-maintained[124] or independent[125]) to discriminate in the ways listed at paragraph 9.69.[126] Thus, faith schools are secured freedom to provide education in accordance with the faiths upon which they are based. For example, a Roman Catholic school which organizes visits for pupils to sites of particular interest to its own faith, such as a cathedral, does not discriminate unlawfully by not arranging trips to sites of significance to the faiths of other pupils.[127] Further, those prohibitions do not apply, so far as relating to religion or belief, to anything done in connection with acts of worship or other religious observance organized by or on behalf of a school (whether or not forming part of the curriculum).[128] This avoids any conflict with the other statutory provisions prescribing the content of the curriculum and religious worship. For example, although a school must allow Jewish or Hindu parents to withdraw their children from daily assemblies which include an element of worship of a mainly Christian character, it will not be discriminating unlawfully against those children by not providing alternative assemblies including Jewish or Hindu worship.[129]

(2) Discrimination in the exercise of public functions

9.71 The Equality Act 2010 exempts from the general prohibition on discrimination or victimization because of religion or belief in the exercise of public functions,[130] anything done in connection with the curriculum of a school;[131] admission to a school which has a religious ethos;[132] acts of worship or other religious observance organized by or on behalf of a school (whether or not forming part of the curriculum),[133] the responsible body of a school which has a religious ethos;[134] transport to or from a school;[135] and the establishment, alteration, or closure of schools.[136] The purpose of the exception is to ensure that policies and practices

---

[117] Equality Act 2010, s 89(2)(b) and (5)(b).
[118] Equality Act 2010, s 89(2)(c) and (5)(c).
[119] Equality Act 2010, s 89(2)(d) and (5)(d).
[120] Equality Act 2010, s 89(2)(e) and (5)(e).
[121] Equality Act 2010, s 89(2)(f) and (5)(f).
[122] Contained in Equality Act 2010, s 89(3).
[123] Equality Act 2010, s 89(10).
[124] ie a foundation or voluntary school designated under SSFA 1998, s 69(3) as having a religious character.
[125] ie a school (other than an alternative provision academy) listed in the register of independent schools for England or for Wales, where the school's entry in the register records that the school has a religious ethos.
[126] Equality Act 2010, Sch 11, para 5.
[127] See Explanatory Notes to the Equality Act 2010, para 868.
[128] Equality Act 2010, Sch 11, para 6.
[129] See Explanatory Notes to the Equality Act 2010, para 870.
[130] Contained in the Equality Act 2010, s 29.
[131] Equality Act 2010, Sch 3, para 11(a).
[132] Equality Act 2010, Sch 3, para 11(b).
[133] Equality Act 2010, Sch 3, para 11(c).
[134] Equality Act 2010, Sch 3, para 11(d).
[135] Equality Act 2010, Sch 3, para 11(e).
[136] Equality Act 2010, Sch 3, para 11(f).

which relate to things which schools are allowed to do under the Act do not become unlawful when carried out by public authorities.

(3) School transport

Local authorities have a duty, in certain cases, to provide free school transport.[137] In other cases they have a discretion as to whether to provide transport for free or on a subsidized basis.[138] In deciding whether to exercise that discretion, as in all its school transport functions,[139] a local authority must have regard to a parent's wish that a child be provided with education at a particular school which is based on the parent's religion or belief,[140] or the wish of pupils themselves if of sixth form age.[141] One of the effects of the exceptions under the Equality Act 2010 highlighted previously, is that an authority would not act unlawfully by having a school transport policy which discriminated in favour of persons of particular religions or beliefs in the provision of free or subsidized transport, so as to allow attendance at a faith school which would not otherwise be possible. Conversely, however, there is nothing to require this. **9.72**

R (T) v Leeds City Council [2002] ELR 91[142] was a challenge to a refusal by Leeds City Council of a request made by three Orthodox Jews for assistance with transport to the nearest Jewish secondary school, which was in Manchester. The Council funded travel for students attending some Church of England and Catholic schools out of its area where such schools were the nearest ones to the students' homes, although there was not an Orthodox Jewish school within a comparable distance to the Christian schools for which the authority provided funding. An argument that the council's refusal to fund transport to the Jewish school was discriminatory on conventional judicial review grounds failed. The Court held that although the council was obliged to consider the wishes of the parents of a child for that child to receive a particular religious education, it had done so, and that did not equate to a duty to give effect to those wishes. No human rights arguments were made in the case. **9.73**

A subsequent refusal to provide free transport to Orthodox Jewish children from Leeds who wished to attend the nearest Orthodox Jewish school in Manchester was then considered in *R (R) v Leeds City Council*.[143] The authority decided that it was inappropriate to provide free transport given the distances involved, the cost, and the fact that there was a school in Leeds which offered Hebrew studies adapted to the demands of the Jewish community among other suitable Leeds schools. That approach was held to be rational on a conventional domestic law basis. In contrast to *R (T)*, referred to at paragraph 9.73, the claimants here also relied on A2P1 of the ECHR, read together with Article 14, in an argument that the Council's policy discriminated on grounds of religion. The Court held, however, that Article 14 was not engaged because A2P1 was not engaged. **9.74**

It is submitted that the court's reasoning on the human rights argument in *R (R) v Leeds City Council* must be open to doubt. First, it is not clear from the judgment on what basis the **9.75**

---

[137] The duty arises only in the case of 'eligible children', as defined in the Education Act 1996, Sch 35B (see s 508B).
[138] Education Act 1996, s 508C
[139] Meaning those under Education Act 1996, ss 508A, 508B, 508C, 508E, 508F, and 509AA.
[140] Education Act 1996, s 509AD(1)(a).
[141] Within the meaning given in Education Act 1996, s 509AC(1).
[142] *R (T) v Leeds City Council* [2002] ELR 91.
[143] *R (R) v Leeds City Council* [2005] EWHC 2495 (Admin), [2006] ELR 25.

Court considered that A2P1 was not engaged (as distinct from breached).[144] Secondly, the Court did not explain, and it is in any event unclear, why the council's policy did not at least fall within the ambit of A2P1, so that it was necessary for the court to undertake an Article 14 analysis. It is submitted that *R (R)* was at least arguably a case of indirect discrimination. The effect of the Council's policy was that whereas Orthodox Jewish families were unable to obtain free transport to any Orthodox Jewish schools, Christian families could benefit from free transport to a choice of Christian schools. In order for this difference in treatment to be justified, it would have had to pursue a legitimate aim and be proportionate. The Court did not address those questions.

E. Admissions

9.76 Religious rights are affected by the law on admissions in two main ways. First, faith schools are given freedom to adopt faith-based admissions criteria in the event that the school is oversubscribed without breaching discrimination legislation. Secondly, the law allows for parents' preferences for particular schools based on religion or belief to be taken into account in admissions decisions. Following a brief overview of the law on admissions, each of these areas will be addressed in turn.

(1) Overview of admissions law

9.77 A school's admission authority is responsible for determining the arrangements for admission of pupils to the school, including the school's admission policy. For community or voluntary controlled schools, the admission authority is the local authority, unless the authority has delegated that function to the school's governing body[145] or contracted it out.[146] For foundation or voluntary aided schools, the admission authority is the governing body.[147] The admission authority for academies is the proprietor of the school.[148] Independent schools lie outside the scope of the admissions legislation, but are still subject to discrimination legislation, as explained later.

9.78 An admission authority must engage in consultation before drawing up its admission arrangements.[149] Objections can be made about variations to admissions arrangements to the Adjudicator (in England)[150] or the Welsh Ministers (in Wales).[151]

9.79 Local authorities must formulate qualifying schemes to coordinate arrangements for all maintained schools in their area except school sixth forms.[152] Local authorities must publish information annually about admission arrangements for maintained schools and academies in their areas.[153]

---

[144] *R (R)* (n 143) para 45 of the Judgment.
[145] SSFA 1998, s 88(1)(a).
[146] Contracting Out (Local Authority Education Functions) (England) Order 2002, SI 2002/928, Sch 2, para 1.
[147] SSFA 1998, s 88(1)(b).
[148] SSFA 1998, s 88(1)(c).
[149] See SSFA 1998, s 88C (England); and School Admissions (Admission Arrangements and Co-ordination of Admission Arrangements) (England) Regulations 2012, SI 2012/8, regs 12–17; SSFA 1998, s 89 (Wales).
[150] SSFA 1998, s 88H; and SI 2012/8 (n 149) regs 21–25.
[151] SSFA 1998, s 90.
[152] SSFA 1998, s 88M (England); s 89B (Wales).
[153] SI 2012/8 (n 149) reg 17; School Information (Wales) Regulations 2011, SI 2011/1944, regs 4–5.

Save in respect of sixth form education,[154] a local authority must make arrangements for a **9.80** parent of a child in the area of the authority to express a preference as to the school at which he wishes education to be provided for his child.[155] If a preference is expressed, the admission authority for a maintained school (and so not an academy) must comply with that preference,[156] unless it would prejudice the provision of efficient education or the efficient use of resources or, if the arrangements for admission to the preferred school are wholly based on selection by reference to ability or aptitude, and are so based with a view to admitting only pupils with high ability or with aptitude, compliance with the preference would be incompatible with selection under those arrangements.[157] An admission authority may not refuse a place on efficiency grounds where the school is undersubscribed. A local authority's arrangements may allow a parent to express a preference for more than one school, but if a parent expresses more than one preference, an admission authority of a school for which one preference has been expressed is not obliged to offer admission where the child has already been offered a place at another preferred school.[158]

Parents of children (or in sixth form cases the child themselves) may appeal against decisions **9.81** refusing admission to a particular school. The admissions authority for the school must arrange the appeal.[159]

It is the duty of local authorities, governing bodies of maintained schools, appeal panels, and **9.82** adjudicators to act in accordance with the codes of practice published from time to time by the Secretary of State.[160] Such codes therefore carry a status akin to law. The present codes are the Schools Admissions Code 2012 and the School Admission Appeals Code 2012, published by the Department of Education on 1 February 2012.

(2) Faith-based admissions criteria

Prior to the introduction of statutory protections against discrimination on grounds of reli- **9.83** gion or belief in the Equality Act 2006, the courts upheld faith-based admission criteria in relation both to faith schools[161] and non-faith schools.[162] The general law is now that in England and Wales, responsible bodies of non-faith state-maintained,[163] and independent schools[164] (including Academies)[165] must not discriminate against or victimize a person in the arrangements they make for deciding who is offered admission as a pupil,[166] as to the terms on which they offer to admit the person as a pupil,[167] or by not admitting the person

---

[154] SSFA 1998, s 86(1ZA).
[155] SSFA 1998, s 86(1).
[156] SSFA 1998, s 86(2).
[157] SSFA 1998, s 86(3).
[158] SSFA 1998, s 86(2A).
[159] SSFA 1998, s 94. For the constitution of appeal panels see School Admissions (Appeals Arrangements) (England) Regulations 2012, SI 2012/9 (England); and Education (Admission Appeals Arrangements) (Wales) Regulations 2005, SI 2005/1398 (Wales).
[160] SSFA 1998, s 84(3).
[161] *R v Governors of the Bishop Challoner Roman Catholic Comprehensive Girls' School and anor, ex p Choudhury* [1992] 3 WLR 99.
[162] *R v Lancashire County Council, ex p Foster* [1995] ELR 33.
[163] Equality Act 2010, s 85(7)(a). The responsible body will be the local authority or the governing body, depending on the type of state-maintained school in question (see s 85(9)(a)).
[164] Equality Act 2010, s 85(7)(b). The responsible body will be the proprietor of the school (see s 85(9)(b)).
[165] Equality Act 2010, s 89(6), read together with Education and Skills Act 2008, ss 92(1) and 168(2) and Education Act 1996, s 463.
[166] Equality Act 2010, s 85(1)(a) and (4)(a) (discrimination and victimization, respectively).
[167] Equality Act 2010, s 85(1)(b) and (4)(b).

as a pupil.[168] However, it is not unlawful for faith schools (whether state-maintained[169] or independent (including academies)[170]) to discriminate in those ways.[171] The effect is that pupils can lawfully be refused admission to faith schools if that refusal is genuinely based on religious criteria (although only if they are oversubscribed).[172]

9.84 Faith-based admissions criteria must not, however, discriminate on prohibited grounds other than religion or belief. This gave rise to an uncomfortable conundrum in *R (E) v Governing Body of JFS and ors*.[173] In that case a father, who was Jewish by birth, wished to send his son to JFS, an oversubscribed voluntary aided Jewish school. Under its oversubscription policy, the school gave priority to children who were recognized as Jewish according to the Office of the Chief Rabbi ('the OCR'). Such recognition was based on matrilineal descent or conversion in accordance with the tenets of Orthodox Judaism. The child's mother had been converted according to non-Orthodox Judaism, and so the child was not Jewish according to the OCR definition. The child was refused a place, and his father sought judicial review of the decision of the school's governing body and the decision of the school's appeal panel upholding it. He argued that the refusal constituted direct discrimination on racial grounds under the Race Relations Act 1976, on the basis that, under section 3 of the 1976 Act, such discrimination embraced discrimination on the grounds of 'ethnic origins'. It was said that the definition of who was a Jew according to the OCR constituted discrimination on grounds of ethnic origins, because it required a focus on the child's descent.

9.85 By a majority of 5 to 4 (Lords Hope, Rodger, Walker, and Brown dissenting), the Supreme Court held that JFS's admissions policy constituted direct race discrimination. The child had been refused admission because of his ethnic origins. It was irrelevant that the admissions arrangements had a benign motive, in that they were based on fundamental tenets of Orthodox Judaism going back many thousands of years.

9.86 By a majority of 6 to 3 (Lords Hope, Rodger, and Brown dissenting), the Court also held that the admission arrangements had constituted indirect discrimination on the basis that, although they pursued the legitimate aim of providing an Orthodox Jewish education to children recognized as being members of the Orthodox Jewish faith, the school had given no consideration to the effect they could have on persons like the claimant's son or whether its aim could be achieved by other means. They could not therefore be regarded as a proportionate means of achieving that legitimate aim.

9.87 It is difficult to suppose that Parliament can have intended the Race Relations Act 1976 to lead to the result arrived at in *R (E) v Governing Body of JFS*. As Lord Rodger, dissenting, observed:

> . . . the decision of the majority means that there can in future be no Jewish faith schools which give preference to children because they are Jewish according to Jewish religious law and belief. Instead, Jewish schools will be forced to apply a concocted test for deciding who is to

---

[168] Equality Act 2010, s 85(1)(c) and (4)(c).

[169] ie a foundation or voluntary school designated under SSFA 1998, s 69(3) as having a religious character.

[170] ie a school (other than an alternative provision academy) listed in the register of independent schools for England or for Wales, where the school's entry in the register records that the school has a religious ethos.

[171] Equality Act 2010, Sch 11, para 5.

[172] See School Admissions Code 2012, para 1.36. Following the repeal of SSFA 1998, s 91 it is no longer possible for faith schools to agree 'special arrangements' with a local authority to keep places empty if they do not have sufficient applications from pupils of their preferred religion (Education Act 2002, s 49).

[173] *R (E) v Governing Body of JFS and ors* [2009] UKSC 15, [2009] 1 WLR 2353.

be admitted. That test might appeal to this secular court but it has no basis whatsoever in the 3,500 years of Jewish law and teaching. The majority's decision leads to such extraordinary results, and produces such manifest discrimination against Jewish schools in comparison with other faith schools, that one can't help feeling that something has gone wrong.[174]

The predominant purpose of legislation fashioned to combat race-based (or ethnic-based) discrimination is surely to protect vulnerable groups, included those the subject of persecution historically, against discrimination.[175] It was surely not to expose such groups to claims of discrimination against them. Yet, as *R (E) v Governing Body of JFS* illustrates, it cannot be assumed that the legislation always affords religious groups a privileged status.

9.88 The issue identified through the *JFS* case may nevertheless be regarded as fairly unique. As Lady Hale pointed out:

> ... as far as we know, no other faith schools in the country adopt descent-based criteria for admission. Other religions allow infants to be admitted as a result of their parents' decision. But they do not apply an ethnic criterion to those parents. The Christian Church will admit children regardless of who their parents are.[176]

9.89 As a consequence of the Supreme Court's ruling, other maintained Orthodox Jewish schools in the United Kingdom had to establish a new test that did not make determinations of Jewish identity based on ethnicity. Such schools have generally now created a test based on the child's religious practice.

9.90 Legislation and the Admissions Code contain further rules about admissions arrangements in faith schools. Admission authorities must ensure that parents can easily understand how any faith-based criteria will be reasonably satisfied,[177] and must have regard to any guidance from the body or person representing the religion or religious denomination when constructing faith-based oversubscription criteria, to the extent that the guidance complies with the Admissions Code itself. They must also consult with the body or person representing the religion or religious denomination when deciding how membership or practice of the faith is to be demonstrated. Church of England schools must, as required by the Diocesan Boards of Education Measure 1991,[178] consult with their diocese about proposed admission arrangements before any public consultation.[179] Further, a faith school may give first priority in their oversubscription criteria to all relevant looked after children, whether or not they are of the same faith as that of the school in accordance with its designation, and must in any event give first priority to all relevant looked after children who are of that faith, and give higher priority to all relevant looked after children not of that faith than to all other children not of that faith.[180]

---

[174] *R (E) v Governing Body of JFS* (n 173) paras 225–226.

[175] For instance the case of *Mandla v Dowell Lee* [1983] 2 AC 548, applied by the Supreme Court in *R (E) v Governing Body of JFS* (n 173) in determining that Jews could constitute an 'ethnic group' for the purposes of the Race Relations Act 1996, concerned the right of Sikh pupils to wear a turban in an independent school. It may be thought unsurprising that, at a time when legislation did not provide protection against discrimination on religious grounds, the concept of discrimination on ethnic grounds was held to extend to religious groups.

[176] *R (E) v Governing Body of JFS* (n 173) para 66. This paragraph has been criticized as betraying a Christian ideology at the heart of the majority's reasoning: see S Mancini, 'To be or not to be Jewish: the UK Supreme Court answers the question' (2010) 6(3) ECL Rev 481, 492.

[177] School Admissions Code 2012, para 1.37.

[178] SI 1991/2.

[179] School Admissions Code 2012, para 1.38.

[180] School Admissions (Admission Arrangements and Co-ordination of Admission Arrangements) (England) Regulations 2012, SI 2012/8, reg 9.

9.91 It was previously the law that state-maintained faith schools could interview parents to assess their religious commitment.[181] This is no longer the case. Save where an interview is for the purpose of assessing suitability for a place at a boarding school, no admission arrangements for a maintained school in England or Wales may require or authorize any interview with an applicant for admission to the school or his parents, where the interview is to be taken into account (to any extent) in determining whether the applicant is to be admitted to the school.[182] The statutory prohibition does not extend to independent schools, including academies.

(3) Preferences for schools based on religion or belief

9.92 Domestic legislation affords no absolute right to education in a faith school. Nor is there a basis for such a right in the second sentence of A2P1.[183] As explained earlier, however, parents may express a preference, under the arrangements adopted by a local authority, for their child to attend a faith school, or a school which best caters for their faith or that of their child. They are entitled to give reasons for the preference(s).[184] Thus they may record the particular reasons why education at the school(s) of choice would best suit their child from a religious perspective.

9.93 The importance of the parents' right to give reasons for their preference where they are based on religion was highlighted in *R (K) v London Borough of Newham*.[185] In that case a Muslim father wished his daughter to attend a single sex school because of his religious convictions, but he was not enabled on the relevant pro forma to express those reasons. The daughter was rejected for admission. The Court held that a local authority was required to establish the reasons for parental preference for a particular school. Specifically, A2P1 required that preference because of religion had to be positively invited as part of arrangements for the making of preferences. That could be achieved by, for example, including a space on the leaflet where a parent could identify the reasons for their preferences. Collins J went as to say that where the reasons were religious convictions on the part of parents, A2P1 required weight to be given to those convictions,[186] although, consistently with the Strasbourg jurisprudence, the case does not decide that religious convictions carry overriding weight.

9.94 A number of cases have considered the role of religion in the meeting of a child's special educational needs (SEN).

9.95 In *R v Secretary of State for Education, ex p E*,[187] a child appealed a decision by the Secretary of State upholding a refusal by a local authority to specify an independent Orthodox Jewish school in her proposed statement of SEN. The Court held that a decision-maker required to make decisions as to what are a child's special educational needs and the provision required to meet those needs must have regard to a child's religion and identity if they are relevant to that child's

---

[181] See eg *Governing Body of the London Oratory School v Schools Adjudicator* [2004] EWHC 3014 (Admin), [2005] ELR 162, which upheld the lawfulness of aspects of a faith school's interview process under the old law.

[182] SSFA 1998, s 88A (England); s 88R (Wales).

[183] See para 9.09. In *Coster v UK* (2001) 33 EHRR 479, para 136, the UK government submitted that A2P1 did not confer a right to be educated at a particular school. The Court did not expressly accept or reject this submission. Such an interpretation was, however, adopted by the Court of Appeal in *S, T and P v Brent LBC* [2002] ELR 556, para 9. See also *Governing Body of the London Oratory School* (n 181) para 58 *per* Jackson J.

[184] SSFA 1998, s 86(1)(b).

[185] *R (K) v London Borough of Newham* [2002] EWHC 405 (Admin).

[186] *R (K) v London Borough of Newham* (n 185) para 38.

[187] *R v Secretary of State for Education, ex p E* [1996] ELR 312.

special educational needs or the manner in which they may be met. On the facts of that case, the Secretary of State had not been entitled to make the assumptions she had about the significance of the Jewish faith to the child's educational needs including without first raising the point as a matter of procedural fairness. The child had an identified need for 'support to encourage a sense of self' which demanded careful consideration of its relationship with the suggested need for a Jewish school. Her decision was accordingly flawed. Similarly, in *A v Special Educational Needs and Disability Tribunal*,[188] a tribunal's failure to identify the impact of a child's Jewishness on the provision required to meet her SEN led the High Court to quash its decision.

In contrast, in *G v London Borough of Barnet*,[189] an appeal by an Orthodox Jew against a deci- **9.96** sion of the then Special Educational Needs Tribunal to name a local authority school instead of a private Jewish school in her statement of SEN was dismissed, on the basis that religious matters had properly been considered in accordance with the then SEN Code of Practice. Ognall J held that a child's religion and identity cannot constitute a special educational need per se.[190]

F. Dress and Symbols in Schools

The issues of religious dress and symbols in a school setting have now given rise to a sig- **9.97** nificant amount of litigation at both domestic and European level. They are not matters addressed in domestic legislation. The outcome of the decided cases has generally turned on the proper application of the relevant provisions of the ECHR.

(1) School uniform and religious dress

The leading domestic case in this area remains *R (Begum) v Headteacher and Governors of* **9.98** *Denbigh High School*.[191] Denbigh High School had a majority of Muslim pupils. In consultation with representatives of the local Muslim community it had designated an alternative uniform based on the *shalwar khameez*, which permitted the wearing of a *hijab* specifically to accommodate local religious and cultural needs. However, the Muslim beliefs of one pupil, Shabina Begum, required her to wear a more covered form of dress, a *jilbab*. She argued that the school's uniform policy breached her right to manifest her religion without unjustified interference under Article 9 ECHR.

A majority of the House of Lords held there had been no interference with her Article 9 right **9.99** given that she had a choice of two alternative schools where she would have been permitted to wear the *jilbab*.[192] The minority held that there was likely to have been an interference on the facts[193] but that it was justified in the circumstances.[194]

---

[188] *A v Special Educational Needs and Disability Tribunal* [2003] EWHC 3368 (Admin), [2004] ELR 293.

[189] *G v London Borough of Barnet* [1998] ELR 480.

[190] *G v London Borough of Barnet* (n 189) 483–4, cited with approval in *R (JW) v Learning Trust* [2009] UKUT 197 (AAC), [2010] ELR 115.

[191] *R (Begum) v Headteacher and Governors of Denbigh High School* [2006] UKHL 15, [2007] 1 AC 100. See generally T Cross and J Beckett, 'Focus on ECHR Article 9: Recent Developments' [2007] Judicial Review 75.

[192] *Begum* (n 191) para 24 *per* Bingham LJ. See also para 50 *per* Hoffmann LJ: 'Article 9 does not require that one should be allowed to manifest one's religion at any time and place of one's choosing ... people sometimes have to suffer some inconvenience for their beliefs'.

[193] See eg *Begum* (n 191) para 41 *per* Lord Nicholls, emphasizing that it would not have been a simple matter for Shabina to move school.

[194] See eg *Begum* (n 191) para 92 *per* Baroness Hale.

9.100 On justification, Lord Bingham placed significant weight on the facts that the school had taken advice, and had been told that its policy conformed with the requirements of mainstream Muslim opinion. He noted that the school had enjoyed a period of harmony and success to which the uniform policy was thought to contribute and that it was feared that acceding to the request to wear the *jilbab* would or might have significant adverse repercussions. In those circumstances it would be 'irresponsible of any court, lacking the experience, background and detailed knowledge of the headteacher, staff and governors, to overrule their judgment on a matter as sensitive as this'.[195]

9.101 Lord Nicholls drew attention to the margin of appreciation given to signatory states in this area and noted that the UK Parliament had considered it right to delegate to individual schools the power to decide whether to impose requirements about school uniforms.[196] Lord Scott similarly suggested that it was 'virtually unarguable' that the decision requiring Shabina to attend school wearing the prescribed school uniform was unlawful as a matter of domestic law.[197]

9.102 Baroness Hale adopted a more nuanced approach to the question of proportionality, recognizing at the outset that the question was more difficult in the case of a young girl than in the case of an adult who wished to manifest his religion in a particular form of dress.[198] However, she also acknowledged the task of schooling as being to educate the young from many and diverse families and communities and to 'promote the ability of people of diverse races, religions and cultures to live together in harmony'.[199] To that end a school uniform could play an important part in easing ethnic, religious, and social divisions. She also recognized a point which might have been taken in the case, namely that the school was a good school, which explained why Shabina wanted to stay there. In that sense her choice may have been arguably constricted.[200] Ultimately she was of the opinion that the school was trying to achieve a balance between conflicting views and to accommodate religious and cultural diversity in allowing girls to wear the *shalwar khameez* and the *hijab*.[201]

9.103 The House of Lords also rejected a further argument that the school had denied the claimant her right to education under A2P1. The interruption in her schooling had occurred as a result of her unwillingness to comply with the school uniform rule to which the school was entitled to adhere, and her failure to secure prompt admission to another school where her religious convictions could be accommodated.[202]

9.104 In *R (X) v Head Teacher and Governors of Y School*,[203] Silber J held, applying *Begum*, that a school's decision to refuse to allow a pupil to wear a *niqab* veil at school did not interfere with her right to manifest her religious beliefs under Article 9 ECHR. The pupil had been offered a place at another selective school, which achieved good academic results, which was easy to get to, and where she would be permitted to wear the *niqab*. In any event the decision was justified under Article 9(2). The Court attached weight to the value of school uniform in

---

[195] *Begum* (n 191) para 34.
[196] *Begum* (n 191) paras 59–64.
[197] *Begum* (n 191) para 83.
[198] *Begum* (n 191) para 94.
[199] *Begum* (n 191) para 97.
[200] *Begum* (n 191) para 97.
[201] *Begum* (n 191) para 98–99.
[202] *Begum* (n 191) see especially para 36 *per* Lord Nicholls, para 69 *per* Lord Hoffmann.
[203] *R (X) v Head Teacher and Governors of Y School* [2007] EWHC 298 (Admin).

encouraging pride in the school, enabling children to feel comfortable in their environment, ensuring that girls of different faiths felt welcome, encouraging a sense of equality and cohesion within the school, and protecting children from social pressures to dress in a particular way. It also considered that important security concerns were involved: allowing girls to wear the *niqab* could permit an unwelcome person to move around the school incognito wearing a *niqab*. It was also possible that pressures might be applied to other Muslim girls to wear the *niqab* if it was a permissible part of the school uniform.[204]

In *R (Playfoot) v Millais School Governing Body*,[205] the school in question had a general ban **9.105** on wearing jewellery, subject to some exceptions for jewellery which was a requirement of the pupil's faith. The claimant was prohibited from wearing a purity ring as a symbol of her commitment to celibacy before marriage. The judge held that Article 9(1) ECHR was not engaged as the act of wearing the purity ring was not intimately linked to the belief in chastity before marriage. The claimant was under no obligation by reason of belief to wear the ring, and was not therefore 'manifesting' her belief by wearing the ring. In the alternative, he held that there was no interference with the claimant's Article 9(1) rights as she voluntarily accepted the uniform policy of the school and there are other means open to her to practice her belief without undue hardship or inconvenience. Finally, he concluded that the aim of the school uniform policy was legitimate and the means used were proportionate.

Subsequent decisions, however, have gone the other way. In *R (Watkins-Singh) v Aberdare* **9.106** *Girls' High School Governors*,[206] a 14-year-old Sikh successfully challenged her school's decision to refuse to allow her to wear the *Kara*, a religious steel bangle, unless she was taught in isolation and kept segregated from the other pupils. The school's uniform policy allowed her to wear only one pair of plain stud earrings and a wristwatch, and she was ultimately excluded for wearing the bangle.

The Court held that the school's decision not to permit her to wear the *Kara* constituted **9.107** indirect discrimination on grounds of religion under the Equality Act 2006 (as well as on grounds of race under the Race Relations Act 1976). The pupil had suffered a detriment because she had been forbidden from wearing an item when she genuinely believed on reasonable grounds that wearing it was a matter of exceptional importance to her religious belief, and the wearing of the item could be shown objectively to be of exceptional importance to her religion, even though it was not an actual requirement. None of the arguments put forward by the school justified the refusal to permit her to wear the *Kara*. The Court considered that the small and unostentatious *Kara*, which was only 5mm wide, was much less visible to the observer than the *niqab* in *R (X)* and the *jihab* in *Begum*.

G v St Gregory's Catholic Science College Governors[207] involved a similar claim of race discrimi- **9.108** nation. There, a secondary school prohibited pupils from wearing their hair in cornrows. An Afro-Caribbean pupil, who had not cut his hair since birth in accordance with his family tradition and wore his hair in cornrows, was turned away on his first day at school.

---

[204] *R (X)* (n 203).
[205] *R (Playfoot) v Millais School Governing Body* [2007] EWHC 1698 (Admin).
[206] *R (Watkins-Singh) v Aberdare Girls' High School Governors* [2008] EWHC 1865 (Admin), [2008] ELR 561.
[207] *G v St Gregory's Catholic Science College Governors* [2011] EWHC 1452 (Admin), [2011] ELR 446.

9.109   The Court held that the pupil had been the subject of indirect discrimination on the grounds of race.[208] The policy constituted a provision, criterion, or practice which put him at a particular disadvantage. Doubting *Watkins-Singh*, the Court held that there was no need for a claimant in an indirect discrimination case to show that the matter prohibited was of exceptional importance to their race. There was evidence that some people of African-Caribbean ethnicity, for reasons based on their culture and ethnicity, regarded the cutting of hair as wrong, and that was sufficient material to establish that there was a group who would be particularly disadvantaged by a refusal to permit them to wear cornrows. In any event the pupil himself had suffered a particular disadvantage by being turned away from school.

9.110   Further, the indirect discrimination was not justified. Where there was a genuine cultural and family practice of not cutting boys' hair and wearing cornrows, an exception to the policy could be made. There was no difference in principle between religious reasons justifying non-compliance and the instant case.

9.111   There have been a number of Strasbourg cases concerning religious dress in educational institutions where the state in question has maintained a policy of secular education in state schools. These cases fall to be contrasted in the context of the United Kingdom, which is not a secular state.

9.112   In *Dahlab v Switzerland*,[209] the ECtHR considered under Article 9 ECHR a prohibition on teachers wearing headscarves in the classroom of state schools in Switzerland. The state required strict denominational neutrality and a clear separation between church and state. The ECtHR held that the restriction was prescribed by law and pursued a legitimate aim, namely the protection of the rights and freedoms of others, public safety, and public order. It further stated that it was difficult to assess the impact on pupils but that it could not be denied that the scarf might have some proselytizing effect and that it was difficult to reconcile the wearing of the scarf with a message of tolerance, respect, and above all equality which teachers were required to convey.

9.113   In *Sahin v Turkey*,[210] the vice-chancellor of Istanbul University issued a circular which banned religious attire and in particular banned students wearing the Islamic headscarf and beard from access to lectures, courses, and tutorials. A female Muslim claimed that the circular infringed Article 9 and A2P1 ECHR, including when read together with Article 14. She argued that she had been entitled to wear the headscarf for four years at the University of Burse, which had not caused any disruption, disturbance, or threat to public order; that the headscarf was not incompatible with principles of secularism; and that it was not applied, apparently, to Jewish skull caps or Christian crucifixes and therefore discriminated against Muslims. The government argued that the principle of secularism was a prerequisite for a liberal democracy and noted that the ban only affected Muslims in the state education system and that the ban on veils and beards was a direct response to previous confrontations between radical groups at the university.

9.114   The Grand Chamber (upholding the earlier decision of the ECtHR) stated that the principle of secularism was fundamental to Turkish society and that a margin of appreciation was

---

[208] The Court rejected a further claim for sex discrimination, made on the basis that the school's uniform policy did allow girls to wear cornrows on the basis that they were conventional.
[209] *Dahlab v Switzerland* (App 42393/98) (2001).
[210] *Sahin v Turkey* (2005) 41 EHRR 8.

particularly appropriate when it comes to the regulation by the state of the wearing of religious symbols in teaching institutions, since rules on the subject vary from one country to another depending on national tradition and there is no uniform European conception of the requirements of the 'protection of the rights of others' and of 'public order'. In dismissing the applicant's claim the ECtHR stated that the interference was based on secular and gender equality.

In *Dogru v France*,[211] a child, F, complained that her expulsion from school due to her refusal **9.115** to remove her Islamic headscarf during physical education lessons was a breach of her right under Article 9 ECHR. Removal of the headscarf had been requested on health and safety grounds. F was subsequently able to continue her education by 'correspondence classes'. F's appeals against the decision to expel her had been unsuccessful at all domestic levels. F submitted that the interference with her Convention rights was not prescribed by law but had mainly taken the form of state opinions, ministerial circulars, and judicial interpretations of case law which were not binding on the courts. Further, she submitted that the restrictions imposed did not pursue a legitimate aim that was necessary in a democratic society.

It was common ground in argument that the restriction imposed upon the child regarding **9.116** the wearing of the headscarf in physical education amounted to an interference with the exercise of her right to manifest her religious belief. The ECtHR nevertheless held that the interference was justified. It reasoned that the conclusion reached by the national authorities that the wearing of the Islamic headscarf was incompatible with sports classes for reasons of health or safety was not unreasonable. The health and safety and attendance rules, for the breach of which the pupil was expelled, embraced principles of secularism and neutrality which it was legitimate for the French government, acting within its margin of appreciation, to impose upon all pupils. It was not within the province of the court, where the ways and means of ensuring respect for internal rules was concerned, to substitute its own vision for that of the appropriate domestic authorities.

(2) Religious symbols in schools

ECHR rights might be engaged when a school displays religious symbols relating to one **9.117** religion but not other religions, where those are strongly represented among the pupils. For example, a display with the Nativity scene at Christmas time but not the Menorah (if there are a number of Jewish pupils) or a cross on a school wall may discriminate against non-Christian pupils and parents who wish to have their religions represented. Different considerations will apply to a school with a religious ethos as opposed to a school without one. However, this area has not given rise to any significant litigation in the United Kingdom to date.

The display of religious symbols in schools remains a controversial topic in other countries. **9.118** The leading case is now *Lautsi v Italy*,[212] in which the Grand Chamber of the ECtHR upheld the practice of state schools in Italy, required by national law since 1860, to affix crucifixes to the wall in school classrooms. In so doing it overturned the decision of the Chamber, which had held that the state had a duty, under A2P1 and Article 9 ECHR, to uphold 'confessional neutrality' in public education.

The Grand Chamber held that the decision whether crucifixes should be present in state **9.119** school classrooms formed part of the state's functions in relation to education and teaching,

---

[211] *Dogru v France* (2009) 49 EHRR 8.
[212] *Lautsi v Italy* (2012) 54 EHRR 3.

and fell within the scope of the second sentence of A2P1. The Court concluded that the crucifix was 'above all a religious symbol', but there was 'no evidence...that the display of a religious symbol on classroom walls may have an influence on pupils'. It could not be asserted, therefore, that it does, or does not, have 'an effect on young persons whose convictions are still in the process of being formed'. The applicants' subjective perception that the display of crucifixes showed a lack of respect for the right to ensure that education and teaching was in conformity with their own philosophical convictions was not sufficient to establish a breach.[213]

9.120   The Italian government had argued that the presence of crucifixes in state school classrooms was a result of Italy's historical development, giving its presence not only a religious connotation but also an identity-linked one: it now corresponded to a tradition which they considered it important to perpetuate. In addition, it was argued that beyond its religious meaning 'the crucifix symbolised the principles and values which formed the foundation of democracy and Western civilisation, and...its presence in classrooms was justifiable on that account'.[214] The Grand Chamber accepted that the decision whether or not to perpetuate a tradition falls within the margin of appreciation of the state, although reference to a tradition cannot relieve a state of its obligation to respect the Convention rights and freedoms.[215] The key issue for the Court was whether the decisions made led to a form of indoctrination.[216]

9.121   Here, there was no indoctrination. The fact that the state's regulations conferred on the country's majority religion 'preponderant visibility in the school environment' was not enough to denote a process of indoctrination.[217] A crucifix on the wall was regarded as an 'essentially passive symbol', and could not be deemed to have an influence on pupils comparable to that of 'didactic speech or participation in religious activities'.[218]

9.122   The Grand Chamber also noted that Italy opened up the school environment in parallel to other religions. Thus it was not forbidden for pupils to wear Islamic headscarves or other symbols or apparel having a religious connotation; alternative arrangements were possible to help schooling fit in with non-majority religious practices; the beginning and end of Ramadan were 'often celebrated' in schools; and optional religious education could be organized in schools for 'all recognised religious creeds'. There was 'nothing to suggest that the authorities were intolerant of pupils who believed in other religions, were non-believers or who held non-religious philosophical convictions'.[219] Further, there was no suggestion that the presence of the crucifix in classrooms had encouraged the development of teaching practices with a proselytizing tendency.[220] In all the circumstances, the Grand Chamber concluded that the decision to keep crucifixes in the classroom fell within the state's margin of appreciation.

---

[213] *Lautsi* (n 212) para 66.
[214] *Lautsi* (n 212) para 67.
[215] *Lautsi* (n 212) para 68.
[216] *Lautsi* (n 212) para 69.
[217] *Lautsi* (n 212) para 71.
[218] *Lautsi* (n 212) para 72.
[219] *Lautsi* (n 212) para 74.
[220] *Lautsi* (n 212) para 74.

10

RELIGIOUS EXPRESSION
AND TOLERATION

A. Introduction

This chapter considers, in parts A and B, the way in which the law controls, and has con- **10.01** trolled, both the expression of religious views and speech or activity which attacks or criticizes religion and matters regarded as sacred by religious believers. Parts C and D outline the way in which the law has sought to accommodate religious beliefs and practices where the application of the general law impinges on religious rights.

B. Blasphemy

The common law offences of blasphemy and blasphemous libel sought essentially to control **10.02** words and acts which tended to endanger society. For historical reasons, including their ecclesiastical origin, the offences were limited to attacks against the doctrines of the established Church. In *Bowman v Secular Society Ltd* Lord Sumner observed that 'the words, as well as acts, which tend to endanger society, differ from time to time...whether a given opinion is a danger to society is a question of the times'.[1] At one time any words challenging or questioning the doctrines of the established Church risked falling foul of the law. Although the offences evolved over the centuries they were never extended to other religions or belief systems other than Christianity.[2]

---

[1] *Bowman v Secular Society Ltd* [1917] AC 406 (HL), 446–447.
[2] See *R v Chief Magistrate Stipendiary Magistrate, ex p Choudhury* [1991] 1 QB 429 (QB). The offence of blasphemy was described by Lord Scarman in *R v Lemon* [1979] AC 617 (HL) as 'shackled by the chains of history'.

10.03   The offences were finally abolished in 2008,[3] by which time the offences of religious hatred were on the statute book.

(1) Origins

10.04   The offences of blasphemy and blasphemous libel were originally the preserve of the ecclesiastical courts, however, by the seventeenth century they were also recognized as offences at common law. The Chief Justice explained in 1676 that blasphemy was 'not only an offence to God and religion, but a crime against the laws, State and Government' punishable in the ordinary courts: 'For to say, religion is a cheat, is to dissolve all those obligations whereby civil societies are preserved'.[4] The emergence of the common law offence was linked to the need to safeguard the 'inner tranquillity of the kingdom'[5] and went hand in hand with the offence of seditious libel. Lord Diplock explained in *R v Lemon*, that 'in the post-Restoration politics of 17th and 18th century England, Church and State were thought to stand or fall together. To cast doubt on the doctrines of the established church or to deny the truth of the Christian faith upon which it was founded was to attack the fabric of society itself'.[6]

10.05   At this time any words challenging or questioning the doctrines of the established church risked falling foul of the law, although the courts were careful to emphasize that 'we do not meddle with any differences of opinion...we interpose only where the very root of Christianity is struck at'.[7] However, by the middle of the nineteenth century the courts had made clear that words attacking the established religion would be blasphemous only if the tone and spirit was that of 'offence, and insult and ridicule'.[8] Discussions carried on in 'a sober and temperate and decent style' would not attract the censure of the law.[9] It came to be recognized that the offensiveness had to reach a certain threshold, described variously as 'contemptuous', 'reviling', 'scurrilous', and 'ludicrous'.[10] In 1922, in the case of *Gott*, it was said that the essence of the crime consisted in the publication of words concerning the Christian religion so scurrilous and offensive as to pass the limits of decent controversy and to be calculated to outrage the feelings of any sympathiser with Christianity.[11]

(2) Application and development in the twentieth and twenty-first centuries

10.06   In *R v Lemon*, a private prosecution was successfully brought against the editor and publishers of a magazine, *Gay News*, for the publication of a poem which purported to describe acts of sodomy and fellatio with the body of Christ after his death, and to ascribe to him during his lifetime promiscuous homosexual practices. On appeal, the House of Lords reviewed the historical development of the offence and authorities and affirmed that the mental element of the offence required only the intent to publish; it was not necessary for the accused to have an intention to blaspheme.[12]

---

[3] Criminal Justice and Immigration Act 2008, s 79.

[4] *Taylor's Case* [1676] 1 Vent 293 (KB).

[5] *Lemon* (n 2) 658 and 662 *per* Lord Scarman.

[6] *Lemon* (n 2) 633.

[7] *Woolston's Case* (1778) 2 Str, 834; *Rex v Williams* (1797) 26 St Tr 654.

[8] *Woolston's Case* (n 7); *Rex v Williams* (n 7).

[9] *Reg v Hetherington* (1840) 4 St Tr NS 563. See also *R v Ramsey and Foote* (1883) 15 Cox 231; and *Bowman v Secular Society Ltd* [1917] AC 406 (HL).

[10] Observation of the ECommHR in *Wingrove v UK* (App 17419/90) (1994) 18 EHRR CD 54 (08/03/1994), quoted in the judgment of the ECtHR at (1997) 24 EHRR 1, para 48.

[11] *Rex v Gott* (1922) 16 Cr App R 87 (as reported in the headnote). See also *Lemon* (n 2) 632, 661–662.

[12] *Lemon* (n 2).

The applicants' complaint to the ECommHR was declared inadmissible.[13] The Commission **10.07** held there was no doubt that there had been an interference with the applicants' freedom of expression guaranteed by Article 10(1); however, the interference satisfied the requirements of Article 10(2). The Commission accepted that the offence was defined with sufficient certainty and complied with the requirement that any restriction must be prescribed by law.[14] It had as its main purpose 'to protect the right of citizens not to be offended in their religious feelings by publications' and so pursued a legitimate aim, namely the protection of the rights of others.[15] As to whether the restriction imposed was necessary in a democratic society, the Commission held that, if it was accepted that the religious feelings of the citizen deserved protection against indecent attacks on matters held sacred by him, then it could also be considered as necessary in a democratic society to stipulate that such attacks, if they attained a certain level of severity, would constitute a criminal offence triable at the request of the offended person. The Commission was satisfied that the offence as laid down in common law satisfied the principle of proportionality.

In *Choudhury* the limits of the offence were tested, in particular its application to religions **10.08** other than Christianity. The case concerned an attempted private prosecution against the author and publishers of *'The Satanic Verses'* on the grounds that they had published 'a blasphemous libel concerning Almighty God (Allah) the Supreme Deity common to all major religions of the world...and the religion of Islam and Christianity'. The magistrate found that the passages complained of did not amount to an attack on Christianity, and since the offence was restricted to the Christian religion, he refused to issue a summons. On appeal the Divisional Court held that while it had been called to examine the claim in the setting of a much changed world and of a society which now contained many adherents other than Christianity, there was no doubt that the offence did not extend to religions other than Christianity.[16] The applicant's complaint to Strasbourg—based on Article 9 ECHR, alone and in conjunction with Article 14—was declared inadmissible.[17]

Criminal prosecution was not the only way the offence was enforced. In *Wingrove* the appli- **10.09** cant's film was refused a classification certificate by the British Board of Film Classification on the ground that it infringed the law of blasphemy. The short film entitled '*Visions of Ecstasy*',

---

[13] *Gay News Ltd and Lemon v UK* (1983) 5 EHRR 123.

[14] The applicants argued that the offence of blasphemy was not defined with sufficient certainty in the common law principles to be applied by the courts. In particular, the requirement only to prove an intent to publish had not been laid down in pre-existing rules of law but was developed by the courts only in the course of proceedings. The Commission held that the courts had not overstepped the limits of what could still be regarded as an acceptable clarification of the law, moreover, the law was accessible to the applicants and its interpretation in this way was reasonably foreseeable with the assistance of appropriate legal advice.

[15] The government invoked three grounds, namely prevention of disorder, protection of morals, and protection of the rights of others. The Commission noted that the public authorities had not considered it necessary to institute criminal proceedings against the applicants for blasphemy or obscenity, so it could not be said that the public interest (prevention of disorder or protection of morals) was so preponderant that it provided the real basis for the interference in the applicants' right to freedom of expression. The justifying ground would therefore primarily have to be sought in the protection of the rights of the private prosecutor.

[16] *R v Chief Magistrate Stipendiary Magistrate, ex p Choudhury* [1991] 1 QB 429 (QB). The Court observed that the anomaly arose from 'the chains of history' (using the words of Lord Scarman in *Lemon* (n 2)). It indicated that even if it were open to the Court to extend the law to cover other religions, it would refrain from doing so and, in its view, the ECHR did not demand such an extension. See, however, the comments of Lord Scarman in *Lemon* (n 2) 658, putting forward a case for legislation extending the offence to protect the religious beliefs and feelings of non-Christians.

[17] *Choudhury v UK* (App 17439/90) (1991), ECommHR.

depicted St Teresa and the figure of Christ and included imagery of a sexual nature. The Board's concern was that for a major proportion of the film's duration that sexual imagery was focused on the figure of Christ. The result was a complete ban on the film's distribution.

10.10   In an application to the ECtHR the applicant complained that the refusal to certify the film violated his freedom of expression. The Court concluded that the interference with the applicant's Article 10(1) rights was justified.[18] The refusal was intended to protect the 'rights of others', and more specifically 'to provide protection against seriously offensive attacks on matters regarded as sacred by Christians'. The Court noted that the English law of blasphemy required a 'high threshold of profanation' which constituted a safeguard against arbitrariness. This, together with the state's margin of appreciation in this area,[19] meant that the reasons relied on by the national authorities to justify the measures could be considered both relevant and sufficient for the purposes of Article 10(2).

10.11   It is notable that, like the Commission in *Gay News v United Kingdom*,[20] the ECtHR in *Wingrove* considered the application of the law of blasphemy (at least in the particular case before it) as essentially aimed at protecting religious sensibilities and therefore the protection of 'rights of others' within the meaning of Article 10(2) ECHR. In *R (Green) v City of Westminster Magistrates' Court*, on the other hand, the Administrative Court held that the gist of the crime was material relating to the Christian religion so scurrilous and offensive in manner 'that it undermines society generally by endangering the peace, depraving public morality, shaking the fabric of society or tending to be a cause of civil strife'.[21] It was common ground that this was an element of the crime.[22] The Court held that this element would not be shown merely because some people of particular sensibility were moved to protest because they were deeply offended. It was necessary that the community or society generally should be threatened.[23] As to Article 10, the Court noted that the protection of freedom of speech must be accorded to the unpopular, tasteless, or offensive as well as to the popular, moderate, or reasoned, unless interference could be justified under Article 10(2). In the Court's view the Article 10(2) basis for the crime was best found in the risk of disorder among, and damage to, the community generally.[24]

10.12   In *Green* a member of a Christian organization had sought to bring a private prosecution for blasphemous libel against the producer of the stage show, '*Jerry Springer: the Opera*', and the Director General of the BBC which had broadcast the work. The claimant's application for judicial review of the district judge's refusal to issue a summons was dismissed. The Court held the judge had been entitled to hold that there was no *prima facie* case of blasphemous libel. Among other things, the play had been performed regularly at theatres for two years without any sign of it undermining society or occasioning civil strife or unrest. There had been no violence or demonstrations. In any event, the Court held that the judge was right to refuse to issue the summons on the basis that the prosecution for blasphemous libel was

---

[18]   *Wingrove v UK* (1997) 24 EHRR 1.
[19]   The ECtHR held that a wider margin of appreciation was generally available to a state when regulating freedom of expression in relation to matters liable to offend intimate personal convictions within the sphere of morals or, especially, religion: *Wingrove* (n 18) para 58.
[20]   See paras 10.06 and 10.07.
[21]   *R (Green) v City of Westminster Magistrates' Court* [2008] EMLR 15 (DC), para 16.
[22]   Upon reviewing the authorities, the Court held that there was ample basis for the common ground.
[23]   *Green* (n 21) para 16.
[24]   *Green* (n 21) para 17.

prevented by section 2(4)(a) of the Theatres Act 1968 and, in respect of the broadcast, the identical provisions in the Broadcasting Act 1990.[25] Section 2(4) of the Theatres Act 1968 prevented a prosecution in respect of a performance or play for an offence at common law where it is the essence of the offence 'that the performance or . . . what was said or done was obscene, indecent, offensive, disgusting or injurious to morality'.

Soon after the decision in *Green*, the offence of blasphemy was abolished. **10.13**

(3) Abolition

In March 2008 the government introduced an amendment to the Criminal Justice and **10.14** Immigration Bill abolishing the offences of blasphemy and blasphemous libel. The government cited two principal reasons: 'First, the law has fallen into disuse and therefore runs the risk of bringing the law as a whole into disrepute. Secondly, we now have new legislation to protect individuals on the grounds of religion and belief. . . .'[26]

The new legislation was the Racial and Religious Hatred Act 2006 (which introduced the **10.15** offences of religious hatred) and the legislation prohibiting discrimination on grounds of religion or belief.[27] That the law had fallen into disuse was evident, according to the government, from the fact that there had been no public prosecutions in almost 90 years and it had been more than 30 years since the last private prosecution. However, the case of *Wingrove* demonstrates that the law was far from a dead letter.[28] Further, the government considered the offences to be 'unworkable in today's society' since:

> . . . they do not protect the individual or groups of people, they do not protect our fundamental rights—indeed, they may conflict with them—and they do not protect the sacred. That last point is very much reinforced by the recent judgment in the Jerry Springer case. . . . whereas the offences of blasphemy and blasphemous libel do not protect the individual or groups of people from harm, the new offences of incitement to religious hatred and discrimination on the grounds of religion and belief—in the provision of goods, services and employment—do.[29]

The amendment was passed, and section 79 of the Criminal Justice and Immigration Act **10.16** 2008, which came into force on 8 July 2008, abolished the 'offences of blasphemy and blasphemous libel under the common law of England and Wales'.

C. Religious Hatred and Other Public Order Offences

The Public Order Act 1986 contains a number of offences which may be used to control **10.17** expression by and against religious adherents. The following are the significant offences:

(1) Using threatening, abusive or insulting words or behaviour likely to cause harassment, alarm, or distress (Public Order Act 1986, Part 1, section 5).

---

[25] Both provisions remain in force.
[26] *Hansard* HL, vol 699, cols 1118–1121 (5 March 2008).
[27] Employment Equality (Religion or Belief) Regulations 2003, SI 2003/1660 and the Equality Act 2006, Pt 2. The provisions can now be found in the Equality Act 2010. See Ch 6.
[28] See paras 10.09 and 10.11.
[29] *Hansard* HL, vol 699, cols 1119–1120 (5 March 2008).

(2) Using threatening, abusive or insulting words or behaviour with the intent to cause harassment, alarm, or distress (Public Order Act 1986, Part 1, section 4A).[30]

(3) Using threatening, abusive, or insulting words or behaviour towards a person with the intent to cause fear or provoke violence (Public Order Act 1986, Part 1, section 4).

(4) Religiously (and racially) aggravated versions of the offences in sections 4, 4A and 5 of the Public Order Act 1986 (Crime and Disorder Act 1998, section 31).

(5) Offences outlawing racial hatred (Public Order Act 1986, Part 3). 'Racial hatred' means 'hatred against a group of persons defined by reference to colour, race, nationality (including citizenship) or ethnic or national origins'.[31] Some religious groups—such as Jews and Sikhs—qualify as racial groups for these purposes.

(6) Offences outlawing hatred against persons on religious grounds (Public Order Act 1986, Part 3A). These offences were introduced by the Racial and Religious Hatred Act 2006, which came into force on 1 October 2007. They are more narrowly drawn than the offence of racial hatred.

(7) Offences outlawing hatred against persons on grounds of sexual orientation (Public Order Act 1986, Part 3A). These offences were introduced by Schedule 16 to the Criminal Justice and Immigration Act 2008, the majority of which came into effect on 23 March 2010.

10.18 There are also other offences which may be used to police and control speech, including religious speech. For example, section 89(2) of the Police Act 1996 makes it an offence to resist or wilfully obstruct a police constable in the execution of his duty. The duties of a constable include the prevention of breaches of the peace.

(1) Religious hatred offences

10.19 The religious hatred offences were introduced by the Racial and Religious Hatred Act 2006 which inserted Part 3A into the Public Order Act 1986. During the passage of the Bill, the government made clear that the legislation was 'about protecting people, not faiths'.[32] Moreover, the scope of the offences, including the inclusion in the legislation of a 'protection of freedom of expression' clause,[33] sends a clear signal that the offences are not intended to protect religious believers against insult or offensive attacks against matters they regard as sacred.

(a) Actus rea *and* mens rea

10.20 The religious hatred offences cover only 'threatening' words, behaviour or material. A person doing the relevant act—whether it is the use of threatening words or behaviour, or the display or publication of threatening material—is guilty of an offence only 'if he intends thereby to stir up religious hatred', ie 'hatred against a group of persons defined by reference to religious belief or lack of religious belief'.[34]

10.21 The various religious hatred offences in Part 3A of the Public Order Act 1986 have these elements in common, but cover different acts and types of communication. It is an offence to use threatening words or behaviour;[35] to display,[36] publish, or distribute written material

---

[30] This offence was introduced by the Criminal Justice and Public Order Act 1994.
[31] Public Order Act 1986, s 17.
[32] *Hansard* HC, vol 435, col 673 (21 June 2005).
[33] Public Order Act 1986, s 29J.
[34] Public Order Act 1986, s 29A.
[35] Public Order Act 1986, s 29B.
[36] Public Order Act 1986, s 29B.

which is threatening;[37] to present or direct the performance of a play which involves the use of threatening words or behaviour;[38] to distribute, show, or play a recording of visual images or sounds which are threatening;[39] to include in a programme service a programme involving threatening visual images or sound;[40] and to possess written material which is threatening, or the recording of visual images or sounds which are threatening, with a view to distribution, publication, etc[41]—provided this is done with the intention of stirring up religious hatred.

The word 'threatening' is to be given its ordinary natural meaning.[42] Unlike other public **10.22** order offences there is no requirement that the person must have intended his words or behaviour to be threatening or to have been aware that they were threatening.[43]

The religious hatred offences have a narrower reach than the racial hatred offences. The **10.23** government's attempts to define the religious hatred offences in the same terms as racial hatred were met with strong opposition and defeated.[44] First, the racial hatred offences cover not only 'threatening' words, behaviour and material but also those which are 'abusive' or 'insulting'. Indeed the protection of freedom of expression clause in Part 3A makes clear that expressions of ridicule, insult, or abuse of particular religions, or the beliefs or practices of their adherents, are not prohibited or restricted.[45] Secondly, a person may be guilty of racial hatred even if he has no intention to stir up racial hatred if, having regard to all the circumstances, racial hatred is likely to be stirred up by his words, behaviour, or any material he displays, etc.[46] Where there is no specific intention to stir up racial hatred, a person is not guilty if he did not intend his words or behaviour, or material to be threatening, abusive, or insulting, and he was not aware that it might be threatening, abusive, or insulting.[47]

It should be noted that a person who uses words or behaviour which, although not 'threat- **10.24** ening', are 'abusive' or 'insulting', may be prosecuted under other public order offences in

---

37 Public Order Act 1986, s 29C.

38 Public Order Act 1986, s 29D.

39 Public Order Act 1986, s 29E.

40 Public Order Act 1986, s 29F.

41 Public Order Act 1986, s 29G.

42 See *Brutus v Cozens* [1973] AC 854 (HL), in which the House of Lords considered the meaning of the word 'insulting' in the Public Order Act 1936, s 5. This made it an offence for a person to use 'threatening, abusive or insulting' behaviour with an intent to provoke a breach of the peace or whereby a breach of peace is likely to be occasioned. It was held that the word 'insulting' should be given its ordinary meaning. Their Lordships refused to define the term any further, and add a gloss to the statutory wording. Lord Reid stated, generally, in relation to the words 'threatening', 'abusive', and 'insulting': 'I see no reason why any of these should be construed as having a specially wide or a specially narrow meaning. They are all limits easily recognisable by the ordinary man.'

43 The offence in the Public Order Act 1986, s 5 (using threatening, abusive or insulting words or behaviour likely to cause harassment, alarm or distress) is established only if a person intended his words or behaviour, or the writing, sign, or other visible representation to be threatening, abusive, or insulting, or was aware that it may be threatening, abusive, or insulting: Public Order Act 1986, s 6(4).

44 The original version of the Racial and Religious Hatred Bill introduced by the government simply inserted the words 'or religious' into the Public Order Act 1986, Pt 3 and the provisions outlawing racial hatred.

45 Public Order Act 1986, s 29J. See paras 10.29–10.30.

46 Public Order Act 1986, ss 18–23.

47 Public Order Act 1986, s 18(5). See also ss 19(2), 20(2), and 21(3).

sections 4 to 5 of the Public Order Act 1986 or the religiously aggravated versions of these offences in section 31 of the Crime and Disorder Act 1998. These offences are considered in the following sections.

(b) The meaning of 'religious hatred'

10.25   'Religious hatred' is defined by section 29A of the Public Order Act 1986 as 'hatred against a group of persons defined by reference to religious belief or lack of religious belief'.

10.26   This does not cover hatred against groups defined by reference to a belief other than a religious one unless it can be said that they are defined by reference to their lack of religious belief, for example atheists and humanists. The phrase 'lack of religious belief' not only covers hatred against persons who lack religious belief, such as atheists, but also those who are targeted because of their lack of belief in a particular religion, or their lack of a particular religious belief.[48] For example, a Muslim group which intends to incite hatred against non-believers (anyone who is not Muslim) will be caught by the religious hatred provisions.

10.27   Importantly, the terms of section 29A of the Public Order Act 1986 make clear that the religious hatred provisions are intended to protect religious groups (or groups defined by their lack of religion), rather than religions. A person is liable only if he intends to stir up hatred against 'a group of persons' and that group is defined by reference to religious belief or lack of religious belief. While the title of Part 3A is 'hatred against persons on religious grounds' this phrase is not replicated in the substance of the provisions. There is no requirement that the hatred which a person intends to stir up must be connected to the group's religious beliefs or lack of religious belief. Therefore, a far right group that enjoins people to punish Muslims for 'taking our jobs', may potentially be caught by the religious hatred provisions. Conversely, a person who attacks the tenets of a particular religion and matters which its followers regard as sacred, will not necessarily intend thereby to stir up hatred against its followers.[49] This is consistent with the government's suggestion that the legislation is about protecting people and not faiths.

10.28   Finally, religious hatred is defined as hatred against 'a group' of persons. This means a person will not be guilty if he intends only to stir up hatred against an individual, even if it is by reason of their religious beliefs or lack of religious belief. For example, a person who in writing about Catholicism's teachings on homosexuality, declares that the world would be a better place without the Pope, will not be guilty of religious hatred if it is shown that he intended only to stir up hatred against the Pope, and not Catholics.[50]

(c) Protection of freedom of expression clause

10.29   Section 29J of the Public Order Act 1986 states:

> Nothing in this Part shall be read or given effect in a way which prohibits or restricts discussion, criticism or expressions of antipathy, dislike, ridicule, insult or abuse of particular religions or the beliefs or practices of their adherents, or of any other belief system or the beliefs or

---

[48] The Explanatory Notes to the Racial and Religious Hatred Act 2006, para 23 state that the offences 'are designed to include hatred against a group where the hatred is not based on the religious beliefs of the group or even on a lack of any religious belief, but based on the fact that the group do not share the particular religious beliefs of the perpetrator'.

[49] See eg the French case of *Houellebecq*, Paris 17eme Chambre Correctionnelle, 22 October 2002, referred to in *Norwood v DPP* [2003] Crim LR 888 (DC), para 26.

[50] Of course, this may well be caught by some other offence.

practices of its adherents, or proselytising or urging adherents of a different religion or belief system to cease practising their religion or belief system.

This section was included to address concerns that the provisions would be used to prevent criticism of religion or religious beliefs and would have a chilling effect on free speech. In fact, the section goes beyond the protection afforded to the right to freedom of expression by Article 10 ECHR as interpreted and applied by Strasbourg. The ECtHR has affirmed that whoever exercises the rights and freedoms enshrined in Article 10(1) undertakes 'duties and responsibilities', as borne out by the wording of Article 10(2).[51] In the context of religious opinions and beliefs, this may include an obligation to avoid, so far as possible, expressions that are gratuitously offensive to others and which do not contribute to any form of public debate capable of furthering progress in human affairs.[52] Section 29J seeks to protect not only genuine criticism and discussion, but also gratuitous abuse, insult, and ridicule. In any case, the section is of little more than symbolic importance since the requirement for words, behaviour, or material to be 'threatening' considerably narrows the scope of the offence. Gratuitous abuse, insult, and ridicule of religious practices and beliefs, or objects of religious veneration which does not exceed this limit will not be caught by the provisions.

10.30

(2) Hatred against persons on grounds of sexual orientation

The Criminal Justice and Immigration Act 2008 extended Part 3A of the Public Order Act 1986 to cover 'hatred on the grounds of sexual orientation'. The offences in sections 29B to 29J of the Public Order Act 1986 now also apply to hatred on grounds of sexual orientation. The *actus reus* and *mens rea* of these offences are the same as the offences of religious hatred. Any words, behaviour, or material must be 'threatening' and a person is guilty only if the relevant act—such as the use of threatening words or behaviour[53]—is done with the intention to stir up hatred on the grounds of sexual orientation. Section 29AB defnines hatred 'on the grounds of sexual orientation' as 'hatred against a group of persons defined by reference to sexual orientation (whether towards persons of the same sex, the opposite sex or both)'.

10.31

The requirement for words and behaviour to be 'threatening' considerably narrows the scope of the offences. Religiously motivated criticism or disapproval of homosexual conduct will not be caught by the provisions unless it goes beyond this limit. Indeed, as in the case of religious hatred, Part 3A includes a protection of freedom of expression clause in section 29JA of the Public Order Act 1986, which states: 'In this Part, for the avoidance of doubt, the discussion or criticism of sexual conduct or practices or the urging of persons to refrain from or modify such conduct or practices shall not be taken of itself to be threatening or intended to stir up hatred.'[54]

10.32

---

[51] *Otto-Preminger Institute v Austria* (1995) 19 EHRR 34, para 49. See further the discussion at para 10.65.

[52] *Otto-Preminger Institute* (n 51) para 49. In a joint dissenting opinion, Judges Palm, Pekkanen, and Makarczyk agreed with this sentiment at least, stating that 'tolerance works both ways and the democratic character of a society will be affected if violent and abusive attacks on the reputation of a religious group are allowed'.

[53] Public Order Act 1986, s 29B.

[54] The relevant amendment to the Criminal Justice and Immigration Bill was introduced by Lord Parker of Waddingdon and is sometimes referred to as the 'Waddington' clause. It came into force on 8 May 2008, some time before the offences themselves came into force on 23 March 2010. The government introduced an amendment during the passage of the Coroners and Justice Bill to remove the clause from the Public Order Act 1986, Pt 3. There was no proposal to remove s 29J, the freedom of expression clause relating to the religious hatred offences. However the government's attempts to remove s 29JA were defeated in the House of Lords and it eventually conceded defeat, stating that it could no longer delay the passage of the Coroners and Justice Bill.

10.33   This was introduced as a result of concerns that the provisions would have a chilling effect on free speech and that mistaken interpretation of the provisions could result in heavy-handed policing. Notably, section 29JA refers to 'sexual conduct or practices' rather than sexual orientation.[55] This is of little more than symbolic importance. On one view, any discussion or criticism of homosexuality can be interpreted as criticism of sexual conduct or practices. In any case, such criticism would only be an offence if it was 'threatening' and done with the requisite intent. The words 'for the avoidance of doubt' make clear that the clause is clarificatory and is not intended to enlarge or narrow the scope of the offences.

10.34   It should be noted that religiously motivated speech which is not 'threatening' may nevertheless be caught by other provisions of the Public Order Act 1986. For example, a preacher who held up a sign with the words 'Stop Immorality' 'Stop Homosexuality' 'Stop Lesbianism' was convicted of displaying an 'insulting' sign causing 'alarm or distress' contrary to section 5 of the Public Order Act 1986.[56] It might be wondered if a similar result would occur today in the light of the statutory clarification by Parliament about protections for free speech for and against religious believers.

(3) Other public order offences and the ECHR

(a) The offences

10.35   There are public order offences, other than the hatred offences, which may be used to either restrict or protect religious speech. These include, in particular, the offences in sections 4 to 5 of the Public Order Act 1986.

10.36   Section 5 provides that a person is guilty of an offence if he uses 'threatening, abusive or insulting' words or behaviour, or disorderly behaviour, or displays any writing, sign, or visible representation which is 'threatening, abusive or insulting' within the hearing or sight of a person 'likely to be caused harassment, alarm or distress thereby'.[57] It is not necessary for the prosecution to prove that anyone was in fact caused harassment, alarm, or distress.[58] As to the mental element, a person must intend his words or behaviour, or the writing, sign, or other visible representation to be threatening, abusive, or insulting, or must be aware that it may be threatening, abusive, or insulting.[59]

10.37   Section 4A contains a more serious offence of a similar kind.[60] A person is guilty of an offence under section 4A if he uses threatening, abusive words or behaviour (or displays such writing, sign, or visible representation) with the 'intent to cause a person harassment, alarm or distress' and 'harassment, alarm or distress' is in fact caused to that person, or another person.[61] There is no requirement that the person must intend his words or behaviour to be threatening, abusive, or insulting, or be aware of that it may be.

10.38   In respect of both offences, it is a defence for the accused to prove that 'his conduct was reasonable' (section 4A(3)(b)). The reasonableness of the accused's conduct is to be judged objectively.[62]

---

[55] The original amendment referred to 'discussions of, criticism of or expressions of antipathy towards, conduct relating to a particular sexual orientation'.

[56] See *Hammond v DPP* [2004] EWHC 69 (Admin).

[57] Public Order Act 1986, s 5(1).

[58] *Norwood* (n 49) para 34.

[59] Public Order Act 1986, s 6(4).

[60] However, both offences are summary only.

[61] Public Order Act 1986, s 4A(1).

[62] *DPP v Clarke* [1991] Cr App R 359 (QB). See the discussion in *Norwood* (n 49)—a case concerning a prosecution for a religious aggravated version of the offence in Public Order Act 1986, s 5—in which Auld LJ

As for section 4, a person is guilty of an offence if he uses towards another person threatening, **10.39** abusive, or insulting words or behaviour (or distributes or displays to another person any such writing, sign, or visible representation) with the intent to cause that person to believe that immediate unlawful violence will be used against them or another, or to provoke the immediate use of violence by that person or another, or whereby that person is likely to believe that such violence is likely to be used or provoked.

All these offences are summary offences. A person convicted of an offence contrary to sec- **10.40** tion 4 and section 4A may be liable to imprisonment for a maximum of six months and/or a fine,[63] whereas the maximum penalty on conviction of a section 5 offence is a fine.[64]

Importantly, section 31 of the Crime and Disorder Act 1998 contains religiously (and **10.41** racially) aggravated versions of these offences.[65] The religiously aggravated versions of the section 4 and 4A offences are triable either way and a person convicted on indictment may face imprisonment for up to two years.[66]

Section 28(1) of the 1998 Act provides that an offence is 'religiously aggravated' (a) if at the **10.42** time of committing the offence, or immediately before or after doing so, the offender demonstrates towards the victim of the offence hostility based on the victim's membership or presumed membership of a religious group,[67] or (b) the offence is wholly or partly motivated by hostility towards members of a religious group based on their membership of that group.[68] For these purposes, 'religious group' is defined as meaning 'a group of persons defined by reference to religious belief or lack of religious belief' (section 28(5)). This is identical to the terms of section 29A of the Public Order Act 1986, which defines 'religious hatred' as hatred against such a group.[69]

In *Norwood v DPP* the accused was convicted of a religiously aggravated offence under sec- **10.43** tion 5(1)(b) of the Public Order Act 1986 when he displayed a poster in the first floor window of his flat with the words: 'Islam out of Britain' and 'Protect the British people', together with a photograph of the twin towers of the Word Trade Center in flames and a crescent and star surrounded by a prohibition sign.[70]

Where an offender is convicted of an offence, other than a religiously aggravated offence **10.44** under the Crime and Disorder Act 1998, and the offence was religiously (or racially)

---

queried whether there was much of a role for the s 5(3) defence once the prosecution had proved the limbs in s 5(1); he stated that if the prosecution proved that an accused's conduct was insulting and that he intended it to be, or was aware that it might be so, it would in most cases follow that his conduct was objectively unreasonable, especially where, in the aggravated form, the prosecution had proved that his conduct was motivated by hostility towards members of a religious group based on their membership of a religious group.

[63] Public Order Act 1986, ss 4(4) and 4A(5).

[64] Public Order Act 1986, s 5(6).

[65] These offences were created by the Anti-Terrorism, Crime and Security Act 2001 and came into force on 14 December 2001.

[66] Crime and Disorder Act 1998, s 31(4). The maximum sentence for a person convicted on indictment of the religious hatred offences is imprisonment for seven years: Public Order Act 1986, s 29L(3).

[67] For these purposes, 'membership' in relation to a religious group includes association with members of that group, and 'presumed' means presumed by the offender: Crime and Disorder Act 1998, s 28(2).

[68] Crime and Disorder Act 1998, s 28(3) makes clear that it is immaterial for the purposes of either s 28(1) (a) or (b) whether or not the offender's hostility is also based, to any extent, on any other factor not mentioned in that paragraph.

[69] For a discussion of the scope of the definition, see paras 10.25–10.28.

[70] *Norwood* (n 49).

aggravated, section 145 of the Criminal Justice Act 2003 provides that the court must treat that as an aggravating factor when sentencing.[71]

10.45 As to aggravation relating to sexual orientation, there are no aggravated versions of the offences in the Public Order Act 1986. However section 146 of the Criminal Justice Act 2003 provides that the court must treat it as an aggravating factor when sentencing an offender for any offence. There is an aggravation relating to sexual orientation when at the time of committing the offence, or immediately before or after doing so, the offender demonstrated towards the victim hostility based on the sexual orientation or presumed sexual orientation of the victim, or the offence was wholly or partly motivated by hostility towards persons who are of a particular sexual orientation.[72]

10.46 Other offences which may be used to control speech, including religious speech, include section 89(2) of the Police Act 1996, which makes it an offence to resist or wilfully obstruct a police constable in the execution of his duty. The duties of a constable include the prevention of breaches of the peace. In *Redmond-Bate v DPP* three Christian fundamentalists preaching about morality, God, and the Bible from the steps of a cathedral attracted a large crowd, some of whom were hostile. Fearing a breach of the peace a police officer asked the preachers to stop and, when they refused to do so, they were arrested for wilfully obstructing the officer in the execution of his duty under section 89(2) of the Police Act 1996. Their appeal against conviction was allowed.[73]

10.47 Having set out the components of the offence,[74] Sedley LJ observed that the question for the constable was whether there was a threat of violence and, if so, from whom it was coming. If the preachers were being so provocative that someone in the crowd, without behaving wholly unreasonably, might be moved to violence, he was entitled to ask them to stop and arrest them if they did not. If the threat of disorder was coming from passers-by who were taking the opportunity to react so as to cause trouble, then it was they and not the preachers who should be asked to desist.

10.48 The Court held that the officer was not justified in apprehending the preachers for breach of the peace. The officer had dealt with those in the crowd who were being disorderly. Nobody was obliged to stop and listen. It was emphasized that 'free speech includes not only the inoffensive but the irritating, the contentious, the eccentric, the heretical, the unwelcome and the provocative provided it does not tend to provoke violence'. Sedley LJ went on to say that:

> Freedom only to speak inoffensively is not worth having. What Speaker's Corner (where the law applies as fully as anywhere else) demonstrates is the tolerance which is both extended by the law to opinion of every kind and expected by the law in the conduct of those who disagree, even strongly, with what they hear. From the condemnation of Socrates to the persecution of modern writers and journalists, our world has seen too many examples of State control of

---

[71] For these purposes, religiously aggravated has the meaning set out in the Crime and Disorder Act 1998, s 28. The Criminal Justice Act 2003, s 145 provides that the court must state in open court that the offence was religiously aggravated.

[72] Criminal Justice Act 2003, s 146(2)(a)(i) and (b)(i).

[73] *Redmond-Bate v DPP* [2000] HRLR 249 (QB).

[74] The Court held that the test of reasonableness of a constable's action is objective in the sense that it is for the court to decide whether in the light of what he knew and perceived at the time, the court is satisfied that it was reasonable to fear an imminent breach of the peace. The next and critical question for the constable, and in turn for the court, is where the threat is coming from—the accused or other people. A constable can only take steps where conduct gives rise to a reasonable apprehension that it will, by interfering with the rights or liberties of others, provoke violence which, though unlawful, would not be entirely unreasonable.

unofficial ideas. A central purpose of the European Convention on Human Rights has been to set close limits to any such assumed power. We in this country continue to owe a debt to the jury which in 1670 refused to convict the Quakers William Penn and William Mead for preaching ideas which offended against State orthodoxy...To proceed, as the Crown Court did, from the fact that the three women were preaching about morality, God and the Bible (the topic not only of sermons preached on every Sunday of the year but of at least one regular daily slot on national radio) to a reasonable apprehension that violence is going to erupt is, with great respect, both illiberal and illogical.[75]

(b) Relationship with Convention rights

The relationship between the offences in sections 4A and 5 of the Public Order Act 1986 and Convention rights—principally Article 10 ECHR—has been considered in a number of cases.[76] **10.49**

It has been held that section 5 of the Public Order Act 1986 is not of itself incompatible with the ECHR.[77] However, when looking at the offences in sections 4A and 5 of the Public Order Act 1986, regard must be had to Convention rights where they are engaged. The accused's right to freedom of expression can be brought into play when considering the reasonableness defence in sections 5(3) and 4A(3)[78] or when determining whether a particular set of facts and circumstances can give rise to a finding that the alleged conduct was 'insulting' within the terms of section 5[79] or, by the same token, 'threatening' or 'abusive'. **10.50**

Prosecutions under sections 4A and 5 of the Public Order Act 1986 tend to engage Article 10 which, it has been emphasized, applies not only to the popular, inoffensive, or moderate, but also the shocking, disturbing, or offensive.[80] The right to freedom of expression is not unqualified. Article 10(2) provides that the exercise of the right may be subject to 'such formalities, conditions, restrictions, or penalties' as are 'necessary in a democratic society' in the interests of 'the prevention of disorder or crime' or 'the protection of the reputation or rights of others' among other things. The restrictions under Article 10(2) must be narrowly construed[81] and the justification for any interference must be convincingly established.[82] **10.51**

In cases concerning religious expression Article 9 ECHR may also be engaged. Article 9 entails the right to manifest one's beliefs by bearing witness to them in words and deeds.[83] In *Connolly* **10.52**

---

[75] *Redmond-Bate* (n 73) paras 20 and 21.

[76] Including *Percy v DPP* [2001] EWHC Admin 1125, *Norwood v DPP* [2003] Crim LR 888 (DC); *Hammond v DPP* [2004] EWHC 69 (Admin).

[77] *Percy* (n 76) para 25. See also *Abdul v DPP* [2011] HRLR 16 (DC), para 55.

[78] In Norwood (n 76) para 35, Auld LJ held that 'the way in which Article 10 intrudes on the operation of a section 5 prosecution is whether the defendant's conduct was objectively reasonable, having regard to all the circumstances, including importantly those for which the Article 10.2 itself provides'. Indeed, Auld LJ stated that 'the mechanics of the Article's operation on a prosecution under it seem to me to be confined to the objective defence of reasonableness in section 5(3)'. See also *Percy* (n 76) para 14 and *Hammond* (n 76) para 21.

[79] *Hammond* (n 76) para 21. The defendant in that case had been convicted of displaying an 'insulting' sign.

[80] Percy (n 76) para 27. See also *Redmond-Bate* (n 73) para 20, *Green* (n 21), and *Otto-Preminger Institute v Austria* (1995) 19 EHRR 24 discussed at paras 10.63–10.65.

[81] *Percy* (n 76); *Norwood* (n 76) para 22.

[82] *Percy* (n 76) paras 14 and 27 and *Abdul* (n 77) para 5, both drawing on *Sunday Times v UK (No 2)* (1992) 14 EHRR 123.

[83] *Kokkinakis v Greece* (1994) 17 EHRR 397. In *Eweida and ors v UK* (2013) 57 EHRR 8, para 94, the ECtHR acknowledged the value to an individual who has made religion a central tenet of his or her life 'to be able to communicate that belief to others'.

it was held that while the importance of freedom of thought, conscience, or religion was not in doubt, it did not follow from the decision in *Kokkinakis* that freedom of religious expression was of higher order than and more worthy of protection than freedom of secular expression enshrined in Article 10.[84] The courts have generally taken the view in religious expression cases that the considerations relevant to Articles 9 and 10 are the same and have tended to consider the matter in the context of Article 10.[85] The fact that the expression constituted a genuine attempt to bear witness may, however, be properly taken into account when assessing whether interference with freedom of expression was justified under Article 10(2).[86]

10.53   As to what justifies interference with the right to freedom of expression, in *Percy v DPP*—a case concerning a conviction under section 5 of the Public Order Act 1986—Hallet J accepted that protecting people from intentionally and gratuitously insulting behaviour which caused them alarm or distress, and preventing 'the denigration of objects of veneration and symbolic importance for one cultural group' were legitimate aims for the purposes of Article 10(2).[87] The object in *Percy* was an American flag at an airbase which the appellant defaced in protest against the use of weapons of mass destruction and American military policy, causing distress to American service personnel and their families. It was accepted that the message she wished to convey was a perfectly lawful political message and it only became insulting because of the manner in which she chose to convey it. While her conduct was insulting, there was found to be little or no risk of disorder.

10.54   Against this background, Hallet J held that in assessing whether prosecution was a proportionate response, relevant factors might include the fact that accused's behaviour went beyond legitimate protest; that the behaviour formed part of an open expression of opinion on a matter of public interest but had become disproportionate and unreasonable; that the accused knew the likely effect of their conduct and chose deliberately to desecrate the national flag, a symbol of some very considerable importance to many; the fact that it had nothing to do with conveying a message or the expression of opinion but amounted to a gratuitous and calculated insult which a number of people at which it was directed found deeply distressing.[88]

---

[84] *Connolly v DPP* [2008] 1 WLR 276 (DC), para 36. There is a hierarchy of different forms of expression in the Strasbourg jurisprudence, with political speech or debates of questions of public interest warranting greater protection than artistic or commercial speech. See also *Kirk Session of Sandown Free Presbyterian Church's Application* [2011] NIQB 26, para 66:

> The nature, purpose and overall context of the expression which is restrained or interfered with by the State will determine the strength and cogency of the justification for the interference required by the Court—interference with political speech rather than commercial or artistic speech requiring the strongest reasons to justify impediments. The nature and purpose of the expression contained in the advertisement was religious, as opposed to commercial, notwithstanding that the applicant paid for the advertisement.

[85] *Hammond* (n 76) para 18; *Connolly* (n 84) para 36; *Kirk Session of Sandown Free Presbyterian Church's Application* (n 84) para 42, in which it was common ground that the issues arising under ECHR, Arts 9(2) and 10(2) were the same.

[86] See eg *Kirk Session of Sandown Free Presbyterian Church's Application* (n 84) paras 69 and 73.

[87] *Percy* (n 76) paras 28 and 30. See also *Connolly* (n 84) para 28; *Kirk Session of Sandown Free Presbyterian Church's Application* (n 84) paras 69, 73 and para 51; *Gay News Ltd* (n 13); *Wingrove v UK Wingrove v UK* (App 17419/90) (1994) 18 EHRR CD 54 (08/03/1994), para 48; *Otto-Preminger Institute* (n 80) para 49, in which the ECtHR acknowledged that it may be considered necessary in certain democratic societies to sanction or prevent improper attacks 'on objects of religious veneration' provided that any formality, condition, or restriction imposed is proportionate to the legitimate aim pursued.

[88] *Percy* (n 76) para 32.

In *Dehal v CPS*, Moses J adopted a more restrictive approach, emphasizing the need to show **10.55** a threat to public order in order to justify the invocation of the criminal law.[89] Mr Dehal had attended his local Sikh Temple for many years, and repeatedly expressed his disagreement with the religious teachings of the establishment which, he asserted, resulted from an incorrect interpretation of the Holy Book. He was prosecuted for an offence contrary to section 4A when he posted a notice in the Temple describing members of the committee, including the President, as a hypocrite, liar, maker of false statements to the police, and a proud, mad dog, among other things. On appeal by way of case stated Mr Dehal relied on his rights under Article 10. His appeal was allowed. Moses J held that it was a fundamental feature of the relationship between Article 10 and section 4 that 'the criminal law should not be invoked unless and until it is established that the conduct which is the subject of the charge amounts to such a threat to public disorder as to require the invocation of the criminal as opposed to the civil law'.[90]

It was held that however insulting and unjustified Mr Dehal's words, a criminal prosecution **10.56** was unlawful as a result of Article 10 unless and until it could be established that such a prosecution was necessary in order to prevent public disorder. The justices had failed to make any such finding, and so the appeal was allowed.[91]

In *Hammond v DPP* the accused's rights under both Articles 10 and 9 ECHR were engaged.[92] **10.57** Mr Hammond was an Evangelical Christian convicted of an offence under section 5 of the Public Order Act 1986 after preaching in a public square while holding a sign bearing the words: 'Stop Immorality', 'Stop Homosexuality', and 'Stop Lesbianism'. He received a hostile reaction from members of the public and was attacked. The justices found that the words displayed on the sign were 'insulting' and caused distress to persons who were present. Mr Hammond had received a similar reaction previously and told the police he knew the sign was insulting; section 6(4) was therefore satisfied. There was found to be no violation of his right to freedom of expression. The interference with his right had the legitimate aim of preventing disorder and was necessary in a democratic society. The words on the sign were directed specifically towards the homosexual and lesbian communities and the justices referred to the need to show tolerance to all sections of the community. The sign was displayed in the town centre on a Saturday afternoon, provoking hostility from members of the public. The justices' found that Mr Hammond's behaviour went beyond legitimate protest, was provoking violence and disorder, and interfered with the rights of others.

The Divisional Court upheld the justices' finding, albeit with some hesitation. May LJ **10.58** accepted that the words on the sign were not expressed in intemperate language; however, it was open to the justices to find that the words were 'insulting' not least because they appeared to relate to homosexuality and lesbianism and immorality. As to whether the defence of reasonableness had been established, May LJ acknowledged the cardinal importance of freedom of expression in a democratic society but held that there were no grounds to interfere with the justices' decision.[93]

---

[89] *Dehal v CPS* [2005] EWHC 2154 (Admin).
[90] *Dehal* (n 89) para 5.
[91] *Dehal* (n 89) para 12. Moses LJ, later in his judgment, referred to the words of the statute the 'Public Order' Act.
[92] *Hammond* (n 76).
[93] *Hammond* (n 76) paras 32, 33.

10.59   In *Abdul v DPP* Davis J suggested that cases such as *Hammond v DPP* went 'close to the limit' of what may justify a prosecution and conviction under section 5 of the Public Order Act 1986.[94] The decision in *Hammond v DPP* can be contrasted with the decision in *Kirk Session of Sandown Free Presbyterian Church's Application*.[95] An adjudication by the Advertising Standards Authority that some of the text used in an advertisement placed by the applicant in the *Belfast News Letter* and headlined 'The Word of God Against Sodomy' was homophobic and likely to cause, and did cause, offence was held to be a violation of the applicant's rights under Article 10 ECHR. The Court acknowledged that the applicant's religious views were offensive to those of a certain sexual orientation, but emphasized that Article 10 protects expressive rights which offend shock or disturb. In finding there had been a disproportionate interference with the applicant's freedom of expression, the Court took into account the context of the impugned advertisement (the annual Gay Pride march), the fact that the advertisement contained no extortion to violence or other illegal activity, and the fact that it constituted a genuine attempt to stand up for their religious beliefs and encouraged others to bear witness.

10.60   A case which engaged Article 17 ECHR was *Norwood v DPP*.[96] Mr Norwood was convicted of committing a religiously aggravated offence under section 5 of the Public Order Act 1986 when he displayed a poster in the window of his flat with the words: 'Islam out of Britain' and 'Protect the British people', together with a photograph of the twin towers of the Word Trade Centre in flames and a crescent and star surrounded by a prohibition sign. The Divisional Court agreed that the display of the poster was 'insulting'. Auld LJ held that 'it could not, on any reasonable basis, be dismissed as merely an intemperate criticism or protest against the tenets of the Muslim religion, as distinct from an unpleasant and insulting attack on its followers generally'.[97] The terms of the poster and its location were, as a matter of common sense, capable of causing harassment, alarm, or distress to passers-by who might see it. That would be the reaction 'of any right-thinking member of society concerned with the preservation of peace and tolerance and the avoidance of any religious and racial tension, as well as to any follower of the Islamic religion'. As to the section 5(3) defence considered alongside Article 10, Auld LJ held that the judge was entitled to find that the appellant's conduct was unreasonable 'having regard to the clear legitimate aim, of which the section itself was a necessary vehicle, to protect the rights of others and/or to prevent crime and disorder'. He observed that there were also 'considerations under Articles 9 and 17, weighing against permitting the appellant to rely on his right under Article 10.1 in the circumstances of this case'.[98]

10.61   Mr Norwood's application to the ECtHR was rejected on the grounds that the display of the poster constituted an act within the meaning of Article 17 ECHR and did not, therefore, enjoy the protection of Article 10.[99]

---

[94] *Abdul* (n 77) para 59.

[95] *Kirk Session of Sandown Free Presbyterian Church's Application* (n 84).

[96] *Norwood* (n 76). Art 17 provides that: 'Nothing in this Convention may be interpreted as implying for any State, group or person any right to engage in any activity or perform any act aimed at the destruction of any of the rights and freedoms set forth herein or at their limitation to a greater extent than is provided for in the Convention.'

[97] *Norwood* (n 76) para 33.

[98] *Norwood* (n 76) para 40. Auld LJ was here agreeing with the submissions of counsel for the respondent/prosecutor which are summarised at para 31: 'As to the prohibition in Article 17 on abuse of rights, Mrs Pitt-Lewis pointed to the right under Article 9 to Islamic people to follow their own religion...'

[99] *Norwood v UK* (2005) 40 EHRR SE11.

(4) Jurisprudence of the ECtHR

Cases involving restrictions on speech with a religious subject matter liable to insult or offend **10.62** religious sensibilities have been characterized by the ECtHR as involving a conflict between the fundamental freedoms guaranteed by Articles 9 and 10 ECHR.[100]

In *Otto-Preminger Institute v Austria*—a case involving a challenge to the seizure of a satiri- **10.63** cal film with a religious subject matter—the majority adopted a generous interpretation of Article 9 in balancing the two apparently conflicting rights. The Court stated that those who choose to exercise the freedom to manifest their religion 'cannot reasonably expect to be exempt from all criticism' and 'must tolerate and accept the denial by others of their religious beliefs and even the propagation by others of doctrines hostile to their faith'. However, the Court went onto say:

> ... the manner in which religious beliefs and doctrines are opposed or denied is a matter which may engage the responsibility of the State, notably its responsibility to ensure the peaceful enjoyment of the right guaranteed under Article 9 to the holders of those beliefs and doctrines. Indeed, in extreme cases the effect of particular methods of opposing or denying religious beliefs can be such as to inhibit those who hold such beliefs from exercising their freedom to hold and express them.[101]

The ECtHR went further, suggesting that Article 9 guaranteed 'respect for the religious feel- **10.64** ings of believers' which could be violated 'by provocative portrayals of objects of religious veneration'.[102] It also referred to 'the *right* of persons *to proper respect* for their freedom of thought, conscience and religion'(emphasis added).[103] In a joint dissenting opinion three of the judges disagreed with the majority, stating that: 'The Convention does not, in terms, guarantee a right to protection of religious feelings. More particularly, such a right cannot be derived from the right to freedom of religion, which in effect includes a right to express views critical of the religious opinions of others.'[104] However, they acknowledged that it may be 'legitimate' for the purposes of Article 10 to protect the religious feelings of certain members of society against criticism. Indeed in *Otto-Preminger Institute* and other cases it has been accepted that laws and measures aimed at protecting citizens from being insulted or offended in their religious feelings pursued a legitimate aim under Article 10(2), namely the protection of the 'rights of others'.[105]

As to Article 10, the ECtHR has affirmed that freedom of expression constitutes one of the **10.65** essential foundations of a democratic society which, subject to Article 10(2), is applicable not only to information or ideas that are favourably received or regarded as inoffensive or

---

[100] See eg *Otto-Preminger Institute v Austria* (1995) 19 EHRR 34, para 55; and *IA v Turkey* (2007) 45 EHRR 30, para 42.

[101] *Otto-Preminger Institute* (n 100) para 47.

[102] *Otto-Preminger Institute* (n 100) para 47. The ECtHR referred to 'The respect for the religious feelings of believers as guaranteed in Article 9 ...'

[103] *Otto-Preminger Institute* (n 100) para 55. See also *Wingrove v UK* (1997) 24 EHRR 1, para 48.

[104] *Otto-Preminger Institute* (n 100) para 6, Joint Dissenting Opinion of Judges Palm, Pekkanen, and Makarczyk. See also the observations of the Administrative Court in *Green* (n 21) para 17: 'it does not seem to us that insulting a man's religious beliefs, deeply held though they are likely to be, will normally amount to an infringement of his Art 9 rights since his right to hold and to practise his religion is generally unaffected by such insults'.

[105] See eg *Gay News Ltd* (n 13); and *Wingrove* (n 103) para 48. In *Chassagnou v France* (1999) 29 EHRR 615, the ECtHR stated that the 'rights of others' included, but were not restricted to the Convention rights of others. See the discussion in *Connolly v DPP* [2008] 1 WLR 276 (DC), paras 23 ff.

a matter of indifference, but also to those that shock, offend, or disturb.[106] The ECtHR has emphasized, however, that whoever exercises the rights and freedoms enshrined in Article 10(1), undertakes 'duties and responsibilities', which is borne out by the wording of Article 10(2) itself.[107] In the context of religious opinions and beliefs, this includes 'an obligation to avoid as far as possible expressions that are gratuitously offensive to others and thus an infringement of their rights, and which therefore do not contribute to any form of public debate capable of furthering human affairs'.[108] That being so, the ECtHR has accepted that, as a matter of principle, it may be considered necessary in certain democratic societies to sanction or even prevent 'improper attacks on objects of religious veneration', provided always that any formality, condition, restriction, or penalty imposed be proportionate to the legitimate aim being pursued.[109] Where speech or material contributes to, and concerns a matter of general or public interest, restrictions on freedom of expression are to be strictly construed.[110]

10.66   In examining whether restrictions on free speech are necessary in a democratic society, the ECtHR extends to states a certain margin of appreciation. It has been held that, whereas there is little scope under Article 10(2) for restriction on political speech or on debates of questions of public interest, states enjoy a wider margin of appreciation when regulating freedom of expression 'in relation to matters liable to offend intimate personal convictions within the sphere of morals or religion'.[111] This has been justified on the basis that there is no uniform European conception of the significance of religion in society[112] or the requirements of 'the protection of the rights of others' in relation to attacks on their religious convictions.[113]

10.67   The following factors may be relevant in assessing whether an interference with the right to freedom of expression is necessary in a democratic society and proportionate to the legitimate aim being pursued: the nature and severity of the penalties imposed;[114] whether the speech concerns a matter of general or public interest;[115] the context in which it was expressed/broadcast/published;[116] and the potential impact of the medium of expression.[117]

---

[106] *Otto-Preminger Institute* (n 100) para 49, citing *Handyside v UK* (1979) 1 EHRR 737.

[107] *Otto-Preminger Institute* (n 100).

[108] *Otto-Preminger Institute* (n 100) para 49.

[109] *Otto-Preminger Institute* (n 100) para 49.

[110] See *Gunduz v Turkey* (2005) 41 EHRR 5; *Giniewski v France* (2007) 45 EHRR 23, para 51.

[111] *Wingrove* (n 103) para 58, followed in, among other cases, *Murphy v Ireland* (2002) 38 EHRR 13; *IA v Turkey* (n 100) para 40; and *Gunduz* (n 110) paras 38 and 39.

[112] *Otto-Preminger Institute* (n 100) para 50.

[113] *Wingrove* (n 103) para 58.

[114] *Gunduz* (n 110) para 42, citing *Skalka v Poland* (2004) 39 EHRR 1; *IA v Turkey* (n 100) para 47, where the ECHtR took into account the fact that the book alleged to contain blasphemous material was not seized and an insignificant fine was imposed; *Giniewski* (n 110) para 55.

[115] *Gunduz* (n 110) para 43; *Giniewski* (n 110) para 51. In *Giniewski* it was found that there had been a violation of the Art 10 rights of the publishing director of a newspaper held liable for making defamatory statements against the Christian community after the newspaper published an article discussing a papal encyclical which suggested that a particular theological doctrine had contributed to anti-Semitism and the Holocaust. Among other things, the ECtHR had regard to the fact that in its view the article contributed to discussion of the various possible reasons behind the extermination of Jews in Europe, which was a question of indisputable public interest in a democratic society.

[116] eg in *Gunduz* (n 110) the ECtHR took into account the fact that the impugned statements by the leader of an Islamist sect were expressed in the course of a pluralistic debate in which the applicant was actively taking part and the fact that his views were counterbalanced by the intervention of other participants in the programme. Moreover, the aim of the programme was to present the sect of which the applicant was the leader.

[117] *Klein v Slovakia* (2010) 50 EHRR 15, para 47.

Finally, it has been held that hate speech is not protected by Article 10 ECHR.[118] In particu- **10.68**
lar, the freedom of expression guaranteed under Article 10 may not be invoked in a sense
contrary to Article 17.[119] In *Norwood v United Kingdom* the applicant had been prosecuted
for displaying a poster with the words 'Islam out of Britain' and 'Protect the British People'
and a photograph of the twin towers of the World Trade Centre in flames. The ECtHR
held that '[s]uch a general and vehement attack against a religious group, linking the group
as a whole with a grave act of terrorism, is incompatible with the values proclaimed by the
Convention, notably tolerance, social peace and non-discrimination'.[120] It concluded that
the applicant's display of the poster constituted an act within the meaning of Article 17
which did not, therefore, enjoy the protection of Article 10.

D. Toleration and Conscientious Objection

(1) Toleration in statute

Where the application of the general law impinges on religious rights, Parliament has in **10.69**
some cases sought to protect those rights by granting specific exemptions from the general
law to accommodate religious beliefs and practices.

(a) Criminal law

Sikhs who wear a turban are exempt from the statutory requirement that motorcyclists **10.70**
wear protective headgear.[121] This exemption was introduced in 1976.[122] Notwithstanding
the importance of road safety, Parliament recognized the need to safeguard the religious
freedom of adherents of the Sikh religion.[123]

Religion can also provide a defence. Where a person is charged with the offence of hav- **10.71**
ing an article with a blade or sharp point in a public place, or on school premises, it is a
defence for him to prove that he had the article with him 'for religious reasons'.[124] This

---

[118] *Jersild v Denmark* (1995) 19 EHRR 1, para 35; *Gunduz* (n 110) In *Gunduz*, the ECtHR examined
whether impugned speech by the leader of an Islamist sect was properly 'hate speech'. It held that the mere fact
of defending Sharia, without calling for violence to establish it, could not be regarded as 'hate speech'.

[119] *Glimmerveen and Hagenbeek v Netherlands* (1982) 4 EHRR 260.

[120] *Norwood* (n 99).

[121] Road Traffic Act 1988, s 16(2).

[122] Motorcyclists Crash Helmets (Religious Exemption) Act 1976.

[123] When introducing the relevant amendment, Lord Avenury stated:

> I think it would be generally agreed that the measures that we take to protect individuals from harm
> are matters of expediency, whereas the freedom of Sikhs to wear the turban…is a fundamental
> question of religious principle. If it is said that the Sikhs can avoid any conflict with the existing law
> by using other means of transport, that is tantamount to saying that we will deny them the freedom
> to engage in certain occupations where the use of a motor-cycle might be incidental to the employ-
> ment, such as the police, the Post Office and certain units of the Armed Forces.

Hansard HL, vol 374, col 1057 (4 October 1976). The exemption provided more generous protection for religious rights than Art 9 ECHR. In *X v UK* (App 7992/77) (1978) the Commission ruled inadmissible a claim
by a Sikh who had been fined for not wearing a helmet before the exemption was introduced. The Commission
held that the obligation to wear a helmet was a necessary safety measure and that any resulting interference with
the applicant's freedom of religion was justified for the protection of health.

[124] Criminal Justice Act 1988, ss 139(5)(b) and 139A(4)(c).

will benefit Sikhs who carry the *kirpan* for religious reasons.[125] In *R v Wang*, the defence was invoked by a defendant found in possession of a curved martial arts sword and a Ghurkha style knife in a public place. He argued that he was a Buddhist and a practitioner of the traditional martial art of Shaolin which required practice with such weapons. However, there was no clear evidence that he intended to practise with the weapons on the day of his arrest. The trial judge found that the defendant had not discharged the burden of proving that he was carrying the weapons for 'religious reasons'. The Court of Appeal agreed, holding that in order for the defence to be made out it was necessary that the religious reason relied on constituted the predominant, if not the only, motivation for being in possession of the weapons in a public place, and that the religious reason specifically motivated the defendant to have those weapons with him on that particular occasion.[126]

(b) Other exemptions

10.72 Other examples of accommodation include the Welfare of Animals (Slaughter or Killing) Regulations 1995 which make specific provision for the slaughter of animals by the Jewish and Muslim method and exempt Jews and Muslims from the general provisions relations to the stunning and killing of animals.[127] Persons of the Jewish religion are also exempted from the prohibition on Sunday trading when a shop occupied by them is closed for the serving of customers on the Jewish Sabbath (Saturday).[128] Sikhs who wear a turban are exempted from any legal requirements to wear a safety helmet while on a construction site.[129]

10.73 Discrimination law also contains a number of religious-based exceptions.[130] For example, an employer can discriminate on grounds of sex or sexual orientation (among other grounds) where employment is 'for the purposes of an organised religion' so as to comply with doctrines of the religion, or so as to avoid conflicting with the strongly held religious convictions of a significant number of the religion's followers.[131] An employer with 'ethos based on religion or belief' can discriminate on grounds of religion or belief, provided certain criteria are met.[132] Religious organizations can also lawfully discriminate on grounds of religion or belief and sexual orientation, for example in the provision of goods and services, but only in carefully defined circumstances.[133]

---

[125] The *kirpan* is a ceremonial sword or dagger carried by adherents of the Sikh religion. It is one of the five 'K's.

[126] *R v Wang* [2003] EWCA Crim 3228. This aspect of the decision was not challenged in the House of Lords. The defendant's conviction was quashed by the House of Lords on other grounds: *R v Wang* [2005] 1 WLR 661 (HL).

[127] Welfare of Animals (Slaughter or Killing) Regulations 1995, SI 1995/731, reg 22 and Sch 12.

[128] Sunday Working Act 1994, Sch 1, para 2(2)(b) and Sch 2, para 8. The general rule in the Sunday Trading Act 1994, which prohibits large shops from opening on Sundays for the serving of retail customers (except for a maximum of 6 hours on Sunday between the hours of 10am and 6pm), does not apply where the shop is occupied by a person of the Jewish religion and that person gives to the local authority for the area a notice that he intends to keep the shop closed for the serving of customers on the Jewish Sabbath.

[129] Employment Act 1989, s 11.

[130] For an overview, see Ch 6.

[131] Equality Act 2010, Sch 9, para 2.

[132] Equality Act 2010, Sch 9, para 3.

[133] Equality Act 2010, Sch 23, para 2.

(2) Conscientious objection

(a) Military service

Conscription existed in Britain between 1916 and 1919, and from 1939 to 1960. Those with a conscientious objection were given an express right by statute to be exempted from military service.[134]   **10.74**

Claims of conscientious objection are now dealt with by an administrative procedure[135] requiring an application to be made to the commanding officer with a right of appeal to the Advisory Committee on Conscientious Objectors.[136]   **10.75**

In *Khan v Royal Airforce Summary Appeal Court*, the Divisional Court considered that the right to invoke conscientious objection was also provided for by legislation relating to the call up of reserve forces, albeit not expressly.[137] The grounds on which a reservist can apply for an exemption are set out in the Reserve Forces (Call Out and Recall) (Exemptions etc) Regulations 1997 and include, as a general catch all, 'any other ground' which ought to be considered 'for compassionate reasons'. In the Court's view this covered claims to conscientious objection.[138]   **10.76**

In *Khan* a medical assistant reservist recalled for service in the run up to the Iraq war failed to report for duty and was convicted of the offence of being absent without leave. He had a conscientious objection to the war in Iraq, believing it to be wrong and against his religion, but had made no application for discharge on the grounds of conscientious objection or, indeed, made any mention of his objection until after his failure to report for duty. The summary appeal court accepted that his objection was genuine (although it noted that he was unable to articulate why his religion did not allow the war in Iraq) but found, having regard to Article 9 ECHR, that it did not provide him with a defence to the charge of being absent without leave.   **10.77**

The Divisional Court agreed that there had been no violation of Mr Khan's Article 9 rights. The mere act of absence did not, on the facts, amount to a manifestation of his belief. Against a background where the call out was on the basis that there might be an exemption on compassionate grounds and the recalled reservist is given repeated opportunities to voice his concerns, it could not be said that Mr Khan had manifested his belief until he had formally informed his service of it.[139] His prosecution was in any case justified under Article 9(2).[140]   **10.78**

---

[134] Military Service Act 1916, s 2(1)(d) and the National Service (Armed Forces) Act 1939, s 5(1). For a more detailed background see *Khan v Royal Airforce Summary Appeal Court* [2004] HRLR 40 (DC), paras 29–32; and *R v Lyons* [2012] 1 WLR 2702, paras 9–11.

[135] eg the procedure for dealing with conscientious objectors in the Royal Air Force is set out 'the Leaflet': see *Khan* (n 134) paras 40–42.

[136] The Advisory Committee on Conscientious Objection (ACCO) is a non-departmental public body which advises the Secretary of State for Defence on all conscientious objection claims. According to its website: 'Many of the conscientious objections are made on religious grounds.'

[137] *Khan* (n 134).

[138] *Khan* (n 134) paras 35 and 53. The Reserve Forces (Call Out and Recall) (Exemptions etc) Regulations 1997, SI 1997/307.

[139] *Khan* (n 134) paras 61–65.

[140] *Khan* (n 134) para 60.

10.79 The Divisional Court observed that the weight of Strasbourg authority suggested that Article 9 read in conjunction with Article 4(3)(b) ECHR[141] did not guarantee a right to refuse military service on conscientious grounds.[142]

10.80 The ECtHR has since departed from earlier authorities and affirmed that Article 9 applies to conscientious objectors. This departure came in *Bayatyan v Armenia* in which the Grand Chamber held that Article 9 should no longer be read in conjunction with Article 4(3)(b) and the applicant's complaint would be assessed solely under Article 9.[143] It went on to state:

> The Court notes that article 9 does not explicitly refer to a right to conscientious objection. However, it considers that opposition to military service, where it is motivated by a serious and insurmountable conflict between the obligation to serve in the army and a person's conscience or his deeply and genuinely held religious or other beliefs, constitutes a conviction or belief of sufficient cogency, seriousness, cohesion and importance to attract the guarantees of article 9…Whether and to what extent objection to military service falls within the ambit of that provision must be assessed in the light of the particular circumstances of the case.[144]

10.81 In *Bayatyan* the applicant was a Jehovah's Witness who for religious reasons refused to perform military service but expressed willingness to perform an alternative civilian service. No alternative being available, the applicant was prosecuted. The ECtHR held that Article 9 applied. The applicant belonged to a religious group whose beliefs include the conviction that service, even unarmed, within the military is to be opposed. His objection to military service was therefore motivated by his religious beliefs, which were genuinely held and were in serious and insurmountable conflict with his obligation to perform military service.[145]

10.82 *Bayatyan* was a case concerning conscription. In *R v Lyons* the court indicated that Article 9 is also capable of applying to a person who has engaged in military service as a volunteer but has subsequently had a change of mind on grounds of conscience.[146] However, the fact that a person has volunteered for military service, and so voluntarily accepted the responsibilities which go with such service, may be highly material when considering the balance to be struck between the individual's conscience and the interest of public safety, the protection of public order and the protection of the rights of others to which Article 9(2) refers.

(b) Other rights of conscientious objection

10.83 The law expressly provides a right of conscientious objection in certain cases.

10.84 The Abortion Act 1967 contains a conscientious objection clause which gives a person a right to refuse 'to participate in any treatment authorised by this Act to which he has a conscientious objection'.[147] It has been held that the right of conscientious objection in section

---

141 This provides that forced or compulsory labour does not include military service.

142 The Commission had in a number of decisions held that Art 9 did not entail a right of conscientious objection: see eg *A v Switzerland* (App 10640/83) (1984); *X v Federal Republic of Germany* (App 8626/79) (1981); *Johansen v Norway* (App 10600/83) (1985). The ECtHR had, however, left the matter open. In *Thlimmenos v Greece* (2001) 31 EHRR 41, the Court had found a violation of Art 9 taken in conjunction with Art 14 where a Jehovah's Witness had been prosecuted for refusing to undergo military service.

143 *Bayatyan v Armenia* (2012) 54 EHRR 15, paras 93–109.

144 *Bayatyan* (n 143) para 110.

145 *Bayatyan* (n 143) para 111. The Court distinguished the applicant's situation from a situation that concerns an obligation which has no specific conscientious implications in itself, such as a general tax obligation.

146 *R v Lyons* [2011] EWCA Crim 2808, para 28.

147 Abortion Act 1967, s 4(1). See further Ch 8, part F.

4(1) extends 'not only to the actual medical or surgical termination but to the whole process of treatment given for that purpose'.[148] The right was successfully invoked by two Roman Catholic midwives who objected to abortions on religious grounds, but whose roles were only supervisory and administrative in nature and did not require direct involvement in the termination process.[149] On the other hand, it has been held that a medical secretary typing a letter referring a patient to a consultant with a view to the termination of the patient's pregnancy was not participating in treatment within the meaning of section 4(1) and was therefore unable to rely on the right.[150]

Importantly, the right of conscientious objection in section 4(1) is not absolute. A person **10.85** who has a conscientious objection to abortion cannot refuse to participate in treatment 'which is necessary to save the life or to prevent grave permanent injury to the physical or mental health of a pregnant woman'.[151]

The Human Fertilisation and Embryology Act 1990 similarly provides that a person is not **10.86** required to participate in any activity governed by the Act—for example research on human embryos and fertility treatment involving the use of donated sperm/eggs and *in vitro* fertilization—to which he has a conscientious objection.[152]

Legislation relating to jobseeker's allowance also makes provision for conscientious objec- **10.87** tion. The legislation requires a person claiming jobseeker's allowance to be available for work;[153] however, a person is permitted to impose restrictions on the nature of employment for which he is available 'by reason of a sincerely held religious belief, or a sincerely held conscientious objection provided he can show that he has reasonable prospects of employment notwithstanding those restrictions'.[154] In *Pattison* it was held that an objection to working in the private sector did not qualify as a conscientious objection sincerely held for the purposes of the legislation.[155] The Court held that Article 9 was not engaged. The terms of the jobseeker's contract followed from the application of a citizen for jobseeker's allowance, something which they are not obliged to do. Accordingly, any restrictions which flowed from the legislative scheme did not necessarily and inherently affect a citizen. Notwithstanding any practical coercion of an unemployed citizen such as the claimant, it was his application for the allowance which brought about the need for him to accept the terms of the job offer.[156]

Under the Juries Act 1974 a person may be excused from jury service if he can show a 'good **10.88** reason'.[157] There is no express right of conscientious objection.[158] In *Siderfin* it was held

---

[148] *Doogan v Greater Glasgow and Clyde Health Board* [2013] SLT 515 (CSIH) para 37.
[149] *Doogan* (n 148).
[150] *Janaway v Salford Area Health Authority* [1988] 3 WLR 1350 (HL).
[151] Abortion Act 1967, s 4(2).
[152] Human Fertilisation and Embryology Act 1990, s 38(1). This provides that 'no person who has a conscientious objection to participating in any activity governed by this Act shall be under any duty, however arising, to do so'.
[153] Jobseekers Act 1995, s 6E.
[154] Jobseeker's Allowance Regulations 1996, SI 1996/207, reg 13(2).
[155] *R (Pattison) v Social Security and Child Support Commissioners* [2004] EWHC 2370 (Admin). The case concerned different provisions under the same legislation, which have since been repealed.
[156] This is comparable to the approach to Art 9 claims in the employment context: *R (Begum) v Headteacher and Governors of Denbigh High School* [2007] 1 AC 100 (HL), para 23. For discussion, see Ch 8, paras 8.59–8.61.
[157] Juries Act 1974, s 9.
[158] Notably the Criminal Justice and Public Order Act 2004 amended the Juries Act 1974 and added to the list of persons excusable as of right: 'A practising member of a religious society or order the tenets or beliefs of

that the existence of a conscientious objection to jury service arising out of a religious belief would, on its own, be unlikely to amount to a 'good reason' for excusal from jury service, but may do so if a person's religious beliefs would be likely to prevent him from performing his duty as a juror.[159] The Court was essentially saying that adherence to a religious belief cannot automatically amount to a 'good reason' and each application has to be determined according to its own facts.[160] This is uncontroversial and would, it is submitted, be the proper approach under Article 9 ECHR.[161]

---

which are incompatible with jury service.' However, this provision was removed by the Criminal Justice Act 2003 with effect from 5 April 2004.

[159] *R v Guildford Crown Court, ex p Siderfin* [1990] 2 QB 683 (QB).

[160] Siderfin (n 159) in particular 695 and 696.

[161] The decision in *Siderfin* preceded the Human Rights Act 1998. Art 9 would now have to be considered when deciding whether a person with a conscientious belief on religious grounds had shown a 'good reason' for excusal from jury service.

11

RELIGION AND THE FAMILY

A. Marriage

(1) Introduction

The ECtHR has held that the right to marry is not a form of expression of thought, con- **11.01**
science, or religion, but is governed specifically by Article 12 ECHR.[1] A similar approach has
been taken by domestic courts, with the result that there is little authority on the compatibility of national marriage legislation with the right to manifest religious belief. Nonetheless,
the plurality of marital rites and requirements under different religions inevitably leads to
occasional discrepancy between religious requirements and the provisions of national legislation. The legislative system either grants legal effect to religious ceremonies if certain requirements are met, or, where the ceremony in question cannot meet those requirements, allows
for parties to undergo a separate civil ceremony to create a union with legal effect.[2] The result
is that parties of all religions are able to fulfil the requirements of their faith and of civil law
when electing to marry, and often on a single occasion.[3]

This section will explore the interaction (or, occasionally, non-interference) between civil and **11.02**
religious marriage in the United Kingdom. It will then consider the way in which national

---

[1] *Khan v UK* (1986) E Com HR 48 DR 253 (App 11579/85).

[2] A recent report by Cardiff University sets out the result of in-depth research into the interaction between
religious marriage and divorce and civil law: G Douglas, N Doe, S Gilliat-Ray, R Sandberg, and A Khan, 'Social
Cohesion and Civil Law: Marriage, Divorce and Religious Courts', Report of a Research Study funded by the
AHRC (Cardiff Law School, June 2011). The full text is available at <http://www.law.cf.ac.uk/clr/Social%20
Cohesion%20and%20Civil%20Law%20Full%20Report.pdf>.

[3] Naturally, where any requirements or permissions under the faith in question are in breach of national
criminal law the parties do not have the option to fulfil them.

and European courts have treated cases where parties claim a breach of their religious rights on the basis that national law has prevented them from marrying, either at all or in the manner they would wish.

(2) The Marriage Act and religious marriages

11.03 Before analysing the interaction of religious and civil marriage in England and Wales, it is important to understand the difference between the two processes. A religious couple may seek to satisfy two distinct sets of requirements in their marriage ceremony. First, it may be important for the couple to satisfy any conditions imposed by their religion, in order that the union will be valid in the eyes of their faith community.[4] Secondly, the couple may also want to ensure that the marriage is valid in the eyes of the law, and to that end the ceremony will need to satisfy the civil requirements. It is entirely possible for a marriage ceremony to be legally valid in the absence of any religious element,[5] and equally possible for a purely religious ceremony to take place which does not have any legal effect.[6]

11.04 Since the Marriage Act of 1836, the legal requirements for a valid marriage in the UK have had no religious content.[7] A man and a woman may marry in England and Wales if they are both 16 years of age and are free to marry.[8] Marriage is prohibited between certain degrees of relationship,[9] and parental consent is required where a party to a marriage is under the age of 18.[10] No person is permitted to be married to more than one person simultaneously.[11] A marriage is valid in the eyes of the state once it has been registered in accordance with the requirements of the 1949 Act,[12] and any marriage must have complied with the civil preliminaries to marriage.[13]

11.05 The lack of religious content in the 1836 Act meant that couples without a religion, or of a religion which was not previously valid for the purpose of legal marriage, could marry for the first time by civil ceremony.[14] However, the Act also recognized and provided for the fact that religious parties would wish to combine the marital rites of their faith with civil registration and recognition. The scheme under the 1949 Act (which substantially re-enacts that under the 1836 Act) sets out the requirements for religious bodies which themselves wish to be able to perform ceremonies which have legal effect. There are two principal conditions: that the

---

[4] eg Jewish marriages must comply with the formal halakhic requirements in order to be valid in the eyes of the religion.

[5] It is only recently (1996) that the number of purely civil marriages have exceeded the number celebrated according to religious rites. See R Probert, 'Forming a Marriage or Civil Partnership' in *Cretney and Probert's Family Law* (Sweet & Maxwell, 2009) 29.

[6] The Marriage Act 1949, s 46, makes provision for post-marriage religious ceremonies which are not themselves valid marriages.

[7] Prior to this, the Lord Hardwicke's Marriage Act 1753 required that a marriage take place according to the rites of the Church of England in order to be legally valid; Jews and Quakers alone were exempt from this requirement.

[8] A person is free to marry if they are single, widowed, or divorced, or if they were in a civil partnership which has been dissolved.

[9] Marriage Act 1949, s 1.

[10] Marriage Act 1949, s 2.

[11] Offences Against the Person Act 1861, s 57.

[12] Marriage Act 1949, s 3.

[13] Those are: that the parties obtain a superintendent registrar's certificate, and that each give notice in person of their intention to marry to the superintendent registrar of the district where they have had their usual place of residence for at least seven days.

[14] See now the Marriage Act 1949, Pt III.

ceremony be conducted on premises which have been registered for the purposes of marriage,[15] and that the celebrant be authorized to conduct the marriage.[16] Jews and Quakers alone are exempted from these requirements: celebration of marriages in these religions is entirely a matter for the religions themselves, and the state requires only that they satisfy the civil requirements previously stated. The question as to whether a refusal to register particular religious premises for the purposes of marriage constitutes a breach of an individual's Article 9 rights is considered in paragraph 11.09.

The provisions under Part III of the Marriage Act 1949 thereby allow individuals in the United Kingdom to marry both in accordance with the requirements of their religion, and in accordance with the requirements of civil law. Whether the religious ceremony can have simultaneous legal effect is a question of registration under section 41 of the Act; in any event, there is nothing in law to prevent parties from performing a religious ceremony followed by a civil ceremony, or vice versa. As long as the religious ceremony does not breach other areas of national law,[17] a couple wishing to perform marital rites particular to a given religion are able to do so.[18]   **11.06**

Failure to comply with the legal requirements will not necessarily render the religious marriage void,[19] but will almost certainly do so where the parties knowingly and wilfully fail to comply with the law.[20] Finally, the fact that religious groups are able to perform religious marriage ceremonies with legal effect does not create marriages that are differentiated by religion. The marriage itself is a civil one in the eyes of the law, albeit performed in accordance with particular religious rites.   **11.07**

(3) Marriage is not a manifestation of religious belief

In *Khan v United Kingdom*,[21] a permission hearing before the ECtHR, the applicant claimed that national legislation making illegal a marriage that was legal under his religion was in breach of his Article 9 rights (among others). The particular facts were that the parties (the 21-year-old male applicant and his 14½-year-old girlfriend) had undergone an Islamic marriage ceremony, after which the applicant was charged with offences under sections 20[22] and 6(1)[23] of the Sexual Offences Act 1956. The applicant claimed that the 1956 legislation   **11.08**

---

[15] Marriage Act 1949, s 41, as amended by the Marriage Acts Amendment Act 1958, s 1(1)(a).

[16] Marriage Act 1949, s 43(1).

[17] See further the discussion of *Khan v UK* at paras 11.08 ff.

[18] Recent research by Cardiff University, by Douglas et al (n 2), has shown that in Muslim communities, it is quite common for a religious ceremony to be held without a subsequent civil marriage. While this is the choice of the parties, such a course can be problematic for women who are treated as mere cohabitants for the purposes of the civil regulation of property division. For detailed analysis, see the discussion in G Douglas, N Doe, S Gilliat-Ray, R Sandberg, and A Khan, 'The Role of Religious Tribunals in Regulating Marriage and Divorce' (June 2012) Child and Family Law Quarterly 139.

[19] See eg the judgment of Evans LJ in *Chief Adjudication Officer v Bath* [2000] 1 FLR 8, FD, where he expressed his willingness to hold that the solemnization of a marriage in premises which could have been registered, by a person who could have been authorized, was valid unless the conditions for nullity were satisfied.

[20] In *Gereis v Yagoub* [1997] 1 FLR 854, a couple were married in a Greek Orthodox Church that had not been registered in accordance with the provisions of the Marriage Act 1949. The parties were aware of this fact and declined to go through the additional civil ceremony which would have been necessary to give their union legal effect. In the circumstances the judge held that the knowing and wilful failure to comply with the law rendered the marriage void.

[21] *Khan* (n 1).

[22] Abduction of a girl from the care of her parent of guardian.

[23] Sexual intercourse with a girl under the age of 16.

prevented him from manifesting his religion through his marriage under Islamic law (which permitted marriage to a girl aged 12 or over without her parents' consent), and thus breached his Article 9 rights. The ECtHR found that the term 'practice' as employed in Article 9(1) ECHR[24] 'does not cover each act which may be motivated or influenced by a religion or belief. While the applicant's religion may allow the marriage of girls at the age of 12, marriage cannot be considered simply as a form of expression of thought, conscience or religion, but is governed specifically by Article 12'.[25] Importantly, this ruling did not simply say that Article 9 rights were engaged, but justified under Article 9(2);[26] the article was not engaged at all in this case. In short, the mere fact that his religion permitted a certain marital practice did not make that practice a manifestation of religion for the purposes of Article 9.

11.09 A similar finding was made by the UK courts in the recent case of *R (Hodkin) v Registrar General*.[27] The Registrar General had refused to register a chapel of the Church of Scientology as a place of worship under section 2 of the Places of Worship Registration Act 1855. Because the Marriage Act 1949 provided that a place could only be used for the solemnization of religious marriage if it was a 'registered building',[28] this meant that the claimant, Louisa Hodkin, could not solemnize her marriage to her fiancé on the premises. The grounds for refusal were that the Registrar General was bound by the decision in *R (Segerdal)*,[29] which had held that the services conducted by Scientology could not be considered religious worship. Ms Hodkin therefore submitted that the legislation interfered with her rights under Articles 9, 12, and 14 ECHR, in that it denied her enjoyment of the right to marry in accordance with her religious beliefs.[30] Ouseley J found that there was 'no interference with the right to marry according to national laws, nor with the right of Scientologists to practise their religion, if such it is. There is no discrimination on the grounds of religion'.[31]

11.10 The judgment in *R v Hodkin* focused primarily on the question of the definition of religion for the purposes of the 1855 Act, rather than on the Convention points raised. However, the fact that national law did not give legal effect to the marriage ceremony of a particular religion did not mean that the claimant was prevented from manifesting her religion.[32] Any particular religious customs, permissions, or rituals associated with marriage are unlikely

---

[24] ECHR, Art 9(1) reads: 'Everyone has the right to freedom of thought, conscience and religion; this right includes freedom to change his religion or belief and freedom, either alone or in community with others and in public or private, and to manifest his religion or belief, in worship, teaching, practice and observance.'

[25] *Khan* (n 1) 255. The Court did not find for the applicant on Art 12 grounds, 'since the right to marry guaranteed under Article 12 is subject to the internal laws governing the exercise of this right'.

[26] ECHR, Art 9(2) reads: 'Freedom to manifest one's religion or beliefs shall be subject only to such limitations as are prescribed by law and are necessary in a democratic society in the interests of public safety, for the protection of public order, health or morals, or the protection of the rights and freedoms of others.'

[27] *R (Hodkin) v Registrar General* [2012] EWCH 3635 (Admin).

[28] Within the Marriage Act 1949, s 26, which in turn depends on the Places of Worship Registration Act 1855, s 2.

[29] In *R (Segerdal) v Registrar General* [1970] 2 QB 697, 709 *per* Buckley LJ, the Court found that services in the Scientologist Booklet of Ceremonies contained no element of worship, having none of the following characteristics: 'submission to the object worshipped, veneration of that object, praise, thanksgiving, prayer, intercession'.

[30] *Segerdal* (n 29) para 89.

[31] *Segerdal* (n 29) para 90.

[32] ECHR, Art 12 in turn would not be breached because the claimant retained a right to undergo a civil marriage ceremony. The case has received permission to appeal, and it is submitted that if the Supreme Court overturns the decision in *Segerdal* and Scientology is able to be redefined as a religion for the purposes of the 1855 Act, any decision not to register the premises would then be unlawful under Art 14.

to be considered sufficiently integral to the manifestation of a religion to engage Article 9 ECHR (as with *Khan v United Kingdom*).

It is nonetheless possible that a claim will succeed which relies on Article 9 in conjunction with Article 14.[33] In *O'Donoghue v United Kingdom*,[34] the applicants complained that their rights under Article 9 had been violated as a Certificate of Approval scheme[35] prevented them from marrying unless they married in the Anglican Church. Relying on Article 14 ECHR, read together with Article 9, they further complained that they were discriminated against in securing the enjoyment of this right. The Court found that the stand-alone allegation under Article 9 was manifestly ill-founded, but that the complaint under Article 14 read in conjunction with Article 9 was admissible. It was held that the applicants had been discriminated against on the grounds of their religion.[36] **11.11**

At the time of writing the Marriage (Same Sex Couples) Bill has not been enacted. **11.12**

B. Civil Partnership

(1) Introduction

The Civil Partnerships Act 2004 (CPA 2004) permits two individuals of the same sex to enter into civil partnerships and to register them with the local Registry Office or other authorized venue. As originally enacted, CPA 2004 imposed two religious restrictions on the formation of civil partnerships. The first prohibited the use of religious services,[37] and the second prohibited the registration of civil partnerships on religious premises.[38] As a result, although the passing of CPA 2004 signalled considerable progress with regard to homosexual individuals' rights under Article 8 (right to family life) and Article 14 (freedom from discrimination) ECHR, those individuals were unable to manifest their religion in any way when celebrating the legal union of their relationship.[39] The Act also respected the rights of individual Registrars, since not every Registrar became a Registrar of Civil Partnerships. A person had to be designated as such a Registrar by the Registration Authority for the relevant area pursuant to section 29 of CPA 2004. **11.13**

The rationale behind the prohibitions was to preserve 'the public perception of civil partnership as a registration procedure'.[40] Furthermore, the provisions mirrored the religious **11.14**

---

[33] The text of ECHR, Art 14 reads: 'The enjoyment of the rights and freedoms set forth in this Convention shall be secured without discrimination on any ground such as sex, race, colour, language, religion, political or other opinion, national or social origin, association with a national minority, property, birth or other status.'

[34] *O'Donoghue and ors v UK* [2011] 1 FLR 1307.

[35] The scheme required certain classes of immigrants to have the approval of the Secretary of State (which could only be secured by means of a fee which the applicants could not afford) before marrying, and had an exception for those whose marriage rites were solemnized according to the rites of the Church of England.

[36] Of course, an allegation of religious discrimination under Art 14 does not require that the article be read in conjunction with Art 9 in order to succeed; see on the same marriage scheme the decision in *R (Baiai) v Secretary of State for the Home Department* [2007] 1 WLR 693.

[37] CPA 2004, s 2(5).

[38] CPA 2004, s 6(1)(b), now repealed. Religious premises were defined as those which were used solely or mainly for religious purposes, or have been so used and not subsequently been used solely or mainly for other purposes (CPA 2004, s 6(2)(a) and (b), now repealed; the definition is preserved in the new s 6A(3C)). CPA 2004, s 93 prohibits the registration of civil partnerships in religious premises in Scotland, and remains in force.

[39] The only available option was to have a 'religious blessing' performed after the registration, but this ceremony could have no legal effect and needed to take place in different premises.

[40] Jacqui Smith, Deputy Minister for Women and Equality, *Hansard* HC, Standing Committee, 3rd sitting, col 102 (21 October 2004).

prohibitions concerning the performance of civil marriage ceremonies,[41] and simultaneously ensured that the rights of religious institutions were themselves were not infringed through a requirement to host ceremonies which were contrary to their beliefs. However, the latter two grounds in particular were criticized because same sex couples did not have a choice between civil and religious marriage as heterosexual couples did, and the right of religious institutions themselves to perform civil partnership ceremonies was interfered with by virtue of the legislation.[42]

11.15 Subsequent to the passage of the Equality Act 2010, legislative protection of religious rights under CPA 2004 has been more concerned with striking a balance between general secular policy, the rights of religious institutions, and the religious rights of individuals.[43] The absolute prohibition against registering civil partnerships on religious premises has been lifted, but this has not resulted in a new obligation: religious institutions are given the freedom to choose whether or not to host registrations.[44] Thus the new amendments do not so much create a right for individuals to register civil partnership in religious premises, but rather an option for religious institutions to apply for registration as a hosting venue.[45] It therefore remains to be seen to what extent individuals of different religions are given a choice under the new legislative scheme.

(2) Religious premises: the changes brought in by the Equality Act 2010

11.16 Section 202 of the Equality Act 2010 provided for amendments to sections 6 and 6A of CPA 2004. In summary, the amendments repealed the provisions prohibiting the registration of civil partnerships on religious premises, and added further provisions to the power to approve premises under section 6A. No amendment was introduced to remove the prohibition on religious services.

11.17 Section 202(2) of the Equality Act 2010 omits section 6(1)(b), which provided that the place at which two people may register as civil partners may not be religious premises. It further omits the definition of religious premises under section 6(2), which is now given in the new section 6A(3C) of CPA 2004. Section 6 as amended therefore simply provides for the fact that the place of registration must be in England and Wales and specified in the notice of proposed civil partnership.[46] Where the registration is conducted under standard procedure, the place must be on approved premises or in a register office.[47]

11.18 Section 6A of CPA 2004 concerns the power to make provision through regulations for the approval by registration authorities of premises for the purposes of section 6(3A)(a), and the amendments add new provisions to clarify the approval of religious premises. The new

---

[41] Marriage Act 1949, s 45A(4): 'No religious service shall be used at any marriage solemnized in the presence of a superintendent registrar.' Applications for the solemnization of civil marriages may only be made in respect of premises that are not religious (Marriages and Civil Partnerships (Approved Premises) Regulations 2005, SI 2005/3168, reg 2C(1).)

[42] Insofar as the religious institutions wished to conduct and register civil partnerships. See eg Minute 23 of the Yearly Meeting of the Religious Society of Friends (Quakers) in Britain at the University of York, 25 July 2009.

[43] By virtue of amendments introduced under the Equality Act, s 202(2).

[44] See eg CPA 2004, s 6A(3A).

[45] Under the procedure in the Marriages and Civil Partnerships (Approved Premises) Regulations 2005, SI 2005/3168 (as amended).

[46] CPA 2004, s 6(1)(a) and (c).

[47] CPA 2004, s 6(3) and (3A).

section 6A(2A) provides for the fact that the new regulations may mean that different premises are approved for the purposes of civil partnerships than are approved for the purposes of civil marriages,[48] while the new section 6A(2B) underlines that provision in relation to the procedure for seeking approval or premises may only be made with the consent of a person specified in the provision. Section 6A(2C) further highlights the flexibility entailed in the power to make regulations: specifically, that regulations may be made in relation to religious premises, which differs from provision in relation to other premises, and that different provisions may be made for different kinds of religious premises.

The new sections 6A(3A), (3B), and (3C) of CPA 2004[49] provide further clarification and **11.19** definition. Section 6A(3A) puts in express terms the fact that nothing under the Act as amended places an obligation on religious organizations to host civil partnerships if they do not wish to do so, while section 6A(3B) defines civil marriage as marriage solemnized other than according to the rites of the Church of England or any other religious usages. Section 6A(3C) preserves the definition of religious premises previously found in section 6(2).

It is clear from the Parliamentary speech accompanying the move for amendment under section **11.20** 202 of the Equality Act 2010 that the focus was on the rights of religious institutions, with a particularly careful view to avoiding the perception of obligation. Lord Alli stated when commenting in support of the proposal:

> Religious freedom means letting the Quakers, the liberal Jews and others host civil partnerships. It means accepting that the Church of England and the Catholic Church should not host civil partnerships if they do not wish to do so ... I believe that people want religion in their lives and many gay and lesbian couples are no different. They want their civil partnership to be held in a place where they can celebrate it with the people with whom they worship. It is a simple act of religious freedom to allow the Quakers, the liberal Jews, the Unitarian Church and others to practise their religion in a way that meets their religious needs.[50]

The speech identifies the rights which the legislation seeks to accommodate.

The bulk of the Equality Act 2010 was brought into force on 1 October 2010. However, **11.21** the amendments under section 202 were not implemented until 11 June 2011[51] and 5 December 2011.[52] This delay was to allow for sufficient public consultation prior to bringing section 202 into force and passing the necessary regulations to implement the changes.[53]

C. Divorce

(1) Introduction

Divorce law concerns itself with two issues: the status of the marriage, and the regulation of **11.22** any dispute over the breakdown of that marriage. For the purposes of marriages conducted

---

[48] Inserted by the Equality Act 2010, s 202(3). It is inevitable that any religious premises approved could not also be approved for the purposes of civil marriages. This section also inserts ss 6(2B) and 6(2C) into the CPA 2004.

[49] Inserted by the Equality Act 2010, s 202(4).

[50] *Hansard* HL, vol 717, col 1426 (2 March 2010).

[51] Equality Act 2010, s 202(3) providing for insertion of ss 6A(2A), (2B) and (2C) into CPA 2004; and s 202(4) of the 2010 Act insofar as it inserts s 6A(3B) and (3C) into CPA 2004.

[52] Equality Act 2010, s 202(2) providing for the omission of ss 6(1)(b) and 6(2) from CPA 2004; and the remainder of s 202(4) of the 2010 Act.

[53] Marriages and Civil Partnerships (Approved Premises) (Amendments) Regulations 2011, SI 2011/2661.

under the rites of a particular religion, there is the additional question of the status of that marriage within the religious community. Although civil courts have exclusive jurisdiction to terminate legal marriages, it is not within their remit to rule that two parties are no longer married in the eyes of their religion. For a determination of this nature, parties will turn to a body which they recognize as a religious authority for that purpose.[54]

11.23 Although this division in function between a person's religious authority and the national legal authority is the same as it is at the inception of a religious marriage, the split role has caused more difficulties when the relationship is being terminated. In principle there is nothing preventing a similar two-stage religious and civil process to determine the conclusion of a marriage for the purposes of the respective spheres;[55] the difficulty lies more in the cases where there is nothing to ensure that both processes have taken place.[56] The division in roles is about more than reaching a conclusion on the status of the marriage: it is often the wish of the parties that the religious authorities regulate the terms of the divorce and any disputes arising under it.

11.24 This section will consider the relationship between the civil and religious termination of marriages; the limited legislative solution devised to cope with disjunction between the legal and religious process; and the interaction between civil and religious authorities where marital disputes are arbitrated.

(2) The relationship between civil and religious termination of marriages

11.25 Recent research has examined the various religious systems of marriage termination, and has found that 'the fundamental rationale for the grant of the religious annulment/divorce is to declare that the religious marriage is over and to enable the parties to remarry within the faith'.[57] This means that for adherents of a particular faith, the marriage will not be fully dissolved until the requirements of that faith (and, if necessary, the faith tribunal) are satisfied. Examples of relevant Tribunals include the Jewish *Beth Din*, the Muslim Sharia Council and the Roman Catholic National Tribunal.[58]

11.26 Research has revealed that in general, the religious courts strongly encourage the parties to obtain a civil divorce prior to seeking a religious determination. Indeed, the Sharia Council considers the obtaining of a civil divorce as conclusive evidence of the parties' view that the marriage is over. Civil law, on the other hand, considers the legal aspects of divorce, nullity, and all other matters arising out of a marriage as creatures of its own jurisdiction, and beyond Section 10A of the Matrimonial Causes Act 1973[59] and voluntary cooperation with religious dispute resolution,[60] has no regard for the stage proceedings have reached with the religious authorities.[61]

---

[54] For a recent case study on the recourse to religious tribunals for determinations of this nature, see G Douglas, N Doe, S Gilliat-Ray, and R Sandberg, 'Marriage and Divorce in Religious Courts: A Case Study' (2011) 41 Family Law 956.

[55] Indeed, while the religious and civil requirements of marriage can very often be fulfilled in one step, there is no mechanism for achieving a religious and a civil divorce simultaneously.

[56] This can result in 'limping divorces' which fall between the religious and civil jurisdictions. The problem is particularly acute in the Jewish community; see paras 11.28 ff.

[57] See Douglas et al (n 2) 45.

[58] For more detailed analysis of the different processes of obtaining religious annulments or divorces, see Douglas et al (n 54).

[59] See paras 11.28–11.30.

[60] See para 11.31.

[61] For a review of the degree to which a civil judge might have regard to the religious courts, see Lord Justice McFarlane, ' "Am I bothered?": The Relevance of Religious Courts to a Civil Judge' (2011) 41 Family Law 946.

Research has concluded that, in the examples studied, the religious courts acknowledged **11.27** the primacy of the civil law and there was no evidence of a desire on the part of the various religious bodies to alter that state of affairs.

(3) Section 10A of the Matrimonial Causes Act 1973

The separation between the civil and religious processes for terminating a marriage causes **11.28** particular problems in the Orthodox Jewish community. Although obtaining a civil divorce means that both parties are free to remarry as far as the state is concerned, a Jewish woman is unable to remarry within her religious community without obtaining a *get* from her husband.[62] This means that until the religious divorce process is completed, she is effectively bound to her husband (and is known as an *agunah* or a 'chained woman').

Section 10A of the Matrimonial Causes Act 1974 was enacted to deal with the difficulty **11.29** faced by Jewish women in these circumstances. Section 10A(1) and (2) read as follows:

(1) This section applies if a decree of divorce has been granted but not made absolute and the parties to the marriage concerned—
(a) were married in accordance with—
(i) the usages of the Jews, or
(ii) any other prescribed religious usages; and
(b) must co-operate if the marriage is to be dissolved in accordance with those usages.
(2) On the application of either party, the court may order that a decree of divorce is not to be made absolute until a declaration made by both parties that they have taken such steps as are required to dissolve the marriage in accordance with those usages is produced to the court.

In essence, the provision allows the county court to make an order refusing to grant the **11.30** decree absolute until a declaration by both parties is produced to the effect that they have taken such steps as are required to dissolve the marriage. The Act is presently confined to the Jewish community. The recent research conducted by Cardiff University explains that the *Beth Din* will not in practice issue the *get* certificate itself until the decree absolute is pronounced; nonetheless, the issue itself simply formalizes the conclusion of the process which the parties have already undergone in order to satisfy the requirements of section 10A.

(4) Alternative dispute resolution with religious bodies

It is an established principle of family law in England and Wales that the jurisdiction of the **11.31** courts cannot be ousted in matters arising from a marriage.[63] This means that there is no form of dispute resolution, secular or otherwise, which can result in a binding agreement between the parties that will be enforced by the courts without consideration.[64]

---

[62] The *get* is a divorce document which the husband must grant of his own free will. It determines that the wife is no longer a married woman and returns to her the legal rights which a husband holds on her behalf during their marriage.

[63] See *Hyman v Hyman* [1929] AC 601, 608 *per* Hailsham LJ.

[64] However, following the premium placed on dispute resolution in the Final Report of the Family Justice Review, November 2011 (available at <https://www.gov.uk/government/uploads/system/uploads/attachment_data/file/217343/family-justice-review-final-report.pdf>), a secular family law arbitration scheme was launched in March 2012. The Institute of Family Law Arbitrators (IFLA) recognizes that parties will need to apply to a court in order to make the terms binding (or to achieve an order in similar terms), but expects that the courts will in general enforce awards made under the scheme.

11.32 There has nonetheless been growing recognition of the usefulness of religious tribunals in regulating matters arising from a dispute.[65] This enables the wishes of the parties to have matters arising out of the marriage regulated in accordance with their religious beliefs to be respected. However, if religious authorities are to take over some of the functions of deciding how a marital dispute should be regulated, the process cannot be brought to a conclusion which would oust the jurisdiction of the civil courts. In a speech entitled 'Equality before the Law', Lord Phillips of Worth Matravers summarized the position as follows:

> There is no reason why principles of Sharia law, or any other religious code, should not be the basis for mediation or other forms of alternative dispute resolution. It must be recognised, however, that any sanctions for a failure to comply with the agreed terms of the mediation would be drawn from the laws of England and Wales. So far as aspects of matrimonial law are concerned, there is a limited precedent for English law to recognise aspects of religious laws, although when it comes to divorce this can only be effected in accordance with the civil law of this country.[66]

11.33 The division of labour is illustrated by a recent judgment. In *AI v MT*,[67] two parties to an orthodox Jewish marriage wished to have the disputes arising out of the breakdown of that marriage resolved by the New York *Beth Din*. After lengthy examination of the manner in which the religious body would seek to arbitrate the dispute, Baker J indicated that he would:

> ... endorse the parties' proposal to refer their disputes to a process of arbitration before the New York *Beth Din* on the basis that the outcome, although likely to carry considerable weight with the court, would not be binding and would not preclude either party from pursuing applications to this court in respect of any of the matters in issue.[68]

11.34 The court continued to monitor the progress of the arbitration, before finally endorsing the reward after consideration of its terms.[69] In making his decision to endorse the award, Baker J stressed the following considerations:

> In this case, having been reassured as to the principles which would be applied by the rabbinical authorities, which so far as the children were concerned were akin to the paramountcy principle on which English children's law is based, the court was content to accept and respect the parents' deeply-held wishes, subject to the proviso that the outcome could not be binding without the court's endorsement. It does not, however, necessarily follow that a court would be content in other cases to endorse a proposal that a dispute concerning children should be referred for determination by another religious authority. Each case will turn on its own facts.[70]

11.35 This judgment reaffirms the fact that civil courts retain ultimate jurisdiction to determine disputes arising out of a marriage, and does nothing to alter the fact that the religious status of divorce has been and will continue to be a matter for religious courts alone. Nonetheless, Baker J's reasoning highlights the use to which the dispute resolution

---

[65] For what is generally considered to be the root of recent debate, see Dr Rowan Williams, 'Civil and Religious Law in England: a religious perspective', delivered on 7 February 2008, available at <http://rowanwilliams.archbishopofcanterbury.org/articles.php/1137/archbishops-lecture-civil-and-religious-law-in-england-a-religious-perspective>.

[66] The speech was given at the East London Muslim Community Centre, 3 July 2008, available at <http://www.judiciary.gov.uk/Resources/JCO/Documents/Speeches/lcj_equality_before_the_law_030708.pdf>.

[67] *AI v MT* [2013] EWHC 100 (Fam) (30 January 2013).

[68] *AI v MT* (n 67) para 15.

[69] *AI v MT* (n 67) paras 26–37, which set out Mr Justice Baker's reasoning for making the decision in helpful detail.

[70] *AI v MT* (n 67) para 33.

procedures of religious courts may be put, whilst stressing in strong terms that the methods of each body would be considered in detail before a court will endorse a proposal to use one. As Baker J put it: 'The parties' devout beliefs have been respected. The outcome was in keeping with English law whilst achieved by a process rooted in the Jewish culture to which the families belong.'[71]

There is more difficulty with those cases where there exists a religious marriage that has never been given legal effect. Over half of the cases dealt with by the Sharia Council in the Cardiff research study involved couples who are not married under English civil law.[72] The women in these marriages had undergone an unregistered *nikah* ceremony, often performed in the home. There was therefore no jurisdiction for the domestic courts in relation to the existence or continuance of the status of their marriage, meaning that when the marriage broke down the civil law could only treat them as cohabitants.[73] **11.36**

There is concern that religious authorities may purport to issue binding determinations with regard to marital disputes. If parties to not apply to the civil courts for enforcement of such an order, it may not come to light that the determination does not have the force of civil law behind it. The Arbitration and Mediation Services (Equality) Bill was introduced into the House of Lords in 2011. It would criminalize any person who 'falsely purports to exercise any of the powers or duties of a court to make legally binding rulings'. At the time of writing, the Bill has not been enacted. **11.37**

D. Upbringing of Children

(1) Introduction

A person with parental responsibility[74] for a child has long had a common law right to determine their religious education.[75] In cases of dispute, however, the extent to which a child's upbringing should be in accordance with a particular religion, or no religion at all, may be determined under the Children Act 1989. **11.38**

Such a dispute might arise under the 1989 Act either in private or public family law proceedings. Private law family proceedings are typically brought by a parent of the child to obtain an order under section 8 of the Children Act 1989 in relation to where the child should live, who should have contact with the child, whether a person with parental responsibility in respect of the child should have that responsibility restricted in some way, or how parental responsibility should be exercised in respect of some specific issue such as where the child should go to school. Public law family proceedings involve the state (in the form of a local authority) seeking a care or supervision order in respect of a child, which they may do if the child is suffering or may suffer significant harm as a result of inadequate parenting.[76] Where **11.39**

---

[71] *AI v MT* (n 67) para 37.
[72] Douglas et al (n 2) 39.
[73] For detailed discussion on this point, see Douglas et al (n 18).
[74] Defined in the Children Act 1989, s 2.
[75] *Andrews v Salt* (1873) 8 Ch App 622. An example of an exercise of parental responsibility in respect of a religious matter in the context of education is the right of a parent to opt their child out of religious education, collective worship, and/or sex education lessons. See Ch 9, paras 9.37 ff.
[76] Children Act 1989, s 31.

a care order is made, the local authority assumes parental responsibility for a child[77] and the child becomes 'looked after' by the authority.[78]

11.40   In any proceedings (private or public) in which a court determines any question with respect to the upbringing of a child, the child's welfare must be the court's paramount consideration.[79] This is known as the 'welfare principle'.[80] The key effect of the welfare principle is that the interests of the child override those of any persons with parental responsibility for him. Another important effect is that, in deciding where the child's interests lie, the voice of the father carries no more weight because he is the father than does the mother's because she is the mother. Prior to the development of the principle,[81] that was not so. Historically, a father alone had a legal right to control and direct the education and bringing up of his children (including in relation to religious matters), and the court would not interfere with him in the exercise of his paternal authority, unless by his gross moral turpitude he forfeited his rights or had by his conduct abdicated his paternal authority.[82]

11.41   The courts construe 'welfare' as embracing religious welfare.[83] But a child's religious welfare is but one of the factors to which the court will have regard in assessing his welfare overall.[84] As Munby LJ explained in *Re G (Children) (Religious Upbringing: Education)* (at para 43):[85]

> Some manifestations of religious practice may be regulated if contrary to a child's welfare. Although a parent's views and wishes as to the child's religious upbringing are of great importance, and will always be seriously regarded by the court, just as the court will always pay great attention to the wishes of a child old enough to be able to express sensible views on the subject of religion, even if not old enough to take a mature decision, they will be given effect to by the court only if and so far as and in such manner as is in accordance with the child's best interests. In matters of religion, as in all other aspects of a child's upbringing, the interests of the child are the paramount consideration.

11.42   In determining issues of a child's religious welfare, it is not for a judge to weigh one religion against another. The court recognizes no religious distinctions and generally speaking passes

---

[77] Children Act 1989, s 33.

[78] Children Act 1989, s 22(1)(a).

[79] Children Act 1989, s 1(1)(a).

[80] Art 3(1) of the Convention on the Rights of the Child (1991) (Cm 1668), adopted on 20 November 1989, similarly provides: 'In all actions concerning children ... the best interests of the child shall be of primary consideration.' The Convention is not part of UK law. Nevertheless it commands and receives the respect of the court: see *Re P (Guidelines and Religious Heritage)* [2000] Fam 15, 42 *per* Ward LJ.

[81] The principle was first put on a statutory basis the Guardianship of Infants Act 1925, s 1. In *Ward v Laverty* [1925] AC 101, Lord Cave LC treated it as established principle (at 108).

[82] *Re Agar-Ellis, Agar-Ellis v Lascelles* (1883) 24 ChD 317. In *J v C* [1970] AC 668, 721, Lord Upjohn, described *Re Agar-Ellis* as the 'dreadful case' where the Court of Appeal 'permitted a monstrously unreasonable father to impose upon his daughter of 17 much unnecessary hardship in the name of his religious faith'.

[83] *Re McGrath (Infants)* [1893] 1 Ch 143, 148 *per* Lindley LJ. Cf UN Convention on the Rights of the Child, Art 14, which provides:

  1. States parties shall respect the right of the child to freedom of thought, conscience and religion.
  2. States parties shall respect the rights and duties of the parents ... to provide direction to the child in the exercise of his or her right in a manner consistent with the evolving capacities of the child.
  3. Freedom to manifest one's religion or beliefs may be subject only to such limitations as are prescribed by law and are necessary to protect public safety, order, health or morals, or the fundamental human rights and freedoms of others.

[84] The proposition is consistent with the ECHR jurisprudence. As Ward LJ said in *Re P (A Minor) (Residence Order: Child's Welfare)* [2000] Fam 15, 43: 'in the jurisprudence of human rights the right to practise one's religion is subservient to the need in a democratic society to put welfare first'.

[85] *Re G (Children) (Religious Upbringing: Education)* [2012] EWCA Civ 1233, [2012] 3 FCR 524.

no judgment on religious beliefs or on the tenets, doctrines, or rules of any particular section of society.[86] All are entitled to equal respect.[87] In principle, therefore, it would be as reasonable on the part of one parent to wish to teach their child the beliefs and practice of one religion as it would be reasonable on the part of the other parent that they should not be taught those practices and beliefs.[88] This is consistent with the jurisprudence of the EHCR.[89] In *Hoffman v Austria*[90] the ECtHR held that a decision of the Supreme Court of Austria upholding a decision to refuse a mother custody because she was a Jehovah's Witness violated Article 8 read together with Article 14 ECHR as unjustified discrimination on the ground of religion.[91] The approach will, however, be different where such beliefs or principles are not 'legally and socially acceptable'[92] or are 'immoral or socially obnoxious'[93] or 'pernicious'.[94]

In addition to the welfare principle, where a court is considering whether to make, vary, or **11.43** discharge a section 8 order (ie in private law proceedings under the Children Act 1989), and the making, variation, or discharge of the order is opposed by any party to the proceedings, the court must have regard in particular to a number of factors which the 1989 Act prescribes, including the ascertainable wishes and feelings of the child concerned (considered in the light of his age and understanding);[95] his physical, emotional, and educational needs;[96] the likely effect on him of any change in his circumstances;[97] and his background and any characteristics of his which the court considers relevant.[98]

In public law proceedings, where a local authority acquires parental responsibility for a child **11.44** under a care order, it does not acquire the power to determine the child's religion.[99] Before

---

[86] *Re R (A Minor) (Residence: Religion)* [1993] 2 FLR 163, 171 *per* Purchas LJ (with whom Balcombe LJ agreed).

[87] *Re G* (n 85) para 36 *per* Munby LJ.

[88] *Re T (Minors) (Custody: Religious Upbringing)* (1981) 2 FLR 239 (a case in which the mother was a Jehovah's Witness), at 244–5:

> Of course, most of us like to play games on Saturdays, to go out to children's parties and to have a quiet Sunday—some of us will go to church, and some of us will not. This appears to be the normal and happy, even though somewhat materialistic, way of life, accepted by the majority of people in our society. It does not follow, however, that it is wrong, or contrary to the welfare of children, that life should be in a narrower sphere, subject to a stricter religious discipline, and without the parties on birthdays and Christmas that seem so important to the rest of us.

[89] See generally *Moscow Branch of the Salvation Army v Russia* (2006) 44 EHRR 912, para 8, where the court said that: 'The State's duty of neutrality and impartiality... is incompatible with any power on the State's part to assess the legitimacy of religious beliefs.'

[90] *Hoffman v Austria* (1993) 17 EHRR 293.

[91] There is some reason to doubt, on human rights grounds, the correctness of the decision of the Court of Appeal in *T v T* (1974) 4 Fam Law 190, upholding a decision refusing custody to a mother who was a Jehovah's Witness in part because the children would not celebrate Christmas. Stamp LJ reasoned, at 191, that the children would be deprived of the 'wholesome joys of life... the charms of crackers and paper hats'. The decision appears justifiable only on the basis that the mother showed signs of mental instability as a matter distinct from her religion. See also *Ismailova v Russia* [2008] 1 FLR 533 (App 37614/02).

[92] *Re R (A Minor)* (n 86) 171 *per* Purchas LJ.

[93] *Re T* (n 88) 244 *per* Scarman LJ.

[94] *Re B and G (Minors) (Custody)* [1985] FLR 134, 157 *per* Latey J. In that case an appeal was dismissed against the decision of a court to award custody of children to their mother over their father over concerns that they would become exposed to scientology, which the judge considered 'corrupt, sinister, and dangerous'.

[95] Children Act 1989, s 1(3)(a).

[96] Children Act 1989, s 1(3)(b).

[97] Children Act 1989, s 1(3)(c).

[98] Children Act 1989, s 1(3)(d).

[99] Children Act 1989, s 33(6)(a).

making any decision with respect to a child whom they are looking after, or proposing to look after, a local authority must give due consideration (among other matters) to the child's religious persuasion.[100]

11.45   Cases concerning the determination of children's religious upbringing in both private and public family law proceedings are considered in the following sections.

(2) Private law cases

11.46   A number of cases have resulted from the breakdown of parents' relationships in a situation where the parents have different religious beliefs or follow different religious observances.

11.47   In *Re R (A Minor) (Residence; Religion)*, a 10-year old boy, who had been brought up in the Exclusive Brethren and whose mother had died, was the subject of a residence and contact dispute between his aunt, some friends who were members of the Brethren, and his father who had been excluded from the sect. The boy identified strongly with the sect's teaching but also wanted to be with his father. The Court of Appeal upheld a decision to grant a residence order to the father and to allow supervised contact with the aunt upon her undertaking not to speak to the child about religious matters.[101]

11.48   In *Re N (A Child) (Religion: Jehovah's Witness)*, an Anglican father applied to restrict the religious practices which the child's mother, who had become a Jehovah's Witness, could undertake with the child. The mother had spent time engaging in house-to-house evangelism with the child, did not celebrate his birthdays or Christmas, and only engaged in social contact with other Jehovah's Witnesses. In making a shared residence order, the court held that a parent's right to enable their child to learn about and experience their religion was not an unconfined right. Where the practice of that religion involved a lifestyle which conflicted with the lifestyle of the other parent and the court was satisfied that that conflict had, or might have, an impact on the child's welfare, the court was entitled to restrict the child's involvement in those practices.[102]

11.49   In *Re G (Children) (Religious Upbringing: Education)*, both the mother and the father were ultra-Orthodox Jews forming part of the Chareidi community, for whom, as Munby LJ recognized, 'every aspect of their lives, every aspect of their being, of who and what they are, [was] governed by a body of what the outsider might characterise as purely religious law'.[103] The Court of Appeal upheld a decision that the best interests of children from an ultra-Orthodox Jewish family could be best served, as in this case their mother wished, by being educated at a school which was orthodox but not ultra-orthodox. Although this would lead to a change in their lifestyle, it would provide them with a wider education and greater career opportunities.

---

[100]   Children Act 1989, s 22(5)(c).

[101]   *Re R (A Minor)* (n 86). cf *Hewison v Hewison* (1977) 7 Fam Law 207, in which the Court expressed concerns about the social isolation which might be faced by children were they to remain living with their father, who was a member of the Brethren.

[102]   *Re N (A Child) (Religion: Jehovah's Witness)* [2011] EWHC 3737 (Fam), [2012] 2 FLR 917. cf *Wright v Wright* (1980) 2 FLR 276, in which the Court dismissed a father's appeal against a decision refusing him access to his child in circumstances where he had not been prepared to undertake not to indoctrinate him as a Jehovah's Witness.

[103]   *Re G (Children)* (n 85) para 18.

In *Re J (Specific Issue Orders: Muslim Upbringing and Circumcision)*,[104] a Muslim father **11.50** wished for a child to be circumcised but a Christian mother did not. The Appeal Court upheld the approach of the trial judge that circumcision at the age of 5, which was not medically necessary, was not in the child's best interests. A similar dispute arose in *Re S (Specific Issue Order: Religion: Circumcision)*,[105] between a Muslim mother and a Hindu (Jain) father, whose children had had a correspondingly mixed heritage. The Court took the view that circumcision once done could not be undone and noted that the Muslim religion, whilst favouring circumcision at 10 years and below, did permit an upper age limit of puberty or later on conversion. It was not in the children's interests to be circumcised yet.

The issue of a child's name may also give rise to dispute based on religion. In *Re S (Change* **11.51** *of Names: Cultural Factors)*,[106] a boy had been born to a Muslim mother who had eloped to Gretna Green with a Sikh man. The boy had been given Sikh names. The woman, who had been ostracized, applied to change all his names on the basis that the Sikh names were a barrier to his acceptance in the Muslim community. The court permitted the boy to be given Muslim middle and last names but refused a formal change of his first name on the basis that it would comprehensively eliminate the Sikh identity.

A change in those who will have parental responsibility for a child may give rise to religious **11.52** issues in a private law context. In *Re P (Guidelines and Religious Heritage)*, a child with Down's syndrome was fostered by Christian parents, but the child's natural parents, who were Orthodox Jews, wished for her to be brought up in their faith. The Court rejected the natural parents' application to vary the child's residence order in the light of the fact, among others, that the child did not have the capacity to understand her religious heritage. It also imposed a restriction preventing the natural parents from making any further residence application without the leave of the Court. An appeal of the natural parents was dismissed, on the basis that the court had acted in accordance with the welfare principle both in refusing the variation application and imposing the restriction. The Court was clear that religious heritage cannot be an overwhelming factor.[107]

Re S, Newcastle City Council v Z[108] concerned the conscientious beliefs held by a devout **11.53** Muslim mother that if her child were adopted, his soul would not get peace when he died, and she would not be able to go on Haj. The question was whether the mother was acting reasonably in withholding consent to adoption for the purposes of section 16(2)(b) of the Adoption Act 1976. The Court adjudged that she was. The mother's religious views called for particular and sensitive consideration, but the question was ultimately whether the advantages of adoption for the child's welfare were sufficiently strong to justify overriding the religious interests of the mother.

(3) Public law cases

As in the private law context, religion has no overriding force as a factor to be taken into **11.54** account in determining a child's welfare when he or she is looked after by a local authority.

---

[104] *Re J (Specific Issue Orders: Muslim Upbringing and Circumcision)* [1999] 2 FLR 678, affirmed in *Re J (Specific Issue Orders: Child's Religious Upbringing and Circumcision)* [2000] 1 FLR 571.
[105] *Re S (Specific Issue Order: Religion: Circumcision)* [2004] EWHC 1282 (Fam), [2005] 1 FLR 236.
[106] *Re S (Change of Names: Cultural Factors)* [2001] 2 FLR 1005.
[107] *Re P (Guidelines and Religious Heritage)* [2000] Fam 15.
[108] *Re S, Newcastle City Council v Z* [2005] EWHC 1490 (Fam), [2007] 1 FLR 861.

As Ryder J has observed, considering the scope of the duty on local authorities to safeguard and promote the welfare of such children under section 22(3)(a) of the Children Act 1989:

> Religious, racial and cultural factors are integral elements of welfare and may on the facts of a particular case provide both the positive and negative factors and context by and within which decisions have to be made. However . . . the law does not give any religious belief or birth-right a pre-eminent place in the balance of factors that compromise welfare . . . Furthermore the safeguarding of the welfare of vulnerable children and adults ought not to be subordinated by the court to any particular religious belief.[109]

11.55   In *Re (Local Authority: Religious Upbringing)*,[110] neither of a boy's parents, who were Muslim, was able to care for him and he was placed with his maternal grandmother, who was Catholic. The care plan said that the boy was to be brought up as a Muslim. The mother subsequently reverted to Catholicism. The father alleged that the local authority had breached section 33(6)(a) of the Children Act 1989, which required the local authority to ensure that the boy was not brought up in any different religious persuasion from that followed by his parents before the care order. The court did not find a breach on the evidence, but commented that the local authority could do more to identify resources in the Muslim community that could assist the grandmother, seeking expert advice, resuming contact between the child and his paternal family, and engaging the father in reviewing the child's care so that he could contribute appropriately.

11.56   In general, the tenets and faith of Jehovah's Witness parents will not prevent the court ordering a child to receive a blood transfusion, even though both the parents and the child vehemently object. In *Re E (A Minor) (Wardship: Medical Treatment)*,[111] a 15-year-old Jehovah's Witness diagnosed with leukaemia and in a critical condition, was made a ward of court by the local authority who sought the Court's permission for him to be treated through blood transfusions. Applying the welfare principle, the Court decided that, notwithstanding the religious convictions of the family, the hospital should be at liberty to give the transfusions. It rejected arguments that, as the boy was close to his sixteenth birthday, his consent to the treatment would be required under section 8 of the Family Law Reform Act 1969, or alternatively that he was competent to decide upon his medical treatment under the test in *Gillick v West Norfolk and Wisbech AHA*,[112] and that it was wrong for the Court to interfere using the interventionist jurisdiction of wardship.

---

[109] *Haringey LBC v C* [2007] 1 FLR 1035, para 36.
[110] *Re (Local Authority: Religious Upbringing)* [2010] EWHC 2503 (Fam), [2011] 1 FLR 615.
[111] *Re E (A Minor) (Wardship: Medical Treatment)* [1993] 1 FLR 386.
[112] *Norfolk and Wisbech AHA* [1986] AC 112. In essence, that children under 16 may have capacity to consent to medical examination and treatment, where they have sufficient maturity and intelligence to understand the nature and implications of the treatment.

12

PROTECTIONS FOR RELIGIOUS RIGHTS IN OTHER AREAS

A. Places of Worship

(1) Introduction

Section 2 of the Places of Worship Registration Act 1855 (PWRA 1855) provides that any **12.01** place of meeting for religious worship of any body or denomination of persons other than the Church of England may be certified in writing to the Registrar General for England and Wales by any person. The Registrar General must then satisfy himself that the place is in fact a place of meeting for religious worship before recording it as such.[1] A place of religious worship must be:

> . . . a place of which the principal use is a place where people come together as a congregation or assembly to do reverence to God. It need not be the God which Christians worship. It may be another God, or an unknown God, but it must be reverence of a deity. There may be exceptions. For instance, Buddhist temples are properly defined as places of meeting for religious worship.[2]

---

[1] In *R (Segerdal) v Registrar General* [1970] 2 QB 697, it fell to the courts to decide whether the Registrar General's duty in recording the registration was purely ministerial, or whether he must first satisfy himself as to the nature of the place certified to him. Lord Denning (at 705) held that the Registrar General only has jurisdiction to record registration where he is so satisfied, first on the basis that to hold otherwise would allow for abuse, and secondly on the basis that PWRA 1855, s 8 conferred a requirement of satisfaction in determining that a place had ceased to be a place of religious worship, which should logically be extended to the initial registration of place.

[2] *Segerdal* (n 1) 707. The Court ultimately found that services in the Scientologist Booklet of Ceremonies contained no element of worship, having none of the following characteristics: 'submission to the object worshipped, veneration of that object, praise, thanksgiving, prayer, intercession': at 709 *per* Buckley LJ.

12.02   Although this is not a compulsory procedure, registration brings certain benefits in terms of exemption from rates and, in certain circumstances, from the requirement to register under the Charities Act 1993.[3] It is also required in order to qualify as a registered building under the Marriage Act 1949,[4] and a place of worship is only brought within the protection of the Ecclesiastical Courts Jurisdiction Act 1960 if it has been registered under the PWRA 1855. The following sections consider to what extent denial of these benefits by virtue of refusing registration could constitute interference with a claimant's Article 9 ECHR rights.

(2) Ratings exemption

12.03   The question of whether refusal of registration under the PWRA 1855 might constitute a breach of Article 9 rights has not yet been decided by the courts. However, the issue has arisen in relation to similar provisions under other legislation. The Local Government Finance Act 1988, for example, provides that those places which are defined as 'places of public worship' are exempt from non-domestic ratings.[5] In *Gallagher (Valuation Officer) v Church of Jesus Christ of Latter-Day Saints*,[6] where a valuation officer had refused to grant such an exemption to a Mormon temple on the grounds that it was only open to a select class of Mormons, the proprietor church claimed that the legislation was in breach of its Article 9 ECHR rights. However, the House of Lords had no difficulty in finding that the liability of the temple to a particular rating would not prevent the Mormons from manifesting their religion, and that therefore the issue was beyond the ambit of Article 9.[7] It seems that any claim for breach of Article 9 rights on the basis of refusal for classification as a particular type of place of worship for the purposes of a rating exemption is unlikely to succeed in the absence of evidence that it prevents the manifestation of the religious belief.

12.04   An alternative route has been to claim for discrimination under Article 14 ECHR. Whether a given religious institution could succeed in arguing that their inability to obtain a rating exemption for their premises on account of the particular requirements of their religion amounted to discrimination would depend on the individual facts of the case. In *Gallagher*, the exemption under Schedule 5 of the Local Government Finance Act 1988 was granted on the ground that a 'place of public worship' provided a public benefit; this was a general requirement of any qualifying place, and it was therefore not the case that the Mormons were being taxed on account of their religion.[8] Even if it could be regarded as a case of indirect discrimination, it was held that it was justified under Parliament's wide discretion in determining what should be regarded as sufficient public benefit to justify exemption from taxation.[9]

(3) Solemnization of marriages

12.05   A recent case considered whether refusal to register a place under PWRA 1855 constituted a breach of the claimant's Article 9 rights (among others) because of the consequence that she could not solemnize her marriage there. In *R (Hodkin) v Registrar General*,[10] the Registrar

---

[3] PWRA 1855, s 3.
[4] Marriage Act 1949, s 26. See para 12.05.
[5] Local Government Finance Act 1988, Sch 5, para 11(1)(a).
[6] *Gallagher (Valuation Officer) v Church of Jesus Christ of Latter-Day Saints* [2008] 1 WLR 1852.
[7] *Gallagher* (n 6) para 13 *per* Hoffmann LJ.
[8] *Gallagher* (n 6) para 13.
[9] *Gallagher* (n 6) para 15.
[10] *R (Hodkin) v Registrar General* [2012] EWCH 3635 (Admin).

General had refused to register a chapel of the Church of Scientology as a place of worship under section 2 of the 1855 Act. Because the Marriage Act 1949 provided that a place could only be used for the solemnization of religious marriage if it was a 'registered building',[11] this meant that the claimant, Louisa Hodkin, could not solemnize her marriage to her fiancé on the premises. The grounds for refusal were that she was bound by the decision in *R (Segerdal)*,[12] which had held that the services conducted by Scientology could not be considered religious worship.[13] Ms Hodkin therefore submitted that the legislation interfered with her rights under Articles 9, 12, and 14 ECHR, in that it denied her enjoyment of the right to marry in accordance with her religious beliefs.[14] Ouseley J found without difficulty that there was 'no interference with the right to marry according to national laws, nor with the right of Scientologists to practise their religion, if such it is'.[15] Therefore there was no obligation to interpret PWRA 1855 any differently from the way in which it had been interpreted in pre-HRA 1998 decisions. It seems as a result of the finding in this case, and as a result of the decision in *R(Gallagher)*,[16] that denial of the substantive benefits incurred through registration under section 2 of PWRA 1855 will not be considered to be interference with a claimant's rights under Article 9.

(4) Ecclesiastical Courts Jurisdiction Act 1860

A further reason for seeking registration under PWRA 1855 is that it is necessary in order **12.06** for a place to be brought under the protection of section 2 of the Ecclesiastical Courts Jurisdiction Act 1860. This section provides that it is a criminal offence to commit 'riotous, violent or indecent behaviour' in the course of lawful liturgical action,[17] and applies not only when those acts are committed during the celebration of 'divine service' but at any time, including in any churchyard or burial ground. In the period 1997 to 2004 there were 78 prosecutions for this offence and 26 convictions;[18] no litigation has arisen as a result of an inability to prosecute through not having been registered under PWRA 1855.

B. Church Courts

Each Diocese of the Church of England has a Consistory Court (in the Diocese of Canterbury **12.07** it is known as the Commissary Court). These courts were constituted under the Ecclesiastical Jurisdiction Measure 1963, and are courts within the meaning of section 6 of HRA 1998.[19] They are presided over by the diocesan chancellor, who is appointed by the bishop and must have seven years' general qualification[20] or hold high judicial office. The chancellor is independent of the bishop.[21]

---

[11] Within the Marriage Act 1949, s 26, which in turn depends on section 2 of the PWRA 1855, s 2.
[12] *R (Segerdal) v Registrar General* [1970] 2 QB 697.
[13] See n 2.
[14] *Segerdal* (n 12) para 89.
[15] *Segerdal* (n 12) para 90.
[16] See para 12.03.
[17] For 'indecency', see *Jones v Catterrall* (1902) 18 TLR 367.
[18] 'Report of the Select Committee on Religious Offences', HL paper 95-I, 10 April 2002, ch 5, para 55.
[19] See Ch 5, para 5.69.
[20] Courts and Legal Services Act 1990.
[21] *Re St Mary's, Barnes* (1982) 1 WLR 531.

12.08   The jurisdiction of these courts concerns the grant or refusal of faculties permitting alterations to the fabric or structure of church buildings and other matters concerning consecrated land, particularly reservation of grave spaces and exhumation. As a result, those cases coming before the Consistory Courts in which Article 9 rights are relied upon tend to concern the exhumation of remains for re-internment in a location appropriate for the deceased's religion.

12.09   In *Re Durrington Cemetery*,[22] a case decided by the Chichester Consistory Court, the Court took Article 9 ECHR into account when granting a faculty permitting the remains of a practising Jew, who had been buried in consecrated ground, to be exhumed for re-internment in a Jewish cemetery. The chancellor held that to refuse the Orthodox Jewish relatives of the buried Jew (Mr Saunders) permission to exhume him and to reinter his remains in a Jewish cemetery would put the Court at risk of acting unlawfully under HRA 1998.[23]

12.10   In *Re Crawley Green Road Cemetery, Luton*,[24] the St Albans Consistory Court granted a humanist widow permission to exhume the remains of her husband (also a humanist) from consecrated ground after hearing that neither she nor her husband had realized that the ground was consecrated. The court recognized that to deny her the right to exhume her husband's ashes would be to act incompatibly with Article 9 ECHR; in particular, with the rights of the widow under that article.[25]

12.11   In faculty cases, an appeal from the Consistory Court is to the Court of Arches (in the Province of Canterbury), presided over by the Dean of Arches, or to the Chancery Court (in the Province of York). If a faculty case involves a matter of doctrine, ritual, or ceremonial, the appeal lies to the Court of Ecclesiastical Causes Reserved (comprising five persons appointed by the Crown).

C. Rituals, Burials, and Ceremonies

(1) Introduction

12.12   There exist in England and Wales common law rights to burial and cremation for all members of each parish. Although every individual thereby accrues rights pertaining to the disposal of their body after death regardless of their religion, the substance of these rights naturally complements the funerary rituals and ceremonies associated with the Church of England and with other main religions in this jurisdiction. Indeed, after the passage of the Cremation Act 1902, any methods of cremating a body other than those prescribed by the Act constituted an offence.[26] Given the variety of practices observed by different religions when disposing of the bodies of the dead, there is considerable scope for Article 9 rights to be interfered with by the restrictions of the 1902 Act. One recent example is the litigation that arose in the context of the Article 9 rights of a Hindu man wishing for his remains to be created on a traditional pyre in direct sunlight.[27] The case was ultimately decided on appeal without reference to Article 9 ECHR, but the reasoning of the Administrative Court at first

---

[22]   *Re Durrington Cemetery* [2001] Fam 33.
[23]   *Durrington Cemetery* (n 22) 37.
[24]   *Re Crawley Green Road Cemetery, Luton* [2001] HRLR 431.
[25]   *Crawley Green* (n 24) para 8.
[26]   Cremation Act 1902, s 8.
[27]   *R (Ghai) v Newcastle City Council* [2011] QB 591.

instance is instructive as to the likely approach of the courts in any future cases of this kind (see paragraphs 12.15–12.20).

(2) Common law rights of burial

The common law position as regards the right of burial is that all parishioners have a right to **12.13** be buried in the parish churchyard or burial ground if there is one which remains open for burials.[28] This right now also applies to cremated remains.[29] A parishioner is one who normally resides in the ecclesiastical parish in question; in addition, a person whose name is on the Church Electoral Roll at the time of death[30] and a person happening to die in the parish also has a right of burial there. If a clergyman refuses to bury the body, it was recognized in *R v Coleridge*[31] that *mandamus* could be granted.

The incumbent may also permit the bodies or cremated remains of others not so qualified to **12.14** be buried in the churchyard, and, in so deciding, he is required to have regard to any general guidance given by the Parochial Church Council with respect to the matter.[32] There is no jurisdiction for the Consistory Court to override this discretion.

(3) Funerary rites of other religions

In *R (Ghai)*,[33] the Administrative Court and then the Court of Appeal considered whether **12.15** open-air funeral pyres were legal under the Cremation Act 1902, and, if they were not, whether this ban was compatible with Article 9 ECHR. The Hindu claimant, Davender Ghai, desired that his remains be cremated following his death on an open-air pyre in accordance with his belief that this was the only way in which the cycle of birth and rebirth could progress. The defendant local authority had refused his application for the provision of land for such an open-air pyre, and Mr Ghai brought proceedings by way of judicial review to challenge that decision.

In the decision at first instance, the Administrative Court held that the Cremation Act 1902 **12.16** did impose a ban on open-air funeral pyres, and that this ban constituted an interference with the claimant's Article 9 rights. However, Cranston J considered that the ban was justifiable in that it pursued a legitimate listed aim under Article 9(2); namely, the protection of public morals.

The case on behalf of the claimant altered in the Court of Appeal, and Mr Ghai contended **12.17** that the religious belief would be satisfied by a cremation within a building using traditional fire and with part of the roof open to permit sunlight on to the body. The Court of Appeal allowed the appeal on the basis that properly analysed, the provisions of the Cremation Act 1902 meant that 'building' was wide enough to permit the construction of a substantial and permanent structure which could be part open at the top. For this reason the decision of the Court of Appeal was on a reasonably narrow point of statutory interpretation. The reasoning of Cranston J at first instance remains important as a guide for the future.

---

[28] *Maidman v Malpas* (1794) 1 Hag Con 205.
[29] Church of England (Miscellaneous Provisions) Measure 1992, s 3.
[30] Church of England (Miscellaneous Provisions) Measure 1976, s 6(1).
[31] *R v Coleridge* (1819) 2 B & Ald.
[32] Church of England (Miscellaneous Provisions) Measure 1976, s 6(2).
[33] *R (Ghai) v Newcastle City Council* [2011] QB 591.

12.18 Cranston J held that the Secretary of State was entitled to conclude that the present legislative framework was consistent with mainstream cultural expectations of persons living in this country, and thereby ensured that likely offence and distress was avoided.[34]

12.19 Cranston J's first finding was that the performance of *anthyesthi sanskara* (open-air cremation) was a manifestation of the claimant's religious belief, and accepted that it was his 'genuine belief, held in good faith' that were he not to be cremated on an open-air funeral pyre, there would be devastating results for him in the afterlife.[35] He then found that this practice was unlawful under the Cremation Act 1902, on the basis that the latter required a cremation to be carried out in a 'building fitted with appliances for the purposes of burning human remains'.[36] The pyre sought by Mr Ghai was unlawful on account of its not being a 'building', and the legislation therefore constituted an interference with his manifestation of his religious belief.

12.20 In considering whether this interference was justified, Cranston J first found that the legislation was pursuing a legitimate aim of protecting public morals and the rights of others, since 'a large proportion of the population of this country would be upset and offended by open air funeral pyres and would find it abhorrent that human remains were being burned in this manner'.[37] It was then necessary to decide whether the manner in which the legitimate aim was pursued was proportionate, and it was held that the legislation struck a 'fair balance' between the rights of the claimant and the interests of society.[38] In coming to this decision, Cranston J had regard to five factors: first, that no blanket interference was imposed;[39] secondly, that the majority of Hindus do not consider open-air burial to be essential;[40] thirdly, that the law on cremation was not rendered outdated by any cultural shifts over the past century;[41] fourthly, that there existed no European consensus in relation to funeral pyres;[42] and finally, that it was no answer to say that a secluded location could avoid any offence being caused.[43]

12.21 Given that the funerary norms in the United Kingdom are restricted to burial and cremation within the meaning of the Cremation Act 1902, it would be surprising if the question does not arise again as to whether legislation interfering with any right under Article 9 to dispose of the body of the deceased a certain way can be justified. The question as to what degree speculative public offence at otherwise harmless activity can constitute justification for a blanket ban on a particular manifestation of religious belief seems in particular need of further investigation.

---

[34] *Ghai* (n 33) para 105.
[35] *Ghai* (n 33) para 123.
[36] Cremation Act 1902, s 2.
[37] *Ghai* (n 33) para 16.
[38] *Ghai* (n 33) paras 115–121. Although individual factors were weighed up in the judgment, Cranston J's conclusion was entirely deferential to the decision-making of elected representatives: 'It is for national authorities to determine whether an individual's Convention rights are outweighed by features which make it offensive to the general public' (para 121). It is worth noting that the conclusion of the balancing exercise was in any event in favour of the defendant.
[39] *Ghai* (n 33) para 116.
[40] *Ghai* (n 33) para 117.
[41] *Ghai* (n 33) para 118.
[42] *Ghai* (n 33) para 119.
[43] *Ghai* (n 33) para 120.

D. Criminal Law

The criminal law interacts with religion and religious rights in a number of ways. This part of the chapter attempts to deal with the most important interactions.
12.22

First, the criminal law protects religious groups against hatred and hostility. The religious hatred offences outlaw the use of threatening words or behaviour, or the publication, distribution, etc of threatening material, with the intention to stir up religious hatred.[44] The offences are not intended to protect religious believers against insult, or offensive attacks on matters they regard as sacred.[45] Abusive or insulting words or behaviour may, however, be caught by the offences in sections 4 to 5 of the Public Order Act 1996. There are religiously aggravated versions of these offences.[46] If, for example, the relevant offence is motivated by hostility towards members of a religious group based on their membership of that group, a person will be guilty of a religiously aggravated offence which attracts a higher penalty than the basic offence.[47] These offences are considered in more detail in Chapter 10.
12.23

Secondly, a person may in some circumstances be prosecuted for expressing religious views. Religious expression may be caught by any number of offences, for example the offences in sections 4A and 5 of the Public Order Act 1986 (which, broadly speaking, prohibit the use of threatening, abusive, or insulting words or behaviour)[48] or the offence of sending letters, etc with intent to cause distress or anxiety in section 1 of Malicious Communications Act 1988.[49] In *Hammond v DPP* an Evangelical Christian preacher was convicted of an offence under section 5 of the Public Order Act 1986 for preaching whilst holding a sign bearing the words 'Stop Immorality', 'Stop Homosexuality', and 'Stop Lesbianism'.[50] In *Dehal v CPS*, another case involving prosecution for religious expression, the court suggested that it was a fundamental feature of the relationship between Article 10 ECHR and section 4A of the Public Order Act 1986 that 'the criminal law should not be invoked unless and until it is established that the conduct which is the subject of the charge amounts to such a threat to public disorder as to require the invocation of the criminal as opposed to the civil law'.[51] It should be noted that hatred against persons on grounds of sexual orientation is now also unlawful. For example, it is an offence to use threatening words or behaviour, or to display threatening material, with the intention of stirring up hatred on grounds of sexual orientation.[52]
12.24

Thirdly, in limited cases the criminal law accommodates religious beliefs and practices by granting religious-based exemptions from the general law. For example Sikhs who wear a turban are exempt from the statutory requirement that motorcyclists wear protective headgear.[53]
12.25

---

[44] Public Order Act 1986, Pt 3A.

[45] See Public Order Act 1986, s 29J.

[46] Crime and Disorder Act 1998, s 31.

[47] Crime and Disorder Act 1998, ss 31(1)(c) and 28(1)(b).

[48] See further Ch 10, part C, section 3.

[49] See eg *Connolly v DPP* [2008] 1 WLR 276 (DC), in which the defendant was a Roman Catholic anti-abortion activist who sent letters containing images of aborted foetuses to pharmacists who sold the 'morning after pill.'

[50] *Hammond v DPP* [2004] EWHC 69 (Admin).

[51] *Dehal v CPS* [2005] EWHC 2154 (Admin), para 5. See further Ch 10.

[52] Public Order Act 1986, s 29B. See generally Pt 3A of the 1986 Act. The offences outlawing hatred against persons on the grounds of sexual orientation were introduced by the Criminal Justice and Immigration Act 2008.

[53] Road Traffic Act 1988, s 16(2).

Moreover, sections 139(5)(b) and 139A(4)(c) of the Criminal Justice Act 1998 provide for a religion-based defence. Where a person is charged with the offence of having an article with a blade or sharp point in a public place or on school premises, it is a defence for him to prove that he had the article with him 'for religious reasons'.

12.26   Acting in accordance with religious beliefs does not generally provide a defence, however. In *Blake v DPP*,[54] a vicar was convicted of criminally damaging a concrete pillar by writing a biblical quotation on it. He appealed on the grounds that he was carrying out the instructions of God, and that God being the ultimate owner of all, was the person entitled to consent to the damage. It was held that belief that one has the authority of God, no matter how strongly or sincerely held, did not amount to a defence under English law. In *R v Taylor* and *R v Andrews* the defendants were Rastafarians who used cannabis for religious purposes. They argued unsuccessfully that their prosecution for drug-related offences infringed their Convention rights including their rights under Article 9.[55] In *R v Senior*,[56] the accused belonged to a sect which objected on religious grounds to calling in medical aid, and to the use of medicine, and so had abstained from providing medical aid and medicine, which were necessary for his child who was seriously ill. The fact that he was acting in accordance with his religious belief provided no defence to a charge of manslaughter.

E. Planning and the Environment

(1) Introduction

12.27   A detailed consideration of the complex legal systems by which the law regulates the use of land for planning and environmental purposes lies beyond the scope of this work. The aim of this section is to highlight the most significant ways in which the law on planning and the environment impacts upon religious freedom. The issue of animal slaughter is dealt with separately, in section H below.

12.28   The planning system is fundamentally concerned with what land should be used for. Religious persons and organizations may wish to change the use of a piece of land to a use connected with their religion (for instance as a site of a place of worship), and/or to develop land for such a purpose. They may require planning permission to do so. Where, as will commonly be the case, the decision on whether or not to grant planning permission falls to a local planning authority, that authority will be bound to determine the application in accordance with the 'development plan' unless 'material considerations' indicate otherwise.[57] The 'development plan' is a statutory concept.[58] Where the statutory plan does not support an application for a use connected with religious practice, the applicant may wish to invoke other material considerations in support of a grant, invoke Article 9 ECHR, and have an eye on compliance with the Public Sector Equality Duty during decision-making. The religious dimension to uses of land may also be relevant in areas of the law such as statutory nuisance, which concern more broadly the use of the environment.

---

[54] *Blake v DPP* [1993] Crim LR 586 (DC).
[55] *R v Taylor* [2002] 1 Cr App R 37 (CA); *R v Andrews* [2004] EWCA Crim 947.
[56] *R v Senior* [1899] 1 QB 283.
[57] Planning and Compulsory Purchase Act 2004, s 38(6).
[58] See Town and Country Planning Act 1990, ss 27, 27A, and 54.

(2) Planning decisions/material considerations

The Government's Planning Policy Statement 1 states that development plan policies should **12.29**
take into account the needs of all the community, including particular requirements relating
to religion (among other matters).[59] 'Diversity and Equality in Planning: A Good Practice
Guide' (ODPM, 2005) provides general guidance but contains no section specifically relating to religious discrimination.

In *Schlesinger v Secretary of State for Communities and Local Government*,[60] an Orthodox Jew **12.30**
sought to quash an inspector's decision refusing planning permission for a loft extension to
her house, which she said she needed because of the size of her family. The inspector had
found that the applicant's personal circumstances were outweighed by the effect the extension would have on the character and appearance of the dwelling and surrounding area.
The applicant argued that the inspector should have been made aware of a policy document
which stated that the local authority should seek to ensure that religious beliefs were taken
into consideration in planning decisions. The court rejected that argument, on the basis that
the policy document had ceased to form part of the statutory development plan at the time
the matter was considered by the inspector.

In *Cherwell District Council v Vadivale* (1991) 6 PAD 433,[61] a planning inspector refused an **12.31**
appeal against the decision of a local planning authority not to grant planning permission
for the continuation of the use of an outhouse as a family Hindu Temple in Oxfordshire.
The building was used by large numbers of visitors, sometimes during antisocial hours,
for a wide range of meetings, celebrations, and festivals. The appellant acknowledged that
the activity at the Temple was not a prerequisite of Hinduism, but a result of his personal choice. The authority was concerned in particular about the general disturbance to
neighbours caused by those functions, and especially the coming and going of cars. Whilst
not 'under-rating' the importance of the appellant's way of life to him and his family, the
inspector found that planning permission should not be granted for the use. In particular,
the appellant's neighbours were 'entitled to expect peace and quiet, especially at weekends
and in the evenings'. Further, the appellant had not been discriminated against on religious grounds; the planning authority had legitimately dealt with the case on its planning
merits.[62]

In *South Bucks and Chiltern District Councils v Gold Hill Baptist Church*,[63] an application **12.32**
was made to erect a new church, with access, car-park, and landscaping on a prominent site
within the Metropolitan Green Belt in a wooded area which had a distinctive rural character.
The application failed. The site was high and prominent, it served as a buffer to the more
open spaces of the green belt and the increased volume of traffic could cause significant harm
to the living environment of the residents.

---

[59] Planning Policy Statement 1, para 16, provides: 'Development plans should promote development that
creates socially inclusive communities including suitable mixes of housing. Plan policies should: . . . take into
account the needs of all the community, including particular requirements relating to age, sex, ethnic background, religion, disability or income.'

[60] *Schlesinger v Secretary of State for Communities and Local Government* [2009] EWHC 973 (Admin).

[61] *Cherwell District Council v Vadivale* (1991) 6 PAD 433.

[62] See also *Brent LBC v Swaminarayan Hindu Mussion* (1987) 2 PAD 327, in which planning permission was
refused for a 'marble temple' of national significance 'with over 600 on-site parking places'.

[63] *South Bucks and Chiltern District Councils v Gold Hill Baptist Church* (1989) 4 PAD 290.

12.33 In *South Cambridgeshire District Council v East Anglian Roman Catholic Diocese*,[64] outline planning permission was refused for the erection of a church to seat 200 to 250 people in a Cambridgeshire village. The successful objections raised by the council were that a church on this site would take away from the general open appearance of the surroundings and that the intended car-park would affect the amenities of neighbours. The inspectors said: 'Noise, disturbance and fumes would be generated at times when the residents could reasonably expect maximum peace and quiet.'

12.34 Applications were granted, though with strict conditions, in *Carrick District Council v The Church of Jesus Christ of Latter Day Saints*[65] and in *East Hampshire District Council v The Waterlooville Trust*.[66] In the former case the application was to convert a former engineering workshop on an industrial site to use for public worship. Although the structure plan policy was to reserve the area for industrial use, this small departure from it was allowed in view of the recession. In the latter case a proposed religious meeting hall for The Brethren, which would be contrary to the structure and local plans for the area because it was development outside a built-up area, was allowed subject to parking, flooding, lighting, drainage, and fencing conditions.

12.35 *The Redeemed Christian Church of God v Lewisham LBC*[67] was an appeal against an enforcement notice prohibiting the continued use of a church as a place of worship. The issue was whether that use compromised the Council's intention to retain the site for employment use as a 'Defined Employment Area' under planning policy. The appellants were critical of the fact that the planning system did not allocate land in development plans specifically for use as places of worship. They pointed out that the absence of such allocated land has put churches at a severe disadvantage in their ability to secure suitable sites, particularly as they are in competition with developers who have substantial funding to pursue other uses. The inspector, whilst expressing his sympathy for this, considered it to be a matter that fell to be resolved through plan formulation and not planning appeals. In the circumstances of the case, the reasons proposed for departing from the allocated use of the land were not sufficiently strong. The unauthorized use of the land as a place of worship could not override the fact that the lawful use of the land was for industrial purposes.

12.36 Such cases are illustrative of the difficulties which religious groups may face in securing planning permission for a change of use. There is no right to a planning permission simply by dint of the fact that it is sought in furtherance of religious practice. However, unmet need for a particular use of land (such as for worship) can be a relevant and, in an appropriate case, determinative material planning consideration. The personal circumstances of an occupier are not to be ignored in the administration of planning control and they can be given direct effect as an exceptional or special circumstance where a specific case can be made out (for example see *Westminster City Council v Great Portland Estates*).[68] The reality is, however, that the planning authority must, as always, perform a delicate balancing act. As the inspector said in the *Brent* case:[69]

> A multi-cultural society must accept the aspirations of different ethnic groups to pursue their religious and cultural activities in appropriate forms of developments. However, the planning

---

[64] *South Cambridgeshire District Council v East Anglian Roman Catholic Diocese* (1986) 1 PAD 498.
[65] *Carrick District Council v The Church of Jesus Christ of Latter Day Saints* (1992) 7 PAD 438.
[66] *East Hampshire District Council v The Waterlooville Trust* (1992) 7 PAD 443.
[67] *The Redeemed Christian Church of God v Lewisham LBC* [2008] PAD 86.
[68] *Westminster City Council v Great Portland Estates* [1985] 1 AC 661, 670.
[69] *Brent LBC v Swaminarayan Hindu Mission* (1987) 2 PAD 327, 328.

system was designed to safeguard the general public interest. The needs of a particular group must be subject to planning policies, otherwise any semblance of control of land use would be continuously sacrificed to minority interests.

In *R (Hackney LBC) v Rottenberg*,[70] a local authority appealed against a decision of a Crown **12.37** Court allowing a Rabbi's appeal against his conviction for six offences of breaching a noise abatement notice relating to activities at a semi-detached house occupied as a school and synagogue. The notice had required him to 'immediately cease shouting chanting and jumping on internal floors to the property'. The Crown Court was not satisfied that the noise at the Rabbi's premises had been sufficiently great to constitute a statutory nuisance. The High Court held that, since the decision as to whether noise constituted a nuisance was a subjective decision, the Crown Court had been entitled to reject the opinion of the Council's environmental health officers to the effect that it was. It was observed, obiter, that in considering whether noise constituted a nuisance and whether there was a reasonable excuse for it, the fact that such noise was created in the course of religious worship, in premises registered and with planning permission for that use, would inevitably be a relevant consideration; however, if the service was conducted in such a way that a court, exercising its own judgment, found that a statutory nuisance existed, then the fact that the nuisance was created in such circumstances would be unlikely to amount to a defence of reasonable excuse, and a prosecution would not be disproportionate.

(3) Planning and Article 9 ECHR

In *Iskcon and ors v United Kingdom*,[71] the International Society for Krishna Consciousness **12.38** Ltd, part of the worldwide promoter of Vayishnavism, the worship of Krishna, alleged that service of a planning enforcement notice prohibiting the use of a manor house for the teaching of Krishna consciousness was disproportionate under Article 9 ECHR. The Commission rejected the complaint as inadmissible. It considered that Article 9 could not be used to circumvent existing planning legislation, provided that adequate weight was given to freedom of religion. The planning inspector, who had heard Iskcon's appeal against the enforcement notice, had done so here.[72] Further, in the circumstances of the case, proportionality did not demand the local planning authority to have dealt with the change of use of the manor house by imposing new conditions on the existing planning permission, rather than issuing an enforcement notice.

In *Vergos v Greece*,[73] the applicant, who belonged to a religious community called 'True **12.39** Orthodox Christians' ('TOC'), complained about a refusal by the Greek Council of State to approve his proposal to build a house of prayer for the community. The proposal would have required amendment to the local plan. Although the ECtHR accepted that the decision had interfered with the complainant's freedom to manifest his religion, the interference was prescribed by law and the refusal had pursued a legitimate aim, namely the protection of public order and the rights and freedoms of others, it decided that there was no breach of Article 9 ECHR. The applicant was the only follower of True Orthodox Christians in his

---

[70] *R (Hackney LBC) v Rottenberg* [2007] EWHC 166 (Admin), [2007] Env LR 24.
[71] *Iskcon and ors v UK* (1994) 18 EHRR CD 133.
[72] The Inspector's decision is reported as *International Society for Krishna Consciousness v Secretary of State and Hertsmere Borough Council* (1992) 64 P & CR 85.
[73] *Vergos v Greece* (2005) 41 EHRR 41.

village, and there was a house of prayer in a neighbouring town which covered the needs of that religious community.

12.40 In contrast, in *Manoussakis v Greece*,[74] Jehovah's Witnesses succeeded in a complaint that their conviction for having established and operated a place of worship without first obtaining authorizations required by domestic law breached Article 9 ECHR. Domestic law empowered the Minister of Education and Religious Affairs to assess, as a criterion which could constitute grounds for refusal of authorization, whether there was a 'real need' for the religious community in question to set up a church; and in practice the Minister could indefinitely defer or refuse authorization without any or any valid explanation. The Court found that Greece had tended to use the possibilities afforded by that power to impose rigid, indeed prohibitive, conditions on the practice of religious beliefs by certain non-orthodox movements. In the circumstances of the case, the Jehovah's Witnesses in question had been convicted in spite of the Minister's not having provided them with an express decision one way or the other. The impugned conviction had such a direct effect on the applicants' freedom of religion that it could not be regarded as proportionate.

12.41 In *Johannische Kirche v Germany*,[75] a Christian religious community claimed that its Article 9 rights had been breached by a refusal to allow it to build a chapel and cemetery on land which had been designated a 'protected zone' for environmental reasons. Since the community's religion was characterized by the belief that after death there was no further difference in social class and that all human beings would be equal before God, it was especially important to it that the cemetery was constructed in a particular way, including that all tombstones had to be laid on their side and be uniform in size. Rejecting the complaint as inadmissible, the ECtHR noted that the prohibition on building in the protected zone applied to persons of any religion and was not simply directed at the applicants. Article 9 ECHR did not afford the applicants a right to build a cemetery on a specially protected site. The refusal of planning permission was proportionate.

12.42 In *Mayor of the City of London v Samede and ors*, the Court granted an order for possession of land occupied by the 'Occupy' protest camp outside St Paul's Cathedral. The camp had resulted in a drop of about two-fifths in the numbers of those worshipping in the cathedral, and about the same fraction had been lost in the number of visitors, an important source of funds for the upkeep of the building and for its ministry. Lindblom J held that the effects of the camp had been such as to interfere seriously with the rights, under Article 9 of the Convention, of those who desired to worship in the cathedral, and took this into account as a factor in favour of granting relief. The nature of the right in Article 9 was, the Court held, 'not that one is entitled to worship only where the activities of others make it comfortable or convenient to do so, or where one is made to go by others in the exercise of their own Convention rights, but where one chooses to worship in accordance with the law'.[76] A challenge was made to the Judge's finding on Article 9 in an unsuccessful application for permission to appeal.[77]

---

[74] *Manoussakis v Greece* (1997) 23 EHRR 387.

[75] *Johannische Kirche v Germany* (App 41754/98) (2001).

[76] *The Mayor of the City of London v Samede and ors* [2012] EWHC 34 (QB), para 162.

[77] See *Samede* (n 76) para 34.

(4) Planning and the public sector equality duty

In exercising their functions in the planning field, as in others, local planning authorities **12.43**
and other public authorities must comply with the public sector equality duty (PSED) in
section 149 of the Equality Act 2010.[78] A general discussion of the PSED can be found elsewhere in this work.[79] A number of the important cases on the scope of the duty have arisen
in the planning context, albeit generally in the context of race rather than religious equality.
Discharge of the PSED is no less onerous in a planning case than it is in others, although
the circumstances in which the authority's performance of the duty has to be scrutinized
will inevitably be different.[80] The court must consider whether due regard has been paid to
the equality duty, and not simply whether the failure to have due regard to that duty was
Wednesbury unreasonable.[81]

In *Baker v Secretary of State for Communities and Local Government*, the Court of Appeal **12.44**
rejected an argument that, in deciding not to grant planning permission for the use of land
as gipsy sites, a planning inspector had failed to have due regard to the need to promote
equality of opportunity between persons of different racial groups as required by the then
section 71(1)(b) of the Race Relations Act 1976. The fact that the relevant sites were on
Green Belt land was a powerful countervailing factor which the inspector was entitled to
balance against the disadvantage suffered by gipsies arising out of the shortage of gipsy sites.
The PSED is not to achieve a result; it is a duty to have regard to the need to achieve the statutory goals,[82] and the question in every case is whether the decision-maker has in substance
had due regard to the relevant statutory need.[83] *Baker* was followed in *R (Isaacs) v Secretary
of State for Communities and Local Government*,[84] in which gipsies appealed against a refusal
of planning permission. Elias J held that, although the inspector had not specifically referred
to his statutory duty to comply with section 71 of the 1976 Act, that did not mean that he
had not taken it into account. In the circumstances of the case, the inspector had had due regard
to the requirements of section 71 by seeking properly to apply the planning policies which had
those considerations in mind.

---

[78] In short that they must have due regard to the need to (a) eliminate discrimination, harassment, victimization and any other conduct that is prohibited by or under this Act; (b) advance equality of opportunity between
persons who share a relevant protected characteristic and persons who do not share it; and (c) foster good relations between persons who share a relevant protected characteristic and persons who do not share it (Equality
Act 2010, s149(1)). 'Religion or belief' is one such protected characteristic (see Equality Act 2010, s 4).

[79] See Ch 6.

[80] *R (Coleman) v Barnet LBC* [2012] EWHC 3725 (Admin), para 71 *per* Lindblom J.

[81] *R (Child Poverty Action Group) v Secretary of State for Work and Pensions* [2011] EWHC 2616 (Admin),
paras 70–72.

[82] *Baker v Secretary of State for Communities and Local Government* [2008] EWCA Civ 141, [2009] PTSR
809, para 31 *per* Dyson LJ. The Court suggested (in paras 90–96) six principles applying to the discharge by a
public authority of its duty to have due regard to the goals set out in the Disability Discrimination Act 1995,
s 49A(1). First, the public authority must be made aware of its duty to have due regard to the identified goals
(para 90). Secondly, the due regard duty must be fulfilled before and at the time that a policy affecting people
with disabilities is being considered by the public authority (para 91). Thirdly, the duty 'must be exercised in
substance, with rigour and with an open mind'. It must be 'integrated within the discharge of the public functions of the authority', which is 'not a question of "ticking boxes"' (para 92). Fourthly, the duty is not delegable
(para 94). Fifthly, the duty is a continuing one (para 95). And sixthly, it is good practice for public authorities
to keep an adequate record 'showing that they had actually considered their disability equality duties and pon-
dered relevant questions' (para 96).

[83] *Baker* (n 82) para 37. See also *R (McCarthy) v Basildon District Council* [2009] EWCA Civ 13, [2009]
BLGR 1013.

[84] *R (Isaacs) v Secretary of State for Communities and Local Government* [2009] EWHC 557 (Admin).

12.45 In *R (Harris) v Haringey LBC*,[85] however, the Court of Appeal held that in granting planning permission for redevelopment of a site in an area made up predominantly of ethnic minority communities, a local authority had failed to discharge its duties under section 71 of the Race Relations Act 1976 because the requirements of section 71 had not formed, in substance, an integral part of the decision-making process. *Baker* and *Isaacs* were distinguished on the basis that they concerned the application of policies whose very purpose was to address the issues addressed in section 71(1). The local authority had engaged in no analysis of the material before it in the context of the duty.

12.46 In *R (Coleman) v Barnet LBC*,[86] the High Court held that a local planning authority had discharged the PSED in section 149 of the Equality Act 2010 in granting planning permission for the development of a school on land on which a garden centre had been situated. The garden centre was used regularly by the disabled and elderly. Lindblom J noted that, in their report, the local authority's officers recognized that the implications of the new proposal for the 2010 Act represented one of the main planning issues on which the members had to concentrate in making their decision. Members were conscious of the particular effects the development was likely to have on those with protected characteristics and conscious that due weight should be given to those effects in the decision that had to be made. The authority's members had in mind each of the needs in section 149(1) and discharged the duty in substance.

F. Charitable Status

12.47 Whether or not a religious body or organization has charitable status can matter a great deal. Whilst charity trustees have the same general powers as private trustees,[87] the common law applies differently to charitable trusts,[88] they are enforced and regulated by certain public authorities, and they are exempt from much taxation.

12.48 Under the Charities Act 2006, a charitable trust must satisfy three main requirements. First, the charitable trust must be for one of the charitable purposes listed in section 2(2) of the 2006 Act, one of which is the 'advancement of religion', or for one of the purposes recognized as charitable under the existing law before the 2006 Act came into force.[89] Secondly, the trust must be for the public benefit.[90] Thirdly, the trust must be for charitable purposes only.[91]

12.49 Whether a particular organization qualifies for charitable status on a religious basis has been the subject of a good deal of case law.

---

[85] *R (Harris) v Haringey LBC* [2010] EWCA Civ 703, [2011] PTSR 931.

[86] *R (Coleman) v Barnet LBC* [2012] EWHC 3725 (Admin).

[87] eg under the Trustee Act 1925 and Trustee Act 2000.

[88] For instance, the rule against perpetuity does not apply to charitable trusts. This means that charitable trusts can exist indefinitely and can accumulate income beyond the period of 21 years which limits private trusts. Charitable trusts can also, by dint of the *cy-pres* doctrine, be varied if they become obsolete. Thus if the purpose of a charitable gift becomes impossible or impractical to carry out, the fund is not held on an automatic resulting trust, as would be the case with a private trust. Rather, the court has the power to re-constitute the settlor's charitable intentions so that an alternative charity is benefited which is in accordance with the settlor's underlying intentions.

[89] Charities Act 2006, s 2(1), (2), (4), and (8).

[90] Charities Act 2006, ss 2(1) and 3.

[91] Charities Act 2006, s 1(1)(a).

Since the nineteenth century, charity law has taken a broad view of the kinds of religion that **12.50** might qualify for charitable status. It declined to make any distinction between one sect and another, and would only draw the line at a sect that would 'inculcate doctrines adverse to the very foundations of all religion' or that were 'subversive of all morality'.[92] The court would not take a view of whether the tenets of a particular creed were sound or not.

This liberal view left open the question of what creeds were to be regarded as religions. The **12.51** Charities Act 2006 has not provided a positive definition. It has added, however, that a religion for charitable purposes can include one that involves belief in more than one god or that does not believe in a god at all.[93] The minimum requirement seems to be some element of faith and worship by the adherents, and the recognition of a supernatural aspect that goes beyond purely intellectual inquiry. Thus in *Re South Place Ethical Society*,[94] it was held that the study of ethical principles and the cultivation of a rational religious sentiment were not charitable on the grounds of advancement of religion (although they were charitable on the grounds of advancement of education).

In *Church of Scientology's Application for Registration as a Charity*,[95] the Charity Commission **12.52** ruled that Scientology was not a religion for charitable purposes. As is well known, Scientology was founded on the research and writings of an individual and has no doctrine concerning God, although it asserts a supreme being to exist. The Commissioners held that it was fatal to the application that Scientology's central practices did not involve a kind of worship involving reverence or veneration, but were based instead on individual instruction akin to counselling. In so holding, the Commissioner applied *R v Registrar General, ex p Segerdal*,[96] in which the Court of Appeal held that, for the purposes of sections 2 and 3 of the PWRA 1855 (which required the Registrar-General to register as places of meeting for religious worship only such places as were in fact used for that purpose), 'religious worship' involved submission to and veneration of a superhuman being. Since the beliefs of Scientologists were concerned with a philosophy of life and of the spirit of man and did not involve submission to or veneration of a divine or superhuman being, their meetings and ceremonies therefore did not consist of 'religious worship'.

In *R (Hodkin) v Registrar General of Births Deaths and Marriages*,[97] the High Court held that **12.53** a registrar had been entitled to refuse to register a chapel owned by a Scientology college as a place of meeting for religious worship on the ground that it was not a place of religious worship under the PWRA 1855, since there had been no significant changes in the beliefs or practices of Scientologists since the decision in *Segerdal*. The claimants relied on changes since that case to the main congregational services of Scientology, which they claimed were services of worship, prayers, and a new form of wedding ceremony. The High Court held that although there was now greater acceptance of Scientology as a religion, the nature of Scientology itself had not changed for the statutory purposes. In the absence of a significant change in the way Scientologists 'worshipped', *Segerdal* remained binding.

---

[92] *Thornton v Howe* (1862) 31 Beav 14, 20; *Re Watson, Hobbs v Smith* [1973] 1 WLR 1472.
[93] Charities Act 2006, s 2(3)(a).
[94] *Re South Place Ethical Society* [1980] 1 WLR 1565.
[95] *Church of Scientology's Application for Registration as a Charity* [2005] WTLR 1151.
[96] *R v Registrar General, ex p Segerdal* [1970] 2 QB 697.
[97] *R (Hodkin) v Registrar General of Births Deaths and Marriages* [2012] EWHC 3635 (Admin).

12.54   The Court further rejected an argument in that case that the Human Rights Act 1998 and the Equality Act 2010 meant that the registration of Buddhist temples but not Scientology chapels as places of worship discriminated against Scientologists. The 1855 Act, it held, discriminated between those places where religion which involved worship undertook that worship and other places, but did not discriminate on the grounds of religion or the enjoyment of the right to freedom of worship, practice, and observance. Similarly, the 2010 Act did not relieve the court from the binding nature of *Segerdal*. Any discrimination that there might have been was required by the 1855 Act and therefore could not contravene the 2010 Act by virtue of section 191 and paragraph 1 of Schedule 22 to the Equality Act 2010.

12.55   Religion is advanced by pastoral and missionary work.[98] Thus trusts for the support of a religious order or community such as a monastery or a convent will advance religion.[99] Schemes to pay stipends or retirement benefits for clergy and their families may qualify for charitable status but not those that provide for ancillary workers in a religious organization.[100]

12.56   If, instead of engaging in good works (for example among the sick and the poor), the object of a religious order is merely sanctification by prayer and pious contemplation, it will lack the necessary element of demonstrable public benefit and so will not be charitable. In *Coats v Gilmour*,[101] the income of a trust fund was given upon trust for the Carmelite Priory. The Carmelite Priory was a convent comprising an association of strictly cloistered and purely contemplative nuns who devoted themselves entirely to worship, prayers, and meditations within the four walls of their cloister, and performed no works, and engaged in no activities whatever for the benefit of anyone outside their own association, but who were regarded, in the belief and teaching of the Roman Catholic Church, as causing, by means of their private worship, prayers, and meditations, the intervention of God to bring about the spiritual improvement of members of the public (both Catholic and non-Catholic) outside those walls, and also as providing an example of self-denial and concentration on the life of the spirit tending to the spiritual edification of such members of the public. The House of Lords held, that neither intercessory prayer nor edification were within the category of public benefit, nor could it be said that, as qualification for admission to the community was not limited to any private group of persons, but was open to any person being a female Roman Catholic who had the necessary vocation, an element of public benefit was thus supplied, because there is no authority to the effect that it can be a valid charitable purpose to assist persons to do something which cannot be shown to have any public utility.

12.57   In *Re Watson (Deceased)*,[102] it was held that a religious charity can only be shown not to be for the public benefit if its doctrines are adverse to the foundations of all religion and subversive of all morality. Two persons were members of a small group of undenominational Christians. From 1942 onwards one largely financed the publication by the other of religious books and tracts. The financier died in 1968 and the author in 1969. By her will one gave the other certain gifts on trust 'for the continuance of the work of God as it has been maintained by

---

[98]   *Church of Scientology's Application for Registration as a Charity* [2005] WTLR 1151, 1117.
[99]   See eg *Re Banfield* [1968] 1 WLR 846.
[100]   *Hester v CIR* (2004) 7 ITELR 420 (New Zealand).
[101]   *Coats v Gilmour* [1949] AC 426.
[102]   *Re Watson (Deceased)* [1973] 1 WLR 1472.

H and myself since 1942 by God's enabling... in propagating the truth as given in the Holy Bible'. Her will provided that the other should provide in his will for a successor, but, as the other had predeceased her, this could not be done. The executor took out a summons to determine whether there was a valid charitable trust. The next-of-kin contended that it failed for impracticability and that there was insufficient evidence of public benefit. Expert evidence showed that the works, while unlikely to extend knowledge of the Christian religion, might confirm the religious opinions of the group for whom they were produced and were certainly not adverse to religion or subversive of morality. Letters from various parts of the world showed that the publications had a certain readership and that the readers were edified by them. Plowman J held that the trust was for the publication and distribution to the public of H's religious works, and was therefore not impracticable; and it was clearly for purposes of a religious nature and so was to be assumed to be for the public benefit unless shown to be adverse to the very foundations of religion and subversive of all morality.

Charity Commission guidance: 'The Advancement of Religion for the Public Benefit' (December 2008) has caused some controversy in its application. There are proceedings before the First Tier Tribunal about whether the Plymouth Brethren should have charitable status, and the matter has been raised in Parliamentary Committees. **12.58**

The celebration of masses for the dead is charitable if they are to be said in public and if the moneys given are to provide stipends for the priests saying the masses.[103] The improvement of musical services in a church,[104] and a gift simply 'for God's work'[105] have also been held charitable. **12.59**

While the upkeep of a particular tomb or vault in a churchyard is not charitable,[106] the repair of the whole churchyard or burial ground is charitable,[107] even if it is restricted to members of a particular religious sect.[108] The repair of all the headstones in a churchyard,[109] or of the churchyard and a specified monument,[110] is also charitable, and so is the upkeep of the whole or any part of a church, including a memorial window,[111] or a specific monument or vault in it.[112] **12.60**

G. Prisons

In *R (Bashir) v The Independent Adjudicator*, a Muslim prisoner undertaking a personal fast was unable to provide a sufficiently large urine sample for the purposes of mandatory drug testing and, as a result, was convicted for failure to obey a lawful order contrary to the Prison Rules. It was found that the requirement to provide a urine sample constituted an interference with his Article 9 rights.[113] The Court rejected the argument that the claimant should **12.61**

---

[103] *Re Caus* [1934] Ch 162; *Re Heatherington* [1990] Ch 1.
[104] *Re Royce* [1940] Ch 514; but cf *Re Woodhams* [1981] 1 WLR 493, 496 (tea for choirboys).
[105] *Re Barker's WT* (1948) 64 TLR 273.
[106] *Hoare v Osborne* (1866) LR 1 Eq 585.
[107] *Re Eighmie* [1935] Ch 524.
[108] *Re Manser* [1905] 1 Ch 68 (Society of Friends).
[109] *Re Pardoe* [1906] 2 Ch 184.
[110] *Re Eighmie* [1935] Ch 524.
[111] *Re King* [1923] 1 Ch 243; *Re Hooper* [1932] 1 Ch 38.
[112] *Hoare v Osbourne* (1866) LR 1 Eq 585.
[113] *R (Bashir) v The Independent Adjudicator* [2011] HRLR 30 (QB).

be treated as having voluntarily accepted the restrictions implicit in a prison environment by committing the offences for which he had been convicted.[114]

12.62   As to Strasbourg jurisprudence, in *Jakóbski v Poland*,[115] it was held that the failure to provide a prisoner with a meat free diet in prison in accordance with his religious precepts violated his rights under Article 9 ECHR. The ECtHR was prepared to accept that a decision to make special arrangements for one prisoner within the system could have financial implications for the custodial institution and therefore indirectly for the quality of treatment of other prisoners. However, it found that the state had failed to strike a fair balance between the interests of the prison authorities and other prisoners, and those of the applicant, namely the right to manifest his religion through the observance of the rules of the Buddhist religion. The Court was not persuaded that the provision of a vegetarian diet would have entailed any disruption to the management of the prison or led to any decline in the standards of the meals to other prisoners. It referred to the recommendation of the Committee of Ministers on the European Prison Rules that prisoners should be provided with food that takes account of their religion.

12.63   In *Kovalkovs v Latvia*,[116] a prisoner complained that he was prevented from adequately performing the fundamental religious rituals of his religion because he was placed in a cell with other prisoners and his incense sticks were taken away. The ECtHR held:

> The Court similarly to its approach in the...Jakóbski case, is also prepared to accept that financial implications for a custodial institution which can have an indirect impact on the quality of treatment of other inmates can serve as a legitimate aim, namely, the protection of the rights and freedoms of others...Another aspect to be taken into account in that regard is other prisoners' wish not to be disturbed by the applicant's performance of religious rituals. Concerning the confiscation of the incense sticks, the legitimate aim is the protection of the rights and freedoms of others and public safety by limiting the types of objects that may be kept in prison cells.

12.64   It concluded that, taking account of the margin of appreciation, the impugned restrictions of the applicant's freedom of religion were proportionate to the legitimate aims sought to be achieved. As to the applicant's wish to perform religious rituals in isolation from other prisoners, what had to be balanced was the degree of interference with the applicant's right to manifest his religion and the rights of other prisoners. The Court noted that the applicant had on at least one occasion been offered alternative premises but had refused. It considered that having to pray, read religious literature and mediate in the presence of others was an inconvenience almost inescapable in prisons, yet one which did not go to the very essence of the freedom to manifest one's religion. As to the burning of incense sticks, the obligation to observe this religious tradition depended on the circumstances of the person in question, which the applicant did not dispute. The burning of sticks, which typically created a powerful odour, could also be disturbing to other prisoners. The Court considered that restricting

---

[114] Bashir (n 115) para 22. The defendant had sought to rely on Lord Bingham's observation in *R (Begum) v Headteacher and Governors of Denbigh High School* [2007] 1 AC 100 (HL), para 23 that:

> The Strasbourg institutions have not been at all ready to find an interference with the right to manifest religious belief in practice or observance where a person has voluntarily accepted an employment or role which does not accommodate that practice or observance and there are other means open to the person to practise or observe his or her religion without undue hardship or inconvenience.

[115] *Jakóbski v Poland* (App 18429/06) (2010).
[116] *Kovalkovs v Lativa* (App 35021/01) (2012).

the list of items permitted for storage in prison cells by excluding items which were not essential for manifesting a prisoner's religion was a proportionate response to the necessity to protect the rights and freedoms of others.

H. Animal Slaughter

Animal slaughter can engage religious rights in a number of ways. First, religious tenets **12.65** may require slaughter to be carried out using a particular method. The Welfare of Animals (Slaughter or Killing) Regulations 1995 makes specific provision for the slaughter of animals by the Jewish and Muslim method and exempts Jews and Muslims from the general provisions relations to the stunning and killing of animals.[117]

In *Jewish Liturgical Association Cha'are Shalom Ve Tsedek v France*,[118] JLA, an Orthodox **12.66** Jewish association, complained of a violation of Article 9 in conjunction with Article 14 ECHR arising from the refusal to grant it approval to carry out ritual slaughter in a manner acceptable to ultra-Orthodox beliefs. The French authorities had refused JLA's application on the basis that ACIP was the organization authorized for this purpose and exempted from the domestic statutory requirement that animals were to be stunned prior to slaughter.

The ECtHR held, by a majority, that by conferring sole authority on ACIP, France had not **12.67** violated JLA's rights under Articles 9 and 14. In appointing ACIP as the only permitted ritual slaughterer, France had given practical effect to its undertaking to ensure that there was no violation of the right to manifest religious beliefs through the observance of rites. Further, the method of slaughter was not in dispute and there was no reason why JLA could not reach agreement with ACIP in relation to the inspection and cleaning processes. JLA also imported meat for its members so that it was not necessary for it to carry out its own slaughtering in France.

Secondly, an animal may have a special religious significance. The case of *R (Swami* **12.68** *Suryananda) v Welsh Ministers*[119] concerned the slaughter of a bullock of special religious significance to the Krishna community in Wales. The community challenged a decision not to except the bullock from a policy of slaughtering cattle testing positive for bovine tuberculosis. The challenge was successful at first instance. Hickinbottom J held that the Welsh Assembly had not properly identified a legitimate objective to be balanced against the rights of the community. An appeal was allowed by the Court of Appeal, which held that the interference with religious rights was justified.

---

[117] Welfare of Animals (Slaughter or Killing) Regulations 1995, SI 1995/731, reg 22 and Sch 12. Derogations from provisions relating to the stunning and killing of animals are permitted by the European Convention for the Protection of Animals for Slaughter [1988] OJ L137/0027–0038 and Council Directive (EC) 93/119.

[118] *Jewish Liturgical Association Cha'are Shalom Ve Tsedek v France* (App 27417/95) (2000) 9 BHRC 27.

[119] *R (Swami Suryananda) v Welsh Ministers* [2007] EWCA Civ 893.

APPENDICES

APPENDIX I

United Nations Standards and Protections

The Universal Declaration of Human Rights (extracts)

Article 2

Everyone is entitled to all the rights and freedoms set forth in this Declaration, without distinction of any kind, such as race, colour, sex, language, religion, political or other opinion, national or social origin, property, birth or other status. Furthermore, no distinction shall be made on the basis of the political, jurisdictional or international status of the country or territory to which a person belongs, whether it be independent, trust, non-self-governing or under any other limitation of sovereignty.

...

Article 18

Everyone has the right to freedom of thought, conscience and religion; this right includes freedom to change his religion or belief, and freedom, either alone or in community with others and in public or private, to manifest his religion or belief in teaching, practice, worship and observance.

International Covenant on Civil and Political Rights (extracts)

Article 2

1. Each State Party to the present Covenant undertakes to respect and to ensure to all individuals within its territory and subject to its jurisdiction the rights recognized in the present Covenant, without distinction of any kind, such as race, colour, sex, language, religion, political or other opinion, national or social origin, property, birth or other status.
2. Where not already provided for by existing legislative or other measures, each State Party to the present Covenant undertakes to take the necessary steps, in accordance with its constitutional processes and with the provisions of the present Covenant, to adopt such legislative or other measures as may be necessary to give effect to the rights recognized in the present Covenant.
3. Each State Party to the present Covenant undertakes:
   (a) To ensure that any person whose rights or freedoms as herein recognized are violated shall have an effective remedy, notwithstanding that the violation has been committed by persons acting in an official capacity;
   (b) To ensure that any person claiming such a remedy shall have his right thereto determined by competent judicial, administrative or legislative authorities, or by any other competent authority provided for by the legal system of the State, and to develop the possibilities of judicial remedy;
   (c) To ensure that the competent authorities shall enforce such remedies when granted.

...

Article 18

1. Everyone shall have the right to freedom of thought, conscience and religion. This right shall include freedom to have or to adopt a religion or belief of his choice, and freedom, either individually or in community with others and in public or private, to manifest his religion or belief in worship, observance, practice and teaching.

2. No one shall be subject to coercion which would impair his freedom to have or to adopt a religion or belief of his choice.

3. Freedom to manifest one's religion or beliefs may be subject only to such limitations as are prescribed by law and are necessary to protect public safety, order, health, or morals or the fundamental rights and freedoms of others.

4. The States Parties to the present Covenant undertake to have respect for the liberty of parents and, when applicable, legal guardians to ensure the religious and moral education of their children in conformity with their own convictions.

…

Article 27

In those States in which ethnic, religious or linguistic minorities exist, persons belonging to such minorities shall not be denied the right, in community with the other members of their group, to enjoy their own culture, to profess and practise their own religion, or to use their own language.

The UN Declaration on the Elimination of All Forms of Intolerance and of Discrimination based on Religion or Belief 1981 (extract)

Article 1

1. Everyone shall have the right to freedom of thought, conscience and religion. This right shall include freedom to have a religion or whatever belief of his choice, and freedom, either individually or in community with others and in public or private, to manifest his religion or belief in worship, observance, practice and teaching.

2. No one shall be subject to coercion which would impair his freedom to have a religion or belief of his choice.

3. Freedom to manifest one's religion or beliefs may be subject only to such limitations as are prescribed by law and are necessary to protect public safety, order, health or morals or the fundamental rights and freedoms of others.

Article 2

1. No one shall be subject to discrimination by any State, institution, group of persons, or person on grounds of religion or other beliefs.

2. For the purposes of the present Declaration, the expression 'intolerance and discrimination based on religion or belief' means any distinction, exclusion, restriction or preference based on religion or belief and having as its purpose or as its effect nullification or impairment of the recognition, enjoyment or exercise of human rights and fundamental freedoms on an equal basis.

Article 3

Discrimination between human beings on grounds of religion or belief constitutes an affront to human dignity and a disavowal of the principles of the Charter of the United Nations, and shall be condemned as a violation of the human rights and fundamental freedoms proclaimed in the Universal Declaration of Human Rights and enunciated in detail in the International Covenants on Human Rights, and as an obstacle to friendly and peaceful relations between nations.

Article 4

1. All States shall take effective measures to prevent and eliminate discrimination on the grounds of religion or belief in the recognition, exercise and enjoyment of human rights and fundamental freedoms in all fields of civil, economic, political, social and cultural life.

2. All States shall make all efforts to enact or rescind legislation where necessary to prohibit any such discrimination, and to take all appropriate measures to combat intolerance on the grounds of religion or other beliefs in this matter.

Article 5

1. The parents or, as the case may be, the legal guardians of the child have the right to organize the life within the family in accordance with their religion or belief and bearing in mind the moral education in which they believe the child should be brought up.

2. Every child shall enjoy the right to have access to education in the matter of religion or belief in accordance with the wishes of his parents or, as the case may be, legal guardians, and shall not be compelled to receive teaching on religion or belief against the wishes of his parents or legal guardians, the best interests of the child being the guiding principle.

3. The child shall be protected from any form of discrimination on the ground of religion or belief. He shall be brought up in a spirit of understanding, tolerance, friendship among peoples, peace and universal brotherhood, respect for freedom of religion or belief of others, and in full consciousness that his energy and talents should be devoted to the service of his fellow men.

4. In the case of a child who is not under the care either of his parents or of legal guardians, due account shall be taken of their expressed wishes or of any other proof of their wishes in the matter of religion or belief, the best interests of the child being the guiding principle.

5. Practices of a religion or beliefs in which a child is brought up must not be injurious to his physical or mental health or to his full development, taking into account article 1, paragraph 3, of the present Declaration.

Article 6

In accordance with article 1 of the present Declaration and subject to the provisions of article 1, paragraph 3, the right to freedom of thought, conscience, religion or belief shall include, inter alia, the following freedoms:

(a) To worship or assemble in connection with a religion or belief, and to establish and maintain places for these purposes;

(b) To establish and maintain appropriate charitable or humanitarian institutions;

(c) To make, acquire and use to an adequate extent the necessary articles and materials related to the rites or customs of a religion or belief;

(d) To write, issue and disseminate relevant publications in these areas;

(e) To teach a religion or belief in places suitable for these purposes;

(f) To solicit and receive voluntary financial and other contributions from individuals and institutions;

(g) To train, appoint, elect or designate by succession appropriate leaders called for by the requirements and standards of any religion or belief;

(h) To observe days of rest and to celebrate holidays and ceremonies in accordance with the precepts of one's religion or belief;

(i) To establish and maintain communications with individuals and communities in matters of religion and belief at the national and international levels.

Article 7

The rights and freedoms set forth in the present Declaration shall be accorded in national legislation in such a manner that everyone shall be able to avail himself of such rights and freedoms in practice.

Article 8

Nothing in the present Declaration shall be construed as restricting or derogating from any right defined in the Universal Declaration of Human Rights and the International Covenants on Human Rights.

The UN Convention on the Rights of the Child (extracts)

Article 2

1. States Parties shall respect and ensure the rights set forth in the present Convention to each child within their jurisdiction without discrimination of any kind, irrespective of the child's or his or

her parent's or legal guardian's race, colour, sex, language, religion, political or other opinion, national, ethnic or social origin, property, disability, birth or other status.

2. States Parties shall take all appropriate measures to ensure that the child is protected against all forms of discrimination or punishment on the basis of the status, activities, expressed opinions, or beliefs of the child's parents, legal guardians, or family members.

...

Article 14

1. States Parties shall respect the right of the child to freedom of thought, conscience and religion.
2. States Parties shall respect the rights and duties of the parents and, when applicable, legal guardians, to provide direction to the child in the exercise of his or her right in a manner consistent with the evolving capacities of the child.
3. Freedom to manifest one's religion or beliefs may be subject only to such limitations as are prescribed by law and are necessary to protect public safety, order, health, or morals or the fundamental rights and freedoms of others.

APPENDIX II

European Standards and Protections

The European Convention on Human Rights (extracts)

Article 9
1. Everyone has the right to freedom of thought, conscience and religion; this right includes freedom to change his religion or belief, and freedom, either alone or in community with others and in public or private, to manifest his religion or belief, in worship, teaching, practice and observance.
2. Freedom to manifest one's religion or beliefs shall be subject only to such limitations as are prescribed by law and are necessary in a democratic society in the interests of public safety, for the protection of public order, health or morals, or the protection of the rights and freedoms of others.

. . .

Article 14
The enjoyment of the rights and freedoms set forth in this Convention shall be secured without discrimination on any ground such as sex, race, colour, language, religion, political or other opinion, national or social origin, association with a national minority, property, birth or other status.

The Treaty on the Functioning of the European Union (extracts)

Article 10
In defining and implementing its policies and activities, the Union shall aim to combat discrimination based on sex, racial or ethnic origin, religion or belief, disability, age or sexual orientation.

. . .

Article 17
1. The Union respects and does not prejudice the status under national law of churches and religious associations or communities in the Member States.
2. The Union equally respects the status under national law of philosophical and non-confessional organisations.
3. Recognising their identity and their specific contribution, the Union shall maintain an open, transparent and regular dialogue with these churches and organisations.

The Charter of Fundamental Rights of the European Union (extracts)

Article 10
Freedom of thought, conscience and religion
1. Everyone has the right to freedom of thought, conscience and religion. This right includes freedom to change religion or belief and freedom, either alone or in community with others and in public or in private, to manifest religion or belief, in worship, teaching, practice and observance.

2. The right to conscientious objection is recognised, in accordance with the national laws governing the exercise of this right.

...

Article 21

Non-discrimination

1. Any discrimination based on any ground such as sex, race, colour, ethnic or social origin, genetic features, language, religion or belief, political or any other opinion, membership of a national minority, property, birth, disability, age or sexual orientation shall be prohibited.
2. Within the scope of application of the Treaties and without prejudice to any of their specific provisions, any discrimination on grounds of nationality shall be prohibited.

Article 22

Cultural, religious and linguistic diversity

The Union shall respect cultural, religious and linguistic diversity.

APPENDIX III

Domestic Standards and Protections

The Human Rights Act 1998 (extracts)

Section 6
(1) It is unlawful for a public authority to act in a way which is incompatible with a Convention right.
(2) Subsection (1) does not apply to an act if—
  (a) as the result of one or more provisions of primary legislation, the authority could not have acted differently; or
  (b) in the case of one or more provisions of, or made under, primary legislation which cannot be read or given effect in a way which is compatible with the Convention rights, the authority was acting so as to give effect to or enforce those provisions.
(3) In this section 'public authority' includes—
  (a) a court or tribunal, and
  (b) any person certain of whose functions are functions of a public nature,
  but does not include either House of Parliament or a person exercising functions in connection with proceedings in Parliament.
(4) …
(5) In relation to a particular act, a person is not a public authority by virtue only of subsection (3)(b) if the nature of the act is private.
(6) 'An act' includes a failure to act but does not include a failure to—
  (a) introduce in, or lay before, Parliament a proposal for legislation; or
  (b) make any primary legislation or remedial order.

…

Section 13
(1) If a court's determination of any question arising under this Act might affect the exercise by a religious organisation (itself or its members collectively) of the Convention right to freedom of thought, conscience and religion, it must have particular regard to the importance of that right.
(2) In this section 'court' includes a tribunal.

PART 2
EQUALITY: KEY CONCEPTS

The Equality Act 2010 (extracts)

Chapter 1
Protected characteristics

4 The protected characteristics
The following characteristics are protected characteristics—
  age;
  disability;
  gender reassignment;

marriage and civil partnership;
pregnancy and maternity;
race;
religion or belief;
sex;
sexual orientation.
...

10 Religion or belief

(1) Religion means any religion and a reference to religion includes a reference to a lack of religion.

(2) Belief means any religious or philosophical belief and a reference to belief includes a reference to a lack of belief.

(3) In relation to the protected characteristic of religion or belief—

    (a) a reference to a person who has a particular protected characteristic is a reference to a person of a particular religion or belief;

    (b) a reference to persons who share a protected characteristic is a reference to persons who are of the same religion or belief.

...

Chapter 2
Prohibited conduct

13 Direct discrimination

(1) A person (A) discriminates against another (B) if, because of a protected characteristic, A treats B less favourably than A treats or would treat others.

...

19 Indirect discrimination

(1) A person (A) discriminates against another (B) if A applies to B a provision, criterion or practice which is discriminatory in relation to a relevant protected characteristic of B's.

(2) For the purposes of subsection (1), a provision, criterion or practice is discriminatory in relation to a relevant protected characteristic of B's if—

    (a) A applies, or would apply, it to persons with whom B does not share the characteristic,

    (b) it puts, or would put, persons with whom B shares the characteristic at a particular disadvantage when compared with persons with whom B does not share it,

    (c) it puts, or would put, B at that disadvantage, and

    (d) A cannot show it to be a proportionate means of achieving a legitimate aim.

(3) The relevant protected characteristics are—

age;
disability;
gender reassignment;
marriage and civil partnership;
race;
religion or belief;
sex;
sexual orientation.

...

23 Comparison by reference to circumstances

(1) On a comparison of cases for the purposes of section 13, 14, or 19 there must be no material difference between the circumstances relating to each case.

...

24 Irrelevance of alleged discriminator's characteristics

(1) For the purpose of establishing a contravention of this Act by virtue of section 13(1), it does not matter whether A has the protected characteristic.

...

25 References to particular strands of discrimination

...

(7) Religious or belief-related discrimination is—
    (a) discrimination within section 13 because of religion or belief;
    (b) discrimination within section 19 where the protected characteristic is religion or belief.

. . .

26 Harassment

(1) A person (A) harasses another (B) if—
    (a) A engages in unwanted conduct related to a relevant protected characteristic, and
    (b) the conduct has the purpose or effect of—
        (i) violating B's dignity, or
        (ii) creating an intimidating, hostile, degrading, humiliating or offensive environment for B.

    . . .

(4) In deciding whether conduct has the effect referred to in subsection (1)(b), each of the following must be taken into account—
    (a) the perception of B;
    (b) the other circumstances of the case;
    (c) whether it is reasonable for the conduct to have that effect.

(5) The relevant protected characteristics are—
    age;
    disability;
    gender reassignment;
    race;
    religion or belief;
    sex;
    sexual orientation.

27 Victimisation

(1) A person (A) victimises another person (B) if A subjects B to a detriment because—
    (a) B does a protected act, or
    (b) A believes that B has done, or may do, a protected act.

(2) Each of the following is a protected act—
    (a) bringing proceedings under this Act;
    (b) giving evidence or information in connection with proceedings under this Act;
    (c) doing any other thing for the purposes of or in connection with this Act;
    (d) making an allegation (whether or not express) that A or another person has contravened this Act.

(3) Giving false evidence or information, or making a false allegation, is not a protected act if the evidence or information is given, or the allegation is made, in bad faith.

(4) This section applies only where the person subjected to a detriment is an individual.

. . .

PART 3

SERVICES AND PUBILC FUNCTIONS

PART 4

PREMISES

PART 5

WORK

PART 6

EDUCATION

PART 7

ASSOCIATIONS

PART 8

PROHIBITED CONDUCT: ANCILLARY

PART 9
ENFORCEMENT

Chapter 1
Introductory

113 Proceedings
(1) Proceedings relating to a contravention of this Act must be brought in accordance with this Part.
(2) Subsection (1) does not apply to proceedings under Part 1 of the Equality Act 2006.
(3) Subsection (1) does not prevent—
    (a) a claim for judicial review;
    (b) proceedings under the Immigration Acts;
    (c) proceedings under the Special Immigration Appeals Commission Act 1997;
    (d) in Scotland, an application to the supervisory jurisdiction of the Court of Session.
(4) This section is subject to any express provision of this Act conferring jurisdiction on a court or tribunal.
...

Chapter 2
Civil courts

114 Jurisdiction
(1) A county court or, in Scotland, the sheriff has jurisdiction to determine a claim relating to—
    (a) a contravention of Part 3 (services and public functions);
    (b) a contravention of Part 4 (premises);
    (c) a contravention of Part 6 (education);
    (d) a contravention of Part 7 (associations);
    (e) a contravention of section 108, 111 or 112 that relates to Part 3, 4, 6 or 7.
(2) Subsection (1)(a) does not apply to a claim within section 115.
(3) Subsection (1)(c) does not apply to a claim within section 116.
(4) Subsection (1)(d) does not apply to a contravention of section 106.
(5) For the purposes of proceedings on a claim within subsection (1)(a)—
    (a) a decision in proceedings on a claim mentioned in section 115(1) that an act is a contravention of Part 3 is binding;
    (b) it does not matter whether the act occurs outside the United Kingdom.
(6) The county court or sheriff—
    (a) must not grant an interim injunction or interdict unless satisfied that no criminal matter would be prejudiced by doing so;
    (b) must grant an application to stay or sist proceedings under subsection (1) on grounds of prejudice to a criminal matter unless satisfied the matter will not be prejudiced.
(7) In proceedings in England and Wales on a claim within subsection (1), the power under section 63(1) of the County Courts Act 1984 (appointment of assessors) must be exercised unless the judge is satisfied that there are good reasons for not doing so.
(8) In proceedings in Scotland on a claim within subsection (1), the power under rule 44.3 of Schedule 1 to the Sheriff Court (Scotland) Act 1907 (appointment of assessors) must be exercised unless the sheriff is satisfied that there are good reasons for not doing so.
(9) The remuneration of an assessor appointed by virtue of subsection (8) is to be at a rate determined by the Lord President of the Court of Session.
...

116 Education cases
(1) A claim is within this section if it may be made to—
    (a) the First-tier Tribunal in accordance with Part 2 of Schedule 17,
    (b) the Special Educational Needs Tribunal for Wales in accordance with Part 2 of that Schedule, or

(c) an Additional Support Needs Tribunal for Scotland in accordance with Part 3 of that Schedule.

(2) A claim is also within this section if it must be made in accordance with appeal arrangements within the meaning of Part 4 of that Schedule.

(3) Schedule 17 (disabled pupils: enforcement) has effect.

...

118 Time limits

(1) Subject to section 140A proceedings on a claim within section 114 may not be brought after the end of—

    (a) the period of 6 months starting with the date of the act to which the claim relates, or

    (b) such other period as the county court or sheriff thinks just and equitable.

    ...

(6) For the purposes of this section—

    (a) conduct extending over a period is to be treated as done at the end of the period;

    (b) failure to do something is to be treated as occurring when the person in question decided on it.

(7) In the absence of evidence to the contrary, a person (P) is to be taken to decide on failure to do something—

    (a) when P does an act inconsistent with doing it, or

    (b) if P does no inconsistent act, on the expiry of the period in which P might reasonably have been expected to do it.

...

119 Remedies

(1) This section applies if a county court or the sheriff finds that there has been a contravention of a provision referred to in section 114(1).

(2) The county court has power to grant any remedy which could be granted by the High Court—

    (a) in proceedings in tort;

    (b) on a claim for judicial review.

    ...

(4) An award of damages may include compensation for injured feelings (whether or not it includes compensation on any other basis).

(5) Subsection (6) applies if the county court or sheriff—

    (a) finds that a contravention of a provision referred to in section 114(1) is established by virtue of section 19, but

    (b) is satisfied that the provision, criterion or practice was not applied with the intention of discriminating against the claimant or pursuer.

(6) The county court or sheriff must not make an award of damages unless it first considers whether to make any other disposal.

(7) The county court or sheriff must not grant a remedy other than an award of damages or the making of a declaration unless satisfied that no criminal matter would be prejudiced by doing so.

Chapter 3
Employment tribunals

120 Jurisdiction

(1) An employment tribunal has, subject to section 121, jurisdiction to determine a complaint relating to—

    (a) a contravention of Part 5 (work);

    (b) a contravention of section 108, 111 or 112 that relates to Part 5.

(2) An employment tribunal has jurisdiction to determine an application by a responsible person (as defined by section 61) for a declaration as to the rights of that person and a worker in relation to a dispute about the effect of a non-discrimination rule.

(3) An employment tribunal also has jurisdiction to determine an application by the trustees or managers of an occupational pension scheme for a declaration as to their rights and those of a member in relation to a dispute about the effect of a non-discrimination rule.

(4) An employment tribunal also has jurisdiction to determine a question that—
  (a) relates to a non-discrimination rule, and
  (b) is referred to the tribunal by virtue of section 122.
(5) In proceedings before an employment tribunal on a complaint relating to a breach of a non-discrimination rule, the employer—
  (a) is to be treated as a party, and
  (b) is accordingly entitled to appear and be heard.
(6) Nothing in this section affects such jurisdiction as the High Court, a county court, the Court of Session or the sheriff has in relation to a non-discrimination rule.
(7) Subsection (1)(a) does not apply to a contravention of section 53 in so far as the act complained of may, by virtue of an enactment, be subject to an appeal or proceedings in the nature of an appeal.
(8) In subsection (1), the references to Part 5 do not include a reference to section 60(1).
...

123 Time limits
(1) Subject to section 140A proceedings on a complaint within section 120 may not be brought after the end of—
  (a) the period of 3 months starting with the date of the act to which the complaint relates, or
  (b) such other period as the employment tribunal thinks just and equitable.
(2) Proceedings may not be brought in reliance on section 121(1) after the end of—
  (a) the period of 6 months starting with the date of the act to which the proceedings relate, or
  (b) such other period as the employment tribunal thinks just and equitable.
(3) For the purposes of this section—
  (a) conduct extending over a period is to be treated as done at the end of the period;
  (b) failure to do something is to be treated as occurring when the person in question decided on it.
(4) In the absence of evidence to the contrary, a person (P) is to be taken to decide on failure to do something—
  (a) when P does an act inconsistent with doing it, or
  (b) if P does no inconsistent act, on the expiry of the period in which P might reasonably have been expected to do it.

124 Remedies: general
(1) This section applies if an employment tribunal finds that there has been a contravention of a provision referred to in section 120(1).
(2) The tribunal may—
  (a) make a declaration as to the rights of the complainant and the respondent in relation to the matters to which the proceedings relate;
  (b) order the respondent to pay compensation to the complainant;
  (c) make an appropriate recommendation.
(3) An appropriate recommendation is a recommendation that within a specified period the respondent takes specified steps for the purpose of obviating or reducing the adverse effect of any matter to which the proceedings relate—
  (a) on the complainant;
  (b) on any other person.
(4) Subsection (5) applies if the tribunal—
  (a) finds that a contravention is established by virtue of section 19, but
  (b) is satisfied that the provision, criterion or practice was not applied with the intention of discriminating against the complainant.
(5) It must not make an order under subsection (2)(b) unless it first considers whether to act under subsection (2)(a) or (c).
(6) The amount of compensation which may be awarded under subsection (2)(b) corresponds to the amount which could be awarded by a county court or the sheriff under section 119.
(7) If a respondent fails, without reasonable excuse, to comply with an appropriate recommendation in so far as it relates to the complainant, the tribunal may—

(a) if an order was made under subsection (2)(b), increase the amount of compensation to be paid;

(b) if no such order was made, make one.

...

Chapter 5
Miscellaneous

136 Burden of proof

(1) This section applies to any proceedings relating to a contravention of this Act.

(2) If there are facts from which the court could decide, in the absence of any other explanation, that a person (A) contravened the provision concerned, the court must hold that the contravention occurred.

(3) But subsection (2) does not apply if A shows that A did not contravene the provision.

...

Part 14
General exceptions

193 Charities

(1) A person does not contravene this Act only by restricting the provision of benefits to persons who share a protected characteristic if—
   (a) the person acts in pursuance of a charitable instrument, and
   (b) the provision of the benefits is within subsection (2).

(2) The provision of benefits is within this subsection if it is—
   (a) a proportionate means of achieving a legitimate aim, or
   (b) for the purpose of preventing or compensating for a disadvantage linked to the protected characteristic.
   ...

(5) It is not a contravention of this Act for a charity to require members, or persons wishing to become members, to make a statement which asserts or implies membership or acceptance of a religion or belief; and for this purpose restricting the access by members to a benefit, facility or service to those who make such a statement is to be treated as imposing such a requirement.

(6) Subsection (5) applies only if—
   (a) the charity, or an organisation of which it is part, first imposed such a requirement before 18 May 2005, and
   (b) the charity or organisation has not ceased since that date to impose such a requirement.

(7) It is not a contravention of section 29 for a person, in relation to an activity which is carried on for the purpose of promoting or supporting a charity, to restrict participation in the activity to persons of one sex.

(8) A charity regulator does not contravene this Act only by exercising a function in relation to a charity in a manner which the regulator thinks is expedient in the interests of the charity, having regard to the charitable instrument.

(9) Subsection (1) does not apply to a contravention of—
   (a) section 39;
   (b) section 40;
   (c) section 41;
   (d) section 55, so far as relating to the provision of vocational training.

(10) Subsection (9) does not apply in relation to disability.

194 Charities: supplementary

(1) This section applies for the purposes of section 193.

(2) That section does not apply to race, so far as relating to colour.

(3) 'Charity'—
   (a) in relation to England and Wales, has the meaning given by section 1(1) of the Charities Act 2011;
   (b) in relation to Scotland, means a body entered in the Scottish Charity Register.

(4) 'Charitable instrument' means an instrument establishing or governing a charity (including an instrument made or having effect before the commencement of this section).

(5) The charity regulators are—

    (a) the Charity Commission for England and Wales;

    (b) the Scottish Charity Regulator.

(6) Section 107(5) applies to references in subsection (5) of section 193 to members, or persons wishing to become members, of a charity.

(7) 'Supported employment' means facilities provided, or in respect of which payments are made, under section 15 of the Disabled Persons (Employment) Act 1944.

...

Schedule 3
Services and public functions: exceptions

Part 2
Education

6

In its application to a local authority in England and Wales, section 29, so far as relating to age discrimination or religious or belief-related discrimination, does not apply to—

(a) the exercise of the authority's functions under section 14 of the Education Act 1996 (provision of schools);

(b) the exercise of its function under section 13 of that Act in so far as it relates to a function of its under section 14 of that Act.

...

11

Section 29, so far as relating to religious or belief-related discrimination, does not apply in relation to anything done in connection with—

(a) the curriculum of a school;

(b) admission to a school which has a religious ethos;

(c) acts of worship or other religious observance organised by or on behalf of a school (whether or not forming part of the curriculum);

(d) the responsible body of a school which has a religious ethos;

(e) transport to or from a school;

(f) the establishment, alteration or closure of schools.

...

Part 3
Health and care

15 Care within the family

A person (A) does not contravene section 29 only by participating in arrangements under which (whether or not for reward) A takes into A's home, and treats as members of A's family, persons requiring particular care and attention.

...

Part 4
Immigration

18 Religion or belief

(1) This paragraph applies in relation to religious or belief-related discrimination.

(2) Section 29 does not apply to a decision within sub-paragraph (3) or anything done for the purposes of or in pursuance of a decision within that sub-paragraph.

(3) A decision is within this sub-paragraph if it is a decision taken in accordance with immigration rules—

    (a) to refuse entry clearance or leave to enter the United Kingdom, or to cancel leave to enter or remain in the United Kingdom, on the grounds that the exclusion of the person from the United Kingdom is conducive to the public good, or

(b) to vary leave to enter or remain in the United Kingdom, or to refuse an application to vary leave to enter or remain in the United Kingdom, on the grounds that it is undesirable to permit the person to remain in the United Kingdom.

(4) Section 29 does not apply to a decision within sub-paragraph (5), or anything done for the purposes of or in pursuance of a decision within that sub-paragraph, if the decision is taken on grounds mentioned in sub-paragraph (6).

(5) A decision is within this sub-paragraph if it is a decision (whether or not taken in accordance with immigration rules) in connection with an application for entry clearance or for leave to enter or remain in the United Kingdom.

(6) The grounds referred to in sub-paragraph (4) are—

(a) the grounds that a person holds an office or post in connection with a religion or belief or provides a service in connection with a religion or belief,

(b) the grounds that a religion or belief is not to be treated in the same way as certain other religions or beliefs, or

(c) the grounds that the exclusion from the United Kingdom of a person to whom paragraph (a) applies is conducive to the public good.

(7) Section 29 does not apply to—

(a) a decision taken, or guidance given, by the Secretary of State in connection with a decision within sub-paragraph (3) or (5);

(b) a decision taken in accordance with guidance given by the Secretary of State in connection with a decision within either of those sub-paragraphs.

...

Part 7
Separate and single services

29 Services relating to religion

(1) A minister does not contravene section 29, so far as relating to sex discrimination, by providing a service only to persons of one sex or separate services for persons of each sex, if—

(a) the service is provided for the purposes of an organised religion,

(b) it is provided at a place which is (permanently or for the time being) occupied or used for those purposes, and

(c) the limited provision of the service is necessary in order to comply with the doctrines of the religion or is for the purpose of avoiding conflict with the strongly held religious convictions of a significant number of the religion's followers.

(2) The reference to a minister is a reference to a minister of religion, or other person, who—

(a) performs functions in connection with the religion, and

(b) holds an office or appointment in, or is accredited, approved or recognised for purposes of, a relevant organisation in relation to the religion.

(3) An organisation is a relevant organisation in relation to a religion if its purpose is—

(a) to practise the religion,

(b) to advance the religion,

(c) to teach the practice or principles of the religion,

(d) to enable persons of the religion to receive benefits, or to engage in activities, within the framework of that religion, or

(e) to foster or maintain good relations between persons of different religions.

(4) But an organisation is not a relevant organisation in relation to a religion if its sole or main purpose is commercial.

...

Schedule 5
Premises: exceptions

1

(1) This paragraph applies to the private disposal of premises by an owner-occupier.

(2) A disposal is a private disposal only if the owner-occupier does not—

(a) use the services of an estate agent for the purpose of disposing of the premises, or

(b) publish (or cause to be published) an advertisement in connection with their disposal.

(3) Section 33(1) applies only in so far as it relates to race.

(4) Section 34(1) does not apply in so far as it relates to—
   (a) religion or belief, or
   (b) sexual orientation.

(5) In this paragraph—

'estate agent' means a person who, by way of profession or trade, provides services for the purpose of—(a) finding premises for persons seeking them, or (b) assisting in the disposal of premises;

'owner-occupier' means a person who—(a) owns an estate or interest in premises, and (b) occupies the whole of them.

. . .

3

(1) This paragraph applies to anything done by a person in relation to the disposal, occupation or management of part of small premises if—
   (a) the person or a relative of that person resides, and intends to continue to reside, in another part of the premises, and
   (b) the premises include parts (other than storage areas and means of access) shared with residents of the premises who are not members of the same household as the resident mentioned in paragraph (a).

(2) Sections 33(1), 34(1) and 35(1) apply only in so far as they relate to race.

(3) Premises are small if—
   (a) the only other persons occupying the accommodation occupied by the resident mentioned in sub-paragraph (1)(a) are members of the same household,
   (b) the premises also include accommodation for at least one other household,
   (c) the accommodation for each of those other households is let, or available for letting, on a separate tenancy or similar agreement, and
   (d) the premises are not normally sufficient to accommodate more than two other households.

(4) Premises are also small if they are not normally sufficient to provide residential accommodation for more than six persons (in addition to the resident mentioned in sub-paragraph (1)(a) and members of the same household).

(5) In this paragraph, 'relative' means—
   (a) spouse or civil partner,
   (b) unmarried partner,
   (c) parent or grandparent,
   (d) child or grandchild (whether or not legitimate),
   (e) the spouse, civil partner or unmarried partner of a child or grandchild,
   (f) brother or sister (whether of full blood or half-blood), or
   (g) a relative within paragraph (c), (d), (e) or (f) whose relationship arises as a result of marriage or civil partnership.

(6) In sub-paragraph (5), a reference to an unmarried partner is a reference to the other member of a couple consisting of—
   (a) a man and a woman who are not married to each other but are living together as husband and wife, or
   (b) two people of the same sex who are not civil partners of each other but are living together as if they were.

. . .

Schedule 9
Work: exceptions

Part 1
Occupational requirements

1 General

(1) A person (A) does not contravene a provision mentioned in sub-paragraph (2) by applying in relation to work a requirement to have a particular protected characteristic, if A shows that, having regard to the nature or context of the work—
   (a) it is an occupational requirement,

    (b) the application of the requirement is a proportionate means of achieving a legitimate aim, and

    (c) the person to whom A applies the requirement does not meet it (or A has reasonable grounds for not being satisfied that the person meets it).

(2) The provisions are—

    (a) section 39(1)(a) or (c) or (2)(b) or (c);

    (b) section 41(1)(b);

    (c) section 44(1)(a) or (c) or (2)(b) or (c);

    (d) section 45(1)(a) or (c) or (2)(b) or (c);

    (e) section 49(3)(a) or (c) or (6)(b) or (c);

    (f) section 50(3)(a) or (c) or (6)(b) or (c);

    (g) section 51(1).

(3) The references in sub-paragraph (1) to a requirement to have a protected characteristic are to be read—

    (a) in the case of gender reassignment, as references to a requirement not to be a transsexual person (and section 7(3) is accordingly to be ignored);

    (b) in the case of marriage and civil partnership, as references to a requirement not to be married or a civil partner (and section 8(2) is accordingly to be ignored).

(4) In the case of a requirement to be of a particular sex, sub-paragraph (1) has effect as if in paragraph (c), the words from '(or' to the end were omitted.

2 Religious requirements relating to sex, marriage etc., sexual orientation

(1) A person (A) does not contravene a provision mentioned in sub-paragraph (2) by applying in relation to employment a requirement to which sub-paragraph (4) applies if A shows that—

    (a) the employment is for the purposes of an organised religion,

    (b) the application of the requirement engages the compliance or non-conflict principle, and

    (c) the person to whom A applies the requirement does not meet it (or A has reasonable grounds for not being satisfied that the person meets it).

(2) The provisions are—

    (a) section 39(1)(a) or (c) or (2)(b) or (c);

    (b) section 49(3)(a) or (c) or (6)(b) or (c);

    (c) section 50(3)(a) or (c) or (6)(b) or (c);

    (d) section 51(1).

(3) A person does not contravene section 53(1) or (2)(a) or (b) by applying in relation to a relevant qualification (within the meaning of that section) a requirement to which sub-paragraph (4) applies if the person shows that—

    (a) the qualification is for the purposes of employment mentioned in sub-paragraph (1)(a), and

    (b) the application of the requirement engages the compliance or non-conflict principle.

(4) This sub-paragraph applies to—

    (a) a requirement to be of a particular sex;

    (b) a requirement not to be a transsexual person;

    (c) a requirement not to be married or a civil partner;

    (d) a requirement not to be married to, or the civil partner of, a person who has a living former spouse or civil partner;

    (e) a requirement relating to circumstances in which a marriage or civil partnership came to an end;

    (f) a requirement related to sexual orientation.

(5) The application of a requirement engages the compliance principle if the requirement is applied so as to comply with the doctrines of the religion.

(6) The application of a requirement engages the non-conflict principle if, because of the nature or context of the employment, the requirement is applied so as to avoid conflicting with the strongly held religious convictions of a significant number of the religion's followers.

(7) A reference to employment includes a reference to an appointment to a personal or public office.

(8) In the case of a requirement within sub-paragraph (4)(a), sub-paragraph (1) has effect as if in paragraph (c) the words from '(or' to the end were omitted.

3 Other requirements relating to religion or belief

A person (A) with an ethos based on religion or belief does not contravene a provision mentioned in paragraph 1(2) by applying in relation to work a requirement to be of a particular religion or belief if A shows that, having regard to that ethos and to the nature or context of the work—

(a) it is an occupational requirement,

(b) the application of the requirement is a proportionate means of achieving a legitimate aim, and

(c) the person to whom A applies the requirement does not meet it (or A has reasonable grounds for not being satisfied that the person meets it).

…

6 Interpretation

(1) This paragraph applies for the purposes of this Part of this Schedule.

(2) A reference to contravening a provision of this Act is a reference to contravening that provision by virtue of section 13.

(3) A reference to work is a reference to employment, contract work, a position as a partner or as a member of an LLP, or an appointment to a personal or public office.

(4) A reference to a person includes a reference to an organisation.

(5) A reference to section 39(2)(b), 44(2)(b), 45(2)(b), 49(6)(b) or 50(6)(b) is to be read as a reference to that provision with the omission of the words ' "or for receiving any other benefit, facility or service" '.

(6) A reference to section 39(2)(c), 44(2)(c), 45(2)(c), 49(6)(c), 50(6)(c), 53(2)(a) or 55(2)(c) (dismissal, etc.) does not include a reference to that provision so far as relating to sex.

(7) The reference to paragraph (b) of section 41(1), so far as relating to sex, is to be read as if that paragraph read—

'(b) by not allowing the worker to do the work.'

…

Schedule 12
Further and higher education exceptions

Part 2
Other exceptions

5 Institutions with a religious ethos

(1) The responsible body of an institution which is designated for the purposes of this paragraph does not contravene section 91(1), so far as relating to religion or belief, if, in the admission of students to a course at the institution—

(a) it gives preference to persons of a particular religion or belief,

(b) it does so to preserve the institution's religious ethos, and

(c) the course is not a course of vocational training.

(2) A Minister of the Crown may by order designate an institution if satisfied that the institution has a religious ethos.

…

Schedule 16
Associations: exceptions

1 Single characteristic associations

(1) An association does not contravene section 101(1) by restricting membership to persons who share a protected characteristic.

(2) An association that restricts membership to persons who share a protected characteristic does not breach section 101(3) by restricting the access by associates to a benefit, facility or service to such persons as share the characteristic.

(3) An association that restricts membership to persons who share a protected characteristic does not breach section 102(1) by inviting as guests, or by permitting to be invited as guests, only such persons as share the characteristic.

(4) Sub-paragraphs (1) to (3), so far as relating to race, do not apply in relation to colour.

(5) This paragraph does not apply to an association that is a registered political party.

...

Schedule 23
General exceptions

2 Organisations relating to religion or belief

(1) This paragraph applies to an organisation the purpose of which is—
  (a) to practise a religion or belief,
  (b) to advance a religion or belief,
  (c) to teach the practice or principles of a religion or belief,
  (d) to enable persons of a religion or belief to receive any benefit, or to engage in any activity, within the framework of that religion or belief, or
  (e) to foster or maintain good relations between persons of different religions or beliefs.

(2) This paragraph does not apply to an organisation whose sole or main purpose is commercial.

(3) The organisation does not contravene Part 3, 4 or 7, so far as relating to religion or belief or sexual orientation, only by restricting—
  (a) membership of the organisation;
  (b) participation in activities undertaken by the organisation or on its behalf or under its auspices;
  (c) the provision of goods, facilities or services in the course of activities undertaken by the organisation or on its behalf or under its auspices;
  (d) the use or disposal of premises owned or controlled by the organisation.

(4) A person does not contravene Part 3, 4 or 7, so far as relating to religion or belief or sexual orientation, only by doing anything mentioned in sub-paragraph (3) on behalf of or under the auspices of the organisation.

(5) A minister does not contravene Part 3, 4 or 7, so far as relating to religion or belief or sexual orientation, only by restricting—
  (a) participation in activities carried on in the performance of the minister's functions in connection with or in respect of the organisation;
  (b) the provision of goods, facilities or services in the course of activities carried on in the performance of the minister's functions in connection with or in respect of the organisation.

(6) Sub-paragraphs (3) to (5) permit a restriction relating to religion or belief only if it is imposed—
  (a) because of the purpose of the organisation, or
  (b) to avoid causing offence, on grounds of the religion or belief to which the organisation relates, to persons of that religion or belief.

(7) Sub-paragraphs (3) to (5) permit a restriction relating to sexual orientation only if it is imposed—
  (a) because it is necessary to comply with the doctrine of the organisation, or
  (b) to avoid conflict with strongly held convictions within sub-paragraph (9).

(8) In sub-paragraph (5), the reference to a minister is a reference to a minister of religion, or other person, who—
  (a) performs functions in connection with a religion or belief to which the organisation relates, and
  (b) holds an office or appointment in, or is accredited, approved or recognised for the purposes of the organisation.

(9) The strongly held convictions are—
  (a) in the case of a religion, the strongly held religious convictions of a significant number of the religion's followers;
  (b) in the case of a belief, the strongly held convictions relating to the belief of a significant number of the belief's followers.

(10) This paragraph does not permit anything which is prohibited by section 29, so far as relating to sexual orientation, if it is done—
  (a) on behalf of a public authority, and
  (b) under the terms of a contract between the organisation and the public authority.

(11) In the application of this paragraph in relation to sexual orientation, sub-paragraph (1)(e) must be ignored.

(12) In the application of this paragraph in relation to sexual orientation, in sub-paragraph (3)(d), 'disposal' does not include disposal of an interest in premises by way of sale if the interest being disposed of is—

    (a) the entirety of the organisation's interest in the premises, or

    (b) the entirety of the interest in respect of which the organisation has power of disposal.

(13) In this paragraph—

    (a) 'disposal' is to be construed in accordance with section 38;

    (b) 'public authority' has the meaning given in section 150(1).

APPENDIX IV

Constitutional Protections Around the World

Australia

The Australian Constitution (extract)

Section 116

The Commonwealth shall not make any law for establishing any religion, or for imposing any religious observance, or for prohibiting the free exercise of any religion, and no religious test shall be required as a qualification for any office or public trust under the Commonwealth.

Human Rights Act 2004 (extracts)

Section 14

Freedom of thought, conscience, religion and belief

(1) Everyone has the right to freedom of thought, conscience and religion. This right includes—
   (a) the freedom to have or to adopt a religion or belief of his or her choice; and
   (b) the freedom to demonstrate his or her religion or belief in worship, observance, practice and teaching, either individually or as part of a community and whether in public or private.
(2) No-one may be coerced in a way that would limit his or her freedom to have or adopt a religion or belief in worship, observance, practice or teaching.

...

Section 27

Anyone who belongs to an ethnic, religious or linguistic minority must not be denied the right, with other members of the minority, to enjoy his or her culture, to declare and practise his or her religion, or to use his or her language.

Canada

The Canadian Charter of Rights and Freedoms (Constitution Act 1982, Part I) (extract)

Section 1

The *Canadian Charter of Rights and Freedoms* guarantees the rights and freedoms set out in it subject only to such reasonable limits prescribed by law as can be demonstrably justified in a free and democratic society.

Section 2

Everyone has the following fundamental freedoms:

(a) Freedom of conscience and religion; ...

India

The Constitution of India (extracts)

Article 14

14. Equality before law.—The State shall not deny to any person equality before the law or the equal protection of the laws within the territory of India.

Article 15

15. Prohibition of discrimination on grounds of religion, race, caste, sex or place of birth—

(1) The State shall not discriminate against any citizen on grounds only of religion, race, caste, sex, place of birth or any of them.

(2) No citizen shall, on grounds only of religion, race, caste, sex, place of birth or any of them, be subject to any disability, liability, restriction or condition with regard to—

(a) access to shops, public restaurants, hotels and places of public entertainment; or

(b) the use of wells, tanks, bathing ghats, roads and places of public resort maintained wholly or partly out of State funds or dedicated to the use of the general public.

(3) Nothing in this article shall prevent the State from making any special provision for women and children.

(4) Nothing in this article or in clause (2) of Article 29 shall prevent the State from making any special provision for the advancement of any socially and educationally backward classes of citizens or for the Scheduled Castes and the Scheduled Tribes.

(5) Nothing in this article or in sub-clause (g) of clause (1) of Article 19 shall prevent the State from making any special provision, by law, for the advancement of any socially and educationally backward classes of citizens or for the Scheduled Castes or the Scheduled Tribes in so far as such special provisions relate to their admission to educational institutions including private educational institutions, whether aided or unaided by the State, other than the minority educational institutions referred to in clause (1) of Article 30.

Article 16

16. Equality of opportunity in matters of public employment—

(1) There shall be equality of opportunity for all citizens in matters relating to employment or appointment to any office under the State.

(2) No citizen shall, on grounds only of religion, race, caste, sex, descent, place of birth, residence or any of them, be ineligible for, or discriminated against in respect of, any employment or office under the State.

(3) Nothing in this article shall prevent Parliament from making any law prescribing, in regard to a class or classes of employment or appointment to an office under the Government of, or any local or other authority within, a State or Union territory, any requirement as to residence within that State or Union territory prior to such employment or appointment.

(4) Nothing in this article shall prevent the State from making any provision for the reservation of appointments or posts in favour of any backward class of citizens which, in the opinion of the State, is not adequately represented in the services under the State.

(4A) Nothing in this article shall prevent the State from making any provision for reservation in matters of promotion, with consequential seniority, to any class or classes of posts in the services under the State in favour of the Scheduled Castes and the Scheduled Tribes which, in the opinion of the State, are not adequately represented in the services under the State.

Article 17

17. Abolition of Untouchability.—

'Untouchability' is abolished and its practice in any form is forbidden. The enforcement of any disability rising out of 'Untouchability' shall be an offence punishable in accordance with law.

. . .

Article 25

25. Freedom of conscience and free profession, practice and propagation of religion.—

(1) Subject to public order, morality and health and to the other provisions of this Part, all persons are equally entitled to freedom of conscience and the right freely to profess, practise and propagate religion.

(2) Nothing in this article shall affect the operation of any existing law or prevent the State from making any law—

    (a) regulating or restricting any economic, financial, political or other secular activity which may be associated with religious practice;

    (b) providing for social welfare and reform or the throwing open of Hindu religious institutions of a public character to all classes and sections of Hindus.

Explanation I.— The wearing and carrying of kirpans shall be deemed to be included in the profession of the Sikh religion.

Explanation II.— In sub-clause (b) of clause (2), the reference to Hindus shall be construed as including a reference to persons professing the Sikh, Jaina or Buddhist religion, and the reference to Hindu religious institutions shall be construed accordingly.

Article 26

26. Freedom to manage religious affairs.—

Subject to public order, morality and health, every religious denomination or any section thereof shall have the right—

(a) to establish and maintain institutions for religious and charitable purposes;

(b) to manage its own affairs in matters of religion;

(c) to own and acquire movable and immovable property; and

(d) to administer such property in accordance with law.

Article 27

27. Freedom as to payment of taxes for promotion of any particular religion.—

No person shall be compelled to pay any taxes, the proceeds of which are specifically appropriated in payment of expenses for the promotion or maintenance of any particular religion or religious denomination.

Article 28

28. Freedom as to attendance at religious instruction or religious worship in certain educational institutions.—

(1) No religious instruction shall be provided in any educational institution wholly maintained out of State funds.

(2) Nothing in clause (1) shall apply to an educational institution which is administered by the State but has been established under any endowment or trust which requires that religious instruction shall be imparted in such institution.

(3) No person attending any educational institution recognised by the State or receiving aid out of State funds shall be required to take part in any religious instruction that may be imparted in such institution or to attend any religious worship that may be conducted in such institution or in any premises attached thereto unless such person or, if such person is a minor, his guardian has given his consent thereto.

. . .

Article 48

48. Organisation of agriculture and animal husbandry.—The State shall endeavour to organise agriculture and animal husbandry on modern and scientific lines and shall, in particular, take steps for preserving and improving the breeds, and prohibiting the slaughter, of cows and calves and other milch and draught cattle.

New Zealand

The New Zealand Bill of Rights Act 1990 (extracts)

Section 13

13 Freedom of thought, conscience, and religion

Everyone has the right to freedom of thought, conscience, religion, and belief, including the right to adopt and to hold opinions without interference.

. . .

Section 15

15 Manifestation of religion and belief

Every person has the right to manifest that person's religion or belief in worship, observance, practice, or teaching, either individually or in community with others, and either in public or in private.

. . .

Section 20

20 Rights of minorities

A person who belongs to an ethnic, religious, or linguistic minority in New Zealand shall not be denied the right, in community with other members of that minority, to enjoy the culture, to profess and practise the religion, or to use the language, of that minority.

Northern Ireland

Northern Ireland Act 1998 (extracts)

Section 24

24 Community law, Convention rights etc.

(1) A Minister or Northern Ireland department has no power to make, confirm or approve any subordinate legislation, or to do any act, so far as the legislation or act—
    (a) is incompatible with any of the Convention rights;
    (b) is incompatible with Community law;
    (c) discriminates against a person or class of person on the ground of religious belief or political opinion;
    (d) in the case of an act, aids or incites another person to discriminate against a person or class of person on that ground; or
    (e) in the case of legislation, modifies an enactment in breach of section 7.

(2) Subsection (1)(c) and (d) does not apply in relation to any act which is unlawful by virtue of the Fair Employment and Treatment (Northern Ireland) Order 1998, or would be unlawful but for some exception made by virtue of Part VIII of that Order.

. . .

Section 75

75 Statutory duty on public authorities.—(1) A public authority shall in carrying out its functions relating to Northern Ireland have due regard to the need to promote equality of opportunity—
    (a) between persons of different religious belief, political opinion, racial group, age, marital status or sexual orientation;
    (b) between men and women generally;
    (c) between persons with a disability and persons without; and
    (d) between persons with dependants and persons without.

(2) Without prejudice to its obligations under subsection (1), a public authority shall in carrying out its functions relating to Northern Ireland have regard to the desirability of promoting good relations between persons of different religious belief, political opinion or racial group.

(3) In this section 'public authority' means—
    (a) any department, corporation or body listed in Schedule 2 to the Parliamentary Commissioner Act 1967 (departments, corporations and bodies subject to investigation) and designated for the purposes of this section by order made by the Secretary of State;
    (b) any body (other than the Equality Commission) listed in Schedule 2 to the Commissioner for Complaints (Northern Ireland) Order 1996 (bodies subject to investigation);
    (c) any department or other authority listed in Schedule 2 to the Ombudsman (Northern Ireland) Order 1996 (departments and other authorities subject to investigation);
    (cc) the Northern Ireland Policing Board, the Chief Constable of the Police Service of Northern Ireland and the Police Ombudsman for Northern Ireland;
    (cd) the Director of Public Prosecutions for Northern Ireland;
    (ce) the Chief Inspector of Criminal Justice in Northern Ireland;
    (cf) the Northern Ireland Law Commission;
    (d) any other person designated for the purposes of this section by order made by the Secretary of State.

(4) Schedule 9 (which makes provision for the enforcement of the duties under this section) shall have effect.

(4A) The references in subsections (1) and (2) and Schedule 9 to the functions of the Director of Public Prosecutions for Northern Ireland do not include any of his functions relating to the prosecution of offences or any of the functions conferred on him by, or in relation to, Part 5 or 8 of the Proceeds of Crime Act 2002 (c. 29) (civil recovery of the proceeds etc. of unlawful conduct, civil recovery investigations and disclosure orders in relation to confiscation investigations).

(5) In this section—

'disability' has the same meaning as in the Disability Discrimination Act 1995; and

'racial group' has the same meaning as in the Race Relations (Northern Ireland) Order 1997.

Section 76

76 Discrimination by public authorities.

(1) It shall be unlawful for a public authority carrying out functions relating to Northern Ireland to discriminate, or to aid or incite another person to discriminate, against a person or class of person on the ground of religious belief or political opinion.

(2) An act which contravenes this section is actionable in Northern Ireland at the instance of any person adversely affected by it; and the court may—

(a) grant damages;

(b) subject to subsection (3) grant an injunction restraining the defendant from committing, causing or permitting further contraventions of this section.

(3) Without prejudice to any other power to grant an injunction, a court may grant an injunction under subsection (2) only if satisfied that the defendant—

(a) contravened this section on the occasion complained of and on more than one previous occasion; and

(b) is likely to contravene this section again unless restrained by an injunction.

(4) This section does not apply in relation to any act or omission which is unlawful by virtue of the [Fair Employment and Treatment (Northern Ireland) Order 1998], or would be unlawful but for some exception made by virtue of [Part VIII of that Order].

(5) Subsection (1) applies to the making, confirmation or approval of subordinate legislation only if—

(a) the legislation contains a provision which discriminates against a person or class of person on the ground of religious belief or political opinion; and

(b) the provision extends only to the whole or any part of Northern Ireland.

(6) Where it is alleged that subsection (1) applies to the making, confirmation or approval of subordinate legislation, subsection (2) shall not apply but the contravention may be relied upon in legal proceedings relating to the validity of the subordinate legislation.

(7) The following are public authorities for the purposes of this section—

(a) a Minister of the Crown;

(b) any department, corporation or body listed in Schedule 2 to the Parliamentary Commissioner Act 1967 (departments, corporations and bodies subject to investigation);

(c) any body listed in Schedule 2 to the Commissioner for Complaints (Northern Ireland) Order 1996 (bodies subject to investigation);

(d) any authority (other than a Northern Ireland department) listed in Schedule 2 to the Ombudsman (Northern Ireland) Order 1996 (departments and other authorities subject to investigation);

(e) the Police Service of Northern Ireland, the Police Service of Northern Ireland Reserve and the Police Ombudsman for Northern Ireland;

(ea) the Director of Public Prosecutions for Northern Ireland;

(f) the Probation Board for Northern Ireland; and

(fa) the Chief Inspector of Criminal Justice in Northern Ireland;

(fb) the Northern Ireland Law Commission;

(g) a universal service provider (within the meaning of the Postal Services Act 2000) so far as carrying out functions in connection with the provision of a universal postal service (within the meaning of that Act).

(8) This section does not apply to a decision of the Director of Public Prosecutions for Northern Ireland not to institute, or to discontinue, criminal proceedings or, where such a decision has been made, to any act done for the purpose of enabling the decision whether to institute or continue the proceedings to be made or for securing that the proceedings are discontinued.

(9) No injunction may be granted in respect of a contravention of this section by the Director of Public Prosecutions for Northern Ireland unless the court is satisfied that it would not prejudice any decision to institute criminal proceedings or any criminal proceedings.

(10) Where a party to proceedings for a contravention of this section applies for a stay of those proceedings on the ground of prejudice to a decision to institute criminal proceedings, or of prejudice to particular criminal proceedings, the court must grant the stay unless it is satisfied that continuance of the proceedings for the contravention would not result in the prejudice alleged.

(11) The reference in subsection (1) to the functions of the Director of Public Prosecutions for Northern Ireland does not include any of the functions conferred on him by, or in relation to, Part 5 or 8 of the Proceeds of Crime Act 2002 (c. 29) (civil recovery of the proceeds etc. of unlawful conduct, civil recovery investigations and disclosure orders in relation to confiscation investigations).

Republic of Ireland

Constitution of Ireland (extracts)

Article 6

1. All powers of government, legislative, executive and judicial, derive, under God, from the people, whose right it is to designate the rulers of the State and, in final appeal, to decide all questions of national policy, according to the requirements of the common good.
2. These powers of government are exercisable only by or on the authority of the organs of State established by this Constitution.

...

Article 42

1. The State acknowledges that the primary and natural educator of the child is the Family and guarantees to respect the inalienable right and duty of parents to provide, according to their means, for the religious and moral, intellectual, physical and social education of their children.
2. Parents shall be free to provide this education in their homes or in private schools or in schools recognised or established by the State.
3. 1 The State shall not oblige parents in violation of their conscience and lawful preference to send their children to schools established by the State, or to any particular type of school designated by the State.

   2 The State shall, however, as guardian of the common good, require in view of actual conditions that the children receive a certain minimum education, moral, intellectual and social.
4. The State shall provide for free primary education and shall endeavour to supplement and give reasonable aid to private and corporate educational initiative, and, when the public good requires it, provide other educational facilities or institutions with due regard, however, for the rights of parents, especially in the matter of religious and moral formation.
5. In exceptional cases, where the parents for physical or moral reasons fail in their duty towards their children, the State as guardian of the common good, by appropriate means shall endeavour to supply the place of the parents, but always with due regard for the natural and imprescriptible rights of the child.

...

Article 44

1. The State acknowledges that the homage of public worship is due to Almighty God. It shall hold His Name in reverence, and shall respect and honour religion.
2. 1° Freedom of conscience and the free profession and practice of religion are, subject to public order and morality, guaranteed to every citizen.

   2° The State guarantees not to endow any religion.

3° The State shall not impose any disabilities or make any discrimination on the ground of religious profession, belief or status.

4° Legislation providing State aid for schools shall not discriminate between schools under the management of different religious denominations, nor be such as to affect prejudicially the right of any child to attend a school receiving public money without attending religious instruction at that school.

5° Every religious denomination shall have the right to manage its own affairs, own, acquire and administer property, movable and immovable, and maintain institutions for religious or charitable purposes.

6° The property of any religious denomination or any educational institution shall not be diverted save for necessary works of public utility and on payment of compensation.

European Convention on Human Rights Act 2003

3.—(1) Subject to any statutory provision (other than this Act) or rule of law, every organ of the State shall perform its functions in a manner compatible with the State's obligations under the Convention provisions.

(2) A person who has suffered injury, loss or damage as a result of a contravention of subsection (1), may, if no other remedy in damages is available, institute proceedings to recover damages in respect of the contravention in the High Court (or, subject to subsection (3), in the Circuit Court) and the Court may award to the person such damages (if any) as it considers appropriate.

(3) The damages recoverable under this section in the Circuit Court shall not exceed the amount standing prescribed, for the time being by law, as the limit of that Court's jurisdiction in tort.

(4) Nothing in this section shall be construed as creating a criminal offence.

(5) (a) Proceedings under this section shall not be brought in respect of any contravention of subsection (1) which arose more than 1 year before the commencement of the proceedings.

(b) The period referred to in paragraph (a) may be extended by order made by the Court if it considers it appropriate to do so in the interests of justice.

South Africa

The Constitution of South Africa (extracts)

Section 15

(1) Everyone has the right to freedom of conscience, religion, thought, belief and opinion.

(2) Religious observances may be conducted at state or state-aided institutions, provided that —
   (a) those observances follow rules made by the appropriate public authorities;
   (b) they are conducted on an equitable basis; and
   (c) attendance at them is free and voluntary.

(3) (a) This section does not prevent legislation recognising —
      (i) marriages concluded under any tradition, or a system of religious, personal or family law; or
      (ii) systems of personal and family law under any tradition, or adhered to by persons professing a particular religion.
   (b) Recognition in terms of paragraph (a) must be consistent with this section and the other provisions of the Constitution.

...

Section 31

(1) Persons belonging to a cultural, religious or linguistic community may not be denied the right, with other members of that community —
   (a) to enjoy their culture, practice their religion and use their language; and
   (b) to form, join and maintain cultural, religious and linguistic associations and other organs of civil society.

(2) The rights in subsection (1) may not be exercised in a manner inconsistent with any provisions of the Bill of Rights.

The United States

The United States Constitution (extract)

Amendment 1

Amendment 1—Freedom of Religion, Press, Expression

Congress shall make no law respecting an establishment of religion, or prohibiting the free exercise thereof; or abridging the freedom of speech, or of the press; or the right of the people peaceably to assemble, and to petition the Government for a redress of grievances.

INDEX